Guide
to
BUDDHIST
RELIGION

The Asian Philosophies and Religions Resource Guides

Guide to BUDDHIST RELIGION

FRANK E. REYNOLDS
with
John Holt and John Strong

Arts Section by
BARDWELL SMITH
with
Holly Waldo and Jonathan Clyde Glass

G.K. HALL & CO.
70 LINCOLN STREET, BOSTON, MASS.

Copyright © 1981 by Foreign Area Materials Center

Library of Congress Cataloging in Publication Data

Reynolds, Frank E
  Guide to Buddhist religion.

  Includes bibliographies and indexes.
  1. Buddhism—Bibliography. I. Strong,
John, 1948-   joint author. II. Holt,
John, 1948-   joint author. III. Title.
Z7860.R48 [BQ4012] 016.2943 79-26809
ISBN 0-8161-7900-X

This publication is printed on permanent/durable acid-free paper
MANUFACTURED IN THE UNITED STATES OF AMERICA

Project on Asian Philosophies and Religions

Sponsoring Organizations

Center for International Programs and Comparative Studies of the New York State Education Department/University of the State of New York

Council for Intercultural Studies and Programs, Inc.

Steering Committee

Kenneth Morgan	Emeritus, Colgate University *Chairman*
Wing-tsit Chan	Chatham College Emeritus, Dartmouth College
David J. Dell	Foreign Area Materials Center Columbia University *Project Manager, 1975-77*
Edith Ehrman	Foreign Area Materials Center *Project Manager, 1971-74*
Robert McDermott	Baruch College, City University of New York
Bardwell Smith	Carleton College
H. Daniel Smith	Syracuse University
Frederick J. Streng	Southern Methodist University

Editorial Coordinators

David J. Dell

Edward S. Haynes

Preparation of this series of guides to resources for the study of Asian philosophies and religions was made possible by a grant from the National Endowment for the Humanities, supplemented through the Endowment's matching funds scheme, with additional financial support from the Ada Howe Kent Foundation, C. T. Shen, and the Council on International and Public Affairs, Inc. None of the above bodies is responsible for the content of these guides which is the responsibility of those listed on the title page.

This project has been undertaken by the Foreign Area Materials Center, State Education Department, University of the State of New York, under the auspices of the Council for Intercultural Studies and Program, 60 East 42nd Street, New York, NY 10017.

IN MEMORY OF
EDITH EHRMAN
1932-1974

Straightway I was 'ware
So weeping, how a mystic shape did move
Behind me, and drew me backward by the hair
And a voice said in mastery while I strove, . . .
'Guess now who holds thee? — 'Death', I said, but there
The silver answer rang . . . 'Not Death, but Love.'

Elizabeth Barrett Browning

Contents

SERIES PREFACE xix

PREFACE xxiii

   1 HISTORICAL DEVELOPMENT OF BUDDHISM 3

     1.1 Pan-Asia 3

     1.2 India 4

       1.2.1 Historical surveys and introductions 4
       1.2.2 Specialized historical studies 6
       1.2.2.1 Early development of Buddhism 6
       1.2.2.2 The Asokan period 7
       1.2.2.3 Post-Mauryan period through the decline 8
       1.2.2.4 Studies focusing on specific regions within India 9
       1.2.2.5 Buddhism in modern India 10

     1.3 Sri Lanka 11

       1.3.1 Historical surveys and introductions 11
       1.3.2 Specialized historical studies 12
       1.3.2.1 Before 1815 12
       1.3.2.2 After 1815 14

     1.4 Burma 15

       1.4.1 Historical surveys and introductions 15
       1.4.2 Specialized historical studies 16

     1.5 Thailand 18

       1.5.1 Historical surveys and introductions 18
       1.5.2 Specialized historical studies 19

     1.6 Cambodia 21

       1.6.1 Historical surveys and introductions 21
       1.6.2 Specialized historical studies 22

     1.7 Laos 23

       1.7.1 Historical surveys and introductions 23
       1.7.2 Specialized historical studies 24

     1.8 Vietnam (Champa and Annam) 24

       1.8.1 Historical surveys and introductions 24
       1.8.2 Specialized historical studies 25

Contents

1.9	Indonesia and Malaya	26
1.9.1	Historical surveys and introductions	26
1.9.2	Specialized historical studies	27
1.10	Central Asia	27
1.10.1	Historical surveys and introductions	27
1.10.2	Specialized historical studies	28
1.11	China	29
1.11.1	Historical surveys and introductions	29
1.11.2	Specialized historical studies	30
1.11.2.1	The introduction of Buddhism into China	30
1.11.2.2	The period of domestication and growth	31
1.11.2.3	Developments under the T'ang and later dynasties	33
1.11.2.4	Buddhism in modern China	35
1.12	Korea	36
1.12.1	Historical surveys and introductions	36
1.12.2	Specialized historical studies	36
1.13	Japan	37
1.13.1	Historical surveys and introductions	37
1.13.2	Specialized historical studies	39
1.13.2.1	Introduction and early development of Buddhism	39
1.13.2.2	The founding of the various sects	40
1.13.2.3	From 1400 to 1868	41
1.13.2.4	Buddhism in modern Japan	41
1.14	Tibet	42
1.14.1	Historical surveys and introductions	42
1.14.2	Specialized historical studies	44
1.14.2.1	Introduction and early development of Buddhism	44
1.14.2.2	Re-introduction of Buddhism and development of the various sects	45
1.14.2.3	Buddhism under the 13th and 14th (present) Dalai Lamas	46
1.15	Nepal and the Himalayan kingdoms	46
1.15.1	Historical surveys and introductions	46
1.15.2	Specialized historical studies	47
1.16	Mongolia	47
1.16.1	Historical surveys and introductions	47
1.16.2	Specialized historical studies	48
1.17	Buddhism in the West	49
2	RELIGIOUS THOUGHT	51
2.1	Surveys and general introductions	51
2.2	Background and context of Buddhist thought in India	52
2.3	Attempted reconstructions of "primitive" Buddhist thought	54
2.4	The Theravada (Hinayana) schools	55
2.4.1	General discussions and surveys	55
2.4.2	The Councils (Rajagrha, Vaisali, Pataliputra)	56
2.4.3	The Sthaviravadin branch (Theravadins, Sarvastivadins, et al.)	57
2.4.4	The Mahasanghikas	58
2.5	The Mahayana schools	59
2.5.1	General discussions and surveys	59
2.5.2	Forerunners and origins of the Mahayana	59
2.5.3	The Madhyamikas	60
2.5.4	Yogacara/Vijnanavada (Fa-hsian/Hosso)	61
2.5.5	Avatamsaka (Hua Yen/Kegon)	63

Contents

2.5.6	T'ien-t'ai/Tendai	64
2.5.7	The Ch'an/Zen schools	64
2.5.8	The Pure Land schools (Ching t'u, Jodo, Shin, etc.)	67
2.5.9	Nichiren	70
2.6	The Tantra-/Mantra-/Vajra-yana schools	70
2.6.1	India and Tibet	70
2.6.2	China and Japan	72
2.7	Discussions of major topics in Buddhist thought	73
2.7.1	Karma and rebirth	73
2.7.2	Duhkha (suffering)	74
2.7.3	Anitya (impermanence) and time	75
2.7.4	Atman/anatman (self and non-self)	75
2.7.5	The Four Noble Truths	77
2.7.6	Pratityasamutpada (dependent origination)	78
2.7.7	Analysis and classification of Dharmas	79
2.7.8	Sunyata (emptiness)	80
2.7.9	The two truths (Paramartha and Samvrtti satya)	81
2.7.10	Tathata (suchness)	82
2.7.11	Tathagatagarbha	82
2.7.12	Alaya-vijnana (store consciousness)	83
2.7.13	Tri-laksana/tri-svabhava (three characteristics: parikalpita, paratantra, parinispanna)	84
2.7.14	Bodhicitta (the mind of enlightenment)	85
2.8	Buddhist thought and the modern world (including: Buddhism and science, Buddhism and communism, etc.)	85
2.8.1	Buddhist periodicals	87
2.9	The West and Buddhist thought (including: Christianity and Buddhism, psychiatry and Buddhism, etc.)	88
3	AUTHORITATIVE TEXTS	92
3.1	Descriptive surveys	92
3.1.1	Buddhist texts as a whole	92
3.1.2	Pali texts	92
3.1.3	Sanskrit texts	93
3.1.4	Tibetan texts	93
3.1.5	Chinese texts	94
3.1.6	Buddhist texts in other languages	95
3.2	Theravada (Hinayana) texts in translation and textual studies	95
3.2.1	Vinaya	95
3.2.1.1	Pali (Theravada) Vinaya texts in translation	95
3.2.1.2	Vinaya texts in translation (other Hinayana schools)	96
3.2.1.3	Vinaya commentaries in translation	97
3.2.1.4	Studies of Vinayana texts	98
3.2.2	Sutra/sutta	98
3.2.2.1	Texts in translation from the Pali (Theravada) Sutta pitaka	98
3.2.2.2	Texts from the Sutra-pitakas of other Hinayana schools	102
3.2.2.3	Translations of commentaries on texts of the Sutta pitaka	103
3.2.2.4	Studies of Sutta pitaka texts	104
3.2.3	Abhidharma/Abhidhamma	104
3.2.3.1	Pali (Theravada) Abhidhamma texts in translation	104
3.2.3.2	Abhidarma texts in translation (other Hinayana schools	106
3.2.3.3	Abhidamma commentaries and manuals in translation	106
3.2.3.4	Studies of Abhidarma texts	107
3.2.4	Other Hinayana texts in translation	108
3.2.4.1	Narrative works (including separate Buddha biographies	108
3.2.4.2	Manuals of teaching and meditation	109
3.2.4.3	Hymns of praise, epistles, and other works in translation	110
3.3	Mahayana texts in translation and textual studies	110
3.3.1	The Perfection of Wisdom (Prajnaparamita) literature	110
3.3.1.1	Prajnaparamita texts in translation	110

Contents

3.3.1.2	Translations of commentaries on Prajnaparamita texts	114
3.3.1.3	Surveys and studies of Prajnaparamita texts	114
3.3.2	Modhyamika texts	115
3.3.2.1	Modhyamika texts in translation	115
3.3.2.2	Studies of Modhyamika texts	119
3.3.3	Yogacara texts	120
3.3.3.1	Translations of Yogacara texts	120
3.3.3.2	Translations of commentaries on Yogacara texts	122
3.3.3.3	Studies of Yogacara texts	123
3.3.4	Avatamsaka/Hua Yen texts	124
3.3.4.1	Avatamsaka/Hua Yen texts in translation	124
3.3.4.2	Studies of Avatamsaka/Hua Yen texts	124
3.3.5	Saddharma Pundarika Sutra (Lotus Sutra)	125
3.3.5.1	Translations of the Saddharma Pundarika Sutra	125
3.3.5.2	Commentaries and Studies on the Saddharma Pundarika Sutra	125
3.3.6	Ch'an/Zen texts	126
3.3.6.1	Translations of Ch'an/Zen "sutras", Koan collections, etc.	126
3.3.6.2	Translations of works by Rinzai (Lin-chi) masters	127
3.3.6.3	Translations of works by Soto (Ts'ao-tung) masters	128
3.3.6.4	Translations of works by other Zen masters	129
3.3.7	Pure Land texts	129
3.3.7.1	Pure Land sutras in translation	129
3.3.7.2	Translations of works of Pure Land patriarchs and abbots	129
3.3.8	Other Mahayana texts in translation	130
3.3.8.1	From Sanskrit	130
3.3.8.2	From Chinese	131
3.3.8.3	From Tibetan	132
3.3.8.4	From other languages	132
3.4	Tantra-/Mantra-/Vajra-yana texts in translation and textual studies	133
3.4.1	Indian texts	133
3.4.2	Tibetan texts	133
3.4.3	Japanese texts	135
3.4.4	Other texts	135
3.5	General anthologies of Buddhist texts	136
4	<u>POPULAR BELIEFS AND LITERATURE</u>	137
4.1	Buddhism and indigenous popular beliefs	137
4.1.1	In South Asia	137
4.1.2	In Southeast Asia	138
4.1.3	In China	139
4.1.4	In Japan	140
4.1.5	In Tibet and other countries	141
4.2	Moral tales, legends, and popular literature	141
4.2.1	Popular sutra segments and passages	141
4.2.2	Jatakas	141
4.2.3	Avadanas and other Buddhist legends	143
4.2.4	Popular literature having a bearing on Buddhism (folk tales, stories, proverbs, etc.)	146
4.3	Poetry and song	147
4.4	Drama, plays, operas (scripts in translation)	149
4.5	The novel and other narrative works (diaries, autobiography, etc.)	150
5	<u>THE ARTS</u> (ART, ARCHITECTURE, DRAMA, MUSIC, DANCE, ETC.)	152
5.1	Asia (general)	152
5.1.1	Bibliographies, encyclopedias, collections, etc.	152
5.1.2	Comparative East-West aesthetics	152
5.1.3	Mythology and symbolism	153
5.1.4	Buddhist art (surveys of several countries)	154

5.2	India	156
5.2.1	Indian Buddhist art (general)	156
5.2.2	Architecture: Stupas, viharas, etc.	158
5.2.3	Sculpture	160
5.2.4	The Mauryan period and the art of Bodhgaya, Bharhut, Sanchi, and Mathura	162
5.2.5	Northwest India, Gandhara, Afghanistan	164
5.2.6	Cave Temples: Ajanta, Ellora, etc.	165
5.2.7	Amaravati, Nagarjunakonda, etc.	167
5.2.8	Later Indian Buddhist art: Gupta, post-Gupta, and Buddhist tantrism	168
5.3	Nepal	170
5.4	Ceylon	171
5.4.1	The art of sacred places (general)	171
5.4.2	Architecture, sculpture, painting	171
5.5	Southeast Asia	173
5.5.1	General surveys	173
5.5.2	Burma	173
5.5.3	Thailand	173
5.5.4	Cambodia	174
5.5.5	Indochina: Laos, Champa, Vietnam	176
5.5.6	Indonesia	176
5.6	Tibet	178
5.7	Central Asia	180
5.8	East Asia: China, Korea, Japan	181
5.9	China	182
5.9.1	Chinese Buddhist art (general)	182
5.9.2	Architecture and sculpture	185
5.9.3	Painting	187
5.9.4	Cave temples: Tun-huang, Lung-men, Maichishan, etc.	189
5.10	Korea	192
5.11	Japan	193
5.11.1	Japanese aesthetics (general)	193
5.11.2	Surveys of Japanese Buddhist art, etc.	193
5.11.3	Architecture	196
5.11.4	Sculpture	198
5.11.5	Painting and calligraphy	200
5.11.6	Zen Buddhist art forms	202
5.11.7	Garden art	203
5.11.8	The way of tea	204
5.12	Music, dance, drama	205
5.12.1	Asia (general)	205
5.12.2	Theatre and drama in Japan	206
5.12.3	Music and dance in Japan	207
6	SOCIAL, POLITICAL, AND ECONOMIC ASPECTS	209
6.1	The Buddhist community	209
6.1.1	The structure of the monastic community	209
6.1.2	Monks and the laity	211
6.1.3	The role and position of women	213
6.1.4	Modern Buddhist organizations	214
6.2	Buddhism and the social order	215
6.2.1	Buddhism in relation to national culture and society	215
6.2.1.1	South and Southeast Asian countries	215
6.2.1.2	Central and East Asian countries	220

6.2.2	Buddhism and politics (including kingship)	222
6.2.2.1	General discussions (including India)	222
6.2.2.2	Sri Lanka	224
6.2.2.3	Burma	225
6.2.2.4	Thailand	227
6.2.2.5	China	227
6.2.2.6	Japan	228
6.2.2.7	Tibet	229
6.2.2.8	Indochina	230
6.2.2.9	Central Asia and other countries	231
6.2.3	Buddhism in relation to family and village life	231
6.2.4	Buddhism in relation to caste	233
6.2.5	Buddhism and education	234
6.2.6	Buddhism and economic activity	236
6.2.7	Buddhism and law	238
7	RELIGIOUS PRACTICES AND RITUALS	240
7.1	Merit-making and rituals of piety	240
7.1.1	General discussions	240
7.1.2	Giving (dana)	241
7.1.3	Veneration of sacred objects (images, relics, stupas, etc.)	242
7.1.4	Repetition of sutras and formulas, prayer, use of rosaries, etc.	243
7.2	Monastic rituals and practices	244
7.2.1	Ordination in the monastic community	244
7.2.2	Daily regimen and monastic routine	245
7.2.3	Chanting of sutras	246
7.2.4	Uposatha rites (including recitation of Patimokkha)	247
7.2.5	Preaching and teaching	248
7.2.6	Building and consecration of monastery or monastic buildings, dedication of new stupa or Buddha image	248
7.3	Calendric rituals and festivals	249
7.3.1	South and Southeast Asia	249
7.3.2	East Asia	250
7.3.3	Tibet, Himalayas, and Central Asia	251
7.4	Life cycle rites	251
7.4.1	General discussions	251
7.4.2	Death and funerals	251
7.5	Magical protection, health and healing	254
7.5.1	Control of natural phenomena	254
7.5.2	Medical practices (including exorcism)	254
7.5.3	Protection (amulets, charms, spells, etc.)	255
7.5.4	Paritta texts	256
7.6	Divination	257
7.7	Royal rituals and cults	257
7.8	Cults and rituals for particular Buddhas, bodhisattvas, deities, nagas, etc.	257
8	IDEAL BEINGS, HAGIOGRAPHY, AND BIOGRAPHY	260
8.1	The Buddha	260
8.1.1	Previous births (jatakas)	260
8.1.2	The final life as Gautama	261
8.1.2.1	Traditional accounts of the life of the Buddha and canonical biographical materials in translation	261
8.1.2.2	Canonical and traditional discussions on the status, powers, and knowledge of the Buddha	263
8.1.2.3	Historical reconstructions of the life of the Buddha	264
8.1.2.4	The Buddha's extended life in relics	267
8.1.3	The Buddha bodies	268

Contents

8.2	Buddhas other than Gautama	270
8.2.1	Previous Buddhas and Pratyeka Buddhas	270
8.2.2	Existing Buddhas (including Dhyani Buddhas)	270
8.3	Bodhisattvas	271
8.3.1	General discussions	271
8.3.2	Avalokitesvara/Kuan yin	272
8.3.3	Tara	273
8.3.4	Maitreya	274
8.3.5	Manjusri	274
8.3.6	Other bodhisattvas	274
8.4	Arhats (including Lohans)	275
8.5	Perfected Yogins: Siddhas	276
8.6	Deities other than Gautama and bodhisattvas	276
8.7	Cakravartins	277
8.8	Bhiksus and the Buddha's disciples	278
8.9	Biography	279
8.9.1	Great Buddhists of India	279
8.9.2	Great Buddhists of Tibet	283
8.9.3	Great Buddhists of China	285
8.9.4	Great Buddhists of Japan	290
8.9.5	Great Buddhists of Southeast Asia and Sri Lanka	292
8.9.6	Great Buddhists of Korea	292
9	MYTHOLOGY (INCLUDING SACRED HISTORY), COSMOLOGY, AND BASIC SYMBOLS	294
9.1	Mythology (including sacred history)	294
9.1.1	General discussions: Cycle and length of kalpas	294
9.1.2	Myths of the renewed creation of the world	294
9.1.3	Myths of the decline of Dharma and of the world	295
9.1.4	The coming of Maitreya and other "eschatological" myths	296
9.1.5	Sacred histories (national, ecclesiastical, doctrinal)	296
9.2	Cosmology (including sacred geography)	298
9.2.1	Introductions and general discussions: Structure and size of the universe	298
9.2.2	The realm of desire (Kamadhatu) and its inhabitants	299
9.2.2.1	General discussions: Mount Meru and the four continents	299
9.2.2.2	Five and/or six gatis (general discussions)	300
9.2.2.3	Hells, and the realms of animals, pretas, and Asuras	300
9.2.2.4	Heavens and gods of the Kamadhatu	302
9.2.2.5	Minor, popular, protective deities of the Kamadhatu (gandharvas, nagas, yaksas, etc.)	302
9.2.3	The realm of form (Rupa dhatu), and the realm without form (Arupa dhatu)	303
9.2.4	Buddha fields (Buddhaksetra)	304
9.2.5	Intermediate states (antarabhava/bardo)	304
9.3	Basic symbols	305
9.3.1	The wheel of Dharma	305
9.3.2	The wheel of life	305
9.3.3	The Lotus	306
9.3.4	Trees	307
9.3.5	Mara and other symbols of evil	307
9.3.6	Stupas	307
9.3.7	Royal symbols	308
9.3.8	The marks of the Mahapurusa	309
9.3.9	Light as a symbol	310
9.3.10	Other symbols	310

Contents

10	SACRED PLACES	312
10.1	Pilgrims' and travellers' accounts	312
10.1.1	India and Central Asia	312
10.1.2	China and Mongolia	313
10.1.3	Tibet and Himalaya	314
10.1.4	Sri Lanka and Southeast Asia	315
10.1.5	Korea and Japan	316
10.2	India	316
10.2.1	General discussions	316
10.2.2	Lumbini and Kapilavastu	318
10.2.3	Bodh Gaya	318
10.2.4	Sarnath	319
10.2.5	Kusinara/Kusinagara	320
10.2.6	Other important sites	320
10.2.6.1	In North India	320
10.2.6.2	In Central India	321
10.2.6.3	In South India	322
10.3	Sri Lanka	322
10.3.1	The royal capitals and their special sites	322
10.3.2	Other important sites	322
10.4	Burma	323
10.4.1	Pagan	323
10.4.2	Other important sites	323
10.5	Thailand	324
10.6	Indochina and Indonesia	324
10.7	Tibet and Himalaya	325
10.8	China	325
10.8.1	General discussions	325
10.8.2	Caves, mountains and other specific sites	326
10.9	Japan and Korea	327
11	SOTERIOLOGICAL EXPERIENCE AND PROCESSES: PATH AND GOAL	328
11.1	Surveys and descriptions of the path	328
11.2	Faith (sraddha) in the three refuges	329
11.3	Moral discipline and ethics	330
11.4	Meditation	332
11.4.1	General surveys and introductions	332
11.4.2	Meditation manuals	333
11.4.3	Subjects of meditation (including Brahma viharas)	334
11.4.4	Mindfulness	335
11.4.5	Concentration and trance states (samadhi, dhyana/jhana)	335
11.4.6	The development of extra-ordinary powers (abhijna, rddhi)	336
11.4.7	The perfection of insight (vipasyana, prajna)	337
11.4.8	Ch'an/Zen methods	338
11.4.8.1	General discussions	338
11.4.8.2	The Koan	340
11.4.8.3	Satori/wu	340
11.4.9	Hua Yen, T'ien-t'ai and other methods	340
11.5	The practice of the perfections (paramitas)	341
11.6	Mantra-/Vajra-/Tantra-yana	341
11.6.1	Tantric practices (Sadhanas)	341
11.6.2	The use of mandalas	343

Contents

11.6.3	The use of sacred sounds and words (mantras, dharanis, sandhabhasa)	344
11.6.4	The use of symbolic gestures (mudras)	345
11.7	Pure Land practices and experiences	346
11.7.1	General discussions: Faith in Amida	346
11.7.2	The Nembutsu	346
11.7.3	Other techniques and expressions (meditative visions of Amitayus, liturgy, hymns, etc.)	347
11.7.4	The Pure Land	347
11.8	Nirvana/Nibbana	348
12	<u>RESEARCH AIDS</u>	351
12.1	Dictionaries	351
12.2	Bibliographies	351
12.3	Encyclopedias	352
<u>INDEXES</u>		355
	AUTHOR/TITLE INDEX	355
	SUBJECT INDEX	397

Series Preface

Asian Philosophies and Religions and the Humanities in America

This guide is one of a series of books on resources for the study of Asian philosophies and religions. The series includes volumes on Chinese, Indian, Islamic, and Buddhist philosophies and religions. Since the preparation of the series has been undertaken as a contribution to advancing humanistic learning in America, it is important to place the study of these traditions in that larger context.

Humanistic scholarship and teaching in America has understandably concentrated on Western civilization of which we are a part. Yet Western civilization has historically drawn significantly upon the humanistic accomplishments of other traditions and has interacted with these traditions. Given the increasing mobility of scholars and students in the second half of the twentieth century and the rapidly advancing technological capacity for communicating ideas in the modern world, this interaction is accelerating as we approach the twenty-first century.

Liberal education for American students in the 1970's and 1980's must reflect not only our human heritage in all of its diversity as it has accumulated through past centuries, but also the nature of the future in its intellectual and cultural as well as economic, social and political dimensions. By the year 2000, a logical future reference point for today's college students who will spend most of their adult lives in the next century, four out of five human beings will live in the "Third World" of Asia, Africa, and Latin America about which we study least in our colleges and universities today.

Numerical distribution of humanity is certainly not the only criterion which should determine the content of humanistic learning in our institutions of higher education. But when orders of magnitude achieve the proportions which, according to most demographic projections, will exist in the year 2000, geographical location of humanity is certainly one criterion which will be applied by today's students in assessing the "relevance" of their undergraduate education to the real world of the future.

The argument becomes all the more compelling when the qualitative aspects of civilizations other than our own are considered. Western man can claim no corner on creative accomplishment, as Hubert Muller has rightly recognized in this passage from The Uses of the Past.

> Stick to Asia, and we get another elementary lesson in humility. Objectively its history looks more important than the history of Europe. . . . It has produced more civilizations, involving a much greater proportion of mankind, over a longer period of time, on a higher level of continuity. As for cultural achievement, we have no universal yardstick; but by one standard on which Western Christendom has prided itself, Asia has been far more creative. It has bred all the higher religions, including Christianity.*

There is little doubt that the rapid growth of student interest in the study of these traditions is the result in part of their search for new value systems in contemporary society. But this interest is also a recognition of other civilizations as being intrinsically worthy of our attention.

Origins of the Project on Asian Philosophies and Religions

The project was initiated in response to this growth of student interest, which began in the 1960's and has persisted in the 1970's, notwithstanding a current general decline in the exponential growth rates in American colleges and universities. Faculty members with specialized training in Asian philosophical and religious traditions, however, are still limited in number and most courses in these subjects are being taught by non-specialists. While the proportion of those with specialized training has certainly increased in recent years, the situation is unlikely to improve greatly due to the ceilings on faculty size which many institutions have imposed because of financial stringency.

The need for a series of authoritative guides to literature in these fields for use in both undergrad-

---

*The Uses of the Past, New York: New American Library, 1954, p. 314.

uate and beginning graduate study of Asian philosophies and religions, which first prompted us to seek support from the National Endowment for the Humanities for the project in 1971, remains just as compelling as the project draws to a close.

Organization of the Project

The project on Asian philosophies and religions was conceived from the beginning as a cooperative venture involving scholars and teachers of these subjects. The key element in the organization of the project has been the project team or working group, a deliberately informal structure with its own leader, working autonomously but within a general conceptual framework developed early in the project by all of those who were involved in the project at that time.

The individual working groups have been linked together by a project steering committee, which has been concerned with the overall organization and implementation of the project. The members of the project steering committee, working group leaders, and other key project personnel are as follows:

Kenneth Morgan, Emeritus, Colgate University (Chairman of the Project Steering Committee)

Wing-tsit Chan, Chatham College and Emeritus, Dartmouth College (Member, Project Steering Committee; Leader of Working Group on Chinese Philosophy and Religion)

Bardwell Smith, Carleton College (Member, Project Steering Committee and Working Group on Buddhist Religion)

H. Daniel Smith, Syracuse University (Member, Project Steering Committee and Working Group on Hinduism)

Robert McDermott, Baruch College, City University of New York (Member, Project Steering Committee and the Working Group on Hinduism)

Thomas Hopkins, Franklin and Marshall College (Leader of the Working Group on Hinduism)

David Ede, Western Michigan University and McGill University (Leader of the Working Group on Islamic Religion)

Karl Potter, University of Washington (Leader of the Working Group on Indian Philosophy)

Frank Reynolds, University of Chicago (Leader of the Working Group on Buddhist Religion)

Kenneth Inada, State University of New York at Buffalo (Leader of the Working Group on Buddhist Philosophy)

Frederick J. Streng, Southern Methodist University (Member, Project Steering Committee and Working Groups on Buddhist Religion and Philosophy)

David Dell (Project Manager, 1975-78 and a Member of the Working Group on Hinduism)

Two characteristics of the project's organization merit mention. One has been the widespread use of other scholars and teachers, in addition to the members of the project steering committee and working groups, in the critical review of preliminary versions of the guides. Reviewers were asked to comment on both commissions and omissions, and their comments were used by the compilers in making revisions. A far more extensive exercise than the customary scholarly review of manuscripts, this process involved well over 200 individuals who contributed immeasurably to improving the quality of the end product.

A similar effort to enlarge participation in the project has been made through discussions at professional meetings about the project among interested scholars and teachers while it was in progress. Over the past four years a dozen such sessions, involving over 300 participants, have been held at both national and regional meetings of the American Academy of Religion and the Association for Asian Studies.

The Classification Scheme and Criteria of Selection for the Guide

Early in the project a conference of most of the key project personnel mentioned above, as well as other members of the project working groups, was held in New York City in June 1972 to develop a common classification scheme and criteria for inclusion of materials in the resource guides.

This task generated lively and intense debate because underlying any classification scheme are the most fundamental issues of conceptualization and periodization in the study of religious and philosophical traditions. The classification schemes for guides in religion and in philosophy have generally been followed by each working group, although there have been inevitable variations. Each of the traditions included in the project has distinctive qualities and characteristics which make it difficult to fit all aspects of all traditions into the same set of categories.

The objective of developing a common set of categories was to facilitate examination of parallel phenomena across traditions. We believe this objective has been at least partially achieved through this series, although we recognize the need for continued refinement before a common set of categories compatible with all the traditions being covered can be evolved.

If developing categories to span diverse religious and philosophical traditions has been difficult, definition and reasonably uniform application of criteria for inclusion of material in the guides has been no easier. The project's basic objective, as originally elaborated at the June 1972 working conference, has been to provide an authoritative guide to the literature, both texts in translation and commentary and analysis, for teachers and advanced undergraduate and beginning graduate students who are not specialized scholars with access to primary texts in their original languages. Because of the limited number of teachers in American colleges and universities who have the necessary language skills, particularly outside their own primary field of scholarly interest, it was expected that the guides would be useful to those teaching in the field who, even though they might have a high level of scholarly specialization on one tradition, would often find it necessary to deal with other traditions in their teaching.

Series Preface

We also sought to achieve some consistency in annotations of entries in the guides. The objective has been to provide short, crisp, critical annotations which would help the user of the guide in identifying material pertinent to his or her interest or most authoritative in its coverage of a particular topic. We recognize, of course, that we have not achieved this objective throughout the entire series of guides encompassing more than 12,000 individual entries.

Because of the difficulties in applying a common set of categories and subcategories to the diverse traditions being covered by the guides, not all categories have been covered in each guide, and in some cases, they have been grouped together as seemed appropriate to the characteristics of a particular tradition. Extensive cross-referencing has been provided to guide the user to related entries in other categories.

The Problem of Availability of Resources in the Guide and the Microform Resource Bank

We realized from the beginning that a series of guides of this character would have little value if the users could not acquire materials listed in the guides. We therefore sought the cooperation of the Institute for Advanced Studies of World Religions, which is engaged in a major effort to develop a collection of resources for the study of world religions in microform, and through the Institute, have established a microform resource bank of material in the guides not readily available from other sources.

Subject to the availability of the material for microfilming and depending upon its copyright status, the Institute is prepared to provide in microform any item included in any of the guides out-of-print or otherwise not readily available, in accordance with its usual schedule of charges. Where an item is already included in the Institute's microform collection, those charges are quite modest, and an effort is being made by the Institute to increase its holding of materials in the guides. Material can also be provided in hard xerographic copy suitable for reproduction for multiple classroom use at an additional charge.

Under the terms of a project agreement with the Institute, the Institute is undertaking the microfilming of some 30,000 pages of material included in these guides. In addition, the Institute already has in its microform collection a substantial number of titles in the fields of Buddhist and Chinese philosophy and religion.

The Institute will from time to time issue lists of material in microform from the guides available in its collections, but as its microform collections are continually being expanded, users are urged to contact the Institute directly to see if a particular title in which they are interested is available:

Institute for Advanced Studies of World
  Religions
Melville Memorial Library
State University of New York
Stony Brook, New York 11794

Acknowledgments

An undertaking of this scope and magnitude, involving such widespread participation, is bound to accumulate a long list of those who have contributed in one way or another to the project. It would be impossible to identify by name all of those who have contributed, and it is hoped that those who are not so identified will nonetheless recognize themselves in the categories which follow and understand that their help, interest, and support are also appreciated.

To begin with, primary thanks must be extended to the members of the project steering committee, the leaders of the various project working groups, and the members of each of the groups. Those responsible for each guide in the series are separately listed on the title page of that volume.

Thanks should also be expressed to the large number of scholars and teachers who served as critical reviewers of preliminary versions of the guides and the many who participated in sessions at regional and national meetings where the guides were subject to further scrutiny and where many constructive suggestions for their improvement were made.

We wish to acknowledge with grateful thanks the generous financial support of the National Endowment for the Humanities, and through its matching fund scheme, additional support from the Ada Howe Kent Foundation, C. T. Shen, and Council for International and Public Affairs, Inc. The patience and understanding of the Endowment's Education Division during the long and protracted period of completion of this project has been particularly noteworthy.

Many institutions have provided support to the project indirectly by making possible participation of their faculty in the various project working groups. In addition, both the South Asia Center at Columbia University and the Institute for Advanced Studies of World Religions have provided special assistance.

The project has been undertaken under the auspices of the Council for Intercultural Studies and Programs by the Foreign Area Materials Center, a project office of the Center for International Programs and Comparative Studies, State Education Department, University of the State of New York. The last-named institution, acting as the agent of the Council for Intercultural Studies and Programs has been responsible for administering the National Endowment for Humanities grant and other financial support received for the project and has contributed extensively out of its own resources throughout the project, particularly in the concluding months, to assure its proper completion. Without the interest and support of key officials in the Center for International Programs and the New York State Education Department, the project could not have been completed.

A particular word of appreciation is in order for Norman Abramowitz of the Center, who succeeded me as Project Director after my resignation from the directorship of the Center in October, 1976 and to whom fell the unenviable task of overcoming administrative and financial obstacles in the final three years

Series Preface

of the project. Appreciation should also be expressed to G. K. Hall and Company, the publishers of this series, and to its editorial staff. Their forbearance, as the manuscripts have been completed over a far longer time than we anticipated, has been exemplary.

Last but certainly not least are the project managers who have carried responsibility from day to day for implementing the project. Perhaps the most difficult and demanding role has been played by David J. Dell who came into the project at midstream and who struggled to assure its orderly completion. He and Edward Haynes have shared responsibility for final preparation of manuscripts for publication as editorial coordinators for the series, with the former handling two (Chinese Philosophy and Hindu Religion) and the latter, the remaining five titles in the series.

Different, but in many ways no less difficult, was the task confronting the interim project director, Josephine Case, who services were kindly made available to the project by the New York Public Library in 1974 and 1975. She responded with dignity and sensitivity to the demands of this task.

But in many ways the most important figure in the project is one who is no longer with us. Edith Ehrman was the Manager of the Foreign Area Materials Center from its inception in 1963, a key figure in the conceptualization of this project, and its manager from the beginning until her untimely death in November, 1974. She was the moving spirit behind the project during its first three years. It is to her memory that this series of guides is dedicated by all those involved in the project who witnessed the extraordinary display of courage borne of her life during her last difficult illness.

Ward Morehouse, Chairman
Editorial and Publications Committee

Preface

The development of a truly comprehensive bibliographical Guide to the Buddhist Religion is, as any scholar in the field knows all too well, an impossible task; and this is true even when, as in the present case, the scope is limited primarily to English-language materials. (Though it was our original intention to limit the bibliography exclusively to materials in English, many French items seemed to be of great importance and interest and have, therefore, been incorporated; on the other hand, with the exception of a few really crucial entries, we have resisted the temptation to include items in other languages.) The extent of the project has, of course, been constrained by the inevitable limitations of time and space. Since it was deemed important to include original annotations, the extent of the references has also been limited by the fact that the research was carried on almost exclusively within the confines of the Joseph Regenstein Library at the University of Chicago. And since the basic research for the bibliography was completed in January, 1975 (tentative plans called for the publication of the book in late 1975), few items published since the early 1970's have been included.

Despite the fact that it is by no means all-inclusive, this bibliography is much more extensive than most, and is organized in a very distinctive way. Therefore a few introductory comments are in order. This bibliography, along with sibling bibliographies dealing with Buddhist Philosophy, Hindu Religion and Hindu Philosophy, Chinese Religion and Chinese Philosophy, and Islam, was undertaken in order to provide a resource for undergraduate teachers of religion; but at the same time those of us who have been involved have nurtured the hope that it might be of some use for those engaged in Buddhological research as well. In addition, those who have sponsored and implemented the bibliography have assumed that the final product would point up older materials which are presently inaccessible and need to be made more available, as well as areas in which new scholarly work needs to be done.

In order to achieve these purposes an original committee composed of myself, Bardwell Smith, and Frederick Streng met with those responsible for preparing the bibliographies dealing with other Asian religions, and established a framework of basic categories to be utilized by all four groups. Our goal was to produce a conceptual schema which would contribute to the development of a more comparative approach to the study of Asian religions without doing violence to the uniqueness of any one of them. The resulting set of twelve major categories, which have proved to be reasonably viable for organizing the Buddhist materials, has provided the basic outline for our table of contents.

This original committee, with the assistance of Alan Miller, then established a preliminary set of subcategories; and following this, the task of actually identifying materials and preparing original annotations was begun. I have been responsible for the work on all sections except Category 5 (The Arts) and have been most ably assisted by John Strong (who took complete charge of the project during a six-month period when I was doing research in Thailand under a Fulbright Hayes Faculty Research Grant), John Holt, and Regina Clifford (who, with the help of Victoria Kennick took responsibility for compiling the author and subject indices). Other graduate students have provided occasional assistance. And a number of established Buddhological scholars including Stephan Beyer, Roger Corless, Byron Earhardt, Mark Ehman, William La Fleur, Charles Prebisch, Nancy Lethcoe, Alan Miller, Daniel Overmeyer, Reginal Ray, and Donald Swearer contributed critical reviews of earlier versions of the manuscript. Category 5 was done separately under the direction of Bardwell Smith who consulted Richard Pilgrim concerning the section on music, drama and dance, and received general assistance from Holly Waldo and Jonathan Clyde Glass.

As the work has proceeded we have been forced to confront the fact that our categories, like any bibliographical categories, are really quite arbitrary. Neither the twelve major categories which we have retained largely intact, nor the subcategories which have undergone innumerable changes, reflect existential wholes. These categories divide the tradition in ways which have aroused protests in our own minds, and will certainly arouse even stronger protests in the minds of others; how can "popular beliefs" be separated from "popular practices," how can "meditation" be separated from "merit-making," how can "nirvana" be included under "soteriological experiences," but not under "religious thought," how can "authoritative texts" be separated from "popular literature," etc. Obviously the problems are legion. However, we trust that those who use the bibliography will recognize that these categories do not so much mark off separate subject matters as indicate different ways

Preface

of approaching what is ultimately the same subject matter--Buddhism itself.

When we turn from the more general organization of the bibliography to the specific sections which compose it, a number of distinctive problems must be noted. Since these problems differ significantly from category to category, I will comment on each one in turn.

1. HISTORICAL DEVELOPMENT. This first segment of the bibliography was one of the most difficult to handle, both in terms of its organization and its specific contents. From the organizational point of view we seriously considered a strictly chronological format in which materials from various areas and countries would be included under a series of time periods extending from the founding of Buddhism to the present. However, it was finally decided that the available sources were so resistant to this kind of approach that a more conservative, basically country-by-country ordering was required. (This typifies a problem which we have faced throughout our entire endeavor--namely the difficulty of trying to encourage new ways of organizing the teaching and study of Buddhism in a bibliography which must necessarily refer to studies which, for the most part, reflect older ways of organizing those same materials.) In regard to content, we quickly became aware that virtually every item in the entire bibliography could, with some degree of appropriateness, be included in one of the various subcategories of this section. Therefore we have limited the entries to those works which describe, in general, the growth and condition of Buddhism in specific geographical areas at particular times; and in the case of each country we have organized our subcategories in roughly chronological fashion. Finally, it is worth noting that many highly relevant works, including a large number which deal with modern historical developments, may be found in Category 6, entitled "Social, Political, and Economic Aspects."

2. RELIGIOUS THOUGHT. The decisions concerning items to be included in this section have been complicated by the fact that a separate group of scholars has been assigned the task of developing a separate bibliography dealing with "Buddhist Philosophy." Therefore we have limited our entries to selected items which mesh with the set of categories which seemed to us to be appropriate for a section on "religious thought" in a bibliography developed from the perspective of religious studies. Those having special interest in Buddhist thought should certainly consult the "Buddhist Philosophy" bibliography which is being organized in terms of categories developed in philosophical studies, and should contain many additional entries.

3. AUTHORITATIVE TEXTS. This section, even though it is basically limited to materials translated into English and French, may seem at first glance to be excessively lengthy. However, more translations have been made than is generally recognized outside the narrow range of professional Buddhologists. It is our conviction that teachers of Buddhism should become more aware of this fact and should utilize these translations more extensively and effectively than is presently the case.

4. POPULAR BELIEFS AND LITERATURE. This section was originally entitled "Popular Literature and Oral Traditions" and then, after much of the work had been done, the heading was revised, first to "Popular Traditions" and finally to "Popular Beliefs and Literature." This final change has resolved some of the difficulties inherent in making appropriate selections, but has left at least two major problems. The first is the difficulty involved in distinguishing religious thought and authoritative texts from popular beliefs and popular literature. The second is the difficulty involved in distinguishing between popular Buddhist beliefs and literature on the one hand, and similar but non-Buddhist beliefs and literature on the other. In the face of these difficulties we have simply used our best judgments on a case-by-case basis.

5. THE ARTS. Because of the fact that this section was compiled separately in another setting, certain differences in procedure were inevitable. Perhaps the most obvious difference that distinguishes the approach taken to the materials in this category is that they are limited to books and monographs. (Professor Smith hopes, at a later date, to compile an annotated bibliography of articles.) It should also be noted that annotations are generally given only on complete books rather than on segments of books listed under appropriate subject headings. In this section, primary attention has been given to painting, sculpture, and architecture (including gardens in China and especially Japan), while less emphasis has been placed on the performing arts (music, dance, and drama). Some attention has been given to Buddhism's indirect influence on the indigenous cultural arts in various areas (for example, on some forms of landscape painting in East Asia), as well as to the intermingling of Buddhist aesthetic expressions and various traditions of folk art. Though the material which has been included covers all levels of analysis and presentation, it is significant that in book form one tends to find a huge amount of repetition at the introductory level, many highly technical studies, and little in between. This clearly suggests an area where more research and writing are needed.

6. SOCIAL, POLITICAL, AND ECONOMIC ASPECTS. This section includes a number of items dealing with the structure and life of the monastic community along with a much larger number of entries concerned with matters often discussed under the rubric of "Buddhism and society." Partially to counterbalance the country-by-country and chronological modes of organizing the materials in the category of "Historical Development" with which this section has very close affinities, we have chosen to divide the entries according to specific types of activity (political, educational, and the like). It should be emphasized that the user of this section should also consult items in Category 1 (Historical Development).

7. RELIGIOUS PRACTICES AND RITUALS. As we have already noted at an earlier point in the discussion, the attempt to distinguish practices from beliefs is bound to run into numerous difficulties. However, it is important to make the distinction, if only because students often take several courses on Buddhism without having any notion of what Buddhists

actually do. The selection of items is by no means complete, but it should introduce teachers and students to the growing body of religio-historical and anthropological literature which highlights the more "practical" aspects of Buddhist life.

8. IDEAL BEINGS, HAGIOGRAPHY, AND BIOGRAPHY. This category has proved to be one of the most fascinating in the entire bibliography, and is one which we hope will be heavily utilized by college and university teachers. The material on the Buddha should alert teachers to the overly romanticized and uncritical presentations of the life of the Buddha included in many commonly used resources and textbooks. Beyond this, the inclusion of "ideal beings," and "biography" (hence Buddhas, the Gautama Buddha, Bodhisattvas, arhats and renowned historical figures) in a single category should suggest a perspective which is more in keeping with traditional modes of Buddhist thought than an organization which clearly separates "mythical" and "historical" figures. It is our conviction that an appropriate selection of the items included in this category could provide the basis for an excellent course or courses in which the entire history of Buddhism would be viewed in terms of the various "biographic images" which the community has generated, transmitted, and transformed.

9. MYTHOLOGY, COSMOLOGY, AND BASIC SYMBOLS. Since there is very little secondary material of real quality on Buddhist mythology and cosmology we have in this section concentrated primarily on references to original materials. Moreover, it should be pointed out that we have taken mythology in a quite "narrow" sense. As we have chosen to use the term here it does not encompass accounts associated with key religious figures (these are included in the "Ideal Beings" category) nor does it encompass accounts associated with sacred places (these are included in the "Sacred Places" category). Rather, it is limited quite specifically to myths which describe the "origins" and "destiny" of the world and of men, and to legends and other chronicle-like materials that are often classified under the rubric of "Sacred History." Since most of the basic symbols of Buddhism are intimately associated with myth and cosmology, references to discussions of them have been incorporated into this section as well.

10. SACRED PLACES. By "sacred places" we generally mean those sites which are considered to be sacred by Buddhists over a broad geographical area, including especially sites which have become destinations for significant numbers of pilgrims. In our actual bibliographic work we have confronted serious difficulties because studies of such sacred places are not numerous, and because practically all of those which do exist have been undertaken from an archaeological and/or artistic point of view rather than from the point of view of a scholar interested in sacred places as such. (See the various references in the appropriate sections of Category 5.) It should be noted that we have tried to compensate for the embarrassing paucity of material in the area by including a number of pilgrims' and travellers' accounts which, despite the fact that they may in some cases be quite naive, often contain much relevant material which can be culled by those who are seriously interested in pursuing the subject. However, our selection of such accounts is quite limited and is included primarily to highlight a type of literature needing further exploration.

11. SOTERIOLOGICAL EXPERIENCE AND PROCESSES. From the very beginning we have been somewhat uneasy about the inclusion of this category. The problem is obviously not with the existence of soteriological experiences and processes in Buddhism, but rather with the advisability of trying to isolate references to them in a separate section of the text. Moreover, a difficulty in identifying appropriate references has arisen because many intrinsically relevant topics have not been treated by scholars in such a way that their soteriological dimensions are highlighted. For example, it proved extremely difficult to locate significant studies which deal with the highly relevant topic of merit-making because the available studies on the subject do not focus on its soteriological dimension. The same proved to be true regarding studies of various Buddhist millenarian traditions. Nevertheless, we believe that if the category is approached with these kinds of qualifications in mind, it can serve a useful purpose.

12. RESEARCH AIDS. In compiling this section we have been highly selective and have included only those major items that are indispensable tools for the teacher of Buddhism or the students in the beginning stages of Buddhological study.

13. THE INDEX. We consider the index--especially the subject index--to be an essential tool for those who wish to use the bibliography in the most effective manner. It has been designed so as to establish a second set of categories, quite different from those which structure the main body of the text; and, as a result, it enables the reader to pursue a wide variety of topics that are not separately identified in the Table of Contents. Obviously the number of references that we have been able to note after each entry has been limited, and the choice among various alternatives has often been quite arbitrary. However, an effort has been made to include enough references to enable the user to obtain a sound introduction to each topic, and to acquire an adequate basis for a more detailed investigation.

During the past eight years this project has had many ups and downs, and at several points its successful completion seemed very remote indeed. Our thanks go to the National Endowment for the Humanities which provided the initial funding, to the Committee on Southern Asian Studies at the University of Chicago which provided a special grant at a very crucial point, and to the Divinity School, University of Chicago, which absorbed many ongoing expenditures for office materials and secretarial help. Our thanks also go to a number of individuals--including especially Kenneth Morgan, David Dell, and Edward Haynes--whose personal commitment to the project enabled it finally to emerge in published form. We can only hope that the contribution this Guide will make to the teaching and study of Buddhism will justify the faith that these institutions and individuals have shown, and the financial and personal investments they have made.

Frank E. Reynolds
University of Chicago

1 Historical Development of Buddhism

1.1　PAN-ASIA

(1) CH'EN, KENNETH KUAN SHENG. <u>Buddhism: The Light of Asia</u>. Woodbury, Conn.: Barron's Educational Series, 1968, 297 pp.

A compact survey of the history, doctrine, and community of Buddhism throughout Asia, which at the same time tries not to neglect its literature, art, ceremonies, and festivals. The result is a work which leaves the beginner introduced to everything but no more than that.

(2) CONZE, EDWARD. <u>Buddhism: Its Essence and Development</u>. New York: Harper, 1959, 212 pp. (Paperback edition: Harper Torchbooks, TB58.)

A fine, doctrinally oriented history of Buddhism which is excellent in its coverage of Indian developments but totally inadequate for China and Japan. It can profitably be used as an undergraduate textbook when adequate time is given to digest the mass of material, and especially when supplemented by R. H. Robinson's <u>The Buddhist Religion</u> (below). It also contains a useful synoptic chart of "Main Dates of Buddhist History."

(3) DUMOULIN, HEINRICH and JOHN C. MARALDO, eds. <u>Buddhism in the Modern World</u>. New York: Collier, 1976, 368 pp.

A newly revised and expanded English translation of <u>Buddhismus der Gegenwart</u> (originally published 1970), this is an anthology of articles on Buddhism as it manifests itself in modern societies. Fifteen Asian countries are treated in brief essays by recognized authorities, and background material is provided in a thirty page treatment of the "Basic Teachings of Buddhism" by Hajime Nakamura.

(4) ELIOT, CHARLES. <u>Hinduism and Buddhism: An Historical Sketch</u>. New York: Barnes and Noble, 1954, 3 vols. (Originally published London: E. Arnold, 1921.)

A dated but still valuable classic which remains one of the few thorough attempts to cover the whole development of Buddhism throughout Asia. Volume 1, pages 129-345 deals with "Pali Buddhism," and volume 2, pages 3-135 with Mahayana. Volume 3, pages 3-408 is entitled "Buddhism outside India" and is especially useful for its coverage of the often neglected histories of Buddhism in Siam, Cambodia, Champa, Java, Central Asia, Korea and Annam. Only Japanese Buddhism, to which Eliot devoted a separate volume (see 1.13.1.[4]), is not covered here.

(5) KITAGAWA, JOSEPH MITSUO. "Buddhism, History of," in <u>The New Encyclopedia Britannica</u>, 15th edition, 1974, vol. 3, pp. 403-414.

A clear, concise and up-to-date survey of the development and spread of Buddhism in India and throughout Asia. Students with no prior knowledge of Buddhism might well start here and go on to use Kitagawa's basic annotated bibliography (pp. 413-414). It is also interesting to compare this article with that of T. W. Rhys-Davids in the 11th edition (1910-1911) of the same encyclopedia (Vol. 4, pp. 742-749). <u>See also</u> Kitagawa's <u>Religions of the East</u> (see 6.1.1.[13]), pp. 155-221.

(6) MORGAN, KENNETH WILLIAM, ed. <u>The Path of the Buddha: Buddhism Interpreted by Buddhists</u>. New York: Ronald Press, 1956, 432 pp.

A collection of chapters written by prominent Buddhists (monks and laymen) from India, Burma, Ceylon, Tibet and Japan. The chapters vary greatly in quality, some focusing on Buddhist history while others concentrate on the development of Buddhist thought, but all together they balance out to make a fair introduction to the spread of Buddhism throughout Asia.

(7) PREBISH, CHARLES S., ed. <u>Buddhism: A Modern Perspective</u>. University Park: Pennsylvania State University Press, 1975, 330 pp.

This work represents a collective effort by former students of Richard Robinson, to provide a basic input for beginning students of Buddhism. The book is composed of forty-five brief chapters on important historical periods of Buddhist history throughout Asia, significant texts, and discussions of major doctrinal importance. Each chapter is followed by a short bibliography; a glossary appears at the back of the book.

(8) ROBINSON, RICHARD H. <u>The Buddhist Religion: A Historical Introduction</u>. Belmont, Calif.: Dickenson, 1970, 136 pp.

A concise, occasionally exceptional, introduction to Buddhism along historical lines. The substantive chapters are "Life and Teachings of Gautama the Buddha" (26 pp.), "Developments of Indian Buddhism" (43 pp., mostly on Mahayana), and "Developments Outside India" (35 pp., mostly on China). While there is a recognition of many Buddhological problems there is no hint of a clear-cut methodology by which these may be approached. In addition, the author often moves back and forth without warning between factual and interpretive material, leaving the reader confused. The book is useful as a textbook but requires the careful guidance of a teacher, who might profitably contrast or supplement it with E. Conze's Buddhism: Its Essence and Development (above). Also contains a topically arranged bibliography.

(9) WAYMAN, ALEX. "Buddhism," in Historia Religionum: Handbook for the Study of the History of Religions. Edited by C. J. Bleeker and George Widengreen. Leiden: Brill, 1971, vol. 2, Religions of the Present, pp. 457-461.

One of the best brief surveys containing much material not readily found in other overviews. Its strength lies primarily in its emphasis on Mahayana and Mantrayana developments.

(10) ZURCHER, ERIK. Buddhism: Its Origin and Spread in Words, Maps and Pictures. London: Routledge and Kegan Paul, 1962, 96 pp.

A short and very simple historical and geographical survey of Buddhism. Useful as a first introduction to the major phases in the spread of Buddhism, but especially valuable for its twenty-three pages of excellent maps in full color.

1.2   INDIA

1.2.1 Historical Surveys and Introductions

(1) BAPAT, PURUSHOTTAM VISHVANATH, ed. 2500 Years of Buddhism. Delhi: Ministry of Information and Broadcasting, 1956, 503 pp.

A series of essays by Indian scholars and others concerned with a myriad of topics within the history of Buddhism. The large number of topics prevents a catalogue listing here; the reader is referred to the table of contents.

(2) BAREAU, ANDRE. "Le Bouddhisme Indien," in Histoire des Religions, 1, Encyclopédie de la Pléiade 29. Paris: Gallimard, 1970, pp. 1146-1215.

A shorter and more popularly oriented survey of Indian Buddhism than Bareau's earlier piece in Les religions de l'Inde (below). Nevertheless, this still makes an effective and well-informed introduction to the subject in all its dimensions.

(3) _____. Les religions de l'Inde. Vol. 3: Bouddhisme, Jaïnisme, religions archaïques. Paris: Payot, 1966, pp. 1-246.

Surveys the history of Buddhism in India, dividing it into "Le Bouddhisme originel," "Le Bouddhisme ancien," "Le Mahayana," and "Le Tantrisme." In each of these periods, Bareau looks at the historical, literary, doctrinal, and communal developments. This makes for a somewhat different and more concise approach than that adopted by Louis Renou and Jean Filliozat in volume 2 of L'Inde classique (see 1.2.2.1.[11]), which might also profitably be consulted.

(4) BASHAM, ARTHUR LLEWELLYN. The Wonder that Was India: A Survey of the Culture of the Indian Sub-Continent Before the Coming of the Muslims. Evergreen Encyclopedia, vol. 1, E-145. New York: Grove Press, 1959, pp. 256-287.

The book as a whole makes a fine introduction to pre-Muslim India. Written from a cultural rather than a chronological perspective, it succeeds in integrating widely varied aspects of life such as society, religion, art, language, etc., into a singular picture of India. The section relating to Buddhism approaches the subject with a broad perspective.

(5) BU-STON RIN-CHEN-GRUB-PA. History of Buddhism (Chos-hnyung). See 1.14.1(2).

(6) Catholic church, Secretariatus pro non-Christianis. Towards the Meeting with Buddhism. Rome: Ancora, 1970, vol. 1, 142 pp.

This short and unfortunately not widely available booklet is the first of a two-volume "directive" published by the Roman Catholic Secretariat for non-Christians. In it Etienne Lamotte concisely outlines the history of Indian Buddhism, thus providing a summary of his monumental researches in the field, which are mostly untranslated into English. He divides this work into four chapters: 1) the Buddhism of Sakyamuni, 2) the Buddhism of the Sravaka, 3) the Buddhism of Mahayana, and 4) the Buddhism of Vajrayana. This is followed by an appendix on Tantric Buddhism by David Snellgrove.

(7) COOMARASWAMY, ANANDA KENTISH. Buddha and the Gospel of Buddhism. New York: Harper and Row, 1964, 369 pp. (Originally published London, 1916; paperback edition: Harper Torchbooks, TB119.)

A highly readable survey of the life of Buddha and the basic teachings seen from a sympathetic point of view. The author, steeped in the tradition of attempting to establish parallels and contrasts with the Christian gospel, treats most facets of Indian Buddhism in a cursory fashion. Good introduction for the elementary student.

India

(8) DUTT, SUKUMAR. *The Buddha and Five After-Centuries*. London: Luzac, 1957, 259 pp.

An ably conceived and worked out volume which provides the introductory student with good discussions of the career of Buddha, the emergence of the Sangha as an institution, Buddhism's evolution in the Asokan era (kingship, stupas, popular practices, and the Bhakti influence), and further developments until the rise of the Mahayana.

(9) KERN, HENDRIK. *Histoire du Bouddhisme dans l'Inde*. Translated by J. Huet. Annales du Musée Guimet. Paris: Leroux, 1901-1903, 2 vols.

Originally published in Dutch in 1882-1884 and translated in those years into German (by H. Jacobi in *Der Buddhismus und Seine Geschichte in Indien*. Leipzig: Harrassowitz, 1882-1884), this classic work is now thoroughly outdated but remains an interesting landmark in the history of Buddhist scholarship. Kern was an extremist of the solar mythology school of interpretation, and his views are pushed especially hard here in section one, which deals with the Buddha. In the other sections, he goes on to treat the Dharma, the Sangha, and the development of the Buddhist Church. For a sampling of Kern's work in English which covers a great deal of material in the space of very few pages, see H. Kern, *Manual of Indian Buddhism* (Strassburg: Karl J. Trübner, 1896), 137 pp.

(10) LAMOTTE, ETIENNE. *Histoire du Bouddhisme indien des origines à l'ère Saka*. (Bibliothèque du Muséon, No. 43.) Louvain: Publications universitaires, 1958, 862 pp.

The most thorough work on the early history of Indian Buddhism. Its footnotes are a mine of references, and its index is a constant tool of the student of Indian Buddhism.

(11) LING, TREVOR. *The Buddha: Buddhist Civilization in India and Ceylon*. Makers of New Worlds. London: Temple Smith, 1973; New York: Scribner, 1973, 287 pp.

This volume could readily be used as a textbook for a course on Buddhism in India and Ceylon. The value of the book is not so much in its profundity, but in the myriad of issues which it raises and considers briefly. Hence, it may serve as a decent source to use as a point of departure.

(12) MAJUMDAR, RAMESH CHANDRA, ed. *The History and Culture of the Indian People*. London: G. Allen and Unwin, 1951; Vol. 2, pp. 365-411; Vol. 3, pp. 368-403; Vol. 4, pp. 258-274; Vol. 5, pp. 404-427.

Taken together, these sections of the monumental *History and Culture* form an adequate survey of Buddhism in India from its beginning until its eclipse in the 12th-13th century. The chapters are also useful for setting the Buddhist developments in the context of Indian history and culture. Volume 2, "The Age of Imperial Unity," includes an article by N. Dutt on the life of the Buddha and the early history of Buddhism, and the pages in volume 3, "The Classical Age," deal with the Hinayana and Mahayana developments. The chapter in volume 4, "The Age of Imperial Kanauj," traces the emergence of "Tantrikism," while volume 5, "The Struggle for Empire," contains an article by N. N. Das Gupta on Tantra and the last phases of Buddhism in India.

(13) SMITH, VINCENT A. *The Oxford History of India*. Third edition. Edited by Percival Spear. Oxford: Oxford University Press, 1958, 898 pp.

A fine standard history of India that is comprehensive in its treatment of the major historical and cultural events which gave shape to Indian life. For other general histories which consider the general historical role of Buddhism, see E. J. Rapson et al., *The Cambridge History of India* (Cambridge: Cambridge University Press, 1922; Delhi: S. Chand, 1958, 6 vols.), which contains a rich bibliography; Louis de la Vallée Poussin, *L'Inde au temps des Mauryas et des barbares, grecs, scythes et Yue-tchi* (Paris: Boccard, 1930); H. G. Rawlinson, *India: A Short Cultural History* (London: Cresset Press, 1965); and *A Concise History of the Indian People* (2nd edition, Oxford, 1961); H. C. Raychaudhuri, *Political History of Ancient India* (6th edition, Calcutta: University of Calcutta, 1953); and R. C. Majumdar, ed., *The Age of Imperial Unity* (Vol. 2 of *The History and Culture of the Indian People* (above)).

(14) TARANATHA. *History of Buddhism in India*. Translated by Lama Chimpa and Alaka Chattopadhyaya. Simla: Indian Institute of Advanced Study, 1970, 472 pp.

An important, scholarly, and quite readable classic, all the more significant because it draws on a number of sources which were subsequently lost. Originally written in Tibetan in 1608, it was long available only in Vasiliev's Russian and Schiefner's German translations (see Taranatha's *Geschichte des Buddhismus in Indien*, translated by Anton Schiefner. St. Petersburg: Eggers, 1869). Now, in English, it should readily provide undergraduates with a fine example of a Buddhist's history of Buddhism.

(15) WARDER, ANTHONY KENNEDY. *Indian Buddhism*. Delhi: Motilal Banarsidass, 1970, 622 pp.

Uses primary texts to provide a detailed doctrinally-oriented history of Buddhism in India. The book's focus is on the development of religious thought. The sociopolitical situation receives occasional attention, cultic practices and popular Buddhism, less. It is useful as a reference work, but not as an introduction to the topic.

1.2.2 Specialized Historical Studies

1.2.2.1 Early Development of Buddhism

See above for relevant sections in general works; for early Buddhist Councils see 2.4.2; for early Buddhist thought see 2.2 and 2.3; for the lives of the Buddha, his disciples and early Buddhist leaders see Category 8.

(1) DREKMEIER, CHARLES. Kingship and Community in Early India. Stanford: Stanford University Press, 1962. 369 pp.

(2) DUTT, NALINAKSHA. Early History of the Spread of Buddhism and the Buddhist Schools. Calcutta Oriental Series, 14. London: Luzac, 1925, pp. 1-192.

A dated but comprehensive survey of the Buddha's ministry and the spread of Buddhism in Kosala, Magadha, and beyond. Gives details on his important disciples, especially those with missionary fervor. Tends to accept texts, myths, legends at face value.

(3) _____. Early Monastic Buddhism. Revised and enlarged edition. Calcutta: Calcutta Oriental Book Agency, 1960, 311 pp.

Discusses the rise of Buddhist monasticism within its historical context, the life of the Buddha as it can be extracted from all sources (which tends to become confusing at times), monastic scholasticism, and the basic organizational features of the monastic system. Good for the intermediate student.

(4) DUTT, SUKUMAR. Buddhist Monks and Monasteries of India: Their History and Their Contribution to Indian Culture. London: Allen and Unwin, 1962, pp. 19-97.

The book as a whole is an important contribution to the history of the Sangha in India. These pages deal specifically with the origin of the Sangha among the larger community of wandering almsmen, and its early development and organization centering around the yearly monsoon rains-retreats. The book is the most recent in a series of Dutt's works which treat this same topic. See also his Early Buddhist Monachism (6.1.1[7]) and The Buddha and Five After-Centuries (1.2.1[8]).

(5) KOSAMBI, DOMODAR DHARMANAND. Ancient India. New York: Pantheon Books, 1965, 243 pp.

Written with Marxist insights and sensitive thinking as to the "main currents of Indian history," of the times in which the Buddhist community was being formed. (See especially Ch. 5, "From Tribe to Society," and Ch. 6, "State and Religion in Greater Magadha.") It is also helpful as an introduction to the topics of Indian prehistory and the Indus Valley civilization. See also Bridget and Raymond Allchin, The Birth of Indian Civilization: India and Pakistan before 500 B.C. (Baltimore: Penguin Books, 1968). For a beautifully illustrated study which stresses continuities well into the Asokan period, see Sir Mortimer Wheeler, Civilizations of the Indus Valley and Beyond (New York: McGraw-Hill, 1966).

(6) LAW, BIMALA CHURN. Historical Gleanings. Calcutta Oriental Series, No. 6.E.2. Calcutta: Thacker, Spink, 1922, 101 pp.

A short volume which consists of six essays, three of which are of historical character, one on the significance of Taxila as a center of Sanskrit and Pali learning, another on the origin and character of the Licchavis of Vaisali and the Buddha's interaction with them, and a third chapter on the Buddha's interaction with the Jains.

(7) _____. Ksatriya Clans in Buddhist India. Calcutta: Thacker, Spink, 1922, 217 pp.

A connected history of the important Ksatriya clans in Northern India at the time of the Buddha, drawing heavily on Buddhist sources. Special emphasis is given here to the tribe of the Licchavis, but substantial attention is also paid to the Videhas, the Mallas, and the Sakyas--the latter, of course, being the clan into which Gotama was born. Law has done substantial work on these clans, and knowledge of their history forms an indispensable perspective for the student of the origins of Buddhism. Other works by Law which might be consulted on this line include his paper on the Licchavis in Journal of the Asiatic Society of Bengal, n.s. 17 (1921), 265-272; his Tribes in Ancient India (Poona: Bhandarkar Oriental Research Institute, 1943), and his The Magadhas in Ancient India (London: Royal Asiatic Society, 1946). See also U. N. Ghoshal, "The Constitution of the Licchavis of Vaisali," Indian Historical Quarterly, 20 (1949), 334-340.

(8) MIZUNO, KOGEN. Primitive Buddhism. Translated, annotated, and compiled by Kosho Yamamoto. The Karin Buddhological Series, No. 2. Ube: The Karin Bunko, 1969, 295 pp.

An introduction to the general topic of Indian Buddhism. Mizuno's work tends to assume knowledge of facets of Japanese Buddhism. This can work as an advantage or disadvantage according to the reader.

(9) MOOKERJI, RADHA KUMUD. Hindu Civilization (From the Earliest Times up to the Establishment of the Mauryan Empire). London: Longmans, Green, 1936, 351 pp.

The social, cultural, and historical setting of India during the Magadha period can be derived from this standard work. For other treatments of the Magadha period of the same nature see B. C. Law, The Magadhas in Ancient India (London: Royal Asiatic Society, 1946), S. C. Chatterjee, Magadha Architecture and Culture (Calcutta: University of Calcutta, 1942), and D. S. Triveda, "The Pre-Mauryan History of Bihar," Journal of the Bihar Research Society, 38 (1952), 147-189.

(10) PANDE, GOVIND CHANDRA. Studies in the Origins of Buddhism. Ancient History Research Series, No. 1. Allahabad: University of Allahabad Press, 1957, 600 pp.

A volume of essays which inquire into the beginnings of Buddhism from all points of view. The reader will find that most of the articles are concerned with the development of Buddhist thought and that they vary greatly in quality. There are, however, several articles of specific interest which are of historical value.

(11) RENOU, LOUIS and JEAN FILLIOZAT. L'Inde classique, Vol. 1: Paris: Payot, 1947; Vol. 2: Paris: Imprimerie nationale, 1953, sections 1929-2386, pp. 315-608.

This portion of this classic work, contributed by Filliozat and Paul Demieville, perceptively treats the rise of Buddhism and the reasons for its consequent spread. Also of great help are appendices on historical chronology and paleography. (An English translation of this work is Classical India, translated by D. S. Pratt [Calcutta, 1959]).

(12) RHYS-DAVIDS, THOMAS WILLIAM. Buddhist India. Third Indian edition. Calcutta: Susil Gupta, 1957, 158 pp. (Originally published London: T. Fisher Unwin; New York: G. P. Putnam, 1903.)

Somewhat dated in its method and content but still a handy survey of the socio-political and economic context of early Buddhism. Drawing mainly on Buddhist texts and archaeological finds, Rhys-Davids devotes separate chapters to "The Kings," "The Clans and Nations," "The Village," "Social Grades," "Town Life," and "Economic Conditions." The work might be profitably supplemented by B. C. Law, "North India in the Sixth Century B.C.," in The History and Culture of the Indian People, edited by R. C. Majumdar (see 1.2.1.[12]), vol. 2, pp. 1-38, which surveys the sixteen great states and the autonomous clans; and by Radha K. Mookerji's section, "Rise of Magadhan Imperialism," which includes discussions of the kingdoms of the Buddhist rulers Bimbisara and Ajatasatru.

(13) VARMA, VISHWANATH PRASAD. Early Buddhism and Its Origins. New Delhi: Munshiram Manoharlal, 1973, pp. 239-382.

A helpful survey, devoting separate chapters to the economic, political, and social foundations of early Buddhism. Includes studies of the economic support to the early Sangha, of Buddhism as an eastern Indian political movement, and of the sociology of Buddhist monachism. A fine introductory piece.

1.2.2.2 The Asokan Period

(1) ASOKA. Edicts. Edited and translated by N. A. Nikam and Richard P. McKeon. Chicago: University of Chicago Press, 1958, 69 pp. (Paperback edition: Phoenix P225, 1966.)

A fine modern translation of the Asokan edicts. Unlike many other editons, the edicts here are not arranged archaeologically but are grouped topically and interpretively to tell a sequential story of the reign of Asoka, portraying him as an appealing and modern monarch. For other editions of the edicts, see E. Hultzsch, The Inscriptions of Asoka (Oxford: Clarendon, 1925); J. Bloch, Les inscriptions d'Asoka (Paris: Société d'Edition les Belles Lettres, 1950); A. C. Woolner, Asoka Text and Glossary (Calcutta: University of Calcutta, 1924); and G. S. Murti and A. N. K. Aiyangar, Edicts of Asoka with English Translation (Adyar: Adyar Library, 1950).

(2) EGGERMONT, PIERRE HERMAN LEONARD. The Chronology of the Reign of Asoka Moriya. Leiden: E. J. Brill, 1956, 222 pp.

A technical and very detailed study of the various sources and traditions concerning the dating of various events in the life of Asoka, which, perhaps questionably, combines legendary materials with Asoka's own edicts. The author's conclusion, presented as "a survey of the res gestae concerning Asoka" which can be regarded as historical, may be found on pp. 180-189. For further references to the life of Asoka, see 8.2.

(3) GOKHALE, BALKRISHNA GOVIND. Buddhism and Asoka. Indian Historical Research Institute, Studies in Indian History, No. 17. Baroda: Padmaja Publications, 1948, Parts I-III, pp. 1-233.

In Part I of his book, Gokhale, making much of the non-Aryan roots of Buddhism, traces and offers support for his view of the evolution of Buddhism from an essentially monastic movement into a "religion of the masses." He emphasizes Asoka's role in this process. Parts II and III deal with the political, social and economic situations under the Mauryans and the Sungas, considering this specifically with respect to Buddhism. For other general studies concerned with Buddhism and Asoka, see Vincent A. Smith, Asoka the Buddhist Emperor of India (see 8.9.1.[19]); Radhakumud Mookerji, Asoka (London: Macmillan, 1928; 3rd revised edition, Delhi: Motilal Banarsidass, 1962); his "The Authenticity of Asokan Legends," in Buddhistic Studies, edited by B. C. Law (see 2.4.2.[7]), pp. 547-558; and V. R. R. Dikshitar, The Mauryan Polity (Madras: University of Madras, 1932). For the relation to Buddhism of the five kings who preceded Asoka, see B. C. Law, "Some Ancient Indian Kings," in Buddhistic Studies, cited above, pp. 186-219. Finally, for an excellent treatment of the significance of Asoka as it has been preserved in legendary materials, see J. Przyluski, La légende de l'empereur Asoka (see 3.2.2.2.[2]), in English as The Legend of Emperor Asoka in Indian and Chinese Texts, translated by Dilip Kumar Biswis (Calcutta: K. L. Mukhopadhyah, 1967).

(4) THAPAR, ROMILA. *Asoka and the Decline of the Mauryas*. Second edition. Delhi: Oxford University Press, 1973, 285 pp. (Originally published Oxford: Clarendon, 1961.)

An attempt to reconstruct historically the life of Asoka, and to set him up as the creator of his own notion of Dhamma. This is followed by a historical survey of the socio-political-economic conditions in the immediate post-Asokan period, with especially helpful accounts of the lives and administrations of the later Mauryas.

1.2.2.3 Post-Mauryan Period through the Decline

(1) CHAVANNES, EDOUARD, trans. "Voyage de Song-Yun dans l'Udyana et le Gandhara (518-522 B.C.)." *Bulletin de l'Ecole française d'Extrême-Orient*, 3 (1903), 379-441.

Chavanne's French translation of the account of Sung Yun's voyage to India at the beginning of the sixth century A.D. is presented here along with a useful introduction and an appendix listing the various Chinese works written about India prior to the T'ang Dynasty. For further reading concerned with Sung Yun, see Chinese Pilgrims in 10.2.1.

(2) DARIAN, STEVEN. "Buddhism in Bihar from the Eighth to the Twelfth Century with Special Reference to Nalanda." *Asiatische Studien/Etudes Asiatiques*, 25 (1971), 335-352.

A worthwhile treatment of an interesting and often neglected period of Buddhist history in India. The author surveys the condition of Buddhism in its homeland and goes on to describe the life of intellectual ferment at the University of Nalanda.

(3) DUTT, NALINAKSHA. *Aspects of Mahayana Buddhism and Its Relation to Hinayana*. Calcutta Oriental Series, No. 23. London: Luzac, 1930, pp. 1-45. Revised and reprinted as *Mahayana Buddhism*. Calcutta, 1973, 304 pp.

These pages contain a succinct and useful overview from the historical point of view of the emergence of Mahayana thought and the critical issues which contributed to their delineation. Dutt sees the chronological development of Buddhism along the lines of a "pure Hinayana," "mixed Hinayana," succeeded finally by the Mahayana (first century A.D. to 300 A.D.).

(4) FA HSIEN. *A Record of Buddhistic Kingdoms: Being an Account by the Chinese Monk Fa-hsien of his Travels in India and Ceylon (A.D. 399-414) in Search of the Buddhist Books of Discipline*. Translated by James Legge. New York: Paragon, Dover, 1965, 123 pp. (Originally published Oxford: Clarendon, 1886.)

This edition remains the best translation of the travels of Fa-hsien. Rich in footnotes and easily readable, it remains a good source for gathering materials concerned with the status of Buddhism in India in the early fifth century A.D. For other translations and editions, or works which detail the travels of Fa-hsien, see 10.2.1.

(5) FOUCHER, ALFRED CHARLES AUGUSTE. *Etude sur l'iconographie bouddhique de l'Inde*. Paris: A. Leroux, 1900-1905; vol. 1, 267 pp.; vol. 2, 114 pp.

This classic work basically represents an attempt to synthesize the artistic and literary materials in order to assess the nature of Buddhism after Nargajuna (Madhyamika, Mantrayana, and Vajrayana). A good work for the intermediate and advanced student.

(6) GHOSH, N. N. "Did Pusyamitra Sunga Persecute the Buddhists?," in *B. C. Law Volume*. Edited by D. R. Bhandarkar et al. Calcutta: The Indian Research Institute, 1945, Pt. 1, pp. 210-217.

The author marshals evidence from epigraphic and literary materials to support his contention that Pusyamitra did indeed carry out an unfavorable policy towards the Buddhists in the Sunga period. For an opposing opinion, see H. C. Raychaudhuri, *Political History of Ancient India* (6th edition, revised and enlarged, Calcutta, 1953).

(7) GOSWAMI, KUNJA GOVINDA. "Buddhism in the Sunga Period," in "Gautama Buddha 25th Centenary Volume." *Indian Historical Quarterly*, 32 (1956), 221-222.

The author examines remains at Bharhut, Sanchi, Sarnath, Bodhgaya, evidences in Bengal and South India to point out that Buddhism flourished during this period even though the Sunga rulers were pro-Brahmanic.

(8) I CHING. *A Record of the Buddhist Religion as Practised in India and the Malay Archipelago (A.D. 671-695)*. Translated by J. Takakusu. Delhi: Munshiram Manoharlal, 1966, 240 pp. (Originally published Oxford: Clarendon, 1896.)

(9) JOSHI, LAL MANI. *Studies in the Buddhistic Culture of India*. Delhi: Motilal Banarsidass, 1967, pp. 18-59.

These pages represent a comprehensive geographical survey of the character of Buddhism during the seventh and eighth centuries in India. The description is drawn from reports of Chinese pilgrims and royal inscriptions. Overall, this chapter is a fine general discussion that can benefit the intermediate student.

(10) LAMOTTE, ETIENNE. "Alexandre et le Bouddhisme." *Bulletin de l'Ecole française d'Extrême-Orient*, 44 (1947-1950), 147-162.

Examines the monuments left by Alexander in India and the significance of the fact that Alexander and allegedly the Buddha frequented the same places in Northwest India, and compares Alexander as a preacher of peace and equality among all men with Mahasammata (the mythic founder of the Sakya clan).

(11) MEUWESE, CATHERINE. L'Inde du Bouddha vue par des pèlerins chinois sous la dynastie Tang (Septième siècle). Paris: Calman-Levy, 1968.

This is an attempt to comprehensively reconstruct the life of India on the basis of the Chinese pilgrims' accounts. The majority of the book is heavily dependent upon Hsuan Tsang's account. Valuable as background source.

(12) MITRA, R. C. The Decline of Buddhism in India. Visva-Bharati Studies, No. 20. Calcutta: Visva-Bharati, 1954, 164 pp.

A work which seeks to explain the reasons for the decline of Buddhism in India. The work begins with the state of Buddhism in the seventh century and continues a region by region account of the decline. The author has chiefly relied on the accounts of the Chinese pilgrims and any available epigraphic materials.

(13) SENGUPTA, SUDHA. "Buddhism in the Classical Age as Revealed by Archeology." Indian Historical Quarterly, 32 (1956), 179-210.

Covers the period from the Gupta rulers to the Palas. The author uses inscriptions and archeological remains in the form of images, shrines, stupas, cave temples, and prayer halls to rebuild a structure of the history of Buddhism during this period. A useful summary for intermediate and advanced students.

(14) WATTERS, THOMAS. On Yuan Chwang's Travels in India 629-645 A.D. Edited by T. W. Rhys-Davids and S. W. Bushell. New York: AMS, 1971, 2 vols. (Originally published London: Royal Asiatic Society, 1904-1905.)

This translation of Hsuan Tsang's Si-Yu-Ki is perhaps the best of its kind, rivalled only by Samuel Beal's translation of the Si-Yu-Ki (Delhi, 1969; New York: Paragon, 1968, 2 vols.). Good material on Buddhism in seventh-century India. For other listings concerned with Hsuan Tsang, see 10.2.1.

(15) WOODCOCK, GEORGE. The Greeks in India. London: Faber and Faber, 1966, pp. 94-114.

The chapter is entitled "The Realm of Menander" and represents a straightforward and well-informed introduction to the question of the Greek and Buddhist influences in Bactria in the second century B.C. See pages 156-186 for an overall discussion of Greek influence on Buddhism. A classical study of the same topic is W. W. Tarn, The Greeks in Bactria and India (2nd edition, Cambridge: Cambridge University Press, 1951). For a study of the conversion to Buddhism of the Greek king Menander, see Alfred Foucher, "A propos de la conversion au Bouddhisme du roi indo-grec Menandre," Mémoires de l'Académie des inscriptions et belles-lettres, 43 (1943), 260-295.

(16) YUSUF, S. M. "The Early Contacts between Islam and Buddhism." University of Ceylon Review, 13, no. 1 (January 1955), 1-28.

The scene of contact between Buddhism and Islam is seventh-century north-west India (presently Afghanistan). After a survey of the rise and decline of Buddhism from Asoka to the seventh century and a survey of the rise of Islam and its movement east, the author attempts to show how Islam was conceptually influenced by Buddhism.

1.2.2.4 Studies Focusing on Specific Regions within India

(1) CHATTERJI, S. K. "Buddhist Survivals in Bengal," in B. C. Law Volume (see 1.2.2.3[6]), Pt. I, pp. 75-87.

An article which may be used by students of all levels. The author has attempted to isolate Buddhist elements of the past which continue to survive in contemporary Bengal. The author excludes the Dharma cult as a vestige of Buddhism, describes the "tantricization" of Hinduism, the modern usage of the terms "Buddha," "Sangha," and "Dharma," and mentions some medieval cults which were probably continuations of Tantric Buddhism.

(2) CHAUDHURY, BINAYENDRANATH. "Pataliputra: Its Importance in the History of Buddhism." Indian Historical Quarterly, 32 (1956), 341-351.

A historical survey of the significance of this city during the pre-Mauryan, Mauryan, Sunga, Gupta, and Harsavardhana periods. The author has made use of the Chinese pilgrims' accounts and findings of modern archeology.

(3) DIKSHITAR, V. R. R. "Buddhism in Andhradesa," in B. C. Law Volume (see 1.2.2.3[6]), Pt. I, pp. 346-353.

These few pages comprise a brief history of Buddhism in the Andhra country from the third century B.C. to the beginning of the fifth century A.D., when it began to decline. The author has relied heavily upon inscriptions at Pratipalapura, Amaravati, Jaggayyapeta, and Nargajunikonda in addition to the descriptions of Fa-Hsien and Hsuan Tsang.

(4) DUTT, NALINAKSHA. "Buddhism in Kashmir," in Gilgit Manuscripts. Edited by Nalinaksha Dutt. Kashmir Series of Texts and Studies. Srinagar-Kashmir, 1939, vol. 1, pp. 3-45.

A short and straightforward history of Buddhism in Kashmir, from the time of Asoka to its demise. Dutt, however, by his own admission, has been generally uncritical of the primary sources on which he is depending.

(5) _____. Development of Buddhism in Uttar Pradesh. Lucknow: Publication Bureau, Government of Uttar Pradesh, 1956, 435 pp.

A rendition of the life of the Buddha, his teachings, the development of the early monastic system, and the important doctrines which made the Sarvastivadins and Sammitiyas unique. Then, the author reviews archeological finds and sites in Uttar Pradesh including the Asokan edicts.

(6) GOKHALE, BALKRISHNA GOVIND. "Theravada Buddhism in Western India." *Journal of the American Oriental Society*, 92 (1972), 230-236.
A study of the history and development of Buddhism in Maharashtra and Gujarat, which effectively correlates literary evidence with archeological findings. Theravada was a minority faith in the region from the second century B.C. to 200 A.D., according to the author.

(7) HASSAIN, F. M. *Buddhist Kashmir*. New Delhi: Light and Life Publications, 1973, 74 pp.
A most elementary essay which provides a skeletal summary of the historical highlights of Buddhism in Kashmir.

(8) KHOSLA, SARLA. *History of Buddhism in Kashmir*. New Delhi: Sagar Publications, 1972, 188 pp.
This volume represents an effort to reconstruct the history of Buddhism in Kashmir based upon literary, epigraphical, and archeological evidences available. Particularly worthy of note are chapters 6-8 which are concerned with monuments, architecture, culture and literature. The rest of the book treats the historical and sociological role assumed by Buddhism in this Indian region.

(9) MURTHY, M. CHIDANANDA. "Buddhism in Karnataka." *Quarterly Journal of the Mythic Society*, 53 (October 1962/January 1963), 124-135.
The author argues against those scholars who contend that Buddhism existed only for a short while in Karnataka. He cites inscriptions which seem to indicate that Buddhism flourished from the Ashokan times up until perhaps the fifteenth century.

(10) NAUDOU, JEAN. *Les bouddhistes kasmiriens au moyen âge*. Annales du Musée Guimet, Bibliothèque d'études, No. 68. Paris: Presses universitaires de France, 1968, 242 pp.
Traces the history of Kashmir as an important center of Buddhism even after its widely supposed decline and virtual disappearance from India. Naudou demonstrates how Buddhism continued to flourish into the fourteenth century (using Bu-Ston's texts). Suitable for the intermediate student.

(11) REYNOLDS, C. H. B. "Buddhism and the Maldivian Language," in *Buddhist Studies in Honour of I. B. Horner*. Edited by L. Cousins, A. Kunst, and K. R. Norman. Dordrecht: Reidel, 1974, pp. 193-198.
The Maldive Islands have been basically Muslim since 1153, but were Buddhist before that. The question of when and where their Buddhism came from has been the subject of a minor debate, which Reynolds reviews and adds to in this article. It is generally conceded that the influence of Sinhalese in the Maldive forms of Buddhism was paramount.

(12) SASTRI, P. S. "The Rise and Growth of Buddhism in Andhra." *Indian Historical Quarterly*, 31 (1955), 68-75.
In these few pages, the author examines literary sources which mention Buddha's activity in the Andhra country and proposes this region as the birthplace of the Mahasanghikas. For further reading concerned with Buddhism in the Andhra region, see G. Bose, "Reconstruction of Andhra Chronology," *Journal of the Asiatic Society of Bombay*, 5 (1939), 1-131; K. Gopalachari, *Early History of the Andhra Country* (Madras: University of Madras, 1941); B. V. K. Rao, *History of the Early Dynasties of the Andhradesa* (Madras, 1942); and V. Ramesam, *Andhra Chronology, 20-1800 A.C.* (Mylapore, 1946).

(13) SIRCAR, DINESH CHANDRA. *Studies in the Religious Life of Ancient and Medieval India*. Delhi: Motilal Banarsidass, 1971, pp. 183-205 and 253-257.
The first selection is concerned with the rise and decline of Buddhism in Bengal based upon historical documents and inscriptions. The latter, an appendix, notes the repudiation of Buddhism by the Candra royal family in Southeast Bengal in the first half of the eleventh century. Good reading for the intermediate student.

1.2.2.5 Buddhism in Modern India

(1) FISKE, ADELE. "Religion and Buddhism among India's New Buddhists." *Social Research*, 36, no. 1 (Spring 1969), 123-157.
The author seriously explores the reasons for the mass conversions to Buddhism which occurred during the movement led by Dr. B. R. Ambedkar. Using data gathered in 1967, the fundamental questions addressed include whether motivations for converting to Buddhism were the result of religious convictions or because of social, political and economic factors; whether this new form of Buddhism is an "authentic expression" of the traditional Buddhist spirit; and how the Ambedkar movement compares with other revitalization movements such as Sokka Gakkai and Black Muslims.

(2) ISAACS, HAROLD P. *India's Ex-Untouchables*. See 6.2.4.(4).

(3) MILLER, ROBERT J. "They will not die Hindus: The Buddhist Conversion of Mahar ex-Untouchables." *Asian Survey*, 7 (September 1967), 637-644.
A summary of the history and character of the Mahar untouchables who have converted to Buddhism and rejected the fundamental principles of Hindu society. The author attempts to

describe the process in which these "ex-untouchables" have gone about constructing their own "social construction of reality."

(4) PRESLER, HENRY. "The Neo-Buddhist Stir in India." India Cultures Quarterly, 21, no. 4 (1964), 1-29.

Provides an overview of the thoughts of Dr. Ambedkar concerning the nature and suitability of Buddhism in relation to India's social problems. The author contends that the conversion of the Mahar untouchable community was a "neo-Buddhist stirring" rather than a genuine religious movement.

(5) ZELLIOT, ELEANOR. "Buddhism and Politics in Maharashtra." See 6.2.4(11).

(6) _____. Dr. Ambedkar and the Mahar Movement. See 6.2.4(12).

(7) _____. "The Revival of Buddhism in India." Asia, 10 (1968), 39-45. See 6.2.4(13).

1.3 SRI LANKA

1.3.1 Historical Surveys and Introductions

(1) ADIKARAM, E. W. Early History of Buddhism in Ceylon. Migoda: D. S. Puswella, 1946, 154 pp.

One of the first scholarly attempts to look at the early history of Ceylonese Buddhism. Based primarily on the Pali commentaries of the fifth century, it does not attempt to trace the history beyond that period, but focuses on what it calls the "corruption" of the Buddhist faith in the first centuries after its introduction to the island. A different view of this early period may be found in W. Rahula's History of Buddhism in Ceylon (below). The use of the commentaries, most of which are unavailable in English, makes the work an essential reference for the advanced student, but of less value to the beginner.

(2) ARASARATNAM, SINNAPPAH. Ceylon. Englewood Cliffs, N.J.: Prentice-Hall, 1964, 182 pp.

The history of Sinhalese Buddhism is inseparable from the history of Sri Lanka. Consequently, much valuable information can be obtained in the more general histories of the island. This work, which is suitable for the beginning student, surveys Ceylonese history, considering especially the interrelations of various ethnic, language and religious groups (Sinhalese, Tamil, Muslim, and Western colonial).

(3) Culavamsa: Being the More Recent Part of the Mahavamsa. Translated by Wilhelm Geiger et al. Pali Text Society Translation Series, Nos. 18, 20. Colombo: Ceylon Government Information Department, 1953, 2 vols.

A late Sinhalese chronicle which attempts to "continue" the account of the Mahavamsa. Part I takes the narrative from the death of King Mahasena to the reign of Parakkamabahu I in the twelfth century. Part II focuses on Parakkamabahu I (pp. 1-124), Parakkambahu II (pp. 143-182), Vijayabahu IV (pp. 183-200), and carries the history of Sinhalese kingship to its demise in 1815. Like the earlier chronicles, the Culavamsa is essential to an understanding of Sinhalese Buddhism and culture.

(4) [Dipavamsa.] The Chronicle of the Island of Ceylon, or the Dipavamsa, a Historical Poem of the 4th Century A.D. Edited by B. C. Law. Ceylon: Saman Press, 1959, 266 pp. (Originally published as a special issue of The Ceylon Historical Journal, 7 [1957-1958].)

The first of the chronicles of Ceylon, written in the fourth century A.D., the Dipavamsa is a historical poem in Pali of considerable importance for an understanding of Buddhism up to the reign of Mahasena. Most of the poem deals with early Indian Buddhism, pre-Buddhist Ceylon, and the origins of Sinhalese Buddhism. It should be read in conjunction with the Mahavamsa, translated by Geiger (below), a chronicle of the next century. For an older and long standard translation of the same text, see Hermann Oldenberg, The Dipavamsa (see 10.3.1[6]).

(5) LING, TREVOR. The Buddha: Buddhist Civilization in India and Ceylon. See 1.2.1(11).

(6) MAHANAMA. The Mahavamsa, or The Great Chronicle of Ceylon. Translated by Wilhelm Geiger et al. London: Luzac, for the Pali Text Society, 1964, 323 pp.

This fifth century chronicle, attributed to a monk named Mahanama, takes the narrative of Sinhalese history from its beginnings up to the reign of Mahasena in the early fourth century. Most of the Mahavamsa deals with the coming of Buddhism to Ceylon during the time of Devanampiyatissa in the third century B.C., and its further establishment under Dutthagamani two centuries later. This document is seminal for an understanding of the early self-image of Sinhalese Buddhism from the standpoint of the orthodox position of the Mahavihara. See also Bardwell L. Smith, "The Ideal Social Order as Portrayed in the Chronicles of Ceylon," in The Two Wheels of Dhamma, edited by Bardwell Smith (below), pp. 31-57.

(7) PARANAVITANA, SENARAT. "Mahayanism in Ceylon." Ceylon Journal of Science, Section G: Archaeology, Ethnography, etc., 2, no. 1 (December 1928), 35-71.

This rare and short contribution by a great Ceylonese scholar is perhaps the only work which concentrates solely on the Mahayana movement in Ceylon. It shows clearly how, historically, Ceylonese Buddhism was affected by all the various doctrinal developments on the Indian mainland, and it argues that a number of

Mahayana bodhisattvas were introduced into Ceylon, and then, under pressure from the Theravada orthodoxy, were disguised and worshipped (to this day) as Hindu deities. A shorter but more available version of the work has appeared as S. Paranavitana, "Mahayanism in Ceylon," in Présence du Bouddhisme (Saigon: France-Asie, 1959), pp. 515-527. A less substantial but historically oriented essay which touches some of the same themes is W. M. K. Wijetunga, "The Spread of Heterodox Doctrines in Early Ceylon," Ceylon Historical Journal, 19 (1969-1970), 16-28.

(8) _____, ed. The University of Ceylon History of Ceylon. Colombo: Ceylon University, 1959-1960. Volume 1 in 2 parts, 409 and 445 pp. Further volumes in progress.

A thorough study of the general history of Sri Lanka from the earliest times until the arrival of the Portuguese in 1505. A scholarly but shorter treatment of the same period is C. W. Nicholas and Senarat Paranavitana, A Concise History of Ceylon (Colombo: Ceylon University, 1961), 357 pp.

(9) PERARA, H. R. Buddhism in Ceylon: Its Past and Its Present. Wheel Publication, No. 100. Kandy: Buddhist Publication Society, 1965, 80 pp.

Sketchy and chauvinistic at times, but one of the few recent complete histories of Ceylonese Buddhism from its beginnings to the present time. It is especially helpful as an introduction to the periods not covered by Adikaram (above) and Rahula (below).

(10) RAHULA, WALPOLA. History of Buddhism in Ceylon: The Anuradhapura Period, 3rd Century B.C.-19th Century A.D. Second edition. Colombo: M. D. Gunasena, 1966, 351 pp. (Originally published 1956.)

The standard work on the topic, suitable as an introduction and remaining valuable as a reference work. However, it deals only with the Anuradhapura period. The first seven chapters examine the origin and development of Buddhism in Ceylon, the next six analyze the monastic life, and the last four deal with lay life, ceremonies and festivals, and the educational system. By far the most interesting chapters are those dealing with monastic life, though helpful material may be found in the other sections as well.

(11) SMITH, BARDWELL L., ed. The Two Wheels of Dhamma: Essays on the Theravada Tradition in India and Ceylon. AAR Studies in Religion, 1972, No. 3. Chambersburg: American Academy of Religion, 1972, 121 pp.

A collection of essays which are useful for understanding the historical development and present condition of Sinhalese Buddhism, especially in its relation to the social order. Frank Reynolds's study of the Indian background highlights the symbiotic relationship in Theravada between the "Wheel of Power" (anacakka) and the "Wheel of Dharma" (dhammacakka). Bardwell Smith continues the theme by examining the concept of an ideal social order as may be found in the Ceylonese Chronicles' view of their own history. The next two essays, by Gananath Obeyesekere and Bardwell Smith, focus on some of the dilemmas of Sinhalese Buddhism in the modern period. They are followed by a bibliographic essay by Frank Reynolds.

1.3.2 Specialized Historical Studies

1.3.2.1 Before 1815

(1) ARIYAPALA, M. B. Society in Mediaeval Ceylon: The State of Society in Ceylon as Depicted in the Saddharma-ratnavaliya and Other Literature of the Thirteenth Century. Colombo: K. V. G. De Silva, 1956, 415 pp.

Suitable primarily for the specialist. Contains three parts, dealing with the political, religious and social aspects of thirteenth century Sinhalese society. Pages 179-249 are especially pertinent to the study of Buddhism. For a more general survey of the Ceylonese culture throughout the same period, see W. Geiger, Culture of Ceylon in Mediaeval Times (below).

(2) DEWARAJA, LORNA SRIMATHIE. A Study of Political, Administrative, and Social Structure of the Kandyan Kingdom of Ceylon, 1707-1760. Colombo: Lake House Investments, 1972, 245 pp.

A detailed scholarly examination of this period. Of particular importance for the study of Sinhalese Buddhism is the chapter on "Religion and the State," pp. 119-149. For the advanced student, this book is very useful.

(3) DHAMMAKITTI. The Dathavamsa: A History of the Tooth-Relic of the Buddha. Edited and translated by Bimala Charan Law. Punjab Sanskrit Series, No. 7. Lahore: Motilal Banarsidass, Punjab Sanskrit Book Depot, 1925, 48 and 68 pp.

The arrival of the tooth relic of the Buddha shortly after the reign of King Mahasena (334-361 A.D.) was an event of capital importance in the history of Ceylonese Buddhism. The Dathavamsa, originally composed in Sinhalese and translated into Pali in the thirteenth century, is a record of events and incidents surrounding the Tooth. A French summary of the text may be found in Victor Goloubew, "Le temple de la Dent à Kandy" (8.1.2.4[10]).

(4) FA HSIEN. A Record of Buddhistic Kingdoms: Being an Account by the Chinese Monk Fa-Hsien of His Travels. See 1.2.2.3(4).

Fa Hsien was one of the few Chinese pilgrims to visit Ceylon, where he remained (mostly at Anuradhapura) for two years, at the beginning of the fifth century. His account remains an important source of information on

Ceylonese Buddhism of that time. For a survey of some of the results of Fa Hsien's visit, see W. Pachow, "Ancient Cultural Relations between Ceylon and China" (1.11.2.3[12]).

(5) FERNANDO, P. EDWIN EBERT. "An Account of the Kandyan Mission sent to Siam in 1750 A.D.," Ceylon Journal of Historical and Social Studies, 2 (1959), 37-83.

An annotated translation of an early account of the mission sent by the Ceylonese king to Siam to request some qualified Buddhist monks to come to Ceylon and restore the higher ordination which had lapsed there. This was not the first such mission--others had been sent to Burma at the end of the seventeenth century (see also D. B. Jayatilake, "Sinhalese Embassies to Arakan," Journal of the Royal Asiatic Society (Ceylon Branch), 35 [1940], 1-6; and P. E. E. Fernando, "The Rakkhanga-Sannas-Curnikava and the Date of the Arrival of Arakanese Monks in Ceylon," University of Ceylon Review, 17 [1959], 41-46. But the 1750 mission was particularly successful, resulting in the arrival of Siamese monks in Ceylon in 1753 and 1755. For a Siamese account of their journey, see E. Lorgeou, "Notice sur un manuscrit siamois contenant la relation de deux missions religieuses envoyées de Siam à Ceylon au milieu du xviii-e siècle," Journal asiatique, 8 (1906), 533-548; or the translation of the Syamavarnanava in P. E. Pieris, "An Account of King Kirti Sri's Embassy to Siam," Journal of the Royal Asiatic Society (Ceylon Branch), 18 (1903), 17-44. For a general survey of the exchange of missions which have remained important landmarks in the history of relations between the various Theravada countries, see S. Paranavitana, "Religious Intercourse Between Ceylon and Siam in the Thirteenth to Fifteenth Centuries" (below).

(6) GEIGER, WILHELM. Culture of Ceylon in Mediaeval Times. Edited by Heinz Bechert. Wiesbaden: O. Harrassowitz, 1960, Pt. III, "King and Government," pp. 111-163.

The third part of this history of Sri Lanka from the death of Mahasena in the fourth century until the coming of the Portuguese in 1505 deals with religious life both in its popular and orthodox forms. The focus is on Buddhism, though Hinduism is also considered briefly. For the advanced student, it is a helpful work for understanding the state of Buddhism during that period.

(7) KALUPAHANA, DAVID J. "Schools of Buddhism in Ceylon." Ceylon Journal of the Humanities, 1, no. 2 (July 1970), 159-190.

A good article that turns out to be a speculative history of the early Buddhist sects in Ceylon. The author contends that the Sthaviravadins were associated with Mahavihara, the Sautrantikas with the Abhayagiri, and the Sarvastivadins and Mahisasakas with the Jetavana.

(8) KNOX, ROBERT. "An Historical Relation of Ceylon." The Ceylon Historical Journal, 6 (1956-1957), 459 pp. (Originally published Glasgow: J. MacLehose, 1911.)

Originally published in 1681, this was the first book in English on Ceylon and remains an important source of information about the culture and religion in Kandy in the seventeenth century. The author was marooned on the island and captured by the Sinhalese and held in Kandy for twenty years, during which time he became thoroughly familiar with the language, people and culture of the court and the capital. The book is his sensitive, observant and fascinating account, which he published after his "miraculous escape" (the Portuguese were of more trouble to him than the Sinhalese). For an abridged version of the work, see E. F. C. Ludowyk, Robert Knox in the Kandyan Kingdom (Oxford University Press, 1948).

(9) LAW, BIMALA CHURN. The Life and Work of Buddhaghosa. See 8.9.1(25).

(10) LIYANAGAMAGE, AMARADASA. The Decline of Polonnaruwa and the Rise of Dambadeniya (circa 1180-1270 A.D.). Colombo: Department of Cultural Affairs, 1968, 213 pp.

For advanced students. An important monograph dealing with a period in Ceylonese history that is relatively unstudied by Western scholars. Has an excellent chapter on the source material for this period, followed by an examination of the disintegration of the Polonnaruwa kingdom and the foundation of the kingdom at Dambadeniya, with special attention given to Vijayabahu III. The last two chapters discuss the reign of Parakramabahu II, the policies of the Tamil invader Magha, and the several Pandya invasions during this period.

(11) LUDOWYK, EVELYN FREDRICK CHARLES. The Footprint of the Buddha. London: Allen and Unwin, 1958, 182 pp.

A beautifully written book presenting through its focus on Sinhalese art and architecture the coming of Buddhism to Ceylon in the third century B.C., its establishment first at Anuradhapura, and its later forms during the Polonnaruwa period. The Sigiriya story is told as well. The narrative is written in a manner making it suitable for both beginner and more advanced student. It is probably one of the more satisfactory introductions to the understanding of Buddhism's interrelationships with the social, political and cultural world of ancient Ceylon.

(12) MALALASEKERA, GEORGE PEIRIS. The Pali Literature of Ceylon. See 3.1.2(7).

(13) MALALGODA, KITSIRI. Buddhism in Sinhalese Society: 1750-1900. Berkeley: University of California Press, 1976, 313 pp.

A study of the fundamental changes that swept through Ceylon during its years of colonization. The author examines the condition of the monastic community during the impact and the evolving phenomenon of "Protestant Buddhism." Highly recommended.

(14) PANDITA, VINCENT. "Buddhism during the Polonnaruwa Period." Ceylon Historical Journal, 4 (1954-1955), 113-129.

A succinct survey of the history of Buddhism in Ceylon from 985-1186 A.D., focusing specifically on the state of the religion during the last phases of the Anuradhapura period and then, in Polonnaruwa, under the reigns of Vijayabahu I (1056-1111) and of the great reformer Parakramabahu I (1153-1186). The article is part of a special number of the journal devoted to the Polonnaruwa period. Also of interest in the same volume are the articles by A. L. Basham, "The Background to the Rise of Parakramabahu I" (pp. 10-22), and B. C. Law, "The Life of King Parakrama Bahu I" (pp. 23-32).

(15) PARANAVITANA, SENARAT. "New Light on the Buddhist Era in Ceylon and Early Sinhalese Chronology." University of Ceylon Review, 18, nos. 3 and 4 (July-October 1960), 129-155.

Paranavitana's article is about the discovery of an inscription which has allowed for a more definitive dating of specific kings' reigns. The article also is concerned with the evidence of dates which can be gleaned from traditional literature in Ceylon. Probably of interest only to the specialist.

(16) _____. "The Religious Intercourse between Ceylon and Siam in the Thirteenth to Fifteenth Centuries." Journal of the Royal Asiatic Society (Ceylon Branch), 32 (1932), 190-212.

The sending of religious missions from one Theravada country to another, generally in order to restore the higher ordination in the country where it had lapsed, represented important landmarks in the Buddhist histories of the various countries. In this article, Paranavitana reviews the exchange of missions between Thailand and Ceylon. For more details, see the annotation of P. E. E. Fernando's article (above).

(17) _____. The Story of Sigiri. Colombo: Lake House Investments, 1972, 153 and 127 pp. (Includes romanized Sanskrit text of Ananda Sthavira's research accounts.)

Translation and commentary of documents in Sanskrit, supposedly prepared by a historian and archaeologist Vajracarya monk named Buddhamitra of Suvarnnapura (Palembana) who spent several years in Ceylon during the reign of Parakramabahu VI (1412-1467) and who received ordination as a member of the Theravada Nikaya while in Ceylon. These documents deal with the reigns of Dhatusena and his sons Kassapa and Moggallana in the fifth and early sixth centuries, centering on the story of the famous Sigiriya rock fortress. These documents tell a fascinating story, but their authenticity has been seriously challenged by several scholars. In any case, they are of interest mainly for the specialist.

1.3.2.2 After 1815

See also under Buddhism and Politics, 6.2.2.2.

(1) Buddhist Committee of Inquiry. The Betrayal of Buddhism: An Abridged Version. Balangoda: Dharmavijaya, 1956, 124 pp. ("The full report is printed in Sinhalese.")

An abridged version of the famous Report of the Buddhist Committee of Inquiry, which in 1956--a year when Buddhist-Sinhalese Nationalism was heightened by the Buddha Jayanti celebrations--reviewed what had happened to Buddhism under British colonial rule and recommended that certain steps be taken by the government to restore Buddhism to its "proper position." This is an important document which is basic to any understanding of Ceylonese Buddhism since independence.

(2) DE SILVA, K. M. "Buddhism and the British Government in Ceylon." Ceylon Historical Journal, 10 (1960-1961), 91-160.

A substantial study of a crucial period in the modern history of Buddhism in Ceylon. During these years (1840-1855), under pressure from Christian evangelical forces at home, the British gradually reneged on the famous Kandyan Convention of 1815, in which they agreed to protect and maintain "the religion of Buddhoo," and thereby left the Buddhist monasteries without any of the customary state support. A shorter study of the same events may be found in Hans-Dieter Evers, "Buddhism and British Colonial Policy in Ceylon, 1815-1875," Asian Studies (Philippines), 2 (1964), 323-333.

(3) DHARMAPALA, ANAGARIKA. Return to Righteousness: A Collection of Speeches, Essays and Letters of the Anagarika Dharmapala. Edited by Ananda Guruge. Colombo, Ceylon: Anagarika Dharmapala Birth Centenary Committee, Ministry of Education and Cultural Affairs, 1965, 875 pp.

A massive collection of speeches, essays and letters by the great late nineteenth century and early twentieth century reformer, the Anagarika Dharmapala, who was the founder of the Maha Bodhi Society and instrumental in the revival of Buddhism in Ceylon at the turn of the century. The writings provide a good primary source on Buddhism in the modern period.

(4) GOKHALE, B. G. "Anagarika Dharmapala: Toward Modernity through Tradition in Ceylon," in Tradition and Change in Theravada Buddhism (see 6.2.1.1[40], pp. 30-39).

(5) SMITH, DONALD EUGENE, ed. South Asian Politics and Religion (see 6.2.4[11]) Part IV, pp. 451-546.

This section is entitled "Ceylon: The Politics of Buddhist Resurgence" and makes a find introduction to the fortunes of some Buddhists in Ceylon during the 1950's and 1960's. It contains two articles by Donald Smith, "The Sinhalese Buddhist Revolution" (pp. 453-488) and "The Political Monks and Monastic Reform" (pp. 489-509), one by A. Jeyaratnam Wilson, "Buddhism in Ceylon Politics, 1960-1965" (pp. 510-530), and one by C. D. S. Siriwardane, "Buddhist Reorganization in Ceylon" (pp. 531-546). Together they make an important and informative collection of essays.

(6) SWEARER, DONALD. "Lay Buddhism and the Buddhist Revival in Ceylon." See 6.1.2(20).

(7) VIJAYAVARDHANA, D. C. The Revolt in the Temple, Composed to Commemorate 2500 Years of The Land, the Race and the Faith. Colombo, Ceylon: Sinha Publications, 1953, 700 pp.

An important manifesto for Buddhist reform and renewal which appeared at a crucial time in the modern history of Ceylonese Buddhism. Attempts to interpret the Buddha's message in light of modern thought, science and socialism.

(8) VIMALAPANDA, TENNAKOON. The State and Religion in Ceylon since 1815. See 6.2.2.2(16).

(9) WEERAMANTRY, LUCIAN G. Assassination of a Prime Minister. Geneva: Studer, 1969, 312 pp.

Full account of the events leading up to the assassination of Prime Minister S. W. R. D. Bandaranaike by a Buddhist monk in the early 1960's, and the immediate aftermath of that event, which was of crucial importance in the history of modern Buddho-Sinhal nationalism.

(10) WICKREMERATNE. L. A. "Religion, Nationalism, and Social Change in Ceylon, 1865-1885." See 6.2.1.1(50).

1.4 BURMA

1.4.1 Historical Surveys and Introductions

(1) APPLETON, G. Buddhism in Burma. Burma Pamphlets, No. 3. Calcutta: Longmans, Green, 1943, 49 pp.

A short, often sketchy, and not very scholarly introduction which does, however, manage to outline the main features and history of the subject. In much the same vein, but of lesser quality, and with an emphasis on Christian-Buddhist dialogue is a pamphlet entitled Buddhism in Burma, edited by G. P. Charles (Rangoon: Commission on Buddhism of the Burma Christian Council, 1955), 70 pp.

(2) COEDES, GEORGES. The Making of South East Asia. Translated by H. M. Wright. Berkeley: University of California Press; London: Routledge and Kegan Paul, 1966, pp. 68-70, 110-117, 181-192. (Originally published as Les peuples de la péninsule indochinoise [Paris: Dunod, 1962].)

Much information on the history of Burmese Buddhism can be gleaned from more general histories of Burma and Southeast Asia. These sections in Coedes's classic form one of the most concise introductions to the history of Burma viewed in the context of Southeast Asia as a whole. For more details, but only up until the early sixteenth century, see the relevant sections of Coedes, The Indianized States of Southeast Asia (1.8.1[2]). For the period after 1500, see the appropriate chapters in D. G. E. Hall, A History of South East Asia (3rd edition New York: St. Martins, 1968). A good, standard, overall history of Burma up until the British conquest is G. E. Harvey, History of Burma (London: F. Cass, 1967; originally published by Longmans Green, o925). For the modern period, see John Cady, A History of Modern Burma (Ithaca: Cornell University Press, 1958).

(3) Hmannan maha yazawintawkyi: The Glass Palace Chronicle of the Kings of Burma. Translated by Pe Maung Tin and G. H. Luce. London, Oxford: H. Milford, 1923, 179 pp.

Early in the nineteenth century, at the request of the king of Burma, a committee of "learned monks, brahmins and ministers" wrote a complete history of the kings of Burma based on all the "credible records" then available. Only a portion of this "Glass Palace Chronicle" has here been translated into English. The early section on Buddhism in India has been omitted, and the translation ends with the fall of Pagan. Still, it remains one of the few works in English in which the Western scholar can gain some idea of the contents of the many various ancient Burmese chronicles on which it is based.

(4) HTIN AUNG, MAUNG. Burmese History before 1287: A Defence of the Chronicles. Oxford: Asoka Society, 1970, 10 + 46 pp.

An attack on the theories of G. H. Luce and a defence of the chronicles insisting that they are historical writings. Chapters in the book cover the "Coming of the Burmese," "Buddhism in Thaton," and a comparison of the lists of kings of Pagan according to the Chronicles and according to the inscriptions compiled by G. H. Luce.

(5) PANNASAMI. The History of the Buddha's Religion (Sasanavamsa). Translated by Bimala Churn Law. Sacred Books of the Buddhists, No. 17. London: Luzac, 1952, 174 pp.

The Sasanavamsa was written in 1861 by an eminent Burmese monk named Pannasami. It was done in the traditional style: like other works of its kind, it begins by dealing, briefly, with the life of the Buddha and the first three Buddhist councils. But its main concern is in tracing the history of the Buddhist religion in Burma--which it does from the time of the Asokan missionaries up to ca. 1850. It thus does for Burma what the Mahavamsa and Culavamsa do for Sri Lanka.

(6) RAY, NIHARRANJAN. An Introduction to the Study of Theravada Buddhism in Burma. Calcutta: University of Calcutta, 1946, 306 pp.

A good standard history of Burmese Buddhism. As its title implies, the focus is primarily on the period from Anawrata and the introduction of Theravada in Pagan in 1057 to the British conquest in the nineteenth century, but some attention is also paid to the early period ("From the alleged Asoka-Mission to the fall of Thaton"). When taken together with Ray's Sanskrit Buddhism in Burma (below), this book forms a good overall study of the subject.

(7) _____. Sanskrit Buddhism in Burma. Amsterdam: H. J. Paris, 1936, 101 pp.

Following up Charles Duroiselle's pioneering article in this field ("The Ari of Burma and Tantric Buddhism," Annual Report of the Archaeological Survey of India [1915-1916], 79-93), Ray tackles the important question of the history of "Sanskrit"--i.e., non-Theravadan--Buddhism in Burma.

1.4.2 Specialized Historical Studies

(1) BA U. My Burma: The Autobiography of a President. New York: Taplinger, 1959, 206 pp.

Although the first half of this book pertains to Ba U's upbringing, the second half contains the perspective of a Western educated elite government worker on the significance of the rebellions of the 1930's, the Japanese occupation, and the final struggles for Burmese independence. Particularly worthwhile is the noting of this western-educated man's considerations of Buddhist contributions to Burma's independence and formation of government.

(2) BUTWELL, RICHARD A. U Nu of Burma. Stanford, Calif.: Stanford University Press, 1963, 301 pp.

This is a biographical study of the man who led the dominant forces towards Burmese independence. There may not be a better source for tracing the intellectual development of the Burmese intelligentsia from the 1930's until 1962. The author has superbly described U Nu's own flirtation with a Buddhist-socialist synthesis. Recommended for both the beginning and the advanced student. For another view of the earlier period of Revolutionary development, see U Maung Maung, Aung San of Burma (The Hague: M. Nijhoff, 1962), 162 pp.

(3) COCHRANE, WILBUR. "Shans and Buddhism of the Northern Canon." Journal of the Royal Asiatic Society (1912), pp. 487-495.

A brief article in which the author takes issue with George Scott by contending that the Shans were probably not introduced to Buddhism by Mahayana followers. Refuting Scott's evidence that this may have been the case, Cochrane argues to the contrary that Buddhism was first introduced via Hinayana adherents to the south. For a rebuttal, see Scott (1.4.2[16]), pp. 496-499.

(4) COLLIS, MAURICE. The Land of the Great Image. New York: A. A. Knopf, 1943, 264 pp.

This discusses Arakan diplomatic and social developments on the basis of the experience of Friar Manrique, who travelled widely through the area in the sixteenth and seventeenth centuries. What is of significance here is that the student can find materials as to how Portuguese pirates were a factor in the defence of Arakan borders from Muslim invaders. Also, Collis recounts how the tooth relic was destroyed in Bombay harbor by the Portuguese. The student is also treated to a description of a Buddhist king's coronation.

(5) CRAWFORD, JOHN. Journal of an Embassy from the Governor General of India to the Court of Ava. Second edition. London: H. Colburn, 1834, 2 vols.

This is the account of a British envoy's journey to secure an agreement with the King of Burma on behalf of British administrators of India. The account is largely a description of the customs and countryside of Burma in the early nineteenth century before the British brought it under colonial control in 1825. Particularly of interest to the student of Buddhism are the chapters which describe the court of the king, monastic life, and the temples in various urban and rural locales.

(6) CROSTHWAITE, CHARLES HAUKES TODD. The Pacification of Burma. London: E. Arnold, 1912, 355 pp.

Crosthwaite's account is concerned with the measures taken to "stabilize" Burma in the three years immediately after its subjugation by the British (Upper Burma was brought under British control in 1885-1886, so the period referred to is 1887 to 1890). Hence, the reader is rewarded with glimpses of the Buddhist as well as governmental state of affairs during this period. Readable and recommended for any student.

(7) FERGUSON, JOHN. "The Quest for Legitimation by Burmese Monks and Kings: The Case Study of the Shwegyin Sect," in Religion and Political Legitimation in Southeast Asia. Edited by Bardwell Smith. Chambersburg: Wilson Books, 1977.

(8) LINGAT, ROBERT. "Evolution of the Conception of Law in Burma and Siam." See 1.5.2(15).

(9) LUCE, G. H. "The Advent of Buddhism to Burma," in *Buddhist Studies in Honour of I. B. Horner* (see 1.2.2.4[11]), pp. 119-138.

A review of the various problems concerned with this question of the introduction of Buddhism to Burma, and a concise statement of Luce's position, which, however, is not going unchallenged by Burmese and other scholars.

(10) _____. "The Ancient Pyu." *Journal of the Burmese Research Society*, 27 (1937), 239-253.

Luce attempts to describe the ancient culture of the Pyu kingdom (ca. 250-1000 A.D.). His description of the religion of the Pyus takes into account Vaishnavism, Mahayanist tendencies, and Theravadan influence, on the basis of archeological remains. But on the basis of Chinese sources, Luce reconstructs the religious (solidly Hinayana) life, the character of dress, musical instruments, and currency of the Pyu period from 700 A.D. to past the year 1000.

(11) _____. "Burma's Debt to Pagan." *Journal of the Burma Research Society*, 22 (1932), 120-127.

This article may well be a suitable place to begin a study of the Pagan period in Burmese history. Luce has simply described the aspects of Pagan Buddhism and the type of economy which prevailed during the period while using the inscriptions as his source of data.

(12) _____. *Old Burma: Early Pagan*. Artibus Asiae, Supplementum, No. 25. New York: J. J. Augustin, 1969-1970, 3 vols.

Excellent presentation of the iconography and inscriptions of Pagan. Luce provides a fluid text to accompany the large number of plates which illustrate scenes from the Buddha's life, symbols, and various postures. Luce is careful throughout to observe the Brahmanical, Mahayanist and Tantric influences. Of use to the student of any level.

(13) MENDELSON, E. MICHAEL. *Sangha and State in Burma: A Study of Monastic Sectarianism and Leadership*. Edited by John Ferguson. Ithaca, N.Y.: Cornell University Press, 1975, 400 pp.

(14) SANGERMANO, VICENTIUS. *A Description of the Burmese Empire, Compiled Chiefly from Burmese Documents*. Translated by William Tandy. Fifth edition. London: Susil Gupta, 1966, 311 pp.

An early and dated, yet valuable general description of Burmese life in the eighteenth century. Included are excellent descriptions of the king and his court, of contemporary manners and customs, of Burmese notions of time and geography, and of the general state of Buddhism during the period.

(15) SARKISYANZ, EMANUAL. *Buddhist Backgrounds of the Burmese Revolution*. The Hague: M. Nijhoff, 1965, 248 pp.

Sarkisyanz traces the political and economic history of Burma in terms of the Buddhist contribution to these two institutions. Hence, the work remains more of an intellectual history of Burmese Buddhism than of anything else. The work is well-done, scholarly, and highly recommended for all students. For another worthwhile source which seeks to establish the significance of Buddhism and Burmese polity, see Donald Eugene Smith, *Religion and Politics in Burma* (Princeton: Princeton University Press, 1965), 350 pp.

(16) SCOTT, JAMES GEORGE. "Buddhism in the Shan States." *Journal of the Royal Asiatic Society* (1911), pp. 917-934; and (1912), p. 496.

A good history of Shan interaction with the other peoples of the area (Thai, Tibetan, etc.). The crux of the article, however, is that Mahayana Buddhism was first introduced to the Shans around the period of Kublai Khan's rule (1250 A.D.) and that this contact with Buddhism constituted the Shans' first consideration of Buddhism.

(17) _____. *The Burman: His Life and Notions*. Third edition. London: Macmillan, 1910, 609 pp. (Originally published 1882).

Although this book is not specifically "historical" in nature, it does attempt to give the reader an overview of everyday Burmese life. The author (who used the pseudonym "Shway Yoe") deftly sketches the typical stages in the life of a Burman from birth to death, providing separate chapters concerning life in the monastery, marriage, tattooing, etc. Also included are chapters on pagodas, images, the Sangha, social customs, the national character and the judicial system. The account is thoroughly concerned with traditional, pre-British Burma and is recommended to any student of Burma and Burmese Buddhism.

(18) STERN, THEODORE. "Ariya and the Golden Book: A Millenarian Buddhist Sect Among the Karen." *Journal of Asian Studies*, 27 (1968), 297-328.

The author compares two millenial movements among the Karen in Burma, one inspired by Buddhist factors and the other motivated by factors present in the indigenous primitive religion. Involved in both millenial movements were American Protestant missionaries who served more or less as catalysts to the events of both movements. The author seeks to examine those specific conditions which in one instance encouraged the attainment of Western goods and styles of life while in the other instance inhibited such an attainment.

(19) TIN, PE MAUNG. "Buddhism in the Inscriptions at Pagan." *Journal of the Burma Research Society*, 26 (1936), 52-70.

This article should be of use to the intermediate and advanced student. Tin attempts a total characterization of Buddhism as it was practiced in the time of Anoratha by ferreting out the significance of key inscriptions preserved. His general conclusion is that although Anoratha is credited with bringing "pure Buddhism" from Thaton, there did remain elements of Vaishnavism during this "golden period." For a study of the character of Buddhism in Burma before Anoratha, *see* Charles Duroiselle, "The Ari of Burma and Tantric Buddhism," *Annual Report of the Archaeological Survey of India (1915-1916)*, pp. 79-93.

1.5 THAILAND

1.5.1 Historical Surveys and Introductions

(1) *Annales du Siam*. Translated by Camille Notton. Paris: C. Lavauzelle, 1926-1939, 4 vols.

Annotated translations of a series of classic historical chronicles from Northern Thai into French. Of interest to the specialist, the work is filled with legendary, historical and mythical accounts, many of them dealing with the foundation of Northern Thai cities. Volume 1 contains the chronicles of Suvanna Khamdeng, of the Mahathera Fa Bot, and of Suvanna Knom Kham. Volume 2 contains a translation of the chronicle of the city of Lamphun. A different account of the history of this important town may be found in Georges Coedes's translation of the *Camadevivamsa* in *Bulletin de l'Ecole française d'Extrême-Orient*, 25 (1925). Volume 3 of the *Annales* contains the chronicle of the city of Chieng Mai, and Volume 4 a set of legends on Siam and Cambodia.

(2) BURIBHAND, LUANG BORIBAL. "Buddhism in Thailand," in *In Commemoration of the Year 2500, Buddhist Era, in Thailand*. Bangkok: C. Wanthanathavi, 1957, pp. 5-21.

A sketch of the history of Buddhism in Thailand, which is especially valuable as an introduction to the four successive layers or spreads of Buddhism into Thailand: as Hinayana, as Mahayana, as Pagan-Hinayana, and as Sinhalese-Hinayana.

(3) COEDES, GEORGES. *The Making of South East Asia* (see 1.4.1[2]), pp. 139-171.

Much information on the context and history of Buddhism in Thailand may be found in the more general histories of Southeast Asia and of Thailand. These pages in Coedes's work treat concisely the history of Thailand. For further details, *see also* the appropriate chapters in Coedes's *The Indianized States of Southeast Asia* (1.8.1[2]); D. G. E. Hall, *A History of South-East Asia* (3rd edition, 1968); or Reginald LeMay, *The Culture of South-East Asia* (London: Allen & Unwin, 1954). A standard history of Thailand (from the earliest beginnings up to and beyond 1781) is William Wood, *A History of Siam* (Revised edition Bangkok: Central Book Depot, 1933), 300 pp. Also, of mixed quality but helpful, are Volumes 3 and 4 of the articles reprinted in *Selected Articles from the Siam Society Journal* (Bangkok: Siam Society, 1959), 13 vols.

(4) ELIOT, CHARLES NORTON EDGECUMBE. *Hinduism and Buddhism: An Historical Sketch* (see 1.1[4]), pp. 78-99.

This chapter, dealing with "Siam" is probably still the most readily available basic introduction to the history of Thai Buddhism in English. It is concise, well-written and includes somewhat dated bibliographic suggestions.

(5) GARD, RICHARD. *The Role of Thailand in World Buddhism*. WFB Books Series, No. 37. Bangkok: World Fellowship of Buddhists, 1971, pp. 1-24.

A brief resume of the study and practice of Buddhism in Thailand today. This article or portion of the book represents an excellent point of departure for any student interested in the general topic of Buddhism in Thailand as the author is known for his bibliographic specialty.

(6) KUSALASAYA, KARUNA. "Buddhism in Siam," in *Présence du Bouddhisme*. Edited by René de Berval. Saigon, 1959, pp. 907-911. (Special No. of *France-Asie*, 16, nos. 153-157 [Feb.-June 1959].)

A sketch of the four "periods" of Buddhism in Thailand: the first period of Hinayana at Nakon Pathom, the second period of Mahayana from Burma and from the South, the third period of Burmese Hinayana in the time of King Anawratha, and the fourth period of Ceylon Buddhism during the twelfth century. A less historical analysis by the same author, dealing with Thai Buddhism past and present, is "Buddhism in Thailand," in *The Wheel*, publication 85-86 (Kandy: Buddhist Publication Society, 1965), 30 pp. *See also* his article "Buddhism: Its Past and Present in Thailand," *Indo-Asian Culture*, 12 (1963), 90-113.

(7) TAMBIAH, STANLEY J. *World Conqueror and World Renouncer*. New York: Cambridge University Press, 1976, 557 pp.

(8) WARD, WILLIAM ALFRED RAE. *A History of Siam*. Revised edition. Bangkok: Central Book Depot, 1933, 300 pp. (Originally published London: T. F. Unwin, 1926.)

A dated, early attempt to write the political and diplomatic history of Siam. Wood lacked the data which is now available concerning Dvarati and other periods of Siamese history. Nevertheless, because his treatment relies upon traditional sources, it remains a useful tool.

(9) WELLS, KENNETH ELMER. Thai Buddhism: Its Rites and Activities. Bangkok: The Christian Bookstore, 1960, 320 pp.

The work is an important source of information on the practices and rituals of Buddhists in Thailand, and has become a standard reference in this field. However, it touches only very incidentally on the history of Buddhism in Thailand (see the "Introduction," pp. iii-viii).

1.5.2 Specialized Historical Studies

(1) AKIN RABIBHADANA. The Organization of Thai Society in the Early Bangkok Period, 1782-1873. Cornell Thailand Project, Interim reports series, No. 12. Cornell University Southeast Asia Program, Data Paper No. 74. Ithaca: Southeast Asia Program, Cornell University, 1969, 247 pp.

This is a study of the social patterns and changes in Thai society before the far-reaching reforms of the late nineteenth century. The study is divided into three parts: 1) a review of the antecedents and history of the social order before the Bangkok period; 2) a description of the social order during the Bangkok period; and 3) an analysis of the process of development and change during this period.

(2) ANUMAN RAJATHON, PHRAYA. Life and Ritual in Old Siam: Three Studies of Thai Life and Customs. Translated and edited by William J. Gedney. New Haven: Human Relations Area File Press, 1961, pp. 65-98.

These pages represent an easily readable account of the role of the "wat," the significance of ordination into the Sangha, and the daily regimen of monastic life in traditional Thai society. The author has also reviewed the major Buddhist feasts and festivals that are still celebrated in contemporary Thailand.

(3) BOCK, CARL. Temples and Elephants: The Narrative of a Journey of Exploration Through Upper Siam and Laos. London: Sampson Low, Marston, Searle and Rivington, 1884, 438 pp.

A dated travel log of an Englishman's trip through Northern Siam and Laos in the 1880's. The extremely detailed table of contents enables the student to pick out the relevant sections pertaining to observations of Buddhist practices and temples as the author encountered them.

(4) BRIGGS, LAWRENCE PALMER. "Dvaravati, The Most Ancient Kingdom of Siam." Journal of the American Oriental Society, 65 (1945), 98-107.

A convenient and concise summary of our knowledge of the culture of the ancient kingdom of Dvaravati, in what eventually became the territory of Thailand. A shorter and earlier discussion of the topic is H. G. Quaritch Wales, "Some Notes on the Kingdrom of Dvaravati," Journal of the Greater India Society, 5 (1938), 24-30.

(5) CHULA, [PRINCE]. Lords of Life: The Paternal Monarchy of Bangkok, 1782-1932, with the Earlier and More Recent History of Thailand. New York: Taplinger; London: Alvin Redman, 1960, 352 pp.

Pages 16-69 attempt a history of Siam from ca. 4000 B.C. to 1767 A.D. which includes an account of the introduction of Buddhism into Siam. The rest of the book is a chapter by chapter account of the royal line of Thai kingship from 1782 to 1932, noting the characteristics and achievements of each of the monarchs. The reader may glean bits of information concerning the status of Buddhism during each of these reigns.

(6) Chulalongkorn the Great: A Volume of Readings. Edited and translated by Prachoom Chomchai. East Asian Cultural Studies Series, No. 8. Tokyo: Centre for East Asian Cultural Studies, 1965, 167 pp.

Basically a biography drawn from Prince Damrong's Chronicle on Rama V's Reign and other texts in Thai, this work provides the student with a "bare bones" account of the sweeping educational, political, economic, and religious reforms carried out under Chulalongkorn in the late decades of the nineteenth century.

(7) COEDES, GEORGES. "Une recension palie des Annales d'Ayuthya." Bulletin de l'Ecole française d'Extrême-Orient, 14 (1914), 1-31.

Coedes has here edited and translated the seventh chapter of the Sangitivamsa, a work written in Pali in 1789 by a monk named Vimaladhamma. The chapter translated deals with the history of the thirty-six (or thirty-three) Buddhist kings of Ayuthya, the Thai capital until 1767.

(8) DAMRONG RAJANUBHAB [PRINCE]. A History of Buddhist Monuments in Siam. Translated by S. Sivaraksa. Siam Society Monograph, No. 2. Bangkok: Siam Society, 1962, 52 pp.

This is an excellent, though dated, study of the introduction and further development of Buddhist scriptures, stupas and images in Siam. The specific study of these elements leads to a broader history of Buddhism in Siam for the intermediate and advanced student.

(9) GERVAISE, NICOLAS. The Natural and Political History of the Kingdom of Siam. Translated by H. S. O'Neill. Bangkok: The "Siam Observer" Press, 1928, 150 pp.

This work, originally written in 1688, represents the first attempt by a westerner to write a history of Siam. The book is divided into three parts describing the geography, religious life, and political history of Siam. Although the work as a whole is restricted by its impressionistic style, the student can still garner valuable information concerning monastic education, special privileges accorded to monks at that time, funeral ceremonies, pagodas, and nuns.

(10) GRISWOLD, ALEXANDER B. King Mongkut of Siam. New York: Asia Society, 1961, 60 pp.
This short work is a treatment of the life and reforms of King Mongkut (1851-1868). The reader should weigh the author's tenuous contention that Mongkut sought to "purify" Buddhism of animistic accretions which were considered "superstitious." Nevertheless, Griswold's work and that of Abbot Moffat, Mongkut, King of Siam (Ithaca: Cornell University Press, 1961) go a long way in dispelling the grotesque and popular image of Mongkut portrayed in Anna and the King of Siam and "The King and I."

(11) _____. Towards a History of Sukhodaya Art. Bangkok: National Museum, 1967, 68 pp.
Though focusing, as its title states, on artistic developments, this work at the same time provides perhaps the best single, short, overview of the history of the Sukhothai kingdom. It is especially important to the specialist for its reevaluation of the role of King Li-t'ai.

(12) LA LOUBERE, SIMON DE. The Kingdom of Siam. Introduction by David K. Wyatt. Oxford in Asia historical reprints. Kuala Lumpur: Oxford University, 1969, 260 pp. (Facsimile of the London edition of 1693.)
Reprint of a translation of a first hand account of Siam in the seventeenth century. La Loubere was an envoy of the French King Louis XIV and originally visited Siam in 1687-88, publishing his account in 1691. It is very interesting to compare what he has to say about Buddhism and Thailand, with the account of Robert Knox, who ten years earlier published his account of twenty years of living stranded in the Kandyan kingdom in Sri Lanka (see 1.3.2.1[8]).

(13) LE MAY, REGINALD. An Asian Arcady: The Land and People of Northern Siam. Cambridge: W. Heffer and Sons, 1926, pp. 1-38 and 123-143.
This book is a rather general and dated attempt to describe the history and culture of the peoples of Northern Thailand. Pages 1-38 recount the political history of Siam (northern) while pages 123-143 contain early relations between Christian missionaries and Buddhists, the story of how Sinhalese Buddhism found its way to Northern Siam, and a cursory description through anecdotes of how Buddhism and animism were practiced in everyday rural life in the early twentieth century.

(14) LINGAT, ROBERT. "La double crise de l'Eglise Bouddhique au Siam, 1767-1851." Cahiers d'Histoire Mondiale, 4 (1958), 402-425.
A summary and analysis of some of the problems faced by and development of Thai Buddhism during the period between the destruction of the old capital of Ayuthia, and the accession of the reformer king Mongkut. Excellent as a background to the modern history of Buddhism in Thailand.

(15) _____. "Evolution of the Conception of Law in Burma and Siam." Journal of the Siam Society, 38, pt. 1 (January 1950), 9-31.
Lingat historically traces the importation of the notion of "dharma" and the "code of Manu" into Burma and Siam taking into account improvisations which resulted in accommodation.

(16) _____. "La vie religieuse du roi Mongkut." Journal of the Siam Society, 20, no. 2 (October 1926), 129-148. (Reprinted in The Siam Society Fiftieth Anniversary Commemorative Publication, 1 [1954], 18-37.)
After sketching the tremendous political and diplomatic advancements completed by King Mongkut and placing him within a proper perspective in Thai history, Lingat proceeds to trace the religious career of the king from his days as a monk to the days of his kingship.

(17) LORGEOU, M. E. "Notice sur un manuscrit siamois contenant la relation de deux missions religieuses envoyées de Siam à Ceylan au milieu du xviii-e siècle." Journal asiatique, 8 (1906), 533-548.
An account of the voyage of the two missions of Siamese monks sent to Ceylon in 1753 and 1755, to restore the higher ordination on that island. For a Ceylonese account of the event, see P. E. E. Fernando, 1.3.2.1(5).

(18) PARANAVITANA, SENARAT. "The Religious Intercourse between Ceylon and Siam in the Thirteenth to Fifteenth Centuries." See 1.3.2.1(16).

(19) RATANAPANYA, THERA. The Sheaf of Garlands of the Epochs of the Conqueror: Being a translation of Jinakalamalipakaranam . . . by N. A. Jayawickrama. Pali Text Society Translation Series, No. 36. London: Published for the Pali Text Society by Luzac, 1968, 235 pp.
The Jinakalamali was written by Ratapanya Thera around 1516 and is an important source of information about the political and religious history of Buddhism in Southeast Asia. As is usual for works of its kind, it starts with a rapid account of the life of the Buddha and the first three Councils. This is followed by a short history of Buddhism in Ceylon, and then by more detailed accounts of the history of Haripunjaya (Lampoon) and Nabbisi (Chiengmai) in Northern Thailand and of the Sinhalese form of Buddhism which was associated with those two centers.

(20) REYNOLDS, FRANK. "The Holy Emerald Jewel: Some Aspects of Buddhist Symbolism and Political Legitimation in Thailand and Laos," in Religion and Political Legitimation, ed. Bardwell Smith (see 1.4.2[7]).

(21) SKINNER, G. WILLIAM and A. THOMAS KIRSCH, eds. Change and Persistence in Thai Society. Ithaca, N.Y.: Cornell University Press, 1975, 386 pp.

A collection of eleven essays focusing upon political, economic and social changes which have taken place in the history of Thailand from the thirteenth century to the present.

(22) SWEARER, DONALD. "Thai Buddhism: Two Responses to Modernity," in Tradition and Change in Theravada Buddhism (see 8.9.5[1]), pp. 78-93.

The two responses to modernity which the author refers to in his title concern two individuals, Buddhadassa and Dhiravamsa. The author first examines the life and work of Buddhadassa and concludes that the figure represents an unusual combination of the archaic and modern Buddhist elements and consequently is seen as an innovator and religious genius. Concluding that Buddhadassa represents the Buddhist reformer, the author goes on to examine the work of Dhiravamsa, a lay meditation teacher in Surrey, England, who has transformed the idiom of Buddhist doctrine into a different mode so that the truth of Buddhism can be appreciated by a Western audience. The author concludes by comparing these two figures using the theoretical work of Bellah.

(23) _____. Wat Haripunjaya. Missoula: Scholars Press, 1976, 94 pp.

(24) "Symposium on Buddhism and Society in Thailand." Journal of Asian Studies, 36, no. 2 (February 1977), 239-326.

This symposium includes articles by Thomas Kirsch on the complexity of Thai religion, by Frank Reynolds on the development of Thai "civic religion," by Charles Keyes on millenarian movements in Thailand, and by Stephen Tobias on the role of Buddhism in Thai-Chinese ethnic relations in a contemporary Thai city. The four articles provide excellent examples of some of the different approaches presently being taken to the study of Thai religion in general and Thai Buddhism in particular; and in so doing they include discussions of historical development and contemporary patterns.

(25) WALES, H. G. QUARITCH. Dvaravati: The Earliest Kingdom of Siam. London: B. Quaritch, 1969, 149 pp.

For the intermediate and advanced student. Wales attempts to give a synthesized statement from the various archeological finds which have been made in the last twenty or thirty years concerning Dvaravati. He discusses historical patterns of migration, artistic influence, the character of Buddhism in the Dvaravati period, and the significance of archeological artifacts. For another of Wales's articles germane to this topic, see "An Early Buddhist Civilization in Eastern Siam," Journal of the Siam Society, 45 (1975), 42-60.

(26) WILSON, DAVID A. Politics in Thailand. Ithaca, N.Y.: Cornell University Press, 1962, 307 pp.

This is a general introductory work, of use to the beginning student. Particularly helpful are the first 110 pages, which deal primarily with the historical background of Thai politics, including discussions of Buddhism's basic influence upon the economic and social structures and an adequate treatment of the relationship between authority and kingship.

1.6   CAMBODIA

1.6.1 Historical Surveys and Introductions

(1) BRIGGS, LAWRENCE PALMER. "The Syncretism of Religions in Southeast Asia, Especially in the Khmer Empire." Journal of the American Oriental Society, 71 (1951), 230-249.

A concise survey of the history of the changing religious emphases in Cambodia, mainly based on the epigraphical material. Read together with Eliot's chapter on Buddhism in Cambodia (below), it makes a fine introduction to the subject.

(2) COEDES, GEORGES. The Making of South East Asia (see 1.4.1[2]), pp. 88-109, 193-203.

Much information on the history and context of Cambodian Buddhism can be gotten out of the more general histories of Cambodia and Southeast Asia. These pages in Coedes's classic form one of the most concise introductions to the whole history of Cambodia in English. For more details, but only up until the early sixteenth century, see the relevant sections of Coedes, The Indianized States of Southeast Asia (see 1.8.1[2]). For the period after 1500, see the appropriate chapters in D. G. E. Hall, A History of South East Asia (3rd edition New York, 1968). Among the general histories of Cambodia are E. F. Aymonier, Le Cambodge (Paris: E. Leroux, 1900-1904), 3 vols., and Georges Maspero, L'empire Khmer (Phnom Penh: 1904), which is especially valid on the Angkor period. In English, perhaps the best rapid introduction to Cambodian history as a whole is Lawrence Palmer Briggs, "A Sketch of Cambodian History," Far Eastern Quarterly, 6 (1947), 345-363.

(3) ELIOT, CHARLES NORTON EDGECUMBE. Hinduism and Buddhism: An Historical Sketch (see 1.1[4]), vol. 3, pp. 100-136.

One of the very few simple, straightforward presentations of the history of Cambodian Buddhism in English. It makes a good introduction to the subject, is readily available, slightly dated but containing basic bibliographic suggestions.

(4) LECLERE, ADHEMARD. Le Buddhisme au Cambodge. Paris: E. Leroux, 1899, 535 pp.
A classic and important work, and one of the few substantial studies of Cambodian Buddhism. It mostly contains descriptions of doctrines and practices, but pages 1-34 do outline the history of Buddhism in that country. Further details of that history may be found in Leclere's more general Histoire du Cambodge depuis le 1-er siècle de notre ère (Paris: P. Geuthner, 1914).

(5) MIGOT, ANDRE. "Le Bouddhisme en Indochine." Bulletin de la Société des études indochinoises, n.s. 21 (1946), 23-38.
A succinct, scholarly survey, focusing primarily on the history of Buddhism in Cambodia and Laos. It makes a fine introduction to the subject for any student who reads French.

(6) PANG KHAT. "Le Bouddhisme au Cambodge," in Présence du Bouddhisme (see 1.5.1[6]), pp. 841-842.
A modern Cambodian monk's view of the development of Buddhism in his own country from its beginnings to the present.

(7) PRATT, JAMES BISSETT. The Pilgrimage of Buddhism and a Buddhist Pilgrimage. New York: Macmillan, 1928, pp. 188-210.
A dated though still useful introductory source for the beginning student. The author speaks in general terms about the introduction of Buddhism into Cambodia and the consequent influences which helped distinguish it from prevalent forms in other countries. The author seems especially interested in contrasting Cambodian thoughts and practices with Siamese.

(8) STEINBERG, DAVID J. et al. Cambodia: Its People, its Society, its Culture. In collaboration with Chester A. Bain et al. Revised by Herbert H. Vreeland. Survey of World Cultures. New Haven: Human Relations Area File Press, 1959, pp. 59-76.
This is perhaps the most elementary of all introductions to the topic of Cambodian Buddhism. The author discusses in the briefest manner, the character of the monks, the organization of the Sangha, the political role of Buddhism, and spirit worship and magic.

1.6.2 Specialized Historical Studies

(1) BEAUCE, THIERRY DE. "Le Cambodge: Bouddhisme et développement." Esprit, 35, 9 (September 1967), 265-279.
A general article describing the political situation in Cambodia and Southeast Asia at the time of Cambodia's independence from colonial powers. The author describes the process of how Buddhism functioned as an integrating factor and basis for the formulation of a politically neutralist position.

(2) BRIGGS, LAWRENCE PALMER. "The Khmer Empire and the Malay Peninsula." Far Eastern Quarterly, 9 (1950), 256-305.
A handy review of the historical relations of Cambodia and its neighbors to the south, including the Indian influences which came in that way. The article covers the Funan period (ca. 150-550), the Chenla period (550-802) and the Anghkor period (802-1431). A more dated discussion of Indian influences may be found in Bijan Raj Chatterji, Indian Cultural Influence in Cambodia (below), which includes a chapter specifically on "The Rise of Buddhism" (pp. 131-170).

(3) BRODRICK, ALAN HOUGHTON. Little Vehicle. New York: Hutchinson, 1949, 266 pp.
Essentially a travelogue of Brodrick's trip through Cambodia and Laos in the late 1930s. The author describes the daily life, architecture of important Buddhist sites, customs, and festivals while trying to portray contemporary life in Indochina. With many fine illustrations. Generally helpful for the modern period.

(4) CHATTERJI, BIJAN RAJ. Indian Cultural Influence in Cambodia. Second revised edition. Calcutta: University of Calcutta, 1964, 288 pp.
A sketch of Hindu influences upon Cambodian politics and literature. The author is careful to include the findings of other scholars (up until 1924) as well as his own interpretations of archeological and epigraphical findings. Of use to the student of all levels.

(5) CHOU, TA KUAN. Notes on the Customs of Cambodia. Translated from the French of Paul Pelliot by J. Gilman d'Arcy Paul. Bangkok: Social Science Association Press, 1967, 41 pp.
This work originally consisted of more than 100 chapters on almost every facet of Cambodian life. Its author was an attendant of a Chinese diplomat of the Yuan dynasty who came to Cambodia in the last years of the thirteenth century. Hence, the reader is provided with descriptions of Angkorian life from a unique perspective. The work may also be found in two other places: Paul Pelliot, "Mémoires sur les coutumes de Cambodge, par Tcheou Ta-Kouan," Bulletin de l'Ecole française d'Extrême-Orient, 2 (1902), 123-177; and Paul Pelliot, ed. and trans., Mémoires sur les coutumes du Cambodge (Paris: Librairie d'Amérique et d'Orient, 1951), 178 pp. The Paris publication is more complete and includes an extended commentary.

(6) DUPONT, PIERRE. "Etudes sur l'Indochine ancienne." Bulletin de l'Ecole française d'Extrême-Orient, 43 (1943-1946), 17-55.
On the basis of inscriptions, Dupont reconstructs the history of the transformation of Tchenla into Angkor Cambodia from the seventh to the ninth century. Recommended for the advanced student.

(7) _____. "La propagation du Bouddhisme indien en Indochine occidentale." *Bulletin de la Société des études indochinoises*, 18 (1943), 93-105.

Perhaps one of the best general surveys available on Buddhism in pre-modern Cambodia. Dupont is careful to use the most important iconographic and epigraphic evidence available at his time to make his composite statement.

(8) FINOT, LOUIS. "Outlines of the History of Buddhism in Indo-China," in *Buddhistic Studies*. Edited by B. C. Law. Calcutta: Thacker, Spink, 1931, pp. 749-767.

An introductory article which seeks to establish the varieties of Buddhism and their introductions into Champa, Funan, and Burma. The author makes copious use of epigraphic and iconographic evidence to establish his findings (notably that only Saivism and Mahayana Buddhism flourished in Champa from the ninth to the thirteenth centuries A.D.).

(9) GARNIER, FRANCIS, trans. "Chronique royale du Cambodge." *Journal asiatique*, 18 (1871), 336-385; 20 (1872), 112-144.

Translations of Cambodian chronicle of the reigns of kings which was brought back by a nineteenth-century French expedition to Indo-China. It is interesting as a piece of first-hand data but covers only the period beginning in 1346.

(10) MAJUMDAR, RAMESH CHANDRA. *Hindu Colonies in the Far East*. Second revised and enlarged edition. Calcutta: K. L. Mukhopadhyay, 1963, pp. 175-206. (Originally published 1944.)

Sketchy history of Cambodia from the time of Funan (ca. 200 A.D.) until the decline of Angkor. The most valuable element of this account is the inclusion of the Cambodian myth of the origin of its own state.

(11) MUS, PAUL. "Angkor vu du Japon." *France-Asie*, 18 (1962), 521-538.

An attempt to assess the political nature of Buddhism as well as the character of the king (as it had been influenced by the bodhisattva motif) in both Cambodia and Japan during the eighth through the twelfth centuries. As is the case with most of Mus's work, this article relies heavily upon sculptures and bas-reliefs as sources. For another account of the same time period in relation to Angkor developments, *see* Mus's "Angkor in the Time of Jayavarman VII," *Indian Arts and Letters*, 11 (1937), 65-75.

(12) POREE-MASPERO, EVELINE. *Etude sur les rites agraires des cambodgiens*. Le monde d'outre-mer passé et présent, first series, No. 14. Paris and The Hague: Mouton, 1962-1969, vol. 3.

The author argues that Buddhism made its first impact in Cambodia during the early centuries of the Christian era, coming from India via land routes across Central Asia, and that during this period, it was expressed in Sanskritic (Sarvastivadin) rather than in Pali form.

(13) *Présence du Cambodge*. Edited by René de Berval. Saigon, 1955, pp. 317-559. (Special number of *France-Asie*, 12, nos. 114-115 [November-December 1955].)

A collection of articles (in French) of varying quality on the geography, history, arts, ethnography, religion, language, literature, folklore, and economy of Cambodia. See in particular Pierre Grison's "Présence historique" and his handy chronological table of the kings of Cambodia (pp. 329-336), Georges Coedes's translation of various royal inscriptions (pp. 483-509), and François Martini's two articles in the section on religion (pp. 409-424).

(14) PURI, B. N. "Buddhism in Ancient Kambujadesa." *Indian Historical Quarterly*, 52, nos. 2-3 (June-September 1956), 313-318.

A summary of the history and character of Buddhism in Cambodia in and around the sixth-eighth centuries. The author relies almost exclusively upon epigraphic sources to make the suggestion that there were two or three waves of Buddhist immigrants which accounted for both its Mahayanist and Theravadanist elements. The author seems to be primarily interested in the fact that Buddhism flourished in a compatible spirit with Brahmanism.

1.7 LAOS

1.7.1 Historical Surveys and Introductions

(1) BERVAL, RENE DE, ed. *Présence du Royaume Lao*. Saigon: 1956, pp. 703-1153. (Special number of *France-Asie*, 12, nos. 118-120 [March-May 1956].)

An important collection of articles on different aspects of Laotian geography, history, art, ethnography, religion, medicine, language, literature, folklore, education, economy, etc., which has been translated into English (but not made readily available) as René de Berval, ed., *Kingdom of Laos: The Land of the Million Elephants and of the White Parasol* (*see* 6.1.1[22]). See in particular: Georges Coedes's "Introduction à l'histoire du Laos" (pp. 711-715), A. R. Mathieu's very handy "Tableau chronologique de l'histoire du Laos" (pp. 724-741), Thao Nhouy Abhay's "Le Bouddhisme lau" (pp. 917-935), and Louis Finot and Auguste Pavie's translations of portions of the "Annales du Lan Xang" (pp. 1047-1076).

(2) COEDES, GEORGES. "Documents sur l'histoire politique et religieuse du Laos occidental." *Bulletin de l'Ecole française d'Extrême Orient*, 25 (1925), 1-201.

A book-size article in which Coedes translates texts pertaining to the history of Buddhism in western Laos from two works: Ratanapanna's chronicle of Buddhism, the *Jinakalamalini* (ca. 1516), and Bodhiramsi's

1.7.1 Laos

Camadevivamsa, which traces the history of the city of Lamphoon from its earliest beginnings. An English translation of the *Jinakalamalipakaranam* may also be found in N. A. Jayawickrama, trans., *The Sheaf of Garlands of the Epochs of the Conqueror* (see 1.5.2[19]).

(3) _____. *The Making of South East Asia* (see 1.4.1[2]), pp. 172-180.

Much information on the history and context of Laotian Buddhism can be derived from more general histories of Laos and Southeast Asia. The above pages in Coedes's basic work form a concise introduction to the whole history of Laos. Further details may be found in D. G. E. Hall, *A History of South East Asia* (3rd edition New York, 1968). A standard history of Laos is Paul LeBoulanger, *Histoire du Laos français: Essai d'une étude chronologique des principautés laotiennes* (Paris: Plon, 1930). Among the very few histories of Laos in English, see the interesting *History of Laos* by Maha Sila Viravong (New York: Paragon Book Reprints, 1964), 147 pp., which is a translation from the Laotian and presents a Laotian's view of his own history. See also M. L. Manich Jumsai, *History of Laos (Including the History of Lannathai, Chiengmai)* (Bangkok: Chalermnit, 1967), 337 pp.

(4) LeBAR, FRANK M. and ADRIENNE SUDDARD, eds. *Laos: Its People, Its Society, Its Culture.* New Haven: Human Relations Area Files Press, 1960, pp. 49-60.

The chapter deals with "religion" and makes a quick introduction, in English, to the relation of Theravada Buddhism to Phi worship, and the non-indigenous religions.

(5) MIGOT, ANDRE. "Le Bouddhisme en Indochine." See 1.6.1(5).

1.7.2 Specialized Historical Studies

(1) BRODRICK, ALAN HOUGHTON. *Little Vehicule: Cambodia & Laos.* See 1.6.2(3).

(2) CONDOMINAS, GEORGES. "Notes dur le Bouddhisme populaire en milieu rural lao." *Archives de sociologie des religions*, 13, no. 25 (January-June 1968), 81-110; and no. 26 (July-December 1968), 111-150.

The best and most comprehensive treatment of Lao Buddhism in the modern period. The author covers the sociological ramifications of the wat as well as its effect upon the economy and education of the community.

(3) FINOT, LOUIS. "Outlines of the History of Buddhism in Indo-China." See 1.6.2(8).

(4) HALPERN, JOEL MARTIN. *Government, Politics, and Social Structure in Laos: A Study of Tradition and Innovation.* Yale University Southeast Asia Studies Monograph Series, No. 4. New Haven: Southeast Asia Studies, Yale University, 1964, distributed by The Cellar Book Shop, Detroit, pp. 49-61.

This short chapter is one of the few treatments of this general topic. Halpern reviews the basic structure and character of the Sangha before discussing the Sangha/state relationship. He stresses that the relationship becomes most emphasized on public occasions (for a detailed study of the phenomenon in Laos, see Reynolds, below). Finally he reviews contemporary relationships between the Sangha and the Pathet Lao and between the Sangha and the monarchy.

(5) LAFONT, PIERRE-BERNARD. "Introduction du Bouddhisme au Laos," in *Présence du Bouddhisme* (see 1.5.1[6]), pp. 889-892.

A brief survey of the early history of Buddhism in Laos, but one of the few available. Lafont argues against the traditional date of 1356 as being too late for the first introduction of Buddhism into the country.

(6) LEVY, PAUL. "Les traces de l'introduction du Bouddhisme à Luang Prabang." *Bulletin de l'Ecole française d'Extrême Orient*, 40 (1940), 411-424.

This is a report on the discovery of four sculptures of the Buddha and a long royal inscription found at Luang Prabang. From these evidences, Levy postulates the introduction of Buddhism (Hinayana form) into Luang Prabang before the fourteenth century.

(7) REYNOLDS, FRANK. "Ritual and Social Hierarchy: An Aspect of Traditional Religion in Buddhist Laos." *History of Religions*, 9, no. 1 (August 1969), 78-89.

This article discusses the function of myth and ritual as categories within the history of religions. Three festivals involving the entire community and concerned with New Year celebrations are investigated with attention to the social significance of the myths and rituals respectively expressed. Reynolds concludes that these festivals express a social idea which reestablishes the "traditional Laotian world."

1.8 VIETNAM (CHAMPA AND ANNAM)

1.8.1 Historical Surveys and Introductions

(1) CADIERE, LEOPOLD MICHEL. *Croyances et pratiques religieuses des vietnamiens.* Publications de la Société des études indochinoises. Second edition Saigon: Imprimerie nouvelle d'Extrême-Orient, 1958, 3 vols.

Entitled, in its first edition, *Croyances et pratiques religieuses des annamites* (Hanoi, 1944-1957), this remains a classic study of popular religion in Vietnam. Volume 1 contains a discussion of the place of Buddhism, including a brief historical sketch of its development in Vietnam.

Vietnam (Champa and Annam)   1.8.2

(2) COEDES, GEORGES. *The Indianized States of Southeast Asia*. Edited by Walter F. Vella. Translated by Susan B. Cowing. Honolulu: East-West Center Press, 1968, 403 pp.

By reading the appropriate sections concerned with Champa, the reader can gain an overall view of the political history of what is now part of Vietnam, from 190 to 1500 A.D. In addition, the author's notes provide the reader with bibliographic information for more specific inquiries.

(3) _____. *The Making of South East Asia* (see 1.4.1[2]), pp. 39-49, 77-87 and 204-217.

Much information on the history and context of Vietnamese Buddhism can be gotten out of the more general histories of Vietnam and Southeast Asia. These pages in Coedes's basic work are a concise introduction to the whole history of Vietnam. Further details may be found in Chapters 8, 9, 22, and 34 of D. G. E. Hall, *A History of South East Asia* (3rd edition New York, 1968). A standard and scholarly history of Vietnam in English is Joseph Buttinger, *The Smaller Dragon* (New York: Praeger, 1958), 535 pp. In French, see, for the South, Georges Maspero, *Le royaume de Champa* (Paris: G. Van Oest, 1928), which was originally published as a series of 11 articles in *T'oung Pao*, 11 (1910), 12 (1911) and 14 (1913), and is a masterful study of the history of Cham culture from its beginnings until the final conquest of the Vietnamese. For the North, a handy survey is L. Cadière, "Tableau chronologique des dynasties annamites," *Bulletin de l'Ecole française d'Extrême-Orient*, 5 (1905), 77-145, as well as Abel Des Michels's translation (from the Chinese) of a seventeenth-century official Vietnamese history, *Les annales impériales de l'Annam* (Paris: Leroux, 1889-1894), which covers the history of the indigenous Vietnamese dynasties during the tenth to seventeenth centuries.

(4) ELIOT, CHARLES NORTON EDGECUMBE. *Hinduism and Buddhism: An Historical Sketch* (see 1.1[4]), vol. 3, pp. 137-150 and pp. 340-344.

These two chapters in Eliot's classic work, one on Champa, the other on Annam, remain perhaps the fullest readily available introduction in English to the history of Buddhism (and Hinduism) in Vietnam.

(5) FINOT, LOUIS. "La religion des Chams d'après les monuments: Etude suivie d'un inventaire sommaire des monuments chams de l'Annam." *Bulletin de l'Ecole française d'Extrême-Orient*, 1 (1901), 12-33.

A concise survey, based on archeological data, of the various religious cults that existed in the kingdom of Champa. Besides Buddhism it deals with Saivite, Vaisnavaite and other sects.

(6) LE HU'O'NG. "Les sectes bouddhiques au Sud Viet-nam." *Samadhi: Cahiers d'Etudes Bouddhiques*, 6, no. 2 (1972), 75-88.

This article consists of a very general overview of the introduction and propagation of Theravada and Mahayana Buddhism in Vietnam. The author then gives brief sketches of the four Vietnamese patriarchs and the eight existing sects.

(7) MAI-THO-TRUYEN, CHANH-TRI. *Le Bouddhisme au Vietnam: Buddhism in Vietnam: Phat-Giao Viet-Nam*. Saigon: Pagoda Xa-Loi, 1962, 105 pp.

A tri-lingual edition, profusely illustrated and slightly expanded, of Mai-Tho-Truyen's article, "Le Bouddhisme au Vietnam," from *Présence du Bouddhisme* (see 1.5.1[6]). It remains one of the few quick sketches of the history and development of Buddhism in Vietnam by a Vietnamese.

(8) MAJUMDAR, RAMESH CHANDRA. *Hindu Colonies in the Far East* (see 1.6.2[10]), pp. 113-174.

These pages contain the history of the "Indianization" of Champa and Annam. The author traces the history of Hindu dynasties, the invasions of the Annamites, military and diplomatic relations with Cambodia and Achina, and the general culture of Champa and Annam with special regard to Indian influences. The scope is introductory, suitable for the beginning student.

(9) THIEN-AN, THICH. *Buddhism and Zen in Vietnam in Relation to the Development of Buddhism in Asia*. Rutland, Vt.: Charles E. Tuttle Co., 1975, 301 pp.

This volume comprises a history of the major developments of Buddhism in Vietnam beginning with the introduction of Chinese Buddhism in the sixth century through the growth and proliferation of the major schools of Buddhism into the seventeenth century. Thich-Thien-An is a western educated Buddhist monk who provides perhaps the best and most accessible account of Buddhism in Vietnam that is currently available.

1.8.2 Specialized Historical Studies

(1) BOISSELIER, JEAN. *La statuaire du Champa: Recherches sur les cultes et l'iconographie*. Publications de l'Ecole française d'Extrême-Orient, No. 54. Paris: L'Ecole française d'Extrême-Orient, 1963, 468 pp.

Though the primary concern of this work is art history in Champa, it may still provide the reader with a sketch of Buddhist influence in particular periods of the history of Champa.

(2) BUTTINGER, JOSEPH. *Vietnam: A Political History*. New York: Praeger, 1968, 565 pp.

Buttinger's book, a combined and abridged edition of his *The Smaller Dragon* (1958) and *Vietnam: A Dragon Embattled* (1967), is concerned with the modern political history of Vietnam and is careful to take into account the intellectual formulations which lie behind political constructions. Hence, the reader

1.8.2 Vietnam (Champa and Annam)

may glean references to Buddhism as the author sees it as a contributor to the making of political events. The author provides a good review of the Buddhist-Diem conflict which came to a head in 1963. This study synthesizes many of the arguments offered elsewhere.

(3) DURAND, MAURICE. "Introduction du Bouddhisme au Vietnam," in Présence du Bouddhisme (see 1.5.1[6]), pp. 797-800.
 A survey of the historical origins of the various Buddhist sects which have flourished in Vietnam, from the beginnings to the seventeenth century.

(4) GIAP, TRAN-VAN. "Le Bouddhisme en Annam des origines au XIIIe siècle." Bulletin de l'Ecole française d'Extrême-Orient, 32 (1932), 191-268.
 An important and classic survey of the much neglected history of Buddhism in Annam during a period of primarily Chinese dominance.

(5) MASPERO, GEORGES, ed. Un empire colonial français: l'Indochine. Paris: G. Van Oest, 1929-1930, pp. 275-296.
 This section of this volume is concerned with the character of Annamite religion. Because of its multifaceted nature, much of the discussion is concerned with Confucian and animistic practices. Nevertheless, this chapter does include discussions of various pagodas and the typical life of "bonzes" (monks). The central theme of the Buddhism among the Annamites seems to be that though Buddhism was patronized as a state religion, it served more as a philosophy of life which inspired religious practices of not always Buddhist origins.

(6) MAYBON, CHARLES and HENRY RUSSIER. Lectures sur l'histoire moderne et contemporaine du pays d'Annam de 1428 à 1926. Revised and corrected edition. Hanoi: Imprimerie d'Extrême-Orient, 1930, 250 pp. (Originally published in 1919 as Lectures sur l'histoire d'Annam depuis l'avènement des Le.)
 A series of lectures which provide the reader with an overview of the political history of Annam. However, references to Buddhism are scattered and limited to its direct influence. For the advanced student.

(7) MUS, PAUL. "Buddhism in Vietnamese History and Society." Jahrbuch des Südasien-Instituts der Universität Heidelberg, 2 (1967-1968), 95-115.
 A perceptive analysis of the historical and ideological background to the coup which overthrew Ngo Dinh Diem in 1963 which fills in many of the questions left unanswered (or untackled) by David Halberstam in his "The Buddhist Crisis in Vietnam" in Vietnam: History, Documents, and Opinions on a Major World Crisis, edited by Marvin E. Gettleman (Greenwich, Conn.: Fawcett Publications, 1965).

(8) NGHIEM-DANG. Vietnam: Politics and Public Administration. Honolulu: East-West Center Press, 1966, 437 pp.
 A lucid and scholarly study which exposes the roots of public administration concepts operative in Vietnamese history back to the earliest of times through Chinese domination and French colonialism. As such, it provides the reader with an excellent study of Vietnam's political history.

(9) NHAT-HANH, THICH. Vietnam: Lotus in a Sea of Fire. New York: Hill and Wang, 1967, 115 pp.
 Primarily concerned with Buddhists in Vietnam, this book is more than a political tract. The author, a Buddhist monk, attempts to put the contemporary Buddhist situation into a historical perspective.

(10) REVERTEGAT, BRUNO. "Le Bouddhisme et les bonzes au Sud-Vietnam." Revue des Deux Mondes, 4 (February 1964), 505-520.
 General article in which the author traces the traditional role played by Buddhism and Buddhist monks in Vietnam in an attempt to understand contemporary activities of monks in the early 1960s.

1.9 INDONESIA AND MALAYA

1.9.1 Historical Surveys and Introductions

(1) COEDES, GEORGES. The Indianized States of Southeast Asia (see 1.8.1[2]), pp. 81-96, 107-109, and 125-132.
 Almost all information in English on the history of Buddhism in Indonesia and Malaya must be gleaned from more general works. The above pages of Coedes's classic work provide a general introduction to the history of the area up to the Moslem conquest. Reference might also be made to D. G. E. Hall, A History of South East Asia (3rd edition New York, 1968), especially chapters 3 and 4.

(2) DAMAIS, LOUIS-CHARLES. "Le Bouddhisme en Indonésie," in Présence du Bouddhisme (see 1.5.1[6]), pp. 813-824.
 One of the few articles devoted exclusively to the history of Buddhism in Indonesia. Short, sketchy, but a good introduction.

(3) ELIOT, CHARLES NORTON EDGECUMBE. Hinduism and Buddhism: An Historical Sketch (see 1.1[4]), pp. 151-187.
 The chapter is entitled "Java and the Malay Archipelago" and remains the fullest easily accessible introduction to the history of Buddhism in that area in English.

(4) MAJUMDAR, RAMESH CHANDRA. Hindu Colonies in the Far East (see 1.6.2[10]), Book II, pp. 17-112.
 General introduction to the history of Indian influence in Indonesia. The author has included separate chapters on the Sailendra empire, the rise of a succession of dynasties

in Java, the introduction of Islam, and Indian cultural vestiges which remain.

(5) POTT, P. H. "Le Bouddhisme de Java et l'ancienne civilisation javanaise," in Conferenze. Serie orientale Roma, No. 5. Roma: Istituto Italiano per il Medio ed Estreme Oriente, 1952, pp. 109-156.

A substantive introduction to the history of Buddhism in Indonesia, which devotes much space to a discussion of its major characteristics and its relationship to Javanese royalty. Richly illustrated.

1.9.2 Specialized Historical Studies

(1) COEDES, GEORGES. "Le Royaume de Çrivijaya." Bulletin de l'Ecole française d'Extrême-Orient, 18 (1918), 1-36.

This is a scholarly treatment intended for advanced students based on an inscription found at Kota Kapur in the early part of the twentieth century. Coedes argues that "Srivijaya" does not refer to a king who reigned in the eighth century, but to an existing kingdom which might have been primarily Buddhist. His placement of that kingdom and some of his theories have been opened to question by recent scholarship.

(2) HOOYKAAS, C. "Buddhism in Bali," in Felicitation Volumes of Southeast Asian Studies Presented to Prince Dhaninivat. Bangkok: Siam Society, 1965, vol. 1, pp. 25-34.

This article is a listing of bibliographical sources for the study of Buddhism in Bali. The author has included a few secondary sources which might be worth looking up. But the bulk of the article lists texts which mention Buddhism. Unfortunately, this article is disappointing because of its lack of focus.

(3) I CHING. A Record of the Buddhist Religion as Practised in India and the Malay Archipelago (A.D. 671-695). See 1.2.2.3(8).

(4) McDOUGAL, COLIN. Buddhism in Malaya. Singapore: D. Moore, 1956, 61 pp.

One of the few treatments available in English concerning the entire topic. The scope of the book is very general and is recommended for the beginning student. The author briefly treats Buddhism historically and calls attention to its remaining vestiges as well as its practice among the Malaysian Chinese. Statistics for the contemporary period.

(5) SARKAR, HIMANSU BHUSHAN. "The Evolution of the Siva-Buddha Cult in Java." Journal of Indian History, 45 (December 1967), 637-646.

A concise historical overview and succinct doctrinal discussion concerned with the evolution of the Siva-Buddha cult in Java.

(6) SASTRI, D. A. NILAKANTA. "Sri Vijaya." Bulletin de l'Ecole française d'Extrême-Orient, 40 (1940), 239-313.

Of benefit to the intermediate or advanced student, the article is basically a composite statement of all scholarship (to its date) concerned with the history of Sri Vijaya. The author has also included a final section on Sri Vijaya art with eight plates of illustrations.

(7) WIJOSUPARTO, R. M. S. "The Role of Buddhism of South India on the Development of Buddhist Thought in Indonesia," in Proceedings of the International Conference of Historians of Asia. Manila, 1962, pp. 211-223.

This article represents an attempt to discern the nature of the Buddhism which was exported to Indonesia from India. By using the treatise Sang Hyand Kamahayanikan, the author offers his speculations.

1.10 CENTRAL ASIA

1.10.1 Historical Surveys and Introductions

(1) BAGCHI, PRABODH CHANDRA. India and Central Asia. Calcutta: National Council of Education, Bengal, 1955, 184 pp.

A book of general scope concerned with the historical and literary backgrounds of India and Central Asia. But more specifically, the author has included discussions of Buddhist culture in Tokharestan, Eastern Iran, and Eastern Turkestan. Unfortunately, these discussions are fragmentary.

(2) BELENITSKII, ALEKSANDR MARKOVICH. Central Asia. Translated by James Hogarth. London: Barrie and Rockliff, Cresset Press, 1969, 251 pp.

This is a treatment of the political, cultural, and economic history of what is today Soviet Central Asia from prehistoric times to the Arab conquest. The author ascribes the transmission of Buddhism to this area as taking place during the Kushan period. Specifically, the author describes two Buddhist temples at Ak-Beshim and a Buddhist monastery at Adehina-Tepe. He has included a good bibliography of research materials concerned with Buddhism in Central Asia, but unfortunately almost all the works are not yet translated from Russian.

(3) ELIOT, CHARLES NORTON EDGECUMBE. Hinduism and Buddhism: An Historical Sketch (see 1.1[4]), pp. 188-222.

A succinct and scholarly treatment of Buddhism in Central Asia. Though somewhat dated, and not as detailed as one might wish, it remains one of the few readily available accounts in English and is an adequate introduction to the history of Buddhism in the area.

(4) LITVINSKY, BORIS ANATOLEVICH. "Outline History of Buddhism in Central Asia," in Kushan Studies in U.S.S.R.: Papers Presented by the Soviet Scholars at the UNESCO Conference on History, Archaeology and Culture of Central Asia in the Kushan Period, Danshanbe,

1.10.1

1968. Soviet Indology Series, No. 3. Calcutta: Indian Studies Past and Present, 1970, pp. 53-132.

Primarily relying upon recent Soviet archeological discoveries which the author contends confirm the historicity of Chinese pilgrims' accounts, the author presents the reader with a superb treatment of the historical development of Buddhism in Western Turkestan from its inception through the period of Muslim conquest. Litvinsky uses the explanatory mode of "the great and little traditions" to elucidate local differences in the variety of Buddhism in Turkestan. The reader is also able to garner further bibliographical notes from this fine work.

(5) SAHA, KSHANIKA. Buddhism and Buddhist Literature in Central Asia. Calcutta: K. L. Mukhopadhyay, 1970, 162 pp.

After Litvinsky's article (above), this is perhaps the most substantial work on Buddhism in Central Asia, and probably the only book on the subject in English. Written by a student of Nalinaksha Dutt, it treats the geography, introduction of Buddhism into the area by Indian monks, manuscript remains and the monastic system. Also includes a short bibliography.

(6) STEIN, MARK AUREL. On Ancient Central-Asian Tracks: Brief Narrative on Three Expeditions in Innermost Asia and Northwestern China. New York: Pantheon, 1964, 290 pp. (Originally published London: Macmillan, 1933.)

Much information about the history and context of Buddhism in Central Asia may be found in the various reports of scientific expeditions to the area. In this work, before describing his travels, the great explorer Sir Aurel Stein summarizes the political and cultural history of Chinese expansion into Central Asia after ca. 150 B.C. Within his narrative he describes the growth of Buddhism in the area and its gradual demise in the tenth century. For another such brief account see the introduction in Albert von Le Coq, Buried Treasures of Chinese Turkestan: An Account of the Activities and Adventures of the Second and Third German Turfan Expeditions (see 10.1.1[8]).

1.10.2 Specialized Historical Studies

(1) ANDREWS, FREDERICK HENRY. Descriptive Catalogue of Antiquities Recovered by Sir Aurel Stein . . . During his Explorations in Central Asia, Kansu and Eastern Iran. Delhi: Manager of Publications, 1935, 445 pp.

The antiquities of Buddhist origin are valuable for the more advanced student interested in shrine sites and burial grounds.

(2) BANERJEE, P. "Central Asia and Its Early Buddhist and Other Remains." The Indo-Asian Culture, 19, no. 4 (October 1970), 18-25.

A discussion of the history and art of the Tarim Basin (Sinkiang) dating from the early centuries of the Christian era to the tenth and eleventh centuries. The author has been attentive to the political developments in China which affected these regions culturally.

(3) BIVAR; DAVID. "The Nomad Empires and the Expansion of Buddhism," in Central Asia. Edited by Gavin Hambly et al. Weidenfeld and Nicolson Universal History. London: Weidenfeld and Nicolson, 1969, pp. 35-48.

This section is primarily a treatment of the political history of Northwest India and Central Asia from the rise of the dynasty of Eucratides to the period of Kushana hegemony. The strength of the article is its general treatment of Central Asia tribes. Its treatment of the expansion of Buddhism into the area is of less value.

(4) BONGARD-LEVIN, G. M. "Buddhist Studies in the USSR and New Archeological Excavations in Soviet Central Asia." East Asian Cultural Studies, 12, nos. 1-4 (March 1973), 11-28.

The article begins with a review of the scholarly contributions of I. P. Minayev, Th. Stcherbatsky and S. F. Oldenberg. The author then describes the results of excavations and expeditions into Central Asia. Finally, he recounts the Russian contributions to the study of Gandharan art and Sogdian inscriptions.

(5) BROUGH, JOHN. "Comments on the Third-Century Shan-shan and the History of Buddhism." Bulletin of the School of Oriental and African Studies, 28 (1965), 582-612.

The bulk of the article is concerned with the dating and contexts of the "Niza documents" which were left by the Central Asian kingdom of Shan-shan. The documents reflect a period when the Buddhist religion was being transmitted from India to China. The disappearance of the Shan-shan community marks a break in the cultural continuity between China and India.

(6) CHEN TSU-LUNG. La vie et les oeuvres de Woutchen (816-895): Contributions à l'histoire culturelle de Touen-houang. See 8.9.3[88]).

(7) GRAY, BASIL. Buddhist Cave Paintings at Tun-huang. London: Faber and Faber; Chicago: University of Chicago Press, 1959, 86 pp.

Though this work is essentially concerned with art, Gray has included a short preface which describes the history of Buddhism in the area.

(8) JAHN, KARL. "Kamalashri-Rashid al-Din's 'Life and Teaching of Buddha': A Source for the Buddhism of the Mongol Period." Central Asiatic Journal, 2 (1956), 81-128.

This apologetic text belonged to the non-Islamicized Mongols of Iran during the late thirteenth and early fourteenth century. With

China

no other extant source of this kind, the work becomes a valuable aid for the understanding of the character of Buddhism in this region during this time. The author critically reviews the content of the document and offers the hypothesis that segments of the Mongolian Kanjur had already been transported into Iran by the early fourteenth century. This thesis is supported by the internal evidence of Kamalashri-Rashid al-Din's text.

(9) KOLARZ, WALTER. Religion in the Soviet Union. New York: St. Martin's, 1961, pp. 448-469.

The author initially sketches historically the series of persecutions and their consequent results for three Buddhist peoples of Central Asia and Mongolia (the Buryat-Mongols, the Kalmucks, and the Tavinians) since 1918. He also includes the ideological arguments which have been used to discredit Buddhism and the manner in which the Soviets have occasionally used Buddhism for political purposes.

(10) KOSHELINKO, G. "The Beginning of Buddhism in Margiana." Acta antigua acadamiae scientiarum Hungaricae, 14 (1966), 175-183.

Koshelenko argues in juxtaposition to Foucher that Buddhism entered Parthia as early as the beginning of the first century A.D. Koshelenko asserts that the growth of Buddhism in the area led to the building of a large stupa which has been excavated and dated by the Soviet archeologist V. M. Masson as ca. second century A.D. In addition, the author cites Chinese sources to support his data.

(11) MIYAMOTO, SHOSON. "The Geographical Expansion of the Indian Cultural Sphere Symbolized by the Metaphor of the Five Rivers of India and the Metaphor of the Four Rivers of Asia." Indogaku Bukkyogaku Kenkyu/Journal of Indian and Buddhist Studies, 16, no. 1 (1967), 474-460 (sic).

A tentative but interesting article associating the five river scheme with Asoka and the four river scheme with Kaniska, and tracing the development and spread of the two schemes in different parts of Asia, with special focus on the movement into Central Asia.

1.11   CHINA

1.11.1 Historical Surveys and Introductions

(1) CH'EN, KENNETH KUAN-SHENG. Buddhism in China: A Historical Survey. Princeton Studies in the History of Religions. Princeton: Princeton University Press, 1964, 560 pp.

A balanced study of the history of Chinese Buddhism with an extensive annotated bibliography. The book is valuable both as an introduction and as a reference work.

(2) _____. The Chinese Transformation of Buddhism. Princeton: Princeton University Press, 1973, 345 pp.

1.11.1

A major study on the much debated question of whether Buddhism influenced or was influenced in China. Written to counterbalance the works that overstress the former position, this is an across-the-board examination of the sinicization of Indian Buddhism, approached from ethical, political, economic, literary and educational perspectives.

(3) _____. "Mahayana Buddhism and Chinese Culture." Asia, 10 (Winter 1968), 11-32.

An overview and condensation of Ch'en's The Chinese Transformation of Buddhism which affords the reader with a quick means of getting acquainted with this broad topic. If the reader is pressed for time, the following articles may be used in lieu of the many introductory volumes available on this general topic of the history of Chinese Buddhism: William T. de Bary, "Buddhism and the Chinese Tradition," Diogenes, 8 (Fall 1964), 102-124; and E. Zurcher, "Buddhism in China" (below).

(4) CHOU, HSIANG-KUANG. A History of Chinese Buddhism. Allahabad: Indo-Chinese Literature Publications, 1955, 264 pp.

A history of Chinese Buddhism by a former lecturer in history at the University of Delhi. The facts are all there, but the book seems to have been written to promote good relations between China and India. The work's final sentences sum up the whole: "An English poet said: 'East is East and West is West and never the twain shall meet.' Yet China in the east and India in the west are spiritually one. The Himalayas divided only to unite."

(5) DE BARY, WILLIAM THEODORE, comp. The Buddhist Tradition in India, China and Japan. New York: Modern Library, 1969, pp. 123-251.

The section on "Buddhism in China" with selections and introductions by the Columbia University team of De Bary, Hakeda, Hurvitz, Chan and Yampolsky makes a good, easy, beginner's introduction, through primary sources, to the early history of Buddhism in China and the formation of the various schools of Chinese Buddhism.

(6) DEMIEVILLE, PAUL. "Le Bouddhisme Chinois," in Encyclopédie de la Pléiade 29: Histoire des Religions 1. Paris: Gallimard, 1970, pp. 1249-1319.

An excellent complement to Ch'en's Buddhism in China, by an eminent Buddhologist. This is the best short substantive introduction to the overall history of Buddhism in China.

(7) HODOUS, LEWIS. Buddhism and Buddhists in China. The World's Living Religions. New York: Macmillan, 1924, 84 pp.

Though dated and in some places factually wrong, this remains a good short introduction to Chinese Buddhism. It touches briefly on the history of Buddhism in China. Such topics as Buddhism and the Peasant, Buddhism and the Family, and Buddhism and Social Life make the book an interesting account of Buddhism in the early twentieth century when the author, a former missionary, observed it.

1.11.1

(8) REICHELT, KARL LUDWIG. *Truth and Tradition in Chinese Buddhism: A Study of Chinese Mahayana Buddhism*. Fourth edition, revised and enlarged. Translated by Kathrina Van Wagenen Bugge. Shanghai: Commercial Press, 1934, 415 pp.

The story of Chinese Buddhism, rather than its history, by a Norwegian Lutheran enthusiast of dialogue. Its scholarship is now dated, but interesting details may still be gleaned from its various chapters. These include the traditional story of the introduction of Buddhism into China, a study of its development during the early centuries, the story of Hsuan Tsang's journey, and chapters on masses for the dead, the Pure Land school, monastic life, pilgrimages, and "Present-day Buddhism in China."

(9) ROBINSON, RICHARD H. "Buddhism: In China and Japan," in *The Concise Encyclopaedia of Living Faiths*. Edited by R. C. Zaehner. London: Hutchinson, 1959, pp. 321-344.

Robinson's section on China is one of the best short first introductions to Chinese Buddhism in English. It is well-written and better, perhaps, than the section on China in Robinson's *The Buddhist Religion* (see 1.1[8]).

(10) TSUKAMOTO, ZENRYU. "Buddhism in China and Korea," in *The Path of the Buddha* (see 1.1[6]), pp. 182-234.

A short introduction to the overall history of Buddhism in China, and one of the few articles of the great Japanese Buddhologist Tsukamoto to be translated into English (by Leon Hurvitz).

(11) WRIGHT, ARTHUR F. *Buddhism in Chinese History*. New York: Atheneum, 1965, 144 pp. (Originally published Stanford, Calif.: Stanford University Press, 1959; paperback edition: Atheneum Paperbacks, No. 77.)

A series of six lectures which are useful as a short introduction to the history of Buddhism in China, especially up to the year 900, but as a reference work it has largely been replaced by Ch'en's *Buddhism in China* (above). For an extended, informative critique of Wright's book, see Richard H. Robinson's review in the *Journal of the American Oriental Society*, 79 (1959), 311-318.

(12) ZURCHER, E. "Buddhism in China," in *The Legacy of China*. Edited by R. Dawson. London, 1964, pp. 56-79.

Good short introduction to the development of Buddhism in China, focusing more on the thought and philosophical aspect of its adaptation and influence there. For an important study of the early period of Chinese Buddhism by the same author, see his *Buddhist Conquest of China* (1.11.2.1[9]).

1.11.2 *Specialized Historical Studies*

1.11.2.1 The Introduction of Buddhism into China

(1) BOSE, PHANINDRA NATH. *The Indian Teachers in China*. Madras: S. Ganesan, 1923, 148 pp.

A survey of the introduction of Buddhism into China and of the continuing role played by Indian Buddhist teachers in the development of Chinese Buddhism. Somewhat chauvinistic but well-documented, and especially useful for its chronological list of over sixty Indian pandits who went to China from the first century to the eleventh.

(2) DEMIEVILLE, PAUL. "La pénétration du Bouddhisme dans la tradition philosophique chinoise." *Cahiers d'histoire mondiale/Journal of World History/Cuadernos de Historia Mundial*, 3 (1956), 19-38.

Very instructive and concise study of some of the difficulties and changes of both Buddhism and Chinese thought as they came into contact. Set within a historical perspective.

(3) DUBS, HOMER H. "The 'Golden Man' of Former Han Time." *T'oung Pao*, 33 (1937), 1-14.

A concise discussion of the capture and worship of a "golden idol" in Western Kansu in 121 B.C. The statue was later claimed to have been an image of the Buddha and thus to have marked one of the first contacts of China with Buddhism. Dubs debates this question. See also the follow-up article by James Roland Ware, "Once more on the 'Golden Man.'" *T'oung Pao*, 34 (1938), 174-178.

(4) GULIK, ROBERT H. VAN. *Siddham: An Essay on the History of Sanskrit Studies in China and Japan*. Sarasvati Vihara Series, No. 36. Nagpur: International Academy of Indian Culture, 1956, 240 pp.

Primarily concerned with the manner in which Sanskrit conceptualizations were incorporated into Chinese thought. In turn, the author considers the conceptual modes of the Chinese language and the consequent effects it had on Buddhist understandings. Also, the author considers the question of translation within the context of important Buddhist works.

(5) MASPERO, HENRI. "Communautés et moines bouddhistes chinois au 2e et 3e siècles." *Bulletin de l'Ecole française d'Extrême-Orient*, 10 (1910), 222-232.

A follow-up on his article on "Le songe et l'ambassade de l'empereur Ming" (below) which argued against the historicity of that early tradition, this article attempts to summarize what is known about the early monastic communities in China in which that legend was formulated. A more specific study of a slightly earlier period, which speculates on the milieu in which the first monasteries in Loyang were organized, may be found in the same author's "Les origines de la communauté bouddhiste de Lo-yang," *Journal asiatique*, 225 (1934), 87-107.

China

(6) ____. *Mélanges posthumes sur les religions et l'histoire de la Chine*. Publications du Musée Guimet. Bibliothèque de diffusion, Nos. 57-59. Paris: Civilisations du Sud, 1950, vol. 1, pp. 195-211.

This section comprises a good introduction to the study of Buddhism's entry into China. The author discusses the then contemporary nature of the Chinese religious spirit and gives reasons for Buddhism's close affinities to Taoism. He ascribes Buddhism's temporary ascendency over Confucianism and Taoism to Buddhism's superior metaphysical system. Of use to the intermediate and advanced student.

(7) ____. "Le songe et l'ambassade de l'empereur Ming: Etude critique des sources." *Bulletin de l'Ecole française d'Extrême-Orient*, 10 (1910), 95-130.

A classical article which questioned the historicity of the traditional explanation of the introduction of Buddhism into China as a result of an expedition sent to India after the first century A.D. Emperor Ming had seen the Buddha in a dream. Through an analysis of a large number of versions of the legend, Maspero concludes that the preface to the "Sutra in 42 Sections" was the original source of the dream and embassy part of the story, and that the Mou Tzu lies at the base of the story of the Buddha statues and of the foundation of the White Horse Monastery. He thus shows the whole legend to be a pious fabrication of the second century Buddhist community in Loyang. For a translation of the Mou Tzu version of the legend with extensive annotations, see Paul Pelliot, "Meou-tseu ou les doutes levés," *T'oung Pao*, 19 (1918-1919), 255-433.

(8) SOPER, ALEXANDER COBURN. *Literary Evidence for Early Buddhist Art in China*. Artibus Asiae, Supplementum, No. 19. Ascona: Artibus Asiae, 1959, 296 pp.

Contains valuable information on the introduction of Buddhism to the masses such as quotations of monks' biographies describing the "discovery" of Asokan Buddha images, "wandering" and "light emitting" images, conflicts with authorities over the use of precious metals, tabulations of the number of occurrences of specific Buddha images in the cave complexes. It is a specialized work which sheds light on the whole period of the beginnings of Buddhism in China.

(9) ZURCHER, ERIK. *The Buddhist Conquest of China: The Spread and Adaptation of Buddhism in Early Medieval China*. Sinica Leidensia, No. 11. Leiden: E. J. Brill, 1959, 2 vols., 468 pp.

This is a technical work, with extensive annotations and very careful and detailed use of historical documents, and not a general survey and not for beginning students. However, its sociological insights, its concern for "gentry Buddhism," etc., and the amount of information it offers make it an indispensable work for any advanced study of Chinese Buddhism, from its beginnings to about 400 A.D.

1.11.2.2 The Period of Domestication and Growth

(1) CH'EN, KENNETH KUAN-SHENG. "Anti-Buddhist Propaganda During the Nan-ch'ao." *Harvard Journal of Asiatic Studies*, 15 (1952), 166-192.

The growth of Buddhism during the period of the Northern and Southern dynasties was not without opposition, but the anti-Buddhist movement took on different forms in the North and in the South. This article discusses the campaign against Buddhism in the South, centering around the figures of Ku Huan (fifth century), who objected to Buddhism as a foreign religion, Fan Chen (fifth century), a Confucian, and Hsun-Chi, who thought Buddhism was undermining the state. In the North, however, the opposition to Buddhism took the form of forceful persecutions under Wei Wu-ti (in 446) and Chou Wu-ti (in 574-577). The background of these Northern developments is studied in Kenneth Ch'en's companion article, "On Some Factors Responsible for the Anti-Buddhist Persecution under the Pei-Ch'ao," *Harvard Journal of Asiatic Studies*, 17 (1954), 261-273.

(2) ____. "Neo-Taoism and the Prajna School during the Wei and Chin Dynasties." *Chinese Culture*, 1 (1957), 33-46.

Concerned with the rise of the Prajna school especially in respect to its utility of the concept of "tao" as an equivalent for "tathata." The author surveys the tendencies (political as well as philosophical) which drew Neo-Taoism and Buddhism together in opposition to Confucianism.

(3) GERNET, JACQUES. *Les aspects économiques du Bouddhisme dans la société chinoise du Ve au Xe siècle*. Publications de l'Ecole française d'Extrême-Orient, No. 39. Saigon: Ecole française d'Extrême-Orient, 1956, 331 pp.

Gernet frequently alludes to the contributions made by Buddhism to agriculture and art, but he is primarily concerned with how Buddhism affected Chinese economy. His general thesis is that the incredible growth in the number of monks, nuns and monasteries during this period greatly strained the Chinese economy for these chief reasons: 1) Depletion of the work force, 2) Cost of alms and monastery construction, 3) Ecclesiastical tax exemption, and 4) Unscrupulous money-lending.

(4) JAN, YUN-HUA, ed. and trans. *A Chronicle of Buddhism in China, 581-960 A.D. (Translations from Monk Chih-p'an's Fo-tsu T'ung-chi)*. Santiniketan: Visva-Bharati, 1966, 121 pp.

The chronicle of Buddhism in China during 581-960 A.D. is a translation and annotation from Fa-yun-chih-lueh, Volume 2 (*A Concise*

Record on the Fate of the Law, which was an abridged version of Chih-p'an's work). Chih-p'an was an orthodox monk of the T'ien-t'ai sect during the thirteenth century who wrote what came to be the accepted history of Buddhism in China which was distributed and printed in various editions up to the present age. Though the chronicle was written about seven hundred years ago, the author's concept of religious history is rather "modern," as he has narrated religious development within the scope of social, political, and cultural perspectives. First-rate source.

(5) LIEBENTHAL, WALTER. "A Biography of Chu Tao-sheng." Monumenta Nipponica, 11 (1955), 64-96.

A straightforward presentation of the life of the monk Tao-sheng (d. 434), an important disciple of Hui-yuan. His biography, especially when supplemented by Liebenthal's "The World Conception of Chu Tao-sheng," Monumenta Nipponica, 12 (1956), 65-103, and 12 (1957), 241-268, makes a fine, informal introduction to Buddhism in North China in the fourth and fifth centuries.

(6) _____. "Chinese Buddhism during the 4th and 5th Centuries." Monumenta Nipponica, 11 (1955), 44-83.

A general description of the religious situation in China at the time of Buddhism's first advances there is followed by a concise account of the initial Chinese misunderstanding of Buddhism, of its subsequent encounters and relations with Taoists and with the Emperor, and of the various sectarian debates that took place. A fine introduction to the period.

(7) LINK, ARTHUR E. "Biography of Shih Tao-an." T'oung Pao, 46 (1958), 1-48.

Annotated translation of the biography of the important Eastern Chin Dynasty monk Shih Tao-an (312-385) taken from the sixth century Kao-seng chuan ("Lives of Eminent Monks") (see 8.9.3[1]). Tao-an's life reflects the growth and changes that Chinese Buddhism was undergoing in the fourth century, and his biography (especially when read in conjunction with the life-stories of Hui-yuan and Tao-sheng --see the Liebenthal articles above) makes a fine, informal introduction to the period.

(8) MATHER, RICHARD B. "Vimalakirti and Gentry Buddhism." History of Religions, 8 (1968), 60-73.

Examines the influence of the Vimalakirti-Nirdesa Sutra on fourth and fifth century gentry Buddhism in the Yangtze Delta area, and attributes its popularity to its flexibility, its support of certain Chinese traditions, and its agreement with current modes of intellectual method. For an examination of the position of the Vimalakirti (and the "Lotus") Sutras in Buddhist art, and a later shift from depicting scenes taken from them to depicting scenes taken from the Pure Land Sutras, see L. Davidson's The Lotus Sutra in Chinese Art (see 5.9.4[3]).

(9) ROBINSON, RICHARD H. Early Madhyamika in India and China. Madison: University of Wisconsin Press, 1967, 347 pp.

Considers the question of how well the early Chinese students of Madhyamika thought understood and were able to use Nagarjuna's ideas and methods. Technical, but very important work in studying the doctrinal introduction of Buddhism to China. Raises a number of important methodological questions in the introduction and provides translations of important Chinese writers in the appendices. See also the annotation in 2.5.3(10).

(10) SENG-CHAO. Chao lun: The Treatises of Seng-chao. Translated and edited by Walter Liebenthal. Second revised edition. Hong Kong: Hong Kong University Press, 1968, 152 pp. (Originally published as The Book of Chao, 1946.)

An annotated translation, with introduction and appendices, of a work of Seng-chao, a one-time disciple of Kumarajiva. The work is essentially philosophical, but a fascinating reflection of the state of thought of fifth century Chinese Buddhism, with its thorough admixture of Taoist and Buddhist insights (so much so that it is hard to decide whether Seng-chao was a Buddhist or a Taoist--and probably wrong to ask the question).

(11) TOKIWA, DAIJO and TADASHI SEKINO. Buddhist Monuments in China. Tokyo: Bukkyo-Shiseki Kenkyu-Kwai, 1926-1931, 5 vols.

Each volume contains a hundred or so pages of text explaining the numerous plates which accompany the volumes in a separate atlas. As a whole, the five volumes attempt to study the history of Buddhist culture during the Sui and T'ang dynasties by means of analysis of the archaeological remains. Based on a series of seven expeditions to China during the first two decades of the twentieth century, the work seems to emphasize the significance of rock caves and the religious life centering around them. In addition, however, the authors have given a fairly comprehensive account of stupas and monasteries which were of great importance. The basic arrangement of the volumes is chronological.

(12) TSUKAMOTO, ZENRYU. "The Sramana Superintendent T'an-yao and His Time." Translated by Galen Eugene Sargent. Monumenta Serica, 16 (1957), 363-396.

After the unsuccessful persecution of 446, Buddhism was restored and placed under the supervision of the Northern Wei Court which appointed a "religious superintendent" in charge of the Buddhist establishment. In this article, Tsukamoto discusses the policies and achievements of the greatest and ablest of these superintendents, T'an-yao, who worked along with the Court to promote the growth of Buddhism. An invaluable source in English on this topic.

(13) WARE, JAMES R. "Wei Shou on Buddhism." *T'oung Pao*, 30 (1933), 100-181.

Wei Shou (506-572) was the author of the Wei shu, or History of the Wei dynasty, at the end of which he added an "Essay on Buddhism and Taoism." The first part of that essay has been translated here, and it makes an interesting first-hand account of sixth century Chinese Buddhism and its understanding of its own historical background.

(14) WRIGHT, ARTHUR FREDERICK. "Biography of the Nun An-ling-shou." *Harvard Journal of Asiatic Studies*, 15 (1952), 193-196.

Translation of the very short biography of the fourth century Chinese nun, taken from Pao Ch'ang's *Lives of Monks* (*Pi-ch'iu-ni chuan*). The biography makes an interesting statement of the conflict between Chinese social morality and the ethics of Buddhism at that time.

(15) _____. "The Formation of Sui Ideology (581-604)," in *Chinese Thought and Institutions*. Edited by John King Fairbank. Comparative Studies of Cultures and Civilizations. Chicago: University of Chicago Press, 1957, pp. 71-104.

Discusses the reasons for Buddhism's revival during the Sui dynasty (581-604). Wright reviews how Wen-Ti, the dynasty's founder, attempted to use Buddhism as a basis to unify Chinese society and at the same time transform it. One fascinating portion of the discussion is concerned with how Wen-Ti appropriated the symbolism of the "cakravartin" in an attempt to identify himself with that Buddhist motif.

(16) _____. "Fo-t'u-teng: A Biography." *Harvard Journal of Asiatic Studies*, 11 (1948), 321-371.

Life story of a monk from Kucha who came to North China during the rather chaotic early fourth century A.D. and, under the patronage of the Shih family, helped lay the foundations for the spread of Buddhism in the North. Informative as an introduction to the period.

(17) _____. "Fu I and the Rejection of Buddhism." *Journal of the History of Ideas*, 12 (1951), 31-47.

An account of the Taoist Fu I (555-639) and of his "Proposals for the Extirpation of Buddhism" which were based on economic, political, nationalistic, social and intellectual arguments but were never accepted in his time. Nevertheless, they provide an interesting glimpse into the Buddhist situation at the time of the reunification of the empire under the Sui, and a convenient summary of most of the points propounded by those who were opposed to Buddhism at any time thereafter.

1.11.2.3 Developments under the T'ang and Later Dynasties

(1) CH'EN, KENNETH KUAN-SHENG. "The Economic Background of the Hui-ch'ang Suppression of Buddhism." *Harvard Journal of Asiatic Studies*, 19 (1956), 67-105.

The events of the great anti-Buddhist persecution of 845 by the Emperor Wu-tsung have been described by Edwin O. Reischauer in *Ennin's Travels in T'ang China* (below, chapter 7). In this article, Ch'en analyses the economic background to that persecution, concluding quite simply that it was caused by the heavy drain on the national economy which the Buddhist monks and their tax-free monasteries represented.

(2) _____. "The Role of Buddhist Monasteries in T'ang China," in *History of Religions*, 3 (February 1976), 203-258.

(3) _____. "The Sale of Monk Certificates During the Sung Dynasty: A Factor in the Decline of Buddhism in China." *Harvard Theological Review*, 49 (1956), 307-327.

It is often assumed that the decline of Buddhism began in the T'ang Dynasty, that it never recovered from the persecution of 845. However, this ignores certain statistics that show it to have been thriving (at times) during the Sung. The question of what caused the final decline of Buddhism, then, must be asked again. In this article, Ch'en suggests that the sale of monk certificates was one of the factors.

(4) CHOU YI-LIANG. "Tantrism in China." *Harvard Journal of Asiatic Studies*, 8 (1945), 241-332.

A classic work examining the introduction and development of Indian Tantric Buddhism into China through the lives and thoughts of three monks of the seventh and eighth centuries, Shan-wu-wei, Vajrabodhi, and Amoghavajra. Essential reading for any student interested in this topic.

(5) EBERHARD, WOLFRAM. "Temple-Building Activities in Medieval and Modern China." *Monumenta Serica*, 23 (1964), 264-318.

An interesting "experimental study" of the changes in patterns of construction and destruction of Buddhist and Taoist temples in China from the seventh to the twentieth century. The purely statistical evidence of the number of temples built seems to indicate that changes in economic conditions were not necessarily a primary determining factor and that it is not true that the fortunes of Buddhism went up and down as those of Taoism went down and up.

(6) ENNIN. *Diary: The Record of a Pilgrimage to China in Search of the Law*. Translated by Edwin O. Reischauer. New York: Ronald Press, 1955, 454 pp. See also 10.1.2.(2).

This is a translation of a diary kept by Ennin, a Japanese Buddhist monk who made an extended pilgrimage to China between the years 838 and 847 A.D. It provides keen insight into the condition of Buddhism and its persecution under the T'ang. The companion volume by Reischauer, <u>Ennin's Travels in T'ang China</u> (below), is a marvelous supplement providing information on China in general and Buddhism in particular during this period.

(7) FUNG YU-LAN. "The Rise of Neo-Confucianism and Its Borrowings from Buddhism and Taoism." Translated by Derk Bodde. <u>Harvard Journal of Asiatic Studies</u>, 7 (1942), 89-125.

This is a translation of Chapter 10 (of Volume 2) of Fung Yu-lan's <u>Chung-Kuo Che hsueh shih</u> (<u>History of Chinese Philosophy</u>, 1941). Pages 89-113 trace very succinctly the influence of Buddhism on the lives and thought of two early protagonists of Neo-Confucianism, Han Yu (768-824) and Li Ao (d. 844). A full treatment of the same subject may be found in Carsun Chang, <u>The Development of Neo-Confucian Thought</u> (New York, 1956). <u>See also</u> Carsun Chang, "Buddhism as Stimulus to Neo-Confucianism," <u>Oriens extremus</u>, 2 (1955), 157-166. For a translation of two of Han-Yu's essays, <u>see</u> Herbert Giles, <u>Gems of Chinese Literature</u> (New York: Paragon, 1965), pp. 115-121 and 124-128 (originally published in 1929).

(8) JAN, YUN-HUA. "Buddhist Relations Between India and Sung China." <u>History of Religions</u>, 6 (1966), 24-42, 135-168.

Discusses the influence of Indian Buddhism on China, with special attention to the matter of translation of texts. Includes a section of translated documents. For an account of Chinese monks traveling to India during the Sung, <u>see</u> E. Huber, "L'Itinéraire du pèlerin Ki-ye dans l'Inde," <u>Bulletin de l'Ecole française d'Extrême-Orient</u>, 2 (1902), 256-257; and F. Chavannes, "L'Itinéraire de Ki-ye," op. cit., 4 (1904), 75-81.

(9) _____, ed. and trans. <u>A Chronicle of Buddhism in China, 581-960 A.D.</u> See 1.11.2.2(4).

(10) KUBO, NORITADA. "Prolegomena on the Study of Controversies Between Buddhists and Taoists in the Yuan Period." <u>Memoirs of the Research Department of the Toyo Bunko</u>, 26 (1968), 39-61.

Kubo's prolegomena consists of a very careful re-examination of the <u>Chih-yuan pien-wei lu</u>, a Buddhist document which in the past has been used by scholars to reconstruct the nature of the Buddhist-Taoist controversy during the Yuan period. The author attempts a critical assessment to uncover errors in accuracy using other sources to dispute its claims. The upshot is that the <u>Chi-yuan pien-wei lu</u> can no longer be regarded as the sole authority concerning the nature and extent of the Buddhist-Taoist controversy.

(11) OVERMEYER, DANIEL L. "Folk-Buddhist Religion: Creation and Eschatology in Medieval China." <u>See</u> 4.1.3(7).

(12) PACHOW, W. "Ancient Cultural Relations between Ceylon and China." <u>The University of Ceylon Review</u>, 12, no. 3 (July 1954), 1-10. See 1.3.2.1(4).

(13) REISCHAUER, EDWIN O. <u>Ennin's Travels in T'ang China</u>. New York: Ronald Press, 1955, 341 pp.

A companion volume to Reischauer's translation of <u>Ennin's Diary</u> (above), this is a highly readable account of the voyage of the Japanese pilgrim Ennin, and of the situation in China during his trip. It is especially useful for its description of the conditions and position of the Buddhist monks in Ch'ang-an in 842-845, just prior to the great persecution of Buddhism by the emperor Wu-tsung.

(14) SARGENT, GALEN EUGENE. "Tchou Hi contre le Bouddhisme," in <u>Mélanges publiés par l'Institut des hautes études chinoises</u>. Bibliothèque de l'Institut de hautes études chinoises, No. 11. Paris: 1957, pp. 1-157.

A discussion of the critique levelled at Buddhism by the eminent Neo-Confucian thinker Tchou Hi (A.D. 1130-1200). Sargent outlines the substance of Tchou Hi's attack, and then translates thirty sections of the critique and two other short essays.

(15) TOKIWA, DAIJO and TADASHI SEKINO. <u>Buddhist Monuments in China</u>. <u>See</u> 1.11.2.2(11).

(16) TWITCHETT, D. C. "Monastic Estates in T'ang China." <u>Asia Minor</u>, n.s. 5 (1956), 123-146.

Twitchett basically asserts that land holding served as the basis of the Sangha's economic power in China. He then recounts how these lands were acquired (chiefly through donation) and how various members of Chinese society used the special status of these lands for their own personal gain. Such abuses brought about serious land reforms which resulted in great losses for the monastic community.

(17) WITTFOGEL, KARL A. and FENG CHIA-SHENG. "History of Chinese Society: Liao (907-1125)." <u>Transactions of the American Philosophical Society</u>, n.s. 36, 1946 (published March 1949), pp. 291-309.

This discussion is one of the few concerned with Buddhism during the Liao period when it was spread to the eastern part of the vast expanses of Inner Asia to Japan and Korea. Specifically, the authors discuss Buddhism's favorable position in relation to the imperial powers of the time and the consequent economic prosperity of many temples. The authors have also included translations of a number of inscriptions. Valuable material for the intermediate to advanced student.

1.11.2.4 Buddhism in Modern China

(1) BUSH, RICHARD C. Religion in Communist China. New York: Abingdon, 1970, pp. 297-347.

This chapter of Bush's volume considers the plight of Buddhism in China from 1949-1969. The author bases his account on refugee reports, government press releases, and Western travelers' accounts. Not a bad introduction. As an alternative, see Donald MacInnis, Religious Policy and Practice in Communist China: A Documentary History (New York: Macmillan, 1972), 392 pp.

(2) CHAO P'U-CH'U. "Buddhism in China," in Présence du Bouddhisme (see 1.5.1[6], pp. 717-730.

A short article on Buddhism in China, its past and its future, by Chao P'u-ch'u, who has been a leading member of the Chinese Buddhist Association since 1953. Also of interest is the Chinese Buddhist Association's Buddhists in New China (Peking, 1956) which consists almost entirely of photographs, with captions, of various Chinese Buddhist sites now being maintained by the Chinese government as national treasures.

(3) KITAGAWA, JOSEPH M. "Buddhism in Taiwan Today." France-Asie, n.s. 18 (July-August 1962), 439-444.

The author notes the fundamental characteristics of Buddhism as found in Taiwan in the early 1960s.

(4) PRATT, JAMES BISSETT. The Pilgrimage of Buddhism and a Buddhist Pilgrimage (see 1.6.1[7]).

For descriptions of Buddhism during the Republican period, various first-hand accounts of Western travellers can be a valuable source, especially for small details and glimpses of particular places or events. These pages of the always-observant James Pratt contain descriptions of temples, monks, laymen, and include a chapter on "The Buddhist Revival in China." Other works which might be consulted include Karl Reichelt, Truth and Tradition in Chinese Buddhism (see 1.11.1[8]); Lewis Hodous, Buddhists and Buddhism in China (see 1.11.1[7]); and the slightly earlier Reginald F. Johnston, Buddhist China (London, 1913). One of the last and best personal accounts of Chinese Buddhism just before the Communist victory is John Blofeld, The Jewel in the Lotus: An Outline of Present Day Buddhism in China (see 10.1.2[1]). Finally, in The Transformed Abbot (London: Lutterworth Press, 1954), Karl Reichelt tells the story of the Taiwanese monk Miao-ch'i (1895-1930) who studied and meditated under the great T'ai Hsu and ended up converting to Christianity; his biography also provides some informal and interesting glimpses into the Buddhism of the Republican era.

(5) WELCH, HOLMES. Buddhism Under Mao. Harvard East Asian Series No. 69. Cambridge, Mass.: Harvard University Press, 1972, 666 pp.

A meticulous work on the history of Chinese Buddhism from the Communist accession in 1949 until the Cultural Revolution in 1966. Drawing heavily on the journal Hsien-tai fo hsueh ("Modern Buddhism"), published for a number of years in Peking, Welch traces the zig-zag pattern of the fortunes of Buddhism under Communist control. For a look at more recent developments, since the Cultural Revolution, see Holmes Welch, "The Buddhists Return," Far Eastern Economic Review (Hong Kong), 81, no. 28 (July 16, 1973), and John Strong and Sarah Strong, "A Post-Cultural Revolution Look at Buddhism," China Quarterly, 44 (April-June 1973).

(6) _____. The Buddhist Revival in China. Harvard East Asian Series, No. 33, Cambridge, Mass.: Harvard University Press, 1968, 385 pp.

Without a doubt, the most detailed study of the history of Chinese Buddhism in the first half of the twentieth century, and the resurgence of Buddhism. It is especially useful when combined with Welch's study of monastic life during the same period, The Practice of Chinese Buddhism, 1900-1950 (see 6.1.1[29]).

(7) WRIGHT, ARTHUR F. "Buddhism in Modern and Contemporary China," in Religion and Change in Contemporary Asia. Edited by Robert F. Spencer. Minneapolis: University of Minnesota Press, 1971, pp. 14-26.

A perceptive but pessimistic survey of the situation of Buddhism in the People's Republic.

(8) YU, DAVID C. "Buddhism in Communist China: Demise or Co-Existence?" Journal of the American Academy of Religion, 39 (1971), 48-61.

A good, quick introduction to the range of scholarly guessing about the situation of Buddhism in China today. Among the views that are surveyed are those of Ernst Benz (Buddhism or Communism, Garden City, N.Y.: Doubleday, 1966, Anchor A515); Kenneth K. S. Ch'en ("Chinese Communist Attitudes toward Buddhism in Chinese History," China Quarterly, 22 [April-June 1965], 14-30); C. K. Yang (Religion in Chinese Society, Berkeley: University of California Press, 1961, pp. 378-404), and Holmes Welch (before the publication of Buddhism under Mao [above] but after the appearance of his "The Re-interpretation of Chinese Buddhism," China Quarterly, 22 [1965], 143-153, and his "Buddhism Since the Cultural Revolution," op. cit., 40 [1969], 127-136). Yu also presents his own view.

1.12 KOREA

1.12.1 Historical Surveys and Introductions

(1) CHUN SHIN-YONG, ed. *Buddhist Culture in Korea*. Seoul: International Cultural Foundation, 1974.

A collection of articles on a variety of topics by leading Korean scholars. Included are pieces on the thought and life of the seventh century scholar Wonthy, on "Buddhist Sculpture in the Silla Period," on "The Publication of Buddhist Scriptures in the Koryo Period," and on the life and thought of a modern Korean Buddhist leader, Han Yong-Woon. The whole gives a multifaceted and overall view of the history of Korean Buddhism which is summed up in the final article, the transcript of a discussion between Suh Kyong-su and Kim Chol-jun on "Korean Buddhism: A Historical Perspective."

(2) CLARK, CHARLES ALLEN. *Religions of Old Korea*. New York: F. H. Revell, 1932, pp. 11-90.

The pages contain a general survey of the history, monasteries, beliefs and practices of Korean Buddhism and are useful as an introduction. More helpful, however, and rich in detail is the author's translation of the Korean scholar Kwon Sang-no's *Choson Pulgyo Yaksa* ("History of Korean Buddhism"), originally written in 1915, but unfortunately available in translation only as a typescript (one at the library of the University of Chicago and one at the Asiatic Society in Seoul).

(3) HAN SANG-RYAN. "The Influence of Buddhism in Korea." *Korea Observer*, 3 (1971), 17-25.

A brief sketch of the history and role of Buddhism in Korea which also gives brief life histories of a number of eminent and original Korean Buddhist thinkers from the seventh to sixteenth centuries. Another short article, also dealing with Buddhist influence on Korea, is F. Ohlinger, "Buddhism in Korean History and Language," *The Korean Repository*, 1 (1892), 101-108.

(4) KAKHUN, comp. *Lives of Eminent Korean Monks: The Haedong Kosung Chon*. Translated by Peter H. Lee. Harvard-Yenching Institute Studies, No. 25. Cambridge, Mass.: Harvard University Press, 1969, 116 pp.

An annotated translation of the *Haedong kosung chon*. Originally compiled by the Korean abbot Kakhun in 1215, this work provides an interesting introduction to Korean Buddhism, through the lives of some of its greatest figures.

(5) KWON SANG-NO. "History of Korean Buddhism." *Korea Journal*, 4, no. 5 (May 1964), 8-14.

An uncritical survey which recounts the introduction of Buddhism into Korea, its rise, and its decline.

(6) PRATT, JAMES BISSETT. *The Pilgrimage of Buddhism and a Buddhist Pilgrimage* (see 1.6.1[7]), pp. 417-435.

A short chapter dealing informally but lucidly with the history of Korean Buddhism and its present (1928) condition. One of the more available sources in English.

(7) STARR, FREDERICK. *Korean Buddhism: History, Condition, Art*. Boston: Marshall Jones, 1918, 104 pp.

Of the three lectures which make up the book, the first deals with the history of Korean Buddhism, while the other two discuss its "condition" and its "art." While not as rich as one might want, the book is one of few specifically on the subject in English.

(8) TROLLOPE, MARK NAPIER. "Introduction to the Study of Buddhism in Corea." *Transactions of the Korean Branch of the Royal Asiatic Society*, 8 (1917), 1-40.

One of the first studies of the subject, it unfortunately devotes most of its space to a simple introduction to the life of Gautama and Buddhist teachings in general, but it does so from a Korean perspective. The article became a standard reference for subsequent studies.

1.12.2 Specialized Historical Studies

(1) AHN, KYE-HYON. "Buddha Images in Korean Tradition." *Korea Journal*, 10 (1970), 7-14, 22.

After very generally contrasting the artistic spirit of Korean images with Indian and Southeast Asian ones, the author proceeds to discuss Amitabha, Alokitesvara, Maitreya, Bhaishajya (the Healing Buddha), and Varocana (the Shining Buddha) and old legends connected with them.

(2) ENCHO TAMURA. "The Influence of Silla Buddhism on Japan during the Asuka Hakuho Period. Translated by Matsuo Hakuning. In *Buddhist Culture in Korea*. Edited by Chun Shin-yong. Seoul: International Cultural Foundation, 1974, pp. 55-79. See 1.13.2.2.

(3) GORDON, ELIZABETH ANNA. "Some Recent Discoveries in Korean Temples and their Relationship to Early Eastern Christianity." *Transactions of the Korean Branch of the Royal Asiatic Society*, 5 (1914), 1-39.

A lively article based on the author's visits to ancient Korean Buddhist temples and study of the early period of Korean Buddhism. A little misguided in what it seeks to emphasize, it nevertheless presents a rare account of the period.

(4) HACKMAN, HEINRICH FRIEDRICH. *Buddhism as a Religion: Its Historical Development and Its Present Conditions*. Probsthain's Oriental Series, No. 2. London: Probsthain, 1910, pp. 257-269.

A standard account of contemporary (1910) Korean Buddhism in which the author briefly describes the character of monks and their monasteries and interaction with laymen. However, the author does describe specific Chinese influences in respect to important Buddhist texts revered by the Koreans. For the beginning student.

(5) JONES, G. H. "Korea's Colossal Image of Buddha." Transactions of the Korean Branch of the Royal Asiatic Society, 1 (1900), 57-70.

A rather simplistic article concerning a giant edifice of the Buddha in rural Korea. The author (or an assistant) gives a free translation of the inscription and then proceeds to describe the image, give a history of Buddhism in the immediate locale, and enumerate various legends concerning the image.

(6) LEDYARD, GARI. "Cultural and Political Aspects of Traditional Korean Buddhism." Asia, 10 (Winter 1968), 46-61.

This article attempts to reevaluate the historical contributions of Buddhism to Korean culture. The author is intent upon contrasting Buddhism as a flexible and heterodox faith with a doctrinaire picture of Confucianism. He tries to show that Buddhism was closer to the national spirit of the Korean peoples (at least until the twelfth century). Specifically, he discusses the Korean style of kingship, the expansion of intellectual thought, and the spirit of nationalism, all as Buddhist contributions. Finally, the author scans the contemporary condition of Buddhism (after six hundred years of suppression by the Yi dynasty), noting the strength of Buddhist institutions.

(7) LEE, PETER H. "Fa-tsang and Visang." See 8.9.3(30).

(8) _____. "The Life of the Korean Poet-Priest Kyunyo." See 8.9.6(4).

(9) LLOYD, ARTHUR. The Creed of Half Japan: Historical Sketches of Japanese Buddhism. London: Smith, Elder, 1911, pp. 168-177.

A brief, dated treatment of the introduction of Buddhism from Korea to Japan. The author speculates about the character of the Buddhism imported and the means of its transportation into Japan.

(10) PALMER, SPENCER J., ed. "The New Religions of Korea." Transactions of the Korea Branch of the Royal Asiatic Society, 43 (1967), 180 pp.

A journal volume dedicated to a number of papers on the topic of new religious movements in Korea. The papers are of varying quality. Among those dealing with the more Buddhistic movements, see Lee Kang-o, "Jingsan-gyo: Its History, Doctrines, and Ritual Practices" (pp. 28-103), and Benjamin Weems, "Ch'ondogyo Enters Its Second Century" (pp. 156-166).

(11) SOK, DO-RYUN. "Modern Sun Buddhism in Korea." Korea Journal, 5, no. 1 (1965), pp. 26-30; no. 2, pp. 27-32; no. 4, pp. 17-22.

These articles pick up where the author's previous series a year before (below) had left off. Generally, the author reviews the basic philosophical and historical changes which characterized Korean Buddhism from the unified Silla period through Buddhism's decline under the Koryo dynasty (913-1392) on to the twentieth century. He discusses the significance of Kyong Song' U in the revival of Buddhism in the last half of the nineteenth century and early twentieth. The activities of Kyong Song' U's disciples are discussed. A bibliography of Korean Buddhism in Korean is appended.

(12) _____. "Sun Buddhism in Korea." Korea Journal, 4, no. 1 (January 1964), 34-40; no. 3 (March 1964), 41-47; 12, no. 4 (April 1964), 32-37; no. 5 (May 1964), 31-36; no. 6 (June 1964), 28-31.

This series of articles by a former Buddhist monk is a review of the history and basic philosophy of the nine emergent Buddhist sects of Korea which appeared during the unified Silla period (668-935).

1.13 JAPAN

1.13.1 Historical Surveys and Introductions

(1) ANESAKI, MASAHARU. History of Japanese Religion, with Special Reference to the Social and Moral Life of the Nation. Rutland, Vt.: C. E. Tuttle, 1963, 423 pp. (Originally published London: K. Paul, Trench, Trubner, 1930).

The history of Japanese Buddhism is inseparable from the history of Japanese religion as a whole. In this classic study, and in his later and shorter Religious Life of the Japanese People (Tokyo, 1938, Revised by Hideo Kishimoto, Tokyo, 1961), Anesaki approaches his subject as a comparative philosopher of religion, emphasizing the capacity of ideas and doctrines to meet the needs of the people at any given time in history, and assuming a blanket Volkgeist for the Japanese people. His treatments of Buddhism in particular tend to picture it as monolithic and primarily doctrinal. Other general works on Japanese religion include the more up-to-date Kitagawa, Religion in Japanese History (below), and Earhart's more introductory Japanese Religion, Unity and Diversity (below).

(2) DE BARY, WILLIAM THEODORE, comp. The Buddhist Tradition in India, China and Japan (see 1.11.1[5]), pp. 255-398.

A collection of texts covering various periods of the history of Japanese Buddhism. Selected mostly from Sources of the Japanese Tradition (New York: Columbia University Press, 1958), with introductory material by de Bary, Yoshito Hakeda, and Ryusaku Tsunoda, they form an adequate first introduction to Japanese Buddhism through primary sources.

(3) EARHART, H. BYRON. Japanese Religion: Unity and Diversity. Second edition. Religious Life of Man Series. Encino, Calif.: Dickenson, 1974, 148 pp. (Originally published 1969.)

An adequate introductory work to Japanese religion. Useful as a textbook and for its annotated basic bibliography, it helps put Japanese Buddhism in the context and perspective of the overall history of religion in Japan (not neglecting folk religion). Other general studies of Japanese religion include Anesaki, History of Japanese Religion (above), and Kitagawa, Religion in Japanese History (below). Earhart also has a companion volume of sources in the same series: Religion in the Japanese Experience: Sources and Interpretations (Encino, Calif.: Dickenson, 1974), 270 pp.

(4) ELIOT, CHARLES NORTON EDGECUMBE. Japanese Buddhism. New York: Barnes and Noble, 1959, 449 pp. (Originally published London: Edward Arnold; New York: Longman's, 1935.)

In 1921, as he was completing his monumental Hinduism and Buddhism, Eliot decided to refrain from writing about Japanese Buddhism as he had just been appointed British ambassador to Tokyo. The result was a fourteen year delay during which the originally planned three chapters became this separate volume, which still remains the standard historical study of the subject. It emphasizes continuity with China and India and is fine in its presentation of historical data, though less so in its survey of the doctrines, and lacking in descriptions of practices or popular beliefs. Still, it is perhaps the best single survey in English.

(5) GRIFFIS, WILLIAM ELLIOT. The Religions of Japan from the Dawn of History to the Era of the Meiji. New York: C. Scribner's Sons, 1896, pp. 153-321.

For years, Griffis's work was considered the standard work in the field. Though it is now dated, it still remains a worthy treatment of the historical and doctrinal development of Buddhism in Japan which gives special attention to the "uniqueness" of the Japanese translation of the faith. A good introduction.

(6) ICHIRO, HORI et al., eds. Japanese Religion: A Survey by the Agency for Cultural Affairs. Tokyo and Palo Alto, Calif.: Kodansha International, 1972, 272 pp.

This edition consists of a general survey with brief historical accounts of each major religious tradition. Its main value to the student of Buddhism lies in its statistical information concerning contemporary membership in various traditions. For the beginning student.

(7) KITAGAWA, JOSEPH M. "The Buddhist Transformation in Japan." History of Religions, 4, no. 2 (Winter 1965), 319-336.

The author identifies two main threads in the Japanese adoption of Buddhism--national and folk. Using this schema, he describes the changing character of Japanese Buddhism through each of Japan's major historical periods up to the present. A good summary of trends and problems for the student of any level.

(8) _____. Religion in Japanese History. New York: Columbia University Press, 1966, 475 pp.

A series of six lectures, drawing on Western and Japanese sources, combining insights on sociology and history of religions, this is one of the standard works on Japanese religion as a whole. For a short presentation of this author's view of Buddhism in Japanese history and his division of it into "National Buddhism" and "Folk Buddhism," see his "The Buddhist Transformation in Japan" (above).

(9) _____. "Religions of Japan," in The Great Asian Religions: An Anthology. By Wing-tsit Chan et al. New York: Macmillan, 1969, pp. 229-290.

A well thought out historical survey of Buddhism in Japanese religious history. The author is careful to point out how Buddhism accommodated itself to Japan's indigenous religious beliefs and practices and how it allied itself with local cultural, social, and political structures. A useful introduction to the history of Japanese Buddhism.

(10) LLOYD, ARTHUR. The Creed of Half Japan: Historical Sketches of Japanese Buddhism (see 1.12.2[9]).

This book is a collection of essays which are rather loosely arranged and somewhat outdated, but informative and interesting. See especially pages 168-381, which trace the history of Buddhism in Japan.

(11) PRATT, JAMES BISSETT. The Pilgrimage of Buddhism and a Buddhist Pilgrimage (see 1.6.1[7]).

Though dated, this section of Pratt's work provides the introductory reader with a decent introduction to the history and doctrinal evolutions of Japanese Buddhism. The reader will also find adequate discussions based on then contemporary scholarship concerning various temples, the character of monks and laymen, Buddhist education and the essential components of the major sects.

(12) REISCHAUER, AUGUST KARL. Studies in Japanese Buddhism. New York: Macmillan, 1917, 361 pp.

Though this contribution is a bit dated and the author seems distressed over contemporary "degeneration" of the faith, the student can still gain from an excellent discussion concerning the Buddhist canon as it is known in Japan.

Japan

(13) RENONDEAU, GASTON and BERNARD FRANK. "Le Bouddhisme Japonais," in Histoire des Religions 1, Encyclopédie de la Pléiade 29. Paris: Gallimard, 1970, pp. 1320-1348.

This account of the development of Buddhism in Japan from its introduction up to the present is useful both as an introduction and overview.

(14) SANSOM, GEORGE BAILEY. A History of Japan. Stanford Studies in the Civilizations of Eastern Asia. Stanford, Calif.: Stanford University Press, 1958-1963, 3 vols.

A monumental history of Japan covering the development of virtually all facets of Japanese life. The great stength of Sansom's work is that he has thoroughly perceived the significance of the role of religion in Japanese history. Although there are other worthy histories of Japan, Sansom's work stands above most. It should be noted that his treatment only runs to 1867.

(15) _____. Japan: A Short Cultural History. Revised edition. New York: Appleton-Century-Crofts, 1962, 558 pp. (Originally published New York, 1931.)

A standard treatment of Japanese cultural history, in which the author has dealt with the medieval history of Buddhism. Sansom is also the author of A History of Japan (above) which is a good resource for placing Buddhism within the entire context of Japanese history.

(16) SAUNDERS, ERNEST DALE. Buddhism in Japan: With an Outline of Its Origins in India. Philadelphia: University of Pennsylvania Press, 1964, 328 pp.

Clear, easily read, but not very inspired doctrinal-historical survey of the history of Japanese Buddhism from its beginnings up to the new religions of the modern day, together with a brief account of Buddhism's Indian and Chinese background. The best section is that which deals with Shingon and the esoteric tradition (pp. 148-178).

(17) SUZUKI, DAISETZ TEITARO. Japanese Buddhism. Tourist Library, No. 21. Tokyo: Board of Tourist Industry, Japanese Government Railways, 1938, 85 pp.

Very sketchy and written in a popular style. The author has done much better elsewhere and so can the reader. No historical treatment of any significance and an emphasis upon Zen make this an unbalanced contribution. Only the beginning student may benefit.

1.13.2 Specialized Historical Studies

1.13.2.1 Introduction and Early Development of Buddhism

(1) ANESAKI, MASAHARU. Prince Shotoku, the Sage Statesman. Tokyo: Boonjudo Publishing House, 1948, 75 pp.

Sensitive to the views that Prince Shotoku was an ardent nationalist or that he was a Buddhist saint, Anesaki has tried to confirm both of these assessments by viewing the prince as a "sage statesman." Shotoku is portrayed as a leader who found Buddhism to be the foundation of his patriotism, using Buddhist ideals to illuminate his policies. The first part of the book is largely biographical, while the second part attempts to equate Shotoku's idealism with the Bodhisattva ideal. A good source for all students.

(2) ENCHO TAMURA. "The Influence of Silla Buddhism on Japan During the Asuka-Hakuho Period," in Buddhist Culture in Korea (see 1.12.2[2]).

Helpful articles on an important and much neglected topic: the importance of the specifically Korean forms of Buddhism in its transmission and establishment in Japan in the sixth and seventh centuries.

(3) KAMSTRA, J. H. Encounter or Syncretism: The Initial Growth of Japanese Buddhism. Leiden: Brill, 1967, 508 pp.

A comprehensive and thorough study of the introduction and early development of Buddhism in Japan. For a short introduction and another view of the same topic, see Zenryu Tsukamoto, "Buddhism in the Asuka-Nara Period" (below).

(4) KIDDER, J. EDWARD. Early Buddhist Japan. Ancient Peoples and Places, No. 78. New York: Praeger, 1972, 212 pp.

A treatment of Japanese history to 794 with special attention to archeological remains such as the Kotun tombs, coins, statuary, ritual sites, and palace sites. Kidder describes Buddhism's interaction with Shinto in terms of Buddhism's access to medical knowledge (this fact filling a gap left by the Shinto aversion to sickness and blood as pollution).

(5) RENONDEAU, GASTON. "La date de l'Introduction du Bouddhisme au Japon." T'oung Pao, 47 (1959), 16-29.

Renondeau suggests, if hesitantly, 538 A.D. as the date, and in so doing presents a useful summary of some of the problems involved in determining when Buddhism was introduced to Japan.

(6) SATOW, ERNEST MASON. "History of the Introduction of Buddhism into Japan." Journal of the Buddhist Text Society of India, 2, no. 3 (1894), 23-30.

An early, dated, bare-bones account of the introduction of the major Buddhist sects into Japan. Suitable for the beginning student.

(7) TSUKAMOTO, ZENRYU. "Buddhism in the Asuka-Nara Period." Translated by Hirano Umeyo. Eastern Buddhist, 7 (1974), 19-36.

A straightforward account of the events surrounding early Buddhism in Japan by an important Japanese scholar. Tsukamoto deals with Shotoku's role, and the influence of the Yamato court, but focuses especially on the significance of the building of the Daibatsu --Great Buddha statue of Vairocana--in Nara.

(8) VISSER, MARINUS WILLEM DE. Ancient Buddhism in Japan: Sutras and Ceremonies in Use in the Seventh and Eighth Centuries A.D. and Their History in Later Times. Buddhica, Nos. 3 and 4. Paris: P. Geuthner, 1928, 2 vols., 763 pp.

This is a study which is very detailed to the point of being an encyclopedic account. An excellent index makes this work an indispensable reference for careful historical work in the early period.

(9) WATSUJI, TETSURO. "The Reception of Buddhism in the Suiko Period." The Eastern Buddhist, 5, no. 1 (May 1972), 47-54.

The author wishes to take issue with the popular theory that when Buddhism was first introduced into Japan by Prince Shotoku, the Buddha was simply worshipped for the sake of "this-world happiness" and that Buddhism had no meaning for the people other than as a "petitionary religion." Instead, he attempts to demonstrate that Buddhism was quickly assimilated into the essential Japanese cultural ethos.

1.13.2.2 The Founding of the Various Sects

See also 2.5 and 8.9.

(1) ANESAKI, MASAHARU. "Honen (born 1133, died 1211), the Pietist Saint of Japanese Buddhism," in Transactions of the Third International Congress for the History of Religions (Oxford, 1908), vol. 1, pp. 122-128.

A brief article which seeks to place Honen's significance in Japanese religious history. It contains a brief biographical sketch and a resume of Honen's fundamental tenets of faith. Useful for the beginning student.

(2) _____. Nichiren the Buddhist Prophet. Cambridge, Mass.: Harvard University Press, 1916, 160 pp.

This is a treatment of Nichiren and his struggles with the then contemporary political regime. Excellent discussion of Nichiren's doctrine. Of use to the student at any level.

(3) ARMSTRONG, ROBERT CORNELL. An Introduction to Japanese Buddhist Sects. Privately printed for Mrs. R. C. Armstrong (Canada), 1950, 350 pp.

Although this source is primarily concerned with the historical evolution of doctrine within each sect, it still contains valuable descriptions of various rituals and meditations. The treatment of Pure Land stands above the others and is of use to the beginning student. See also Armstrong's Buddhism and Buddhists in Japan (New York: Macmillan; London: S.P.C.K., 1927), 144 pp.

(4) BLOOM, ALFRED. The Life of Shinran Shonin: The Journey to Self-Acceptance. Leiden: E. J. Brill, 1968, 62 pp.

An account of the emergence of Shinran as leader of the Shin sect. Because of the few historical studies available in western languages on this important figure, Bloom's work looms as a major contribution since his work is based almost entirely upon Japanese sources. The reader is treated to excellent discussions of controversial matters relevant to historical scholarship concerned with Shinran.

(5) BOHNER, HERMANN. "Kobo Daishi." Monumenta Nipponica, 6 (1943), 266-313.

This is probably the best scholarly treatment available concerning the life and thought of Kobo Daishi. The author has examined available primary sources in order to present this composite account. The article is in German; for another good treatment of Kobo Daishi, see U. A. Casal, "The Saintly Kobo Daishi in Popular Lore," Folklore Studies, 18 (1959), 95-144.

(6) DUMOULIN, HEINRICH. A History of Zen Buddhism. Translated by Paul Peachey. New York: McGraw-Hill, 1965, 335 pp. (Originally published New York: Pantheon Books, 1963; McGraw-Hill Paperbacks in Religion and Philosophy).

This is the standard historical work on Zen Buddhism by a Western interpreter. Chapters 9-14 are specifically concerned with Zen in Japan (as opposed to Chan in China).

(7) FUJIKAWA, ASAKO. Daughter of Shinran. Tokyo: Hokuseido Press, 1964, 60 pp.

Brief treatment based almost entirely upon secondary sources which seeks to treat historically the importance of Kakushin-ni, Shinran's daughter, who was responsible for some of the first organizational efforts for the Shin sect.

(8) HAKEDA, YOSHITO. Kukai: Major Works. See 2.6.2(4).

(9) INOUE, MITSUSADA. "Eizon Ninsho and the Saidai-ji Order." Acta Asiatica, 20 (March 1971), 77-103.

The author details the attempt of Eizon and the Saidi-ji order to carry out the propagation of Buddhist precepts in response to the popularization of Nembutsu (as preached by Shinran and Hone) during the Kamakura period.

(10) NANJIO, BUNYIU, comp. and trans. A Short History of the Twelve Japanese Buddhist Sects. Tokyo: Bukkyo-sho-ei-yaku-shuppan-sha, 1886, 172 pp.

This is basically a translation of a well-known traditional account of the various historical and doctrinal developments of the Buddhist sects. It amounts to a rather uncritical survey. Its value remains its traditional mode.

(11) PETZOLD, BRUNO. "Dengyo Daishi (767-822): The Founder of the Japanese Tendai Sect." *Young East*, 2 (1926), 5-16.

Overly sympathetic and perhaps too brief, this article is still a useful account of Saicho, who brought Tendai Buddhism to Japan in 804 A.D.

(12) SHUNJO. *Honen, the Buddhist Saint: His Life and Teaching*. See 2.5.8(19).

(13) STEINILBER-OBERLIN, E. *The Buddhist Sects of Japan: Their History, Philosophical Doctrines and Sanctuaries*. Translated by Marc Loge. London: G. Allen and Unwin, 1938, 303 pp.

The author describes this work as a philosophical inquiry into basic tenets of the various Japanese Buddhist sects. However, what evolves is an overly-sympathetic treatment of each of the schools with references to the basic texts, the "centers" of each sect, and romanticized discussions with various representatives from each sect. The reader is further cautioned to be aware of over-simplified comparisons with western philosophic tradition.

(14) UI, HAKUJU. "A Study of Japanese Tendai Buddhism," in *Philosophical Studies of Japan*. Edited by The Japanese National Commission for UNESCO. Tokyo, 1959, vol. 1, pp. 33-74.

Though the focus of this article is primarily philosophical, the reader is able to see the historical development of Tendai thought from its beginning to the contemporary period. Of use to the intermediate student.

(15) YAMAMOTO, KOSHO. *An Introduction to Shin Buddhism*. Oyama: The Karinbunko, 1963, 328 pp.

In general, the entire work is a worthy introduction to the study of Shin. Its historical import lies in the author's treatment of the life and teachings of Shinran which can be used as a supplement to Alfred Bloom's works (above).

1.13.2.3 From 1400 to 1868

(1) BELLAH, ROBERT NEELLY. *Tokugawa Religion: The Values of Pre-Industrial Japan*. Glencoe, Ill.: Free Press, 1957, 249 pp.

A scholarly work concerning the role of religion as a value creating system which has consequences in the economic realm. A classical application of Weberian thought which is of value to any student.

(2) RATTI, OSCAR and ADELE WESTBROOK. *Secrets of the Samurai: A Study of the Martial Arts of Feudal Japan*. Rutland, Vt.: C. E. Tuttle, 1973, pp. 445-459.

These pages discuss the effects of Confucianism, Taoism, and Buddhism upon the moral and ethical conduct of the Samurai. The authors contend that the general Buddhist influence upon the Samurai was more aesthetic than ethical (that the Samurai renounced desire not in order to attain nirvana, but in order to become perfect warriors). More specifically, the authors detail the relationship between Zen and Bujutsu. A good source to begin a study of this topic in general. For additional reading, see Kaiten Nukariya, *The Religion of the Samurai* (London: Luzac, 1913).

(3) SUGIHIRA, SHIZUTOSHI. "Rennyo Shonin, the Great Teacher of Shin Buddhism," *Eastern Buddhist*, 8, no. 1 (May 1949), 5-35.

In this article, the reader will find ten important epistles of Rennyo Shonin (1415-1499) and a short biographical sketch which includes an account of his leadership in restoring Shin following its decline. The doctrinal significance of Rennyo's teaching is also adequately discussed. A good source for the intermediate student.

(4) YAMPOLSKY, PHILIP B., trans. *The Zen Master Hakuin: Selected Writings*. (Records of civilization: Sources and Studies, No. 86) New York: Columbia University Press, 1971, 253 pp.

1.13.2.4 Buddhism in Modern Japan

See also 6.2.2.6.

(1) COOKE, GERALD. "Traditional Buddhist Sects and Modernization in Japan." *Japan Journal of Religious Studies*, 1, no. 4 (December 1974), 267-330.

The author first summarizes the prevailing notion among some scholars that the traditional Buddhist sects in Japan are nothing more than "funeral Buddhism" today. He goes on to ask the question concerned with the type of efforts being made to revive the traditional sects and notes "signs of life" among Zen, Shinshu, and Shingon Buddhism.

(2) HAMMER, RAYMOND. *Japan's Religious Ferment: Christian Presence amid Faiths Old and New*. Christian Presence Series. New York: Oxford University Press, 1962, pp. 33-71 and 120-134.

The first set of pages represents the author's attempt to make a coherent presentation of the history of Buddhism in Japan from its introduction well into its domestication. The other pages outline the author's view of the Buddhist response to Japanese modernity.

(3) KITAGAWA, JOSEPH M. "The Contemporary Religious Situation in Japan." Japanese Religions, 2, nos. 2-3 (May 1961), 24-42.

A brief survey of the dominant religious trends in Japan during the last one hundred years. The reader will be able to glean a general notion concerning the place of Buddhism in Japanese society. Suitable for the beginning student.

(4) KIYOTA, MINORU. "Buddhism in Postwar Japan: A Critical Survey." Monumenta Nipponica, 24 (1969), 113-136.

A useful survey taken mostly from Japanese sources setting the contemporary situation of Japanese Buddhism in historical perspective.

(5) ____. "Meiji Buddhism: Religion and Patriotism." See 6.2.2.6(8).

(6) MURATA, KIYOAKI. Japan's New Buddhism: An Objective Account of Soka Gakkai. New York: Walker/Weatherhill, 1969, 194 pp.

An account of the history of Soka Gakkai to the contemporary period by a Japanese journalist. It is written in a straightforward manner and based upon sound sources and recent scholarship. The bibliography is extensive but most works cited are in Japanese. Of good use to the intermediate student.

(7) OFFNER, CLARK B. and HENRY VAN STRAELEN. Modern Japanese Religions, with Special Emphasis Upon Their Doctrines of Healing. New York: Twayne; Leiden: E. J. Brill, 1963, 296 pp.

An evaluation concerning the causes which have yielded the rise of the "new religions" in modern Japan. The authors have included detailed accounts of various methods of "healing," and as a whole the book is sound in terms of description.

(8) OKAKURA, KAKUZO. The Book of Tea. Edited by Everett F. Bleiler. New York: Dover, 1964, pp. 47-69. (Originally published New York: Fox, Duffield, 1906.)

These pages are generally concerned with the connections between Zen and Tea. The author sees Zen as the successor of Taoism in a religious trend toward increasing individuation whereby Taoism furnished a basis of aesthetic ideals and Zen converted these ideals into the practical sphere. Intended for the student at the elementary level.

(9) WHITE, JAMES W. The Sokagakkai and Mass Society. See 6.2.2.6(11).

1.14 TIBET

1.14.1 Historical Surveys and Introductions

(1) BELL, CHARLES. The Religion of Tibet. Oxford: Clarendon, 1968, 235 pp. (Originally published 1931.)

A standard work, somewhat dated in its method, but still a good account of the beginning and growth of Buddhism in Tibet, with special focus on religious personalities, and the role of monks in government. Written in a style easy enough for those with little or no previous knowledge of Tibetan Buddhism.

(2) BU-STON RIN-CHEN-GRUB-PA. History of Buddhism (Chos-hnyung). Translated by E. Obermiller. Materialien zur Kunde des Buddismus, nos. 18-19. Heidelberg: O. Harrassowitz, 1931-1932, 2 vols.

A fourteenth century work which includes, in its second volume, a narrative of the life of the Buddha, an account of the "rehearsals of the Scripture," biographies of Buddhist teachers, and a history of Buddhism in Tibet --doctrinal as well as chronological. It is a classic and important source of our knowledge of the history of Tibetan Buddhism.

(3) DAS, SARAT CHANDRA. "Rise and Progress of Buddhism in Tibet." Journal of the Asiatic Society of Bengal, 51 (1882), 1-14.

This is a translation of part of the second book of an eighteenth century text, the Grub mTha' Sel-kyi me long, and makes a good, concise example of a Tibetan's own view of the history of Buddhism in his country.

(4) ELIOT, CHARLES NORTON EDGECUMBE. Hinduism and Buddhism: An Historical Sketch (see 1.1[4]), vol. 3, pp. 345-401.

A very good starting point for the introductory student of Tibetan Buddhism. The reader will find succinct and well-done treatments of the history of Buddhism in Tibet, the canon, the uniqueness of Lamaism and the major points of controversy between the Red and Yellow Hats.

(5) GOS LO-TSA-BA. The Blue Annals. Edited and translated by George N. Roerich. Royal Asiatic Society of Bengal Monograph Series, No. 7. Calcutta: Royal Asiatic Society of Bengal, 1949-1953, 2 vols., 1275 pp.

A translation of Gos lo-tra-ba's Deb-ther-sngon pa, an important classic history of the origin, development and spread of Buddhism in Tibet, which fortunately is now available as a reprint (Delhi: Motilal Banarsidass, 1976).

(6) HOFFMAN, HELMUT. The Religions of Tibet. Translated by Edward Fitzgerald. New York: Macmillan, 1961, 199 pp.

A translation of Die Religionen Tibets, which remains one of the standard general works and is especially valuable for its coverage of the changing historical relationship of Buddhism and the Bon religion.

(7) JIVAKA, LOBSANG. "Le Bouddhisme tibétain: Un bref historique." Translated by Françoise Cayrac. France-Asie, 21, no. 188 (Winter 1966-1967), 197-205.

An excellent article which begins by outlining the basic differences which arose between the Theravada and Mahayana sects and the historical consequences this had for Tibetan Buddhism. The author then goes on to highlight the important figures and events from King Srong-btsan-gam-po to Tsong-khapa, noting the significance of each for the development of the tradition. Probably the best short summary available. For another worthy summary in English, see Li An-che, "Tibetan Religion," in Forgotten Religions, edited by Vergilus Ferm (Freeport, New York: Books for Libraries Press, 1970), pp. 251-269; and William Weedonn, "Tibetan Buddhism, a Perspective," Philosophy East and West, 17 (1967), 167-172.

(8) LALOU, MARCELLE. Les religions du Tibet. Mythes et religions, No. 35. Paris: Presses universitaires de France, 1957, 101 pp.
  Lalou traces very concisely the development of Buddhism (and Bon) in Tibet, from its introduction to the Gelugpa ascendancy. A good introduction for students who read French.

(9) LI, T'IEH-CHENG. Tibet, Today and Yesterday. Revised edition. New York: Bookman Associates, 1960, 324 pp. (Originally published as The Historical Status of Tibet. New York: King's Crown Press, 1956.)
  A treatment of Tibet's political history especially in its references to the modern period. Three chapters are concerned with the nature of the Panchen Lama and there is a copious treatment of the Dalai Lama's role in Tibetan history.

(10) SHAKABPA, TSEPON W. D. Tibet: A Political History. New Haven: Yale University Press, 1967, 369 pp.
  Shakabpa's work was inspired by his nationalist convictions that Tibet has historically been ignored as a sovereign and independent country. This, he claims, resulted from the fact that the world did not fully understand the true nature of governments led by a religious figure (Dalai Lama) and Tibet's historical sovereignty through the Mongol and Manchu periods. Hence, his history is written primarily to establish as historical fact the traditionally misunderstood independence of Tibet. Relying upon indigenous historical accounts as well as Western scholarship, he has provided the reader (both beginning student and advanced) with an excellent account of Tibetan political history from the earliest times to the contemporary period.

(11) SNELLGROVE, DAVID and HUGH RICHARDSON. A Cultural History of Tibet. London: Weidenfeld and Nicolson, 1968, 291 pp.
  Any general history of Tibet will deal with the history of Tibetan Buddhism. This work, richly illustrated, combines the views of two prominent English Tibetologists and is significant for its methodological independence from early monastic studies. Other general works containing much information on the history and context of Tibetan Buddhism include Charles Bell, Tibet Past and Present (Oxford, 1927), Stein's Tibetan Civilization (below), and, for the views of a Tibetan political leader anxious to stress Tibet's relations with India (as opposed to China), Shakabpa's Tibet: A Political History (above).

(12) STEIN, ROLF ALFRED. Tibetan Civilization. Translated by J. E. Stapleton Driver. Stanford, Calif.: Stanford University Press, 1972, 333 pp.
  This is probably the best place to start for the student who has had no previous experience with Tibetan life. Stein (whose first edition of this book was published in French in 1962) neatly outlines Tibetan history, characterizes society in general, and treats the religion and customs concisely, sensitively and accurately.

(13) THUBTEN JIGME NORBU and COLIN M. TURNBULL. Tibet. Harmondsworth: Penguin Books, 1972, 359 pp. (Also published London: Chatto and Windus, 1969; New York: Simon and Schuster, 1968.)
  This work is a Tibetan's history of his country written from a traditional point of view. The reader is provided with a history of the introduction and establishment of Buddhism in Tibet as well as the character of monastic rule. Useful reading if accompanied by a scholarly historical corrective.

(14) TUCCI, GIUSEPPE, trans. Deb t'er dmar ro gsar ma Tibetan Chronicles by bSod nams grags pa. Serie Orientale Roma, No. 24. Rome: Istituto Italiano per el medio ed estremo Orientale, 1971, 245 pp.
  Tibetan text with English translation of a historical chronicle compiled by the fifteenth and sixteenth century bSod nams grags pa, and not to be confused with the better known "Red Annals," which has a similar title. Tucci has begun his translation with Chapter 3, "The Royal Genealogies of Tibet," omitting unfortunately Chapters 1 and 2 on the royal genealogies of India and Sambhala.

(15) _____. Tibet: Land of Snows. Translated by J. E. Stapleton Driver. New York: Stein and Day, 1967, pp. 64-97.
  This section contains a very good introduction to the topic of Tibetan Buddhism in general. The author discusses Buddhism's Tibetan history, meditative practices, monasteries, while providing the reader with beautiful illustrations. Excellent for the beginning student.

(16) _____. "The Validity of Tibetan Historical Tradition," in India Antiqua. Edited by Frederik David Kan Bosch et al. Leiden: E. J. Brill for Kern Institute, 1947, pp. 309-322.
  This article consists of an examination of the more authoritative Lamaistic historical works in light of more recently published documents. Specifically, Tucci examines two historical traditions, attempting to see if

these traditions relied upon parallel sources or sources dependent upon the Tun Huang texts. He concludes that the Sa Skya traditions embody information parallel to information in the Tun Huang texts while another Tibetan historical tradition is dependent upon Chinese sources. Tucci has included a chart to help the reader unravel his findings. For the advanced student.

(17) WADDELL, LAURENCE AUSTINE. Tibetan Buddhism, with Its Mystic Cults, Symbolism and Mythology, and in Its Relation to Indian Buddhism. New York: Dover Publications, 1972, 598 pp. (Reprint of The Buddhism of Tibet, 1895.)

For years, this work was considered by many as the basic handbook of Tibetan Buddhism. However, recent scholarship has tended to discredit some of Waddell's historical reconstructions of the history of Buddhism in Tibet, as well as some interpretation grounded in Western and Christian assumptions. Nevertheless, the work remains one of the best general sources available on Tibetan Buddhism in general because of its detailed cataloging of monastic dress, ritual implements, symbolism, etc.

1.14.2 Specialized Historical Studies

1.14.2.1 Introduction and Early Development of Buddhism

(1) BACOT, JACQUES, FREDERICK WILLIAM THOMAS and CHARLES TOUSSAINT, eds. and trans. Documents de Touen-Houang relatifs à l'histoire du Tibet. Annales du Musée Guimet, Bibliothèque d'études, No. 51. Paris: P. Geuthner, 1940, 204 pp.

This edition is for those students seeking primary sources for the early historical period of Tun-huang. The material includes annals, genealogies, and chronicles. In Tibetan, with French or English translations.

(2) DEMIEVILLE, PAUL. Le concile de Lhasa: Une controverse sur le quiétisme entre bouddhistes de l'Inde et de la Chine au VIIIe siècle de l'ère chrétienne. Bibliothèque de l'Institut des hautes études chinoises, No. 7. Paris: Presses universitaires de France, 1952, 398 pp.

Contains translations and discussions of various accounts of the Great Debate held in Tibet during the reign of Khri-Srong-lDe-bCan between Chinese and Indian Buddhist masters. For the intermediate and advanced student.

(3) FRANCKE, A. H. Antiquities of India and Tibet. Vol. 2: The Chronicles of Ladakh and Minor Chronicles. Calcutta: Superintendent of Government Printing, 1926, 310 pp.

Traces the history of Ladakh from its beginnings up to the modern period. Though presently part of India, Ladakh is still culturally Tibetan, and, as a preface to the tracing of its own history, the La-dvag-rgyal-rabs, translated here, deals with the early line of Tibetan kings, providing some interesting information on that subject. The reader should beware, however, of Francke's particular prejudices which make him see Ladakh itself as the locus centrum of the ancient Tibetan monarchy. In this regard, an almost indispensable aid to the reading of Francke's translation is Petech's "A Study on the Chronicles of Ladakh" (below).

(4) HAARH, ERIK. The Yar-Lun Dynasty: A Study With Particular Regard to the Contribution by Myths and Legends to the History of Ancient Tibet and the Origin and Nature of Its Kings. Copenhagen: G. E. C. Gad's Forlag, 1969, 481 pp.

Important and well-conceived work concerned with the myths and legends connected with the history of ancient Tibet and the origin and nature of its kings. Of use primarily to the intermediate and advanced student.

(5) KVARNE, PER. "Aspects of the Origin of the Buddhist Tradition in Tibet." Numen, 19 (1972), 22-40.

Using manuscripts found at Tun-huang as well as Lamaist literature (philosophical and historical), the author addresses the following problems: 1) the differences between Buddhism and the indigenous Bon religion; 2) the relationship of Bon and Buddhism to dharma in the religious history of Tibet; and 3) the introduction of Buddhism into Tibet.

(6) LI AN-CHE. "Rnin-ma-pa: The Early Form of Lamaism." Journal of the Royal Asiatic Society (1948), pp. 142-163.

An introductory article concerned with the historical background and unique qualities of the "red sect." The author explains how the "red sect" has divided Buddhism into nine categories in order to explain the variations; portrays the academic organization of the sect as being divided between doctrinal instruction and practical training; and depicts the actual program of study carried out in the sect's "teaching college."

(7) PETECH, LUCIANO. "A Study on the Chronicles of Ladakh." Indian Historical Quarterly, 13 (1937), supplement; and 15 (1939), pp. 1-38; supplement, pp. 39-189. See 1.14.2.1(3).

(8) RICHARDSON, HUGH E. "Tibetan Inscriptions at Zva-hi Lha Khan." Journal of the Royal Asiatic Society (1952), pp. 133-154; and (1953), pp. 1-12.

The author begins by presenting a brief historical sketch of the area around the chapel in which these inscriptions were found. But the basic thrust of the article centers around the historical significance of the inscriptions for arguments concerned with Tibetan history in the eighth and ninth centuries. Scholarly article for the advanced student.

(9) SNELLGROVE, DAVID L. Buddhist Himalaya: Travels and Studies in Quest of the Origins and Nature of Tibetan Religion. New York: Philosophical Library; Oxford: Bruno Cassirer, 1957, pp. 121-165.

These pages represent a general discussion concerned with the early myths of kings, the historical line of Tibetan kingship, the political rise to power of Tibet as a nation, and the introduction of Buddhism into Tibet, as well as chapters on Tantric Buddhism in India. Of use to the beginning student.

(10) TUCCI, GIUSEPPE, ed. Minor Buddhist Texts. Serie Orientale Roma, No. 9. Rome: Istituto per il Medio ed Estremo Oriente, 1958, Pt. 2, First Phavanakrama of Kamalasila: Sanscrit and Tibetan Texts with Introd. and English Summary, 288 pp.

A detailed account of the Lhasa debate using Tibetan historical materials with a Sanskrit edition and English summary of the first of Kamalasila's texts on the gradual path to Buddhahood. Authoritative and of use to the advanced student.

(11) _____. The Tombs of the Tibetan Kings. Serie Orientale Roma, No. 1. Rome: Istituto Italiano per il Medio ed Estremo Oriente, 1950, 117 pp.

A monograph on the inscriptions and tombs of the early Tibetan kings of the Yarlung Valley. It is essential reading for those students concerned with the very beginnings of Buddhism in its Tibetan translation and in its initial relationships to the old Bon religion.

(12) _____. "The Wives of Sron btsan sgam po." Oriens Extremus, 9 (1962), 121-126.

Tucci raises a critical skepticism about the legends concerning the wives of this illustrious Tibetan Buddhist king. See also Jacques Bacot, "Le mariage chinois du roi tibétain Sron bcan sgan po," Mélanges Chinois et Bouddhiques, 3 (1934-1935), 1-60.

1.14.2.2 Re-introduction of Buddhism and Development of the Various Sects

(1) AHMAD, ZAHIRUDDIN. Sino-Tibetan Relations in the Seventeenth Century. Serie orientale Roma, No. 40. Rome: Istituto Italiano per il Medio ed Estremo Oriente, 1970.

A sober and detailed account of the stormy relations between the Tibetans, Mongols, and Chinese. The reader witnesses the diplomatic skill of the fifth Dalai Lama as he gathers the reins of power to the Dge-lugs-pa sect. Of use to the intermediate and advanced student.

(2) CASSINELLI, C. W. and ROBERT B. EKVALL. A Tibetan Principality: The Political System of Sa skya. See 6.2.2.7(3).

(3) CHATTOPADHYAYA, ALAKA. Atisa and Tibet: Life and Works of Dipamkara Srijnana in Relation to the History and Religion of Tibet. Calcutta: Indian Studies Past and Present, 1967, 593 pp.

An authoritative account concerned with the historical figure of Atisa which yields insight into his historical period both in Tibet and in India. The author has catalogued Atisa's works and the author's appendices include sources helpful to the study of Lang Darmai's persecution of Buddhism, the coming of Santiraksita to Tibet, and the significance of Padmasambhava. For the intermediate student.

(4) DAS, SARAT CHANDRA. "Life of Sum pa Khanpo also styled Yeses Dpal hbyor, the author of the Rehumig (Chronological Table)." See 8.9.2(20).

(5) LI AN-CHE. "The Bkah-Brgyud Sect of Lamaism." Journal of the American Oriental Society, 69 (1949), 51-59.

An article concerned with the general characteristics of the "white sect." The author traces the line of traditional patriarchs back to the Buddha along two lines. He then outlines the characteristics of subsects, the significance of Milarepa, the importance of the "great hand seal" to liberation, the basic teachings of the sect, and the grades of lamas. Good article for the intermediate student.

(6) PETECH, LUCIANO. China and Tibet in the Early 18th Century: History of the Establishment of Chinese Protectorate in Tibet. Monographes du T'oung Pao, No. 1. Leiden: E. J. Brill, 1950, 286 pp.

An historical account of the remarkable events leading up to the establishment of the Chinese protectorate in Tibet. Very detailed and of value to the intermediate and advanced student.

(7) RAS-CHUN. Tibet's Great Yogi, Milarepa: A Biography from the Tibetan, being the Jetsun-Kahbum, or Biographical History of Jetsun-Milarepa. Translated by Lama Kazi Dawa-Samaup. Edited by W. Y. Evans-Wentz. Second edition. London: Oxford, 1958, 315 pp. (Originally published 1928; condensed version: The Life of Milarepa, Tibet's Great Yogi. London: J. Murray, 1962, 174 pp.)

A translation of a popular biography of the well-known "Saint" Milarepa. This should be one of the first books considered by the introductory student of Tibetan Buddhism. For further reading on Milarepa, see Sir Humphrey Clark, trans., The Message of Milarepa (London: J. Murray, 1958), 106 pp.; Garma C. C. Chang, trans. and ed., The Hundred Thousand Songs of Milarepa (see 4.3[12]), 2 vols.; and especially Jacques Bacot, Milarepa (see 8.9.2[10]).

1.14.2.2   Tibet

(8) RICHARDSON, HUGH E. "The Karma-pa Sect: A Historical Note." *Journal of the Royal Asiatic Society* (1958), pp. 139-164; and (1959), pp. 1-18.

Basically an attempt to sketch historically (but not in a comprehensive fashion) the periods in the sect's history by examining incidents in the relations of its principal lamas, especially Zva-nag-pa, with Mongolia and China. The second section is an appendix of translated and transliterated historical documents.

(9) RUEGG, DAVID SERFORT. "The Jo nan pas: A School of Buddhist Ontologists according to the Grub mtha' sel gyi me lon." *Journal of the American Oriental Society*, 83, no. 1 (January-March 1963), 73-91.

This article represents an examination of the basic ontological speculation of the Jo nan pa school which flourished in Tibet from the thirteenth to the seventeenth centuries. The unique feature of this philosophic school was the contention that there exists an eternal element which is substantially permanent and absolute--a very typically un-Buddhist position. The author traces the history of the doctrine and discusses its significance within the context of Madyamika thought.

(10) TUCCI, GIUSEPPE. "Tibetan Notes 2: The Diffusion of the Yellow Church in Western Tibet and the Kings of Guge." *Harvard Journal of Asiatic Studies*, 12 (1949), 477-496.

An attempt to fill in the gaps in our information about the history of Gelupga influence in the regions of Ladakh and Western Tibet. Helpful, but for advanced and interested students only.

(11) _____. *Tibetan Painted Scrolls*. Translated by Virginia Vacca. Rome: Libreria dello Stato, 1949, 2 vols., 798 pp.

Although Tucci's masterpiece is primarily concerned with technical and artistic features of the painted scrolls, the first section of the work contains a cultural and religious history of Tibet covering the period of 1200-1700 A.D. Within this account, Tucci highlights the conflicts between the Red and Yellow Hat sects, the significance of the Saskya pa administration, and the Vajrayana doctrine of time which is crucial to an understanding of Tibetan Buddhism. Excellent for the student of any level.

1.14.2.3 Buddhism under the Thirteenth and Fourteenth (Present) Dalai Lamas

(1) BELL, CHARLES ALFRED. *Portrait of the Dalai Lama*. London: Collins, 1946, 414 pp.

A biographical treatment of the life and accomplishments of the thirteenth Dalai Lama (1876-1933) which offers the reader a sympathetic view concerning the religious and political developments of the same period. An adequate treatment by a noted scholar. For another treatment of the same Dalai Lama, see Tokan Tada, *The Thirteenth Dalai Lama* (Tokyo: Center for East Asian Cultural Studies, 1965), 115 pp.

(2) GELDER, STUART and ROMA GELDER. *The Timely Rain: Travels in New Tibet*. London: Hutchinson, 1964, 248 pp.

This book is the result of a trip that this husband and wife team made to Tibet in 1962 with the consent of the Chinese government. The title refers to a poem written by the Dalai Lama describing the coming to power of Chairman Mao. The significance of this book, then, lies in its pro-Chinese account of the events which preceded the Dalai Lama's flight in 1959. For another account of the same era from a different perspective, see Rinchen Dolma Taring, *Daughter of Tibet* (London: J. Murray, 1970), 280 pp.

(3) NGAWANG LOBSANG YISHEY TENZING GYATSO, 14th Dalai Lama. *My Land and My People*. Edited by David Howarth. New York: McGraw-Hill, 1962, 271 pp.

This autobiography of the Dalai Lama contains his view of his relationship to the Chinese before his exile and also his view of the exile itself.

(4) *Tibetans in Exile, 1959-1969: A Report on Ten Years of Rehabilitation in India*. Compiled by the Office of H. H. Dalai Lama. Dharamsala, India: Bureau of H. H. the Dalai Lama, 1969, 366 pp.

This report covers the first ten years of exile for Tibetans who fled to India. It remains an important source of information on these exiles as it describes all facets of their lives and problems in India. Especially of worth is the chapter entitled "Culture and Religion."

1.15 NEPAL AND THE HIMALAYAN KINGDOMS

1.15.1 Historical Surveys and Introductions

(1) FURER-HAIMENDORF, CHRISTOPH VON. *The Sherpas of Nepal: Buddhist Highlanders*. Berkeley: University of California, 1964, 298 pp.

A comprehensive study of Sherpa society drawn from vast experience, which displays a clear understanding of the history and character of Buddhism in Nepal.

(2) MORRIS, JOHN. *Living with Lepchas: A Book About the Sikkim Himalayas*. London: W. Heinemann, 1938, 312 pp.

An ethnographical study of the Lepchas in Jongu, including an account of the origin of the Lepcha people, the role of Lamaism within their society, as well as a general portrayal of the customs of that society. Good introduction.

(3) RAHUL, RAM. *Modern Bhutan*. Delhi: Vikas Publications, 1971, 173 pp.

An historical sketch of Bhutan from the earliest times to the present. The author sets aside a chapter to discuss the history, sects, and sociological role of Buddhism in Bhutan. For a more complete history of Bhutan, but with a little less treatment of Buddhism, see Nagendra Singh, Bhutan (New Delhi: Thomson Press, 1972). For further reading, see V. H. Coelho, Sikkim and Bhutan (New Delhi: Indian Council for Cultural Relations, 1970).

(4) SNELLGROVE, DAVID L. Buddhist Himalaya (see 1.14.2.1[9]), pp. 91-120.
The chapter, though not presented in strictly historical form, represents a substantial account of Buddhism in the kingdom of Nepal.

(5) SWARAMAMURTI, C. "Buddhism in Sikkim, Ladakh, and Bhutan." The Light of Buddha, 5 (1960), 34-38.
Brief article which seeks to discuss the organization, chief monasteries, and important rites in these countries. For introductory use.

(6) TAN 'DZIN CHOS RGYAL. Lho'i chos-'by-ung: Religious History of the South (=Bhutan=). Translated by Kazi Dawasamdup. Annotated by Turrell V. Wylie. (A History of Bhutan from the 7th Century A.D. to the 18th Century A.D.). Historical Reproductions, 1969, n.p.
A reproduction, in limited edition, of the manuscript of a translation of this important religious history of Bhutanese Buddhism. The translation is by Kazi Dawasamdup, the translator of the Tibetan Book of the Dead and other works, edited by W. Y. Evans Wentz. The manuscript is in severe need of editing, but can be profitably read in its present state, especially with Wylie's introduction, notes and index.

(7) WADDELL, LAURENCE AUSTINE. Tibetan Buddhism, with Its Mystic Cults, Symbolism and Mythology, and in Its Relation to Indian Buddhism. See 1.14.1(17).
Scattered references to Sikkim and Bhutan can be gleaned from this work concerning the introduction of Buddhism into these countries. For other references which briefly treat Buddhism in these countries, see Gunther Schulemann, Geschichte der Dalai-Lamas (Leipzig: O. Harrassowitz, 1958), 519 pp; Marco Pallis, Peaks and Lamas (Revised edition New York: Knopf, 1949); and Alexandra David-Neel, With Mystics and Magicians in Tibet (London: Lane, 1931), 320 pp.

(8) ZETLAND, LAWRENCE JOHN LUMLEY DUNDAS, 2nd Marquis of. Lands of the Thunderbolt. London: Constable, 1923, 267 pp.
Weaves together a narrative account of the Marquis's travels through Sikkim, Bhutan, and Chumbi in the 1920s and his intense interest in Buddhism as it is practiced in the Himalayan kingdoms. He has included a good rendition of Padma Sambhava's role in Sikkimese Buddhism and focuses on Lamaism as he saw it practiced in Sikkim. Also included is an account of the uniqueness of Buddhism in Bhutan.

1.15.2 Specialized Historical Studies

(1) ROCK, JOSEPH F. "Excerpts from a History of Sikkim." Anthropos, 48 (1953), 925-948.
The "History of Sikkim" is a traditional history put together by the King and Queen of Sikkim in the early part of the twentieth century. It was translated into English by a Sikkimese lama. It was this translation which Rock discovered. The excerpts published here are basically legendary accounts, and few relate specifically to Buddhism. However, there is a brief allusion to Padma Sambhava as the physical father of the line of divine Sikkimese teachers. Further, there are brief accounts of a number of Buddhist figures who transmitted their teachings to the Sikkimese.

1.16 MONGOLIA

1.16.1 Historical Surveys and Introductions

(1) BAWDEN, CHARLES R., ed. The Jebtsundamba Khutukhtus of Urga. Asiatische Forschungen, No. 9. Wiesbaden: O. Harrassowitz, 1961, 91 pp.
Text and translation of an account of the eight incarnations of the supreme ecclesiastical dignitary of the Khalkha Mongols. The eight incarnations span the years 1635-1924, and the stories of their lives are filled with many irreplaceable historical and religious details.

(2) BISCHOFF, F. A. "Preliminary Report on a Mongol Buddhist Text on Christian Teaching." Transactions of the International Conference of Orientalists in Japan, 7 (1962), 22-26.
An account of a text which Bischoff found among Mongolian nomads, called "The Sutra called Irradiant Manifesto." It is a very short, syncretic work beginning with an injunction that the faithful can find enlightenment in a Church in Moscow called "Irradiant Migayal Nikolai Kristos, Son of God," and ending with the blessing "Sarva mangalam, om mani padme hum."

(3) CH'ANG-CH'UN. The Travels of an Alchemist: The Journey of the Taoist Ch'ang-ch'un from China to the Hindukush at the Summons of Chingiz Khan, recorded by his disciple Li Chih-ch'ang. Translated by Arthur Waley. London: G. Routledge and Sons, 1931, pp. 5-33.
In this translation of an account of a journey made by a Taoist who was summoned from China by Genghis Khan, Waley has included an excellent introduction in which he discusses the relationship of Genghis Khan to

the Buddhists. Waley claims that the earliest form of Buddhism to which the Mongols were drawn was that of Chan. For an article which claims that Genghis Khan was neither a convert to Tibetan Buddhism nor influenced by Zen, but practiced a strange religion of monotheism mixed with shamanistic beliefs, see E. Dora Earthy, "The Religion of Genghis Khan (A.D. 1162-1227)," Numen, 2 (1955), 228-232.

(4) DAS, SARAT CHANDRA. "Rise and Progress of Buddhism in Mongolia (Hor)." Journal of the Asiatic Society of Bengal, 51 (1882), 58-75.

Text and translation of the eleventh book of the eighteenth century Grub mThah Sel-kyi Me-long, which deals in a remarkably concise way with the introduction of Buddhism into Mongolia by Sakya Pandita and its subsequent history there. The article has been reprinted as Chapter 7 of Das's Contributions on the Religion and History of Tibet (New Delhi: Manjusri, 1970), and represents one of the few "native sources" on Mongolian Buddhism available in translation. Another such source, which may be found in German translation, is the early nineteenth century Hor-chos byung by Jigs-med nam-mkha, translated in Volume 2 of Georg Huth, Geschichte de Buddhismus in der Mongolei (Strassburg: Trübner, 1892-1896). On this latter text, however, see the argument made by George Roerich that the author of the work was not Jigs-med nam-mkha but Gu-sri dKah-bcu Sud-dhi A-yu-warta (George M. Roerich, "The Author of the Hor-chos-hbyun," Journal of the Royal Asiatic Society [1946], 192-198).

(5) GROUSSET, RENE. The Empire of the Steppes: A History of Central Asia. Translated by Naomi Walford. New Brunswick, N.J.: Rutgers University Press, 1970, 687 pp.

An excellent source book which historically examines this vast geographical area from the earliest times until the eighteenth century. The treatment of Mongolian history is perhaps the most comprehensive one available in English published recently. For a study which is concentrated on the nineteenth and twentieth centuries, see Charles R. Bawden, The Modern History of Mongolia (London: Weidenfeld and Nicolson, 1968), 460 pp., which includes an excellent treatment of Buddhism as a state religion in the early twentieth century. These two works should be among the first consulted in any study of Mongolian history.

(6) HARLEZ, CHARLES J. DE. La religion nationale des Tartares orientaux: Mandchous et Mongols. Brussels: Académie Royal des sciences, des lettres et des beaux-arts de Belgique, 1887, 216 pp.

An early treatment of the religion of the Asian pastoral peoples. After surveying the indigenous religion of the Tartars and Mongols respectively, the author treats the introduction to and influence of Buddhism on each respective culture. In turn, the author discusses the transformation of Buddhism as a result of its assimilation.

(7) MILLER, ROBERT JAMES. Monasteries and Culture Change in Inner Mongolia. Asiatische Forschungen, No. 2. Wiesbaden: O. Harrassowitz, 1959, pp. 1-10.

The book as a whole presents an anthropological view of the history and social role of Buddhist monasteries in Mongolia and is of more general interest than its title might imply. See especially the first chapter, entitled "The Foundation of Lamaist Inner Mongolia," which deals concisely with the "two conversions" (sixteenth century and thirteenth century) of the Mongols to Buddhism.

(8) SERRUYS, HENRY. "Early Lamaism in Mongolia." Oriens extremus, 10 (1963), 181-216; and 13 (1966), 165-173.

A brief but thorough survey of pre-Yuan Mongolian Buddhism--perhaps the best quick introduction in English.

1.16.2 Specialized Historical Studies

(1) Altan Tobci. The Mongol Chronicle, Altan Tobci. Göttinger asiatische Forschungen, No. 5. Translated and edited by Charles Bawden. Wiesbaden: O. Harrassowitz, 1955, 205 pp.

With the exception of the Secret History of the Mongols (translated into French by Paul Pelliot as Histoire secrète des Mongols [Paris, 1949]), the Altan Tobci is the earliest known historical work in the Mongol language. Composed in the seventeenth century, it offers a striking picture of the "fierce and unsubtle" character of Mongol life. Further, we have a history replete with Buddhist trappings and offering a Mongolian Buddhist view of history. Genghis Khan is seen as "a benevolent patriarch fulfilling the commands of the Buddha." Excellent source for the advanced student.

(2) CHANDRA, LOKESH. "Buddhism in Mongolia." Indo-Asian Culture, 8 (1960), 266-275.

An informative account of a visit which Lokesh Chandra (a knowledgeable Indian scholar) made to Buddhist centers in Ulan Bator and other places in Outer Mongolia in 1957.

(3) DAWSON, CHRISTOPHER HENRY, ed. Mission to Asia: Narratives and Letters of the Franciscan Missionaries in Mongolia and China in the Thirteenth and Fourteenth Centuries. New York: Harper and Row, 1966, 246 pp. (Originally published as The Mongol Mission. London: Sheed and Ward, 1955; paperback edition: (Harper Torchbooks, The Cathedral Library, TB315L.)

Translations of documents relating to the Franciscan missions to the Khan in the thirteenth and fourteenth centuries. Essential background information on Mongolian Buddhism (and Islam) of the time, and how it was (mis)-understood by the Christians. For example,

"Om Mani padme hum . . . [means] O God, Thou knowest, so one of them translated it for me." Includes interesting extras such as a recipe for fermented mare's milk.

(4) JAGCHID, SECHIN. "Buddhism in Mongolia after the Collapse of the Yuan Dynasty." Mongolia Society Bulletin, 10, no. 1 (Spring 1971), 48-63.

Jagchid's article presents a new twist to an old problem. While others (e.g., Robert Miller, Monasteries and Culture Change in Inner Mongolia (above), have argued that Lamaism died out following the collapse of the Yuan dynasty, Jagchid argues in this article, with the aid of Chinese sources, that although Buddhism declined considerably between 1368 and the conversion of Altan Khan in 1578, it nevertheless continued to exist in Mongolia, honored and revered by the Oirad Mongol leaders.

(5) KOLARZ, WALTER. Religion in the Soviet Union (see 1.10.2[9]), pp. 448-469.

(6) LATTIMORE, OWEN. "Religion and Revolution in Mongolia." Modern Asian Studies, 1 (1967), 81-94.

Recounts the history of major Mongolian political transactions from Ming times to the present. Lattimore is very careful to note the general effects of Mongolia's dealings with the Manchus and Tibetans on Lamaism. The article is also valuable because it tells the story of the demise of Lamaism after the 1921 revolution. It incorporates sources not previously available to Western scholars which only recently have been published by the Peoples' Republic of Mongolia.

(7) NATSAGDORJI, SH. "The Introduction of Buddhism into Mongolia." Translated by John R. Krueger. Mongolia Society Bulletin, 7 (1968), 1-12.

Examines the question of Buddhism's introduction into Mongolia. The author considers the history of Buddhism's first penetration in three historical stages: the period of the Great Empire in Mongolia (mainly the thirteenth century) under Genghis Khan, Godan Khan, Kublai Khan, etc.; the period of feudal decay; and the period of Mongol submission to Manchu authority.

(8) POPPE, NICHOLAS. "The Destruction of Buddhism in the USSR." Bulletin, Institute for the Study of the USSR, 3, no. 7 (July 1956), 14-20.

The author begins his article by outlining the roles played by lamas in the traditional societies of the Buryat and Kalmyk peoples. He then goes on to describe the events which led to the destruction of Buddhism among the Kalmyks and their transportation to the trans-Ural region. The discussion then moves to the Soviet policy of destroying "relics of feudalism" which resulted in the removal of Buddhist elements in Buryat culture so that

"no large monastery buildings remain today in Mongolia."

(9) RACHEWILTZ, IGOR DE. "Yeh-Lu Ch'u-Ts'ai (1189-1243): Buddhist Idealist and Confucian Statesman," in Confucian Personalities. Edited by Arthur F. Wright and Denis Twitchett. Stanford Studies in the Civilizations of Eastern Asia. Stanford, Calif.: Stanford University Press, 1962, pp. 189-216.

A fascinating biographical study of a man who combined Confucian and Buddhist qualities in his job as secretary-astrologer to Genghis Khan, and chief of the secretariat under Ogodei Khan.

(10) SCHRAM, LOUIS M. J. The Monguors of the Kansu-Tibetan Frontier. 3 Parts: Part I, Their Origin, History, and Social Organization, 138 pp.; Part II, Their Religious Life, 164 pp.; Part III, Records of the Monguor Clan: History of the Monguors in Huangchung and the Chronicles of the Lu Family, 116 pp. Transactions of the American Philosophical Society, n.s. 44, no. 1 (April 1954); 47, no. 21 (March 1957); and 51, no. 3 (May 1961).

Part Two, which is of most interest here, represents a detailed and thorough account of the religion of a Mongol group, placed in historical and cultural context with reference to both Tibetan and Chinese influences.

1.17 BUDDHISM IN THE WEST

See also 2.9.

(1) BERVAL, RENE DE, ed. Présence du Bouddhisme (see 1.5.1[6]), pp. 913-958.

In these pages, Max Hoppe, Adrian Peel, Narada Mahathera, E. Barbarin, Christmas Humphreys, and C. F. Knight have contributed brief articles (mostly in English) on the history of Buddhism in Germany, Belgium, the United States, France, England, and Australia.

(2) CHARTERS, ANN. Kerouac: A Biography. San Francisco: Straight Arrow Books, 1973, 416 pp. (Paperback edition: New York: Warner, 1974.)

An important source for the study of "beat" Buddhism of the 1950s.

(3) CHRISTY, ARTHUR. The Orient in American Transcendentalism: A Study of Emerson, Thoreau, and Alcott. Columbia University Studies in English and Comparative Literature. New York: Columbia University Press, 1932, 382 pp.

A pioneer work, the highlight of which is ten pages on the reception in America of Arnold's The Light of Asia.

(4) Eminent Orientalists: Indian, European, American. Madras: G. A. Natesan, 1922, 378 pp.

Brief biographies of twenty-five orientalists, nine of them Buddhologists.

(5) HUMPRHEYS, CHRISTMAS. Sixty Years of Buddhism in England (1907-1967): A History and a Survey. London: Buddhist Society, 1968, 84 pp.

A historical survey of the development of the Buddhist Society in England which highlights important events such as the first English Bhikkhu, important visitors, and significant publications.

(6) HUNTER, LOUISE H. Buddhism in Hawaii: Its Impact on a Yankee Community. Honolulu: University of Hawaii Press, 1971, 266 pp.

Concerned with the history and problems of Buddhism in the Hawaiian community. The student should have facility in Japanese if he or she is going to tackle this general subject, since all significant bibliographical references are in that language.

(7) IGGLEDEN, R. E. W. "Short Survey of Buddhism in the West." The Maha Bodhi, 77, nos. 11-12 (November-December 1969), 366-370.

A brief review of British scholarship of Buddhism and the founding of the Sangha in Great Britain.

(8) JONG, J. W. DE. "A Brief History of Buddhist Studies in Europe and America." Eastern Buddhist, n.s. 7 (May 1974), 56-106.

This excellent summary of Buddhology is continued by De Jong in the following issue of The Eastern Buddhist (October 1974), pp. 49-82. It is sufficiently detailed to serve not only as a history but as an annotated bibliography of principal works of Western Buddhist scholarship.

(9) KEROUAC, JOHN (JACK). The Dharma Bums. New York: New American Library, 1959, 192 pp. (Paperback edition: Signet D1718.)

Thinly fictionalized account of Kerouac's participation in West-Coast "beat" Buddhism, with portraits of Gary Snyder, Kenneth Rexroth, Allen Ginsberg, et al.

(10) KITAGAWA, JOSEPH. "Buddhism in America." Japanese Religions, 5, no. 1 (July 1967), 32-57.

The author begins his article by summarizing the prevailing religious ethos of America and notes that Eastern culture and religion are being taken more seriously in many quarters of American society. After drawing a distinction between those who practice religion and those who study it, the author reviews the past efforts of Western and American scholars to provide sound scholarship on the topic of Buddhism. Finally, the author takes note of the history of institutionalized Buddhism in America. A good survey.

(11) LACH, DONALD FREDERICK. Asia in the Making of Europe. Chicago: University of Chicago Press, 1965, vol. 1, The Century of Discovery.

Frequent references to Western contacts with Buddhism particularly by Jesuit missionaries. Indispensable history of East-West relations in the sixteenth century.

(12) LAYMAN, EMMA McCLOY. Buddhism in America. Chicago: Nelson-Hall Publishers, 1976, 343 pp.

Layman's attempt to study the Buddhist phenomena in America includes a survey of the major communities in historical and contemporary contexts. The reader will find helpful chapters on Pure Land, Zen, Tantric, Nichiren Shoshu, and other Buddhist sects in addition to a discussion concerned with how American culture has influenced Buddhist expression. Finally, author addresses the issues of Buddhism and psychology, Buddhism and Christianity, the future of Buddhism in America, and the special attraction of Buddhism for Americans.

(13) LELAND, C. G., trans. and C. F. Neumann, ed. Fusang or the Discovery of America by Chinese Buddhist Priests in the Fifth Century. New York: Barnes and Noble, 1972. (Originally published in 1875.)

Incredible as it may sound, the authors have attempted to build a case for the discovery of America by Buddhist priests in the fifth century. The book includes a translation of a narrative authored by a fifth century Chinese monk who was sent "East" by imperial decree to spread the Buddha's teaching. Neumann follows with notes and remarks in an attempt to correlate Fusang with America. Also included are a discussion about Neumann's theories, the navigational possibilities for such a journey, and American antiquities which bear similarities to those found in China.

(14) MACKENZIE, DONALD ALEXANDER. Buddhism in Pre-Christian Britain. London and Glasgow: Blackie, 1928, 178 pp.

An early attempt to make some sense out of the undoubted resemblances between European and Indian mythology and iconography.

(15) NYANASATTA, C. THERA. "Buddhism in the West." The Maha Bodhi, 75, no. 3 (March 1967), 74-82; and 75, no. 4 (April 1967), 105-110.

A good survey of the history of early European scholarship concerned with Buddhism and also a brief survey of Buddhist monasteries in the West.

(16) WATTS, ALAN WILSON. In My Own Way: An Autobiography, 1915-1965. New York: Pantheon, 1972, 400 pp.

Christmas and Aileen Humphreys, Ruth Fuller and Sokei-an Sasaki, Gary Snyder, C. G. Jung, and Aldous Huxley are some of the more prominent characters in Watts' autobiographical kaleidoscope of world Zen.

2 Religious Thought

2.1 SURVEYS AND GENERAL INTRODUCTIONS

(1) CONZE, EDWARD. Buddhist Thought in India: Three Phases of Buddhist Philosophy. Ann Arbor: University of Michigan Press, 1967, 302 pp. (Originally published Ann Arbor: Ann Arbor Paperbacks, 1962.)

A survey of "Archaic Buddhism," "The Sthaviras," and "The Mahayana" (with short chapters on the later logicians and the Tantras). This book is a basic study of the development of Buddhist thought in India and the bases of Buddhist thought in the rest of Asia. However, it might be noted, the work is intended as a sequel to the same author's Buddhist Meditation (see 2.7.5[2]), and that portions of the book are so condensed as to make them very difficult; Conze's more general and elementary Buddhism: Its Essence and Development (see 1.1[2]) is sometimes useful as an introduction to it.

(2) DUTT, NALINAKSHA. Aspects of Mahayana Buddhism and Its Relation to Hinayana. See 1.2.2.3(3).

A study of the rise and background of Mahayana and also of its cardinal teachings such as the Bodhisattva stages, the doctrine of the tri-kaya and the conception of the two truths. For a good, brief statement of Dutt's views, see "Emergence of Mahayana Buddhism" in The Cultural Heritage of India (Calcutta: Ramakrishna Mission, 1958), vol. 1, pp. 503-517.

(3) FOX, DOUGLAS A. The Vagrant Lotus. Philadelphia: Westminster Press, 1973.

A simple overall introduction to Buddhist philosophy, popularly oriented for Westerners who are well grounded in neither Buddhism nor philosophy. The section on philosophy is preceded by a short historical introduction.

(4) FUJIYOSHI, JIKAI. "The Spirit of Criticism in Buddhism." Journal of Indian and Buddhist Studies, 10, no. 1 (January 1962), pp. 7-12.

This brief article is valuable for its general presentation of the basic Buddhist perspective on life, the role of religion in life, and the Buddhist approach to scholarship. For other brief presentations concerned with these general issues, see G. P. Malalasekera, "The Buddhist Point of View," in Humanism and Education in East and West (Paris: UNESCO, 1953), pp. 133-148; and Buddha Prakash, "The Buddhist Methodology," Buddha Jayanti Special Issue of Journal of the Bihar Research Society, 1 (1956), pp. 35-46.

(5) GUENTHER, HERBERT. Buddhist Philosophy in Theory and Practice. Berkeley, Calif.: Shambala, 1971, 240 pp.

Not as encompassing as the title would lead one to expect, Guenther's treatment of the basic philosophical problems within a Buddhist tradition is actually limited to a specifically Tibetan perspective which he has derived from two Tibetan sources.

(6) JAYATILLEKE, KASHI NATH. The Message of the Buddha. Edited by Ninian Smart. New York: Free Press, 1976, 260 pp.

Worthwhile introduction to the crucial issues of Buddhist speculative thought. The author addresses himself to such issues as Karma, conditioned genesis, morality, mind, etc.

(7) KALUPAHANA, DAVID. Buddhist Philosophy: A Historical Analysis. Honolulu: University of Hawaii Press, 1976, 188 pp.

The chief purpose of this work is to prove that early Buddhist philosophy was empiricist and antimetaphysical. In this light, the author attempts to provide a historical analysis of such concepts as karma, causality, morality, and nirvana. Having provided these analyses, useful sketches of the development of the Mahayana, Madhyamika, and Yogacara schools follow. An interesting chapter on the relationship between early Buddhism and Zen concludes the volume. A worthwhile effort of use to most students.

(8) KEITH, ARTHUR BERRIEDALE. Buddhist Philosophy in India and Ceylon. Fourth edition. The Chowkhamba Sanskrit Studies, No. 26. Varanasi: Chowkhamba, 1963, 339 pp. (Originally published Oxford: Clarendon, 1923.)

A dated but still useful classic. Parts I and II, dealing with "Buddhism in the Pali Canon" and "Developments in the Hinayana," are the most substantial. Parts III and IV on "The Philosophy of the Mahayana" and

2.1 Surveys and General Introductions

"Buddhist Logic" are sketchier. There is no coverage of Vajrayana developments.

(9) MORGAN, KENNETH WILLIAM, ed. The Path of the Buddha: Buddhism Interpreted by Buddhists (see 1.1[6]), pp. 67-112, 153-181, 364-400.

Taken together, these chapters form an adequate introduction to the history of Buddhist thought, and a good introduction to the way in which some important contemporary Buddhists think. Chapter 2 is by U Thittila and covers "The Fundamental Principles of Theravada Buddhism." Chapter 4, by Susumu Yamaguchi, deals with the "Development of Mahayana Buddhist Beliefs," and Chapter 8, by Hajime Nakamura, deals with "Unity and Diversity in Buddhism."

(10) RAHULA, WALPOLA. What the Buddha Taught. Revised edition. Bedford: G. Fraser, 1967, 151 pp. (Originally published 1959.)

Based almost exclusively on Pali texts, this is a clear and concise exposition of what Rahula thought the Buddha taught. As such it forms an excellent introduction not to Buddhist doctrine but to the teachings of the Theravadins.

(11) STCHERBATSKY, FEDOR IPPOLITOVICH. Buddhist Logic. New York: Dover, 1962, vol. 1, pp. 3-14. (Originally published Leningrad, 1930-1932.)

In these few pages, Stcherbatsky outlines his view of the "three periods" of Buddhist philosophy--"Pluralism," "Monism," and "Idealism"--which, he claims, correspond to the late Buddhist theory of the three "Swingings of the Wheel of the Law." Stcherbatsky's two other principal works, The Central Conception of Buddhism (see 2.7.7[11]) and The Conception of Buddhist Nirvana (see 2.5.3[12]), essentially dealt with periods one and two. His vast and difficult Buddhist Logic, which is basic to any serious study of the development of Buddhist thought, essentially focuses on period three. Using the works of Dharmakirti, Dignaga and their commentators, it gives a detailed exposition of their system. The second volume consists almost entirely of translation from their original works.

(12) SUZUKI, DAISETZ TEITARO. Outlines of Mahayana Buddhism. New York: Schocken, 1963, 383 pp. (Originally published 1907.)

Still a useful and readable work. It is organized topically rather than historically or textually and is helpful for that very reason. Another presentation of the same author's views may be found in his On Indian Mahayana Buddhism (see 2.5.5[6]), where his approach is edited and introduced by E. Conze.

(13) TAKAKUSU, JUNJIRO. The Essentials of Buddhist Philosophy. Edited by Wing-tsit Chan and Charles A. Moore. Westport, Conn.: Greenwood Press, 1973, 221 pp. (Reprint of the third edition, 1956; originally published 1947.)

One of the few attempts in English to approach the whole of Buddhist thought from the Japanese perspective. Claiming that in Japan, the whole of Buddhist doctrine--Theravada and Mahayana--has been preserved in the various sects, Takakusu attempts to differentiate these sects from a strictly philosophical point of view. See page 18 for an interesting "philosophical classification" of Buddhist sects. The work is difficult and recommended for advanced students only. A shorter version of his basic views may be found in Junjiro Takakusu, "Buddhism as a Philosophy of 'Thusness'" (see 2.7.10[5]).

(14) THOMAS, EDWARD JOSEPH. The History of Buddhist Thought. Second edition. The History of Civilization. New York: Barnes and Noble, 1963, 316 pp. (Originally published 1933.)

A standard and important study of early Buddhist thought based principally on Pali materials. It never moves out of India, however, and is less inspired in its treatment of the later doctrines.

(15) WARDER, ANTHONY KENNEDY. Indian Buddhism (see 1.2.1[15]), pp. 81-106, 288-513.

Taken together, these chapters form a thorough and fine survey of the history and development of Buddhist thought in India, based on the texts of all the schools. Chapter 4 uses the Vaisali summary of teachings to present "The Doctrine of the Buddha." Chapters 9-12 cover, in turn, the eighteen schools, Mahayana and Madhyamika, Idealism and late Mahayana and Mantrayana.

2.2 BACKGROUND AND CONTEXT OF BUDDHIST THOUGHT IN INDIA

(1) BARUA, BENIMADHAB. A History of Pre-Buddhist Indian Philosophy. Delhi: Motilal Banarsidass, 1970, 444 pp. (Originally published 1921.)

A standard work which is especially useful for its lucid delineation of pre-Buddhist heterodox teachings which influenced the development of early Buddhist thought.

(2) BARUA, PROMODE RANJAN. Early Buddhism and the Brahmanical Doctrines. Dacca: Asiatic Society of Pakistan, 1968, 166 pp.

An attempt to look at how Buddhism developed and changed some of the doctrines it "took over" from the Brahmanic tradition. The work focuses on the questions of the doctrine of atman, on the problem of caste, on sacrifice and rituals, and on the gods and the Brahma-viharas.

(3) BASHAM, ARTHUR LLEWELLYN. History and Doctrines of the Ajivikas: A Vanished Indian Religion. London: Luzac, 1951, 304 pp.

A scholarly work on a sect which grew out of the Brahmanical tradition approximately at the same time as Buddhism. Useful in establishing the cultural and ideological framework of the sixth century B.C. Many of the sources which the author employs in the reconstruction are Buddhist.

(4) CHANDRA, PRATAP. "Was Early Buddhism Influenced by the Upanisads?" *Philosophy East and West*, 21 (1971), 317-324.

The author begins by surveying the issues and opinions that have led some scholars to believe Buddhism was dependent upon Upanishadic thought for its theory of renunciation. The author, however, contends that the Buddha was not aware of Upanishadic texts or thought. He makes this assertion because the Pali texts do not make mention of the Upanishads. For another short treatment of this topic, see M. S. R. Anjaneyulu, "The Buddha and Upanishadic Thought." *Aryan Path*, 38 (June 1967), 252-255.

(5) DASGUPTA, SURENDRANATH. *A History of Indian Philosophy*. Cambridge: Cambridge University Press, 1922-1955, vol. 1, 528 pp.

An effective survey of the philosophy of India by an important Indian scholar, giving the historical context of the rise of Buddhist thought and also its interactions with various schools of Indian philosophy (Samkhya, Yoga, Vedanta, etc.). A standard reference work.

(6) DUTT, NALINAKSHA. "Brahmanism and Buddhism." *Bulletin of Tibetology*, 7 (1970), 7-11.

Discusses how Buddhism understood the following Upanishadic terms: Brahma and Brahmana, atman and brahman, and pudgalvada.

(7) FOZDAR, JAMSHED K. *The God of Buddha*. New York: Asia Publishing, 1973. 184 pp.

A questionable attempt by the author to compare sayings of the Buddha on a variety of topics to quotations found in Hindu scriptures. The intent of all of this is to support the thesis that "the Buddha was familiar with most, if not all of the Hindu scriptures."

(8) JAINI, PADMANABH S. "Sramanas: Their Conflict with Brahmanical Society," in *Chapters in Indian Civilization*. Edited by Joseph Walter Elder. Dubuque: Kendall Hunt (Rev. ed.) 1970. 2 vols. Vol. 1, pp. 39-81.

Read together with J. A. B. van Buitenen's "Vedic and Upanisadic Bases of Indian Civilization," which immediately precedes it in the same volume (pp. 1-38), this chapter forms a fine introduction to the ideological context in which Buddhism arose.

(9) JAYATILLEKE, KULATISSA NANDA. *Early Buddhist Theory of Knowledge*. London: G. Allen and Unwin, 1963. 519 pp. Chapters 1-5 (pp. 21-276).

A difficult, but rewarding study of epistemologies contemporary with early Buddhist thought. Chapters 1-3 cover the Vedic and Upanishadic traditions, the Materialists, the Sceptics, the Ajivikas, and the Jains.

(10) DE JONG, J. W. "The Background of Early Buddhism." *Journal of Indian and Buddhist Studies*, 12, no. 1 (1964), 34-47.

Concise introductory account of the background of early Buddhism's basic doctrines (karma, ahisma, etc.), in the context of the socio-political milieu of the time. Compares Buddhist views to the Jain and Brahmanical interpretations of the same concepts. Sees Buddhism as a creative synthesis of Aryan and non-Aryan conceptions.

(11) LAW, BIMALA CHURN. *Historical Gleanings* (see 1.2.2.1[6]), pp. 9-42, 76-95.

Chapter 2 contains a concise list of over thirty "Wandering Teachers in Buddha's time" together with their principal topics of discussion and references to them in the Pali Canon. Chapter 3 deals more specifically with the influence of the five heretical teachers on Jainism and Buddhism. Chapter 6 looks at the relationship between the Buddha and the Jains.

(12) MIZUNO, KOGEN. *Primitive Buddhism* (see 1.2.2.1[8]), pp. 46-91.

A straightforward account of Indian "thoughts and thinkers" in the Buddha's time. This is one of the few such works that is not overly dependent on the Pali traditions.

(13) PANDE, GOVIND CHANDRA. *Studies in the Origins of Buddhism* (see 1.2.2.1[10]), pp. 541-557.

This chapter, entitled "Early Buddhism in Relation to Its Rivals and Forerunners," tries hard to be precise about what Buddhism's contacts were with Jainism, Samkhya, and the Vedic tradition, and to conclude what doctrines were borrowed from whom.

(14) RHYS-DAVIDS, CAROLINE AUGUSTA FOLEY. "The Relations Between Early Buddhism and Brahmanism." *Indian Historical Quarterly*, 10 (1934), 274-287.

Tries to show that Buddhism was based on the religious beliefs (but not on the rituals) of Brahmanism, and that these differences in external expression slowly caused a "drifting apart" in the tenets.

(15) SASTRI, PANDIT N. AIYASAWANI. "Sramana or Non-Brahmanical Sects," in *The Cultural Heritage of India*. Second edition, revised and enlarged. Calcutta: Ramakrishna Mission Institute of Culture, 1953-1962, vol. 1 (1958), "The Early Phases," pp. 389-399. (Originally published 1937.)

A lucid article devoted solely to the "lesser wellknown" heterodox schools at the time of the Buddha: Purana Kassapa and the Akriyavadins; Pakudha Kaccayana and the Anuvadins; Makkhali Gosala and the Ajivikas; Ajita Kesakambalin and the Materialists; and Sanjaya Belatthiputta and the Sceptics.

(16) STCHERBATSKY, FEDOR IPPOLITOVICH. *Buddhist Logic* (see 2.1[11]), vol. 1, pp. 15-27.

The section entitled "The Place of Buddhist Logic in the History of Indian Philosophy," contains a very helpful resume of the relation of Buddhist thought to 1) the Materialism, 2) the Jains, 3) the evolutionism of Samkhya, 4) Yoga, 5) the Monism of the Upanisads, 6) the realism of the Mimamsakas, and 7) the realism of Nyaya-Vaisesika.

(17) UPADHYAYA, KASHI NATH. *Early Buddhism and the Bhagavadgita*. Delhi: Motilal Banarsidass, 1971, 567 pp.

A comparison of the Bhagavad Gita to early Buddhism with respect to chronology, sources, epistemology, metaphysics, and ethics.

(18) VARMA, VISHWANATH PRASAD. *Early Buddhism and Its Origins*. See 1.2.2.1(13).

Surveys all aspects of early Buddhism and keeps in mind the Indian context--both the religious and the sociological one. For a condensed version of the first few chapters, see V. P. Varma, "The Vedic Religion and the Origins of Buddhism," *Journal of the Bihar Research Society*, 46 (1960), 276-308.

(19) WARDER, ANTHONY KENNEDY. "On the Relationships Between Early Buddhism and Other Contemporary Systems." *Bulletin of the School of Oriental and African Studies*, 18 (1956), 43-63.

Contains a bibliography on the "Contemporary Systems." May be supplemented by the briefer account in the same author's *Indian Buddhism* (see 1.2.1[15]), pp. 31-42.

2.3 ATTEMPTED RECONSTRUCTIONS OF "PRIMITIVE" BUDDHIST THOUGHT

(1) CONZE, EDWARD. *Buddhist Thought in India* (see 2.1[1]), pp. 17-118.

Conze abandons the attempt to recover "Original Buddhism," and instead comes up with a convincing portrait of "Archaic Buddhism" which he places c. 300-250 B.C. See first of all Chapter 2, "The Problem of Original Buddhism" (pp. 31-33). A fine discussion of the scholarly controversy about early Buddhism and an outline of some of the difficulties involved in its reconstruction may also be found in the same author's "Recent Progress in Buddhist Studies," in *Thirty Years of Buddhist Studies* (see 2.5.1[5]), pp. 1-32.

(2) FALK, MARYLA. *Nama-rupa and Dharma-rupa: Origin and Aspects of an Ancient Indian Conception*. Calcutta: University of Calcutta, 1943, 222 pp.

An important work for the understanding of "pre-canonical" Buddhism, containing numerous bold speculations on the thought-world in which Gautama lived.

(3) JENNINGS, J. G. *The Vedantic Buddhism of the Buddha*. London: Oxford, 1947, 679 pp.

The nature of this volume is indicated by its subtitle: "A collection of historical texts translated from the original Pali." Its purpose is to assert the Vedantic quality of the Pali canon and to try to delineate it into earlier/later strata of composition.

(4) JOSHI, LALMANI. *Studies in the Buddhist Culture of India*. See 1.2.2.3(9).

An attempt to account for the Buddhist culture of seventh and eighth century A.D. India from a philosophical context. Includes discussion of most of the major schools and thinkers, concentrating heavily on authorship, dates, etc.

(5) KEITH, ARTHUR BERRIEDALE. "Pre-Canonical Buddhism." *Indian Historical Quarterly*, 12 (1936), 1-20.

An important article in the on-going debate about "primitive Buddhism" by one of the opponents of the primacy of the Pali Canon.

(6) MIZUNO, KOGEN. *Primitive Buddhism*. See 1.2.2.1(8).

After the Meiji era, the knowledge of the Pali Canon through Western scholarship led to the investigation of "Genshi Bukkyo" or "Primitive Buddhism"--that antedating the separation of the Vehicles--in Japan. This is a Japanese scholar's investigation of the characteristics and intellectual life of this primitive Buddhism.

(7) PANDE, GOVIND CHANDRA. *Studies in the Origins of Buddhism*. See 1.2.2.1(10).

A massive scholarly attempt to dig back through the Pali texts. Part 1 tackles the crucial question of Chronology in the various nikayas of the Pali Canon. Part 2 reviews the historical and cultural background of Early Buddhism, before discussing, in Part 3, all the principal doctrines that have been commonly assigned to an "original Buddhism."

(8) REGAMEY, CONSTANTIN. "Le problème du bouddhisme primitif et les derniers travaux de Stanislaw Schayer." *Rocznik Orjentalistyczny*, 21 (1957), 37-58.

A discussion of the scholarly debate carried on between the "Franco-Belgian" school (La Vallée Poussin, Przyluski, Keith, etc.) and the "Anglo-Germans" (Rhys-Davids, Oldenberg, Winternitz, etc.) on what constituted "Primitive Buddhism." The article clarifies and summarizes the various positions, shows what turns the debate took after World War Two, and calls attention to the important articles of Stanislaw Schayer: "Precanonical Buddhism" and "New Contributions to the Problem of Pre-hinayanistic Buddhism," which remained mostly buried in journals: *Archív Orientální*, 7 (1935), 121-132, and *Polski Biuletyn Orientalistyczny*, 1 (1937), 8-17.

(9) RHYS-DAVIDS, CAROLINE AUGUSTA FOLEY. *Sakya or Buddhist Origins*. London: K. Paul, Trench, Trubner, 1931, 444 pp.

In the latter portion of her long career, Rhys-Davids claimed repeatedly that the original "Sakya" teachings of "Gotama the Man" had been betrayed by the monastically biased suttas, and that it was possible to get back to them only by "winnowing the older grain from the later chaff." However, it has been pointed out that her efforts resulted in a Gotama who bore a strange resemblance to a Ramakrishna or a Gandhi and whose teachings had more in common with Tagore's Religion of Man than with any known Buddhist texts. Her position, therefore, has been much criticized and has become a sort of curious landmark in the history of scholarship. Other presentations of her argument may be found in Gotama the Man (see 8.1.2.3[25]), A Manual of Buddhism (New York: Macmillan, 1932), and What Was the Original Gospel in Buddhism? (London: Epworth, 1938).

(10) SCHAYER, STANISLAUS. "Pre-canonical Buddhism." Archív Orientální (1935), pp. 121-132.
Schayer argues for the antiquity of the three major strands of early Buddhist thought: Abhidharma, Madhyamika dialectic, and "mind-only."

(11) STCHERBATSKY, FEDOR IPPOLITOVICH. Buddhist Logic (see 2.1[11]), vol. 1, pp. 3-7.
Perhaps the most concise of all Stcherbatsky's descriptions of Primitive Buddhism, which, in his own words "can hardly be said to represent a religion."

(12) _____. "The Doctrine of the Buddha." Bulletin of the School of Oriental and African Studies (1930-32), pp. 867-896.
In this important article the author attempted to summarize his own views with respect to the problems of the teachings of Buddha Sakyamuni. Essentially, he argues that the Buddha preached a doctrine which anticipates much of later abhidharmic thought.

(13) WARDER, ANTHONY KENNEDY. "On the Relationships Between Early Buddhism and Other Contemporary Systems." See 2.2(19).
An intelligent and interesting attempt to describe the views of Primitive Buddhism by considering its similarities and oppositions to non-Buddhist systems of thought, rather than by trying to trace the original doctrine back through the history of the schools of Buddhism itself.

(14) WINTERNITZ, MORIZ. "Problems of Buddhism." Visva-Bharati Quarterly, 2 (1936), 41-60.
A critique of C. A. F. Rhys-Davids's methods and conclusions about what constituted "Original Buddhism." Nevertheless Winternitz believes it is not impossible to get back to a picture of "what the Buddha taught," and concludes that one of those teachings was "active love."

2.4   THE THERAVADA (HINAYANA) SCHOOLS

2.4.1 General Discussions and Surveys

(1) BAPAT, PURUSHOTTAM VISHVANATH, ed. 2500 Years of Buddhism (see 1.2.1[1]), pp. 97-120.
A concise article which lists the major schools one by one, summarizes what is known of them, and offers a chart to explain their relationships (based on Bareau). May be used as a quick introduction to the subject.

(2) BAREAU, ANDRE. Les Sectes bouddhiques du petit véhicule. Publications de l'Ecole française d'Extrême-Orient, No. 38. Saigon: Ecole française d'Extrême-Orient, 1955, 310 pp.
A classic, scholarly work on the subject of the historical and doctrinal development of the eighteen sects of Theravada Buddhism. It should be consulted by all students especially interested in the topic. Even non-French readers can profit from Bareau's chart on p. 30.

(3) _____. "Trois traités sur les sectes bouddhiques attribués à Vasumitra, Bhavya et Vinitadeva." Journal Asiatique, 242 (1954), 229-266.
A French translation of three short treatises which constitute one of our principal original sources on the various doctrines of the Theravada schools. The first is Vasumitra's important Samayabhedoparacanacakra ("Cycle de la formation des schismes"); for an English translation see Jiryo Masuda, "Origin and Doctrines of Early Indian Buddhist Schools," Asia Major, 2 (1925), 1-78. The second and third (found in Journal Asiatique, 244 [1956], 167-200) are Bhavya's Nikayabhedavibhangavyakhyana ("L'Explication des divisions entre les sectes"), a German translation of which is in Max Walleser, Die Buddhistische Philosophie in Ihrer Geschichtlichen Entwicklung (Heidelberg: K. Winter, 1904-1927), 4 vols., Bd. 4 (1927): "Die Sekten des Alten Buddhismus, and Vinitadeva's Samayabhedoparacanacakre-nikayabhedopadarsanasamgraha (Le compendium descriptif des divisions des sectes dans le cycle de la formation des schismes)."

(4) DEMIEVILLE, PAUL. "L'Origine des sectes bouddhiques d'après Paramartha." Mélanges chinois et bouddhiques, 1 (1931), 15-64.
A French translation of the portions of Ki Tsang's (549-623) "Profound Meaning of the Three Sastras" (San louen hiuan yi) which pertain to the development and doctrines of the early schools of Buddhism in India. This is accompanied by a translation of fragments from Paramartha's sixth century commentary on Vasumitra's treatise, which is one of our main sources of information on the early Hinaya sects. An important article for students doing specific research on the topic.

(5) DUTT, NALINAKSHA. Buddhist Sects in India. Calcutta: Mukhopadhyay, 1970, 317 pp.

Based primarily on articles previously published in the Indian Historical Quarterly, 1937-1940 (vols. 13, 14, 15), this book is a fine, doctrinally-oriented study of the eighteen Theravada schools. It is especially useful for those who cannot read Bareau's Les sectes bouddhiques du petit véhicule (above).

(6) DUTT, SUKUMAR. The Buddha and Five After-Centuries (see 1.2.1[8]), pp. 123-140.

The chapter makes a good short introduction to the rise of "Sects and Schools" in the Theravada, and one of the few that comes at the question sociologically (as well as doctrinally).

(7) Kathavatthu: Points of Controversy: or Subjects of Discourse. Translated by Shwe Zan Aung and C. A. F. Rhys-Davids. Translation Series, No. 5. London: Pali Text Society, 1915, 416 pp.

The whole of the Katha-vatthu sheds much light (in its own Abhidhammic way) on the positions taken by the various Theravada schools on various points of doctrine. The book is presented from a Theravada standpoint, but the arguments of the other schools come out in the debates. These "heretical" positions are also conveniently grouped by Rhys-Davids in her tables of contents, and her three charts show various understandings of the development of the schisms. The "Prefatory Notes," though dated, are also noteworthy.

(8) KIMURA, RYUKAN. Introduction to the History of Early Buddhist Schools. Calcutta: Calcutta University Press, 1925, pp. 88-128.

A classic, now surpassed by Bareau's Les sectes bouddhiques (above), but still very valuable as "an introduction" and for its discussion of some of the issues involved in the splitting of the Sangha.

(9) LAMOTTE, ETIENNE. Histoire du bouddhisme indien: des origines à l'ère Saka (see 1.2.1[10]), pp. 571-705.

A masterful look at the origins, development and accomplishments of the early sects (among the latter were the geographical and linguistic spread of Buddhism and the progress in Abhidharma studies). See especially pp. 584-606 where, rather than trying to draw any conclusions on the filiation of the sects, Lamotte simply and clearly presents various traditional theories. See p. 571, n. 1 for an extensive bibliography.

(10) MASUDA, JIRYO. Origin and Doctrines of Early Indian Buddhist Schools. Leipzig: Verlag der Asia Major, 1925, 78 pp.

Somewhat dated, but very useful for those who cannot read French (i.e., Bareau or Lamotte). It is basically a translation of Hsuan Tsang's rendition of Vasumitra's treatise on the schools, but Masuda's copious and scholarly notes, based on a wide range of original materials, make it an important source of information on the subject.

(11) NYANATILOKA THERA. Guide to the Abhidhamma Pitaka. Third edition. Kandy: Buddhist Publication Society, 1971, pp. 60-87.

Contains a summary of the important issues raised in the Katha-Vatthu, noting the various positions argued by respective early schools.

(12) RHYS-DAVIDS, THOMAS WILLIAM. "The Sects of the Buddhists." Journal of the Royal Asiatic Society (1891), pp. 409-422.

An outdated article, but convenient for its tabular review of the Theravada traditions concerning the eighteen schools (see also W. Geiger's translation of The Mahavamsa [London: Oxford University Press, 1912], Ch. 5, "The Third Council," pp. 26-50), and its handy listings of the sects mentioned by the Chinese travelers Fa Hsien and Hsuan Tsang. This is continued as "Schools of Buddhist Belief" in Journal of the Royal Asiatic Society (1892), pp. 1-37, by a table of the Theravada sects according to Tibetan traditions (see also W. W. Rockhill, The Life of the Buddha [see 3.2.1.2(11)], pp. 182ff., and E. Obermiller's translation of Bu Ston's History of Buddhism [see 1.14.1(2)], pp. 97-100); and a synopsis of positions of different schools as found in the Kathavatthu (above). A later statement of Rhys-Davids' position may be found in his "Sects (Buddhists)" in Encyclopaedia of Religion and Ethics (see 1.15.1[9]), vol. 2, pp. 307-309.

(13) TAKAKUSU, JUNJIRO. The Essentials of Buddhist Philosophy (see 2.1[13]), pp. 57-80.

Two chapters in which Takakusu (looking back from a Japanese perspective) analyzes and summarizes the two main streams of Theravadan philosophy; the Sarvastivadins (actually the Vaibhasikas) which he identifies with the Japanese Kusha school and calls "realism," and the Sautrantikas (Satyasiddhi or the Jojitsu school) which he calls the Nihilist or Non-ens school. In both cases, Takakusu introduces the school and traces its history and philosophy and relation to other viewpoints.

(14) WARDER, ANTHONY KENNEDY. Indian Buddhism (see 1.2.1[15]), pp. 288-351.

The chapter entitled "The Eighteen Schools," focuses on the geographical spread and literary achievements of the various schools, rather than their doctrinal differences. See also Warder's bibliography, pp. 523-533, for a clear listing of what text belongs to which school.

2.4.2 The Councils (Rajagrha, Vaisali, Pataliputra)

(1) BAREAU, ANDRE. Les Premiers Conciles Bouddhiques. Annales du Musée Guimet, Bibliothèque d'études, No. 60. Paris: Presses Universitaires de France, 1958, 150 pp.

The Theravada (Hinayana) Schools

The classic work on the subject. Bareau has made an exhaustive analysis of the sources and then presented, in a methodical and strikingly clear way, his findings concerning the first four councils. (He argues there were two of them held at Pataliputra.)

(2) DEMIEVILLE, PAUL. "A Propos du concile de Vaisali." T'oung pao, 40 (1951), 239-296.

This is essentially a critique and discussion of Hofinger's book on the same subject (below) in which Demieville presents his views and doubts about the historicity of the second Buddhist council.

(3) DUTT, NALINAKSHA. "The Second Buddhist Council." Indian Historical Quarterly, 35 (1959), 45-56.

The only work in English specifically on the Council at Vaisali. Dutt questions Hofinger and Bareau's assumption of the antiquity of the Mahasanghika and Mulasarvastivadin Vinayas in their reconstruction of the events of the second Council. For a critique of Dutt, see Prebish's review article (below).

(4) FRANKE, RUDOLF OTTO. "The Buddhist Councils at Rajagaha and Vesali as Alleged in Cullavamsa, 11, 12." Translated by C. A. F. Rhys-Davids in Journal of the Pali Text Society (1908), pp. 1-80.

An old, now dated work which examines the Pali account of the first two Councils and questions the historicity of both of them.

(5) HOFINGER, MARCEL. Etude sur le Concile de Vaisali. Bibliothèque du Muséon, No. 20. Louvain: Bureaux du Muséon, 1946, 300 pp.

A thorough and important study, containing translations of the Chinese and Pali sources dealing with the second council. Hofinger concludes the council was historical, and unlike Bareau, sees in it a tension between the Western schools (Sthaviravadins) and the Eastern (Mahasanghikas).

(6) LA VALLEE POUSSIN, LOUIS DE. "The Buddhist Councils." Indian Antiquary, 37 (1908), 1-18 and 81-106.

A translation of his "Les Premiers Conciles Bouddhiques," Le Muséon, 6 (1905), 213-323, this is an old article but still one of the few studies in English where most of the major original sources are set down. The article deals only with the Councils of Rajagrha and Vaisali; a later statement of La Vallée Poussin's position, together with a study of the "Councils of the two Asokas," may be found in Encyclopaedia of Religion and Ethics (see 1.15.1[9]), "Councils (Buddhist)," vol. 4, pp. 179-185.

(7) MAJUMDAR, RAMESH CHANDRA. "The Buddhist Councils," in Buddhistic Studies. Edited by Bimala Churn Law. Calcutta: Thacker, Spink, 1931, pp. 26-72.

Majumdar's article is superseded by the more specific studies presented by scholars since the time of this publication. Unlike Bareau, Majumdar takes the historical authenticity of the First Council at Rajagrha perhaps a bit too seriously. This leads one to suspect that the remainder of his survey lacks the thrust of historical-critical analysis. Nevertheless, Majumdar's article provides the reader with a neat, fairly comprehensive, and readable summary.

(8) PREBISH, CHARLES. "A Review of Scholarship on the Buddhist Councils." Journal of Asian Studies, 35 (1974), 239-254.

A survey of the questions and conclusions of the major scholarly works on the subject. The article lucidly summarizes the events of each council and should be the place to begin any study of this topic.

(9) PRZYLUSKI, JEAN. Le Concile de Rajagrha: Introduction à l'Histoire des Canons et des Sectes Bouddhiques. Buddhica. Documents et travaux pour l'étude du bouddhisme, 1 sér.: Mémoires, No. 2. Paris: P. Geuthner, 1926-1928, 432 pp.

A classic work which is a valuable source of information concerning the first council at Rajagrha as it contains partial translations of the relevant material taken from the various sutras, commentaries, avadanas, and Vinayas. The last section, however, in which he discusses the myth of Gavampati, the expulsion of Ananda, the history of the first sects and the formation of the canon, is colored by Przyluski's own scholarly eccentricities.

(10) TSUKAMATO, KEISHO. "Mahakasyapa's Precedence to Ananda in the Rajagrha Council." Indogaku Bukkyogaku Kenkyu/Journal of Indian and Buddhist Studies, 11, no. 2 (1963), 824-817 (sic).

Short, useful tabulation of the different accounts of the events of the first council, compiled from twenty different Sanskrit, Pali and Chinese sources. Specific attention is then paid to the listings of Ananda's faults and to his relationship with Mahakasyapa. This is followed by a bibliography of Western works on the First Council classified into those which support and those which oppose its historicity.

2.4.3 The Sthaviravadin Branch (Theravadins, Sarvastivadins, et al.)

See also 2.4.1.

(1) BANERJEE, ANUKUL CHANDRA. Sarvastivada Literature. Calcutta: K. L. Mukhopadhyay, 1957, 271 pp. See also 3.1.3(1).

(2) CARTER, JOHN ROSS. "Dharma as a Religious Concept: A Brief Investigation of Its History in the Western Academic Tradition and Its Centrality within the Sinhalese Theravada Tradition." Journal of the American Academy of Religion, 44, no. 4 (December 1976), 661-674.

In the second half of this article Carter identifies Dhamma as the religious concept which is most central to the Theravada tradition; and he begins to spell out some of the crucial aspects of that concept as these were articulated in the Sinhalese commentaries.

(3) CONZE, EDWARD. Buddhist Thought in India (see 2.1[1]), pp. 119-191.
This introduction to the different schools of the Sthaviravada branch approaches the subject not school by school but by focusing on certain key issues of doctrinal debate which arose between the various schools.

(4) DUTT, NALINAKSHA. "Doctrines of the Sammitiya School of Buddhism." Indian Historical Quarterly, 15 (1939), 90-100.
An outline, compiled from various sources (mostly the Katha-vatthu), of the doctrinal position of the Sammitiyas (sometimes called the Vatsiputriyas), who formed one of the branches of the Sthaviravadins.

(5) HALDAR, ARUNA. "Doctrine of Sarvastivada in the Light of Modern Philosophy and Psychology." Journal of the Asiatic Society of Calcutta, 8 (1966), 51-63.
The title of the article is a bit misleading as most of the article is a well-done straightforward presentation of the basic conceptions employed in Sarvastivadin doctrine including space, time, dharma, matter and mind. The author's basic contention seems to be that Sarvastivadin thought cannot be easily categorized as a "realism" or an "idealism."

(6) LAMOTTE, ETIENNE, ed. and trans. "Le traité de l'acte de Vasubandhu: Karmasiddhiprakarana." Mélanges chinois et bouddhiques, 4 (1935-1936), Introduction, pp. 151-171.
Concise presentation of the doctrines of the Sarvastivadin--Vaibhasikas, the Vatsiputriya--Sammitiyas and the Sautrantikas, with specific reference to their views on the nature of karma. Some of the details of Lamotte's findings have been questioned by Susumu Yamaguchi whose study, Kusha-ron no genten Kaimei (Kyoto: Hozokan, 1955), in Japanese, of the Karmasiddhiprakarana has been summarized in Giuseppe Morichini, "The Spiritual Struggle of Vasubandhu and his Karmasiddhiprakarana." East and West, 6 (1955), 31-33.

(7) LA VALLEE POUSSIN, LOUIS DE. "Sautrantikas," in Encyclopaedia of Religion and Ethics (see 1.15.1[9]), vol. 2, pp. 213-214.
A short review of the Sautrantikas and their doctrines and position in Buddhist thought.

(8) PRZYLUSKI, JEAN. "Darstantika, Sautrantika and Sarvastivadin." Indian Historical Quarterly, 16 (1940), 246-254.
In this article, Przyluski examines these three schools and attempts to show them as being three stages of an evolution in doctrinal and textual attitudes.

(9) RAHULA, WALPOLA. What the Buddha Taught. See 2.1(10).

(10) TAKAKUSU, JUNJIRO. "On the Abhidharma Literature of the Sarvastivadins." Journal of the Pali Text Society (1904-1905), pp. 67-146.
A valuable survey of Sarvastivada Abhidharma literature, including an analysis of all seven Sarvastivada Abhidharma works and reviews of the contents of important works connected to the Sarvastivadin school. The essay should be read in conjunction with passages from the Theravadin Abhidhamma (a totally different text), and/or introductory material on Abhidharma philosophy.

(11) _____. "Sarvastivadins," in Encyclopaedia of Religion and Ethics (see 1.15.1[9]), vol. 2, pp. 198-200.
A concise introductory article which does not neglect the spread of Sarvastivadin doctrines outside of India.

2.4.4 The Mahasanghikas

(1) CONZE, EDWARD. Buddhist Thought in India (see 2.1[1]), pp. 195-200.
A concise consideration of the Mahasanghikas as the forerunners of the Mahayana, with a chart of their subjects.

(2) DUTT, NALINAKSHA. "Doctrines of the Mahasanghika School of Buddhism." Indian Historical Quarterly, 13 (1937), 549-580; and 14 (1938), 110-113.
A compendium of what was then known about the Mahasanghikas, drawing heavily on the Katha Vatthu and the work of J. Masuda.

(3) LAMOTTE, ETIENNE. "Buddhist Controversy over the Five Propositions." Indian Historical Quarterly, 32 (1956), 148-162.
An English version of what may be found in French in the same author's Histoire du Bouddhisme Indien (see 1.2.1[10]), pp. 500-516. Discusses the origins of the Mahasanghikas by examining the sources on the "Five Points" concerning the nature of Arhat, and in dealing with the question of the authorship of those five points examines the traditions of the "Two Mahadevas."

(4) LA VALLEE POUSSIN, LOUIS DE. "The Five Points of Mahadeva and the Kathavatthu." Journal of the Royal Asiatic Society (1910), pp. 413-423.
An early listing of the different traditions regarding Mahadeva's "Five Points" concerning the nature of the Arhat, which are said to lie at the origin of the Mahasanghika schism. The author was the first to identify the "Five Points" with certain heretical tenets listed in the Kathavatthu.

The Mahayana Schools

(5) *The Mahavastu.* Translated by J. J. Jones. Sacred Books of the Buddhists, Nos. 16, 18, 19. London: Luzac, 1949-1956, 3 vol.s

The text claims to be the Vinaya of the Lokattara-vadin sect of the Mahasanghikas, but it is not very helpful in reconstructing their doctrines. See also 3.2.1.2(5).

(6) WARDER, ANTHONY KENNEDY. *Indian Buddhism* (see 1.2.1[15]), pp. 212-218.

A concise discussion of the first schism between Sthaviravadins and Mahasanghikas, with a look at the origins of the latter.

2.5 THE MAHAYANA SCHOOLS

2.5.1 General Discussions and Surveys

(1) ARMSTRONG, ROBERT CORNELL. *An Introduction to Japanese Buddhist Sects.* See 1.13.2.2(3).

(2) BAPAT, PURUSHOTTAM VISHVANATH, ed. *2500 Years of Buddhism* (see 1.2.1[1]), pp. 120-136.

These pages survey the major Mahayana schools in India, China, and Japan, describing them one by one and giving a chart to illustrate their development. Useful as a quick introduction to the subject.

(3) CHAN, WING-TSIT, trans. and ed. *A Source Book in Chinese Philosophy.* Princeton: Princeton University Press, 1963.

Chan has included many articles worthy of reference in this compendium. The reader may well profit from the following chapters: "The Seven Early Buddhist Schools," pp. 336-342, "Seng-chao's Doctrine of Reality," pp. 343-356, "The Philosophy of Emptiness: Chi-tsang of the Three-Treatise School," pp. 357-369, "Buddhist Idealism: Hsuan Tsang of the Consciousness-Only School," pp. 370-395, "The Tien-t'ai Philosophy of Perfect Harmony," pp. 396-405, and "The Zen School of Sudden Enlightenment," pp. 425-449.

(4) CONZE, EDWARD. *Buddhist Thought in India* (see 2.1[1]), pp. 195-274.

After a survey of the "Doctrines common to all Mahayanists," Conze lucidly discusses "The Madhyamikas" and "The Yogacarins." This may be the best currently available introduction to the bases of Mahayana thought, but deals with none of the developments outside of India.

(5) _____. *Thirty Years of Buddhist Studies: Selected Essays.* Columbia, S.C.: University of South Carolina Press, 1968, pp. 48-86. (Also published in *The Concise Encyclopaedia of Living Faiths* [see 1.11.1(9)], pp. 296-320.)

These pages contain a superlative survey of Mahayana Buddhism--the reasons for its success, its ontological concerns, doctrines, soteriological ideals, mythologies--a work that sets the horizon for all students.

(6) HANAYAMA, SHINSHO. "Buddhism of the One Great Vehicle (Mahayana)," in *Essays in East-West Philosophy: An Attempt at World Synthesis.* Edited by Charles A. Moore. Honolulu: University of Hawaii, 1951, pp. 196-210.

This article is one of several adquate treatments aimed at instructing the reader to a general understanding of Mahayana thought. For two other useful articles of similar scope, see Hajime Nakamura, "A Critical Appraisal of Mahayana and Esoteric Buddhism," *Acta Asiatica*, 6 (1964), 57-88, and 7: 36-94, which provides descriptions of important Mahayana texts; and Susumu Yamaguchi, "Development of Mahayana Buddhist Beliefs," in *The Path of the Buddha* (see 1.1[6]), pp. 153-181.

(7) ROBINSON, RICHARD H. *The Buddhist Religion: A Historical Introduction* (see 1.1[8]), pp. 49-107.

A concise survey of the rise of the Mahayana and of the history and doctrines of the various Chinese and Japanese schools.

(8) SUZUKI, BEATRICE LANE. *Mahayana Buddhism: A Brief Outline.* New York: Macmillan, 1969, 158 pp. (Paperback.)

A short overview of the teachings of Mahayana which are the common ground of the various schools, this book is in many ways better for introductory purposes, than many of the works of the author's husband.

(9) SUZUKI, DAISETZ TEITARO. *Outlines of Mahayana Buddhism.* See 2.1(12).

(10) TAKAKUSU, JUNJIRO. *The Essentials of Buddhist Philosophy.* See 2.1(13).

2.5.2 Forerunners and Origins of the Mahayana

(1) CONZE, EDWARD. *Buddhist Thought in India* (see 2.1[1]), pp. 195-204.

(2) _____. *The Prajnaparamita Literature.* The Hague: Mouton, 1960, pp. 9-17.

Conze argues for a South Indian origin of the Prajnaparamita literature and Mahayana in general. See also, in the same line, his *Buddhism: Its Essence and Development* (1.1[2]), pp. 123-125.

(3) DUTT, NALINAKSHA. *Aspects of Mahayana Buddhism and Its Relation to Hinayana* (see 1.2.2.3[3]), pp. 1-80.

Two helpful chapters, one dealing with the political and cultural background of Mahayana, the other with "Mahayanic traces in the Nikayas" of the Pali Canon. Useful as an introduction.

(4) HALDAR, JNANRANJAN. *Links between Early and Later Buddhist Mythology.* Calcutta: K. L. Mukhopadhyaya, 1972, 45 pp.

Attempts to show how early (Pali Hinayana) mythology is reflected in later (Mahayana) literature. The author examines eleven motifs (including bodhisattva, heaven, hell, gods, and the Buddha's body) to illustrate his thesis.

(5) HIRAKAWA, AKIRA. "The Rise of Mahayana Buddhism and Its Relationship to the Worship of Stupas." Memoirs of the Toyo Bunkyo Research Department, 22 (1963), 57-106. See also 7.1.3(8).

(6) KEITH, ARTHUR BERRIEDALE. Buddhist Philosophy in India and Ceylon (see 2.1[8]).
Contains Keith's view on the formerly much debated question of the non-Indian origins of the Mahayana movement. Gives footnote references to other works dealing with this question.

(7) LAMOTTE, ETIENNE. "Sur la Formation du Mahayana," in Asiatica: Festschrift Friedrich Weller. Leipzig: O. Harrassowitz, 1954, pp. 377-96.
Excellent and authoritative survey of the beginnings of Mahayana which reviews the traditional "indigenous" legends about its origin as well as the scholarly debate on its "Southern" or "Northern" beginnings.

(8) MUS, PAUL. Barabudur: Esquisse d'une Histoire du Bouddhisme fondée sur la critique archéologique des textes. Hanoi: Imprimerie d'Extrême-Orient, 1935, vol. 1, pp. 45-48.
These pages contain a concise presentation of Mus's understanding of the origins of the Mahayana as the stabilization of a development already expressed in "primitive" Buddhism, and not as a departure from or reaction against it.

2.5.3 The Madhyamikas

See also 2.5.1 and 2.7. Cross references to authoritative texts are in 3.3.2.7.

(1) BHATTACHARYA, KARUNA. "Sankara's Criticism of Nagarjuna." Journal of the Indian Academy of Philosophy, 1 (1961-1962), 53-64.
In this article, the author builds a case to defend Shankara's understanding and critique of Nagarjuna's philosophy. In short, he agrees with Shankara that Nagarjuna's assertion that "everything is non-existent or void" is sheer nonsense. The reader should bring his own understanding of Nagarjuna's philosophy to this article in order to make his own decision.

(2) CONZE, EDWARD. Buddhist Thought in India (see 2.1[1]), pp. 238-249.
Short introduction to the theories of the Madhyamika school. Its description of a meditation on emptiness may be useful for putting those theories into the context of practice.

(3) GARD, RICHARD A. "The Madhyamika in Korea." Journal of Indian and Buddhist Studies, 7, no. 2 (1959), 60-78.
Study of the development and the significance of the Madhyamika school in Korea, a subject much neglected by Western scholars.

(4) _____. "Why Did the Madhyamika Decline?" Indogaku Bukkyogaku Kenkyo, 5 (1957), 623-618 (sic).
Asks more questions than it answers, but presents a good summary of some of the problems encountered by late Madhyamika in India, Tibet, China, Korea, and Japan.

(5) KATZ, NATHAN. "An Appraisal of the Svatantrika-Prasanghika Debates: Ca. 52-795 CE." Philosophy East and West, 26, no. 3 (July 1976).
An appeal for more serious consideration of the positions of Bhavaviveka, Santiraksita and Kamalasila in studies of Madhyamika. Also included is a reappraisal of the bSamyas debates (792-774) which were instrumental, the author contends, in establishing a Svatantrika norm for early forms of Tibetan Buddhism.

(6) LA VALLEE POUSSIN, LOUIS DE. "Reflexions sur le Madhyamika." Mélanges Chinois et Bouddhiques, 2 (1933), 4-59.
This is one of La Vallée Poussin's articles in his long vacillating debate with Stcherbatsky and others about how to interpret Nagarjuna. His focus here is on "suchness" and "dependent origination" as basic concepts for understanding Indian Madhyamika. A presentation of his view in English, but much more general and introductory, is his article "Madhyamika," in Hastings' Encyclopaedia of Religion and Ethics (see 1.15.1[9]), vol. 8, pp. 235-37.

(7) MURTI, TIRUPATTUR RAMASESHAYYER VANKATACHALA. The Central Philosophy of Buddhism: A Study of the Madhyamika System. Second edition. London: G. Allen and Unwin, 1960, 372 pp.
The first thorough study of Madhyamika philosophy in English. It is an important insightful interpretation which looks at Nagarjuna through the lenses of Candrakirti and Stcherbatsky. It also (unfortunately at times) seeks to draw parallels and comparisons with Kantian categories.

(8) PANDEYA, RAM CHANDRA. "The Madhyamika Philosophy: A New Approach." Philosophy East and West, 14 (1964), 3-24.
A presentation of the fundamental conceptions operative in Madhyamika philosophical thought. The author concludes his remarks by referring to Madhyamika as an "analytical zeroism" rather than as an absolutism, realism, idealism, or empiricism.

(9) RAMANAN, K. VENKATA. Nagarjuna's Philosophy as Presented in the Maha-prajnaparamita-sastra. Rutland, Vt.: published for the Harvard Yenching Institute by C. E. Tuttle, 1966, 409 pp.

This work is useful as one of the few analyses in English of the huge Chinese text of the Maha-Prajnaparamita-Sastra. The author wishes thereby to reinterpret the thought of Nagarjuna which, he believes, has been seen too much in the light of the Mulamadhyamikarikas. In so doing, however, he discards the arguments against Nagarjuna's authorship of the Sastra. A clear, concise statement of Venkata Ramanan's position may be found in his "A Fresh Appraisal of the Madhyamika Philosophy," Visvabharati Quarterly, 27 (1961-62), 230-238.

(10) ROBINSON, RICHARD H. Early Madhyamika in India and China. See 1.11.2.2(9).

An important turning point in the study of Madhyamika, which is terse, difficult to read, ground-breaking, and brilliant. Essentially the work is a study of the background of the Chinese Three Treatises School (San Lun). Chapter 2 (pp. 21-70) contains a description of the basic features of Nagarjuna's system with a brief section on his mysticism. Chapters 3-6 (pp. 71-161) deal with Kumarajiva, Hui-Yuan, Seng-jui, and Seng-chao and their role in transmitting and interpreting Madhyamika thought to China. Chapter 8 (pp. 162-73) discusses in the guise of an epilogue, the lineage of the Old Three Treatise Sect. Pp. 177-232 contain translations of ten relevant "documents."

(11) _____. "Madhyamika," in Chapters in Indian Civilization (see 2.2[8]), vol. 1, pp. 202-210.

A concise introduction to the Madhyamika system, which tries not to cut any corners off the topic.

(12) STCHERBATSKY, FEDOR IPPOLITOVICH. The Conception of Buddhist Nirvana. Revised and enlarged edition. Varanasi: Bharatiya Vidya Parkashan, 1968, 1 vol., various pagination. (Originally published Leningrad, 1927.)

Written as a response to de La Vallée Poussin's Nirvana (see 11.2[4]), this work also contains Stcherbatsky's interpretation of the thought of Nagarjuna, in response to Poussin's views on Madhyamika, in part of the great ongoing Russo-Belgian debate.

(13) STRENG, FREDERICK J. Emptiness: A Study in Religious Meaning. Nashville: Abingdon Press, 1967, 252 pp. See also 2.7.8(10).

(14) TAKAKUSU, JUNJIRO. The Essentials of Buddhist Philosophy (see 2.1[13]).

Most short surveys of Madhyamika thought focus on the Indian origins and development of the school. In this chapter, Takakusu looks instead from the perspective of China and Japan where the basic Madhyamika views were taken up by the San-lun (Sanron or Three-treatises) school.

(15) WARDER, ANTHONY KENNEDY. Indian Buddhism (see 1.2.1[15]), pp. 373-422, 540-542.

An extensive, textually oriented discussion of the Madhyamikas and their position within the Mahayana. Pages 540-542 contain a bibliography of the works of Nagarjuna, Aryadeva, Sthiramati, and others. See for cross reference the entire section on Madhyamika in "Authoritative Texts," Category 3.

(16) WAYMAN, ALEX. "Contributions to the Madhyamika School of Buddhism." Journal of the American Oriental Society, 89 (1969), 141-152.

This article is essentially a review of Streng's Emptiness (above). Wayman's basic criticisms include a new translation of a passage which is a key to an understanding of Nagarjuna's "middle path."

2.5.4 Yogacara/Vijnanavada (Fa-hsian/Hosso)

See also Authoritative Texts, 3.3.3 and in Ideal Beings, under Vasubandhu, Asanga, etc., and in 2.7 under Alayavijnana, tri-laksana. . . . See also relevant sections of the works listed under 2.5.1.

(1) BHATTACHARYA, VIDHUSEKHARA. "Evolution of Vijnanavada." Indian Historical Quarterly, 10 (1934), 1-11.

A brief article in which the author argues for the origins and first expressions of Vijnanavada philosophy in the Upanisads.

(2) CHATTERJEE, ASHOK KUMAR. The Yogacara Idealism. Banaras Hindu University Darsana series, No. 3. Varanasi: Banaras Hindu University, 1962, 309 pp.

A not always successful attempt to apply some of the insights of T. R. V. Murti to the Vijnanavada school. However, it is the only full-length overall study of the subject in English. See also Wayman's review article (below).

(3) CONZE, EDWARD. Buddhist Thought in India (see 2.1[1]), pp. 250-260.

This concise introduction to the principal doctrines of the Yogacarins may sometimes be made easier by supplementing it with Chapter 7 (pp. 161-173) of the same author's Buddhism: Its Essence and Development (see 1.1[2]).

(4) DASGUPTA, SURENDRANATH. Indian Idealism. Cambridge: Cambridge University Press, 1969, pp. 76-148. (First published 1933.)

In these two chapters entitled "Buddhist Idealism," Dasgupta examines the doctrines of the Yogacarins and seeks to trace their origins in the Upanishads. A less successful but shorter attempt to do the same thing is Vidhusekhara Bhattacharya's "Evolution of Vijnanavada" (above).

(5) FUNG, YU-LAN. A History of Chinese Philosophy. Translated by Derk Bodde. Princeton: Princeton University Press, 1952-53, vol. 2, pp. 299-338.

A discussion of the principal doctrines set forth in the Ch'eng-Wei-shih-lun (Vijnaptimatra Siddhi) of Hsuan Tsang, the importer, interpreter, and establisher of the Yogacara (Fa-hsiang) school in China. Selections from and introductions to that text may also be found in English in Wing-Tsit Chan's A Source Book in Chinese Philosophy (see 2.5.1[3]), pp. 374-395; and William T. de Bary, ed., Sources of Chinese Tradition (see 2.5.8[7]), pp. 346-349.

(6) HAMILTON, CLARENCE H. "Hsuan Chuang and the Wei Shih Philosophy." Journal of the American Oriental Society, 51 (1931), 291-308.

A good summary introduction to the important topic of the role of the Chinese Pilgrim Hsuan Tsang in not only bringing but also interpreting Vijnanavada philosophy to China.

(7) HATTORI, MASAAKI. Dignaga on Perception, Being the Pratyaksaparicccheda of Dignaga's Pramanasamuccava. Harvard Oriental Series, No. 47. Cambridge, Mass.: Harvard University Press, 1968, 265 pp. See also 3.3.3.1(14).

(8) HSUAN TSANG. Ch'eng Wei-shih Lun: The Doctrine of Mere-Consciousness. Translated by Wei Tat. Hong Kong: Ch'eng Wei-shih Lun Publication Committee, 1973, 818 pp. See also 3.3.3.2(3).

(9) LEVI, SYLVAIN. Un Système de Philosophie Bouddhique: Matériaux pour l'étude du système Vijnaptimatra. Bibliothèque de l'Ecole des Hautes Etudes, Sciences Historiques et Philosophiques, fasc. 260. Paris: H. Champion, 1932, 206 pp.

At the time of the translation into Japanese of Hsuan Tsang's Vijnaptimatrata Siddhi (the systematic presentation of Vijnanavada doctrines), Prof. Shimaji wrote a scholarly and authoritative "Introduction" to the work. Here (pp. 15-42) it is translated into French by Paul Demieville as "Historique du Système Vijnaptimatra." It is preceded by Levi's "Analyse Resumée du Système Vijnaptimatra" (pp. 1-14), and followed by his translation of Vasubandhu's Vimsatika and Trimsika (see 3.3). The volume is rounded off by some translations of Edouard Chavannes dealing with the Alaya-vijnana.

(10) MATILAL, BIMAL KRISHNA. "A Critique of Buddhist Idealism," in Buddhist Studies in Honour of I. B. Horner (see 1.2.2.4[11]), pp. 139-169.

A clearly written attempt to differentiate the peculiarities of Yogacara from other sorts of idealism, together with a presentation of various arguments against Yogacara made by such realists as Kumarila, Jayanta, and Bhasarvajna, and ending with Matilal's own objections to the Yogacara system stated in purely philosophical terms.

(11) MAY, JACQUES. "La philosophie bouddhique idéaliste." Asiatische Studien, 25 (1971), 265-323.

Excellent and comprehensive survey of the history and doctrines of the Yogacara school, from a philosophical point of view.

(12) RAHULA, WALPOLA. "Asanga," in Encyclopaedia of Buddhism. Edited by G. P. Malalasekera. Colombo: Government of Ceylon, 1961--. In progress. Issued in parts. Vol. 2, fasc. 1 (1966), pp. 133-146. See also 8.9.1(9).

(13) ROBINSON, RICHARD H. "Vijnanavada," in Chapters in Indian Civilization (see 2.2[8]), pp. 210-216.

This introduction to the difficult theories of this school sets them in the context of the whole of Indian philosophy.

(14) STCHERBATSKY, FEDOR IPPOLITOVICH. Buddhist Logic. See 2.1(11).

A thorough and classic presentation of the "third period of Buddhist philosophy" (idealism), focusing on the logical theories of the school of Dignaga, Dharmakirti, and others.

(15) SUZUKI, DAISETZ TEITARO. "Philosophy of the Yogacara." Le Muséon, n.s. 5 (1904), 370-386.

An adequate introduction to the major doctrines of the Yogacara school. As it is topically arranged, however, it might well be supplemented by works which give either textual or historical contexts of these doctrines (e.g., Robinson or Warder, above and below). Much the same sort of presentation may be found in Suzuki's later article, "The Psychological School of Mahayana Buddhism," The Eastern Buddhist, 2 (1922), 105-128. A fuller and finer discussion of certain of the Yogacara theories is in his Studies in the Lankavatara Sutra (see 3.3.3.3[3]), esp. pp. 153-201.

(16) TAKAKUSU, JUNJIRO. The Essentials of Buddhist Philosophy. See 2.1(13).

Under the title of "The Hosso School," Takakusu traces the whole history and philosophy of the idealist, Yogacara stream of Buddhist thought, in a very neat, concise, but somewhat difficult summary fashion.

(17) TRIPATHI, CHHOTE LAL. The Problem of Knowledge in Yogacara Buddhism. Varanasi: Bharat-Bharati, 1972, 396 pp.

A highly technical, full-length study of Dignaga's epistemology, which questions the often too facile comparisons of Dignaga's views with those of Hume, Kant, and Wittgenstein.

(18) TUCCI, GIUSEPPE. On Some Aspects of the Doctrines of Maitreya and Asanga. Calcutta University Readership Lectures. Calcutta: University of Calcutta, 1930, 81 pp.

A set of five somewhat technical and condensed lectures on the beginnings of logic in the early Yogacara school. A more general lecture by the same author is "The Idealistic School in Buddhism," Dacca University Bulletin, 12 (Oxford University Press, 1926).

(19) UEDA, YOSHIFUMI. "Two Main Streams of Thought in Yogacara Philosophy." Philosophy East and West, 17 (1967), 155-165.

This article consists of a discussion of the differing interpretations handed down from the Yogacara masters, Vasubandhu and Asanga. The article will benefit the intermediate and advanced student.

(20) WARDER, ANTHONY KENNEDY. Indian Buddhism (see 1.2.1[15]), pp. 423-462.

The chapter is entitled "Idealism and the Theory of Knowledge" and contains a textually oriented discussion of the history and doctrines of the Yogacarins. See also pp. 542-544 for a listing of the original works of the school, and, for cross reference, see also the Authoritative Texts section on Yogacara, Category 3.3.

(21) WAYMAN, ALEX. "The Yogacara Idealism." Philosophy East and West, 15 (1965), 65-73.

This article consists of a critical review of Chatterjee's The Yogacara Idealism (above). Wayman concludes that "Chatterjee's book is still worth reading as a philosophical exegesis of what was traditionally held, principally by non-Yogacarins, to be the Yogacara position."

2.5.5 Avatamsaka (Hua Yen/Kegon)

See also relevant portions of works listed under 2.5.1. See also under Authoritative Texts, 3.3.4.

(1) CHANG, GARMA CH'ENG-CHI. The Buddhist Teaching of Totality: The Philosophy of Hua Yen Buddhism. University Park: Pennsylvania State University Press, 1971, 270 pp.

The Hua Yen or Avatamsaka School of Buddhism has been much neglected in Western classes. This book, the only one in English solely on Hua Yen, can be recommended as an introduction to the principal teachings of the school. It is written clearly in an informal, personal style which reflects Chang's almost evangelistic enthusiasm for the Hua Yen teachings. It is also a scholarly work--the opening section deals with "the Realm of Totality," Part 2 traces the foundation of Hua Yen in the doctrines of Emptiness, Totality, and Mind Only, and Part 3 contains a number of translations from Hua Yen texts.

(2) FUNG, YU-LAN. A History of Chinese Philosophy (see 2.5.4[5]), pp. 339-359.

A discussion of some of the doctrines of Hua Yen philosophy based on Fa-tsang's Essay on the Gold Lion. The text of the "Essay" may be found (with brief introductions) in Wing-tsit Chan's A Source Book in Chinese Philosophy (see 2.5.1[3]), pp. 409-414; and in William Theodore De Bary, ed., Sources of Chinese Tradition (see 2.5.8[7]), pp. 369-373. See also Chang, The Buddhist Teaching of Totality (above).

(3) KARUNATILLAKE, W. S. "Avatamsaka School," in Encyclopaedia of Buddhism (see 2.5.4[12]), vol. 2, fasc. 3 (1967), pp. 432-435.

A concise introduction to the history and basic doctrines of the Avatamsaka school in China and Japan. It is followed by a longer discussion and analysis of the "Avatamsaka Sutra" by Kao Kuan-ju (pp. 435-446).

(4) STEINILBER-OBERLIN, EAMILE. The Buddhist Sects of Japan (see 1.13.2.2[13]), pp. 58-73.

Entitled "The Kegon Sect," this chapter is a highly romantic description of the author's visit to the Todaiji Temple in Nara, the traditional center of Kegon in Japan. Nevertheless, it contains an informal and personal introduction to the teachings of the sect, including quotations from the Kegonkyo (Avatamsaka Sutra).

(5) SUZUKI, DAISETZ TEITARO. Essays in Zen Buddhism: Third Series (see 2.5.7[20]), pp. 1-185.

This was, for a long time, the only substantial account of some of the Avatamsaka's doctrines in English, and it remains the only treatment of the mutual influences of Zen and the Gandhavyuha. However, the focus remains on the Zen side, and, generally speaking, it has been surpassed by Suzuki's more recently published article in On Indian Mahayana Buddhism (below) and Chang's The Buddhist Teaching of Totality (above).

(6) _____. On Indian Mahayana Buddhism. New York: Harper and Row, 1968, pp. 147-226. (Paperback edition: Harper Torchbooks, TB 1403.)

This is the only substantive article in English on the Gandavyuha (the portion of the Avatamsaka Sutra which deals with Sudhana's pilgrimage). Suzuki's discussion is excellent, though his interpretation tends to be overly philosophical. Large segments of the Gandavyuha are translated or paraphrased. The essay goes a long way toward filling some of the gaps in our knowledge concerning the development of a most important school.

(7) TAKAKUSU, JUNJIRO. The Essentials of Buddhist Philosophy (see 2.1[13]), pp. 108-126.

A fine summary survey of the history and doctrines of the Kegon (Avatamsaka, Hua Yen) philosophy which Takakusu calls "Totalism." Perhaps the best short philosophically oriented introduction to the subject in English.

2.5.6 T'ien-t'ai/Tendai

See also under Soteriological Experience and Processes, 9.4.9.

(1) ARMSTRONG, ROBERT CORNELL. "The Doctrine of the Tendai Sect." Eastern Buddhist, 3 (1924), 32-54.

A basic and introductory survey of Tendai doctrines in Japan, including the so-called "Eight Teachings" and the classification scheme of the "Five Periods" of the Buddha Dharma (with Tendai, of course, the last). The same material is covered in the author's An Introduction to Japanese Buddhist Sects (see 1.13.2.2[3]), pp. 132-165.

(2) FUNG, YU-LAN. A History of Chinese Philosophy (see 2.5.4[5]), vol. 2, pp. 360-386.

A discussion of a number of T'ien-t'ai doctrines as they are set forth in Hui-ssu's Mahayana Method of Cessation and Contemplation (Ta-ch'eng Chih-huan Fa Men). Hui-ssu was the teacher of Chih-I (Chih-k'ai), the recognized founder of T'ien-t'ai in China. Excerpts from his treatise may also be found translated in Wing-tsit Chan's A Source Book in Chinese Philosophy (see 2.5.1[3]), pp. 398-405, and William Theodore De Bary's Sources of Chinese Tradition (see 2.5.8[7]), where they are included among a number of other selections dealing with T'ien-t'ai (pp. 349-68).

(3) HURVITZ, LEON NAHUM. Chih I (538-597): An Introduction to the Life and Ideas of a Chinese Buddhist Monk. Mélanges Chinois et Bouddhiques, No. 12. Brussels: Institut Belge des Hautes Etudes Chinoises, 1962, 372 pp.

This is the most thorough of the very few works in English dealing with the patriarch Chih I and T'ien-t'ai Buddhism. All students specifically interested in T'ien-t'ai should consult it. The book is in three parts: 1) a historical survey of Chinese Buddhism prior to Chih I, 2) an account of his life, and 3) an outline of his doctrines (including his view of the "Lotus Sutra" and understanding of the five periods of the Buddha Dharma). The work is unfortunately out of print, but available in dissertation format from University Microfilms, Ann Arbor, Michigan (Columbia University Ph.D., 1959).

(4) KIYOTA, MINORU. "The Structure and Meaning of Tendai Thought." Transactions of the International Conference of Orientalists in Japan, 5 (1960), 69-83.

A fine concise introduction to Tendai thought, focusing on the meditation side of Tendai and the practical application of its doctrines (Tendai Shikan).

(5) PETZOLD, BRUNO. "The Chinese Tendai Teaching." The Eastern Buddhist, 4 (1928), 299-347.

A substantive introduction to Chinese T'ien-t'ai doctrines. Presents the philosophy of the school from three points of view: 1) as a synthesis of the whole Buddhist teaching, 2) as a pure theory of metaphysics, and 3) as a practical teaching. Petzold's charts are also very helpful in showing the interrelationships of the various doctrines.

(6) TAKAKUSU, JUNJIRO. The Essentials of Buddhist Philosophy (see 2.1[13]), pp. 126-142.

A substantive and fine philosophically oriented survey of Tendai (T'ien-t'ai), which Takakusu presents as the "school of phenomenology." Authoritative, concise, and more than introductory.

(7) TAMURA, YOSHIRO. "The New Buddhism of Kamakura and Nichiren." Acta Asiatica, 20 (1971), 45-57.

The author posits that the Tendai concept of "original enlightenment," which was brought to Japan by Saicho, was the basis of Buddhist thought in the Kamakura period. After explaining the meaning of this Tendai concept which is predicated upon an "absolute monism," the author continues his article by illustrating how Shinran attempted to unify Honen's "relative dualism" into an "absolute monism," how Dogen attempted to synthesize "absolute monism" and "relative monism," and how Nichiren was able to successfully accomplish what Dogen set out to do.

(8) UI, HAKUJU. "A Study of Japanese Tendai Buddhism." See 1.13.2.2(14).

2.5.7 The Ch'an/Zen Schools

See also Authoritative Texts, 3.3.6 and Soteriological Experience and Processes under 11.4.8.

(1) BLYTH, REGINALD HORACE. Zen and Zen Classics. Tokyo: Hokuseido Press, 1960-70, 5 vols.

Blyth uses numerous anecdotes to trace the history of Zen which, as he puts it, is "the history of moments" and "cannot be an account of development, systematization, criticism, modification, replacement, and so forth." The result is that the reader is left with many fine stories and a need for a look at Heinrich Dumoulin's A History of Zen Buddhism (below). Volume 1 looks at a number of moments from the Upanishads to Hui-neng, Volume 2 is on the history of the Seigen Branch, Volume 3 on that of the Nangaku Branch, Volume 4 translates and comments upon the Mumonkan, and Volume 5 is entitled "Twenty-five Zen Essays."

(2) DE BARY, WILLIAM THEODORE, comp. The Buddhist Tradition in India, China and Japan (see 1.11.1[5]), pp. 207-240, 355-398.

The introductory essays together with the selections of Ch'an and Zen in this anthology form a fine first orientation to the subject. The section dealing with Ch'an (pp. 207-240) includes excerpts from the "Platform Sutra of the Sixth Patriarch," from a sermon by Lin-Chi, and some anecdotes about Ts'ao-shan. The chapter on Zen (pp. 355-398) contains selections from the writings of Eisai, Dogen, Takuan, and Hakuin.

(3) DOGEN. *A Primer of Soto Zen*. Translated by Reiho Masunaga. London: Routledge and Kegan Paul, 1972, 119 pp. See also 3.3.6.3.

(4) DUMOULIN, HEINRICH. *The Development of Chinese Zen after the Sixth Patriarch in the Light of Mumonkan*. Translated by Ruth Fuller Sasaki. New York: First Zen Institute of America, 1953, 146 pp.

Possibly the best short survey of the history of Ch'an after Hui-neng. It looks at the "Golden Age" of Zen during the T'ang, traces the origins of the "Five Houses" of Zen, and then looks at the development of the Koan in the Sung. It also includes convenient "genealogical" charts of the successions of Zen Masters of the T'ang and Sung dynasties.

(5) _____. *A History of Zen Buddhism*. See 1.13.2.2(6).

The best available history of Zen in English, treating the subject mostly in doctrinal terms. Chapters 5-8 deal with Ch'an, 9-14 with Zen. Chapters 1-4 sketch the "Indian Background" somewhat misleadingly. For an alternative to Father Dumoulin's view of Zen as "natural mysticism," see the work of his colleague at Sophia University, William Johnston, S.J., *The Still Point: Reflections on Zen and Christian Mysticism* (New York: Harper and Row, 1971), pp. 121-141. (Paperback edition: Perennial P227.)

(6) FOX, DOUGLAS. "Zen and Ethics: Dogen's Synthesis." *Philosophy East and West*, 21 (1971), 33-42.

A good article in which the author sketches the Zen approach to ethics. Specifically, the author attempts to show how Dogen related Zen subjectivism and Mahayana ontology to the problem of "value," and to the relationship between "being" and "doing."

(7) FRODSHAM, J. D. "Hsieh Ling-yun's Contributions to Mediaeval Chinese Buddhism," in *International Association of Historians of Asia: Second Biennial Conference Proceedings*. Taipei, 1963, pp. 27-55.

A competent study of the life and thought of Hsieh (a Chinese poet who lived from 383-433 A.D.). The author attempts to show how Hsieh, an early adherent to the doctrine of "instantaneous enlightenment," was able to grasp the spirit of Buddhism and formulate it within Chinese modes of thought.

(8) GERNET, JACQUES. "Biographie du Maître Chen-houei du Ho-tso (668-760): Contribution à l'histoire de l'école du Dhyana." *Journal Asiatique*, 239 (1951), 29-68.

An article complementing the same author's translation of the *Entretiens du Maître de Dhyana Chen-houei* (see Authoritative Texts 3.3.5) which is of interest for the early history of Ch'an. Chen-houei (Shen-hui) was a disciple of the Sixth Patriarch Hui-neng. For his doctrinal position in defense of Sudden Enlightenment, see the "appendix" of this article, pp. 60-68; see also Walter Liebenthal's "The Sermon of Shen-hui," *Asia Major*, 3 (1952), 132-155.

(9) HISAMATSU, SHIN'ICHI. "The Characteristics of Oriental Nothingness." Translated by Richard DeMartino. *Philosophical Studies of Japan*, 2 (1960), 65-97.

A philosophical investigation of "Mu," which the author claims is the core of Buddhism and the essence of Zen. The essay seeks to clarify levels of meanings intrinsic to "Mu" and to distinguish its Zen uses from Western notions of emptiness and negation.

(10) HOANG THI BICH. *Etude et Traduction du Gakudo-yojin-shu: Recueil de l'application de l'esprit à l'étude de la voie du maître de Zen, Dogen*. Centre de recherches d'histoire et de philologie de la 4e section de l'Ecole pratique des hautes études, No. 2. Hautes études orientales, No. 4. Geneva: Librairie Droz, 1973, 224 pp.

A fully annotated translation of the thirteenth century founder of Soto Zen in Japan, Dogen's second-most important doctrinal work. This is preceded by a critical study of the text, and by a general introduction to Zen and Ch'an thought in China and in Japan.

(11) HU SHIH. "Development of Zen Buddhism in China." *Chinese Social and Political Science Review*, 15 (1931), 475-505.

Hu Shih and D. T. Suzuki carried on a long and interesting debate on the question of the value of "history" in the understanding of Zen. This article provides a good summary of Hu Shih's position. For D. T. Suzuki's position in the debate, see Zen: A Reply to Hu Shih," *Philosophy East and West*, 3 (1953), 25-46. (This follows the article by Hu Shih in the same issue, pp. 3-24, entitled "Ch'an (Zen) Buddhism in China: Its History and Method.")

(12) HYERS, CONRAD. *Zen and the Comic Spirit*. Philadelphia: Westminster; and London: Rider, 1974, 192 pp.

A unique study of Zen and Zen masters, focusing on the notions of irony involved in behavior and techniques of instruction.

(13) JAN, YUN-HUA. "Tsung-mi: His Analysis of Ch'an Buddhism." *T'oung Pao*, 58 (1972), 1-54. See also 8.9.3(82).

(14) KENNETT, JIYU. *Selling Water by the River: A Manual of Zen Training*. New York: Pantheon Books, 1972, 317 pp. (Vintage paperback.)

This effort represents an apologetic approach to the history and character of Soto Zen. After reviewing the fundamental understandings essential to Zen ("zazan," "koan," etc.), the author presents a series of translations of treatises which outline the teachings of Dogan and Keigan.

(15) LALOU, MARCELLE. "Document tibétain sur l'expansion du Dhyana chinois." Journal Asiatique, 1939, pp. 505-523.

Scholarly article focusing on the brief inscriptions found at Tun Huang (Cave of the Thousand Buddhas). The author discusses the historical significance of the find before going on to a detailed analysis of the doctrinal and orthographic significance. Of use to the advanced student.

(16) LU K'UAN-YU (CHARLES LUK), comp. Ch'an and Zen Teaching. London: Rider, 1960-1962, 3 vols. ("Series").

Anthologies of uneven quality and interest, which, however, make a number of texts available in English for the first time. Series 1 translates and introduces some of the late Hsu Yun's discourses, excerpts from the Imperial Selection of Ch'an Sayings (Yu Hsuan Yu Lu), and two pieces by the sixteenth century Ch'an Master Han Shan. Series 2 is largely devoted to the stories of the founders of the Five Ch'an Sects, taken from The Transmission of the Lamp. Series 3 contains the Sutra of the Sixth Patriarch, Yung Chia's Song of Enlightenment, and the Sutra of Complete Enlightenment.

(17) MASUNAGA, REIHO. The Soto Approach to Zen. Tokyo: Layman Buddhist Society Press, 1958, pp. 1-80.

Four chapters giving the general background of the place of Zen within Buddhism, and then, more specifically, the place of Dogen and Soto within Zen. It is a helpful introduction which is followed in the same book by selections from Dogen's writings.

(18) SHIBATA, MASUMI. Les Maîtres du Zen au Japon. Paris: Maisonneuve and Larose, 1969, 246 pp.

This book seeks to cover the whole history of Japanese Zen through a series of sketches of the lives and teachings of eminent Zen masters. It helps fill a gap in the Westerner's knowledge of Zen after the Kamakura, because, unlike so many studies, it does not stop with Eisai and Dogen, but goes on to deal with Keizan (b. 1268), O-to-kan (i.e., Emio, b. 1235?), Daito (b. 1282), Kannan, and others down through D. T. Suzuki and Hisamatsu Shin'ichi of this century.

(19) SOK, DO-RYUN. "Modern Sun Buddhism in Korea." See 1.12.2(11).

(20) SUZUKI, DAISETZ TEITARO. Essays in Zen Buddhism. First Series. New York: Grove Press, 1961, 387 pp. (First published London: Luzac, 1927; Paperback edition: Evergreen Original E-309.) Second series. Edited by Christmas Humphreys. New York: S. Weiser, 1971, 367 pp. (First published London: Luzac, 1933.) Third Series. New York: S. Weiser, 1970, 396 pp. (First published London: Luzac, 1934.)

A classic collection of essays of varying quality, which remains a basic reference work for the student of Zen thought. Where the First series is more on Zen in general, the Second is largely devoted to studies of the koan exercise, and the Third deals with Zen and the Gandavyuha, the Prajnaparamita literature, and Japanese culture.

(21) _____. Manual of Zen Buddhism. New York: Grove Press, 1960, 192 pp. (First publishied Kyoto: The Eastern Buddhist Society, 1935; Paperback edition: Evergreen Original E-231.)

A useful collection of excerpts from a variety of texts--some, like the sayings of Chinese masters, clearly in the Zen tradition; others, like the Lankavatara Sutra, which can be read in the Zen style. Of major interest, however, are the translations of the principal gathas, dharanis, and sutras which are used regularly in Zen rituals in Japan.

(22) _____. Zen Buddhism: Selected Writings. Edited by William Barrett. Garden City: Doubleday, 1956, 294 pp. (Paperback edition: Doubleday Anchor Books A90.)

This selection of passages from a number of Suzuki's works forms a fine introduction to Suzuki and a fair introduction to Zen. Students wanting more of both might also refer to the same author's An Introduction to Zen Buddhism (London: Rider, 1969), which contains a foreword by C. G. Jung; Living by Zen (London: Rider, 1950); The Field of Zen (New York: Harper and Row, 1970), a posthumous selection of Suzuki's talks and notes made by Christmas Humphreys; and The Zen Doctrine of No Mind (London: Rider, 1969). The Eastern Buddhist (1921-1939), edited by Dr. Suzuki, contains numerous articles on Zen by him of varying quality; and The Eastern Buddhist, n.s. 2 (1967) contains a number of interesting articles in his memory and a bibliography of his major works. See also, for cross reference, the annotations of his Essays in Zen Buddhism (above), and his Manual of Zen Buddhism (above).

(23) TAKAKUSU, JUNJIRO. The Essentials of Buddhist Philosophy (see 2.1[13]), pp. 153-166.

A brief but valuable discussion of the philosophy of Zen, which Takakusu classifies together with Avatamsaka (Kegon), Tendai, and Shingon as a school of "undifferentiated intuitionism" as opposed to Shin, Nichiren, and Ritsu (Vinaya) which he sees as schools of "differentiated intuitionism."

(24) TAMAKI, KOSHIRO. "The Position of Dogen in the History of Buddhist Thought." Acta Asiatica, 20 (March 1971), 7-24.

The author first explains "zenzo" (dhyana) as a means for fostering independent and original thought that leads to "prajna" (wisdom). He then attempts to illustrate how Dogen's thought relates not only to the Chinese thought of T'ien-t'ai, Chan, and Hua-yen, but also how it relates to other Japanese Kamakura leaders such as Nichiren and Shinran.

(25) TAO-YUAN, SHIH. *Original Teachings of Ch'an Buddhism, Selected from the Transmission of the Lamp*. Translated with introductions by Chang Chung-yan. New York: Pantheon, 1969. (Paperback edition: Vintage, 1971.)

An important contribution to the understanding of Ch'an. The author introduces and translates the stories and sayings of nineteen Ch'an masters from *The Transmission of the Lamp*, one of the earliest records of Ch'an Buddhism, compiled by Tao-yuan in 1004 A.D. The masters selected represent the viewpoints of early Ch'an and of all of the "Five Schools," and they are grouped together as such. Other "Transmission Stories" may be found in Lu K'uan Yu (Charles Luk), *Ch'an and Zen Teachings* (above) and Jiyu Kennett, *Selling Water by the River* (above).

(26) WU, CHING-HSIUNG (JOHN C. H. WU). *The Golden Age of Zen*. Taipei: National War College in cooperation with the Committee on the compilation of the Chinese Library, 1967, distributed by Paragon Book Gallery, New York, 332 pp.

A Chinese convert to Catholicism looks back and traces the background to and the rise of the "Five Houses" of Ch'an during the T'ang dynasty. It can be used to supplement either Heinrich Dumoulin's *The Development of Chinese Zen* (above), or Series 2 of Lu K'uan Yu's *Ch'an and Zen Teaching* (above). The introduction by Thomas Merton gives some insights on Christianity and Zen.

(27) YAMPOLSKY, PHILIP B., trans. *The Zen Master Hakuin: Selected Writings*. See 1.13.2.3(4).

Primarily a collection of long pastoral letters by the famous seventeenth and eighteenth century Japanese Zen mystic, poet, and painter. Good, short introduction. Especially valuable for insight into the interaction between Zen thought and historical conditions at the time in Japan.

2.5.8 The Pure Land Schools (Ching t'u, Jodo, Shin, etc.)

See also 11.7 and 3.3.7.1.

(1) ANDREWS, ALLAN A. *The Teachings Essential for Rebirth: A Study of Genshin's Ojoyoshu*. Tokyo: Sophia University, 1973, 133 pp.

Genshin was one of the early advocates of the worship of Amida and the Nembutsu within Japanese Tendai. His work, which is here summarized, translated, and discussed, describes the torments of hell, the beauties of the Pure Land, and the advantages of the Nembutsu. It was influential in the formative period of the Japanese Pure Land sects. Another study of it may be found in A. K. Reischauer, "Genshin's Ojoyoshu," *Transactions of the Asiatic Society of Japan*, 2, no. 7 (1930), 16-97.

(2) BANDO, SHOJUN. "Myoe's Criticism of Honen's Doctrine." *The Eastern Buddhist*, 7, no. 1 (May 1974), 37-54.

The Pure Land reformation brought on by Honen did not go unchallenged in religious philosophical circles. One of the most important critics of Honen's doctrines was Myoe Shonin (1173-1232), a mystic and scholar who mixed Avatamsaka and Tantric practices and was specifically opposed to Honen's denigration of the necessity to develop bodhicitta. This and some of his other objections are examined in this article.

(3) _____. "Shinran's Indebtedness to T'an-luan." *The Eastern Buddhist*, 4, no. 1 (May 1971), 72-87.

The author begins his article with a discussion of Shinran's position in regard to Pure Land thought. He points out that Shinran equated T'an-luan's thought as expounded in his Jodo Ronchu with the thought expressed in Vasubandhu's Treatise on the Pure Land.

(4) BLOOM, ALFRED. *Shinran's Gospel of Pure Grace*. Association for Asian Studies, Monographs and papers, No. 20. Tucson: The University of Arizona Press, 1965, 97 pp.

A good treatment of Shinran's teachings, with an account of the seven patriarchs of Shin. It is brief, clearly written and well organized, and touches on both the philosophical aspects of Shinran's thought and on his teachings as presented to the people.

(5) "The Ching-t'u Shih-i-lun (Ten Doubts Concerning the Pure Land)." Translated by Leo Pruden. *The Eastern Buddhist*, n.s. 6 (1973), 126-157.

An introduction to and translation of a short eighth century Chinese catechism, traditionally but erroneously thought to be a minor work of Chih-i, the founder of T'ien-t'ai. The "Doubts" raise and answer questions concerning the nature and direction of the Pure Land and its attainment by the common laypeople, but they are most interesting for what they reveal about the doctrinal and intellectual milieu in which early Chinese Pure Land (Ching-t'u) was beginning to evolve.

(6) CORLESS, ROGER. "Monotheistic Elements in Early Pure Land Buddhism." *Religion: Journal of Religion and Religions*, 6 no. 2 (Autumn 1976), 176-189.

A few brief observations on various ways in which Amitabha does and does not conform to Western ideas of a monotheistic deity.

(7) DE BARY, WILLIAM THEODORE, ed. *Sources of Chinese Tradition*. Records of Civilization. Sources and Studies, No. 55. Introduction to Oriental Civilizations. New York: Columbia University Press, 1960, pp. 374-386.

A brief introduction to Chinese Pure Land Buddhism (Ching-t'u), reflecting its close association with T'ien-t'ai teachings. Selections are from the patriarch T'an-luan's (476-542) commentary to Vasubandhu's "Essay on Rebirth," and from Tao-ch'o's (d. 645) "Compendium on the Happy Land." For further materials on T'an-luan, his life and work and role in early Chinese Pure Land, see Roger J. Corless, "T'an-luan's Commentary on the Pure Land Discourse," University of Wisconsin Ph.D. dissertation, 1973; and Hsiao Ching-fen, "The Life and Teachings of T'an-luan," Princeton Theological Seminary Th.D. dissertation, 1967. Both are available through University Microfilms, Ann Arbor, Michigan.

(8) FUJIMOTO, RYUKO. *An Outline of the Triple Sutra of Shin Buddhism*. Kyoto: Honpa Hongwanji Press, 1955, 1960, 2 vols.

These two volumes represent expositions of the "Larger Sutra" and the "Meditation Sutra" by a contemporary Shinshu writer. The author seeks to relate the teachings of those two works to Pali tradition, Zen, and contemporary problems of an existential nature.

(9) FUJIWARA, RYUSETSU. *The Way to Nirvana*. Tokyo: Kyoiku Shincho Sha, 1974, 223 pp.

This presents an assessment of Shan-tao's (Zendo) thought, and traces the evolution of that thought from an emphasis on quiet meditation to an emphasis upon vocal use.

(10) HAYASHIMA, KYOSHO. "From Sakyamuni (Gotama Buddha) to Shinran, Founder of the Denomination of Jodo-Shinshu." *Acta Asiatica*, 20 (1971), 25-44.

In this article, the author attempts to show how the notion of "marga" (way) evolved from the time of the Buddha in India to the time of Shinran in Japan. In this manner, the author hopes to show how Shinran's followers were able to accept the exhortation to have faith in the mercy of Amitabha.

(11) ISHIDA, MITSYKI. "Tendai Elements in the Doctrinal Systems of Honen's Disciples." *Journal of Indian and Buddhist Studies*, 2, no. 2 (1963), 74-79.

Honen's background at the headquarters of the Tendai sect on Mount Miei is well known. This unfortunately short article discusses some of the Tendai doctrines which continued to be used by some of Honen's disciples--Ryukan, Shoku, Kosai, and Bencho--when engaged in doctrinal disputes in the defense of Jodo Buddhism.

(12) LIEBENTHAL, WALTER. "Shih Hui-yuan's Buddhism as Set Forth in His Writings." *Journal of the American Oriental Society*, 70 (1950), 243-259. See also 8.9.3(47).

(13) OKUSA, YEJITSU. *Principal Teachings of the True Sect of Pure Land*. Tokyo: The Asakusa Hongwanji, 1910, 65 + 44 pp.

General account of Shin Buddhist teachings from an apologetic viewpoint. Includes an account of the history of Shinshu which is heavily dependent on legend and undocumented tradition.

(14) ONO, GENMYO. "On the Pure Land Doctrine of Tz'u-min." *The Eastern Buddhist*, 5 (1930), 200-210.

A short but interesting article on a subject rarely touched upon in English: the life and teachings of Tz'u-min (Hui jih) (680-748 A.D.). Tz'u-min came to be an ardent believer in Amitabha during his extended pilgrimage to India and returned to China to found one of the three principal branches of Chinese Pure Land Buddhism.

(15) REISCHAUER, AUGUST KARL. "A Catechism of the Shin Sect (Buddhism)." *Transactions of the Asiatic Society of Japan*, 38 (1912), 333-395.

English translation of a manual apparently in use among Shin Buddhists at the turn of the century. It is very useful for reference, but no background is given on the text itself.

(16) RENNYO. *The Words of St. Rennyo*. Translated and annotated by Kosho Yamamoto. Ube: Karinbunko, 1968, 196 pp.

Rennyo was the eighth abbot of Shin Buddhism, and his writings are an orthodox exposition of Shinran's teachings. Translated here into what is sometimes painful English are the *Rennyoshonin-Goichicaiki Kikigaki* (a collection of his sayings), and the *Anjin-ketsujosho* (a work dealing with the doctrine of the Other-Power). Other translations of some of Rennyo's works may be found in James Troup, "The Gobunsho or Ofumi of Rennyo Shonin," *Transactions of the Asiatic Society of Japan*, 17 (1889), 101-143; and in Shizutoshi Sugihira, "Rennyo Shonin, The Great Teacher of Shin Buddhism" (see 1.13.2.3[3]).

(17) SASAKI, GESSHO. *A Study of Shin Buddhism*. Kyoto: Eastern Buddhist Society, 1925, 145 pp.

A fair introduction to the teachings of Shin Buddhism which attempts to set the doctrines within the overall framework of the Mahayana, and tries to show how Shin is "The True Sect" of Buddhism (as vs. Jodo, for example). Most of the chapters were originally published in *The Eastern Buddhist*, 1 (1921), 38-46 and 167-179; 2 (1922), 154-162 and 236-259; and 3 (1924), 195-205. A presentation along lines similar to Sasaki's may be found in Susumu Yamaguchi, *Dynamic Buddha and Static Buddha*, translated by Shoko Watanabe (Tokyo: Risosha, 1958).

(18) SHINRAN. *The Private Letters of Shinran Shonin*. Translated by Kosho Yamamoto. Tokyo: Okazakiya Shoten, 1956, 115 pp.

A translation of the Mattosho and the Shinranshonin-Goshosokushu--two important collections of letters, most from Shinran to his disciples but also some by those disciples, which indicate the significant problems of doctrine and practice faced by Shin Buddhism in its early formative years. Especially interesting are Shinran's references to the various heterodox viewpoints within Shin Buddhism.

(19) SHUNJO, HOIN. Honen the Buddhist Saint: His Life and Teaching. Translated, introduced, with explanatory and critical notes by Harper H. Coates and Ryugaku Ishizuka. Kyoto: Chionin, 1925, xciv, 955 pp.

The classic work on the Honen and the Jodo School and its branches, amply covering his life, his doctrines, and those of his followers and disciples. Coates and Ishizuka's introduction and notes are very useful and make the work invaluable for anyone interested in Jodo, a sect which has not received the same scholarly attention as Shin.

(20) SUGIHIRA, SHIZUTOSHI. "A Study in the Pure Land Doctrine, as Interpreted by Shoku, the Founder of the Seizan Branch of the Pure Land Sect." The Eastern Buddhist, 5 (1929), 80-101.

One of the few articles in English on the Seizan branch of Pure Land Buddhism which was founded by Honen's disciple Zennebo (Shoku), and which held a semi-radical understanding of faith and Nembutsu. Sugihira's chart (p. 83) of the various sects of Pure Land and their principal tenets is also quite useful. A more limited exposition of one aspect of Shoku's teaching is the same author's "The Pure Land Doctrine as Illustrated in the 'Plain Wood' Nembutsu," The Eastern Buddhist, 6 (1932), 23-39. Also on Zennebo's doctrines, see Shunjo's Honen, the Buddhist Saint (above).

(21) SUZUKI, BEATRICE LANE. "Honen Shonin and the Jodo Ideal." The Eastern Buddhist, 1 (1921-1922), 316-336.

An attempt to answer philosophically (not historically) the question: "How much of the Pure Land idea is deducible from the teaching of 'Primitive Buddhism,' or from the personality of Sakyamuni Buddha himself?"

(22) SUZUKI, DAISETZ TEITARO. Collected Writings on Shin Buddhism. Kyoto: Shinshu-Otani, 1973, 261 pp.

This volume brings together many of Suzuki's articles which earlier appeared in The Eastern Buddhist. It includes a translation of Godensho (the life of Shinran) and the Tannisho.

(23) _____. A Miscellany on the Shin Teaching of Buddhism. Kyoto: Shinshu Otaniha Shumusho, 1949, 151 pp.

A fairly good, rather detailed treatment of Shin philosophical views with some attempt to trace the history of the sect's principal doctrines, and an extended comparison of Shin with Christianity which is not really helpful and sometimes misleading. Also included are translations and discussions of some of Shinran's songs (wasan) by Beatrice Lane Suzuki, and Kakunyo's Tract on Steadily Holding to the Faith' (Shuji), translated by Kensho Yokogawa, Chapter 1 ("The Shin Sect of Buddhism"). The wasan and the tract originally appeared in The Eastern Buddhist, 7 (1939), 227-284, 285-295, and 363-375.

(24) TAKAHASHI, TAKEICHI and JUNJO IZUMIDA. Shinranism in Mahayana Buddhism and the Modern World. Los Angeles: privately printed, 1932, 249 pp.

An attempt to portray Shin teachings as the most appropriate religion for contemporary times (1930s). The work can be helpful as an introduction, but suffers from being highly apologetic and attempting too much--an introduction of all of Buddhism to Westerners, from a Shin point of view.

(25) TSUNODA, RYUSAKU, ed. Sources of the Japanese Tradition. Compiled by Ryusaku Tsunoda, William Theodore De Bary, and Donald Keene. Records of Civilization: sources and studies, No. 54. Introduction to Oriental civilizations. New York: Columbia University Press, 1958, pp. 190-218.

Fine introductory essays and selection of texts from Ippen, Genshin, Honen, and Shinran to show the beginnings of Amidism within Mahayana Buddhism and its sectarian establishment in Japan. A good first introduction to the subject.

(26) UTSUKI, NISHU. The Shin Sect: A School of Mahayana Buddhism, Its Teaching, Brief History, and Present-Day Conditions. Kyoto: Publication Bureau of Buddhist Books, Hompa Hoganji, 1937, 45 pp.

A brief outline of the teachings of the Shin school, and the history of its two major subsects (with notes on the eight minor ones). The work was published by the sect itself and is useful (if available). However, it gives no interpretation of the position of Shin within Japanese Buddhism.

(27) YAMAMOTO, KOSHO. An Introduction to Shin Buddhism. See 1.13.2.2(15).

A scholarly and well organized survey of Shin doctrines, suitable for easy reference. The work also includes a survey of historical background and of materials available to the scholar.

(28) _____, ed. The Shinshu Seitin: The Holy Scripture of Shinshu. Second edition. Honolulu: Honpa Hongwanji Mission of Hawaii, 1961, 524 pp.

Translations of Sutras, Shastras, and Epistles supporting the Shinshu doctrinal position. About a third of the book is composed of doctrinal summaries, a glossary, and a bibliography. Basically, it is a useful anthology since it brings together disparate material, sometimes translating it for the first time into English. But the style is puzzling and requires effort on the part of the reader.

(29) YANAGI, SOETSU. "Ippen Shonin." The Eastern Buddhist, n.s. 6, no. 2 (October 1973), 33-57.

A recent article on the life and teachings of Ippen (1239-89), the founder of the Ji subsect of the Seizan branch of the Pure Land school. Ippen was a spiritual grandson of Honen's disciple Shoku. He deemphasized the scholastic interpretation and exegesis of the Nembutsu and the question of faith, and stressed simply the practice. His view is perhaps best illustrated by the fact that he burned all his writings just before his death, leaving behind him only the six syllables "Namu-Amida-butsu." Another study of his thought may be found in Shizutoshi Sugihira, "The Teaching of Ippen Shonin (1239-1289)" (see 11.7.2[6]).

2.5.9 Nichiren

(1) ANESAKI, MASAHARU. Nichiren, the Buddhist Prophet. See 1.13.2.2(2).

The classic work on the life and teachings of Nichiren in English. It is old and somewhat apologetic, but still the standard reference. Its approach is from the viewpoint of religious psychology and it includes translations of some of his works. Brief excerpts from it may be found in William Theodore De Bary, ed., The Buddhist Tradition in India, China, and Japan (see 1.11.1[5]), pp. 345-354.

(2) LLOYD, ARTHUR. The Creed of Half Japan (see 1.12.2[9]), pp. 287-328.

These pages contain one of the first treatments in English of Nichiren's life and doctrines, and it is still valuable today (especially for its substantial translation of his famous essay, the Rissho Ankoku Ron--a treatise on the "Establishment of the Legitimate Teaching for the Security of the Country" which Nichiren wrote to the Kamakura Regent in 1260, and which got him into trouble for prophesying doom and dire times for Japan unless all sects were suppressed in favor of the "Lotus Sutra." A complete French translation of the work may be found in Gaston Renondeau, "Le 'Traité sur l'Etat' de Nichiren," T'oung Pao, 40 (1950), 123-198, where it is followed by translations of eight of Nichiren's letters.

(3) NICHIREN. The Awakening to the Truth, or "Kaimokusho." Translated by Ryokui Ehara. Tokyo: The International Buddhist Society, 1941, 122 pp.

The only complete English translation of one of Nichiren's most important works. Though he never wrote a systematic presentation of his doctrine, the Kaimokusho, written in exile on Sado Island in 1271, perhaps comes closest, dealing as it does with three of Nichiren's basic dogmas--the superiority of the Lotus Sutra, the certainty of final salvation for all, and the eternality of the Buddha. The work also reflects the polemical spirit of its author. A French translation of it may be found in Gaston Renondeau, La Doctrine de Nichiren (below), pp. 53-206.

(4) RENONDEAU, GASTON. La Doctrine de Nichiren. Publications de Musée Guimet Bibliothèque d'études, No. 58. Paris: Presses Universitaires de France, 1953, 332 pp.

An important study of Nichiren, and one of the few in Western languages devoted specifically to his religious thought and contributions to Buddhist doctrine. The significance of the work is reinforced by the annotated French translation of six of Nichiren's works: the Kaimokusho ("Le traité qui ouvre les yeux") (for an English translation see Nichiren's The Awakening to the Truth, above); the Kwanjin Honzon sho ("L'introspection révèle l'objet fondamental de notre vénération"); Hokke Shuyo Sho ("Traité sur l'essentiel du Lotus"); and three letters to his disciples, the "Sho Ho Jisso Sho," the "Somoku Jobutsu Kuketsu," and the letter to Shijo Kingo.

(5) SATOMI, KISHIO. Japanese Civilization, Its Significance and Realization: Nichirenism and the Japanese National Principles. Trubner's oriental series. London: K. Paul, Trench, Trubner, 1923, 238 pp.

A fairly detailed exposition for Westerners of the doctrines of Nichiren, written in the spirit of Nichiren by one who believes "Nichirenism" to be "the religion of the future and for ever"--the past ages not having been "ready to be Nichirenized." It is, however, the most substantial work of this genre. A sketchier example of the same type is the Rev. Nitto Kobayashi's The Doctrines of Nichiren (Tokyo: Kelly and Walsh, 1893).

(6) TAKAKUSU, JUNJIRO. The Essentials of Buddhist Philosophy (see 2.1[13]), pp. 176-184.

One of the few concise attempts to treat Nichiren Buddhism philosophically in relation to the rest of Mahayana Buddhism. Takakusu considers it as a school of "Lotus pietism" akin to Jodo and Shin (Amita pietism) and Ritsu (disciplinary formalism)--all of them being schools of "differentiated intuitionism."

2.6 THE TANTRA-/MANTRA-/VAJRA-YANA SCHOOLS

See also under Authoritative Texts: 3.4. See also under Soteriological Experience and Processes, 11.6.

2.6.1 India and Tibet

(1) BHARATI, AGEHANANDA. The Tantric Tradition. London: Rider, 1965, pp. 13-40.

Tantra-/Mantra-/Vajra-Vana Schools

The chapter is entitled "The Philosophical Content of Tantra" and is an attempt to be precise about the relationship of "the Tantric Tradition" (both Hindu and Buddhist) to the main lines of Hindu and Buddhist thought. Not a bad introduction to the subject.

(2) BHATTACHARYYA, BENOYTOSH. An Introduction to Buddhist Esoterism. The Chowkhamba Sanskrit Studies, vol. 46. Varanasi: Chowkhamba Sanskrit Series Office, 1964, 184 pp. (Originally published Oxford University Press, 1932.)

Based largely on the author's work on the Sadhanamala and other Tantric texts, this book is a handy compilation of his views on the history, doctrines, and practices of Vajrayana Buddhism. It is mostly a reworking of some of his previous articles: the 177-page "introduction" to Vol. 2 of his edition of the Sadhanamala (see 11.6.1[5]); his The Indian Buddhist Iconography (see 5.2.8[4]); his introduction to his edition of Two Vajrayana Works (see 3.4.4[1]); and his "Origins and Development of Vajrayana," Indian Historical Quarterly, 3 (1927), 733-46.

(3) BLOFELD, JOHN. The Tantric Mysticism of Tibet: A Practical Guide. New York: E. P. Dutton, 1970, pp. 1-68.

Although the book as a whole attempts to be a practical guide to Tantric meditation, these two initial chapters form a good, simple introduction to the basic doctrines behind the Tibetan Vajrayana. Chapter one is very introductory, chapter two discusses the Vajrayana's Mahayana setting.

(4) BOLLE, KEES W. "Devotion and Tantra." Studies of Esoteric Buddhism and Tantrism. Koyasan University (1965), pp. 217-228.

One of the few studies to tackle the question of the relationship of the Tantric practitioner to the general stream of Indian Bhakti.

(5) DASGUPTA, SHASHIBHUSAN. An Introduction to Tantric Buddhism. Berkeley, Calif.: Shambala, 1974, 211 pp. (Originally published Calcutta: Calcutta University Press, 1958.)

A book which is not without its problems (see the "foreword" by H. V. Guenther), but useful as a substantial introduction which seeks to trace the gradual transformation of Mahayanic ideas into what the author calls "The Theological Position of the Tantric Buddhists" (pp. 77-144).

(6) _____. Obscure Religious Cults. Revised edition Calcutta: K. L. Mukhopadhyay, 1962, pp. 3-109. (Originally published 1946.)

Part 1 of this book represents the classical discussion in English of "The Buddhist Sahajiya Cult"--a late offshoot of Tantric Buddhism in Bengal--as it is found in songs (Caryapadas and dohas) of its practitioners. See in particular chapter two on the philosophical standpoint of the caryapadas, and chapter three on the general religious outlook of the Sahajiyas.

(7) DGE-LEGS-DPAL-BZAN PO. Mkhas grub rje's Fundamentals of the Buddhist Tantras. Translated by Ferdinand D. Lessing and Alex Wayman, with original text and annotation. Indo-Iranian monographs, No. 8. The Hague: Mouton, 1968, 382 pp.

Translation and rich annotation from the Tibetan of the Rgyud sde spyihi rnam par gzag pa rgyas brjod, written by the early fifteenth century master-scholar mKhas grub rje. It is a summary by a close disciple of Tibetan tantric orthodox philosophy and practice. The importance of the work to Western scholars is enhanced by the accurate translation (with accompanying Tibetan), extensive notes and thorough index.

(8) DUTT, NALINAKSHA. "Tantric Buddhism." Bulletin of Tibetology, 1, no. 2 (October 1964), 5-16.

An article for the reader short on time and needing a quick overview of this complicated topic. The author presents an adequate summary of the development of Tantrism in the Buddhist context and some of the most important principles of practice. For another brief but adequate treatment which supplements Dutt's article, see Lama Anagarika Govinda, "Principles of Buddhist Tantrism," Bulletin of Tibetology, 2, no. 1 (1965), 9-16.

(9) GOVINDA, ANAGARIKA BRAHMACARI. Foundations of Tibetan Mysticism, According to the Esoteric Teachings of the Great Mantra, Om Mani Padme Hum. New York: S. Weiser, 1969, 311 pp. (First published New York: Dutton, 1959.)

Ostensibly a grand exegisis of the mantra "Om Mani Padme Hum," this book, misleadingly at times, looks like a simple introduction to the teachings of Tibetan Vajrayana, but it is much more than that: it embodies the bka-rgyud-pa teachings of Govinda's guru, Tro-mo Ge-bshes Rin-po-che, and demands of its reader a certain amount of previous knowledge. A short simple article by the same author which seeks to give a general idea of Tantric Buddhism and the differences between it and Hindu Tantrism may be found on pp. 360-376 of P. V. Bapat, ed., 2500 Years of Buddhism (see 1.2.1[1]), in which one should ignore the misleading "Introductory" on pp. 358-360.

(10) GUENTHER, HERBERT V. The Tantric View of Life. The Clear Light Series. Berkeley, Calif.: Shambala, 1972, 168 pp.

Perhaps the best introduction to the views of this prolific author on Tibetan Tantric Buddhism. Guenther touches on all of his favorite points and his use of non-standard equivalents for Buddhist technical terms (which has long annoyed orientalists unable to follow him) is here mitigated by the inclusion in parentheses of the Sanskrit and/or

2.6.1

Tibetan. For other presentations of his views on Tantra in general, see his "The Philosophical Background of the Buddhist Tantris," Journal of Oriental Studies, 5 (1959-60), 45-46, which focuses on the Mahamudra but is a helpful introduction to Guenther's methods and views; Chapter 5 (pp. 51-73) of Tibetan Buddhism without Mystification (see 3.4.2[9]); and Guenther's Life and Teaching of Naropa (see 3.4.2[6]), pp. 112-123.

(11) SNELLGROVE, DAVID L., ed. and trans. The Hevajra Tantra: A Critical Study. London, New York: Oxford University Press, 1959, vol. 1, Introduction and translation. See also 3.4.1(4).

(12) TUCCI, GIUSEPPE. Tibetan Painted Scrolls (see 1.14.2.2[11]), vol. 1, pp. 209-249.
   The section entitled "The Religious Ideas of Vajrayana" is a masterful survey of the literature and doctrines of Tibetan Tantric tradition. Among its many gems it contains the clearest discussions of the doctrinal differences between the four classes of Tantra: the Kriya, Carya, Yoga, and Anuttara. Unfortunately, it is not available outside of the massive tomes of Tibetan Painted Scrolls.

(13) WANGYAL, GESHE THUPTEN, comp. The Door of Liberation. Prefatory note by Tenzin Gyatshe, the 14th Dalai Lama. New York: Girodias Associates, distributed by L. Stuart, 1973, 323 pp.

(14) WARDER, ANTHONY KENNEDY. Indian Buddhism (see 1.2.1[15]), pp. 482-502.
   A brief but useful textual history of the Mantrayana in India. For a listing of Mantrayana texts in Sanskrit, see the bibliographic sections on pp. 551-553.

(15) WAYMAN, ALEX. The Buddhist Tantras: Light on Indo-Tibetan Esotericism. New York: S. Weiser, 1973, 247 pp.
   An important collection of essays which makes readily available a number of articles, some previously published by Wayman in journals. The essays, dealing with Tantric texts and thoughts, are organized into three parts: "Introductions," "Foundations of the Buddhist Tantra," and "Special Studies." They will most likely baffle the student who has had no previous acquaintance with Tantric Buddhism but are a challenge and important source to the one who has.

2.6.2 China and Japan

(1) CHOU YI-LIANG. "Tantrism in China." See 1.11.2.3(4).
   A classic work examining the introduction and development of Indian Tantric Buddhism in China through the lives and thought of three monks of the seventh and eighth centuries: Shan-wu-wei, Vajrabodhi, and Amoghavajra. Essential reading for any student interested in this topic.

(2) EARHART, H. BYRON. "Shugendo, the Tradition of En no Gyoja, and Mikkyo Influence," in Studies of Esoteric Buddhism and Tantrism. Koyasan University, 1965, pp. 297-317.
   A study of the influence of Esoteric (Mikkyo) beliefs on the figure of En no Gyoja, the traditional founder of Shugendo in Japan.

(3) KITAGAWA, JOSEPH M. "Master and Savior," in Studies of Esoteric Buddhism and Tantrism. Koyasan University, 1965. See also 8.9.4(19).

(4) KUKAI. Major Works. Translated, with an account of his life and a study of his thought, by Yoshito S. Hakeda. Records of Civilization: sources and studies, No. 87. New York: Columbia University Press, 1972, 303 pp.
   This book is probably the place for any student to begin a study of the life and thought of Kukai, the founder of Shingon Buddhism in Japan. It also includes translations of eight of Kukai's important works.

(5) LLOYD, ARTHUR. "Development of Japanese Buddhism." Transactions of the Asiatic Society of Japan, 22 (1894), 382-405.
   Ch. 6 of this lengthy "article" on the history of Japanese Buddhism deals with the basic doctrines of the Shingon school. It is somewhat dated but still substantial, and can be a viable introduction to the topic.

(6) MATSUNAGA, YUKEI. "Tantric Buddhism and Shingon Buddhism." The Eastern Buddhist, 2 (1969), 1-14.
   A brief outline of Shingon and Indo-Tibetan Tantric doctrines and practices which argues that they are structurally similar and have essentially the same origins.

(7) SAUNDERS, ERNEST DALE. Mudra: A Study of Symbolic Gestures in Japanese Buddhist Sculpture. Bollingen series, No. 58. New York: Pantheon, 1960, 296 pp. See also 5.11.4(16) and 11.6.4(6).

(8) TAJIMA, RYUJUN. Les Deux Grands Mandalas et la Doctrine de l'Esoterisme Shingon. Bulletin de la Maison Franco-Japonaise. Nouv. sér., t. 6. Paris: Presses Universitaires de France, 1959, 352 pp.
   Pages 215-323 deal systematically, concisely, and authoritatively with the basic Shingon doctrines. This is preceded by a detailed analysis of Shingon's two principal mandalas, the Mahakaruna-garbha and the Vajradhatu, which, respectively, are "pictorial summaries" of the doctrines contained in Shingon's two principal authoritative texts--the Mahavairocana-sutra and the Sarvatathagatatattvasamgraha-sutra. The author is a "late archbishop" of the Shingon sect.

Discussions of Major Topics in Buddhist Thought

(9) _____. Etude sur le Mahavairocana-sutra (Dainichikyo). Paris: Maisonneuve, 1936, 186 pp. See also 3.4.3(3).

2.7 DISCUSSIONS OF MAJOR TOPICS IN BUDDHIST THOUGHT

For Nirvana, see 11.8. For problems in Faith-oriented schools, see 11.7. For problems in Tantric schools, see 11.6. See also the treatment of these topics in the appropriate sections of the more general works listed in 2.1, 2.4.1, and 2.5.1.

2.7.1 Karma and Rebirth

(1) COOMARASWAMY, ANANDA KENTISH. "Rebirth and Omniscience in Pali Buddhism." Indian Culture, 3 (1936), 19-33.

An example of an early polemical article on the meaning of the doctrine of rebirth in early Buddhism. Coomaraswamy disputes C. A. F. Rhys-Davids' various views, and contends that early Buddhism at no time had a doctrine of reincarnation, but only one of transmigration.

(2) FOUCHER, ALFRED, ed. Les Vies Antérieures du Bouddha, d'après les Textes et les Monuments de l'Inde. Publications du Musée Guimet. Bibliothèque de Diffusion, No. 61. Paris: Presses Universitaires de France, 1955, pp. 11-62.

As preface to his selection of Jataka tales, Foucher gives a clearly written, popularly oriented introduction to the doctrines of karma and rebirth. It is suggestively divided into three parts: "La Théorie Indienne de la Transmigration," "Transmigration et Bouddhisme," and "Bouddhisme et Transmigration."

(3) GAUTHIOT, ROBERT and PAUL PELLIOT, trans. Le Sutra des Causes et des Effets du Bien et du Mal. Mission Pelliot en Asie Centrale, ser. in-4, 2. Paris: Geuthner, 1920-1928, vol. 2, fasc. 1, 66 pp. See also 3.3.8.4(4).

(4) HUMPHREYS, CHRISTMAS. The Way of Action: A Working Philosophy for Western Life. Baltimore, Md.: Penguin, 1971, 195 pp. (First published London: G. Allen and Unwin, 1960; paperback edition: Pelican A1390.)

A popularized and highly interpretative book for Westerners by the head of the Buddhist Society in London. Humphreys attempts to combine his view of the Theravada doctrine of Karma with his understanding of the spirit of Zen and Taoism, all to formulate "an entire and sufficient working philosophy of life . . . devised about the right doing of the act in hand, whatever it may be." A good example of what can happen to the doctrine of karma.

(5) "Kathavatthu." Points of Controversy, or Subjects of Discourse: being a translation of the Katha-vatthu from the Abhidhammapitaka (see 2.4.1[7]), pp. 205-210, 283-285, 314-315.

These passages of the Katha-vatthu deal with various questions that arose in the early Sangha concerning the workings of karma. These include: whether karma causes old age and death, whether the actions of Aryans are also subject to karma, how karma acts upon the embryo, whether "everything" is really due to karma. The student who is plagued by any of these questions might look here for the answers which certain Buddhists brought to them.

(6) KING, WINSTON. "Split Selves and Fractured Karma," in Studies on Asia. Lincoln: University of Nebraska Press, 1964, pp. 175-186.

A well-written discussion putting forth a new analysis of the karmic theory. King raises the possibility of karmic individuality splitting into new karmic entities.

(7) LAMOTTE, ETIENNE, ed. and trans. "Le Traité de l'Acte de Vasubandhu: Karmasiddhiprakarana." See 2.4.3(6).

A translation of a rather technical and abstruse treatise on the mechanics of the law of karma. Lamotte's introduction, however, is very convenient for its summaries of the understandings of karma of the various philosophical schools: the Sarvastivadin-Vaibhasikas, the Vatsiputriya-Sammitiyas, the Sautrantikas, the Vijnanavadins, and the Madhyamikas. An interesting and recent study of the same text may be found in Stefan Anacker, "Vasubandhu's Karmasiddhiprakarana and the Problem of the Highest Meditations," Philosophy East and West, 22 (1972), 247-258.

(8) LA VALLEE POUSSIN, LOUIS DE. "Death and Disposal of the Dead (Buddhist)," in Encyclopaedia of Religion and Ethics (see 1.15.1[9]), vol. 4, pp. 446-449.

Excellent short article on Buddhist views of the inevitability of death, and the process of rebirth which follows.

(9) _____. The Way to Nirvana: Six Lectures on Ancient Buddhism as a Discipline of Salvation. Hibbett Lectures, 2nd series, 1916. Cambridge: The University Press, 1917, pp. 57-106.

The two chapters make a fine and substantial introduction to the history of the Buddhist doctrine of karma--including its relationship to the Jain and Brahmanic views--and to the mechanics of karma as conceived by the Buddhists. It is one of the few writings by La Vallée Poussin in English on the subject and represents the middle stage in his changing views. For his earlier opinions, see his "La négation de l'âme et la doctrine de l'acte," Journal Asiatique (1903), 357-450. For his later position, see pp. 119-218 of his Morale Bouddhique (Paris: Nouvelle Librairie Nationale, 1927). See also the very helpful article by Maryla Falk, "Nairatmya and Karman: The Life-long Problem of Louis de la Vallée Poussin's Thought," Indian Historical Quarterly 16 (1940), 647-682 (also included in the Louis de la Vallée Poussin Memorial Volume, edited by Narendra Nath Law (see 2.7.4[4]), pp. 429-464.

(10) LAW, BIMALA CHURN. "Karma," in The Cultural Heritage of India. Second edition, revised and enlarged. Calcutta: Ramakrishna Mission, Institute of Culture, 1953-1962, vol. 1 (1958), pp. 537-546. (First published in 1937.)

A convenient review of the Buddhist doctrine of karma in its historical context. Law first examines the Brahmanic background, then surveys the way in which the Buddhist understanding of karma diverged from this, looks at different classifications of kinds of karma, and provides an instructive comparison with the Jain views of the subject.

(11) LEE, ORLAN. "From Acts--to Non-Action--to Acts: The Dialectical Basis for Social Withdrawal or Commitment to This World in the Buddhist Reformation." History of Religions, 6 (1967), 273-302.

This article is basically an historical analysis of early Buddhism in terms of the emphasis placed upon action and withdrawal. Lee's thesis seems to be heavily influenced by the thought of Paul Mus as the contention is made that Buddhism represented a return to action in response to asceticism and world renunciation.

(12) NARADA, THERA. "Karma or the Buddhist Law of Causation," in B. C. Law Volume (see 1.2.2.3[6]), vol. 2, pp. 158-175.

A very simple introduction to the topic of the workings of karma, and a good example of a common modern Buddhist view of karma as providing the raison d'être for the inequality which exists in the world. An older and longer essay by the author on the same topic is The Buddhist Doctrine of Re-birth (Colombo, 1936). In the same vein is Nyanatiloka Mahathera, Karma and Rebirth (Kandy, Ceylon: Buddhist Publication Society, 1959).

(13) "Payasi Suttanta," in Dialogues of the Buddha. Translated by T. W. Rhys-Davids. Sacred Books of the Buddhists, vols. 2-4. London: published for the Pali Text Society by Luzac, 1971-1973, vol. 2, pp. 347-374. (First published 1899-1921.)

In this sutta, a chieftain named Payasi presents a whole series of reasons showing why he does not believe in karma and rebirth. Each of his arguments is refuted by the monk Kumara Kassapa. The sutta is, therefore, a useful example of the early Buddhist arguments in favor of rebirth. At the same time, it strikes a curiously contemporary note: many of Payasi's arguments and experiments have also been carried on in modern times.

(14) SASAKI, GENJUN KIDEMARU. "The Concept of Kamma in Buddhist Philosophy." Oriens Extremus, 3 (1956), 185-204.

The problem of the apparent incompatibility of the two doctrines of karma (action) and anatman (non-self) is one which has long preoccupied Buddhologists. In this article, Sasaki provides a scholarly and philosophical discussion of the issues involved, based primarily on Pali materials. A shorter discussion of the same problem which attempts some comparison with pre-Socratic philosophies is Hajime Nakamura, "The Kinetic Existence of the Individual." Philosophy East and West, 1 (1951), 33-39.

(15) VARMA, V. P. "The Origins and Sociology of the Early Buddhist Philosophy of Moral Determinism." Philosophy East and West, 13 (1963), 25-47.

The author begins by identifying the concept of karma as a type of moral determinism. He then proceeds to trace its evolution as a concept through the Vedas, Brahmanas, and Upanishads. Concerning the origin of the concept, Varma offers a variety of explanations on anthropological, sociological, and political grounds. Finally, he attempts to illustrate how the concept was utilized by Buddha as an explanation for the individual's plight in life. Varma sees the consequent sociological significance of the promulgation of karma as being a contributing factor to conservatism and individualism.

(16) WARREN, HENRY CLARKE. Buddhism in Translations. Eighth issue. Harvard Oriental series, vol. 3. Cambridge, Mass.: Harvard University Press, 1922, pp. 209-274.

The chapter is entitled "Karma and Rebirth" and contains a judicious selection of Pali texts to illustrate the subject. It forms a convenient introduction, especially when paired with Chapter 9 (pp. 107-118) of Edward Joseph Thomas, The History of Buddhist Thought (see 2.1[14]).

2.7.2 Duhkha (Suffering)

(1) CONZE, EDWARD. Buddhism: Its Essence and Development (see 1.1[2]), pp. 43-48.

An introduction to the meaning and implications of the doctrine of duhkha, which Conze translates as "ill." The beginning student should read it before the somewhat more technical passage on "ill" in Conze's Buddhist Thought in India (see 2.1[1]), pp. 34-36.

(2) "Kathavatthu." Points of Controversy (see 2.4.1[7]), pp. 127-129 and 315-317.

The nature and meaning of Suffering (duhkha) was a topic of debate among the early Buddhists as well. These two passages from the Pali Kathavatthu illustrate some of the arguments and controversies. The first ends by pointing out that duhkha does not necessarily mean there are no pleasures at all in life, and the second deals with the question of whether duhkha only concerns the senses.

Discussions of Major Topics in Buddhist Thought

(3) RAHULA, WALPOLA. "Duhkha-Satya." *Indian Historical Quarterly*, 32 (1956), 249-253.

This article on the first Noble Truth covers almost exactly the same ground as chapter two of the same author's *What the Buddha Taught* (see 2.1[10]), and either the article or the chapter may be used as a lucid introduction to the doctrine of duhkha as seen in the Pali Texts. Rahula follows Buddhaghosa in distinguishing between Dukkha as ordinary suffering (dukkha-dukkha), dukkha as suffering produced by change (viparinama-dukkha), and dukkha as inherent in the conditioned states (samkhara-dukkha). The discussion of this last aspect leads him also into a survey of the five skandhas.

2.7.3 Anitya (Impermanence) and Time

(1) CONZE, EDWARD. *Buddhist Thought in India* (see 2.1[1]), pp. 34, 134-143, 205-208.

The section entitled "The analysis of impermanence" surveys the development of the doctrine of anicca--its relationship to the speculations about the duration of a moment (ksana) and about the nature of the three times (past, present, and future)--and how this led within the Sthaviravadin branch to certain pseudo-permanentist positions such as those of the Sarvastivadins. Pages 205-208 give a glimpse of the Mahayana discussions of permanence and impermanence, based primarily on the Lankavatara Sutra.

(2) "Kathavatthu." *Points of Controversy* (see 2.4.1[7]), pp. 84-110.

In this, the fifth book of the Theravadin Abhidamma, the debate turns to the topic of the nature of time. The thrust of the argument is against the Sarvastivadins who claim that the past and the future actually exist. It is interesting to compare this with the debate in the *Vijnanakaya* (Book 4 of the *Sarvastivadin Abhidharma*), in which the Theravadin Maudgalyana is defeated and the existence of the past and the future is soundly established. (See the translation in Louis de La Vallée Poussin, "La Controverse du Temps et du Pudgala dans le Vijnanakaya." *Etudes Asiatiques*, 1 (1925), 343-376.

(3) LA VALLEE POUSSIN, LOUIS DE. "Documents d'Abhidharma, la Controverse du Temps." *Mélanges Chinois et Bouddhiques*, 5 (1937), 7-158.

The question of the nature of the three times (past, present, and future) is an offshoot of discussions about the doctrine of impermanence (anicca) and has long been an important and controversial subject of debate among the various Buddhist schools. In this article, de La Vallée Poussin has translated passages relevant to this issue from the Vibhasa and from Sanghabhandra's commentary on the Abhidharmakosa. He also adds a few comments on the Vaibhasika and Sautrantika views of the "instant" or "moment" (ksana)--a topic also discussed by him in "Notes sur le 'moment' des Bouddhistes," *Rocznik Orjentalistyczny*, 8 (1931), 1-9. See also Appendix 1 of Theodore Stcherbatsky, *The Central Conception of Buddhism* (see 2.7.7[11]), pp. 76-91.

(4) MIYAMOTO, SHOSON. "Time and Eternity in Buddhism." *Journal of Indian and Buddhist Studies*, 7, no. 2 (1959), 3-18.

Approaches the theory of impermanence through an analysis of the notion of time as it has been perceived within the Buddhist tradition.

(5) NYANAMOLI, BHIKKHU. "Anicca," in *Encyclopaedia of Buddhism* (see 2.5.4[12]), vol. 1, fasc. 4 (1965), pp. 657-663.

A useful survey of the teaching of impermanence, containing many quotes of sources and passages, mostly from the Pali Canon. Nyanamoli's interpretation of anicca under the threefold aspect of "change," "formation," and "recognizable pattern" is instructive. Also helpful is his discussion of impermanence as a subject of meditation.

(6) *The Three Basic Facts of Existence: 1. Impermanence*. The Wheel publication, Nos. 186/187. Kandy, Ceylon: Buddhist Publication Society, 1973, 73 pp.

A collection of essays of varying quality on this subject, many of them by Western Theravada monks. Included are: Piyadassi Thera, "The Facts of Impermanence" (pp. 1-12); Bhikkhu Nanajivako, "Aniccam--The Buddhist Theory of Impermanence" (pp. 13-38); Y. Karundasa, "The Buddhist Doctrine of Anicca" (pp. 44-56); and Bhikkhu Nanamoli, "Anicca According to Theravada" (pp. 57-73). The book as a whole provides a good introduction to the ways in which modern Theravadins are conceiving and presenting their views on this doctrine.

2.7.4 Atman and Anatman (Self and Not-Self)

(1) BHATTACHARYA, KAMALESWAR. *L'Atman-Brahman dans le Bouddhisme Ancien*. Publications de l'Ecole Française d'Extrême-Orient, No. 90. Paris: Ecole Française d'Extrême-Orient, 1973, 183 pp.

A study of the various early views of the Buddhist notion of Atman and Anatman in relation to the Upanishadic views of Atman-Brahman. The author concludes that the Buddha did not deny the Upanishadic Atman but affirmed it indirectly, and suggests the correspondence Brahman=Atman=Dharma=Buddha=Nirvana.

(2) CHOWDURY, R. P. "Interpretation of the 'Anatta' Doctrine of Buddhism." *Indian Historical Quarterly*, 31 (1955), 52-67.

A good, simple introduction to the view that the doctrine of Anatman was not intended as a doctrine of no-self (i.e., that there is no self) but as a technique of combating false notions and misinterpretations of what the self is. In the same vein, see the article by I. B. Horner, "Atta and Anatta," Middle Way, 45 (1970), 66-70, which argues that only false views of the self--not the self-- are to be rejected; and see Roger Gunter-Jones's "The Meaning and Use of the Anatta-Concept," Middle Way, 44 (1969), 65-69, which sees anatta not as a statement of philosophic truth but as an aid to attainment of self-knowledge.

(3) CONZE, EDWARD. Buddhist Thought in India (see 2.1[1]), pp. 122-134.

These pages may serve as an introduction to the early doctrinal disputes that arose concerning the status of the Self. Conze discusses the position of the Pudgalavadins, and touches on the tendencies in various Buddhist schools to find "personal continuities." The presentation, however, may be a bit too condensed for the beginning student and might well be introduced by Chapter 6 of Rahula's What the Buddha Taught (below).

(4) FALK, MARYLA. "Nairatmya and Karman: The Life-long Problem of Louis de La Vallée Poussin's Thought," in Louis de La Vallée Poussin Memorial Volume. Edited by Navendra Nath Law. Calcutta: Calcutta Oriental Press, 1940, pp. 429-64.

Uses the changing opinions of La Vallée Poussin on the subject to review some of the major difficulties involved in the interpretation of the doctrine of anatman. Falk then goes beyond La Vallée Poussin with her own discussion of Buddhist and Upanisadic understandings of atman, maintaining that "Buddhistic nairatmya is no more a denial of the reality of Atman than Upanishadic nairatmya: it is a denial of the immanence of atman in contingent existence."

(5) Kathavatthu: Points of Controversy (see 2.4.1[7]), pp. 1-63.

This first section of the canonical Kathavatthu consists of a lengthy debate between a Theravadin and a Pudgalavadin on the question of the existence of the personal entity or ego. The problems that arise are sometimes real, sometimes contrived, and the debate shows the extent to which such questions were entered into. This sometimes makes for rather painful reading, especially for the beginning student, but the student who is inclined towards scholastic logic and interested in this question should definitely take a look at it. For a Sarvastivadin account of the debate, see the French translation of the "Pudgala-skandhaka" which is Part 2 of Devasarman's Vijnanakaya (Book 4 of the Sarvastivadin Abhidharma) in Louis de La Vallée Poussin, "La Controverse du Temps et du Pudgala dans le Vijnanakaya," Etudes Asiatiques, 1 (1925), 76-343.

(6) LA VALLEE POUSSIN, LOUIS DE. "The Atman in the Pali Canon." Indian Culture, 2 (1936), 821-824.

This article was La Vallée Poussin's last publication on the doctrine of the Atman. In it, he attempts (again) to solve what he sees as the incompatibility between the philosophical doctrine of anatman and "faith in transmigration and a beatific Nirvana." The solution involves a tracing of a duality of views concerning a Self connected to karmic reality and one which is not. An earlier stage on the question in de La Vallée Poussin's thought may be found in chapter 2 (pp. 30-56) of his The Way to Nirvana (see 2.7.1[9]).

(7) MALALASEKERA, GEORGE PEIRIS. "Anatta," in Encyclopaedia of Buddhism (see 2.5.4[12]), vol. 1, fasc. 4 (1965), pp. 567-576.

A thorough and enlightening treatment by a renowned scholar. Background of the atman-anatman controversy is discussed and Malalasekera's position is set forth and based chiefly on the Pali suttas, the Vinaya and the Milindapanha.

(8) _____. "The Status of the Individual in Theravada Buddhism." Philosophy East and West, 14 (1964), 145-156.

A presentation of the Buddha's view in the Pali Canon of what man really is and what man should make of his life in order to achieve the supreme value that life can afford.

(9) NAGARJUNA. Le Traité de la Grande Vertu de Sagesse (Mahaprajnaparamitasastra). Translated by Etienne Lamotte. Bibliothèque du Museon, No. 18. Louvain: Bureau de Museon, 1944-49, vol. 2 (1949), pp. 735-750.

The debate on the nature of the self and of the doctrine of anatman was continued by the Mahayanists in the context of Sunyata. These pages of Nagarjuna's vast commentarial work are a good example of this. For a short poetical statement of the Madhyamika position, see also Santideva's "Bodhicaryavatara," translated by Marion Matics, in Entering the Path of Enlightenment (see 3.3.2.1[28]), pp. 216 ff. For a later, full scholastic treatment which presents and discusses the views on Atman of the various Indian Schools of philosophy and then of the Vatsiputriyas (refuting them all), see the translation of Santaraksita's Tattvasamgraha by Ganganatha Jha (see 3.3.2.1[11]), vol. 1, pp. 139-226.

(10) RAHULA, WALPOLA. What the Buddha Taught (see 2.1[10]), pp. 51-66.

The chapter is entitled "The Doctrine of No-Soul: Anatta" and gives a good, lucid, and simple introduction to that doctrine, based primarily on Pali materials. It is especially helpful for the beginning student, and useful for its relating the anatman doctrine to the analysis of the five skandhas and the theory of pratityasamutpada.

Discussions of Major Topics in Buddhist Thought

(11) STCHERBATSKY, FEDOR IPPOLITOVICH. The Soul Theory of the Buddhists. Translated by the author. Varanasi: Bharatiya Vidya Prakasan, 1970, 122 pp. (Originally published St. Petersburg.)

A translation of chapter nine of Vasubandhu's Abhidharmakosa with a short introduction by Stcherbatsky. The chapter is sometimes considered to be a sort of appendix to Vasubandhu's work and contains a scholastic refutation of the pudgalavadin theory of the Self, and an espousal of the doctrine of anatman. A French translation of it may also be found in Louis de La Vallée Poussin, trans., L'Abhidharmakosa de Vasubandhu (see 3.2.3.2[4]), vol. 5, pp. 227-302.

(12) UEDA, YOSHIFUMI. "Thinking in Buddhist Philosophy." Philosophical Studies of Japan, 5 (1964), 69-94.

The author compares the basic starting points of Western and Buddhist philosophy. He contends that whereas the West began with the fundamental question "What is?," Buddhist philosophy began its quest with the fundamental question "What is the self?" He goes on to describe how Gautama arrived at the doctrine of "no-self" and how Nagarjuna, Chih-i, Dogen, as well as the thinkers of Yogacara also articulated the doctrine.

2.7.5 The Four Noble Truths

(1) ASANGA. Le Compendium de la Super-Doctrine (Philosophie): Abhidharmasamuccaya. Translated and annotated by Walpola Rahula. Publications de l'Ecole Française d'Extrême-Orient, vol. 78. Paris: Ecole Française d'Extrême-Orient, 1971, pp. 59-130.

In this important Mahayana Abhidharma text, Asanga (one of the founders of the Yogacara school) gives a sort of Abhidharmic summary of his teachings, including, in these pages, his analysis of the four Noble Truths. The text is very analytical and technical, and should be looked at only by the advanced student who wants a full, philosophical, Mahayanist view of the subject.

(2) CONZE, EDWARD. Buddhist Meditation. Ethical and religious classics of East and West, No. 13. London: Allen and Unwin, 1956, pp. 142-146.

One of the most readily available accounts of the important listing of the sixteen aspects of the Four Noble Truths. Conze presents, without comment, four versions of the listing, which became important in meditation.

(3) GOVINDA, ANAGARIKA BRAHMACARI. The Psychological Attitude of Early Buddhist Philosophy, and Its Systematic Representation According to Abhidhamma Tradition. London: Rider, 1961, pp. 45-75.

This third part of Govinda's book is entitled "The Four Noble Truths as Starting Point and Logical Frame of Bhuddhist Philosophy" and treats the Truths from a psychological-metaphysical point of view with interesting interpretations of the correspondences between the Four Truths, the Eightfold Noble Path, the Twelve Phases of Dependent Origination, etc. Not intended for beginning students.

(4) JONES, J. GARRETT. "The Four Truths and the Three Marks." Religion: A Journal of Religion and Religions, 20, no. 6 (August 1976), 190-195.

A short discussion which reviews some previous interpretations and then goes on to demonstrate the way these two formulations of Buddhist doctrines mesh.

(5) LA VALLEE POUSSIN, LOUIS DE. "Vyadhisutra on the Four Aryasatyas." Journal of the Royal Asiatic Society (1903), pp. 578-580.

A very short article giving additional information for Hendrik Kern's view in his Manual of Indian Buddhism (see 1.2.1[9]) that the doctrine of the Four Noble Truths was a borrowing from the four cardinal articles of Indian medicine applied to the spiritual healing of mankind. Specifically, he quotes a number of passages from the Lalitavistara and the Bodhicaryavatara which picture the Buddha as a great physician, and, more importantly, he signals a passage in the Abhidharmakosa which refers to an otherwise unknown Vyadhisutra in which the comparison between the four Noble Truths and the medical phases of disease, diagnosis, cure, and medicine is explicitly made. Interesting, but undeveloped, and of specialized interest.

(6) PANDE, GOVIND CHANDRA. Studies in the Origins of Buddhism (see 1.2.2.1[10]), pp. 397-400.

Pande argues against E. J. Thomas and others (see Thomas' The History of Buddhist Thought [2.1(14)], p. 42) that the Four Noble Truths were probably not part of "original Buddhism." But his pages are also valuable for their references to the different views--of texts and of modern scholars--on the Noble Truths. Included in the discussion are the positions of various Abhidhamma texts, of C. A. F. Rhys-Davids, of Samuel Beal, and of Stcherbatsky (see Stcherbatsky's iconoclastic comments on the four noble truths--"they contain, in reality, no doctrine at all"--in his Conception of Buddhist Nirvana [2.5.3(12)], pp. 90-91).

(7) RAHULA, WALPOLA. What the Buddha Taught (see 2.1[10]), pp. 16-50.

Perhaps still the best simple introduction for the beginning student who wants only to know what the Four Noble Truths are, and who is totally uninterested in whether the Buddha actually taught them, or in how the doctrine developed and changed and was used over the centuries.

2.7.6 Pratityasamutpada (Dependent Origination)

(1) BANERJEE, A. C. "Pratityasamutpada." *Indian Historical Quarterly*, 32 (1956), 261-264.

An exposition of the doctrine of pratityasamutpada, based on Pali texts and seeking to list summarily what is meant by each of the twelve steps of the formula. Its brevity, however, makes it more useful as a review than as an introduction.

(2) BARUA, B. M. "Pratitya-samutpada as Basic Concept of Buddhist Thought," in *B. C. Law Volume* (see 1.2.2.3[6]), vol. 1, pp. 574-589.

A good survey of the different understandings of the doctrine of pratitya-samutpada, which does not limit itself to the Pali texts and the *Abhidharmakosa* but goes on to discuss the views on the subject of the *Lankavatara* and of Nagarjuna. It assumes, however, some previous acquaintance with the doctrine.

(3) CHATTERJEE, H. "Pratityasamutpada." *Annals of the Bhandarkar Oriental Research Institute at Poona*, 37 (1954), 313-318.

Concise and helpful introduction to the relationship of the doctrine of pratityasamutpada to the Four Noble Truths, and also its connection with Samkhya. Includes also a brief account of how the doctrine was interpreted by Theravadans and Mahayanists.

(4) CONZE, EDWARD. *Buddhist Thought in India* (see 2.1[1]), pp. 156-158.

An excellent and concise introduction to the topic of Pratityasamutpada which, unfortunately, is too condensed for the beginning student. It will need to be supplemented at least by pages 152-157 of Conze's *Buddhist Meditation* (see 2.7.5[2]) (*Buddhist Thought in India* was always intended as a sequel to that book); and it might be best to obtain first a more general background to the subject in Edward Joseph Thomas, *The History of Buddhist Thought* (see 2.1[14]), pp. 58-70; and then a more textually oriented overview in A. K. Warder, *Indian Buddhism* (see 1.2.1[15]), pp. 107-117.

(5) FOUCHER, ALFRED CHARLES AUGUSTE. *The Life of the Buddha According to the Ancient Texts and Monuments of India*. Abridged translation by Simone Brangier Boas. Middletown, Conn.: Wesleyan University Press, 1963, pp. 116-126. See also 2.7.1(2).

Useful for putting the doctrine of pratityasamutpada in the context of the enlightenment experience of the Buddha, and also for its highlighting of the key role played by ignorance (avidya) in the chain of becoming.

(6) HARTMANN, GERDA. "Symbols of the Nidanas in Tibetan Drawings of the 'Wheel of Life.'" *Journal of the American Oriental Society*, 60 (1940), 356-360. See also 9.3.2(3).

(7) LAW, BIMALA CHURN. "Formulation of Pratityasamutpada." *Journal of the Royal Asiatic Society* (1937), pp. 287-292.

A useful discussion of and introduction to the two basic ways of "going through" the formula of Pratityasamutpada: anuloma ("in the genetic order," illustrating causation), and patiloma ("in the order of cessation"). The first way is associated with the second noble truth, and the second way with the third.

(8) "Maha-nidana Suttanta," in *Dialogues of the Buddha*. Translated by T. W. Rhys-Davids (see 2.7.1[13]), vol. 2, pp. 42-70.

The "Maha-nidana sutta" is one of the classic expositions of the doctrine of Paticcasamuppada in the Pali Canon, and constitutes one of the important sources on the doctrine. Another canonical treatment is "The Kindred Sayings on Cause" in the *Samyutta Nikaya* (*The Book of Kindred Sayings*), translated by C. A. F. Rhys-Davids and F. L. Woodward (see 2.7.7[10]), vol. 2, pp. 1-94, which comes at the list of the twelve nidanas again and again from different angles and repeats it almost ad nauseam.

(9) OLTRAMARE, PAUL JEAN. *La Formule Bouddhique des Douze Causes: Son sens originel et son interpretation théologique*. Geneva: Georg, 1909, 52 pp.

A dated but still valuable survey of the development of the doctrine of pratityasamutpada which seeks to isolate the original meaning of the term and present also the interpretations made by the Abhidhamma doctors. Also useful for its survey of the early scholarship on the subject.

(10) STRENG, FREDERICK J. *Emptiness* (see 2.5.3[13]), pp. 58-68.

It has often been pointed out that the entire Madhyamika system is but a radical reinterpretation of the doctrine of pratityasamutpada. In this chapter of his study of the basic doctrine of Nagarjuna, Streng attempts to show in what way pratityasamutpada and sunyata were related in the Madhyamika system. Students interested in this topic might also check the views of T. R. V. Murti in *The Central Philosophy of Buddhism* (see 2.5.3[7]), pp. 7 ff.; the more advanced should look at Candrakirti's own comments in his *Prasannapada*, translated in F. I. Stcherbatsky, *The Conception of Buddhist Nirvana* (see 2.5.3[12]), pp. 124 ff.

(11) WAYMAN, ALEX. "Buddhist Dependent Origination." *History of Religions*, 10 (1971), 185-203.

An insightful, detailed, and fairly technical article which examines concepts of dependent origination in classic Buddhist texts and argues that there is a "western" and "eastern" tradition in early Buddhism. The article includes also a discussion of the relationship between early Buddhist and Upanishadic concepts of understanding the nature of existence.

Discussions of Major Topics in Buddhist Thought

2.7.7 Analysis and Classification of Dharmas

Abhidhamma

Many of the Abhidhamma texts are devoted primarily to vast analyses and classifications of dharmas, starting usually with the skandhas, the ayatanas, and the dhatus, and going on from there. These include, among others: Books 1, 2, 3, and 7 of the Pali Abhidhamma (Dhammasangani, Vibhanga, Dhatu-Katha, and Patthana), see Asanga's Abhidharmasamuccaya, translated by Walpola Rahula, Vasubandhu's Abhidharmakosa, translated by de La Vallée Poussin (see 3.2.3.2[4]), and Anuruddha's manual, the Abhidhammatthasangaha, translated by C. A. F. Rhys-Davids (see 2.7.5[1]). These volumes are mammoth compositions, often tedious, and for advanced and interested students only. See appropriate citations in Sections 3.1 and 3.2.

(1) BAREAU, ANDRE. L'Absolu en Philosophie Bouddhique: Evolution de la Notion d'Asamskrita. Paris: Centre de Documentation Universitaire, 1951, 307 pp.

This is primarily a textual study devoted to tracing the theory of asamskrta dharmas in Theravadin, Sarvastivadin, Madhyamika, Yogacara and other materials. For the advanced and interested student only. A shorter study of the same topic by Bareau is his "L'Absolu dans le bouddhisme," in Entretiens 1955 (Pondichéry: Institut Français d'Indologie, 1956), pp. 37-43.

(2) CONZE, EDWARD. Buddhist Thought in India (see 2.1[1]), pp. 92-116, 220-235.

Chapter 7, entitled "Dharman and Dharmas," is a fine but difficult discussion of some of the meanings of the word Dharma, with special emphasis on its meaning as a "truly real event." Chapter 8 is a somewhat easier discussion of the pan-Buddhist classification of dharmas into the five skandhas (heaps), twelve ayatanas (sense-fields), and eighteen dhatus (elements). After reading these two chapters, the student should check pp. 220-225 for the Mahayana interpretations of the notion of Dharmas.

(3) _____. "The Ontology of the Prajnaparamita." Philosophy East and West, 3 (1953), 117-129.

A concise consideration of the nature of dharmas from a Perfection of Wisdom/Madhyamika point of view.

(4) GOVINDA, ANAGARIKA BRAHMACARI. The Psychological Attitude of Early Buddhist Philosophy and Its Systematic Representation According to Abhidhamma Tradition (see 2.7.5[3]), pp. 77-176.

This, the second half of Govinda's book, deals with the systematic Abhidhamma representation of consciousness, the factors of consciousness, and its functions, from a Theravada standpoint. The subject is a difficult one, and only the advanced and interested student should tackle Govinda's many helpful listings and charts.

(5) GUENTHER, HERBERT V. Philosophy and Psychology in the Abhidharma. Berkeley: Shambala Publications, 1976, 270 pp. (Originally published 1957.)

This presents various Abhidharma discussions of the nature of the mind, meditation, perception, interpretation, and the path to enlightenment, using representative works of Buddhaghosa (Theravadin), Vasubandhu (Sautrantika) and Asanga (Yogacara).

(6) LAMOTTE, ETIENNE. Histoire du Bouddhisme Indien: Des origines à l'ère Saka (see 1.2.1[10]), pp. 658-668.

A handy listing and discussion of the Theravada method of classifying all dharmas into eighty-one samskrta dharmas and one asamskrta dharma. The list is based on the Abhidhammattha-sangaha and divides the samskrta dharmas into matter (rupa), mentals (cetasika) and mind (citta). Lamotte then compares this with the Sarvastivadin list of seventy-one samskrta and three asamskrta dharmas, the former being divided into matter, mentals, mind, and viprayuktasamskaras which are disjoined from both matter and mind.

(7) LA VALLEE POUSSIN, LOUIS DE. "Documents d'Abhidharma," in Bulletin de l'Ecole française d'Extrême-Orient, 30 (1930), 1-28, 247-298.

The asamskrta dharmas are an important category of dharmas (the members of which vary according to different schools). In these pages, La Vallée Poussin presents a selection of Abhidharma texts dealing with the asamskrta dharmas, nirvana, akasa, pratisankhya-nirodha, and apratisankhyanirodha (the two basic types of cessation). For advanced and interested students only.

(8) NYAYA-TARKATIRTHA, A. D. "Nirodha-Satya." Indian Historical Quarterly, 32 (1956), 254-260.

Useful introduction to the study of various Abhidharma schools' views of two of the unconstituted (asamskrta) dharmas: pratisamkhya and apratisamkhya nirodha, which refer to two types of cessation. For advanced and interested students.

(9) RANASINGHE, C. P. The Buddha's Explanation of the Universe. Colombo: Lanka Bauddha Mandalaya Fund, 1957, 414 pp.

Not very inspiring, but popularly-oriented presentation of Abhidhamma classifications and explanations, based exclusively on the Pali texts.

(10) Samyutta Nikaya: The Book of Kindred Sayings. Pali Text Society Translation Series, Nos. 7, 10, 13, 14, 16. Translated by C. A. F. Rhys-Davids and F. L. Woodward. London: published for the Pali Text Society by Luzac, 1950-1956, vol. 3 (1954), pp. 1-154. (Originally published 1917-30.)

This section of the Samyutta Nikaya is entitled "The Kindred Sayings on Elements" and contains numerous statements (some of which have become "classic") on the theory of the Five Skandhas. It forms a good example of a Pali canonical treatment of this subject.

(11) STCHERBATSKY, THEODORE (FEDOR IPPOLITOVICH). The Central Conception of Buddhism and the Meaning of the Word "Dharma." Fourth edition. Delhi: Indological Book House, 1970, 99 pp. (Originally published 1923.)

The classic treatment of the subject of dharmas, it remains an excellent and concise exposition. Drawing mainly on Vasubandhu's Abhidharmakosa, Stcherbatsky presents, in a detailed but comprehensible outline, the important features in the Abhidharma analysis of the nature of existence--i.e., its being composed of dharmas. He begins with the skandhas, ayatanas, and dhatus, but also treats the more complex classifications, and throughout there is the emphasis that the basis of Buddhism as a salvation religion is to be found in this ontology. His "Tables of the Elements according to the Sarvastivadins" (Appendix 2) are also extremely helpful. For a critique of his views, see A. B. Keith, "Doctrine of the Buddha," Bulletin of the School of Oriental Studies, 6 (1931), 393-404.

(12) _____. "The 'Dharmas' of the Buddhists and the 'Gunas' of the Samkhyas." Indian Historical Quarterly, 10 (1934), 737-760.

Written as a response to Vidhushekhara Bhattacharya, The Basic Conception of Buddhism. Calcutta: University of Calcutta, 1934. This article contains a summary of Stcherbatsky's argument in favor of the centrality of the notion of dharma, and, at the same time, a comparison of that notion with the gunas of the Samkhyas.

(13) WARREN, HENRY CLARKE. Buddhism in Translations (see 2.7.1[16]), pp. 487-496 (Appendix).

This appendix forms a convenient and readily available table of what the five skandhas consist of. The lists are based on the Visuddhimagga, and should be compared at least to the Sarvastivadin tables which may be found in Appendix 2 of Stcherbatsky's Central Conception of Buddhism (above). Especially valuable here is a complete listing of the eighty-nine types of consciousness.

2.7.8 Sunyata (Emptiness)

(1) BHATTACHARYA, AJIT RANJAN. "Brahman of Sankara and Sunyata of Madhyamikas." Indian Historical Quarterly, 32 (1956), 270-285.

One of the more balanced and thorough attempts to make a comparison of the notions of the Absolute of Vedanta and Madhyamika. The discussion is carried on only at the philosophical level. A short, somewhat different view of the same topic may be found in T. R. V. Murti, The Central Philosophy of Buddhism pp. 236-238 (see below).

(2) CONZE, EDWARD. Buddhism: Its Essence and Development (see 1.1[2]), pp. 130-135.

Almost all of the more general books on Buddhist thought contain sections on the doctrine of Sunyata. These pages contain a concise, clear, and readily available introduction to the subject. It is especially helpful in showing the relation of emptiness to the progression of the anatman doctrine from the egolessness of persons to the egolessness of dharmas. Other treatments of the subject may be found in Richard H. Robinson, The Buddhist Religion (see 1.1[8]), pp. 51-54; and in Daisetz Teitaro Suzuki, Outlines of Mahayana Buddhism (see 2.1[12]), pp. 173-179.

(3) _____. Buddhist Thought in India (see 2.1[1]), pp. 242-249.

These pages give a concise description of a meditation which distinguishes thirty-two kinds of "Emptiness" corresponding to the five levels of insight implied in the final mantra (gate, gate, paragate, parasamgate, bodhi svaha) of the Heart Sutra. The passage is not for beginning students, but is well worth studying in conjunction with the "Heart Sutra," which is itself a classic and popular statement of the doctrine of Sunyata. It is also best to read these pages while checking at the same time Conze's index (under "Emptiness") for references throughout the book to various stages and aspects of that doctrine.

(4) HAMILTON, CLARENCE H. "Encounter with Reality in Buddhist Madhyamika Philosophy." Journal of Bible and Religion, 26 (1958), 13-22.

A simple, short introduction to the meaning of Emptiness in the thought of Nagarjuna, with some attention paid to pointing to Western parallels. Useful for the beginning student who has little familiarity with Buddhist philosophy.

(5) JONG, J. W. DE. "Le Problème de l'absolu dans l'école Madhyamika." Revue Philosophique de la France et de l'Etranger, 140 (1950), 323-337.

A study of the interrelated doctrines of Sunyata, of svabhava, and of the two levels of truth. De Jong also critiques the views of Schayer and of Stcherbatsky, and emphasizes that the "real" meaning of Sunyata lies in mystical rather than philosophical insights.

(6) Majjhimanikaya, the Collection of the Middle Length Sayings. Translated by Isaline Blew Horner. Pali Text Society Translation Series, Nos. 29-31. London: published for the Pali Text Society by Luzac, 1954-1959, vol. 3, pp. 147-152 ("Culasunnatasutta"), and 152-162 ("Mahasunnatasutta").

These two short suttas of the Majjhima Nikaya are of interest and importance in that they are canonical Theravada treatments of the doctrine of Sunyata (Emptiness).

Discussions of Major Topics in Buddhist Thought

(7) MAY, JACQUES. "La philosophie bouddhique de la vacuité." <u>Studia Philosophica</u>, 18 (1958), 123-37.

An excellent introduction to the notion of Sunyata for the student of Western philosophy who is unfamiliar with Indian thought. The same student might also find useful another article by May, "Kant et le Madhyamika," <u>Indo-Iranian Journal</u>, 3 (1959), 102-111. This is a critique of T. R. V. Murti's <u>Central Philosophy of Buddhism</u> (below).

(8) MURTI, TIRUPATTUR RAMASESHAYYER VENKATACHALA. <u>The Central Philosophy of Buddhism: A Study of the Madhyamika System</u>. See 2.5.3(7).

Check the references in the index under "Sunya" for discussions of such topics as the relationship of Sunyata to the Middle Path doctrine, the notion of Pratityasamutpada, Nirvana, the Tathagata, bodhicitta, and karuna, and especially pp. 329-334 for Murti's conclusion: "Sunyata is Absolutism, not Nihilism or Positivism."

(9) OBERMILLER, EUGENE. "A Study of the Twenty Aspects of Sunyata Based on Haribhadra's Abhisamayalamkaraloka and the Pancavimsatisahasrika." <u>Indian Historical Quarterly</u>, 9 (1933), 170-187.

A rather technical study based primarily on the views of Haribhadra, but interesting as an illustration of the development and elaboration of the doctrine of Sunyata in the later phases of Madhyamika thought. A quick introduction to the same topic may be found in Murti's <u>The Central Philosophy of Buddhism</u> (above), "Appendix: A Note on the Twenty Modes of Sunyata," pp. 352-356.

(10) STRENG, FREDERICK J. <u>Emptiness</u>. See 2.5.3(13).

One of the most complete recent studies of Nagarjuna's notion of Sunyata, supported by the first complete English translation of his <u>Mulamadhyamakakarikas</u> and his <u>Vigrahavyavartani</u>. The concept of Sunyata, superficially "nihilist," is studied against the background of the dynamic process of at once apprehending and fabricating the ultimate and transforming truth--and as a means of communication of this truth. The study includes a very helpful bibliography.

(11) TENZIN GYATSO, THE 14TH DALAI LAMA (BSTANDZIN RGYA-MTSHO). "The Key to the Middle Way: A Treatise on the Realisation of Emptiness," in his <u>The Buddhism of Tibet and the Key to the Middle Way</u>. Translated by Jeffrey Hopkins and Lati Rimpoche with Anne Klein. The Wisdom of Tibet series, No. 1. New York: Harper and Row, 1975, pp. 49-89.

Insightful and scholarly exposition by the present Dalai Lama of the doctrine of emptiness and its meaning in both its philosophical and spiritual dimension. The Dalai Lama illustrates his explanation, which is based on the Tibetan oral tradition, with well chosen quotes from sutras and commentaries. Altogether it makes a fine introduction to the topic of emptiness, and one which is worth returning to.

2.7.9 <u>The Two Truths (Paramartha satya and Samvrtti satya)</u>

(1) BHAVAVIVEKA. <u>Madhyamarthasamgraha</u>. Translated by N. Aiyaswami Sastri as "Madhyamarthasamgraha of Bhavaviveka." <u>Journal of Oriental Research</u> (Madras), 5 (1931), 41-49.

A very short text of only eleven stanzas, but useful for summarizing Bhavaviveka's understanding of the two truths, and of the different types of Samvrtti satya. Translated from the Tibetan.

(2) DUTT, NALINAKSHA. <u>Aspects of Mahayana Buddhism</u> (see 1.2.2.3[3]), pp. 255-293.

The chapter is entitled "Conception of the Truth" and contains a discussion of the doctrine of the Two Truths (paramartha satya and samvrti satya) which is set in the broader context of a discussion of Truth (including the four Noble Truths, the three laksanas of the Yogacarins, etc.). Helpful for the student already acquainted with the main lines of Mahayana thought.

(3) LA VALLEE POUSSIN, LOUIS DE. "Les deux, les quatre, les trois vérités." <u>Mélanges Chinois et Bouddhiques</u>, 5 (1936-1937), 159-187.

The doctrine of the two truths (samvrti and paramartha satya) is one of the hallmarks of Mahayana Buddhism. In this article, de La Vallée Poussin translates some passages from Theravada works which shed some light on the development of that doctrine. It is only for advanced students concerned with this topic.

(4) MURTI, TIRUPATTUR RAMASESHAYYER VENKATACHALA. <u>The Central Philosophy of Buddhism</u> (see 2.5.3[7]), pp. 243-255.

Though the doctrine of the two truths (paramartha and samvrti satya) may not have been an originally Mahayanist or even Buddhist doctrine, it did become a vital part of the Madhyamika system. In these pages, Murti provides a good survey of what it meant to Nagarjuna and the subsequent philosophers of the Madhyamika school.

(5) SANTIDEVA. <u>Entering the Path of Enlightenment: The Bodhicaryavatara of the Buddhist Poet Santideva</u>. Translated by Marion L. Matics. New York: Macmillan, 1970, pp. 107-123, 211 ff. (Paperback edition: Macmillan 08760; published also under title <u>The Path of Light</u>.)

In his "guide" to his translation of Santideva's classic work, Matics has provided what is perhaps the best, easily available, introduction to the Madhyamika doctrine of the two truths. He touches on some of the ethical and metaphysical problems raised by the doctrine, and discusses its relationship to the notions of maya (illusion) and emptiness. This should be read in conjunction with the text of the <u>Bodhicaryavatara</u>, Chapter 9, verse 2 ff., which is translated on pp. 211 ff.

(6) SPRUNG, MERVIN, ed. <u>The Problem of Two Truths in Buddhism and Vedanta</u>. Dordrecht: Reidel, 1973, pp. 1-88.

These pages represent six contributions in article form which are concerned with the problem of "samvrti" and "paramartha" in Madhyamika thought. All papers are concerned with the manner in which Madhyamika understands the relationship between the two concepts, but each paper varies according to specific implications of the understanding. Includes articles by Frederick Streng, T. R. V. Murti, A. K. Warder, and others. Makes a fine introduction to various understandings of the subject.

(7) STRENG, FREDERICK J. <u>Emptiness</u> (<u>see</u> 2.5.3[13]), pp. 39-40, 144-146.

Discussion and introduction to Nagarjuna's understanding of the two truths—paramartha satya, which Streng translates as "highest truth," and samvrti satya, "practical truth." Pages 39-40 are more introductory in nature than pages 144-46. Streng's view specifically on the two truths has been criticized in Alex Wayman's review article, "Contributions to the Madhyamika School of Buddhism" (<u>see</u> 2.5.3[15]); <u>see</u> especially pp. 147-150.

(8) SUZUKI, DAISETZ. <u>Outlines of Mahayana Buddhism</u> (<u>see</u> 2.1[12]), pp. 94-98.

A somewhat dated introduction to the doctrine of the two truths—paramartha satya which Suzuki translates as "transcendental truth," and samvrti satya, "conditional truth"—but nevertheless important because, in his discussion, Suzuki follows the Lankavatara Sutra, which is the only major sutra to discuss the two truths in the context of the three laksanas ("characteristics"): parikalpita, paratantra, parinispanna. <u>See also</u> D. T. Suzuki, <u>Studies in the Lankavatara Sutra</u> (<u>see</u> 3.3.3.3[3]), pp. 163-165.

2.7.10 Tathata (Suchness)

(1) <u>Astasahasrika Prajnaparamita: The Perfection of Wisdom in Eight Thousand Lines and Its Verse Summary</u>. Translated by Edward Conze. Wheel series, No. 1. Bolinas: Four Seasons Foundation, 1973, distributed by Book People, Berkeley, Calif., pp. 193-199.

Conze has called this chapter on Suchness (tathata) the "culminating point" of the whole <u>Astasahasrika Prajnaparamita</u>. In it, Subhuti outdoes himself in his attempt to describe suchness (so well that the earth quakes and many beings are saved). Then, discussions follow on the relationship of suchness, skill in means, enlightenment, and emptiness. The same passage may be found on pages 113-120 of E. Conze, trans., <u>Astasahasrika Prajnaparamita</u> (Calcutta: The Asiatic Society, 1958).

(2) CONZE, EDWARD. <u>Buddhist Thought in India</u> (<u>see</u> 2.1[1]), pp. 225-230.

A short, condensed discussion of the doctrine of suchness (tathata) and its relation to other designations and synonyms for the absolute. Check also Conze's index under "suchness" for references throughout the work.

(3) LA VALLEE POUSSIN, LOUIS DE. "Notes sur la Tathata ou Dharmata," in <u>Vasubandhu. Vijnaptimatratasiddhi (La Siddhi de Hiuan-Tsang)</u>. Translated by La Vallée Poussin. Buddhica-- Documents et Travaux, Nos. 5, 7. Paris: Geuthner, 1929, vol. 2, pp. 743-61 (Appendix 2).

A fine survey of sources dealing with the doctrines of suchness, and arranged according to various philosophical schools and textual traditions. Of great help, but only for the advanced student.

(4) SUZUKI, DAISETZ TEITARO. <u>Outlines of Mahayana Buddhism</u> (<u>see</u> 2.1[12]), pp. 99-124.

Somewhat dated, this remains a valuable introduction and survey of the doctrine of Suchness. A shorter introduction of the same topic presenting much the same view may be found in Beatrice Lane Suzuki, <u>Mahayana Buddhism</u> (<u>see</u> 2.5.1[8]), pp. 42-48.

(5) TAKAKUSU, JUNJIRO. "Buddhism as a Philosophy of 'Thusness,'" in <u>Philosophy East and West</u>. Edited by Charles Alexander Moore. Princeton: Princeton University Press, 1944, pp. 69-108.

A difficult but extremely helpful article which posits Tathata as "the ultimate foundation of Buddhist thought concerning the real state of all that exists," and relates the doctrine to almost all the other major doctrines of Hinayana in a very perceptive fashion. It also compares the Upanishads, based on Thatness (tattva), with Buddhism, based on Thusness (Tathata). Not for the beginning student.

(6) TAKASAKI, JIKIDO. "Dharmata, Dharmadhatu, Dharmakaya, and Buddhadhatu." <u>Journal of Indian and Buddhist Studies</u>, 14, no. 2 (1966), 78-94.

A textually oriented study of some of the various modes of conceiving the structure of Ultimate Value in Mahayana Buddhist thought.

2.7.11 Tathagatagarbha

(1) DUTT, NALINAKSHA. "Tathagatagarbha." <u>Indian Historical Quarterly</u>, 33 (1957), 26-39.

A helpful introduction to the concept and a good first discussion of the meaning of the term. Perhaps beginning students interested in the subject should start here.

Discussions of Major Topics in Buddhist Thought

(2) RUEGG, DAVID SEYFORT. La Théorie du Tathagatagarbha et du Gotra. Publications de l'Ecole Française d'Extrême-Orient, No. 70. Paris: Ecole Française d'Extrême-Orient, 1969, 531 pp.

Subtitled "Etudes sur la Soteriologie et la Gnoseologie du Bouddhisme," this is a most thorough, scholarly, and technical study of the Tathagatagarbha theory and its intimate connection to the important doctrine of the gotra ("spiritual lineage") in Mahayana literature. It will benefit only those well acquainted with these theories, and should not be used as an introduction to the subject. For a brief article by the same author comparing the notions of Tathagatagarbha and Paramartha, see Ruegg's "On the knowability and expressibility of Absolute Reality in Buddhism," Journal of Indian and Buddhist Studies, 20, no. 1 (1971), 1-7.

(3) _____. Le Traité du Tathagatagarbha de Buston Rin Chen Grub, traduction du De bzin gsegs pa'i snin po gsal zin mdzes par byed pa'i rgyan. Publications de l'Ecole Française d'Extrême-Orient, No. 88. Paris, 1973, 162 pp.

Authoritative translation of a treatise on the Tathagathagarbha theory by the fourteenth century Tibetan scholar Bu ston, who himself cites a number of authoritative sources, some of which are not now extant.

(4) "Srimalasutra." The Lion's Roar of Queen Srimala: A Buddhist Scripture on the Tathagatagarbha Theory. Translated, with introduction and notes by Alex Wayman and Hideko Wayman. New York: Columbia University Press, 1974, 142 pp.

The Srimalasutra which the Waymans have translated here is one of the earlier sutras dealing with the Tathagatagarbha theory (see in particular, pp. 96-98). Translation of the lost Sanskrit work was made from a collation of the Chinese, Japanese, and Tibetan versions, and passages cited in other Sanskrit works. The Waymans' introduction (especially pp. 42-55) makes their book an especially valuable, sharp introduction to the study of this topic. In it, they discuss, very concisely, the doctrinal and textual history of the doctrine, and its relations to the concepts of Sunyata and Alayavijnana.

(5) SUZUKI, DAISETZ TEITARO. Outlines of Mahayana Buddhism (see 2.1[12]), pp. 125-139.

In this chapter, entitled "The Tathagatagarbha and the Alaya-vijnana," Suzuki tends to identify the two terms, seeing the latter as a particularized expression of the former. In so doing he is following the leads of the Lankavatara Sutra and the Awakening of Faith, both of which identify the two. See also D. T. Suzuki, Studies in the Lankavatara Sutra (see 3.3.3.3[3]), pp. 261-263. It should be pointed out, however, that in India the two theories were distinguished, as may be seen in the earlier Srimalasutra (see Waymans' translation above, p. 53).

(6) TAKASAKI, JIKIDO. A Study on the Ratnagotravibhaga (Uttaratantra): Being a Treatise on the Tathagatagarbha Theory of Mahayana Buddhism. Serie orientale Roma, No. 33. Rome: Istituto Italiano per il Medio ed Estremo Oriente, 1966, 439 pp.

The Ratnagotravibhaga is the principal Mahayana sutra dealing with the theory of the Tathagatagarbha. (See especially pp. 196-98 and 294-304 of the translation.) Takasaki's introduction is one of the more thorough accounts of the theory in English. (See especially pp. 32-44, "Genealogy of the Tathagatagarbha Theory," and pp. 20-31, "Keypoint of the Discourse.") Altogether, the book makes perhaps the best substantial introduction to the subject. See also Jikido Takasaki, "The Tathagatagarbha Theory in the Mahaparinirvana Sutra," Journal of Indian and Buddhist Studies, 19, no. 2 (1971), 1-10.

2.7.12 Alaya-vijnana (Store Consciousness)

(1) "Araya," in Hobogiren: Dictionnaire Encyclopédique du Bouddhisme d'après les Sources Chinoises et Japonaises. Edited by Paul Demieville. Tokyo: Maison Franco-Japonaise, 1929- . Incomplete. Issued in fascicles. Fasc. 1, pp. 35-37.

Excellent survey of the concept of alaya in Mahayana, and, interestingly, in Hinayana texts. It is especially helpful for references to Chinese materials that have not been translated. The article is part of the masterful and authoritative encyclopedia of Chinese and Japanese Buddhism.

(2) CONZE, EDWARD. Buddhism: Its Essence and Development (see 1.1[2]), pp. 168-71.

In these pages, Conze presents some of his strong views on the alaya-vijnana as just one of many manifestations of a general trend to retain some kind of belief in a self or a soul. See also his Buddhist Thought in India (see 2.1[1]), pp. 133-34, where he calls the store-consciousness a "conceptual monstrosity" and a "fine example of running with the hare, and hunting with the hounds."

(3) FUKAURA, SEIBUN. "Alaya-Vijnana," in Encyclopaedia of Buddhism (see 2.5.4[12]), vol. 1, fasc. 3 (1964), pp. 382-388.

Solid introduction and survey of the doctrine of the store-consciousness (alaya-vijnana) and one of the few which touches upon its development in various Chinese sects.

(4) HSUAN TSANG. Ch'eng Wei-shih Lun (The Doctrine of Mere-Consciousness) (see 2.5.4[8]), pp. 105-251.

This section of Hsuan Tsang's major compendium of Yogacara doctrines deals thoroughly with the eighth consciousness, the Alaya-vijnana. The same passage may be found in de La Vallée Poussin's annotated French translation of the same text, the Vijnaptimatrata siddhi: La Siddhi de Hiuan Tsang (see 3.3.3.2[6]), vol. 1, pp. 94-220.

(5) LAMOTTE, ETIENNE. "L'Alayavijnana (Le Réceptacle) dans le Mahayanasamgraha. Asanga et ses Commentateurs (Ch. 2)." Mélanges Chinois et Bouddhiques, 3 (1934-1935), 169-255.

This chapter, which Lamotte has translated and introduced here, is probably the most thorough abhidharmic treatment of the doctrine of the store-consciousness (alaya-vijnana). It is divided into four sections--synonyms of the term, characteristics, demonstrations, and types of it. The same passage may also be found in Mahayanasamgraha, edited and translated by Lamotte as La Somme du Grand Véhicule d'Asanga (see 3.3.3.1[3]).

(6) LA VALLEE POUSSIN, LOUIS DE. "Note sur l'Alayavijnana." Mélanges Chinois et Bouddhiques, 3 (1934-1935), 145-168.

Written as an introduction to Lamotte's translation of the chapter on alayavijnana of the Mahayanasamgraha, this is one of the more thorough surveys of the notion of store-consciousness and represents the summation of de La Vallée Poussin's views on this subject. Of help especially to the advanced student.

(7) LEVI, SYLVAIN. Un Système de Philosophie Bouddhique: Matériaux pour l'Etude du Système Vijnaptimatra (see 2.5.4[9]), pp. 125-173.

The section is entitled "La Notation du Trefonds (alayavijnana)," and consists of a French translation of excerpts from Fa yun's Fan yi ming yi tsi, a twelfth century lexicon of Sanskrit words used in the Chinese canon. The translation is of the article dealing with alaya and contains many quotations from many Chinese texts dealing with this doctrine. A rich source for the advanced student.

(8) SUZUKI, DAISETZ TEITARO. Outlines of Mahayana Buddhism (see 2.1[12]), pp. 125-139.

A discussion of the relation of the doctrines of alaya-vijnana (which Suzuki translates here as "All-conserving Soul") and tathagata-garbha. In his interpretation, Suzuki follows the later Mahayana sutras which tend to identify the two doctrines. There are indications, however, that at one time the two doctrines were quite distinct. See Alex and Hideko Wayman, trans., The Lion's Roar of Queen Srimala (see 2.7.11[4]).

(9) WEINSTEIN, STANLEY. "The Alaya-vijnana in Early Yogacara Buddhism." Transactions of the International Conference of Orientalists in Japan, 3 (1958), 46-58.

Study of the doctrine of storehouse consciousness focusing on its interpretation in the Samdhinirmocana sutra and in Dharmapala's Vijnaptimatrata siddhi, and comparing the two.

2.7.13 Tri-laksana/tri-svabhava (Three Characteristics: Parikalpita, Paratantra, Parinispanna)

(1) CONZE, EDWARD. Buddhist Thought in India (see 2.1[1]), pp. 257-260.

The section is entitled "The Three Kinds of Own-Being," and contains an introduction to the topic of the trilaksana or trisvabhava. Parikalpita is seen as "the imagined," paratantra as "the interdependent" and parinispanna as "the absolute." The discussion is set in an overall consideration of Yogacara doctrines.

(2) HSUAN TSANG. Ch'eng Wei-shih Lun (see) 2.5.4[8]), pp. 621-668.

This section of Hsuan Tsang's major compendium of Yogacara doctrines deals with the doctrine of the three natures or characteristics. It touches on definition, relation to Asamskrta dharmas, etc. The same passage may be found in de La Vallée Poussin's annotated translation of the text, Vijnaptimatrata siddhi: La Siddhi de Hiuan Tsang (see 3.3.3.2[6]), vol. 2, pp. 514-561.

(3) KIYOTA, MINORU. "The Three Modes of Encompassing in the Vijnaptimatrata System." Journal of Indian and Buddhist Studies, 10, no. 1 (1962), 19-24.

Short and rather abstract but nevertheless helpful discussion of the Yogacara trilaksana doctrine, subtitled "Their correlated meaning in the Structural Totality of the Human Consciousness.

(4) Lankavatarasutra: A Mahayana Text. Translated by Daisetz Teitaro Suzuki. London: Routledge, 1932, pp. 59-60, 112-114, and 193-197.

Comparatively few Mahayana sutras discuss the Yogacara doctrine of the three marks (tri-laksana or tri-svabhava). These pages in the Lankavatara sutra are perhaps the most readily available example of a textual treatment of the topic. Another, more substantial one may be found in the Samdhinirmocana Sutra: L'Explication des Mystères, translated by Etienne Lamotte (see 3.3.3.1[17]), pp. 188-208.

(5) SUZUKI, DAISETZ TEITARO. Outlines of Mahayana Buddhism (see 2.1[12]), pp. 87-94.

A concise and clear discussion of the Yogacara trilaksana (three marks) doctrine from the epistemological point of view as three forms of knowledge. Suzuki translates parikalpita as "illusion," paratantra as "relative knowledge," and parinispanna as "absolute knowledge." However, it should be paired with the discussion in Conze (above). Another discussion of the same topic by the same author may be found in Suzuki's Studies in the Lankavatara Sutra (see 3.3.3.3[3]), pp. 157-163.

(6) Trisvabhāvanirdeśa. Translated by Louis de La Vallée Poussin. In "Le Petit Traité de Vasubandhu-Nāgārjuna sur les Trois Natures." Mélanges Chinois et Bouddhiques, 2 (1932-1933), 147-161. See 3.3.3.1[19].

2.7.14 Bodhicitta. (The Mind of Enlightenment)

(1) ABE, MASAO. "Dogen on Buddha Nature." The Eastern Buddhist, 4, no. 1 (May 1971), 28-71.

A thorough and insightful study of the founder of Soto Zen and his particular interpretation of the Mahayana doctrine of Buddha nature.

(2) BHADANTA SANTI, BHIKSHU. "Fa Fu T'i Hsin Ching Lun: Bodhicittotpada-sutra-sastra of Vasubandhu." Visva-Bharati Annals, 2 (1949), i-xviii, 207-243.

In these pages Bhadanta Santi has translated into Sanskrit a Chinese text dealing with the awakening of Bodhicitta which is one of the important sources on this topic. The preface to his translation is in English and provides a summary of the text and an argument for the theory of Bodhicitta as central to any understanding of the Mahayana and as homologizeable with Brahman of the Upanisads and Nirvana of the Hinayanists.

(3) BLOFELD, JOHN EATON CALTHORPE. The Tantric Mysticism of Tibet: A Practical Guide (see 2.6.1[3]), pp. 157-159.

A concise treatment of the generation of Bodhicitta (the thought of enlightenment) as a preliminary to general Buddhist practice, according to the Tibetan system. This "awakening" is an important stage in practice. See also Lama Anagarika Brahmacari Govinda, Foundations of Tibetan Mysticism (see 2.6.1[9]), p. 274.

(4) DASGUPTA, SHASHIBHUSAN. An Introduction to Tantric Buddhism (see 2.6.1[5]), pp. 162-173.

The section is entitled "The Production of Bodhicitta and Its Regulation" and represents a thorough introduction to the Tantric interpretation and understanding of Bodhicitta. Reviewing various tantric texts, and following the distinction between paramartha-satya (absolute truth) and samvrti satya ("provisional truth"), Dasgupta distinguishes between two aspects of Bodhicitta: the one absolute aspect as "all-pervading incorporeal Mahasukha," and the other the phenomenal, physical aspect as semen virile. Check also the index under "Bodhicitta" for references throughout the book.

(5) NANAYAKKARA, S. K. "Bodhicitta," in Encyclopaedia of Buddhism (see 2.5.4[12]), vol. 3, fasc. 2 (1972), pp. 184-189.

Probably the best short introduction to the doctrine of the mind of enlightenment (bodhicitta). It points to the implicit presence of the doctrine in certain Theravada texts, describes its formulation along ethical and metaphysical lines in the Mahayana, and ends with the Tantric interpretations. Helpful quotations are given throughout from various untranslated texts such as the Bodhicittotpada-sutra-sastra.

(6) SANTIDEVA. Entering the Path of Enlightenment: The Bodhicaryavatara of the Buddhist Poet Santideva (see 2.7.9[5]), pp. 33-39, 143 ff.

On pages 33-39 of his "Guide" to his translation of the Bodhicaryavatara, Matics gives a very useful summary of the Mahayanist interpretation of the "arising of the thought of enlightenment (bodhicitta)." Indeed Santideva's work itself (see pp. 143 ff.) begins with "praising the thought of enlightenment."

(7) SUZUKI, DAISETZ TEITARO. Outlines of Mahayana Buddhism (see 2.1[12]), pp. 294-307.

Somewhat dated but helpful introduction to the meaning of Bodhicitta (which Suzuki translates as "intelligence-heart") in Mahayana Buddhism, most especially in the thought of Nagarjuna and Sthiramati.

2.8 BUDDHIST THOUGHT AND THE MODERN WORLD (INCLUDING: BUDDHISM AND SCIENCE, BUDDHISM AND COMMUNISM, ETC.)

(1) BENZ, ERNST. Buddhism or Communism: Which Holds the Future of Asia? Translated by Richard and Clara Winston. Garden City, N.Y.: Doubleday, 1966, 185 pp. (Paperback edition: Anchor Books, A515.)

A lively though not terribly profound discussion which introduces the reader to the revival of Buddhism in India, Ceylon, and Burma, and to such topics as "Ecumenical Buddhism," "Social and Political Teachings of Buddhism," "Buddhism and Modern Science," and "The Buddhist Critique of Communism."

(2) BUDDHADASA, BHIKKHU. Toward the Truth. Edited by Donald K. Swearer. Philadelphia: Westminster Press, 1971, 189 pp.

Buddhadasa, considered by some to be the foremost thinker in modern Thai Buddhism, explains his interpretation of the Buddha-Dharma as a practical system, open to all. As an interpreter of Buddhism, Buddhadasa has particular appeal in his ability to relate the ancient truths of Buddhism to modern man's experience.

(3) CH'EN, KENNETH KUAN SHENG. Buddhism: The Light of Asia (see 1.1[1]), pp. 268-282.

The chapter is entitled "Buddhism in the Modern World" and makes a fine short introduction to the topics of "Buddhism and Communism," "Buddhism and Science," "Buddhism and Race," and "Buddhism and War and Peace."

(4) DE SILVA, S. P. A Scientific Rationalization of Buddhism. Colombo: Metro Printers, 1969, 187 pp.

This is one example among several attempts by contemporary Buddhists to exalt the teachings of Buddhism as being in complete accord with the message of modern science. Its conclusion: "Buddhism stands unique in that not a single facet of its teaching can be disproved or even rationally doubted. Unless somewhat fanatical or languidly complacent, few persons can embrace any other religious system."

(5) DHARMAPALA, ANAGARIKA. Return to Righteousness: A Collection of Speeches, Essays and Letters. See 1.3.2.2(3). Ministry of Education and Cultural Affairs, 1965, 875 pp.

Collected works of the founder of the Mahabodhi Society.

(6) DUMOULIN, HEINRICH. Buddhism in the Modern World. See 1.1(3).

(7) FROMM, ERICH. "Psychoanalysis and Zen." Psychologia, 3, no. 2 (June 1960), 79-99.

Compares and contrasts the use of Zen meditation and psychoanalysis.

(8) GURUGE, ANANDA W. P. Facets of Buddhism. Colombo: Swabhasha Prakashakayo, 1967, 132 pp.

A set of essays on such topics as "Buddhism in the Modern World," "Buddhism and Other Religions," ("The Future of Buddhism"), "Toward World Buddhism," etc.

(9) HIRAI, TOMIO. Psychophysiology of Zen. Tokyo: Igaku Shoin, 1974, 147 pp.

A treatment of Zen in terms of its psychosomatic effects as measured by pulse rate, brain waves, etc.

(10) JATAVA, D. R. The Buddha and Karl Marx. Agra: Phoenix Publishing House, 1968, 236 pp.

Heavily influenced by the thought of Ambedkar and taking an apologetic stance, the author fundamentally interprets Buddhism as the doctrine of "dynamic realism." By interpreting Buddhism in this way, the author makes the claim that Buddhism is not only spiritualistic, but materialistic as well. He sets out to make comparisons on this basis to the thought of Karl Marx.

(11) JAYATILLEKE, KULATISSA NANDA. Buddhist Attitude to Other Religions. Dona Alphina Ratnayake Trust Lecture, No. 12. Colombo: Public Trustee Department, 1966, 27 pp.

The thesis of this short essay is that the outlook of Buddhism towards other religions is one of "critical tolerance." The author believes that this outlook allowed Buddhism to combine missionary zeal with a tolerance which contributed heavily toward its successful spread.

(12) _____. "Buddhist Relativity and the One-World Concept," in Religious Pluralism and the World Community: Interfaith and Intercultural Communication. Edited by Edward Jabra Jurji. Studies in the history of religions, No. 15. Leiden: E. J. Brill, 1969, pp. 43-78.

This broadly conceived article discusses the manner in which Buddhism can contribute to a world of religious pluralism by providing a model for a moral order. This can be achieved, the author contends, through a proper understanding of the Buddhist notion of relativity, which he then attempts to explain.

(13) JAYEWARDENE, JUNIUS RICHARD. Buddhism and Marxism, and Other Buddhist Essays. Third edition. London: East and West, 1957, pp. 1-14.

(14) KING, WINSTON LEE. A Thousand Lives Away: Buddhism in Contemporary Burma. Cambridge, Mass.: Harvard University Press, 1964, pp. 114-46.

The chapter is entitled "Theravada Buddhism Encounters Science" and represents an excellent introduction to the topic, based primarily on Burmese materials.

(15) LING, TREVOR. Buddha, Marx, and God. New York: St. Martin's Press, 1966, Part 3, "Marxism and Religion," pp. 87-172.

In this section of Ling's book, the author reviews the historical encounters between Buddhism and Marxism in Southeast Asia, the Soviet Union, and China, sketches the Marxist critique of Buddhism, raises the question of whether Marxism is itself a religion, and notes the possibilities for the coexistence of Buddhism and Marxism. Overall, a good introduction to the topic.

(16) SANKRITYAYAN, RAHUL et al. Buddhism: The Marxist Approach. Delhi: People's Publishing House, 1970, 86 pp.

A series of articles by a number of Indian scholars concerned with Buddhist-Marxist dialogue. The articles touch on early Buddhist doctrine, Buddhist dialectics, Buddhist Art, etc., in order to point to a number of parallels and contrasts between the two ideologies.

(17) STORY, FRANCIS. The Case for Rebirth. The Wheel Publications, Nos. 12, 13. Kandy, Ceylon: Buddhist Publication Society, 1959, 70 pp.

In some circles, the impact of Western science has made the doctrines of karma and rebirth seem stumbling blocks. This, in turn, has resulted in numerous writings by "Modern Buddhists" which aim at showing how karma and rebirth are really compatible and verifiable by science. This pamphlet by Francis Story (Anagarika Sugatananda) is one of the better examples of this. A short summary of the argument may be found in Winston Lee King's A Thousand Lives Away (above).

(18) SWEARER, DONALD K. Buddhism in Transition. Philadelphia: Westminster Press, 1970, pp. 95-120.

Swearer singles out two important Thai Buddhists for a discussion of the direction of modern Asian Buddhism and an attempt to answer the question of "resurgence or reformation?" He presents the works and views of, first, Phra Maha Sila, an educational administrator, combining traditional and modern aspects of the Sangha, and, second, of Buddhadasa Bhikkhu, whom Swearer considers the most significant thinker within contemporary Thai Buddhism and a genuine innovator.

(19) VIJAYAVARDHANA, D. C. The Revolt in the Temple, Composed to Commemorate 2500 Years of the Land, the Race and the Faith. See 1.3.2.2(7).

(20) WELCH, HOLMES. Buddhism under Mao (see 1.11.2.4[5]), pp. 267-297.

The chapter is entitled "Interpreting Buddhist Doctrine" and contains an informative though not very sympathetic account of some of the ways in which Chinese Socialist Buddhists have sought to look at Buddhist teachings in a new light.

(21) WETTIMUNY, R. G. DE S. Buddhism and Its Relation to Religion and Science. Colombo: M. D. Gunasena, 1962, 380 pp.

This book by a Ceylonese Buddhist takes a middle ground in the contemporary debate among Buddhist intellectuals about the relationship of their religion to science. The thesis here is that Buddhism goes both between and beyond religious dogma and Western scientism.

(22) WICKRAMASINGHE, MARTIN. Buddhism and Culture. Dehiwala, Ceylon: Tissar Poth Prakasakayo, 1964, 202 pp.

This book presents a contemporary Ceylonese Buddhist's argument against the views of some of his fellow intellectuals that "Buddhism is a scientific religion." The following quote (p. 8) tells most of the story: "Most of our educated Buddhists and monks who succumbed to the glamour of Anglican and Brahminical rationalism accepted rational interpretation of their religion. The Buddha rejected reason definitely in relation to the truth of religion. Truth of religion is to be experienced by intuition."

2.8.1 Buddhist Periodicals

One of the ways of approaching the range and scope of modern Buddhist thought is in the pages of the numerous publications (journals, newspapers, annuals) of Buddhist groups around the world. Generally speaking, the articles they contain vary widely in quality and may or may not treat upon contemporary issues and concerns. The following list is in no way complete and includes periodicals which may or may not have ceased publication. (For a list which includes scholarly publications, see category 12.)

(1) Buddhist India:--A Fortnightly Gazette. Calcutta, 1928-1935.

(2) Cat's Yawn. New York: First Zen Institute of America, 13 issues, July 1940-July 1941.

(3) Kalpa: Journal of the Cambridge University Buddhist Society. St. John's College, Cambridge, England, 1962- .

(4) The Light of the Dhamma. Rangoon: Union of Burma Buddha Sasana Council, 1952- .

(5) The Light of Dharma (quarterly). The Buddhist Mission, San Francisco, Calif., 1901-1907.

(6) The Maha Bodhi:--International Buddhist Monthly. Founded by Anagarika Dharmapala. Colombo (now published in Calcutta) Mahabodhi Society, 1892- .

(7) The Middle Way:--Journal of the Buddhist Society. London, 1925- .

(8) La Pensée Bouddhique:--Bulletin des Amis du Bouddhisme. Paris, 1939-1942, 1944- .

(9) Samadhi: Cahiers d'Etudes Bouddhiques. Brussels: Institut Belge des Hautes Etudes Bouddhiques, Centre d'Etudes Bouddhiques Ananda, 1966- .

(10) Visakhapuja: An Organ for Dissemination of the Buddha's Teaching (annual). Bangkok: Buddhist Association of Thailand, 1950- .

(11) The Wheel. Kandy, Ceylon: Buddhist Publication Society, 1958- . Also called Wheel Publication.

(12) World Buddhism: The International Buddhist Newsmagazine (monthly). Colombo, Ceylon: 1952- . Also publishes the World Buddhism Vesak Annual, Dehiwela, Ceylon.

(13) Young East: Japanese Buddhist Quarterly. Tokyo, first edited by Junjiro Takakusu, 1925-1930, 1934-1941, n.s. 1952- .

2.9 THE WEST AND BUDDHIST THOUGHT (INCLUDING: CHRISTIANITY AND BUDDHISM, PSYCHIATRY AND BUDDHISM, ETC.)

See also 1.17.

(1) ABE, MASAO. "Zen and Nietzsche." The Eastern Buddhist, 6, no. 2 (October 1973), 14-32.

An attempt to understand Nietzsche's statement that "God is a lie," the problem of death in Nietzschean thought, and the "will to power," in the Zen perspective.

(2) AMES, VAN METER. *Zen and American Thought*. Honolulu: University of Hawaii Press, 1962, 293 pp.

Ames claims one does not have to go East to find Zen, but only has to discover it in Tom Paine, in the Boston Tea Party, in Jefferson (who "had the sense of oneness with land and man that Zen teaches"), in Emerson ("an American bodhisattva"), in the Taoist Thoreau, in Whitman, etc. A more insightful attempt to do the same with English thought is Reginald H. Blyth's *Zen in English Literature and Oriental Classics* (below).

(3) BARBORKA, GEOFFREY A. *H. P. Blavatsky, Tibet and Tulku*. Adyar: Theosophical Publishing House, 1966.

Among the various uncritical, theosophical biographies of Blavatsky, this one has the advantage of concentrating on the alleged relationship between her and esoteric Tibetan Buddhism.

(4) BERRY, THOMAS STERLING. *Christianity and Buddhism: A Comparison and a Contrast*. Donnellan lectures, 1889-1890. London: Society for Promoting Christian Knowledge, 1891, 256 pp.

There exists a host of books, largely by Christian missionaries, which seeks to compare and contrast Buddhism with Christianity. The quality of these varies greatly. Among others that might be mentioned are the following: Joseph Estlin Carpenter, *Buddhism and Christianity: A Contrast and a Parallel* (New York: G. Doran, 1923); Archibald Scott, *Buddhism and Christianity: A Parallel and a Contrast* (Edinburgh: Douglas, 1890); Bryan de Kretser, *Man in Buddhism and Christianity* (Calcutta: YMCA Publishing House, 1954); and S. Kellogg, *The Light of Asia and the Light of the World* (London: Macmillan, 1895).

(5) BLYTH, REGINALD HORACE. *Zen in English Literature and Oriental Classics*. New York: E. P. Dutton, 1960, 446 pp. (Paperback edition: Everyman, D57.)

A misleading title. Blyth demonstrates the obvious--that the writings of Wordsworth, Shelley, Cervantes (!), etc. have less Zen than some Japanese and Chinese poetry. Interesting only because of Blyth's expertise in Eastern literature and his unusual approach to Zen.

(6) BREAR, DOUGLAS. "Early Assumptions in Western Buddhist Studies." *Religion: A Journal of Religion and Religions*, 5, pt. 2 (Autumn 1975), 136-159.

A substantial discussion which gives an interesting overview of the "image" of Buddhism generated by the earliest Western Buddhologists.

(7) CARPENTER, FREDERIC IVES. *Emerson and Asia*. Cambridge, Mass.: Harvard University Press, 1930, pp. 146-150.

Emerson's comparative incomprehension of Buddhism, "the one Indian doctrine to which he ever expressed a decided aversion," is examined by Carpenter, who does not seem to understand it much better than Emerson did.

(8) CHARTERS, ANN. *Kerouac: A Biography*. See 1.17(2).

An important source for the study of "beat" Buddhism of the 1950s.

(9) CHRISTY, ARTHUR. *The Orient in American Transcendentalism: A Study of Emerson, Thoreau, and Alcott*. See 1.17(3).

A pioneer work, the highlight of which is ten pages on the reception of Arnold's *The Light of Asia* in America.

(10) CONZE, EDWARD. "Buddhist Philosophy and Its European Parallels." *Philosophy East and West*, 13 (1963), 9-23.

Conze begins his article with an interpretation of what he considers to be the primary existential tenets of Buddhism. He follows this discussion with the assertion that a "perennial philosophy" kept both Eastern and Western philosophical traditions in relative concert until around 1450. Having made this assertion, Conze contends that the "perennial philosophy" as it was articulated in India was marked by the two specific features of yoga and karma. Thus, he goes on to discuss parallels to these features as they have appeared in Greek skepticism, Western ascetic and mystical thinkers such as Meister Eckhart and Schopenhauer.

(11) _____. "Buddhist Prajna and Greek Sophia." *Religion: A Journal of Religion and Religions*, 5, pt. 2 (Autumn 1975), 160-167.

This article compares the notions of "Wisdom" in the Buddhist and Greek traditions. It extends the discussion in the similarly titled chapter in his *Thirty Years of Buddhist Studies* (below); but still only skims the surface of the topic.

(12) _____. *Thirty Years of Buddhist Studies: Selected Essays* (see 2.5.1[5]), pp. 210-242.

Two essays which outline the real and false parallels to Buddhism in Western Philosophy. After providing an exemplary comparativist study of the Mediterranean Sophia and the Mahayana Prajnaparamita, Conze goes on to deal with the spurious or only partial parallels such as Kant, Bergson, the Existentialists, David Hume, etc., and the more recent misunderstandings of the Beat and post-Beat generations.

(13) DAUER, DOROTHEA W. *Schopenhauer as Transmitter of Buddhist Ideas*. European University papers. Series 1: German language and literature, No. 15. Berne: Lang, 1969, 39 pp.

This essay is aimed at comparing Schopenhauer's thought to the primary concepts elucidated by Gautama. The author compares such topics as the soul, time, atheism, and ethics, all within the context of Gautama's four noble truths. As all of the quotes attributed to Schopenhauer have not been translated, the reader will need facility with German before tackling this essay.

(14) EDMUNDS, ALBERT JOSEPH. Buddhist and Christian Gospels, Now First Compared from the Originals. Fourth edition. Philadelphia: Innes, 1908-1909; London: Luzac, 1906, 2 vols.
A substantial attempt to compile a "Gospel parallel" with texts chosen from the Bible and the Pali Tipitaka (by Edmunds) and from the Chinese Tripitaka (by Anesaki). In the same vein, but shorter, is Karl von Hase, New Testament Parallels in Buddhistic Literature (New York: Eaton and Mains, 1907).

(15) ELLWOOD, ROBERT S. "Percival Lowell's Journey to the East." Sewanee Review, 78 (1970), 285-309.
A study of the growth of Lowell's thought under the impact of Buddhism and Japanese culture.

(16) Eminent Orientalists, Indian, European, American. See 1.17(4).
Brief biographies of twenty-five orientalists, nine of them Buddhologists.

(17) FOX, DOUGLAS A. "Soteriology in Jodo Shin and Christianity." Contemporary Religions in Japan, 9, nos. 1-2 (March-June 1967), 30-51.
A discussion of leading Jodo Shin soteriological concepts and then an attempt to show their uniqueness as well as their evident correspondences with comparable Christian ideas.

(18) FROMM, ERICH, ed. Zen Buddhism and Psychoanalysis. New York: Grove Press, 1963, 180 pp. (Paperback edition: Evergreen Books.)
Essays by the three authors (Fromm, Richard De Martino, and D. T. Suzuki) which attempt to place Zen in the Western context of psychotherapy and its goals. Of interest primarily to the student of psychology, but also useful as a general introduction. Fromm and De Martino, however, are already understanding Zen through Suzuki's eyes, and all three sometimes allow distortion of Zen principles to fit Western categories.

(19) GLASENAPP, HELMUTH. Buddhism and Christianity. The Wheel Publication, No. 16. Kandy, Ceylon: Buddhist Publication Society, 1963, 42 pp.
Short essay retrieved from two articles first published in German in 1949 and 1950 in which the author reviews general parallels between Buddhism and Christianity with regard to the human condition and salvation.

(20) GODDARD, DWIGHT. Was Jesus Influenced by Buddhism? A Comparative Study of the Lives and Thoughts of Gautama and Jesus. Thetford, Vt., 1927, 249 pp.
One of the concerns (especially of the older scholarship) dealing with the topic of Christianity and Buddhism has been the question of the influence of the latter on the former. At least in this work by Goddard, the question mark remains. Other books on this subject include Arthur Lillie, The Influence of Buddhism on Primitive Christianity (New York: Scribner, 1893); and Charles Francis Aiken, The Dhamma of Gotama the Buddha and the Gospel of Jesus the Christ (Boston: Marlier, 1900). For perhaps the most extreme work along this line, which argues that the Synoptic Gospels were a transparent attempt to attach "the highest teaching of Buddha with the crudest religious idea of the Old Testament" and that "Jesus" = "Jushu" = "Jishnu"--one of the names of the Buddha, see Swami Sankarananda, The Western Buddhism of Christianity (Calcutta: N. Maharaj, 1956).

(21) HEARN, LAFCADIO. Gleanings in Buddha-Fields. Boston, New York: Houghton, Mifflin, 1897, 296 pp.
One of Hearn's most popular books. His Vedantist interpretation of Nirvana in the chapter by that name (which took him over three years to write) is a classic among Western popularizations of Buddhism.

(22) _____. Japan: An Attempt at Interpretation. New York: Macmillan, 1904, 541 pp.
Hearn's chapter, "The Higher Buddhism," is his most mature attempt to relate Buddhism to Herbert Spencer and evolution. An influential and popular book.

(23) _____. Oriental Articles. Edited by Ichiro Nishizaki. Tokyo: Hokuseido Press, 1950, 260 pp. (Originally published 1939.)
These articles (all from the 1880s) include a number of journalistic accounts of Buddhism, the most interesting of which derides the Ceylonese sage Sumangala. A short article on anti-Buddhist Christian hysteria is also entertaining.

(24) INADA, KENNETH. "Whitehead's 'Actual Entity' and the Buddha's Anatman." Philosophy East and West, 21 (1971), 303-316.
A well done effort in which the author first focuses upon Whitehead's concept of "actual entity" and then upon the Buddha's notion of "anatman." The author actually constructs a lively dialogue in his final section when he specifically compares the two conceptions.

(25) JACKSON, CARL T. "The Orient in Post-Bellum American Thought: Three Pioneer Popularizers." American Quarterly, 22 (Spring 1970), 67-81.
A study of the works on oriental religion by James Freeman Clarke, Samuel Johnson, and Moncure Conway.

(26) JONG, JAN WILLEM DE. "A Brief History of Buddhist Studies in Europe and America." See 1.17(8).

This excellent summary of Buddhology is continued by de Jong in the following issue of The Eastern Buddhist (October 1974), pp. 49-82. It is sufficiently detailed to serve not only as a history but as an annotated bibliography of principal works of Western Buddhist scholarship.

(27) KEROUAC, JACK. The Dharma Bums. See 1.17(9).

Thinly fictionalized account of Kerouac's participation in West-Coast "beat" Buddhism with portraits of Gary Snyder, Kenneth Rexroth, Allen Ginsberg, et al.

(28) KING, WINSTON LEE. Buddhism and Christianity: Some Bridges to Understanding. Philadelphia: Westminster Press, 1962, 240 pp.

This book takes seriously the difficulties of dialogue, and is a well-informed attempt to discuss together topics such as "Love: Christian and Buddhist," "Christian Guilt and Buddhist Dukkha," "Christian Prayer and Buddhist Meditation," etc. Helpful as an introduction.

(29) LACH, DONALD FREDERICK. Asia in the Making of Europe. See 1.17(11).

Frequent references to Western contacts with Buddhism, particularly by Jesuit missionaries. Indispensable history of East-West relations in the sixteenth century.

(30) LANCASHIRE, DOUGLAS. "Buddhist Reaction to Christianity in Late Ming China." Journal of the Oriental Society of Australia, 6 (1968-1969), 82-103.

The author reviews the response of Chinese Buddhists to the missionary propagations and doctrinal attacks of Matteo Ricci. Specifically, the responses attempt to refute Ricci's allegations that the doctrine of void was absurd, that the Buddhist concepts of Heaven and Hell were distorted versions of the Christian concepts, that metempsychosis originally springs from the thought of Pythagoras, and that animals can be legitimately killed because they were made as part of the dominion of man.

(31) LOWELL, PERCIVAL. The Soul of the Far East. New York: Houghton, Mifflin, 1888, 226 pp.

"Nirvana . . . has wrapped Far Eastern Asia in its winding sheet." Comparison between the supposedly decadent, selfless, and unimaginative East and the progressive West by a noted linguist and astronomer who later predicted the discovery of the planet Pluto.

(32) LUBAC, HENRI DE. La Rencontre du Bouddhisme et de l'Occident. Théologie, No. 24. Paris: Aubier, 1952, 285 pp.

A straightforward historical survey of the contacts of the West (i.e., Christianity) and Buddhism from antiquity up to the present, concluding with a useful survey chapter entitled "Le Bouddhisme et la pensée européenne." Helpful to supplement Guy Welbon's The Buddhist Nirvana and Its Western Interpreters (below).

(33) MERTON, THOMAS. Mystics and Zen Masters. New York: Farrar, Strauss and Giroux, 1967, 303 pp.

Father Thomas Merton was a renowned Catholic contemplative who sought to build bridges of understanding between Christian meditation and prayer and Buddhist (especially Zen) meditation. All of his works are written in a personal line. See also his posthumously published diary, The Asian Journal of Thomas Merton (New York: New Directions, 1973). But Merton has not been the only Catholic contemplative to write on these matters. Among the others, see Dom Aelred Graham, Conversations: Christian and Buddhist (New York: Harcourt, Brace & World, 1968); William Johnston, Christian Zen (New York: Harper and Row, 1971); and H. M. Enomiya Lassalle, Zen Meditation for Christians (Lasalle, Ill.: Open Court, 1974).

(34) Philosophy East and West, 25, no. 4 (October 1975), entire issue.

Six well-done pieces comparing the philosophical notions of A. N. Whitehead with those of Buddhist thought appear in the same issue of Philosophy East and West. These papers, originally presented at a Honolulu conference on the subject held in October 1974, include: Jay McDaniel and John B. Cobb, Jr., "Introduction: Conference on Mahayana Buddhism and Whitehead," pp. 393-406; Charles Hartshorne, "Whitehead's Differences from Buddhism," pp. 407-414; Masao Abe, "Mahayana Buddhism and Whitehead: A View by a Lay Student of Whitehead's Philosophy," pp. 415-428; Frederick Streng, "Metaphysics, Negative Dialectic, and the Expression of the Inexpressible," pp. 429-448; Robert F. Olson, "Whitehead, Madhyamika, and the Prajnaparamita," pp. 449-464; and Kenneth Inada, "The Metaphysics of the Buddhist Experience and the Whiteheadian Encounter," pp. 465-488. In addition to these articles, see also John Cobb, Jr. and Ryusei Takeda, "'Mosa-Dharma' and Prehension: Nagarjuna and Whitehead Compared," Process Studies, 4, no. 1 (Spring 1974), 26-36; and Thomas J. J. Altizer, "The Buddhist Ground of the Whiteheadian God," Process Studies, 5, no. 4 (Winter 1975).

(35) RAY, REGINALD. "Demystifying Demystification," Shambala Review of Books and Ideas, 4, nos. 1-2 (Winter 1976), 48-49.

This article uses the occasion of a review of Crystal Mirror 4 to raise the question of the extent to which Western psychological models are adequate for interpreting Tibetan Buddhism. The author concludes that such models have their value in "demystifying" the Tibetan Tantra, but that they are of little value and, if used too rigorously, distort a tradition that in many ways is alien to Western psychological modes of thought.

(36) SAIGUSA, MITSUYOSHI. "Henri Bergson and Buddhist Thought." Philosophical Studies of Japan, 9 (1969), 79-101.

This essay is concerned with Bergson's direct references to Buddhism and the accuracy of his understanding of Buddhist thought in regard to perception, memory, etc.

(37) SAUNDERS, KENNETH JAMES. Buddhist Ideals: A Study in Comparative Religion. Madras: Christian Literature Society for India, 1912, 179 pp.

The search for parallels between Buddhism and Christianity has been one avenue of approach of scholars who are sympathetic to both religions and who do not want to argue for the influence or superiority of one or the other. Saunders' work contains comparisons of the biographies of the Buddha and Christ, of Asoka and St. Paul and discussions of Hope and Faith, and Metta and Christian Love. Other works which point to Christian-Buddhist parallels include chapter four of Thomas J. J. Altizer, Oriental Mysticism and Biblical Eschatology (Philadelphia: Westminster Press, 1961), pp. 113-15; and, from a Japanese point of view, Fumio Masutani, A Comparative Study of Buddhism and Christianity (4th edition. Tokyo: CIIB Press, 1965). Arthur Osborne, Buddhism and Christianity in the Light of Hinduism (London: Rider, 1959) argues that the two are complementary religions.

(38) SCHWAB, RAYMOND. La Renaissance Orientale. Bibliothèque Historique. Paris: Payot, 1950, 526 pp.

History of nineteenth century orientalism including an interesting examination of Buddhist influence on French literature.

(39) SINGH, BHUPAL. A Survey of Anglo-Indian Fiction. London: Oxford University Press, 1934, 344 pp.

A good starting point for a study of Theravada Buddhism in English-language fiction. A twenty-six page bibliography of Anglo-Indian fiction to 1932 is included.

(40) SUZUKI, DAISETZ TEITARO. Mysticism: Christian and Buddhist. The Eastern and Western Way. New York: Harper and Row, 1971, 240 pp. (Originally published 1957; paperback edition: Perennial Library, P218.)

A useful attempt to make East-West comparisons of Zen and Buddhist thought with the mysticism of Meister Eckhardt.

(41) UMEHARA, RAKESHI. "Heidegger and Buddhism." Philosophy East and West, 20 (1970), 271-281.

This article directly discusses the notion of "being" as it was articulated by Gautama and then Dogen. The author continues by comparing these notions to Heidegger. This entire edition of Philosophy East and West is devoted to a variety of comparisons between Buddhist thought and Heidegger. If the reader is interested in the topic, he may benefit from some of the other articles.

(42) WATTS, ALAN WILSON. In My Own Way: An Autobiography, 1915-1965. See 1.17(16).

Christmas and Aileen Humphreys, Ruth Fuller and Sokei-an Sasaki, Gary Snyder, C. G. Jung, and Aldous Huxley are some of the more prominent characters in Watts' autobiographical kaleidoscope of world Zen.

(43) WELBON, GUY RICHARD. The Buddhist Nirvana and Its Western Interpreters. Chicago: University of Chicago Press, 1968, 320 pp. See also 11.8(15).

(44) WILKINSON, WILLIAM CLEAVER. Edwin Arnold as Poetizer and as Paganizer. New York: Funk and Wagnalls, 1884, 177 pp.

Wilkinson, a Baptist Minister and Professor at the University of Chicago, compares Arnold's The Light of Asia with more scholarly books on the life of the Buddha, derides Buddhism and ridicules Arnold's verse.

(45) WILLIAMS, GERTRUDE LEAVENWORTH. Priestess of the Occult, Madame Blavatsky. New York: A. A. Knopf, 1946, 345 pp.

A non-Theosophical biography of Blavatsky. More concerned with exposing her impostures than with examining her attitude toward Buddhism.

3 Authoritative Texts

3.1 DESCRIPTIVE SURVEYS

3.1.1 Buddhist Texts as a Whole

(1) BAREAU, ANDRE. Les Religions de l'Inde (see 1.2.1[3]), pp. 30-40, 93-106. 150-168, 203-206.

Bareau has divided his overall study of Buddhism in India into four "periods," original Buddhism, ancient Buddhism, Mahayana, and Tantrism. In each of these periods, he devotes one section to "Littérature." Taken together, these sections make a handy descriptive survey of Buddhists texts--at least those composed in India.

(2) BEAUTRIX, PIERRE. Bibliographie du Bouddhisme. Volume 1: Editions de Textes. Publications de l'Institut Belge des Hautes Etudes Bouddhiques. Série "Bibliographies," No. 2. Bruxelles: Institut Belge des Hautes Etudes Bouddhiques, 1970, 206 pp.

Probably the most complete listing of editions of Buddhist texts in all the various languages. However, it does not include translations (a second volume with translations listed is supposed to appear). It does add, however, various lists of catalogues of books and manuscripts, with separate listings for catalogs of manuscripts in Chinese, Manchu, Mongolian, Pali, Sanskrit, Thai, Tibetan, and of the Tun Huang finds.

(3) FILLIOZAT, JEAN and PAUL DEMIEVILLE. "Le Bouddhisme, 1. Les Sources," in L'Inde Classique. Edited by Louis Renou and Jean Filliozat. 2 vols. Paris: Payot and Ecole Française d'Extrême-Orient, 1947, 1953, vol. 2, pp. 324-463.

Most of the second volume of this classic work concerns Buddhist literature, and represents an authoritative and systematic survey of both the Pali and Sanskrit Buddhist material. Though portions of it could be updated (for example the section on Tantra), it is by no means outdated, and remains valuable both as an introduction and as a reference work. As the focus is on Indian Buddhist literature, the Tibetan and Chinese texts are treated only complementally. Some attempt is also made to place the Buddhist material, literally and historically, in the context of the whole of Indian literature.

3.1.2 Pali Texts

(1) BODE, MABEL HAYNES. The Pali Literature of Burma. London: Royal Asiatic Society of Great Britain and Ireland, 1966, 119 pp. (First published in 1909.)

Bode presents a concise and technical survey of the Pali literature of Burma, covering both the early and the modern periods (twelfth to nineteenth centuries). She also discusses the introduction of the Tipitaka into Burma and the rise of Pali scholarship in Upper Burma.

(2) COEDES, GEORGES. "Note sur les Ouvrages Palis Composés en Pays Thai." Bulletin de l'Ecole française d'Extrême-Orient, 15 (1915), 39-46.

This is a short but handy survey of the Pali works written in Thailand. Included are: some fifteenth century grammatical sub-commentaries on Buddhaghosa's works, a short life of the Buddha, Dhammakitti's Saddhamasangaha (a history of Buddhist councils), Ratanapanna's Jinakalamalini (1516?), and Vimaladhamma's Sangitivamsa (1789) (both histories of Buddhism, especially in Siam), and most noteworthy perhaps, Sirimangala's Mangaladipani (1524), which is an important commentary on the Kangalasutta.

(3) GEIGER, WILHELM. Pali Literature and Language. Translated by Batakrishna Ghosh. Second edition. Delhi: Oriental Books Reprint Corp., 1943, Part 1, pp. 8-58.

The value of this masterful survey lies in its conciseness. In the space of fifty pages, the whole of Pali literature, both canonical and non-canonical, is "covered." This makes it good as an introduction and even better as a review. The student interested in more details should either consult the more comprehensive works of Winternitz, Law, and Malalasekera, or the texts themselves.

(4) JAYAWICKRAMA, N. A. "Buddhaghosa and the Traditional Classifications of the Pali Canon." University of Ceylon Review, 17 (1959), 1-17.

Short discussion of the various systems of classification of the texts implicit in the canon itself and of the difficulties in making comparisons between them.

Descriptive Surveys

(5) LAFONT, PIERRE-BERNARD. "Les écritures du Pali au Laos." Bulletin de l'Ecole française d'Extrême-Orient (1962), pp. 395-405.

A short but adequate survey of the history and use of Pali literature by the Laotian Buddhist community.

(6) LAW, BIMALA CHURN. A History of Pali Literature. London: K. Paul, Trench, Trubner, 1933, 2 vols.

Volume one is a very useful reference work, the bulk of which consists of fairly detailed purely descriptive summaries of the whole Pali Canon, basket by basket, and book by book. Not to be neglected, however, are the introduction (which contains a discussion of the history of the Pali language), and Chapter 1, in which Law presents his own relative chronology for the Canonical books. In this regard see also Law's "Chronology of the Pali Canon," Annals of the Bhandarkar Oriental Research Institute, 12 (1931), 171-201. Volume two attempts to give a work-by-work descriptive analysis of all non-canonical Pali literature. The largest section is devoted to the commentaries of Buddhadatta, Buddhaghosa, and Dhammapala, but other chapters deal with the Milindapanna, the Ceylonese chronicles, and various grammars, manuals, literary pieces, etc. Most useful, of course, are the summaries of those texts which have not been translated.

(7) MALALASEKERA, GEORGE PEIRIS. The Pali Literature of Ceylon. London: Royal Asiatic Society of Great Britain and Ireland, 1928, 329 pp.

This book covers the entire history of the Pali literature composed in Ceylon (commentaries, chronicles, etc.). Thus it does not have to deal directly with the Tipitaka, the Milindapanna, etc. This allows it to have a direction, unity and focus which make it not only a descriptive analysis of Ceylonese Pali literature, but a valuable literary history of Ceylonese Buddhism itself. The work is a classic and a must for any student interested in either of these two fields.

(8) SADDHATISSA, H. "Pali Literature of Thailand," in Buddhist Studies in Honour of I. B. Horner (see 1.2.2.4[11]), pp. 211-225.

A very handy review of all known original Pali compositions in Thailand which are listed and discussed in the chronological order of their composition. Updates the work on the same subject by Coedes (above).

3.1.3 Sanskrit Texts

(1) BANERJEE, ANUKUL CHANDRA. Sarvastivada Literature. See 2.4.3(1).

A useful survey of the Sanskrit works (and their translations thereof) of this important school. The book is in two parts--the first reviews what is known about Sarvastivada literature in general: the agamas, the Vinaya, and the Abhidharma; the second part contains a detailed study of a part of the Sarvastivada Vinaya, the Vinayavastu.

(2) BROUGH, JOHN. "The Language of the Buddhist Sanskrit Texts." Bulletin of the School of Oriental and African Studies (1954), pp. 351-375.

This is a technical article in which the author reviews the contributions of Franklin Edgerton and suggests that Buddhist Sanskrit not be modified to conform to classical Sanskrit; but that instead Buddhist Sanskrit ought to be reckoned with in its own right.

(3) CUENDET, GEORGES. "Textes sanscrits bouddhiques d'Asie centrale." Bulletin de la Société suisse des Amis de l'Extrême-Orient, 2 (1940), 35-41.

A very short but interesting article on the discovery and meaning of the Buddhist Sanskrit texts that were being found in Central Asia. See also Pavel Poucha, "Indian Literature in Central Asia," Archív Orientální (Prague), 2 (1930), 27-38.

(4) FILLIOZAT, JEAN. "Le Bouddhisme, 1. Les Sources," in L'Inde Classique (see 1.2.2.1[11]), vol. 2, pp. 361-388.

Excellent descriptive survey of the whole of Sanskrit Buddhist literature with summaries of specific texts. More up-to-date than Winternitz's History of Indian Literature (see 3.1.1[5]), which, however, is in English.

(5) MITRA, RAJENDRALALA. The Sanskrit Buddhist Literature of Nepal. Calcutta: Asiatic Society of Bengal, 1882, 340 pp.

A descriptive analysis of the finds of Buddhist texts made by Brian Hodgson. These texts formed the basis of Eugène Burnouf's classic Introduction à l'Histoire du Bouddhisme Indien (2nd edition Paris: Maisonneuve, 1876), 586 pp., which contains on pages 29-254 a massive "Description de la Collection des Livres du Nepal," including translations of passages of many of them.

3.1.4 Tibetan Texts

(1) BADARAEV, BAL-DORZHI. "Notes on a List of the Various Editions of the Kanjur." Acta Orientalia, B (1968), 339-351.

This article contains a manuscript anonymously authored and translated by Badaraev. The significance of this manuscript "lies in the fact that it contributes to the comparative examination of the structural components of the Kanjur in the various editions, each of them providing something new as compared to the previous one."

(2) BANERJEE, ANUKUL CHANDRA. "Abhidharma Texts in Tibetan." Indian Historical Quarterly, 28 (1952), 372-378.

The author begins his article with a brief, general description of Abhidharma texts and

3.1.4 Descriptive Surveys

then provides a listing of Abhidharma texts found in Tibetan. Brief annotations accompany the listings.

(3) BELL, CHARLES ALFRED. The Religion of Tibet (see 1.14.1[1]), pp. 193-218.

In the section entitled "Sources," Bell presents a good first introductory survey to the religious literature found in Tibet.

(4) CH'EN, KENNETH K. S. "The Tibetan Tripitaka." Harvard Journal of Asiatic Studies, 9 (1946), 53-62.

Translation of an article by the Japanese scholar Mochizuki, with extensive annotations added by Ch'en. It forms a convenient survey and study of the various editions of the Kanjur and Tanjur, including notes on their present locations. For a review of the article and some complementary information, see Giuseppe Tucci, "The Tibetan Tripitaka," Harvard Journal of Asiatic Studies, 12 (1949), 477-481.

(5) CSOMA, SANDOR [ALEXANDER]. "Analyse du Kandjour: Recueil des Livre Sacres au Tibet." Translated and annotated by Leon Feer. Annales du Musée Guimet, 2 (1881), 131-555.

An extremely useful descriptive analysis of the Tibetan Bka' 'gyur, its divisions, and major texts. The work was translated into French from the original English by Leon Feer, but that English edition is not widely available and is missing Feer's helpful annotations and additions.

(6) FILLIOZAT, JEAN. "Le Bouddhisme: 1. Les Sources," in L'Inde Classique (see 3.1.3[4]), vol. 2, pp. 388-397.

A concise descriptive survey, not of the whole of Tibetan religious literature, but of those texts which were translated into Tibetan from Sanskrit.

(7) GRINSTEAD, E. D. "The Manuscript Kanjur in the British Museum." Asia Major, n.s. 13 (1967), pp. 48-70.

This article consists of a cataloguing of the Kanjur manuscript now in the British Museum. The cataloguing is in accord with the Tibetan Tripitika and the Tohoku and Otani catalogues.

(8) KOLMAS, JOSEF. "Notes on the Kanjur and Tanjur in Prague." Archiv Orientální, 30 (1962), 314-317.

A brief article in which the author lists the subject order of the Tibetan Kanjur and Tanjur which is currently in the possession of the library of the Oriental Institute of the Czechoslovak Academy of Sciences, Prague.

(9) TUCCI, GIUSEPPE. "A Brief History of Tibetan Religious Literature from the XIIth to the Beginning of the XVIIIth Century," in his Tibetan Painted Scrolls (see 1.14.2.2[11]), vol. 1, pp. 94-138.

Excellent historical survey of Tibetan religious texts, unfortunately hidden away in the unwieldy mammoth folios of Tibetan Painted Scrolls. It should be complemented, however, by a discussion of the literature before this period, which may be found in Marcelle Lalou, "Contribution à la bibliographie du Kanjur et du Tanjur: Les textes bouddhiques au temps du roi Khri-sron-ldebcan," Journal Asiatique, 241 (1933), 313-353.

3.1.5 Chinese Texts

(1) CH'EN, KENNETH K. S. Buddhism in China: A Historical Survey (see 1.11.1[1]), pp. 365-386.

A fine introduction to the topic of "The Chinese Tripitaka." Deals with translation techniques and problems, and with different catalogues and editions of the Chinese canon. Excellent starting place for study of the whole subject, with a long bibliography listed (for Chapter 13) at the back of the book, pp. 538-539.

(2) DEMIEVILLE, PAUL. "Le Bouddhisme: 1. Les Sources," in L'Inde Classique (see 1.2.2.1[11]), pp. 398-463.

A superb description of Chinese Buddhist literature, especially for its bearing on the study of Indian Buddhism. Includes summaries and analyses of many Chinese texts. Fine as a substantial introduction to the subject.

(3) _____, ed. Hobogiren: Dictionnaire Encyclopédique du Bouddhisme d'après les Sources Chinoises et Japonaises (see 2.7.12[1]), Fascicule Annexe (1931), pp. 11-202.

The last publication of the Franco-Japanese encyclopaedia of Buddhism before work started again was this listing of 2,184 works in the Taisho Tripitaka, together with their Sanskrit titles, names of authors and/or translators. This is followed by a handy table of authors and translators giving their dates when known.

(4) FACHOW, W. "Development of Tripitaka-Translations in China," in B. C. Law Volume (see 1.2.2.3[6]), pp. 66-74.

Very clear and concise outline of the method and three historical stages of translation of Buddhist texts into Chinese, which must be understood for a proper perspective on the Chinese canon. See also on this question Robert Hans Van Gulik, Siddham: An Essay on the History of Sanskrit Studies in China and Japan (Nagpur: International Academy of Indian Culture, 1956), 240 pp. (see 1.11.2.1[4]).

(5) GILES, LIONEL. Descriptive Catalogue of the Chinese Manuscripts from Tunhuang in the British Museum. London: Trustees of the British Museum, 1957, Part 1, pp. 1-216.

A list of over six thousand items pertaining to Buddhism, discovered in the Tun huang caves.

Theravada (Hinayana) Texts

(6) MIURA, ISSHU. Zen Dust: The History of the Koan and Koan Study in Rinzai (Lin-Chi) Zen. New York: Harcourt, Brace and World, 1966, pp. 333-479.

These pages contain a tremendously helpful survey, mostly of Chinese and Japanese Buddhist works, with substantial descriptions of them, discussions of important passages, listings of translations, cross-references to other versions or divisions. The bibliography was undertaken "in the hope of broadening the western reader's acquaintance with Buddhist literature . . . and to make it easier for him to identify texts, their authors and translators . . ." and it does just that.

3.1.6 Buddhist Texts in Other Languages

(1) CHANDRA, LOKESH. "A Conspectus of the Mongolian Tanjur." Ural-altaische Jahrbucher, 33 (1961), 36-40.

A conspectus of all of the 226 volumes of the Mongolian Tanjur which is in Ulan Bator. The author lists references to Rinchen's descriptive catalogue of the Mongolian Tanjur and also to P. Cordier's Catalogue du fonds tibétain, parts two and three.

(2) FINOT, LOUIS. "Recherches sur la littérature laotienne." Bulletin de l'Ecole française d'Extrême-Orient, 17 (1917), 1-221.

This article is one of the first and few surveys of the whole of Laotian literature, including basic texts, paritta, grammar, non-canonical material and commentaries, tales, novels, histories, and legends. It is followed by a bibliography of 1163 Laotian manuscripts.

(3) GODAKUMBURA, C. E. Sinhalese Literature. Colombo: Colombo Apothecaries, 1955, 376 pp.

The author divides his book into sections according to the types of literature considered, i.e., prose, poetry, popular literature, and scientific literature. The value of the book is that it provides an effective summary of the topics written about by Sinhalese authors because Godakumbura emphasizes the content of the literature rather than form or style. Combined with the historical survey of Sinhalese literature in the first part of the book, the author's approach is ideal for getting acquainted with the classics of Sinhalese literature.

(4) LECLERE, ADHEMARD. Les Livres Sacrés du Cambodge. Annales du Musée Guimet, Bibliothèque d'Etudes, Vol. 20. Paris: Leroux, 1906, 340 pp.

Any student interested in Cambodian sacred texts should become acquainted with Leclere's French translations of many of them, and descriptions of even more.

(5) PAIK, NAK CHOON (GEORGE PAIK). "Tripitaka Koreana." Transactions of the Korean Branch of the Royal Asiatic Society, 32 (1951), 62-78. (Reprinted Seoul: Dong Kook University, 1957.)

A brief description of the printing and edition of the "Sam Chong" or Tripitaka in Korea, without, however, a list of its contents.

(6) PHIMMASONE, PHOUVANG. "La Littérature bouddhique lao," in Présence du Bouddhisme. See 1.5.1(6).

A short descriptive survey of canonical and non-canonical texts and also of treatises and manuals, preserved in Loas. Some of the works are in Pali, others in Laotian. See also the same author's "Les textes bouddhiques de la littérature laotienne," La Persée Bouddhique, 3 (1950), 12-16. For a more detailed treatment, see Louis Finot, Recherches sur la littérature laotienne (above).

(7) QUENEAU, RAYMOND, ed. Histoire des littératures. Paris: Gallimard, 1955-58, 3 vols., Encyclopédie de la Pléiade, 1, 3, 7. Vol. 1 (1955), Littératures Anciennes Orientales et Orales, pp. 1318-1394.

Five useful survey articles dealing with literatures of Southeast Asian countries, which touch on Buddhist works, though not only on them. Included are three articles by Solange Bernard-Thierry, "Littérature birmane," pp. 1384-94; "Littérature cambodgienne," pp. 1353-61; "Littérature laotienne," pp. 1343-52; and K. Sibunruang, "Littérature siamoise," pp. 1362-83; and Maurice Durand, "Littérature vietnamienne," pp. 1318-1342.

3.2 THERAVADA (HINAYANA) TEXTS IN TRANSLATION AND TEXTUAL STUDIES

3.2.1 Vinaya

3.2.1.1 Pali (Theravada) Vinaya Texts in Translation

Outline of Pali Vinaya pitaka

1. Sutta-vibhanga (including patimokkha).
   a. Mahavibhanca (rules for monks)
   b. Bhikhuni-vibbanca (rules for nuns)

2. Khandhaka
   a. Mahavagga
   b. Cullavagga

3. Parivara

(1) Vinaya pitaka. Translated by Isaline Blew Horner as The Book of the Discipline. London: Oxford University Press, 1938-1942, 6 vols. Vol. 1-3, Luzac and Co., 1951-1966; vol. 4-6, Sacred Books of the Buddhists, Nos. 10, 11, 13, 14, 20, and 25.

This is the only complete translation of the Pali Vinaya into English. Done over a period of twenty-eight years, it is, as C. A. F. Rhys-Davids put it, "a labour of love." Vols. one-three (the Sutta-vibhanga) contain the rules, explanations and commentary of the

3.2.1.1 Theravada (Hinayana) Texts

Patimokkha code. In Vols. four-five may be found the Mahavagga and the Cullavagga; and Vol. six consists of the Parivara which rather dryly classifies all the rules. But the Vinaya is much more than a "code of disciplinary rules."

(2) _____. Partial translation by T. W. Rhys-Davids and Hermann Oldenberg in Vinaya Texts. Oxford: Clarendon Press, 1882-85. Sacred Books of the East, vols. 13, 17, 20. (Reprinted 1965 by Motilal Banarsidass, Delhi.)

Fluent and readily available translation of the Patimokkha (below), Cullavagga (below). For full translation see the work of Horner (above).

(3) Sutta-vibhanga. Translated by Horner in Vols. 1-3 of Vinaya pitaka The Book of the Discipline (above).

The sutta-vibhanga is organized around the 227 rules of personal conduct for monks (the Patimokkha) which is one of the oldest portions of the whole of Buddhist literature. These rules are divided into eight groups according to the severity of the penalty incurred for violating them. Each rule (and each exception to it), is accompanied by an anecdote explaining the original reason for its formulation. These anecdotes are a rich source of information on the lives of early Buddhists. The last volume of the Sutta-vibhanga contains the additional rules for nuns (the Bikkhuni-vibhanga) and is important in any consideration of the Buddhist attitude towards women.

(4) The Patimokkha. Translated by Rhys-Davids and Oldenberg in Vinaya Texts (above), vol. 1, pp. 1-69.

The 227 Patimokkha rules for monks represent the core of the Sutta-vibhanga and one of the most ancient portions of the Pali Canon. The list is still recited twice a month (on Uposatha days) by the assembled Sangha, and so is important morally, disciplinarily, and ritually. These rules should not be studied apart from the anecdotes and contextual material which may be found in Horner's translation of the Sutta-vibhanga. However, excerpted as they are here from the mass of that material, they form a handy reference list of the monks' code. The additional rules for nuns do not appear in this translation.

(5) The Mahavagga. Translated by Horner in Vinaya Pitaka, The Book of the Discipline, vol. 4 (above). Also translated by Rhys-Davids and Oldenberg in Vinaya Texts (above), vol. 1, p. 71, vol. 2, p. 325.

In the Mahavagga ("Great Division") regulations dealing with such things as the preceptor-pupil relationship, the Uposatha ceremony, the rains retreat, robes, medicine, and various procedural matters of the Sangha are all set forth with anecdotes and contextual material. One of the longest of these contextual stories is the opening narrative dealing with the events immediately following the Buddha's enlightenment. This is an extremely important piece of the Buddha's sacred biography. The translation by Oldenberg and Rhys-Davids is older (1880s) but in freer and looser language than that of Horner, which is more literal, thorough, and preceded by a valuable introduction.

(6) The Cullavagga. Translated by Isaline Blew Horner in Vinaya pitaka, The Book of the Discipline, vol. 5 (above). Also translated by Rhys-Davids and Oldenberg in Vinaya Texts (above), vol. 2, p. 327; vol. 3, p. 414.

The Cullavagga ("Lesser Division") continues to set out the rules and regulations for monastic life with the same concern for detail as the Mahavagga. In addition, it contains much historical and legendary material. Especially noteworthy in this regard are the last two sections which deal with the councils of Rajagaha and Vesali; the section on schism in the Sangha (which includes the story of Devadatta); and the section on nuns which tells of the Buddha's acceptance of women into the order and the conditions imposed on them.

(7) The Parivara. Translated by Isaline Blew Horner in Vinaya-pitaka, The Book of the Discipline, vol. 6 (above).

The Parivara is the last major division of the Vinayapitaka, and by far the dryest of the three. The book tries to summarize and reiterate all of the regulations of the monastic life, but it does so in a "list-style," devoid of any contextual or anecdotal material. This makes for rather painful reading, especially for anyone not already familiar with the rest of the Vinaya. As I. B. Horner put it in her helpful introduction to this work: "It would be possible to fathom the Parivara without either the Suttavibhanga or the Khandakas. . . . To follow it is another matter."

3.2.1.2 Vinaya Texts in Translation (Other Hinayana Schools)

(1) Anavataptagatha. Translated by Marcel Hofinger as Le Congrès du Lac Anavatapta: Vies de Sains Bouddhiques. 1: Légendes des Anciens (Sthaviravadana). Bibliothèque du Muséon, Vol. 34. Louvain: Publications Universitaires, Institut Orientaliste, 1954, 346 pp.

Hofinger has here translated into French (with Chinese and Tibetan editions of the text), the Anavataptagatha, a work which is part of the Vinaya of the Mulasarvastivada school and which deals principally with thirty-six legends about famous elders (sthaviravadana).

(2) FILLIOZAT, JEAN and HORYU KUNO. "Fragments du Vinaya des Sarvastivadin." Journal Asiatique, 230 (1938), 21-64.

Edition of six very short fragments of the original Sanskrit text of the Vinaya of the Sarvastivadins, with translations into French supported by the parallel passages of the Chinese version. Of interest only to the advanced student.

(3) HOERNLE, A. F. RUDOLF, ed. and trans. Manuscript Remains of Buddhist Literature Found in Eastern Turkestan. Oxford: Clarendon Press, 1916, pp. 4-16, 166-175, 357-365.

These pages of Hoernle's collection contain texts and translations of two unidentified Sanskrit fragments dealing with monastic regulations (pp. 4-16), of a Sanskrit work on technical vinaya terms (pp. 166-175), and, translated into French from the Kuchean by Sylvain Levi, some fragments of the Sarvastivadin Pratimoksa (pp. 357-365).

(4) Kathinavastu. Translated by Kun Chang in A Comparative Study of the Kathinavastu. Indo-Iranian Monographs, Vol. 1. Gravenhage: Mouton, 1957, 120 pp.

This important work, comparing the sections of the different Vinayas dealing with the regulations about monastic dress, also contains an English translation of that section (the Kathinavastu) as found in the Vinaya of the Mulasarvastivadins.

(5) Mahavastu. Translated by J. J. Jones. London: Luzac, 1949-1956, 3 vols. Sacred Books of the Buddhists, vols. 16, 18, 19.

The Mahavastu calls itself the Vinayapitaka of the Lokottarvadins (a subschool of the Mahasanghikas), but it contains none of the rules characteristic of a Vinaya. It is, rather, a loose compilation of histories, legends, and Jatakas which deal with the figure of the Buddha, written in "mixed Sanskrit" and may date anywhere from the Second century B.C. to the Fourth century A.D. Interesting in its own right, it is also important because its contents often bear comparison with Pali versions of the same stories, and because, though still a Theravada text, its flavor and thought reflect the movement towards the Mahayana.

(6) PACHOW, W. and RAMAKANTA MISHRA. "The Pratimoksa Sutra of the Mahasanghikas." Journal of the Ganganath Research Institute, 9, parts 2-4 (1952), 239-260.

Translation and explanation of the Mahasanghika's Pratimoksa Sutra. The authors have also provided a rule by rule comparison with Pali and Sarvastivadin Pratimoksa Sutras.

(7) Pratimoksa. Translated by Samuel Beal in A Catena of Buddhist Scriptures from the Chinese. London: Trubner, 1871, pp. 204-239.

An almost complete translation of the Chinese version of the Dharmagupta Pratimoksa. It contains 250 rules and regulations which are organized into the same basic categories as the Pali Patimokkha (which, however, has but 227 rules). It is interesting to compare this also with the Sarvastivadin version of the Pratimoksa, translated by E. Huber (below) and the Mulasarvastivadin version, translated by Vidyabhusana (below).

(8) _____. Translated by Edouard Huber in "Le Pratimoksasutra des Sarvastivadins." By Louis Finot and Edouard Huber. Journal Asiatique, 2 (1913), 465-558.

A translation into French of Kumarjiva's early Fifth century rendition of the Sarvastivadin version of the Pratimoksa, together with an edition of the original Sanskrit text that was found in Kucha and a table of concordances between the text and ceremonies of the Pratimoksa and the Pali Patimokkha. It is also interesting to compare this with the Dharmagupta version of the Pratimoksa translated by S. Beal (above), and with the Mulasarvastivadin version, translated by Vidyabhusana (below). A few Kuchean fragments of this same Sarvastivadin text have been edited and translated in Hoernle's Manuscript Remains of Buddhist Literature Found In Eastern Turkestan (above).

(9) _____. Translated by Satis Chandra Vidyabhushan in his "So-sor-thar-pa, or, A Code of Buddhist Monastic Laws, being the Tibetan version of Pratimoksa of the Mulasarvastivadin School." Journal of the Asiatic Society of Bengal, n.s. li (1915), 29-139.

Tibetan text and translation of the Mulasarvastivadin Pratimoksa, which contains two hundred and fifty-eight rules and regulations for monks. Vidyabhushan has also added a brief introduction and a table of parallels with the rules of the Pali Patimokkha. It is also interesting to compare this text with Huber's translation of the Sarvastivadin version (above), and with Samuel Beal's translation of the Dharmagupta version (above). A summary of the Tibetan version here translated may also be found in Sandor Csoma, "Analyse du Kandjour," Annales du Musée Guimet, 2 (1881), 131-577. (3.1.4[5])

(10) PREBISH, CHARLES S., ed. Buddhist Monastic Discipline: The Sanskrit Pratimoksa Sutras of the Mahasamghikas and Mulasarvastivadins. IASWR Series. University Park: Pennsylvania State University Press, 1975, 156 pp. See also 3.2.1.4(7).

(11) ROCKHILL, W. WOODVILLE. The Life of the Buddha and the Early History of His Order. London: Trubner, 1884, pp. 1-180. See also 8.1.2.1(23).

3.2.1.3 Vinaya Commentaries in Translation

(1) BUDDHAGHOSA. Samantapasadika, introductory chapter, "The Bahiranidana." Translated by N. A. Jayawickrama as The Inception of Discipline and the Vinayanidana. Sacred Books of the Buddhists, Vol. 21. London: Luzac, 1962, 222 pp.

"The Bahiranidana" is the introductory chapter to the Vinaya Commentary (Samantapasadika) which Buddhaghosa completed c. A.D. 430. In it he seeks to establish the authenticity of the Vinaya by linking it back to the Buddha through a direct line of transmission. It is thus not so much a part of the commentary as a presentation of the orthodox Theravada accounts of the first Three Councils (at which the Vinaya was recited), of the lines of succession of Vinaya teachers, and of the establishment and early history of Buddhism in Ceylon.

3.2.1.4 Studies of Vinaya Texts

(1) BANERJEE, ANUKUL CHANDRA. _Sarvastivada Literature_ (see 2.4.3[1]), pp. 28-50, 79-246.
Pages 28-50 contain a handy survey of the Vinaya of the Sarvastivadin school based on the Tibetan texts. Pages 79-246 give a much more detailed "analytical study" of one of the major parts of that Vinaya, the _Vinayavastu_. See also 2.4.3 and 3.1.3.

(2) _____. "The Vinayapitaka--Tibetan Version." _Calcutta Review_, 118 (1951), 162-166.
A brief descriptive survey of the thirteen volumes of the _'dul.ba._ or Tibetan Vinaya, which seems to be based on that of the Mulasarvastivadins.

(3) DUTT, NALINAKSHA, ed. and trans. _Gilgit Manuscripts_ (see 1.2.2.4[4]), vol. 3 (in four parts).
The third volume of Dutt's _Gilgit Manuscripts_ contains texts and summary translations of substantial portions of the Mulasarvastivadin _Vinayavastu_. See Vol. 3, Part 1, pp. 1-37 for the _Bhaisajyavastu_; Part 2, pp. xv-xxii for sections on robes and cloth and acts; Part 3, pp. ix-xix for a number of shorter texts including the _Pudgalavastu_; and Part 4, pp. vii-xxiv for other fragments. For a much more detailed study of the first half of the Sarvastivadin _Vinayavastu_ according to the Tibetan text, see Banerjee, _Sarvastivada Literature_ (above), pp. 79-246.

(4) FINOT, LOUIS. "Mahaparinibbanasutta et Cullavagga." _Indian Historical Quarterly_, 8 (1932), 241-246. See also 3.2.2.4(4).

(5) FRAUWALLNER, ERICH. _The Earliest Vinaya and the Beginnings of Buddhist Literature_. Serie Orientale Roma, Vol. 8. Roma: Istituto Italiano per il Medio ed Estremo Oriente, 1956, 218 pp.
A very important comparative study of six extant versions of the Vinaya, and a fine example of a much needed text-critical approach. By correlating the Vinayas of the different schools and what we know of the history of the schisms that resulted in those schools, Frauwallner draws important conclusions about which sections of the Vinaya are the oldest and when they were drawn up.

(6) PACHOW, W. _A Comparative Study of the Pratimoksa on the Basis of Its Chinese, Tibetan, Sanskrit and Pali Versions_. Sino-Indian Studies, 4. Sino-Indian Cultural Society, 1955, 219 pp.

A thorough scholarly work which analyzes the various pratimoksas in Sanskrit, Pali, Tibetan and Chinese, and, using the Sarvastivadin version as a standard, tabulates all the differences in the various lists of rules and regulations. Pachow concludes that the essential portions of the texts were probably established during the lifetime of the Buddha, and that the Mahasanghika version seems to be the oldest.

(7) PREBISH, CHARLES S., ed. _Buddhist Monastic Discipline: The Sanskrit Pratimoksa Sutras of the Mahasamghikas and Mulasarvastivadins_. See 3.2.1.2(10).
Prebish's volume marks an important contribution to the study of _Pratimoksha_ texts. He has included English translations, with a copious amount of notes, of the _Pratimoksha_ texts of Mulasarvastivadins and the Mahasamghikas. In addition, the first chapter comprises an effective collation of the major secondary sources concerned with the history and function of the _Pratimoksha_ rules. Hence, this first chapter is probably the finest available introduction to the study of Buddhist monastic discipline. For further discussion, see the same author's "The Pratimoksha Puzzle: Fact versus Fantasy," _Journal of the American Oriental Society_, 94 (1974), 168-176.

3.2.2 _Sutra/sutta_

3.2.2.1 Texts in Translation from the Pali (Theravada) Sutta pitaka

Outline of the Pali _Sutta pitaka_

1. _Digha-nikaya_

2. _Majjhima-nikaya_

3. _Samyutta-nikaya_

4. _Anguttara-nikaya_

5. _Khuddaka-nikaya_
   a. _Khuddaka-patha_
   b. _Dhammapada_
   c. _Udana_
   d. _Itivuttaka_
   e. _Sutta-nipata_
   f. _Vimana-vatthu_
   g. _Peta-vatthu_
   h. _Thera-gatha_
   i. _Theri-gatha_
   j. _Jataka_
   k. _Nidessa_ (not translated)
   l. _Patisambhida-magga_ (not translated)
   m. _Apadana_ (not translated)
   n. _Buddhavamsa_
   o. _Cariya-pitaka_

Works sometimes considered canonical outside of Sri Lanka:
   p. _Milindapanha_
   q. _Petakopadesa_
   r. _Nettippakarana_

Theravada (Hinayana) Texts

(1) Anguttara Nikaya. Translated by F. L. Woodward and E. M. Hare as The Book of Gradual Sayings. Pali Text Society Translation Series, Nos. 22, 24, 25, 26, 27. London: Luzac, 1951-55, 5 vols. (First published 1932-1936 by Oxford University Press.)

The Anguttara is a sort of "bonus Nikaya"; it contains little that is doctrinally essential (and not found elsewhere), but much that is interesting for its details or style of presentation. The hundreds of short discourses are arranged according to numerical progression, i.e., in the Book of Ones, of Twos, or Threes . . . etc., things are viewed as being of one, of two, of three kinds . . . etc. This mode of arrangement may have been mnemonically useful, but it makes things difficult for the modern reader used to more topically ordered presentation. There is no quick way to discover the many small gems hidden in the mass of material; and only students who are advanced enough to know a gem when they see one are likely to profit much from their reading.

(2) Buddhavamsa. Translated by Bimala Churn Law as "Buddhavamsa: The Lineage of the Buddhas," in Minor Anthologies of the Pali Canon, Part 3. London: Oxford University Press, 1938, pp. 1-88. Also translated by Isaline Blew Horner as "Buddhavamsa: Chronicle of Buddhas," in Minor Anthologies of the Pali Canon, Part 3. Sacred Books of the Buddhists, No. 31. London: Luzac, 1975.

The Buddhavamsa is the fourteenth Book of the Khuddaka-nikaya. It gives, in short, the histories of twenty-four previous Buddhas.

(3) Cariya pitaka. Translated by Bimala Churn Law as "Cariya-pitaka: The Collection of Ways of Conduct," in Minor Anthologies of the Pali Canon, Part 3. Sacred Books of the Buddhists, No. 9. London: Oxford University Press, 1938, pp. 95-127.
Also translated by Isaline Blew Horner as "Cariya-pitaka: Basket of Conduct," in Minor Anthologies of the Pali Canon, Part 3. Sacred Books of the Buddhists, No. 31. London: Luzac, 1975.

The Cariya-pitaka is the fifteenth Book of the Khuddaka-nikaya and one of the latest works of the Pali Canon. It is a collection of Jatakas (retold in verse) intended to illustrate a number of actions characteristic of a bodhisattva's career.

Dhammapada. Book 2 of the Khuddaka-nikaya

Many scholars attempt a translation of the Dhammapada at some leisurely moment in their academic lives--almost as many as do the Bhagavad gita. The work has been consistently popular both in Buddhist countries and in the West. It has Chinese, Tibetan, Gandhari, Sogdian and Kuchean versions, and the commentary on it (Dhammapadathakatha, translated by Burlingame, see 4.2.2[2]) has long been a source of stories and illustrations for Buddhist sermons. In Europe, it has been translated numerous times into the various languages, even into Latin (Michael Viggo Fausboll [Havniae, 1855?], 470 pp.) and even set to music. The translations listed below are all complete and in English and represent but a few of the many available.

(4) Dhammapada. Translated by Irving Babbitt. New York: New Directions, 1965, 122 pp. (Originally published London and New York, 1936; paperback edition: New Directions: NDP 188.)

Now available in paperback, this translation is based on Max Müller's text and translation and is followed by an interesting essay, "Buddha and the Occident."

(5) _____. Translated by C. A. F. Rhys-Davids as Dhammapada: Verses on Dhamma. Sacred Books of the Buddhists, No. 7. London: Oxford University Press, 1931, 165 pp.

Translated as part of the Minor Anthologies of the Pali Canon series, this edition by Rhys-Davids is handy for giving both the Pali text and the English translation on facing pages.

(6) _____. Translated by P. Lal. New York: Farrar, Straus and Giroux, 1967, 184 pp.

Reputedly the most "poetic" translation, the author hopes to have "transcreated" in some places rather than merely translated.

(7) _____. Translated by Friedrich Max Müller. Sacred Books of the East, Vol. 10, Part 1. Delhi: Motilal Banarsidass, 1965, 95 pp. (First published Oxford University Press, 1881.)

Annotated translation with an introduction on the dating of the text, and correspondences with Chinese and Tibetan sources. Max Müller's translation is of Fausboll's edition of the text and was done in consultation of the translations by Burnouf, Gogerly, Fausboll, Upham, Weber, et al.

(8) _____. Translated by Narada Thera. Third edition. Calcutta: Maha Bodhi Society of India, 1970, 359 pp. (First published 1940.)

Translation by a well versed Theravada monk-scholar, with Pali text romanized, notes, and his own commentary.

(9) _____. Translated by Sarvepalli Radhakrishnan. London: Oxford University Press, 1966, 194 pp. (First published 1950.)

This translation, by the eminent Indian philosopher-statesman, is done in the spirit of bringing East and West closer, in an effort to contribute to a common spiritual heritage for "modern" man. Each of the verses is given in the original Pali (romanized) and followed by a readable yet literal rendering.

(10) Digha Nikaya, in Dialogues of the Buddha. Translated by T. W. Rhys-Davids. See 2.7.1(13).

In the four other Nikayas, the student usually has to "shop around" to find the important and interesting suttas. In the Digha

Nikaya he does not: such a large percentage of its thirty-four comparatively long suttas are "classics" that he cannot possibly miss them. Here, among others, are the Brahmajala-, the Samannaphala-, the Mahasatipatthana-, the Cakkavatti Sinhanada- suttas, and of course the Mahaparinibbana sutta (which every student should read). In this translation, each sutta is preceded by an introduction which is interesting for its information on the text and for its reflecting the state of late nineteenth century Buddhist scholarship.

(11) Itivuttaka. Translated by Frank L. Woodward as "Itivuttaka: As it was said," in Minor Anthologies of the Pali Canon, Part 2. Sacred Books of the Buddhists, Vol. 8. London: Oxford University Press, 1948, pp. 115-199.

The Itivuttaka (Book 4 of the Khuddaka Nikaya) is so-called because it purports to report 112 short sutras "as they were said" by the Buddha. In them, the monks are exhorted to disciplined and ethical activities. The scheme of arrangement of the Itivuttaka is akin to that of the Anguttara Nikaya with its categories of "the Ones," "the Twos," "the Threes," etc.

(12) Jataka. Translated under the editorship of E. B. Cowell as The Jataka; or, Stories of the Buddha's Former Births. UNESCO collection of representative works. London: Published for the Pali Text Society by Luzac, 1969, 7 vols. in 3. (Originally published 1895-1913 in 6 vols. and index.)

Only the verses were (supposedly) uttered by the Buddha, but the 547 stories that go with them are considered to be extra-canonical. See also 3.2.2.3.

(13) Khuddaka-patha. Translated by C. A. F. Rhys-Davids in The Minor Anthologies of the Pali Canon, Part 1. Sacred Books of the Buddhists, vol. 7. London: Oxford University Press, 1931, pp. 140-159.

The Khuddaka-patha is the first book of the Khuddaka Nikaya and the shortest book in the whole Pali canon. It seems to have been used as a sort of monastic primer.

(14) ____. Translated by Bhikkhu Nanamoli as The Minor Readings in the Minor Readings, Khuddakapatha, and The Illustrator of Ultimate Meaning, Paramatthajotika. Pali Text Society Translation Series, No. 32. London: Luzac, 1960, 342 pp.

Nanamoli's translation of the short Khuddaka patha is pretty much equal in quality to that of Rhys-Davids (above). However, it does have the advantage of being accompanied by a translation of Buddhaghosa's (?) Paramatthojotika, which is a commentary on the text (see under 3.2.2.3).

(15) Majjhima Nikaya. Translated by Robert Chalmers as Further Dialogues of the Buddha.

Sacred Books of the Buddhists, Vols. 5-6. London: Oxford University Press, 1926-1927, 2 vols.

The 152 suttas of the Majjhima Nikaya are arranged in three groups of fifty suttas (+2) and contain a wide variety of teachings and doctrinal discussions. Some passages are insignificant and dry, while others are important and exciting. Among them, these can be mentioned: No. 26, which deals with the Buddha's own quest for enlightenment; No. 63, the questions of Malunkyaputta; Nos. 71-73, which contain important dialogues with Vacchagotta. But the interested student should shop around. Chalmers's rather free translation reads very smoothly; unfortunately, it is almost devoid of notes and his introduction is not very useful.

(16) ____. Translated by Isaline Blew Horner as The Middle Length Sayings. Pali Text Society Translation series, Nos. 29-31. London: Luzac, 1954-1959, 3 vols.

The suttas of the Majjhima Nikaya are difficult to summarize because of the "wide variety" of material they contain. Horner's introductions to each of her volumes help orient the student in this regard; and her footnotes and cross-references in the text are useful for the more advanced student. Her translation is more precise and literal than that of Chalmers (above). This makes it more dependable, but at the same time less readable.

(17) Milindapanha. Translated by Isaline Blew Horner as Milinda's Questions. Sacred Books of the Buddhists, Vols. 22-23. London: Luzac, 1963-1964, 2 vols.

A thorough translation of this important text which is considered canonical in some countries (e.g., Burma). Not as fluent reading as Rhys-Davids' translation, but nevertheless important for the serious student doing a paper on the text. The latter should also consult Paul Demieville's "Les Versions Chinoises du Milindapanha" (see 3.2.2.4[2]), in which there is a French translation from the Chinese of the so-called "Sutra du Bhiksu Nagasena."

(18) ____. Translated by T. W. Rhys-Davids as The Questions of King Milinda. Sacred Books of the East, Vols. 35, 36. Delhi: Motilal Banarsidass, 1965, 2 vols. (Originally published 1890-1894 by Oxford University Press.)

This authoritative and semi-canonical work, which was written in Northern India, became very popular in Theravada lands. It contains a series of dialogues on doctrinal and other matters between the Ven. Nagasena and the King Milinda (Menander). It is further useful as a source on the relationship between Sangha and State in its time. Finally, the book has enjoyed a curious popularity among Western students of Buddhism, perhaps because the "Greek" Milinda asks the sort of questions

Theravada (Hinayana) Texts

we might have asked. This translation by Rhys-Davids reads better than that by Horner (above) but is older and less literal and careful.

(19) Nettippakarana. Translated by Bhikkhu Nanamoli as The Guide, Netti-ppakaranam. Pali Text Society Translation Series, No. 33. London: Luzac, 1962, 325 pp.

Translation with introduction and notes of a Pali work which is traditionally attributed to the Buddha's disciple Maha Kaccana, but is clearly later than that. The work seems to be a revised and improved version of the Petakopadesa (q.v.), and, like that work, seeks to set out the methods for writing commentaries and explaining canonical works. It is not a commentary itself but a "guide for commentators." As Nanamoli puts it, "it deals with scaffolding, not with architecture." It is also easy to see why the Sinhalese refused to accept this work as canonical, although it was so at times in other Theravada countries, such as Burma.

(20) Petakopadesa. Translated by Bhikkhu Nanamoli as The Pitaka-Disclosure, Petakopadesa. Pali Text Society Translation Series, No. 35. London: Luzac, 1964, 402 pp.

Translation with introduction and notes of a Pali work which is traditionally attributed to the Buddha's disciple Maha Kaccana, but is clearly later than that. The work is slightly older than the Nettippakarana (q.v.), which is akin to it, and, like that work, it sets the rules for the writing of commentaries on canonical works. It is easy to see why the Sinhalese refused to accept this work as canonical, although it was so in other Theravada countries, such as Burma.

(21) Peta vatthu. Translated by Henry Snyder Gehman as "Peta vatthu: Stories of the Departed," in Minor Anthologies of the Pali Canon, Part 4. Sacred Books of the Buddhists, No. 12. London: Luzac, 1942, 250 pp. Second edition 1974. Sacred Books of the Buddhists, No. 30.

The Peta vatthu is the seventh book of the Khuddaka Nikaya. It is a complementary work to the Vimana vatthu, telling, as it does, stories about pretas (the so-called "hungry ghosts") and their sufferings. Its main thrust is to prescribe the leading of the ethical life by illustrating the consequences of bad karma. Like the Vimana vatthu (below) it has long been neglected by Western scholarship.

(22) Samyutta Nikaya. Translated by C. A. F. Rhys-Davids, in The Book of Kindred Sayings or Grouped Suttas. See 2.7.7(10).

The Samyutta Nikaya has been called "a woodland to wander in not unrewarded." This is true; many discoveries can be made there; but the student should know what he is looking at and for before undertaking the journey. The hundreds of relatively short sutras are topically arranged into fifty-six groups which cover the whole Buddhist gamut of "psycho-ethical" Buddhist morality and practice.

(23) Sutta-Nipata. Translated by Robert Chalmers as Buddha's Teachings. Harvard Oriental Series, Vol. 37. Cambridge, Mass.: Harvard University Press, 1932, 300 pp.

The Sutta-nipata (Book 5 of the Khuddaka Nikaya) owes its fame and importance to being perhaps the most ancient book of the Pali Canon. This edition of it very usefully gives the Pali text with translation on the facing page. See also the translations of the same text by Fausboll and by Hare (below).

(24) _____. Translated by V. Fausboll as part 2 of The Dhammapada and the Sutta-Nipata. Sacred Books of the East, No. 10. Translated by F. Max Müller and V. Fausboll. Delhi: Motilal Banarsidass, 1965, 2 vols. in 1, 99, and 224 pp. (Originally published 1881 by Oxford University Press.)

Translation of this, the fifth book of the Khuddaka nikaya, with an introduction discussing the great antiquity and possible date of the text. See also the translations by Chalmers (above) and by Hare (below).

(25) _____. Translated by E. M. Hare as Woven Cadences of Early Buddhists, Sutta-nipata. Second edition. Sacred Books of the Buddhists, Vol. 15. London: Oxford University Press, 1948, 229 pp.

This translation from the Pali comes with very helpful index and table of concordances with passages in other Pali canonical works. There exists also a commentary on the Sutta-nipata, a portion of which has been translated into English by Ria Kloppenborg in her The Paccekabuddha, A Buddhist Ascetic (see: 8.2.1[5]). See also the translations of the Sutta-nipata by Chalmers and Fausboll (above).

(26) Theragatha. Translated by C. A. F. Rhys-Davids as Psalms of the Brethren. Pali Text Society Translation Series, No. 4. Second edition. London: Luzac, 1937, 446 pp. (Reprinted 1964) and bound with Therigatha as Psalms of the Early Buddhists.) Also translated by K. R. Norman as The Elders' Verses 1, Theragatha. Pali Text Society Translation Series, No. 38. London: Luzac, 1969, 319 pp.

The Theragatha is the eighth book of the Khuddaka Nikaya. It contains 264 poems or songs which are arranged in order of increasing length, and, here, accompanied by excerpts from Dhammapala's commentary. Many of these verses are comparatively ancient and hence form an important source on the lives and religious aspirations of the early Buddhist monks. The "Psalms" are full of human vitality and make the Dhamma "come alive." However, the student should proceed very cautiously before using any one of them as historical source material on any individual thera. Norman's new translation much surpasses that of Rhys-Davids and should be used in its stead.

(27) Therigatha. Translated by C. A. F. Rhys-Davids as Psalms of the Sisters. Pali Text Society Translation Series, No. 1. London: H. Frowde, 1909, 200 pp. (Reprinted 1964 by Luzac and bound with Theragatha as Psalms of the Early Buddhists, above.) Also translated by K. R. Norman as The Elders' Verses ll, Therigatha. Pali Text Society Translation Series, No. 40. London: Luzac, 1971, 199 pp.

The Therigatha is a collection of seventy-three poems or songs uttered by various bhik-paratively ancient. They are important 1) for their literary value, 2) as expressions of religious striving and experience, 3) as illustrative of the forces leading or driving women to enter the early Buddhist order. Each psalm is prefaced by a passage from Dhammapala's commentary which states the occasion for its utterance. The whole collection is preceded by a valuable introduction and followed by an appendix of verses from the Samyutta-nikaya, in which the sisters deal successfully with Mara. Norman's new translation much surpasses that of Rhys-Davids and should be used in its stead.

(28) Udana. Translated by Frank L. Woodward as "Udana: Verses of Uplift," in Minor Anthologies of the Pali Canon, Part 2. Sacred Books of the Buddhists, Vol. 8. London: Oxford University Press, 1948, pp. 1-114. (Originally published 1935.)

The Udana constitutes the third book of the Khuddaka-nikaya. It is a collection of eighty inspired verses reportedly uttered by the Buddha himself. Each verse is preceded by a short anecdote which more or less sets forth the occasion for the utterance. These anecdotes are often more filled with human interest than the verses themselves.

(29) _____. Translated by D. M. Strong as The Udana, or, The Solemn Utterances of the Buddha. London: Luzac, 1902, 129 pp.

Strong's translation of this relatively short book of the Khuddaka nikaya has been superseded by that of Woodward (above). Students who use it, however, should be wary of Strong's then-current enthusiasms for Buddhism based on scientific and evolutionary biases.

(30) Vimana vatthu. Translated by Jean W. Kennedy as "Vimana vatthu: Stories of the Mansions," in Minor Anthologies of the Pali Canon, Part 4. Sacred Books of the Buddhists, No. 12. London: Luzac, 1942, 250 pp. Also translated by I. B. Horner under the same title in 1974 edition of Minor Anthologies of the Pali Canon, Part 4. Sacred Books of the Buddhists, No. 30.

The Vimana vatthu is the sixth book of the Khuddaka Nikaya. It is a collection of stories about Buddhist heavens and about the people who were reborn there through meritorious action. Along with the Peta vatthu (below), its main thrust is to prescribe the making of merit and the leading of the ethical life. Unfortunately, it has long been neglected by Western scholarship in favor of more "major" and "philosophical" books.

3.2.2.2 Texts from the Sutra-pitakas of Other Hinayana Schools

(1) Arthapada sutra. Translated by P. V. Bapat as "The Arthapada sutra." Visva Bharati Annals, 1 (1945), 135-227; 3 (1950), 1-109.

The Arthapada sutra, the Chinese text of which has been translated here, was originally rendered into that language by the Scythian Che-Kien c. 225 A.D. Fragments of the original Sanskrit entitled the Arthavargiya, have been found but are of little help in determining to which school the text belongs. In any case, it is clear that it corresponds to the Pali Atthakavagga, a very old collection of Pali suttas which became incorporated into the fourteenth section of the Suttanipata. See also the discussion of the sutra in Bhapat's "Introduction," which follows his translation on pp. 79-109.

(2) Asokavadana. Translated by Jean Przyluski in La Légende de l'Empereur Açoka dans les Textes Indiens et Chinois. Annales du Musée Guimet. Bibliothèque d'Etudes, t. 31. Paris: P. Geuthner, 1923, 459 pp.

French translation of a collection of avadanas about the Emperor Asoka which the Sarvastivadins (at least in the Chinese canon) incorporated into the Ksudraka section of the Sutra pitaka. See also 4.2.2.

(3) Avadanasataka. Translated by Leon Feer as Avadana-cataka: Cent Légendes Bouddhiques. Annales du Musée Guimet, No. 18. Paris: Leroux, 1891, xxxviii, 496 pp.

French translation of a collection of avadanas which was incorporated into the Ksudraka texts of the Sarvastivadin Sutra pitaka.

(4) AVALOKITASIMHA. Dharmasamuccaya. Translated by Lin Li-Kouang as Dharmasamuccaya: Compendium de la Loi. Annales de Musée Guimet, Bibliothèque d'Etudes, . 53. Paris: Adrien Maisonneuve, 1946, 1969 and 1973, 3 vols. Vols 2 and 3 with revisions by André Bareau, J. W. de Jong and Paul Demieville.

A complete French translation with editions of the Sanskrit, Tibetan and Chinese texts, of the 2549 stanzas taken by Avalokitasimha from the vast Sanskrit Mulasarvastivadin sutra of the second to third century A.D., the Saddharma-smrtyupasthana-sutra. Only the stanzas which have been translated here and which are contemporary and akin in form to the Dhammapada and Udanavarga have survived in Sanskrit. The Sutra itself is

Theravada (Hinayana) Texts

extant only in the Chinese and Tibetan and has not been translated. See, however, the study of it by Lin Li-kouang, L'Aide-mémoire de la Vraie Loi (Paris: A. Maisonneuve, 1949), 384 pp.

(5) Fa chu ching (Chinese version of Dhammapada). Translated by Samuel Beal as Dhammapada, with Accompanying Narratives. Third edition Varanasi: Indological Book House, 1971, 104 pp. (First published London: Trubner, 1878, as Texts from the Buddhist Canon Commonly Known as Dhammapada, with Accompanying Narratives, 176 pp.)

A translation, with introduction, of the Chinese version of the Dhammapada which is interesting for having seventy-nine verses more than the 423 contained in the Pali texts. These verses have quite clearly been added to the beginning and the end of the original version.

(6) HOERNLE, A. F. RUDOLF, ed. and trans. Manuscript Remains of Buddhist Literature Found in Eastern Turkestan (see 3.2.1.2[3]), pp. 16-52.

Text and translation of a number of fragments of Sanskrit Sutras, most of them probably from the Sarvastivadin tradition. Included are the Samgiti and Atanatiya sutras of the Dirgha-agama, the Upali and Suka sutras of the Madhyama-agama, and the Pravarana, Candropama, and Sakti sutras of the Samyukta-agama.

(7) PAULY, BERNARD. "Fragments Sanskrits de Haute Asie." Journal Asiatique, 245 (1957), 280-307.

Description of a few fragments of a Sanskrit sutra corresponding to the Pali Dasuttarasutta of the Dighanikaya, and translations of a Turfan Sanskrit manuscript entitled the Samghastotrastava ("L'Hymne à la gloire de la Communauté"), and of very small fragments of the Vaisaligathastava, a hymn in praise of the Buddha and the seven Tathagatas.

(8) "Sigalovada-sutta." Translated by Bhadanta Pannasiri. Visva Bharati Annals, 3 (1950), 150-228.

The Sigalovada sutta, the Pali version of which is contained in Digha Nikaya 3, is famous for being the "Vinaya of the Laity" containing as it does a dialogue in which the Buddha instructs a householder on his religious and social duties. The sutta is found in four translations in the Chinese canon, all of which are translated here and compared and contrasted with the Pali text.

(9) Srimala-devi-simhanada-sutra. Translated by Alex and Hideko Wayman as The Lion's Roar of Queen Srimala: A Buddhist Scripture on the Tathagatagarbha Theory. New York: Columbia University Press, 1974, 142 pp. See also 3.3.2.1(31).

(10) Udanavarga. Translated by William Woodville Rockhill as Udanavarga: A Collection of Verses from the Buddhist Canon. Trubner's Oriental Series. London: Trubner, 1883, 224 pp.

The Udanavarga (said to have been compiled by Dharmatrata), is the Sarvastivadin version of the Dhammapada. The Sanskrit was translated into Tibetan and incorporated into the bkay 'gyur, from which Rockhill rendered it into English, with occasional notes from the commentary of Prajnavarman.

(11) WALDSCHMIDT, ERNST. "A Fragment from the Samyuktagama." Adyar Library Bulletin, 20 (1956), 213-228.

One of the few articles which the reader will find concerning the Samyuktagama which is available in English. Waldschmidt does an admirable job placing the significance of the fragment within its correct context.

(12) _____. "Sutra 25 of the Nidanasamyukta." Bulletin of the School of Oriental and African Studies, 20 (1957), 569-579.

Text and translation of a fragmentary Sanskrit work found in Turkestan which appears to be the last sutra in the Nidanasamyukta, one of the important "chapters" of the Samyuktagama (which corresponds to the Pali Samyuttanikaya).

3.2.2.3 Translations of Commentaries on Texts of the Sutta Pitaka

(1) BUDDHAGHOSA(?). Paramatthajotika. Translated by Bhikkhu Nanamoli as The Illustrator of Ultimate Meaning in the Minor Readings, Khuddaka-patha, and the Illustrator of Ultimate Meaning, Paramatthajotika. Pali Text Society Translation Series, No. 32. London: Luzac, 1960, 342 pp.

The Khuddakapattha is the first book of the Pali Khuddaka nikaya, and the Paramatthajotika is Buddhaghosa's (?) commentary on it. The commentary itself contains no new doctrinal points, but the student doing a paper on Buddhaghosa might want to take a look at it, making sure to note first the pros and cons of Buddhaghosa's authorship which are weighed by Bhikkhu Nanamoli in his introduction.

(2) Dhammapadatthakatha. Translated by Eugene Watson Burlingame as Buddhist Legends. London: Luzac, 1969, 3 vols. (Originally published 1921 by Harvard University Press; Harvard Oriental Series, Vols. 28-30.) See also 4.2.3(13).

(3) Jatakatthakatha. Translated under the editorship of E. B. Cowell as The Jatakas, Stories of the Buddha's Former Births. See 3.2.2.1(12). See also 4.2.2(6).

(4) LEVI, SYLVAIN, ed. and trans. Fragments des textes Koutchéens. Cahiers de la Société

3.2.2.3   Theravada (Hinayana) Texts

Asiatique, No. 2. Paris: Imprimerie Nationale, 1933, pp. 66-77.

These pages of Levi's collection contain texts and translations of fragments of two Kuchean texts: the Udanastotra and the Udanalamkara, both of which appear to be Sarvastivadin commentaries on the Sanskrit Udanavarga and akin in style to the Pali Dhammapada commentary.

3.2.2.4 Studies of Sutta pitaka texts

(1) BARUA, DIPAK KUMAR. *An Analytical Study of Four Nikayas*. Calcutta: Rabindra Bharati University, 1971, 626 pp.

A massive study of all the Pali nikayas except the Khuddaka nikaya, which can be extremely useful at times. After a general discussion of the compilation of the four nikayas and a helpful tabulation of it in comparison to the Chinese agamas, the author divides and discusses the suttas of the four collections into "Discourses to the laity," "Discourses on Sila, samadhi, and panna," "Discussions on secular matters," and "Historical and geographical materials."

(2) DEMIEVILLE, PAUL. "Les Versions Chinoises du Milindapanha." *Bulletin de l'Ecole française d'Extrême-Orient*, 24 (1924), 1-258.

A book-size article containing a thorough analysis of the Chinese versions of the Questions of King Milinda (see Milindapanha under 3.2.2.1), including a history of the various Chinese translations, a comparison of these with the Pali version, some notes on the figures of King Menander and Nagasena, and a French translation of the "Sutra of bhiksu Nagasena," which exists only in the Chinese. Of great help to students doing research on the Milindapanha.

(3) DUTT, NALINAKSHA. "The Brahmajala Sutta in the light of Nagarjuna's expositions." *Indian Historical Quarterly*, 8 (1932), 706-746.

The Brahmajaia sutta, which appears in Digha Nikaya I, contains a list of sixty-two heterodox views which the Buddha rejects. The list is commonly used to present a sort of "bird's eye view" of non-Buddhistic opinions of that time; but, in this interesting article, Dutt disputes the notion that this was the sutta's purpose, claiming instead that its main object was to draw up a list of the possible theories which could hamper a monk in his meditation, and that the famous sixty-two views represent a systematic exposition of the mental experiences of a monk.

(4) FINOT, LOUIS. "Mahaparinibbanasutta et Cullavagga." See 3.2.1.4(4).

A classic article in which Finot claims that these two texts originally formed a single narrative which was then split up so as to include the part containing utterances of the Buddha (the Mahaparinibbana sutta) in the Sutta pitaka, and the part containing rules and events that took place after the Buddha's death in the Vinaya. Finot's position quickly received support from Tibetan evidence presented by E. Obermiller in "The Account of the Buddha's Nirvana and the First Councils according to the Vinayaksudraka," *Indian Historical Quarterly*, 8 (1932), 781-784.

(5) LAMOTTE, ETIENNE. "Khuddaka-nikaya and Ksudrakapitaka." *East and West*, 7 (1957), 341-348.

A concise history of the formation of the collections of so-called "minor texts" in the canons of the various Theravada sects, and of the debates on what and what not to include in them. The problems that arose, according to Lamotte, reflect an ancient and early uncertainty about whether or not certain texts were the word of the Buddha. See also Etienne Lamotte, "Problèmes concernant les textes canoniques mineurs," *Journal Asiatique* (1956), pp. 249-264.

(6) LAW, BIMALA CHURN. "Tirukkural et Dhammapada, Etude Comparative." *Journal Asiatique* (1952), pp. 37-52.

An interesting attempt to make a comparison between the Dhammapada and one of the basic sacred texts of the Tamils, the Tirukkural. Unfortunately, Law's original English article was never published, except translated here into French.

(7) MUKHERJEE, PRABHAT KUMAR. "The Dhammapada and the Udanavarga." *Indian Historical Quarterly*, 2 (1935), 741-760.

A quite helpful survey of the various versions of the Udanavarga (=Sanskrit Dharmapada) in its Chinese translations and Tibetan translation. All these versions are then tabulated for parallel passages and compared with the Pali Dhammapada.

(8) PANDE, GOVIND CHANDRA. *Studies in the Origins of Buddhism* (see 1.2.2.1[10]), pp. 1-247.

One of the finest discussions of the complexity and different layers of materials in the Pali Canon. The Abhidhamma and Vinaya are treated briefly, but then the author proceeds to a full analysis of the Nikayas and how they were formed. The discussion is exceedingly well documented and, for this reason, may be difficult to follow at times; but it deals with questions which must be taken into consideration in any serious handling of the texts of the Sutta pitaka.

3.2.3   Abhidharma/Abhidhamma

3.2.3.1 Pali (Theravada) Abhidhamma Texts in Translation

Outline of Pali Abhidhamma pitaka

1. Dhamma-sangani
2. Vibhanga
3. Dhatu-katha

Theravada (Hinayana) Texts

4. Puggala-pannatti
5. Katha-vatthu
6. Yamaka (not translated)
7. Patthana

(1) Dhamma-Sangani. Translated by Caroline Rhys-Davids as A Buddhist Manual of Psychological Ethics of the Fourth Century B.C. Oriental Translation Fund, New Series, Vol. 12. London: Royal Asiatic Society, 1900, xcv, 393 pp. Third edition. Pali Text Society Translation Series, No. 41. London: Luzac, 1974.

The Dhamma-sangani is the first book of the Abhidhamma pitaka and is said to date back to some time before the third century B.C. One of its aims is to enumerate and classify into various schemes and lists all Dharmas, i.e., all states of consciousness, all phenomena. It does so in a dry way which does not generally appeal to western readers; but then, the Dhamma-sangani is not meant to be "read"; it is a manual for advanced monks and is supposed to be studied, learned and meditated upon. It is the sort of thing that only becomes "exciting" after it has at least partly been mastered. A commentary on the Dhamma-sangani by Buddhaghosa, the Atthasalini (The Expositor), has been translated into English (see 3.2.3.3[3]).

(2) Vibhanga. Translated by U. Thittila as The Book of Analysis. Pali Text Society Translation Series, No. 39. London: Luzac, 1969, lxxviii, 573 pp.

In many ways, the Vibhanga (Book II of the Abhidhamma pitaka) is a companion volume to the Dhammasangani; yet it approaches its material differently. The subjects dealt with include the skandhas, the ayatanas, the eighteen dhatus, the four truths, Dependent origination, Mindfulness, the Path, the Jhanas, etc. These are primarily analyzed a) according to the suttas, and b) according to the Abidhamma. The comparison of these two ways of analyzing the above topics gives, in a nutshell, some idea of the whole nature and thrust of the Abidhamma movement. R. E. Iggleden's "Introduction" (pp. xv-lxxi) is also quite helpful.

(3) Dhatu Katha. Translated by U. Narada as Discourse on Elements (Dhatu-Katha). Pali Text Society Translation Series, No. 34. London: Luzac, 1962, xlviii, 155 pp.

The Dhatu-katha (Book III of the Abhidhamma pitaka) 1) is intended for advanced monks (or students) only; 2) is not only supposed to be studied but also meditated upon; 3) has the aim of dispelling wrong views of atman. Essentially, it consists of complex dealings with 371 subjects of inquiry--the topics of the Vibhanga, and the triplets and couplets of the Dhammasangani (and others). All of these are classified, unclassified, associated and disassociated with each other and with the Five Skandhas, the Twelve Ayatanas and the Eighteen Dhatus. The student should definitely consult the helpful "Preface" (pp. ix-xxix), the "Introduction" (pp. xxxi-xlv), and U. Narada's famous Abhidhamma charts: they do not make things easy but do make them studiable.

(4) Puggala Pannatti. Translated by Bimala Churn Law as Designation of Human Types, Puggala-pannatti. Pali Text Society Translation Series, No. 12. London: Luzac, 1969, 111 pp. (First published 1924 by Oxford University Press.)

The Puggala Pannatti (Book IV of the Abhidhamma pitaka) attempts to classify different types of human personalities, by using the (often artificial) "Anguttara method" of organization--into groups of Ones, of Twos, of Threes, etc. Thus, for example, in the Threes, we find similes or definitions about: the blind, the one-eyed, and the two-eyed man; the foul-mouthed, the flower-speaker, and the honey-tongued man; the despairing, the hopeful, and the above-hope man; etc. None of this is very enlightening and perhaps of value mostly for the Pali scholar on the hunt for elucidations of specific terms.

(5) Katha vatthu. Translated by Shwe Zan Aung and C. A. F. Rhys-Davids as Points of Controversy, or Subjects of Discourse. Pali Text Society Translation Series, No. 5. London: Luzac, 1969, 416 pp. (Originally published London: H. Milford, 1915.)

The Katha-vatthu (Book 5 of the Abhidhamma pitaka) is a very important source on the history and development of Buddhist thought. Said to have been first recited at the Third Council to deal with newly arisen controversial doctrines, it represents the Theravada attempt to fill the doctrinal "loopholes" opened up by non-Theravadins. The book will be of little interest to the beginning student; it assumes a basic knowledge of the sutras. But the more advanced might find it worth exploring--a task made much easier by Rhys-Davids' introduction and indices. A commentary on the text, the Kathavatthup pakarana Atthakatha, ascribed to Buddhaghosa, has been translated by B. C. Law as The Debates Commentary (see 3.2.3.3 under Buddhaghosa).

(6) Patthana. Translated by U. Narada as Conditional Relations, Patthana. Pali Text Society Translation Series, No. 37. London: Luzac, 1969, cxxxi, 526 pp.

It is said that one of the prerequisites for fully comprehending the Patthana is omniscience; let the student therefore be warned. In any case, no hardy westerner should even open this seventh book of the Abhidhamma before reading the Dhammasangani and the Dhatukatha. Essentially, the Patthana takes the twenty-two triplets and 100 couplets of the Dhammasangani, and relates them to the twenty-four conditions--by four methods, under seven headings, and also under positive, negative, positive-negative and negative-positive aspects. It then asks and answers questions, the possible permutations of which number nearly 405 billion. Narada's excellent introduction is indispensable for seeing the total scheme: his five hundred pages of translation represent only a small portion of the entire work.

3.2.3.2 Abhidharma Texts in Translation (Other Hinayana Schools)

(1) Abhidharmakosa-karika. Edited and translated by N. Aiyaswami Sastri. Indian Historical Quarterly, 29 (1953), pp. 111-120, 242-259, 363-377.

Translation of only the first of the nine chapters of this text, which the Chinese and Tibetans attributed to Vasubandhu, and which was translated into Chinese by Hsuan Tsang c. 651. The text as a whole is a Sarvastivadin collection of over 600 stanzas which are explained in the Abhidharmakosa. Only the section on the dhatus has been translated here.

(2) Asraya-prajnaptisastra. Translated by K. Venkataramanan as "Sammitiya-nikaya-sastra." Visva-Bharat Annals, 5 (1953), 155-242.

Translation of one of the very few extant Sammitiya texts. This one, an anonymous Abhidharma work first translated into Chinese in the Fifth century, is interesting for its reflection of the Sammitiya's own particular understanding of the workings of karma and the nature of the self.

(3) DEMIEVILLE, PAUL. "Un Fragment Sanskrit de l'Abhidharma des Sarvastivadin." Journal Asiatique, 249 (1961), 461-475.

Edition of Bernard Pauly's fragments (found in Kucha) of the Sanskrit text of the Jnanaprasthana, a Sarvastivadin Abhidharma work attributed to Katyayaniputra with a facing translation into French of the corresponding passages from Hsuan Tsang's Chinese rendition of the text.

(4) VASUBANDHU. Abhidharmakosa. Translated by Louis de La Vallée Poussin as L'Abhidharmakosa de Vasubandhu. Paris: P. Geuthner, 1923-1931, 6 vols. Nouv. édition anasiatique présentée par Etienne Lamotte, Mélanges Chinois et Bouddhiques, No. 16 (1971).

It is hard to overestimate the importance the Abhidharmakosa has had among scholarly-minded Buddhists. Though written by Vasubandhu (fifth century A.D.) along Sautrantika lines, it has been a textbook and authority on Abhidharmic questions for all schools, Hinayanist and Mahayanist alike, in India, China, and Tibet. The work's contents are impossible to summarize; but, roughly: Chapters 1-2 analyze the dhatus and the indriyas; Chapter 3, cosmology; Chapters 4-5, karma and the klesas; Chapter 6, the Path; Chapters 7-8, the jhanas and dhyanas; and Chapter 9 refutes the pudgalavadin theory of self. This well-annotated edition is a reprint of La Vallée Poussin's translation (Paris: P. Geuthner, 1923-1931), and is based largely on Hsuan Tsang's Chinese translation of the text. Since that time, the original Sanskrit text has been found.

(5) _____. Karmasiddhiprakarana. Translated by Etienne Lamotte as "Le Traité de l'Acte de Vasubandhu." See 2.4.3(6).

The Karmasiddhiprakarana, which is here translated into French, is a relatively short treatise dealing primarily with the mechanisms of the law of Karma. It should interest those who are looking for a rather technical and abhidharmic debate on the workings of cause and effect. The Chinese and Tibetans both classify it as a Mahayanist work, but its own argument espouses the Sautrantika viewpoint; it seems safe to say, therefore, that its author is "Vasubanhu of the Abhidharmakosa," i.e., before his "conversion" to the Yogacara school.

3.2.3.3 Abhidhamma Commentaries and Manuals in Translation

(1) ANURUDDHA. Abhidhammattha-sangaha. Translated by Shwe Zan Aung and revised by C. A. F. Rhys-Davids as Compendium of Philosophy. Pali Text Society Translation Series, No. 2. London: Luzac, 1910, 298 pp. (Reprinted 1972.)

The classic translation of a work which is undoubtedly the most important Theravada compendium of Abhidhamma teachings. It was composed in the tenth century (?) by the monk Anuruddha and since then has been used in Ceylon and in Burma as a primer of philosophy and psychology. However, its highly condensed contents make it a difficult work, especially for the beginning student. Parts 1-5 of its nine parts deal with various analyses of the different kinds of consciousness. Parts 6-9 deal respectively with Matter, Categories, Relations, and Stations of Religious Exercise. All this is preceded by Shwe Zan Aung's helpful 76-page introduction. There is another translation of the work by Narada Thera (below).

(2) _____. Abhidhammattha-sangaha. Translated by Narada Thera as A Manual of Abhidamma. Second revised edition. Kandy, Ceylon: Buddhist Publication Society, 1968, 451 pp. (First published Colombo: Vajirarama, 1956-1957 in 2 vols.)

Not as readily available as Shwe Zan Aung's translation (above), but helpful for being printed alongside the original Pali text, and for Narada's notes which bring a Sinhalese perspective (where Aung's bring a Burmese). Roughly, volume 1 deals with the analysis of nama (mind, mentals, etc.) and volume 2 with that of rupa (matter); in the

Theravada (Hinayana) Texts

process most of the main Buddhist doctrines undergo a terse Abhidhammic treatment.

(3) BUDDHAGHOSA. Atthasalini. Translated by Pe Maung Tin as The Expositor. Pali Text Society Translation Series, Nos. 8-9. London: Oxford University Press, 1920-1921, 2 vols. (Reprinted as The Expositor Atthasalini, London, 1958.)

The Atthasalini is Buddhaghosa's commentary on the Dhammasangani (Book I of the Abhidhamma pitaka), and should be consulted in any detailed study of that work. At the same time, it is more than just a commentary, for, in addition to word definitions and explanations, it contains self-standing discourses (e.g., the "discourse on Kamma"). The importance and meaning of the work will only be grasped by students who are advanced enough to be interested in and ready for its contents, except, perhaps, for the "Introductory Discourse" in which Buddhaghosa presents some "historical" and contextual material valuable for all students.

(4) BUDDHAGHOSA(?). Kathavatthuppakarana-Atthakatha. Translated by Bimala Churn Law as The Debates Commentary. Pali Text Society Translation Series, No. 28. London: Luzac, 1969, 248 pp. (First published 1940.)

The Kathavatthu, Book 5 of the Pali Abhidhamma (see 3.2.3.1), is an important source of information on the history of Buddhist doctrine. The Kathavatthuppakarana-Atthakatha is an important commentary on that text. Generally ascribed to Buddhaghosa, its helpfulness lies primarily in providing the details as to who the different factions involved in the debates were. It should be noted, however, that many of its major points have been footnoted in C. A. F. Rhys-Davids' translation of the Kathavatthu itself.

3.2.3.4 Studies of Abhidharma Texts

See also "The Analysis and Classification of Dharmas" in 2.7.7.

(1) AUNG, SHWE ZAN. "Abhidhamma Literature in Burma." Journal of the Pali Text Society (1910-1912), pp. 112-132.

Admirable overview of the Abhidhamma literature in use by the Burmese Sangha. The author makes it clear which books of the Abhidhamma are emphasized and notes the significance of Burmese interpretations of the materials. Recommended for the elementary student.

(2) BAREAU, ANDRE. "Les Origines du Sariputrabhidharmastra." Muséon, 63 (1950), 69-75.

A thorough study of a Hinayana Sanskrit Abhidharma treatise which appears to parallel the Pali Vibhanga in its contents and intent. Bareau concludes, not without hesitation, that it is a text of the Dharmaguptaka school.

(3) BUDDHAGHOSA. Atthasalini. Translated by Pe Maung Tin as The Expositor Atthasalini (see 3.2.3.3[3]), vol. 1, pp. 1-45.

In this "Introductory Discourse" to his commentary on the first book of the Abhidhamma (Dhammasangani), Buddhaghosa presents some very interesting information about the legendary origins of the whole Abhidhamma pitaka --who and what it was intended for, how it is divided, what its relationship is to the other pitakas. This is the sort of passage which interested students might as well read here rather than paraphrased in a work by some modern scholar.

(4) DUTT, NALINAKSHA. "The Dhammasangani." Indian Historical Quarterly, 15 (1939), 345-372.

Helpful, straightforward outline and exposition of the contents and approach of the Dhammasangani, the first book of the Pali Abhidhamma. Designed to make the reading and studying of that text easier.

(5) GOVINDA, ANAGARIKA BRAHMACARI. The Psychological Attitude of Early Buddhist Philosophy, and Its Systematic Representation According to Abhidhamma Tradition. See 2.7.5(3).

(6) LA VALLEE POUSSIN, LOUIS DE. "Documents d'Abhidharma, traduits et annotés." Mélanges Chinois et Bouddhiques, 1 (1931/1932), 65-109.

Study of Abhidharma texts, mostly of the Sarvastivadin school, with an eye for what they say about the profession of faith in the Buddha, Dharma, and Sangha. See also 11.2(5).

(7) _____. "Documents d'Abhidharma." See 2.7.7(7).

(8) NYANAPONIKA, THERA. Abhidhamma Studies: Researches in Buddhist Psychology. Island Hermitage publication no. 2. Colombo: Frewin, 1949, 87 pp.

A set of essays on Abhidhamma problems. The first one has a helpful description of two of the Abhidhamma's methods: analysis, as illustrated by the Dhammasangani, and investigation of relations, as seen in the Patthana. The other essays include studies of specific topics in the Dhammasangani.

(9) NYANATILOKA. Guide to the Abhidhamma-Pitaka: Being a Synopsis of the Philosophical Collection Belonging to the Buddhist Pali Canon, followed by an essay on the Paticca-Samuppada. See 2.4.1(11).

Second edition of a book which has become almost indispensable for a serious study of Pali Abhidhammas. Its helpful abstracts, summaries, and valuable synoptic tables make it a fine introduction to this literature as well as a later reference book. The work also contains an essay by Nyanatiloka on the doctrine of paticca samuppada.

3.2.3.4

(10) STCHERBATSKY, FEDOR IPPOLITOVICH. The Central Conception of Buddhism and the Meaning of the Word Dharma. See 2.7.7(11).

(11) TAKAKUSU, J. "Chinese Translations of the Milinda Panha." Journal of the Royal Asiatic Society (1896), pp. 1-21. See also 8.9.1(36).

(12) TAKAKUSU, JUNJIRO. "On the Abhidharma Literature of the Sarvastivadins." See 2.4.3(10).
    A very helpful introductory survey of the Abhidharma works of this school which have been preserved in the Tibetan and Chinese canons. Includes analyses of the contents of the seven basic Abhidharma works of the Sarvastivadins (each of which is assigned an author) beginning with Katyayaniputra's Jnanaprasthana, a Sanskrit fragment of which has been translated into French (see 3.2.3.2[3]). Also included in the discussion are some other important philosophical works connected with the Sarvastivadin school. A much shorter survey of the Sarvastivadin Abhidharma works, which amounts to hardly more than a listing of their Sanskrit and Tibetan titles but is helpful for quick reference, may be found in Anukul Chandra Banerjee, "Abhidharma Texts in Tibetan" (see 3.1.4[2]), pp. 372-378, or on pp. 51-75 of his more substantial Sarvastivada Literature (see 2.4.3[1]).

3.2.4 Other Hinayana Texts in Translation

3.2.4.1 Narrative Works (Including Separate Buddha Biographies)

See also Biography of the Buddha in Category 8. For National and Ecclesiastical Histories see in Category 9.

(1) Abhiniskramanasutra. Translated by Samuel Beal as The Romantic Legend of Sakya Buddha. London: Trubner, 1875, 295 pp.
    Translation of a Buddha biography reputed to reflect the views of the Dharmaguptaka school in whose canon it may or may not have been included. This translation is from the extant Chinese version.

(2) ASVAGHOSHA. Saundarananda. Edited and translated by E. H. Johnston. Punjab University Oriental Publications. London: H. Milford, 1928, 175 pp.
    Translation of a long poem (short epic) by the great second century Buddhist poet Asvaghosha about the conversion of "Nanda the Handsome," whom the Buddha convinced to become a monk by promising him pleasurable union with heavenly maidens. He gets Nirvana instead. The first two of the eighteen chapters have also been translated into French by A. Baston in "Le Saundrananda Kavya d'Acvaghosa," Journal Asiatique, 19 (1912), 79-100.

Theravada (Hinayana) Texts

(3) _____. Buddhacarita. Translation of Dharmaraksha's Chinese version by Samuel Beal as The Fo-sho-hing-tsan-king: A Life of Buddha by Asvaghosha Bodhisattva. Delhi: Motilal Banarsidass, 1968, 380 pp. (First published 1883 by Oxford University Press, Sacred Books of the East, Vol. 19.)
    This is the English rendition of Dharmaraksha's fifth century translation of Asvaghosha's life of the Buddha (Buddha carita). Asvaghosha was a second century Theravadan poet whose work nevertheless reflects certain Mahayanist tendencies and was popular in Mahayana lands. Unlike the extant Sanskrit original which contains only seventeen chapters--stopping at the sermon in Sarnath--this Chinese version is a complete biography, and its twenty-eight chapters cover all the major events in the Buddha's life, from his birth to the disposal of his relics. It can also be recommended as a work of the highest literary quality.

(4) _____. Buddhacarita. Translated by E. B. Cowell as "The Buddhacarita of Asvaghosha." Part 1 of Buddhist Mahayana Texts. Edited by E. B. Cowell, F. Max Müller and J. Takakusu. Delhi: Motilal Banarsidass, 1972, 208 pp. (First published 1894 by Oxford University Press, Sacred Books of the East, Vol. 49.)
    Although his work has here been translated in a set of Mahayana texts, Asvaghosha himself was a Theravadan (probably belonging to a subsect of the Mahasanghikas). His poems, however, especially this one on the life of the Buddha, are the work of a great Indian bard rather than of a sectarian and were popular in all schools. Cowell has here translated the seventeen extant chapters of the Sanskrit text (the last four of which are of debatable authorship).

(5) _____. Buddhacarita. Translated by Edward Hamilton Johnston as The Buddhacarita or, Acts of the Buddha. Punjab University Oriental Publications, No. 32. Calcutta: Baptist Mission Press, 1936, 2 vols. Part 1, Trans. of Chs. 1-14.
    The Sanskrit original of the Buddhacarita (second century A.D.) is an incomplete biography of the Buddha, containing only seventeen chapters, the last four of which are not even Asvaghosha's. Johnston's authoritative translation, therefore, stops at Chapter 14, with the Buddha's enlightenment. It may be compared with Cowell's older but still more readily available translation of all seventeen chapters of the same text. It should also be complemented by Beal's English rendition of Dharmaraksha's fifth century Chinese translation, which contains a full twenty-eight chapters. Johnston has also translated the extra chapters from the Tibetan in "The Buddha's Mission and Last Journey (Buddhacarita xv to xxviii)," Acta Orientalia, 15 (1937), 1-128.

Theravada (Hinayana) Texts

(6) **Jinacarita**. Translated by William Henry Denham Rouse as "Jinacarita." Journal of the Pali Text Society (1904-1905), pp. 1-65.
Text (pp. 1-32) and translation (pp. 33-65) of a Pali work which praises the Buddha by recounting his life and deeds. The work is attributed to the Sinhalese author Vanaratana Medhankara who flourished in the late thirteenth century. It thus is interesting for showing developments in the formulation of the biography of the Buddha. Another translation has been made by Charles Duroiselle as The Career of the Conqueror (Rangoon: British Burma Press, 1906), 197 pp.

(7) **Mahavastu**. Translated by J. J. Jones. See 3.2.1.2(5).

3.2.4.2 Manuals of Teaching and Meditation

See also 11.4.2.

(1) BUDDHAGHOSA. **Visuddhimagga**. Translated by Bhikkhu Nanamoli as The Path of Purification. Second edition. Colombo: A. Semage, 1964, 885 pp. Also translated by Pe Maung Tin as The Path of Purity. (First published 1923, 1929, and 1931 by Luzac, London, as Pali Text Society Translation Series, nos. 11, 17 and 21; reissued as a single volume, 1971, 907 pp.)
The Visuddhimagga, the magnum opus of the great fifth century exegetist Buddhaghosa, has enjoyed a tremendous reputation among Theravada Buddhists. On the one hand, it is a detailed meditation manual full of practical advice and instruction. On the other hand, it is an authoritative reference work which systematizes and summarizes the whole of the Buddha's teachings. It classically presents the Path to Nirvana centering on three topics: sila ("virtue"), samadhi ("concentration"), and panna (understanding--wisdom). Throughout it is a model of clarity; it is only because of its length and detail that it has not generally been used in undergraduate classes; but for the interested and advanced student it can become an exciting and important book. Pe Maung Tin's translation is different in style from that of Bhikkhu Nanamoli, whose 1956 rendition of the text as The Path of Purification has been used in this bibliography, and is, on the whole, easier to read. Both, however, have their merits and demerits.

(2) **Yogavacara's Manual**. Translated by Frank L. Woodward as Manual of a Mystic. London: Luzac, 1962, 159 pp. (First published 1916 by H. Milford. Pali Text Society Translation Series, no. 6.)
The original influence of this eighteenth century Ceylonese meditation manual is difficult to assess; clearly its early publication and translation by the Pali Text Society have given it a more widespread fame than it might have attained on its own. Perhaps its final importance lies not so much in its contents per se as in what they reveal about the history and development of Theravada meditation; when compared to much earlier meditation discourses, they reflect a definite, quasi-tantric, yogic influence. D. B. Jayatilaka's appendix is also helpful in setting the text in its historical framework.

(3) SAMGHARAKSA. **Yogacarabhumi**. Partial translation by Paul Demieville in "Le Yogacarabhumi de Sangharaksa." Bulletin de l'Ecole française d'Extrême-Orient, 44 (1954), 340-436.
Sangharaksa was a Sarvastivadin, contemporary and perhaps teacher of King Kanishka. The Yogacarabhumi (not to be confused with Asanga's great work of the same name) is his treatise on meditation. The Sanskrit original is lost and the Chinese translation has received a sort of Mahayanist appendix. Tao-an, one of the great figures of Chinese Buddhism in the fourth century, wrote a preface to this work, which reflects the popularity it had in China. See Arthur E. Link, "Shyh Daw-an's preface to Sangharaksa's Yogacarabhumi sutra and the problem of Buddho-Taoist Terminology in Early Chinese Buddhism," Journal of the American Oriental Society, 77 (1957), 1-14.

(4) **Traibhumi Brah R'van**. Translated by Charles Archaimbault, with Georges Coedes, as Les Trois Mondes. UNESCO collection of representative works, Thailand series. Publications de l'Ecole française d'Extrême-Orient, vol. 89. Paris: A. Maisonneuve, 1973, 294 pp.
French translation of a Thai text which is one of the basic Theravada manuals of cosmological concerns, dealing primarily with the kama, rupa, and arupa realms of existence. An English translation by Frank and Mani Reynolds is due to appear soon.

(5) UPATISSA. **Vimuttimagga**. Translated by N. R. M. Ehara, Soma Thera and Kheminda Thera as The Path of Freedom-Vinuttimagga. Colombo: D. Roland D. Weerasuria, 1961, 1xi + 362 pp.
The Vimuttimagga is a meditation manual with an interesting history. Upatissa's Pali original, now lost, was translated into Chinese by Sanghapala (sixth century), and then (here) retranslated into English by three Ceylonese monks. The work is shorter and earlier than the Visuddhimagga, but so similar in structure and content that it is hard to believe Buddhaghosa did not have it before him when he wrote the latter work. Both are organized around the foci of Sila, Samadhi and Panna; both deal with the thirteen Austerities, the forty Subjects of Meditation, the Four Noble Truths and the fruits of the Path. The Vimuttimagga, however, devotes comparatively more space to practical instruction and less to doctrinal exegesis.

3.2.4.3　　　　　　　　　　　　　　　　　　　　　　　　　　　　　　　Theravada (Hinayana) Texts

3.2.4.3 Hymns of Praise, Epistles and Other Works in Translation

(1) MATRCETA. Maharajakanikalekha. Translated by Frederick William Thomas in "Matriceta and the Maharajakanikalekha." Indian Antiquary, 32 (1903), 345-360.

Translation with introduction and facing edited Tibetan text of a letter addressed to King Kanishka and signed by the poet Matrceta (second century A.D.). It consists of eighty-five better known letters to a king by the great philosopher Nagarjuna (see also 3.3.2.1). On the whole genre of these letters, see Sylvain Levi, "Kaniska et Satavahana," Journal Asiatique (1936), 63-121.

(2) _____. Satapancasatka. Translated by David Roy Shackleton-Bailey as The Satapancasatka of Matrceta. Cambridge: University Press, 1951, 237 pp.

Introduction to and annotated translation of the second century A.D. poet Matrceta's "Hymn in 150 verses." The hymn was popular in all Buddhist schools and consists of praises of the Buddha and of his exploits as a Bodhisattva. For a discussion of the original title of the work and an argument that it was actually called the Prasadapratibha, see David Roy Shackleton-Bailey, "A Note on the Titles of Three Buddhist Stotras," Journal of the Royal Asiatic Society (1948), pp. 55-60. The work has also been translated in a much "freer style" by Stephan Beyer in his The Buddhist Experience: Sources and Interpretations. (Encino, Calif.: Dickenson, 1974), pp. 1-6.

(3) _____. Varnarhavarna Stotra. Translated by David Roy Shackleton-Bailey as "The Varnarhavarna Stotra of Matrceta." Bulletin of the School of Oriental and African Studies, 13 (1950), 671-701, 809-810; and 13 (1951), 947-1003.

Sometimes called the "Hymn of 400 verses," this was a popular work in praise of the Buddha by the famous second century poet Matrceta, who seems to have been originally a worshipper of Siva.

(4) Vajrasuci. Translated by Sujitkumar Mukhopadhyaya as The Vajrasuci of Asvaghosa. Second edition, revised. Visva-Bharati Research Publication. Santiniketan: R. Ray, 1960, 63 pp. (First published 1950.)

An English translation with a study of the Sanskrit text and Chinese version of a short text which claims to be by the great second century poet Asvaghosa but is clearly not. The text was first translated as long ago as 1829 by Brian Hodgson; it is a rather powerful Buddhist attack on the whole Indian caste system and has enjoyed moments of popularity among scholars who share its sentiments. Another translation of it has been made by S. K. Mukherjee, "The Vajrasuci of Asvaghosa," Visva-Bharati Annals, 2 (1949), 125-184.

3.3　MAHAYANA TEXTS IN TRANSLATION AND TEXTUAL STUDIES

3.3.1　The Perfection of Wisdom (Prajnaparamita) Literature

3.3.1.1 Prajnaparamita Texts in Translation

Outline of Prajnaparamita literature

Large sutras:
- in 100,000 lines = Satasahasrika prajnaparamita (only brief excerpts in translation)
- in 25,000 lines = Pancavimsatisaharika prajnaparamita
- in 18,000 lines = Dasasahasrika prajnaparamita (not translated)
- in 8,000 lines = Astasahasrika prajnaparamita

Its verse summary = Prajnaparamita-ratnagunasamcayagtha

Middling sutras:
- in 2,500 lines = Suvikrantavikrami-pariprocha prajnaparamita
- in 700 lines = Saptasatika prajnaparamita
- in 500 lines = Parcasatika prajnaparamita

Short sutras:
- in 300 lines = Vajracchedika prajnaparamita ("Diamond Sutra")
- in 25 or 14 lines = Prajnaparamita hrdaya ("Heart Sutra")
- The Perfection of Wisdom in a Few Words = Svalpaksara prajnaparamita
- The Perfection of Wisdom for Kausika = Kausika prajnaparamita

Special texts:
- The Questions of Nagasri = Nagasri-pariprocha prajnaparamita
- The Sutra on Perfect Wisdom which explains how Benevolent kings may protect their countries = Ninno prajnaparamita

Tantric texts:
- in 150 lines = Adhyardhasatika prajnaparamita
- The 108 Names of Perfect Wisdom = Prajnaparamita nama-asiasaiaka
- The 25 Doors to Perfect Wisdom = Pancavimsati-prajnaparamita-mukha
- The Blessed Perfection of Wisdom, in One Letter
- The Perfect Wisdom and the Five Bodhisattvas

(1) Adhyardhasatika prajnaparamita. Translated by Edward Conze as "The Perfection of Wisdom in 150 lines," in his The Short Prajnaparamita Texts. London: Luzac, pp. 184-195.

Also known as the Prajnaparamita-naya-satapancasatika, this "Perfection of Wisdom sutra in 150 lines" is the most substantial of the clearly tantric prajnaparamita texts. It is thought to have been written c. 600 A.D. and was translated six times into Chinese,

Mahayana Texts

once into Tibetan and also into Khotanese (the latter version being translated into German by Ernst Leumann in his "Die Nordarischen Abschnitte des Adhyardhasatika-Prajna-Paramita." _Journal of Taisho University_, 6-7 (1930), 47-87). Conze's translation is of the Sanskrit version and previously appeared in _Studies of Esoteric Buddhism and Tantrism_ (Koyasan: Koyasan University, 1965), pp. 101-115.

(2) _Astadasasahasrika prajnaparamita-sutra_. Chapters 55-70 translated by Edward Conze in his _The Gilgit Manuscript of the Astadasasa hasrikapra-jnaparamita_. Serie Orientale Roma, Vol. 26. Roma: Istituto Italiano per il Medio ed Estremo Oriente, 1962, 390 pp.

This "Perfection of Wisdom in 18,000 lines" is the smallest of the three large _Prajnaparamita_ texts which were composed in the first few centuries of our era. The chapters edited and translated here were the only ones found (by Giuseppe Tucci) in Northern Pakistan. Their contents (which deal with the Seventh-Ninth Bodhisattva bhumis) correspond to the fifth chapter of the _Abhisamayalankara_. Not for beginning students.

(3) _Astasahasrika Prajnaparamita_. Translated by Edward L. Conze in his _The Perfection of Wisdom in Eight Thousand Lines & Its Verse Summary_. Wheel series, No. 1. Balinas: Four Seasons Foundation, 1973, 325 pp.

The Perfection of Wisdom in 8,000 Lines is one of the oldest and most basic texts of the _Prajnaparamita_ literature. Its contents are not easy to summarize as they touch on many topics; but throughout them runs the theme of reaction against the Athidharma of the Theravadans, coupled with an espousal of the aim and path of Bodhisattvahood, i.e., perfecting wisdom for the sake of all sentient beings; and a lively interest in Absolute. Conze's translation, which has cut out the original's tangles of redundancies, gives this important text the readability it really deserves in any language. It is here preceded by a translation of its verse summary, the _Prajnaparamita-ratnaguna-samcayagatha_ (below). It was originally translated without the verse summary and published in Calcutta by The Asiatic Society in 1958. Two of the commentaries on the text have been translated: Kambalapada's _Navasloki_ and Dignaga's _Prajnaparamita pindartha_ (see 3.3.1.2[3]).

(4) "The Blessed Perfection of Wisdom, the Mother of All the Tathagatas, in One Letter." Translated by Edward Conze in his _The Short Prajnaparamita Texts_ (above), p. 201.

The most condensed of all Perfection of Wisdom sutras in which the Buddha teaches the Prajnaparamita to Ananda in one letter: A.

"Diamond Sutra"

See under _Vajracchedika prajnaparamita-sutra_

"Heart Sutra"

See under _Prajnaparamita-hrdaya-sutra_

(5) _Kausika prajnaparamita-sutra_. Translated by Edward Conze as "The Perfection of Wisdom for Kausika" in his _The Short Prajnaparamita Texts_ (above), pp. 157-159.

The "Perfection of Wisdom for Kausika" (Indra) is sometimes considered to be a Tantric _prajnaparamita_ text. But the Tibetan version, on which Conze has based this translation, omits many of the additional mantras found in the Central Asian Sanskrit text and in the Chinese; thus Conze classifies it simply as a summary of perfection of wisdom teachings, in which the "level of instruction is on a pretty elementary level."

(6) _Nagasri-pariprccha prajnaparamita sutra_. Selections translated by L. Lancaster as "The Questions of Nagasri," in _The Short Prajnaparamita Texts_ (above), pp. 160-164.

Translation of about one-tenth of an interesting perfection of wisdom sutra (one of the so-called "special texts"), in which the Bodhisattva Manjusri explains the perfectly wise way of going on a begging round and of eating the food thus collected.

(7) _Ninno Prajnaparamita-sutra_. Summary translation by Edward Conze, Richard Robinson and L. Lancaster as "The Sutra on Perfect Wisdom, which explains how Benevolent Kings may protect their Countries" in _The Short Prajnaparamita Texts_ (above), pp. 165-183.

Summary translation of a so-called "Special Prajnaparamita text" which is known as the _Ninno kyo_, and is an important example of the Perfection of Wisdom's concern for social affairs and worldly matters. It was twice rendered into Chinese; once by Kumarajiva (c. 400) and once by the Tantric Amoghavajra. An extensive account of the text, which was one of the most important Buddhist sutras in Japan (at least in the court) from the seventh to the thirteenth centuries, has been given by M. W. deVisser in his _Ancient Buddhism in Japan_ (see 1.13.2.1[8]), vol. 1, pp. 116-189.

(8) _Pancasatika Prajnaparamita-sutra_. Translated by Edward Conze as "The Perfection of Wisdom in 500 Lines," in his _The Short Prajnaparamita Texts_ (above), pp. 108-121.

This medium size perfection of wisdom text was translated from the Tibetan, as it is extant only in that language. It is quite different in style than the slightly larger "Perfection of Wisdom in 700 Lines," and consists largely of a teaching on form (rupa) and the other skandhas, pronounced by the Buddha to Subhuti.

(9) _Pancavimsati-prajnaparamita-mukha_. Translated by Edward Conze as "The 25 Doors to Perfect Wisdom" in his _The Short Prajnaparamita Texts_ (above), pp. 199-200.

Translation of a very short tantric perfection of wisdom text in which the Buddha tells the Great Bodhisattva Vajrapani the names of the "25 doors" to the Perfection of Wisdom.

(10) "Perfect Wisdom and the Five Bodhisattvas." Translated by Edward Conze in his The Short Prajnaparamita Texts (above), pp. 148-153.

Under this heading Conze has translated from the Tibetan five very short treatises on the Perfection of Wisdom which most likely should be classified as tantric texts. They were composed after 750 A.D., and each one concerns a different bodhisattva, viz. Suryagarbha, Candragarbha, Samantabhadra, Vajrapani, and Vajraketu. They are followed by the translation of a slightly longer text, also from the Tibetan, under the title of "The Holy and Blessed Perfection of Wisdom in 50 Lines," pp. 154-156.

(11) Prajnaparamita-hrdaya-sutra. Translated by Edward Conze as "The Heart Sutra" in his Buddhist Wisdom Books. London: G. Allen and Unwin, 1958, pp. 75-107.

The "Heart Sutra" is probably the most famous and popular of all the Prajnaparamita texts, and its importance in the rituals and in the minds of the Buddhists of China and Japan is hard to overestimate. There are two versions of it: a longer one in twenty-five slokas and a shorter and earlier one in fourteen. It is the latter that is translated here alongside the Sanskrit text, with a masterful commentary by Conze. ("The Diamond Sutra"--see under Vajracchedika below--is included in this volume.) Note also the now famous erroneous claim on p. 106 that "gate" in the famous mantra "Gate, gate, Paragate, Parasamgate Bodhi Svaha," is a feminine locative; of this mistake, Conze has since said "This howler has given so much joy to my detractors that I am almost glad to have made it." For a translation of both the short and the longer version by Conze, see also his The Short Prajnaparamita Texts (above), pp. 140-143.

(12) Parajnaparamita-hrdaya-sutra. Translated by Friedrich Max Müller in Buddhist Mahayana Texts. Edited by E. B. Cowell, Max Müller and J. Takakusu. Delhi: Motilal Banarsidass, 1965, 2 vols. in 1. (First published 1894 by Oxford University Press, Sacred Books of the East, Vol. 49, Part 2, pp. 145-154.)

Translations with a short introduction, of the two versions of the "Heart Sutra," the larger and the smaller Prajnaparamita-hrdaya. The longer version which is the later one merely adds a few contextual paragraphs to the earlier and shorter version, which was probably composed in the fourth century A.D.

(13) _____. Translated by Daisetz Teitaro Suzuki in his Manual of Zen Buddhism (see 2.5.7[21]), pp. 27-32.

Chinese text and English translation of the "Heart Sutra," with, importantly, the transliteration of the way the text is recited still today in Japanese Zen temples (in words which are a combination of the original Sanskrit and Chinese sounds and attempt to be meaningful at the same time). This transliteration (and the Chinese text) were unfortunately omitted in the paperback edition of the book. There are many other translations of the Chinese text; among them: Hannya Shaku's rendition of Kumarajiva's (c. 400) version, along with an edition of the Sanskrit and Tibetan texts, in The Eastern Buddhist, 2 (1922-1923), 163-175; Shao-chang Lee's translation of Hsuan Tsang (seventh cent.) version as "The Essence of Transcendental Wisdom," Journal of the North China Branch of the Royal Asiatic Society, 65 (1934), 150-151. See also Samuel Beal's translation in his Catena of Buddhist Scriptures from the Chinese (see 3.2.1.2[7]), pp. 282-284, which gives the Chinese transliteration of the sutra's famous mantra.

(14) _____. Translated by Jacques Bacot in his Le Bouddha. Paris: Presses Universitaires de France, 1947, pp. 86-88.

Translation into French of the Tibetan text of the "Heart Sutra." For a somewhat eccentric translation of the same Tibetan version, but one into English, see Walter Yeeling Evans-Wentz, Tibetan Yoga and the Secret Doctrines (see 3.4.2[4]), pp. 355-359, where it is translated under the title "The Path of Transcendental Wisdom: the Yoga of the Voidness." For other translations of the Tibetan text, see also that of Alexandra David-Neel in her La Connaissance Transcendente d'après le Texte et les Commenaires Tibétains (below), pp. 95-101; and that of Leon Feer in his Fragments Extraits du Kandjour (see 3.5[5]), pp. 177-179.

(15) _____. Translated by Charles Joseph de Harlez. Journal Asiatique, 8, no. 18 (1891), 440-509, 445-446.

French translation of the Manchu version of the "Heart Sutra." See also the same author's translation in Wiener Zeitschrift für die Kunde des Morgenländes, 11 (1897), 209-230.

(16) Prajnaparamita-nama-astasataka. Translated by Edward Conze as "The 108 Names of Perfect Wisdom" in his The Short Prajnaparamita Texts (above), pp. 196-198.

A short, tantric litany which addresses Perfect Wisdom and recites its 108 epithets. It is interesting to compare this devotional hymn with that addressing the 108 Names of Tara, also translated by Conze in his Buddhist Texts Trhough the Ages (below), pp. 196-202.

(17) Prajnaparamita-ratnagunasamcayagatha. Translated by Edward Conze as "Verses on the Perfection of Wisdom" in his The Perfection of Wisdom in Eight Thousand Lines and Its Verse Summary (above), pp. 1-73.

Mahayana Texts

Translation of the verse text which sums up large portions of the Astasahasrika (the Perfection of Wisdom in Eight Thousand lines --one of the basic Prajnaparamita texts). Conze includes references to the parallel passages in the two works. The Ratnaguna was also translated by Conze as "Verses on the Accumulation of Precious Qualities" in Indo-Asian Studies, Part 1, edited by Raghu Vira (New Delhi: International Academy of Indian Culture, 1963), pp. 126-178.

(18) Saptasatika prajnaparamita-sutra. Translated by Edward Conze as "The Perfection of Wisdom in 700 Lines" in his The Short Prajnaparamita Texts (above), pp. 79-107.

Translation of a medium size Perfection of Wisdom sutra which consists mostly of a dialogue between the Buddha and the Bodhisattva Manjusri.

(19) Satasahasrika prajnaparamita-sutra. Partial translation by Edward Conze in his Buddhist Texts Through the Ages. New York: Harper and Row, 1964, pp. 145, 153-154, 174-175. (Paperback edition: Harper Torchbook, TB 113.)

Translations of a very few selected excerpts from the Perfection of Wisdom in 100,000 lines--the largest of the large Prajnaparamita texts. The passages are taken from Book 9, Book 45, f. 119, and Book 53, ff. 279-283. In addition to this, a short fragment of the sutra has been translated into French from the Chinese in Chavannes and Sylvain Levi, "Un fragment en chinois de la Satasahasrika Prajnaparamita," in Manuscript Remains of Buddhist Literature Found in Eastern Turkestan (see 3.2.1.2[3]), pp. 390-395.

(20) Suvikrantavikrami-pariprccha prajnaparamita-sutra. Translated by Edward Conze as "The Questions of Suvikrantavikramin" in his The Short Prajnaparamita Texts (above), pp. 1-78.

Also known as the "Perfection of Wisdom in 2,500 Lines," this was the last composed of the full-scale Prajnaparamita texts, dating sometime before the middle of the seventh century A.D. It owes its title to its being a conversation on the doctrine between the Tagagata and other enlightened beings in which the Bodhisattva Suvikrantavikramin takes a part.

(21) Svalpaksara prajnaparamita-sutra. Translated by Edward Conze as "The Perfection of Wisdom in a Few Words," in his The Short Prajnaparamita Texts (above), pp. 144-147.

Conze considers the "Perfection of Wisdom in a Few Words" to be a not-very-subtle counterpart to the "Heart Sutra" which reflects slightly more Tantric influence in its mantras. Conze has here translated the Sanskrit text, with reference to the Chinese and Tibetan variations.

(22) Vajracchedika prajnaparamita-sutra. Translated by Edward Conze as "The Diamond Sutra" in his Buddhist Wisdom Books (above), pp. 15-74.

The Vajracchedika prajnaparamita, also known as the "Diamond sutra," is a perfection of wisdom text in 300 lines. It is here translated along with the "Heart Sutra" with masterful notes and explanations by Conze. The Vajracchedika, like the "Heart Sutra," contains the essential teachings of the larger prajnaparamitas, but, unlike it, it is itself long enough to give an idea of the style and method of those larger texts. It is hard to overstate the importance and position these two sutras have had in the Buddhist world, especially in China and Japan. Their brevity has made them popular for recitation in ritual; and their depth of thought has won them the reverence of the laity and made them bases for further teaching and study. Conze has also done a more literal translation of it: Vajracchedika Prajnaparamita. Serie Orientale Roma, No. 13 (Roma: Istituto Italiano per il Medio ed Estremo Oriente, 1957). The work was translated into numerous Asian languages, from which it has been rerendered into English or French (see translations below). It has also received numerous commentaries among which those of Asanga and of Han Shan have been translated. See also 3.3.1.2.

(23) _____. Translated by Friedrich Max Müller as "The Vagrakkhedika, or Diamond Cutter," in Buddhist Mahayana Texts (above), part 2, pp. 111-144.

Older translation than that of Conze (above), but still readily available and long one of the standard renditions of the text. It is also preceded by an introduction in which Müller gives the history of the text and of its translations into Chinese, Tibetan, Mongolian and Manchu.

(24) _____. Translated by Samuel Beal as "Vajra-chhedika, the Kin Kong King, or Diamond Sutra." Journal of the Royal Asiatic Society, n.s. 1 (1865), 1-24.

An old but not a bad translation of the Diamond Sutra from the Chinese.

(25) _____. Translated by Alexandra David-Neel in her La Connaissance Transcendente d'après le Texte et les Commentaire Tibétains. Paris: Adyar, 1958, pp. 150-171.

A somewhat casual translation into French of the "Diamond Sutra," but of the Tibetan text, by the great French adventurer and Tibetologist, David-Neel.

(26) _____. Translated by Nicholas Poppe in his Three Mongolian Versions of the Vajracchedika Prajnaparamita Texts. Asiatische Forschungen, No. 35. Wiesbaden: Otto Harrassowitz, 1971, 256 pp.

Translation with notes and glossaries of the Mongolian version(s) of the "Diamond Sutra."

(27) _____. Translated by Sten Konow in *Manuscript Remains of Buddhist Literature Found in Eastern Turkestan* (see 3.2.1.2[3]), pp. 214-356.

Translation of the "Diamond Sutra" from the Khotanese with edition of the text preceded by a long introduction by Konow.

3.3.1.2 Translations of Commentaries on Prajnaparamita Texts

(1) *Abhisamayalankara-nama-prajnaparamitopadesa-sastra*. Translated by Edward Conze as *Abhisamayalankara*. Serie Orientale Roma, Vol. 6. Roma: Istituto Italiano per il Medio ed Estremo Oriente, 1954, 223 pp.

The *Abhisamayalankara* is a commentary on the large *Prajnaparamita* (in 25,000 lines). A disputed tradition assigns its authorship to Asanga, but Conze considers it to be a product of the Yogacara-Svatantrika-Madhyamika school. In any case, it became a very influential text, especially in Tibet. Its importance lies in its being a table of contents to the large *Prajnaparamita* which gives, at the same time, a new organization and intelligibility to that sutra, by relating it to the important Mahayana tradition of the fivefold path to Buddha-hood. It is not an easy text, and no undergraduate should read it without consulting pages 100-110 of Conze's *The Prajnaparamita Literature* (see 2.5.2[2]), or, alternatively, his "Maitreya's Abhisamayalankara," *East and West*, 5 (1954), 192-197.

(2) ASANGA. *Trisatikayah prajnaparamitayah Karika Saptatih*. Translated by Giuseppe Tucci in his *Minor Buddhist Texts, Part 1* (see 1.14.2.1[10]), pp. 3-128.

Tucci discovered the Sanskrit manuscript of this commentary on the "Diamond Sutra"; he then proceeded to edit it, together with its Tibetan and Chinese parallels and then translated it into English (pp. 93 ff.). The work, although attributed to the great Yogacarin Asanga, remains a "minor text." Most of its contents have been taken account of by Edward Conze in his own "commentary" on the "Diamond Sutra" (cf. his *Buddhist Wisdom Books*, see 3.3.1.1[11]), so only students who are deeply involved in a detailed study of that sutra need look into this work.

(3) DIGNAGA. *Prajnaparamitapindartha*. Translated by Giuseppe Tucci as "The Prajnaparamita pindartha of Dignaga," *Journal of the Royal Asiatic Society* (1947), pp. 53-75.

This is a commentary on "Perfection of Wisdom in 8,000 Lines." See 3.3.1.1(3).

(4) FA TSANG. *A Commentary on the Heart Sutra*. Translated by Garma C. C. Chang in his *The Buddhist Teaching of Totality*. University Park: Pennsylvania State University Press, 1971, pp. 197-206.

For a commentary of the *Prajnaparamita Hrdaya* or "Heart Sutra" from an Avatamsaka/Hua yen perspective, this work by the third Hua Yen patriarch Fa Tsang (643-712) should be consulted. The translation is only a partial one and is, at places, a rather free rendition of the original text, which appears in the Taisho Tripitaka.

(5) KUKAI. *The Secret Key to the Heart Sutra*. Translated from the *Hannya Shingyo hiken* by Yoshito S. Hakeda in his *Kukai: Major Works* (see 2.6.2[4]), pp. 262-275.

For a commentary on the *Prajnaparamita Hrdaya* or "Heart Sutra" from a Shingon-Mantrayana perspective, interested students should consult this work by the Japanese founder of the school, Kukai or Kobo Daishi (774-835).

(6) *Mahaprajnaparamitasastra*. Translated by Etienne Lamotte as *Le Traité de la Grande Vertu de Sagesse de Nagarjuna, Mahaprajnaparamitasastra*. Bibliothèque du Muséon, No. 18, Vols. 1 and 2; Publication de l'Institut Orientaliste, No. 2, Vol. 3. Louvain: Bureaux du Muséon, 1944-1970, 3 vols., 1753 pp.

This is a commentary on "Perfection of Wisdom in 25,000 Lines." See 3.3.2.1.

(7) PRASASTRASENA. *Arya-prajnaparamita-hrdaya-tika*. Translated by Edward Conze in "Prasastrasena's Arya-prajnaparamita-hrdaya-tika," in *Buddhist Studies in Honour of I. B. Horner* (see 1.2.2.4[11]), pp. 51-61.

Translation of a concise and straightforward commentary on the "Heart Sutra" from a basically Madhyamika standpoint with some Yogacara perspectives added. This is one of the seven Indian commentaries on the "Heart Sutra" preserved in the Tibetan Tanjur.

3.3.1.3 Surveys and Studies of Prajnaparamita Texts

(1) BEAUTRIX, PIERRE. *Bibliographie de la Littérature Prajnaparamita*. Publications de l'Institut Belge des Hautes Etudes Bouddhiques. Série Bibliographies, No. 3. Bruxelles: Institut Belge des Hautes Etudes Bouddhiques, 1971, 58 pp.

A fairly complete and helpful bibliography of editions, translations, and articles on *Prajnaparamita* texts, preceded by a short preface by Etienne Lamotte.

(2) CONZE, EDWARD. *The Prajnaparamita Literature*. See 2.5.2(2).

This authoritative survey by the scholar who has made the Perfection-of-Wisdom literature his special field, is immensely useful both as an introduction and as a reference work. It contains a concise history of the vast *Prajnaparamita* literature, followed by a scholarly and complete annotated bibliography. It is a must for anyone wishing to study the whole range of this literature.

Mahayana Texts

(3) HANAYAMA, SHOYU. "A Summary of Various Research on the Prajnaparamita Literature by Japanese Scholars." Acta Asiatica, 10 (1966), 16-93.

Most of the scholarly textual research being done on the Perfection of Wisdom literature is in Japanese. This substantial article on what Japanese scholars are doing and thinking with regard to Prajnaparamita texts and thought is an attempt to bridge the linguistic gap that keeps Western students unaware of this material, which they should at least be congnizant of, if they cannot take it into account.

(4) OBERMILLER, E. "The Doctrine of Prajnaparamita as Exposed in the Abhisamayalankara of Maitreya." Acta Orientalia, 11 (1932), 1-133, 334-354.

Early, but still useful introduction and study of the important Abhisamayalankara, which has now been translated by E. Conze. (See under 3.3.1.2[1].)

3.3.2 Madhyamika Texts

3.3.2.1 Madhyamika Texts in Translation

(1) Abhisamayalankara. Translated by Edward Conze. See 3.3.1.2(1).

(2) ARYADEVA (?). Hastavalaprakarana. Translated by Frederick William Thomas and H. Ui in "The Hand Treatise." Journal of the Royal Asiatic Society (1918), pp. 267-310. See also 3.3.3.1(10).

(3) ____. Satasastra. Translated by Giuseppe Tucci in his Pre-Dignaga Buddhist Texts on Logic from Chinese Sources. Gaekwad's Oriental Series, No. 49. Baroda: Oriental Institute, 1929, pp. 1-91.

Translation from Chinese and Tibetan of a polemical work by Arya Deva, the great disciple of Nagarjuna, in which he carries on Nagarjuna's critique of philosophical systems, turning his attention to the Samkhyas, Vaisesikas, Jains, and others. The Satasastra is closely related to Aryadeva's major work, the Catuhsataka, the extant Chinese chapters of which have been translated also by Giuseppe Tucci, but into Italian. See his "La versione cinese del catuhsataka di Aryadeva confrontata col testo sanscrito e la tradizione tibetana," Rivista degli Studi Orientali, 10 (1923-1925), 521-590.

(4) Bhavasamkrantisutra. Translated by N. Aiyaswami Sastri in Journal of Oriental Research (Madras), 5 (1931), 246-260.

Translation of a very short Mahayana text dealing with the transitoriness of karma. Candrakirti, who quotes it in his Madhyamakavatara, claims it as a Madhyamika text. Sastri, in addition to his translation, has here attempted to restore the Sanskrit text.

(5) BHAVAVIVEKA. Karatalaratna. Translated from Hsuan Tsang's Chinese translation by Louis de La Vallée Poussin as "Le Joyau dans la Main." Mélanges Chinois et Bouddhiques, 2 (1932/1933), 68-138.

De La Vallée Poussin has here translated into French Hsuan Tsang's Chinese rendition of Bhavaviveka's "Jewel in the Hand." Bhavaviveka was a Madhyamika philosopher of the Svatantrika-Sautrantika variety, and his work was part of the ongoing philosophical debate which centered on the doctrine of Emptiness. His arguments are rough going, and only for students who have a firm footing in Buddhist philosophy.

(6) ____. Madhyamarthasamgraha. Translated by N. Aiyaswami Sastri as "Madhyamarthasamgraha of Bhavaviveka." See 2.7.9(1).

A very short text of only eleven stanzas, but very useful, giving Bhavaviveka's understanding of the Madhyamika doctrine of the two truth levels. Sastri has tried to restore the Sanskrit text from the Tibetan and has given a translation into English.

(7) CANDRAKIRTI. Madhyamakavatara. Partial translation by Louis de La Vallée Poussin in "Madhyamakavatara, Introduction au traité du Milieu." Le Muséon, 8 (1907), 249-317; 11 (1910), 217-358; 12 (1911), 236-328.

French translation of the first six chapters of the great sixth-seventh century philosopher Candrakirti's introduction to the Madhyamika. The work is a masterful and important but often neglected, treatise outlining the Bodhisattva path and Buddhist doctrine as seen from the Madhyamika viewpoint. Unfortunately, de La Vallée Poussin seems never to have finished his translation. After finishing this "Introduction," Candrakirti then went on to write his commentary on Nagarjuna's Karikas, the Prasannapada Madhyamakavrtti (below).

(8) ____. Prasannapada Madhyamakavrtti.

This important commentary on Nagarjuna's Mulamadhyamaka karikas (below) is one of the basic texts of the Madhyamika school, by one of its most sophisticated scholars. It has been completely translated into Western languages, but its twenty-seven chapters are spread out in various books, in English, French and German: Chs. 1 and 25 have been translated into English in Fedor Stcherbatsky, The Conception of Buddhist Nirvana (see 2.5.3[12]), pp. 110-329. These two chapters are probably the most important of the work, the first containing the famous critique of causality which reduced all previous theories ad absurdum; the 25th dealing with the question of Nirvana. Chs. 5 and 12-16 have been translated into German by Stanislas Schayer in Ausgewahlte Kapitel aus der Prasannapada (Krakow: Polska Akademia Umiejetnosci, 1931), 126 pp. Ch. 10 has also been translated by Stanislaus Schayer into German in "Feuer und Brennstoff," Rocznik Orientalistyczny, 7

(1929), 26-52. Chs. 2-4, 6-9, 11, 23-24, and 26-27 may be found in a well-annotated French translation by Jacques May, Candrakirti Prasannapada Madhyamakavrtti, Collection Jean Przyluski, t. 2 (Paris: A. Maisonneuve, 1959), 539 pp. The chapters make a good exposition of the "middle-way method" of rejecting the extremes of realism and nihilism, but, because May translated them only because they had not previously been translated, the work as a whole betrays a certain disunity.
Ch. 17, which deals with the doctrine of karma, has been translated by Etienne Lamotte in "Madhyamakavrtti--XVIIe Chapitre: Examen de l'Acte et du Fruit," Mélanges Chinois et Bouddhiques, 4 (1935/1936), 265-288. And Chs. 18-22, which contain important discussions on the nature of the Self, of time, of causality, and of the Tathagata, have been translated into French by J. W. de Jong in Cinq Chapitres de la Prasannapada, Buddhica, t. 9 (Paris: Geuthner, 1949), 165 pp.

(9) COSGI ODSIR. Bodistw-a cari-a Awatar-un Tayilbur. Translated by Francis Woodman Cleaves as "The Bodistw-a cari-a awatar-un Tayilbur of 1312." Harvard Journal of Asiatic Studies, 17 (1954), 1-129.
Introduction, texts and translation of a fourteenth century Mongolian commentary on Chapter 10 of Santideva's Bodhicaryavatara. Fortunately this fragment, which was the only one to be discovered, covers the important last section of Santideva's work, for a translation of which see below (3.3.2.1[26]).

(10) Dvadasamukhasastra. Translated by N. A. Sastri as "Dvadasamukhasastra of Nagarjuna." Visva Bharati Annals, 6 (1954), 167-231.
The Dvadasamukhasastra, also known as the Dvadasadvarasastra, is a short manual on Madhyamika philosophy which was most likely composed by a disciple of Nagarjuna variously known as Naga, Nagarjuna II, or Nagabodhi, and often confused with his master. The text is extant only in the Chinese, which Sastri has here translated along with an attempted reconstruction of the Sanskrit text.

(11) KAMALASILA. Tattvasamgrahapanjika. Translated by Ganganatha Jha in The Tattvasangraha of Santaraksita, with the Commentary of Kamalasila. Gaekwad's Oriental Series, Nos. 80, 83. Baroda: Oriental Institute, 1937-1939, 2 vols, 1593 pp.
Commentary on Santaraksita's Tattvasamgraha and translated alongside it (below).

(12) Mahaprajnaparamitopadesa. Translated by Etienne Lamotte as Le Traité de la Grande Vertu de Sagesse de Nagarjuna (Mahaprajnaparamitasastra) (see 3.3.1.2[6]), vol. 3.
The Mahaprajnaparamita(upadesa)sastra, though attributed to the philosopher Nagarjuna, was probably the work of a fourth century Indian monk who converted to the Madhyamika from the Sarvastivada. It is a work of overwhelming size, scope, and richness.

Lamotte's seventeen hundred pages translate into French only half of Kumarajiva's Chinese text, and Kumarajiva reputedly translated only a tenth of the original Sanskrit (which has long since been lost). The work is a commentary on the Prajnaparamita Sutra in 25,000 lines, but its author was using the exegetical format only as a tool; his real aim was to give the Madhyamika reply to the Abhidharma of the Sarvastivadins; the result is a truly inexhaustible source of information on the Mahayana system in full bloom. Coupled with Lamotte's wealth of cross-references and footnotes it becomes a work of prime importance for reference purposes in the study of the Indian and Tibetan Mahayana, but, unfortunately, because of its size and style, most undergraduates will not have the time to profit very much from it directly.

(13) Mahayana-Vimsaka. Translated by Susumu Yamaguchi as "Nagarjuna's Mahayana-Vimsaka." The Eastern Buddhist, 4 (1927), 56-72, 169-176.
Annotated translation from the Tibetan of the very short (twenty-three verses) Mahayanavimsaka, a work traditionally attributed to Nagarjuna but probably dating from around the seventh century A.D. For an edition of the Tibetan and Chinese texts, a reconstruction of the Sanskrit and a different English translation, see Vidhushekhara Bhattacharya, ed. and trans., Mahayanavimsaka (Calcutta, 1931), 44 pp.; also Visvabharati Quarterly, 8 (1930-1931), 107-150.

(14) NAGARJUNA. Catuhstava. Translated by Louis de La Vallée Poussin as "Les Quatres Odes de Nagarjuna." Le Muséon, 32 (1913), 1-18.
There seems to be no reason to doubt Nagarjuna's authorship of these four short hymns of praise (although some scholars will point out there is no proof of it either). The four, which are here translated into French (along with a publication of the Tibetan text), are: the Nirupamastava ("Louange de l'incomparable"), Lokatitastava ("Louange de celui qui a depassé le monde"), Cittavajrastava ("Louange du Diamant de Pensée") and Paramarthastava ("Louange véritable"). The four make a good example of the more "religious" devotional side of the great philosopher. Two of them, the first and the last, have also been translated into English by Giuseppe Tucci (below).

(15) _____. _____. Partial translation by Giuseppe Tucci in "Two Hymns of the Catuhstava of Nagarjuna." Journal of the Royal Asiatic Society (1932), pp. 309-325.
Translation of two of the four hymns that make up Nagarjuna's Catuhstava, taken from a Sanskrit manuscript brought back by Tucci from Nepal. The two are the Nirupamyastava and the Paramarthastava. See, however, Tucci's brief introduction, in which he discusses the relationship of the four hymns to the four bodies

of the Buddha and concludes that, taken all together, the Catuhstava "codifies the Buddhology of Nagarjuna." For a translation of all four hymns from the Tibetan, see the French rendition by de La Vallée Poussin (above).

Nagarjuna(?), Mahaprajnaparamitasastra

See under Mahaprajnaparamitasastra

(16) NAGARJUNA. Mulamadhyamakakarikas. Translated by Frederick J. Streng in his Emptiness (see 2.5.3[13]), pp. 181-220.

The only complete English translation of the Mulamadhyamakakarikas, perhaps Nagarjuna's most important work, in which he radically reinterprets some basic notions of Buddhism, and presents the fundamental insights of the Madhyamika school. The text is here divested of its important commentarial jacket, the Prasannapada of Candrakirti.

(17) _____. Ratnavali. Partial translation by Giuseppe Tucci in "The Ratnavali of Nagarjuna." Journal of the Royal Asiatic Society (1934), pp. 307-325; (1936), pp. 237-252, 423-435.

The Ratnavali, like the Suhrllekha, is one of Nagarjuna's more "poetical" works and is likewise addressed to a king (a literary genre which seems to have caught on in the early centuries A.D.). There seems to be no reason to doubt its claim to be a work of the great Madhyamika philosopher, and it does, in fact, expound a bit more on philosophy than the Suhrllekha. Tucci has here edited the extant portions of the Sanskrit text (Chapter 1, 2 and parts of Chapter 4) and translated them into English.

(18) _____. Suhrilekha. Translated by Stephan Beyer in his The Buddhist Experience: Sources and Interpretations. Encino, Calif.: Dickenson, 1974, pp. 10-18.

The Suhrilekha, translated here as "A letter to a friend," is commonly ascribed to the great Madhyamika philosopher Nagarjuna. It is a short work of 123 stanzas in which Nagarjuna gives some practical political advice to a king, often thought to have been Kanishka, other times perhaps Udayibhadra. The text is extant only in the Tibetan, and has been translated into English at least three times. Beyer's is by far the most readily accessible, but for comparative purposes, see also H. Wenzel, "Nagarjuna's 'Friendly Epistle,'" Journal of the Pali Text Society (1886), pp. 17-32; and Suhrilekha, "The Letter of Kindheartedness, tr. by Ven Thubten Kalzang Rimpoche, Bhikkhu Nagasena and Bhikkhu Khantipalo" in The Wisdom Gone Beyond. Bangkok: Social Science Association Press of Thailand, 1966, pp. 13-44.

(19) _____. Vigrahavyavartani. Translated by Kamaleswar Bhattacharya in "The Dialectical Method of Nagarjuna." Journal of Indian Philosophy, 1 (1972), 217-261.

Complete English translation of the Sanskrit text of this short but important work by Nagarjuna. Unlike Streng's translation in his Emptiness (above), this also includes Nagarjuna's own commentary on the verses.

(20) _____. _____. Translated by Frederick J. Streng in his Emptiness (see 2.5.3[13]), pp. 221-227.

The most readily available translation of this important work by Nagarjuna, presented here as "Averting the Arguments" in the appendix of Streng's helpful study of the Madhyamika notion of Emptiness. However, Streng's translation is only of the seventy verses of the text and does not include Nagarjuna's autocommentary on them (for which see the translations by Giuseppe Tucci or by Susumu Yamaguchi). The Vigrahavyavartani is a concise example of how Nagarjuna reduces the notions of self-existence (svabhava) to absurdity, and explains quite well how, after destroying the "positions" of others, he adopts no "position" himself.

(21) _____. _____. Translated by Giuseppe Tucci in his Pre-Dignaga Buddhist Texts on Logic from Chinese Sources (above).

English translation of this important treatise of Nagarjuna, based on the Chinese and Tibetan versions. See also the annotation to Frederick Streng's translation (above).

(22) _____. _____. Translated by Susumu Yamaguchi as "Traité de Nagarjuna pour écarter les vaines discussions Vigraha-vyavartani." Journal Asiatique, 215 (1929), 1-86.

French translation of the Tibetan text which includes both the verses "Averting the Arguments" and Nagarjuna's autocommentary on them. This is preceded by Yamaguchi's long introduction and followed by extensive notes. For an English translation, see the works of Tucci and Streng (above).

(23) Ratnagotravibhaga Mahayana-Uttaratantra. Translated by E. Obermiller as "The Sublime Science of the Great Vehicle to Salvation, Being a Manual of Buddhist Monism." Acta Orientalia, 9 (1931), 81-306.

Introduction, Tibetan text and annotated translation of this work, which, though assigned to the Bodhisattva Maitreya and commented on by Asanga, is clearly a Madhyamika work, and one of the most important sources on the doctrine of the Tathagatagarbha. The text, which is now generally assigned to one Sthiramati (or Saramati), has been studied and translated more recently by Jikido Takasaki (below). For a study of one aspect of the work, see also David Seyfort Ruegg, La Théorie du Tathagatagarbha et du Gotra (see 2.7.11[2]), part 11.

(24) _____. Translated by Jikido Takasaki in *A Study on the Ratnagotravibhaga*. See 2.7.11(6).

The Ratnagotravibhaga Uttarantantra is a Prasangika (Madhyamika) work, traditionally assigned to the Bodhisattva Maitreya, but thought by some to be the work of Sthiramati (not to be confused with the Yogacarin of the same name) who is sometimes called Saramati. One of the major thrusts of the work is its concern with the doctrine of the Tathagatagarbha. It has here been translated into English with extensive introductions and notes by Takasaki. An older translation of it has been made by E. Obermiller (above).

(25) SANTARAKSITA. Tattvasamgraha. Translated by Ganganatha Jha as *The Tattvasangraha of Santaraksita, with the Commentary of Kamalasila* (above).

Santaraksita was an eighth century follower of the Bhavaviveka, and though much influenced by Dharmakirti's epistemology, may be considered as within the Madhyamika camp. Together with his pupil Kamalasila, whose commentary on the Tattvasamgraha has been translated here along with the text, he was preeminently responsible for the definitive introduction of Buddhism into Tibet. The Tattvasamgraha itself is a mammoth critique of all of Indian philosophy, centered around the discussions of twenty-six different topics, and conluding that all that can remain is the Pratitya samutpada doctrine as interpreted by Nagarjuna. For courageous and interested students only.

(26) SANTIDEVA. Bodhicaryavatara. Translated by Lionel David Barnett as *The Path of Light*. Wisdom of the East Series. London: Murray, 1909, 107 pp.

This 1909 translation of Santideva's Bodhicaryavatara is incomplete (omitting, for example, large portions of the important chapter on the Perfection of Wisdom), and its "Introduction" and "Notes" are now somewhat dated; so it cannot be recommended in the face of Matics's new (1970) rendition (below). Still, what has been translated is not badly done, and the appendix (pp. 103-107) contains a handy translation of the twenty-eight stanzas (karikas) which summarize Santideva's other work, the Siksha-samuccaya.

(27) _____. _____. Translated by Louis de La Vallée Poussin as *Bodhicaryavatara: Introduction à la Pratique des Futurs Bouddhas*. Paris: Blond, 1907, 144 pp.

Marion Matics's 1970 translation of Santideva's Bodhicaryavatara (below) should not completely eclipse de La Vallée Poussin's 1907 French rendition of the same text. The latter's work, especially his general introduction and his copious notes, retain much of their original value.

(28) _____. _____. Translated by Marion L. Matics as *Entering the Path of Enlightenment*. New York: Macmillan, 1970, 318 pp. (Published also under title *The Path of Light*.)

The work of Santideva, the prominent Madhyamika philosopher and poet of the eighth century, contains very little that is doc-runners, Nagarjuna, Aryadeva, Buddhapalita, and Candrakirti. But he restates their positions concisely and clearly, and, here in the Bodhicaryavatara, he sets them in a religiously real framework, emphasizing the development of Bodhicitta and the Bodhisattva path. Matics's fine translation (in paperback), which is preceded by a lucid "Guide to the Text," might well be used as an introduction-piece to the study of Indian or Tibetan Mahayana. See also N. Aiyaswami Sastri, "Epitome of the Bodhicaryavatara with Its Panjika," *Adyar Library Bulletin*, 17 (1950), 36-441.

(29) _____. _____. Translated by Nicholas Poppe in "A Fragment of the Bodhicaryavatara from Olon Sume." *Harvard Journal of Asiatic Studies*, 17 (1954), 411-418.

Discussion, translation and study of a fragment of Chapter 9 of the Mongolian version of Santideva's Bodhicaryavatara, which was brought back by a Japanese expedition to Olon Sume in Inner Mongolia. A fragment of a Mongolian commentary on Chapter 10 of the same work has been translated by Francis W. Cleaves (above, under Cosgi Odsir, *Bodistw-a cari-a Awatar-un Tayilbur*).

(30) _____. Siksasamuccaya. Translated by Cecil Bendall and W. H. D. Rouse as *Siksha-samuccaya: A Compendium of Buddhist Doctrine*. Delhi: Motilal Banarsidass, 1971, 328 pp. (First published 1922.)

If in the Bodhicaryavatara the eighth century Prasangika Santideva gave vent to his poetic talents, in the Siksha-samuccaya it is his scholarly side that appears. The core of the work consists of twenty-seven mnemonic stanzas (karikas) which reflect an orthodox Madhyamika doctrine and deal mostly with Bodhicitta and the Bodhisattva Path. Structured around these are numerous quotations from over 100 other Buddhist works, some of which are no longer extant. These make the Siksha-samuccaya an early and important anthology of Buddhist texts. This sole English translation unfortunately suffers from an overdose of King James Biblical English.

(31) Srimala-devi-simhapada-sutra. Translated by Alex and Hideko Wayman as *The Lion's Roar of Queen Srimala: A Buddhist Scripture on the Tathagatagarbha Theory*. See 3.2.2.2(9).

A masterful translation with notes and a very helpful introduction of an important early Mahayana sutra which deals with the doctrine of the tathagatagarbha. The translation is based on the Tibetan, Chinese and Japanese renditions and also on the extant Sanskrit fragments. The Waymans consider the text to be a product of some of the late Mahasanghika schools which flourished in the Andhra region in the third century; but, though composed by these Theravadans, the sutra, which features a dialogue between the Buddha and a Buddhist queen, Srimala, attained its fame and popularity among Mahayanists. Indeed, it may be said to reflect some of the concerns of the Madhyamikas at this time, and even to point to certain trends (such as that of the Tathagatagarbha doctrine) which will eventually break away from the Madhyamika.

(32) Suramgamasamadhisutra. Translated by R. E. Emmerick as The Khotanese Surangamasamadhisutra. London Oriental Series, Vol. 23. London: Oxford University Press, 1970, 134 pp.

Annotated edition and translation of substantial Khotanese fragments of this sutra, the Chinese version of which has been translated by Etienne Lamotte (below). Emmerick has also edited the Tibetan text on which he relies to fill in the lacunae in his manuscripts.

(33) _____. Translated by Etienne Lamotte as "La Concentration de la Marche Héroïque." Mélanges Chinois et Bouddhiques, 13 (1965), 1-308.

The Suramgamasamadhisutra (not to be confused with the Suramgama sutra of the seventh century) enjoyed an early popularity in China (where it was translated over ten times) and in Tibet. The Sanskrit original is now lost. Its main subject matter, the "samadhi of the Hero's March," is expounded by the Buddha, who enlists the aid of Matyabhimukha, a tenth stage Bodhisattva who more or less resembles the layman Vimalakirti of the Vimalakirtinirdesa sutra. Lamotte classified the work as a Madhyamika text because of its dependence on the doctrines of that school. His translation and introduction are (as usual) masterful and authoritative. The Khotanese version of the sutra has been translated into English by R. E. Emmerick (above).

(34) Vimalakirti Nirdesa sutra. Translated by Etienne Lamotte as L'Enseignement de Vimalakirti. Bibliothèque du Muséon, Vol. 51. Louvain: Publications Universitaires, 1962, 488 pp.

Lu K'uan Yu's English translation of the Vimalakirti Sutra is of Kumarajiva's fifth century Chinese version of the text. This authoritative French translation by Etienne Lamotte is based on the Tibetan text and on Hsuan Tsang's later (seventh century) but fuller version. The Sanskrit original (apart from a few quotations in other works), is lost. Lamotte's work, as always, contains copious cross-references and a definitive "Introduction" giving the history, sources, date, and concordances of the text. Also noteworthy is Paul Demieville's "Appendix" (pp. 438-455) on Vimalakirti in China.

(35) _____. Translated by Lu K'uan Yu (Charles Luk) as The Vimalakirti Nirdesa Sutra Wei Mo Chieh So Shuo China. The Clear Light Series. Berkeley, Calif.: Shambala, 1972, 168 pp.

The Vimalakirti Nirdesa Sutra is a marvelous gem of Mahayana literature, and perhaps, readily available now in English, it can be used in undergraduate classes as an introduction-piece to the Madhyamika or even the Mahayana as a whole. Composed in Sanskrit in the Second Century, the sutra attained its real popularity in translation; Tibetan and Chinese Buddhists were won over by its vivacious and humorous stories about Vimalakirti's miraculous exploits, iconoclastic activities, and practical application of Madhyamika philosophy. Luk's translation is of Kumarajiva's rendition; for a full scholarly treatment of the text and its history, see the "Introduction" to Lamotte's authoritative French translation (above). Readers of English only might also want to supplement Luk's sometimes erratic translation by reference to that of Hokei Idzumi (below).

(36) _____. Translated by Hokei Idzumi as "Vimalakirti's Discourse on Emancipation." The Eastern Buddhist, 2 (1922-1923), 358-366; 3 (1924-1925), 55-69, 138-153, 224-242, 336-349; 4 (1926-1928), 48-55, 177-190, 348-366.

A complete English translation of this extremely popular Mahayana sutra, which may readily be used as a supplement to and comparison with more recent translations. The pages in Eastern Buddhist, Vol. 2, contain an introduction to the text; those in Vols. 3 and 4 a chapter by chapter translation. Readers of French should consult Etienne Lamotte's fully annotated and authoritative translation.

3.3.2.2 Studies of Madhyamika Texts

See also under 2.7.8 in Religious Thought

(1) HIKATO, RYUSHO. "On the Author of Ta-chic-tu-lun" in his "Introductory Essay" in his edition of Suvikranta-vikrama Parinrccha Prajnaparamita Sutra. Fukuoka, Japan: Kyushu University, 1958, 142 pp.

A helpful article which discusses the authorship (attributed to Nagarjuna) of the Ta-chic-tu-lun (Mahaprajnaparamitopadesa) currently being translated by Etienne Lamotte (see 3.3.2.1[12]). Hikato analyzes three kinds of passages in the text: those clearly not Nagarjuna's, those probably his, and those which are questionable.

(2) MURTI, TIRUPATTUR RAMASESHAYYER VENKATACHALA. The Central Philosophy of Buddhism: A Study of the Madhyamika System (see 2.5.3[7]), pp. 87-103.

The section is entitled "The Madhyamika Schools and Literature" and contains a short, straightforward introductory survey of the literature of the major Madhyamika philosophers from 150-800 A.D. Basically, Murti distinguishes four periods: 1) Nagarjuna and Arya Deva in the second century, 2) Buddhapalita and Bhavaviveka in the fifth century, 3) Candrakirti (seventh century), and Santideva (eighth century), and 4) a syncretism of Yogacara with Santaraksita and Kamalasila.

(3) OBERMILLER, E. "A Study of the Twenty Aspects of Sunyata based on Haribhadra's Abhisamayalam-karaloka and the Pancavimsatisahasrika." See 2.7.8(9).

(4) RAMANAN, VENKATA E., ed. Nagarjuna's Philosophy as Presented in the Maha-prajna-paramita-Sastra. See 2.5.3(9).

(5) ROBINSON, RICHARD H. Early Madhyamika in India and China. See 1.11.2.2(9).

(6) VIDYABHUSANA, SATIS CHANDRA. "A Descriptive List of Works on the Madhyamika Philosophy." Journal of the Asiatic Society of Bengal, 4 (1908), 367-379.
A useful listing of works that can be classified as Madhyamika, only the titles of the works have not been romanized and appear only in Devanagari and Tibetan script.

3.3.3 Yogacara Texts

3.3.3.1 Translations of Yogacara Texts

(1) ASANGA. Abhidharmasamuccaya. Translated by Walpola Rahula as Le Compendium de la Super-Doctrine Philosophie, Abhidharmasamuccava d'Asanga. Publications de l'Ecole française d'Extrême-Orient, Vol. 78. Paris: Ecole française d'Extrême-Orient, 1971, 236 pp.
This is a French translation of an important Mahayanist Abhidharma text: the Abhidharmasamuccaya, in which Asanga (the founder of the Yogacara school) gives a sort of Abhidharmic resume of his teachings. In its style, and degree of analysis, it is akin to the Dhatu-katha (Book III of the Theravada Abhidharma), and like that work, it should be tackled only by interested or advanced students.

Asanga, Bodhisattvabhumi

See under Asanga, Yogacarabhumi-sastra

(2) ASANGA. Madhyantavibhanga. Translated by Fedor Stcherbatsky as Madhyanta-Vibhanga: Discourse on Discrimination between Middle and Extremes Ascribed to Bodhisattva Maitreya. Soviet Indology Series, No. 5. Bibliotheca Buddhica Reprint, vol. 30. Leningrad: Bibliotheca Buddhica, 1936. (Reprinted in Indian Studies Past and Present. Calcutta, 1971, 223 pp. Distributed by Lawrence Verry, Mystic, Conn.)
The verses of the Madhyanta-Vibhanga were composed by "Asanga-Maitreya"; the prose commentary was written by Vasubandhu; and there is a further tika (sub-commentary) by Sthiramati. Taken all together, these make up an important text of the Yogacara school. It is a polemical work which attacks what it considers to be the extreme of nihilism of the Madhyamika on the one hand, and the extreme of realism of the Sarvastivada on the other. Only the important first chapter on Lakshana (characteristics) has been translated here.

(3) _____. Mahayanasamgraha. Translated by Etienne Lamotte as La Somme du Grand Véhicule d'Asanga Mahayanasamgraha. Bibliothèque du Muséon, No. 7. Vol. 2. Louvain: Bureaux du Muséon, 1938-1939, 2 vols. in 4.
Translation of a basic and classic manual of Yogacara doctrines, now extant only in Tibetan and Chinese. The first volume contains the editions of those texts, the second, a French translation together with helpful and thorough annotations.

(4) _____. Mahayanasutralankara. Translated by Sylvain Levi as Asanga: Mahayana-sutralamkara. Exposé de la Doctrine du Grand Véhicule selon le Système Yogacara. Paris: H. Champion, 1907-1911, 2 vols. Bibliothèque de l'Ecole des Hautes Etudes. Sciences historiques et philologiques, fasc. 159, 190. Tome 1: Text. Tome 2: Translation, Introduction, Index.
In 1898, when Sylvain Levi was in Nepal, he discovered Asanga's Mahayanasutralamkara by accident when looking for Asvaghosha's Sutralamkara. The result was this edition and now quite outdated French translation of this major text in the Yogacara tradition. (There is no English translation.) The first part contains a rather standard presentation of the Bodhisattva path, and the second part examines specific points in the light of the Yogacara philosophy, and discourses on some of the principal doctrines of that school. It is not Asanga's most lucid work and should be tackled only by well-advanced students who are very interested in Yogacara.

Asanga, Paramartha gatha

See under Asanga, Yogacarabhumi-sastra

Asanga, Sravakabhum

See under Asanga, Yogacarabhumi-sastra

(5) ASANGA. Trisatikayah prajnaparamitayah Karika Saptatih. Translated by Giuseppe Tucci in his Minor Buddhist Texts, Part 1. Roma: Istituto Italiano per il Medio ed Estremo Oriente, 1956, pp. 3-128.

(6) _____. Yogacarabhumi sastra. Partial translation by Alex Wayman in his Analysis of the Sravakabhumi Manuscript. University of California Publications in Classical Philology, Vol. 17. Berkeley: University of California Press, 1961, pp. 58-134, 163-185. Summary translation of other portions by Cecil Bendall and Louis de La Vallée Poussin in "Bodhisattva-Bhumi: A Textbook of the Yogacara School," Le Muséon, 6 (1905), 38-52;

Mahayana Texts

and 7 (1906), 213-230 (in English); and 12 (1911), 155-191 (in French).

Asanga's Yogacarabhumi, only parts of which are still extant in Sanskrit but which was completely translated into Tibetan and Chinese, can only be described as gigantic. One of the longest of all Buddhist works, it gives an encyclopedic and fully-developed treatment of the Path, and was for the Yogacarins what the Mahaprajnaparamitopadesa (see 3.3.2.1[12]) was for the Madhyamikas. The work is divided into five sections, the first of which, the Bhumivastu, is as long as the other four combined. This Bhumivastu, in turn, is divided into seventeen bhumis or stages in the yogin's progression to Buddhahood. The thirteenth of these is the Sravakabhumi (summarily translated by Wayman on pp. 58-134); the fifteenth is the Bodhisattvabhumi, summarized by Bendall and de La Vallée Poussin. Wayman, on pp. 163-185, has also given an edition and translation of the Paramartha gatha, which is a small portion of Bhumi No. eleven, the Cintamayi-bhumi.

(7) DHARMAKIRTI. Nyayabindu. Translated by Fedor I. Stcherbatsky in his Buddhist Logic (see 2.1[11]), vol. 2.

A very short but concise manual of philosophy by the great seventh century Buddhist logician and philosopher, Dharmakirti, a follower and reinterpreter of Dignaga. The work is translated here along with the commentary (tika) on it by the important eighth century Kashmiri commentator Dharmottara. The work has also been translated within M. Gangopadhyaya's English translation of another eighth century commentary on it, Vinitadeva's Nyayabindu-tika, for which see 3.3.3.2(7).

(8) _____. Pramanavarttika. Partial translation by S. Mookerjee and Hojun Nagasaki in The Pramanavarttikam of Dharmakirti. Nalanda: Nava Nalanda Mahavihara, 1964, 134 pp.

Annotated translation of the first of the four chapters of Dharmakirti's Pramanavarttika. This is nominally a commentary on a work by Dignaga, the Pramanasamuccaya, but in actuality is perhaps Dharmakirti's most important work in which he treats such topics as inference, perception, and epistemology. See also 3.3.3.2(1).

(9) DIGNAGA. Alambanapariksa. Translated by Susumu Yamaguchi as "Dignaga: Examen de l'objet de la connaissance," Journal Asiatique, 214 (1929), 1-65.

Annotated translation with an edition of the Tibetan and Chinese texts of the late fourth century philosopher Dignaga's short but technical treatise on the analysis of sense objects. His critique leads him to the conclusion that objects have no reality apart from consciousness. For a brief discussion of the work see Stcherbatsky, Buddhist Logic (see 2.1[11]), pp. 518-520.

3.3.3.1

(10) _____ (?). Hastavalaprakarana. Translated by Frederick William Thomas and H. Ui as "The Hand Treatise." See 3.3.2.1(2).

The Chinese text of this short treatise, which discusses the famous simile of the reality of a perception which confuses a rope and a snake, ascribes its authorship to Dignaga. The Tibetan text, however, claims it is the work of the Madhyamika Aryadeva. F. W. Thomas, who has here edited the Tibetan text, along with an English translation, also thinks it is Aryadeva's work. H. Ui, who has here edited the Chinese text, does not express himself on this matter. T. R. V. Murti, in his Central Philosophy of Buddhism (see 2.5.3[7]), says it is clearly Aryadeva's. A. K. Warder, in his Indian Buddhism (see 1.2.1[15]), claims it is Dignaga's. Either way, the debate on the authorship is an interesting reflection of the text's own nonsectarian outlook.

(11) _____. Hetucakranirnaya. Translated by Durgacharan Chatterji in "Hetucakranirnaya." Indian Historical Quarterly, 9 (1933), 266-272, 511-514.

A translation of the Tibetan text and reconstruction of the Sanskrit of this short work by Dignaga which is also sometimes called the Hetucakradamaru. The work is a technical logician's manual on principles of inference and proof.

(12) _____. Prajnaparamitapindartha. Translated by Bhikkhu Pasadiko in The Wisdom Gone Beyond. Bangkok: Social Science Association Press of Thailand, 1966, pp. 89-106.

See the annotation under the translation by Giuseppe Tucci (below).

(13) _____. _____. Translated by Giuseppe Tucci as "The Prajnaparamitapindartha of Dignaga." Journal of the Royal Asiatic Society (1947), pp. 53-75. See 3.3.1.2(3).

English translation (together with the Sanskrit and Tibetan texts) of a short work in fifty-eight verses by the great Buddhist logician Dignaga (fourth century). The work tries to be an epitome of the "Perfection of Wisdom in 8,000 Lines," and it fairly well summarizes the Yogacara schools' understanding of the meaning of the prajnaparamita. It is also one of the few works of Dignaga that is still extant in Sanskrit.

(14) _____. Pramanasamuccaya. Partial translation by Masaaki Hattori in Dignaga on Perception: Being the Pratyakasaparicccheda of Dignaga's Pramanasamuccaya. See 2.5.4(7).

Translation and explanation of the Sanskrit fragments and the Tibetan version of the great logician Dignaga's (c. 480-540) first chapter of his greatest work, the Pramanasamuccaya. This is preceded on pages 1-12 by a concise and helpful introduction, "Dignaga and His Works."

(15) Lankavatarasutra. Translated by Daisetz Teitaro Suzuki as The Lankavatara Sutra. London: G. Routledge, 1932, 300 pp.

Suzuki has emphasized the Lankavatarasutra's relationship to the Zen sect, but it is also an important source of information about the Yogacara. The notion of "Mind Only," which is here set in the system of the "eight vijnanas," is a recurring theme. At the same time, the sutra touches on many other teachings, but in a rather chaotic manner which betrays its nature as a casually compiled memorandum of Mahayana doctrines, and makes for uneven reading. Still, it is worthwhile to plumb its depths, and in so doing the interested student should consult Suzuki's companion volume Studies in the Lankavatara Sutra (see 3.3.3.3[3]).

(16) RATNAKIRTI. Ksanabhangasiddhih Vyatirekatmika. Translated by A. C. Senape McDermott in An Eleventh-Century Buddhist Logic of Exists. Foundations of Language, Supplementary series, Vol. 11. Dordrecht: D. Reidel, 1970, 88 pp.

Translation of a work by Ratnakirti (eleventh century), a late representative of a Yogacarin tradition running through Dignaga, Dharmakirti, and Ranakirti's own teacher, Jnanasrimitra. Interesting mainly as an illustration of the later developments of the school and the kind of solipsistic idealism espoused and argued for by some at this time.

(17) Samdhinirmocanasutra. Translated by Etienne Lamotte as Samdhinirmocana Sutra: L'Explication des Mystères. Université de Louvain, Recueil de travaux, 2e série, 34e fasc. Paris: Maisonneuve, 1935, 278 pp.

The Sanskrit original of the Samdhinirmocana Sutra is lost; this French translation is based on the Tibetan version; there is, as yet, no English rendition. The sutra is important because it reflects a transition between the Prajnaparamita- and the Yogacara-literature. It already contains the important doctrine of the Three characteristics of phenomena (Dharmalaksana), and refers to the alayavijnana (storehouse consciousness); it served as a source of inspiration and authority to the founders of the Yogacara school. The text itself is tough; it is not a unified work, and the never easy Yogacara doctrines mark it "for advanced students only."

(18) VASUBANDHU. Trimsika karika prakarana. Translated by Sylvain Levi as "La Trentaine," in his Matériaux pour l'Etude du Système Vijnaptimatra. Bibliothèque de l'Ecole des Hautes Etudes. Sciences historiques et philologiques, 260 fasc. Paris: Honoré Champion, 1932, pp. 61-123.

Translation of the "treatise in thirty stanzas" of Vasubandhu, one of the important early figures of the Yogacara school. The treatise, which became popular as a textbook summarizing the major points of Vijnanavada doctrine, was the subject of ten famous commentaries, one of which--that of Sthiramati--has been translated here along with the text. Altogether, these commentaries became the basis of the monumental Vijnaptimatrata siddhi compiled by Hsuan Tsang and translated into French by de La Vallée Poussin (see 3.3.3.2[6]).

(19) _____. Trisvabhavanirdesa. Translated by Louis de La Vallée Poussin as "Le Petit Traité de Vasubandhu-Nagarjuna sur les Trois Natures." Mélanges Chinois et Bouddhiques, 2 (1932-1933), 147-161.

In this article, de La Vallée Poussin has edited and translated into French the Tibetan and Sanskrit texts of a very short work (thirty Karikas), the Trisvabhavanirdesa, which is variously attributed to Vasubandhu or Nagarjuna (but is more likely the former's). The text is not insignificant; it presents a very concise statement of the important Yogacara doctrine of the three svabhavas or laksanas.

(20) _____. Vimsika karika prakarana. Translated by Clarence Herbert Hamilton in his Wei Shih Er Lun, or, The Treatise in Twenty Stanzas on Representation-Only. American Oriental Series, Vol. 13. New Haven: American Oriental Society, 1938, 82 pp.

English translation of Hsuan Tsang's Chinese rendition of this short but important treatise by Vasubandhu, one of the fathers of the Yogacara system. See also the translations by de La Vallée Poussin and Sylvain Levi (below).

(21) _____. _____. Translated by Louis de La Vallée Poussin as "Traité des Vingt Slokas." Le Muséon, 13 (1912), 53-90.

Tibetan text and French translation of this short work by one of the founders of the Yogacara school. See also the translations by Levi (below) and Hamilton (above).

(22) _____. _____. Translated by Sylvain Levi as "La Vingtaine" in his Matériaux pour l'Etude du Système Vijnaptimatra (above), pp. 43-59.

Translation of Vasubandhu's twenty stanzas and prose autocommentary, which together form a short polemical text arguing for the doctrine of "mind only" against the views of other schools. It is often paired with Vasubandhu's Trimsika in thirty verses, but is less systematic. It has also been translated by de La Vallée Poussin and by Hamilton.

3.3.3.2 Translations of Commentaries on Yogacara Texts

(1) DHARMAKIRTI. Pramanavarttika. Partial translation by S. Mookerjee and Hojun Nagasaki in The Pramanavarttikam of Dharmakirti. See 3.3.3.1(8).

Mahyana Texts

(2) DHARMOTTARA. Nyayabindutika. Translated by Fedor Stcherbatsky in his Buddhist Logic (see 2.1[11]), vol. 2.
Translation of this commentary along with the text of Dharmakirti's Nyayabindu (see 3.3.3.1[7]).

(3) HSUAN TSANG. Ch'eng Wei-shih Lun: The Doctrine of Mere-Consciousness. See 2.5.4(8).
English translation of the work otherwise known as the Vijnaptimatrata siddhi (below) and translated into French by de La Vallée Poussin as La Siddhi de Hiuan Tsang. This is the monumental systematization of Yogacara doctrines which Hsuan Tsang compiled on the basis of ten Sanskrit commentaries on Vasubandhu's Trimsika (see 3.3.3.1[18]). As such it is an important source book on Vijnanavada doctrines, and Wei Tat's translation, though it does not contain the wealth of annotations to be found in de La Vallée Poussin's, has the advantage of having the Chinese text on facing pages.

(4) STHIRAMATI. Madhyantavibhagatika. Translated by David Lasar Friedmann as Sthiramati, Madhyantavibhagatika: Analysis of the Middle Path and the Extremes. Utrecht: Rijksuniversiteit te Leiden, 1937, 143 pp.
A translation of Sthiramati's subcommentary on the first chapter (dealing with Laksana--characteristics) of Asanga's important Yogacara polemical work, the Madhyanta-vibhanga. It is for advanced and philosophically-inclined students only and should be read in conjunction with that work. Also translated by Stcherbatsky along with his translation of Asanga's Madhyanta-vibhanga (above).

(5) VASUBANDHU. Madhyantavibhangabhasya. Translated by Fedor Stcherbatsky in Madhyanta-Vibhanga. See 3.3.3.1(2).
Translation of this commentary along with the text of Asanga's Madhyanta-vibhanga.

(6) Vijnaptimatratasiddhi. Translated by Louis de La Vallée Poussin as Vijnaptimatratasiddhi: La Siddhi de Hiuan-Tsang. Buddhica, ser. 1, t., 1-5. Paris: Geuthner, 1928-1929, 2 vols., 820 pp.
The Vijnaptimatratasiddhi is one of the monumental works of the Yogacara school. In format, a Chinese synthesis of Sanskrit commentaries on Vasubandhu's Trimsika, it is actually a systematic presentation of Vijnanavada doctrines and arguments. In many ways, it is to the Yogacara school what the Abhidharmakosa is to the Sarvastivadins. It discusses all the classic Buddhist questions--Atman, Karma, Consciousness, the Path, etc.--but dwells particularly on the special Yogacarin concerns of the Alayvijnana, the Manas, and the three laksanas. For brave and advanced students only. Short selections from the text may also be found in English translation in Wing-tsit Chan, A Source Book in Chinese Philosophy (see 2.5.1[3]), pp. 374-395; and in William Theodore de Bary, ed.,

Sources of Chinese Tradition (see 2.5.8[7]), pp. 346-349.

(7) VINITADEVA. Nyayabindu-tika. Translated by Mrinalkanti Gangopadhyaya. Calcutta: Indian Studies: Past and Present, 1971, distributed by K. L. Mukhopadhyaya, Calcutta, 245 pp.
Translation of Vinitadeva's (c. 700 A.D.) commentary on the great philosopher-logician Dharmakirti's very short but comprehensive and difficult manual, the Nyayabindu. Includes a reconstruction of the Sanskrit text from the extant Tibetan. English translation also contains the text of Dharmakirti's work.

3.3.3.3 Studies of Yogacara Texts

See also under Religious Thought in 2.5.4.

(1) LEVI, SYLVAIN. Un Système de Philosophie Bouddhique: Matériaux Pour l'Etude du Système Vijnaptimatra. See 2.5.4(9).

(2) STCHERBATSKY, FEDOR. "La littérature Yogacara d'après Bouston." Le Muséon, 6 (1905), 144-155.
A dated but still helpful and short review of the Tibetan historian Bu-ston's somewhat complex classification of Yogacara literature.

(3) SUZUKI, DAISETZ TEITARO. Studies in the Lankavatara Sutra. London: Routledge, 1930, 464 pp.
This volume of essays on the Lankavatara is a companion to Suzuki's translation of that work and is important to anyone interested in the history of the text and some of its principal doctrines. At the same time, it makes a helpful, scholarly introduction to the whole teaching of Mahayana Buddhism in its developed stages.

(4) WAYMAN, ALEX. Analysis of the Sravakabhumi Manuscript. See 3.3.3.1(6).
Essentially the published version of Wayman's doctoral dissertation, this work is very helpful not only as a study of the language, style and thought of the Sravakabhumi, but also as an introduction to the huge Yogacarabhumi and its place in the life and works of Asanga. For a more introductory survey, see Wayman's article "A Report on the Sravaka-bhumi . . ." (below).

(5) _____. "A Report on the Sravaka-bhumi and its author Asanga." Journal of the Bihar Research Society, 42 (1956), 316-329.
The Sravaka-bhumi is one of the sections of Asanga's encyclopedic Yogacara-bhumi. In this article, Wayman discusses the Sravaka-bhumi in light of what he takes to be a generic class of Buddhist texts named Yogacara-bhumi, and in this connection deals with the question of authorship (Maitreyanatha, Asanga, etc.) of the text. A more detailed, analytical study of one section of the Sravaka-bhumi (the

"hetu-vidya") may be found in Alex Wayman, "The Rules of Debate according to Asanga," *Journal of the American Oriental Society*, 78 (1958), 29-40.

3.3.4 Avatamsaka/Hua Yen Texts

3.3.4.1 Avatamsaka/Hua Yen Texts in Translation

(1) *Avatamsaka Sutra*. Partial translation by Garma C. C. Chang in his *The Buddhist Teaching of Totality* (see 3.3.1.2[4]), pp. 187-196.
 The *Avatamsaka Sutra* (*Hua-yen ching* or *Kegon kyo*) is great both in size and importance and has never been completely translated into English. Chang has here given a translation of part of Chapter 31 of Buddhabhadra's (359-429) Chinese rendition which deals with the vows of the Bodhisattva Samantabhadra, which Chang has selected to illustrate the style and contents of the text as a whole.

(2) _____. Partial translation by Daisetz Teitaro Suzuki. *The Eastern Buddhist*, 1 (1921), 1-13, 147-155, 237-242, 282-290.
 The *Avatamsaka Sutra* (*Hua-yen ching*, *kegon-kyo*) in Buddhabhadra's fourth century version contains a total of thirty-four chapters in sixty chuan. In these pages, Daisetz Teitaro Suzuki has translated into English the epitomized translation of the first eight of those chapters, which was prepared by two Japanese scholars, Shugaku Yamabe and Chizen Akanuma. It forms a helpful introduction to the text, but unfortunately never seems to have been completed.

(3) FA-TSANG. *Chin-shih-tzu chang*. Translated by Garma C. C. Chang as "Treatise on the Golden Lion," in *The Buddhist Teaching of Totality* (see 3.3.1.2[4]), pp. 224-230.
 Translation of the third Hua Yen patriarch, Fa Tsang's (643-712) famous lecture on the Golden Lion, which he reportedly gave to the Empress Wu in order to explain Avatamsaka doctrines. It has remained one of the most popular works of Hua Yen philosophy and has been translated several times into English. See for example Wing-tsit Chan, *Source Book in Chinese Philosophy* (see 2.5.1[3]); and William Theodore De Bary, ed., *Sources of Chinese Tradition* (see 2.5.8[7]), pp. 369-373.

(4) _____. *A Commentary on the Heart Sutra*. Translated by Garma C. C. Chang in his *The Buddhist Teaching of Totality* (see 3.3.1.2[4]), pp. 197-206.

(5) TU SHUN. *Fa Chieh Kuan*. Translated by Garma C. C. Chang as "On the Meditation of Dharmadhatu" in his *The Buddhist Teaching of Totality* (see 3.3.1.2[4]), pp. 207-223.
 Example of an Avatamsaka meditation text written by the founder of the Hua Yen school in China, Tu Shun (557-640). The meditation follows three stages, Meditation on Emptiness, on the Non-obstruction of Li and Shih, and on All-Embracing Totality. Unfortunately, the translation is not annotated.

(6) SUZUKI, DAISETZ TEITARO. *On Indian Mahayana Buddhism* (see 2.5.5[6]), pp. 147-226. See also 3.3.4.2(7).

3.3.4.2 Studies of Avatamsaka/Hua Yen Texts

See also Religious Thought under 2.5.5

(1) CHANG, GARMA C. C. *The Buddhist Teaching of Totality: The Philosophy of Hwa Yen Buddhism*. See 3.3.1.2(4).

(2) CSOMA, SANDOR (ALEXANDER). "Analyse du Kandjour: Recueil des Livres Sacres au Tibet." See 3.1.4(5).
 These pages contain a brief analysis (in French) of the contents of the *Avatamsaka* (*Phal Chen*) section of the Tibetan Canon.

(3) KAO KUAN-JU. "Avatamsaka Sutra," in *Encyclopedia of Buddhism* (see 2.5.4[12]), vol. 11, fasc. 3 (1967), pp. 435-436.
 A substantive and scholarly introduction to and discussion of this important and vast Mahayana work with a helpful analysis of the contents of the text.

(4) MIURA, ISSHU and RUTH FULLER SASAKI. *Zen Dust: The History of the Koan and Koan Study in Rinzai lin-Chi Zen* (see 3.1.5[6]), pp. 337-341.
 A helpful, descriptive survey of the different Chinese translations of the Avatamsaka Sutra and related texts. Includes discussions of Buddhabhadra's version in sixty chuan, of Siksananda's in eighty chuan, and of Prajna's in forty chuan.

(5) SUZUKI, BEATRICE LANE. "An Outline of the Avatamsakasutra." *Eastern Buddhist*, 6 (1934), 279-286.
 A helpful, short, first introductory discussion of this monumental Mahayana sutra. In the same genre but more scholarly is Kao Kuan-ja's "Avatamsaka Sutra" (above). For an even shorter outline, but more recent and helpful for showing the relations between the Avatamsaka, the Gandavyuha and the Dasabhumika, see Beatrice Lane Suzuki, *Mahayana Buddhism* (see 2.5.1[8]), pp. 102-108.

(6) SUZUKI, DAISETZ TEITARO. *Essays in Zen Buddhism, Third Series* (see 2.5.7[20]), pp. 1-185.
 Long the only substantial study of the *Avatamsaka* and *Gandavyuha sutras*, this series of four essays is still valuable, although for introductory purposes, the student should look rather at Suzuki's chapter in his *On Indian Mahayana Buddhism* (below). In these chapters, Suzuki discusses especially the *Gandavyuha*'s relation to Zen, translating several passages from it to support his views.

(7) _____. On Indian Mahayana Buddhism (see 2.5.5[6]), pp. 147-226.

This chapter, a posthumously published collection of writings by D. T. Suzuki, very ably edited by Edward Conze, contains a fine, and perhaps the only substantive discussion in English on the Gandavyuha--that portion of the Avatamsaka Sutra which deals with Sudhana's pilgrimage. Large segments of the text are translated or paraphrased, and this makes it a much better introduction to the subject than Suzuki's rather rambling four essays on Zen and the Gandavyuha published in his Essays in Zen Buddhism, Third Series (above), pp. 1-185.

3.3.5 Saddharma Pundarika Sutra (Lotus Sutra)

3.3.5.1 Translations of the Saddharma Pundarika Sutra

(1) Kuan-p'u-hsien-p'u-sa-hsing-fa-ching. Translated by Kojiro Miyasaka, with revisions by Pier P. Del Campana, as "The Sutra of Meditation on the Bodhisattva Universal Virtue" in The Three Fold Lotus Sutra. New York: Weatherhill, 1975, pp. 345-370.

Translations of a short work from the Chinese (Japanese title: Kanfugen Gyo) which has traditionally been associated with the "Lotus Sutra" in a sort of triad of related works. Popularly known as "The closing sutra," it was first translated into Chinese by Dharmamitra, although the Sanskrit original is now lost.

(2) Saddharmapundarika sutra. Translated by H. Kern as The Saddharma-Pundarika or The Lotus of the True Law. Delhi: Motilal Banarsidass, 1965, xliii, 454 pp. (First published 1884 by Oxford University Press, Sacred Books of the East, Vol. 21.)

It is difficult to overestimate the importance and popularity the "Lotus Sutra" has had among the Buddhists of China and Japan. With its parables and prophecies, its doctrine of ekayana (one vehicle), with its full-blown Buddhology and splendid descriptions of hosts of bodhisattvas and miraculous events, it has become an object of fervent devotion. Kern's translation (available in Dover paperback), which is based on the Sanskrit text, is still the standard one, and is preceded by a helpful fifty page introduction. The sutra, known as the Fa-hua ching in Chinese (hoke kyo in Japanese) or more fully as the Miao-fa-lien-hua ching (Myoho renge kyo), was first translated from the Sanskrit by Kumarajiva, c. 400 A.D., whose version has been partially translated into English by W. E. Soothill and brought more up to date by Schiffer (both below).

(3) _____. Translated by Eugene Burnout as Le Lotus de la Bonne Loi. Paris: Imprimerie Nationale, 1852, 897 pp.

A now-classic French translation, with extensive annotations, of the Sanskrit text of the "Lotus Sutra" by the greatest of the early Western Buddhologists. See the English translation of the same text by H. Kern (above).

(4) _____. Partial translation by William Edward Soothill as The Lotus of the Wonderful Law or the Lotus Gospel. Oxford: Clarendon Press, 1930, 275 pp.

An incomplete and somewhat weak translation by W. E. Soothill (who was much assisted by Bunno Kato) of Kumarajiva's Chinese rendition (406 A.D.) of the "Lotus Sutra" (Miao-fa lien-hua ching). The translation has been revised and completed by Wilhelm Schiffer and newly published by Rissho Kosei-kai, one of the new religions of Japan (below).

(5) _____. Translated by Bunno Kato and revised by William Edward Soothill, and revised with notes by Wilhelm Schiffer as Myoho-Renge-Kyo: The Sutra of the Lotus Flower of the Wonderful Law. Tokyo: Rissho Kosei-kai, 1971, 440 pp.

A translation of Kumarajiva's Chinese rendition of the "Lotus Sutra" (Miao-fa lien-hua ching; Myoho Renge Kyo in Japanese) with Schiffer's revision and completion and annotations make it a great improvement on Soothill and Kato's 1930 translation, on which it is based. Published by one of the "new relitions" of Japan. For a full translation of the Sanskrit manuscript see the work by Kern (above). This same version with further revisions by Yoshiro Tamura may also be found in The Three Fold Lotus Sutra (below), pp. 31-344.

(6) Wu-liang-i-ching. Translated by Yoshiro Tamura, revised by Wilhelm Schiffer and Pier P. Del Campana as "The Sutra of Innumerable Meanings" in The Three Fold Lotus Sutra. New York: Weatherhill, 1975, pp. 3-27.

Translation of a short work, the Wu-liang-i-ching (Japanese, Muryogi-kyo), which is closely related to the "Lotus." Popularly known as "the opening sutra," it was first translated into Chinese by Dharmajatayasas, although the Sanskrit original is now lost. It forms an interesting introductory piece to Kumarajiva's translation of the "Lotus," which follows it in this volume.

3.3.5.2 Commentaries and Studies on the Saddharma Pundarika Sutra

(1) DUTT, NALINAKSHA. "Manuscripts of the Saddharmapundarikasutra--their linguistic peculiarities." Indian Historical Quarterly, 29 (1953), 133-148.

A helpful introductory survey and description of the various manuscript versions of the "Lotus Sutra" from Nepal, Central Asia, Gilgit, and China. This is followed by a discussion of the dating of the original, which Dutt places at the second or first century A.D. For more details on the various manuscripts of the "Lotus," with a bibliography of all materials relevant to them (including the many in Japanese), see Akira Yuyama, A Bibliography of the Sanskrit Texts of the Saddharmapundarika sutra. Oriental Monograph Series, No. 5. (Canberra: Australian National University Press, 1970), 115 pp.

(2) LA VALLEE POUSSIN, LOUIS DE. "Lotus of the True Law," in Encyclopaedia of Religion and Ethics (see 1.15.1[9]), vol. 8, pp. 145-146.

A short but helpful introduction to the Saddharmapundarika sutra as a most representative work of Mahayana literature.

(3) MUS, PAUL. "Le Bouddha Paré: Son Origine Indienne." Bulletin de l'Ecole française d'Extrême-Orient, 28 (1926), 153-280.

A rich, insightful and difficult study of the position and role of Sakyamuni in Mahayana Buddhism, in the course of which Mus offers a reinterpretation of the whole of the Saddharma pundarika, its organization, intent and many layers of meaning, drawing in particular on the iconographic representation of scenes taken from it. For advanced students only.

(4) NICHIREN. The Awakening to the Truth; or Kaimokusho. Translated by Ryozui Ehara. Tokyo: The International Buddhist Society, 1941, 122 pp.

(5) _____. Hokke-Shuyo-Sho. Translated by Gaston Renondeau as "Traité sur l'Essential du Lotus," in his La Doctrine de Nichiren (see 2.5.9[4]), pp. 293-316.

The "Lotus Sutra" is absolutely central to the doctrine and faith of Nichiren Buddhism; this centrality is well reflected in this semi-exegetical "hymn of praise" of the "Lotus Sutra" written by Nichiren himself.

(6) TODA, JOSEI. Lecture on the Sutra, Hoben and Juryo chapters. Third edition. Tokyo: Seikyo Press, 1968, 305 pp.

Translation of a missionary lecture on two chapters of the "Lotus Sutra" by a vice president of Soka Gakkai, a "new religion" offshoot of Nichiren Buddhism in which the "Lotus Sutra" and its praise in the mantra "Namu Myoho Renge Kyo" occupy central roles.

3.3.6 Ch'an/Zen Texts

3.3.6.1 Translations of Ch'an Zen Sutras, Koan Collections, etc.

(1) Chao-lun. Translated by Walter Liebenthal as The Book of Chao. Monumenta Serica, Monograph No. 13. Peking: Catholic University of Peking, 1948, 195 pp.

The Book of Chao is a compilation of the writings of the Buddhist (or Taoist?) Seng-chao (374-414), said to have been a disciple of the great translator Kumarajiva. His work became important in the "Three Treatises School" (San-lun) and was also of great popularity among the Ch'an and Hua-yen schools.

(2) Ch'uan-teng lu. Partial translation by Chang Chung-yuan in Original Teachings of Ch'an Buddhism Selected from the Transmission of the Lamp. New York: Pantheon, 1969. (Paperback edition: Vintage, 1971, 333 pp.)

The Ch'uan-teng lu or Transmission of the Lamp is a collection of biographies and teachings of Ch'an monks and patriarchs beginning with the seven Buddhas of the past and ending with men contemporary with the time of the compiler of the collection, Tao-yuan, who lived towards the end of the tenth century. The text claims to contain the biographies of 1701 patriarchs and monks in all, but actually gives them for only 960 men, nineteen of the more substantial and interesting of which have been translated here. Portions of the text have also been translated by Lu K'uan Yu in his Ch'an and Zen Teaching, Second Series (see 2.5.7[16]).

Hekigan Roku
See 3.3.6.1(8).

(3) Lankavatarasutra. Translated by Daisetz Teitaro Suzuki as The Lankavatara Sutra. See 3.3.3.1(15).

(4) Liu-tsu t'an-ching. Translated by Wing-tsit Chan as The Platform Scripture. Asian Institute Translations, No. 3. New York: St. John's University Press, 1963, 193 pp.

A fine translation of the Tun Huang manuscript of the "Platform Sutra" which is often attributed to the Sixth Patriarch of Ch'an Buddhism, Hui-neng. For a translation which is different in style, see that of Yampolsky (below).

(5) _____. Translated by Lu K'uan Yu as "The Altar Sutra of the Sixth Patriarch" in Ch'an and Zen Teaching, Third Series (see 2.5.7[16]), pp. 15-102.

Where Yampolsky and Chan translated the Tun Huang manuscript of this "Platform Sutra," Lu K'uan Yu has here rendered the Yuan text into English.

(6) _____. Translated by Wong mu-lam as The Sutra of Wei-lang (or Hui-neng). Edited by Christmas Humphreys. London: Published for the Buddhist Society by Luzac, 1947, 128 pp. (First published 1944.)

Like that of Lu K'uan Yu (above), this translation of the so-called "Platform Sutra" is based on the Yuan text (and not the Tun Huang manuscript translated by Yampolsky and by Chan). Substantial portions of Wong's translation also appeared in Dwight Goddard, ed., A Buddhist Bible (see 3.5[6]), pp. 497-558.

(7) _____. Translated by Philip B. Yampolsky as The Platform Sutra of the Sixth Patriarch. Records of Civilization: Sources and Studies,

Mahayana Texts

No. 76. New York: Columbia University Press, 1967, 212 pp.

This fine translation of the "Platform Sutra" is an excellent means for any student to become acquainted with the life of Hui-Neng (the sixth Patriarch of the Southern School of Ch'an) and the teachings of Ch'an/Zen in general. It is preceded by Yampolsky's helpful introduction and followed by an edition of the Chinese Tun-Huan manuscript. For a different translation of the same text, see that of Chan (above).

Mumonkan

See Wu-men-kuan (below)

(8) Pi-yen lu. Edited and translated by R. D. M. Shaw as The Blue Cliff Records: Hekigan Roku, Containing 100 Stories of Zen Masters of Ancient China. London: M. Joseph, 1961, 299 pp.

The Hekigan Roku (Pi-yen- u) is a famous collection of Zen koans, compiled about a hundred years earlier than the Mumonkan. It should be looked at by any student interested in Zen koans. Unfortunately, this, the only English translation, is not readily available and not very well done. The work has also been translated into German by Wilhelm Gundert in Bi-yan-lu: Meister Yuan-wu's Niederschrift von der Smaragdenen Felswand (Munich: C. Hanser, 1963-   , in process).

"The Platform Sutra"

See Liu-tsu t'an-ching (above)

(9) Shih-niu-t'u sung. Translated by Nyogen Senzaki and Paul Reps as "Ten Bulls" in Zen Flesh, Zen Bones: A Collection of Zen and Pre-Zen Writings. Compiled by Paul Reps. New York: Doubleday, 1961, pp. 131-155. (Originally published Tokyo and Rutland, Vt.: Tuttle, 1957; paperback edition: Anchor A233.)

A short text comprising ten verses and ten pictures on finding and bringing home the bull. Popular illustration of Zen.

(10) ____. Translated by Daisetz Teitaro Suzuki as "The Ten Oxherding Pictures" in Manual of Zen Buddhism (see 2.5.7[21]), pp. 127-144.

For annotation see Shih-niu-t'u sung, translated by Nyogen Senzaki and Paul Reps (above).

(11) Wu-men-kuan. Translated by Reginald Horace Blyth in his Zen and Zen Classics (see 2.5.7[1]), vol. 4 (1966), The Mumonkan.

The Wu-men-kuan, better known by its Japanese title of Mumonkan, is an important Sung Dynasty collection of forty-eight Zen koans, with commentary by Mumon. Each koan (beginning with the celebrated "Joshu's Mu") is here introduced, translated, and chattered about by Blyth, whose own commentary varies from the helpful and charming to the detrimental and annoying. For alternative translations see Ogata and Reps (below).

(12) ____. Translated by Sohaku Ogata as "The Mu Mon Kwan: The Gateless Barrier to Zen Experience" in his Zen for the West. London: Rider, 1959, pp. 79-133.

For annotation of the work, see Wu-men-kuan, translated by Reginald Horace Blyth (above).

(13) ____. Translated by Paul Reps and Nyogen Senzaki as "The Gateless Gate" in Zen Flesh, Zen Bones: A Collection of Zen and Pre-Zen Writings (above), pp. 83-129.

For annotation of the work, see Wu-men-kuan, translated by R. H. Blyth (above).

3.3.6.2 Translations of Works by Rinzai (Lin-Chi) Masters

(1) Bankei Zenji Goroku. Translated by Norman Waddell as "The Zen Sermons of Bankei Yotaku." The Eastern Buddhist, 6, no. 2 (1973), 129-151; 7, no. 1 (1974), 124-141; and 7, no. 2 (1974), 83-107.

Translation of a series of informal talks given on Zen subjects by the seventeenth century master Bankei, often considered to be a sort of predecessor to the great master Hakuin.

(2) GERNET, JACQUES. Entretiens du Maître de Dhyana Chen-houei du Ho-tso, 668, 760. Publications de l'Ecole française d'Extrême-Orient, Vol. 31. Hanoi: Ecole française d'Extrême-Orient, 126 pp.

Shen-hui (670-762) was a famous master of the Southern School of Ch'an and a strong advocate of the doctrine of Sudden Enlightenment. A set of his known writings was edited by Hu Shin in 1930 and published under the title Shen hui ho-shang i-chi. Of these, three have been translated into French by Gernet: a treatise establishing the True and the False according to the Southern School of Bodhidharma on pp. 81-105; a "Eulogy on the Wisdom by Which there is Sudden Awakening to No-Birth" on pp. 106-110; and a long but untitled piece on pp. 5-80. Gernet has also written a study of all these texts in his "Complément aux Entretiens du Maître de Dhyana Chen-houei," Bulletin de l'Ecole française d'Extrême-Orient, 54 (1954), 453-466, and a "Biographie du Maître Chen-Houei du Ho-tso" (see 2.5.7[8]).

(3) HAKUIN ZENJI. Yasen Kanna. Translated by R. D. M. Shaw and William Schiffer as "A Chat on a Boat in the Evening." Monumenta Nipponica, 13 (1957), 101-127.

An interesting piece by the great Japanese Zen Master, Hakuin (eighteenth century), valuable for its description of "Zen sickness" (a result of overzealous striving on the part of novices) and for its method of cure.

(4) ____. Zazen Wasan. Translated by Isshu Miura and Ruth Fuller Sasaki as "Song of Zen" in Zen Dust: The History of the Koan and Koan Study in Rinzai, Lin-chi, Zen (see 3.1.5[6]), pp. 251-253.

Translation of the famous "Song of Zazen" by the great Rinzain master, Hakuin (eighteenth century) which has become a standard piece in all handbooks used for sutra chanting in Japanese Zen temples.

(5) HAN SHAN. Pan-jp po-lo-mi-to hsin-ching chih-shuo. Translated by Lu K'uan Yu as "A Straight Talk on the Heart Sutra" in his Ch'an and Zen Teaching, First Series (see 2.5.7[16]), pp. 207-223.

A commentary on the "Heart Sutra" (see 3.3.1.1[11], ff.) by Han Shan, a Chinese Ch'an master of the seventeenth century. The work is one illustration of textual exegesis of the more traditional type in the Ch'an school.

(6) _____. Chin-kang chueh-i. Translated by Lu K'uan Yu as "The Diamond Cutter of Doubts" in his Ch'an and Zen Teaching, First Series (see 2.5.7[16]), pp. 147-206.

This commentary on the "Diamond Sutra" (see 3.3.1.1[22], ff.) was written in 1616 by Han Shan, a Ch'an Master of the Ming Dynasty. Like Vasubandhu, Han Shan thinks the key to understanding the Sutra is to discover the hidden questions which Subhuti had in mind, but which were never expressed in words, because the all-seeing Buddha knew and answered them before Subhuti had a chance to verbalize them. The work is interesting as a commentary and as an illustration of the practice of textual exegesis--which Westerners often forget to associate with the Ch'an school.

(7) Huang-po Tuan-chi ch'an-shih Wan-ling lu. Translated by John Blofeld as The Wan-ling Record in the Zen Teaching of Huang-po on the Transmission of Mind. London: Rider, 1958, pp. 67-132.

English translation of a series of sermons by the Ch'an master Huang Po (Obaku in Japanese), who died ca. 850 A.D. Traditionally, the compilation of these sermons and anecdotes about the master is said to have been done by P'ei Hsiu, while he was governor of Wan-ling in Kiangsi province, and hence the work is known as "The Wan-ling Record."

(8) P'ang chu-shih yu-lu. Translated by Ruth Fuller Sasaki, Yoshitaka Iriya, and Dana R. Fraser as The Recorded Sayings of Layman P'ang. New York: Weatherhill, 1971, 109 pp.

A translation of a collection of anecdotes and verses of a lay Ch'an master of the eighth century, compiled after his death by his friend the prefect Yu Ti. It became a famous and popular work in China.

(9) Tun-wu ju-tao yao-men lun. Translated by John Blofeld as The Zen Teaching of Hui Hai on Sudden Illumination. London: Rider, 1962, 160 pp.

The Tun-wu ju-tao yao-men lun (in Japanese, Tongo nyudo yomon ron), literally "On the Essentials for Entering Tao through Sudden Awakening," is attributed to the Ch'an master Ta-chu Hui Hai of the T'ang dynasty. The first part presents the doctrine of sudden enlightenment through a series of questions and answers; the second part contains a number of sermons by the master, many of which contain quotations from Mahayana scriptures. The present text of the work was edited and compiled by a T'ien-t'ai monk, Miao-hsieh, of the Ming dynasty.

(10) YAMPOLSKY, PHILIP B., trans. The Zen Master Hakuin: Selected Writings. See 1.13.2.3(4).

Fascinating essays and letters by Hakuin (1686-1769), a Rinzai master who revived Zen practices at a low point in their history. Contains direct and personal writings that describe Hakuin's own struggles; also, his own discussion of the "Sound of a Single Hand Clapping"--perhaps the most famous of his koans.

3.3.6.3 Translations of Works by Soto (Ts'ao-tung) Masters

(1) DOGEN. Gakudoyojin-shu. Translated by Hoang-Thi-Bich as "Recueil de l'Application de l'Esprit à l'Etude de la Voie" in his Etude et Traduction de Gakudoyojin-shu (see 2.5.7[10]), pp. 109-175.

Next to the Shobogenzo, this is perhaps Dogen's most important doctrinal work and is certainly much shorter, written as it is in just ten chapters. The fully annotated French translation here is preceded by a study of the text and by a placing of it in the historical context of Dogen's life and of Soto Zen in Japan.

(2) _____. Shobogenzo. Translation of selected chapters by Reiho Masunaga in his The Soto Approach to Zen (see 2.5.7[17]), pp. 81-90, 91-99, 125-132, 133-161.

Translations of portions of this collection of works by Dogen, the founder of Japanese Soto Zen, written over a period of twenty-three years (1231-1253) and compiled by his disciple Ejo. They include "Uji," in which Dogen gives his views on time; "Shoji," on life and death; "Genjokoan," on the koan expressed in daily life; and "Bendowa," on zazen. Other translations of selections from the Shobogenzo may be found in Jiyu Kennett, Selling Water by the River: A Manual of Zen Training (see 2.5.7[14]), pp. 73-158.

(3) _____. Shobogenzo Zuimonki. Translated by Reiho Masunaga as A Primer of Soto Zen. London: Routledge and Kegan Paul, 1972, 119 pp.

Translation of a popular collection of anecdotes, sermons, sayings, and instructions by the Japanese Zen master Dogen, the thirteenth century founder of Soto in Japan. Not to be confused with the much larger work by Dogen, the Shobogenzo (above).

(4) TUNG-SHAN. Pao-ching San-Mei. Translated by Reiho Masunaga in his The Soto Approach to Zen (see 2.5.7[17]), pp. 188-192.

Mahayana Texts

Translation of the Pao-ching San-Mei, better known in Japan as the Hokyozammai, a short work in ninety-four lines written by Tung-shan (Tozan), one of the founders of the Chinese Ts-ao-tung (Soto) sect. The work is still chanted daily in Japanese Soto temples and is a presentation of the famous "Five Ranks" of Soto Zen. The text has also been translated by Lu K'uan Yu in his Ch'an and Zen Teachings, Second Series (see 2.5.7[16]), pp. 149-154.

(5) _____. _____. Translated by Lu K'uan Yu in his Ch'an and Zen Teachings, Second Series (see 2.5.7[16]), pp. 149-154.
Translation of the Pao-ching San Mei (Hokyozammai) by Tung-shan (Tozan) one of the founders of the Ts'ao-tung (Soto) sect in China. Has an advantage over the Masunaga translation (above) in that it is accompanied by a diagram illustrating the relations denoted in the "Five Ranks" of Soto Zen which it expounds. Furthermore, this translation, though not always reliable, is preceded by a translation of Tung-shan's shorter work, the Wu-wei sung (Goi no ju), known as the "Verses on the Five Ranks" (pp. 137-138).

(6) _____. Wu-wei sung. Translated by Isshu Miura and Ruth Fuller Sasaki as "Tozan Ryokai's Verses on the Five Ranks" in Zen Dust: The History of the Koan and Koan Study in Rinzai (Lin-chi) Zen (see 3.1.5[6]), pp. 67-72.
Translation of the very short "Verses on the Five Ranks" of Soto Zen, known in Chinese as Wu-wei sung and in Japanese as Goi no ju, by the ninth century co-founder of the Ts'ao-tung (Soto) sect in China, Tung-shan (Tozan). It is very succinct and abstruse and is translated along with Hakuin's commentary on it. Another English translation may be found in Lu K'uan Yu, Ch'an and Zen Teaching, Second Series (see 2.5.7[16]), pp. 137-138.

(7) YAMPOLSKY, PHILIP B., trans. The Zen Master Hakuin: Selected Writings. See 1.13.2.3(4).
Fascinating essays and letters by Hakuin (1686-1769), a Rinzai master who revived Zen practices at a low point in their history. Contains direct and personal writings that describe Hakuin's own struggles; also, his own discussion of the "Sound of a Single Hand Clapping"--perhaps the most famous of his koans.

3.3.6.4 Translations of Works by Other Zen Masters

(1) TETSUGEN. "Sermon sur le Bouddhisme Zen." Translated by Masumi Shibata in Présence du Bouddhisme (see 1.5.1[6]), pp. 633-653.
Translation into French of part of a sermon by the seventeenth-century master Tetsugen, who belonged to the Obaku sect of Zen. The contrast between this and the works of Rinzai and Soto masters is noteworthy.

3.3.7 Pure Land Texts

3.3.7.1 Pure Land Sutras in Translation

(1) Amitayur-Dhyana-Sutra. Translated by J. Takakusu as "The Sutra of the Meditation on Amitayus" in Buddhist Mahayana Texts (see 3.3.1.1[12]), Part 2, pp. 161-201.
Standard translation of one of the basic Pure Land sutras which is very popular in Japan. In it, the Buddha tells Queen Vaidehi the several ways of getting to the Pure Land and instructs her in meditation techniques (including chanting the Nembutsu and visualization) which will enable her to get a glimpse of that Western paradise. For a study of the visualization technique as explained by Shan Tao in his commentary on this sutra, see Julian F. Pas, "Shan Tao's Interpretation of the Meditative Vision of the Buddha Amitayus," History of Religions, 14 (1974), 96-116.

(2) Sukhavati vyuha. Translated by F. Max Müller as "The Smaller Sukhavati-vyuha" in Buddhist Mahayana Texts (see 3.3.1.1[12]), Part 2, pp. 89-103.
The standard translation of the shorter Sanskrit text of the Sukhavati-vyuha--the one that was translated into Chinese by Kumarajiva in 402 A.D. The chief speakers in the sutra are the Buddha and Sariputra. It is interesting to make a close comparison between the contents of this text and those of the Larger Sukhavati-vyuha; both became fundamental texts in the Pure Land School.

(3) _____. Translated by F. Max Müller as "The Larger Sukhavati-vyuha" in Buddhist Mahayana Texts (see 3.3.1.1[12]), Part 2, pp. 1-75.
The standard translation of the longer Sanskrit text of the Sukhavati vyuha--the one that was translated into Chinese by Sanghavarman in the third century. The chief speakers in the sutra are the Buddha, Ananda and Ajita, and it contains descriptions of Sukhavati, the Western "Land of Bliss" of the Buddha Amitabha, and instructions on how to get there. This became one of the very basic texts of the Pure Land sects in Japan and China.

3.3.7.2 Translations of Works of Pure Land Patriarchs and Abbots

(1) The Ching-t'u Shih-i-lun. Translated by Leo Pruden as "Ten Doubts Concerning the Pure Land." The Eastern Buddhist, n.s. 6 (1973), 126-157. See also 11.7.4(7).

(2) GENSHIN. Ojoyoshu. Translated by Allan A. Andrews in The Teachings Essential for Rebirth. See 2.5.8(1).

(3) RENNYO. Anjinketsujosho. Translated by Kosho Yamamoto in The Words of St. Rennyo. Ube: Karinbunko, 1968, 196 pp.
A short work by Rennyo, the eighth abbot of Shin Buddhism, who lived in the fifteenth

century. This is a treatise dealing solely with the doctrine of other power and with faith.

(4) Rennyoshonin-Goichidaiki-kikigaki. Translated by Kosho Yamamoto in The Words of St. Rennyo (above).
A mélange of memoirs about Rennyo (eighth abbot of Shin Buddhism in Japan) and of some of his sayings, compiled by one of his followers probably some time around 1585.

(5) SHINRAN. The Kyo Gyo Shisho. Translated and annotated by Hisao Inagaki, Kosho Yukawa and Thomas R. Okano. Ryukoku Translation Series, Vol. 5. Kyoto: Ryukoku Translation Center, Ryukoku University, 1966, 247 pp.
This is a translation of one of Shinran's (1173-1262) most important works, his "Teaching, Practice, Faith and Enlightenment." The many quotations Shinran makes to support his arguments have been omitted in translation, and the result is a concise bare-bones presentation of the fundamental Shin position.

(6) _____. Mattosho. Translated by Kosho Yamamoto in The Private Letters of Shinran Shonin. Tokyo: Okazakiya Shoten, 1956, pp. 3-53.
Translation of the Mattosho, a collection of Shinran's letters to his followers, containing spiritual advice to his followers and disciples. This is followed by the translation of a similar collection, the Shinranshonin Goshosokushu.

(7) _____. Shuji. Translated by Kensho Yokagawa as "The Tract on Steadily Holding to the Faith" in Daisetz Teitaro Suzuki, A Miscellany on the Shin Teaching of Buddhism. See 2.5.8(23).
Translation of a short work containing sayings of Shinran on the teachings of his school, compiled by Kakunyo (1270-1351). The same translation appeared also in The Eastern Buddhist, 7 (1939), 363-375.

(8) _____. Wasan. Translated by Beatrice Lane Suzuki as "The Songs of Shinran Shonin" in A Miscellany on the Shin Teaching of Buddhism (see 2.5.8[23]), pp. 122-135.
Translation of some of Shinran's songs in praise of Amitabha with an explanatory "Afterword." The translation originally appeared in The Eastern Buddhist, 7 (1939), 285-295.

3.3.8 Other Mahayana Texts in Translation

See also under 4.2. Popular Literature

3.3.8.1 Other Mahayana Texts Translated from the Sanskrit

(1) Bhaisajyagurusutra. Translated by Nalinaksha Dutt in Gilgit Manuscripts (see 1.2.2.4[4]), vol. 1, pp. 47-57.
An almost complete translation of this very popular sutra in which the Buddha Bhaisajyaguru takes twelve vows to assist and succor sentient beings. The sutra also gives ritual instructions for worshippers of Bhaisajyaguru.

(2) Lalita Vistara. Translated by Philippe Edouard Foucaux as Développement des Jeux. Annales du Musée Guimet, t. 6, 19. Paris: E. Leroux, 1884-1892, 2 vols. Vol. 1: French translation; Vol. 2: Notes, variants and index.
The Lalita Vistara is one of the most important and widespread Mahayana biographies of the Buddha. Composed in Sanskrit (prose) and mixed Sanskrit (verse), probably over a long period of time, its contents generally run parallel to the Pali biographical material—except that they are much embellished with "supernatural" and "miraculous" events. Thus, the Buddha rarely does anything alone, unaccompanied by myriads of heavenly beings. This old but dependable translation by Foucaux is the only complete translation in a Western language. See also under Category 8 for other partial translations.

(3) MAJUMDER, PRABHAS CHANDRA. "The Karandavyuha; Its Metrical Version." Indian Historical Quarterly, 24 (1948), 293-299.
A summary of the verse version of this Mahayana sutra which describes the exploits of Avalokitesvara, with a discussion of its various translations into Chinese and Tibetan and its relation to the prose version of the same work.

(4) Pratimalaksanam. Translated by Jitendra Nath Banerjee. Journal of the Department of Letters, Calcutta University, 23 (1933) 2, 84 pp.
Translation of a fascinating late Indian Sanskrit text on the measurements of the Buddha image, with extensive notes about the relationship of the text to iconography. The work is also known as the SamyakSambuddhabhasita Pratimalaksanam.

(5) PYTHON, PIERRE. Vinaya-viniscaya-Upali-pariprccha: Enquête d'Upali pour une exégèse de la discipline. Paris: Adrien Maisonneuve, 1973, 224 pp.
Includes translation of the Upali-pariprccha, one of the important texts included in the great Mahayana Ratnakuta collection. The work deals with questions of discipline and conduct proper for Bodhisattvas, who here are given their own pratimoksa code.

(6) Rastrapalapariprccha. Translated by Jacob Ensink as The Question of Rastrapala. Zwolle: Van de Erven J. J. Tijl, 1952, 140 pp.
Translation of a very early (budding) Mahayana text which has become part of the great Ratnakuta sections in the Tibetan and Chinese canons and is one of the few works in that class still extant in the Sanskrit. The text deals with the notion of bodhisattva and even bodhicitta in the Mahayana sense, though it does so by using illustrations from jataka stories.

Mahayana Texts

(7) Samadhirajasutra. Partial translation by Constantin Regamey in his Three Chapters from the Samadhirajusutra. Publications of the Oriental Commission, No. 1. Warsaw: The Warsaw Society of Sciences and Letters, 1938, 113 pp.

The Samadhirajasutra (translated into Chinese in the fourth century) is an important Mahayana text which is much quoted by such authors as Candrakirti and Santideva. Its subject is samadhi but it is not a meditation manual. Rather, it explains various samadhis by illustrating them with stories. Only three chapters have been translated here, along with the edited Sanskrit and Tibetan texts.

(8) Suvarnabhasottamasutra. Translated by R. E. Emmerick as The Sutra of Golden Light. Sacred Books of the Buddhists, Vol. 27. London: Luzac and Co., 1970, 108 pp.

The Suvarnabhasottamasutra (sometimes called the Suvarnaprabhasa sutra) is a short and widely popular Mahayana text which was translated twice into Chinese (in the fifth and eighth centuries), three times into Tibetan, and into Khotanese, Sogdian, Hsihsia, and Uignur. It is a medley of jatakas, of popular presentation of philosophical and ethical doctrines, of exhortations to praise the Buddhas, and of medical advice and dharanis to use in the case of illness.

3.3.8.2 Other Mahayana Texts Translated from the Chinese

(1) The Awakening of Faith Attributed to Asvaghosa. Translated by Yoshito S. Hakeda. New York: Columbia University Press, 1967, 128 pp.

The postulated Sanskrit original of the "Awakening of Faith in the Mahayana" (Mahayanasraddhotpada-sastra) has never been found. This fine translation (preceded by a valuable introduction) is based on Paramartha's sixth century Chinese version. The text is not the work of the second century poet Asvaghosha, but probably dates from the fifth or sixth centuries. Widely influential in China and Japan, it is a sort of epitome of all Mahayana philosophy, and, in its own pan-Mahayana doctrine, succinctly synthesizes a little Madhyamika and a lot of Vijnanavada with a developed and philosophical Buddhology, and exhortations to Faith and other practices. For an important study of the sutra, see also Walter Liebenthal, "New Light on the Mahayana-Sraddhotpada Sastra," T'oung Pao, 46 (1958), 155-216.

(2) "Awakening of Faith." Translated by Daisetz Teitaro Suzuki as Asvaghosha's Discourse on the Awakening of Faith in the Mahayana. Chicago: Open Court, 1900, 160 pp.

This is one of Suzuki's early translations; it is now quite dated, and students will have a much happier time with Hakeda's 1967 rendition. Still, at least two points about Suzuki's work should be noted: 1) It is the only English translation of Siksananda's eighth century Chinese version; the other English renditions are all based on Paramartha's sixth century version. 2) Suzuki mistakenly accepts the second century poet Asvogosha as the original author of the work; but in so doing, he includes, in his introduction, an unnecessary but otherwise valuable compendium of information about that figure.

(3) Buddhadhyana-samadhi-sagara-sutra. Translation of Chapter 9 of the Chinese version by Paul Demieville in "Notes sur le fragment sogdien du Buddhadhyanasamadhisagara-sutra." By Emile Benveniste and Paul Demieville. Journal Asiatique, 223 (1933), 193-248.

The work as a whole is a sort of meditation manual, the Chinese title of which Demieville translates as "Sutra de la mer de Samadhi de la contemplation du Buddha." The original was first translated into Chinese by Buddhabhadra in the fifth century. Chapter 9, which is translated here following some notes by Benveniste on the discovered Sogdian fragments of the text, deals with the contemplation of Buddha images.

(4) Chao-lun. Translated by Walter Liebenthal as The Book of Chao. See 3.3.6.1(1).

The Book of Chao is a compilation of the writings of the Buddhist (or Taoist?) Sengchao (374-414), said to have been a disciple of the great translator Kumarajiva. His work became important in the "Three Treatises School" (San-lun) and was also of great popularity among the Ch'an and Hua-yen schools.

(5) Gandistotra. Translated by E. J. Johnston as "The Lauds of the Gong." Indian Antiquary, 62 (1933), 61-70. See also 7.2.3(2).

(6) LEVI, SYLVAIN and EDOUARD CHAVANNES. "Les Seize Arhat protecteurs de la Loi." Journal Asiatique, 8 (1916), 5-50, 189-304.

These pages contain a French translation of Hsuan Tsang's Chinese rendition of Nandimitra's "Relation sur la Durée de la Loi." Nandimitra was a native of Ceylon who lived ca. the third century A.D., and his work is an important source of information on the subject of the sixteen lohan (arhats) who became so popular in China. The work has also been translated into English by Li Yung-hsi as "A Record of the Abiding of the Dharma" in The Sixteen Arhats and the Eighteen Arhats, compiled by the Shan Shih Buddhist Institute (Peking: Buddhist Association of China, distributed by China Books and Periodicals, Chicago, 1961).

(7) Mahaparinirvana sutra. Translated by Kosho Yamamoto as The Mahayana Mahaparinirvana-Sutra. Karin Buddhological Series. Ube City: Karinbunko, 1974, 3 vols.

3.3.8.2

A complete, annotated, English translation of this large important Mahayana text, not to be confused with the Mahaparinibbana sutta of the Pali canon. Unfortunately, the translator's English is not of the best quality, which makes for trouble, sometimes, in understanding the already difficult work. Extracts from this sutra may also be found in translation in Samuel Beal, A Catena of Buddhist Scriptures from the Chinese (see 3.2.1.2[7]), pp. 160-172 and 173-188.

(8) Sutralamkara. Translated by Edouard Huber as Asvaghosa, Sutralamkara. Paris: E. Leroux, 1908, 496 pp.

The Sanskrit original of the Sutralamkara (attributed to Asvaghosa) has been lost. Huber has here translated Kumarajiva's Chinese rendition of the text (ca. 410). The work is a rich collection in verse and prose of moral tales and legends illustrative of proper and noble conduct. For a study of the question of the authorship of the work, see E. J. Thomas, "Asvaghosa and alamkara," Indian Culture, 13 (1947), 143-146.

(9) Ssu-shih-erh-chang-ching. Translated by Samuel Beal as "The Sutra of Forty-two Sections" in his A Catena of Buddhist Scriptures from the Chinese (see 3.2.1.2[7]), pp. 186-203.

The "Sutra in 42 Sections" is important for being one of the earliest sutras to have been introduced (?) into China (c. 70 A.D.). It is a very short work containing forty-two ethical and disciplinary points of advice. Another translation of it may be found in Seven Shaku, Sermons of a Buddhist Abbot, translated by Daisetz Teitaro Suzuki (Chicago: Open Court, 1906), 220 pp. For an important discussion of the probable nature of the original version of the sutra see T'ang Yong-t'ung, "The Editions of the Ssu-shih-erh-chang-ching," translated by James R. Ware, Harvard Journal of Asiatic Studies, 1 (1936), 147-155.

3.3.8.3 Other Mahayana Texts Translated from the Tibetan

(1) RUEGG, DAVID SEYFORT. Le Traité du tathagatagarbha de Buston Rin chen grub: Traduction du De bzin gsegs pa'i snin po gsal zin mdzes par byed pa'i rayan. See 2.7.11(3).

(2) sGAM PO PA, Jewel Ornament of Liberation. Translated by Herbert V. Guenther. Clear Light series. Berkeley: Shambala, 1971. 333 pp. See also 11.1(4).

(3) THOMAS, FREDERICK WILLIAM, trans. Tibetan Literary Texts and Documents Concerning Chinese Turkestan. Oriental Translation Fund, n.s., vols. 32, 37, 40, 41. London: Luzac, 1935-1963, 4 vols.

Some of these texts are extracted from the Tibetan Canon; others were found by Sir Aurel Stein in Chinese Turkestan itself. Most are of interest to specialized students only.

(4) TSONG KHAPA. The Graded Course to Enlightenment. Translated by Sherpa Tulku, Khamlung Tulku, and Alexander Berzin. Upper Dharamsala: Secretariat of H. H. the Dalai Lama, 1971, 32 pp.

This rare booklet is a translation of the "Lam-gyi-Rim-mdu-tsam-du-bsTappa," a letter which the great fourteenth century Tibetan reformer Tsong Kha wrote to a friend. In it, he summarizes very neatly the main points of his teachings on the Lam Rim.

(5) WAYMAN, ALEX. "Introduction to Tson Kha pa's Lam rim chen mo." Phi Theta Annual, 3 (1952), 51-82.

A good introduction to the most famous work of Tsong Kha pa, in which he gives in great detail an analysis of all the steps on the path. In this article, Wayman gives the historical background and an outline of the text.

3.3.8.4 Other Mahayana Texts Translated from Other Languages

(1) Aparimitayuh sutra. Translated by Sten Konow in Manuscript Remains of Buddhist Literature Found in Eastern Turkestan (see 3.2.1.2[3]), pp. 289-329.

A translation from the Khotanese version of a long dharani which is an invocation of the Buddha and a praise of his qualities, paralleled by editions of the Khotanese, Sanskrit and Tibetan texts.

(2) BAILEY, H. W., trans. "The Pradaksina-sutra of Chang Tsiang-kuin," in Buddhist Studies in Honour of I. B. Horner (see 1.2.2.4[11]), pp. 15-18. See also 7.1.3(3).

(3) BENVENISTE, EMILE, ed. and trans. Textes Sogdiens. Mission Pelliot en Asie centrale. Serie in quarto, No. 3. Paris: P. Geuthner, 1940, 280 pp.

In this edition and translation with notes of Sogdian texts into French, Benveniste has included many fragments of Buddhist works which had been translated into Sogdian from the Chinese. Among them there are, on pages 3-58, a long unidentified text on the interdiction to eat meat and consume alcohol which contains a long quote from the Lankavatara Sutra; on pages 74-81, the short Dirghanakha sutra, translated as "Sutra du religieux Ongles-Long"; on pages 82-92, a fragment of the Bhaisajyaguru vaiduryaprabhatathagata sutra dealing with the Buddha of Medicine; on pages 105-115, an interesting hymn calling on the 108 names of Avalokitesvara (Avolokites-varasyana-mastasatakastotra), and a large number of small unidentified fragments.

(4) GAUTHIOT, ROBERT and PAUL PELLIOT, trans. Le Sutra des Causes et des Effets du Bien et du Mal. See 2.7.1(3).

Tantra-/Mantra-/Vajra-yana Texts

Text and translation of the Sogdian version of the Shan-o-yin-ching, an apocryphal Chinese sutra on the workings of karma, written before 695 A.D. It puts forward and seeks to explain the differences between men on the basis of specific actions committed by them in past lives. It especially seeks the causes of particular physical traits in the workings of the individual's karma.

(5) Jatakastava. Translated by Mark J. Dresden in "The Jatakastava or Praise of the Buddha's Former Births." Transactions of the American Philosophical Society, n.s. 45 (1955), 397-588. See also 4.2.2(5).

(6) POPPE, NICHOLAS, trans. The Twelve Deeds of Buddha. Studies on Asia, No. 16. Seattle: University of Washington Press, 1968, 173, 65 pp.

What Poppe presents in this book is the sole surviving second volume of a Mongolian translation of a now lost Tibetan abbreviated version of the Lalitavistara. Even so, it is an important and interesting text: 1) as a "rare specimen of early Mongolian Buddhist literature"; and 2) as a concise narrative of the events in the Buddha's life from the time of his Great Departure to his defeat of the Evil One under the Bodhi tree.

3.4   TANTRA-/MANTRA-/VAJRA-YANA TEXTS IN TRANSLATION AND TEXTUAL STUDIES

See also in Religious Thought under 2.6.

See also in Soteriological Experience and Processes under 11.6.

3.4.1   Indian Texts

(1) Adhyardhasatika prajnaparamita. Translated by Edward Conze as "The Perfection of Wisdom in 150 Lines." See 3.3.1.1(1).

(2) BHATTACHARYYA, BENOYTOSH, ed. Guhyasamaja Tantra or Tathagataguhyaka. Gaekwad's Oriental Series No. 53. Baroda: Oriental Institute, 1931, pp. ix-xxxviii.

In this preface to his edition of this important Sanskrit Tantra, Bhattacharyya gives a fine and fairly detailed synopsis of the text, which, in the absence of any translation, is of great use to the Western student. Also important are Giuseppe Tucci's comments on Bhattacharyya's edition, based on his own knowledge of the Tibetan material, and found in Giuseppe Tucci, "Some Glosses upon the Guhyasamaja," Mélanges Chinois et Bouddhiques, 3 (1934/1935), 339-353.

(3) Hevajrasekaprakriya. Translated by Louis Finot in "Manuscrits sanskrits de Sadhanas retrouvés en Chine," Journal Asiatique, 225 (1934), 31-48.

Translation of an anonymous tantric text dealing with the cult and liturgy of Heruka and his consort. This is followed by a number of shorter texts on the same theme, all of which were found in the original Sanskrit in Western China.

(4) The Hevajra Tantra: A Critical Study. Translated by D. L. Snellgrove. See 2.6.1(11).

Very few of the Buddhist tantras have been translated into English. The Hevajra is an anuttarayoga-tantra which was "revealed" by the teacher Saroruha (eighth-ninth century). Like many works of its kind, it is largely devoted to practical instructions in the performance of sadhanas, use of mantras and mandalas. Snellgrove's fine translation which is preceded by an excellent introduction may well be recommended as a starting point for the student interested in Tantric texts and practices. Second volume has edition of Tibetan and Sanskrit text.

(5) Kincitvistara Tara Sadhana. Translated by Edward Conze in his Buddhist Meditation (see 2.7.5[2]), pp. 133-139.

A translation of one of the Sadhanas (that of Tara) which is included in the Sadhanamala, a large collection of such texts. The free translation of the same text may be found in Benoytosh Bhattacharyya, An Introduction to Buddhist Esoterism (see 2.6.1[2]), pp. 104-108, and in the same author's The Indian Buddhist Iconography. (See 5.2.8[4]).

(6) Pancavimsati-prajnaparamita-mukha. Translated by Edward Conze as "The 25 Doors to Perfect Wisdom." See 3.3.1.1(9).

(7) Vidhisamgraha. Translated by Louis Finot in "Manuscrits sanskrits de sadhanas retrouvés en Chine" (above), pp. 62-78.

The Vidhisamgraha is an anthology of at least seven short liturgical and meditative texts dealing with the cult of Heruka and his consort. All of them have been translated here by Finot. They include works by the seventh century Luyi and Advayavajra.

(8) WARDER, ANTHONY KENNEDY. Indian Buddhism (see 1.2.1[15]), pp. 482-502.

These pages contain a brief but useful survey of the Indian Mantrayana texts, and a discussion of their division into Kriya-, Carya-, Yoga-, and Anuttarayoga-tantras.

3.4.2   Tibetan Vajrayana Texts in Translation and Textual Studies

(1) Arya Mahabala-nama-mahayanasutra. Translated by F. A. Bischoff. Buddhica Première série: Mémoires, t. 10. Paris: P. Geuthner, 1958, 126 pp.

In spite of its title of Mahayanasutra, this work, the Tibetan and Chinese versions of which Bischoff has here edited and translated into French, is clearly a Mantrayana text. It primarily concerns the figure of Mahabala, a fierce deity associated with Vajrapani. Not for beginning students.

(2) EVANS-WENTZ, WALTER YEELING, ed. The Tibetan Book of the Dead, or The After-Death Experiences on the Bardo Plane, According to Lama Kazi Dawa-Samdup's English Rendering. Third edition. London: Oxford University Press, 1960, 249 pp. (Paperback edition: Galaxy GB39.)

An English rendition of the Tibetan Bardo Thodol, a ritual and doctrinal text dealing with the passage through the intermediate state between death and birth. The work has enjoyed a tremendous popularity in certain circles in the West, but its original import and place within Tibetan Buddhism is hard to estimate. The translation, which can hardly be called authoritative, is preceded by Evans-Wentz's long introduction, which is frustratingly unhelpful. Students would do better to use Francesca Freemantle and Chogyam Trungpa's recent translation (below) instead.

(3) _____. The Tibetan Book of the Great Liberation. Translated by S. W. Laden-la, Karma Sumdhon Paul, Lobzang Mingyur Dorje, and Kazi Dawa-Samdup, with psychological commentary by C. G. Jung. London: Oxford University Press, 1954, 261 pp.

The book as a whole is a strange Evans-Wentzian conglomeration of general information, misguided emphases, and occasional fascinating details. The text referred to in the title occupies only about sixty pages and is said to be the "Yoga of Knowing the Mind in its Nakedness," one of a series of Yogic treatises connected to the Bardo Thodol or "Book of the Dead." It is preceded by a valuable but all too short biography of its supposed author, Padma Sambhava.

(4) _____. Tibetan Yoga and Secret Doctrines. Second edition. London: Oxford University Press, 1958, 389 pp. (First published 1935; Oxford paperback, 1967.) See also 11.6.1(12).

(5) FREEMANTLE, FRANCESCA and CHOGYAM TRUNGPA, trans. The Tibetan Book of the Dead: The Liberation through Hearing in the Bardo. Berkeley: Shambhala, 1975, 176 pp.

New translation of the Tibetan Bardo Thodol, which deals with the experiences of the dead in the intermediate state and which should replace the now outdated rendition of Dawa Samdup and Evans-Wentz (above), although students might still wish to consult the latter for its foreword by C. G. Jung and Anagarika Govinda. Freemantle and Chogyam Trungpa's translation is also preceded by useful preface and introduction by the two translators.

(6) GUENTHER, HERBERT V. The Life and Teaching of Naropa. UNESCO Collection of representative works, Tibetan series. Oxford: Clarendon Press, 1963, pp. 131-249. (Paperback edition, 1971.) See also 11.6.1(14).

(7) _____, trans. The Royal Song of Saraha: A Study in the History of Buddhist Thought. Seattle: University of Washington Press, 1969, 214 pp.

Guenther has here translated the very short Mantrayana work, the "King Dohas" of Sarana, and two commentaries on it: one by the eleventh century Nepalese Skye Med bDe Chen, and a second by Karma Phrin las pa, a fifteenth century bKa' brGyud pa lama. The student who has become used to technical Buddhist terms will have to get used to Guenther's way of translating them before he can gain full profit from the book: for example, the three "bodies" of the Buddha (Dharma-, Sambhoga- and Nirmana-kaya) are here rendered as the "three existential norms: noetic, communicative and authentic being."

(8) _____, trans. sGam-po-pa: The Jewel Ornament of Liberation (see 3.3.8.3[2]). See also 11.1(4).

(9) _____. Tibetan Buddhism Without Mystification: The Buddhist Way from Original Tibetan Sources. Leiden: E. J. Brill, 1966, 204 pp. Pp. 92-148. See also 11.6.1(15).

(10) Manjusrimulakalpa. Chapters 2 and 3 translated by Ariane MacDonald in Le Mandala du Manjusrimulakalpa. Paris: A. Maisonneuve, 1962, 190 pp. Collection Jean Przyluski, t. 3. Chapters 4-7 translated by Marcelle Lalou in Iconographie des Etoffes Peintes (Pata) dans le Manjusrimulakalpa. Paris: P. Geuthner, 1930, 116 pp. Buddhica, No. 6.

One of the major later tantras, probably composed in the eighth century and translated here on the basis of its Tibetan text. Chapters 2 and 3 describe the rites and visualizations involved in making the text's mandala. Chapters 4-7 set forth the rites and techniques associated with making a pata (painting on cloth, as vs. a mandala drawn on the ground).

(11) PAD-MA DKAR-PO. Chos-rje 'brug-pa'i lugs-kyi phyag-rgya chen-po lhan-cig skyes-sbyor-gyi khrid-yig. Translated by Stephan Beyer as "Manual of the Spontaneous Great Symbol" in his The Buddhist Experience: Sources and Interpretations (see 3.3.2.1[18]), pp. 155-161.

Translation of a work by a sixteenth century Tibetan tantric explaining the methods and aims of Mahamudra techniques. (See also 11.6.1[1].)

(12) _____. Mgon-po mchod-pa. Translated by Stephan Beyer as "The Worship of the Fierce Lord" in his The Buddhist Experience: Sources and Interpretations (see 3.3.2.1[18]), pp. 124-130.

Translation of a sixteenth century Tibetan monk's evocation of a "terrifying deity." (See also 11.6.1[1].)

Tantra-/Mantra-/Vajra-yana Texts   3.4.4

(13) _____. Snyan-rgyud yid bzhin nor-bu'i bskeyd-pa'i rim-pa rgyas-pa 'dod-pa'i re-skong znes bya-ba. Translated by Stephan Beyer as "The Process of Generation of the Wishing Gem of the Ear-Whispered Teachings" in his The Buddhist Experience: Sources and Interpretations (see 3.3.2.1[18]), pp. 140-154.

Translation of a Tantric text by a sixteenth century Tibetan adept, chosen by Beyer to illustrate the manner and technique by which "The Meditator Becomes the God." (See also 11.6.1[1].)

(14) Prajnaparamita-nama-astasataka. Translated by Edward Conze as "The 108 Names of Perfect Wisdom" (see 3.3.1.1[16]).

3.4.3 Japanese Vajrayana Texts in Translation and Textual Studies

(1) HAKEDA, YOSHITO S., trans. Kukai: Major Works (see 2.6.2[4]), pp. 101-275.

This section of Hakeda's excellent book on Kukai contains complete or substantial translations of eight of Kukai's major works. These include: "The Difference between Exoteric and Esoteric Buddhism" (Benkenmitsu nikyo ron), "Attaining Enlightenment in this Very Existence" (Sokushin jobutsu gi), "The Meanings of Sound, Word, and Reality" (Shoji jisso gi), "The Meaning of the Word Hum" (Unji gi). Not included in this selection is the monumental "Ten Stages of Development of Mind" (Jushin ron).

(2) KIYOTA, MINORU. "Introduction to the Hizo-Hoyaku, A Classical Text on Japanese Buddhist Esoterism." Transactions of the International Conference of Orientalists in Japan, 6 (1961), 75-87.

Outline and study of the Hizo-hoyaku, a ten chapter doctrinal work by Kukai, which places esoterism within the structure of Buddhist doctrines and systematizes it as a distinct school of Japanese Buddhism.

(3) TAJIMA, RYUJUN. Etude sur le Mahavairocana Sutra: Dainichikyo. See 2.6.2(9).

Important study of one of the two basic texts of Shingon Buddhism, known in Japan as the Dainichikyo, by a late "archbishop" of Shingon. The work contains a translation of Chapter 1 and summaries of the contents of Chapters 2-31. More information may be found in the same author's study of the mandalas associated with this text. For this, see Ryujun Tajima, Les Deux Grands Mandalas et la Doctrine de l'Esoterisme Shingon (see 2.6.2[8]).

3.4.4 Other Vajrayana Texts in Translation and Textual Studies

(1) BHATTACHARYYA, BENOYTOSH, ed. Two Vairayana Works: Prajnopayaviniscayasiddhi and Jnanasiddhi. Gaekwad's Oriental Series, No. 44. Baroda: Oriental Institute, 1929, xxi, 118 pp.

Edition of the Sanskrit text of these two Vajrayana works, the one by the late seventh century master, Anangavajra, and the other by his disciple, Indrabhuti. The text is preceded by a helpful summary of the teachings of both texts, and by a study of their authorship.

(2) DE, SUSKIT KUMAR. "The Buddhist Tantric Literature, Sanskrit, of Bengal." New Indian Antiquary, 1 (1938), 1-23.

Bengal was always one of the centers of Indian Buddhist Tantric practices. This article forms a helpful survey of the specifically tantric literature composed and found in that area.

(3) LALOU, MARCELLE. "Manjusrimulakalpa et Taramulakalpa." Harvard Journal of Asiatic Studies, 1 (1936), 327-349.

Analysis and comparison and table of concordances of the Tibetan texts of these two iconographic and meditational works. Chapters 2-7 of the first of these texts have been translated into French by Ariane MacDonald in Le Mandala du Manjusrimulakalpa (see 3.4.2[10], chapters 2-3), and by Marcelle Lalou in his Iconographie des Etoffes Peintes (see 3.4.2[10]), chapters 4-7.

(4) SNELLGROVE, DAVID L., trans. "Saraha's Treasury of Songs" in Buddhist Texts Through the Ages (see 3.3.1.1[19]), pp. 224-239.

This is a complete translation from the original Apabhramsa of the so-called "People's Dohas" of Saraha (ninth century), who was one of the eighty-four Siddhas ("perfect ones"). It is not to be confused with the "Royal Dohas" of Saraha, translated by Herbert Guenther. Because it is short, and readily available, and summarizes many important tantric notions, the "People's Dohas" is often used as an introductory reading in classes that touch but briefly on the Mantrayana.

(5) WAYMAN, ALEX. "Analysis of the Tantric Section of the Kanjur Correlated to Tanjur Exegesis" in his The Buddhist Tantras: Light on Indo-Tibetan Esotericism (see 2.6.1[15]), pp. 233-239. (Originally published in Indo-Asian Studies, Part 1. Edited by Raghu Vira. New Delhi: International Academy of Indian Culture, 1963, pp. 118-125.)

This brief article provides an outline of the Tantric works in the Tibetan canon and is very useful for seeing which works are Annuttara-yoga tantras, yoga tantras, carya tantras or Kriya tantras.

3.5 GENERAL ANTHOLOGIES OF BUDDHIST TEXTS

(1) BEAL, SAMUEL. A Catena of Buddhist Scriptures from the Chinese. See 3.2.1.2(7).

This old anthology is important mainly for the role it played in "opening up the Chinese Canon" to a whole generation of students; and today in spite of its Christian, diffusionist and sun-symbolist biases, it is still a useful book. Among those works partially or wholly translated are: Wang Puh's (650 A.D.) biography of the Buddha; some extracts from the Mahaparinirvana Sutra; the "Sutra of Forty-Two Sections"; the Chinese Pratimoksha; the so-called "Daily Manual of the Shaman"; and some T'ien-t'ai, Pure Land, and "Lotus Sutra" selections.

(2) BEYER, STEPHAN. The Buddhist Experience: Sources and Interpretations. See 3.3.2.1(18).

Translations not only from all major Buddhist traditions, but including cultic and popular material as well. This is a fine companion to Robinson's The Buddhist Religion (see 1.1[8]), which appeared in the same "Religious Life of Man" Series and should go a long way towards pointing new orientations and directions for the overall study of Buddhism as a religion. Makes a fine supplement to Conze's Buddhist Texts through the Ages (below).

(3) CONZE, EDWARD, ed. Buddhist Texts through the Ages. See 3.3.1.1(19).

If anthologies must be used, this one (available in paperback) is one of the best--especially for courses focusing primarily on Buddhist thought. The material covered includes translations from the Pali, Sanskrit, Chinese, Tibetan and Apabhramsa; and the collaboration of Conze, Snellgrove, Horner, and Waley, each a specialist in his or her own field, has meant this anthology has avoided the pitfall of overemphasis on one particular area or aspect of Buddhist studies.

(4) DE BARY, WILLIAM THEODORE, ed. The Buddhist Tradition in India, China and Japan. See 1.11.1(5).

Essentially this anthology brings together excerpts pertaining to Buddhism from the three Columbia University anthologies, the sources of the Indian, Chinese, and Japanese traditions, thereby omitting Tibet, Southeast Asia, Central Asia, and Korea. Each selection is introduced by a few comments from one of the editors.

(5) FEER, LEON, trans. Fragments Extraits du Kandjour. Annales du Musée Guimet, No. 5. Paris: E. Leroux, 1883, 577 pp.

In this book, Leon Feer did for the Tibetan Canon what Henry Clarke Warren was to do for the Pali Canon in his Buddhism in Translations (below); he selected important passages from the bKan Gyur and arranged them topically. These topics include: "history" of the Buddha and some disciples; "discipline" (vinaya); "dogma"; "morality"; "transmigration"; and "mantras."

(6) GODDARD, DWIGHT, ed. A Buddhist Bible. (Paperback edition: Beacon BP 357; First published 1938.)

Unlike most anthologies, Goddard's Buddhist Bible does not present short excerpts from many texts, but a few whole texts in translation. (These, however, have often been "edited.") The selection includes material from Pali, Sanskrit, Chinese, Tibetan, and Modern sources, and for many years was a very influential book in Western classrooms. It is now outdated.

(7) HAMILTON, CLARENCE HERBERT, ed. Buddhism: A Religion of Infinite Compassion. Indianapolis: Bobbs-Merrill, 1962, 189 pp. (First published New York: Liberal Arts Press, 1952.)

This was one of the first anthologies to try to span the whole of Buddhist literature: Pali, Sanskrit, Chinese, Tibetan and Japanese. Useful in its day, it was, however, almost immediately superseded by Edward Conze's Buddhist Texts through the Ages (above).

(8) WARREN, HENRY CLARKE, trans. Buddhism in Translations. See 2.7.1(16).

This collection of translations of Pali materials has probably introduced more students to Buddhist texts than any other book. It is a classic which can still be highly recommended for introductory courses; but two of its limitations should be remembered: 1) It is an anthology; and 2) It deals only with Theravada Buddhism. It is also available in paperback.

4 Popular Beliefs and Literature

4.1 BUDDHISM AND INDIGENOUS POPULAR BELIEFS

See also: 7.3, Calendric Rituals and Festivals; 7.4, Life Cycle Rites; and 7.5, Magical Protection, Health and Healing, etc.

4.1.1 Buddhism and Popular Beliefs in South Asia

(1) AMES, MICHAEL M. "Buddha and the Dancing Goblins: A Theory of Magic and Religion." American Anthropologist, 66 (1964), 75-82.
  Interesting analysis of magic and religion in Ceylon. Ames argues that the popular magic rituals are transitional devices that mediate between the profane world and sacred Buddhist concerns.

(2) _____. "Magical-animism and Buddhism: A Structural Analysis of the Sinhalese Religious Systems," in Religion in South Asia. Edited by Edward B. Harper. Seattle: University of Washington Press, 1964, 199 pp. (Originally published Journal of Asian Studies, 23, special issue [1964], 21-52.)
  A preliminary attempt to subject the total Sinhala religious system to sociological analysis. Ames interestingly describes the dominant ideals of Sinhalese religion, clarifies the role various types of Buddhist beliefs play in it, shows how they are put into practice, and suggests some of the problems their implementation poses.

(3) _____. "Ritual Prestations and the Structure of the Sinhalese Pantheon," in Anthropological Studies in Theravada Buddhism. Edited by Manning Nash. Southeast Asia Studies. Cultural Report Series, No. 13. New Haven: Yale University, 1966, pp. 27-50.
  Ames analyses the structure of the Sinhala pantheon through the dichotomy of reciprocal (expressive) and non-reciprocal (instrumental) rituals. Non-reciprocal transactional units form the network of bonds in the Buddhist moral community while reciprocal units form a therapeutic relationship between the magician and his clientele. Ritual transactions determine a spirit's status in the pantheon.

(4) BLOSS, LOWELL W. "The Buddha and the Naga: A Study in Buddhist Folk Religiosity." History of Religions, 13 (1973), 36-53.
  One of the few specific studies of Buddhism and popular beliefs in early India. Focusing on the role and meaning of the naga, or snake-folk-fertility figure, the author seeks to explicate the symbolism and significance of its incorporation into Buddhist myths and legends.

(5) EVERS, HANS-DIETER. "Buddha and the Seven Gods: The Dual Organization of a Temple in Central Ceylon." Journal of Asian Studies, 27 (1968), 541-550.
  Detailed description of the dual organization of a Sinhala temple in order to show the intimate connection of worship of the Buddha with that of other deities.

(6) FALK, NANCY E. "Wilderness and Kingship in Ancient South Asia." History of Religions, 13 (1973), 1-15.
  Falk touches on Buddhist legends and other material as she focuses on the various symbolisms of "the wilderness" in its relation to the important "civilized" figure of the king, and deals with the role of caityas, yaksas, relics, and other "folk" motifs in this relationship. An interesting way of approaching the question of the relationship of Buddhism and indigenous popular beliefs throughout India and South Asia.

(7) GOMBRICH, RICHARD FRANCIS. Precept and Practice: Traditional Buddhism in the Rural Highlands of Ceylon. Oxford: Clarendon Press, 1971, 366 pp.
  Important contribution to the study of popular Buddhism in Sri Lanka. Gombrich explores the problem of the relationship between what contemporary Sinhala Buddhists do, what they believe they do, and the norms expressed in the Pali canon and commentaries. The whole makes an ambitious project which is carried out from an anthropological perspective by a professor of Pali and Sanskrit at Cambridge.

(8) LEACH, EDMUND RONALD. "Pulleyar and the Lord Buddha: An Aspect of Religious Syncretism in Ceylon." Psychoanalysis and the Psychoanalytic Review, 49 (1962), 80-102.

Fascinating article analyzing a specific example of syncretism between the Hindu and Sinhala Buddhist traditions. Leach studies the figure Ganesha in his Hindu and Sinhalese aspects.

(9) OBEYESEKERE, GANANATH. "The Great Tradition and the Little in the Perspective of Sinhalese Buddhism." *Journal of Asian Studies*, 22 (1963), 139-153.

Description of Sinhala Buddhism at the village level with an eye to its relation with the great community of Theravada "priests, theologians and literary men." Obeyesekere recognizes the importance of the great tradition but shows how the little tradition at the village level is a "whole" though not an "isolate."

(10) YALMAN, NUR. "On Some Binary Categories in Sinhalese Religious Thought." *Transactions of the New York Academy of Sciences*, Second series, 24 (1962), 408-420.

Yalman applies the structuralist approach to the study of ritual and Sinhala categories of the supernatural. In analyzing the Buddhist complex and its relationship to the devale complex, Yalman finds important categorical oppositions in pure-impure, birth-death, concern with other world-concern with this world.

4.1.2 Buddhism and Popular Beliefs in Southeast Asia

(1) BROHM, JOHN. "Buddhism and Animism in a Burmese Village." *Journal of Asian Studies*, 22 (1963), 155-167.

A study of religion at the village level, in which Brohm objects to speaking of "animists or Buddhists" or even of "animism and Buddhism," but argues that Buddhism is a form of animism (in a Burmese village).

(2) BROWN, R. GRANT. "The Pre-Buddhist Religion of the Burmese." *Folk-Lore*, 32 (1921), 77-100.

A straightforward description of what the author considers to be indigenous religious "survivals" among Buddhists in Burma. Includes discussions of animism, the twenty-seven nats, tree-worship, snake-worship, sacrifice, and rain-making.

(3) CADIERE, LEOPOLD MICHEL. *Croyances et Pratiques Religieuses des Vietnamiens.* See 1.8.1(1).

Easily the most extensive and detailed treatment of popular religion in Vietnam. Volume 1 discusses Buddhism and its relationship to spirit cults, to Confucianism and to Taoism, family religion, various historical imperial cults and funerary practices, and religious and magical manifestations that took place during a 1908 cholera epidemic. Volume 2 includes discussions of the cult of trees and of stones, popular beliefs in Quang-Binh province and Nguon-so'n valley and traditions surrounding the ancient capital of Hue. Volume 3 contains two sections dealing with "popular Vietnamese philosophy" devoted to cosmology and conceptions of the human body.

(4) CHOTISUKHARAT, SANGUAN. "Supernatural Beliefs and Practices in Chungmai." *Journal of the Siam Society*, 59 (1971), 211-231.

The thrust of this well-done article seems to be the importance of the teritorial distribution of shrines and cults associated with specific shrines. The author describes ceremonies and propitiations associated with the "central post" of Chiengmai, the courting and placation of spirits associated with other shrines, the dance of the "ant ghost," rituals of healing, and the considerations that go into the building of a house.

(5) *Génies, Anges et Démons*. Sources Orientales, No. 8. Paris: Editions du Seuil, 1971, 430 pp.

A collection of articles on genies, angels and demons throughout Asia, some of which touch upon Buddhism, brought together as volume 8 of the Sources Orientales series. See in particular Pierre Lafont, "Génies, Anges, et Démons en Asie du Sud-Est," pp. 343-382; and Denise Bernot, "Les nats de Birmanie," pp. 295-342.

(6) HTIN AUNG, U. *Folk Elements in Burmese Buddhism.* London: Oxford University Press, 1962, 140 pp.

A short study of the folk cults which the author claims were flourishing in Burma prior to the predominance of Theravada Buddhism in the eleventh century, and of their persistence within the practices and beliefs of Burmese Buddhism of the present day.

(7) KING, WINSTON LEE. *A Thousand Lives Away: Buddhism in Contemporary Burma.* See 2.8(14).

In this chapter of his book on contemporary Burmese Buddhism, King seeks to clarify the relationship between "folk religion," "pagoda religion," "scriptural orthodoxy," etc., by placing them and other practices in a hierarchical structure ascending towards Nibbana. The title of the chapter is "Buddhism: High, Low, and Medium."

(8) MALALGODA, KITSIRI. "Millennialism in Relation to Buddhism." *Comparative Studies in Society and History*, 42 (1970), 424-441.

The author begins his article by reviewing the thought of Max Weber in relation to theodicy. He then attempts to show how Buddhism has assimilated and accommodated animism in such a way that belief in deities has supplanted the theory of karmic retribution as an explanation for the "state of being." The consequent result is popular belief in magic and in saviors. The author then goes on to survey millennial developments as they have been related to events in the Jatakas, Maitreya, arhats, and cakravartins. The entire article is intended to dispel the notion that millennialism does not play an important role in Theravada Buddhism. A good article to read

Popular Beliefs and Literature

Buddhism and Indigenous Popular Beliefs

in conjunction with Melford E. Spiro's books and articles on the subject.

(9) MENDELSON, E. MICHAEL. "The King of the Weaving Mountain." Journal of the Royal Central Asian Society, 48 (1961), 229-237.

Mendelson's study of a "gaing," mystical sect, in Burma, is an important contribution to the study of popular Buddhist millenarian movements. Mendelson's observations are perceptive in discerning the various occult and Buddhist elements in the gaings.

(10) _____. "A Messianic Buddhist Association in Upper Burma." Bulletin of the School of Oriental and African Studies, 24 (1961), 560-580.

Detailed description of the building and ceremonies of the Maheikdi gaing, a group whose millenarian expectations are to be fulfilled with the coming of the future Buddha Maitreya. Also provides some comparative materials in his discussion of the movement.

(11) _____. "Observations on a Tour in the Region of Mount Popa, Central Burma." France-Asie, 19, no. 179 (1963), 780-807.

An excellent description of a gaing, millenarian cult, at Mount Popa. Mendelson describes the interweaving of nat spirits and the Buddha, the weikza (magician/alchemist), and the belief in a coming cakravartin and the importance of Maitreya in this popular millenarian cult.

(12) _____. "The Uses of Religious Skepticism in Modern Burma." Diogenes, 41 (1963), 94-116.

Intriguing study of the nature of Burmese religious authority based upon a case study involving beliefs about nats. Mendelson states that he is not interested so much in the beliefs themselves as in the way in which people manipulate them for reasons which are not always entirely religious.

(13) NASH, JUNE C. "Living with Nats: An Analysis of Animism in Burman Village Social Relations," in Anthropological Studies in Theravada Buddhism (see 4.1.1[3]), pp. 117-136.

Nash shows how the nat cult is perpetuated by obligations inherited at the levels of family, village and region. She further discusses how the system is articulated within dominant Theravada beliefs and practices.

(14) NASH, MANNING. The Golden Road to Modernity: Village Life in Contemporary Burma. New York: Wiley, 1965, 333 pp.

From an anthropological viewpoint, Nash presents a good analysis and description of the popular beliefs and ritual system in a village in Burma. He discusses the nats, spirits, and the predictive, divinatory, and curing systems, viewing Buddhism and the popular beliefs as a coherent whole.

4.1.3

(15) SPIRO, MELFORD E. Burmese Supernaturalism: A Study in the Explanation and Reduction of Suffering. Prentice-Hall College Anthropology Series. Englewood Cliffs: Prentice-Hall, 1967, 300 pp.

Comprehensive anthropological account of Burmese "supernaturalism" including its relation to Buddhism. Develops a typology of belief systems in conjunction with an analysis of the supernatural practitioner's role. For a review article of the work, see Chandra Jayawardena, "The Psychology of Burmese Supernaturalism," Oceania, 41 (1970), 12-19.

(16) TAMBIAH, STANLEY J. Buddhism and the Spirit Cults in North-East Thailand. Cambridge Studies in Social Anthropology, No. 2. Cambridge: Cambridge University Press, 1970. 388 pp.

An important and fine anthropological study of the Buddhist religion and its relationship to popular beliefs in a Northeastern Thai village. Tambiah describes the religious "kaleidoscope" primarily through the interaction of four ritual complexes: 1) rites performed by Buddhist monks; 2) the sukhwan rituals concerning personal spirits and performed by village elders; 3) the cult of guardian deities of the village; 4) rites addressed to malevolent spirits.

4.1.3 Buddhism and Popular Beliefs in China

(1) CHAO WEI-PANG. "Secret Religious Societies in North China in the Ming Dynasty." Folklore Studies (Peking), 7 (1948), 95-115.

Buddhism was an important element in the formation of many of these groups, which are case studies in how the Indian tradition came to be appropriated at the popular level in China. They were also prime carriers of the Mahayana message of salvation to the common people.

(2) CH'EN, KENNETH K. S. Buddhism in China: A Historical Survey (see 1.11.1[1]), pp. 426-433.

Chapter 10, pages 258-296, gives a good summary and introduction to "orthodox lay religion" in China, emphasizing the importance of Buddhist temples at the popular level. Pages 426-433 deal with two of the so-called secret societies which were very important Buddhistic groups of a more heretical but equally popular nature: the Maitreya Society of the Sung Dynasty, and the White Lotus Society of the Yuan, Ming, and Ch'ing.

(3) DORE, HENRI. Researches into Chinese Superstitions. Translated by M. Kennelly et al. Shanghai: T'usewei Press, 1914-1938, 13 vols.

This massive work, "profusely illustrated," is rich in illustration and examples but very weak on interpretation. Fr. Dore deals with the Chinese Buddhist pantheon as understood at the popular level in vol. 6, pp. 89-233, and vols. 7-8, pp. 235-716.

4.1.3

(4) HSU, FRANCIS L. K. <u>Under the Ancestors' Shadow: Chinese Culture and Personality</u>. New York: Columbia University Press, 1948, 317 pp.

Important treatment of Chinese popular religion and ancestral cult, based on village studies in 1941-1943. See, in particular, pp. 167-199 for evidence of the Buddhist role in village life.

(5) MASPERO, HENRI. "The Mythology of Modern China," in <u>Asiatic Mythology</u>. Edited by Joseph Hackin. London: G. C. Harrap, 1932, pp. 252-384.

A lucid presentation of Chinese mythological and religious beliefs and concerns, this essay is of fundamental importance for a background to and an understanding of the place of Buddhism in Chinese popular religion.

(6) MURAMATSU, YUJI. "Some Themes in Chinese Rebel Ideologies," in <u>The Confucian Persuasion</u>. Edited by Arthur F. Wright. Stanford Studies in the Civilizations of Eastern Asia. Stanford: Stanford University Press, 1960, pp. 241-267.

A good introduction to the topic of Buddhist Taoist and Shamanistic influences in inspiring and solidifying some of the mass rebellions that have occurred throughout Chinese history. A good historical survey of some of these same "rebel ideologies" and movements prior to the mid-nineteenth century may be found in Vincent Yu-chung Shih, <u>The Taiping Ideology: Its Sources, Interpretations and Influences</u> (Seattle: University of Washington Press, 1967), pp. 329-389. (This chapter is based on an earlier article by the same author entitled "Some Chinese Rebel Ideologies," <u>T'oung Pao</u>, 44 [1956], 150-226.)

(7) OVERMEYER, DANIEL L. "Folk-Buddhist Religion: Creation and Eschatology in Medieval China." <u>History of Religions</u>, 12 (1972), 42-70.

A fine study of the beliefs of folk-Buddhist sects in the Ming and Ch'ing periods (1368-1911).

4.1.4 <u>Buddhism and Popular Beliefs in Japan</u>

(1) EARHART, H. BYRON. <u>A Religious Study of the Mount Haguro Sect of Shugendo: An Example of Japanese Mountain Religion</u>. A Monumenta Nipponica Monograph. Tokyo: Sophia University, 1970, 212 pp.

A study of the historical development and religious dynamics of a particular sect of Shugendo, an interesting popular movement within Japanese religion which combines esoteric Buddhist practices and views with Japanese folk religious beliefs--especially those surrounding sacred mountains. This is the best study of this important topic in English.

Buddhism and Indigenous Popular Beliefs

(2) _____. "Shugendo, the Traditions of En no gyoja, and Mikkyo Influence." <u>See</u> 2.6.2(2).

A discussion of the ways in which popular traditions about Shugendo's "founder" (En no gyoja) have been transformed under the impact of esoteric Buddhism in Japan. <u>See also</u> 2.6.2(2).

(3) EMBREE, JOHN FEE. <u>Suye Mura: A Japanese Village</u>. Chicago: University of Chicago Press, 1964, pp. 221-298. (Originally published 1939; paperback edition: Phoenix Books P173.)

The book as a whole is a classic sociological study of a Japanese village. Chapter 7 deals with "religion," and makes a good introduction to the ways in which Buddhism and Shinto interact in the popular religious observances and beliefs of the villagers throughout the calendar year.

(4) HORI, ICHIRO. <u>Folk Religion in Japan: Continuity and Change</u>. Edited by Joseph M. Kitagawa and Alan L. Miller. Haskell lectures on History of Religion, New series, No. 1. Chicago: University of Chicago Press, 1968, 278 pp.

These were the 1965 Haskell lectures at the University of Chicago, and they have become one of the basic studies in the field of Japanese folk religion. For Buddhist elements and influences in that folk religion, see, in particular, Chapter 3, "Nembutsu as Folk Religion."

(5) _____. "On the Concept of Hijiri (Holy-Man)." <u>Numen</u>, 5 (1958), 128-160, 199-232.

The Hijiri in Japan were unofficial reformers of institutionalized Buddhism and figured prominently as leaders of popular Buddhist movements. What Hori does, then, in this article, is to trace the whole history and development of Japanese Popular Buddhism by focusing on the role of these key figures. This makes a good introduction to the topic of popular traditions within Japanese Buddhism, especially when read in conjunction with the more specialized study by H. Byron Earhart, <u>A Religious Study of the Mount Haguro Sect of Shugendo: An Example of Japanese Mountain Religion</u> (above).

(6) MATSUNAGA, ALICIA. <u>The Buddhist Philosophy of Assimilation: The Historical Development of the Honji-Suijaku Theory</u>. A Monumenta Nipponica Monograph. Rutland, Vt.: C. E. Tuttle, 1969, 310 pp. <u>See also</u> 6.2.1.2(16).

(7) TAKEDA, CHOSHU. "Ancestor Worship: An Important Historic and Social Factor in Japanese Folk Buddhism," in <u>Proceedings of the VIIIth International Congress of Anthropological and Ethnographical Sciences, 1968, Tokyo and Kyoto</u>. Tokyo: Science Council of Japan, 1970, vol. 3, pp. 123-125.

The author attributes the success of Buddhism among the popular masses in Japan to

Moral Tales, Legends, and Popular Literature

its ability to merge with a uniquely Japanese type of ancestor worship.

4.1.5 Buddhism and Popular Beliefs in Tibet and Other Countries

(1) FURER-HAIMENDORF, CHRISTOPH VON. *Morals and Merit: A Study of Values and Social Controls in South Asian Societies.* The Nature of Human Society Series. Chicago: University of Chicago Press, 1967, 239 pp.

This work deals with the whole range of moral ethos and the relation between Hindu, Buddhist and indigenous popular elements. Especially interesting for the student of Buddhism is the chapter which compares the moral ethos in Sherpa society with that among Buddhists in Sri Lanka.

(2) GIMARET, DANIEL. "Bouddha et les Bouddhistes dan la Tradition Musulmane." *Journal Asiatique*, 257 (1969), 273-316.

A very fine article in which the author surveys the diverse traditions about the Buddha found among the Muslims of Iran and adjacent areas. The author concerns himself with those traditions which speak of "avatars" of d'al-Budd and Budasf. Finally, he treats the references to the Sumaniyyas which the author equates as references to Buddhists.

(3) NEBESKY-WOJKOWITZ, RENE DE. *Oracles and Demons of Tibet: The Cult and Iconography of the Tibetan Protective Deities.* La Haye: Mouton, 1956, 666 pp. See also 9.2.2.5(8).

(4) WADDELL, LAWRENCE AUSTINE. "Demonolatry in Sikhim Lamaism." *The Indian Antiquary*, 25 (1894), 197-215.

Though dated in its attitude and methodology, this article, by one who had much first-hand acquaintance with the Sikkimese and with Tibetan Buddhism, describes with a fair amount of detail the position of gods, demons, etc., in the Buddhism of Sikkim, with an emphasis on their function in rites and rituals.

4.2 MORAL TALES, LEGENDS, AND POPULAR LITERATURE

4.2.1 Popular Sutra Segments and Passages

See also 7.5.4.

(1) BARUA, DIPAK KUMAR. *An Analytical Study of Four Nikayas.* See 3.2.2.4(1), pp. 64-120.

The chapter is entitled "Discourses to the Laity" and contains what is undoubtedly one of the most thorough studies of passages in the first four Pali nikayas which may be considered to be directed towards the laity. After an introductory discussion and an attempt at defining gahapati and Upasaka, the author goes on to discuss "Ethical," "Religious" and "Secular" discourses of the Buddha to the laity, and then concludes with a brief comparison of them with Jaina discourses. Very helpful for bibliographic references to passages in the Digha, Majjhima, Samyutta and Anguttara nikayas.

(2) HRDLICKOVA, V. "The First Translations of Buddhist Sutras into Chinese Literature and Their Place in the Development of Storytelling." *Archív Orientální*, 26 (1958), 114-144.

A very good article in which the author traces the development of forms of storytelling from the sermon in the temple to the story-telling in the marketplace. In order to accomplish this, the author discusses translations of Buddhist sutras into Chinese during the period from the Han Dynasty to the end of the Sui.

(3) JAWORSKI, JAN. "L'Avalambanasutra de la Terre Pure." *Monumenta Serica*, 1 (1935), 82-107. (See also 9.2.2.3[6].)

(4) *Prajnaparamita-hrdaya-sutra.* Translated by Edward Conze as "The Heart Sutra" (see 3.3.1.1[11]).

(5) ROBINSON, RICHARD H., ed. and trans. *Chinese Buddhist Verse.* London: Murray, 1954, 85 pp. (Wisdom of the East Series.)

A fine sampling of popular Buddhist hymns and poems, most of which are taken from sutras or from the writings of Chinese patriarchs. Includes excerpts from the *Buddhacarita*, the *Dharmapada*, the *Vimalakirti Nirdesa Sutra*, the *Avatamsaka*, the *Saddharmapundarika Sutra*, and some of the works of Shan Tao and Hui Neng. These are all intended to document a spiritual movement in terms of the contents of the popular hymns it produced.

(6) *Saddharma pundarika.* Translated by H. Kern as *The Lotus of the True Law.* Delhi: Motilal Banarsidass, 1965, 454 pp. (Sacred Books of the East, Vol. 21.) Originally published by Oxford University Press, 1884.

The "Lotus" is full of passages which were of special popular appeal and instruction to the laity. For example, see the particularly famous "parable of the burning house" (pp. 72-81). See also the chapter on spells (pp. 370-375) and the numerous descriptions of magical feats and miraculous displays.

(7) *Suvarnabhasottamusutra.* Translated by R. E. Emmerick as *The Sutra of Golden Light.* See 3.3.8.1(8).

(8) *Vimalakirti Nirdesa sutra.* Translated by Etienne Lamotte as *L'Enseignement de Vimalakirti.* See 3.3.2.1(34).

4.2.2 Jatakas

(1) ARYASURA. *Jatakamala.* Translated by J. S. Speyer as *The Gatakamala, or Garland of Birth Stories.* Sacred Books of the Buddhists, Vol. 1. London: Henry Frowde, 1895, 350 pp.

4.2.2

The <u>Jatakamala</u> is a series of thirty-four well-known and popular jatakas (birth-stories of the Buddha), selected and retold by Aryasura, a Mahayanist whose dates are unknown. The selection was primarily intended as sermons illustrating and inspiring moral conduct and virtue.

(2) BURLINGAME, EUGENE WATSON, trans. and ed. <u>The Grateful Elephant and Other Stories</u>. New Haven: Yale University Press, 1923, 172 pp.

A children's book with fine translations of twenty-six Pali stories, almost all of which are taken from the Pali.

(3) FEER, LEON. "Les Jatakas dan les mémoires de Hiouen-Thsang," in <u>Actes du Onzième Congrès International des Orientalistes</u>. Paris, 1898-1899, vol. 1, section 1, pp. 151-169.

A convenient noting of the Jataka tales recounted by the Chinese pilgrim Hsuan Tsang relative to some of the spots he visited in India. This makes it a source of oral versions of the jatakas, as Hsuan Tsang claims merely to be recounting what was told him at each place. Feer has given the parallel canonical story in each case.

(4) FOUCHER, ALFRED. <u>Les Vies Antérieures du Bouddha, d'après les textes et les monuments de l'Inde</u>. See 2.7.1(2); see also 8.1.1(5).

(5) <u>Jatakastava</u>. Translated by Mark J. Dresden in "The Jatakastava or 'Praise of the Buddha's Former Birth.'" <u>See</u> 3.3.8.4(5).

After some technical grammatical notes, Dresden gives the Khotanese text and a translation of the Tun Huang manuscript. The text is interesting in that it recounts certain Jatakas and great deeds of the Buddha in order to praise him, and was originally translated into Khotanese from Sanskrit, specifically to make it more accessible to the laity. Dresden also gives a table of parallels between these stories and the Jatakas of the Pali canon.

(6) <u>Jatakatthakatha</u>. Incomplete translation as <u>The Jataka or Stories of the Buddha's Former Births</u>. Edited by E. B. Cowell. <u>See</u> 3.2.2.1(12).

According to Buddhist tradition, only the verses of the Jatakas are canonical and belong in the <u>Khuddaka nikaya</u>. The stories themselves (about five hundred of them) are considered commentaries. All of the stories have been translated here by this team of scholars. However, the long introduction to them, the <u>Nidanakatha</u>, has not. This is an important biography of the Buddha up to his enlightenment, and may be found translated by T. W. Rhys-Davids and Robert Childers in Rhys-Davids's <u>Buddhist Birth Stories</u> (London: Trubner, 1880), 347 pp. Cowell considered the <u>Nidanakatha</u> to be basically not related to the Jataka tales themselves—an opinion which needs serious reconsideration.

Moral Tales, Legends, and Popular Literature

(7) LANE, GEORGE S. "The Tocharian Punyavantajataka." <u>Journal of the American Oriental Society</u>, 67 (1947), 33-53.

"Tocharian" text and translation of an interesting jataka which is paralleled also by stories in the <u>Mahavastu</u> and in the <u>Bhadrakalpavadana</u>.

(8) LAW, BIMALA CHURN. "Some Observations on the Jatakas." <u>Journal of the Royal Asiatic Society</u> (1939), pp. 241-251.

A short but helpful article which discusses the sources, origins and aims of the jatakas. Limited, however, to the Pali versions of the stories.

(9) <u>Mahajjatakamala</u>. Partial translation by M. E. Lang as "La Mahajjatakamala." <u>Journal Asiatique</u>, 19 (1912), 511-550.

Translation of two fragments from what was once a voluminous collection of jatakas closely related to Aryasura's <u>Jatakamala</u>. The stories, whose Sanskrit text is also given, are called "The Potter" and "The Slave" and are paralleled by passages in the <u>Mahavastu</u> and the <u>Majjhima nikaya</u>.

(10) d'OLDENBURG, SERGE. "On the Buddhist Jatakas." <u>Journal of the Royal Asiatic Society</u>, 25 (1893), 301-356.

A substantial survey, translated from the Russian by H. Wenzel, of the various collections of Jataka texts, including the <u>Jatakamala</u> and the texts contained in the <u>Mahavastu</u>. By an important Russian Buddhologist. Also includes an extensive bibliography of the nineteenth century work done on the jatakas.

(11) PE WIN, U LU. "The Jatakas in Burma," in <u>Ba Shin</u>. Edited by Jean Boisselier and A. B. Griswold. Essays Offered to G. H. Luce. Artibus Asiae. Supplementum 23. Ascona: Artibus Asiae, 1966, 2 vols.

The author sets the scope of his article by posing the question as to why the Jatakas are so profuse and conspicuous in Burmese temples. The answer is rather stock: that the Burmese believe that the Jatakas represent the Buddha in previous births. However, he goes on to give other reasons for the places of specific illustrations.

(12) <u>Vessantara Jataka</u>. Translated by Emile Benveniste as <u>Vessantara Jataka</u>. Mission Pelliot en Asie Centrale, No. 4. Paris: Geuthner, 1946, 137 pp.

Edition and translation into French of the Sogdian text of this most popular of jatakas. It is interesting to compare this Sogdian version with those in the various other Buddhist languages. An older, less authoritative translation of the same text may be found in Robert Gauthiot, "Une Version sogdienne du Vessantara Jataka," <u>Journal Asiatique</u>, 19 (1912), 163-193 and 429-510. <u>See also</u> Ilya Gerschevitch, "On the Sogdian Vessantara Jataka" (<u>see</u> 8.1.1[7]); and

Moral Tales, Legends, and Popular Literature

especially L. Alsdorf, "Bemerkungen zum Vessantara Jataka," Wiener Zeitschrift für die Kunde Süd- und Ostasiens, 1 (1957), 1-70.

4.2.3 Avadanas and Other Buddhist Legends

See 8.1 for biography and autobiography.

(1) Anavataptagatha. Translated by Marcel Hofinger as Le Congrès du Lac Anavatapta (Vies de Saints Bouddhiques). See 3.2.1.2(1).
Legends of thirty-six theras, contained in the Vinaya of Mulasarvastivadins.

(2) Asokavadana. Translated by Jean Przyluski as La Légende de l'Empereur Asoka dans les Textes Indiens et Chinois. See 3.2.2.2(2).
The avadana of the Emperor Asoka was one of the earliest, most popular, and most important of the Buddhist avadanas. It contains a whole cycle of stories about the deeds and misdeeds of this third century B.C. king and makes for an interesting comparison with the image of him as we derive it from his Edicts and Rock Inscriptions. Part 1 of this book contains Przyluski's important, though sometimes misguided, discussions of the legend itself. Part 2 contains his translation of the A-yu-wang-chuan, which is one of the Chinese renditions of the text. Part 1 has been translated into English by Dilip Kumar Biswas in Jean Przyluski, The Legend of Emperor Asoka in Indian and Chinese Texts (Calcutta: K. L. Mukhopadhyay, 1967), 252 pp. Substantial portions of the Sanskrit text of the Asokavadana were translated into French by Eugène Burnouf in his Introduction à l'Histoire du Buddhisme Indien (2nd edition Paris: Maisonneuve, 1896), 586 pp.

(3) ASVAGHOSA. Sutralamkara. Translated by Edouard Huber. See 3.3.8.2(8).
A French translation of Kumarjiva's Chinese rendition (ca. 410 A.D.) of the Sutralamkara, attributed to Asvaghosa, who is often thought to have been an advisor to King Kanishka. The Sanskrit original has been lost. The work, as we have it, is a rich collection in verse and prose of moral tales and popular legends illustrative of proper and noble conduct.

(4) Avadana-sataka. Translated by Leon Feer as Avadana-çataka: Cent Légendes Bouddhiques. See 3.2.2.2(3).
Translation of one of the important early collections of avadanas, probably compiled by the Sarvastivadin school. Feer's helpful discussion of the organization of the text, of its relationship to other avadana collections (most of which are untranslated), and of the nature of the whole genre of avadana literature should be supplemented by the remarks of Kanga Takahata in his introduction to his edition of the Ratna-malavadana (Tokyo: Toyo Bunko, 1954). Feer has also written a series of articles based on his study of the Avadanasataka: "Etudes Bouddhiques," Journal Asiatique, 14 (1879), 141-189, 273-307; 16 (1880), 486-514; 17 (1881), 515-550; 18 (1881), 460-498; 19 (1882); 328-360; n.s. 1 (1883), 407-440; and 3 (1884), 5-41, 109-140.

(5) BAILEY, H. W. "Kanaiska." Journal of the Royal Asiatic Society (1942), pp. 14-28, 250.
A translation of fragments of the Khotanese version of the legend of King Kaniska, including the story of his great stupa and Sangharama which are mentioned by the Chinese pilgrims and by Alberuni.

(6) BARUCH, WILLY. "Le cinquante-deuxième chapitre du mJans-blun (Sutra du Sage et du Fou)." Journal Asiatique, 243 (1955), 339-366.
The mJans blun, which has been translated into German by I. J. Schmidt as Der Weise und der Tor (Leipzig: Leopold Voss, 1843), is a collection of Buddhist legends contained in the bKah 'gyur, but has been preserved in Chinese and in a sixteenth century Mongolian translation. Baruch has here edited the Mongolian text and translated the Chinese.

(7) BODE, MABEL. "The Legend of Ratthapala in the Pali, Apadana and Buddhaghosa's Commentary," in Mélanges d'Indienisme offerts à Sylvain Levi. Paris: E. Leroux, 1911, pp. 183-192.
Discussion of the legend of Ratthapala (Skt. Rastrapala), the Buddha's disciple who became known as a paradigm of faith. The legend explains how he earned that designation. Includes text and translation of the Pali Ratthapala apadana.

(8) Bya chos rin-chen 'phren-ba. Translated by Edward Conze as The Buddha's Law among the Birds. Oxford: Cassirer, 1955, 65 pp.
A charming tale, translated from the Tibetan, about the practice and preaching of the good Dharma in the animal kingdom.

(9) CHAVANNES, EDOUARD, ed. and trans. Cinq Cents Contes et Apologues Extraits du Tripitaka Chinois. Paris: E. Leroux, 1910-1934. 4 vols.
An extremely important resource for non-Chinese readers. Chavannes has selected and translated five hundred legends, tales, stories, avadanas, etc., all of which were included in various parts of the vast Chinese canon, and in Volume 4 has provided a very helpful topical index to them. Readers who want a smaller dosage of these kinds of stories should refer to the twenty-five tales selected by Chavannes in his Contes et Légendes du Bouddhisme Chinois (Paris: Bossard, 1921), 220 pp.

(10) CH'EN, KENNETH K. S. "A propos the Mendhaka Story." Harvard Journal of Asiatic Studies, 16 (1953), 374-403.
Translation and comparison of the Sanskrit, Chinese and Tibetan texts of an avadana which

was first partially translated by Eugène Burnouf in his Introduction à l'Histoire du Bouddhisme Indien (2nd edition Paris: Maisonneuve, 1876), pp. 169-172, and which appears in different versions in the Divyavadana, the Mulasarvastivada Vinaya, the Pali Vinaya and the Dhammapada commentary.

(11) _____. "A Study of the Svagata Story in the Divyavadana in its Sanskrit, Pali, Tibetan, and Chinese Versions." Harvard Journal of Asiatic Studies, 9 (1947), 207-314.

A textual study of different versions of a story, the Taisho Tripitaka text of which is translated. The legend of Svagata is closely connected to the interdictions on the drinking of intoxicating beverages and is interesting in its own right, although Ch'en is using it to make some technical points about the various recensions in which it appears.

(12) DENIS, EUGENE. "L'Origine Cingalaise du P'rah Malay," in Felicitation Volumes of Southeast-Asian Studies Presented to His Highness Prince Dhaninivat. Bangkok: Siam Society, 1965, vol. 2, pp. 329-338.

One of the very few articles in a Western language on the important and extremely popular P'rah Malay, a Thai Buddhist text which tells of visits to the hells and to the various heavens.

(13) Dhammapadatthakatha. Translated by Eugene Watson Burlingame as Buddhist Legends. See 3.2.2.3(2).

A full translation, with introduction and synopses of the stories, of the Pali commentary on the Dhammapada. The work is sometimes ascribed to Buddhaghosa, although Burlingame argues it is anonymous. The commentary consists almost entirely of illustrative stories, many of which parallel the tales of the Jataka commentary, and other texts as well. These stories often form the basis for sermons preached by monks in Theravada countries.

(14) EBERHARD, WOLFRAM. Guilt and Sin in Traditional China. Berkeley: University of California Press, 1967, 141 pp. See also 11.3(5).

(15) GOMBRICH, RICHARD. "Feminine Elements in Sinhalese Buddhism." Wiener Zeitschrift für die Kunde Südasiens, 16 (1972), 67-93. See also 8.1.1(8).

(16) HAMILTON, JAMES RUSSELL, ed. and trans. Le Conte Bouddhique du Bon et du Mauvais Prince en Version Ouigoure. Mission Paul Pelliot, Documents conservés à la Bibliothèque Nationale, No. 3. Paris: Editions du Centre Nationale de la Recherche Scientifique, 1971, 204 pp.

A definitive scholarly annotated edition and translation of the Uighur text of a widespread and popular tale of two brothers who embark on a sea voyage. The same version has been translated unsatisfactorily twice previously: Clement Huart, "Le Conte Bouddhique des Deux Frères, en Langue Turque et en Caractères Ouigours," Journal Asiatique, 3 (1914), 5-57; and Paul Pelliot, "La Version ouigoure de l'histoire des Princes Kalyanamkara et Papamkara," T'oung Pao, 15 (1914), 225-272. For a translation of the Tibetan version, see Anton von Schiefner, Tibetan Tales (London: Routledge, 1925), pp. 279-285. For a translation of the Chinese version, see Edouard Chavannes, "Une version chinoise de conte bouddhique de Kalyanamkara et Papamkara," T'oung Pao, 15 (1914), 469-500.

(17) HRDLICKOVA, V. "The First Translations of Buddhist Sutras in Chinese Literature and Their Place in the Development of Story-telling." See 4.2.1(2).

An interesting and helpful article dealing with the importance and influence both of sutras on Buddhist pien-wen (avadanas) and of popular literature on Buddhist sutras.

(18) HTIN AUNG, U., ed. and trans. Burmese Monk's Tales. New York: Columbia University Press, 1966, 181 pp.

The translator has collected and translated a fascinating group of tales which were first told during the dark decade of Burmese history (1876-85), the eve of the British conquest of Burma. The author of the tales, the Thingazar Sayadaw, improvised them on the spot to supplement his formal sermons centered on the Jatakas. The monk's tales are a new literary form modeled on the Burmese folk tale but dealing with the problems of laity and clergy of his day. They attempt to draw attention to the religious controversies of his time, often in a satirical manner.

(19) Karma-sataka. Briefly translated by Leon Feer in "Le Karma-sataka." Journal Asiatique, 17 (1901), 53-100, 257-315, 410-486.

Introduction to and substantial French summaries of the over one hundred avadanas of the Karma-sataka, a collection (the text of which is extant only in the Tibetan bKa' 'gyur) which Feer thinks was supposed to rival the similar Sarvastivadin collection, the Avadana-sataka. The legends, which vary in quality and interest, tell stories of merit making.

(20) LEVI, SYLVAIN. "Les Elements de Formation du Divyavadana." T'oung Pao, 8 (1907), 105-122.

In agreement with Edouard Huber ("Les Sources du Divyavadana," Bulletin de l'Ecole française d'Extrême-Orient, 6 [1906], 1-37), Sylvain Levi seeks to show that the collection of legends known as the Divyavadana (untranslated) was based on the stories of the Vinaya of the Mulasarvastivadins. For an opposite view, see Jean Przyluski's article "Fables in the Vinaya Pitaka of the Sarvastivadin School," Indian Historical Quarterly, 5 (1929), 1-5, in which he argues that the Vinaya stories were based on an old collection of stories similar to the Divyavadana.

Moral Tales, Legends, and Popular Literature

(21) LIENHARD; SIEGFRIED, trans. Manicudavadanoddhrta: A Buddhist re-birth story in the Nevari language. Stockholm Oriental Series, No. 4. Stockholm: Almqvist and Wiksell, 1968.
　Translation of a Nevari uddhrta (extract) of an avadana which was widespread and popular in India and recently in Nepal.

(22) Manicudavadana. Edited and translated by Ratna Handurukande in The Manicudavadana and Lokananda. Sacred Books of the Buddhists, No. 24. London: Luzac, 1967, pp. 1-193.
　The story of the bodhisattva Manicuda is an avadana (legend) which is presented in the manner of a Jataka retelling some former lives of the Buddha. It extolls the virtue of selfless giving (dana) for the sake of the enlightenment of all beings. The only dated manuscript of the popular story is of the late eighteenth century, but it is clearly based on much earlier material (fourth-eleventh centuries?). Handuru-kande has here edited a prose and a verse version of the story and translated it.

(23) NAKAMURA, KYOKO MOTOMOCHI, trans. "Miraculous Stories from the Japanese: The Nihon Ryoiki of the Monk Kyokai," in Buddhist Tradition. Harvard-Yenching Institute. Monograph No. 20. Cambridge, Mass.: Harvard University Press, 1973, 325 pp.
　An important contribution to the study of specifically Buddhist popular legends in Japan. The work contains a substantial introduction to and well-annotated translation of the Nihon ryoiki, one of the earliest Japanese collections of Buddhist tales, compiled by a ninth century monastic named Kyokai. The introduction provides an excellent review of Kyokai's life and background.

(24) PRUSEK, JAROSLAV. "The Narrators of Buddhist Scriptures and Religious Tales in the Sung Period." Archív Orientální, 10 (1938), 375-389.
　An interesting study of one type of Chinese story-teller thriving around the capital of Hangchow in Sung times: the specialist in religious tales. Within this group, Prusek distinguishes two classes: the mere narrators of Buddhist legends and the real creators of new and original works, which he discusses as being at the origins of the Chinese novel.

(25) PRZYLUSKI, JEAN and MARCELLE LALOU. "Récits Populaires et Contes Bouddhiques." Journal Asiatique, 228 (1936), 177-191.
　Study of two stories found both in the Avadana-sataka and in the Karmasataka (for both of which, see above). The two stories tell of daughters of kings of Benares who become Arhatis. Przyluski and Lalou seek to show how the form and tradition of this genre was very loose and open to change.

(26) ROGERS, HENRY THOMAS, trans. Buddhaghosha's Parables. London: Trubner, 1870, clxxii, 206 pp.
　A translation of twenty-nine Burmese legends, at least fifteen of which seem to be late Burmese versions of stories from the Dhammapada commentary (and thus not by Buddhaghosa). An old and dated collection.

(27) SCHIEFNER, F. ANTON VON, trans. Tibetan Tales, Derived from Indian Sources: Translated from the Tibetan of the Kahgyur. Done into English from the German by W. R. S. Ralston. New edition. London: G. Routledge, 1926, lxv, 368 pp. (Originally published 1882.)
　A collection of tales, selected and translated from the bKa' gyur (the Tibetan Tripitaka). Many of the stories are animal fables, or jatakas, and most are derived from Indian sources. For a selection of tales from the Chinese Tripitaka, see Edouard Chavannes, Cinq Cents Contes et Apologues Extraits du Tripitaka Chinois (see 4.2.3[9]).

(28) WALEY, ARTHUR, ed. and trans. Ballads and Stories from Tun-Huang: An Anthology. New York: Macmillan, 1960, 273 pp.
　Anthology of works gathered from Tun-huang in 1900, and given a lively translation by Arthur Waley. Includes Buddhist legendary tales (pien wen), in particular the very popular story of Moggallana's (Mu-lien) descent into hell to visit his mother. Also contains ballads, stories, and legendary expansions of Buddhist texts. Altogether a good introduction to popular Buddhist literature in China.

(29) WARE, JAMES R. "Studies in the Divyavadana." Journal of the American Oriental Society, 48 (1928), 159-165; 49 (1929), 40-51; and Harvard Journal of Asiatic Studies, 3 (1938), 47-67.
　Analysis, discussion, and translation of three of the stories from the Divyavadana, one of the earliest compendiums of Buddhist avadanas. Part 1, the Sukarikavadana; Part 2, the Danadhikara mahayanasutra; and Part 3, the preamble to the Samgharaksitavadana, the text of which may be found translated in Eugène Burnouf, Introduction à l'Histoire du Bouddhisme Indien (Second edition Paris: Maisonneuve, 1876), pp. 280-299.

(30) WOODWARD, FRANK LEE, trans. Buddhist Stories. Adyar: Theosophical Publishing House, 1925, 140 pp.
　Fine translations of Pali Buddhist legends, most of which are taken from the Dhammapada commentary, but some also from canonical texts, and some from the Jatakas. The collection is designed to illustrate popular understanding of Buddhist ethics.

4.2.4   Moral Tales, Legends, and Popular Literature

4.2.4 Popular Literature Having a Bearing on Buddhism (Folk Tales, Stories, Proverbs, etc.)

(1) BROUGH, JOHN. "Legends of Khotan and Nepal." Bulletin of the School of Oriental and African Studies, 12 (1948), 333-339.
Interesting study of some of the remarkable parallels between local legends in those two areas and of the implications of these on the development of the Buddhist tradition there.

(2) CHEN SHOU-YI. Chinese Literature: A Historical Introduction. New York: Ronald Press, 1961, 665 pp.
By checking the entries under "Buddhism" in the index, the student can trace historically the streams of Buddhist thought running through Chinese literature. A helpful source.

(3) DAVID-NEEL, ALEXANDRA and LAMA YONGDEN. The Superhuman Life of Gesar of Ling. New York: Kendall, 1934, 390 pp.
This book should not be thought of as a "translation" of the important Tibet epic of Gesar, but rather as another and new version in the cycle of sagas surrounding the figure of that king. As with a number of David-Neel's books, the end is weaker than the beginning: she seems to run out of steam. Still, it is the only book in English on this epic, a partial French translation of which may be found in Rolf Alfred Stein, L'Epopée Tibétaine de Gesar dans sa Version Lamaïque de Ling (below).

(4) DAVID-NEEL, ALEXANDRA, ed. and trans. "Le Roman du Bosquet dans Lotus," in her Textes Tibétains Inédits. Paris: La Colombe, 1952, pp. 7-30.
A French translation of a popular and charming Tibetan parable about the misadventures of two bumble bees who are neglectful of their meditation. This is followed by a series of maxims attributed to a Raja of Bhutan.

(5) DORSON, RICHARD MERCER. Folk Legends of Japan. Rutland, Vt.: C. E. Tuttle, 1962, 256 pp.
A collection of translations of short local Japanese stories and legends. See especially Part One, which deals with "Priests, Temples, and Shrines" and contains a number of interesting legends dealing with famous places and persons in Japanese Buddhism.

(6) EBERHARD, WOLFRAM, ed. and trans. Folktales of China. Revised edition. Chicago: University of Chicago Press, 1965, 267 pp. (Originally published 1937 as Chinese Fairy Tales and Folk Tales.)
A good selection, reliable translations. Includes interesting portrayals of Buddhist monks as magicians, disguised deities, etc. Several of these tales illustrate how Buddhism is understood at popular levels.

(7) HTIN AUNG, U., ed. and trans. Burmese Monk's Tales. See 4.2.3(18).

(8) LAI, T'IEN-CH'ANG, ed. and trans. Selected Chinese Sayings. Third revised edition. Hong Kong: University Bookstore, University of Hong Kong, 1966, 191 pp. (Originally published 1960.)
Chinese and English texts of many of the better known proverbs, alphabetically arranged, some of which show Buddhist influence. Sources of the sayings are usually provided. See also the same author's More Chinese Sayings (Kowloon: Swindon, 1972), 86 pp.

(9) MacDONALD, A. W., trans. Matériaux pour l'Etude de la Littérature Populaire Tibétaine. Annales du Musée Guimet, Bibliothèque d'Etudes, No. 72. Paris: Presses Universitaires de France, 1967, 324 pp.
In this book for specialists and interested students, MacDonald has edited and translated into French the "twenty-one religious stories of the gold Vetala," which deal with stories about corpses and should be of interest to the Buddhologist, folklorist, and historian of religions.

(10) MAYER, FANNY HAGIN. "Religious Elements in Japanese Folk Tales," in Studies in Japanese Culture. Edited by Joseph Roggendorf. Tokyo: Sophia University, 1963, 276 pp.
A brief survey of some of the religious themes that are popular within Japanese stories and tales. Treats, in particular, the roles of the Buddhist figures Kannon (Avalokitesvara) and Jizo (Ksitigarbha), as well as Shinto and other figures.

(11) PARMENTIER, HENRI. "Sentences et Proverbes Cambodgiens." Bulletin de l'Ecole française d'Extrême-Orient, 15 (1915), 47-71.
A selection of two hundred and fifty short Cambodian proverbs and aphorisms, many of them bearing on Buddhist subjects. Published here for the first time and translated into French.

(12) PLOPPER, CLIFFORD H. Chinese Religion Seen Through the Proverb. Second edition. Shanghai: Shanghai Modern Publishing House, 1935, 381 pp. (Originally published 1926.)
A unique account of Chinese Buddhism, as seen through and in various popular proverbs and sayings. An interesting and different way of approaching and understanding Chinese Buddhism.

(13) P'U SUNG-LING. Liao Chai Chih i. Translated by Herbert Allan Giles as Strange Stories from a Chinese Studio. London: T. De la Rue, 1880, 2 vols.
A seventeenth century collection of traditional stories, most showing the influence of popular beliefs, some depicting Buddhist monks and nuns.

(14) REYNOLDS, C. H. B., ed. An Anthology of Sinhalese Literature up to 1815. Translated by W. G. Archer and others. UNESCO collec-

Poetry and Song

tion of representative works, Sinhalese series. London: Allen and Unwin, 1970, 377 pp.

A selection of new translations into English of Sinhala literature beginning with fragments dating back to the sixth through ninth centuries. It continues with the great prose works of the twelfth to fourteenth centuries and the beautiful poems of the fifteenth and sixteenth centuries. The anthology ranges from Buddhist teachings on Nirvana to tales of the disciplinary habits of Ceylonese schoolmasters and includes extracts from the best-known writers of ancient Ceylon. Designed mainly for the advanced student of the subject.

(15) SOYMIE, MICHEL. "L'Entrevue de Confucius et de Hiang T'o." *Journal Asiatique*, 242 (1954), 311-392.

Analysis and translation of various Tibetan, Chinese, Mongolian, Siamese and Japanese versions of a tale about the encounters of Confucius and a wise little boy named Hiang t'o who outdoes him on the high road. This very popular, originally Chinese, story has been adapted and Buddha-ized in an interesting way, but only in the Mongolian version.

(16) STEIN, ROLF ALFRED. *L'Epopée Tibétaine de Gesar dans sa version Lamaïque de Ling*. Annales du Musée Guimet, Bibliothèque d'Etudes, No. 61. Paris: Presses Universitaires de France, 1956, 399 pp.

Tibetan text and translation of the first part of this very popular and important "national epic" of Tibet, with helpful introduction and indices showing heavy lamaist reinterpretations in the text itself. The story of King Gesar, who in this version is an incarnation of a bodhisattva, provides an excellent and entertaining introduction to the ways in which popular, shamanistic, and Buddhist elements were combined in Tibetan folk beliefs. For an important, scholarly study which is crucial for putting the Gesar saga in perspective, see Rolf Alfred Stein, *Recherches sur l'Epopée et le Barde au Tibet*. Bibliothèque de l'Institut des Hautes Etudes Chinoises, No. 13. (Paris: Presses Universitaires de France, 1959), 647 pp.

(17) *T'ai-shang kan-ying p'ien*. Translated by Paul Carus and Daisetz Teitaro Suzuki as *Treatise of the Exalted One on Response and Retribution*. Chicago: Open Court Press, 1906, 139 pp.

A popular morality book oriented toward Taoist deities, but showing strong Buddhist influence in its understanding of karmic retribution.

(18) WICKRAMASINGHE, MARTIN. *Landmarks of Sinhalese Literature*. Translated by Ediriweera R. Sarach-chandra. Second revised edition. Colombo: M. D. Gunasena, 1963, 211 pp.

A critical study of the principal works of Sinhala literature by a modern novelist, short story writer, and critic. Worthwhile for both initial and more advanced examination of the material. Helps to provide insight into the role of Sinhala literature, alongside the Pali writings, in the transmission of Buddhism.

4.3 POETRY AND SONG

(1) BLYTH, REGINALD H. *Haiku*. Tokyo: Hokuseido, 1950-1952, 4 vols.

Undoubtedly the most substantial collection of Haiku in English, which has the advantage of giving the Japanese text of the verses as well. Blyth has added his own sometimes rambling, sometimes perceptive commentary and has divided his tetralogy into vol.1, "Eastern Culture," vol. 2, "Spring," vol. 3, "Summer-Autumn," and vol. 4, "Autumn-Winter." Blyth is also careful, in several instances, to point to the Buddhist background and references in many of the haiku.

(2) DAVID-NEEL, ALEXANDRA, trans. *Textes Tibétains Inédits*. See 4.2.4(4).

In addition to some of the love songs of the Sixth Dalai Lama, these pages contain a folk song from the region around Lop Nor, a song said to have been improvised by King Ti Srong de tsan at the consecration of the Samye monastery, and some philosophical poems attributed to the Indian yogi Sharapa.

(3) DUNCAN, MARION HERBERT. *Love Songs and Proverbs of Tibet*. London: Mitre Press, 1961, 239 pp.

A light book on the love poetry and proverbs of Tibet, some very old and traditional, some contemporary, many expressing Buddhist and popular sentiments. Most of the book consists of translations, but Duncan has also provided an interesting and helpful introduction on the characteristics of Tibetan poetry and proverbs.

(4) HAN SHAN. *Cold Mountain*. Translated by Burton Watson. UNESCO Collection of Representative Works, Chinese Series. New York: Columbia University Press, 1970, 118 pp.

One hundred poems attributed to the somewhat elusive T'ang Dynasty Ch'an poet-recluse Han Shan are here given a fine translation and make a good introduction to the poetic literature not only of this poet but of the emerging Ch'an sect in China.

(5) HEARN, LAFCADIO. "Buddhist Allusions in Japanese Folk-songs," in his *Gleanings in Buddha-fields: Studies of Hand and Soul in the Far East* (see 2.9[21]), pp. 185-210.

A romantic and popular yet sensitive and interesting treatment of this topic, by one of the turn of the century popularizers of Japanese culture in the West.

(6) LaFLEUR, WILLIAM R. "Saigyo and the Buddhist Value of Nature." *History of Religions*, 13 (1973-1974), 93-128, 227-248.

Discussion of the twelfth century Japanese monk-poet Saigyo, and of the Japanese development of Buddhist doctrine which set the stage for his affirmation of the natural world as the highest Buddhist reality.

(7) LEVY, HOWARD S., trans. *Translations from Po Chu-i's Collected Works*. New York: Paragon, 1971, 2 vols.

While not a "Buddhist poet," the great T'ang dynasty poet Po-Chu-i (772-846) was interested in Buddhism and sometimes refers to Buddhist themes in his work. On this, see, for example, pages 74-89 of volume 1: "Aging and Death." Arthur Waley has also translated a number of Po Chu-i's poems in his *Chinese Poems* (London: G. Allen and Unwin, 1946), pp. 120-199. See, for example, "Realizing the Futility of Life," "Taoism and Buddhism," etc. For a more general study of the background of this poet, see Arthur Waley, *The Life and Times of Po Chu-i* (London: G. Allen and Unwin, 1949), 238 pp. For a view of his relation to Buddhism, see Kenneth K. S. Ch'en, *The Chinese Transformation of Buddhism* (1.11.1[2]), pp. 179-239. For a translation of his biography from the Hsin T'ang Shu, see E. Feifel, "Biography of Po Chu-i," *Monumenta Serica*, 17 (1958), 255-311.

(8) LIENHARD, SIEGFRIED, trans. *Nevarigitimanjari: Religious and Secular Poetry of the Nevars of the Kathmandu Valley*. Stockholm Oriental Studies, No. 10. Stockholm: Almqvist and Wiksell, 1974, 332 pp.

Newari text and translation of a hundred poems and songs, many of which refer to Buddhist figures of legends. See especially the poems beginning with "Buddha descends to Lumbini," and the epic songs inspired by various jatakas and avadanas.

(9) MATHER, RICHARD. "The Landscape Buddhism of the Fifth Century Poet Hsieh Ling-yun." *Journal of Asian Studies*, 18 (1958), 67-79.

Interesting account of the life and work of Hsieh Ling-yun, the originator of "landscape poetry," a form later brought near to perfection by poets such as Wang Wei (699-759) and having its roots in a Buddhist inspired identification of natural and spiritual phenomena. Mather also traces Hsieh's connections with the "White Lotus Society." For a scholarly study of the whole life and work of Hsieh Ling-yun, see J. D. Frodsham, *The Murmuring Stream* (Kuala Lumpur: The University of Malaya Press, 1967, distr. by Oxford University Press), 2 vols.

(10) MATSUO, BASHO. *Back Roads to Far Towns: Basho's Oku-no-Hosomichi*. Translated by Cid Corman and Kamaike Susumu. New York: Grossman, distributed by Viking Press, 1968, 173 pp.

Idiosyncratic and somewhat cryptic translations of a poetic diary written during his travel/pilgrimage by Japan's master of haiku, Basho. Both the prose and poetry are influenced by the Buddhist faith of the poet. Japanese text and English translation on facing pages.

(11) _____. *The Narrow Road to the Deep North, and Other Travel Sketches*. Translated by Nobuyuki Yuasa. Harmondsworth: Penguin, 1966, 167 pp.

Autobiographical account of meditative travels by the famous Haiku poet Basho. Includes many examples of Basho's art, suffused with Zen attitudes. Besides the "Narrow Road to the Deep North" (Oku-no-Hosomichi), the translator has included some of Basho's other travel sketches, "The Records of a Weather Exposed Skeleton," and "A Visit to the Kashima Shrine."

(12) *Mila mgur 'bum*. Translated by Garma C. C. Chang as *The Hundred Thousand Songs of Milarepa*. Abridged edition. New York: Harper and Row, 1970, 301 pp. (Complete edition published New Hyde Park, N.Y.: University Books, 1962, 2 vols.)

Helpfully annotated translation of the songs of the great Tibetan mystic-yogin Milarepa, which are strung together with narrative episodes of his life. Songs were very popular in Tibet. See 8.1.2 for accounts of the life of Milarepa.

(13) MIYAZAWA, KENJI. *Spring and Asura*. Translated by Hiroaki Sato. Floating World Modern Poets Series. Chicago: Chicago Review Press, 1973, 104 pp.

Fine translations of selected poems of Miyazawa Kenji (1896-1933), a well-known Japanese modern poet who was a devout Nichiren Buddhist. His religious spirit is reflected in his verse as well as in his "children's stories," sixteen of which have been translated by John Bester in *Winds from Afar* (Tokyo and Palo Alto: Kodansha International, distributed by Harper and Row, 1972.)

(14) MORRELL, ROBERT E. "The Buddhist Poetry in the Goshuishu." *Monumenta Nipponica*, 28 (1973), 87-100.

Study and translation of the nineteen "Poems on the Teaching of Sakyamuni" (shakkyoka) in the "Later Collection of Gleanings" (*Goshuishu*), an eleventh century compilation by Fujiwara Michitoshi (1047-95) of over twelve hundred poems.

(15) NIELSON, THOMAS P. *The T'ang Poet-Monk Chiao-jan*. Occasional Paper, No. 3. Tempe: Center for Asian Studies, Arizona State University, 1972, 65 pp.

Interesting study of a T'ang dynasty poet, Chiao-jan (734-799), who was a Buddhist monk and wrote both secular and religious poetry.

(16) ROBINSON, G. W., trans. *Poems of Wang Wei*. Harmondsworth: Penguin, 1973, 144 pp.

A useful and fine selection and translation of some of the poems of this T'ang Dynasty poet, with some introductory notes on his relationship to Buddhism.

(17) ROBINSON, RICHARD H., ed. and trans. *Chinese Buddhist Verse*. See 4.2.1(5).

Drama, Plays, Operas

(18) STEIN, ROLF ALFRED, trans. *Vie et Chants de 'Brug-Pa Kun-Legs le Yogin*. Collection UNESCO d'oeuvres représentatives. Paris: G. P. Maisonneuve et Larose, 1972, 446 pp.

A fine work by an important Tibetologist on the life and songs of the great Tibetan "mad" yogin, 'Brug-pa Kun-legs, who has often been compared to the better-known Milarepa.

(19) TAKAHASHI, SHINKICHI. *Afterimages: Zen Poems*. Selected and translated by Lucien Stryk and Takashi Ikemoto. Chicago: Swallow Press, 1970, 127 pp.

Translation of selected poems by a relatively unknown but interesting modern poet who was influenced in his youth by dadaism and then, under the influence of Master Shizan Ashikaga, became a conscious proponent of Zen views in poetry.

(20) TUCCI, GIUSEPPE, ed. and trans. *Tibetan Folk Songs from Gyantse and Western Tibet*. Second edition, revised and enlarged. Artibus Asiae Supplementum, No. 22. Ascona: Artibus Asiae, 1966, 200 pp. (Originally published 1949.)

An excellent monograph on the folksongs around the region of Gyangtse which includes Tibetan texts and translations, and a discussion of the nature of Tibetan folksongs and the importance of the marriage songs for insight into the popular beliefs and customs which differ from one region to another.

(21) WAI-LIM YIP, trans. *Hiding the Universe: Poems by Wang Wei*. New York: Grossman, 1972, 131 pp.

Striking but sometimes strange translations of this Chinese T'ang dynasty poet whose verse was very much formed by Buddhism as well as by the Taoism which receives the emphasis in the translator's introduction.

(22) WU, CHI-YU. "A Study of Han-shan." *T'oung Pao*, 45 (1957), 392-450.

A detailed analysis of the dates, life, and work of this rather elusive T'ang poet. Wu concludes that he was actually the Buddhist monk Chih-yen (577-654).

4.4 DRAMA, PLAYS, OPERAS
(Scripts in Translation)

(1) ARLINGTON, LEWIS CHARLES and HAROLD ACTON, eds. and trans. *Famous Chinese Plays*. Peking: H. Vetch, 1937, 443 pp.

Summaries of thirty-three traditional opera plots, with selections from the dialogue. A few of these plays deal directly with Buddhist themes, such as "Buddha's Temple" and "A Nun Craves Worldly Vanities."

(2) BACOT, JACQUES. *Three Tibetan Mysteries*. Translated by H. I. Woolf. Broadway translations. New York: E. P. Dutton, 1923, 267 pp.

A popular presentation, easily read, with some introductory notes, of three mystery dramas, *Tchrimekundan*, *Djroazanmo*, and *Nansal*. These plays were commonly performed by monks in Tibetan monasteries.

(3) _____, ed. and trans. *Zuginima*. Cahiers de la Société Asiatique, No. 14. Paris: Imprimerie Nationale, 1957, 2 vols. in 1.

Introduction, translation into French, and notes to a cursive manuscript of a Tibetan Buddhist morality play based on Indian folklore themes. The title of the work is *Gzugs-kyi ni-ma*.

(4) *Dri med kun ldan-gye rnam-thar*. Translated by Jacques Bacot as "Drimedkundan, une version Tibétaine Dialoguée du Vessantara Jataka." *Journal Asiatique*, 4 (1914), 221-305.

Translation of a Tibetan dramatic version of the ever-popular Vessantara Jataka.

(5) DUNCAN, MARION HERBERT. *Harvest Festival Dramas of Tibet*. Hong Kong: Orient Publishing Co., 1955, 271 pp.

A sound and well-written account of the preparation for and production of these dramas, many of which are Tibetan "mystery plays" and translated Indian tales, the intent of which is to further the growth of Buddhism and strengthen opposition to Bon. Contains translations of three of these plays with helpful footnotes. For further examples of this genre, see also Marion Herbert Duncan, *More Harvest Festival Dramas of Tibet* (London: Mitre Press, 1967), 123 pp.

(6) GAMBLE, SYDNEY D. *Chinese Village Plays from the Ting Hsien Region*. Amsterdam: Philo, 1970, 762 pp.

An excellent collection of forty-eight operas performed in rural areas of north China, collected in the first half of the twentieth century. Religious beliefs referred to in the plays are all from the syncretic popular tradition, of which Buddhism was of course a part.

(7) KURATA, HYAKUZO. *The Priest and His Disciples*. Translated by Glenn W. Shaw. Tokyo: The Hokuseido Press, 1922, 246 pp.

A translation of Kurata's *Shukke to Sono Deshi*, "a story of religion and love woven about the lives of Shinran Shonin and his disciples." First published in 1918, but more a reading play than for actual performance.

(8) *Lokananda*. Edited and translated by Ratna Handurukande in *The Manicudavadana and Lokananda* (see 4.2.3[22]), pp. 194-298.

The *Lokananda* is a drama in five acts based on the legend of the Bodhisattva Manicuda (for which, see "Manicudavadana" under 4.2.3). It is said to be the work of Candragomin (seventh century A.D.), but now exists only in its Tibetan translation, which has been included in the *bsTan 'Gyur*. Handurukande has here edited the Tibetan text of the play with a scholarly introduction and a detailed English synopsis.

4.4 Drama, Plays, Opera

(9) SARACHCHANDRA, EDIRIWEERA R. The Folk Drama of Ceylon. Second edition. Colombo: Department of Cultural Affairs, 1966, 180 pp. (Originally published 1952.)

A scholarly treatment of the development and present expression of various types of Sinhalese folk plays placed in the historic and cultural contexts of Sinhala Buddhism, folk religion and diverse Hindu and other Indian influences. Of use mainly to the advanced student, though it is a work basic to the subject. Helps to show how various religious forms are incorporated into dramatic portrayals and thus provides further insight into the several frameworks within which Buddhism, as well as other religions, can be seen.

(10) SHIVELY, DONALD H. "Buddhahood for the Non-Sentient: A Theme in No Plays." Harvard Journal of Asiatic Studies, 20 (1957), 135-161.

An interesting analysis of No drama to demonstrate that in them the possibility of Buddhahood is extended to animals and plants as well as to man.

(11) WADDELL, LAURENCE AUSTINE. Tibetan Buddhism: With Its Mystic Cults, Symbolism and Mythology, and in Its Relation to Indian Buddhism (see 1.14.1[17]), pp. 515-565.

Views the mystery plays as remnants of primitive, cannibalistic Tibet. A detailed account of a play and its preparations. Sacred drama based on the Jatakas and popular Tibetan legends, with an account of a few famous ones.

(12) WALEY, ARTHUR, trans. The No Plays of Japan. New York: Grove Press, 1957, 319 pp. (Originally published London: G. Allen and Unwin, 1921; paperback edition: Evergreen E62.)

Buddhist ideas weave in and out of many No plays: see the "Note on Buddhism," pp. 57-59. Nineteen examples, plus a few summaries, put into English with minimum rubrics. Useful, but the student who is not somewhat familiar with the actual genre of performance of No plays will probably derive little from the bare scripts.

4.5 THE NOVEL AND OTHER NARRATIVE WORKS
(Diaries, Autobiography, etc.)

For biographies, see under 8.

(1) BRAZELL, KAREN, trans. The Confessions of Lady Nijo. New York: Doubleday, 1973, 288 pp. (Paperback edition: Anchor books.)

Prize-winning translation of the very personal diaries of a medieval Japanese court woman whose distress concerning her life caused her to become a Buddhist nun. Fascinating reading. Taken from a recently discovered manuscript.

(2) FAIRWEATHER, IAN, trans. The Drunken Buddha. Brisbane: University of Queensland Press, 1965, 161 pp.

Translation of a Chinese novel based on the true life of the Buddhist Tao-chi of the Sung. The official title of the work is Tao chi Tui t'u Chi-tun chian hua.

(3) HAKEDA, Y. S. "The Religious Novel of Kukai." Monumenta Nipponica, 20 (1965), 283-297.

A discussion of Kukai's (the founder of Japanese Shingon Buddhism) first major work, the Sango-shiki ("Indications to the Three Teachings"). The novel is a story of three characters, Kimo ("Tortoise hair"), a Confucianist; Kyobu ("Nothingness"), a Taoist, and Kamei Kotsuji ("Mendicant"), a Buddhist, who have a dramatized debate concerning the merits of their three respective traditions.

(4) KURATA, HYAKUZO. Shinran. Translated by Umeyo Hirano. Tokyo: Cultural Interchange Institute for Buddhists, 1964, 250 pp.

Historical novel about the life of Shinran, by a Pure Land Buddhist author, originally published in 1936, and receiving the "Imprimatur" of the Higashi Honganji hierarchy.

(5) MISHIMA, YUKIO. The Temple of the Golden Pavilion. Translated by Ivan Morris. New York: Knopf, 1959, 262 pp. (Also published New York: Berkeley, 1971, a Berkeley Medallion book.)

This novel, by one of Japan's most renowned contemporary novelists, the late Yukio Mishima, was inspired by the act of arson which destroyed the Golden Pavilion at the Kinkakuji Zen temple in Kyoto. The book, however, is more Mishima than Zen.

(6) MORRIS, IVAN, ed. and trans. The Pillow Book of Sei Shonagon. Records of Civilization, Sources and Studies, No. 77. New York: Columbia University Press, 1967, 2 vols. (Also published Penguin, 1970.)

Full English translation, with extensive notes and useful appendices, of a great Heian classic, second only to the Tale of Genji (below) in fame. Together with that work, it is an important source for providing one view of the court context in which Buddhism was trying to operate in Heian Japan.

(7) MURASAKI, SHIKIBU. The Tale of Genji: A Novel in Six Parts. Translated by Arthur Waley. New York: Modern Library, 1960, 1135 pp. (Also published Tokyo: C. E. Tuttle, 1970, 2 vols.)

The most famous of the Heian classics by a lady of the court. Waley's translation is "liberal" and not always complete, but it makes for easy reading, despite the book's length. Together with Ivan Morris's translation of The Pillow Book of Sei Shonagon (above) this provides one view of the Japanese court context in which Heian Buddhism was, in part, operating.

The Novel and Other Narrative Works

(8) NIWA, FUMIO. *The Buddha Tree.* Translated by Kenneth Strong. UNESCO Collection of Contemporary Works. Rutland, Vt.: C. E. Tuttle, 1971, 380 pp.

An interesting novel by one of Japan's most prolific contemporary writers. It portrays with great detail, in a way far from flattering, the life and personal struggles of a Shin priest in a post-war Japanese temple of the True Pure Land School. The author himself was formerly a Buddhist priest.

(9) PRAMOJ, KUKRIT. *Red Bamboo.* Bangkok: Progress Bookstore, 1961, 205 pp.

One of the few modern popular Thai novels that have been translated into English. It depicts the life in a small Thai village, which is in, if not quite of, the modern world, and centers around the figure of Bhikkhu Krang, the abbot of Red Bamboo Monastery. The work, however, is based on an Italian novel about a priest. The author has since become Prime Minister of Thailand.

(10) TAKEYAMA, MICHIO. *Harp of Burma.* Translated by Howard Hibbett. UNESCO Collection of Contemporary Works. Rutland, Vt.: C. E. Tuttle, 1966, 132 pp.

Fine and moving novel about a Japanese soldier who refuses to leave war-torn Burma with the rest of his regiment, but decides to become a Burmese Buddhist monk.

(11) TSAO, HSUEH-CHIN. *Dream of the Red Chamber.* Translated by Chi-chen Wang. New York: Twayne, 1958, 574 pp. (An abridged edition was published Garden City: Doubleday, 1958, 329 pp.)

An important eighteenth century Chinese novel which was heavily influenced by Buddhism, and has been translated by Wang Chi-chen. A new and fine translation is being prepared by David Hawkes. For the first chapters, *see* his *The Story of the Stone.*

(12) WU, CHENG-EN. *Hsi-yu chi* ("Journey to the West"). Translated by Arthur Waley as *Monkey.* London: Allen and Unwin, 1965, 305 pp. (Originally published 1942.)

A famous sixteenth century Chinese novel based on the pilgrimage of the T'ang monk Hsuan Tsang to India. It is a rich source of information on popular Buddhism, but unfortunately Waley's condensed and only partial translation omits some of the most interesting religious material. For a fuller French translation (but still omitting most of the verse), see Louis Avenol, trans., *Si Yeou Ki ou Le Voyage en Occident* (Paris: Editions du Seuil, 1957), 2 vols. A complete English translation by Anthony Yu (*The Journey to the West*) is being published by the University of Chicago Press. For an analysis of some of the sources of the novel, see Glen Dudbridge, *The Hsi-yu Chi: A Study of Antecedents of the Sixteenth Century Chinese Novel* (Cambridge: Cambridge University Press, 1970), 219 pp.

(13) YOSHIDA, KENKO. *Essays in Idleness: The Tsure-zuregusa of Kendo.* Translated by Donald Keene. Records of Civilization, Sources and Studies, No. 78. New York: Columbia University Press, 1967, 213 pp.

Valuable translation of a fourteenth century priest's classic "jottings" on life, religion, beauty, and "the impermanence of all things." An important work for the nexus between Buddhism and aesthetics in the Japanese sensibility.

5 The Arts
Art, Architecture, Drama, Music, Dance, Etc.

5.1 ASIA (General)

5.1.1 Bibliographies, Encyclopedias, Collections, etc.

(1) *Bibliographie Bouddhique*. See 12.2(6).

Extremely helpful annotated bibliography of western (and some eastern) language publications (both books and articles) on Buddhism and Buddhist-related subjects published annually between 1928 and 1958. Each volume contains a separate section for "Art, Archéologie, Epigraphie." While for the most part the journal is in French, some of the annotations appear in English. Titles of Japanese language sources are given in English translation. Of immense value to the intermediate and advanced student.

(2) *Mélanges chinois et bouddhiques*. L'Institut belge des Hautes Etudes chinois, place of publication and publisher vary, I+ (July 1932--).

Highly valuable series presenting rather specialized articles on Buddhism and Buddhist-related topics by leading experts in the field such as P. Demieville, Arthur Waley, L. de La Vallée Poussin, M. Lalou, G. Tucci, and numerous others. Many of the articles, some in English as well as French, are of book length (200-500 pages) and occupy an entire volume or more. Of specific relevance to art/architecture are Combaz, "L'Evolution du Stupa en Asie," and Pierre Ryckmans, "Les 'Propos sur la Peinture' de Shitao: traduction et commentaire." Most volumes contain bibliographic notes and some, annotated bibliographies. The back cover of each volume provides a complete index of all the articles and authors published in all previous issues. For the advanced student.

(3) *Encyclopedia of World Art*. New York: McGraw Hill, 1958-1968, 15 vols.

Contains an excellent collection of essays on Buddhist and Buddhist related arts by such eminent scholars as Tucci, Bussagli, Jan Fontein and many others. Treatments are of quite surprising depth, detail and thoroughness for an encyclopedia which covers Western art as well. Index in vol. 15.

(4) BERVAL, RENE DE, ed. "Présence du Bouddhisme." See 1.5.1(6).

An exciting and diverse collection of essays by eminent Buddhist scholars of the time (Paul Mus, Giuseppe Tucci, Senart, Paranavitana, Walpole Rahula, et al.) replete with one hundred and ten clear black and white plates of works from all Buddhist countries. Numerous maps include those detailing the spread of Buddhism throughout Asia, and an itinerary of Chinese pilgrims in India. The only essay directly relevant to art is Jeannine Auboyer, "Bilan de l'art et de la culture bouddhique in Asie" (ten pages). However, the numerous plates and rather specialized essays may be of use. An eighteen page glossary gives definitions of Sanskrit terms in French with Chinese characters. The forty-four page bibliography gives five pages to Buddhist art and architecture.

(5) ROWLAND, BENJAMIN. *The Harvard Outline and Reading Lists for Oriental Art*. Third revised edition. Cambridge, Mass.: Harvard, 1967.

Helpful rather extensive outline of major periods and figures in the art history of India, Kashmir, Nepal, Tibet, Ceylon, Siam, Indonesia, Iran, Central Asia, China, and Japan (27 pages). There is a twenty-eight page reading list of relevant periodicals, books and articles arranged according to country.

5.1.2 Comparative East-West Aesthetics

(1) BURCKHARDT, TITUS. *Sacred Art in East and West: Its Principles and Methods*. Translated by Lord Northbourne. London: Perennial Books, 1967, 160 pp., 25 black and white illustrations.

An interesting collection of seven essays on the art of five great traditions (Hinduism, Christianity, Islam, Buddhism, and Taoism). Those on Eastern themes include: "The Genesis of the Hindu Temple," "The Image of the Buddha," "Landscape in Far Eastern Art," principally Ch'an and Buddhist influences. Little of a comparative nature is attempted. Essays are provocative on the introductory level.

Asia (General)

(2) COMBAZ, GISBERT. L'Inde et L'Orient classique. Paris: Librairie Orientaliste Paul Geuthner, 1937, 2 vols. Vol. 1, 265 pp.; vol. 2, 51 pp., 165 plates.

Considers the possible relationships of Indian art to that of "Occidental" Asia (Iran, Mesopotamia, Asiatic Greece, the Roman Empire, Syria, and Sassanian Iran). The second volume (of drawings) compares motifs in these areas. No index, but the extensive section on sculpture considers Bharhut, Sanchi, Gandhara, Mathura, Amaravati, and fourth-fifth century India in general. Somewhat obsolete. For intermediate or advanced levels.

(3) COOMARASWAMY, ANANDA K. Christian and Oriental Philosophy of Art. New York: Dover Publications, 1956, 148 pp. (Originally published as Why Exhibit Works of Art, London, 1943.)

This is a collection of brief essays primarily on the nature and function of art. Includes chapters such as "Why Exhibit Works of Art?," "Is Art a Superstition or Way of Life?," "Beauty and Truth." A weighty thirty page chapter attempts to explain and compare the general philosophies of Oriental and Christian art. Sporadic references to Buddhism. No index.

(4) MERILLAT, HERBERT C. Sculpture in East and West. New York: Dodd, Mead, and Co., 1973, 272 pp., 187 black and white illustrations.

Devotes separate one hundred page sections to European and Asian (mostly Buddhist) sculpture. Only in brief conclusion are comparisons between East and West suggested. Covers Indian, Chinese, Japanese and Southeat Asian sculpture, attempting to capture the main characteristics only. Includes a glossary of foreign terms, a chronological table spanning Europe and Asia, a good index, and a general introduction. Pleasant reading.

(5) ROWLAND, BENJAMIN. Art in East and West. Cambridge, Mass.: Harvard, 1954, 144 pp., 62 black and white illustrations. (Paperback edition: Boston: Beacon, 1964.)

Consists of approximately thirty pairs of works of art, one Eastern, one Western. The subjects are arranged in categories of figures, landscapes, birds-beasts-flowers, still lifes. The first two are particularly concerned with Buddhist art, and the index provides specific further references. The volume is not intent on determining which style of art most influenced the other. The plates are well selected, and the comparisons sophisticated and imaginative, suggestive of new interpretations and themes of Eastern and Western art.

5.1.3 Mythology and Symbolism

(1) BOSCH, F. D. K. The Golden Germ: An Introduction to Indian Symbolism. See 9.3.3(1).

Ventures into the field of Indian symbolism in order to interpret Indian art, rather than merely classifying it. Relates symbols to the "golden germ" or "principle of life." Focuses on the symbol of Indian monster heads, but discusses other symbols, notably the tree. Emphasis is on sculpture. Plates are small and unexceptional but selected for specific purposes. A highly valuable, advanced level book on a specialized topic.

(2) COOMARASWAMY, ANANDA K. The Transformation of Nature in Art. Cambridge, Mass.: Harvard, 1934, 245 pp. (Reprinted New York: Dover Publications, 1956.)

See especially Chapter 1 for an important general statement on the arts of Asia, as they are influenced by Buddhism.

(3) HACKIN, J., et al. Asiatic Mythology. See 4.1.3(5).

Covers mythology from Persia and Central Asia to Japan. Includes forty pages on Buddhism in India, forty pages on Lamaism, thirty-seven pages on Buddhism in Japan, smaller sections on Buddhism in China, Indochina, and Central Asia. The text includes a brief sketch of the history and beliefs of Buddhists in particular areas, then centers principally on sacred figures and historical personages. The format is somewhat scattered. Plates are profuse and complement text, but are of mediocre quality. A good table of contents makes inquiries possible.

(4) HAVELL, E. B. The Himalayas in Indian Art. London: John Murray, 1924, xiv, 94 pp., 24 black and white plates.

Mainly considers the symbolic role of the Himalayas in Indian art. While the book concentrates on Hindu art, Chapter 3, "The Mountain Deified," treats briefly such topics as the Gandharan School, the derivation of the yogic Buddha image from a pre-Buddhistic archetype, the Buddha as the Universal Pillar, the relic casket of Kanishka and its Himalayan substitutes.

(5) ZIMMER, HEINRICH. The Art of Indian Asia. Completed and edited by Joseph Campbell. Second edition. Bollingen Series 29. New York: Pantheon, 1964, 2 vols. Vol. I, 465 pp., approx. 60 illustrations; vol. II, 614 plates.

Comprehensive survey of Indian art related to the symbolism and meaning of Indian mythology. Pages 158-230 discuss the symbolism of the lotus, 231-257 treat early Buddhist architecture, 325-352 analyze Bharhut, Mathura, Gandhara, Amaravati, Bodhgaya. Touches on Southeast Asia and Himalayan countries. Includes maps and chronological charts, and a copious index, replete with references to Buddhism. Plates in Volume II are large and detailed.

(6) _____. Myths and Symbols in Indian Art and Civilization. See 9.2.2.5(13).

Consists of papers and notes compiled after Zimmer's death. Most of the work deals with

Hindu topics, but there is a ten page section on the serpent as supporter of Vishnu and Buddha. Includes a good index with sporadic references to Buddhism but no extended discussion. Touches on Tibet and Southeast Asia. Plates are unexceptional. A well written introductory book, but with little relevance to Buddhism except as an account of the general Indian scene in which Buddhism flourished.

5.1.4 Buddhist Art (Surveys of Several Countries)

(1) BINYON, LAURENCE. The Spirit of Man in Asian Art. New York: Dover, 1965, 217 pp., 70 black and white plates. (Originally published Cambridge, Mass., 1935.)

Originally a series of lectures delivered at Harvard University in 1933-1934. The introduction cites general contrasts between European and Asian art. Lecture 2 deals specifically with early Indian art and the impact of Buddhism on Chinese art and thought. Lecture 3 details the conception of landscape art in China in reference to Taoism and Zen. Altogether, covers Persian, Indian, Chinese, and Japanese art. A dated but worthwhile interpretation.

(2) Boston Museum of Fine Arts, Boston, Mass. The Arts of India and Nepal: The Nasli and Alice Heeramaneck Collection. New York: October House, 1966, 185 pp., 282 plates.

One hundred and nine plates of sculpture, 173 plates of painting and minor arts, mostly black and white. Contains only ten pages of introductory text, but extensive descriptions of plates which, though small, are well done. Plates of Buddhist art must be sought individually. A few are in each subheading. Emphasis is on northern and central India with a few Nepalese and Tibetan works scattered throughout.

(3) COOMARASWAMY, ANANDA K. The Arts and Crafts of India and Ceylon. New York: Noonday, 1964, 259 pp., 225 black and white illustrations. (Originally published Edinburgh and London: Foulis, 1913.)

Combines Hindu and Buddhist art in one section, pp. 5-209, and makes a point of discussing them together, showing how they were closely related. The inadequate index makes it difficult to locate specific references to Buddhist art. They are scattered throughout, especially in chapters on architecture, painting and sculpture. Touches on Nepal, Java, and Cambodia. Plates are small and indistinct.

(4) _____. History of Indian and Indonesian Art. New York: Dover, 1965, 295 pp., 400 illustrations. (Originally published New York: Weyhe, 1927.)

Treatment extends from Chinese Turkestan through the Himalayan countries, India, Southeast Asia, and Indonesia. A wide ranging book arranged chronologically and geographically, with references to Buddhism scattered throughout. Includes a superb index and extensive bibliography. An intermediate work, heavy on details but short on analysis. Plates are extensive, with emphasis on sculpture, but are mediocre in quality.

(5) FOCILLON, HENRI. L'Art Bouddhique. Paris: Henri Laurens, 1921, xvi, 164 pp., 24 black and white plates.

Written in French. Includes a sixteen-page introductory essay on "Art et Religion," sixty-eight pages on "Les Origines" (in India), forty-one pages discussing "L'Idéalisme et Positivisme en Chine," and forty-four pages on "L'Art Bouddhique et le Génie Japonais." Illustrations are unexceptional. The text gives some insights to the intermediate student, though the interpretations are now rather dated. The author was a noted art historican of the early twentieth century.

(6) GRISWOLD, ALEXANDER, CHEWON KIM, and PETER H. POTT. The Art of Burma, Korea, Tibet. Art of the World Series. New York: Crown, 1964, 277 pp., 70 color plates, 57 figures, maps, chronological tables.

Forty-seven pages, ten plates, and thirty figures for Burma. Eighty-six pages, thirty plates, and fourteen figures for Korea. Eighty-seven plates and thirteen figures for Tibet. The whole Burmese section relates to Buddhist art, with chapters on Pagan, cetiyas, ornamentation, and cave temple iconography. Korean art from the Stone Age onward is discussed and organized into chapters on kingdoms and dynasties. The first thirty pages of the Tibetan section discuss the history of Western interest in Tibetan art and the history of Buddhism in Tibet. The remaining fifty-six pages are organized into sections on various art forms, from ritual objects to sculpture and various forms of painting. The Tibetan section is particularly interesting and comprehensive; there are fewer Buddhist references on Korea. The volume is well indexed, with an eight-page bibliography and chronological tables.

(7) HARTEL, HERBERT and JEANNINE AUBOYER. Indien und Südostasien. Propylean Kunstgeschichte, No. 16. Berlin: Propylean Verlag, 1971, 369 pp., 408 plates, 61 figures.

A good general introduction to the art of India and Southeast Asia written by Herbert Hartel, Director of the Museum für Indische Kunst in Berlin, and Jeannine Auboyer, Conservateur en Chef at the Musée Guimet. The main attraction of the book is its excellent illustrations, which include a good sampling of early Indian terracottas, and bronzes, some of which were excavated by Professor Hartel at the site of Sonkh in Mathura district. Due to Professor Hartel's interests, a few recently excavated pieces are included, as well as many pieces from the Museum für Indische Kunst in Berlin. The selection of plates is not the group found in most standard survey books.

Asia (General)

(8) LEE, SHERMAN E. *A History of Far Eastern Art*. Third edition. Englewood Cliffs, N.J.: Prentice-Hall and Harry N. Abrams, 1973, 527 pp., 656 black and white illustrations, 60 color plates.

Despite its title, this volume attempts to provide an introduction to all of Asian art from the Indus Valley civilization and pre-Shang China through the Japanese Tokugawa period. Includes extensive sections on India, Southeast Asia, Indonesia, and Korea. References to and illustrations of Buddhist art naturally form a current throughout the book, with 176 pages discussing the "International Influence of Buddhist Art." Provides a map showing the main sites of Buddhist arts and trade routes, and chronological tables of art periods in all areas. There is a twelve-page bibliography which is extremely helpful. Probably the most comprehensive introduction to a vast subject.

(9) MUNSTERBERG, HUGO. *Art of India and Southeast Asia*. New York: Harry N. Abrams, 1970, 263 pp., approx. 250 illustrations.

Includes a brief section on early Buddhist art of India, twenty-four pages on Buddhist art under the Kushans, with various sections on Buddhist art of Afghanistan and Central Asia, art of Nepal and Tibet, Ceylon, Indonesia, Burma, Thailand, Cambodia and Viet Nam. Standard examples are quite well reproduced. Includes a helpful introductory bibliography, and an excellent pictorial introduction with brief text providing the bare historical essentials.

(10) Musée Guimet. *Guide-Catalogue du Musée Guimet: Les Collections Bouddhiques*. Paris and Bruxelles: G. Van Oest, 1923, 175 pp., 24 black and white plates.

Divided essentially into four parts dealing with Central India and Gandhara, Turkestan, Buddhist China (the Wei and the T'ang Dynasties), and Tibet. The Central India section deals with the first Buddhist monuments and Greco-Indian art. Under Turkestan are discussed Tourfan and Tun-huang. The China section deals with Yun-kang and Lung-men, while under Tibet an historical outline and discussions of painting, bronzes, and ritual objects are presented. Contains clear plates and a relatively sophisticated text. There is a nine-page bibliography, helpful but understandably dated, and a twenty-seven page glossary.

(11) ROSS, NANCY WILSON. *Three Ways of Ancient Wisdom: Hinduism, Buddhism, Zen*. New York: Simon and Schuster, 1966, 222 pp., 124 black and white illustrations.

A popularized explanation of religious philosophies and arts of the three religious traditions. Twenty pages are devoted to pictures (mostly Buddha images) and descriptions of Buddhist art without any geographic, chronological or thematic order. Another twenty pages on Zen art (mostly painting) display the same characteristics--simple and unordered. Includes an adequate index and plates. Designed to acquaint Americans with Eastern religions and their arts, the volume is strictly introductory.

(12) ROWLAND, BENJAMIN. *The Wall-Paintings of India, Central Asia, and Ceylon*. Boston: Merrymount, 1938, 94 pp., 30 color and 6 black and white plates.

Ananda Coomaraswamy begins the book with a forty-page introduction on the nature of Buddhist art--primarily, how one can best appreciate it. Rowland then briefly describes the paintings of Miran, Bamiyan, Ajanta, Bagh, Ceylon. Comparisons between regions are made throughout and the conclusion attempts to summarize the impact of India on Far Eastern painting. Plates are quite appealing.

(13) SECKEL, DIETRICH. *The Art of Buddhism*. Translated by Ann E. Keep. Art of the World Series. New York: Crown, 1964, 331 pp., including approx. 65 color and 35 black and white plates and 73 figures.

In seventy-five pages, Seckel describes the development and expansion of Buddhist art throughout Asia. Another one hundred seventy pages describe particular types of art forms: stupas, pagodas, temples, monasteries, Buddha-images, hierarchy of sacred figures, narrative works, symbolism and ornamentation. Plates are good and are accompanied by maps and chronological tables. Despite the vastness of the subject, the material is comprehensive and coherent on the introductory level.

(14) SMITH, VINCENT A. *A History of Fine Art in India and Ceylon*. Edited by Karl Khandavali. Third edition, revised and enlarged. Bombay: Taraporevala, 1962, 219 pp., 5 color and 194 black and white plates.

An introductory work, including chapters on Indian art from post-Mauryan time through the Gupta empire when Buddhist art flourished, Ceylon, Java, Central Asia, Tibet and Nepal. There is no single chapter on Buddhist art.

(15) SPEISER, WERNER. *Oriental Architecture in Colour: Islam, Indian, Far Eastern*. London: Thames and Hudson, 1965, 504 pp., 112 plates, 32 plans.

Pictures constitute the core of this broad study. Architectural sites in Southeast Asia, as well as in India, China, and Japan, included. Stupas and temples make their appearance, but Buddhist art is not especially emphasized. Some sketches of temple plans.

(16) VOGEL, JEAN PHILIPPE. *Buddhist Art in India, Ceylon, and Java*. Translated by A. J. Barnou. Oxford: Clarendon Press, 1936, 115 pp., 39 black and white plates.

The author intends this rather brief handbook "to give a historical outline of Indo-Buddhist art, to sketch its various successive schools in their main characteristics, and to trace their mutual relationship." Topics include monuments of Asoka and the national school of sculpture of Central India, the Graeco-Buddhist art of Gandhara, Mathura sculpture under the Kushans, South Indian art of Amaravati, the Gupta Golden Age, Buddhist cave temples, aftermath and decline, Buddhist art of Ceylon, Buddhist art of Java. A four-page bibliography helpful for older sources. The black and white pictures are fair.

5.2 INDIA

5.2.1 Indian Buddhist Art (General)

(1) AGRAWALA, VASUDEVA S. Indian Art: A History of Indian Art from the Earliest Times up to the Third Century A.D. Varanasi: Prithivi Prakashan, 1965, 389 pp., 139 black and white illustrations, 251 line-drawing plates.

An extensive discussion of Buddhist art during these time periods. Eight pages are devoted to the Saisunaga-Nanda period, twenty-five pages to Mauryan art (including sections on Ashokan pillars, architecture of Pataliputra, etc.), fifty-five pages to Sunga-Kanva art (extensive discussion of the origin of the Buddha image). Fifteen pages are devoted to Gandhavra art, thirty pages to stupas of the Andhra-Satavahana period, sixteen pages to Indian terracottas, eleven pages to symbols and icons. The author attempts to deal with art and architecture "as part of a single scheme, as the builders of the monuments actually conceived them," thereby departing from previous treatments. A very important study.

(2) Archaeological Survey of India. Archaeological Remains: Monuments and Museums. 2 vols. New Delhi: Director General of Archaeology, Government of India, 1964, 2 vols. Vol. 1, 190 pp., 58 black and white plates; vol. 2, 188 pp., 38 black and white plates.

A chronological treatment of significant remaining monuments of India contributed to by several eminent scholars. Beginning with proto-historic remains, the first part contains chapters on remains of historical cities, Northern Buddhist monuments (Krishna Deva), Southern Buddhist monuments (K. R. Srinivasan) and Northern Temples (Krishna Deva). Volume 2 discusses Southern temples, Islamic monuments and museums, supplying the index for both volumes. Quite a successful collection of a large amount of significant material in which Buddhist works maintain an important place.

(3) BANERJI, ADRIS. Origins of Early Buddhist Church Art. Calcutta Sanskrit College Research Series, No. 56. Calcutta: Sanskrit College, 1967, 58 pp.

Treats the history of Buddhist art, beginning with the historical background of Buddhism with special reference to Asoka, through the Gandharan and Mathura schools and the development of the cult image. Each topic is summarized briefly, but in a compact style.

(4) BUSSAGLI, MARIO and CALEMBUS SIVARAMA-MURTI. 5000 Years of Indian Art. New York: Harry Abrams, 1971, 335 pp., 397 color illustrations.

Over half of the ten chapters, spanning Indian history from the Indus Valley to the Gupta empire and including Indian influences on Central and Southeast Asia, relate to Buddhist art. Sanchi, Mathura, Gandhara, and Gupta art are well covered, with emphasis on sculpture and architecture. An excellent intermediate and advanced level book with perceptive analysis rather than mere description. Includes a fine index and exquisite photos.

(5) CODRINGTON, KENNETH DE BURGH. Ancient India. London: Ernest Benn, 1926, 65 pp., 76 plates.

A large portion of this book concentrates on the Buddhist art of India through Gupta times. Although much of the material has been updated in later texts, the book is still valuable in that it reproduces some works of art not found in other books, as well as informative photographs of some of the Buddhist caves in the pre-restoration state.

(6) COOMARASWAMY, ANANDA K. Introduction to Indian Art. Edited by Mrs. Ananda K. Coomaraswamy. Second edition. Delhi: Munshiram Manoharlal, 1969, 104 pp., 44 black and white plates.

A rudimentary chronological survey of Indian art from antiquity to the nineteenth century. Chapters 6-10 and 15 refer to Buddhist art from the time of the Buddha through the Gupta empire as well as medieval Buddhist painting. The book is admirably readable for introductory students, but not at all comprehensive. Includes a competent index. The first and last chapters make general comparisons between Indian and Western art. Plates, approximately seventeen of which are on Buddhist art, are mediocre.

(7) DATTA, BUPENDRANATH. Indian Art and Its Relation to Culture. Calcutta: Nababharat, 1956, 114 pp., 19 black and white plates.

Reviews aspects of Indian art with respect to their ancient heritage and their reflection of Indian social conditions. Pages 34-42 only cover Buddhist art up to the Scythian period. The plates are mediocre, and the text strictly introductory.

(8) GOETZ, HERMANN. The Art of India. Second edition. Art of the World Series. New York: Crown Publishers, 1964, 283 pp., approx. 72 color illustrations.

Includes introductory essays on the nature of Indian art. Further chapters are divided into early, classic, medieval Hindu, Islamic and modern Indian art periods. Topics in Buddhist art and architecture are discussed frequently in relevant sections but seldom for more than a few paragraphs. A sixteen-page chronology parallels events in Central and East Asia, India, Greater India, the Mediterranean, and Southwestern Asia. A seven-page select bibliography is extremely helpful and complete. Includes a three-page glossary of technical names, and an excellent introduction.

(9) GROUSSET, RENE. The Civilization of India. Translated by Catherine Alison Phillips. New York: Tudor, 1939, 404 pp., 246 figures. (Originally published as Tome 2, L'Inde: Les Civilisations de l'Orient. New York: Alfred A. Knopf, 1931.)

The bulk of the book discusses Indian culture from the Indus Valley to medieval Hinduism. Approximately one hundred forty pages are devoted to the life of the Buddha and Buddhist art up to the Gupta period. The Buddhist element in India's influence on Southeast Asia is also discussed in Chapter 2. Plates are mediocre. Includes no index.

(10) GRUNWEDEL, ALBERT. Buddhist Art in India. Translated by A. C. Gibson. Revised and enlarged by James Burgess. London: Susil Gupta, 1965, 228 pp., 154 illustrations. (Originally published London: B. Quaritch, 1901.)

A very thorough introduction to a large subject by a noted authority. The chapters include: 1) a discussion of Indian art forms and civilization, including early Buddhist art; 2) a more detailed analysis of early Indian styles of art, with attention to a large number of motives; 3) a focus upon Gandharan sculpture in all its varieties; and 4) a concentration upon the representation of the Buddha figure and of bodhisattvas. Somewhat dated but still helpful. Intermediate level.

(11) HAVELL, ERNEST B. The Art Heritage of India. Revised and edited by Pramod Chandra. Bombay: D. B. Taraporevala, 1964, 199 pp., 18 color and 207 black and white plates.

A crucial book when first published and still an interesting contribution to the field. While most of the text deals with Hindu art forms, there is much on Buddhist stupas, sculpture, and mural painting. One chapter examines Bharhut, Sanchi, and Amaravati, while another deals with Borobudur. Contains a solid introduction.

(12) _____. A Handbook of Indian Art. New York: E. P. Dutton, 1920, 222 pp., 79 black and white plates.

Conveniently arranged for access to information pertaining to Buddhist art. The first fifty-six pages discuss the stupa from its origins through the Asokan and Buddhist periods. In regard to sculpture, there is a short section on the Buddha as guru and king. The section on painting barely touches on Ajanta. Plates are small but generally sharp. A simple introductory work, rather outdated.

(13) KRAMRISCH, STELLA. The Art of India. Third revised edition. London: Phaidon, 1965, 231 pp., including 8 color and 156 black and white plates, 29 illustrations.

The text provides a brief definitive survey of Indian art. Emphasizes spiritual themes of Indian art, rather than merely describing the works. Includes scattered references to Buddhism throughout. See especially pages 32-34. Plates are arranged in roughly chronological order, accompanied by lengthy comments. Stresses architecture and sculpture. A highly valuable essay on the general philosophical/mythical themes of Indian art.

(14) _____. Indian Sculpture. Calcutta: Y.M.C.A. Publishing House, 1933, 236 pp., 116 illustrations, 1 map.

The art of India is usually discussed from the point of view of history, epigraphy, iconography, and other disciplines related to art history. This is the only survey of Indian art which successfully interprets and differentiates the various schools of art by means of careful stylistic analysis.

(15) MISRA, G. S. P. The Age of Vinaya. New Delhi: Munshiram Manoharlal, 1969, 298 pp.

Reviews all aspects of the early vinaya (monastic discipline) in the context of Buddhist thought as a whole and Indian social conditions of the time. Most of the book is concerned with religious and social aspects, but one chapter on art and architecture briefly discusses urban, domestic and religious architecture of the sixth to the fourth century B.C., as well as sculpture and painting. The bulk of the material is derived from the Vinaya Pitaka. The volume includes a good bibliography on Buddhist and non-Buddhist sources and is well organized and well written.

(16) MUKHERJEE, RADHAKAMAL. The Cosmic Art of India. Bombay: Allied Publishers, 1965, 227 pp., 192 black and white illustrations.

This book attempts to capture the whole spirit of Indian art, emphasizing its uniqueness and its transcendent vision. Among the nine chapters are ones on form and composition, themes and symbols, and transcendent norms of beauty. There is no attempt to separate Buddhist art from the rest of Indian art, but an excellent index guides the reader to specific references to Buddhist art forms. Contains a glossary of foreign terms. Plates from all over Asia are small but sharp. The author tends to overgeneralize about the metaphysical nature of Indian life and its relation to art, but this perspective still produces a valuable, well-written work.

(17) _____. The Culture and Art of India. New York: Praeger, 1959, 447 pp., 54 black and white illustrations.

Reviews culture of India from the Indus civilization to independence from Britain. Pages 74-234 discuss the millennium from the time of the Buddha to the spread of Buddhism through Asia and Southeast Asia to Japan. Although treating a very extensive subject, the book is astute and well written. Emphasis is on history and conveying a sense of the general Indian "spirit." The work makes few references to specific works of art; it contains a good time chart and index. Plates are undistinguished.

(18) _____. The Flowering of Indian Art. London: Asia Publishing House, 1964, 303 pp., 76 black and white illustrations.

Altogether about eighty pages on Buddhist art covering such topics as humanism and lyricism in classic Buddhist sculpture, Buddhist art throughout Asia, and the contemplative universal man in Gupta art. Includes uncommon illustrations with paragraph-long descriptions and an excellent but concise bibliography of major works on Indian and Indic art.

(19) PAL, PRATAPADITYA, ed. Aspects of Indian Art. Leiden: E. J. Brill, 1972, 171 pp., 107 plates, 24 figures.

A collection of papers presented in a symposium at the Los Angeles County Museum in October 1970, including numerous short essays by various experts on aspects of Indian art: the cultural relationship between Gandhara and Mathura (by van Lohuizen-de Leeuw), Western Indian sculpture and the so-called Gupta influence (U. P. Shah), a brief history of Ajanta (W. Spink), "The Five Protective Goddesses of Buddhism" (D. C. Bhattacharyya), and "Nepali Sculptures--New Discoveries." Essays are brief but provocative.

(20) RAY, NIHARRANJAN. Maurya and Sunga Art. Second edition. Calcutta: Ramakrishna Maitra, 1965, 123 pp., including 45 black and white plates.

Discusses these periods from the sociological standpoint, focusing on the causes and circumstances which conditioned this art, rather than its form and technique. In particular, the author attempts to explain the great differences between the arts of the two periods. Also includes chapters on specific forms of art-columns, cave animal figures. There are frequent references to Buddhism, but the only extended discussion occurs in the chapter on Asokan ideology.

(21) ROWLAND, BENJAMIN. The Art and Architecture of India. See 10.2.1(16).

Discusses Indian art from prehistoric times to the nineteenth century. Arrangement is both chronological and geographical, with the bulk of the Buddhist material found in parts two to four, which cover the Maurya periods, Romano-Indian art in Northwest India, and the Golden age and the end of Buddhist art in India. Further attention to Buddhist art is given in discussions of the art of the Himalayan region and Southeast Asia. Contains thorough descriptions of famous works as well as general cultural background, and good plates. An important book.

5.2.2 Architecture: Stupas, Viharas, etc.

(1) AGRAWALA, PRITHIVI KUMAR. Gupta Temple Architecture. Varanasi: Prithivi, Prakashan, 1968, 108 pp., 30 black and white plates, 85 illustrations.

Essentially, a description of Gupta temple architecture as a whole with more detailed treatment of specific examples, both Hindu and Buddhist. Arranged in sections which deal with early tradition and beginnings, temple architecture in the Gupta period, Gupta temple door frames, pillars and sculpture, and a "Further Estimate" of the architecture. Important Buddhist sites touched upon include the Bodhgaya temple, Sanchi, and certain Amaravati pillars. Appendices include a classification chart of Gupta and allied architecture, a chronological chart of early dated North Indian temples to 800 A.D., and an outline of the evolution of Ganga-Yamuna figures and their position on early temple entrances. Gives a good impression of Buddhist architecture as a part of the larger Gupta architectural tradition.

(2) BHATTACHARYA, TARAPADA. The Canons of Indian Art. Second edition. Calcutta: Firma K. I. Mukhapadhyay, 1963, 506 pp. (Originally published as A Study on Vastuvidya, 1947.)

Extensive analysis of the development of the Vastuvidya, an ancient Indian text on architecture. Also discusses the general development of Indian architecture from Vedic to medieval times. Contains several chapters on specific topics like the mithuna, door, bricks, etc., and only a few pages on Buddhist art which essentially argue that Buddhist architectural forms like the stupa and chaitya were adaptations of Hindu forms.

(3) BROWN, PERCY. Indian Architecture (Buddhist and Hindu Periods). Fifth edition Bombay: Taraporevala, 1965, 216 pp., 164 plates.

Ranges widely over Indian architecture from the Indus Valley to the tenth century and touches on Sinhalese and Southeast Asian architecture as well. About ten chapters focusing on Buddhist art from the early rock-cut viharas and stupas to later Mahayana and South Indian Buddhist architecture. There are further references to Buddhism in chapters on Kashmir, Nepal, Ceylon and Southeast Asia. Chapters are brief but concisely written and informative.

(4) CHATTERJEE, SRIS CHANDRA. Magadha Architecture and Culture. Calcutta: Calcutta University Press, 1942, 112 pp., 30 plates.

In this survey of the Magadha architecture, only twenty-five pages are devoted to the one thousand years between Gautama and Nalanda. In rather simple fashion, the author praises the glories of Indian architecture rather than actually describing specific architectural monuments. Plates are poor quality.

(5) COMBAZ, GISBERT. "L'Evolution du stupa en Asie." See 9.3.6(3).

This article examines the architectural forms, symbolism, sculpture and worship of stupas throughout Asia, including brief chapters for each country. A comprehensive study which covers many architectural details, and valuable because it organizes considerable information and crosscultural comparisons (in one series of the article).

(6) COOMARASWAMY, ANANDA K. "Early Indian Architecture." Eastern Art, 2 (1930), 209-242; and 3 (1931), 181-217.

This three part article discusses early Indian architecture as represented on early Buddhist reliefs and as described in Pali literature. The author attempts to reconstruct the wooden prototypes upon which some of these reliefs were based. The headings for the individual sections are: Cities and City-Gates, etc., Bodhigarhas, and Palaces.

(7) DUTT, SUKUMAR. Buddhist Monks and Monasteries of India. See 1.2.2.1(4).

A well-written work in which Dutt examines the history of the Buddhist sangha in India, not simply as an expression of religious faith but as a cultural institution. There are five main sections: the primitive sangha, Asokan period, Gupta age, eminent monk-scholars, monastic universities; and a bibliography. The volume is well indexed, though without explicit references to Buddhist art.

(8) FERGUSSON, JAMES. History of Indian and Eastern Architecture. See 10.2.1(10).

More than half of Volume 1 is devoted to Buddhist architecture of India, Ceylon, and the Himalayas. Includes specific sections on stambhas, stupas, rails, caitya halls, and viharas. Volume 2 includes seventy pages on Southeast Asia and only fifty pages on Chinese and Japanese architecture. The text lacks a general analysis of Buddhist art, but the descriptions of sites are exceedingly detailed, full of statistics and measurements. Includes an excellent index, and is well-suited as a reference work.

(9) GANGOLY, O. C. Indian Architecture. Second revised edition. Bombay: Kutib, 1965, 72 pp. and 109 black and white illustrations.

Proceeds chronologically through the history of Indian architecture. There are references to Buddhism throughout, but Buddhist architecture is discussed only in the first twenty-five pages. There is no index or table of contents.

(10) HAVELL, ERNEST B. The Ancient and Medieval Architecture of India. London: John Murray, 1915, 230 pp., 83 black and white plates, 63 text illustrations.

There are few references to Buddhism in this book, though it does touch on Buddhist topics: stupas, lotuses, caitya-grihas, viharas, Mauryan and Gupta art. Breaks with Fergusson's classification and chronology. Contains mediocre plates and a poor index.

(11) HIRAKAWA, AKIRA. "The Rise of Mahayana Buddhism and Its Relation to the Worship of Stupas." See 2.5.2(5).

An extremely important article dealing with the textual/doctrinal background of the development of the most significant Buddhist architectural form, the stupa, in India. The text is rather technical, dealing not primarily with art history but with textual references and attitudes toward stupa worship. Chinese character equivalents are provided for all Sanskrit terms, and extensive notes include Japanese and Chinese sources.

(12) MITRA, DEBALA. Buddhist Monuments. See 10.2.1(14).

Covers over sixty-eight sites of Buddhist monuments in India, Pakistan, and Nepal. The first twenty pages review the life of the Buddha and history of Buddhism. Pages 21-56 analyze architectural forms such as the stupa, monastery, caitya-griha, and temple. The next 200 pages describe the sites, arranged geographically and conveniently listed in the table of contents. Includes a bibliography, map. A valuable work for the review of architectural forms and quick references to little-known sites.

(13) SARKAR, H. Studies in Early Buddhist Architecture of India. Delhi: Munshiram Manoharlal, 1966, 120 pp., 13 black and white plates.

The author discusses both how the Buddhists adopted various building plans such as elliptical, apsidal, circular and quadrilateral, for their stupas and monasteries, and how archaeological evidence may provide insight into the development of doctrinal divisions among Buddhists. Also contains chapters on the excavations at Taxila and Nagarjunakonda.

(14) SWANN, WINN. Lost Cities of Asia. New York: G. P. Putnam's Sons, 1966, 103 color and black and white plates, 18 maps and figures.

Discusses Pagan, Angkor, and, in Ceylon, Anuradhpura, Sigiriya, Polonnaruwa. Much of the text is devoted to the history of these sites rather than detailed artistic analysis. Emphasis is on architecture and sculpture. Nearly half the plates are in color and are excellent.

5.2.3 Sculpture

(1) BACHHOFER, LUDWIG. *Early Indian Sculpture*. New York: Hacker Art Books, 1972, 137 pp., 161 black and white plates. (Originally published New York: Pegasus Press, 1929, 2 vols.)

A valuable study despite the fact that more recent work has been done in some of the areas dealt with. Deals with the Mauryan period, then early sculpture in India, followed by an examination of Gandhara, Mathura, Bharkut, Sanchi, Sarnath, Bodh Gaya, Karli, Amaravati, Udayagiri, Taxila, Kabul, and Hadda. The focus is entirely on Buddhist art throughout, though other forms of art are considered as each site is discussed.

(2) CHANDRA, PRAMOD. *Stone Sculpture in the Allahabad Museum*. American Institute of Indian Studies, Publication No. 2. Poona: Dr. R. J. Miller, 1970, 211 pp., 173 black and white plates.

A brief review of the history of Indian art followed by one hundred thirty-eight pages of description of plates, glossary of Indian words, and concordance of holdings of the Allahabad Museum. The volume is well-indexed, with a good table of contents. Plates are extensive and detailed, divided into five chronological categories ranging from third century B.C. to fourteenth century A.D. and subdivided according to their geographical location. Plates are extremely important.

(3) COOMARASWAMY, ANANDA K. *Elements of Buddhist Iconography*. See 9.3.1(4).

An important work. Studies briefly the tree of life, earth-lotus, word-wheel, lotus throne and fiery pillar symbols. Attempts to trace these symbols back through the aniconic period of the Brahmanical Vedas to the Rig-Veda itself, thereby establishing them as elements in a universal Indian symbolism expressive of universal Indian theological concepts. Thirty-two pages of extensive notes supplement the text as do the rather detailed descriptions of the forty-four photographs. Contains no index or bibliography. Although somewhat dated, this is an excellent monograph.

(4) _____. *The Origin of the Buddha Image*. New Delhi: Munshiram Manoharial, 1972, 42 pp., 73 black and white illustrations. (Originally published in *Art Bulletin*, 9 (1926-1927), 287-329.)

A carefully balanced argument against a Greek origin for the Buddha image at Gandhara. The author prefers to locate the first Buddha image at Mathura and dates it no more than fifty years prior to the reign of Kanishka. Plates are of only fair quality, but are well-selected. Includes no table of contents or index.

(5) _____. *Yaksas*. See 9.2.2.5(2).

Part 1 traces the history of yaksa worship to pre-Aryan times and recounts the impact it might have had on Buddhism and Hinduism. Rather than regarding this form of worship as primitive animism, the author views it as a sophisticated religious system which fell into disfavor and lower status. Part 2 expands on the relationship of yaksas and water cosmology. Includes little direct reference to art works. Plates are mediocre but relevant. Unfortunately, there is no index nor table of contents. A provocative, well-written account of a specialized subject.

(6) DANI, AHMED HASAN. *Buddhist Sculpture in East Pakistan*. Karachi: Department of Archaeology, Government of Pakistan, 1959, (approx. 50 pp.), 47 black and white plates.

This brief introductory text relies mainly on its illustrations, drawn exclusively from the museums at Dacca and Rajshahi and the excavations at Parhapur and Mainamati and all belonging to the "Bengal School of Art." The text devotes one or two paragraphs each to Buddhist monasteries, royal patrons, internal and external influences, characteristics of Buddhist art, the Gupta tradition, etc. The evolution of the Buddhist pantheon is given ten pages. Includes no table of contents or index. This is a field in which little is published, and the volume contains unusual plates.

(7) DENECK, M. M. and W. and B. FORMAN. *Indian Sculpture*. Translated by Iris Urwin. London: Spring Books, 1962, 35 pp., 264 black and white plates.

Begins with a brief account of Indian history and its art, including its influence on Khmer and Kham art, and includes a short history of Buddhism and its art. Plates are arranged roughly chronologically. Approximately 100 of them depict Buddhist art. Description of plates is cursory. The major value of the book is in the plates, which are large, full of detail and well-presented.

(8) FERGUSSON, JAMES. *Tree and Serpent Worship*. Delhi: Oriental Publishers, 1971, 247 pp., 99 black and white plates. (Originally published London: Indian Museum, 1868.)

To impress the reader with the prevalence of tree and serpent worship, Fergusson devotes a lengthy introductory essay to the history of its practice throughout the Western world and Asia. He inserts a brief chapter on general characteristics of Buddhist architecture before discussing Sanchi and Amaravati in terms of their histories, ethnographies and sculpture. Includes lengthy descriptions of old, rather blurred plates. An interesting book with detailed descriptions of the two stupas.

(9) FOUCHER, ALFRED. The Beginnings of Buddhist Art and Other Essays in Indian and Central Asian Archaeology. Translated by L. A. Thomas and F. W. Thomas. Revised edition. Varanasi: Indological Book House, 1972, 316 pp., 50 black and white plates. (Originally published Paris: P. Geunther, 1917.)

A collection of nine separate essays on Buddhist art. Among them are: the beginnings of Buddhist art, the Eastern Gate of Sanchi, Buddhist art in Java. Several essays discuss the contact between Buddhist and Mediterranean art: the Greek origin of the Buddha image, the tutelary pair in Gaul in India, the Buddhist Madonna. Plates are blurry but have lengthy descriptions. Contains a good index, and a coherent, well-written introductory essay, but needs to be seen in the perspective of recent scholarship.

(10) _____. Etudes sur l'art bouddhique de l'Inde. Tokyo: Maison Franco-Japonaise, 1928, pp. 88, paie 149.

A series of lectures in both French and Japanese. The first three (an iconographical sketch of Buddhist art in India, the origins of the Buddha image, and an account of a visit to Angkor) are in both languages. The fourth, the itinerary of Hsuan-tsang in Afghanistan, is in Japanese only. Contains three maps of Northwest India; no index; valuable summaries of the knowledge of these topics as of the 1920s. See also 1.2.2.3(5).

(11) _____. The Life of the Buddha. See 2.7.6(5).

A scholarly account of the Buddha's life which presents him as both human and divine. Information is drawn mainly from ancient texts, but the introduction discusses how the author used works of art to trace the life of the Buddha. The book is detailed, well-written, with no index, good plates.

(12) _____. On the Iconography of the Buddha's Nativity. See 9.3.3(3).

A close examination of the iconography of the bas-relief at Sanchi to determine which symbol has been used to represent the Buddha in the nativity scene: the lotus, the zodiac sign of the bull, the elephant of conception, or the gateway and horse of the Great Renunciation. Foucher decides in favor of the lotus and traces the evolution of the motif up to the appearance of the Buddha image. (Edgerton, by the way, disagrees in his review of the monograph.) Plates are carefully selected and described to illustrate the evolution of the symbols.

(13) GANGOLY, O. C. The Antiquity of the Buddha Image: The Cult of the Buddha. Calcutta: Bani Publishers, 1965, 21 pp., 10 figures, 2 black and white plates. (Originally published in Ostasiatische Zeitschrift, neue Folge, 14 [1938], 41-59.)

Brief, direct account of the origin of the cult of the Buddha image and the conditions which accompanied it, particularly the popular desire for image worship. Information is drawn from many ancient sutras.

(14) GETTY, ALICE. The Gods of Northern Buddhism. See 8.3.1(6).

A useful though dated book on Mahayana Buddhist iconography. Contains a thirty-page introductory essay on the history of Buddhism and Buddhist art. Sixteen chapters cover various forms of Buddhas, bodhisattvas, and divinities from India, China, Tibet, Mongolia, and Japan. Each chapter is introduced by a table of names of various manifestations. Plates are small but sharp and helpful, and the book is well-indexed.

(15) HALLADE, MADELEINE. Etudes d'art indien: la composition dans les reliefs de l'Inde. Paris: Librairie d'Amérique et d'Orient, Adrien-Maisonneuve, 1942, 197 pp., 338 drawings, 8 black and white plates.

Intensive and rather technical, the book is divided into two sections, one dealing with pre-Guptan art (including Sanchi, Bharhut, Bodh-gaya, Greco-Buddhist art), and Guptan, post-Guptan period, discussing the parallel evolution of Buddhist and Hindu sculpture during this period. Extensive sketches well illustrate major points. This work is specialized, and relies on discussion of specific sites.

(16) HAVELL, ENREST B. Indian Sculpture and Painting. Second edition. London: John Murray, 1928, 288 pp., 78 black and white and color plates.

Approaches Indian art thematically, with chapters on the divine ideal, myth and metaphysics, etc. One of the first attempts to abandon European prejudices in evaluating Indian art. A few pages of each section are devoted to Buddhist art. There are separate chapters on Borobodur and the human ideal in sculptures of Bharhut, Sanchi, and Amaravati, and some chapters on history and schools of art as they spread to Southeast Asia. The index is poor.

(17) LAW, BIMALA CHURN. Heaven and Hell in Buddhist Perspective. See 9.2.2.3(8).

Though not directly concerned with art, this contains many vivid descriptions of Buddhist heavens and hell, especially from Pali literature. Helpful for establishing the textual background for subsequent artistic representation. Contains no illustrations.

(18) MALLMAN, MARIE-THERESE DE. Introduction à l'étude d'Avalokiteçvara. See 8.3.2(8).

An exhaustive study of Avalokitesvara in India with major sections discussing: the texts utilized, the name of Avalokitesvara, the place of Avalokitesvara in Indian religious thought, a chronological study of Indian images of Avalokitesvara, and a stylistic study of images of the deity. Includes an eleven-page bibliography and clear and helpful black and white illustrations. Clearly a definitive work about a problem in regard to which Paul Mus, in his introduction, states, "Le problème entier du Grand Véhicule y est lié." Highly specialized.

(19) Ministry of Information and Broadcasting, Government of India. The Way of the Buddha. Delhi: Publications Division, Ministry of Broadcasting and Information, Government of India, 1956, 330 pp., extensively illustrated.

A pictorial work divided into seven sections: background, the bodhisattva's life, the Buddha's message, growth of Buddhism, Buddhist pantheon, spread of Buddhism abroad, enduring influence of Buddhism. The notes on the plates include generalized historic information. The numerous pictures from Southeast Asia, emphasizing sculpture, are well done and helpful, arranged chronologically to suggest the evolution of artistic expression.

(20) ROWLAND, BENJAMIN. The Evolution of the Buddha Image. New York: Asia Society, 1963, 146 pp., 68 black and white plates, 15 figures.

An important brief introduction to the development of the Buddha image from India, through Southeast Asia, China, and Japan.

5.2.4 The Mauryan Period and the Art of Bodhgaya, Bharhut, Sanchi, and Mathura

(1) AGRAWALA, VASUDEVA S. Masterpieces of Mathura Sculpture. Varanasi: Prithivi Prakashan, 1965, 27 pp., 16 black and white plates.

A brief introduction recounts the synthesis of Indian, Iranian, and Hellenistic influences which created the Mathura school of art. The basic features of the Mathura school, as well as its history, are discussed. Plates are of adequate quality, but are too few to convey the richness of Mathura sculpture. There is no table of contents, bibliography, nor index. A simple but good introduction to the subject.

(2) BARUA, BENIMADHAB. Bharhut. Indian Research Institute Publications. Fine Arts Series, Nos. 1-3. Calcutta: Indian Research Institute, 1934-1937, 3 vols. Vol. 1, Stone as a Story Teller, 1934, 103 pp. Vol. 2, Jataka Scenes, 1934, 178 pp. Vol. 3, Aspects of Life and Art, 1937, 94 pp., 97 plates.

At present, this is the most complete study of the Buddhist stupa at Bharhut. The author describes the physical aspects of the monument as well as the known historical information gathered from its inscriptions. An elaborate discussion identifies the scenes from the life of the Buddha, the jatakas, the symbolism of individual motifs represented and the symbolism of the stupa as a whole.

(3) _____. Gaya and Buddha-Gaya. See 10.2.3(1).

Volume 2 contains the last four parts of this five part series, almost exclusively devoted to old shrines at Bodh-gaya. One part presents general description, another deals with inscriptions, a third with bas-reliefs and art, and a fourth presents plates. Makes no attempt to be comprehensive or artistically descriptive but only to indicate the earliest landmarks of the shrines. Specialized text.

(4) BHATTACHARYA, TARAPADA. The Bodhgaya Temple. See 10.2.3(3).

A brief account of the history of the area around Bodhgaya from Vedic times through the medieval period. Discusses Bodhgaya as an ancient sacred spot for Hindus as well as Buddhists. For the intermediate student with previous knowledge of both religions. Contains no index or bibliography.

(5) CHANDRA, RAMPRASAD. The Beginnings of Art in Eastern India: With Special Reference to Sculptures in the Indian Museum, Calcutta. Memoirs of the Archaeological Survey of India, No. 30. Calcutta: Government of India, Central Publications Branch, 1927, 54 pp., 7 plates.

For many years, this book remained the basic introduction to the beginnings of Buddhist art during the Maurya period. The author discusses the Mauryan period from a religious and historical point of view. He develops theories concerning the relationship to Persepolitan antecedents of the Mauryan palace at Pataliputra and one of the so-called "Asokan" pillars, which carry edicts attesting to King Asoka's conversion to Buddhism. Later Mauryan and early Sunga art is also considered.

(6) COOMARASWAMY, ANANDA K. La Sculpture de Bodhgaya. Ars Asiatica, No. 18. Paris: Les Editions d'Art et d'Histoire, 1935, 72 pp., 60 plates, 2 maps, 15 figures.

Sixty large pages discuss in detail the history of the enclosure of Bodhgaya, the architecture of various sites, scenes of past lives of the Buddha, and inscriptions, with a section for subjects not exclusively Buddhist. The extensive black and white plates are quite clear. A good, rather detailed, overview of Bodhgaya sculpture.

(7) _____. Les Sculptures de Bharhut. See 10.2.6.1(1).

After a brief historical introduction, the text centers on the iconography of the Buddha at Bharhut. The work as a whole, however, is devoted to extensive discussion of the plates with references to relevant jatakas. A good visual and textual presentation of important themes in the iconography of Bharhut, albeit brief.

(8) CUNNINGHAM, ALEXANDER. Mahabodhi. See 10.2.3(6).

Detailed architectural description of the Mahabodhi Temple at Bodhgaya. Includes discussions of railings, monuments, seals, additions and restorations, sculptures, arches and vaults, etc., and a twenty-two page review of

Indo-Scythian, Chinese and Burmese inscriptions. The introduction has a chronology of progress in development of sites from the third century B.C. to contemporary times. Plates are old and blurred but those of seals, inscriptions and ground plans are interesting.

(9) _____. The Stupa of Bharhut. See 10.2.6.1(2).

A work of central importance by a noted figure who was the discoverer of the Great Stupa at Bharhut in 1873. The work describes in great detail the stupa itself and the various forms of sculpture connected with it: superhuman beings (yakshas, devas, nagas, apsarases), human beings, animals, trees and fruits, sculptured scenes (from the jatakas and from historical incidents), objects of worship (e.g., relics), decorative ornaments, other Buddhist buildings, miscellaneous objects and inscriptions. Crucial to the field.

(10) DHAVALIKAR, M. K. Sanchi: A Cultural History. See 10.2.6.2(2).

After a short introduction to the history and architecture of Sanchi, the author devotes the book to describing the "cultural material" depicted in Sanchi sculpture: personal ornaments, hair styles, costumes, furniture, etc. Each subject is treated very briefly, with no attempt to coordinate the material into a coherent picture. Less on Buddhist art than on general aspects of culture depicted in Buddhist art.

(11) IRWIN, JOHN. "Asokan Pillars: A Reassessment of the Evidence." Burlington Magazine, 115 (1973), 706-720.

The origins of Indian Monumental Art are traditionally traced to the Maurya period, at which time the so-called "asokan" pillars are generally believed to have been erected. This is the first in a series of articles which attempts to assign some of these pillars to a much earlier date and ascribes their original function to pre-Buddhist beliefs.

(12) MAISEY, F. C. Sanchi and Its Remains. See 10.2.6.2(4).

Begins with one hundred fifty pages describing Sanchi: the various stupas, gateways, chaityas, viharas, pillars, inscriptions, and other remains. Concluding chapters contest the then commonly accepted dates of Sakyamuni, Asoka, and Sanchi, attempting to prove that they are more recent. An unexceptional text and illustrations with no index.

(13) MARSHALL, JOHN. A Guide to Sanchi. See 10.2.6.2(5).

Essentially a guide book, but of great value for the serious student as well. Discusses the area's topography, historical and artistic development, the Great Stupa, pillars, other temples and stupas on the main terrace, southern and eastern areas, Stupa 2, and other remains. A ten-page appendix provides a sketch of the Buddha's life with reference to Sanchi sculptures. A worthy introduction; includes two maps.

(14) MARSHALL, JOHN and ALFRED FOUCHER. The Monuments of Sanchi. See 10.2.6.2(6).

The combined effort of Sir John Marshall, Alfred Foucher, and M. G. Majumdar, as epigrapher, has produced the most complete study of the monuments of Sanchi. These are carefully described and are considered from the points of view of their history, style, iconographic schemes, and inscriptions. Ground plans and elevations, as well as rubbings of the inscriptions are provided. The descriptions of the plates are fully cross indexed to the relevant sections in Volume 1.

(15) MITRA, RAJENDRALALA. Buddha Gaya. See 10.2.3(7).

Although one hundred years old, this book is thorough, with twenty pages on the community of Buddhagaya, thirty pages on the account of the Buddha's penance, fifty-five pages on architectural remains, sixty pages on sculpture, fifty pages on inscriptions, and twenty pages on the chronology of the sites. Plates are old and somewhat unattractive, but there are several maps and sketches of ground plans which prove helpful. A rather dry, detailed book which reads like the account of an archaeological excavation and is suited to the more advanced student.

(16) MYER, PRUDENCE. "The Great Temple at Bodh-Gaya." Art Bulletin, 40 (1958), 277-298.

An extremely detailed study of the various reconstructions of the Mahabodhi temple at Bodh-Gaya.

(17) RAY, NIHARRANJAN. Maurya and Sunga Art. See 5.2.1(20).

(18) VAN LOHUIZEN-DE LEEUW, J. E. The "Scythian" Period: An Approach to the History, Art, Epigraphy, and Paleography of North India from the First Century B.C. to the Third Century A.D. Leiden: E. J. Brill, 1949, 435 pp., 40 plates.

A highly technical book examining the art of Gandhara and Mathura from the points of view of epigraphy, paleography, and style. Advanced.

(19) VOGEL, JEAN PHILIPPE. La Sculpture de Mathura. Ars Asiatica, No. 15. Paris and Bruxelles: G. Van Oest, 1930, 131 pp., 60 plates.

Includes some general geographical and historical background material. Features the Mathuran art during the Kushan Dynasty, the mingling of Oriental and Occidental influences, sections on sacred edifices, images, bas-reliefs, and decorative motifs. Plates are quite comprehensive and well described; there is a good bibliography.

5.2.5　Northwest India, Gandhara, Afghanistan

(1) BARTHOUX, JULES. Les Fouilles de Hadda. Mémoires de la délégation archéologique française en Afghanistan, Nos. 4 and 6. 2 vols. Vol. 1, Stupas and Sites. Paris: Les Editions d'Art et d'Histoire, 1933, 208 pp., 7 plans. Vol. 2. Figures et Figurines: Album Photographique. Paris and Bruxelles: Les Editions G. Van Oest, 1930, 26 pp., 112 plates.

The excavation reports of the various monastic units at Hadda (Afghanistan), well known for the abundant production of masterful works in the medium of stucco. The dates of these works are highly controversial.

(2) DEYDIER, HENRI. Contribution à l'étude de l'art du Gandhara. Paris: Librairie d'Amérique et d'Orient, Adrien-Maisonneuve, 1950, 318 pp.

An exhaustive study of Gandharan art, recommending books and articles and reporting most recent findings, arranged around geographic areas such as Gandhara, Kapica, Oddiyana, Taxila, Hadda, Kashmir, Bamiyan and Bactria. Within each area, various topics such as locality, iconography, etc. are discussed. Extensive sections are devoted to the dating of Gandharan art according to inscriptions of the Kushans. Several maps and an index of authors' names, as well as historical, geographic, iconographic, and Chinese word indices.

(3) FOUCHER, ALFRED. L'Art gréco-bouddhique du Gandhara. See 9.2.2.5(3).

Volume 1 contains introduction, discussion of buildings and bas-reliefs under which the following headings are treated: the stupa (34 pages), the vihara (47 pages), the development and the decoration of the sangharama (58 pages), the legends of the bodhisattva (70 pages), the transformation of bodhisattva into Buddha (100 pages), the Buddha's career (75 pages), the Buddha's death (29 pages), and a general review of legendary material (25 pages). Includes a map of Peshawar district. Volume 2 deals with the general categories of images, history and conclusion. Images are discussed in terms of the inferior deities (91 pages), the higher castes (73 pages), the outside castes (73 pages), a general review of images (60 pages), the evolution of the Gandhara school (105 pages), the origins of the Gandhara school (65 pages), the influence of the Gandhara school (75 pages), historical resume (64 pages), and sixty-three pages of conclusion. Obviously, a comprehensive and definitive work although somewhat dated in certain areas.

(4) _____. Les Bas-reliefs du stupa de Sikri (Gandhara). Paris: Imprimerie Nationale, 1903, 146 pp., 13 illustrations.

The stupa of Sikri, presently in the Lahore Museum, was found with its drum decoration complete. This small book describes and identifies the iconographic scheme of this monument.

(5) GODARD, ANDRE and JOSEPH HACKIN. Les Antiquités bouddhiques de Bamiyan. Mémoires de la délégation archéologique française en Afghanistan, No. 2. Paris: G. Van Oest, 1928, 113 pp., 48 black and white plates.

The book opens with a brief summary of the history of research at Bamiyan, then includes descriptions of the large Buddha images and a fifteen-page discussion of the paintings. The next chapter, with approximately twenty sketches, describes the caves. Following a ten-page section on the Sassanid paintings of Dokhtar-i-Noshirwan, there are copies of previous travellers' accounts of Bamiyan. Plates are large and comprehensive, a few in color. Presents preliminary research on the subject.

(6) GRUNWEDEL, ALBERT. Buddhist Art in India. See 5.2.1(10).

(7) HALLADE, MADELEINE. Gandharan Art of North India and the Graeco-Buddhist Tradition in India, Persia and Central Asia. Translated by Diana Imber. New York: Harry N. Abrams, 1968, 266 pp., including 24 color and 179 black and white plates, 5 figures.

Impressive analysis which examines the cultural and geographical background of the area before focusing on Gandharan art in terms of the schist school, stucco school and Indo-Sassanian art. Proceeds to discuss the impact of Gandhara on all Asian art. Includes a glossary, maps, chronological tables, and a good index, as well as specific sections on representations of the Buddha and bodhisattvas, and marvellous plates. Features sculpture but also touches on painting and jewelry. The text is simple but valuable for all students.

(8) INGHOLT, HARALD and ISLAY LYONS. Gandharan Art in Pakistan. Hamden, Conn.: Archon Books, 1971, 203 pp., 577 black and white illustrations. (Originally published New York: Pantheon Books, 1957.)

Deals exclusively with Buddhist sculpture. The actual text is a forty-one page introduction of questionable value. The remaining 162 pages consist of a detailed descriptive catalogue of the 571 plates. The plates and their descriptions form the core of the book. Intermediate-advanced.

(9) KHAN, F. A. Architecture and Art Treasures in Pakistan. Karachi: Elite Publishers, 1969.

Considers the archeological heritage of Pakistan. Pages 69-128 on Buddhist period (third century B.C.-seventh century A.D.) of West Pakistan and pages 158-173 on Buddhist period (third century B.C.-eleventh century A.D.) of East Pakistan. Text is of an introductory nature, with emphasis on architecture and sculpture. Combined with numerous black and white and color illustrations, it conveys a sense of the whole culture of the period. Plates are well done and uncommon. Includes a glossary.

(10) MARSHALL, JOHN. The Buddhist Art of Gandhara. Memoirs of the Department of Archaeology in Pakistan, No. 1. Cambridge: Cambridge University Press, 1960, 118 pp., 111 black and white plates.

This is a key work by a central figure in South Asian archaeology. Marshall traces the beginnings, the growth, the maturity, and the late maturity of Gandharan art.

(11) _____. A Guide to Taxila. Fourth edition. Cambridge: Cambridge University Press, 1960, 196 pp., 22 plates, 15 figures.

A thorough discussion of Taxila presented in terms of such topics as topography, history, artistic influences, the Dharmarajika stupa, Buddhist remains in the glen of Giri, the stupa of Kunala, Kunala, Sirkap, Jandial, Jaulian, and Bhamala, and the Bhir Mound. Numerous maps, site and architectural plans included, as well as unusual and appropriate plates. An indispensable work for the student of Taxila.

(12) MEUNIE. Shotorak. Mémoires de la délégation archéologique française en Afghanistan, No. 10. Paris: Les Editions d'Art et d'Histoire, 1942, 77 pp., 42 plates.

The excavation reports of the Buddhist site of Shotorak (Afghanistan), believed to have been the place where the Kushan King Kanishka housed hostages from China during the summer. The finds include works of both schist and stucco, many representing the later phases of Gandharan art.

(13) ROSENFIELD, JOHN M. The Dynastic Arts of the Kushans. Berkeley and Los Angeles: University of California Press, 1967, 377 pp., approx. 500 illustrations.

Contains limited but easily found material on the Kushans' contact with Buddhism. Pages 27-38 discuss Kanishka as a patron of Buddhism. Pages 215-250 treat Kushan figures as donors and devotees of Buddhist sculpture. Chapters on Mathura also mention Buddhist influences. Plates are comprehensive and detailed. Excellent index and multi-lingual bibliography are included. Emphasizes sculpture.

(14) ROWLAND, BENJAMIN. Ancient Art from Afghanistan. New York: The Asia Society, 1966, 144 pp., including 111 black and white illustrations.

Material is divided into art discoveries from specific archaeological excavations; sections on Paitava and Shotorak, Hadda, Bamiyan, Kabul, and Fondukistan are related to Buddhist art. Text is very brief but descriptions of plates often extensive. Plates are small but well-done and display many pieces not seen in other books.

(15) _____. Art in Afghanistan. London: Allen Lane, The Penguin Press, 1971, 93 pp., 214 black and white illustrations.

Covers a wide range of Afghanistan's art: classical, Buddhist, Hindu and Islamic; but features Buddhist art. Contains eleven brief chapters on particular periods of Afghanistan's art and locations such as Gandhara, Hadda, Bamiyan, and Fondukistan. Plates, almost exclusively of sculpture, are good, sometimes with lengthy commentaries.

(16) _____. Gandharan Sculpture from Pakistan Museums. New York: Asia Society, 1960, 64 pp., including 65 black and white illustrations.

Helpful short account of the history and styles of Gandharan art. Approximately seventeen pages of text, some devoted to the Buddha image. Also briefly describes the development of bodhisattva images, reliefs, stucco, painting, and architecture. Plates are often full-page and well-done but lack thorough descriptions. A convenient way to familiarize oneself with the essentials of Gandharan art.

(17) VAN LOHUIZEN-DE LEEUW, J. E. The "Scythian" Period. See 5.2.4(18).

5.2.6 Cave Temples: Ajanta, Ellora, etc.

(1) ANAND, MULK RAJ. Ajanta. Bombay: Marg Publications, 1971, 59 pp., including 31 color and black and white plates.

A short presentation of technical developments as traced in wall paintings of Ajanta from Caves 9 and 10 (the earliest) through 16, 17, to 1 and 2. Brief treatment of the discovery of the caves, Buddhist imagery, development of style and Hinayana to Mahayana caves. Mostly consists of specific plates and relatively extensive notes discussing style, iconography, and corresponding jataka where appropriate. Slim but good introduction.

(2) BURGESS, JAMES. Notes on the Buddha Rock-Temples of Ajanta, Their Paintings and Sculptures and on the Paintings of the Bagh Caves, Modern Bauddha Mythology, etc. Archaeological Survey of Western India, No. 9. Bombay: Government Central Press, 1879, 111 pp., 31 plates.

Highly technical. Sanskrit text of inscriptions and, occasionally, their romanizations scattered throughout. Detailed descriptions with some reproductions of the caves and paintings of Ajanta from Cave 1 to 29. Appendix includes essay on the Buddha mythology of Nepal and extensive copies of the Sanskrit inscriptions of Buddhist caves other than Ajanta. An old but detailed and still valuable study.

(3) _____. Report on the Buddhist Cave Temples and Their Inscriptions. See 10.2.1(4).

Results of the fourth, fifth, and sixth seasons' operations of the Archaeological Survey of Western India, 1876-1877, 1877-1878, 1878-1879. Supplementary to the volume The Cave Temples of India (see 10.2.1[9]). Consists of discussion and description of architectural detail and inscriptions of major Buddhist caves. Ajanta is concentrated on, but various other locations are dealt with as well. Drawings and plates consist mainly of architectural plans and copies of inscriptions. Highly specialized.

(4) DEHEJIA, VIDYA. Early Buddhist Rock Temples. Ithaca, N.Y.: Cornell University Press, 1972, 240 pp., 90 black and white illustrations, maps, 5 figures, 11 tables.

Examines the formative phase of rock architecture in India from its beginnings to c. 200 A.D. The author attempts to establish a clear chronology of the evolution of the rock temples by comparing the sequences suggested by historical records, paleography, architecture and sculpture. Includes chapters on historical and geographical information, paleography, inscriptions, architecture, sculpture, painting, and social-economic craft organization. Paleography study is particularly good. Extensive tables on paleography, coins, inscriptions, chronology. Plates are adequate. A valuable book.

(5) DEY, MUKUL. My Pilgrimages to Ajanta and Bagh. Introduced by L. Binyon. Second edition. Bombay: Oxford University Press, 1950, 185 pp., 56 plates.

Sees Ajanta and Bagh through the eyes of a young artist on pilgrimage there in 1918 and 1919. Recounts his travelling adventures as well as his impressions of the art, especially the paintings. Plates are small but sharp. Written for popular consumption.

(6) FERGUSSON, JAMES and JAMES BURGESS. The Cave Temples of India. See 10.2.1(9).

Historical information is dated but a thorough description of the caves is given. Minimal analysis of artistic styles. Pages 55-86 discuss cave temples at Hathi Gumpha, Kathiawar, South Konkan, Karle and the vicinity of the Bor Ghat, Junnar, Nasik, Ajanta, Kanheri, Bagh, Elura, Aurangabad. Plates consist of hand sketches and ground plans, but are detailed and helpful.

(7) GOLOUBEW, VICTOR. D'Ajanta: Les Peintures de la Première Grotte. Ars Asiatica, No. 10. Paris and Bruxelles: G. Van Oest, 1927, 48 pp., 66 black and white plates.

Twenty-five pages of general introductory text. Discusses the history of the paintings and the history of their study by Westerners. Included is a short section on the techniques employed in the wall paintings. Ground plans are also included.

(8) GUPTE, RAMESH SHANKAR. Ajanta, Ellora and Aurangabad Caves. See 10.2.6.2(3).

The book is conveniently arranged: thirty pages on the story and teachings of the Buddha and of Buddhist iconography; a twenty-page discussion of architectural forms of Ajanta; and fifty pages describing thirty Ajanta caves. Also, a twenty-page description of twelve Buddhist caves of Ellora and a brief account of inscriptions from all sites. Includes glossaries of technical words and names. Plates are small and somewhat blurred, the style rather dry.

(9) _____. The Iconography of the Buddhist Sculptures (Caves) of Ellora. Aurangabad: Shri M. B. Chitnis, Registrar, Marathwada University, 1964, 164 pp., 20 black and white plates.

Originally a Ph.D. thesis submitted to Marathwada University. The Buddhist sculptues of Ellora had, up until the author's study, been relatively neglected by scholars and many had remained unidentified. Gupte provides an exhaustive treatment of the subject replete with economic and historical background, descriptions of the Buddhist sculptures, tables of asanas and mudras of the Buddha, cave by cave presentation of the asanas of the Buddha, discussion of the bodhisattvas and Buddha Saktis, symbols, flying figures, dress, ornaments, etc. Photographs are fair. Includes two maps, a two-page glossary of technical terms, a four-page helpful bibliography. Somewhat technical treatment of Buddhist iconography of a period dominated by Vajrayana.

(10) KRAMRISCH, STELLA. A Survey of Painting in the Deccan. London: The India Society, 1937, 233 pp., 24 plates.

Part one of this book deals with a relative sequence and carefully reasoned visual descriptions of the Buddhist cave paintings at Ajanta.

(11) LEVINE, DEBORAH BROWN. "Aurangabad: A Stylistic Analysis." Artibus Asiae, 28 (1966), 175-188, 21 plates.

An important study of the development of the Buddhist iconography and style of the rock-cut caves at Aurangabad. These caves are divided into two groups--those influenced by the later Mahayana caves at Ajanta and those influenced by Elephanta and Ellora.

(12) MARSHALL, JOHN, et al. The Bagh Caves in Gwalior State. London: The India Society, 1927, 78 pp., 27 plates.

In brief sections, John Marshall describes the general architectural features of the six caves as well as including a word on the painting. Ph. Vogel discusses the sculpture and iconographical aspect of the paintings. James Cousins comments on the aesthetic and topographical factors. B. B. Havell and M. B. Garde also contribute. The plates are adequate and include many detailed architectural sketches and a map of the Malwa region. Simple introduction.

(13) SINGH, MADANJEET. Ajanta. New York: Macmillan, 1965, 189 pp., 82 black and white plates, 22 figures.

Consists largely of magnificent plates which speak for themselves. Most are in color and even reveal some of the nuances of the brushwork. Approximately sixty pages of text review the history and social conditions of the development of Buddhism as well as the evolution of painting styles. Appendix includes extensive description of Caves 1, 2, 6, 9, 10, 16, 17. Contains approximately twenty short anecdotes about the Buddha's life which are depicted in the cave paintings. Imaginatively written.

(14) SPINK, WALTER. Ajanta to Ellora. Bombay: Marg Publications, for the Center for South and Southeast Asian Studies, University of Michigan, 1967, 67 pp., including 175 black and white illustrations.

Approximately thirteen pages of text, not counting extensive descriptions of plates. Text provides history of the caves and discussion of their artistic styles. Plates are of sculpture and are conveniently divided into categories of ground plans and pillars, Buddha images, female figures, doorways, dwarfs, guardians, old men, pilasters, and seated couples. Includes time graphs for excavations of caves.

(15) TAKATA, OSAMU. Ajanta. Tokyo: Heibonsha, 1971, 115 pp., 179 plates, 38 illustrations.

Although this book is in Japanese and cannot be read by most students in the West, it is still highly recommended for its exquisite plates of the Buddhist cave temples at Ajanta.

(16) YAZDANI, GHULAM. Ajanta. London: Oxford, 1930-1955. 4 vols. text, 4 vols. accompanying plates. (Texts: vol. 1, 1930, 55 pp.; vol. 2, 70 pp., 8 black and white plates; vol. 3, 1946, 100 pp., 9 black and white plates; vol. 4, 1955, 130 pp., 5 black and white plates. Plates: vol. 1, 16 color, 4 black and white plates; vol. 2, 18 color, 31 black and white plates; vol. 3, 17 color, 57 black and white plates; vol. 4, 17 color, 65 black and white plates.)

Each volume focuses on architectural features and/or wall paintings of specified caves. Text consists mainly of description, particularly identifying characters in the paintings, rather than stylistic analysis. Several appendices with detailed explanations of the inscriptions, with plates of inscriptions, are included. Volume 4 treats briefly the political-social context in which the caves were originally excavated. Well indexed. The most comprehensive treatment of the subject.

5.2.7 Amaravati, Nagarjunakonda, etc.

(1) BARRETT, DOUGLAS. Sculptures from Amaravati in the British Museum. London: The Trustees of the British Museum, 1954, 76 pp., 48 black and white plates.

Fifty pages of text, with brief accounts of the early history of the Deccan, the Satavahana Dynasty, and the discovery of the Amaravati stupa. The next thirty pages describe the form of the stupa and the style of the sculptures and the Buddha images at Amaravati. Plates are large and well done. An excellent book regarding the essentials of the Amaravati stupa.

(2) BURGESS, JAMES. The Buddhist Stupas of Amaravati and Jaggayyapeta. See 10.2.6.3(2).

This book presents the results of the James Burgess survey of Amaravati and Jaggayyapeta in 1882. Although most of the material on Amaravati is easily accessible in more recent works, it remains essential for its discussions and illustrations of the works from Jaggayyapeta.

(3) FERGUSSON, JAMES. Tree and Serpent Worship. See 5.2.3(8).

(4) LONGHURST, A. H. The Buddhist Antiquities of Nagarjunakonda, Madras Presidency. See 10.2.6.3(3).

The first half of the text describes the locality and history of the area. Next is a discussion of the following architectural forms: temples, monasteries, stupas, carved steles, cornice stones. The last half of the text explains twenty-five episodes from Buddhist lore depicted on the bas-reliefs at Nagarjunakonda. The plates are extensive and sharp. An easily read account of a major site.

(5) RAMACHANDRAN, T. N. Buddhist Sculptures from a Stupa Near Goli Village. Bulletin of the Madras Government Museum, N.S. No. 1, part 1. Madras: Superintendent, Government Press, 1929, 44 pp., 12 plates.

The basic site report of Goli village, a Buddhist site belonging to the later phases of the art of Andhra Pradesh. Gives a detailed account of the various jatakas represented and compares them to other versions found at Amaravati.

(6) _____. Nagarjunakonda, 1938. Memoirs of the Archaeological Survey of India, No. 71. Delhi: Manager of Publications, 1953, 46 pp., 38 black and white plates.

A specialized study presenting the finds of the Indian Archaeological Department's excavations in the Nagarjunakonda area conducted in 1938. Discussion includes general introduction, previous history (brief mention of inscriptions, chaityas, viharas, stupas) and recent excavations. Sanskrit inscriptions (Nagarjunakonda, Jaggayyapeta, and Gummididurru), and coins. Two appendices discuss the significant Mandhatu Jataka and provide a comparison of relevant Buddhist sects. A significant publication.

5.2.7

(7) RAMACHANDRA RAO, P. R. The Art of Nagarjunikonda. Madras: Rachana, 1956, 150 pp., 56 black and white plates, 4 floor plans.

Brief but quite valuable study on a rarely dealt with location of great significance for Buddhism. The many black and white illustrations successfully supplement the text. Many plates deal with symbolism of the mithuna (embracing couple) indicating interpenetration of Hindu and Buddhist motifs. Discussion centers on Nagarjuna, the Iksvakus, the benefactresses, the heritage of Amaravati, architecture, and the monuments. Plans of viharas presented as well. An important work, at the intermediate to advanced level.

(8) REA, ALEXANDER. South Indian Buddhist Antiquities. Archaeological Survey of India, New Imperial Series, No. 15 and Archaeological Survey of Southern India, No. 6. Varanasi: Indological Book House, 1969, 51 pp., 47 black and white plates. (Originally published Madras: Superintendent, Government Press, 1894.)

Self-contained short essays on various archaeological finds from Bhattiprolu, Gudivada, Ghantasala, and Amaravati, all in the Krishna District existing during the Andhra Dynasty. The notes are fairly detailed descriptively, but contain little artistic analysis except for a brief introduction comparing various methods of stupa construction within south India. No historical or cultural background is included, yet this is an important book on South Indian Buddhist architecture.

(9) SIVARAMAMURTI, CALEMBUS. Amaravati Sculptures in the Madras Government Museum. Madras: Superintendent, Government Press, 1942, 376 pp., 65 plates.

This book remains the most thorough study of the Amaravati stupa. Although in blurred plates, it illustrates all the major works from that site now preserved in the Madras Government Museum. The works are arranged chronologically and adhere to the most traditional chronology of the site, illustrating works from c. 200 B.C.-100 B.C. to works from c. 200 A.D.-250 A.D. A careful study is made of the individual motifs represented on the sculptures. There is a lengthy discussion on the life of the Buddha and the jataka tales represented on the Amaravati stones. Transliterations and translations of the basic inscriptions found at the site are also included.

(10) STERN, PHILIPPE and MIREILLE BENISTI. Evolution du style indien d'Amaravati. Publication du Musée Guimet, Recherches et Documents d'Art et d'Archéologie, No. 7. Paris: Presses Universitaires de France, 1961, 116 pp., 58 plates.

This book deals with a chronology of the Amaravati stupa and concentrates most specifically on the stylistic evolution of the individual motifs.

5.2.8 Later Indian Buddhist Art: Gupta, Post-Gupta, and Buddhist Tantrism

(1) AGRAWALA, PRITHIVI KUMAR. Gupta Temple Architecture. See 5.2.2(1).

Essentially, a description and discussion of Gupta temple architecture as a whole with more detailed treatment of specific significant examples, both Hindu and Buddhist. Arranged in sections which deal with early tradition and beginnings, temple architecture in the Gupta period, Gupta temple door-frames, pillars and sculpture and a "Further Estimate" of the architecture. Important Buddhist sites touched upon include the Bodhgaya temple, Sanchi, and certain Amaravati pillars. Appendices include a classification chart of Gupta and allied architecture, a chronological chart of early dated North Indian temples to 800 A.D., and an outline of the evolution of Ganga-Yamuna figures and their position on early temple entrances. Gives a good impression of Buddhist architecture as a part of the larger architectural tradition. At the introductory to intermediate levels.

(2) AGRAWALA, VASUDEVA S. Gupta Art. Lucknow: U. P. Historical Society, 1948, 38 pp., 28 black and white illustrations.

A brief introduction to Gupta art covering iconography, terracottas, sculpture, architecture, and painting. Both Hindu and Buddhist art are discussed, but there is no index and rather poor plates. Helpful, though introductory.

(3) BANERJI, R. D. Eastern School of Medieval Sculpture. Archaeological Survey of India, New Imperial Series, No. 47. Delhi: Manager of Publications, 1933, 203 pp., 96 plates.

This book is most important for its numerous illustrations of works from the Pala-Sena period, including many books from the important Buddhist site of learning at Nalanda. Many inscribed and dated images are published, frequently with a separate illustration of the inscription. Although the book deals with iconographic rather than stylistic features, the reader is given sufficient visual material to observe the stylistic interchange between Buddhist and Hindu works of the period.

(4) BHATTACHARYYA, BENOYTOSH. The Indian Buddhist Iconography. See 8.3.1(1).

A thorough, systematic study of the pantheon of Indian Vajrayana. The material is meticulously arranged into numerous categories. A forty-two page introduction on Vajrayana is followed by extensive descriptions of images. Categories consist of Buddhas, bodhisattvas, gods, goddesses, emanations, etc. The illustrations are small and mediocre in quality. Appendix is included, with drawings and descriptions of 108 forms of Avalokitesvara; the volume is well-indexed.

An advanced level book, helpful primarily for research and reference purposes.

(5) _____. An Introduction to Buddhist Esoterism. See 2.6.1(2).
Written by a convinced believer in Tantra. The author writes a sympathetic account of the origins, tenets, worship and pantheon of Tantrism and dwells on tantra as a scientific form of magic and a source of valuable psychic knowledge. Includes discussion of Buddhist Tantra, but nothing directly to do with Buddhist art. An unusual approach, at the intermediate level.

(6) BHATTASALI, NALINI KANTA. Iconography of the Buddhist and Brahmanical Sculptures in the Dacca Museum. Dacca: Rai S. N. Bhadra Bahadur, 1929, 274 pp., 79 black and white plates.
The first third of this museum catalogue is concerned mainly with the iconography of the Buddhist art of the Pala-Sena period housed in the Dacca Museum. The book is careful to mention inscriptions and their translations when possible.

(7) CUNNINGHAM, ALEXANDER. Mahabodhi. See 10.2.3(6).

(8) HARLE, J. C. Gupta Sculpture: Indian Sculpture of the Fourth to Sixth Centuries A.D. Oxford: Clarendon Press, 1964, 57 pp., 149 plates.
As the Gupta period represents the zenith of both Hindu and Buddhist art, the Buddhist works are rarely treated independently. Dr. Harle's book is as yet the finest monograph on the period, extensively illustrating works both in stone and terracotta. Those particularly interested in detailed data concerning the Buddhist works should consult the extensive notes on the relevant plates and the excellent bibliography given therein.

(9) KRAMRISCH, STELLA. "Die Figurale Plastik der Guptazeit." Wiener Bieträge zur Kunst und Kulturgeschichte Asiens, 5 (1929/1930), 15-39.
Although recent scholarship has changed some of the dates given in this article, it still remains the basic study of the evolution of Gupta sculpture.

(10) _____. "Pala and Sena Sculptures." Rupam, 40 (1929), 107-126, with 55 illustrations in 15 plates.
Establishes a basic chronology of Pala and Sena art illustrating numerous works of prime importance to Buddhism. Although recent study has caused a change in chronology of some of the works, this article still remains the basic reference on the subject. Advanced level.

(11) PAL, PRATAPADITYA. Bronzes of Kashmir. New York: Hacker Art Books, 1975, 255 pp., 120 plates.
This is the first book which gathers into one collection many of the finest bronzes of Kashmir, which was the focal point of Northern Buddhism from the seventh century onwards. Brahmanical and Buddhist bronzes are treated separately, and stylistic sources and influences are taken into account for both. Bronzes from the neighboring regions such as Swat are included for comparative purposes. An excellent bibliography is included for further reference.

(12) POTT, P. H. Yoga and Tantra: Their Interrelation and Their Significance for Indian Archaeology. See 11.6.2(10).
Originally published in 1946 by E. J. Brill, Leiden, as Yoga en Tantra: in hunne beteekenis de Indischeea archaeologie. This is a study which aims at determining to what extent a knowledge of the concepts of yoga and tantra may aid in understanding Indian archaeology. Chapters are of twenty to thirty pages each on yoga, yantra, symbols of Lamaist ritual, the sacred cemeteries of Nepal, pantheons in Java and Bali. An interesting conclusion directly explores the question motivating the work. Includes interesting black and white photographs of sculpture, contemporary yogins, and participants in rites. Intermediate level.

(13) RAMACHANDRAN, T. N. The Nagapattinam and Other Buddhist Bronzes in the Madras Museum. Bulletin of the Madras Government Museum, N.S. 7, no. 1. Madras: Superintendent, Government Press, 1954, 150 pp., 30 plates.
Although Hindu bronzes of South India are well known and highly treasured, Buddhist bronzes from that region generally receive little notice. This monograph on the Buddhist bronzes from Nagapattinam is essential for an understanding of the continuation of the Buddhist tradition in the South through the later part of the Cola period.

(14) RAWSON, PHILIP. The Art of Tantra. Greenwich, Conn.: New York Graphic Society, 1973, 197 pp., 176 black and white color illustrations.
A highly successful introductory presentation of the art of Tantra, both Hindu and Buddhist, replete with numerous effective illustrations. Serves to suggest the interpenetration of Buddhist and Hindu motifs and conceptions which occurred in Tantra. Main topics discussed are: fundamental attitudes, historical characteristics, sex and logic, basic ceremonies and images, mantra and yantra, sexual transformation, Krishna and aesthetics, graveyards and horror, cosmograms, the subtle body, doubling and development, and the one. The appendix includes a brief translation of the Kamakalavilasa.

(15) _____. Tantra. Second revised edition. London: Arts Council of Great Britain, 1972, 148 pp., including 511 color and black and white plates.

Approximately thirty pages of text provide a sophisticated account of Tantra. A six-page introduction discusses history and philosophy of Tantra in general. In conjunction with particular sets of plates, there are briefer essays on specific topics: puja, mantras, etc. Plates are small but comprehensive and interesting. No table of contents, no index. Treats Tantra primarily as a Hindu school. Advanced.

(16) ROSENFIELD, JOHN. "On the Dated Carvings of Sarnath." Artibus Asiae, 26 (1963), 16-26. t+ 1.

This is a very important essay on the Buddha images at Sarnath. Rosenfield not only presents a relatively convincing chronology of the best known Buddha images of Sarnath, but also alludes to the psychological and spiritual values contained within these images.

(17) ROY CHOUDHURY, P. C. Temples and Legends of Bengal. Bombay: Bharatiya Vidya Bhavan, 1967, 167 pp., 12 black and white plates.

Essentially a collection of descriptions and discussions of the major temples of Bengal accompanied, where significant, with description of the important related gods and legends. Primarily concerned with Hindu temples and deities but gives some tangential reference to Buddhism in the case of some temples which serve both Hindu and Buddhist deities (the Tibetan temple at Bhotbagan). Gives a good picture of the background into which Buddhism fits and, more significantly, from which Tantrism emerged. No index. Introductory.

(18) SAHNI, DAYA RAM and JEAN PHILLIPE VOGEL. Catalogue of the Museum of Archaeology at Sarnath. Calcutta: Superintendent, Government Press, 1914, 328 pp., 29 plates.

A summary history of Sarnath (the ancient site of the Deer Park in which the Buddha conducted his first sermon) is given as well as a history of the excavations of the site. The illustrated works include the most important of the Buddha images and narrative reliefs as well as the Mauryan lion capital from Sarnath, works from the Sunga period, the well known Kushan image dedicated by Friar Bala in the third year of the reign of Kanishka, and several works from the medieval period. When available, translations of inscriptions are given.

(19) SANKALIA, H. D. The University of Nalanda. See 6.2.5(24).

Discusses the Buddhist University of Nalanda from a historical and religious point of view with a brief chapter on its art and architecture.

(20) SINGH, MADANJEET. Himalayan Art. UNESCO Art Books. Greenwich, Conn.: New York Graphic Society, 1968, 295 pp., including 140 color plates and 33 figures.

Vajrayana is the dominant school of Buddhism discussed in this introductory work. The book is organized into geographic areas: Ladakh, Lahaul and Spiti, Siwalik ranges, Nepal, Sikkhim, Bhutan, with some history. One must consult a detailed index for references to Buddhist art or Buddhist influences. The emphasis is on sculptures; the level is introductory.

(21) WEINER, SHEILA L. "From Gupta to Pala Sculpture." Artibus Asiae, 25 (1962), 167-192.

The transition between the Gupta and Pala styles of art is extremely difficult to trace due to a sparsity of dated works from this time. Sheila Weiner has attempted to set up a chronology for this period. Although one may disagree with some of the sequences, this article does help to familiarize the reader with the basic monuments, problems, and bibliography of the period.

5.3 NEPAL

(1) BERNIER, RONALD M. The Temples of Nepal: An Introductory Survey. Kathmandu: Voice of Nepal, 1970. 239 pp., 32 black and white plates.

A basic study of a new field of interest, including highly detailed descriptions of specific temples. There is little attempt to place these temples historically, due primarily to difficulties in dating. Chapters include general historical and religious background sketches, discussion of elements of Nepalese temple architecture, and separate chapters on the monuments of Patan, Bhaktapur, Kathmandu, and selected others. A four-page bibliography includes most major works on Nepal; and the volume contains a three-page name-location index of Nepali temples. Specialized but not overly technical.

(2) KRAMRISCH, STELLA. The Art of Nepal. New York: The Asia Society, 1964, 159 pp., extensively illustrated.

An exhibition catalogue of the first major show of Nepalese art in the West. The focus of the thirty-page text is on the international position of Nepalese art, including its impact on Tibet, and India's dominant impact on it. The history of Nepalese art through the nineteenth century is surveyed. Excellent plates include sculpture and painting.

(3) PAL, PRATAPADITYA. The Arts of Nepal. Part 1, Sculpture. Leiden/Köln: E. J. Brill, 1974, 186 pp., 300 illustrations.

This textbook is the first in a series of three volumes to be followed by a volume on painting, and a volume on the architecture of Nepal. The text gives historical background, a corpus of dated material, a discussion of the stylistic problems involved, and separate chapters on Buddhist and Hindu icons. An excellent bibliography is included for further research.

(4) _____. *Nepal: Where the Gods Are Young.* New York: The Asia Society, 1975, 136 pp., 97 illustrations.

Catalogue of an exhibition of Nepalese art, including mostly works from American collections. This exhibition shows the newly created vast interest in the collecting of Nepalese art, and contributes new information to the present state of scholarship.

(5) WALDSCHMIDT, ERNEST and ROSE WALDSCHMIDT. *Nepal: Art Treasures from the Himalayas.* Translated by David Wilson. New York: Universe Books, 1970, 160 pp., including 82 color and black and white plates.

Approximately thirty pages of text provide a good introduction to the geography, history, religions, and arts of Nepal. The descriptions of plates are also lengthy and informative. Plates are of superior quality showing mostly sculpture and painting. Well-written compact introduction.

5.4 CEYLON

5.4.1 The Art of Sacred Places (General)

(1) BENY, ROLOFF and JOHN LINDSAY OPIE. *Island Ceylon.* New York: Viking Press, 1970, 224 pp., including 102 color and black and white plates.

Superb plates provide an enthralling glimpse of the scenery, culture, and people of Ceylon. Approximately fifty pages of text include brief reflective introductions to the essentials of Buddhism and the meaning of the Buddha-image. Descriptions of plates are also poetic and informative. Exceptional series of plates on Polonnaruwa. Text is simple and thoughtful and may inspire any student to further study.

(2) LUDOWYK, EVELYN FREDERICK CHARLES. *The Footprint of the Buddha.* See 1.3.2(11).

A study of the Buddhist monuments of Ceylon (especially Mihintale, Anuradhpura, Sigiriya, and Polonnaruwa) and an attempt to link this artistic heritage with the influence of Buddhism on Sinhalese civilization. Exceptionally well written. A perceptive account of the broad historical features. Intended for the general reader.

(3) MITTON, G. E. *The Lost Cities of Ceylon.* London: John Murray, 1917. (Originally published 1916.) 256 pp., 38 plates, 4 maps.

Through a discussion of specific cities, this book gives an excellent sense of the place, both historically and visually, of Buddhism in Ceylonese tradition. Not a direct study of art per se, but uses architecture and sculpture as sources for historical understanding. Intermediate.

(4) PARANAVITANA, SENARAT. *The God of Adam's Peak.* See 10.3.2(2).

An interesting study of the Ceylonese peak which is venerated as the footprint of the Buddha by Buddhists, of Adam by Muslims, and of Siva by Hindus. The author attempts to support the identity of the Buddhist god Saman (Pali, Sumana) of the peak, one of the four deities protecting the Island and its Buddhist religion, with the god Yama. Sections deal with Adam's Peak in history and literature, Saman, the God of Adam's Peak who is the same as Yama, characteristics and iconography of Saman compared with those of Yama, Samiddhi Sumana and Mahakala, aspects of Saman or Yama, divinities associated with Saman, an ancient Sinhala King as an embodiment of Yama, and Yama and Agastya. Includes helpful plates. An unusual and important study.

(5) RAVEN-HART, R. *Ceylon: History in Stone.* See 10.3.1(7).

Although intended as a detailed guide for the visitor, this work has a great historical emphasis, Buddhism playing a large part. Discusses Mihintale and Anuradhapura with their monasteries, Adam's Peak, Alu-vihara, etc. Interesting approach giving a sense of Buddhism's place in Sinhalese history, but not viewed from a scholarly perspective. Introductory level.

(6) WEERASOORIYA, HUBERT E. *Voices in Stones: A Book on Anuradhapura.* Fort Galle, Ceylon: Ruhunu Books, 1958, 102 pp., 15 black and white illustrations.

Deals briefly with those ancient Anuradhapura monuments which are more important historically, leading to conjecture about the past. Unusual plates are rather poorly reproduced. The work is interesting and informative but often deteriorates into a kind of romanticism. Nevertheless, an interesting introduction.

5.4.2 Architecture, Sculpture, Painting

(1) Arts Council of Ceylon. *Art and Architecture of Ceylon.* Introduced by S. Paranavitana. Ceylon: Arts Council of Ceylon, 1954, 84 pp., 46 black and white plates.

Only fifteen pages of text. Discusses the political history of the period (eleventh-twelfth century), Ceylon's emancipation from Chola rule, and the establishment of Polonnaruwa as a capital. Painting, sculpture and architecture at Polonnaruwa are briefly described. The work is too brief to be thorough.

(2) DEVENDRA, D. T. *The Buddha Image and Ceylon.* Colombo: K. V. G. De Silva, 1957, 92 pp., 29 black and white plates.

The author argues that the Buddha-image in Ceylon has not yet received adequate study and that the Buddha image may have originated there. This is deduced from ancient Sinhalese inscriptions and the style of Buddhist sculpture in Ceylon which never hesitated to portray images. Includes a table of measurements of ten Sinhalese Buddha images. Plates are sometimes blurred, but give an adequate impression of the types of Buddha images in Ceylon. An interesting though highly debatable thesis.

(3) _____. Classical Sinhalese Sculpture: C. 300 B.C.-A.D. 1000. London: Alec Tiranti, 1958, 48 pp., 128 figures, map.

Brief, highly introductory presentation of Buddhist sculpture as it developed around Anuradhapura. Short chapters give a general historical background of Sinhalese art and Buddhism, then treat "Anuradhapura, the First Phase," "Early Sculpture," "The Buddha Image," "Figure Sculpture," and "Animal and Other Subjects." A general chronological table of major rulers' reigns and a very elementary glossary are included. Photographs are clear and good.

(4) MODE, HEINZ. Die buddhistische Plastik auf Ceylon. Leipzig: E. A. Seeman, 1963, 145 pp., 175 illustrations.

An analysis of various art forms associated with the major ancient sites in Ceylon. Examines architecture, ornamental motifs, symbols associated with both Buddhist and folk tradition, as well as a thorough study of Buddha images. A solid piece of work for the nonbeginner.

(5) MUDIYANSE, NANDASENA. The Art and Architecture of the Gampola Period (1341-1415 A.D.). Colombo: M. D. Gunasena, 1960, 190 pp., 49 figures, numerous architectural plans and diagrams.

An archaeological investigation of a hitherto unstudied field, originally a thesis submitted for the M.A. degree at the University of Ceylon. Divided into five sections: historical; sites of the period: their history and traditions; architectural; sculptural; and inscriptions. Appendix provides texts of inscriptions and their translations. Includes no bibliography. Highly specialized, but not overly technical.

(6) _____. Mahayana Monuments in Ceylon. Colombo: M. D. Gunasena, 1967, 135 pp., 39 black and white plates.

The first twenty-three pages review history of Mahayana in Ceylon politics and literature. Contains chapters on stone, metal sculpture, and epigraphy; an appendix on Tantric influences; poor plates but a good index. A competent but dry intermediate level book.

(7) PARANAVITANA, SENARAT. Art of the Ancient Sinhalese. Colombo: Lake House Investments, 1971, 29 pp., 112 black and white and a few color illustrations.

Brief, highly introductory presentation of Sinhalese sculpture and painting. The many black and white illustrations are clear and work effectively with the text. An additional fifteen pages of notes on the plates give extensive description of each. A good visual introduction for the beginner.

(8) _____. The Stupa in Ceylon. Memoirs of the Archaeological Survey of Ceylon, No. 5. Colombo: Ceylon Government Press, 1946, 105 pp., 22 black and white plates.

A highly significant attempt to trace the evolution of the stupa in Ceylon through comparison of the remains of actual Sinhalese dagobas with Pali and Sinhalese literary references. The author considers the relationship of Sinhalese monuments as well. An indispensable study. Intermediate-advanced level.

(9) University of Ceylon. History of Ceylon. Colombo: Ceylon University Press, 1959 and 1960, vol. 1, parts 1 and 2, 910 pp., 50 black and white plates.

A major contribution to the understanding of the history of Ceylon. Roughly sixty pages of these two volumes deal with architecture, sculpture and painting. These are scholarly, reliable treatments even though not exhaustive. Both Hindu and Buddhist art are discussed, with more emphasis on the latter. Approximately equal treatment is given to art forms of the Anuradhapura period (third century B.C. to tenth century A.D.) and to art during the succeeding periods up to the beginning of colonialism in 1505. For the serious student.

(10) WICKRAMASINGHE, MARTIN. Buddhism and Art. Colombo: M. D. Gunasena, 1972, 176 pp., including 109 figures.

A series of interpretive essays complemented by photographs and drawings of Sinhalese Buddhist sculpture. Essays include "Buddhism and Art," "Symbolism and Originality," "Dehumanized Art: Old and New," and "Human Comedy in Sculpture." The book concentrates on India and Ceylon, and is concerned with the "spirit" of Buddhism as it relates to art. Introductory, not scholarly.

(11) WIJESEKERA, NANADEVA. Early Sinhalese Painting. Maharagama: Saman Press, 1959, 107 pp., 30 black and white plates.

Surveys the history of Sinhalese painting to the twelfth century and the sociological conditions in which it developed. Two schools of Sinhalese painting are identified and studied. Fully discusses the interaction between Indian and Sinhalese styles, stressing the uniqueness of the latter. Includes brief sections on iconography and subject matter, technique and material, style and artists, and extended descriptions of paintings at Sigiriya, Hindagala, Dumbulagala, Anuradhapura, Polonnaruwa. Plates are only fair, often blurred. A carefully organized, intermediate level work.

(12) _____. Early Sinhalese Sculpture. Colombo: M. D. Gunasena, 1962, 256 pp., 82 black and white plates.

After presenting the historical and sociological background of Sinhalese sculpture and its study, the author presents an extensive analysis of the sculpture itself. He examines its evolution, subject matter and iconography, material and technique, Buddha figure and style. There are detailed descriptions of certain specimens, but not of most, and a good index. Plates are mediocre. An exhaustive well-organized study, at the advanced level.

5.5 SOUTHEAST ASIA

5.5.1 General Surveys

(1) FREDRIC, LOUIS. The Arts of Southeast Asia. Translated by Arnold Rosin. New York: Harry Abrams, 1965, 435 pp., including 454 black and white plates.

Reviews briefly the history and styles of art in Ceylon and focuses on mainland Southeast Asia and Indonesia. The text provides brief introductions for each area. There are references to Buddhism throughout, but these are not lengthy. Excellent plates of sculpture and architecture are included, with extended commentaries. Visually stunning.

(2) RAWSON, PHILIP. The Art of Southeast Asia. New York: Praeger, 1967, 288 pp., 251 illustrations.

An introduction which divides Southeast Asia into six regions and covers each (including Java and Bali) briefly. Angkor receives the most comprehensive examination, with approximately equal treatment of Hindu and Buddhist influences. Excellent plates some in color.

5.5.2 Burma

(1) LUCE, GORDON H. Old Burma-Early Pagan. See 1.4.2(12).

An extensive three-volume work detailing the founding of the Burmese city Pagan, its rise to architectural and political glory, and its ultimate weakening as a political center. Volume 1 consists of three sections: a history based on original inscriptions and other records; iconography, which seeks to relate the arts of early Pagan to those of Buddhist India; and architecture, in which chief buildings of specific regions are described and discussed extensively. Volume 2 contains a catalogue of the plates, a sixteen-page bibliography, index of proper and place names, index of Pagan sites, subject and character index of Chinese words, botanical index, old Burma calendar, names, titles, and regnal dates of the kings of Pagan, and maps. Volume 3 contains plates of architecture, sculpture, and painting. Ground plans are included. An important study of Pagan in the eleventh and twelfth centuries.

(2) WALES, HORACE GEOFFREY QUARITCH. Early Burma-Old Siam. London: B. Quaritch, 1973, 188 pp., 39 black and white plates.

A review of the cultural history of Burma and Thailand from antiquity through the Middle Ages. The author comments on the political history of the area and the impact of the Singhalese and the Indian cultures. Each country is treated separately and comparisons are confined to a brief conclusion. A general, simple introduction.

5.5.3 Thailand

(1) BOWIE, THEODORE, ed. The Arts of Thailand. Bloomington: Indiana University Press, 1960, 219 pp., including 163 black and white illustrations.

A series of essays by noted scholars of Thai art, as well as a catalogue of an exhibition held in the U.S. between 1960 and 1962. Approximately sixty pages of text deal primarily with Buddhist artistic expression. Covers the sixth to the twentieth centuries with chapters on Dvaravati, Khmer period (school of Lopburi), Sukhodaya, Northern Siam, U Tong, Ayudhya, Tonpuri, Bangkok. These treat architecture and sculpture and are well written. A separate seven-page essay on Thai painting. Plates are often small, but distinct and well arranged. A good introduction.

(2) BOWIE, THEODORE, M. C. SUBHADRIS DISKUL, and A. B. GRISWOLD. The Sculpture of Thailand. New York: The Asia Society, 1972, 137 pp., including 80 black and white illustrations.

This book was prepared for an exhibition of Thai sculpture in the U.S. Except for a ten-page introductory essay on the Buddha image, the book consists of eighty chronologically arranged plates and often lengthy commentaries. Many figures illustrate the Buddha or bodhisattvas, as well as Hindu and popular deities. An introductory level treatment with tasteful photos.

(3) BRUCE, HELEN. Nine Temples of Bangkok. Bangkok: Progress Book Store, 1960, 137 pp., including 54 black and white plates.

Approximately half of the eighty pages of text provides a basic introduction to the history of Buddhism in Thailand. Discussion of the temples is purely descriptive, with some historical information included, but negligible artistic analysis. Plates effectively convey the artistic splendor of the temples. A glossary is provided. Well written on an introductory popular level.

(4) CHAND, EMCEE and KHIEN YIMSIRI. Thai Monumental Bronzes. Bangkok: printed privately by the authors, 1956, 96 pp., 99 black and white plates.

An interesting study dealing exclusively with Buddhist works which suggests that the Sri Vijaya art of Borobodur was closely related to the early art of Northern Siam. Separate sections deal with the Indian prototypes, pre-Thai images, three Thai schools, iconographical features, early Chieng San (soft type), Sukothai High Classic, Walkers and Sleepers, later Chieng San (stiff type), Ayudhya and U-Thong, and monumental bronzes. Plates support the text well.

(5) COEDES, GEORGES. Les Collections archéologiques du Musée National de Bangkok. Ars Asiatica, No. 12. Paris and Bruxelles: G. Van Oest, 1928, 36 pp., 40 black and white plates.

An attempt to present a balanced sample of the works contained in the archaeological section of the Bangkok Museum, representing diverse Siamese archaeological periods from the pre-Khmer (fifth century A.D.) era through the "Siamese" era beginning in the thirteenth century. An attempt is made to stress less well-known works of art of which the museum is the sole possessor: pre-Khmer statues, sculptures from the Malaysian Peninsula and such Buddhist images as form a transition between Khmer and modern Siamese styles. Each plate is accompanied by a lengthy explanation. Also included are essays on Siamese archaeology, as illustrated by the collection and the history of the museum itself. An unusual and important work.

(6) DOEHRING, KARL. Buddhistische Tempelangen in Siam. Bangkok: Asia Publishing House, 1920, 3 vols. Vol. 1, 348 pp., vol. 2, 90 plates with descriptions; vol. 3, 90 plates with descriptions.

An important early study, now somewhat superseded. The focus of the work is primarily on temples in the Bangkok area. The volumes examine architecture, sculpture, ornamentation and overall temple sites. A valuable analysis for the advanced student.

(7) GRISWOLD, A. B. Dated Buddha Images of Northern Siam. Artibus Asiae Supplementum, No. 16. Ascona: Artibus Asiae, 1957, 79 pp., 57 black and white plates.

Provides a general discussion of the Buddha image, its history in Siam, and problems arising out of the attempt to date certain figures. The appendix includes sketches and brief discussion of various types of hand and foot patterns, curls, ear lobes, robe and cuff designs relevant to dating. The rest is a catalogue of dated images accompanied by descriptions of varying lengths and black and white photographs. Specialized but not overly technical.

(8) LE MAY, REGINALD. A Concise History of Buddhist Art in Siam. See 10.5(5).
Le May outlines the development of Buddhist art in Siam over fifteen centuries and evaluates the impact of Indian, Chinese, and indigenous factors. He divides his material chronologically with chapters on the Dvaravati period, the Kingdom of Sri Vijaya, Funan, the Khmer period, Chiengsen school, the rise of Tai, Suk'otai, and schools of U'T'ong, Lopburi and Ayudhya. Includes over 200 small, often indistinct photos, and an excellent bibliography.

(9) SALMONY, ALFRED. Sculpture in Siam. London: Ernest Benn, 1925, 52 pp., 70 plates.

Twelve brief chapters survey the history of immigrations in Siam, as well as chronology and form and material of Siamese sculpture. The author also describes specific sculptures found in Llgor, Prapatom, Sawankolok, Lopburi, Pitsanulok, Sukothai, Ayuthia. The book is quite short but helpful on an intermediate level.

(10) WALES, H. G. QUARITCH. Dvaravati: The Earliest Kingdom in Siam. See 1.5.2(25).

The author attempts to incorporate new archaeological evidence in studying this earliest kingdom in the time period from the sixth to the eleventh centuries A.D., approaching the question of the differentiation of the cultures of Indianized Southeast Asia. Buddhist art and architecture, sculpture, etc. are heavily relied on. The clear photographs supplement the text effectively, including some unusual items. A good, non-technical introduction to this period.

(11) WARREN, WILLIAM. The House on the Klong. New York: Walker/Weatherhill, 1969, 87 pp., including 86 color and black and white plates.

A collection of excellent plates of the artwork in the house of James Thompson of Bangkok. The collection includes sculpture, ceramics, and painting, much of it Buddhist, against a background of a tastefully decorated house and gardens.

(12) WRAY, ELIZABETH, CLARE ROSENFIELD and DOROTHY BAILEY. Ten Lives of the Buddha: Siamese Temple Paintings and Jataka Tales. New York: Weatherhill, 1972, 154 pp., 32 color plates, 5 black and white figures, 2 maps.

Consists of a retelling of ten of the most important and frequently heard Thai jataka-tales accompanied by color photographs of the wall-paintings which illustrate them. Although the text is on an introductory level, many of the photographs of these paintings have never been published before, so the work is meaningful to the specialist as well. See also 8.1.1(16).

5.5.4 Cambodia

(1) AUDRIC, JOHN. Angkor and the Khmer Empire. London: Robert Hale, 1972, 207 pp., 23 black and white plates.

An interesting study of Khmer political history with discussion of Angkor art and architecture in this context. Illustrations include many helpful diagrams of temple sites and structures. A popular but helpful introduction to the subject.

(2) BOISSELIER, JEAN. La Statuaire khmère et son évolution. Saigon: Ecole française d'Extrême-Orient, 1955. 2 vols. Vol. 1, 322 pp. Vol. 2, 12 pp., and 114 plates.

(Publications de l'Ecole française d'Extrême-Orient, No. 37.)

Deals with the evolution of Khmer sculpture in such terms as costume (masculine, feminine, and Buddhist), coiffures, anatomy, materials, etc. Buddhist statues dealt with passim in specific sections (11 pages on Buddhist costume). Part 2 gives the specific characteristics of the diverse styles and proposes a chronology. Black and white photographs include many examples of Buddhist statuary. An important work, highly specialized. Advanced.

(3) COEDES, GEORGES. Angkor. 2nd edition, translated and edited by Emily Floyd Gardiner. Hong Kong: Oxford University Press, 1963, 116 pp., including 24 black and white plates.

Emphasizes religious and historical setting of Angkor. An interesting fifteen-page chapter on architectural symbolism. Little stylistic analysis. Written somewhat like a guidebook.

(4) GITEAU, MADELEINE. Le Bornage rituel des temples bouddhiques au Cambodge. See 7.2.6(2).

An important study on a rite of great significance in Cambodian Buddhism, yet rarely dealt with up to the present. Though not primarily concerned with art, illustrates many photographs of the actual boundary-stones, sketches of temple plans, and drawings of Buddhist statues and artistic motives. Fifty-two pages devoted to the rites, 47 pages to the texts therein employed, and 48 pages discussing "Evolution artistique de la feuille de sima." Specialized but not overly technical.

(5) _____. Khmer Sculpture and the Angkor Civilization. Translated by Diana Imber. New York: Harry Abrams, 1965, 301 pp., including 24 color, 100 black and white plates, and 135 figures.

Divided into sections of introductory background material, then focuses on stone, bronze, and wood sculpture. The influences on Buddhism and Hinduism are seen in their interrelationship, but only a few short chapters on specifically Buddhist sculptural forms are included. Also, maps, ground plans of Angkor, and a comparative chronology of all Asia. Plates are good. Covers pre- and post-Angkor Wat in an introductory style.

(6) GROSLIER, BERNARD and JACQUES ARTHAUD. Angkor: Art and Civilization. Translated by Ernshaw Smith. 2nd rev. ed. New York: Praeger, 1966, 236 pp., including 6 color and 115 black and white illustrations.

Approximately 70 pages of text treat background and history of the development and downfall of Angkor. Artistic analysis is not highly technical, but descriptive, with few explicit references to Buddhism. Appendix includes summary of major styles. Chronological table from second to thirteenth century. Good plates and illustrations of ground plans. No index.

(7) GROSLIER, GEORGE, ed. Arts et archéologie khmers. Vol. 1, parts 1-4. Vol. 2, parts 1-3. Paris: Ancienne Maison Challamel, 1921-1926. Vol. 1 (1921-1923): 486 pp., 32 plates. Vol. 2 (1924-1926): 348 pp., 35 plates.

Both volumes consist of a series of essays about aspects of Khmer and Cambodian art by experts of the time. Each volume has a table of contents, but no subject index, so topics of relevance to Buddhism are difficult to locate. Volume 1 pays scant attention to Buddhism. However, the many black and white plates of temples, craftwork, etc., include two statues of Buddhas with short descriptions. Gives a good general, if non-specific background. Volume 2 is much more relevant to Buddhism with a long section on "Les Empreintes du 'Pied de Buddha' d'Angkor Wat" and a shorter "Essai sur le Buddha Khmer" accompanied by many helpful black and white plates. An extremely important work, highly specialized and advanced.

(8) LEE, SHERMAN E. Ancient Cambodian Sculpture. New York: The Asia Society, 1969, 115 pp., including 81 color and black and white illustrations.

Fifteen pages of text accompany the pictures of an exhibition of Cambodian sculpture. A thoughtful introduction to the subject. Surveys the history of Cambodia from the seventh to the thirteenth century. Focuses on Angkor and treats both Hindu and Buddhist influences. Includes maps and chronological tables. Extensive description of plates, 10 of which are in color.

(9) MARCHAL, HENRI. Guide to Angkor. Saigon: Société des Editions d'Extrême Asie, 1930, 237 pp., 16 plates.

Designed primarily as a guide to the various monuments of Angkor, but gives an excellent physical description with detailed enough explanation to be meaningful even to those who cannot visit the site. Dated, but quaintly so.

(10) _____. Les Temples d'Angkor. 3rd ed. Paris: Albert Guillot, 1955, 181 pp., extensively illustrated.

An exciting introduction by an important author. Lack of table of contents and index, however, impedes search for topics of specifically Buddhist nature. Sections include a legendary account of the construction of the temple, discussion of monumental and artistic discoveries of Cambodia, scientific study of Cambodia's past, chronological evolution of the Khmer style, decor and ornamentation, sculpture en ronde bosse. Hindu art motifs predominate. A very successful introduction, both visually and textually.

5.5.4

(11) MYRDAL, JAN and GUN KESSLE. Angkor: An Essay on Art and Imperialism. Translated by Paul Britten Austin. New York: Pantheon, 1970, 167 pp., extensively illustrated.

Approximately 50 pages of text describe the history of Angkor. Written in an unusual style in support of the Vietnamese Liberation Front. Plates are not exceptional, but do depict some unusual details.

(12) PARMENTIER, HENRI. L'Art Khmer classique: monuments du quadrant nord-est. Paris: Les Editions d'Art et d'Histoire, 1939. 2 vols. Vol. 1, 364 pp., 72 plates, 49 figures. Vol. 2, 10 pp., 73 plates. (Publications de l'Ecole française d'Extrême-Orient, No. 29 bis.)

An impressive work which examines in detail the pre-Angkorian architectural and sculptural remains primarily from Northeast Cambodia. Extensive descriptions of Ko Kher, Wat Phu, Prasat Khna Sen Kev and the temple of Prah Vihar, in addition to other sites which, for the most part, preceded the arrival of Buddhism. Volume 2 contains sketches of architectural and sculptural features and groundplans. Intermediate to advanced.

(13) STERN, PHILIPPE. Les Monuments Khmers du style du Bayon et Jayavarman VII. Paris: Presses Universitaires de France, 1965, 267 pp., 15 plans, 211 figures. (Publications du Musée Guimet, Recherches et Documents d'Art et d'Archéologie, No. 9.)

Highly specialized exhaustive treatment of the subject. Book is structured around evolution of motives, study by monuments, and a chronological exposition of the obtained results. Jayavarman VII was a Buddhist, so references to Buddhism are scattered throughout. Unfortunately, there is no subject index, but one index of monuments and one of motives. A six-page bibliography of French sources. Good black and white plates include architectural plans of temple ensembles. Indispensable for advanced work in this area.

5.5.5 Indochina: Laos, Champa, Vietnam

(1) BEZACIER, LOUIS. L'Art vietnamien. Paris: Editions de l'Union française, 1955, 236 pp., 33 figures, 29 plates.

Re-edition of Essais sur l'art annamite, published in September 1944 in Hanoi. A rather extensive treatment of Buddhist topics. Includes seventeen pages on religious architecture, twelve pages on the Buddhist pagoda at "Ninh-phuc" at But-thap, sixteen pages on the ancient pagoda "Van-Phuc" at Phat trich, twenty-four pages on the pantheon of the Buddhist pagodas at Tonkin, and twenty pages delineating the major epochs in Vietnamese art history. Includes an index of Vietnamese names of Buddhist divinities and an index of monuments, as well as a three-page bibliography of French publications on Vietnam.

An in-depth and unique study, unparalleled in English. For the intermediate or advanced student.

(2) BOISSELIER, JEAN. La Statuaire du Champa. See 1.8.2(1).

A comprehensive account of the sculpture of Champa from ancient times through the fifteenth century. Very little is explicitly devoted to Buddhist arts. The main specific reference is the brief treatment of the Buddhist sculpture of Dong-Duxong. A commendable index offers other references. Plates are small, maps helpful.

(3) GROSLIER, BERNARD PHILIPPE. The Art of Indochina. Translated by George Lawrence. Art of the World Series. New York: Crown, 1962, 261 pp., including 63 color plates and 39 sketched figures.

Discusses the synthesis of native Chinese and Indian artistic styles from pre-history to the European conquest. A vast subject, but competently covered with much political-cultural history as well. Emphasizes architectural monuments and sculptures. Contains good plates, maps, and chronological tables. An interesting introduction with a good deal on Buddhist art.

(4) PARMENTIER, HENRI. L'Art du Laos. Publications de l'Ecole française d'Extrême-Orient, No. 35. Paris: Imprimerie nationale, 1954, 2 vols. Vol. 1, 364 pp., text; vol. 2, 51 maps and sketches, 145 photographs.

A definitive work by an important scholar. Extensive, technical discussion of pagoda and wat architecture, with Volume 2 supplying plans and sketches. Twenty pages are devoted to the Buddha image, with many illustrations of Buddhist sculpture in Volume 2. Indispensable to the study of Laotian sculpture and architecture.

(5) STERN, PHILIPPE. L'Art du Champa (Ancien Annam) et son évolution. Publication du Musée Guimet, Etudes et Documents d'Art et d'Archéologie, No. 3. Paris: Adrien Maisonneuve, 1942, 122 pp., 164 plates.

Intensive, rather technical study of the development of and influences (Indian, Khmer) upon ancient Annamese sculpture and architecture. Contains no special reference to Buddhism and no index. Intermediate-advanced level.

5.5.6 Indonesia

(1) DE KLEEN, TYRA. Mudras: The Ritual Hand-poses of the Buddha Priests and the Shiva Priests of Bali. Introduced by A. J. D. Campbell. New foreword by Omar V. Garrison. New Hyde Park, N.Y.: University Books, 1970, 42 pp., 62 pp. illustrations. (Originally published New York: E. P. Dutton, 1924.)

Well-written introduction to a rarely treated specialized topic. Ten pages of text on Buddhist priests consist of the author's observations from a visit to Bali in 1920. A very simple explanation of mudras and mantras. Sketches are detailed and informative in addition to being helpfully described.

(2) FONTEIN, JAN. *The Pilgrimage of Sudhana: A Study of the Gandavyuha Illustrations in China, Japan, and Java.* See 5.8(4).

(3) FONTEIN, JAN, R. SOEKMONO, and SATYAWATI SULEIMAN. *Ancient Indonesian Art of the Central and Eastern Javanese Periods.* New York: The Asia Society, 1971, 160 pp., including 111 black and white illustrations.

Basically an exhibition catalogue of Indonesian sculpture. A brief introductory text surveys the impact of Indian culture on Javanese architecture and sculpture in the Central Javanese period beginning in the eighth century and the Eastern Javanese period beginning in the tenth century and divided into three dynastic eras. Another essay describes the basic characteristics of the differences between the tjandi architecture of Central Java, and the more slender tall architecture of Eastern Java. References to Buddhist art are scattered throughout, with little substantive discussion of it.

(4) GANGOLY, O. C. *The Art of Java.* Second revised edition. Calcutta: A. N. Gangoly, 1967, 26 pp., 51 black and white plates, 11 figures.

The book focuses on the dominance of Indian art forms in Java. Pages 3-12 provide the bulk of the material on Buddhist art in Java (post fifth century). A dense, intermediate level text, with concentration on history rather than extensive analysis of artistic styles, and emphasis on architecture and sculpture. Contains no index. Plates and figures are mediocre. Includes a five-page bibliography.

(5) HOLT, CLAIRE. *Art in Indonesia.* Ithaca, N.Y.: Cornell University Press, 1967, 355 pp., 200 illustrations.

A standard survey of the art of Indonesia, with an historical section including Indian and Buddhist influences (Chapter 2), and descriptive sections focusing on dance (Chapter 4), Wayang puppets (Chapter 5), and dance/drama (Chapter 6) of especially Java and Bali. See also Appendix 3 for translations of eight Wayang plays, and the rather complete bibliography on pages 323-338.

(6) KEMPERS, A. J. BERNET. *Ancient Indonesian Art.* Cambridge, Mass.: Harvard University Press, 1959, 124 pp., 353 black and white plates.

The author considers his book a pictorial archive. The 353 plates are accompanied by eighty pages of description. A brief introduction summarizes the emergence and development of ancient Indonesian art, the Hindu-Indonesian contacts, and finally the arrival of Islam after the thirteenth century. An introductory text, good for browsing. Some of the plate descriptions are quite comprehensive. Includes a five-page bibliography.

(7) KROM, N. J., ed. *The Life of the Buddha on the Stupa of Barabudur According to the Lalitavistara Text.* See 8.1.2.4(14).

A thorough and well-organized examination of the 120 scenes from the life of the Buddha carved in relief on the base of the stupa of Barabudur. Photographs and descriptions of scenes are juxtaposed with appropriate verses from the Lalitavistara text, which was used by the original sculptor. Basically a description, lacking overall analysis. Contains no table of contents, index, or bibliography.

(8) MUS, PAUL. *Barabudur: Esquisse d'une histoire du Bouddhisme fondée sur la critique archéologique des textes.* See 2.5.2(8).

A work of monumental importance, which is of value for many sections of this bibliography and not simply for the study of one Indonesian stupa. There are three main sections. A 300-page foreword deals with the methods, results, and implications of his work on Barabudur for the study of Buddhism as a whole, stressing, in particular, the Indian sources. The main part of the two volumes is sub-titled "Les Origines du stupa et la transmigration, Essai d'archéologie religieuse comparée" and is subdivided into six sections. These are: architectural interpretations, religious interpretations, the symbolism of Barabudur, the problem of the five directions, the cosmic value of the stupa, and the beginnings of Mahayana Buddhology. Mus also includes a one hundred page appendix on the Seven Steps of the Buddha and the Doctrine of the Pure Lands. While advanced in nature, this book is of seminal value to Buddhist studies in general, and Buddhist art in particular.

(9) SIVARAMAMURTI, CALEMBUS. *Le Stupa du Barabudur.* Publication du Musée Guimet, Recherches et documents d'art et d'archéologie, No. 8. Paris: Presses Universitaires de France, 1961, 78 pp., 42 black and white plates.

Briefly but systematically examines the basic features of Barabudur: the base, identity of sculptures, royal emblems, rites and costumes, and other motives. Essentially concerned with the Indian, rather than Javanese, style of the monuments. Little background is included, but the work is reflective and well organized. Introductory level.

(10) WAGNER, FRITZ. *Indonesia: The Art of an Island Group.* Translated by Ann E. Keep. Art of the World Series. New York: Crown, 1959, 257 pp., including 60 color plates, 35 figures and maps.

Covers Indonesian art from Neolithic to modern times, with little on Buddhist impact.

The index contains a few references. Chapter 9 explains the Buddhist and Hindu influence in simple, introductory fashion. Focuses on several tjandis and Barabudur. Contains a few plates on Buddhist art, and a chronological table. Strictly introductory.

5.6 TIBET

(1) BERNARD, THEOS. *Land of a Thousand Buddhas*. London: Rider and Company, 1950, 320 pp., 65 illustrations. See also 10.1.3(1).

Essentially an account of the author's experiences in Tibet, including his initiation as a Buddhist "White Lama." Although not a scholarly study of Buddhist art, the text contains many references to the function, not only of Buddhism, but of Buddhist art in the lives of the people. Black and white photographs contain several unusual examples of Buddhist temples and art. An intriguing, if non-scholarly introduction.

(2) BEYER, STEPHAN. *The Cult of Tara: Magic and Ritual in Tibet*. See 7.1.1(2).

Impressive, sophisticated account of Tibetan religious ritual. Emphasizes unique complementary relation of ritual and magic in Tibetan religious practice. Includes hymns, mantras and descriptions of ritual, but also a discussion of general structure of ritual. Focuses on rituals involved in worship of Tara. Extremely well-indexed, with sixteen pages of bibliography. Plates depict contemporary ritual scenes. A specialized topic, written on an advanced level, but with little direct discussion of art work.

(3) BRYNER, EDNA. *Thirteen Tibetan Tankas*. See 8.1.1(2).

Presents an identification of the scenes on thirteen Tibetan tankas with the stories of Arya Sura's *Jatakamala* ("Garland of Birth Stories") and a study of the stories on those tankas, rich in historical information. Contains a twenty-four-page general discussion of Tibetan art and teaching, forty-four pages detailing the stories of the scenes on the tankas, ten pages discussing two Tibetan scriptures: the Kanjur and the Tanjur. The remaining fifty-three pages discuss the famous "Feeding the Tigress" jataka and three jatakas from the Kanjur. No index or bibliography is included. All levels will find something of meaning here.

(4) CHAPMAN, F. SPENCER. *Lhasa: The Holy City*. London: Chatto and Windus, 1938, 342 pp., 10 color and approx. 120 black and white plates.

Written by an explorer who accompanied a British expedition to Lhasa in 1937, this resembles a diary of travels and describes all facets of Tibetan life. Includes a ten-page chapter on Potala and a twenty-page chapter on monasteries. Written for popular consumption, with no scholarly pretension. Plates are vivid.

(5) EKVALL, ROBERT B. *Religious Observances in Tibet: Patterns and Functions*. See 7.1.1(5).

A study of daily practices and attitudes in Tibetan religion. Includes twenty- to fifty-page chapters on the Tibetan's subjective response, faith, verbalized religion, offerings, salutations, circumambulation, divination and religious work, with minimal treatment of Tibetan art forms, however. See index. Includes a good bibliography. Advanced level.

(6) GORDON, ANTOINETTE. *The Iconography of Tibetan Lamaism*. Second revised edition. Rutland, Vt.: Charles E. Tuttle, 1959, 131 pp., approx. 200 black and white illustrations.

The book consists primarily of general illustrations with detailed commentaries organized into chapters on sacred images (Buddhas, bodhisattvas, divinities, guardians) and also on topics such as ritual objects, mudras, thangkas. Emphasis is on thorough treatment of sacred images. Includes an eight-page bibliography. A comprehensive, introductory survey.

(7) _____. *Tibetan Religious Art*. Second edition. New York: Paragon Books, 1963, 104 pp., including approx. 95 black and white illustrations. (Originally published New York: Columbia University Press, 1952.)

A simple introductory book, with a brief account of Buddhism and Lamaism followed by brief general discussion of sacred pantheon. The bulk of the book is thirty-five pages on temple paintings and twenty-two pages on sculpted images. Shorter chapters are on minor arts. Plates are extensive, particularly for the minor arts, but small. Those for paintings are unexceptional in quality.

(8) GRISWOLD, ALEXANDER, CHEWON KIM, and PETER H. POTT. *The Art of Burma, Korea, Tibet*. See 5.1.4(6).

(9) HOFFMAN, HELMUT. *Symbolik der Tibetischen Religionen und das Schamanismus*. Stuttgart: Anton Hiersman, 1967, 173 pp.

A valuable analysis of the symbolism of Lamaism, Bon religion and Shamanism. Important for the understanding of the ways in which these traditions influenced each other iconographically and in ritualistic practice. Intermediate level.

(10) HUMMEL, SIEGBERT. *Die Lamaistische Kunst in der Umwelt von Tibet*. Leipzig: Otto Harrassowitz, 1955, 149 pp., 110 black and white illustrations, 1 map.

A careful study of the various forms of Buddhist art inspired by the Tibetan tradition as these appeared in China, Mongolia, the Soviet Union, Southeast Asia, and the Himalayan kingdoms of Bhutan, Sikkim, and Nepal. Important for the study of how indigenous folk art influenced and coexisted alongside Buddhist art. Advanced level.

(11) _____. *Geschichte der Tibetischen Kunst*. Leipzig: Otto Harrassowitz, 1953, 123 pp., 124 black and white illustrations.

An excellent study of the history of Tibetan art. Considers in detail the influences upon this art of various countries. The intermingling of folk art, non-Buddhist Indian art, and Buddhist art is part of the work's value. Advanced level.

(12) JISL, LUMIR. *Tibetan Art*. Translated by Ilse Gottheiner. London: Spring Books, 1957, 40 pp., 112 color and black and white plates.

A very brief and simple book which examines the relation of Tibetan art and religion. One hundred twelve marvellous large black and white and color photos of architecture, sculpture, painting, pottery, ritual objects, masks, pageantry, people, landscapes. Strictly introductory.

(13) LALOU, MARCELLE. *Iconographie des étoffes peintes (pata) dans le Manjusrimulakalpa*. See 3.4.2(10).

A translation and discussion of parts of the *Manjusrimulakalpa* (described by the author as the "Buddhist encyclopedia of the Mahayana school") in which the making of pata is described in minute detail. Pata are quadrangular pieces of fringed cotton on which are painted images of Buddhist saints subsequently disposed in a hierarchical order and regarded as magical. After a helpful introduction, the author presents translations of the rites for creating various kinds of pata (superior, middle, small, simplified) and, in several appendices, actual rules for painting, order, color, and location. Plates are drawings showing location of figures. Tibetan text is supplied in romanized letters. Limited and specialized, but interesting. Advanced.

(14) NEBESKY-WOJKOWITZ, RENE DE. *Oracles and Demons of Tibet: The Cult and Iconography of the Tibetan Protective Deities*. See 4.1.5(3).

An extremely significant work, divided essentially into two parts: the iconography of the protective deities (340 pp.) and the cult of the protective deities (213 pp.). The first part discusses the respective iconographies of specific groups, types and individual deities. Part 2 deals with sacrificial objects and offerings, thread-crosses and thread-cross ceremonies, worship of dharmapalas, Tibetan oracles, the State Oracle, methods of divination, Tibetan weathermakers, destructive magic, protection against evil, and shamanism. A highly specialized, advanced text.

(15) PAL, PRATAPADITYA. *The Art of Tibet*. New York: The Asia Society, 1969, 163 pp., including 119 illustrations, 16 text figures.

Forty-six pages of text provide simple coverage of Tibetan history and art. There are brief sections on religion, pantheon, artist and patron, materials and techniques, sculpture, painting, and an essay by Eleanor Olson on meditations and rituals. Plates are sharp and have lengthy descriptions. There are several color plates. An easy introduction.

(16) PAL, PRATAPADITYA and HSIEN-CH'I TSENG. *Lamaist Art, The Aesthetics of Harmony*. Boston: Museum of Fine Arts, 1969, 56 pp., 76 black and white illustrations.

Contains a twenty-nine-page introduction on the history of Lamaism, Lamaist imagery, and the artistic milieu. General, but readable and stimulating. Plates of painting, sculpture, and ritual objects are sharp, and there are extended descriptions of the plates. Recommended for introductory level.

(17) PALLIS, MARCO. *Peaks and Lamas*. Fourth edition. London: Cassel and Co., 1946, approx. 100 illustrations, 2 maps.

Essentially the story of the author's two Himalayan journeys. With no pretensions of being a scholarly treatment, the book does contain a twenty-three-page section on "the symbolism of Tantra," sixteen pages describing traditional painting lessons in which the student learns to paint the Buddha, and forty pages devoted exclusively to Tibetan art, its relation to doctrine, present state, and future dangers. An important first-hand account with much valuable information. Introductory and intermediate levels.

(18) SCHLAGINTWEIT, EMIL. *Buddhism in Tibet*. London: Susil Gupta, 1968, 403 pp., approx. 50 pp. of black and white hand sketches. (Originally published London: Trubner, 1863.)

An account of Tibetan Buddhism as it appeared to Europeans of the mid-nineteenth century. Includes a history of all Buddhism and Tibet, and a description of priesthood and worship practices. Pages 177-216 describe religious monuments and representations of the deities. There are no photographs, some sketches of sacred texts. Appendices include table with transliteration of Tibetan alphabet and forty-page list of books and journals of Buddhism. Introductory level, interesting for browsing.

(19) SCHMID, TONI. *The Eighty-Five Siddhas*. See 8.5(3).

An advanced book which treats the specialized subject of the eighty-five siddhas (saints, perfected ones) worshipped and invoked by the Vajrayanists of Tibet. Each siddha is listed along with an inscription in one of thirteen scrolls in conjunction with a thanka. This book contains a translation of each inscription and plate of each thanka. Included are three excursii, being translations of other scrolls found in the region. Helpful indices of personal names.

(20) TUCCI, GIUSEPPE. *Gyantse ed i suoi Monasteri (Gyantse and Its Monasteries)*. Rome: Reale Accademia D'Italia, 1941. Vol. 4 of *Indo-Tibetica*, published in 3 separately-bound parts. Part 1, 302 pp.; part 2, 330 pp.; part 3, 397 figures.

This work is the fourth volume of Tucci's monumental work on the monasteries of Tibet, concentrating on those of central Tibet, especially in or near Gyantse with particular emphasis on the temples of Kumbum. The fourth volume of a larger work, it is published in three separately bound parts which are interrelated and cross-referenced. Part 1, "General Description of the Stupas," is a history and description of the major temples of the Man region of central Tibet, including specifically those of Samuda, Salu, Iwang, Shonang, Gyantse, and Kumbum. Part 2 gives the original Tibetan texts and their translation into Italian. Where there have been "errors" in the original text, Tucci reproduces them, giving his "corrections" along with philological and historical explanations as to why the errors occurred. Part 3 consists solely of maps and photographs, poorly clued into the text.

Part 1 is much more than a description of the temples studied. The first four chapters are an analysis of the temples of Kumbum. An almost unique characteristic of this temple is that the paintings and sculpture are signed by the individual artists. From the Buddhist point of view, Tucci considers this practice a "sin" because signing a work of art "inflates" the ego rather than "deflating" it. Tucci is particularly interested in the role of a mandala and its relation to an art form. The whole temple of Kumbum is a mandala of a tantric cycle based on the specific works of Bu ston, and the smaller chapels are "sub-mandalas" thereof. Tucci produces an impressive synthesis of religious analysis and art criticism which draws on the tradition of Italian art criticism. However, he seems to have been able to break out of some of its more ossified features. A most impressive work, at an advanced level.

(21) _____. *Shrines of a Thousand Buddhas*. See 10.7(5).

Diary of Tucci's travels through Western Tibet, observing and studying many monasteries, texts, and works of art previously unknown. Not a scholarly account, but provides descriptions of all aspects of Tibetan life and emphasizes their religion with its art work. Plates are bleak but interesting, revealing more about Tibetan life than art. A good introductory work for one who wants to get a feel of the country before studying its art work.

(22) _____. *Tibet: Land of Snows*. See 1.14.1(15).

Methodically surveys Tibetan history, politics, and culture, with one chapter on art. Among the best brief treatments of the influences and general characteristics of all Tibetan art. Approximately one-third of the plates are in color. All are well done. For the student with some previous knowledge of Tibetan culture.

(23) WADDELL, L. A. *The Buddhism of Tibet of Lamaism*. London: W. H. Allen, 1895, 598 pp., including approx. 200 black and white plates and figures.

Treats Tibetan Buddhism in full. Includes sixty-five pages on buildings, ninety-five pages on mythology and gods, providing most material on Buddhist art. Rather antiquated, but full of detailed information. Plates and figures are not good. Includes a good chronological table from the time of the Buddha to the nineteenth century, and an index. Intermediate level.

5.7 CENTRAL ASIA

(1) BUSSAGLI, MARIO. *Painting of Central Asia*. Geneva: Skira, 1963, 136 pp., including approx. 75 color plates and 6 black and white illustrations.

Focuses on the triangular area between Gandhara, the Aral Sea and Sinkiang. This area of the silk road was influenced by many styles of art. The Buddhist impact is never singled out for substantive discussion, though it is frequently referred to. Chapters are included on Miran, Khotan, Turfan, Pjandzikent, and Sogdiana. Almost exclusively concerned with wall-paintings. Includes excellent plates. A valuable introduction.

(2) RICE, TAMARA TALBOT. *Ancient Arts of Central Asia*. Praeger World of Art Series. New York: Praeger, 1965, 288 pp., 252 illustrations, including maps.

Covers 4000 years of Central Asian art. Includes a chapter on Eastern Turkestan in the Roman and Buddhist periods, and scattered references to Buddhist art in a chapter on Bactria and Northwest India as well. Brief discussion of impact of trade and politics on various schools of art, with copious but unexceptional pictures and time table. Introductory level.

(3) ROWLAND, BENJAMIN. *The Art of Central Asia*. Art of the World Series. New York: Crown, 1970, 232 pp., including 56 color plates, 35 black and white photographs, 80 figures, map.

Covers considerable material quickly but coherently. Emphasis is on painting and sculpture, with short chapters on Gandhara and Miran. Thirty pages on Western Turkestan (Bactria), forty pages on Afghanistan, eighty pages on Serindia, and a short chapter on the Tun-huang caves. Includes a comparative chronological table. Plates and figures are helpful and well done. Of use both to introductory and intermediate level students.

(4) _____. *The Wall Paintings of India, Central Asia, and Ceylon*. See 5.1.4(12).

East Asia: China, Korea, Japan

(5) SIREN, OSVALD. "Central Asian Influences in Chinese Painting of T'ang." See 5.9.3(10).

(6) SOPER, ALEXANDER. "Northern Wei and Northern Liang in Kansu." See 5.9.4(13).

(7) STEIN, AUREL. Ancient Khotan: Detailed Report of the Archaeological Explorations in Chinese Turkestan. Oxford: Clarendon Press, 1907, 2 vols. Vol. 1, 621 pp., 72 illustrations; vol. 2, 119 plates, 1 map.

5.8 EAST ASIA: CHINA, KOREA, JAPAN

(1) BUHOT, JEAN. Chinese and Japanese Art: With Sections on Korea and Vietnam. Translated by Remy Inglis Hall. Edited by Charles McCurdy. New York: Praeger, 1967, 428 pp., 63 drawings, 46 black and white illustrations.

Buddhism dealt with passim and in short, specialized sections devoted to such topics as T'ang Buddhist sculpture, T'ang Buddhist architecture, Sung and Yuan Buddhist sculpture, jatakas, etc. Twenty-three pages are devoted exclusively to Buddhist art in Central Asia. The pages dealing with Korean art lightly touch on Buddhist buildings and sculpture. There is no separate section for Viet Nam. A standard general introduction to East Asian art, touching on Buddhism briefly and superficially. A good bibliography is divided according to topics. A valuable chronological table is appended, outlining and juxtaposing important historical stages and events in the art of these areas.

(2) Chinese, Korean, and Japanese Sculpture in the Avery Brundage Collection, Asian Art Museum of San Francisco. Edited by Réne-Yvon Lefébre d'Argence and Diana Turner, with contributions by the staff of the Asian Art Museum of San Francisco and Alexander C. Soper. San Francisco: Asian Art Museum of San Francisco, 1974, 459 pp., 288 plates.

One of the major collections of Asian art in the West, including substantial holdings in Buddhist art. Amongst the major pieces in the collection is the earliest known dated Buddha image produced in China. Pieces are well illustrated, often with many views. The documentation includes inscriptions and translations whenever possible. The collection comprises a broad chronological scope, a wide variety of iconographic types, and a broad variety of media. Includes extensive documentation, bibliography, glossary of terms. Inscriptions are fully recorded in Chinese and Japanese.

(3) EDMUNDS, WILL H. Pointers and Clues to the Subjects of Chinese and Japanese Art. London: Sampson Low, Marston, and Co., 1934, 725 pp., 6 pp. drawings.

A general detailed glossary includes sixty pages on Buddhist subjects with Sanskrit, Chinese, and Japanese equivalents for terms as well as rather extensive definitions. Does not provide Chinese characters. The sections on Chinese and Japanese subjects also include many Buddhist figures. Motifs, themes, and scenes indicative of certain artists and subjects are also detailed. Chronological tables are given for emperors of both Chinese and Japanese dynasties. Helpful especially for the connoisseur.

(4) FONTEIN, JAN. The Pilgrimage of Sudhana: A Study of the Gandavyuha Illustrations in China, Japan and Java. The Hague: Mouton, 1967, 229 pp., 63 black and white illustrations.

A study whose aim is "to describe and catalogue the great variety of works of art which all have the story of the Gandavyuha as their common source of inspiration and to study some iconographical and other art historical problems which arise upon closer scrutiny of this material." In addition to a summary of the Gandavyuha text, discussions of its Chinese translations, Gandavyuha and Avatamsaka doctrines, and major sections devoted to Sudhana's pilgrimage in Chinese, Japanese, and Barabudur's art also provided. Extensive notes and bibliography are included. An appendix provides a detailed romanized Sanskrit and Chinese character list of Sudhana's kalyanamitras and the corresponding stages of sanctification. A specialized, advanced text.

(5) FONTEIN, JAN and ROSE HEMPEL. China, Korea, Japan. Propylean Kunstgeschichte, No. 17. Berlin: Propylean Verlag, 1968, 362 pp., 400 plates, 33 figures, maps.

A good general survey of the arts of China, Japan, and Korea. A large percentage of the Chinese Buddhist material, aside from site photographs, is presently in Western museums, while most of the Japanese material is presently in Japan, and the Korean material in Korea. A catalogue of the plates is contained at the end of the book. This contains numerous references to other works.

(6) LEE, SHERMAN E. A History of Far Eastern Art. See 5.1.4(8).

(7) MUNSTERBERG, HUGO. Art of the Far East. New York: Harry N. Abrams, 1968, 264 pp., extensively illustrated.

Traces the history of the art of the Far East from China through Korea to Japan. The limited text is clearly secondary to the profuse illustrations, which offer examples of Buddhist sculpture, painting, and architecture. Includes sections entitled "Far Eastern Art under Buddhist Inspiration," "Japanese Art under Zen Inspiration," and "Korean and Japanese Art under Buddhist Inspiration." All sections rely heavily on pictures. An excellent visual introduction to the famous masterpieces of Buddhist art and architecture in these three countries with just enough text to tie the pictures together in the broadest historical outline.

(8) SECKEL, DIETRICH. *The Art of Buddhism*. See 5.1.4(13).

(9) SOPER, ALEXANDER C. *Chinese, Korean, and Japanese Bronzes: A Catalogue of the Auriti Collection Donated to ISMEO and Preserved in the Museo Nazionale d'Arte Orientale in Rome*. Serie Orientale Roma, No. 35. Rome: Istituto Italiano per il Medio ed Estremo Oriente, 1966, xii, 79 pp., 86 illustrations.

A catalogue of early Buddhist bronzes (mostly mirrors). The majority of these bronzes are dated by inscription. The plates include clear photographs of the inscriptions. A translation of the texts is provided. Individual catalogue entries include iconographic identification, comparative material, as well as an extensive bibliography. About thirty-five of these bronzes are from China, about ten from Korea, and the remainder from Japan. Useful for the serious student.

(10) SWANN, PETER C. *Arts of China, Korea, and Japan*. New York: Praeger, 1963, 285 pp., including 259 illustrations.

As the text states about itself, "a very general introduction to a vast subject--An ABC so to speak of three great civilizations of East Asia." The history of East Asian art is dealt with in an historical fashion moving from China through Korea and Japan. The many color and black and white illustrations provide excellent if standard examples of general stages and styles of Asian art. While no specific section is devoted to Buddhism alone, the place of Buddhism in the spread and development of various genres and styles constitutes a major theme of the book. Many famous Buddhist paintings and statues are included in the illustrations. Architecture is not dealt with. An excellent introductory outline which, by its own definition, can be no more than cursory.

(11) VISSER, M. W. DE. *The Arhats in China and Japan*. Berlin: Oesterheld and Co., 1923, 215 pp., 16 black and white plates.

A specialized study dealing with the grouping of the 500 Arhats in China and Japan and the art relating not only to the 500 Arhats, but the special group of the sixteen and eighteen Arhats as well. The work is divided into sections discussing the name and qualities of an arhat, the 500 Arhats in India, China, and Japan (separate sections for each country), the sixteen and eighteen arhats in India, China and Japan, legends about arhats found in Chinese biographical sources, the ceremonies of the Soto (Zen) sect in honor of the sixteen Arhats. For each country, artistic sources (caves, paintings, sculpture, etc.), as well as textual sources, are used and discussed extensively. An important comprehensive study at the intermediate to advanced level.

(12) _____. *The Bodhisattva Akasagarbha in Japan and China*. See 7.8(15).

Originally designed to be published in book form as a sequel to the author's important work on Ti-tsang wang (Kshitigarbha, Jizo), but prevented from completion by the author's death. This text represents the completed introduction to the work, including chapters discussing akasa (ether or space, the fifth of the elements) and, most extensively, sutras and ceremonies which relate to the bodhisattva Akasagarbha. Although iconographical studies are not directly contained, the work provides a good background for associations with the god. Chinese characters are supplied for all terms. A very important work, at the intermediate to advanced level.

(13) _____. *The Bodhisattva Ti-tsang (Jizo) in China and Japan*. See 7.8(16).

A highly specialized study divided into three major sections treating: "Kshitigarbha According to the Sutras, and His Cult in India, Tibet, and Turkestan," "Ti-tsang in China," and "Jizo in Japan." Fair photographs and some drawings reveal diverse artistic renditions of the god. Chinese characters accompany all important names. The most competent treatment of the subject in a Western language, by a noted scholar. Advanced level.

(14) _____. *The Dragon in China and Japan*. See 9.2.2.5(12).

A unique specialized study investigating the conceptions and legends associated with the dragon as expressive of Indian influences brought to China and, in turn, Indian and Chinese influences transmitted to Japan, along with Buddhism in both cases but not necessarily expressive of Buddhist doctrines. A thirty-five-page introduction discusses "The Naga in Buddhism, with Regard to His Identification with the Chinese Dragon." Subsequent sections discuss the dragon in the Chinese classics, myths and legends, use by Wu-ist priests and in Buddhist rain ceremonies, temples of dragon-kings. Of more direct relevance to Buddhism is the section on Japan in which numerous pages deal with dragon legends and dragon-associated temples. Specialized, but highly readable. Chinese characters are supplied for important terms and names. A very important work, at the intermediate to advanced level.

5.9 CHINA

5.9.1 Chinese Buddhist Art (General)

(1) CARTER, DAGNY. *Four Thousand Years of China's Art*. Revised edition. New York: The Ronald Press Co., 1951, xix, 358 pp., including 210 black and white illustrations.

Within the context of a larger history of Chinese art from the stone age to Ch'ing, several sections deal directly with Buddhist topics (Buddhism in India and Gandharan art, Buddhism's entry into China, cave temples and early Buddhist sculpture, Chinese Buddhist influence on Japan, etc.) as well as various Buddhist topics (influence of Ch'an). Black and white illustrations include photographs of stupas, monasteries and gardens, pagodas, Buddhist statuary, paintings, etc. Touches upon architecture as well. Gives a good sense of the place of Buddhism in the growth of Chinese art. Relevant on the introductory and intermediate levels. A helpful bibliography divided according to topics is included.

(2) COHEN, JOAN LEBOLD and JEROME ALAN COHEN. China Today and Her Ancient Treasures. New York: Harry N. Abrams, 1974, 399 pp., 357 color and black and white illustrations.

Contains recent photographs of the major cave sites which reflect the efforts of the Chinese to restore the sites to their original condition.

(3) GROUSSET, RENE. Chinese Art and Culture. Translated by Haakon Chevalier. New York: Oreon Press, 1959, xxii, 331 pp., 64 plates.

The introduction provides a general essay on aspects of Chinese culture. The rest of the text is a history of China, as well as of Chinese art, from the Neolithic age to modern times. Approximately thirty-five pages are devoted to Buddhism in pre-T'ang China, as well as fourteen pages to T'ang Buddhism. The stress is on historical and cultural developments as they relate to art. This gives a good sense of Buddhism as an historical as well as an artistic phenomenon. An extremely comprehensive introduction, also valuable on the intermediate level.

(4) _____. The Civilization of the East. Vol. 3, China. New York: Alfred Knopf, 1934, 363 pp., 269 black and white plates.

Traces the history of Chinese art from prehistoric China through the Ch'ing dynasty. One hundred pages are devoted to Buddhist influence on China, concentrating mainly on Wei, Sui, and T'ang art; also three chapters are devoted to Greco-Roman, Gupta, and Iranian influence in Central Asia. Contains no index or bibliography. Plates are only fair. Introductory and intermediate levels.

(5) HAJEK, LUBOR. Chinese Art. London: Spring Books, 1959, 86 pp., 232 plates.

The author calls attention to some important results of "new" (post-1950) research work in China. The text is concerned with bronzes, ceramics, pottery, sculptures, painting, and minor arts. The brevity of the text permits only cursory discussions of Buddhist sculpture and painting. Many lovely black and white photographs of seldom illustrated Buddhist statues are included. Not for the advanced student, but for the general reader.

(6) HANSFORD, HOWARD S. A Glossary of Chinese Art and Archaeology. China Society Sinological Series, No. 4. London: The China Society, 1954, iv, 104 pp., 8 pp. of illustrations.

Highly specialized. Gives characters, then romanization and English definition. Illustrations consist of drawings of specific shapes of various vessels. The sculpture section includes divisions devoted to Buddhist terminology, bodhisattvas and arhats, divine beings and Buddhist iconography. Helpful to the advanced student with some Chinese or Japanese language training.

(7) KADOKAWA, SHOTEN, ed. A Pictorial Encyclopedia of the Oriental Arts: China. New York: Crown, 1969, vols. 1-2. Vol. 1, 32 pp., 193 illustrations; vol. 2, 31 pp., 177 illustrations.

Approximately twenty-five pages of text provide a lean introduction to the history of Chinese art from the Yin to the Ch'ing dyanasties. Plates, however, are thorough and well-done, though rather small. Approximately one-third are in color, none is thoroughly described.

(8) LEE, SHERMAN E. and WAI-KAM HO. Chinese Art Under the Mongols: The Yuan Dynasty (1279-1368). Cleveland: Cleveland Museum of Art, 1968, 403 pp., 306 illustrations.

Contains two essays, one by Sherman Lee on the nonpictorial art of the Yuan Dynasty and one by Wai-kam Ho on Chinese art under the Mongols, in addition to a catalogue with extensive notes on an exhibition of Yuan art presented at the Cleveland Museum of Art. Various references to Buddhist symbols, motifs, and influences appear throughout the text. Exhibition photographs include many statues of Buddhas and bodhisattvas along with woodblock prints and paintings of Buddhist subjects. The detailed notes make this work an excellent reference source on the art of this period. An intermediate or advanced text.

(9) LION-GOLDSCHMIDT, DAISY and JEAN-CLAUDE MOREAU-GOBARD. Chinese Art. Third American edition. Translated by Diana Imber. New York: Universe Books, 1962, 425 pp., including 198 color and black and white plates.

Contains four brief essays on bronze, jade, stone sculpture, and ceramics. Each essay attempts to establish a chronology of the development of art as well as describe the basic techniques and motifs. Reference to Buddhist art is confined, for the most part, to the section on sculpture. Plates are exceptional and fully described, few in color. A helpful introduction, with powerful visual impact.

(10) MUNSTERBERG, HUGO. A Short History of Chinese Art. New York: Philosophical Library, 1949, 227 pp., 50 plates.

Spans the millennia from prehistoric art to the Ch'ing dynasty. Brief sections are devoted to Buddhist art in the Six Dynasties, Sui, T'ang, and Sung periods. Plates are of poor quality. Very introductory.

(11) Royal India Society, London. Studies in Chinese Art and Some Indian Influences. London: The India Society, 1936, 64 pp., 39 plates.

A series of essays by four outstanding scholars. Hackin describes the synthesis of foreign influences that shaped Buddhist art in Central Asia. Siren explains Indian influences on Chinese sculpture. Paul Pelliot describes the royal tombs of An-yang. Langdon Warner presents a general approach to Chinese sculpture. All are excellent, short introductions to their topics, particularly Pelliot's and Siren's, whose subjects are more limited. There is no index. Plates unexceptional.

(12) SECKEL, DIETRICH. The Art of Buddhism. See 5.1.4(13).

(13) SICKMAN, LAURENCE and ALEXANDER SOPER. The Art and Architecture of China. Third edition. Pelican History of Art. Baltimore: Penguin Books, 1968, 350 pp., 190 black and white plates, 2 maps, 1 chronological table.

Attempts a history of Chinese art from the beginning to the Ch'ing dynasty. Divided into two parts: "Painting and Sculpture" (by Sickman) and "Architecture" (by Soper). Deals with Buddhist sculpture from Yuh-kang through the T'ang, T'ang Buddhist painting, Ch'an Buddhist painters. The architecture section treats Buddhist architecture, T'ang masonry pagodas, Todai-ji, Horyu-ji, and other Chinese and Japanese Buddhist architectural sites in about thirty pages. Black and white plates include many Buddhist statues, pagodas, etc. Includes an excellent, detailed bibliography. An important comprehensive work, at the introductory and intermediate levels.

(14) SIREN, OSVALD. A History of Early Chinese Art. New York: Hacker Art Books, 1970, 4 vols. in 2. Vol. 1, 75 pp., 108 plates; vol. 2, 82 pp., 20 plates; vol. 3, 75 pp., 128 plates; vol. 4, 77 pp., 120 plates. (Originally published London: Ernest Benn, 1929-1930.)

An extensive work of four volumes, of which the first two volumes (dealing with "the Prehistoric and Pre-Han" and "Han Period" respectively) have little to do with Buddhism. Volume 3, devoted to sculpture, gives specific discussion of Buddhist sculpture of the Northern Wei period, Buddhist sculpture of the Northern Ch'i and Sui periods, Buddhist sculpture of the T'ang, and sculpture after the T'ang, accompanied by extensive black and white plates referred to in the text. Volume 4, devoted to architecture, gives numerous examples and some lengthy discussion of Buddhist architecture under the topics of walls, sacrificial altars, constructive features, and buildings in mud, brick, and stone. Fourteen pages are devoted to pagodas. "Notes on Historical Evolution" provide architectural plans and discussion of Nara (Japan's) Yakushiji. Extensive black and white plates illuminate text. All of the sections but that on sculpture are badly dated.

(15) SMITH, BRADLEY and WAN-GO WENG. China: A History in Art. New York: Harper and Row, 1973, 296 pp., including approx. 249 color illustrations.

An excellent pictorial introduction to both Chinese history and Chinese art with a brief introduction to Chinese history by Dirk Bodde and an introduction to Chinese art by Nelson Wu. Executed in a chronological fashion around major themes of each era (i.e., beginning 1100 B.C. as "Legends into History," 220-581 as "Darkness and Light," etc.) from the beginning of Chinese art through 1949. Each section begins with two clear concise chronologies--one of historical and one of artistic "major events." Buddhism is dealt with in several sections. For the beginner.

(16) SOPER, ALEXANDER COBURN. Literary Evidence for Early Buddhist Art in China. See 1.11.2.1(8).

A specialized study, translating from Chinese sources those sections relevant to Buddhism of Omura Seigai's encyclopedic history of Chinese sculpture. 122 pages are devoted to the chronological development from the Eastern Han to Northern Chou. Some material is added (e.g., on contemporary painting). Attention is devoted to inscriptions, to iconography of Buddhas, bodhisattvas, and minor beings. Miracles, materials, and sizes, and best known Indian images are also dealt with in separate sections. Five extremely helpful indices, one of Chinese names and places, providing characters, one Japanese and Korean, one Sanskrit, and one of number groups (five bodhisattvas, seven Buddhas, etc.) and one miscellaneous. A definitive work on the advanced level.

(17) SPEISER, WERNER. The Art of China: Spirit and Society. Translated by George Lawrence. Art of the World Series. New York: Crown, 1960, 256 pp., including 68 illustrations, 13 p. table of most important artists and events.

Attempts to treat the vast subject of China's art history with a sensitivity to epochs and to present uncommon illustrations. Buddhism is dealt with passim, but not exhaustively. Includes one interesting set of drawings of the stylistic development of seated Buddhist figures from 460-750 A.D., after S. Mizuno (pp. 120-121), and several color plates of Buddhist figures. A detailed and complete introduction.

(18) SULLIVAN, MICHAEL. The Arts of China. Berkeley: University of California Press, 1973, 264 pp., 235 illustrations, 34 diagrams and maps.

A standard introduction to the entire history of Chinese art featuring the standard pictures. Attempts to incorporate the new

China

archaeological discoveries of 1972. A limited, standard treatment of Ch'an and Buddhist artists passim. A few pages are devoted to the spread of Buddhism, Buddhist sculpture, and architecture to China.

(19) ____. An Introduction to Chinese Art. Berkeley: University of California Press, 1961, 223 pp., 151 illustrations.

A standard introduction to the entire history of Chinese art. Many familiar works appear among the large black and white (some color) plates but are rather successfully presented. Buddhism and Ch'an are mentioned where historically important (Sui-T'ang era, etc.) but no special sections are devoted to the topics. Map on page 105 gives location of major Buddhist monuments in China. Places little stress on Buddhist art.

(20) WILLETS, WILLIAM. Chinese Art. Paperback edition. London: Penguin Books, 1958, 2 vols. bound together, 802 pp., 64 plates.

Encyclopaedic in scope. Attempts to cover the history of all Chinese arts and crafts, arranged by topic (pottery, painting, architecture, etc.). A seventy-five page sculpture section is dominated by Buddhist topics, including treatment of the beginnings of Buddhism and Buddhist sculpture in China, the Buddha image at Mathura, the development of Buddhist doctrine and its effect on Chinese Buddhist sculpture. The architecture section includes information on pagodas. Buddhist artists are mentioned in the section on painting and calligraphy. A comprehensive treatment, especially of Buddhist sculpture. Intermediate level.

(21) ____. Foundations of Chinese Art from Neolithic Pottery to Modern Architecture. London: Thames and Hudson, 1965, 456 pp., including 264 black and white and some color illustrations.

Revised, abridged, and rewritten version of Willets' 1958 publication, Chinese Art (above). Attempts a lighter style with newer data than the earlier work. The sculpture section with plates devotes almost fifty-five pages to Buddhist sculpture. A chart gives characteristics of specific Buddhas and bodhisattva figures in terms of asana, mudra, support, attendants, etc. Includes large, clear illustrations of many important sculptures. A visual improvement over the earlier work. The bibliography is not limited to Buddhist topics. Comprehensive treatment at the intermediate level.

5.9.2 Architecture and Sculpture

(1) ASHTON, LEIGH. An Introduction to the Study of Chinese Sculpture. London: Ernest Benn, 1924, 113 pp., 63 black and white plates.

Spans Chinese history from the "Dark Ages" to the Ming. One chapter discusses the early history of Buddhism and another examines

5.9.2

Buddhist bronze statuettes from the fifth to the tenth century. Elsewhere, there are intermittent references to Buddhism. A poor index makes these difficult to locate. Good plates. Simple introductory essays, somewhat dated.

(2) BUNKER, EMMA C. "Early Chinese Representations of Vimalakirti." Artibus Asiae, 30 (1968), 28-52, 11 figures.

Discusses the sculptural representations of Vimalakirti drawn from the Vimalakirti-nirdesa sutra, during the Six Dynasties period from its earliest known appearance in the fifth century through the sixth century. An appendix at the end of the article lists additional Six Dynasty representations of the Vimalakirti-nirdesa sutra.

(3) CHAVANNES, EDOUARD. Six monuments de la sculpture chinoise. Ars Asiatica, No. 2. Bruxelles: Librairie d'art et d'histoire, G. Van Oest, 1914, 40 pp., 52 black and white plates.

Among the six monuments described, five are Buddhist steles and bas-reliefs from the sixth and seventh centuries. Priority is given to an analysis of the inscriptions which are reproduced in Chinese characters and translated. Full-page plates reveal excellent detail, even of the inscriptions. Specialized, advanced level.

(4) Chinese, Korean, and Japanese Sculpture in the Avery Brundage Collection, Asian Art Museum of San Francisco. See 5.8(2).

(5) ECKE, GUSTAVE and PAUL DEMIEVILLE. The Twin Pagodas of Zayton: A Study of Later Buddhist Sculpture in China. See 10.8.2(3).

Presents data concerning the iconography and sculpture of the twin Sung-style pagodas at Ch'uan-chou, the ancient Zayton, in the province of Fu-chien. The introduction, by Gustave Ecke, includes a general discussion of Zayton, the architecture of the pagodas, the sculpture, notes, and bibliography. Demieville's section deals with iconography and history divided into separate sections on the Western and Eastern Pagoda, also discussing the K'ai-yuan temple, stupas and votive pillars, and Buddhist architects and foreign monks in Ch'uan-chou. An important specialized study, informative not only on the subject of the twin temples, but about Ch'uan-chou itself as an important center of foreign intercourse. Advanced level.

(6) GRISWOLD, ALEXANDER B. "Prolegomena to the Study of the Buddha's Dress in Chinese Sculpture." Artibus Asiae, 26 (1963), 335-348, 12 figures.

Instead of discussing the dress of the Buddha purely in terms of artistic convention, Griswold illustrates how the Chinese based their drapery style on the art of Gandhara, and shows how it is linked with present day Theravadin practice, as well as with the Pali vinaya.

(7) GROOT, J. J. M. DE. Der Thupa: Das heiligste Heiligtum des Buddhismus in China. Berlin: Verlag der Akademie der Wissenschaften, 1919, 92 pp., 6 plates.

An important though brief and somewhat dated analysis of a relatively untouched subject in Chinese Buddhism by a well-known authority on religion in China. Emphasis is on the symbolic meaning of the pagoda in China, as distinguished from its artistic design and details. An index is included. Advanced level.

(8) LESSING, FERDINAND D. Yung-Ho-Kung: An Iconography of Lamaist Cathedral in Peking. See 7.5.3(3).

Discusses the structure, iconography, and rituals of this lamaist temple in Peking. Contains detailed descriptions of the structure and decoration of various halls and courts as well as series of images. Also describes four rites performed there. Includes figures and a table which clarify the understanding of symbols, pronunciation, etc. Reads like a categorization of terms rather than an analytical essay. Plates are sharp, and include pictures of rituals. Chinese characters are provided throughout. No index is included. Highly specialized.

(9) MATSUBARA, SABURO. Chugoku bukkyo chokoku-shi kenkyu, zotei (Chinese Buddhist Sculpture, A Study Based on Bronze and Stone Statuettes Other than Works from Cave Temples). Tokyo: Yoshikawa, 1966, 8, 306 pp. 312 plates.

Contains a series of essays and plates covering the period from circa 470-750 A.D. All in Japanese, but the plates are of use.

(10) MIZUNO, SEIICHI. Bronze and Stone Sculpture in China: From the Yin to the T'ang Dynasty (Chugoku no Chokohu). Translated by Yuichi Kajiyama and Burton Watson. Tokyo: Nihon Keizai, 1960, 38 pp. English text, 77 pp. Japanese text, 10 color plates, 130 black and white plates, 153 figures.

A collection of the works presented at the Exhibition of Ancient Chinese Sculpture held in Tokyo in 1959, with some additions. The brief English text provides a short introduction to the history of Buddhist sculpture in China, Buddhist images of the early period, Buddhist figures of the period of the sixteen states, the pre-Yun-kang period, the Yun-kang period, the Lung-men period, the period of Hsiang-t'ang-shan, Buddhist sculpture in the Sui, and T'ang Buddhist sculpture. Although the Japanese text and illustrations cover all of early Chinese sculptural history, the English text deals only with the period of predominant Buddhist inspiration. A brief but important introductory text.

(11) MUNSTERBERG, HUGO. Chinese Buddhist Bronzes. Rutland, Vt.: Charles E. Tuttle, 1967, 192 pp., including 130 black and white plates.

Moves from an assertion of the prominence of bronzes among Chinese Buddhist sculpture to deal briefly, in separate sections, with the introduction of Buddhist imagery into China, Chinese materials and techniques, images of seated and standing Buddhas, as well as images of various Buddhas of the past, bodhisattvas, arhats and donors, inscriptions and dates, collections, auction prices and forgeries. Two appendices provide lists of major dated Chinese Buddhist bronzes and museums and art galleries. While supported by pertinent illustrations, each section is extremely brief. Includes a limited but directed (Chinese Buddhist Sculpture) bibliography. A very general and uncritical introduction to a rather specialized subject.

(12) PRIP-MOLLER, J. Chinese Buddhist Monasteries. See 7.2.1(7).

With his architectural background, Prip-Moller focuses on the functional, architectural layout of Chinese Buddhist monasteries, especially in the Yangtze Valley. He has separate chapters for the central axes, lateral groups, ordination unit, and monks' offices, as well as two chapters on the monastery Hui Chu Ssu. The book includes 366 excellent detailed explanatory sketches and black and white photographs which are highly suggestive of monastic life in the 1930s. Also includes four blueprint sketches of Hui Chu Ssu. An extremely valuable, well written history of Chinese Buddhist monasteries as well as daily monastic life.

(13) SICKMAN, LAURENCE and ALEXANDER SOPER. The Art and Architecture of China. See 5.9.1(13).

(14) SIREN, OSVALD. Chinese Sculpture from the Fifth to the Fourteenth Century. Hacker Art Books, 1970, vol. 1, 166 pp. text; vols. 2-4, 623 plates. (Originally published London: Ernest Benn, 1925, in 4 vols.)

Concentrates on Buddhist sculpture of North China. The text mainly is an explanation of the plates, including only the most necessary historical and iconographical information. The material constitutes a large and representative selection. Plates and plate descriptions are arranged chronologically from the Western Tsin to the Yuan, while the text concentrates on the evolution of style in terms of "the archaic period," "the transition period," "the period of maturity," and "the period of decadence and reflorescence," with an additional section on general iconographic remarks. A very important work for the student of Chinese sculpture. Intermediate level.

(15) SOPER, ALEXANDER. Chinese, Korean, and Japanese Bronzes. See 5.8(9).

(16) _____. "Japanese Evidence for the History of Architecture and Iconography of Chinese Buddhism." Monumenta Serica, 4 (1940), 638-678.

A description of the journey through South China and to Japan of the mid-eighth-century Chinese missionary Chien-chin, founder of Toshadaiji at Nara.

(17) _____. "Some Late Chinese Bronze Images (Eighth to Fourteenth Centuries) in the Avery Brundage Collection, M. H. de Young Museum, San Francisco." *Artibus Asiae*, 31 (1969), 32-54, 27 figures.

A critical discussion with extensive documentation of iconographic and stylistic features of some Chinese Buddhist bronzes in the Asian Art Museum of San Francisco.

(18) _____. "Two Stelae and a Pagoda on the Central Peak of Mt. Sung." *Archives of the Chinese Art Society of America*, 16 (1962), 41-48, 3 figures.

Discusses two stelae and a pagoda which have been preserved on Mt. Sung in Honan Province. Both stelae are dated 535 A.D. One of the two is contrasted to a work formerly in the collection of C. T. Loo. Mt. Sung is a famous Buddhist site which flourished during the Six Dynasties Period.

(19) _____. "A 'Wei Style' Bronze from Chekiang." *Artibus Asiae*, 13 (1960), 213-219, 8 figures.

Discusses an extremely rare example of a bronze bodhisattva discovered in 1956 in Chekiang. The bronze reflects the Buddhist metal working techniques of that period.

(20) TOKIWA, DAIJO and TADASHI SEKINO. *Shina Bukkyo Shiseki* (Buddhist Monuments in China). See 1.11.2.2(11).

A major collection of Buddhist monuments in situ, including descriptive texts of plates. Works include pagodas, statues, stelae, stone pillars inscribed with sutras, rock shrines with stone relief figures, and grottoes. Part 1 deals with important objects at Lo-yang, Shensi, and Chi-nan. Part 2 deals with historical relics and sites at Lu Shan, Su Chou, Yun-kang, Lung-men, Kung Hsien and Sung Shan. Part 3 covers sites and relics in Shan-hsi, T'ien Lung Shan, Hsiang-t'ang Shan, Lung Shan, Fang Shan and Pao Shan. Part 4 includes historical sites and objects in Nanking, Nan-Yueh, Ching Chou, T'ien-t'ai Shan, Ch'ing Chou and Cheng-ting. Part 5 deals with W'u-t'ai Shan, Hang-Chou, Ningpo, Pu-to Shan and Peking.

(21) WARNER, LANGDON. "A Tun-huang Statue in the Fogg Museum, Cambridge, Mass., with Chinese and Japanese Parallels." *Art Studies*, 4 (1926), 29-40, 18 illustrations.

The introduction to this article recounts the desecration of the Tun-huang caves after their rediscovery by Aurel Stein. The core of the article deals with the rare clay figure from Tun-huang presented to the museum as a result of the expedition in January 1925. The discussion of the work is mainly technical and stylistic, showing close parallels in Japan, as well as in China.

5.9.3 Painting

(1) ACKER, W. R. B. "Notes on Wall Paintings in the Buddhist and Taoist Temples of the Two Capitals and the Provinces," in *Some T'ang and Pre-T'ang Texts and Chinese Painting*. By Li-Tai Ming Hua Chi. Leiden, 1954, Ch. 3, sect. 4.

A description of Buddhist and Taoist wall paintings referring to their artist, iconography and quality. An extremely important literary source for early Buddhist material. Almost all the paintings referred to in this text were destroyed in the mid-ninth century, while others apparently fell into the hands of art lovers who kept them in their homes. The text was written by the mid-ninth-century author Chang Yen-Yuan.

(2) BRIESSEN, FRITZ VAN. *The Way of the Brush: Painting Techniques of China and Japan*. Rutland, Vt.: Charles E. Tuttle, 1962, 329 pp., including 284 black and white illustrations.

The majority of the book is on Chinese painting--its cultural position, elements, subjects, techniques, and principles. Part 2, "Notes on Technical Matters," consists of thirteen brief essays, including a comparison of China and Japan. A few references to Ch'an and a short section on Tun-huang comprise the book's treatment of Buddhist impact on Chinese painting. Valuable appendices include a glossary of art terms, a chronological table which lists the order of prominent painters, and an explanation of specific art symbols. Plates are good. A well-written intermediate level survey.

(3) BULLING, ANNELIESE. "Buddhist Temples in the T'ang Period." See 10.8.1(2).

A reconstruction of T'ang Buddhist temples, palaces and other buildings based on cave paintings and banners from Tun-huang.

(4) CAHILL, JAMES. *Chinese Painting*. Geneva: Skira, 1960, 211 pp., approx. 106 color plates.

An excellent introduction to the subject with excellent color plates. No specific section is devoted to Buddhism; however, many Buddhist artists and influences are discussed passim and in the section on "The Literati and Ch'an Painters of the Sung Dynasty." Although not primarily focused on Buddhism, a superlative introduction to Chinese painting, contributed to by unusually good plates.

(5) CHAPIN, HELEN B. *A Long Roll of Buddhist Images*. Revised by Alexander C. Soper. Foreword and excursus on the text of Man Chao T'u Chuan by Alexander C. Soper. Ascona: Artibus Asiae, 1972, 142 pp., 58 pages of plates. (Originally published in *Artibus Asiae*, 32 [1970], 5-41, 159-199, 259-306; and 33 [1971], 75-142.)

The "long roll" is a painting, some fifty-one feet of paper, presenting by ink drawings and color, a series of Buddhist deities in 102 sections, ranging from a single figure to a large group. As an inscription makes clear, the work was done around 1175 A.D., chiefly by one artist, presumably an expert Chinese, by order of the king of the small state of Ta Li (corresponding to modern Yunan province). The scroll was part of the former Chinese collection in Peking, and is now housed in the National Palace Museum, Taipei. Its chief importance is as a witness to the broad eclecticism of the Buddhism practiced in the frontier regions between China, the Southeast Asian kingdoms, and Tibet. The work was introduced to the West by Helen Chapin in the Journal of the Indian Society of Oriental Art, 1936-1938, unfortunately in incomplete form and very poorly illustrated. The Soper contribution is primarily an amplified study of the scroll's richest feature, its kaleidoscope of Buddhist iconography, now fully illustrated. The book contains, in addition, a report on a much shorter and simpler anonymous handscroll which retells a legend concerning the origin of the Yunanese kingdom in the seventh century. This also had been published by Chapin, as an article in the Harvard Journal of Asiatic Studies in 1944. She knew then only the painting with its short subtitles, and had not the separate scroll of the text that makes a fully coherent treatment possible. (Both legend scrolls are now relatively accessible in the Fujii Yurinkan Museum in Kyoto.)

(6) COHN, WILLIAM. Chinese Painting. Second edition. London: Phaidon, 1950, 112 pp., 224 black and white plates, 5 color plates, 46 additional plates included in pagination.

A brief survey of Chinese art from the beginning to the end of the Ch'ing. Twenty pages are devoted to religious and court painting of the Sui-T'ang era. This work touches on the influence of Ch'an in the Sung and Yuan. A cursory introduction, but one in which Buddhist influence remains a recurring, if superficially rendered, theme. The selected bibliography is almost complete regarding works published prior to 1950. For the beginning student.

(7) FONG, WEN. The Lohans and a Bridge to Heaven. Freer Gallery of Art, Occasional Papers, 3, no. 1. Washington: The Smithsonian Institution, 1958, 64 pp., 18 pp. black and white plates.

A specialized study centering on two Buddhist paintings owned by the Freer Gallery of Art which were identified in 1954 as coming from a famous Chinese set formerly owned by the Japanese temple Daitoku-ji. Included are brief discussions of the cult of lohans (arhats), the rock bridge at the T'ien-t'ai mountain, the lohans at the rock-bridge, lohans in Mahayanism, a list of Chinese, Japanese, and Sanskrit names and terms in Chinese characters. A seven-page bibliography is included. An important, specialized, but readable study. Intermediate-advanced level.

(8) FONTEIN, JAN and MONEY HICKMAN. Zen Painting and Calligraphy. See 5.11.6(3).

(9) NAGAHIRO, T. "On Wei-ch'ih I-seng." Oriental Art (Summer 1955), pp. 70-74.

Considered one of the most renowned painters of the T'ang dynasty, although his work is known only through literary source material. He painted the walls of Buddhist temples and the article names the temples he is supposed to have painted at. Some of the descriptions in this article are discussed in the Li-Tai Ming Hua Chi by Chang Yen-Yuan (see above, under Acker) as well as other literary sources.

(10) SIREN, OSVALD. "Central Asian Influences in Chinese Painting of T'ang." Arts Asiatiques, 3 (1956), 4-21, 12 figures.

Considers Central Asian influences on both Buddhist and secular Chinese painting, particularly in the T'ang dynasty.

(11) _____. Chinese Painting: Leading Masters and Principles. Part 1. London: Lund Humphries, 1956, 3 vols. Vol. 1, 235 pp., 18 figures; vol. 2, 95 pp.; vol. 3, xviii plus 372 plates.

Volume 1 is organized chronologically from antiquity through early Sung. Volume 2 deals solely with the Sung. Volume 3 contains the plates pertaining to the first two volumes. Except for an admirable chapter on the Ch'an painters in Volume 2, references to Buddhism, which is not mentioned in the index, are hard to find. Volume 2 contains an annotated history of paintings arranged according to dynasty and reproductions of paintings by Chinese artists. It does not provide Chinese characters except in appendices. A vast number of attractive plates are assembled in Volume 3. An authoritative, intermediate level book in which both the leading masters and their works are well covered.

(12) _____. A History of Early Chinese Paintings. London: The Medici Society, 1933, 2 vols. Vol. 1, 138 pp., 100 black and white plates; vol. 2, 161 pp., 126 black and white plates.

Volume 1, Han to the Beginning of Sung, is basically a chronological treatment of the period. Buddhist artists and works are mentioned in specific sections such as: Tun-huang, religious painting in the T'ang, several pages each on Wu Tao-tzu, Wang-wei, Yen Li-pen, Li Ssu-hsun, Li Chao-tao, the rise of Ch'an Buddhism, centers of art in the Five Dynasties period, and characteristics and leading masters of Sung monochrome landscapes. Volume 2 contains, among numerous references to Buddhist art, pages on Li Lung-mien and other Buddhist painters with brief discussion of Ch'an in the Southern Sung and other topics of relevance to Buddhism. Generally superseded by his 1956 book (above).

(13) SOPER, ALEXANDER C. "Early Buddhist Attitudes Toward the Art of Painting." Art Bulletin, 32 (June 1950), 1947-151.

A translation of various Chinese-Buddhist texts regarding the question of pre-Tantric image making in Buddhism.

(14) _____, trans. and annotator. Kuo Jo-hsu's Experiences in Painting (T'u Hua Chien-wen Chih). Washington: American Council of Learned Societies, 1951, 216 pp., plus Chinese facsimile of text.

An annotated translation of an eleventh century history of Chinese painting by an eminent authority. Refers to numerous Buddhist artists in his history, which deals with late T'ang, Five Dynasties, and Sung Masters. Extensive footnotes provide Chinese characters for names. Separate indices are provided for Chinese names, Chinese book titles, non-Chinese names, and Chinese technical terms. Highly specialized.

(15) _____. "Representations of Famous Images at Tun-huang." Artibus Asiae, 24 (1965), 349-364, 9 figures.

Discusses a fragmentary Buddhist silk painting from Tun-huang in the British Museum, with emphasis on problems of iconography and sources. The other half of this painting is in the National Museum in New Delhi. According to Soper, the majority of the figures are Theravadan in type.

(16) _____. "T'ang Ch'ao Ming Hua Lu: Celebrated Painters of the T'ang Dynasty by Chu Ching hsuan of T'ang." Artibus Asiae, 21 (1958), 204-230.

One of the two major literary sources of T'ang dynasty painting including descriptions of Buddhist paintings of the time. This is a revised version of the text by Soper which first appeared in the Archives of the Chinese Art Society of America, 4 (1950), 5-28.

(17) STEIN, AUREL. Serindia. See 5.7(10).

(18) SWANN, PETER C. Chinese Painting. Paris: Pierre Tisne, 1958, 154 pp., 61 color illustrations.

An introductory work which attempts to give an outline of the history of Chinese painting, to discuss some essentials of technique, to indicate some of the fundamental ideas at the basis and to reproduce (in color) some major masterpieces in Chinese and European collections. Chapters are arranged in dynastic order from the beginning to the Ch'ing. Buddhism and Buddhist artists are mentioned passim, but lack of a subject index (only an artist's name index is provided) makes spotting specifically Buddhist-related subjects difficult for the beginner. The color plates are unusually lovely.

(19) WALEY, ARTHUR. An Introduction to the Study of Chinese Paintings. London: Ernest Benn, 1923, 262 pp., 50 plates.

Actually a series of essays on the time from the Chou Dynasty to the Yuan, with chapters on symbolic motifs, calligraphy, and prominent painters and works. The work addresses itself to the history of Chinese art traditions and tastes, rather than analysis of individual paintings. Has commendable introductory discussions of Zen and Buddhism in the Han and T'ang. Plates are somewhat blurred, with few in color. Lively, but badly dated.

(20) WHITE, WILLIAM CHARLES. Chinese Temple Frescoes. Royal Ontario Museum of Archaeology, Museum Studies, No. 3. Toronto: University of Toronto Press, 1940, 230 pp., including 76 black and white illustrations.

Confines itself to three thirteenth century temple frescoes from South Shansi. The first pages provide a general introduction to Chinese wall-painting of the period, examining the history, locations, techniques, masterter painters and common subjects. The last pages give detailed descriptions of three frescoes, two Taoist and one Buddhist, depicting the Paradise of Maitreya. For the most part in these descriptions, the author merely identifies the figures and the stories behind the picture. In White's own words, "No attempt has been made to deal with the frescoes from the standpoint of art." Fair plates, a few in color. A standard introductory work, aside from the descriptions of particular frescoes.

5.9.4 Cave Temples: Tun-huang, Lung-men, Maichi-shan, etc.

(1) AKIYAMA, TERUKAZU and SABURO MATSUBARA. Arts of China. Vol. 2: Buddhist Cave Temples, New Researches. See 10.8.2(1).

An excellent exposure to Buddhist cave art. Includes an essay on the Tun-huang caves and their wall paintings by Akiyama, and an article on Buddhist sculpture by Matsubara. An informative description is devoted to each plate. Includes a chronology dating materials for the Tun-huang caves, and an extensive map showing the locations of Chinese Buddhist sites. Plates are arranged according to location with a section for Buddhist sculpture now in China other than cave figures and a very short section on Kizil, Bezelik, and Toyuk Ravine and Tibet. An excellent treatment.

(2) CHEN TSU-LUNG. "Table de concordance des numérotages des Grottes de Touen-houang." Journal Asiatique, 250 (1962), 257-276.

A concordance of various numbering systems for the Tun-huang caves.

(3) DAVIDSON, J. LeROY. The Lotus Sutra in Chinese Art. Yale Studies in the History of Art, No. 8. New Haven: Yale University Press, 1954, ix, 105 pp., 41 plates.

A specialized study which attempts in historical fashion to view cultural, philosophical, and religious transformations within China through tracing changes in the use of the important "Lotus Sutra" in art. Includes such topics as the relation of the Buddhist conquest of China to the image, the "Lotus Sutra" in cave temples, the paradise cults, sectarianism and decline. A unique and valuable study for intermediate and advanced students.

(4) GRAY, BASIL. Buddhist Cave Paintings at Tun-huang. See 1.10.2(7).

Only about twenty pages of text, well written (but uneven in factual accuracy) covering the history of the area, influence of Central Asian Buddhist paintings, the landscape elements in the cave paintings, and the technique of the wall paintings. The remainder of the volume provides extensive commentary on the plates, approximately half of which are in color, but all excellent.

(5) HSIEH CHIH-LU. Tung-huang I-shu Hsu-lu (Collection of Materials for the Study of the Tun-huang Caves). Peking: Shanghai Press, 1955.

Historical preface and detailed description/inventory of the caves. Uses own numbering system providing chart for cross references to Pelliot's and the Tun-huang Institute's. In Chinese, but with useful illustrations.

(6) Kung-hsien Shih-k'u-ssu (The Cave Temples at Kung-hsien). Peking: Wen Wu Press, 1963, 66 pp., 347 plates, 77 illustrations.

A major publication, in Chinese, with good photographs and drawings of one of the important Buddhist cave sites in North China during the Six Dynasties period in North China. See also Akiyama and Matsubara, Arts of China, Vol. 2 (5.9.4[1]).

(7) MIZUNO, SEIICHI and TOSHIO NAGAHIRO. The Buddhist Cave Temples of Hsiang-T'ang-ssu on the Frontier of Honan and Hopei. Kyoto: Toho-bunka-gakuin Kyoto Kenkyusho, 1937, 10 pp. English text, 77 pp. Japanese text, 66 plates, 88 figures.

A book valuable for its photographs of reliefs and sculptures from both the North and South caves of Hsiang-t'ang-ssu. Both Northern Ch'i and Sui periods are represented. The photographic collection is accompanied by a highly useful set of ground and elevation plans of the caves, and by rubbings of inscriptions and certain decorative motifs. A brief introduction in English (otherwise Japanese text) outlines the content and major characteristics of each Buddhist cave. Although this publication is not an exhaustive photographic study of Hsiang-t'ang-ssu, it is the best to date and provides photographs that are not available in other texts.

(8) ____. A Study of the Buddhist Cave Temples at Lung-men, Ho-nan. Tokyo: Zauho Press, 1941, 257 pp. (17 pp. English text), 103 plates of illustrations, 10 plates of rubbings. (Publication of the Toho-Bunka-Kenkyusho.)

Appendices in Japanese cover Buddhism under the Northern Wei and a corpus of Lung-men inscriptions. Photographic coverage and descriptions are excellent but relatively meagre, since the author's visit was a brief one.

(9) ____. Yun-kang: The Buddhist Cave Temples of the Fifth Century A.D. in Northern China. Kyoto: Jimbunkagaku Kenkyusho, Kyoto University, 1951-1956, 16 vols. in 32.

Exhaustive coverage of the site. Each large cave shrine is typically allotted one volume of plates and one volume of text. Each text volume is in Japanese, with a complete English translation, and contains descriptions of the caves and scale drawings. Also an essay on some general topic, e.g., iconography, ornament, cave forms and their evolution, Western influence, etc.

(10) PELLIOT, PAUL. Les Grottes de Touen-houang. Paris: Librairie Paul Geuthner, 1920-1924, 6 vols., 375 plates.

The present collection of plates presents the visual results of a survey of the Tun-huang caves conducted by Paul Pelliot from February to May in 1908. The plates published in this series represent the first large group of plates of this important Buddhist site along the Chinese silk-route. There is no accompanying text to these plates, but Pelliot's notes taken during this expedition were found after his death in 1945 and may eventually be published. The numbering system for the caves used by Pelliot in this book is not the same as the one currently in use by the Tun-huang Cultural Research Institute established in 1944. However, a concordance and a chronology of the major caves may be found in Akiyama and Matsubara, Arts of China (above), Vol. 2, pp. 242-244. The dated caves extend from 353 A.D. to 1035 A.D.

(11) SILVA, ANIL DE. The Art of Chinese Landscape Painting in the Caves of Tun-huang. Art of the World Series. New York: Crown, 1967, 240 pp., including 90 color and black and white plates.

Features the development of landscape painting in the frescoes of Tun-huang from the fourth to eleventh centuries. Provides a good introduction to a broad subject. Chronological tables correlate histories of Europe and Asia.

(12) SOPER, ALEXANDER C. "Imperial Cave-Chapels of the Northern Dynasties: Donors, Beneficiaries, Dates." Artibus Asiae, 28 (1966), 241-270, 12 figures, 6 plates.

Establishes links between the large cave shrines of major Buddhist sites and specific rulers. Summarizes his earlier work on Yun-kang and Lung-men, discussed in his "South Chinese Influence on the Buddhist Art of the Six Dynasties" (below). Expands his discussion to include Kung-hsien, T'ien Lung-shan, and Hsiang T'ang-shan. The last portion of the article is devoted to a chronology of the caves.

(13) _____. "Northern Wei and Northern Liang in Kansu." Artibus Asiae, 21 (1958), 131-164, 20 figures.

Establishes a chronology of Chinese and Central Asian cave painting based on historical evidence and the style of the draped scarf. Traces forms of drapery back to Classical, Sassanian, and Indian prototypes.

(14) _____. "South Chinese Influence on the Buddhist Art of the Six Dynasties." Bulletin of the Museum of Far Eastern Antiquities, 32 (1960), 47-112, 18 plates.

A highly useful article and requisite reading for a proper understanding of the history and art history of Six Dynasties Buddhism. As the title of the article suggests, South Chinese rather than North Chinese influences on the Buddhist art of the Six Dynasties are traced. Although the bulk of the Buddhist monuments derives from the North (e.g., Yun-kang, Lung-men, Hsiang T'ang Shan) the author is able to demonstrate, through use of literary, historical, and newly discovered art historical evidence, that southern Buddhist art fostered at the courts of Nanking was the primary force of inspiration for Buddhist styles and standards of the Six Dynasties period. Southern Buddhist art produced under the Chin, Sung, S. Ch'i, and Liang regimes includes literary evidence referring to such southern masters as T'ai Kuei as well as surviving sculptures from Mouhsien and Wan-fo-ssu site in Szechwan province. Two phases of South Chinese influences which brought northern Buddhist arts to maturity are noted. The first phase is just after 480 A.D. and the second is in the third quarter of the sixth century. The article is outlined according to the following subtitles: "Continuity and New Flowering in the South," "The Dark Ages in the North," "Yun-kang and the Sinicizing Style," "The Southern Ch'i Style and Its Continuation," and "The Indian Strain in Liang and Northern Ch'i Remains."

(15) SULLIVAN, MICHAEL. The Cave Temples of Maichishan. See 10.8.2(11).

Outlines the history and describes the art styles of Maichishan. Forty more pages deal with the plates, which are nearly all black and white, but large and well presented. Includes map of Buddhist cave temples in Northwest China. Provides a good visual impression and competent introduction to the subject.

(16) SWANN, PETER C. Chinese Monumental Art. New York: The Viking Press, 1963, 276 pp., including 157 color and black and white plates.

An attempt to link into a coherent whole the important photographic documents brought back from China by two photographers, François Herbert-Stevens and Claude Arthaud. Includes an introduction on Buddhism, and sections on Yun-kang, Lung-men, Tun-huang, and Mai-chi-Shan with a brief appendix on sources of Buddhist art. Various secular arts are discussed as well. Includes excellent photos; strictly introductory.

(17) TOKIWA, DAIJO and SEKINO TADASHI. Shina Bukkyo Shiseki (Buddhist Monuments in China). See 1.11.2.2(11).

(18) Tun-huang Pi-hua. Peking: Wen Wu Press, 1959, 17 pp., 213 plates.

Moderately good reproductions from photographs (chiefly black and white). A very important supplement to Pelliot's Les Grottes de Touen-houang (above). In Chinese.

(19) VANDERSTRAPPEN, HARRY and MARILYN RHIE. "The Sculpture of T'ien Lung-shan: Reconstruction and Dating." Artibus Asiae, 27, No. 3 (1965), 189-210, 111-220, 84 figures.

An important Buddhist cave site in Central Shansi which flourished in the late Six Dynasties Period, mid to late sixth centuries, and saw a resurgence in the early eighth century or T'ang dynasty. Some of the finest examples of mature T'ang dynasty style Buddhist sculpture came from the site. The site was rediscovered by the Japanese in the early decades of the twelfth century. Soon thereafter, the caves were almost totally destroyed and the majority of the sculptures found their way to private and public collections in the West and Japan. Part 1 of the article reconstructs the major caves matching site photographs with fragments available in various collections, while Part 2 discusses problems of dating.

(20) VINCENT, IRENE VONGEHR. The Sacred Oasis: Caves of the Thousand Buddhas. See 10.1.2(8).

The story of a young American woman's visit to Tun-huang. Describes the history of Buddhism's expansion into China and the history of the caves. No in-depth artistic analysis, but pleasant reading for a popular introduction.

(21) WALEY, ARTHUR. A Catalogue of Paintings Recovered from Tun-huang by Sir Aurel Stein. London: Trustees of the British Museum and the Government of India, 1931, 328 pp.

Carefully describes the paintings and fragments stored both at the British Museum and in New Delhi. Inscriptions are presented in their original language and translated. The valuable introduction contains brief essays on iconography, specific motives of the paintings and other topics. Highly specialized, advanced.

(22) WARNER, LANGDON. <u>Buddhist Wall-paintings</u>. Cambridge, Mass.: Harvard-Radcliffe Fine Arts Series, 33 pp., 45 black and white plates.

The author is complementing work done by Sir Aurel Stein so restricts himself solely to Cave 5 at Wan Fo Hsia cave complex near Tun-huang. Describes the geography, purpose and techniques used in painting, as well as the major sources in painting. Plates are large and helpful. A specialized intermediate level book.

(23) _____. "A Tun-huang Statue in the Fogg Museum, Cambridge, Mass." <u>See</u> 5.9.2(21).

5.10 KOREA

(1) BUHOT, JEAN. <u>Chinese and Japanese Art with Sections on Korea and Vietnam</u>. <u>See</u> 5.8(1).

(2) <u>Bukkokuji Temple and Sekkutsu-an Cave in Keishu, Chosen</u>. Service of Antiquities, Government-General of Chosen, Remains of Korean Art Treasures, Vol. 1. Keijo: Government of Korea, 1938, 6 pp., 76 plates.

The Sekkutsu-an cave is the most important remaining work of Buddhist art in Korea which reflects T'ang dynasty influence from China both in style and in iconography. This work is the only major source for a study of the Sekkutsu-an cave, which is also known by the name Sokulam. While the text is in Japanese, the quality of the plates makes this volume of use. The list of plates is in English and Japanese.

(3) CHAPIN, HELEN B. "A Little Known Temple in South Korea and Its Treasures." <u>Artibus Asiae</u>, 11 (1948), 189-195, 6 figures.

Preliminary description of a small Buddhist temple which dates from Korea's golden age of Buddhist art, the Silla Period (668-935), an age of Buddhist art which flourished under royal patronage and Chinese Buddhist influence. Includes a description of the temple and identification of the main images. An interesting observation by the author is that Koreans did not always follow iconographic rules.

(4) <u>Chinese, Korean, and Japanese Sculptures in the Avery Brundage Collection, Asian Art Museum of San Francisco</u>. <u>See</u> 5.8(2).

(5) ECKHARDT, ANDREAS. <u>A History of Korean Art</u>. Translated by J. M. Kindersley and M. A. Oxon. 225 pp., 506 illustrations.

A thorough and important introduction to an area still little dealt with. A section is devoted to Buddhist sculpture, another discusses the specific topic of sculpture and pagoda art. Extensive black and white illustrations include photographs of Korean Buddhist priests, temples, sculptures, altars, pagodas, etc. Sculpture section provides classification of various divinities. Korean names with corresponding Chinese characters. Relevant on the intermediate level as well as introductory, though now dated.

(6) FONTEIN, JAN and ROSE HEMPEL. <u>China, Korea, Japan</u>. <u>See</u> 5.8(5).

(7) KADOKAWA SHOTEN, ed. <u>A Pictorial Encyclopedia of the Oriental Arts: Korea</u>. New York: Crown, 1969, 28 pp., 129 illustrations.

Due to the brevity of the text which provides a general history of Korean art and Korea's relation to the rest of Asia, Buddhist art cannot be dealt with separately or extensively. However, the excellent illustrations which constitute the core of the book, contain many examples of Korean Buddhist temples, statues, pagodas, etc. No index or bibliography. Clearly introductory, but highly valuable for its pictures.

(8) KIM, CHEWON. <u>The Arts of Korea</u>. London: Thames and Hudson, 1966, 284 pp., including 24 color, 262 black and white plates.

Most of the book discusses ceramics, bronze, gold, and lacquer works, with sporadic references to Buddhism throughout. Part 3 addresses itself to Buddhist sculpture, roughly from the sixth to eleventh centuries, for the most part describing outstanding pieces. Included are several good maps, a glossary of foreign terms, a comparative chronology of Korea, China, and Japan, and large, attractive plates. A simple, general introduction.

(9) _____. "The Stone Pagoda of Kuo Huang Li in South Korea." <u>Artibus Asiae</u>, 13 (1950), 25-38, 15 figures.

A discussion of a pagoda near the small town of Kyongju in South Korea, the ancient capital of the Silla Dynasty. Besides discussing this pagoda and its reliefs in detail, the author also covers the development of pagoda construction in Korea, which, according to literary references, began in the fourth century A.D.

(10) _____. "Treasures from the Songyimsa Temple in Southern Korea." <u>Artibus Asiae</u>, 22 (1959), 95-112, 22 figures.

Detailed discussion of a little known Buddhist temple called Songyimsa in Southern Korea, originally built in the Great Silla Period (668-935), originally a large temple compound with many buildings. Today, two wooden structures which house images and a brick pagoda remain. The poor condition of the brick pagoda (probably seventh century) warranted extensive restoration, and during this process interesting relics were found—particularly a gilt bronze shrine which contained the sarira (relics of the Buddha's body). This is the first object of this kind found in Korea.

Japan

(11) KIM, CHEWON and WONG-YONG KIM. Treasures of Korean Art: 2000 Years of Ceramics, Sculptures, and Jeweled Arts. New York: Abrams, 1966, 283 pp., 24 color, 101 black and white plates, 11 drawings and ink rubbings.

An inviting visual and textual introduction with extremely good plates. Buddhist works are dealt with in one section specifically devoted to Buddhist sculpture of the Three Kingdoms, the Great Silla, the Koryu, and Yi periods. Many Buddhist statues appear in the plates. An excellent comprehensive introduction to the art of an area infrequently treated in Western language, with special relevance to Buddhist art.

(12) Masterpieces of Korean Art: An Exhibition under the Auspices of the Government of the Republic of Korea. 1957, 182 pp., 187 illustrations.

Catalogue of an exhibition of Korean art works which were exhibited in several of the major museums in the United States. Although the majority of the works in this exhibition are secular, Plates 26-50 illustrate works which are important to Buddhism. The majority of these works are in bronze and date from the sixth through the fourteenth century. The descriptive material is minimal, but the plates clearly demonstrate the stylistic developments of Korean art of the time.

(13) McCUNE, EVELYN. The Arts of Korea: An Illustrated History. Rutland, Vt.: Charles E. Tuttle, 1962, 452 pp., 314 illustrations.

"This book is the first attempt in English to present a chronological account of the sweep of Korean art, and it is the first attempt to present the subject in a nonscholarly way for the use of the ordinary reader," as the text describes itself. No separate section is devoted to Buddhist art, yet the influence, introduction, official adoption, etc. of Buddhist art, as well as specific Buddhas and bodhisattvas are dealt with in many places passim. The extensive black and white (and a few color) illustrations are dominated by Buddhist subjects such as pagodas, statues, temples, paintings, etc. An excellent introduction replete with many examples of Buddhist art objects, perhaps the most comprehensive treatment yet in English.

(14) SECKEL, DIETRICH. The Art of Buddhism. See 5.1.4(13).

(15) SOPER, ALEXANDER C. Chinese, Korean, and Japanese Bronzes. See 5.8(9).

(16) SWANN, PETER C. Arts of China, Korea, and Japan. See 5.8(10).

5.11 JAPAN

5.11.1 Japanese Aesthetics (General)

(1) ANESAKI, MASAHARU. Buddhist Art in Its Relation to Buddhist Ideals: With Special Reference to Buddhism in Japan. London: John Murray, 1916, 73 pp., 47 black and white plates.

Comprised of four lectures given by the author at the Boston Museum of Fine Arts in 1914. The essays deal with the life of the Buddha, the beginning of Buddhist religion and art, the Buddhist ideal of communion in Japanese art, Buddhist cosmotheism and the symbolism of its art, and Buddhist naturalism and individualism: the transition from religious to secular arts. Plates are fair and now familiar. Understandably dated, but by a noted scholar early in this century. Introductory level.

5.11.2 Surveys of Japanese Buddhist Art, etc.

(1) Art Treasures from Japan. National Commission for Protection of Cultural Properties and Participating Museums in the U.S.A. and Dominion of Canada. Tokyo: Kodansha, 1965, 196 pp., including 120 illustrations.

Written to accompany a Japanese collection exhibited in the U.S. and Canada, it includes plates of sculpture, painting, calligraphy, and minor arts. Most of the plates are black and white, for the most part unexceptional in quality. A brief introduction surveys history of Japanese art from pre-Buddhist times to the nineteenth century. Not one of the better books of this sort.

(2) BUHOT, JEAN. Histoire des arts du Japon. Vol. 1: Des Origines à 1350. Annales du Musée Guimet, Bibliothèque d'art, n.s. 5, Paris: Van Oest, Editions d'art et d'histoire, 1949, 270 pp., 88 black and white plates, 7 maps.

A general history of Japanese art up to 1350. Of relevance to Buddhism is a section delineating the major epochs of Japanese history, their era names and their sexagesimal computation. Includes sections on the Japanese adoption of Buddhism and Chinese civilization, on the Fujiwara epoch, and on the Kamakura era. The index gives characters, romanized reading, French definition, and page numbers of terms in the text. Photographs are fair. Introductory to intermediate level.

(3) Catalogue of Art Treasures of Ten Great Temples of Nara (Nanto Judaiji Okagami). Second edition. Tokyo: Otsuka Kogeisha, 1932-1934, 25 vols.

Extensive coverage of individual temples and their contents including maps and plans. Full text in Japanese, resume in English. Volumes include: 1-12, The Horyuji Temple, 12 pt.; 13. The Yakushiji Temple; 14-15. The

Kofukuji Temple, pt. 1-2; 16-17, 18^2. The Todaiji Temple, pt. 1-3; 18^1. The Gangoji Temple; 19. The Hokkeji Temple; 20. The Shinyakushiji Temple, The Daianji Temple; 21-22. The Toshodaiji Temple, pt. 1-2; 23-25. The Saidaiji Temple.

(4) HARADA, JIRO. A Glimpse of Japanese Ideals: Lectures on Japanese Art and Culture. Kokusai Bunka Shinkokai, Publications Series A, No. 9. Tokyo: Kokusai Bunka Shinkokai, 1937, 239 pp., 144 plates.

A series of lectures delivered at museums and universities and designed to introduce Americans to aspects of Japanese art and aesthetics at a time when much less was known by the general public. Of specific relevance to Buddhism are: "Some Characteristics of the Japanese Which Have Influenced Their Art," "Certain Ideals and Characteristics of Japanese Art" (which discusses Zen), "Japanese Architecture" (dealing mainly with Buddhist temples), "Japanese Gardens," "Noh Drama," and "Cha-no-yu as a Cultural Institution." Highly interpretive, and introductory.

(5) KADOKAWA SHOTEN, ed. A Pictorial Encyclopedia of Oriental Arts: Japan. New York: Crown, 1969, 4 vols., 128 pp., 1025 plates.

A very comprehensive encyclopedia of pictures of painting, sculpture, and architecture. The text provides the barest introduction to the chronologically arranged periods of Japanese art from prehistory to the twentieth century. Glossary in each volume. The primary value is in the plates, of which approximately one-third are in color. However, none is thoroughly described.

(6) LOUIS-FREDERIC (pseud.). Japan: Art and Civilization. New York: Harry Abrams, 1969, 504 pp., including 430 black and white illustrations.

An ambitious work which examines Japanese culture in chronological periods ranging from prehistory to the Tokugawa regime which ended in 1868. Attempts to capture the "evolution of the spirit of the Japanese as a whole." Each period has brief subsections on architecture, painting, sculpture, as well as literary and political conditions. From the sixth century onward, the Buddhist element is heavily represented. Excellent plates which are well described suggest the great diversity of Japanese artistic styles. A thoughtful, comprehensive introduction.

(7) MUNSTERBERG, HUGO. The Arts of Japan: An Illustrated History. Rutland, Vt.: Charles E. Tuttle, 1957, 186 pp., 11 color, 109 half-tone plates.

A capable introduction attempting to fill the need for a history of Japanese art which includes crafts as well as fine arts. Deals extensively with Buddhist subjects. Chapters discuss: beginnings of Buddhist art in Nara, the art of the Nara period, with approximately the same number of pages on each period of Japanese art history through modern Japan. Each chapter (period) is divided into brief sections on painting, sculpture, architecture, and crafts. Plates are familiar, but fittingly illustrative. Gives a good, if elementary, sense of Buddhism in Japan's art history.

(8) MURASE, MIYEKO. Japanese Art: Selections from the Mary and Jackson Burke Collection. New York: A. Colish, 1975, 347 pp., 103 illustrations.

The catalogue of an exhibition held at the Metropolitan Museum of Art in New York. Although only a small portion of this catalogue deals with Buddhist sculpture and painting, the excellent descriptive entries and bibliography make it a very useful research tool. Each of the 103 pieces in this catalogue is fully illustrated and documented.

(9) NOMA, SEIROKU. The Arts of Japan. Tokyo: Kodansha, 1966, 2 vols. Vol. 1. Ancient and Medieval. Translated and adapted by John Rosenfield. 236 pp., 198 illustrations. Vol. 2. Late Medieval. Translated and adapted by Glen T. Webb, 299 pp., 232 illustrations.

Volume 1 moves historically from art remains of forest and village life through the successive art periods to the Zen temples of Kyoto. An essay on each period is accompanied by extensive illustrations with rather detailed captions. Buddhist art and architecture are touched upon in most chapters. One section is devoted to Zen temples of Kyoto. Includes a glossary of Sanskrit and Japanese words; a chronology of Japanese art until 1568; maps of Japan, Nara, Kyoto, and Kamakura and environs. Volume 2 is less concerned with Buddhist art than the earlier volume. However, it does contain a chapter on the arts of the tea ceremony. Includes several plates of Nishi-hongan-ji. Also includes a history of Japanese art from the sixteenth century and an index to both volumes at the end of the work. Good pictures, directed text, broad sweep. Introductory to intermediate level.

(10) PAINE, ROBERT TREAT and ALEXANDER COBURN SOPER. The Art and Architecture of Japan. See 10.9(4).

This book is divided into two sections. The first is by Paine and deals with painting and sculpture, focusing on Buddhist subjects in several chapters moving from the introduction of Buddhism (Asuka Period) through the popularization of Buddhism (Kamakura period). Buddhist topics are later touched upon in sections on the Muromachi renaissance of Chinese traditions and passim. Soper's architecture section deals extensively with Buddhist architecture of all periods, especially the Buddhist architecture of Asuka and Nara, Heian, and Kamakura periods. Includes an extensive bibliography and notes, glossary of terms, chronological table, and two maps. The numerous black and white plates are quite helpful. The most comprehensive and detailed introduction to the subject with a wealth of material of relevance to Buddhism, and sophisticated enough for the intermediate student as well.

(11) PIER, GARRETT CHATFIELD. Temple Treasures of Japan. New York: Frederic Fairchild Sherman, 1914, 334 pp., 59 plates.

A general introductory discussion of the treasures owned by numerous famous temples of Japan, divided according to geographical location: sections on the temples of Tokyo, Nikko, Nara, Uji, Kamakura, Kyoto and Koyansan. The work is interesting in employing the temple by temple approach, but not an indepth treatment. Contains no table of contents. Black and white photographs are unexceptional. Objects may now have been moved to temple or city museums.

(12) ROSENFIELD, JOHN M. Japanese Arts of the Heian Period: 794-1185. New York: The Asia Society, 1968, 135 pp., 57 illustrations.

The catalogue of an exhibition presented at the Asia House Gallery in 1967 and the Fogg Museum in 1968. About three pages of text apiece give a cursory introduction to esoteric Buddhist arts, the classic Buddhist tradition, the arts of the Pure Land creed, and the arts of the court. Deals almost exclusively with Buddhist art. The black and white plates and lengthy descriptions form the core of the work. As exhibition catalogues go, an excellent one for the study of Heian Buddhist art. Introductory to intermediate level.

(13) ROSENFIELD, JOHN M. and SHUJIRO SHIMADA. Traditions of Japanese Art: Selections from the Kimiko and John Powers Collection. Cambridge, Mass.: Fogg Art Museum, Harvard University Press, 1970, 393 pp., including 153 black and white and color illustrations.

General essays introduce each section. Those relevant to Buddhism are "Japanese Buddhist Arts: Ancient Epoch (500-1200 A.D.)," "Japanese Buddhist Arts: The Middle Ages (1200-1600 A.D.)," "Arts Related to the Zen Sect." There are separate sections on suiboku-ga, tea ceremony ceramics, and zenga. Each plate within the sections is accompanied by a description and explanation which forms a text in itself. An excellent scholarly, as well as visual, presentation. Introductory.

(14) SHOSOIN JIMUSHO, Nara, Japan. Treasures of the Shosoin. Tokyo: Asahi Shimbun Publishing Co., 110 color plates with captions, 9 pp. outline of the Shosoin, 91 pp. detailed explanation of plates.

An excellent representation of the major works in one of the most important collections of East Asian arts and crafts. One short section is devoted to Buddhist dedicatory records and one short section deals with Buddhist pictures and ritual objects. Remaining sections include one covering music and dance (though not specifically Buddhist), but most deal with secular arts, such as textiles, interior furnishings, arms, personal ornaments, etc. Contains excellent plates. Buddhist material is limited but unusual. Introductory and intermediate levels.

(15) SMITH, BRADLEY. Japan: A History in Art. New York: Simon and Schuster, 1964, 295 pp., including approx. 180 color illustrations.

Limited text, highly dependent upon beautiful color illustrations. Two brief introductory essays, one by Marius B. Jansen and one by Nagatake Asano, attempt a broad outline of Japanese history and art. The text is arranged according to the generally accepted time periods from the Archaic period to the Meiji. Buddhism and Buddhist illustrations are stressed in the sections on the Nara through the Kamakura eras. Excellent illustrations, elementary text. Introductory.

(16) SWANN, PETER C. The Art of Japan: From the Jomon to the Tokugawa. Art of the World Series. New York: Crown, 1966, 238 pp., 63 illustrations, 60 plates.

A thorough introduction to all aspects of Japanese art from pre-Buddhist times to the Tokugawa period. Both in plates and in detail, a vast improvement over the author's previous work on Japan (An Introduction to the Arts of Japan, below). Contains profuse illustrations of Buddhist sculpture, painting, and architecture with comprehensive discussion in the pages which move from the Asuka to the Ashikaga period, as well as scattered references to Buddhist topics in other sections. Color plates are familiar, but beautifully reproduced. Includes a good bibliography and chronological table paralleling Japanese, Chinese, and Korean art history. Excellent for conveying a sense of the place of Buddhist art in Japanese art history.

(17) _____. An Introduction to the Arts of Japan. Oxford: Bruno Cassirer, 1958, 213 pp., 168 black and white plates.

This book attempts to fill what the author sensed as a "gap" of his time by trying "to reassess Japanese art in the light of our vastly expanded knowledge of all the arts of the East." Includes crafts as well as arts, treated in an historical fashion in chapters moving from pre-sixth century Japanese art through the Edo period. Buddhist art is treated fairly extensively in the relevant periods (Nara, Heian, Kamakura, especially) with many reproductions of Buddhist works among the generally unexceptional plates. The unusual appendix gives alphabetical lists of the Chinese characters which form the names of the most important Japanese color print masters.

(18) TAKI, SEIICHI. *Japanese Fine Art*. Translated by Kazutomo Takehashi. Tokyo: The Fuzambe Publishers and Booksellers, 1931, 163 pp., 70 black and white plates.

Attempts to balance what the author interpreted as a problem of his time--Western interest only in Japanese art "curiosities"-- with a well rounded introduction to Japanese fine arts as a whole. Chapters provide discussion of the characteristics of Japanese sculpture, the characteristics of Japanese architecture, a historical sketch of Japanese painting. Buddhist art is emphasized throughout. A dated by competent introduction.

(19) TSUDA, NORITAKE. *Handbook of Japanese Art*. Second edition. Tokyo: Sanseido, 1936, 525 pp., 345 illustrations, 10 color plates.

Although an older work, this provides a detailed introduction greatly concerned with Buddhism. Part 1 (History) includes pages devoted to early Buddhist art, on Buddhist art under T'ang artistic influence, on esoteric art, on the arts of the court, on Kamakura art with a section devoted to Zen inspired art of the Muromachi period. Part 2 consists of a comprehensive guide to numerous temples and museums around Nara, Kyoto, Kamakura, and Tokyo, proving a pleasant "modern" balance to the history section. Well illustrated with black and white reproductions of the old favorites. A comprehensive introduction.

(20) VISSER, M. W. DE. *Ancient Buddhism in Japan*. See 1.13.2.1(8).

Both volumes begin with a chronological list of sutras used in the seventh and eighth centuries. No translations of the sutras are included, but there is a detailed description of festivals and ceremonies which accompanied religious holidays, such as the Buddha's birth, August lights, etc. Volume 2 focuses on the "Lotus Sutra," Konkyomyokyo, Yakushikyo, Shichi-Butsu-Yakushikyo, Kegon, Nehan, Yuimakyo, Bommokyo and Issaikyo. An index is included in Volume 2. A highly advanced, specialized book.

(21) WARNER, LANGDON. *The Enduring Art of Japan*. Fifth printing. New York: Grove Press, 1958, 113 pp., 92 black and white plates.

A successful introduction to the history of Japanese art which places great emphasis on the cultural and historical transformations underlying artistic changes. Sections relevant to Buddhism include: early Buddhism, Fujiwara, Kamakura, Ashikaga art, the transformation of nature in art, and tea, gardens, and Zen. A helpful introduction for the beginner.

5.11.3 Architecture

(1) ALEX, WILLIAM. *Japanese Architecture*. The Great Age of World Architecture. New York: George Braziller, 1963, 127 pp., 154 black and white illustrations.

A brief general introduction to the history of Japanese architecture with good plates illustrating important themes and styles. The role of Buddhism is touched on in many places and dealt with exclusively in a brief section. Slim, but successful.

(2) BLASER, WERNER. *Japanese Temples and Tea-houses*. New York: F. W. Dodge Corporation, 1956, 155 pp., extensively illustrated.

Not intended as an art historical work. Contains some text, but mostly drawings and some quite nice photographs, and brief discussion of numerous famous temples, tea houses, and even some Shinto sites. The author attempts to take as his theme "the elements which provide the immediate inspiration of these structures" in a visual sense. Unfortunately, there is no table of contents or index. An aesthetically pleasing introduction.

(3) DREXLER, ARTHUR. *The Architecture of Japan*. New York: Museum of Modern Art, 1955, 286 pp., profusely illustrated.

While not focused exclusively on Buddhist architecture per se, the book gives a general sense of the historical, cultural, aesthetic and structural/design background of many diverse types of Japanese architecture in which numerous Buddhist examples appear. Provides a good visual sense of Buddhist architecture as part of Japanese architecture as a whole, but does not delve extensively into its unique aspects. The text is very general. An interesting introduction.

(4) FUTAGAWA, YUKIO. *The Roots of Japanese Architecture: A Photographic Quest*. New York: Harper and Row, 1963, 207 pp., including 128 plates.

Photography by Futagawa, text and commentaries by Teiji Itoh, foreword by Isamu Noguchi. This book is mainly plates, including many of Buddhist temples and gardens. The brief text lightly mentions Zen aesthetics but does not deal with Buddhist topics exhaustively. Each of the large photographs has a paragraph-long description in addition to the text. Gives a sense of participation of Buddhist architecture in the larger Japanese architectural aesthetic tradition. An excellent visual introduction to traditional Japanese architecture.

(5) KIDDER, J. EDWARD. *Early Buddhist Japan*. See 1.13.2.1(4).

Deals with the archaeology of the early centuries of Buddhism in Japan. Of particular relevance to Buddhism are the pages devoted to a discussion of specific Asuka and Nara era temples, to burial practices and relic-cults (including a discussion of pagodas), and to stone carvings and monuments (with section on the Asuka Niimasu Shrine). With clear, unusual, black and white plates. A thorough but not overly specialized introduction.

(6) _____. *Japanese Temples: Sculpture, Paintings, Gardens, and Architecture.* See 10.9(3).

Dominated by large, sensitive photographs of temples, gardens, etc. An introduction deals with the history of Buddhist buildings from Buddhism's introduction to temples and gardens of the Ashikaga rulers. Subsequent sections discuss the fourteen major Buddhist temples and gardens with historical essays and extensive pictures. The main bibliography is of Japanese sources. Unusual in treating the history of individual temples and extensive photographs. Intermediate level.

(7) KIRBY, JOHN B., JR. *From Castle to Teahouse: Japanese Architecture of the Momoyama Period.* Rutland, Vt.: Charles E. Tuttle, 1962, 222 pp., including 268 illustrations.

Discusses the basic forms of the period (castle, Shoin mansion, sukiya teahouse, paintings, gardens, and gates), then deals with specific examples including buildings and gates in many Buddhist temple complexes (Nishi Hongan-ji, Daitoku-ji, Nanzen-ji, etc.). Although many Buddhist temple structures are mentioned and illustrated, the uniquely Momoyama architecture was not primarily religious. Further, extensive plates limit the text to a general and brief discussion. Specialized, but not technical. Introductory to intermediate level.

(8) OOKA, MINORU. *Temples of Nara and Their Art.* Translated by Dennis Lishka. Heibonsha Survey of Japanese Art. New York: Weatherhill; Tokyo: Heibonsha, 1973, 184 pp., including 207 black and white illustrations.

Briefly discusses, through numerous pictures and text, the dawn of Japanese Buddhist culture, specific temples of ancient Nara, temple architecture of the Nara period, the emergence of post-Nara period temples (mountain temples) and Heian temple architecture, reconstruction and reformation, Kamakura temple architecture and "the waning of a long tradition" (decline of temple power and temple architecture of the Muromachi and afterwards). Includes several interesting charts, architectural plans, one "lineage of temple compound layouts" and one pictorial chronology of the evolution of temple architecture styles. A good introduction, heavily dependent on illustrations.

(9) PAINE, ROBERT TREAT and ALEXANDER SOPER. *The Art and Architecture of Japan.* See 10.9(4).

(10) SADLER, ARTHUR. *A Short History of Japanese Architecture.* Second edition. Rutland, Vt.: Charles E. Tuttle, 1963, 140 pp., 123 plates.

A sound textual and visual introduction to the development of Japanese architecture in a chronological treatment from 600 B.C. through the Edo period. Predominant treatment is given to Buddhist architecture, particularly temples. Many black and white illustrations include numerous architectural plans and drawings of important temples and pagodas. Appendices include a list of numbers and plates in Amunuma's *Illustrations of Japanese Architecture* (*Nippon Kenchikushi Zuroku*), a glossary of Japanese architectural terms with kanji, plus a comparative table with major historical dates for India, China, Korea, and Japan. A thorough and detailed work. Introductory to intermediate level.

(11) SAWA, TAKAAKI. *Art in Japanese Esoteric Buddhism.* Translated by Richard L. Gage. Heibonsha Survey of Japanese Art. New York: Weatherhill; Tokyo: Heibonsha, 1972, 151 pp., including 180 black and white and color illustrations.

A good visual introduction to this topic with a rather general text divided into such topics as the esoteric art of the ancient period, esoteric sculpture and painting of the Heian period, the spread of esoteric art, and the world of the mandala. The section "Famous Esoteric Temples" treats briefly but individually seven famous temples (To-ji, Enryaku-ji, Daigo-ji, etc.). The section on "Some Aspects of Esoteric Deities" discusses specific esoteric deities, different types of Kannon, and Shinto gods in the esoteric pantheon. The heavy reliance on pictures is extremely helpful to the student who has never visited Japan, yet leaves little room for textual depth. On the whole, an extremely effective introduction to the subject.

(12) SOPER, ALEXANDER COBURN III. *The Evolution of Buddhist Architecture in Japan.* Princeton: Princeton University Press, 1942, 330 pp., 211 black and white figures.

Essentially, a history of Buddhist architecture from the Asuka through the Edo periods. Pages are devoted to history and stylistic detail of each period. The numerous plates include architectural plans, close-ups, and drawings of brackets as well as photographs of significant structures. All Chinese and Japanese words and names are accompanied by their characters. The bibliography mainly cites Chinese and Japanese sources. Among the definitive works in English.

(13) TAUT, BRUNO. *Houses and People of Japan.* London: John Gifford, Ltd., 1938, 318 pp., 551 illustrations, some color.

A very general introduction to the relationship between certain tendencies in Japanese architecture and Japanese civilization, at a time when much less was known about the Orient by Westerners. In the process, it produces a sensitive portrait of the Japan of the author's day. Buddhist influences appear throughout, but one chapter ("Gods and Demigods") is devoted exclusively to Buddhism. A sensitive humanistic treatment, explicating the relationship of Japanese architecture to Japanese life.

(14) Tokyo National Museum. Pageant of Japanese Art. Edited by Staff Members of the Tokyo National Museum. Vol. 6: Architecture and Gardens. Tokyo: Toyo Bunko Co., 1952, 50 plates, 73 figures.

A good general survey of the history of Japanese architecture and gardens from the primitive period (pre-Buddhist) through the Edo period. The text deals with major secular and Buddhist developments. Includes a useful glossary of terms and appendices of detailed drawings and architectural elements. The text includes: "Primitive Architecture" (earlier dwellings and Shinto architecture), "Architecture and Gardens of the Ancient Periods" (Buddhist architecture in the Asuka and Nara periods, changes in the form of Buddhist monasteries caused by the rise of Esoteric Buddhism and the Pure Land Faith, the development of Shinto architecture, the development of palace and residential architecture, Gardens of the Heian period, and the undercurrent of Japanese architecture), and "Architecture and Gardens of the Middle and Early Modern Ages" (introduction, the importation of new styles in the Kamakura period, Buddhist architecture during and after the Momoyama period, Shinto architecture during and after the Kamakura period, changes in residential architecture, the development of the "Tea Ceremony" and its influence, gardens during and after the Middle Ages, the development of castle architecture, and the development of cities and their architecture).

5.11.4 Sculpture

(1) Chinese, Korean, and Japanese Sculpture in the Avery Brundage Collection, Asian Art Museum of San Francisco. See 5.8(2).

(2) HENDERSON, GREGORY and LEON HURVITZ. "The Buddha of Seiryoji: New Finds and New Theory." Artibus Asiae, 19 (1956), 5-55, 9 plates, 16 figures.

The introduction by Leon Hurvitz deals with the historical background of Chonen. The remainder of the article deals with the Sakyamuni image of Seiryoji (A.D. 985), which is "probably the most important, best-documented and best-preserved sculpture now existing which represents the school and tradition of Buddhist sculpture connected with the sacred Udayana image of the living Buddha of which Hsuan-tsang brought a copy to the court at Ch'ang-an" in China. The interior of the Buddha contained several documents as well as fragments of textile which shed light on Buddhism of the time as well as textiles used during the Sung dynasty.

(3) KIDDER, J. EDWARD, JR. Masterpieces of Japanese Sculpture. Revised edition. Rutland, Vt.: Charles E. Tuttle, 1961, 328 pp., including 199 black and white plates.

A chronologically arranged survey of Japanese art from prehistoric times to the Kamakura period (1333). The text is basically a guide to the plates, which are magnificent, often full-page, with close-ups or different views of the same piece. Most of the plates depict Buddhist art. All are accompanied by ample commentaries. Includes a glossary of iconographical, biographical, geographical and historical terms. Introductory to intermediate level.

(4) KUNO, TAKESHI. A Guide to Japanese Sculpture. Tokyo: Maruyama, 1963, 69 pp. text, 100 plates, 37 pp. appendices.

A good brief introduction in English by a member of the Tokyo Museum staff.

(5) _____, ed. Kanto chokoku no kenkyu (A Study of the History of Japanese Sculpture in the Kanto District). Tokyo: Gakuseisha, 1964, 416 pp. Japanese text, 12 page English summary, 30 plates, 218 illustrations in text.

Deals with works around Tokyo and farther northeast. Includes numerous pieces, most previously unpublished. The introduction gives a brief summary of the history of Japanese sculpture. The excellent plates make this volume of special value, even though most of the text is in Japanese.

(6) LEE, SHERMAN E. "Six of the 500 Rakan." Art Quarterly, 10 (1948), 124-132, 10 figures.

While most of the art historical literature deals with the early tradition and the beginning of Buddhist art in Japan, Sherman Lee published a series of statues of rakan (arhats) dating to the seventeenth century in order to emphasize the chronological span of Buddhist production in Japan.

(7) McCALLUM, DONALD F. "The Sculpture of Enku." Part 1. "The Early Period." Oriental Art, 20 (1974), 174-191, 19 figures. Part 2. "The Mature Period." Oriental Art, 20 (1974), 400-413, 11 figures.

As McCallum mentions, "considerations of Japanese Buddhist sculpture usually end in the Kamakura period, the monuments produced after that time being dismissed as derivative and decadent." This two-part article discusses the sculpture of a seventeenth century Buddhist monk, Enku, and considers Enku's work within the context of Japanese work as a whole.

(8) MORAN, SHERWOOD F. "Ashura: A Dry Lacquer Sculpture of the Nara Period." Artibus Asiae, 27 (1964), 93-133, 12 figures.

A discussion of the best known representation of this deity in Japan. The article considers the structural characteristics of this dry lacquer figure as well as the stylistic and iconographic issues. Includes a valuable discussion of the various dry lacquer techniques.

(9) _____. "Certain Features of Kichijoten Statue in Kondo, Horyuji." Artibus Asiae, 20 (1957), 111-122, 3 plates, 9 figures, line drawings.

A careful scrutiny of the wooden statue of Kichijoten of the Fujiwara period, ranked by Moran as one of the four or five best examples of wooden sculpture of this period. Reflects stylistically and structurally a transition between two periods.

(10) _____. "Early Heian Sculpture at Its Best: Three Outstanding Examples." Artibus Asiae, 34 (1972), 119-161, 20 figures.

A detailed study of three outstanding examples of Early Heian wooden sculpture: two Juichimen Kannons, one in Kogenji, Shiga Prefecture, and another in Hokkeji, Nara, and the Nyoirin Kannon, Kanshinji, Osaka Prefecture. Such Kannons achieved a new level of popularity with the growth of esoteric Buddhist sects in the early Heian period. Besides an extensive discussion of the structure of each image, attention is also given to iconographic and stylistic questions.

(11) _____. "The Statue of Miroku Bosatsu of Chuguji." Artibus Asiae, 21 (1958), 179-202, 4 plates, 5 linecut figures.

A detailed study of a key monument in the development of early Japanese Buddhist sculpture. A primarily descriptive article concerning structural features of this wooden figure. Some notice is given to art historical issues, iconography and dating, and Chinese and Korean prototypes for this type of image. This article, as well as the other articles by Moran included in this bibliography, are often the only extensive articles available in English on the subject.

(12) _____. "Structural Features of Clay Sculpture of the Nara Period." Artibus Asiae, 23 (1960), 41-66, 7 plates, 9 figures, line cut drawings.

The use of clay sculpture in Japan reached its greatest technical and artistic perfection in the Nara period (eighth century). Moran's article is a detailed discussion of the development of clay sculpture and its structural features. Consideration is given to the prototypes of clay sculpture in China. Includes an appendix of Chinese literary sources referring to clay images.

(13) MORI, HISASHI. Sculpture of the Kamakura Period. Translated by Katherine Eickmann. Heibonsha Survey of Japanese Art. New York: Weatherhill; Tokyo: Heibonsha, 1974, 174 pp., 169 illustrations.

Exclusively concerned with Buddhist works, approached through a discussion of the Kamakura sculptor Unkei, his apprentices and descendants, the two Jokei's and Kaikei. In addition, considers more general aspects of Kamakura Buddhist sculpture such as the influences of Zen, the Nara Busshi, and Sung dynasty style. Quite good illustrations occupy the major portion of the book. An enticing introduction.

(14) NOMA, SEIROKU, ed. Early Japanese Bronze Sculpture. Tokyo: Takeuchi Shoten, 1964, 42 pp., 126 plates.

Part of the text is in Japanese and English. Notes on the plates are in Japanese only. The most valuable part of this book are the numerous plates including excellent details of small Buddhist bronzes of the Asuka and Nara periods. The English text gives a brief introduction to the function, history and technique of these images.

(15) NOMA, SEIROKU and JIRO HARADA. Masterpieces of Japanese Art. Vol. 3. Sculpture and Art Crafts. Tokyo: Bunka Koryu Kurabu, 1948, 21 pp., 70 black and white plates.

A very cursory introductory essay on the history subjects, materials, and techniques of Japanese sculpture and art crafts. Plates include many bodhisattvas and gods. Descriptions give a good sense of familiarity with who these gods are, but the text is not directed and the pictures are poor.

(16) SAUNDERS, ERNEST DALE. Mudra: A Study of Symbolic Gestures in Japanese Buddhist Sculpture. See 2.6.2(7).

A specialized study intended as "an aid to the student of iconography in organizing in a general way the common symbolic gestures that occur in Far Eastern Art." Discusses rites, contribution to Tantrism, origins and first representations of mudra as well as devoting space to the eight principal mudras, providing their Chinese, Japanese, and Sanskrit names with Chinese characters. Secondary mudras, asanas, and significant iconographical attributes also are given separate sections. Extended notes are intended for the specialist, while the text itself may be read as an introduction to the subject. A pictorial index of mudra gives names and photographic illustrations. Contains an extensive bibliography, and clear black and white plates. An essential work for the student of Buddhist iconography.

(17) SOPER, ALEXANDER C. Chinese, Korean, and Japanese Bronzes. See 5.8(9).

(18) _____. "Notes on Horyuji and the Sculpture of the 'Suiko Period.'" Art Bulletin, 33 (June 1951), 77-94, 12 illustrations.

Articulates the arguments for the dating of the Yakushi Buddha and the Shaka triad in the Golden Hall of Horyuji. See also Soper's review of Mizuno Seiichi, Horyuji (Nihon no bijutsu, No. 4), in Artibus Asiae, 28 (1966), which is an examination of Mizuno's views on the same subject.

(19) Tokyo National Museum. Pageant of Japanese Art. Edited by Staff Members of the Tokyo National Museum. Vol. 3: Sculpture. Tokyo: Toyo Bunka, 1952, 117 pp., 50 plates, 69 figures.

An excellent general survey in English of the development of Buddhist sculpture from the Asuka period through the Kamakura period. Impeccable factually, it includes both a general introduction and individual descriptions of pieces.

(20) WARNER, LANGDON. *The Craft of the Japanese Sculptor*. New York: McFarlane, Warde, McFarlane and The Japanese Society, 1936, 55 pp., 85 black and white plates.

A limited text, but the place of Buddhism is central. Divided according to standard Japanese artistic period divisions. The most extensive section is on the Kamakura period. Includes numerous fairly good plates of Buddhist objects as well as Noh masks and puppet heads. Intended as an introduction for the general reader.

(21) _____. *Japanese Sculpture of the Suiko Period*. Publications of the Cleveland Museum of Art. New Haven: The Cleveland Museum of Art by Yale University Press, 1923, 80 pp., 145 plates.

The text is ingratiating but erratic. Most of the pieces illustrated post-date the "Suiko" period in a literal sense.

(22) _____. *Japanese Sculpture of the Tempyo Period: Masterpieces of the Eighth Century*. Cambridge, Mass.: Harvard University Press, 1964, 165 pp., 217 black and white plates. (Originally published in 2 vols. by Harvard University Press, 1959.)

The rather brief text deals extensively with Buddhism. Includes pages on Buddhism and the arts, on T'ang China and Tempyo Japan, and on Abbot Ganjin, among other aspects of the sculpture of the period. Includes lists of deities and saints with Japanese, Sanskrit, and Chinese (characters) names and plate references, and a list of main Japanese sutras, Chinese characters, and Sanskrit names. Extensive but unexceptional black and white illustrations and lengthy descriptions of each plate are included. A rather specialized study.

(23) WATSON, WILLIAM. *Sculpture of Japan: From the Fifth to the Fifteenth Century*. London: The Studio, Ltd., 1959, 39 pp., 87 black and white plates.

Basing his commentary, where possible, on the illustrations provided in the plates, the author provides a brief introduction to the function of Buddhist sculpture as well as the religious and symbolic significance and attributes of the gods. In addition to the sections devoted to the Asuka, early Nara, later Nara, Heian, and Kamakura periods, the author includes notes on iconography. The large black and white plates are rather good. A successful introduction.

5.11.5 Painting and Calligraphy

(1) AKIYAMA, TERUKAZU. *Japanese Painting*. Lausanne: Albert Skira, 1961, 217 pp., approx. 86 color illustrations.

An attempt "to trace and illustrate the long development of Japanese painting in the light of the latest results of art scholarship in Japan itself." Avoids traditional time divisions (Nara, Heian, etc.) in the attempt to retain the unity of the different types of painting. Sections relevant to Buddhism include those on the introduction of Buddhist painting and the assimilation of T'ang style, on "Buddhist Painting of Japanese Inspiration," and on "The Renewed Influence of Chinese Art and the Development of Monochrone Painting." Includes a chronological table, two maps, and an extensive index. Color plates of familiar masterpieces are exquisite. One of the best general introductions to Japanese painting in English.

(2) ARMBRUSTER, GISELA. *Das Shigisan engi emaki; ein japanisches Rollbild aus dem 12. Jahrhundert*. Mitteilungen der Gesellschaft für Natur- und Volkerkunde Ostasiens, Bd. 40. Hamburg: O. Harrassowitz, 1959, v. 290, 34 pp., 76 pp. of plates.

A dissertation written at Heidelberg regarding one of the most celebrated Yamato-e scroll paintings. Armbruster deals with the style and history of the scroll, which represents stories of the Buddhist monk Myoren. The scroll was painted in a period of transition between the Late Heian and Kamakura. See also the review by Alexander Soper in *Artibus Asiae*, 23 (1960), 257-259.

(3) AUBOYER, JEANNINE. *Les Influences et les réminiscences étrangères au Kondo du Horyuji*. Publications du Musée Guimet, Documents d'Art et Archéologie, t. 2. Paris: Librairie Orientaliste Paul Geuthner, 1941, 140 pp. text, 48 black and white plates.

A valuable and systematic, though short, study of the wall paintings in the Kondo of the important Nara period temple, Horyuji (now destroyed by fire). Focus is on the Buddha figures, the bodhisattvas, the other diverse figures of a religious nature, and a number of motifs (landscapes, lion figures, the lotus symbol, and the nimbus or aureole). The final part considers a variety of foreign influences on these paintings--Indian, Iranian, Chinese, and Central Asian. Includes a bibliography suitable for the more advanced student.

(4) IENAGA, SABURO. *Painting in the Yamato Style*. Translated by John M. Shields. Heibonsha Survey of Japanese Art, No. 10. New York: Weatherhill, 1973, 162 pp., 152 illustrations.

A competent introduction to the subject with references throughout to Buddhist sects, themes, and influences, but no index. The subjects dealt with are: the origins of

Yamato painting, Yamato painting during the Heian period, four-seasons painting, picture scrolls, Yamato painting from the Middle Ages, and Yamato painting. A detailed study.

(5) ISHIDA, MOSAKU. *Japanese Buddhist Prints*. New York: Harry N. Abrams, 1964, 195 pp., including 32 color and 162 black and white plates.

In a few pages, the author introduces the reader to the early history and development of print making, prints of Buddhist scriptures, prints on fans and decorated paper, and block-printed sacred images. Includes a list of all prints that can be dated and a glossary of foreign terms. Color plates are excellent and have lengthy commentaries. A good short introduction to a specialized subject.

(6) MORAN, SHERWOOD. "The Death of the Buddha, A Painting at Koyasan." *Artibus Asiae*, 36 (1974), 97-146, 16 figures.

A detailed discussion of a famous Japanese painting of the death of the Buddha or Parinirvana of the Buddha, a popular subject vividly represented in Japanese painting. Includes extensive analysis of the physical properties and condition of the painting as well as an iconographic study of the entire work.

(7) NAITO, TOICHIRO. *The Wall Paintings of Horyu-ji*. Translated and edited by William R. B. Acker and Benjamin Rowland. American Council of Learned Studies in Chinese and Related Civilizations, No. 5. 316 pp., 85 black and white plates in separate binding.

A specialized study by Naito preceded by an essay by Rowland relating the Horyu-ji frescoes to Indian and Central Asian painting and religion. Naito's text deals with the four paradise scenes on the four large walls, the eight bodhisattvas on the small wall sections, the origins and the date of the Horyu-ji paintings. Two rather brief appendices discuss the symbol of the wheel and the Buddha's footprint. Includes an extensive bibliography of Japanese sources. A definitive work. Advanced level.

(8) OKUDAIRA, HIDEO. *Narrative Picture Scrolls*. Translated and adapted with an introduction by Elizabeth ten Grotenhuis. Arts of Japan Series, No. 5. New York: Weatherhill; Tokyo: Shibundo, 1973, 151 pp., 122 illustrations.

Relying heavily on profuse illustrations, approaches emaki from five points of view: the emaki and Yamato-e, historical development, emaki as an art form, emaki as historical mirrors, and selected individual emaki. As Buddhist themes were highly significant in this art, many important examples are discussed, but this is clearly not an exhaustive treatment. Unfortunately, there is no index. Excellent plates, limited text, alluring introduction.

(9) ROSENFIELD, JOHN. *Japanese Arts of the Heian Period: 794-1185*. See 5.11.2(12).

(10) SECKEL, DIETRICH. *Emakimono: The Art of the Japanese Painted Hand Scroll*. Translated by J. Maxwell Brownjohn. New York: Pantheon Books, 1959, 238 pp., 68 color, 29 black and white figures.

After a general introduction discussing the various aspects of the art of emakimono, the main portion of the work consists of color reproductions of several of the most important emaki, many of which are on Buddhist themes and their accompanying texts. Illustrations are exceptionally good. A good introduction to the subject both visually and textually.

(11) Shosoin Jimusho, Nara, Japan. *Treasures of the Shosoin*. See 5.11.2(14).

(12) SOPER, ALEXANDER C. "The Fire in the Horyuji Kondo." *Oriental Art*, 2 (Autumn 1949), 67-68, 1 illustration.

Describes the damage done to the frescoes in the Horyuji Kondo in January 1942.

(13) _____. "A Pictorial Biography of Prince Shotoku." *Bulletin of the Metropolitan Museum of Art*, 25 (January 1967), 197-215, 16 figures.

The article concerns a hanging scroll in the Metropolitan Museum of Art, New York, illustrating the life of Prince Shotoku, great patron of Buddhism and Buddhist art in Japan. By the Heian period, he became the center of a cult and was incorporated into the Buddhist pantheon. His unique position was based on the belief that he was a reincarnation of a great Chinese Zen master. Soper discusses the historical circumstances and basis for his cult, as well as the resulting cycle of paintings, of which this scroll in the Metropolitan Museum is an early fourteenth century example.

(14) TAKATA, OSAMU, AKIYAMA TERUKAZU, and YANAGISAWA TAKA. *Takao Mandara* (The Ryokai Mandara of the Jingoji, Kyoto: Garbhadhatu Mandala and Vajradhatu Mandala, the Oldest Mandala Paintings of Esoteric Buddhism in Japan). Tokyo: Yoshikawa Kobunkan, 1967. Text volume: 118 pp. Japanese text, 2 pp. English summary. Plate volume: 24 sketches, 100 plates.

A discussion and illustrations of the oldest surviving paired mandala in Japan, housed at Jingoji, one of the most important temples of the Shingon sect of Buddhism. These mandalas were supposedly drawn under the direction of Kukai in imitation of another pair of mandalas which were given to him by his teacher Huei-Kuo in Ch'ang-an, the capital of China in 805 A.D. See also the review by Alexander Soper in *Artibus Asiae*, 32 (1970), 90-93. Since the text is mostly in Japanese, the plates will be of greater use.

(15) TANAKA, ICHIMATSU. *Japanese Ink Painting: Shubun to Sesshu*. Translated by Bruce Darling. Heibonsha Survey of Japanese Art. New York: Weatherhill, 1972, 175 pp., 175 black and white and color illustrations.

An introductory work which stresses the role of Buddhist and, later, Zen influences on this painting genre in terms of such topics as "The Art of the Ancient Period," Secession from the Chinese Cultural Sphere," "New Trends in Buddhist Painting," and "From Devotional to Purely Aesthetic Painting." Priests and Zen adherents are discussed briefly in short sections on "Josetsu and the Shokoku-ji" and "Shubun, the Enigmatic Master." Unfortunately, there is no index, so specifically Buddhist-related subjects may not be approached directly. A competent introduction.

(16) TODA, KENJI. "The Shitennoji Albums of Painted Fans." *Ars Orientalis*, 4 (1961), 323-328, 13 figures.

An article concerning a group of paintings on fan-shaped paper. On the paper is a series of paintings of the common people of Japan in Yamato-e style. On top of this is written the texts of the Buddhist sutra Hokke-kyo.

(17) Tokyo National Museum. *Pageant of Japanese Art*. Edited by Staff Members of the Tokyo National Museum. Vol. 1: *Paintings*. Tokyo: Toyo Bunka, 1952, 111 pp., 50 plates, 76 illustrations.

A good general survey of Japanese painting from its beginnings through the Kamakura period. The text includes: 1. The Asuka Period, 556-645 (the introduction of Buddhism and the origin of religious painting). 2. The Nara Period, 645-794 (the introduction and development of the T'ang style). 3. The Heian Period, 794-1184 (the introduction of the new Buddhism and changes in painting styles, and the origins of Yamato-e). 4. The Kamakura Period, 1185-1333 (the main trends of the Kamakura period and their effect on painting styles, changes in the subject matter of Buddhist painting, realism in portraiture, the development of scroll painting, and man and nature in Kamakura painting). A list and explanation of plates are also included.

(18) United Nations Educational, Scientific, and Cultural Organization. *Japan: Ancient Buddhist Paintings*. UNESCO World Art Series, No. 11. Greenwich, Conn.: The New York Graphic Society, 1959, 25 pp., 32 color plates, 4 black and white illustrations.

Begins with brief introductory essays on the early history and impact of Buddhist art in Japan. Paintings of the seventh-twelfth centuries (images of the Buddha and other sacred figures, nature scenes and paintings on fans) are represented in attractive full-length plates which, however, lack full description. At the introductory level, with plates ideal for quick browsing.

(19) VIRA, RAGHU and LOKESH CHANDRA, eds. *Sanskrit Bijas and Mantras in Japan*. Sata-Pitaka series, Indo-Asian Literatures, Vol. 39. New Delhi: International Academy of Indian Culture, 1965, 11 pp. text, 59 facsimiles.

Essentially a reproduction of the Asharajo, a collection of the calligraphic masterpieces of the eminences of Japan's cultural history (such as Kobo-daishi) who left behind a treasure of bijas, varnapatha, and entire mantras, compiled by the monk Sogen in 1837. All five fascicles are reproduced, numbered into fifty-nine sections for easy reference. Includes examples attributed to Kakai, Saicho, Amoghavajra (eighth century), etc. Advanced level.

5.11.6 Zen Buddhist Art Forms

(1) AWAKAWA, YASUICHI. *Zen Painting*. Translated by John Bester. Tokyo: Kodansha, 1970, 184 pp., 140 illustrations.

A pleasant introduction to Zen and Zen painting, saying the usual things. The numerous black and white illustrations accompanied by paragraph length descriptions fittingly augment the text with familiar reproductions. Includes biographical sketches of the major artists. A competent presentation by an important Japanese figure.

(2) DRAEGER, DONN F. *Classical Budo*. The Martial Arts and Ways of Japan, Vol. 2. New York: Weatherhill, 1973, 127 pp.

One of the few competent sources in English on the Buddhistic contribution to the martial arts. See especially the first four chapters emphasizing the historical and religious influences of Buddhism.

(3) FONTEIN, JAN and MONEY L. HICKMAN. *Zen Painting and Calligraphy*. Boston: Museum of Fine Arts, 1970, LIV, 173 pp., 126 illustrations.

Based upon an exhibition of Ch'an and Zen arts held at the Boston Museum of Fine Arts in 1970, this book includes a wide range of works dating from China's Sung and Yuan periods and Japan's Kamakura and Muromachi periods (landscapes, paintings of monks, portraits, birds and animals, and calligraphy). The text treats the development of Ch'an thought and Ch'an related art from its beginnings in China through the Zen art of the Japanese Edo period. The excellent black and white catalogue reproductions are each accompanied by extensive, sometimes page-long, descriptions. An excellent, unusually direct introduction to the history of Ch'an/Zen art in the two countries.

(4) HASUMI, TOSHIMITSU. *Zen in Japanese Art*. New York: Philosophical Library, 1962, 113 pp., 4 illustrations.

In the tradition of D. T. Suzuki, Hasumi tends to see Zen primarily as a mode of spiritual experience which underlies and informs most of the classical traditional arts of Japan. Similarly, he tends to overemphasize Zen's role, but nonetheless fairly, clearly and insightfully expresses Zen's impact on and relation to the arts.

(5) HERRIGEL, EUGEN. Zen in the Art of Archery. New York: Pantheon Books, 1953, 109 pp.

A provocative and helpful book for seeing in concrete terms the relation of Zen to archery and, by extension, to all the martial and fine arts. A classic.

(6) HISAMATSU, SHIN'ICHI. Zen and the Fine Arts. Translated by Gishin Tokiwa. Tokyo: Kodansha, 1971, 400 pp., 276 illustrations.

An exposition of the spirit of Zen itself as well as its relationship to many Japanese arts (tea, Noh, sculpture, painting) by an eminent scholar of both philosophy and aesthetics. By Japanese standards, perhaps the definitive work on Zen aesthetics. The numerous black and white plates give clear examples of the author's at times abstract points. While it may seem overly subjective to Western readers, it reflects Japanese attitudes and scholarly approaches to both Zen and aesthetics. An important work, at the introductory to intermediate levels.

(7) KISHIMOTO, HIDEO. "The Immediacy of Zen Experience and Its Cultural Background." See 11.4.8.3(2).

This emphasizes Zen experience as an underlying model and motif for the traditional Japanese arts and culture. It suggests the important relationship between aesthetic and religious sensitivity in Japan.

(8) LEACH, BERNARD. Kenzan and His Tradition: The Lives and Times of Koetsu, Sotatsu, Korin and Kenzan. London: Faber and Faber, 1966, 167 pp., 96 plates.

An intriguing account of two late Ashikaga and two early Tokugawa ceramicists and the Genroku era which lay between their births. The influence of Zen Buddhism, tea ceremony, Noh drama, etc. is dealt with in several places, as Kenzan himself was a student of Zen. Includes some of Kenzan's diaries. Written by a potter, not an art historian. A capable treatment of an unusual subject. Introductory to intermediate levels.

(9) MUNSTERBERG, HUGO. Zen and Oriental Art. Rutland, Vt.: Charles E. Tuttle, 1965, 147 pp., including 53 black and white plates.

Attempts to explore the relationship between Zen Buddhism and traditional Chinese and Japanese visual arts. Some treatment of Zen-influenced modern arts is contained as well. Includes discussion of the origin and nature of Zen Buddhism, the introduction and development of Zen in Japan, cha-no-yu and Zen, Zen in Japanese architecture, Zen in Japanese gardens, and Zen and modern art. Plates are of famous works and sites. Introductory.

(10) READ, HERBERT. "Suzuki: Zen and Art." The Eastern Buddhist, n.s. 2 (1967), 19-28.

A succinct statement reflecting D. T. Suzuki's contribution to the important relation of Zen and the arts, as well as making its own points about this relationship.

(11) SATO, GIEI and ESHIN NISHIMURA. Unsui: A Diary of Zen Monastic Life. See 7.2.2(11).

Although not about "Buddhist Art" per se, it portrays various aspects of Rinzai Zen Buddhist monastic life in a series of amusing color drawings executed by a contemporary Buddhist priest. An entertaining pictorial introduction to Zen life which may be regarded as an example of "modern" Zen art, serving to humanize the often unnatural image of Zen life.

(12) SUZUKI, DAISETZ T. Sengai: The Zen Master. Greenwich, Conn.: New York Graphic Society, 1971, 191 pp., 119 black and white plates.

A collection of reproductions of ink drawings by the eighteenth century zen master Sengai, accompanied by Dr. Suzuki's text and explanatory notes. Sengai's work was related to both the scholarly bunjinga and haiga or "limited aphoristic poem and sketch" movements. Clear plates are accompanied by easily readable copies of the Chinese characters drawn by Sengai. The text is informative about Zen in general as well as about Sengai. Introductory to intermediate levels.

(13) _____. Zen and Japanese Culture. See 6.2.1.2(20).

An interesting series of essays which attempt to show the relationship of Zen to diverse aspects of Japanese culture: art culture in general, Confucianism, the samurai, swordsmanship, Haiku, tea, etc. Appendices include a translation of the Noh play "Yamauba." While considered overly idealistic by some, this still represents a significant interpretation of the relationship of Zen and the Japanese arts by an important figure. Plates introduce one to the "classics" of Zen art. Introductory.

5.11.7 Garden Art

(1) HAYAKAWA, MASAO. The Garden Art of Japan. The Heibonsha Survey of Art. New York: Weatherhill, 1973, 173 pp., 159 illustrations.

This book is among the better books on the garden art of Japan. It is generally sensitive to the religious meanings and influences on that art, and treats the specifically Buddhist influences, particularly in chapters three and four. However, the text is limited, and for the most part descriptive. Introductory.

(2) ITO, TEIJI. The Japanese Garden: An Approach to Nature. New Haven: Yale University Press, 1972, 205 pp., 105 illustrations.

The book attempts to show Japanese attitudes toward nature as mirrored through garden art. Seven types of gardens are discussed. The paradise garden and dry garden sections are devoted almost exclusively to esoteric and Zen Buddhism respectively. The section on tea gardens also stresses Zen influence. Includes sensitive color photographs and a glossary-index. An excellent introduction to garden aesthetics.

(3) ____. *Space and Illusion in the Japanese Garden*. Translated by Ralph Friedrich and Masajiro Shimamura. New York: Weatherhill; Kyoto: Tankosha, 1973, 229 pp., 103 mostly black and white photographs.

Discusses borrowed-landscape and small courtyard (enclosed) gardens. Although tea gardens are presented in an incidental role, and most of the gardens discussed are from private homes, restaurants, etc., several temple gardens are included in the photographs and text with a short discussion of Zen court gardens. The sense of intermingling of Japanese religious and aesthetic ideals is conveyed throughout. Contains no index or bibliography. An enticing introduction to two types of Japanese gardens, relevant on the intermediate level as well.

(4) KOKUSAI BUNKA SHINKOKAI. *Tradition of Japanese Garden*. Second edition. Tokyo: Kokusai Bunka Shinkokai; distributed by East West Center Press, Honolulu, 1963, 185 pp., including 140 black and white color plates.

Two brief essays on general aspects of Japanese gardens, followed by 140 plates, with more detailed notes on a number of important gardens. Not for the advanced student.

(5) KUCK, LORAINE. *The World of the Japanese Garden: From Chinese Originals to Modern Landscape Art*. New York: Walker/Weatherhill, 1963, 414 pp., including 205 black and white and color illustrations.

A comprehensive treatment of Japanese garden art done rather historically. Contains a discussion of the Chinese origins of Japanese gardens from the Nara era to modern developments. In addition to chapters discussing specific temple gardens (Saihoji, Tenryuji, etc.), the text deals with such topics as Zen gardens, Ryoanji, and impressionism in Buddhist landscapes. Includes a helpful bibliography, extensive notes, and tasteful photographs. Perhaps the most comprehensive introduction in English, relevant on the intermediate level as well.

(6) SAITO, KATSUO and SAIDAIJI WADA. *Magic of Trees and Stones: Secrets of Japanese Gardening*. New York: Japanese Publications Trading Co., 1970, 282 pp., including 200 figures, some black and white plates.

The book touches on Buddhism in several places. Some temple gardens are dealt with, but these are not primarily concerned with Buddhism. An excellent technical study of many aspects of gardens and their construction. The appendix includes lists of garden trees and plants, a glossary, and a two-page bibliography of Japanese garden books in English.

(7) TAKAKUWA, GISEI. *Japanese Garden Revisited*. Rutland, Vt.: Charles E. Tuttle, 1973, 161 pp., including 65 black and white figures, extensive color illustrations.

Although a few pages are devoted to a discussion of the history, aesthetics, and materials involved in a Japanese garden, the book consists mainly of extensive color photographs of important gardens. Intended to provide a good visual introduction to such topics as dry-landscape and pond gardens, and special themes (Buddhist Paradise, Tea-house paths, waterfalls and streams, and the like). Contains exquisite pictures, limited text.

5.11.8 <u>The Way of Tea</u>

(1) CASTILE, RAND. *The Way of Tea*. New York: Weatherhill, 1971, 329 pp., including 189 black and white illustrations.

A comprehensive, well presented study of aspects of the tea ceremony and tea culture in general. Discusses the history of tea, beginning in China with an extensive discussion of Sen no Rikye, including post-Rikye tea history. In a section on "The Tea Setting" tea gardens and tea architecture are discussed. Other sections discuss various major and minor tea utensils and the practice of tea (nonprofessional, professional, and special professional studies). A brief appendix gives descriptions of selected tea huts and rooms. A most successful and thorough introduction.

(2) FUJIOKA, RYOICHI. *Tea Ceremony Utensils*. Translated and adapted by Louise Allison Cort. Arts of Japan, No. 3. New York: Weatherhill, 1973, 142 pp., including 204 black and white and color plates.

Originally published in Japan as *Chadogu by Shibundo* in Tokyo, 1968. An effective and much needed presentation. Unusual in that it concentrates not on aesthetics or the history of tea, but on the implements themselves. Separate sections are devoted to the tea ceremony as a whole, the tea bowl, tea caddy and tea-leaf jar, tea scoop, kettle and lid rest, fresh-water jar and waste-water jar, flower container, incense and hearth utensils, utensils of the kaiseki meal, boxes for the tea ceremony utensils, and glossary. A good introduction to the physical accoutrements of tea culture.

(3) HAYASHIYA, T., M. NAKAMURA and S. HAYASHIYA. *Japanese Arts and the Tea Ceremony*. Translated by Joseph P. Macadam. The Heibonsha Survey of Japanese Art, No. 15. New York: Weatherhill, 1974, 186 pp., including 198 black and white and color illustrations.

Discusses all aspects of the tea ceremony in sections on: origin, types (formal, semi-formal, informal), suki (artistic taste), rusticity, refined, tea as a work of art, the design of the tea garden and tea house, etc. Historical as well as aesthetic issues are broached under these categories. The real heart of the book is the extensive and well done photographs of tea bowls, houses (and their architectural plans), and related arts. An excellent introduction, specialized enough for intermediate students as well.

(4) HISAMATSU, SHIN'ICHI. "The Nature of Sado Culture." *The Eastern Buddhist*, n.s. 3 (1970), 9-19.

An analysis of the "tea way" as a paradigmatic model for a whole system of Zen-based cultural forms in Japan. Hisamatsu is a major authority in the field of Zen and the arts.

(5) LEE, SHERMAN E. *Tea Taste in Japanese Art*. New York: The Asia Society, 1963, 111 pp., 65 black and white and color plates.

Essentially, the catalogue of an exhibition which attempts to deal not with the general arts of the tea ceremony or complete history of the art but "with the general taste for Chinese and Japanese art displayed during the earlier and more creative development of tea ceremony and of tea taste." The work basically consists of an introductory text, dealing with aspects of tea aesthetics, lovely plates of paintings, pottery and utensils associated with tea, and a description of the plates. A unique and attractive introduction not only to tea as an art, but to the related strain of sensitivity underlying numerous Japanese arts.

(6) OKAKURA, KAKUZO. *The Book of Tea*. See 1.13.2.4(8).

An attempt to introduce the "spirit" of tea, as well as some general facts and legends of the art, to Westerners at a time when little was known about such things. Provides general discussion of tea as "the cup of humanity," the schools of tea, Taoism and Zen, the tea-room, art appreciation, flowers and tea masters. While the style may strike the modern reader as romanticized, it provides a good reminder of Japanese perception of the pure ideals of tea, often besmirched in reality. Introductory.

(7) SADLER, ARTHUR LINDSAY. *Cha-no-yu: The Japanese Tea Ceremony*. Rutland, Vt.: Charles E. Tuttle, 1962, 265 pp., 23 plates, numerous small unnumbered drawings. (Originally published Kobe: J. L. Thompson and Co., 1933.)

Among the most comprehensive studies of tea and tea-related arts to appear in a Western language, if not the most comprehensive one. Chapter 1 deals with the various material aspects of the tea ceremony touching on aesthetics. Chapter 2, the major portion of the book, discusses major tea masters and important events associated with tea. Chapter 3 briefly notes miscellaneous interesting topics such as characteristic names of tea houses with Chinese characters and a genealogy of tea masters from Naomi to the present. An excellent introduction, with material for the intermediate level as well.

(8) TANAKA, SEN'O. *The Tea Ceremony*. Tokyo: Kodansha, 1973, 214 pp., including 84 black and white and color illustrations, 2 tea-room plans.

A general introduction to aspects of tea art covering the early history of tea, tea masters and tea styles, aesthetics of tea, temae, performance of a tea ceremony, tea architecture, and tea gardens. Some of the color plates are rather nice. Appendices include extensive notes to plates, a list with paragraph length descriptions of important tea houses, a glossary of tea terms, and a chronological chart of important events in tea history. A standard work with helpful appendices.

5.12 MUSIC, DANCE, DRAMA

5.12.1 Asia (General)

(1) BOWERS, FAUBION. *Theater in the East: A Survey of Asian Dance and Drama*. Evergreen Encyclopedia, Vol. 8. New York: Grove Press, 1950, 374 pp., extensive black and white illustrations.

A competent and very general coverage of these arts in all of Asia. Brief references to Buddhist literature are to be found on pages 4-6 (India), 85-105 (Ceylon), 167-168 (Cambodia), 275 (China), and 325-331 (Japan).

(2) BRANDON, JAMES R. *Theater in Southeast Asia*. Cambridge, Mass.: Harvard University Press, 1967, 370 pp., 73 illustrations, 6 maps, 3 figures, 17 tables.

A very helpful survey of theater, and one reflective of the part that Buddhism has played in a highly complex cultural/religious mixture of these traditions (see especially pages 23ff., 98ff., 281ff.). The book has both historical and typological treatments, and shows that the performing arts in general are part and parcel of each other.

(3) DE ZOETE, BERYL. *Dance and Magic Drama in Ceylon*. London: Faber and Faber, 1957, 237 pp., 38 illustrations.

A kind of diary travelogue by a noted and perceptive student of South Asian dance and drama. The focus of the book is first-hand descriptions of performances in Ceylon. See the index for specific references to Buddhism as it plays such an important part in Sinhalese arts.

5.12.1   Music, Dance, Drama

(4) HSIUNG, SHIH-I. "Drama," in China. Edited by H. F. McNair. Berkeley: University of California Press, 1946, pp. 372-385.

A convenient summary of drama (including music and dance), with a nod to the Buddhist influences on that tradition.

(5) HTIN AUNG, MAUNG. Burmese Drama. London: Oxford University Press, 1937, 258 pp.

A competent but older survey of the history and nature of Burmese drama. See the index for references to Buddhism and Jataka tales as they influence the dramas.

(6) JERSTAD, LUTHER G. Mani-Rimdu: Sherpa Dance-Drama. Seattle: University of Washington Press, 1969, 192 pp., 22 photographs, 6 figures.

An excellent source filling an important gap in information both about Tibetan/Nepalese Buddhist performing arts, and also about Buddhist performing arts in China (Chapter 3). Note the good bibliography at the end of the book. The Mani-Rimdu is a tantric dance/drama performed at Buddhist monasteries and among the Sherpa peoples of Northeast Nepal.

(7) KEITH, ARTHUR BERRIEDALE. The Sanskrit Drama. Oxford: Clarendon Press, 1924, 405 pp.

Although the bulk of Sanskrit drama is oriented to Hinduism, Keith includes a brief discussion of Buddhism and drama in India (pp. 42 ff.) and a chapter on the dramatic literature of Ashvaghosha (Chapter 3).

5.12.2 Theater and Drama (Japan)

(1) ARAKI, JAMES T. The Ballad-Drama of Medieval Japan. Berkeley: University of California Press, 1964, 289 pp., 10 line cuts, 3 black and white plates.

While the particular theme of this study is not necessarily Buddhist, the author treats important Buddhist and Buddhist-related performing arts which are antecedents to his subject. See especially the sections on gagaku, gigaku, and bugaku (pp. 26-46).

(2) GOLAY, JACQUELINE. "Pathos and Farce: Zato Plays of the Kyogen Repertoire." Monumenta Nipponica, 28 (1973), 139-149.

A careful discussion of a little discussed drama form, the plots of which have been influenced by Buddhist ideas and ideals.

(3) GUNJI, MASAKUTSU. Kabuki. Tokyo: Kodansha, 1969, 265 pp., 464 illustrations.

The brief text includes essays on the spirit of Kabuki, its history, Kabuki actors, plays and playwrights, production, performances, stages and audiences. The real core of the work consists of the profuse illustrations of all aspects of Kabuki and scenes from many plays. Includes a list of plays, a general chronology of Kabuki, and extensive actors' chronology. An excellent visual introduction with helpful text, useful also for the intermediate student.

(4) HIRANO, UMEYO, trans. Buddhist Plays from Japanese Literature. Tokyo: The CIIB, 1962, 103 pp., illustrated.

Translation of several plays by modern writers whose plots and themes carry Buddhist ideas and influences.

(5) KEENE, DONALD. Landscapes and Portraits: Appreciations of Japanese Culture. Tokyo: Kodansha, 1971, 343 pp., illustrated.

This book is a collection of articles by this noted authority on Japanese literature and culture. Of particular interest are the sections on Japanese aesthetics and Japanese drama, both of which come under heavy Buddhist influence.

(6) _____. No: The Classical Theater of Japan. Tokyo: Kodansha, 1966, 112 pp., 21 illustrations.

Buddhist elements in No are discussed in scattered places in the text. Includes beautiful plates and excellent text. Chapters on the pleasure of No (which gives a sense of religious aesthetic dimensions of No), the history of No and Kyogen (with sections on Yoshimitsu, Kannami, and Zeami), the background for performances, the role of music and dance in the plays, and the stage and its properties. A small record accompanying the book gives the sounds of actual No performances (Funa Benkei). An excellent and well-rounded introduction, with meaning for the intermediate student as well.

(7) _____, ed. Twenty Plays of the No Theatre. New York: Columbia University Press, 1970, 336 pp., line-cut illustrations.

Recent translations of No plays under the guidance of an authority in the field. The texts of almost all the plays reflect the important influence of Buddhism on the plot content and ideas.

(8) NOBURI, ASAJI. A Philosophy of the Japanese Noh Drama: An Excerpt from My Book of Noh. Tokyo: Tokushima, 1964, 18 pp.

A book not readily available, but one which is very good in relating No to the aesthetic and poetic tradition as that tradition reflects a Buddhist influence on the arts. Especially good is his discussion of yugen and myo, as these terms capture a kind of Buddhist "meta-aesthetic."

(9) NOGAMI, TOYOICHIRO. Zeami and His Theories on Noh. Translated by Ryozo Matsumoto. Hinoki, 1955, 89 pp., 19 black and white illustrations, 2 color plates.

This is an abridged translation of a larger work in Japanese. Its strength and relevance lie in its discussion of the Buddhist-influenced aesthetic of No. Of particular importance is his extended discussion of the term yugen, but also of other major themes in the aesthetic ideals of No.

(10) O'NEILL, PATRICK GEOFFREY. Early No Drama: Its Background, Character, and Development, 1300-1450. London: Lund Humphries, 1958.

An authoritative history of the early No indicating some of the Buddhist factors that played a part, though also showing the importance of Shinto and folk influence.

(11) PILGRIM, RICHARD. "Some Aspects of Kokuro in Zeami." Monumenta Nipponica, 24 (1969), 393-401.

Shows the Buddhist influence on the theory of performance and the aesthetics of No.

(12) ____. "Zeami and the Way of No." History of Religions, 12 (November 1972), 136-148.

An attempt to relate Zeami's vision of training and mastery in No--a vision heavily influenced by Buddhism--to general "Way arts" in Japan.

(13) RENONDEAU, GASTON. Le Bouddhisme dans les No. Tokyo: Publications de la Maison Franco-Japonaise, 1950, Series B, Tome 3.

One of the very few monographs in Western languages whose sole concern is Buddhist influences and elements in a major performing art in the Far East. An important and authoritative study showing both the general ethos of Buddhist thought informing the world of No, and the particular instances in the practice and plays of No.

(14) SHIVELY, DONALD H. "Buddhahood for the Nonsentient: A Theme in No Plays." See 4.4(10).

An interesting article tracing one particular Buddhist theme through several No plays.

(15) SUZUKI, BEATRICE L. Nogaku: Japanese No Plays. New York: E. P. Dutton, 1932, 124 pp.

In addition to the translation of several plays, there is a good introduction to the aesthetics of No and the religious influences on it. See particularly pages 39-47 for Buddhist influences.

(16) WALEY, ARTHUR. The No Plays of Japan. See 4.4(12).

A long-time standard introduction to No. While his translations of the plays form the focus of the book, note his introduction for special reference to Buddhism (pp. 57-59).

5.12.3 Music and Dance (Japan)

(1) GARFIAS, ROBERT. Gagaku: The Music and Dances of the Japanese Imperial Household. New York: Theater Arts Book, 1959, unpaginated, illustrated.

Though strictly speaking not Buddhist, gagaku and bugaku are ancient Chinese and Japanese ceremonial performing arts which have functioned importantly at Buddhist festivals and rituals. This book is a standard survey of these arts.

(2) GULIK, R. H. VAN. "The Lore of the Chinese Lute." Monumenta Nipponica, 2 (1939), 75-99; and 3 (1940), 127-176, illustrated.

Although the focus here is on the "zither" (ch'in) and its place in China, the article indicates the underlying ideology of playing the lute and shows the relation of this to Buddhism and Taoism.

(3) HARICH-SCHNEIDER, ETA. "Roei: The Medieval Court Songs of Japan." Monumenta Nipponica, 13 (1957-1958), 1-40; 14 (1958), 91-118; 14 (1958-1959), 73-109; 15 (1959-1960), 207-216, illustrations.

A major study by an authority on ancient Japanese music. While the focus is not on Buddhism, this long article does indicate the important effect of Buddhism on music, and the importance of Buddhism as a bearer of Chinese culture to Japan.

(4) HONDA, YASUJI. "Yamabushi Kagura and Bangaku: Performances in the Japanese Middle Ages and Contemporary Folk Performances." Educational Theater Journal (May 1974), 192-208, 4 plates.

An authoritative interpretation of Yamabushi kagura as the latter is an example of folk-Buddhist influences on the folk arts.

(5) HORI, ICHIRO. Folk Religion in Japan: Continuity and Change. See 4.1.4(4).

Excellent indications here of the points at which folk Buddhism joins and influences the folk religions and cultural traditions of music and dance. See especially pages 117-139, 212-215 on nembutsu-odori and shamanistic folk arts.

(6) KAUFMAN, WALTER. "The Mudras in Samavedic Chant and Other Probable Relationships to Go-on Hakase of the Shomyo of Japan." Ethnomusicology, 11 (1967), 161-169, 2 figures.

A brief technical article, but one which suggests an interesting relation between the rise and fall of pitch in Samavedic chant, and that of certain kinds of Buddhist chant in Japan.

(7) KISHIBE, SHIGEO. The Traditional Music of Japan. Series on Japanese Life and Culture, No. 12. Tokyo: Kukai Bunka Shinkokai, 1969, 57 pp., 87 plates.

A summary description of several musical forms in Japan, including such Buddhist-related music as gagaku, shomyo, and no. Descriptions tend to be musically technical and very brief.

(8) MALM, WILLIAM P. Japanese Music and Musical Instruments. Rutland, Vt.: Charles E. Tuttle, 1959, 299 pp., 89 black and white and color illustrations, 42 figures.

5.12.3   Music, Dance, Drama

    The standard treatment of Japanese music in English. See especially pages 64-74 on Buddhist music, but also references to the influence of Buddhism on other musical forms in Japan such as No, shakuhachi, and biwa music.

(9) NISHITSUNOI, MASAYOSHI. "Religious Music and Drama in Japan," in Proceedings: IXth International Congress for the History of Religions. Tokyo, 1958, pp. 375-381.
    A brief but authoritative survey of the main lines of development in religious music and drama. While the focus is Shinto-related forms, aspects of Buddhist music and drama are also mentioned as they play a part.

(10) TANABE, HISAO. Japanese Music. Third edition. Tokyo: Kokusai Bunka Shinkokai, 1959, 74 pp., illustrated.
    A short survey of various forms of Japanese music. See especially pages 21-31 for descriptions of Buddhist music (shomyo), and Buddhist influenced music (shakuhachi, biwa, and No).

6 Social, Political, and Economic Aspects

6.1 THE BUDDHIST COMMUNITY

6.1.1 The Structure of the Monastic Community

(1) BAREAU, ANDRE. "Quelques ermitages et centres de méditation bouddhiques au Cambodge." Bulletin de l'Ecole française d'Extrême-Orient, 56 (1969), 11-28.

Monks in present-day Theravada countries who are serious in their pursuit of meditation are in the habit of retreating from regular monastic life to live in more secluded hermitages. In this short article, Bareau examines some of the forest hermitages (arannaka) of Cambodia and discusses the lives of the meditators in them.

(2) BECHERT, HEINZ. "Theravada Buddhist Sangha: Some General Observations on Historical and Political Factors." Journal of Asian Studies, 29, No. 4 (August 1970), 761-778.

The author discusses concepts of Buddhist historiography, the establishment of the Sangha and Asokan political ideology, historical changes of the structure of the Sangha in Ceylon and Burma, "ideal structure" of the Sangha as revealed in the Vinaya in comparison with modern Sangha structure, and the contemporary political nature of the monastic institution.

(3) DE, G. Democracy in the Buddhist Sangha. Calcutta: Calcutta University, 1955, 120 pp.

In this work, intended for the specialist but also of use to the beginner, De traces the growth of democracy in relation to the framing of the Vinaya rules within the Sangha. The chief theme seems to be the assertion that majority rule always has been the way in which the Sangha has operated its own affairs.

(4) DUTT, NALINAKSHA. Buddhist Sects in India. See 2.4.1(5).

The primary thrust of this effort is to distinguish the doctrinal differences which existed between the early Buddhist sects. However, there is one particularly noteworthy chapter (pages 37-50) in which the author addresses the problem of disruptive forces within the early Sangha community. Here the reader will find a discussion of the structure of the community at that time and reasons for its split into sects.

(5) _____. Early Monastic Buddhism. See 1.2.2.1(3).

Though this work is most concerned with the philosophical considerations in regard to the path to nirvana, the reader is able to glean a picture of the early monastic community's character as it is envisioned in the canonical works. See especially pages 95-132, where the author gives an account of the Buddha's missionary activities.

(6) DUTT, SUKUMAR. Buddhist Monks and Monasteries in India. See 1.2.2.1(4).

This work marks the culmination of the fine scholarly career of this Indian scholar. The scope of the book is the historical development of the monastic community in India from its inception to its disappearance. The reader will find lucid discussions concerning the structure of the community; the evolution of the most important rituals; the interaction with the laity, and the laity's role in contributing to the success of the community; the rise of the monasteries as Indian universities; and the causes for the decline and disappearance of Buddhism in India. Highly recommended for the intermediate student.

(7) _____. Early Buddhist Monachism. London: K. Paul, Trench, and Trubner, 1924, 196 pp.

When this book was written, it included much of the scholarly work already accomplished in the field of early monastic Buddhism, for the author is at pains to discuss the variety of theories concerned with the rise of sramanas--the forerunners of the Buddhist and Jain communities. There are also worthwhile discussions of the Vinaya and the Pattimokka ritual. Recommended for the intermediate student.

(8) EKVALL, ROBERT B. "Three Categories of Inmates within Tibetan Monasteries: Status and Function." Central Asiatic Journal, 5, 3 (1959-1960), 206-220.

This article is an attempt to assess the character and status of "yellow sect" monks in their relationships with each other and with society at large. The three categories referred to in the article's title are Ekvall's device to distinguish between monks who are considered "emanation bodies," "School ones," and "priest rebels." The author evaluates each of these categories with respect to doctrinal status, origins, duties, sanctions and regulations. A good article for the intermediate or advanced student.

(9) EVERS, HANS-DIETER. "Kinship and Property Rites in a Buddhist Monastery in Central Ceylon." American Anthropologist, 69, no. 6 (December 1967), 703-710.

This should be of interest to the specialized or advanced student interested in Sinhala Buddhism. Evers here focuses in upon the practice of "ordination lineage" as a means to transfer property. After a sketch of the organization of the Sangha and how an abbot is succeeded, Evers offers his thesis that "a monk selects a relative as his pupil only if he controls temple property that the pupil might inherit." He supplies a valuable bibliography concerned with the same topic.

(10) HIRAKAWA, AKIRA. "The Two-Fold Structure of the Buddhist Sangha." Journal of the Oriental Institute (Baroda), 16 (December 1966), 131-137.

An interesting discussion based on Pali Vinaya sources concerning a comparison of the Sammuthibhutasamgha and the Caluddisasamgha. The author asserts that the former represents those monks who live within the boundaries of the vihara while the latter represent an ideal community which is "open in all directions," boundless, universal, and timeless.

(11) JOSEPH, MARIETTA B. "The Viharas of the Kathmandu Valley." Oriental Art, 18, no. 2 (Summer 1971), 121-144.

A study on the viharas of the Kathmandu Valley from which the author concludes that form and function of the vihara have continued to exist even though Buddhist monasticism has decayed considerably. She attributes this fact to desire of the "new priest class" to maintain identity with forebears of the tradition. Practically, form and function continued traditionally because of the abilities of the priests to use the format of the monastery to fit the needs of family residence.

(12) KERN, HENDRIK. Manual of Indian Buddhism (see 1.2.1[9]), pp. 73-101.

Within these pages is Kern's classic study; the author is basically concerned with the worship life and the monastic rules of the Sangha. Kern provides the reader with discussions on admission to the order and ordination, the Pattimokka ritual, the mendicant's accessories, the veneration of relics, the various kinds of sanctuaries, and the major holidays and festivals.

(13) KITAGAWA, JOSEPH. Religions of the East. Philadelphia: Westminster Press, 1968, pp. 155-221.

In this short and elementary introduction to Buddhism, the author is careful to relate the role of the Sangha to individuals (kings) and to the surrounding social order. A good place to start, as an overall view is easily attained.

(14) LAMOTTE, ETIENNE, trans. Le Traité de la Grande Vertu de Sagesse de Nagarjuna (Mahaprajnaparamitasastra) (see 3.3.1.2[6]), vol. 1, pp. 198-203.

These pages include a number of etymologies of the word "bhiksu," followed by a brief discussion of the four kinds of assemblies of bhiksus (sanghas). For another discussion of this by Lamotte, see his Histoire du Bouddhisme indien (see 1.2.1[10]) the section entitled "L'idéal du moine," pp. 66-68.

(15) LAW, B. C. "A Short Account of the Wandering Ascetics (Parivrajakas) in India in the Sixth Century B.C." Journal of the Bihar Research Society, 53 (1967), 17-26.

An introductory article in which the author generally characterizes the life style and practices of the paribbajakas as can be derived from the Pali texts.

(16) LECLERE, ADHEMARD. Le Bouddhisme au Cambodge (see 1.6.1[4]), pp. 389-428.

Leclere's chapter on the Sangha outlines the authority structure of the community from the individual monasteries to the national level. From a discussion of a monk's confessional, the author reviews the basic regimentation of the Bhikku's routine.

(17) LESTER, ROBERT. Theravada Buddhism in Southeast Asia. Ann Arbor: University of Michigan Press, 1973, pp. 47-65, 83-129.

In these chapters of this introductory work, Lester sketches the ideal of the monk as it has been developed in canonical writings and attempts to correlate this ideal with everyday practice. He also attempts to present a coherent picture of the structure of the Sangha and the king's relation to it.

(18) MARTINI, FRANCIS. "Le bonze cambodgien" and "Organisation du clergé bouddhique," in Présence du Cambodge. Edited by René de Berval (see 1.6.2[13]), and France-Asie, 12, no. 114-115 (special numbers), pp. 409-424.

Two short articles which make a fine introduction to the question of the structure of the Sangha in Cambodia. May be profitably read in conjunction with Bareau's article on hermitages and meditation centers in Cambodia (above).

(19) MASPERO, HENRI. "Communautés et moines bouddhistes chinois au IIe et IIIe siècles." See 1.11.2.1(5).

(20) "Le monastère bouddhique de Tep Pranam à Oudong." Bulletin de l'Ecole française d'Extrême-Orient, 56 (1969), 29-56.

A four-part article on a Cambodian monastery forty-five kilometers from Phnom Penh, prepared by a group of students from the Faculté Royale d'Archéologie de Phnom Penh. It treats descriptively the Vihara, the Monastery, legends about its pagoda, and the laymen in the surrounding countryside and their relationship to it. A follow-up article may be found in "Le vénerable chef de la pagode de Tep Pranam," in the next volume of the Bulletin, 57 (1970), 127-154.

(21) NIYOGI, PUSHPA. "Organization of Buddhist Monasteries in Ancient Bengal and Bihara." Journal of Indian History, 51, No. 3 (December 1973), 531-538.

A descriptive article in which the author has used the accounts of Fa-hsien, Hsuan Tsang, and I Ching as well as the Vinaya and epigraphic information to summarize the organization of Buddhist monastic life in India.

(22) PATHOUMXAD, KROUGH. "Organization of the Sangha," in Kingdom of Laos. Edited by René de Berval. Saigon: France-Asie, 1959, pp. 257-267.

A good overall treatment of the Buddhist Sangha in Laos with respect to monastic hierarchy, daily regimen, education, admittance, ordination, and rituals.

(23) PERRY, EDMUND F. and SHANTA RATNAYAKA. The Sangha of the Tri-ratana. Evanston, Ill.: Religion and Ethics Institute, 1974.

A general study of the Buddhist monastic community including discussions of rites, daily regimen, disciplinary code, and general role in Buddhist society.

(24) RAHULA, WALPOLA. History of Buddhism in Ceylon (see 1.3.1[10]), pp. 112-216.

In this study of the structure and administration of the Sinhala Sangha in its classical period, Rahula has also detailed the daily routines of the monks, characterized their communal and individual duties to the Sangha and the community at large, and sketched the peak events of a monk's career.

(25) SANGHARAKSITA, BHIKSU. The Three Jewels. New York: Rider, 1967, pp. 149-261.

An introductory discussion concerned with the basic life of the Sangha as it was expressed in rituals, its regimen, and interaction with the community at large. The role and practices of the laity and the popular forms of worship and ritual which developed are also treated. Suitable to begin the study of the Buddhist community.

(26) SHASTRI, AJAY M. An Outline of Early Buddhism. Varanasi: Indological Book House, 1965, pp. 112-150.

An account of the formation of the Sangha (both the order of monks and the order of nuns) on the basis of canonical literature, inscriptions, paintings, and pilgrims' accounts. There is also a discussion of what constituted the order of the Sangha (local or collective). A good source of canonical references to the life of the Sangha in its Indian development.

(27) SINGH, MADAN MOHAN. "Life in the Buddhist Monastery During the 6th Century B.C." Journal of the Bihar Research Society, 40 (1954), 131-154.

This article contains a picture of the early Buddhist monastic life as it has been portrayed in the Jatakas, the Cullavagga and other early sources. The author depicts the rite of ordination, the Sangha authority structure, and dress, and considers the problem of Bhikkunis. Whether there were Buddhist monasteries at all in the sixty century B.C. is a highly debatable question.

(28) WELCH, HOLMES. "Dharma Scrolls and the Succession of Abbots in Chinese Monasteries." T'oung Pao, 50 (1963), 93-149.

This is for the advanced or specialized student. Welch accounts for the nature of the "dharma scroll," its importance for abbots, and the selecting of worthy monks for succession.

(29) _____. The Practice of Chinese Buddhism, 1900-1950. Cambridge, Mass.: Harvard University Press, 1967, pp. 3-245.

The whole of Part 1, entitled "Monastic Institutions," makes a very fine in-depth introduction to the structure of the monastic community in China. See especially the chapters on "The People of the Monastery," "Hereditary and Branch Temples," "The Abbot," and "The Economy of the Monastery."

(30) YALMAN, NUR. "The Ascetic Buddhist Monks of Ceylon." Ethnology, 1 (1962), 315-328.

This article is concerned with the "Tapasa" monks who profess strict adherence to "the Buddha's original teachings." Thus, they reject the ways of the established Sangha and temple life. Yalman compares this sect with orthodox practices and Sangha structure. But before doing so, he describes the "Tapasa" organization, the symbolism of "bones," initiation, and dress. Finally, he examines the motivations of asceticism, and its place in societies.

6.1.2 Monks and the Laity

(1) BAREAU, ANDRE. La vie et l'organisation des communautés bouddhiques modernes de Ceylan. Pondichéry: Institut français d'indologie, 1957, 90 pp.

This is a concise and lucid study of the modern community in Ceylon which is valuable to the intermediate and the advanced student. The author compares the modern with the ancient monastery, describes the modern cult, and places the individual monastery in respect to the larger monastic community.

(2) BARUA, D. K. "Buddhism and Lay Worshippers." The Maha Bodhi, 74, nos. 3-4 (March-April 1966), 38-44.

A rather straightforward review of the activities performed by the laity as presented in the Pali Canon. The author outlines these activities as taking refuge, observing sila, listening to the Uposatha, offering robes, taking pilgrimage, and performing stupa veneration.

(3) _____. "Secular Discourses of Buddha to the Laity." The Mahabodhi, 74, nos. 1-2 (January-February 1966), 10-14.

This article is basically an uncritical review of the Buddha's discourses to the laity as they are presented in the Sigalovada Suttanta and other Suttas.

(4) BUNNAG, JANE. Buddhist Monk, Buddhist Layman? Cambridge: Cambridge University Press, 1973, 219 pp.

Based upon field observation, this study represents an attempt by a contemporary anthropologist to study the basic roles played by the monk, layman, and the wat. Though her findings are based upon data collected in a rural Thai village, Bunnag is at pains to make generalizations from her analyses. This book is recommended for the intermediate student.

(5) CONZE, EDWARD. Buddhism: Its Essence and Development (see 1.1[2]), pp. 70-88.

This is one of the best introductory treatments of lay Buddhism to which the beginning student can be directed. Conze sketches the place of laity within the Buddhist community as a whole, the services offered by the Sangha to the laity, and the influences wielded by the laity in the actual practice of Buddhism.

(6) DUTT, NALINAKSHA. "The Place of the Laity in Early Buddhism." The Indian Historical Quarterly, 21 (1945), 163-183.

A good discussion of the activities and responsibilities of the Buddhist laity as it can be discerned in the canonical materials. Dutt summarizes the discourses of the Buddha delivered to the laity, the moral precepts observed, the role of the laity as the "supplier" of the Sangha, and finally, whether a lay devotee could become an arhat.

(7) DUTT, SUKUMAR. Buddhist Monks and Monasteries in India. See also 1.2.2.1(4).

(8) GOKHALE, B. G. Buddhism and Asoka (see 1.2.2.2[3]), pp. 25-27.

These pages represent a historical treatment of the development of the position of the layman in relation to the Sangha, from the earliest beginnings to the time of Asoka.

(9) _____. "The Early Buddhist Elite." Journal of Indian History, 43, no. 2 (August 1965), 391-402.

In this article, Gokhale seeks to establish the role played by an elite group of Buddhists who chiefly contributed to developing dogma, practices, and missionary endeavors from 500 B.C. to 200 B.C. The author mainly draws his data from the Pali Canon, specifically the Thera and Theri Gathas.

(10) INGERSOLL, JASPER. "The Priest Role in Central Village Thailand," in Anthropological Studies in Theravada Buddhism. New Haven: Yale Southeast Asia Studies, 1966, pp. 51-76.

This article centers on the role of the priest in Thai village religious life and the general features of Thai village religious life which can be discerned from a study of this important role. Ingersoll divides his analysis into five parts: the priest's duties, his relationships with other priests and with laymen, norms regulating his role, the basic value concerns of his role, and the sources of his training. A good article for the advanced student.

(11) KRISHNAN, Y. "Was It Permissible for a Samnyasi (Monk) to Revert to Lay Life?" Annals of the Bhandarkar Oriental Institute Society, 50 (1969), 75-89.

The author seeks to show that it was acceptable for a sannyasin or a bhikshu to leave the monastic community permanently and not be hindered by a negative stigma in the countries outside of India. This, however, was not the case in India. The author then attempts to explain why it became permissible to leave the Sangha in Ceylon, Burma, China, and Tibet.

(12) LA VALLEE POUSSIN, LOUIS DE. "Les fidèles laïcs ou Upasaka." Bulletin de la Classe des Lettres et de Sciences Morales et Politiques, Académie Royale des Sciences, des Lettres, et Beaux Arts de Belgique (1925), pp. 15-34.

The author begins his discussion of the general structure of the early Buddhist community by surveying the traditional roles of the monk, layman, nun, and laywoman. He then goes on to note the importance of the five cardinal precepts appropriate to the laity and notes their merit-making practices. The entire article is drawn from canonical sources.

(13) LESTER, ROBERT. Theravada Buddhism in Southeast Asia (see 6.1.1[17]), pp. 130-150.

This chapter gives a brief characterization of the laity's relationship to the practice of Buddhism. It can be of use to the beginning student. Lester surveys the ritual aspect, popular beliefs, and Buddhist-influenced political organizations and activities.

(14) MORGAN, F. BRUCE. "Vocation of Monk and Layman: Signs of Change in Thai Buddhist Ethics," in Tradition and Change in Theravada Buddhism (see 6.2.1.1[40]), pp. 68-77. See also 11.3(14).

(15) OBEYESEKERE, GANANATH. "Sin, Theodicy, and Salvation," in Dialectic in Practical Religion. Edited by Edmund Leach. London: Cambridge, 1968, pp. 7-40.

The author implies that the pious life which is exhibited in the Pali and Sanskrit scriptures and achieved to some extent by some monastic recluses is not a mode of existence which could be adhered to by the general body of a religious congregation. Hence, the monk serves as a reminder to the laity not of what the layman should be, but of what he cannot hope to be.

(16) PACHOW, W. "Legal Dealings between the Buddhist Sangha and the Laity." All-India Oriental Conference: Nagpur University, Thirteenth Session, 1946, pp. 352-357.

Through the use of two illustrations taken from the Buddhist canon, Pachow seeks to show the nature of Buddhist law as it is concerned with dealings between Bhikhus and laymen. The first illustration shows that the Buddhist law punishes monks much more severely than the laity (which points to the conclusion drawn by Pachow that Upasakas are not counted as members of the order). The second illustration demonstrates that the law does not deal harshly with the laity because of the Sangha's economic dependence upon lay support.

(17) SADLER, A. W. "Engakuji and Kenchoji: Reflections on the Social Morphology of Two Kamakura Temples." Eastern Buddhist, 3, no. 1 (June 1970), 97-107.

After studying the Engakuji monastery structurally, the author determines that the first level of the monastery represents the presence of the Buddha, the middle level symbolizes the Dharma, and the upper level the Sangha. His determinations are aided by a functional study of the respective floors. At Kenchoji, the author proposes that the distinct building complexes within the monastery represent monastic and lay styles of life. Another grouping of buildings within the monastery represents the interaction between the monks and laity.

(18) _____. "Pagoda and Monastery: Reflections on the Social Morphology of Burmese Buddhism." Journal of Asian and African Studies, 5, no. 1 (October 1970), 282-292.

A well done article conceived of within the context of Durkheimian categories of thought. Correspondingly, the author finds two distinct levels of religious activities associated with the two types of building, one reflecting primarily lay activities and the other reflecting monastic interests.

(19) Sigalovada Suttanta, Digha Nikaya. Translated by T. W. and C. A. F. Rhys-Davids. London: H. Frowde, Oxford University Press, 1899-1921, pp. 168-184.

The Sigalovada has been called "the Vinaya of the Householder." It sets forth a series of ethical standards to be followed in the whole gamut of social relationships. In examining these, students should be especially mindful of the social background of Buddhism in its nascent development.

(20) SWEARER, DONALD K. "Lay Buddhism and the Buddhist Revival in Ceylon." Journal of the American Academy of Religion, 38, No. 3 (September 1970), 255-275.

The major concern of this article is with the forms that the lay Buddhist revival has taken in Ceylon. After giving a historical background, Swearer discusses the types of relationships existing between the monk and laymen, and the revival's effect upon education, social welfare, nationalism, and "internationalism."

(21) THAN, U AUNG. "Relation Between the Sangha and State and Laity." Journal of the Burma Research Society, 48, no. 1 (June 1965), 1-7.

This is brief but useful, recounting the traditional relationships between these three entities. It should be used by the beginning student. Than sketches the historical development of these relationships from the time of Buddha, through Asoka, early Sinhala Buddhist history, Pagan, Pegu, and Ava.

6.1.3 The Role and Position of Women

(1) BHAGVAT, D. N. Early Buddhist Jursprudence. Poona: Oriental Books Agency, 1939, pp. 158-190.

These pages discuss the traditional role of women as it can be discerned from the Vinaya. The author thus details the participation of bhikkhunis in the rites of Uposatha, Kathina, Pavarana, and Ovada (a rough equivalent to the Pratimoksa ceremony of the monks).

(2) BODE, MABEL. "Women Leaders of the Buddhist Reformation." Journal of the Royal Asiatic Society (1893), pp. 517-566, 763-798.

The text and translation of the stories of thirteen bhikkhunis famous in early Buddhism. Taken from the "Manoratha Purani" (Wish-Fulfiller)--Buddhaghosa's commentary on the Anguttara Nikaya. A helpful look at these relevant texts which are as yet not translated elsewhere.

(3) DHIRASEKARA, JOTHIYA. "Women and the Religious Order of the Buddha." The Maha Bodhi, 75, nos. 5-6 (May-June 1967), 154-161.

A general article in which the author begins by noting the hostile attitude toward women as presented in the Pali Canon. But the author goes on to note more congenial references and sketches the role of women in the religious community in general. Finally, the point is made that women were considered as possible candidates for arhatship.

(4) DUTT, SUKUMAR. Buddhist Monks and Monasteries in India (see 1.2.2.1[4]), pp. 126-137.

In these few pages, Dutt details the contributions of a long line of royal ladies of the Iksvaka dynasty to the construction and maintenance of the large monastic complex at Nargajuna/Konda during the post-Satavahana period.

6.1.3

(5) FOUCHER, ALFRED. Les Vies Antérieures du Bouddha (see 2.7.1[2]), pp. 157-195.
A useful discussion of and organization of the Jataka tales which reflect various (usually derogatory) attitudes towards women. Two chapters are devoted to this subject: "Le Bodhisattva et les Femmes" and "Le Bodhisattva-Femme."

(6) HORNER, ISALINE BLEW. Women Under Primitive Buddhism. New York: E. P. Dutton, 1930, 391 pp.
This is one of the few treatments of the role played by women in either classical, medieval or contemporary times. This eminent scholar, who was concurrently head of the Pali Text Society and translator of the Vinaya, has gathered her material from the canonical literature, the Jatakas, the Milindapanha, the Cullavagga and the Bhikkhuni-Khandhaka, in an effort to show that the status of women was probably in better accord with the Buddha than has been traditionally noted. She has divided her work into two basic parts. Part 1 is concerned with the laywomen and how they functioned as Buddhists within the roles of mother, daughter, wife, widow, etc., and Part 2 treats the almswomen, their admission, rules, psalms, and routines.

(7) RHYS-DAVIDS, CAROLINE AUGUSTA FOLEY. Psalms of the Early Buddhists. Part I: Psalms of the Sisters (Therigatha). See 3.2.2.1(27).
From the content of the Therigatha, the reader is able to discern some of the concerns of the sisters. However, it should be stressed that some knowledge of the early community is a necessary prerequisite for a full comprehension and utilization of these psalms.

(8) TALIM, M. V. "Buddhist Nuns and Disciplinary Rules." Journal of the University of Bombay, 34, no. 2 (September 1965), 98-137.
The author makes the point that the practice of renunciation among women was a fairly widespread facet of religious life during the Sramana period. She reviews the traditional causes for renunciation, why the Buddha was reluctant to admit women to the Sangha, and the monastic routine of the nuns. Finally, the author compares the rules of the nuns to the Pratimoksa rules of the monks.

(9) WEERARATNE, AMARASIRI. "The Bhikkhuni Order in Ceylon." The Maha Bodhi, 78, nos. 10-11 (October-November 1970), 333-337.
This brief article represents an attempt to reconstruct a history of the order of nuns in Ceylon by making use of references to their activities in Pali literature and Ceylonese traditional historical materials (Mahavamsa and Culavamsa).

6.1.4 Modern Buddhist Organizations

(1) BENZ, ERNST. Buddhism or Communism--Which Holds the Future of Asia? See 2.8(1).
Contains discussions of a number of modern Buddhist associations throughout Asia.

(2) BLOFELD, JOHN. Mahayana Buddhism in Southeast Asia. Singapore: Asia Pacific Press, 1971, pp. 40-47.
Brief discussions of a neglected topic: lay associations of Mahayana Buddhists in Singapore, Malaysia and Thailand, where they are a minority religion.

(3) CHAO P'U CH'U. "Buddhism in China." See 1.11.2.4(2).
Chao has long been a leading member of the new Chinese Buddhist Association, which has been the government's facility for handling the affairs of Chinese Buddhism. In this article, he describes some of the specific functions of this agency.

(4) SWEARER, DONALD K. Buddhism in Transition (see 2.8[18]), pp. 55-62.
A good though not lengthy introduction to Buddhist lay associations and their relationship to nationalism in contemporary Asia. He singles out for discussion the Young Men's Buddhist Association in Ceylon and Burma. In East Asia, he attempts to present the political philosophy of Soka Gakkai as a lay association of Nichiren-shu.

(5) WELCH, HOLMES. "Buddhist Organizations in Hong Kong." Journal of the Hong Kong Branch of the Royal Asiatic Society (1960-1961), pp. 98-114.
A good overview of the condition of Buddhism, both monastic and lay, in Hong Kong as of 1960. The author ably describes the organization of the Sangha, its sources of revenue, its governmental supervision, and the lay Buddhist organizations. Welch concludes that Buddhist organizations in Hong Kong do not play the economic, political, and cultural roles of their counterparts in Southeast Asia. However, he contends that he saw evidence of a revitalization of faith among the laity which had been sparked by a few very able monks.

(6) _____. The Buddhist Revival in China (see 1.11.2.4[6]), pp. 23-52, 72-86.
The chapter entitled "The Lay Buddhist Movement" contains much information on Chinese Buddhist organizations in the modern era. But see also references throughout the book. For the continuation of the activities of the Chinese Buddhist Association after 1950, see Holmes Welch, Buddhism under Mao (1.11.2.4[5]), especially the appendix for its role in the World Fellowship of Buddhism.

6.2 BUDDHISM AND THE SOCIAL ORDER

6.2.1 Buddhism in Relation to National Culture and Society

6.2.1.1 South and Southeast Asian Countries

(1) AMES, MICHAEL. "Ideological and Social Change in Ceylon." Human Organization, 22, no. 1 (Spring 1963), 45-63.

The author describes the changes which occurred within Ceylon causing a revitalization and transformation of Sinhala Buddhism in the 1950s and 1960s. First he characterizes the traditional religious system and then reviews the various groups of special interests primarily concerned with Buddhist transformation. Finally he outlines the ideological reinterpretations of Buddhism and consequent reformist activities which took place.

(2) BECHERT, HEINZ. Buddhismus: Staat und Gesellschaft in den Ländern des Theravāda-Buddhismus. Frankfurt: A. Metzner, 1966; Wiesbaden: O. Harrassowitz, 1967, 1973, 3 vols.

This work is the most thorough and most important study of the whole relationship between Theravada Buddhism and the social order. The first volume deals primarily with the basic questions and background, specifically in relation to Ceylon. The second volume concerns Burma, Cambodia, Laos, and Thailand, with an excursus on Vietnam. Volume 3 consists of a 2,000 item bibliography on the field.

(3) _____. "Religionssoziologie und Struktur des südasiatischen Buddhismus," in International Yearbook for the Sociology of Religion, Vol. 4, Essays on Research in the Sociology of Religion. Cologne and Opladen: Westdeutscher Verlag, 1968, pp. 251-295.

This is a study which covers some of the same ground which Bechert covers in other contexts, but includes also some very important comparisons of the relationship of Buddhism and society and Buddhism and folk religion in Ceylon on the one hand and Burma on the other.

(4) _____. "Sangha, State, Society, 'Nation': Persistence of Traditions in 'Post-Traditional' Societies." Daedalus (Winter 1973), pp. 85-95.

The author proposes that if the student of Buddhism is to understand the contemporary role of Buddhism in Southeast Asian countries, he must be able to discern the marked changes which the religion has undergone in its historical transmission. Bechert sees these marked changes as stages of development in which Buddhism can be seen to have existed in canonical, traditional, and modern forms. The thrust of his article is a survey of these marked changes in various Theravada countries.

(5) Buddhist Committee of Inquiry. The Betrayal of Buddhism. See 1.3.2.2(1).

This is an abridged report (the full one is in Sinhalese) of the contemporary state of Buddhism in Ceylon. The title refers to the broken British promise, from the Convention in Kandy in 1815, to protect Buddhism. The report is comprehensive in nature as it attempts to discern the social, economic, and political conditions as they have had effect on the Sangha.

(6) Digha Nkaya (Dialogues of the Buddha). Translated by T. W. Rhys-Davids (see 2.7.1[13]), vol. I, pp. 3-26 (Part I of the Brahmajala sutta).

The first portion of the Brahmajala sutta deals with Buddhist "moralities," listing numerous games, sports, "low arts," etc., which "Brahmins and some recluses" practice, but which the Buddha does not. These lists are important to the student who seeks material on the daily life and culture of the early times and the Buddha's relationship to them.

(7) EBIHARA, MAY. "Interrelations Between Buddhism and Social Systems in Cambodian Peasant Culture," in Anthropological Studies in Theravada Buddhism. New Haven, Conn.: Yale Southeast Asia Studies, 1966, pp. 175-196.

This is perhaps the most general article (in terms of scope) included within this volume and, as such, it may be a suitable piece for the beginning student. Ebihara first outlines the general ecclesiastical structure of Cambodian Buddhism, then discusses merit-making practices and the way in which these practices and Buddhist thought influence the economic life of the typical Cambodian village. She then looks at the influence of Buddhism in relation to group leadership and group formation and concludes with a discussion of the role of the temple as a social focal point.

(8) ELLAWALA, H. Social History of Early Ceylon. Colombo: Department of Cultural Affairs, 1969, 180 pp.

This book is useful to both beginning and advanced students. It focuses on the early period of Ceylonese history, reviewing the character of the caste institution, the family organization, the nature of various occupations, and finally the effects of Buddhism upon the traditional society.

(9) EMBREE, JOHN F. "Thailand--A Loosely Structured Social System." American Anthropologist, 52, no. 2 (April-June 1950), 181-193.

This article seems to have spurred the many subsequent articles which have dealt with the concept of the "loosely structured" Thai society theory. As such, it should be read by those who plan to test the veracity of this concept. In terms of content,

Embree's article is actually of the most general nature, as he attempts to support his "loosely structured" theory with somewhat vague observations in an attempt to document the "highly individualistic character" of the Thai.

(10) EVERS, HANS-DIETER. "The Buddhist Sangha in Ceylon and Thailand." Sociologus, 18, no. 1 (1969), 20-35.

This article, which is best suited for the advanced student, begins with a discussion of the social characteristics of the Sangha as a formal organization, carefully noting its goals. Evers then portrays certain aspects of the Sinhala and Thai social structures, hoping later to establish the respective impacts upon the Sangha in each country. He proposes that the central difference between the social structures in Thailand and Ceylon is a result of the presence of castes in Ceylon and the characteristically "loosely structured" system of Thailand. Surprisingly, he is able to arrive at the conclusion that "the more formalized and strict the structure of a society, the less formalized and strict is the structure of formal organizations. . . ."

(11) _____. Monks, Priests and Peasants: A Study of Buddhism and the Social Structure in Central Ceylon. Leiden: E. J. Brill, 1972, 136 pp.

A monograph on the interrelationship between the vihara, the devale, and the palace systems, which developed in and around the royal temple of Lankatilaka outside Kandy about the fourteenth century. Separate chapters deal with the social organization (involving secular and religious temple administration), the religious organization (ritual) and the economic organization (temple lands and temple services). The study shows the contrasting values which distinguish the three systems and the interdependence between them as a result of a clear division of labor. Intended for the advanced student.

(12) GEIGER, WILHELM. Culture of Ceylon in Medieval Times. See 1.3.2(6).

Primarily for the advanced student, this volume covers the period from 362 to 1505 A.D. The first of three principal parts deals with the social organization, including the caste system, family structure and domestic life, the nature of village and town life, recreational and artistic activities, educational and literary development, and economic life. The second major section thoroughly treats the political sphere, especially kingship, the royal court, and royal duties, while the final section deals with religious life, in both its popular and more orthodox aspects. While this work has been challenged by later studies, it remains a major contribution.

(13) GOKHALE, B. G. "The Buddhist Social Ideals." Indian Historical Quarterly, 32 (1956), 141-147.

In this article, Gokhale concisely describes the early evolution of the Sangha as a force within society. Relying exclusively upon canonical literature, he not only sketches the primary social ideals espoused by the early Buddhists, but also attempts to show how the Sangha became "the custodian of moral and spiritual values of society."

(14) GOMBRICH, RICHARD F. Precept and Practice: Traditional Buddhism in the Rural Highlands of Ceylon. See 4.1.1(7).

(15) HANKS, L. M., JR. "Merit and Power in the Thai Social Order." American Anthropologist, 64, no. 6 (December 1962), 1246-1261.

Hanks' article may serve as a good introduction to the Buddhist influence upon the Thai social order. The author begins by establishing the connection between the cosmic hierarchy and the social hierarchy, both based upon the notion of merit. He then notes the possibility of social mobility through the accumulation of merit or the possession of power. Finally, he takes into account the social function of education and makes the observation that acquired skills (intellectual or mechanical) are insignia of a higher social ranking.

(16) KEYES, CHARLES. "Buddhism and National Integration in Thailand." Journal of Asian Studies, 30, no. 3 (May 1971), 551-567.

This is an article for the student interested in Buddhism's effect upon the national life of a country. Keyes' article is primarily concerned with the Thai government's attempt to use Buddhism as a factor in unifying of the various ethnic peoples in Thailand from the nineteenth century to the present.

(17) KIYOTA, MINORU. "Buddhism and Social Change in Southeast Asia." Transactions of the International Conference of Orientalists in Japan, 14 (1969), 66-83.

A good article in which the author asserts that as the West provides an infrastructure model for modernization, Buddhist countries will be required to restate a formula which meets the traditional understanding of the masses of people in order to cope with the problems of socio-cultural change. The article provides a good introduction to the general topic of Buddhism and social change.

(18) KOSAMBI, D. D. The Culture and Civilization of Ancient India in Historical Outline. Delhi: Vikas Publications, 1970, pp. 96-198.

These pages of Kosambi's outstanding treatment of the historical development of Indian society are concerned with the impact of Buddha and his followers. Though the reader should take into account the author's philosophy of history, which is rooted in dialectical materialism, this treatment is one of the finest.

(19) LeBAR, FRANK and ADRIENNE SUDDARD, eds. Laos: Its People, Its Society, Its Culture. See 1.7.1(4).

As a book in the series produced by the Human Relations Area File, the scope and depth of this edition are necessarily introductory. The reader is acquainted with the basic facts of Lao history, politics, social structure, economy, geography and religion, in order to provide a basis for further and more specific inquiry. Though the discussion of Lao religion is cursory and not of much value to the more advanced student, discussions relating to values, polity, art, economy and education are careful to note the general significance of Buddhist influence.

(20) LECLERE, ADHEMARD. Le Bouddhisme au Cambodge (see 1.6.1[4]), pp. 497-529.

This section of Leclère's work is concerned with the expressions of Buddhist social ethics in Cambodian Buddhism. The author discusses within this context the ethical standard of the Buddhist king, the virtues to be practiced by the laity, and the etiquette involved in family life.

(21) LeMAY, REGINALD. The Culture of South-East Asia. London: G. Allen and Unwin, 1954, 217 pp.

Though the author proves his basic familiarity with the politics and economy of Southeast Asia, this introductory work relies heavily upon a history of Buddhist art. Indeed, LeMay has provided the reader with 215 plates, and seems intent upon conveying the underlying principles of Buddhist spiritualism as they are revealed through the art and architecture of pagodas, temples and monasteries. From this perspective, he succeeds in generally demonstrating the influence of Buddhism upon the creative talents of the Burmese, Cambodians, Thai, Mons, and Javanese.

(22) LING, TREVOR. "The Social Dimension of Theravada Buddhism in Burma." The Hibbert Journal, 60, no. 239 (July 1962), 314-322.

Suitable for the beginning student, Ling's article is a basic and simple discussion of a "contemplative" religion's effects upon the society of Burma. The author emphasizes the historical role played by the Sangha and the social dimension embodied in the Dhamma.

(23) MOERMAN, MICHAEL. "Ban Ping's Temple: The Center of a 'Loosely Structured' Society," in Anthropological Studies in Theravada Buddhism. New Haven, Conn.: Yale Southeast Asia Studies, 1966, pp. 137-174.

This article should be read by all students who are interested in the "loosely structured" society concept originally offered by John Embree in 1950 (above), for this author challenges the accuracy of the concept by positing that temples serve as a binding force in village Thailand.

(24) MORGAN, KENNETH. "The Buddhists: The Problem and the Promise." Asia, 4 (Winter 1966), 72-84.

This article may be read by the beginning student interested in the question of political and social involvement of Buddhist monks. Morgan introduces the elementary and basic problem of the Buddha's pronouncements on renunciation and the phenomenon of "engaged Buddhism."

(25) MULDER, J. A. NIELS. "A Comparative Note on the Thai and Javanese World View as Expressed by Religious Practice and Belief." Journal of the Siam Society, 56, no. 2 (1970), 79-86.

Mulder posits and compares Theravadan and Javanese world views and concludes that the differences help to explain the great appropriation of modernizing trends which has occurred in Thailand as opposed to Java.

(26) _____. Monks, Merit and Motivation: Buddhism and National Development in Thailand. Second edition. DeKalb: Northern Illinois University Press, 1973, 58 pp.

This is a study which seeks to view the functions of Buddhism in behavioral terms while at the same time attempting to analyze roles and policies in relation to underlying social patterns and processes. Hence, the author investigates the motivational character of merit making, while also discussing the monk's position in society as an individual and the Sangha's position within the total social hierarchy.

(27) O'NEILL, HERBERT. "Religious Influence in Thai Culture." Religions, 39 (April 1942), 12-17.

This brief article is suitable as an introduction to this very broad topic. The author makes general statements concerning the syncretism of Theravada Buddhism and animism, Buddhist influence upon the fine arts (including drama and temple architecture), the Buddhist style of education, and general revelations concerning Buddhist history that have been discovered through archeological finds.

(28) PARDUE, PETER. Buddhism: A Historical Introduction to Buddhist Values and the Social and Political Forms They Have Assumed in Asia. New York: Macmillan, 1971, 203 pp.

This book is a broad survey intended for the beginning student. The author pays a great deal of attention to sociological theory and is influenced by the analysis of Max Weber.

(29) PERARA, E. "Sinhala Culture and Buddhism." New Orient, 3, no. 5 (October 1962), 129-134.

Perara's article seems to be mistitled, as it is generally concerned with pre-Buddhist Sinhala culture. As such, it serves as an introductory, yet worthwhile survey of indigenous language, art, religion and social structure. Against this major backdrop, Perara discusses the religion of Asoka in its own scope and briefly sketches its reception and consequenct transformation of Sinhala culture.

(30) PFANNER, DAVID. "The Buddhist Monk in Rural Burmese Society," in *Anthropological Studies in Theravada Buddhism*. New Haven, Conn.: Yale Southeast Asia Studies, 1966, pp. 77-96.

Pfanner's study includes a detailed examination of the Burmese monk's activities, the social character of his relationships, values, and recruitment. At the end of the article, the reader will find a valuable comparison of the role of the Buddhist monk and the role of the "nat" specialist. This article is for the more advanced student.

(31) PIERIS, RALPH. *Sinhalese Social Organization: The Kandyan Period*. Colombo: Ceylon University Press, 1956, 311 pp.

A basic, yet detailed, study of Sinhala civilization as it existed in the Kandyan period at the lowest level of social structure. It may be utilized by the beginning or advanced student, but because of its sociological bent it is most useful for those interested in "permanent" institutions such as marriage, land tenure, revenue and economy, and government.

(32) PIKER, STEVEN. "Buddhism and Modernization in Contemporary Thailand," in *Tradition and Change in Theravada Buddhism* (see 6.2.1.1[40]), pp. 51-67.

A highly analytical essay which examines "The Project for Encouraging the Participation of Monks in Community Development" in Thailand. From his examination, the author argues that reverence for monks in rural Thai society is not a given, but the result of earned respect on an individual basis, and that although monks may attain some success as leaders of community development programs, the long-run result will be a dilution of veneration villagers now extend to monks. The result of the entire project will entail a lessening of Thai Buddhism's influence in Thai polity and a corresponding decline in Thai national stability.

(33) _____. "Comments on the Integration of Thai Religion." *Ethos*, 1 (1973), 298-320.

In this article, the author applies the "projective institution hypothesis" and attempts to argue the following: 1) practices (principally Buddhist) of Thai villagers express "personality dispositions" and are widespread, other beliefs and practices also reflect personality dispositions of more restrictive distribution; 2) that the variable distribution of personality dispositions is in part plausibly interpreted by variations in child-rearing practices; and 3) that the persistence of village religion is dependent in part upon precisely this psychological diversity among villagers.

(34) RAHULA, WALPOLA. *History of Buddhism in Ceylon* (see 1.3.1[10]), pp. 230-250.

This chapter of Rahula's work consists of a discussion of the social aspects of Buddhist Ceylon. The author provides a lucid analysis of Buddhism in relation to the caste system, the power of the king, and the vocations and customs of the laity.

(35) RATNAPALA, NANDASENA, ed. and trans. *The Katikavatas*. Munich: R. Kitzinger, 1971, 316 pp.

A critical edition, translation and annotation of the laws of the Buddhist order of Ceylon from the twelfth to the eighteenth centuries. Part I deals with the texts of the Katikavatas and Part II is a historical study of this material, including its importance in the religious, cultural, social, and political history of Ceylon.

(36) REYNOLDS, FRANK. "Buddhism as Universal Religion and as Civic Religion: Some Observations on a Tour of Four Contemporary Buddhist Centers in Central Thailand." *Journal of the Siam Society*, 63, no. 1 (January 1975), 28-43.

Reynolds deals with the symbolism of four Buddhist complexes which draw a continuing stream of visitors from all over Thailand. He concludes that in two cases this symbolism expresses an understanding of Buddhism as a universal religion while in the other two cases the symbolism expresses an understanding of Buddhism as a civic religion whose community is constituted by the Thai nation.

(37) _____. "Ritual and Social Hierarchy: An Aspect of Traditional Religion in Buddhist Laos." See 1.7.2(7).

Reynolds' article may be read by the advanced student of Buddhism or by the more general reader interested in the function of myth and ritual as functional categories within the history of religions. Essentially, this is an investigation of three festivals which involve the entire community and are concerned with New Year celebrations, with attention given to the social significance of their myths and rituals. The author concludes that these festivals express a social ideal which re-establishes the "traditional Laotian world."

(38) SARACHCHANDRA, EDIRIWEERA R. "Traditional Values and the Modernization of a Buddhist Society: The Case of Ceylon," in *Religion and Progress in Modern Asia*. Edited by Robert Bellah. New York: Free Press, 1965, pp. 109-123.

This article is introductory in nature and scope, as the author intends his conclusions to be representative of all Theravada countries. He begins by sketching the traditional nature of Sinhala Buddhism, emphasizing that Buddhism never became intertwined with folk religion and hence became a higher religion of the elite culture while still being practiced at the village level. Finally the

(39) SMITH, BARDWELL L. "Toward a Buddhist Anthropology: The Problem of the Secular." *Journal of the American Academy of Religion*, 36, no. 3 (September 1968), 203-216.

In this five-part article, the author succinctly examines the case of Ceylon since 1956 as being an instance of "increasing self-examination," the inherent problems with developing a social ethic within a "nibbana-oriented Buddhism," changes within Buddhism in respect to doctrine, monastic organization and practice, the "proneness of Buddhism" to this-worldly orientations, and the secular challenge to Buddhism. This article may be read by the student interested in contemporary problems of Buddhism in the modern world.

(40) _____, ed. *Tradition and Change in Theravada Buddhism. Essays on Ceylon and Thailand in the 19th and 20th Centuries*. Contributions to Asian Studies, Vol. 4. Leiden: E. J. Brill, 1973, 104 pp.

Of a total of eight essays, four deal with Ceylon (including a bibliographical essay by Frank Reynolds concerning Buddhism in Ceylon and Thailand in the last two centuries). The three other chapters dealing with Ceylon are by Hans Bechert: "Contradictions in Sinhalese Buddhism," "British Ceylon: A Neglected Aspect of the Nationalist Movement," and by B. G. Gokhale: "Anagarika Dharmapala: Toward Modernity through Tradition in Ceylon." This book is for the specialist.

(41) _____. *The Two Wheels of Dhamma: Essays on the Theravada Tradition in India and Ceylon*. See 1.3.1(11).

Intended for the advanced student, but of use to the beginning student as well, this work includes five essays (one of bibliographic nature). The first, by Frank Reynolds, is concerned with the emergence of Buddhism in India and the relationship between kingship and dhamma, especially in the Asokan experience. The next, by Bardwell Smith, continues this theme by examining the concept of an ideal social order as this may be perceived in the Ceylon chronicles. The third and fourth essays, by Grananath Obeysekere and Smith respectively, deal with the contemporary period in Ceylon and focus on the tensions and dilemmas appearing in Sinhalese Buddhism in relationship to social and political change.

(42) SPIRO, MELFORD E. *Buddhism and Society: A Great Tradition and Its Burmese Vicissitudes*. New York: Harper and Row, 1970, 510 pp.

A major sociological attempt to deal with the whole question of Buddhism's relation to society, using Burma as the primary context and example. The work is not without its difficulties, among which is the author's understanding of the various strands—Nibbanic, kammatic, apotropaic, etc.—of Buddhism which he distinguishes. Still, it remains a significant contribution to the realities of the relationship between Buddhism and the social-cultural order.

(43) SWEARER, DONALD. *Buddhism in Transition*. See 2.8(18).

This is an introductory work to Buddhism and change in Asia. The author covers subjects ranging from Buddhism's resurgence as a political force to its role in social ethics and education.

(44) TAMBIAH, STANLEY J. "Buddhism and This Worldly Activity." *Modern Asian Studies*, 7, no. 1 (1973).

A succinct article in which Tambiah re-evaluates the Weber hypothesis on the relation of Buddhism and social action, and tries out his own understanding of this issue.

(45) _____. "The Persistence and Transformation of Tradition in Southeast Asia, with Special Reference to Thailand." *Daedalus* (Winter 1973), pp. 55-84.

The author addresses the problem of how traditional institutions have endured and continued to play an important role in Theravada socieities. After briefly summarizing the manner in which Buddhism has been related to the political structures of Ceylon, Thailand, and Burma traditionally, the author specifically focuses upon how Thailand has responded to modern Western impact. He characterizes the Thai response as a new ideology based upon Buddhism and notes how Buddhism has been used as an instrument to help unify the country, and the opportunities the monastic community has provided for geographical and societal mobility as well as serving as a channel for the intellectual aspirations of the peasants.

(46) VARMA, VISHWANATH PRASAD. *Early Buddhism and Its Origins* (see 1.2.2.1[13]), pp. 329-408.

A survey devoting separate chapters to the economic, political, and social foundations of early Buddhism. A fine introduction to this topic.

(47) WAGLE, N. K. "Social Groups and Ranking: An Aspect of Ancient Indian Social Life Derived from the Pali Canonical Texts." *Journal of Orient*, 10 (1967), 278-316.

An attempt to reconstruct the social hierarchy of Indian society during the time of the writing of the Pali canons. The author has tried to accomplish this by analyzing the forms of salutations, the terms of addresses, and the terms of references used in the canons.

(48) WARDER, A. K. *Indian Buddhism* (see 1.2.1[15]), pp. 157-200.

This chapter of Warder's work serves as a good introduction to the general topic of Buddhism and society. Using the Pali canons, Warder presents the Buddhist version of the evolution of society with reference to "the ideal society," the makings of "good government," and the Buddha's specific teachings to the laity including the duties and responsibilities of the "uposaka."

(49) WEBER, MAX. The Religion of India: The Sociology of Hinduism and Buddhism. Translated and edited by Hans Girth and Don Martindale. New York: Free Press, 1958, pp. 204-290, 329-343.

This is Weber's famous attempt to apply theories arrived at in The Protestant Ethic and the Spirit of Capitalism to the religion of the Buddha. After surveying the historical roots of Buddhism, its doctrine, practices, and expansion, Weber concludes that Buddhism cannot generate rational economic activity and thus attempts to explain the lack of capitalistic enterprise where Buddhism prevailed. Such a thesis has spawned scores of books which have either defended or rejected Weber's bypothesis. For two classic responses of pro and con nature, see Robert Bellah's Tokugawa Religion (1.13.2.3[1]) and E. Sarkisyanz's Buddhist Backgrounds of Burmese Revolution (1.4.2[15]) respectively.

(50) WICKREMERATNE, L. A. "Religion, Nationalism, and Social Change in Ceylon, 1865-1885." Journal of the Royal Asiatic Society of Great Britain and Ireland (1969), pp. 123-150.

A fine article which comprises and effective study of the role played by Col. H. S. Olcott (one of the two founders of the Theosophical Society) in the Buddhist revival of the late nineteenth century. The author has described the specific events and social circumstances which led to the situation by which Olcott could act as a catalyst for advocating change.

6.2.1.2 Central and East Asian Countries

(1) ANESAKI, MASAHARU. "The Foundation of Buddhist Culture in Japan." Monumenta Nipponica, 6, no. 1/2 (1943), 1-12.

This article represents a presentation of Buddhist ideals as they were conceived by Shotoku Taishi, the seventh century prince who articulated a relationship between religion and the state.

(2) CHAN, WING-TSIT. Religious Trends in Modern China. New York: Columbia University Press, 1953, pp. 54-135.

These pages represent a good starting point for the student interested in gaining an overview or a summary statement of the status of Buddhism from the late nineteenth century to 1950. Chan covers the major shifts in internal reform of organization and doctrinal thought.

(3) _____. "Wang Yang-ming's Criticism of Buddhism," in World Perspectives in Philosophy, Religion, and Culture. Edited by Ran Jee Singh. Patna: Bharati Bhawan, 1968, pp. 31-47.

A very good article in which the author seeks to demonstrate that although Wang Yang-ming (1472-1529 A.D.) was somewhat influenced by Buddhist thought, he was probably more critical of and less receptive to Buddhism than is generally accepted.

(4) CH'EN, KENNETH K. S. The Chinese Transformation of Buddhism. See 1.11.1(2).

(5) _____. "Mahayana Buddhism and Chinese Culture." See 1.11.1(3).

This article is a synthesis of Ch'en's very useful work on Buddhism in China, and may serve as a point of departure for the student interested in this general topic. Ch'en first recounts Buddhism's delayed introduction into Chinese society (due to the strength of Confucianism) and attributes its eventual success to its adaptability to Chinese traditions (particularly its compatibility with "filial piety"). He then demonstrates Buddhism's influence upon Chinese literature, which became more imaginative, and language (its phonetic influence), admits contributions to Chinese science (calandrical rites, astronomy, and medicine), art (the emphasis upon nature), and philosophy (the Neo-Confucian interpretation of traditional concepts in light of Buddhist understanding).

(6) CHENEY, GEORGE. The Pre-revolutionary Culture of Outer Mongolia. Bloomington, Ind.: The Mongolia Society, 1968, 99 pp.

Cheney's work is of an introductory nature, to be read by those students with no previous acquaintance in the field. He does, however, provide a useful bibliograpy for further work. Though he only briefly alludes to Lamaism's influence on the political and class structure, and the economy of Mongolia, his treatment of Mongolian education (pp. 52-56) provides the reader with a decent accounting of Buddhist education as compared to secular education. There are also scattered references to the role of the Lama (economic and social) and the monastery (economic and political) throughout the essay.

(7) CHUN SHIN-YONG, ed. Buddhist Culture in Korea. See 1.12.1(1).

(8) FURER-HAIMENDORF, CHRISTOPH VON. "The Role of the Monastery in Sherpa Society." Ethnologica, 2 (1910), 11-28.

An article which seeks to account for the high esteem accorded to monasticism in Sherpa society. The author has noted the recent resurgence in Buddhism's popularity by recounting the establishment and development of a specific monastery in a Sherpa village. From this specific study, he then makes generalizations concerning the social character of monks, the stages in their careers, and the structure of authority within the monastery.

Finally, analysis of the function is offered, stressing the performance of rites and the opportunity of education as the chief roles.

(9) HU SHIH. "Buddhist Influence on Chinese Religious Life." Chinese Social and Political Science Review, 9 (1925), 142-150.

This is an introductory article which could be read by the beginning student. The author concerns himself with the unique changes which Buddhism brought to and instilled in Chinese religious life, and he underscores the radical difference between the Buddhist conception of the soul and Taoist and Confucian conceptions.

(10) _____. "The Indianization of China: A Case Study in Cultural Borrowing," in Independence, Convergence and Borrowing in Institutions, Thought and Art. Cambridge, Mass.: Harvard University Press, 1937, pp. 219-247.

Hu Shih's address, which was subsequently printed as a chapter in this book, serves as the point of contention for Kenneth Ch'en in his The Chinese Transformation of Buddhism (see 1.11.1[2]). Hu Shih had contended that the Chinese culture owed as much to Buddhism (which he claimed "Indianized" China) as it did to any other single element in the formation of its cultural heritage. This is an invaluable article for the student interested in cultural transformation, as the author has taken a decided and debatable stand.

(11) KITAGAWA, JOSEPH M. Religion in Japanese History. See 1.13.1(8).

This is one of the best introductions to the life of religion and the role it has played in Japanese history. Pages 131-340, in which the author concerns himself with the information of a "religious ethos" of Japan, are especially worthwhile.

(12) _____. "Religions of Japan." See 1.13.1(9).

Within the space of forty pages, the reader is treated to a well thought out historical survey of Buddhism in Japanese religious history. The author is careful to point out how Buddhism accommodated itself to Japan's indigenous religious beliefs and practices and how it allied itself with local cultural, social, and political structures. An excellent introduction to the history of Japanese Buddhism.

(13) _____. Religions of the East (see 6.1.1[13]), pp. 278-304.

Chapter Six of Kitagawa's survey of Asian religions is entitled "Japanese Religion and the National Community" and includes enough material on Buddhism to make it a useful introduction to the subject of Buddhism's relation to Japanese national culture and society.

(14) _____. "Religious and Cultural Ethos of Modern Japan." Asian Studies, 2, no. 3 (December 1964), 334-352.

In this excellent composite statement, Kitagawa first briefly characterizes the nature of Tokugawa Japan and the sweeping changes ushered in by the Meiji restoration. He then depicts how the "back to the pristine past" movement resulted in anti-Buddhist sentiments and a decline in Buddhist influence. Finally, he sketches the ways in which "sect Shinto," Buddhism, Confucianism, and Christianity encountered the problems of "immanental theocracy" and modernity, taking time to note that by siding with the conservative forces of society, Buddhism opposed movements in the direction of modernity.

(15) MATHER, RICHARD B. "The Conflict of Buddhism with Native Chinese Ideology." The Review of Religion, 20, nos. 1-2 (November 1955), 25-37.

An article investigating conflict between Buddhist spirituality and the Chinese world view. Mather points out that the adherence to a doctrine which emphasized "otherworldliness" by monks and nuns forced them to repudiate the Chinese view of a monistic harmony. By such a repudiation, the monks and nuns neglected certain "worldly" obligations of Chinese society and thus posed a threat to the state. Mather goes on to discuss the ramifications of this conflict in social, economic, political, cultural, metaphysical, and moral terms.

(16) MATSUNAGA, ALICIA. The Buddhist Philosophy of Assimilation. See 4.1.4(6).

Catalogues the interaction between Buddhism and indigenous cults through China to Japan and argues for a philosophy of "assimilation" (whereby Buddhism assumes the best and leaves behind the rest of what the indigenous tradition has to offer). Though this main thesis is controversial, the book presents a wealth of material on Buddhas, Bodhisattvas and lesser entities unavailable to the reader who lacks facility in Japanese. Unfortunately, the work is filled with misprints, such that even the woefully incomplete errata sheet is in error. For a cogent critique of it, see Kazumitsu Kato, "A Reflection on the Question of a Philosophy of Assimilation in Buddhism," Journal of the American Oriental Society, 93 (1973), 328-334.

(17) MIKISABURO, MORI. "Chuang Tzu and Buddhism." The Eastern Buddhist, n.s. 5, no. 2 (October 1972), 44-69.

The author begins by outlining the fundamental principles of Chuang-tzu's thought. He then goes on to note that Taoist thought overpowered Confucian thought during the same time period as Buddhism (third to tenth centuries A.D.). The course of events, according to the author, led to a mutual confluence of thought which was largely responsible for the rise of the Pure Land and Chan schools of thought. He finishes by comparing the affinities of both schools to Chuang Tzu.

6.2.1.2   Buddhism and the Social Order

(18) MILLER, BEATRICE D. "The Web of Tibetan Monasticism." Journal of Asian Studies, 20, no. 2 (February 1961), 197-203.

The central thesis of this article, which is useful for the beginning and intermediate student, is that the institution of monasticism is responsible for the cohesiveness of Tibetan society. Miller discusses how the various sects "cross-fertilize" each other through various means and how, as a result, there is no one center of power within the Sangha as a whole. This lends itself to a very curious power structure which involves the relationship between the Sangha as a whole and the Dalai Lama.

(19) MILLER, ROBERT J. Monasteries and Culture Change in Inner Mongolia. See 1.16.1(7).

This excellent treatment of Lamaism in Inner Mongolia is written from the standpoint of cultural anthropology and may be appropriated by students of all levels. Its central argument contends that the Lamaist monastic system entered Inner Mongolia at a time when new social structures were sorely needed to hold the Mongolian society in balance. Miller is careful to point out that Lamaism not only altered the socio-political and economic bases of Mongolian society, but that it too was altered in the process. He has scrupulously examined the scarce materials available and relies heavily upon Russian, Chinese and Japanese reports.

(20) SUZUKI, D. T. Zen and Japanese Culture. Princeton: Princeton University Press, 1959, 476 pp.

After Suzuki explains, in brief fashion, what Zen is, he discusses various aspects of Japanese culture which Zen has influenced: "haiku," the tea ceremony, the cult of swordsmanship, and the Japanese appreciation of nature. Other chapters are concerned with the relationship between Zen and Confucianism, Zen and the Samurai, and Zen and Japanese art. The text is easily readable and is recommended for the beginning student.

(21) WATSUJI TETSURO. "The Reception of Buddhism in the Suiko Period." See 1.13.2.1(9).

(22) WELCH, HOLMES. The Buddhist Revival in China. See 1.11.2.4(6).

The whole book is a mine of information about various aspects of the relationship of Buddhism and society in China from the late nineteenth century until 1950. See especially the chapters on the lay Buddhism movement, on Tai hsu, on social action by the sangha, and on sangha and state. For developments since after 1950, consult the author's Buddhism under Mao (1.11.2.4[5]).

(23) WRIGHT, ARTHUR F. "Buddhism and Chinese Culture: Phases of Interaction." Journal of Asian Studies, 17, no. 1 (November 1957), 17-42.

Wright breaks down the acculturation of Buddhism into four basic historical periods and describes in general terms the interactions within each period. As such, this is a most useful article for the beginning student of the history of China or the beginning to intermediate student of Buddhism.

(24) _____. "Buddhism in Modern and Contemporary China." See 1.11.2.4(7).

This is a handy article for the beginning student. The author discusses four ways in which Buddhism was used by the thinkers and programmers of modern China and how each of these ways failed to be successful: Buddhism as a possible state religion, Buddhism as a "lay ethic or social gospel," Buddhism as a common bond with other emergent Asian peoples, and Buddhism as a source of Chinese nationalism.

(25) _____. "Fu I and the Rejection of Buddhism." See 1.11.2.2(17).

A very fine article which discusses the life and the arguments of Fu I, who emphatically called for the rejection of Buddhism during the early years of the T'ang dynasty. Wright outlines the basic arguments and catalogues them according to economic, political, social, psychological, and intellectual bases. The author concludes that the rejection of Fu I's arguments reveals the prevailing attitudes of the court and gentry of the early T'ang.

(26) YANG, MING-CHE. "China Reinterprets Buddhism." Free China Review, 18 (December 1968), 27-32.

A brief article giving an overview of how Buddhism was influenced by such traditionally Chinese concepts as filial piety.

(27) ZURCHER, ERIK. The Buddhist Conquest of China. See 1.11.2.1(9).

6.2.2 Buddhism and Politics (including Kingship)

6.2.2.1 Buddhism and Politics: General Discussions, Including India

(1) BARUA, D. K. "Origin of State: A Buddhist Approach." Maha Bodhi, 75 (1967), 390-393.

In this brief article, Barua traces the origin of state back to the episode of Mahasummata (the fall from the perfect society). Unfortunately, the article is marred by his attempt to compare the early Buddhist concepts of polity with those of Hobbes, Rousseau, and Locke.

(2) BASHAM, A. L. "Society and State in Theravada Buddhism," in Sources of Indian Tradition. Edited by William T. deBary. New York: Columbia University Press, 1958, pp. 127-153.

A fine introductory essay which discusses the Buddhist theory of the origins of the world (society and state), the ideal of government, and the nature of kingship as exemplified in the rule of Asoka.

(3) GARD, RICHARD. "Buddhism and Political Power," in The Ethics of Power. Edited by Harold D. Lasswell and Harlan Cleveland. New York: Harper and Bros., 1962, pp. 38-70.

A good place to begin a study concerned with the relationship of Buddhism to politics. The author organizes his article into sections concerned with the mutual influences which have resulted from the relationship of Buddhism and politics in both the past and present situations.

(4) GHOSHAL, U. N. "The Ancient Indian Republic and Mixed Constitution from the Sixth Century B.C. to the Third Century A.D.," in his Studies in Indian History and Culture. Bombay: Orient Longmans, 1957, pp. 360-405.

These pages address the importance of the term "sangha" and its implications in a political context.

(5) _____. A History of Indian Political Ideas. Bombay: Oxford University Press, 1959.

Ghoshal's effort may serve as a good introduction to the topic of "Buddhist political thought." The author deals specifically with Buddhist political thought arranged according to texts and approximate time periods. Hence, the reader will find discussions of the topic based upon literature from the Jatakas and Pali canon covering the period of 600-325 B.C. (pp. 62-79), from Sanskrit canonical and non-canonical sources covering 325 B.C. to 320 A.D. (pp. 258-309) and from the works of Buddhist poets and philosophers covering 320 A.D. to 800 A.D. (pp. 337-349).

(6) _____. "Principle of Kings' Righteousness in the Pali Canon and the Jataka Commentary." Indian Historical Quarterly, 32, nos. 2-3 (June-September 1956), 196-204. See also 6.2.7(4).

(7) GOKHALE, B. G. "Dhamma as a Political Concept in Early Buddhism." Journal of Indian History, 44 (August 1944), 249-261.

The author shows how the "legal act" was incorporated by the Buddhists and how the Buddhists consequently moralized the "legal act." Gokhale spends most of the article ferreting out the implications of a "moralized legal act" for the power of the state.

(8) _____. "The Early Buddhist View of the State." Journal of the American Oriental Society, 89, no. 4 (October-December 1969), 731-738.

An effective summary of the fundamental concepts of the role of the king from the Buddhist point of view. The author emphasizes the type of relationship which ideally or traditionally was to exist between the king and the Sangha.

(9) HEINE-GELDERN, ROBERT. Conceptions of State and Kingship in Southeast Asia. Southeast Asia Program Data Paper, No. 18. Ithaca, N.Y.: Cornell University Press, 1956, 10 pp.

In this classic article (also found in The Far Eastern Quarterly, 1, no. 1), Heine-Geldern explores the microcosm-macrocosm cosmological relationship and the symbolism of royal regalia, and attempts a workable typology of kingship in Southeast Asian countries. It should be read by all students interested in the topic.

(10) JAYASWAL, KASHI PRASAD. "Republican Origin of the Buddhist Sangha and Republics in Buddhist Literature," in his Hindu Polity. Third edition. Bangalore: Bangalore Printing and Publishing Co., 1955, pp. 40-48.

A sketchy, uncritical piece, drawing upon the Pali canon, in which the author discusses the manner in which the powerful ruling families of the Buddha's time (Sakyas, Licchavis, etc.) governed.

(11) KITAGAWA, JOSEPH. "Buddhism and Asian Politics." Asian Survey, 2, no. 5 (July 1962), 1-11.

Kitagawa's article may serve as an excellent starting point for any student interested in the question of Buddhism and politics in Asia. Not only has the author reviewed Buddhism's beginnings in the political sphere (the Asokan welfare state and its ramifications), but he has also brought to mind the influence and specific lack of influence which Buddhism has had on the traditional politics of Cambodia, Burma, and China. His basic contention is that although Buddhism has been a vital force in the formation of various national identities and continues to inform social and political attitudes in Asia, it must be considered as just one of many factors which have been ultimately responsible for the historical course of East Asia.

(12) LESTER, ROBERT. Theravada Buddhism in Southeast Asia. See 6.1.1(17).

(13) McKEON, RICHARD and N. A. NIKAM, eds. The Edicts of Asoka. Chicago: The University of Chicago Press, 1966, 69 pp. See also 1.2.2.2(1).

(14) MITRA, R. C. The Decline of Buddhism in India. See 1.2.2.3(12).

(15) SARKISYANZ, EMANUEL. "The Social Ethics of Buddhism and Socio-economic Order of Southeast Asia." Asian and African Studies, 6 (1970), 7-21.

This article represents the author's generalization of his Buddhist Backgrounds of the Burmese Revolution (see 1.4.2[15]). It is his contention that the Asokan ideal of kingship (welfare state) provided an ideal which generated a particular mode of economy.

(16) SCHECTER, JERROLD. The New Face of Buddha. New York: Coward-McCann, 1967, 300 pp.

Schecter believes that Buddhism is the ultimate source of Asian values. He sees the "new involvement" of Buddhism in the political life of Asia as a variation on the old Buddhist-State theme. Though he recognizes Buddhism as a "pan-Asian force," he concedes that its strength does not lie in its international character but in its historical role within each nation. Hence, the organization of his book is based upon separate studies of the respective Buddhist countries (four chapters, however, are given to Vietnam) and the specific role Buddhism now plays in the contemporary political life of each. As a whole, Schecter's book is a worthwhile source for the beginning student.

(17) _____. "The New Face of Buddhism in Asia." Asia, 10 (Winter 1968), 81-90.

Schecter's article is a composite statement of his book with the same title. Generally, he contends that Buddhism is now the most important rallying force for Asian identity and nationalism. To shore this up, he surveys the politicization of the monastic orders in Vietnam and Burma, interprets Bandaranaike's conversion to Buddhism as a political statement, sees the attempts to identify the King of Thailand with Buddhism as a means of combating communist influence, translates Sihanouk's neutralism as a "Buddhist middle way," and surveys the militant Soka Gakkai's struggle for power in Japan. If read with Kitagawa's article in this same issue, a more balanced view of Buddhism's role can be gained.

(18) SMITH, DONALD EUGENE. Religion and Political Development. Boston: Little, Brown, 1970, 298 pp.

This is a good introduction to the general topic of religion and politics. Because the author's more specific interest lies in Southeast Asian political structures, there are many discussions of traditional Buddhist governments.

(19) SPIRO, MELFORD. Buddhism and Society (see 6.2.1.1[42]), pp. 378-395.

This chapter is concerned with the historical relationship between the Sangha and the State. Spiro underlines the king's role of purifier and protector and the consequent control the king was able to exercise over it. The king, in turn, was given the opportunity to gain even more merit by sustaining his duties and obligations towards the Sangha.

(20) VARMA, V. P. Studies in Hindu Political Thought and Its Metaphysical Foundations. Delhi: Motilal Banarsidass, 1959, pp. 114-119, 174-185.

In the first set of pages, Varma deals with the Buddhist metaphysic which supports the Buddhist conception of dharma. In the second set of pages, he offers some speculations as to the nature of the psychological foundations of the Buddhist theory of Kingship.

6.2.2.2 Buddhism and Politics: Sri Lanka

(1) ARIYAPALA, M. B. Society in Mediaeval Ceylon. See 1.3.2.1(1).

Designed for use by the specialist, this volume consists of three parts, dealing with the political, religious and social aspects of thirteenth century Sinhala society.

(2) BECHERT, HEINZ. "Buddhism and Mass Politics in Burma and Ceylon," in Religion and Political Modernization. Edited by Donald E. Smith. New Haven, Conn.: Yale University Press, 1974, pp. 147-167.

A fine analysis of the activities of Buddhist monks and laymen in the political milieux of Burma and Ceylon. This article could well be the best brief introduction to this topic.

(3) Buddhist Committee of Inquiry. The Betrayal of Buddhism. See 1.3.2.2(1).

(4) DE SILVA, K. M. "Buddhism and the British Government in Ceylon 1840-55." See 1.3.2.2(2).

(5) EVERS, HANS-DIETER. "Buddhism and the British Colonial Policy in Ceylon, 1815-1875." Asian Studies, 2, no. 3 (December 1964), 323-333.

A very good article tracing the beginnings of a conflict which continued to be a problem in Ceylonese politics. Evers is here dealing with the problem of monastic land tenure and the British "protection" of these lands, monasteries, and the very religion itself.

(6) _____. "The Buddhist Sangha in Ceylon and Thailand." See 6.2.1.1(10).

(7) GOKHALE, B. C. "Anagarika Dharmapala: Toward Modernity through Tradition in Ceylon." See 1.3.2.2(4).

An effective study of the contributions and influences of Dharmapala, the nineteenth and twentieth century Sinhalese Buddhist monk who vociferously argued for the superiority, utility, and revival of Buddhism as the driving force in forging Sinhalese national consciousness.

(8) HETTIARACHCHY, TILAK. History of Kingship in Ceylon up to the Fourth Century A.D. Colombo: Lake House Investments, 1972, 200 pp.

This is suitable for both advanced and beginning students. It is concerned with the origins and early development of kingship in Ceylon, with attention given to the Indian roots. Separate chapters examine the significance of royal titles, the formation and division of the nobility, the court and various officers of the king, the relationship between the king and the Sangha, the widening authority of the king over the centuries, and the extent and limitation of royal power. While some of this ground is covered better elsewhere, this volume remains the best summary statement and explores sources not always treated by others. Also, it is the best analysis in print of the king-Sangha relationship.

(9) KEARNEY, ROBERT. "Sinhalese Nationalism and Social Conflict in Ceylon." Pacific Affairs, 37, no. 2 (Summer 1964), 125-136.

This seeks to account for the reasons leading to tensions and conflict between ethnic and religious groups during the rise of Sinhalese nationalism, since the 1948 revolution. The author recounts the demands of the Buddhist majority which further alienated the elite and caused bitter conflict with the Tamil-speaking community.

(10) LEACH, EDMUND. "Buddhism in the Post-Colonial Political Order in Burma and Ceylon." Daedalus (Winter 1973), pp. 29-54.

A useful account of Buddhist influences on contemporary Burmese and Sinhalese political events.

(11) RAHULA, WALPOLA. History of Buddhism in Ceylon. See 1.3.1(10).

(12) SARACHCHANDRA, E. R. "Traditional Values and the Modernization of a Buddhist Society: The Case of Ceylon." See 6.2.1.1(38).

A basic impressionistic overview of the role played by Buddhism in Ceylon's struggle for independence and national integration.

(13) SMITH, DONALD E. "The Political Monks of Burma and Ceylon." Asia, 10 (Winter 1968), 3-10.

This is a light treatment of the political activities of monks in these two Theravada countries. Smith first mentions briefly the uprisings led by monks against the British in the 1920s and 1930s, and also the actions of monks which surrounded the state-religion issue in Burma. He then recounts the partnership of Bandaranaike and Buddharakkhita, which helped to transform Ceylon culturally but then degenerated into Buddhist fanaticism and the assassination of Bandaranaike. Finally, he considers the basic problems which confront the political monk: extremism, political clout but political ineptitude, and the basic philosophical quandary of the monks' involvement in mundane matters.

(14) _____, ed. South Asian Politics and Religion (see 6.2.4[11]), pp. 451-546.

This section is concerned with the political resurgence of Buddhism in Ceylon from 1948 until the early 1960s. It consists of four articles (two of these by Smith) which discuss the general political history of Ceylon as it traditionally has been known, the leadership of Bandaranaike, the national significance of the Buddha Jayanti, the effects of the All-Ceylon Buddhist Committee of Inquiry, and its publication The Betrayal of Buddhism, on education and political elections, the role of political monks and consequently monastic reform, and the Buddhist-Marxist coalition. Suitable for all students.

(15) VIJAYAVARDHANA, D. C. The Revolt in the Temple. See 1.3.2.2(7).

(16) VIMALAPANDA, TENNAKOON. The State and Religion in Ceylon since 1815. Colombo: M. D. Gunasena, 1971, 264 pp.

A collection of documents and comments which seek to make the case against the British of reneging on their promise to protect Buddhism in Ceylon (made at the time of the Kandyan Convention in 1815). This is a somewhat disordered and chauvinistic book, but it contains material of importance to advanced students interested in early modern Buddhism in Ceylon. Another book by the same author in the same vein is Buddhism in Ceylon under the Christian Powers and the Educational and Religious Policy of the British Government in Ceylon 1797-1832.

(17) WRIGGINS, W. HOWARD. Ceylon: Dilemmas of a New Nation. Princeton: Princeton University Press, 1960, 483 pp.

A major work, dealing principally with the economic and political aspects of modern Ceylon. In conjunction with political affairs, the author examines the relationship between religious revival and cultural nationalism (pages 169-270 are of special interest here). In general, this is "a comprehensive and authoritative account of the historical, economic, cultural and religious matrix within which political behavior occurs." For the advanced student and the beginner as well, this could be the best treatment of its kind.

6.2.2.3 Buddhism and Politics: Burma

(1) BADGLEY, JOHN. "Theravada Polity of Burma." Tonan Ajia Kenkyu, 2, no. 4 (March 1965), 52-75.

This is a good article for beginning to advanced students. After reviewing the cosmological microcosm-macrocosm relationship, Badgley explores the structure of Burmese monarchy using these categories: usurper-occult monarch, hereditary-legal monarch, and the constitutional basis for monarchy. Then, after briefly reviewing the nature of Burmese political history, he discusses the political character and function of monastic education and Theravada values.

(2) BECHERT, HEINZ. "Buddhism and Mass Politics in Burma and Ceylon." See 6.2.2.2(2).

(3) CADY, JOHN. Political Institutions of Old Burma. Southeast Asia Data Paper, No. 12. Ithaca, N.Y.: Cornell University, 1954, 6 pp.

This brief account by a well known historian reviews the basic elements of the Burmese political bureaucracy prior to British colonialism. Cady describes the structure of the king's court, the symbols of royalty, and the administrative aspects (diplomacy, local government, military, etc.) of the king's government, while being careful to note Chinese and Indian influences. Introductory in scope and content.

(4) KING, WINSTON. "Buddhism and Political Power in Burma." Studies on Asia, 3 (1962), 9-19.

This particular article may serve as an introduction to the topic of Buddhism and politics in Burma. King succinctly describes the significance of the mythos of sacred Buddhist kingship in Burmese history, the consequent desacralization of government resulting from British colonialism, the Buddhist-socialism of the revolutionary leader Aung San, and U Nu's abortive attempt to resacralize government and attain "loka nibbana" by establishing a thoroughly Buddhist interpretation of socialist ideology.

(5) LEACH, EDMUND. "Buddhism in the Post-Colonial Political Order of Burma and Ceylon." See 6.2.2.2(10).

(6) MAUNG, MAUNG. Burma and General Ne Win. London: Asia, 1969, pp. 306-309.

In these few pages, the reader is able to perceive Ne Win's attitude concerning the place of Buddhism in his socialist Burma. Maung uses extensive quotes from The Burmese Way to Socialism in order to underscore Ne Win's contention that Buddhism and politics must be kept apart.

(7) MENDELSON, E. MICHAEL. "Buddhism and the Burmese Establishment." Archives de sociologie des religions, 17 (1972), 85-95.

This is an article for the advanced reader on the Buddhist Sangha in the milieu of contemporary Burmese politics. Mendelson's chief contention is that the government of U Nu, while portraying the Buddhist revival in Burma as purely a religious phenomenon, actually sought to gain ascendency over the Sangha in order more effectively to lead the Burmese to a path of modernization informed by traditional values.

(8) SARKISYANZ, EMANUEL. Buddhist Backgrounds of the Burmese Revolution. See 1.4.2(15).

A scholarly treatment that is useful for beginning and advanced students. Sarkisyanz reviews the political history of Burma and traces its political and economic institutions (as well as the Sangha) back to the legends of Asoka. Specifically, his account of the rise of Buddhism in the early twentieth century is recommended. A basic contention within this work, contrary to Max Weber, is that Buddhism is capable of generating rational economic activity.

(9) _____. "On the Place of U Nu's Socialism in Burma's History of Ideas." Studies on Asia, 2 (1961), 53-62.

This brief article is a condensed version of Sarkisyanz's Buddhist Backgrounds of the Burmese Revolution (above). As such, it is valuable to the advanced student as well as the beginner. Sarkisyanz's contention is that U Nu's socialism is a modern expression of the Buddhist ethos of kingship, the motif of the Future King, and the myth of the Padeytha Tree. For added evidence, Sarkisyanz points to the suspicion which U Nu aroused in the educated elite of Burma.

(10) SMITH, DONALD EUGENE. "Political Monks of Burma and Ceylon." See 6.2.2.2(13).

(11) STARGARDT, JANIC. "Social and Religious Aspects of Royal Power in Medieval Burma." Journal of the Economic and Social History of the Orient, 13 (1970), 289-308.

Using the inscriptions at Myinkaba, the Shwegizon Pagoda at Pagan, the Shwesandaw inscription at Prome and the Tharaba Gate inscriptions at Pagan, the author has tried to reconstruct political history (including social and religious events which had political ramifications during the reign of Kyansittha, 1084-1112). This article is useful for the intermediate and the advanced student.

(12) THAN, U AUNG. "Relation between Sangha and State and Laity." See 6.1.2(21).

(13) THAUNG, U. "Burmese Kingship in Theory and Practice during the Reign of Mindon." Journal of the Burma Research Society, 42, no. 2 (December 1959), 171-185.

This article reviews the traditional Indian theory of the origins of kingship, the role of the king as protector of the religion, and his relationship to the people at large, and describes a coronation and a typical king's day.

(14) TOTTEN, GEORGE. "Buddhism and Socialism in Japan and Burma." Comparative Studies in Society and History, 2, no. 3 (April 1969), 293-304. See also 6.2.2.6(10).

(15) TRAEGER, FRANK. Burma: From Kingdom to Republic: A Historical and Political Analysis. New York: Praeger, 1966, 455 pp.

A very general but informative political history of Burma from the period of colonization to the mid-1960s. Traeger's use of sources provides a number of bases on which to continue further reading. Particularly significant for the reader interested in the relationship between politics and Buddhism in Burma during the twentieth century are the chapters concerned with nationalism (pp. 43-67), independence (pp. 68-91), and the insurrections which followed independence (pp. 95-

139). Traeger is careful to note the political contributions of Buddhism in the nationalist movement and in the insurrection period following independence.

(16) VON DER MEHDEN, FRED. "The Changing Pattern of Religion and Politics in Burma." Studies on Asia, 2 (1961), 63-73.

Von der Mehden's article is a valuable piece for those students interested in contemporary political developments in Burma. He is mainly concerned with the amount of influence exercised by the Sangha from the 1920s to the U Nu government of 1960, and seeks to understand why the Sangha enjoyed great influence in the prerevolution years and then increasingly declined in political importance.

6.2.2.4 Buddhism and Politics: Thailand

(1) DHANINIVAT, H. H. PRINCE. Monarchical Protection of the Buddhist Church in Siam. Bangkok: World Fellowship of Buddhists, 1964, 15 pp.

A short essay prublished in pamphlet form which includes the ten edicts issued by King Rama I between 1782 and 1801 which effectively define the king's relationship to the Sangha. Prince Dhaninivat includes a running commentary on each of the edicts and mentions other measures of "constructive protection" which have been instituted by subsequent Thai kings.

(2) EVERS, HANS-DIETER. "The Buddhist Sangha in Ceylon and Thailand." See 6.2.1.1(10).

(3) ISHII, YONEO. "Thailand: Church and State." Asian Survey, 8, no. 10, 864-871.

This brief article provides a general history of the Sangha's relation to the government in the last forty years. Ishii outlines the bureaucratic structure of the Sangha and underscores the important role Buddhism has played in supporting Thailand's traditional values in the twentieth century.

(4) KEMP, JEREMY. Aspects of Siamese Kingship in the Seventeenth Century. Bangkok: Social Science Assoc., 1969, 61 pp.

A good short summary of this subject, based largely on European writings about Thailand at the time.

(5) REYNOLDS, FRANK E. "Sacral Kingship and National Development: The Case of Thailand," in Tradition and Change in Theravada Buddhism (see 6.2.1.1[40]), pp. 40-50.

The author focuses upon the transformation which has taken place in the interaction between a sacral kingship and the overall national development in Thailand from the period of the first modern intrusions in the early nineteenth century up to the present time.

(6) WALES, H. G. Q. Ancient Siamese Government and Administration. London: B. Quaritch, 1934, 263 pp.

This is an overview of ancient Thai civilization, although the primary intent of the author was to discern the nature of the government and the structure and function of the administrative system. It may be of use to the beginning or advanced student.

(7) WILSON, DAVID. Politics in Thailand. See 1.5.2(26).

This is a general introductory work, of use to the beginning student. Particularly helpful are the first 110 pages, which deal primarily with the historical background of Thai politics, including discussions of Buddhism's basic influence upon the economic and social structures and an adequate treatment of the relationship between authority and kingship.

6.2.2.5 Buddhism and Politics: China

(1) CH'EN, KENNETH. "Anti-Buddhist Propaganda during the Nan-ch'ao." See 1.11.2.2(1).

The growth of Buddhism during the period of the Northern and Southern dynasties was not without opposition, but the anti-Buddhist movement took on different forms in the North and in the South. This article discusses the campaign against Buddhism in the South, centering around the figures of Ku Huan (fifth century) who objected to Buddhism as a foreign religion, Fan Chen (fifth century), a Confucian, and Hsun-Chi, who thought Buddhism was undermining the state. In the North, however, the opposition to Buddhism took the form of forceful persecutions under Wei Wu-ti (in 446) and Chou Wu-ti (in 574-577). The background of these Northern developments is studied in Ch'en's companion article, "On Some Factors Responsible for the Anti-Buddhist Persecution under the Pei-Ch'ao," Harvard Journal of Asiatic Studies, 17 (1954), 261-273.

(2) _____. "Political Life," in The Chinese Transformation of Buddhism (see 1.11.1[2]), pp. 65-124.

The general thrust of this chapter deals with the political Sinicization of the Sangha. In the first part, Ch'en reveals how the Sangha first declared its apolitical nature in China. Then he reviews the conflicts which developed between the Sangha and state, when the state attempted to exercise control over monks. Finally, Ch'en demonstrates how the Buddhist monks gradually became actively involved in the state's political programs.

(3) GROOT, JOHN J. M. DE. "Militant Spirit of the Buddhist Clergy in China." T'oung Pao, Series 1, 2, no. 2 (June 1891), 127-139.

The author begins this article with a review of Buddhist militarism as it has been mentioned in traditional Chinese histories during the period of 532-1628 A.D. This review is followed by an outline of the Buddhist precepts against the taking of human life. Finally, the author explains how the Bodhisattva doctrine of salvation was used to justify this type of action and served as a motivation: as the Bodhisattva gives up his own life to quest for the salvation of others, so too were Buddhists urged to fight for the safe-keeping of the Sam-Pao (Triratna).

(4) _____. Sectarianism and Religious Persecution in China. Amsterdam: J. Muller, 1903-1904, 2 vols. Vol. 1, pp. 1-136.

These pages deal with state opposition to Buddhism and related popular sects and the author has included copious quotes from Chinese sources. However, it needs to be supplemented by other material (see Ch'en, above).

(5) HURVITZ, LEON. "Render Unto Caesar." Sino-Indian Studies, 5, nos. 3-4 (1957), 96-114.

This article, of interest to the more advanced student, consists of a study of Hui-yuan's famous defense of Buddhist independence from normal Chinese forms of political submission in 403 A.D.

(6) WELCH, HOLMES. Buddhism Under Mao. See 1.11.2.4(5).

(7) WITTFOGEL, KARL and FENG CHIA-SHENG. "Religion under the Liao Dynasty." The Review of Religion, 12, no. 4 (1948), 355-374.

An article in which the authors emphasize the neglected fact that Buddhism was never persecuted under the Liao dynasty (a northern Chinese regime from 907-1125 A.D.). The major importance of this was that Buddhism was allowed to spread into the vast expanses of Inner Mongolia. The authors go on to show how Buddhism became acculturated to Liao society and played important sociological and economic roles.

(8) WRIGHT, A. F. "The Formation of Sui Ideology." See 1.11.2.2(15).

A study of the history of Buddhism in its relationship to Chinese religions during the years of 581-604 (Sui dynasty). The author perceptively describes how Buddhism, Taoism, and Confucianism were part of the process towards this end. He speculates that perhaps Buddhism helped to "contribute to the breaking-down of cultural and racial and regional barriers."

6.2.2.6 Buddhism and Politics: Japan

(1) BELLAH, ROBERT. Tokugawa Religion: The Values of Pre-Industrial Japan. See 1.13.2.3(1).

This is a first-rate sociological analysis of the Tokugawa period, of good use to beginning and intermediate students. Bellah first argues that political loyalties are more responsible for the generation of societal values than economic determinants. He then suggests that Buddhism chiefly, but also Confucianism and Shinto, bears the same relationship to economics in Japan as Protestantism bears to capitalism in Europe and America.

(2) BLACKER, CARMEN. "Le Soka Gakkai japonais." Archives de sociologie des religions, 17 (1972), 63-67.

This is a brief article that serves as an adequate introduction to the history of the Soka Gakkai movement. Blacker traces the sect's political ideology back to the saint Nichiren while also taking into account the international political factors which provided a fertile ground for the evolution of such a movement in modern Japan.

(3) BRETT, CECIL. "The Priest-Emperor Concept in Japanese Political Thought." The Indian Journal of Political Science, 23, no. 1 (January-March 1962), 17-28.

This may be used as an introduction to the topic of "kingship in Japan." The author sets out to describe some of the sacred symbolism which has been appropriated by the Japanese imperial institution to legitimate itself, describing not only the Buddhist influence, but the Shinto and Confucian influences as well.

(4) DEMIEVILLE, PAUL. "Le Bouddhisme et la guerre." Mélanges publiés par l'Institut des Hautes Etudes Chinoises, 1 (1957), 347-385.

An excellent study of the history of Buddhism in its relationship to wars which focuses on the Japanese context. The author attempts to discern if the militarization of Buddhism in Japan is unique to the history of Buddhism, how the militarization of Buddhism can be reconciled to the cardinal rule which prohibits the taking of life, and what social, economic and political factors led to militarization.

(5) FUJIWARA, HIROTATSU. I Denounce Soka Gakkai. Translated by Worth C. Grant. Tokyo: Nishin Hodo, 1970, 287 pp.

Translation of a now famous polemical work which sought to expose Soka Gakkai and Komeito's alleged underhand practices. The author indulges in invectives, which makes the work more interesting in itself than as scholarly analysis.

(6) IENAGA, SABURO. "Japan's Modernization and Buddhism." Contemporary Religions in Japan, 6, no. 1 (March 1965), 1-41.

A very general article which could be useful to the beginning student. The author seems to be generally pessimistic about the future of Buddhism in a modern technological society: after tracing the political role played by Buddhism in feudal times and its decline in the Meiji period, he suggests that Buddhism's future lies not so much in a political role as in a return to its spiritual message.

(7) INGRAM, PAUL. "Soka Gakkai and the Komeito: Buddhism and Political Power in Japan." Contemporary Religions in Japan, 10, nos. 3-4 (September-December 1969), 155-180.

This article contends that faith is understood by the Soka Gakkai primarily in terms of social and political power. Ingram asserts that this doctrine of faith is held necessary in order for the sect to believe it can accomplish worldwide conversion to the teaching of Nichiren.

(8) KIYOTA, MINORU. "Meiji Buddhism: Religion and Patriotism." See 1.13.2.4(5).

This is an excellent summary of the plight of Buddhism during the Meiji period, 1868-1900. Kiyota begins by reviewing the events leading up to the Shinto-Buddhist Separation Policy which resulted in a persecution of Buddhism and its disestablishment from social, political, and economic positions of power. He discusses the two forces which led the attack on Buddhism: the Hirata school of Shintoism and the Mito school of Confucianism; then traces the movements within Buddhism (especially its attack upon Christianity) which helped to improve its position within Japanese political circles. Finally, he shows how Buddhism failed to join with the more liberal components of Japanese society, which endeavored to promote parliamentary government, civil rights, and progressive socail actions around the turn of the century. (This had the effect of leaving Buddhism out of the mainstream of Japanese progressive thought.)

(9) PALMER, ARVIN. Buddhist Politics: Japan's Clean Government Party. The Hague: M. Nijhoff, 1971, 98 pp.

A good study of the nature of the Sokagakkai in relation to its religious beginnings and contemporary Japanese politics. The author has three basic propositions: 1) the Sokagakkai and the Komeito (its political arm) are intertwined to such a level that they are virtually impossible to separate; 2) the Komeito is composed of a constituency which has either been alienated by or not adequately represented by other Japanese political parties; and 3) the Sokagakkai represents an authoritarian alternative to the maturing Japanese democratic political system.

(10) TOTTEN, GEORGE O. "Buddhism and Socialism in Japan and Burma." See 6.2.2.3(14).

In this brief but well done article, the author attempts to find the reasons why the Burmese socialists (such as U Nu) were Buddhists and why the Japanese socialists were not. He arrives at the general conclusion that this is because the Burmese were nationalists first and socialists second, and that the Japanese were socialists first and nationalists second. Although this sounds simplistic, the author endeavors to show why, historically, this is the case. As a result, this is one of the few good articles on the topic of Buddhism and Marxism.

(11) WHITE, JAMES W. The Sokagakkai and Mass Society. Stanford, Calif.: Stanford University Press, 1970, 376 pp.

Possibly the best available work concerned with the Sokagakkai as a political force; the student can gain immeasurably by reading it in conjunction with William Kornhauser's The Politics of Mass Society and Seymour Lipset's Political Man. In analyzing the Sokagakkai, the author uses the model of "mass-movement" developed by Kornhauser. This model of political activity is held to be subversive in nature to existing political institutions. Hence, White seeks to find the social and political background which spawned the Sokagakkai, using the concept of alienation (from individual self, from society qua mankind, and from concrete political institutions) to aid in his explanation. Having covered this theoretical ground, he examines the movement's development and contemporary state, its psychological attitudes and the possible consequences of the movement in the Japanese political system.

6.2.2.7 Buddhism and Politics: Tibet

(1) BELL, CHARLES. The Religion of Tibet (see 1.14.1[1]), pp. 169-192.

Under the headings "The Power of the Monasteries," "Priests as Civil and Military Officers," and "A Diety as King," Bell, who was a long-time friend of the thirteenth Dalai Lama, attempts to describe the actual working relationships between Buddhism and political authority as he personally observed them.

(2) CARRASCO, PEDRO. Land and Polity in Tibet. Seattle: University of Washington Press, 1959, pp. 78-140.

Consists of a neatly organized and lightly written sketch of the ecclesiastic role in land tenure, politics, social relations, and economics in Tibet from 1792-1951. It can be put to good use by the beginning student.

(3) CASSINELLE, C. W. and ROBERT B. EKVALL. A Tibetan Principality: The Political System of Sa skya. See 1.14.2.2(2).

(4) HOFFMAN, HELMUT. Die Religionen Tibets. Munich: K. Alber, 1956, pp. 126-181.

These chapters of Hoffman's book (which is also available in an English translation, see 1.14.1[6]), trace the rise and development of the "king-priest phenomenon" in its historical Tibetan context. As such, it is a general treatment which could be used as an adequate point of departure.

(5) RAHUL, RAM. The Government and Politics of Tibet. Delhi: Vikas Publications, 1969, 160 pp.

Because the entire structure of political and social life in Tibet is tied up with the land system, rights over land imply many types of social obligations and political functions. This fine work describes the roles played by the government headed by the Dalai Lama, the aristocracy, and the monasteries in determining the economic, social and political institutions of traditional Tibet. The reader will find an excellent chapter on the Dalai Lama as an institution. Other works which treat these topics in a less direct fashion include: Hugh Richardson, Tibet and Its History; Luciano Petech, Aristocracy and Government in Tibet; Thubten Jigme Norbu and Colin Turnbull, Tibet (see 1.14.1[13]); and C. W. Cassinelle and Robert B. Ekvall, A Tibetan Principality: The Political System of Sa sKya (above).

(6) ROCKHILL, WILLIAM W. "The Dalai Lamas of Lhasa and Their Relations with the Manchu Emperors of China, 1644-1908." T'oung Pao, Series 2, no. 11 (1910), 1-104.

Written from a strictly historical point of view using both traditional and critical sources, this early article gives an easily readable and effective description of the diplomatic relations between the Dalai Lamas of Tibet and the Manchus and Mongols during the period indicated.

(7) SHAKABPA, TSEPON. Tibet: A Political History. See 1.14.1(10).

Shakabpa's work was inspired by his own nationalist convictions that Tibet has historically been ignored as a sovereign and independent country. This, he claims, resulted from the fact that the world did not fully understand the true nature of governments led by a religious figure (Dalai Lama) and Tibet's historical sovereignty through the Mongol and Manchu periods. Hence, his history is written primarily to establish as historical fact the traditionally misunderstood independence of Tibet. Relying upon indigenous historical accounts as well as western scholarship, he has provided both the beginning and advanced student with an excellent account of Tibetan political history from the earliest times to the present.

(8) SNELLGROVE, D. L. "The Notion of Divine Kingship in Tantric Buddhism," in The Sacral Kingship: Contributions to the Central Theme of the VIIIth International Congress for the History of Religions (Rome, April 1955). Leiden: E. J. Brill, 1959, pp. 204-218.

This article is intended for the advanced or specialized student. The author has made copious use of tantric literature, citing and explaining the significance of references to the nature of kingship in Tantric Buddhism.

6.2.2.8 Buddhism and Politics: Indochina

(1) BEAUCE, THIERRY DE. "Le Cambodge: Bouddhisme et développement." See 1.6.2(1).

(2) HALPERN, JOEL M. Government, Politics, and Social Structure in Laos (see 1.7.2[4]), pp. 49-61.

The author treats the basic structure and character of the Sangha before discussing the Sangha-State relationship. He stresses that the relationship becomes most emphasized on public occasions. For a detailed study of this phenomenon in Laos, see Reynolds, "Ritual and Social Hierarchy" (1.7.2[7]). Finally, he reviews contemporary relationships between the Sangha and the Pathet Lao, and the Sangha and the monarchy.

(3) MUS, PAUL. "Angkor vu du Japon." See 1.6.2(11).

Mus's article consists of an attempt to assess the political nature of Buddhism as well as the character of the king (as it had been influenced by the bodhisattva motif) in both Cambodia and Japan from the eighth through the twelfth centuries. As with most of his work, Mus relies heavily upon sculptures and bas-reliefs as sources. For another rendering of the same time period in relation to Angkor developments, see Mus's "Angkor in the Time of Jayavarman VII," Indian Arts and Letters, 11 (1937), 65-75.

(4) _____. "Buddhism in Vietnamese History and Society." See 1.8.2(7).

A perceptive analysis of the historical and ideological background to the coup which overthrew Nho Dinh Diem in 1963. Fills in many of the questions left unanswered (or unaddressed) by David Halberstam in his "The Buddhist Crisis in Vietnam," in Vietnam: History, Documents, and Opinions on a Major World Crisis, edited by Marvin E. Gettleman (Greenwich, Conn.: Fawcett Publications, 1965), 448 pp.

(5) NHAT HANH, THICH. Vietnam, Lotus in a Sea of Fire. See 1.8.2(9).

(6) REVERTEGAT, BRUNO. "Bouddhisme et les bonzes au Sud-Vietnam." See 1.8.2(10).

(7) SACKS, I. MILTON. "Some Religious Components in Vietnamese Politics," in Religion and Change in Contemporary Asia (see 1.11.2.4[7]), pp. 44-66.

Sacks briefly characterizes the traditional relationships between the various religions of Vietnam and the state authority. He notes the historical stronghold of Confucianism as a favored system, then analyzes the recently rising significance of Cao Dai, Hoa Hao, and Buddhism in their respective political activities.

(8) SCIGLIANO, ROBERT. "Vietnam: Politics and Religion." Asian Survey, 4, no. 1 (January 1964), 666-673.

Scigliano's article concerns the Buddhist conflicts which led to the downfall of the ruling Ngo Dinh family in Vietnam in the early 1960s. For an article which more broadly characterizes the Sangha during this crucial period, see Charles Joiner, "South Vietnam's Buddhist Crises: Organization for Charity, Dissidence, and Unity," Asian Survey, 4, no. 7 (July 1964), 915-929.

(9) THIERRY, SOLANGE. "La personne sacrée du roi dans la littérature populaire cambodgienne," in The Sacral Kingship (see 6.2.2.7[8]), pp. 219-230.

This is an excellent article which should be read in conjunction with M. Coedes' "Le culte de la royauté divinisée, source d'inspiration des grands monuments du Cambodge ancien," in vol. I of Conferenz (Rome: Istituto per il Medio ed Estremo Oriente). Thierry has shown how the royal and divine character of the Cambodian kings was perpetuated in Cambodian novels and stories.

6.2.2.9 Buddhism and Politics: Central Asia and Other Countries

(1) LATTIMORE, OWEN. "Religion and Revolution in Mongolia." See 1.16.2(6).

An excellent article recounting the history of major Mongolian political transactions from Ming times to the present. Lattimore is very careful to note the general effects of Mongolia's dealings with the Manchus and Tibetans on Lamaism and tells the story of the demise of Lamaism after the 1921 revolution. He has incorporated sources not previously available to western scholars which have recently been published by the Peoples' Republic of Mongolia.

(2) LEDYARD, GARI. "Cultural and Political Aspects of Traditional Korean Buddhism." See 1.12.2(6).

A cursory attempt to re-evaluate the historical contributions of Buddhism to Korean culture. The author is intent upon contrasting Buddhism, as a flexible and heterodox faith, with a doctrinaire picture of Confucianism and consequently tries to show that Buddhism was closer to the national spirit of the Korean peoples (at least until the twelfth century). He discusses specifically the Korean style of kingship, the expansion of intellectual thought, and the spirit of nationalism, all as Buddhist contributions. Finally, he scans the contemporary condition of Buddhism (after 600 years of suppression under the Yi dynasty), noting the strength of Buddhist educational institutions.

(3) RAHUL, R. "The Role of Lamas in Central Asian Politics." Central Asiatic Journal, 12, no. 4 (1969), 209-227.

An excellent article for the advanced student. The author proceeds from north to south ("owing to the historical spread of Buddhism") to appraise the role of religious hierarchs in the political affairs of Tibet, Sikkim, Bhutan, Siberia, and Mongolia.

(4) SARKISYANZ, E. "Communism and Utopianism in Central Asia." The Review of Politics, 20, no. 4 (October 1958), 623-633.

The author seeks comparisons between the Buddhist ideals of utopia and the communist hope of a classless society.

6.2.3 Buddhism in Relation to Family and Village Life

See also 6.2.1.1 and 6.2.1.2.

(1) BINSTED, G. C. "Life in a Khalkha Steppe Lamasery." Journal of the Royal Asiatic Society (1914), pp. 847-900.

This is a rather informal article which recounts the events of a trip taken by Binsted in 1913 which included a week's stay in a Mongolian Lamasery. The article is rich in description of temple architecture, lamaistic rituals, lama life style, musical instruments, boy lamas and lama doctors.

(2) BOUTSAVATH, VONGSAVANH and GEORGE CHAPELIER. "Lao Popular Buddhism and Community Development." The Journal of the Siam Society, 61, no. 2 (July 1973), 1-38.

This article is basically a report on and an advocation of the use of monks to further community development in rural Laos. Though not overly substantive, it is of some interest because it is co-authored by the Laotian government official who was responsible for rural development in the late 1960s and early 1970s, and a UN advisor who assisted him in his work.

(3) BURR, ANGELA. "Religious Institutional Diversity, Social Structure and Conceptual Unity: Islam and Buddhism in a Southern Thai Coastal Fishing Village." Journal of the Siam Society, 60, no. 2 (1972), 183-216.

This article challenges some of the stereotypes of Buddhism and Islam by focusing on the way in which these religions operate in a southern Thai village where they coexist. The study is important because it provides material and a perspective on an important but neglected aspect of southeast Asian religions and their interaction.

(4) CH'EN, KENNETH. "Filial Piety in Chinese Buddhism." Harvard Journal of Asiatic Studies, 28 (1968), 81-97.

Like all of Ch'en's works, this article proves useful to students of all levels. Ch'en reviews the Buddhist accommodation to Chinese ideas and mores, especially the concept and practice of filial piety. Next, he recounts various sutras which claim that their spiritual interpretation of filial piety is superior to the Confucian conception.

(5) CONDOMINAS, GEORGES. "Notes sur le Bouddhisme populaire en milieu rural Lao." See 1.7.2(2).

Condominas' work is a comprehensive treatment of Lao Buddhism in the modern period. The author covers the sociological ramifications of the wat as well as its effect upon the economy and education of the community.

(6) EMBREE, JOHN F. Suye Mura (see 4.1.4[3]), pp. 221-298.

(7) GOMBRICH, RICHARD F. Precept and Practice: Traditional Buddhism in the Rural Highlands of Ceylon. See 4.1.1(7).

This is a work of importance by a philologist who looks at the problem of religious change while utilizing the perspectives of a variety of disciplines. Although the book is based upon field work in a Sinhalese village, it is intended as a study of traditional Theravada Buddhism. Gombrich covers such topics as the basic Buddhist vocabulary, the concept of "total responsibility," the ethic of "intention," the "monastic ideal and the decline of Buddhism," and caste in the monastery. Suitable for the advanced student.

(8) HSU, FRANCIS L. K. Under the Ancestors' Shadow (see 4.1.3[4]), pp. 167-199.

These pages of this classic work on Chinese popular religion deal specifically with the role of Buddhism in daily life at the village level.

(9) INGERSOLL, JASPER. "The Priest Role in Central Village Thailand." See 6.1.2(10).

(10) INGERSOLL, JASPER and DAVID PFANNER. "Theravada Buddhism and Village Economic Behavior: Burmese and Thai Comparison." Journal of Asian Studies, 21, no. 3 (May 1962), 341-361.

First selecting two separate communities in two distinct countries, the authors each consider the following: The role of monk or priest within the community, the effect of doctrinal and moral norms upon economic activity, the economic consequences of religious activities, and the relationship between the religious roles and the economic activities in respect to economic development. Having completed these discussions within the context of their own studies, the two authors compare their results.

(11) KLAUSNER, WILLIAM J. "Popular Buddhism in Northeast Thailand," in Cross-Cultural Understanding: Epistemology in Anthropology. Edited by F. S. C. Northrop and Helen H. Livingston. New York: Harper and Row, 1964, pp. 71-92.

An introductory article giving an overview of how Buddhism plays a vital role in rural village life in Thailand. The author describes such topics as the entrance into monkhood, monk involvement in secular affairs, the lay conception of the monk's role, the lay conception of "doctrinal Buddhism," and the influence of Brahmanical and animist elements in village Buddhism.

(12) LING, R. "Buddhist Factors in Population Growth and Control: A Survey Based on Thailand and Ceylon." Population Studies, 23, no. 1 (March 1969), 53-60.

As the author points out, Buddhist doctrines and institutions do not directly encourage the procreation of children in Southeast Asian countries, though fertility rates are quite high there. The first part of this paper seeks to establish that there are significant factors within the structure of Buddhist culture which indirectly might lead to high fertility rates. The second half surveys Buddhist attitudes toward birth control measures.

(13) MOERMAN, MICHAEL. "Ban Ping's Temple: The Center of a 'Loosely Structured' Society." See 6.2.1.1(23).

(14) MORIOKA, KIYOMA. "Buddhist Orders and the Japanese Family System." Orient/West, 7, no. 1 (January 1962), 55-59.

In this brief but well written article, Morioka demonstrates how the social organization of the Japanese Buddhist orders were patterned after "ie seido" (the traditional family system in Japan). He discusses the three-fold connotation of the word "tera," which at the same time signifies temple, juridical person (in this case a religious person), and the residents of a temple compound. He also brings to light the factors of heredity and the ranking of temples which played a part in the life of the Japanese Sangha. As he draws parallels between the family system and the Sangha on the basis of these factors, he also demonstrates how the structure of the monastic orders changed as the structure of the Japanese family changed.

(15) NASH, JUNE. "Living with Nats: An Analysis of Animism in Village Social Relations." See 4.1.2(13).

The author attempts to study the role of "nats" as it affects everyday social relations. She shows how nat cults are perpetuated through inherited obligations passed on through the family, village or regional level, how relationships between "nats" are reflected in relationships between villages, and how concern with "soul crises" is resolved through Buddhist ritual rather than in nat propitiation.

(16) NASH, MANNING. The Golden Road to Modernity (see 4.1.2[14]), pp. 104-165.

This section of Nash's excellent study of contemporary life in a Burmese village consists of a description of Buddhism as an integral part of the daily routines of the villagers. Nash concentrates on the effects of Buddhism on the organization of the village and the economic role which it plays.

(17) NIEHOFF, ARTHUR. "Theravada Buddhism: A Vehicle for Technical Change." Human Organization, 23 (Summer 1964), 108-122.

This is a very general characterization of the role of the monk in a contemporary Laotian village. Niehoff reviews the traditional debate between the "other-worldliness" espoused in canonical Buddhism and the "this-worldly" activities of the Sangha in village life. However, he is primarily interested in suggesting that the Sangha offers the best organizational means for completing all kinds of projects (from education to sewer construction) in Laotian villages, while noting that the United States will not fund foreign aid projects which are in any way connected with religious activities. Thus he points to a basic U.S. misunderstanding of Laotian social structure and the consequent missed opportunities for effective foreign-aid supported projects.

(18) PIKER, STEVEN. "The Relationship of Belief Systems to Behavior in Rural Thai Society." Asian Survey, 7, no. 5 (May 1968), 384-399.

This is an excellent article in which the author argues a correspondence between the content of magio-animism and the Buddhist doctrine of karma (retribution and merit) and activity in mundane situations.

(19) TAMBIAH, S. J. "The Ideology of Merit and the Social Correlates of Buddhism in a Thai Village," in Dialectic in Practical Religion (see 6.1.2[15]), pp. 41-121.

Tambiah's excellent paper is predicated on the thesis that village Buddhism in Thailand consists of a cult for the living rather than a "theology for the dead or dying." The paper also demonstrates Malinowski's contention that "the components of a religious system are meaningful not only because of internal coherence but because of their practical integration with the secular life of the religious congregation." Tambiah's analysis of merit follows these same lines. Intended for the specialist.

6.2.4 Buddhism in Relation to Caste

See also 6.2.1.1 for general discussions of Buddhism as a caste.

(1) Digha Nikaya (Dialogues of the Buddha). Translated by T. W. Rhys-Davids (see 2.7.1[13]). Vol. I, pp. 98-136 (The Ambattha Sutta); 137-159 (The Sonadanda Sutta).

Both of these suttas contain valuable material on the relationship of early Buddhism to the caste system. The student should also look at Rhys-Davids' introduction to the Ambattha Sutta, where his position on the question is evident.

(2) FISKE, ADELE. "Religion and Buddhism among India's New Buddhists." See 1.2.2.5(1).

(3) GOMBRICH, RICHARD. Precept and Practice: Traditional Buddhism in the Rural Highlands of Ceylon (see 4.1.1[7]), pp. 294-317.

Gombrich offers a valuable picture of the influence of caste on the life of the monks and the laity. Suitable for beginning and intermediate students.

(4) ISAACS, HAROLD R. India's Ex-Untouchables. New York: J. Day, 1965, 188 pp.

This sympathetic treatment presents the alternatives available to the disenfranchised untouchable castes in India at the time of its political independence. Isaacs treats specifically the dramatic exit from Hinduism to Buddhism of a notable number of untouchables.

(5) JAYATILLEKE, K. N. Aspects of Buddhist Social Philosophy. Wheel Series Publication Nos. 128/129. Kandy: Buddhist Publication, 1969, 50 pp.

This publication consists of two essays of an apologetic nature. In the first, Jayatilleke attempts to refute the criticisms of Theravada made by Arnold Toynbee in his An Historian's Approach to Religion. The second is a response to S. Radhakrishnan, who contends that both "the Gita and Buddhism attempt to relax the rigours of caste." Jayatilleke argues that this case can be made only for Buddhism.

(6) KRISHNAN, Y. "Was There Any Conflict Between the Brahmins and the Buddhists?" Indian Historical Quarterly, 30 (1954), 167-177.

This article contends that, contrary to what most historians and Buddhologists have argued, little (if any) animosity existed between the two groups. The author contends that: 1) the caste system as we know it did not exist in Buddha's time; 2) the Buddha never directly challenged the caste system; 3) Brahmins, as well as the Buddha, challenged social classification by birth; 4) numerous cases within Sanskrit and Pali literature depict cordial relations; and 5) Sankara admired the Buddha.

(7) MILLER, ROBERT J. "They will not die Hindus: the Buddhist Conversion of Mahar ex-Untouchables." See 1.2.2.5(3).

(8) MUKHOPADYAYA, SUJITKUMAR, trans. The Vajrasuci of Asvaghosa. See 3.2.4.3(4).

The Vajrasuci is a very short but powerful attack on Brahmins and the whole Indian caste system. First translated by B. H. Hodgson in 1829, it has enjoyed moments of popularity among scholars who share its sentiments. It is probably safer to say that its author and date are unknown than to believe its own claim that it is the work of the second-century poet Asvaghosa.

(9) PRESLER, HENRY. "The Neo-Buddhist Stir in India." See 1.2.2.4(4).

(10) RAHULA, WALPOLA. History of Buddhism in Ceylon. See 1.3.1(10).

(11) ZELLIOT, ELEANOR. "Buddhism and Politics in Maharashtra," in South Asian Politics and Religion. Edited by Donald Eugene Smith. Princeton: Princeton University Press, 1966, pp. 191-212.

This is a very good representation of the political and social currents which led to the "untouchable" Mahar caste's final disenchantment with caste-Hinduism and their opting in 1956, under the leadership of Ambedkar, for Buddhism.

(12) _____. Dr. Ambedkar and the Mahar Movement. Philadelphia: University of Pennsylvania Press, 1969, 304 pp.

This is the most complete study of the Mahar caste (one of the "untouchable" castes of Maharashtra, numbering around three hundred thousand) and their efforts since the 1890s to gain acceptance and a semblance of equality. The author reviews the caste's attempts at "temple entry," "sanskritization," the leadership of Ambedkar, and the conversion to Buddhism.

(13) _____. "The Revival of Buddhism in India." Asia, 10 (Winter 1968), 33-45.

This brief article is chiefly concerned with the activities of B. R. Ambedkar, which consequently led to large number of "untouchables" converting to Buddhism from the 1930s through the 1950s. Zelliot raises important questions concerning the social and political future of Buddhism as a force in Indian society.

6.2.5 Buddhism and Education

(1) ARIYAPALA, M. B. Society in Mediaeval Ceylon (see 1.3.2.1[1]), pp. 269-280.

These pages constitute Ariyapala's treatment of education as it was practiced in Ceylon during the mediaeval period. As such, it is a useful introduction and sketch that can be used to supplement Rahula's comments and also the essays in Education in Ceylon (below).

(2) AYABE, TSUNEO. "Dek Wat and Thai Education: the Case of Tambon Ban Khem." Translated by Edward Tiffany and Toshikazu Ari. The Journal of the Siam Society, 61, 2 (July 1973), 39-52.

A look at the youngsters of Thailand who live in Buddhist temples where they do services while carrying on their schooling in the temple or elsewhere.

(3) BAPAT, P. V. 2500 Years of Buddhism (see 1.2.1[1]), pp. 176-194.

In this chapter, Bapat reviews the basic training of the monk, a general history of "Buddhist education" in India, and the influences wielded by the "great Indian universities" of the early Buddhist period.

(4) BETHEL, DAYLE M. Makiguchi: The Value Creator. Revolutionary Japanese Educator and Founder of Soka Gakkai. New York and Tokyo: Weatherhill, 1973, 174 pp.

A helpful but not very critical examination of the educational theories and policies of the founder of Sokagakkai. Especially useful for its information on the life and career of Makiguchi.

(5) CAMPBELL, ALEXANDER. "Education in Burma." Royal Society of Arts Journal, 94, no. 4719 (7 June 1946), 438-448.

At the time he wrote this, the author was serving as Director of Public Instruction in Burma. He sketches the traditional history of education in Burma, characterizing "the existing native schools." Perhaps its most interesting facet is its appraisal of the British attempt to utilize the monastic-run schools for "public instruction."

(6) CH'EN, KENNETH. "Educational and Social Life," in The Chinese Transformation of Buddhism (see 1.11.1[2]), pp. 240-303.

In this chapter Ch'en discusses how Buddhism adapted itself to the daily lives of the common people. He reviews how the teaching and propagation of the faith were carried out by means of lectures, debates, dramas, religious festivals, vegetarian festivals on days of fasting, the establishment of Buddhist societies consisting of laity, and charitable activities of individual monks and monasteries. Finally, Ch'en wants to say that the monastery and temple became close to the heart of Chinese life.

(7) COREA, J. C. A. "One Hundred Years of Education in Ceylon." Modern Asian Studies, 3, no. 2 (April 1969), 151-175.

Corea's article is a historical review of the progress made in all forms of education in Ceylon in the last hundred years. The most relevant portions of the article for the student of Buddhism discuss the influence of economic factors, the missionary monopoly of English schools, and the religious movement (Buddhist) which led to an end of the denominational system of education in Ceylon.

(8) Education in Ceylon (From the Sixth Century B.C. to the Present Day). Colombo: Ministry of Education and Cultural Affairs, 1969, 3 vols.

This splendid three volume effort consists of a collection of essays on the history and character of education in Ceylon. The reader's attention is specifically called to the articles by E. W. Adikaram, "Introduction of Buddhism and Its Influence upon Learning" (pp. 9-18); S. Paravitana, "The Mahavihara and Other Ancient Seats of Learning" (pp. 51-60); M. B. Ariyapala, "Life and Aspirations of the People as Conditioned by Their Education" (pp. 139-153); D. Arampatta, "Religious Education" (pp. 965-974); and P. B. J. Hewawasam, "The Buddhist Tradition" (pp. 1107-1130).

(9) GOKHALE, B. G. Buddhism and Asoka (see 1.2.2.2[3]), pp. 260-265.

In this brief chapter, Gokhale offers the reader one of the few treatments available concerning Buddhist influence on Indian education.

Buddhism and the Social Order

(10) HANKS, L. M. "Merit and Power in the Thai Social Order. See 6.2.1.1(15).

(11) HICKEY, G. E. and H. P. VO. "Religion and Education," in Area Handbook on Laos. Edited by Norton S. Ginsburg. New Haven, Conn.: Human Relations Area File, 1955, pp. 156-177.

In the first section of the article, the reader will find a general description of the basic Buddhist celebrations observed, the organization of the Sangha hierarchy, and the traditional role of the monk in Lao society. Then the traditional educational function of the monk is detailed, with a concluding section on the traditional and contemporary curricula of modern Lao schools.

(12) JAYASEKERA, U. D. Early History of Education in Ceylon. Colombo: Department of Cultural Affairs, 1969, 208 pp.

Suitable for beginning and advanced students, this selection deals with the early period of Ceylonese history up to Mahasena (fourth century A.D.). Only one chapter, pages 70-96, treats religious backgrounds of education, but other sections of the book examine the educational institutions, the curriculum, methods of teaching, and the prominent "theras" who are mentioned in the literature as outstanding teachers. Since the Sangha was solely responsible for most education until the fourth century A.D., the student primarily interested in Sinhalese Buddhism can profit handsomely from this discussion.

(13) JAYAWEERA, SWARNA. "Religious Organizations and the State in Ceylonese Education." Comparative Education Review, 12, no. 2 (June 1968), 159-170.

A good scholarly treatment of the British educational policy in Ceylon prior to the 1948 revolution. The author characterizes the "dual system" of education which favored Christian operated schools at the expense of Buddhist and Hindu schools.

(14) JOSHI, LALMANI. Studies in the Buddhistic Culture of India (see 1.2.2.3[9]), pp. 154-178.

This chapter contains a worthwhile overview of Buddhist educational practices in Indian monasteries during the seventh and eighth centuries. Joshi covers the subjects of study, the daily regimen of the student-monks, and the major universities.

(15) KEAY, F. B. Ancient Indian Education. London: Oxford University, 1918, pp. 87-113.

These pages represent a concise description of Buddhist education in India, especially during the fifth to seventh centuries. The author has relied almost exclusively upon the accounts of I Ching, Hsuan Tsang, and Fa-Hien. Though a bit dated, this piece is still useful as an introduction.

(16) LI AN-CHE. "The Lamasery as an Educational Institution." Asiatic Review, 46, no. 165 (January 1950), 915-922.

The author has chosen the Lamasery at Labrang as an exemplary model on which to build generalizations concerning education in Tibetan monasteries. In a straightforward manner, he discusses admissions policies, academic activities, including examinations and degrees, discipline, and opportunities for further study for the teachers. On the whole, it is a good characterization.

(17) _____. "Rnin-ma-pa: The Early Form of Lamaism." See 1.14.2.1(6).

An introductory article concerned with the historical background and unique qualities of the "red sect." The author explains how the "red sect" has divided Buddhism into nine categories in order to explain the variations; portrays the academic organization of the sect as being divided between doctrinal instruction and practical training; and depicts the actual program of study carried out in the sect's "teaching college."

(18) MALALASEKERA, G. P. "The Influence of Buddhism on Education in Ceylon," in Religions of the Empire. Edited by William L. Hare. London: Duckworth, 1925, pp. 160-175.

A rather impressionistic effort in which the author hails education as the greatest service rendered by the monasteries of Ceylon. He outlines the "principles of life" emphasized in monastic education and the manner in which these principles were imparted. Finally, he notes the changes brought about by the coming of the Western powers.

(19) MILLER, MARGARET. "Educational Practices of Tibetan Lama Training." Asian Folklore Studies, 16 (1957), 188-267.

An article in which the author assumes that the reader has a prior knowledge of Tibetan meditation and doctrine. The bulk of the article is concerned with the methods employed in a lama's training, the types of educational facilities in use, the character of the curriculum, and the entire educational environment. Also includes sections which attempt to discern the role of the lama in Tibetan society, the variety of careers open to the trained lama, requirements for entrance into a Lamasery, and the discipline designed for maintenance of the monastery as a community.

(20) MISRA, S. S. P. "The Ideal of Education in Early Buddhism." Journal of the Gujarat Research Society, 29 (January 1967), 21-24.

On the basis of the Vinaya texts, the author attempts to identify the proper relationship between teacher and student and the role of the educator in the Buddhist society in India. The central point of this article seems to be that there was a correlation between the popularization of education in India and the growth of Buddhism in society.

(21) MOOKERJI, RADHA KUMUD. Ancient Indian Education (Brahmanical and Buddhist). London: Macmillan, 1947, part 2, pp. 347-610.

These pages, without doubt, contain the finest comprehensive treatment of Buddhist education in India. The reader will find discussions of the character of Buddhist education in all phases of its history in India and attempts to identify the causes of significant changes.

(22) OPPER, CONRAD. "Educational Development in Thailand." Asia, 3 (1965), 72-88.

A simple article dealing with the historical development of education in Thailand. Opper first sketches the character of Buddhist education in Thailand and notes the transitions which occurred as a result of the spread of Catholic and Protestant missions. He then emphasizes the roles played by King Chulalongkorn and Prince Damrong in the modernization of the Thai educational system.

(23) RAHULA, WALPOLA. History of Buddhism in Ceylon (see 1.3.1[10]), pp. 287-302.

One of the few accounts of Buddhist education in ancient Ceylon, this chapter consists of a concise statement concerning the aims, curriculum, and instructional practices of monastic education.

(24) SANKALIA, H. D. The University of Nalanda. Madras: B. G. Paul, 1934, 259 pp.

This volume comprises a complete history and characterization of the University of Nalanda, from its inception to its destruction. The author devotes chapters to the University's illustrious alumni, the student life, the curriculum, etc.

(25) SASTRI, K. A. N. "Nalanda." Journal of the Madras University, 13 (1941), 147-202.

This article attempts to say everything relevant about Nalanda but ends up saying little of specific importance. The author has utilized the descriptions of I Ching and Hsuan Tsang to ground his discussion in respected sources.

(26) TAPINGKAE, AMNUAY, ed. Education in Thailand: Some Thai Perspectives. Washington: U.S. Government Printing Office, 1973, 118 pp.

This is a useful little volume containing various articles on a myriad of topics relating to traditional and contemporary Thai education. Generally, the articles fall into three categories: the role of education in Thai society, the situation and education of teachers, and the status of the university system. Specifically, there are two excellent, though brief, articles on "The Buddhist Theories of the Learner and of the Teacher," and "Some Principles of Education in Buddhism." For an excellent treatment of Thai education in the early twentieth century, see also David K. Wyatt, The Politics of Reformation in Thailand: Education in the Reign of King Chulalonghorn (New Haven, Conn.: Yale University Press, 1969), 425 pp.

(27) THOMAS, E. J. "Buddhist Education in Pali and Sanskrit Schools," in Buddhistic Studies (see 2.4.2[7]), pp. 220-235.

An attempt to reconstruct, from various Sanskrit and Pali texts, a picture of the ideal courses of study followed in Indian monasteries and Buddhist universities. The article is designed to supplement the knowledge of Buddhist education derived from the accounts of Chinese pilgrims. It in turn can be supplemented, especially for information on the early period, by Radhakumud Mookerjee, "Ancient Indian Education from the Jatakas," on pages 236-256 of the same volume.

(28) WELCH, HOLMES. The Buddhist Revival in China (see 1.11.2.4[6]), pp. 103-121.

This chapter, devoted to Buddhist education, provides a fine introduction to the subject for China, with special attention to the modern developments.

6.2.6 Buddhism and Economic Activity

(1) AYAL, ELIEZER B. "Value Systems and Economic Development in Japan and Thailand." Journal of Social Issues, 19, no. 1 (January 1936), 35-51.

The author's fundamental thesis is that changes in political and social institutions will not bring about economic change unless the fundamental human values in a society are conducive to economic development. Hence, Ayal sees the function of the value system as twofold: it can provide goals which in some way might lead to economic activity, and it must sanction the nature of economic activity. Having established this, he goes on to discuss the manner in which Buddhism has informed the value systems of Japan and Thailand.

(2) BELLAH, ROBERT. Tokugawa Religion: The Values of Pre-Industrial Japan. See 1.13.2.3(1).

(3) CARRASCO, PEDRO. Land and Polity in Tibet. See 6.2.2.7(2).

(4) CH'EN, KENNETH. "The Economic Background of the Hui-ch'ang Suppression of Buddhism." See 1.11.2.3(1).

(5) _____. "Economic Life," in The Chinese Transformation of Buddhism (see 1.11.1[2]), pp. 125-178.

In this chapter, Ch'en describes the role which the Buddhist monasteries played in the industrial and commercial life of T'ang China. He points out that the Sangha's economic powers sometimes became quite great and that its power basis was the ownership of land. Ch'en hints at a connection between the wealth of a monastery and the scope of its activities.

Buddhism and the Social Order

(6) EBIHARA, MAY. "Interrelations between Buddhism and Social Systems in Cambodian Peasant Culture." See 6.2.1(7).

(7) EVERS, HANS-DIETER. "Buddhism and the British Colonial Policy in Ceylon, 1815-1875." See 6.2.2.2(5).

(8) _____. "Kinship and Property Rights in a Buddhist Monastery in Central Ceylon." See 6.1.1(9).

(9) _____. "Monastic Landlordism in Ceylon." Journal of Asian Studies, 28, no. 4 (August 1969), 685-692.
In this brief article, the author finds that the driving force behind the development of monastic land ownership is the factor of merit accumulation (by donating land to the Sangha, the laity accumulate merit). Having established this, Evers reviews the present use and status of monastic-owned lands in contemporary Ceylon. Suitable for the intermediate and advanced student.

(10) _____. Monks, Priests, and Peasants. See 6.2.1.1(11).

(11) GERNET, JACQUES. Les aspects économiques du Bouddhisme dans la société chinoise du Ve au Xe siècle. See 1.11.2.2(3).
Gernet frequently alludes to the contributions made by Buddhism to agriculture and art, but he is primarily concerned with how Buddhism affected Chinese economy. His general thesis is that the incredible growth in the number of monks, nuns and monasteries during this period greatly strained the Chinese economy, for these chief reasons: 1) depletion of the work force; 2) cost of alms and monastery construction; 3) ecclesiastical tax exemptions; and 4) unscrupulous money-lending.

(12) INGERSOLL, JASPER and DAVID PFANNER. "Theravada Buddhism and Village Economic Behavior." See 6.2.3(10).

(13) JOSHI, LALMANI. Studies in the Buddhistic Culture of India (see 1.2.2.3[9]), pp. 83-93.
Joshi provides the reader with an interesting view of the economics of monasticism by reviewing records of endowments given by various kings and patrons in seventh and eighth century India.

(14) LUCE, G. H. "Economic Life of the Early Burman." Journal of the Burma Research Society, 30, no. 1 (April 1940), 283-335.
Luce's article is directed to those readers who might be primarily interested in the daily life of the Burmese of the Pagan period. Using the Pagan inscriptions as his source, Luce attempts to reconstruct the nature of Burmese agriculture, taxation, and economic transactions.

(15) MAUNG, MYA. "Cultural Value and Economic Change in Burma." Asian Survey, 4, no. 3 (March 1964), 757-764.
This is a well written general article which seeks to evaluate the impact of Buddhist cultural values on the Burmese attitude toward material goods, the availability of opportunities for economic growth, and the stimulation of effort in that direction.

(16) MILLER, ROBERT. "Buddhist Monastic Economy: The Jisa Mechanism." Comparative Studies in Society and History, 3 (1960-1961), 427-438.
In this good article for the advanced student, Miller is concerned with the "mechanism" by which gifts (by laymen or monks) are transferred into merit. This mechanism is the "jisa," which the author explains as the basis for all economic activities engaged in by the Sangha. He also points out the relationships spawned by such a mechanism and gives specific examples of its operation in Bhutan, Sikkim, and Inner and Outer Mongolia. On pages 439-442 of the same journal, George Murphy argues that "jisa" must not be misconstrued as the basis of monastic economic activity, but should be seen as one segment within the total monastic finance system. Finally, André Bareau follows Murphy in the same issue (pp. 443-449) and reviews the nature of institutions analogous to "jisa" which were operative in the early economies of monastic institutions of India, Ceylon, and China. He draws his information from old canons and scriptures.

(17) NASH, MANNING. The Golden Road to Modernity. See 4.1.2(14).

(18) PIERIS, RALPH. Sinhalese Social Organization: The Kandyan Period. See 6.2.1.1(31).

(19) SARKISYANZ, EMANUEL. Buddhist Backgrounds of the Burmese Revolution. See 1.4.2(15).

(20) _____. "The Social Ethics of Buddhism and the Socio-economic Order of Southeast Asia." See 6.2.2.1(15).

(21) SPIRO, MELFORD. "Buddhism and Economic Action in Burma." American Anthropologist, 68, no. 5 (October 1966), 1163-1173.
This is an excellent though brief article, useful for both beginning and advanced students. Spiro's chief thesis is that because the Buddhist concepts of rebirth, karma, merit, and charity have indelibly impressed Burmese behavior, the Burmese will typically invest their money in religious activities as a means of improving their own lot soteriologically and socially.

(22) TWITCHETT, DENNIS W. "Monastic Estates in T'ang China." See 1.11.2.3(16).
A piece intended for the advanced student. Twitchett asserts that land-holding served as

the basis of the Sangha's economic power in China. He then recounts how these lands were acquired (chiefly through donation) and how various members of Chinese society used the special status of these lands for their own personal gain. These abuses brought about serious land reform which resulted in great losses for the monastic community.

(23) _____. "The Monasteries and China's Economy in Medieval Times." *Bulletin of the School of Oriental and African Studies*, 19 (1957), 526-549.

A well done technical article for the advanced student. Twitchett relies heavily upon Gernet's *Les aspects économiques du Bouddhisme dans la société chinoise du Ve au Xe siècle* (above) and takes other secondary sources into account as he sketches the monastic involvement with land, currency, crops, and industry.

(24) WRIGGINS, W. HOWARD. *Ceylon: Dilemmas of a New Nation.* See 6.2.2.2(17).

(25) WRIGHT, ARTHUR F. "The Economic Role of Buddhism in China." *Journal of Asian Studies*, 16, no. 3 (May 1957), 408-414.

A critical review of Jacques Gernet's *Les aspects économiques du Bouddhisme dans la société chinoise du Ve au Xe siècle* (above).

(26) YANG, LIEN-SHENG. "Buddhist Monasteries and Four Money Raising Institutions in China." *Harvard Journal of Asiatic Studies*, 13 (1950), 174-191.

An article intended for the specialist and the advanced student. The author reviews four money-raising institutions which originated in, or had very close connections with, Buddhist monasteries and temples: the pawnshop, mutual financing, auctions, and lotteries.

6.2.7 Buddhism and Law

(1) AUNG, HLA U. "Some Aspects of Marriage under Burmese Buddhist Law and Malayan Muslim Law." *Journal of the Burma Research Society*, 48, no. 2 (December 1965), 1-15.

Aung's article is a comparison of Burmese Buddhist law and Malayan Muslim law on the following aspects of marriage: age, consent, consanguinity, "kufu" (equal social status), "maskahwin" (dowry), mixed marriages, polygamy, etc. Aung ends his article with the recommendations that Burmese women be accorded more rights and that the legal practice of polygamy be abolished.

(2) BHAGVAT, D. N. *Early Buddhist Jurisprudence.* See 6.1.3(1).

Though this volume is dated, it may still serve the purposes of an analysis and history of the development of Vinaya precepts. The title may seem a little misleading; but the author considers the Vinaya as jurisprudence because it carried with it the sanction of the state. The author seeks to trace the evolution of and account for the consequent promulgation of the Vinaya precepts. Particularly worthy of note is the section in which he considers the nature of Vinaya legal proceedings and the principles underlying the Buddhist idea of penalty or punishment.

(3) FURNIVALL, JOHN S. "Manu in Burma: Some Burmese Dhammathats." *Journal of the Burma Research Society*, 30 (1940), 351-370.

A good article which attempts to trace the spread of Manu through his various Buddhist and Hindu incarnations. An effective survey of the development of Manu literature in Burma.

(4) GHOSHAL, U. N. "Principle of Kings' Righteousness in the Pali Canon and Jataka Commentary." See 6.2.2.1(6).

A study of the king's righteousness which allows him to rule effectively and legitimately. The author draws upon the Jatakas and the *Cakkavatti Sihanada Sutta* to ferret out the significance of the concept of "World-ruler" and its consequences.

(5) HORNER, I. B., trans. *The Book of Discipline (Vinaya-Pitaka).* See 3.2.1.1(1).

(6) HTIN AUNG, MAUNG. "Customary Law in Burma," in *Southeast Asia in the Coming World.* Edited by Philip Thayer. Baltimore: Johns Hopkins, 1953, pp. 203-216.

A summary of the evolution of Burmese law with specific attention given to the Hindu, Buddhist and British influences.

(7) JARDINE, JOHN. "Buddhist Law." *Asiatic Review*, 34, no. 8 (October 1897), 367-375.

A brief characterization of Buddhist law suitable as an introduction to this general topic. Jardine lightly traces Burmese Buddhist law in terms of its history and organization as well as its "contemporary applications."

(8) LEE, O., comp. *Cases under Burmese Law: The Development of the Anglo-Burmese Interpretation (1874-1906).* Cleveland: Case Western Reserve University, 1971, 127 pp.

A collection of law cases tried before Burmese courts in the above period. All cases pertain to rulings on the subject of inheritance. A translation of the digest of appropriate laws cited in the cases accompanies.

(9) LINGAT, ROBERT. "The Buddhist Manu or the Propagation of Hindu Law in Hinayanist Indochina." *Annals of the Bhandarkar Oriental Research Institute*, 30, nos. 3-4 (1949), 281-297.

The author demonstrates how the Dhammasatthams functioned in the same way for the Theravada countries of Southeast Asia as the Dharmashastras did for the peoples of India.

Buddhism and the Social Order

(10) _____. "La conception du droit dans l'Indochine Hinayaniste." Bulletin de l'Ecole française d'Extrême-Orient, 44 (1947-1950), 163-187.

This article may be the best source available on the conception of law in Southeast Asian Theravada Buddhist countries. The author traces the history of the concept of law and discusses the origins of "dhammasattham." The second part of the article is an overview of Burmese Buddhist juridical literature.

(11) _____. "Evolution of the Conception of Law in Burma and Siam." See 1.5.2(15).

An excellent article tracing the development of the Burmese and Thai legal concepts from the Indian notion of dharma. The author has successfully shown how Indian conceptions of law were adopted and secularized, first by the Burmese and then by the Thai.

(12) _____. "Vinaya et droit laïque." Bulletin de l'Ecole française d'Extrême-Orient, 37, no. 2 (n.d.), 415-477.

Lingat's article is of paramount importance to the advanced student concerned with the conflicts between religious law based upon the Vinaya (and intended for the maintenance of the Sangha) and the secular law. In particular, Lingat examines the problem of Bhikkhus marrying and leaving their spouses and the legal problem of ownership of Bhikkhu possessions.

(13) LUTTER, HENRY M. A Manual of Buddhist Law. Second edition. Mandalay: Star of Burma Press, 1894, 76 pp.

Lutter's edition is really a compilation of Major Spark's Code of Burmese Law, which was itself compiled in 1860. This second edition contains the Buddhist laws concerning marriage, adultery, divorce, property, parental authority, and adoption.

(14) MEHTA, RATILAL. "Crime and Punishment in the Jatakas." The Indian Historical Quarterly, 12, no. 3 (September 1936), 432-442.

The author sketches the "ideal of justice" as it can be gleaned from various Jatakas. Specifically, he examines the role of the king as the "Head of Justice," looks at the nature of cases that are tried, and discusses the acts which constitute a crime. Finally, he considers the nature of punishments meted out for certain transgressions.

(15) NAKAMURA, HAJIME. "The Indian and Buddhist Concept of Law," in Religious Pluralism and World Community: Interfaith and Intercultural Communication (see 2.8[12]), pp. 131-174.

The author discusses the Buddhist notion of law, not in the traditional sense of jurisprudence but in terms of divine, moral and natural law. The discussion centers on the multifaceted nature of dharma.

(16) PACHOW, W. "Legal Dealings between the Buddhist Sangha and the Laity." See 6.1.2(16).

(17) WIGMORE, JOHN HENRY. "The Buddhist Branch," in his A Panorama of the World's Legal Systems. Washington: Washington Law Book Co., 1928, pp. 224-242.

A historical overview of the development of law administration in India, Burma, and Siam. It should be used only as an introduction to the topic of Buddhist law.

7 Religious Practices and Rituals

For meditation, tantric practices and Pure Land practices, see Category 11, Soteriological Experience and Processes. For dance and music, see Category 5, The Arts.

7.1 MERIT-MAKING AND RITUALS OF PIETY

For moral observances, see 11.3, Moral Discipline and Ethics, and 7.2.4, Uposatha Rites. For taking the three refuges, see 11.2. For pilgrimage, see Category 10, Sacred Places. For meditation, see 11.4, Meditation.

7.1.1 General Discussions

(1) BAREAU, ANDRE. "Les idées sous-jacentes aux pratiques cultuelles bouddhiques dans le Cambodge actuel." Wiener Zeitschrift für die Kunde Süd- und Ost-Asiens, 12-13 (1968-1969), 23-32 (E. Frauwallner Festschrift).
   A fine concise study of the ideological and metaphysical backdrops to the Theravada cultic and ritual practices, based on ritual formulas commonly in use in modern Cambodia.

(2) BEYER, STEPHAN. The Cult of Tara: Magic and Ritual in Tibet. Berkeley: University of California Press, 1973, 542 pp. See 7.8(2).

(3) DAVIS, RICHARD. "Tolerance and Intolerance of Ambiguity in Northern Thai Myth and Ritual." Ethnology, 13, no. 2 (1974), 1-24.
   A fine, solid anthropological work, which makes a unique contribution to the literature on Northern Thai Buddhism and works out a sophisticated interpretation of the relationship of myth and ritual.

(4) DICKSON, J. F. "Notes Illustrative of Buddhism as the Daily Religion of the Buddhists of Ceylon, and Some Account of Their Ceremonies before and after Death." Journal of the Royal Asiatic Society (Ceylon Branch), 8 (1884), 203-236.
   Includes excellent descriptions of nineteenth century performances of everyday ceremonies such as giving, keeping moral precepts, transferring merit, listening to preaching, etc. Dickson gives both the Pali and an English translation of the ritual texts involved in these rites--a "hope that [t]his work can be read as a complement" to his own Precept and Practice (below).

(5) EKVALL, ROBERT B. Religious Observances in Tibet. Chicago: University of Chicago Press, 1964, 313 pp.
   A detailed, chapter-by-chapter description of Tibetan "rituals of piety," based primarily on the author's personal acquaintance with religious observances in Amdo (Northeastern Tibet). Included in the discussion are "offering" (mchod pa), "salutation" (phyag), circumambulation (bskor ba), and "verbalized religion" (chos 'don), the latter including the use of chants, of prayer wheels, rosaries, sacred formulas, etc.

(6) GOMBRICH, RICHARD. "Merit Transfer in Sinhalese Buddhism: A Case Study in the Interaction between Doctrine and Practice." History of Religions, 11 (1971), 203-219.
   Intended for the more advanced student, Gombrich's article is an attempt to show that "merit transfer" has been rationalized to conform to canonical doctrine. Hence, he traces this evolution through the interpretation of ritual as it has been laid out in ancient texts. For another noteworthy article on the same topic, see G. P. Malalasekere, "Transference of Merit in Ceylonese Buddhism," Philosophy East and West, 17 (1967), 85-90.

(7) _____. Precept and Practice (see 4.1.1[7]), pp. 214-243.
   An illuminating discussion of some of the doctrines and practices by which Buddhists in Central Ceylon find "loopholes" in a rigid interpretation of the doctrines of karma and the practice of merit-making. Included are examinations of the practices based on the doctrine of "superseded karma" (ahosi kamma), of the "religious wish" (prarthana), and of the "transference of merit" (patti and pattanumodana).

(8) NASH, MANNING. "Ritual and Ceremonial Cycle in Upper Burma," in Anthropological Studies of Theravada Buddhism (see 4.1.1[3]), pp. 97-115.
   Nash tries to provide a generalized scheme to account for any ritual and ceremonial

cycle. He sees a dichotomy between communal rites performed by Buddhist specialists oriented towards ultimate ends and individual rites in the hands of nonspecialists oriented towards immediate-crisis ends. Communal rites are obligatory and transcend local organization while "nat" rites are personal, village-structured and regional.

(9) OBEYESEKERE, GANANATH. "Structure of a Sinhalese Ritual." Ceylon Journal of Historical and Social Studies, 1 (1958).

An interesting functional analysis of Sinhalese social structure which focuses upon the form of ritual grouping known as udupila and yatipila which was a feature of Sinhala social organization in almost every part of the island at one time.

(10) SPIRO, MELFORD. Buddhism and Society (see 6.2.1.1[42]), pp. 92-113.

Merit-making comes under what Spiro calls "Kammatic Buddhism" (as distinguished from Nibbanic and Apotropaic Buddhism), and he sees it as a sort of soteriologically second-class practice. His discussion, however, based on Burmese materials, of the "means for acquiring merit" is very helpful, and includes some interesting charts (based on the answers of Burmese villagers) of the acts deemed most demeritorious. These charts might be compared with those provided for northeastern Thailand by Tambiah in his Buddhism and the Spirit Cults (below).

(11) TAMBIAH, STANLEY J. Buddhism and the Spirit Cults in North-East Thailand (see 4.1.2[16]), pp. 143-151.

An anthropological discussion of the ideology and practice of merit-making ("Thambun") among villagers in Northeastern Thailand. Includes an interesting table of the villagers' ranking of seven different common merit-making acts. For a similar table based on the answers of Burmese villagers, see Spiro, Buddhism and Society (above).

(12) TIN, PE MAUNG. Buddhist Devotion and Meditation. London: S.P.C.K., 1964, pp. 3-66.

This first section of the book deals with Buddhist devotion in Burma, and contains a number of prayers, praises, and descriptions of "rituals of piety" commonly practiced in that country.

(13) WELCH, HOLMES H. The Practice of Chinese Buddhism 1900-1950 (see 6.1.1[29]), pp. 357-394.

The chapter, entitled "The Lay Buddhist," makes a fine introduction to lay life in China in all its variety. Includes discussions of temple worship, pilgrimage, meritorious practices, and acts of taking refuge and observing lay vows.

7.1.2 Giving (dana)

(1) BECHERT, HEINZ. Some Remarks on the Kathina Rite." Journal of the Bihar Research Society, 54 (1968), 319-329.

A description of early Buddhist practices of offering new robes to the Sangha and the rites that go along with it, based on texts of the Pali Vinaya. For a more technical study of the Kathina rite texts, see Kun Chang, A Comparative Study of the Kathinavastu (3.2.1.2[4]). For a discussion of the contemporary festival as it takes place in Thailand, see Kaufman, Bangkhuad (below).

(2) KAUFMAN, HOWARD KEVA. Bangkhuad, A Community Study in Thailand. Locust Valley, N.Y.: J. J. Augustin, 1960, pp. 185-189.

A fine description of the Thai festival and ceremonies of Thaud Kathin, the first celebration after the end of the rainy season and traditionally the occasion for the laity to give new cloth to the monks. Other descriptions of the festival may be found in John Blofeld, "Tod Kathin," Holiday Time in Thailand, 5, no. 3 (July-September 1964), 23-31; H. G. Quaritch Wales, Siamese State Ceremonies (7.7[6]), pp. 200-212; and Kenneth Wells, Thai Buddhism (below, pp. 105ff.). For a discussion of the traditional ceremony as found in the Vinaya texts, see Bechert, "Some Remarks on the Kathina Rite" (above). For a discussion of the economics and social relations involved in the Thot Kathin, see Jane Bunnag, Buddhist Monk, Buddhist Layman (6.1.2[4]) pp. 113-120.

(3) SPIRO, MELFORD. Buddhism and Society (see 6.2.1.1[42]), pp. 103-111.

Giving (dana) is the meritorious act par excellence. In these pages, based on Burmese materials, Spiro describes the various forms which giving can take. A fine introduction to the subject.

(4) VISSER, MARINUS WILLEM DE. Ancient Buddhism in Japan (see 1.13.2.1[8]), pp. 27-44.

A historical discussion of what de Visser calls "Maigre Entertainments of Monks and Nuns" in seventh to ninth century Japan. Provides some interesting first-hand accounts of these large-scale feasts held for the Sangha, generally sponsored by the imperial family.

(5) WELLS, KENNETH E. Thai Buddhism, Its Rites and Activities (see 1.5.1[9]), pp. 91-109.

The Rainy Season (Vassa in Thailand) is a time for the giving of special offerings by the laity. This chapter describes among others the ceremonies of giving of robes, honey, and medicines, and also describes the Loi Katong festival of giving lights, which is held just after the end of the rainy season. Other descriptions of these ceremonies in Thailand may be found in Chapters 17-18 of Ernest Young, The Kingdom of the Yellow Robe (see 7.2.5[8]).

7.1.3 <u>Veneration of Sacred Objects (including images of the Buddha, relics, stupas, etc.)</u>

<u>See also</u> Category 10, Sacred Places, and Category 9, Mythology, Cosmology and Basic Symbols.

(1) ANESAKI, MASAHARU. <u>Nichiren, the Buddhist Prophet</u> (see 1.13.2.2[2]), pp. 46 ff.

A good treatment, with an original translation from Nichiren himself, of veneration of the "Lotus Sutra," the Great Mandala and the Holy See.

(2) BAGCHI, B. C. "The Eight Great Caityas and Their Cult." <u>Indian Historical Quarterly</u>, 17 (1941), 223-235.

The eight stupas marking the major events in the life of the Buddha became, very early, important centers of pilgrimage and cult. They have remained so. As examples of the later cult paid to these eight caityas, Bagchi has translated here a Chinese text praising them (the <u>Fo shuo pa ta ling t'a hao king</u>, or <u>Buddhabhasita-asta-mahacaitya-nama-sutra</u>), and two Tibetan texts from the <u>bstan-'gyur</u>, describing the worship of them. (Both texts are entitled <u>Gnas chen po brgyad kyi mchod rten la bstod pa</u>, or <u>Astamaha sthana caitya-stotra</u>.) <u>See also</u> on this praise: Sylvain Levi, "Une poésie inconnue du roi Harsa Siladitva," <u>Actes du Dixième Congrès International des Orientalistes</u>, 1 (1894), 187-203.

(3) BAILEY, H. W. "The Pradaksina-sutra of Chang Tsiang-kuin." <u>See</u> 3.3.8.4(2).

A translation of a very short Khotanese text on the advantages of reverencing and circumambulating Buddha images and stupas. Other material on pradaksina may be found in <u>Semitic and Oriental Studies Presented to W. Popper</u>, 1951, pp. 345-354.

(4) BAREAU, ANDRE. "La Construction et le culte du Stupa d'après le Vinayapitaka." <u>See</u> 9.3.6(1).

(5) EKVALL, ROBERT B. <u>Religious Observances in Tibet</u>. <u>See</u> 7.1.1(5).

(6) GHINE, OHN [DAVID MAURICE]. "The Botatung Pagoda." <u>The Light of Dhamma</u>, 1, no. 2 (1953), 5-7.

A fascinating, almost suspenseful account of the discovery of a hair relic of the Buddha in the ruins of the Botatung pagoda, which was destroyed by the Royal Air Force during the war. Includes an account of the ceremonies at the opening of the casket.

(7) GUPTA, KESAB CHANDRA. "Relics of Sariputta and Moggallana Arahans: Their Return Home and Welcome," in <u>Diamond Jubilee Souvenir of the Maha Bodhi Society</u>. Calcutta: Maha Bodhi Society, 1952, pp. 201-204.

A short article giving a pietistic history of the relics of two of the Buddha's major disciples, and an account of the ceremonies when they were returned to India from the Victoria and Albert Museum in London.

(8) HIRAKAWA, AKIRA. "The Rise of Mahayana Buddhism and Its Relationship to the Worship of Stupas." <u>See</u> 2.5.2(5).

Hirakawa sees the stupa as the one origin of Mahayana, but his article contains much scholarly information on Buddhist cultic practices in India.

(9) HOCART, A. M. <u>The Temple of the Tooth in Kandy</u>. Memoirs of the Archaeological Survey of Ceylon, No. 4. London: Luzac, 1931, 40 pp.

An important study of the story and ritual of what is perhaps the most famous of the relics of the Buddha, the Tooth relic in Kandy, one of the former capitals of Sri Lanka. For another study of the same, see Victor Goloubew, "Le temple de la dent à Kandy," <u>Bulletin de l'Ecole française d'Extrême-Orient</u>, 32 (1932), 442-474.

(10) I-CHING. <u>A Record of the Buddhist Religion</u> (see 1.2.2.3[8]), pp. 140-152.

Two chapters in I-Ching's descriptions of Buddhist practices as he observed them during his late-seventh-century pilgrimage to India deal specifically with the manners of venerating holy objects. Chapter 30 treats, in a rather confused manner, the question of circumambulation (pradaksina), while Chapter 31 presents the more interesting "Rules of Decorum in Cleansing the Sacred Object of Worship."

(11) LESSING, FERDINAND D. "Structure and Meaning of the Rite Called the Bath of Buddha According to Tibetan and Chinese Sources," in <u>Studia Serica Bernhard Karlgren dedicata</u>. Edited by Soren Egerod and Else Glahn. Copenhagen: Ejnar Munksgaard, 1959, pp. 159-171.

The best description in English of the rite of "Bathing (the statue of) the Buddha" (in Chinese, Yu-fo; in Sanskrit, Buddhasnana). Includes an excellent synopsis of the ritual, and a translation of the Tibetan text of the ceremony. In China, the rite was one in which both monks and laymen participated. For a photograph of a woman "bathing the Buddha" in Hong Kong, <u>see</u> Holmes Welch, <u>The Practice of Chinese Buddhism</u> (6.1.1[29]), p. 368.

(12) PERERA, ARTHUR A. "The Daily Ritual at the Dalada Maligava." <u>Ceylon Antiquary and Literary Register</u>, 6 (1920-1921), 67-68.

A simple, straightforward account, without any interpretation attempted, of what takes place every day at the Temple of the Buddha's Tooth Relic in Kandy, Ceylon. For a more generalized work on the same shrine, <u>see</u> Hocart's <u>The Temple of the Tooth</u> (above).

(13) <u>Saddharma pundarika Sutra</u>. Translated by H. Kern as <u>The Lotus of the True Law</u> (see 4.2.1[6]), pp. 227-254.

The "Lotus Sutra" has a number of chapters (for example, this one on the "Apparition of a Stupa") which vividly describe the Buddhist

Merit-Making and Rituals of Piety

7.1.4 Repetition of Sutras and Formulas, Prayer, Use of Rosaries

See also 7.5.3, Protection, and 7.5.4, Paritta Texts.

(1) BOYER, MARTHA and JIKAI FUJIYOSHI. "Omizutori, One of Japan's Oldest Buddhist Ceremonies." Eastern Buddhist, 3, no. 1 (June 1970), 67-96.
  A good article which provides the reader with an outline of the Omizutori ceremony, an annual rite instituted by imperial decree in 752 and carried out to the present day. Omizutori (the taking of water) is based upon the text of "The Way of the Eleven-Headed Kannon" and implies that Buddhist priests may repent their sins and intensify their piety by means of an eleven-headed Kannon-image enshrined in the Nigatsu-so (Hall of the Second Month).

(2) CLARK, CHARLES ALLEN. Religions of Old Korea (see 1.12.1[2]), pp. 286-287.
  Translation of the Yunchoo-kyung, "Classic of the Buddhist Rosary," copied from E. B. Landis, "The Classic of the Buddhist Rosary," Korean Repository, 2 (1895), 23-25. The text tells how to tell 108 beads.

(3) EKVALL, ROBERT B. Religious Observances in Tibet. See 7.1.1(5).

(4) I-CHING. A Record of the Buddhist Religion (see 1.2.2.3[8]), pp. 152-166.
  This chapter of the Chinese pilgrim I-Ching's account of Buddhist practices in India and the Malayan archipelago is entitled "The Ceremony of Chanting," and is especially interesting for the details it provides on this aspect of ritual as it was carried out at Nalanda in the late seventh century A.D.

(5) JAMES, J. M. "Descriptive notes on the rosaries (jiu-dzu) as used by the Different Sects of Buddhism in Japan." Transactions of the Asiatic Society of Japan, 9 (1881), 173-182.
  A helpful article which gives a straightforward description, first of the "sho-zoku-jiu-dzu," a rosary used by all sects, and then of the special rosaries of the Tendai, Shingon, Jodo, Zen and Shin sects.

(6) LALOU, MARCELLE. "Deux Prières de Caravaniers Tibétains." Mélanges Chinois et Bouddhiques, 8 (1946-1947), 217-223.
  Lalou has here translated into French two very short texts that were among the documents found in Tung huang. They are both popular prayers which were used by merchants on the trade route, and reflect the popular side of the Mantrayana.

(7) LECLERE, ADHEMARD. Le Bouddhisme au Cambodge (see 1.6.1[4]), pp. 418-420.
  A short description of the Cambodian Phkom or rosary of 108 beads, and of its use. Unfortunately lacking in details.

(8) MATRCETA. Satapancasatka. Translated by David Roy Shackleton-Bailey as The Satapancasatka of Matrceta. See 3.2.4.3(2).

(9) _____. Varnarhavarna Stotra. Translated by David Roy Shackleton-Bailey as "The Varnarhavarna Stotra of Matrceta." See 3.2.4.3(3).

(10) SERRUYS, HENRY. "A Mongol Lamaist Prayer: Undusun bsang, Incense Offering of Origin." Monumenta Serica, 28 (1969), 321-418.
  A photostat edition, transliteration, and translation into English of a fascinating "prayer" consisting of invocations to various deities and Buddhas and requests for boons.

(11) SUZUKI, BEATRICE LANE. "Ceremonies for Lay Disciples at Koya-san." Eastern Buddhist, 6 (1932-1935), 157-175.
  A description of three ceremonies available both to priests and laymen at the Endzuritsuji Vinaya Temple on Mt. Koya, the headquarters of the Japanese Shingon sect. The three are: The Bosatsukai (Bodhisattva Sila, or ceremony of taking the Bodhisattva vows), the Sanzenbutsumyo (a ritual of paying homage to and calling the names and dharanis of three hundred Buddhas), and the Ango ceremony, which takes place around July 16th.

(12) WADDELL, L. A. "Lamaic Rosaries: Their Kinds and Uses." Journal of the Asiatic Society of Bengal, 61 (1892), 24-33.
  A short but informative description of the various types of Tibetan Buddhist rosaries, the materials they are made out of, and some of the mantras uttered when telling them. A summary of this article may be found in L. A. Waddell, Tibetan Buddhism (New York: Dover, 1972), pp. 202-211.

(13) WELCH, HOLMES. The Practice of Chinese Buddhism, 1900-1950 (see 6.1.1[29]), pp. 89-104.
  This chapter, entitled "The Buddha Recitation Hall," provides a fine introduction to this important practice of contemporary Chinese Buddhism.

(14) WELLS, KENNETH E. Thai Buddhism, Its Rites and Activities (see 1.5.1[9]), pp. 47-53.
  Four times a month, on Wan Phra, Thai laymen and women attend the ceremonies taking place in the monastery. These pages contain a good description of the laity's participation in these rituals.

7.2 MONASTIC RITUALS AND PRACTICES

7.2.1 Ordination in the Monastic Community (novitiate, full membership, higher authoritative ranks)

(1) BUNNAG, JANE. *Buddhist Monk, Buddhist Layman* (see 6.1.2[4]), pp. 165-179.
  In a section entitled "The Ordination Ceremony: its organization and implication," Bunnag describes relationships between the people who participated in a particular ordination ceremony held in Thailand on July 2, 1967. For a description of the actual rites of the ordination ceremony itself in Thailand, see Wells, *Thai Buddhism* (below).

(2) I-CHING. *A Record of the Buddhist Religion* (see 1.2.2.3[8]), pp. 95-107.
  An interesting first-hand account of an ordination ceremony based on the Mulasarvastivada Vinaya as the pilgrim I-Ching observed it in the late seventh century A.D. in India. Even more valuable is that he correlates his observations with what he knows of the ordination ceremonies of the time back home in China.

(3) LAFONT, PIERRE-BERNARD and PIERRE BITARD. "Ordination de deux dignitaires bouddhiques 'Tay Lu,'" *Bulletin de la Société des études indochinoises*, 32 (1957), 199-221.
  A fascinating description of a specific ordination ceremony in Northern Laos on February 7, 1955 for the promotion of two monks to a higher ecclesiastical rank. The ritual involves an interesting, highly symbolic, procession through the forest.

(4) LECLERE, ADHEMARD. *Le Bouddhisme au Cambodge* (see 1.6.1[4]), pp. 405-412.
  A concise, straightforward, turn-of-the-century description of the ordination ceremony of a Cambodian monk.

(5) LEVY, PAUL. *Buddhism: A Mystery Religion?* London: University of London, 1957; New York: Schocken, 1968, 119 pp.
  An imaginative series of lectures presenting and calling for the study of Buddhist ordination ceremonies. Levy's interpretation, unfortunately, is at times reckless, generally over-dependent on Przyluski's work on the Council of Rajagriha, and saved only by the question-mark in the title. However, advanced students might find it interesting.

(6) MENDELSON, E. MICHAEL. "Initiation and Paradox of Power: A Sociological Approach," in *Initiation*. Edited by C. J. Bleeker. Leiden: E. J. Brill, 1965, pp. 214-222.
  Using the data of Burmese Buddhism, Mendelson attempts to discern the efficacy of reciprocity involved in initiation rites among Buddhist participants. His fundamental thesis is that initiation into the Sangha provides the individual with an "enhancement." This "enhancement" can be compared to the function of ritual as seen by those who ascribe to the "rites de passage" theory. Mendelson sees his theory of enhancement as more congruent to the overall enhancement which Buddhism provides for its Theravada monks.

(7) PRIP-MOLLER, J. *Chinese Buddhist Monasteries*. Copenhagen: G. E. O. Gads Forlag, 1937, pp. 297-352.
  Chapter 5 of Prip-Moller's magnificent book on Chinese monasteries is entitled "The Ordination Unit, Its Ceremonies and Its Development," and remains one of the most detailed descriptive treatments of all phases of the ordination of Chinese monks. Marvellously illustrated, it is unfortunately not readily available.

(8) SANGHARAKSITA BHIKSU. "Ordination and Initiation in the Three Yanas of Buddhism." *Indo-Asian Culture*, 8 (1960), 246-265.
  A reprint of an article from *Middle Way*, 24 (1959), 94-104, this makes a good, overall introduction to the topic. Rather than comparing the different texts of the pratimoksa, Sangharaksita compares the Hinayana Upasampada (ordination) and its patimokkha pratimoksa of 227 of 250 precepts, with the Mahayana Boddisattva Samvara and its bodhisattva precepts (bodhisattva sila), and with Vajrayana Abhiseka and its Samaya vows.

(9) SPIRO, MELFORD. *Buddhism and Society* (see 6.2.1.1[42]), pp. 290-292.
  A concise, contemporary description of an ordination ceremony witnessed by Spiro in Burma. Other, longer, earlier descriptions of such occasions in Burma may be found in Vincentius Sangermano, *The Burmese Empire a Hundred Years Ago* (Westminster: A. Constable, 1893), pp. 124-128, and in Paul A. Bigandet, *The Life or Legend of Gaudama, the Buddha of the Burmese* (London: Trubner, 1912), pp. 275-281. Chapter 10 of *Buddhism and Society* gives a description of the boys' initiation or ordination (shin byu) in Burma.

(10) SUZUKI, DAISETZ TEITARO. *The Training of the Zen Buddhist Monk*. New York: University Books, 1966, pp. 3-19. (Originally published 1934.)
  A somewhat romanticized account of the arrival of a Zen monk and his acceptance into a monastery after a period of waiting. The chapter is entitled "Initiation."

(11) TAMBIAH, STANLEY J. *Buddhism and the Spirit Cults in North-East Thailand* (see 4.1.2[16]), pp. 103-115.
  A concise introduction to three rites as they are practiced in Northeastern Thailand: the ordination and de-robing of a monk, and the rite of honoring the monk. The latter is a ritual organized by the villagers themselves which marks a monk's passage from one grade and title to another.

Monastic Rituals and Practices

(12) Vinaya pitaka. Translated by I. B. Horner as The Book of the Discipline (see 3.2.1.1[1]), Vol. 4.

The first Khandaka of the Mahavagga (contained in this volume) presents, in a legendary-historical framework, the basic regulations dealing with the ordination of monks into the Sangha. This serves to give a "canonical perspective" on these practices. The same passage may be found in a different translation in T. W. Rhys-Davids and H. Oldenberg, Vinaya Texts (see 3.2.1.1[2]), vol. 1.

(13) WADDELL, L. AUSTINE. Tibetan Buddhism (see 1.14.1[17]), pp. 169-187.

A good description of the processes of entering the Sangha in Tibet, and of ceremonies connected with the novitiate, with ordination, and with the attainment of higher ecclesiastical grades.

(14) WARREN, HENRY CLARKE. Buddhism in Translations (see 2.7.1[16]), pp. 393-401.

In this passage of his anthology, Warren reprints an 1874 article by J. F. Dickson containing an eyewitness account of an ordination ceremony in Central Ceylon, and a translation of the Upasampada Kammavaca, a manual which sets forth the Theravada manner of ordination both to the novitiate and to the full monastic community. The passage is concise, worthwhile, and above all readily available. Originally published as J. F. Dickson, "Ordination in Theravada Buddhism," Journal of the Royal Asiatic Society of Great Britain and Ireland, 7 (1874-1875), 1-16. Also published in The Wheel, 56 (Kandy: Buddhist Publication Society, 1963). The Upasampada Kammavaca translation has also been published in Richard Gard, Buddhism (see 7.2.2[5]), pp. 158-166.

(15) WELCH, HOLMES H. The Practice of Chinese Buddhism 1900-1950 (see 6.1.1[29]), pp. 247-303.

The chapter, entitled "Entering the Sangha," contains excellent detailed discussions of the tonsure ceremony, of receiving a new name, and of full ordination as a monk. It also discusses in some detail the practice of burning moxa scars (hsiang-pa) onto the initiate's scalp.

(16) WELLS, KENNETH E. Thai Buddhism, Its Rites and Activities (see 1.5.1[9]), pp. 118-131.

The section is entitled "Entering the Monastic Order" and contains a good description of the Thai rituals connected with the various stages of this process. Also given are translations of the various texts and chants of the rites. For an account of a specific ordination ceremony in Thailand and a description of all the expenditures and various social duties and obligations surrounding the occasion, and an estimate of its social significance, see Jane Bunnag, Buddhist Monk, Buddhist Layman (above), pp. 165-179.

7.2.2

(17) WIEGER, LEON. Bouddhisme chinois. Hou Chien Fu: Imprimerie de la Mission catholique, 1910, pp. 147-207.

These pages contain a convenient compilation of the texts (translated into French) taken from the vinayas of various schools, describing the rites of reception into the community of a layman taking five or eight precepts, of a male and a female novice, or monks and nuns.

7.2.2 Daily Regimen and Monastic Routine

See also 6.2.3, Buddhism in Relation to Family and Village Life.

(1) BAREAU, ANDRE. La vie et l'organisation des communautés bouddhiques modernes de Ceylan (see 6.1.2[1]), pp. 60-69.

The chapter is entitled "La vie des moines" and contains a straightforward account of the daily routine of monks in Ceylon today. Bareau presents a typical daily schedule, discusses monastic dress and food and possessions as well as the "spiritual activities." Another first-hand report of this type, dating from last century, may be found in Reginald S. Copleston, Buddhism Primitive and Present in Magadha and Ceylon (London: Longmans, Green, 1892), pp. 427 ff.

(2) BEAL, SAMUEL, trans. A Catena of Buddhist Scriptures from the Chinese (see 3.2.1.2[7]), pp. 239-244.

These pages contain a translation of a very short "Daily Manual of the Shaman," which sets forth a number of short verses, hymns, gathas, dharanis, etc., which the monk ("shaman") is to recite at various times during the day. For example: on awakening, on hearing the temple bell, on drinking water, when spreading out the mat, when bowing to the Buddha, when worshipping a stupa, etc. It is a good example of advanced regimentation of the day's activities.

(3) BLOFELD, JOHN. Mahayana Buddhism in Southeast Asia (see 6.1.4[2]), pp. 26-39.

The section is entitled "Monks and Nuns" and contains a short description of the monastic life of Chinese Buddhists in Southeast Asia, including daily activities, liturgy, funerals, etc.

(4) DAVID-NEEL, ALEXANDRA. Magic and Mystery in Tibet. Kingsport: Penguin Books, 1971, pp. 90-131.

Under the title "A Famous Tibetan Monastery," the intrepid French explorer David-Neel gives a vivid firsthand account of life in the Kum-bum monastery, which she generalizes to encompass all monastery life in Tibet. Daily ritual, food, organization, and study are portrayed, and also a short account of the miraculous tree of Tsong Khapa from which Kum-bum derives its celebrity.

7.2.2 Monastic Rituals and Practices

(5) GARD, RICHARD A., ed. *Buddhism*. New York: G. Braziller, 1961, pp. 178-202.

In this section of his general book on Buddhism, Gard has included three articles of interest: "Life in a Thai Theravada Monastery" by Phra Kaveevorayan; "Life in a Japanese Mahayana Monastery," from D. T. Suzuki's *The Training of the Zen Buddhist Monk* (see 7.2.1[10]); and "Life in a Tibetan Vajrayana Monastery," by Chang Chen-chi. This is an invitation to comparison.

(6) GOMBRICH, RICHARD. *Precept and Practice* (see 4.1.1[7]), pp. 269-293.

An illuminating discussion of the relationship between monastic ideals, monks' understanding of those ideals, and the actual lives, routines, and practices of Buddhist monks in Central Ceylon.

(7) I-CHING. *A Record of the Buddhist Religion*. See 1.2.2.3(8).

The entire book (the real title of which should be translated as A Record of Buddhist Practices Sent Home from the Southern Sea) forms an important firsthand report on monastic practices in India and the Malay Archipelago during the late seventh century A.D. I-Ching covers a range of monastic customs and rituals and correlates them to the rules established in the Mulasarvastivada vinaya, and to the usual practices with which he was familiar in China. For a view of monastic life as seen by the Chinese pilgrim Fa-hsien almost three hundred years earlier, see Thich Minh Chau, "Monastic Life in India in the 5th Century as Seen by Fa-Hsien," *Journal of the Bihar Research Society*, 47 (1961), 65-71.

(8) LECLERE, ADHEMARD. *Le Bouddhisme au Cambodge* (see 1.6.1.[4]), pp. 421-427.

A concise, straightforward description of the average day of the average Cambodian monk —when he gets up, goes out begging, eats, sleeps, etc.—based on turn-of-the-century observations.

(9) PRIP-MOLLER, J. *Chinese Buddhist Monasteries* (see 7.2.1[7]), pp. 353-384.

Chapter 6 of Prip-Moller's magnificent book is entitled "Monk's Offices and Daily Life in the Monasteries," and makes a useful supplementary source of information to Welch's more recent *Practice of Chinese Buddhism 1900-1950* (below).

(10) RAHULA, WALPOLA. *History of Buddhism in Ceylon* (see 1.3.1[10]), pp. 173-198.

The chapter is entitled "The Monastic Life: Its Activities" and represents Rahula's view of the daily life of monks in ancient Ceylon, based on scattered references in numerous sources. For an account of modern life in Ceylonese monasteries, see André Bareau (above).

(11) SATO, GIEI and NISHIMURA ESHIN. *Unsui: A Diary of Zen Monastic Life*. Edited by Bardwell Smith. Honolulu: University Press of Hawaii, 1973.

A lively, instructive, and straightforward account of life in a Zen monastery in Japan, illustrated by a series of delightful drawings.

(12) SUZUKI, DAISETZ TEITARO. *The Training of the Zen Buddhist Monk*. See 7.2.1(10).

Suzuki's description of Japanese Zen monastic life is heavily interlaced with sayings from and stories about the great Zen masters. Though no distinction is made among different schools of Zen in Japan, a certain picture of a daily regimen does emerge successfully. Suzuki describes it as a "life of humility" (chapter 2), "of labor" (chapter 3), "of service" (chapter 4), "of prayer and gratitude" (chapter 5), and "of meditation" (chapter 6). His appendix also contains very useful translations of various gathas uttered during the course of daily activities, and of rules regulating the daily routine, the lodging room, the bathroom, etc.

(13) TAMBIAH, STANLEY J. *Buddhism and the Spirit Cults in North-East Thailand* (see 4.1.2[16]), pp. 116-140.

Under the title "The Monastic Routine and Its Rewards," Tambiah has given a concise, well-rounded description of day-to-day life in the wat (monastery) of Phraan Muan village in Northeastern Thailand. Includes a list of "chants frequently memorized and recited by novices and monks."

(14) WELCH, HOLMES H. *The Practice of Chinese Buddhism 1900-1950* (see 6.1.1[29]), pp. 105-128.

The chapter, entitled "Observance of the Rules," makes a good introduction to the question of the following of monastic rules and regulations in China, in the twentieth century. It gives some details on clothing, hygiene, sexual activity, and also touches on the question of attitudes towards "heterodox practices" such as geomancy (feng-shui), divination, and the practice of medicine.

(15) WELLS, KENNETH E. *Thai Buddhism, Its Rites and Activities* (see 1.5.1[9]), pp. 131-139.

Under the title "The Life and Duties of a Bhikkhu," Wells provides a concise description of the regimen of Thai monastic life. He also includes a discussion of the ceremonies for leaving the Sangha (for a novice and for a bhikkhu).

7.2.3 Chanting of Sutras

(1) BEAL, SAMUEL, trans. "Daily Manual of the Shaman," in *A Catena of Buddhist Scriptures from the Chinese* (see 3.2.1.2[7]), pp. 239-244.

Monastic Rituals and Practices

(2) <u>Gandistotra</u>. Translated by E. J. Johnston as "The Lauds of the Gong." See 3.3.8.2(5).

Translation from the Chinese of a ritual text which was to be chanted during the striking of the monastery "gong" or gand. The text includes a lengthy praise of the Buddha and his defeat of Mara.

(3) <u>Standard Buddhist Gathas and Services</u>. Kyoto: Publications Bureau of Buddhist Books, Hompa Honganji, 1940, 217 pp.

One of the very few books of its kind, this work gives the Japanese and English texts of the main gathas and ceremonies--especially those of the Pure Land School. It is furthermore probably unique in providing musical notation along with the texts.

(4) SUZUKI, BEATRICE LANE. "Ceremonies for Lay Buddhists at Koya-San." See 7.1.4(11).

(5) SUZUKI, DAISETZ TEITARO. <u>Manual of Zen Buddhism</u>. See 2.5.7(21).

The first part of Suzuki's <u>Manual</u> contains a very useful collection of the principal gathas, dharanis and sutras which are used regularly in Zen rituals in Japan. The original Kyoto edition contains, in addition to a translation of these, the originals, and transliterations of the way they are actually chanted (the Chinese characters being pronounced in such a way that they reflect the original Sanskrit sound and yet retain some meaning). The Grove Press edition, unfortunately, gives only the translations.

(6) _____. <u>The Training of the Zen Buddhist Monk</u> (see 7.2.1[10]), appendix.

Contains very useful translations of the various gathas and segments of sutras supposed to be uttered by monks during the course of daily activities (on awakening, meal time, etc.).

(7) VISSER, MARINUS WILLEM DE. <u>Ancient Buddhism in Japan</u> (see 1.13.2.1[8]), pp. 3-26.

A list and brief discussion of the Buddhist sutras in use in seventh century Japan on different ceremonial occasions. Gives specific historical information on the times in which they were used.

(8) WADDELL, L. AUSTINE. <u>Tibetan Buddhism</u> (see 1.14.1[17]), pp. 420-449.

Though dated in its method and attitude, this chapter contains much valuable information on Tibetan monastic "worship and ritual." But the beginning student had better gain some previous perspective on these "facts," in, for example Stephan Beyer, <u>The Cult of Tara</u> (see 7.8[2]).

(9) WELLS, KENNETH E. <u>Thai Buddhism, Its Rites and Activities</u> (see 1.5.1[9]), pp. 41-47, 53-61, 261-262.

A good description of the daily morning and evening worship in Thai Buddhist monasteries, which, except on Uposatha days, are not usually attended by the laity. Pages 261-262 give a handy list of the chants for morning and evening ceremonies.

7.2.4 Uposatha Rites (including recitation of the Patimokkha)

(1) DICKSON, J. F. "The Patimokkha, being the Buddhist Office of the Confession of Priests." <u>Journal of the Royal Asiatic Society</u>, 8 (1875-1876), 62-130.

A dated but still helpful and detailed description of the ceremony of reciting the Patimokkha as observed in central Ceylon by the author a century ago. The whole Pali text of the original is translated as well as an extensively annotated text and translation of the Patimokkha itself.

(2) GROOT, J. J. M. DE. <u>Le Code du Mahayana en Chine</u>. Amsterdam: J. Muller, 1893, pp. 173-185.

A full description of the Uposatha ceremonies as observed by de Groot in Chinese monasteries. The confession of faults and the reading of the 250 pratimoksa rules of the Chinese Brahmajala Sutra (designed for Boddhisattvas rather than Arhats) which de Groot has translated on pages 14-88.

(3) I-CHING. <u>A Record of the Buddhist Religion</u> (see 1.2.2.3[8]), pp. 35-53.

Valuable firsthand account of the way Uposatha rites were practiced in "India and the Southern Sea" during the late seventh century A.D. by the Chinese pilgrim-scholar I-Ching.

(4) LECLERE, ADHEMARD. <u>Le Bouddhisme au Cambodge</u> (see 1.6.1[4]), pp. 428-432.

A brief but straightforward description of the Uposatha rites as they took place in Cambodian monasteries at the turn of the century.

(5) NANAMOLI, trans. <u>The Patimokkha</u>. Bangkok: Social Science Association Press of Thailand, 1966, 119 pp.

Clearly the best source for the study of the ritual recitation of the <u>Patimokkha</u> by Theravada monks. It gives (on facing pages) the Pali text and an English translation. It includes not only the 227 rules of the order but also the <u>Pubbacikkam</u> (preliminary functions: "invitation to the recitation," "counting of the bikkhus," etc.) and, in an appendix, the "Suttas and Gathas usually chanted at the end of the recitation of the Patimokkha."

(6) PACHOW, W. <u>A Comparative Study of the Pratimoksa</u>. See 3.2.1.4(6).

(7) PRZYLUSKI, JEAN. "Uposatha." <u>Indian Historical Quarterly</u>, 12 (1936), 383-390.

A characteristically imaginative article in which Przyluski argues for neo-Babylonian over Vedic influences on the Buddhist choice of calendar days for the performance of the Uposatha ceremonies.

7.2.4

(8) RHYS-DAVIDS, T. W. and HERMANN OLDENBERG. Vinaya Texts (see 3.2.1.1[2]), vol. 1, pp. 1-69, 239-297.
This volume of Vinaya Texts contains both the rules of the Patimokkha (pp. 1-69) as they are recited at the Uposatha ceremony, and also the important second section of the Mahavagga (pp. 239-297), which deals with the monastic regulations concerning the Uposatha rites.

(9) ROBERTSON, ALEC. The Triple Gem and the Uposatha: Buddhist Ethics and Culture. Colombo: Colombo Apothecaries' Co., 1971, 183 pp.
A study of the beliefs and practices which have come to be associated with the Uposatha ceremony. Perhaps the most valuable facet of this book is the fact that the author has relied almost exclusively upon canonical and commentary literature. Hence, the reader is presented with an annotated catalogue of canonical references to Uposatha.

(10) WELLS, KENNETH E. Thai Buddhism, Its Rites and Activities (see 1.5.1[9]), pp. 107-109.
A brief description of the chants and rituals of the fortnightly monastic Uposatha Day ceremonies, at which time the 227 Patimokkha rules are recited, and breaches of them are confessed.

7.2.5 Preaching and Teaching

See also 6.2.5, Buddhism and Education.

(1) DAVIDSON, J. LE ROY. "Traces of Buddhist Evangelism in Early Chinese Art." Artibus Asiae, 11 (1948), 251-265.
Discussion and illustration of various portrayals of preaching in the "Lotus Sutra" and the Vimalakirti Sutra in Buddhist art-- an important medium for the popularization and expression of Buddhism in China.

(2) DUTT, NALINAKSHA. Early Monastic Buddhism (see 1.2.2.1[3]), pp. 124-134.
In this section, Dutt summarizes the teaching techniques employed by the Buddha to convert followers and to amplify his dharma to his disciples.

(3) GROOT, J. J. M. DE. Le Code du Mahayana en Chine (see 7.2.4[2]), pp. 133-143.
The chapter is entitled "Prédication de la Loi--propagande" and contains detailed descriptions of the Dharma in Chinese monasteries. Included are discussions of the different classes and titles of preachers, the different times and occasions for sermons, the symbolism of the preacher's fly whisk, etc.

(4) HOFINGER, MARCEL. "L'Action missionnaire du Bouddhisme ancien: fondement doctrinal, formes et méthodes de la prédication." Studia missionalia, 12 (1962), 11-34.

Monastic Rituals and Practices

A short but helpful study of early Buddhist preaching techniques in all their variety: systematic or occasional preaching, missionary rounds, instruction at rains-retreats and in monasteries, of elites and of masses, conversion by example, etc.

(5) HTIN AUNG, U, ed. and trans. Burmese Monk's Tales. See 4.2.3(18).
Htin Aung has collected and translated a fascinating group of tales which were first told during the dark decade of Burmese history (1876-1885), the eve of the British conquest of Burma. The author of the tales, the Thingazar Sayadaw, improvised them on the spot to supplement his formal sermons centered on the Jatakas. The monk's tales are a new literary form modeled on the Burmese folk tale but dealing with the problems of laity and clergy of his day. They attempt to draw attention to the religious controversies of his time, often in a satirical manner.

(6) PRUSEK, JAROSLAV. "Narrators of Buddhist Scriptures and Religious Tales in the Sung Period." See 4.2.3(24).

(7) TADA KANAI. Shudo Kowa. Translated by Arthur Lloyd as The Praises of Amida. Yokohama: Kelly and Walsh, 1907, 140 pp.
Translation of seven contemporary sermons by a Shin priest, which treat various topics of Pure Land concern and seek to be relevant to turn-of-the-century Japanese needs.

(8) YOUNG, ERNEST. The Kingdom of the Yellow Robe. London: A. Constable, 1907, pp. 316 ff.
A good description of the content and practice of the Thet Maha Chat or "Preaching of the Story of the Great Birth" as it takes place in Thailand.

7.2.6 Building and Consecration of Monastery or Monastic Buildings (establishing the boundaries [sima], dedication of new stupa or Buddha image)

(1) BAREAU, ANDRE. La vie et l'organisation des communautés bouddhiques modernes de Ceylan (see 6.1.2[1]), pp. 57-59.
A very brief, firsthand account of the dedication of a new monastery in Central Ceylon. The ceremony, which is described, includes the painting of the new images of the Buddha by the entire community of the laity.

(2) GITEAU, MADELEINE. Le Bornage Rituel des Temples Bouddhiques au Cambodge. Paris: Ecole française d'Extrême-Orient, 1969, 152 pp.
An excellent and fascinating study of the rites of establishing the boundaries (sima) and setting the boundary markers either for a new monastery, or simply for a new monastic building. Also includes an iconographic stylistic study of the boundary markers themselves.

Calendric Rituals and Festivals   7.3.1

(3) GOMBRICH, RICHARD. "The Consecration of a Buddhist Image." Journal of Asian Studies, 26 (1966), 23-36.

A fascinating firsthand account and discussion of a Ceylonese festival and ceremony for the consecration of a new Buddha image. The festival of the setting of the "eyes" of the new image, which is popularly known as netra pinkama, is a very important ceremony replete with danger and ceremonial symbolism which transforms an ordinary statue into a sacred image of the Buddha, worthy of honor and worship.

(4) LECLERE, ADHEMARD. Le Bouddhisme au Cambodge (see 1.6.1[4]), pp. 370-372.

A fascinating, though brief, turn-of-the-century description of the dedication of a new monastery in Cambodia and the placing of the various sima stones.

(5) WELLS, KENNETH E. Thai Buddhism, Its Rites and Activities (see 1.5.1[9]), pp. 141-145, 74-90.

Pages 141-145 contain a description of the extremely important practice of setting out the sima or boundary of the site on which a monastery is to be built. This is followed by a ceremony of consecration of the soil, which Wells describes in full. Pages 74-90 set out the various dedication rituals which accompany the completion of construction of new monastic buildings.

7.3   CALENDRIC RITUALS AND FESTIVALS

7.3.1 South and Southeast Asia

(1) ANUMAN RAJATHON, PHRAYA. Life and Ritual in Old Siam (see 1.5.2[2]), pp. 65-98.

(2) ARCHAIMBAULT, CHARLES. "La Fête du T'at à Luoang Prabang," in Essays Offered to G. H. Luce. Edited by Ba Shin, Jean Boisselier, and A. B. Griswold. Artibus Asiae, Supplement 23, 1 (1966), 5-47.

This article is a rich, detailed interpretation of a major ceremony incorporating Buddhist, civic, and indigenous traditions. Archaimbault has provided a parallel study in "La Fête du T'at à S'ieng Khwang," Artibus Asiae, 24, 3-4 (1961), 187-199. Also, Frank Reynolds has treated this festival in the broader context of Buddhist-oriented calendric rites in Luang Prabang. See his "Ritual and Social Hierarchy in Buddhist Laos" (1.7.2[7]).

(3) DASSANAYAKE, M. B. The Kandy Esala Perahera. Colombo: Lake House, 1970, 32 pp.

A study of the origins and development and a description of the magnificent pageantry of the Esala Perahera, Ceylon's prime festival, which takes place in summer in Kandy, and surrounds the cult of the Buddha's Tooth relic enshrined there. The work supplements and to an extent replaces that of Richard Aluwihare, The Kandy Perahera (Colombo:

Gunasena, 1964). See also A. M. Hocart, The Temple of the Tooth (7.1.3[9]).

(4) DEYDIER, HENRI. Introduction à la connaissance du Laos. Saigon: Imprimerie française d'Outre-Mer, 1952, pp. 33-47.

The chapter is entitled "Cérémonies et fêtes religieuses" and makes a handy introductory survey to the Laotian calendar and religious festivals, Buddhist and otherwise.

(5) JINARATANA, MAHASTHAVIRA NELUWE. "Buddhist Festivals." Maha Bodhi, 72 (1964), 158-163.

An attempt by a Ceylonese monk to give a concise presentation of pan-Buddhist festivals, which ends up being pretty much a Theravadan list. However, he does include an interesting picture of an ecumenical ceremony held in memory of John F. Kennedy.

(6) KEYES, CHARLES F. "Buddhist Pilgrimage Centers and the Twelve Year Cycle: Northern Thai Moral Orders in Space and Time." See 10.5(4).

(7) LECLERE, ADHEMARD. Le Bouddhisme au Cambodge (see 1.6.1[4]), pp. 363-381.

The section is entitled "Les fêtes religieuses," and surveys very concisely the year's festivals in Cambodia, beginning with the New Year. Extra details on some of these may be found in Guy Poree and Eveline Maspero, Moeurs et coutumes des Khmers (Paris: Payot, 1938), pp. 152-166.

(8) _____. Cambodge: Festes Civiles et Religieuses. Paris: E. Bouillon, 1895, 308 pp.

This book is a classic compilation of materials which remains indispensable for the student of religious life in traditional Cambodian society.

(9) MARTINI, G. "Valukacetiya." Bulletin de l'Ecole française d'Extrême-Orient, 57 (1970), 155-168.

A short and interesting analytical article on the practice throughout Buddhist Southeast Asia of building mountains out of sand, with a cosmological significance, at New Year's time.

(10) NGINN, PIERRE S., MARIE-DANIEL FAURE, and THAU NHOUY ABHAY. "Fêtes religieuses," in Présence du Royaume Lao (see 1.7.1[11]), pp. 446-471.

Five articles on five Laotian religious festivals by three competent observers. Included are descriptions of New Year's, of Bang-fay (Fêtes des Fusées), of entering and leaving the rainy season, of That Luang (full moon of the twelfth month), and of the boun Pha-vet during which the whole Vessantara jataka is recited by the monks.

(11) PARANAVITANA, SENARAT. "Buddhist Revivals in Ceylon," in Buddhistic Studies (see 2.4.2[7]), pp. 529-546.

7.3.1   *Religious Practices and Rituals*   Calendric Rituals and Festivals

A concise review of various Sinhala Buddhist rites, both as practiced today and as recorded in the Ceylonese Chronicles. Includes discussions of ceremonies connected with stupas (such as that of renewing the stupa's whitewash), of the cult of the Tooth Relic, of causing rainfall, of a festival for Ananda, and of bathing the Bodhi Tree.

(12) POREE-MASPERO, EVELINE. Etude sur les Rites Agraires des Cambodgiens. See 1.6.2(12).

This is a very detailed, usually dry study which deals at points with important Buddhist rites. See Volume 1 for the discussion of the New Year rites involving the construction of sand pagodas, Volume 2 for the discussion of the festival of the waters and its connection with relic cults, and Volume 3 for the discussion of the rainy season "retreat" of the monks. Both the manner of presentation and the detail with which the material is presented mark this as a study for more advanced students only.

(13) SENEVIRATNE, H. L. "The Asala Perahara in Kandy." Ceylon Journal of Historical and Social Studies, 6 (1963), 169-180.

A fine study of the background, history and evolution of the annual festival held for the Tooth Relic of the Buddha in Kandy, Central Ceylon.

(14) SPIRO, MELFORD. Buddhism and Society (see 6.2.1.1[42]), pp. 209-231.

A concise and clear introduction to Buddhist calendrical rituals in Burma. It covers the daily, weekly, monthly and annual cycles. For a more poetic description of many of the same festivals, see H. Fielding Hall, The Soul of a People (London: Macmillan, 1907), pp. 152-168.

(15) TAMBIAH, STANLEY J. Buddhism and the Spirit Cults in North-East Thailand (see 4.1.2[16]), pp. 152-178.

A good discussion of the calendar of collective rituals and festivals which are connected to the wat (monastery) in a village in Northeastern Thailand. Tambiah seeks to show the intimate linkage of these wat rites to the phases of the agricultural cycle.

(16) WELLS, KENNETH E. Thai Buddhism, Its Rites and Activities (see 1.5.1[9]), pp. 179-206.

A survey of the various seasonal ceremonies in Thailand, including a discussion of the role of Buddhist monks in them. Covered are the New Year ceremonies, the various agricultural ceremonies connected with the growth of rice, the King's birthday, Chulalongkorn Day, Constitution Day, etc. The observances for each occasion are described, together with translations of the sutras and texts recited. A shorter, somewhat older presentation of much of the same material may be found in G. E. Gerini, "Festivals and Fasts (Siamese)," in Encyclopedia of Religion, edited by James Hastings (see 1.15.1[9]), vol. 5, pp. 885-890.

7.3.2 East Asia

(1) BOWNAS, GEOFFREY. Japanese Rainmaking and Other Folk Practices. London: Allen and Unwin, 1963, 175 pp.

A popular, anecdotal introduction to the most important Japanese festivals of the year, most of which intermix Buddhist, Shinto and other elements. Treats New Year's, Bon festival, etc. Only Chapter 6 deals with the rainmaking of the title.

(2) BOYER, MARTHA and JIKAI FUJIYOSHI. "Omizutori, One of Japan's Oldest Buddhist Ceremonies." See 7.1.4(1).

(3) CH'EN, KENNETH. Buddhism in China (see 1.11.1[1]), pp. 275-285.

A fine introduction to the topic of Buddhist festivals as they were held in China. Includes descriptions of the Lantern Festival, the Festival of the Buddha's Birthday, the Ullambana or avalambana or All-Souls' Feast, and the great Vegetarian Feast.

(4) DUYVENDAK, J. J. L. "The Buddhistic Festival of the All-Souls in China and Japan." Acta orientalia, 5 (1926), 39-48.

History, description, and discussion of the extremely popular "All-Souls" day, which occurred in the seventh month in China. The festival, which was based on the legend of the visit of Moggallana to the Buddhist hells, involves ceremonies of giving and merit-transfer to relieve the sufferings of the inhabitants of those hells. In China, this became intimately connected to the ethic of filial piety. Duyvendak also makes a comparison between the Chinese festival and the Bon celebrations in Japan. For a translation into French of the story of Moggallana's visit, see Jan Jaworski, "L'Avalambanasutra de la Terre Pure" (4.2.1[3]).

(5) EBERHARD, WOLFRAM. Chinese Festivals. New York: H. Schuman, 1952, 152 pp.

The most useful chapter is entitled "The Buddhist Calendar" and simply lists, chronologically, the various festivals which took place when Eberhard was in China. These include national celebrations and festivals for celestial beings, for Buddhas and Bodhisattvas and for "characters in Chinese Buddhist History." Unfortunately no detailed description of them is given. Much the same kind of treatment may be found in E. Lamairesse, L'Empire chinois: Le Bouddhisme en Chine et au Tibet (Paris: G. Carre, 1894), pp. 190-209.

(6) GROOT, J. J. M. DE. Les fêtes annuellement célébrées à Emoui (Amoy). Annales du Musée Guimet, Nos. 11-12. Paris: E. Leroux, 1886, 830 pp.

A monumental study of popular Chinese festivals as they were observed by the author in the port city of Amoy in the nineteenth century. De Groot deals with all the celebrations during the course of the calendar year, including those influenced or determined by Buddhism. The work is too detailed and dated to be a good introduction but makes a valuable source for the specialized student.

(7) HEYMAN, ALAN. "Lunar Leap Year Offers Buddhist Ceremonial Music and Dance." Korea Journal, 6, no. 7 (July 1966), 32-34.

A description and explanation of the dances, music, and musical instruments used in the Lunar Leap Year festival.

(8) VISSER, MARINUS WILLEM DE. Ancient Buddhism in Japan (see 1.13.2.1[8]), pp. 45-57, 190-248.

The three chapters describe various periodical festivals as they took place in seventh to ninth century Japan, citing specific occasions from the records. Chapter 3 deals with the yearly "festival of the Buddha's birth"; Chapter 6 with the quinquennial great festival of merit, the Musha-daie (Pancavarsika), and with the Hojoe or Meetings for the liberation of sentient beings; and Chapter 7 considers various festivals of lights and lanterns, including the Mando-e in August and the Sento-e or "Festival of Ten Thousand Lanterns."

7.3.3 Tibet, Himalayas, and Central Asia

(1) ANDERSON, MARY M. The Festivals of Nepal. London: Allen and Unwin, 1971, 288 pp.

A beautifully illustrated, substantial presentation of thirty-six different Nepalese festivals occurring throughout the calendar year. Helpful for seeing the place of Buddhist festivals and Buddhist influences on Hindu and other festivals in Nepal.

(2) MILLER, ROBERT and BEATRICE MILLER. "On Two Bhutanese New Year's Celebrations." American Anthropologist, 58 (1956), 179-183.

A brief description and discussion of the archery contests at the "Cultivator's New Year" among the Bhutias in West Bengal, and of the minimal role which lamas play in these New Year celebrations (as opposed to Sikkim, where they participate more fully).

(3) SCHRAM, LOUIS M. J. The Monguors of the Kansu-Tibetan Border (see 1.16.2[10]), pp. 139-148.

Under the heading "Various Public Rites," Schram describes the Monguors' ceremonies at New Year's, springtime, autumn, etc., with their combinations of Taoist, Lamaist, and Shamanic themes.

7.4 LIFE CYCLE RITES

7.4.1 General Discussions

(1) BARUA, RABINDRA BIJAY. "The Marriage Ceremony of the Buddhists." Maha Bodhi, 73 (1965), 245-250.

An attempt to argue that although monks do not generally participate in the marriage ceremonies of Buddhists, there are certain specifically Buddhist elements in these. Includes a discussion of the Vinaya's attitude towards these ceremonies.

(2) BROUGH, JOHN. "Nepalese Buddhist Rituals." Bulletin of the School of Oriental and African Studies, 12 (1948), 668-676.

A translation of a short Nepalese text, outlining the chief daily, monthly, and yearly rites of Buddhism in that country. This is followed by a description of the thirteen rituals of the life cycle from the first viewing of the child and the cutting of the umbilical cord to the funeral ceremonies.

(3) HTIN AUNG, MAUNG. "Burmese Initiation Ceremonies." Journal of the Burma Research Society, 36, no. 1 (1953), 77-87.

A good history and description of the Burmese shin byu--the ceremony of entering the Sangha (for a period of time whose length varies), which virtually every Burmese boy goes through before adulthood. A more readily available discussion of the same ceremony is given by Melford Spiro (below). In another account of the shin byu, Htin Aung seeks to trace the survival of pre-Buddhist folk elements in the ceremony: see his Folk Elements in Burmese Buddhism (4.1.2[6]), pp. 115-124.

(4) SPIRO, MELFORD E. Buddhism and Society (see 6.2.1.1[42]), pp. 232-254.

This chapter deals with all the life-cycle rituals in the life of the average Burmese which involve Buddhist elements, but concentrates especially on the important shin-byu, or boy's initiation ceremony. For another description of the shin-byu, see Htin Aung (above).

(5) WELLS, KENNETH E. Thai Buddhism, Its Rites and Activities (see 1.5.1[9]), pp. 155-163.

A brief description of Buddhist participation in wedding ceremonies, tonsure ceremonies, housewarming, and birthday ceremonies. For other descriptions of some of the same life-cycle rites in Thailand, see Ernest Young, The Kingdom of the Yellow Robe (7.2.5[8]), chapters 4-5.

7.4.2 Death and Funerals

(1) ARCHAIMBAULT, CHARLES. "Contributions à l'Etude du Rituel Funéraire Lao." The Journal of the Siam Society, 51, no. 1 (July 1963), 1-57.

Most aspects of the rituals which Archaimbault describes in great detail are not specifically Buddhist, but Buddhist personages, texts and ideas do play a significant role. In the second half of the article Archaimbault provides a translation of the local text in which the "first king" of the present cosmic era gives brief instructions for the funerals of those who have died various kinds of unusual deaths.

(2) ASHIKAGA, ENSHO. "The Festival for the Spirits of the Dead in Japan." Western Folklore, 9 (1950), 217-228.

A good introduction to the history and ceremonies of the Japanese Bon Festival (or All Souls Day or Festival of Lanterns). The festival, which has its roots in China and the story of the visit of Moggallana (Maudgalyayana or Mulien) to his mother in hell, is a time when the faithful seek to benefit the dead, especially their own ancestors.

(3) BOURLET, A. "Funerailles chez les Thay." Anthropos, 8 (1913), 40-46.

This article constitutes a fine description of the preparation and execution of a Buddhist funeral rite in its rural Thai context in the early part of the twentieth century.

(4) FILLIOZAT, JEAN. "La mort volontaire par le feu et la tradition bouddhique indienne." Journal Asiatique, 251 (1963), 21-51.

The author begins his study by reviewing Gernet's discussion of the same topic (below). He then goes on to discuss suicide by fire as an act of devotion according to the "Lotus Sutra" and according to Buddhaghosha. Filliozat's was one of several articles inspired by the actual fiery suicides of Vietnamese monks in the early 1960s. For another, see André Migot, "Le suicide par le feu des religieux bouddhistes vietnamiens," Guerre et Paix, 1 (1967), 18-27.

(5) FREEMANTLE, FRANCESCA and CHÖGYAM TRUNGPA, trans. The Tibetan Book of the Dead. See 3.4.2(5).

(6) GERNET, JACQUES. "Les Suicides par le feu chez les bouddhistes chinois du Vème au Xème siècle," in Mélanges. Paris: Université de Paris, Institut des hautes études chinoises, 1960, vol. 2, pp. 527-528.

A fascinating compilation of the places and dates of Buddhist monks' suicides by fire in China over a period of five centuries, based primarily on biographies of monks, relevant portions of which are translated. Gernet traces the influence of the Pure Land and indigenous Chinese beliefs on the practices of partial autocremation (of fingers and arms).

(7) GROOT, J. J. M. DE. "Buddhist Masses for the Dead in Amoy," in Actes du sixième congrès international des orientalistes. Leiden, 1885, Part 4, section 4, pp. 1-120.

A detailed description of ceremonies, rituals and liturgies connected with death and disposal of the body. Also includes discussions of offerings to the dead and of the burning of paper money. A good supplement to the introduction to these topics that may be found in Holmes Welch, The Practice of Chinese Buddhism (see 6.1.1[29]), chapter 7. (See also annotation to this chapter, below.)

(8) HEYMAN, ALAN. "Historical Document in Sound: Korean Buddhist Ceremony Recorded in Its Entirety." Korea Journal, 8, no. 7 (July 1968), 36-38.

A nice description, however brief, of the Yong San Jae--a memorial service for the dead which lasts for three days. The author describes the songs, dances, and processions.

(9) HOLCK, FREDRICK, ed. Death and Eastern Thought. Nashville and New York: Abingdon Press, 1974, pp. 114-141, 198-225.

This book contains two excellent essays dealing with Buddhism. In a chapter entitled "The Heterodox Systems" Roy Amore gives a fine overview of Indian Buddhist beliefs and practices related to death. In the final chapter, entitled "Japan," William LaFleur provides a fascinating account of the development of a specifically Japanese Buddhist orientation toward death in which Zen and aesthetic themes are emphasized.

(10) HORI ICHIRO. "Self-mummified Buddhas in Japan: An Aspect of the Shugen-do ('mountain asceticism') Sect." History of Religions, 1 (1962), 222-242.

An historical inquiry into the background and religious context of the six mummified figures discovered at Shugendo temples in 1961. Hori argues that the Shingon school at Mt. Koya was a significant, if indirect, influence on the beliefs and practices of the group involved.

(11) JAN, YUN-HUA. "Buddhist Self-immolation in Medieval China." History of Religions, 4 (1965), 243-265.

Discusses the motives, sources of inspiration, and attitudes toward the practice of self-immolation during the period in which Buddhism flourished in China. The claim is made that the attitudes towards the practice reflect a more practical view founded on religious sentiment.

(12) KING, WINSTON. "Practicing Dying: The Samurai-Zen Death Techniques of Suzuki-Shosan," in Religious Encounters with Death. Edited by Frank Reynolds. University Park: Pennsylvania State University Press, 1976.

This article deals in a very fascinating way with meditation on death as advocated by an important figure in classical Japanese Buddhism. It is written in a highly readable style and is an authoritative treatment of the subject.

(13) LAMOTTE, ETIENNE. "Le suicide religieux dans le bouddhisme ancien." Bulletin de la Classe des Lettres et des Sciences Morales et Politiques, Académie de Belgique, 5, no. 51 (1965), 156-168.

A very fine article in which the author discusses the modes of suicide prevalent among Buddhists. Though he is quick to point out that suicide is an act which brings on the same horror for observers whether they be Buddhists or Westerners, Lamotte explains that the suicidal act may be considered a noble act among the Buddhists when seen from the point of view of karmic retribution. The author then reviews the explanations of suicide as they have been understood within the Buddhist context: 1) suicide is warranted for arhats who have conquered their passions; 2) it is an acceptable act by those who wish to give their bodies to others to aid in their salvation quests; and 3) it is an acceptable act done out of veneration for the Buddha.

(14) LECLERE, ADHEMARD. Les crémations et les rites funéraires au Cambodge. Hanoi: F. H. Schneider, 1907, 154 pp.

A rich source of information on Cambodian funerary customs. Leclere starts off with an account of the Buddha's funeral, and ends with a full, firsthand description of the cremation of the Cambodian king Noroudam.

(15) LLOYD, A. "Death and the Disposal of the Dead (Japanese)," in Encyclopedia of Religion and Ethics. Edited by James Hastings. (See 1.15.1[9], vol. 4, pp. 485-497.)

A substantial and very helpful article. After surveying Shinto attitudes toward death, Lloyd then goes on to give fairly detailed description of Buddhist funerary ceremonies (including liturgy, sutras chanted, etc.) as practiced by the following sects: Zen, Shingon, Tendai, Jodo, Shin, and Nichiren. Excellent for comparison of different practices within Japanese Buddhism.

(16) NEBESKY-WOJKOWITZ, RENE. "Ancient funeral ceremonies of the Lepchas." The Eastern Anthropologist, 5 (1951), 27-40.

An attempt to dig below the syncretism of the Nying ma pa funerary practices and indigenous Sikkimese Lepcha elements, and determine which is which.

(17) REICHELT, KARL LUDVIG. Truth and Tradition in Chinese Buddhism (see 1.11.1[8]), chapter 4, pp. 77-126.

The chapter is entitled "The Origin and Development of Masses for the Dead," and contains a detailed though dated discussion of the history of Chinese funerary ceremonies. Reichelt also touches upon the matter of a possible Nestorian influence on the Chinese development, and considers briefly the "Feast for the Wandering Souls" and various legends concerning karmic retribution. The whole is colored by Reichelt's enthusiasm for seeing parallels between Buddhism and Christianity.

For more detailed descriptions of the actual ceremonies involved in the "masses," see de Groot, "Buddhist Masses for the Dead in Amoy" (above).

(18) SCHRAM, LOUIS M. J. The Mongours of the Kansu-Tibetan Frontier (see 1.16.2[10]), pp. 139-148.

Description of the Mongours' ceremonies for the dying and the dead, and their various methods for disposing of the corpses. Interesting for the combination of Lamaist, Confucianist and Shamanic practices.

(19) SPIRO, MELFORD. Buddhism and Society (see 6.2.1.1[42]), pp. 248-254.

A short but good escription of Buddhism's part in ceremonies surrounding death and burial in Burma. An older, alternative source on the same subject is Kyaw Dun, "Burmese Funeral Rites," Journal of the Burmese Research Society, 7 (1917), 85-88.

(20) TAMBIAH, STANLEY J. Buddhism and the Spirit Cults in North-East Thailand (see 4.1.2[16]), pp. 179-194.

The chapter is entitled "Death, Mortuary Rites, and the Path to Rebirth" and contains a fine description of all the practices associated with death among Buddhist villagers in Northeastern Thailand. See also, as a sort of urban counterpart to this, pages 163-178 of Wells, Thai Buddhism (below).

(21) VISSER, MARINUS WILLEM DE. Ancient Buddhism in Japan (see 1.13.2.1[8]), pp. 58-115.

Descriptions of seventh and eighth century Japanese Buddhist festivals for the dead, including a lengthy section on various ceremonies and practices to relieve the sufferings of the pretas (hungry ghosts), a description of the Chinese "All-Souls day," and a comparison of it with the Bon festival in Japan.

(22) WELCH, HOLMES H. The Practice of Chinese Buddhism 1900-1950 (see 6.1.1[29]), pp. 179-206.

The chapter is entitled "The Rites for the Dead" and makes an excellent introduction to these ceremonies, which, in East Asia, were preeminently the domain of Buddhist monks. Welch also provides interesting views of the commercialization surrounding these rites. For further details on the rituals themselves, see de Groot (above).

(23) WELLS, KENNETH E. Thai Buddhism, Its Rites and Activities (see 1.5.1[9]), pp. 163-178, 246-254.

A detailed description of Thai funeral rites, and of the participation of Buddhist monks in them. Includes an interesting discussion of the use of Abhidharma texts at funerals, and translations of a number of "funeral chants." Pages 246-254 contain translations of some additional "Sutras for funerals." For a fine anthropological study of practices associated with death in

Northeast Thailand, see pages 179-194 of Tambiah (above).

(24) WYLIE, TURRELL. "Mortuary Customs at Sa-skya, Tibet." *Harvard Journal of Asiatic Studies*, 25 (1964-1965), 229-242.

    A specific study of local funeral customs of the region of Sa-skya in Central Tibet, preceded by a concise and handy introduction discussing the five basic Tibetan modes of disposal of the corpse: interment, water burial, cremation, vulture-disposal and desiccation.

(25) YETTS, W. PERCEVAL. "Notes on the Disposal of Buddhist Dead in China." *Journal of the Royal Asiatic Society* (1911), 699-725.

    A helpful article which focuses on the disposal of the bodies of Buddhist monks. Yetts discusses the three ways of cremation, burial, and preservation by drying, giving details on the preparation and clothing of the corpse, but nothing on ceremonials associated with this. Includes interesting photographs of a "dried priest" at P'u-k'ou and of a "spurious dried priest" at Wu-ch'ang.

7.5 MAGICAL PROTECTION, HEALTH AND HEALING

7.5.1 Control of Natural Phenomena (rain-making, etc.)

(1) ARCHAIMBAULT, CHARLES. "Les rites pour l'obtention de la pluie à Luong Prabang (observés en juillet, 1954)." *Bulletin de la Société des études indochinoises*, 43 (1968), 199-217.

    A fine detailed and fascinating firsthand account of a successful series of rain-making ceremonies in Laos. Includes details about the involvement and role of Buddhist monks and laymen qua Buddhists in the ceremonies.

(2) BITARD, PIERRE. "Le monde du sorcier au Cambodge," in *Le Monde du Sorcier*. Edited by du Seuil. Paris: Sources Orientales, 1966, pp. 305-328.

    A descriptive study of rural Cambodian beliefs and practices regarding spirits, sorcerers, and demons. The author outlines the power of these beings and the methods employed by peasants to combat their effects.

(3) BOWNAS, GEOFFREY. *Japanese Rainmaking and Other Folk Practices* (see 7.3.2[1]), chapter 6.

(4) GRANT BROWN, R. "Rain-making in Burma." *Man*, 8 (1908), 145-146.

    A very short description of various attempts at rain-making in Upland Burma, including the "Water festival," tug-of-war contests, and ceremonies associated with Shin Upagod (Upagupta). Contains an interesting photograph of a raft with an image of Upagupta which is sent floating down the river and is worshipped by villagers all along the way.

(5) GROOT, J. J. M. DE. *Le code du Mahayana en Chine* (see 7.2.4[2]), pp. 148-159.

    Presentation and translation of Sutras used in China to ask for rain, for good weather, and to combat the attacks of grasshoppers.

(6) SCHRAM, LOUIS M. J. *The Mongours of the Kansu-Tibetan Frontier* (see 1.16.2[10]), pp. 97-104.

    Discussions of the many different public rites--Taoist, Buddhist and other--in use among the Mongours to combat the plague of hailstorms.

(7) WELLS, KENNETH E. *Thai Buddhism, Its Rites and Activities* (see 1.5.1[9]), pp. 190-194.

    A good description of the Phra Raja Bidhi Barunasatr, a Thai Buddhist ceremony for the invocation of rain. Included is a translation of a gatha asking for rain.

7.5.2 Medical Practices (including exorcism)

(1) *Dvadasa graha santi*. Translated by P. C. Bagchi as "New Materials for the Study of the Kumaratantra of Ravana." *Indian Culture*, 7 (1940-1941), 269-286.

    The *Ravanakumara tantra* is a non-Buddhist Sanskrit text concerning the symptoms and cures of children's diseases. It has been translated by Jean Filliozat as "Le Kumaratantra de Ravana," *Journal asiatique* (1935), pp. 1-66. The text which Bagchi has presented here is a Chinese and Buddhistic version of that same text and includes fascinating descriptions of the use of mandalas and magical formulas in the cures prescribed.

(2) FILLIOZAT, JEAN. "Un chapitre du rgyud-bzi sur les bases de la santé et des maladies," in *Asiatica* (Festschrift Friedrich Weller. Leipzig: O. Harrassowitz, 1954, pp. 93-102.

    Translation of one chapter of the *Amrtahrdaya*, popularly known in Tibet as the *rgyud bzi* ("Four Tantras"), a text which is both an invocation of Bhaisajyaguru and an explanation of the principles of Indian medicine as they were applied in Tibet.

(3) HALPERN, JOEL. "Traditional Medicine and the Role of the Phi in Laos." *Eastern Anthropologist*, 16, no. 3 (1963), 191-200.

    A fine treatment by an acknowledged expert. The article is a rarity on a neglected subject and provides the reader with a basic description of both methods and materials of traditional medical practices as well as the role of the medicine man.

(4) OBEYESEKERE, GANANATH. "The Ritual Drama of the Sanni Demons: Collective Representatives of Disease in Ceylon." *Comparative Studies in Society and History*, 11, no. 2 (April 1969), 174-216.

Magical Protection, Health and Healing

Sanni demons are thought to cause disease, and the ritual which is concerned with them is an attempt to exorcise them. The author has deftly analyzed the significance of the myth from the perspective of "role generalization." Particularly interesting is the discussion of the significance of the obscenities aimed at the Buddha and guardian spirits. An excellent article.

(5) Suvarnabhasottamasutra. Translated by R. E. Emmerick as The Sutra of Golden Light (see 3.3.8.1[8]), pp. 44-48, 73-77.
A good example of a Mahayana sutra's concern with the problems of health and healing. In the first passage (pp. 44-48), the goddess Sarasvati gives some medical advice and spells to be used when bathing. The second passage (pp. 73-77) is called the "Chapter on Healing Illness" and contains the interesting story of the doctor Jatimdhara.

(6) TAMBIAH, STANLEY J. Buddhism and the Spirit Cults in North-East Thailand (see 4.1.2[16]), pp. 312-336.
These two chapters deal with afflictions caused by malevolent spirits and ritual exorcism among villagers in Northeastern Thailand. Rather than trying to contrast the practice of exorcism with Buddhism, Tambiah seeks to elucidate the relationship between the two.

(7) VEITH, ILZA and ATSUMI MINAMI. "A Buddhist Prayer Against Sickness." History of Religions, 5 (1966), 239-249.
A ten-page article on a six-page Chinese/Japanese sutra prescribing a curative technique for piles. Includes a two-page summary of Nara and Heian medicine, but no real interpretation of the copiously translated text.

(8) VISSER, MARINUS WILLEM DE. Ancient Buddhism in Japan (see 1.13.2.1[8]), pp. 293-308.

(9) WAYMAN, ALEX. "The Concept of Poison in Buddhism." Oriens Extremus, 10 (1957), 107-109.
A brief article which shows the Buddhist understanding of poison as being psychological and physical--the three poisons of greed, hatred and delusion corresponding with the three bodily poisons of wind, bile and phlegm.

(10) WIRZ, PAUL. Exorcism and the Art of Healing in Ceylon. Leiden: E. J. Brill, 1954, 253 pp.
Includes description of a great number of ceremonies and exorcist practices still in use in Sri Lanka, including, on pages 235-237, a discussion of the place and role of Buddhism in these rites.

(11) YALMAN, NUR. "The Structuring of Sinhalese Healing Rituals," in Religion in South Asia (see 4.1.1[2]), pp. 115-150.
A structural analysis of Sinhala healing rituals in which Yalman distinguishes the opposition between purity and pollution as basic to all Sinhala rituals. He describes and analyzes the variety of Central Ceylonese healing rituals, including those performed by Buddhist monks (such as Pirit) and those performed by other ritual specialists and involving drumming and dancing (such as the Bali rite).

(12) YASHPAL. "Surgery and Medicine in the Days of Gautama." Indian Historical Quarterly, 25 (1949), 102-109.
A survey of the Pali texts to see what they reveal about the state of medicine of that time. The author is struck by some of the advanced techniques to which they bear witness. The article is especially useful to the generalist when complemented by Baijnath Puri, "Medicine and Surgery between the First and Third Centuries A.D.," Indian Culture, 13 (1947), 182-185, which includes surveys of the data found in later Buddhist texts such as the Lalitavistara, the Saddharmapundarika, and the works of Asvaghosa. For a more specialized study along these lines, see P. K. Gode, "Massage in Ancient and Medieval India between B.C. 1000 and A.D. 1900," Annals of the Bhandarkar Oriental Research Institute, 36 (1955), 85-113, which includes discussion of Buddhist texts in this regard.

7.5.3 Protection (amulets, charms, spells, etc.)

(1) BEYER, STEPHAN. The Buddhist Experience (see 3.3.2.1[8]), pp. 130-139.
A selection of passages dealing with charms, spells, exorcisms, etc. Included is a "charm against snakes" taken from the Cullavagga, a discussion about the validity of magic spells excerpted from the Milindapanha, and translation of two Tibetan texts illustrating the use of protective spells--one called the "Mantra of Red Copper Beak," the other a spell book taken from the bka' 'gyur.

(2) LALOU, MARCELLE. "Notes à propos d'une amulette de Touen Houang: Les litanies de Tara et la Sitatapatradharani." Mélanges chinois et bouddhiques, 4 (1936), 135-149.
An interesting description of a protective amulet found in Tun Huang, with a translation of the invocation and praise of Tara that was inscribed on it.

(3) LESSING, FERDINAND D. Yung-ho-kung. Reports from the Scientific Expedition to the Northwestern Provinces of China, No. 8. Stockholm: Eegers, 1942, vol. 1, pp. 150-161.
A detailed description, with photographs, of the Lamaist "Burnt Offering" (Homa sbyin sreg), which according to Lessing may have four purposes--propitiating deities, increasing prosperity, subduing demons, overpowering enemies. The ceremony was a common and important one in Tibet. For another description of it in relation to the goddess Tara, see Stephan Beyer, The Cult of Tara (7.8[2]), pp. 264-275.

7.5.3 Magical Protection, Health and Healing

(4) LEVI, SYLVAIN. "Le catalogue géographique des Yaksas dans le Mahamayuri." *Journal asiatique* (1915), pp. 20-138.

An extensive discussion of the Mahamayuri, one of five famous Mahayana "Sutras of protection." The work is filled with mantras, but at the same time includes an invocation of a whole series of popular deities, group by group, including the seven bodhi trees of the seven previous Buddhas, the four Maharajas, the son of Kubera, the yaksas protecting the cities, the twenty-eight Mahayaksasenapati, the dharmabrother of Vaisravana, the 109 nagaraja, Brahman Indra, etc.

(5) NEBESKY-WOJKOWITZ, R. and GEOFFREY GORER. "The Use of Thread-Crosses in Lepcha Lamaist Ceremonies." *The Eastern Anthropologist*, 4 (1950), 65-87.

Describes the ceremonial use of mdos (thread-crosses) by lamas in Sikkim. They were used to catch demons, to "house" deities, or simply as offerings in various rituals, mainly in those combatting illness and bad weather. Also describes their use in the bi-annual ceremony for the god of the great Sikkimese mountain Kanchenjunga. For a short description of the use of thread-crosses at the other end of the lamaist world in Yung-ho-kung monastery in Peking, see Lessing, *Yung-ho-kung* (above), Appendix 3, pp. 148-149.

(6) POREE-MASPERO, EVELINE. "La Cérémonie de l'appel des esprits vitaux chez les cambodgiens." *Bulletin de l'Ecole française d'Extrême-Orient*, 45 (1951), 145-183.

Description of the rite of calling on local spirits which takes place in Cambodia on the occasion of the ordination of new monks into the Sangha (as well as at other occasions, such as disease and sickness, etc.).

(7) SOURYS-ROLLAND, A. "Les procédés magiques d'immunisation chez les cambodgiens." *Bulletin de la Société des études indochinoises*, 26 (1951), 175-187.

Description of the various methods used by Cambodians for protection against disease and harm. Includes discussions of talismans, magical formulas, tattoos, elixir, and a reproduction of a "magical scarf" inscribed with parittas and images of the Buddha.

(8) WADDELL, L. AUSTINE. *Tibetan Buddhism* (see 1.14.1[17]), pp. 400-408.

A convenient discussion, with illustrations, of various kinds of Tibetan talismans and charms used for magical protection. Includes descriptions of edible charms on paper, of larger "general charms," of charms against bullets, animals, domestic troubles, cooking smells, cholera, plagues, scorpions, dog-bite, eagles, etc.

7.5.4 Paritta Texts

(1) *Atanatiya sutta*, in the *Digha Nikaya*. Translated by T. W. Rhys-Davids and Catherine A. F. Rhys-Davids as *Dialogues of the Buddha* (see 2.7.1[13]), vol. 3, pp. 185-197.

An example of a Pali canonical presentation and explanation of the use of a paritta for protection and for the warding off of evil.

(2) FEER, LEON, trans. "Extraits du Paritta --textes et commentaires en Pali." *Journal Asiatique*, 18 (1871), 225-335.

Translation of Pali canonical and commentarial texts used as "pirit" in Ceylon. The selection of the particular texts and the edition of the Pali were made by M. Grimplot.

(3) GOGERLY, DANIEL JOHN. *Ceylon Buddhism*. London: K. Paul, Trench, Trubner, 1908, pp. 327-393.

A translation of a "pirit book" which contains the paritta (pirit in Sinhalese) texts used during rituals of exorcism and protection at a monastery near Colombo. Gogerly's translation is preceded by a description of the rite, which, when done on behalf of a whole village, involves seven days of continuous recitation. (It is much shorter when performed for the benefit of individuals.)

(4) LaFUENTE, MARGUERITE, trans. *Pirit Nula: Le fil de Pirit*. Paris: A. Maisonneuve, 1941, 85 pp.

Under the Sinhalese title of "Pirit Nula," LaFuente has translated, from the Pali, some of the parittas most commonly used in Theravada countries. She also offers an unpretentious but helpful classification of parittas into "Suttas de protection" (e.g., the *Mahamangala sutta*), "Suttas de direction" (e.g., the *Sigalovada sutta*), and "Suttas d'enseignement" (e.g., the *Dhammacakkappavattana sutta*).

(5) SPIRO, MELFORD. *Buddhism and Society* (see 6.2.1.1[42]), chapters 6 and 11.

The first of these two chapters deals with what Spiro calls "apotropaic Buddhism," i.e., a religion of magical protection, and traces its canonical and "theological" basis in paritta. The other chapter concerns "crisis rituals" and includes translations of several parittas that are commonly used in Burma. Together, they make a good introduction to the Burmese use of these Buddhist rituals.

(6) TAMBIAH, STANLEY J. *Buddhism and the Spirit Cults in North-East Thailand* (see 4.1.2[16]), pp. 199-222.

A fine discussion of the use of paritta in Northeastern Thailand. Includes descriptions of the use of certain paritta and translations of those most frequently recited in Thailand.

(7) WELLS, KENNETH E. *Thai Buddhism, Its Rites and Activities* (see 1.5.1[9]), pp. 240-246.

Translation of a number of parittas in frequent use in Thailand, and also of the Sado Phra Gro Parittas which are used once a year at the king's birthday ceremonies.

Cults and Rituals for Buddhas, Bodhisattvas, etc.

7.6 DIVINATION

(1) BACOT, JACQUES. "La table des présages signifiés par l'éclair." Journal asiatique (1913), 445-449.

Text and translation of a fascinating divination table, which gives a set of various interpretations of the omen of a flash of lightning, depending on the time of day and quarter of the sky in which this takes place. However, B. Laufer, in "Bird Divination among the Tibetans," T'oung Pao, 15 (1914), 1-110, has shown that the table does not refer to lightning flashes but to the calls of birds. Laufer also gives an annotated translation of another divination text, the Bya-rog-gi skad brtag-par bya-ba (Examination of the sounds of crows), which is fascinating in its own right.

(2) EKVALL, ROBERT B. Religious Observances in Tibet. See 7.1.1(5).

See the chapter on the more popular and practical uses of divination (mo) and the prominent part it plays in the daily life of the Tibetan nomad of Amdo (northeastern Tibet).

(3) NEBESKY-WOJKOWITZ, RENE. "Tibetan Drum Divination: 'Ngamo.'" Ethnos, 17 (1952), 149-157.

A good description of this form of divination among the Lepchas in Sikkim. Also touches on the religious ceremonies and practices associated with it.

(4) STEIN, ROLF. "Trente-trois fiches de divination tibétaines." Harvard Journal of Asiatic Studies, 4 (1939), 297-371.

A French translation and description of a set of divination slips which the great Tibetologist Stein found in the British Museum. Each slip is inscribed with a readily recognizable picture and a written fortune or horoscope. For another example of a different kind of divination in Tibet, see A. Rona Tas, "Taly Stick and Divination Dice in the Iconography of Lha-mo," Acta orientalia, 6 (1956), 163-177. See also Bacot (above).

(5) WADDELL, L. AUSTINE. Tibetan Buddhism (see 1.14.1[17]), pp. 450-474.

The chapter is entitled "Astrology and Divination," and although Waddell's methodology is at times questionable, he does present a substantial amount of data on the Tibetan time system and its connection with astrology, on the use of trigrams for divination, horoscopes, and various other methods of divination.

7.7 ROYAL RITUALS AND CULTS

(1) BRODBECK, JEAN-CLAUDE. "L'Intronisation du Prince Héritier de Thailande." Bulletin de la Société des Etudes Indochinoises, n.s. 48 (1973), 559-576.

A short description of the investiture of the Thai crown prince which took place on December 28, 1972. The ceremony is a recent one based on Western patterns but combines them with distinctly Buddhist elements.

(2) COEDES, GEORGES. "Le culte de la royauté divinisée, source d'inspiration des grands monuments du Cambodge ancien," in Conferenze Istituto Italiano per il Medio ed Estremo Oriente. Serie orientale Roma, No. 5. Rome, 1952, pp. 1-23.

Surveys the influence and connection of ancient Indian royal ritualism, cult and symbolism and the architecture of the great Cambodian capitals. A somewhat wider perspective on this subject may be found in H. G. Quaritch Wales, The Mountain of God (see 10.6[8]).

(3) GEIGER, WILHELM. Culture of Ceylon in Medieval Times (see 1.3.2.1[6]), pp. 111-117.

In these pages, Geiger discusses the right of kingship and the inauguration of the king in medieval Ceylon. Included are concise discussions of the qualifications of persons entitled to kingship, peculiar body marks of a future king, and also those of his mother, laws of succession within the royal family, and the inauguration (abhiseka) of a new king.

(4) THIERRY, S. "La personne sacrée du Roi dans la littérature populaire Cambodgienne." See 6.2.2.8(9).

(5) VISSER, MARINUS WILLEM DE. Ancient Buddhism in Japan (see 1.13.2.1[8]), pp. 116-189.

The chapter is entitled "The Ninnokyo or Sutra of the Benevolent Kings, and the Ninno-e, based thereon." It contains a description of the ancient Japanese imperial performance of the Ninno-e ceremony which was intended for the protection and benevolence of the whole country.

(6) WALES, H. G. QUARITCH. Siamese State Ceremonies. London: B. Quaritch, 1931, 326 pp.

A useful collection of royal cermonies in Thailand, with an attempt to study their history and function. Included are ceremonies of installation, ceremonies closely connected with kingship, and ceremonies relating to agriculture.

7.8 CULTS AND RITUALS FOR PARTICULAR BUDDHAS, BODHISATTVAS, DEITIES, NAGAS, ETC.

(1) BEAL, SAMUEL, trans. "The Liturgy of Kwan-yin," in A Catena of Buddhist Scriptures from the Chinese (see 3.2.1.2[7]), pp. 396-400.

This section of Beal's Catena contains a liturgical manual giving instructions and texts for devotions to the Goddess of Mercy (Kuan-yin/Avalokitesvara). It is preceded by the "Imperial Preface to the Liturgical

7.8   Cults and Rituals for Buddhas, Bodhisattvas, etc.

Services of the Great Compassionate Kwan-yin," which was written by Yung Loh of the Ming Dynasty in 1412.

(2) BEYER, STEPHAN. *The Cult of Tara: Magic and Ritual in Tibet*. See 7.1.1(2).

Unquestionably the most thorough work in English on the cult and rituals associated with the goddess Tara, giving full descriptions of ritual practices, explanations, interpretations, and translations of cultic texts. At the same time, the work is more than just a study of the cult of Tara, and seeks to illuminate the basic ritual structures and patterns that underlie other Tibetan rituals as well.

(3) *Bhaisajyagurusutra*. Translated by Nalinaksha Dutt in *Gilgit Manuscripts* (see 1.2.2.4[4]), vol. 1, pp. 47-57.

(4) BHATTACHARYYA, BENOYTOSH. "The Cult of Bhutadharma." *Proceedings and Transactions of the Sixth All-India Oriental Conference* (1930), pp. 349-370. See 8.6(1).

(5) KARAMBELKAR, V. W. "Matsyendranatha and his Yogini Cult." *Indian Historical Quarterly*, 31 (1955), 362-374.

A discussion of the role and place of Matsyendranatha in Nepal, a syncretic deity whom Hindus regard as Vishnu and Buddhists as Avalokitesvara. A more specific discussion of the yearly Matsyendranatha festival held in Kathmandu may be found in M. Lobsiger-Dellenbach, "La construction du char de Petan (Nepal)," *Etudes asiatiques*, nos. 3-4 (1953), pp. 99-121.

(6) LALOU, MARCELLE. "Le culte des naga et la thérapeutique." *Journal asiatique*, 230 (1938), 1-19.

Text and translation of an important Tibetan ritual work dealing with methods of controlling nagas, the *Klu'i gdon-las grol-bar-byed-pa sbrul 'jin gsan-po* (Secret qui saisit le serpent, pour délivrer de l'emprise des naga). Also includes a description of a puja to eight nagas.

(7) LESSING, FERDINAND D. "Bodhisattva Confucius." *Oriens*, 10 (1957), 131-139.

A short article dealing with Chinese Lamaist cult incorporating Confucius into the Buddhist pantheon. Gives examples of Buddhist invocation of Confucius.

(8) _____. *Yung-ho-kung* (see 7.5.3[3]), vol. 1, pp. 139-147.

A description of the cult of Vaisravana, the God of Wealth, as it was carried out in the "Rite of Conjuring up Prosperity" at the Yung-ho-kung "Lamaist Cathedral" in Peking.

(9) ROCK, JOSEPH F. *The Na-khi Naga Cult and Related Ceremonies*. Serie Orientale Roma, No. 4. Rome: Istituto Italiano per il Medio ed Estremo-Oriente, 1952, 806 pp., 58 plates.

Extensive and detailed descriptions of Na-khi religious rituals, with their interesting combination of Buddhist, Bon, and other elements. Rock's point of focus is the Ssu Ddu gy ceremony or great Naga Cult.

(10) SHASTRI, HIRANANDA. *The Origin and Cult of Tara*. Memoirs of the Archaeological Survey of India, No. 20. Calcutta: Government of India Press, 1925, 28 pp.

A historical-iconographic study of Tara, which claims that her popularity grew in India around the fifth to seventh centuries A.D. when she came to India from Tibet. See also 7.8(2).

(11) SIRCAR, D. C., ed. *The Sakti Cult and Tara*. Calcutta: University of Calcutta, 1967, pp. 107-168.

A series of papers of widely varying quality on the iconography and cult of Tara, presented to a seminar at the University of Calcutta in 1967 by K. K. Dasgupta, D. C. Sircar, D. C. Bhattacharya, N. N. Bhattarcharya, A. K. Bhattacharya, and S. Chattopadhyay.

(12) SUZUKI, DAISETZ TEITARO. "The Cult of Kwannon." *The Eastern Buddhist*, 6 (1932-1935), 339-353.

A description of the cult of Kwannon (Kuan Yin, Avalokitesvara) in China as observed by Suzuki during his trip there in 1934. He distinguishes the cult of Kwannon and that of Amida in terms of orientation towards this-worldly and other-worldly concerns.

(13) VAN GULIK, R. H. *Hayagriva: The Mantrayanic Aspect of Horse-Cult in China and Japan*. Leiden: E. J. Brill, 1935, 105 pp.

A major work on the figure of Hayagriva, this traces the evolution of the cult and its relation to indigenous Chinese and Japanese horse-cults, and attempts to relate it to Mantrayanic concepts (so that, for example, the neigh of the horse equals the mantra of Hayagriva, etc.).

(14) VISSER, MARINUS WILLEM DE. *Ancient Buddhism in Japan* (see 1.13.2.[8]), pp. 293-308, 309-317, 318-350.

The first set of pages offers a survey of the occasions on which the Yakushi-kekwa or "Rites of Repentance in Worship of the Buddha Bhaisajyaguru" were performed in Japan between the years 686 (or 744) and 842 A.D. Bhaisajyaguru is the so-called "Buddha of Medicine," and these ceremonies were generally performed at the time of a sickness in the imperial family. The second set of pages is a survey of the occasions on which the Kich-ijo-Kekwa or Sembo (rites of repentance in worship of Sri Devi [Laksmi]) were performed in Japan between A.D. 739 and 1068. Laksmi was the goddess of felicity or fortune, and the Buddhist ceremony in her honor was largely based on the Suvarna-prabhasa Sutra and was generally held at the request of the emperor. The final set of pages is a substantial discussion of the Amida-kekwa, or rites of repentance in worship of the Buddha Amitabha in Japan from A.D. 782 to the present day. It includes a background survey of the cult of Amitabha in China and in Japan, and is helpful for emphasizing the cultic and ritual aspects of Pure Land Buddhism.

(15) _____. The Bodhisattva Akasagarbha (Kokuzo) in China and Japan. Vehandlingen der Koninklijke Akademie van Wetenschappen, No. 30. Amsterdam: Koninklijke Akademie van Wetenschappen, 1931, 47 pp.

After a brief survey of the notion of space (Akasa) in Buddhism, Visser goes on to describe the "Sutras and ceremonial rules with regard to the bodhisattva Akasagarbha," and gives summaries of a number of relevant legends, texts, dharanis, meditations, etc., all related to this important (though secondary) bodhisattva.

(16) _____. The Bodhisattva Ti-tsang (Jizo) in China and Japan. Berlin: Oesterheld, 1914, 181 pp.

An important study of the important bodhisattva Ksitigarbha (Ti-tang or Jizo) and of his history and cult in China and Japan, this includes a discussion of the very popular "cult of the six Jizos," which involved worship at six shrines for six Ksitigarbhas who were protectors of the six different realms of rebirth.

(17) WADDELL, L. AUSTINE. "The Indian Buddhist Cult of Avalokita and His Consort Tara 'the Saviouress,' Illustrated from the Remains in Magadha." Journal of the Royal Asiatic Society (1894), pp. 51-89.

A dated article but still useful for its translations of some ritual texts, especially in praise of Tara, and for its listing of different forms of Tara and of Avalokitesvara.

(18) WAYMAN, ALEX. "The Twenty-One Praises of Tara: A Syncretism of Saivism and Buddhism." Journal of the Bihar Research Society, 45 (1959), 36-43.

Translation of a short text in praise of Tara taken from the Sarvatathagatamatrtaravisvakarmabhavatantranama, which reflects her "syncretic" nature.

8 Ideal Beings, Hagiography, and Biography

8.1   THE BUDDHA

8.1.1   Previous Births (Jatakas)

(1) ARYASURA. Jatakamala. Translated by J. S. Speyer as The Gatakamala or Garland of Birth Stories. See 4.2.2(1).

(2) BRYNER, EDNA. Thirteen Tibetan Tankas. Denver: Falcon's Wing Press, 1956, 155 pp.
    This book is generally a description of thirteen Tankas--banner paintings--and an elaboration of their themes, which are taken from the Jatakas.

(3) Cariya pitaka. Translated by Bimala Churn Law as "Cariya-pitaka: The Collection of Ways of Conduct." See 3.2.2.1(3).

(4) FEER, M. L. A Study of the Jatakas. Translated by G. M. Foulkes. Calcutta: Susil Gupta, 1963, 126 pp.
    This is a study of the Jatakas held to be the most important by the Theravada school. The author compares various renditions of specific Jatakas and also organizes Jatakas into categories suitable to analysis. A translation from the original French.

(5) FOUCHER, ALFRED. Les Vies Antérieures du Bouddha. See 2.7.1(2).
    A fine discussion of numerous Jataka tales organizing them into different types, the broader categories being "Fables," "Fabliaux," and "Contes." This makes a good introduction to the subject but should be complemented by an actual reading of the tales. The work is charmingly illustrated by Jeannine Auboyer.

(6) FRANCIS, H. T. and E. J. THOMAS, trans. and eds. Jataka Tales. Bombay: Jaico, 1957, 313 pp. (Originally published Cambridge: University Press, 1916.)
    A fine and an interesting selection of Jataka stories by two eminent Pali scholars who also participated in the complete translation of the tales edited by E. B. Cowell. This selection makes a fine introduction to the jataka genre for students who do not wish to go through the whole six volumes of Cowell's work.

(7) GERSCHEVITCH, ILYA. "On the Sogdian Vessantara Jataka." Journal of the Royal Asiatic Society of Great Britain (1942) pp. 97-101.
    This is a brief textual study of an old manuscript of this particular Jataka. The author offers little in the way of interpretation.

(8) GOMBRICH, RICHARD. "Feminine Elements in Sinhalese Buddhism." See 4.2.3(15).
    An unusual article, the second part of which presents and translates a popular Sinhalese poem entitled "Manopranidhanaye Sivpada," which tells of an episode in one of the Buddha's lives before he took his formal vow under the previous Buddha Dipamkara (a period which is not dealt with in the canonical and commentarial jatakas). In this life, the bodhisattva saves his mother from a shipwreck and then is said to "receive Buddhahood" from her and to formulate a mental vow for enlightenment in her presence (manopranidhana). This whole section is preceded by an interesting discussion of the "Buddha Mother" notion as found in the medieval Sanskritized Sinhalese manuscript the Matr Upamava (mother simile), in which the Buddha is compared to a mother, the Dharma to milk, and the Sangha to suckling babes. The whole makes a very useful discussion of feminine symbolism in Sinhalese Buddhism, based not on canonical and commentarial texts but on the more popular literature.

(9) Jatakastava. Translated by Mark J. Dresden in "The Jatakastava or Praise of Buddha's Former Births." See 3.3.8.4(5).

(10) Jatakatthakatha. Edited and translated by E. B. Cowell et al. as The Jataka or Stories of the Buddha's Former Births. See 3.2.2.1(12).
    The basic, standard translation of the Jataka stories from the Pali tradition. Excellent indices allow the reader to select appropriate Jatakas for specific purposes. Does not include the Nidanakatha, the long introduction to the work.

(11) LAW, BIMALA CHURN. "Some Observations on the Jatakas." See 4.2.2(8).

A short but helpful discussion of the sources, origins, and aims of the Jatakas, limited to the Pali versions. For a brief overview of the form and style of the same Jataka literature, see Rhys-Davids, Buddhist India (below), pp. 189-209.

(12) Mahavastu. Translated by J. J. Jones as The Mahavastu. See 3.2.1.2(5).

Many Buddha biographies incorporate Jataka stories to illustrate certain events in the Buddha's life with reference to his deeds in past lives. The Mahavastu is a prime example of this: throughout its pages, the reader may find the texts of various Jatakas, which may be fruitfully compared with versions found in other canons or languages.

(13) NAGARJUNA. Catuhstava. Partially translated by Giuseppe Tucci in "Two Hymns of the Catuhstava of Nagarjuna." See 3.3.2.1(15).

(14) RHYS-DAVIDS, T. W. Buddhist India (see 1.2.2.1[12]), pp. 189-209.

This general discussion of the form and style of Jataka literature, according to the scholarship of the late nineteenth and early twentieth centuries, remains worthy and provides the reader with an overview.

(15) Vessantara Jataka. See 4.2.2(12).

(16) WRAY, ELIZABETH, CLARE ROSENFELD, and DOROTHY BAILY. Ten Lives of the Buddha: Siamese Temple Painting and Jataka Tales. New York and Tokyo: Weatherhill, 1972.

Telling of the last ten lives of the Buddha before his life as Gotama. The work is beautifully illustrated with Joe D. Wray's photographs of murals in various Thai temples.

8.1.2 The Final Life as Gautama

8.1.2.1 Traditional Accounts of the Life of the Buddha and Canonical Biographical Materials in Translation

(1) Abhiniskramana Sutra. Translated by Samuel Beal as The Romantic Legend of Sakya-Buddha. See 3.2.4.1(1).

Translation of a Chinese Buddha-biography which claims to date at least to a Sanskrit original of the sixth century A.D.; the precise sect affiliation is difficult to determine. The colophon claims that the Mahasanghikas call it the Mahavastu, the Sarvastivadins call it the Lalitavistara, while the Kasyapas and the Dharmaguptas give it other names.

(2) ALABASTER, HENRY, trans. The Wheel of the Law. London: Trubner, 1871, pp. 76-241.

An annotated translation from a Thai text of the life of the Buddha, the "Pathomma Somphothiyan or first (festival) of omniscience." Interesting primarily as a Thai national source on the Buddha's life, this should be compared to the Cambodian work translated by Adhemard Leclere (below).

(3) ASVAGHOSHA. Buddhacarita. Translated by Edward Hamilton Johnston as The Buddhacarita or Acts of the Buddha. See 3.2.4.1(5).

The Sanskrit original of the Buddhacarita (second century A.D.) is an incomplete biography of the Buddha, containing only seventeen chapters, the last four of which are not even Asvaghosha's. Johnston's authoritative translation, therefore, stops at Chapter 14, with the Buddha's enlightenment. It may be compared with Cowell's older but still more readily available translation of all seventeen chapters of the same text. It should also be complemented by Beal's English rendition of Dharmaraksha's fifth century Chinese translation, which contains all twenty-eight chapters.

(4) AUNG, SHWE ZAN and C. A. F. RHYS-DAVIDS, trans. Points of Controversy (Katha-vatthu) (see 3.2.3.1[5]), pp. 164-170, 323-326, 353-355, 366-367.

These pages from one of the seven books of the Abhidharma are concerned with various controversies that arose in relation to the nature of the Buddha. They include the resolution of such problems as: whether the Buddha's speech was supramundane, whether his compassions also implied passion, whether his excrements were fragrant, etc. Comparativist students might also be interested in the Theravada refutation of the "docetic" view that the Buddha actually stayed in Tushita heaven during his early ministry and only sent a "phantom" body to be born on earth.

(5) BEAL, SAMUEL, trans. The Fo-Sho-Hing-Tsan-King. See 3.2.4.1(3).

This volume represents Beal's translation from the Chinese of Asvaghosha's Buddhacarita, which was originally written in Sanskrit. The Buddhacarita contains little common to the other sacred biographies of the Buddha except for the well known and central events of his life. The biography covers the period up to the session of the first council and generally follows the Pali tradition. The Buddha is depicted as a human being who achieved his perfection as a result of his accumulated merit from past lives.

(6) _____. "Text and Commentary of the Memorial of Sakya Buddha Tathagata by Wong Puh." Journal of the Royal Asiatic Society, 20 (1863), 135-220.

Translation of a seventh century Chinese text which consists of summary paragraphs on the life of the Buddha, each of which is followed by a commentary which often sheds interesting lights on contemporary Chinese traditions. The text, without the commentary, has also been translated by Beal as "Memorials of the Complete Inspiration of the Tathagata" in his A Catena of Buddhist Scriptures from the Chinese (see 3.2.1.2[7]), pp. 126-142.

(7) BIGANDET, PAUL. The Life or Legend of Gaudama the Buddha of the Burmese. Fourth

edition. London: Kegan Paul, Trench, Trubner, 1911, 2 vols.

The first edition of this work by Bishop Bigandet appeared in 1858 and tells the story of the life of the Buddha as he learned it from the Burmese. Not a scholarly work, but interesting and important for its translation and preservation of mid-nineteenth century Burmese traditions and sources.

(8) BUDDHARAKKHITA. Jinalankara. Translated by James Gray as Embellishments of Buddha. London: Luzac, 1894, 112 pp.

A translation of a Pali hymn of debatable antiquity which praises the Buddha and at the same time traces his biography in 250 stanzas.

(9) BU-STON. History of Buddhism (Chos 'byung) (see 1.14.1[2]), vol. 2, pp. 1-72.

At the head of his "History of Buddhism in India and Tibet," the fourteenth century Tibetan historian Bu sTon includes a "Life of the Buddha" which describes his biography in terms of the "Twelve Acts of the Buddha." The account of the first eleven of these is based on the Lalitavistara, while that of the twelfth is taken from the Vinaya ksudraka as found in the Kangyur.

(10) COWELL, E. B. "The Buddha-karita of Asvaghonosha." See 3.2.4.1(4).

Cowell's translation of Asvaghosha's biography of the Buddha is an earlier translation than the one offered by Johnston (above). Hence it does not contain the valuable notes of the latter's work. Still, it remains a fine translation and has been reissued as a paperback, which makes it the most available translation. Further, unlike Johnston's edition, Cowell's contains four additional chapters which were added by Amritananda, a nineteenth century Nepalese scholar.

(11) EDWARDES, MICHAEL, ed. A Life of the Buddha from a Burmese Manuscript. London: The Folio Society, 1959, 188 pp.

An edition and, in some places, a retranslation of Chester Bennett, trans., "Life of Gaudama--A Translation from the Burmese Book Entitled Ma-la-len-ga-ra Wottou," Journal of the American Oriental Society, 3 (1852), 1-164. Edwardes checked Bennett's translation with an early nineteenth century manuscript which he acquired in 1946, and in some places corrected it. The work is interesting for much the same reasons as is that of Paul Bigandet (above), with which it can be compared.

(12) FOUCAUX, PHILIPPE EDOUARD, trans. Le Lalita Vistara. Paris: E. Leroux, 1884-1892, 2 vols.

Foucaux's translation of the Lalitavistara brings to the reader a fine presentation of the most systematic sacred biography of the Buddha. The Lalitavistara, originally written in a hybrid form of Sanskrit and as a text of the Sarvastivadins, uses bold imagery and descriptive accounts in poetry and prose in order to produce faith in and devotion for the Buddha.

(13) HORNER, ISALINE BLEW, trans. Majjhima Nikaya (see 3.2.2.1[16]), vol. 1, pp. 203-219.

These pages represent the Ariyapariyesana-sutta (Discourse on the Ariyan Quest), which contains an "autobiographical" account of Gautama's search for enlightenment. Of special interest is the Buddha's account of his learning experiences under Alara Kalama and Uddaka Ramaputta.

(14) _____. Vinayapitaka. London: Oxford, 1938-1942, and Luzac, 1951-1966, vol. 4, pp. 1-57. (Also published in Sacred Books of the Buddhists, Vol. 14.)

This opening narrative of the Mahavagga relates a series of events immediately following his enlightenment at Bodh Gaya: his decision to preach the doctrine, the first sermon at Sarnath, the story of the young noble, Yasa, etc. As a part of the Vinaya, the entire Mahavagga represents an extremely important source for the study of the life of the Buddha, since it is constitutive of some of the oldest Buddhist materials we have. A different translation of the Mahavagga may be found in the Sacred Books of the East, Volumes 13 and 17.

(15) Jinacarita. Translated by W. H. D. Rouse. See 3.2.4.1(6).

Text (pp. 1-32) and translation (pp. 33-66) of a Pali work which praises the Buddha by recounting his life and deeds. The work is attributed to the Sinhalese author Vanaratana Medhankara, who lived in the late thirteenth century. It is interesting for showing developments in the formulation of the biography of the Buddha. Another translation has been made by Charles Duroiselle as The Career of the Conqueror (Rangoon: British Burma Press, 1906).

(16) JONES, J. J., trans. The Mahavastu. See 3.2.1.2(5).

Written originally in hybrid Sanskrit and covering over 1300 pages in print, the Mahavastu claims to be the Vinaya of the Lokotaravada branch of the Mahasanghikas. By and large, it lacks systematic cohesion and is generally a rather confused mass of legends and historical facts. All three volumes contain accounts of the life of the Buddha at various stages of his existence; but as the descriptions of the Buddha's career overlap chronologically, it remains a difficult piece to read or use as a whole.

(17) KERN, HENDRIK, trans. Saddharma-Pundarika or the Lotus of the True Law (see 3.3.5.1[12]), pp. 298-310.

This chapter of Kern's translation, which was first published in 1884, represents the Mahayanist contention that the Buddha attained full enlightenment hundreds of aeons before his earthly birth and ministry.

(18) KLAPROTH, JULIUS HEINRICH, trans. "Vie de Bouddha d'après les livres mongols." Journal asiatique, 4 (1824), 9-23, 65-79.

Very early translation of an account of the life of the Buddha drawn from unspecified Mongolian sources. Makes for interesting comparison with other early nineteenth century lives of the Buddha.

(19) LAW, BIMALA CHURN, trans. Buddhavamsa. See 3.2.2.1(2).

The Buddhavamsa is the fourteenth book of the Khuddaka-nikaya. It gives, in short, the histories of twenty-four previous Buddhas, ending with that of the "present" Buddha Gautama. The most important story (also found elsewhere) is probably that of the "first" Buddha Dipankara, under whom Gautama (who was then the Brahman Sumedha) resolved to become a Buddha. The Buddhavamsa is interesting because it is one of the latest books of the Pali Canon and, though still canonical, reflects some of the changes that were taking place within Buddhism.

(20) LECLERE, ADHEMARD, trans. Les livres sacrés du Cambodge (see 3.1.6[4]), pp. 13-114.

In these pages, Leclere has translated into French the Preas Pathama Sampothiau, a short yet complete biography of the Buddha which has enjoyed great popularity in Cambodia.

(21) MITRA, RAJENDRALALA, trans. The Lalitavistara, or Memoirs of the Early Life of Sakya Sinha. Calcutta: Asiatic Society of Bombay, 1831-1836, 233 pp.

This English translation of the Lalitavistara is not only rather poorly done, it is incomplete, containing only fifteen out of twenty-seven chapters of the text. (A second volume which was to complete it never appeared). To his translation Mitra has added copious notes, some of them interesting (but perhaps unreliable), others now quaintly out of date. Students who read French should definitely use Foucaux's complete translation (above).

(22) RHYS-DAVIDS, T. W. and C. A. F. RHYS-DAVIDS, trans. "The Maha-parinibbana sutta," Digha Nikaya (Dialogues of the Buddha) (see 2.7.1[13]), vol. 3, pp. 71-191.

The sutta is the longest and probably the most important in the Digha Nikaya. Though it is a composite work containing very early and also comparatively late material, it still holds together as a single literary masterpiece. It contains a fascinating record of the last days of the Buddha's early ministry and summaries of his doctrines and exhortations.

(23) ROCKHILL, W. WOODVILLE. The Life of the Buddha (see 3.2.1.2[11]), pp. 1-180.

Translation from the Tibetan Vinaya ('Dul wa) of the Mulasarvastivadins of a long complete biography of the Buddha. The work is divided into five chapters: the history of the world from the time of its renovation up until the reign of Suddhodana (the Buddha's father), the reign of Suddhodana until the start of the Buddha's ministry, the life of the Buddha from the start of his ministry until the reign of Ajatasatru, his life from then until his death, and the history of the Buddhist sangha during the 110 years following the Buddha's death.

(24) WANG PUH. Shing Tan ki. Translated by Samuel Beal in A Catena of Buddhist Scriptures from the Chinese (see 3.2.1.2[7]), pp. 126-142.

This work, which Beal translates as "Memorials of the Complete Inspiration of the Tathagata," was written during the period of the T'ang dynasty around 650 A.D. Though very brief, it seems to follow closely the schematization of the Lalitavistara and may even be a summary of it.

(25) WIEGER, LEON, trans. "Les Vies Chinoises du Buddha: Récit de l'Apparition sur Terre du Buddha des Sakya," in Buddhisme. Sien-Hsien: Imprimerie de la Mission Catholique, 1913, vol. 2.

Text and translation of a full biography of the Buddha, compiled during the Ming dynasty by Pao ch'ung. The text is a fascinating example of the retroactive influence of Chinese concepts on the life story of the Buddha. Certain episodes are elaborated or invented to make him a more filial son, or, out of conformity to T'ien t'ai and other tranditions, he is made to preach first the Avatamsaka sutra immediately after his enlightenment. Also, episodes from the Pure Land Sutras and various avadanas are inserted into his biography. The translation is followed by a set of about 150 drawings made in 1808 and designed to illustrate the text.

8.1.2.2 Canonical and Traditional Discussions on the Status, Powers, and Knowledge of the Buddha

(1) BAREAU, ANDRE. "The Superhuman Personality of the Buddha and Its Symbolism in the Mahaparinirvanasutra of the Dharmaguptaka," in Myths and Symbols: Studies in Honor of Mircea Eliade. Edited by Joseph M. Kitagawa and Charles H. Long. Chicago: University of Chicago Press, 1969, pp. 9-21.

An interesting and useful treatment of the gradually increasing docetic character of the Buddha as reflected in this Dharmagupta version of the Mahaparinirvana sutra. Deals also with the importance of cakravartin symbolism in this context.

(2) CONZE, EDWARD. Astasahasrika Prajnaparamita. Calcutta: Asiatic Society, 1958, pp. 93-100, 216-219.

The first set of these pages represents the Prajnaparamita's view of the powers and knowledge of the Tathagata. The second set, in true Prajnaparamita style, attacks the well-known double etymology of "tathagata," claiming that Tathagatas certainly do not come from anywhere, nor do they go anywhere. "Suchness" does not move.

(3) FOUCAUX, PHILIPPE, trans. Le Lalita Vistara (see 8.1.2.1[12]), vol. 1, pp. 95-99, 106-109.

Many authoritative texts contain a listing of the thirty-two major marks of the Mahapurusa (great being)--a status shared by both Buddhas and Cakravartins. It is rarer, however, to find the list of the eighty minor markings of the Mahapurusa. Both lists are contained in the first set of pages. The second set contains a story concerned with the divinity of the Buddha. The story is that as a young boy the Buddha is brought by his parents to worship at a temple of the gods: upon entering, all of the statues of the deities fall off their pedestals at the feet of the Buddha.

(4) FOUCHER, ALFRED. "Le grand miracle du Buddha à Sravasti." Journal asiatique, 13 (1909), 1-72.

An important early iconographic and textual study of the "miracle" performed by the Buddha at Sravasti, in which he magically multiplies his form thousands of times, and preaches the law and converts many beings,

(5) JAINI, PADMANABH S. "Buddha's Prolongation of Life." Bulletin of the School of Oriental and African Studies, 21 (1958), 546-552.

A short discussion of the Buddha's reputed power to live out a whole kalpa, though he did not because Ananda neglected to ask him to do so. Touches on the role which the belief in this power of the Buddha had in the rise of a more developed Buddhology.

(6) _____. "On the Sarvajnatva (Omniscience) of Mahavira and the Buddha," in Buddhist Studies in Honour of I. B. Horner (see 1.2.2.4[11]), pp. 71-91.

An interesting comparative study of Buddhist and Jain traditions about their respective founders' powers of omniscience. The author attempts to be precise about just what omniscience entails in the two religions-- something which he finds more difficult in the case of Buddhism.

(7) LAMOTTE, ETIENNE. "Passions and Impregnations of the Passions in Buddhism," in Buddhist Studies in Honour of I. B. Horner (see 1.2.2.4[11]), pp. 91-104.

A discussion of the differences between Buddhas on the one hand and arhats and pratyekabuddhas on the other in terms of which klesas (defilements or "passions") they have eliminated. Buddhas have eliminated all of them, while arhats, though they have eliminated the klesas, still retain the lingering "impregnations of the passions" (klesa-vasama).

(8) _____. Le traité de la grande vertu de sagesse de Nagarjuna (see 3.3.1.2[6]), vol. 1, pp. 115-161.

This chapter contains an explanation and etymology of the word "Bhagavat"--one of the principal titles of the Buddha. This is followed by briefer explanations of about a dozen other epithets of the Buddha.

(9) _____. Le traité de la grande vertu de sagesse de Nagarjuna (see 3.3.1.2[6]), vol. 3, pp. 1340-1361.

This passage describes the practice of "Buddhanusmrti"--the remembrance and contemplation of the Buddha's titles, marks, characteristics, etc.

(10) NAGAO, GADJIN. "On the Theory of the Buddha-Body." Eastern Buddhist, 6, no. 1 (May 1973), 25-53.

The author traces the development of the concepts of the three bodies of Buddha and attempts to show how these concepts were used in philosophic speculation.

(11) SUZUKI, D. T. Outlines of Mahayana Buddhism (see 2.1[12]), pp. 242-310.

The author presents the Mahayana conceptions of the Buddha and also deals with the problems of Trikaya and Karuna.

(12) _____. Studies in the Lankavatara Sutra (see 3.3.3.3[3]), pp. 308-338.

Suzuki discusses the doctrine of the three bodies of the Buddha and especially emphasizes the various Chinese epithets of the three bodies. This is a clear exposition of the concept.

8.1.2.3 Historical Reconstructions of the Life of the Buddha

There are innumerable accounts of the life of the Buddha which can be found in any book which deals with the subject of "religions of the world" or with Buddhism in an introductory fashion. In addition, many books which attempt to describe the role of Buddhism in Indian history will also include an account of the life of the Buddha. Below, the reader will find a few representative treatments of the Buddha's life, including the most important studies.

(1) AMBEDKAR, B. R. The Buddha and His Dhamma. Bombay: Siddharth College Publication, 1957, 599 pp.

An interesting reinterpretation of the life of the Buddha by the leader of thousands of Indian "untouchables" who converted to Buddhism after Indian independence. Although the book could perhaps be better entitled "Ambedkar and His Dhamma," it is an exciting example of the practical use of sacred biography in the world today.

(2) BAPAT, P. V., ed. 2500 Years of Buddhism (see 1.2.1[1]), pp. 20-24.

A short sketch contributed by C. V. Joshi, which consists of a rather standard narration

The Buddha

of the highlights of the Buddha's life and teachings.

(3) BAREAU, ANDRE. "La Date du Nirvana." *Journal asiatique*, 241 (1953), 27-62.

A concise, scholarly, and authoritative discussion of the problem of dating the Buddha's death. Bareau presents and analyzes the various sources and gives an extremely helpful table of the different traditions involved. He concludes by placing the Buddha's Nirvana around 480 B.C.

(4) _____. "La Jeunesse du Bouddha dans les Sutrapitaka et les Vinayapitaka Anciens." *Bulletin de l'Ecole française d'Extrême-Orient*, 61 (1974), 199-274.

A scholarly discussion and translation of all the texts related to the Buddha's birth and youth--a period which is not covered by Bareau's monumental *Recherches sur la Biographie du Bouddha* (below). For an earlier discussion on this topic which gives a detailed study of the account of Sakyamuni's youth as found in the Mahisasaka and Dharmaguptaka Vinayas see André Bareau, "La légende de la jeunesse du Bouddha dans les Vinayapitaka anciens," *Oriens Extremus*, 9 (1962), 6-33.

(5) _____. *Recherches sur la Biographie du Bouddha dans les Sutrapitaka et les Vinayapitaka Anciens*. Publications de l'Ecole française d'Extrême-Orient, Nos. 53 and 77. Paris, 1963, 1971.

An indispensable aid to serious work on the overall tradition about the life of the Buddha. Bareau has translated and compared texts from the Vinayas and sutras of various schools, dealing with all the traditional incidents in the life of the Buddha. Volume 1 treats the period from his quest for enlightenment up to the conversion of Sariputra and Maudgalyayana, and Volume 2 deals with the last months of the Buddha's life, his parinirvana and funerary ceremonies.

(6) BREWSTER, E. H. *The Life of Gotama the Buddha*. London: Kegan Paul, Trench, and Trubner, 1926, 243 pp.

One of a number of "reconstructions" of the life of the Buddha based exclusively and rather uncritically on selected passages from the Pali Texts. There are many other works in this genre, among which two should perhaps be mentioned here: Henry Clarke Warren, *Buddhism in Translations* (see 2.7.1[16]), ch. 1; and Kenneth J. Saunders, *Gotama Buddha, A Biography* (New York: Association Press, 1920).

(7) CONZE, EDWARD. *Buddhist Scriptures*. Baltimore: Penguin, 1968, pp. 19-68.

A simple but effective introduction to the legends concerned with the life of Gautama. Chapter 1, which deals with "the Buddha's previous lives," offers a good sampling of the range of Jatakas. Also, the reader will find an adequate treatment of the life of the Buddha with many selections taken from Ashvagosha's *Buddhacarita*.

(8) DUTT, NALINAKSHA. *Early Monastic Buddhism* (see 1.2.2.1[3]), pp. 77-132.

Using the Mahavastu, the Buddhacarita, the Lalitavistara, and Gilgit manuscripts, Dutt has woven together a rather one-dimensional account of the life of the Buddha. The value of this presentation is that it contains a "who's who" of the Buddha's converts which goes a long way toward explaining how the Buddhist community conceived of the early monastic community.

(9) DUTT, SUKUMAR. *The Buddha and Five After-Centuries* (see 1.2.1[8]), pp. 3-56.

This is an easily readable account in which the author attempts a type of "quest for the historical Buddha." The result is a rather informative discussion of the specific circumstances (social, political, and religious) which probably existed during the period of the life of the Buddha. By trying to extract data from the Buddhist legends concerning the life of the Buddha, the reader is presented with "historical" fragments which might be likened to pieces of wreckage. Nevertheless, Dutt's attempt at a reconstruction is probably as credible as any other.

(10) ELIADE, MIRCEA. *From Primitives to Zen*. London: Collins, 1967, pp. 423-527.

Eliade provides textual materials concerned with Gautama's asceticism, his great departure, his masters, his proclamation of the path following his enlightenment, his decision to preach, and his remembrance of past lives.

(11) FILLIOZAT, JEAN. "La vie du Bouddha," in *L'Inde Classique* (see 1.2.2.1[11]), pp. 463-492.

A fine survey of scholarship and a straightforward presentation of the life of the Buddha based on all available sources, by a great French Indologist.

(12) FOUCAUX, PHILIPPE EDOUARD. *Histoire du Bouddha Sakya-mouni*. Paris: Ernest Leroux, 1874, 208 pp.

A well written if somewhat romanticized biography which tries to combine Sanskrit, Tibetan, and Pali sources.

(13) FOUCHER, ALFRED. *Etude sur l'iconographie bouddhique de l'Inde* (see 1.2.2.3[5]), vol. 1, pp. 65-93; vol. 2, pp. 15-21.

These sections are concerned with the relative humanity and divinity ascribed to the historical Sakyamuni Buddha and to the other Buddhas of later Mahayana Indian Buddhism.

(14) _____. *The Life of the Buddha*. See 2.7.6(5).

This is an edited version of Foucher's *La vie du Bouddha* (Paris, 1949). Still, it remains perhaps the best "life of Buddha" treatment available in English. Foucher has relied upon the Mahavastu, the Buddhacarita, and the Lalitavistara to give the reader a composite picture of the life of the Buddha from representative traditions. He also includes many stories from the Jatakas and an introduction to the character and significance of the eight major pilgrimage sites in India.

(15) FRAUWALLNER, ERICH. "The Historical Data We Possess on the Person and the Doctrine of the Buddha." East and West, 7 (1957), 309-312.

A short introduction to the problem of scientific historical knowledge of the life of the Buddha. Frauwallner's answer to the question "what can we know for sure?" is cautious but not pessimistic.

(16) GEDEN, A. S. "The Life of the Buddha," in Encyclopedia of Religion and Ethics (see 1.15.1[9]), vol. 2, pp. 881-885.

This brief article uses the Pali sources and some archeological findings and is good for a quick overview or general review.

(17) HEROLD, A. FERDINAND. The Life of Buddha. Translated by Paul Blum. Tokyo: Charles E. Tuttle Co., 1954. (Originally published 1927.)

A reconstructed narration of the life of the Buddha based exclusively on Sanskrit sources--the Lalitavistara, the Buddhacarita, and the Avadanasataka. It is interesting to compare it with the books based on the Pali canon, such as that of Brewster (above).

(18) LAMOTTE, ETIENNE. "La légende du Bouddha." Revue de l'Histoire des Religions, 134 (1948), 37-71.

An article which is really two studies in one. First is a survey of the various Western interpretations of the Buddha biography, outlining the mythological explanation of Senart and Kern, the rationalist position of Oldenberg and Rhys-Davids, and the pragmatic attitude of A. Barth and Keith. This is followed by a study of the "successive stages" in the development of the legend of the Buddha, listing biographical fragments in sutras and in vinayas, separate but incomplete "lives," complete lives, etc. For another account by the same author, see his Histoire du Bouddhisme Indien (1.2.1[10]), pp. 713-789.

(19) LAW, BIMALA CHURN. "Buddha's Activities at Anga-Magadha." Journal of the Bihar Research Society, special volume (1956), 32.

One of Law's series of articles attempting to compile (mainly from the Pali sources) a record of what the Buddha did in particular geographical regions or places. Others include: "The Buddha's Activities at Kasi Kosala," Journal of Indian History, 34 (1956), 139-71; and "The Buddha's Activities at Vaisali," Journal of Indian History, 35 (1957), 7-36.

(20) OLDENBERG, HERMAN. Buddha: His Life, His Order, His Doctrine. Varanasi: Indological Book House, 1971, pp. 71-203.

Originally published in the 1880s by the early great philologist, this work, though dated, remains a valuable source of information concerning the life of the Buddha as it is presented in the Pali texts.

(21) PERI, NOEL. "Les femmes de Sakya-muni." Bulletin de l'Ecole française d'Extrême-Orient, 18 (1918), 1-37.

The author examines canonical sources and various biographies of the Buddha in an attempt to discern how many wives the Buddha left behind at his Great Departure. Somehow, the author concludes that Buddha had been married three times.

(22) POPPE, NICHOLAS, trans. The Twelve Deeds of the Buddha. See 3.3.8.4(6).

What Poppe presents in this book is the sole surviving second volume of a Mongolian translation of a now lost Tibetan abbreviated version of the Lalitavistara. Even so, it is an important and interesting text: 1) as a "rare specimen of early Mongolian-Buddhist literature," and 2) as a concise narrative of the events in the Buddha's life from the time of his Great Departure to his defeat of the Evil One under the Bodhi tree.

(23) PRZYLUSKI, JEAN. "Le Parinirvana et les Funérailles du Bouddha." Journal asiatique, 11 (1918), 485-526; 12 (1918), 401-56; 13 (1919), 365-430; and 15 (1920), 5-54.

A series of articles in which Przyluski offers his own interesting interpretation of the Buddha's last days and cremation. Valuable today especially for its presentation and translation of relevant texts. It consists of four chapters: 1) "Les stances de lamentation," 2) "Le dernier voyage du Bouddha," 3) "Vêtements de religieux et vêtements de rois," 4) "Les éléments rituels dans les funérailles du Bouddha."

(24) REYNOLDS, FRANK. "The Many Lives of Buddha: A Study of Sacred Biography and Theravada Tradition," in The Biographical Process: Studies in the History and Psychology of Religion. Edited by Frank Reynolds. Religion and Reason Series, No. 11. The Hague: Mouton, 1976, pp. 37-61.

This article deals with the formation of the biography of the Buddha in the early tradition including both the "classical biography" and "biographical chronicles" such as the Mahavamsa. It also traces the development of these biographical traditions in the later Theravada tradition, ending with comments on the Buddha biography in modern Theravada countries.

(25) RHYS-DAVIDS, CAROLINE AUGUSTA FOLEY. Gotama the Man. London: Luzac, 1928, 302 pp.

Rhys-Davids' reconstruction (or construction) of an "autobiography" of the Buddha who here tells his own story and preaches his own message "out of which grew the cults known as Buddhism." Interesting mostly as a period piece, and as an example of a particular phase of the scholarship of Buddhism.

(26) ROBINSON, RICHARD. The Buddhist Religion (see 1.1[8]), pp. 10-35.
This chapter offers a summary of the Buddha's life and teachings, with attention given to the historical background of the period. It could be a useful reading for undergraduates in an introductory course.

(27) ROCKHILL, WOODVILLE. The Life of the Buddha and the Early History of His Order (see 3.2.1.2[11]), pp. 1-147.
This work is primarily a translation of derivations from Tibetan works in the Bkah-hGyur and bStan-hGyur. Consequently, the reader is treated to a rendition of the Buddha's life which is rarely presented in courses on Buddhism. Rockhill, however, has seen fit also to use the popular secondary sources of his time (Rhys-Davids, Hardy, Beal, etc.) to comment upon the story as it progresses.

(28) SENART, EMILE. Essai sur la Légende du Bouddha. Second edition. Paris: Ernest Leroux, 1882, 496 pp.
Senart, an advocate of the old solar interpretation of the legend and life of the Buddha, pushes his interpretation throughout this work. Still, the book is a classic and remains useful for its discussion of various symbols and themes (cakravartin's wheel, Mahapurusa's marks, etc.) which are all too often left untouched. For another "solar interpretation" of the Buddha's life, see Hendrik Kern, Histoire du Bouddhisme dans l'Inde (1.2.1[9]), pp. 19-291.

(29) SENGUPTA, P. C. "Dates of Principal Events in the Buddha's Life." Indian Historical Quarterly, 32 (1956), 124-128.
A misguided but interesting attempt to prove the correctness of the Ceylon-Burma tradition of the date (and exact time) of the Buddha's Nirvana, based on elaborate scientific astronomical and solar calculations. Interesting compared to attempts to calculate the date of creation, etc. in the Christian tradition.

(30) THOMAS, EDWARD J. The Life of the Buddha as Legend and History. London: Kegan Paul, Trench and Trubner, 1927, 297 pp.
Thomas's volume on the life of the Buddha remains one of the standard works on the subject and a suitable introductory work. Generally it is clearly written and can easily be read as a companion to the same author's History of Buddhist Thought (see 2.1[14]) which also contains a brief sketch of the Buddha's life (pp. 133-152).

(31) WARDER, A. K. Indian Buddhism (see 1.2.1[15]), pp. 43-80.
A brief but fairly comprehensive rendition of the life of the Buddha, based upon the canonical sources.

(32) WILSON, H. H. "Buddha and Buddhism." Journal of the Royal Asiatic Society, 16 (1856), 248 ff.
An early attempt at interpreting the life of the Buddha which is now thoroughly outdated, but interesting for its view of the Buddha's biography as an allegorical resume of the Samkhya system of philosophy.

8.1.2.4 The Buddha's Extended Life in Relics

(1) BAREAU, ANDRE. "Le Parinirvana du Bouddha et la naissance de la religion bouddhique." Bulletin de l'Ecole française d'Extrême-Orient, 61 (1974), 275-299.
A study of the rise of the cult of the Buddha in the first decades following his parinirvana, and of the role of the laity in using relics, caityas, trees, and stupas, as the objects of a veneration directed towards the departed Buddha.

(2) BARUA, B. M. "Stupa and Tomb." India Historic Quarterly, 2 (1926), 16-27.
A study of the relationship between the Buddhist stupa and non-Buddhist burial traditions. Barua first reviews the origins of the stupa in ancient Indian practice and then shows how Buddhism incorporated this tradition. He relies heavily upon canonical sources to show the Buddhist incorporation.

(3) BEAL, SAMUEL, trans. The Fo-Sho-Hing-Tsan-King (see 3.2.4[3]), pp. 324-328.
This section of Asvaghosha's Buddhacarita contains an important account of the war which was caused by the division of the Buddha's relics.

(4) BHATTACHARYYA, BENOYTOSH. "Iconography of Heruka." Indian Culture, 2, no. 1 (July 1935), 23-36.
The author presents a useful summary of some of the various forms assumed by this tantric deity in iconographic representation.

(5) The Buddha's Tooth Relic Pagoda. Peking: Buddhist Association of China, 1966.
This rare pamphlet was published following the completion of construction of the New Tooth Relic Pagoda in the hills to the west of Peking in the 1960s. The pamphlet contains many illustrations of the pagoda and the tooth relic itself.

(6) CONZE, EDWARD, trans. Astasahasrika Prajnaparamita (see 8.1.2.2[2]), pp. 35-38.
This brief passage neatly sums up the Prajnaparamita's attitude towards the worship of the Buddha's relics. The basic attitude is that the relics are really of secondary importance and that wisdom is primary.

(7) Dathavamsa. Translated by Bimala Churn Law as The Dathavamsa (A History of the Tooth-Relic of the Buddha). Lahore: Motilal Banarsidass, 1925. See also 9.1.5(4).

(8) DUTT, SUKUMAR. The Buddha and Five After-Centuries (see 1.2.1[8]), pp. 163-197.

This part of Dutt's work is a general study of the rise and use of Stupas by Buddhists. Dutt sees the phenomenon as a contribution of "folk religion" to higher religion and notes the canonical sanctions of the stupa as the practice was absorbed into the tradition. He shows how various aspects of the Buddha's personality and his previous lives were depicted in the artistic expressions of the stupas. Further, he shows how these expressions concerning the nature of the Buddha were altered under the influence of Bhakti devotionalism.

(9) FINOT, LOUIS. "Notes on the Singhalese Tradition Relative to Buddha's Relics." Indian Culture, 1 (1935), 567-572.

A fascinating discussion of the Ceylon chronicle's accounts of the coming of early Buddha relics to the island, especially that concerning the collar bone and bowl relic in Dipavamsa, Chapter 15. It is one of the few critical studies of these sources.

(10) GOLOUBEW, VICTOR. "La temple de la dent à Kandy." Bulletin de l'Ecole française d'Extrême-Orient, 32 (1932), 441-474.

Goloubew's article should be read as a supplement to Hocart's The Temple of the Tooth (below), as it mentions some aspects of the cult worship which are omitted in Hocart's account. It is suitable for the intermediate and advanced student.

(11) HIRAKAWA, A. "Rise of Mahayana Buddhism and Its Relation to the Worship of Stupas." See 2.5.2(5).

This article is concerned with the evolution and growth of the practice of stupa worship in early Indian Mahayana Buddhism.

(12) HOCART, A. M. The Temple of the Tooth in Kandy. See 7.1.3(9).

Though it suffers from brevity, Hocart's study remains a worthwhile investment for any student interested in cult worship in Southeast Asia. The author succinctly outlines the history of the temple, describes its architecture (mostly by means of drawings), depicts the various rituals conducted at the temple, and attempts to compare the plan of the temple with other Sinhalese temples and with Western monasteries.

(13) JAYAWICKRAMA, N. A., trans. The Inception of Discipline and the Vinayanidana: Being a Translation and Edition of the Bahiranidana of Buddhaghosa's Samantapasadika, the Vinaya Commentary (see 3.2.1.3[1]), pp. 74-88.

In this portion of Buddhaghosha's commentary on the Vinaya, the reader will find a request by the Theravadins for and the reception of a branch of the Bodhi Tree. The branch was, of course, brought from Bodh Gaya and transplanted at Anuradhapura.

(14) KROM, NICOLAS J. The Life of the Buddha on the Stupa of Barabudur according to the Lalitavistara. The Hague: M. Nijhoff, 1926, 131 pp.

Krom's work basically consists of 120 plates reproducing the famous series of reliefs of the life of the Buddha found on the first gallery of the stupa of Borobudur. Each plate is described, and accompanied by a translation of a passage from the Lalitavistara which Krom believes the reliefs illustrate. Overall, this work is not a bad way to become acquainted with the Lalitavistara and with the most important narrative series of panels at Borobudur.

(15) PRZYLUSKI, JEAN. "Le partage des reliques du Bouddha." Mélanges Chinois et Bouddhiques, 4 (1936), 341-367.

Translations and discussions of Chinese vinaya texts and other legendary materials relevant to the dividing of the Buddha's relics immediately after his death as well as again later under Asoka. A helpful sequel to Przyluski's longer and more important "Le Parinirvana et les funérailles du Buddha" (see 8.1.2.3[22]).

(16) RHYS-DAVIDS, T. W. "Asoka and the Buddha Relics." Journal of the Royal Asiatic Society (1907), pp. 397-410.

8.1.3 The Buddha Bodies

(1) AKANUMA, CHIZEN. "The Triple Body of the Buddha." The Eastern Buddhist, 2 (1922), 1-29.

Chizen traces the development of Asanga's formulation of the tri-kaya from a doctrine of two bodies, emphasizing the role of popular religion.

(2) ANESAKI, MASAHARU. "Docetism," in Encyclopaedia of Religion and Ethics (see 1.15.1[9]), vol. 4, pp. 835-840.

A classic article which traces the "Buddhist tendency towards docetic ideas" from the early Theravada through the Mantrayana, including the development of the various doctrines concerning the bodies of the Buddha. Terminologically dated but still a valuable survey and introduction.

(3) CHAVANNES, EDOUARD. "Les Inscriptions Chinoises de Bodh-gaya." Revue de l'Histoire des Religions, 34 (1896), 1-58.

The tri-kaya is here shown as the subject of religious devotion and worship rather than philosophical discourse. Chavannes translates a hymn of praise to the three bodies

The Buddha

left as an inscription by Chinese pilgrims to Bodh-gaya. This is supplemented with translated passages from the Chinese Buddhist Canon also praising the tri-kaya.

(4) COEDES, GEORGES. "Dhammakaya." *Adyar Library Bulletin*, 20 (1956), 248-286.

An introduction (in French and English) and edition of a fascinating short Pali text entitled the *Dhammakayassa Atthavannana*. Each of the text's thirty paragraphs presents a single tenet of Buddhist doctrine and relates it to a part of the Buddha's body.

(5) DEMIEVILLE, PAUL. "Busshin," in *Hobogirin*. Tokyo: Maison Franco-Japonaise, 1930, Fasc. 2, pp. 174-185.

A survey of the development of the doctrines of the Buddha's bodies (Busshin means Buddha-kaya) in Hinayana and Mahayana schools with a special section on its interpretation in China. The article is especially useful for its many references to original materials.

(6) GUENTHER, HERBERT V. "The Psychology of the Three Kayas." *Uttara Bharati*, 2 (1955), 37-50.

Quoting Tibetan texts, Guenther tries to show that the three Kayas represent three different levels of experience.

(7) LA VALLEE POUSSIN, LOUIS DE. "Studies in Buddhist Dogma: The Three Bodies of a Buddha (Trikaya)." *Journal of the Royal Asiatic Society* (1906), pp. 943-977.

A survey of the evolution of the trikaya doctrine dealing in turn with the Dharmakaya, the Sambhogakaya, and the Nirmanakaya, tracing the origins, antecedents and development of each and their relationship to one another. The discussion here is at a philosophical and exegetical level. For a treatment that takes into account the more popular aspect (worship and praise of the three bodies) as well as later elaboration of doctrines of four and five bodies, see de La Vallée Poussin's "Notes sur les Corps du Bouddha," in *Vijnaptimatra Siddhi (La Siddhi de Hiuan Tsang* (3.3.3.2[6]), vol. 2, pp. 762-813 (App. III).

(8) MacDONALD, ALEXANDRE W. "La notion du sambhogakaya à la lumière de quelques faits ethnographiques." *Journal asiatique*, 243 (1955), 228-239.

One of the few discussions of the Sambhogakaya that gets away from philosophical and textual analysis. MacDonald reviews the relationship of food and power and communal eating in India and elsewhere, suggesting that the word "sambhuj" and its derivative "sambhoga" imply "eating together," and the Sambhogakaya refers to a communal body. MacDonald relies heavily on certain suggestions by Paul Mus in his *Barabudur* (see 2.5.2[8]), vol. 1, p. 264, and also in his "La Communion de l'Eglise dans le Buddha selon les textes pali," *Journal asiatique*, 228 (1936), 299-300.

(9) MASSON-OURSEL, PAUL. "Les Trois Corps du Bouddha." *Journal asiatique*, 2, no. 1 (1913), 581-618.

Dissatisfied with the interpretations of Suzuki (below) and de La Vallée Poussin (above), Masson-Oursel argues that the trikaya doctrine was largely the result of a double process of speculative divination and then contingent humanization. In his presentation, he pays more attention than they do to the Sambhogakaya, and also suggests possible Persian and neo-Platonic influences on the doctrine. He notes certain parallels with the Samkhya system and the Hindu trimurti. He also insists that even though the notion of the Dharmakaya rapidly took on ontological significance, it never lost its original meaning of "the Body of the Dharma."

(10) MUS, PAUL. "Le Bouddha Paré: Son origine indienne. Sakyamuni dans le Mahayanisme Moyen." See 3.3.5.2(3).

Mus, taking off on the search for the origins of a particular iconographic form, gives a new interpretation to the whole of the *Lotus Sutra* and, in the process, gives insights into the figure, nature and purpose of the Sambhogakaya and its relationship with the other bodies. This should be read with caution and is recommended for advanced students only.

(11) NAGAO, GADJIN. "On the Theory of Buddhabody (Buddha-kaya)." See 8.1.2.2(10).

An introduction to the Trikaya subject, tracing its development and its significance for religious philosophy.

(12) NAGARJUNA. *Catuhstava*. Partially translated by Giuseppe Tucci in "Two hymns of the Catuhstava of Nagarjuna." See 3.3.2.1(15).

(13) ROCKHILL, WILLIAM WOODVILLE. *The Life of the Buddha, and the Early History of His Order* (see 3.2.1.2[11]), pp. 200-202.

In these pages Rockhill translates a short sutra from the Tibetan bMah 'gyur dealing with the kayatraya (three bodies). The sutra is a conversation between the Buddha and Ksitigarbha in which the former gives various similes to explain the nature of each of his three bodies.

(14) STEIN, OTTO. "Notes on the Trikaya-Doctrine," in *Jha Commemoration Volume*. Poona Oriental Series, No. 39. Poona: Oriental Book Agency, 1937, pp. 389-398.

Stein sees the tri-kaya doctrine as one of the bridges from Hinayana to Mahayana, and so devotes the first portion of the article to a presentation of passages from the Pali Nikayas dealing with "kaya."

(15) SUZUKI, DAISETZ TEITARO. *Outlines of Mahayana Buddhism* (see 2.1[12]), chapters 9-10, pp. 217-276.

A somewhat dated, but still useful survey. For another discussion of the trikaya by

Suzuki, which is especially valuable for its tabulation of the various Chinese epithets of the three bodies, see his Studies in the Lankavatara Sutra (3.3.3.3[3]), pp. 308-338.

8.2 BUDDHAS OTHER THAN GAUTAMA

8.2.1 Previous Buddhas and Pratyeka Buddhas

(1) Asokavadana. Translated by Jean Przyluski as La légende de l'empereur Asoka. See 3.2.2.2(2).

Check the index for references to pratyekabuddhas, especially the important story of Upagupta's encounter with 500 pratyekabuddhas on Mount Urumunda. This particular legend gave rise to later scholastic debate about the nature of the pratyekabuddha (see Vasubandhu, Abhidharmakosa, translated by L. de La Vallée Poussin [3.2.3.2(4)], pp. 194 ff.).

(2) Avadana-Sataka. Translated by Leon Feer as Avadanaçataka, cent légendes (bouddhiques) (see 3.2.2.2[3]), pp. 91-111.

These pages, which make up one of the divisions of the Avadana-Sataka, contain a set of ten legends concerning pratyekabuddhas and specific acts of merit which lead to pratyekabodhi. They provide good examples of some of the legends that surround this figure.

(3) DORE, HENRY. Researches into Chinese Superstitions (see 4.1.3[3]), vol. 6, pp. 89-120.

A substantial article on the legends about and position of the former Buddha Dipamkara within Chinese Buddhism. Dore's is a dated treatment, but very useful for specific information of this kind.

(4) JONES, J. J., trans. The Mahavastu (see 3.2.1.2[5]), vol. 1, pp. 108-112, 152-207.

The first section includes a list of the 500 Buddhas which preceded Gautama, while the second section gives the history of two of these: Dipamkara and Mangala.

(5) KLOPPENBORG, RIA. The Paccekabuddha, Buddhist Ascetic. Leiden: E. J. Brill, 1974, 129 pp.

As the only book on the subject of the Paccekabuddha, this is especially valuable for bringing together a lot of material from the Pali canonical and commentarial literature, most notably the first translation of the stories about paccekabuddhas found in the commentary to the Khaggavisanasutta of the Suttanipata. However, the author does not touch on any of the Sanskrit and Mahayana traditions concerning the pratyekabuddha.

(6) LAMOTTE, ETIENNE, trans. Le traité de la grande vertu de sagesse de Nagarjuna (see 3.3.1.2[6]), vol. 1, pp. 531-557.

This passage contains the Mahayanist argument for the existence of a plurality of Buddhas and a refutation of the theory that Gautama was the only Buddha.

(7) LA VALLEE POUSSIN, LOUIS DE. "Adi Buddha," in Encyclopedia of Religion and Ethics (see 1.15.1[9]), vol. 1, pp. 93-100.

A fairly extended discussion concerned with this important figure of the Vajrayana school. The reader can glean some hints of Adi Buddha's implication for the problem of whether there was a mode of theism in this school of Buddhism.

(8) _____. "Pratyekabuddha," in Encyclopedia of Religion and Ethics (see 1.15.1[9]), vol. 10.

This is still a useful introduction to the concept and figure of the pratyekabuddha, especially in the Sanskrit literature. It makes a good complement to Ria Kloppenborg's book (above), which concentrates on the Pali texts.

(9) RHYS-DAVIDS, T. W. and C. A. F. RHYS-DAVIDS, trans. Digha Nikaya (Dialogues of the Buddha (see 2.7.1[13]), vol. 2, pp. 1-41.

These pages contain the "Mahapadana Sutta," which discusses the history of six Buddhas prior to Gautama.

8.2.2 Existing Buddhas (including Dhyani Buddhas)

(1) "Aksobhya," in Encyclopaedia of Buddhism (see 2.5.4[12]), vol. 1, pp. 363-368.

A very helpful article based on materials supplied by Zenkhyo Nakagawa and D. T. Devendra. For a listing of sutras and sources (most untranslated) useful for the study of this "dhyani" Buddha, see Hobogirin (Tokyo, 1929), s.v. "Ashuku."

(2) "Amita," in Encylopaedia of Buddhism (see 2.5.4[12]), vol. 1, pp. 434-463.

An excellent series of useful articles on this important Buddha of the Western Paradise. An introductory piece by G. P. Malalasekera is followed by articles on "The Appellations of Amita" by Kenryu Tsukinowa, on the cult of Amita by Jushin Ikemoto, and on Amita art by Ryogaku Tsumoto.

(3) Bhaisajyagurusutra. Translated by Nalinaksha Dutt in Gilgit Manuscripts (see 1.2.2.4[4]), vol. 1, pp. 47-57.

(4) FREEMANTLE, FRANCESCA and CHOGYAM TRUNGPA, trans. The Tibetan Book of the Dead (see 3.4.2[5]), pp. 15-22.

The first five days of the Bardo-intermediate state experience involve successive visions of the five Dhyani Buddhas, which are described and discussed here by Chogyam Trungpa in his introduction.

(5) KANAOKA, SHUYU. "Vairocana in Tathagata Form." Indogaku Bukkyogaku Kenkyu/Journal of Indian and Buddhist Studies, 13, no. 2 (1965), 821-814 (sic).

A short article arguing for distinction between the forms of Vairocana as a Dhyani Buddha and also in the guide of a bodhisattva.

Bodhisattvas

(6) KARIYANWASAM, A. G. S. "Amoghasiddhi," in Encyclopaedia of Buddhism (see 2.5.4[12]), vol. 1, pp. 478-482.

A short but very helpful article specifically on the characteristics and position of the "dhyani" Buddha.

(7) MIBU, TAISHUN. "On the Theory of Five Buddhas in Guhyasamaja-tantra." Indogaku Bukkyogaku Kenkyu/Journal of Indian and Buddhist Studies, 21, no. 2 (1973), 1053-1039 (sic).

A technical discussion of various arrangements and groupings of the five dhyani Buddhas in this important Tantric text, opposing the "Aksobhya family" to the "Vairocana family."

(8) MUS, PAUL. Barabudur (see 2.5.2[8]), vol. 2, pp. 435-474.

Sections xiii-b to xvi of Mus's monumental Barabudur deal specifically with various aspects of the scheme of the five "dhyani" Buddhas. See especially "Les cinq sens et les cinq Buddhas," "Pancendriya," and "Des cinq Agni aux cinq Jinas." In many ways, they represent the final outcome of his work, and readers should be familiar with that in order to put these passages in their proper perspective.

(9) NANAYAKKARA, S. K. "Bhaisajyaguru," in Encyclopaedia of Buddhism (see 2.5.4[12]), vol. 2, pp. 661-666.

A helpful and fairly substantial article on this important "Buddha of Medicine" known as Yakushi Nyorai in Japan and Yo-shih-fu in China. For a translation of a text which invokes Bhaisajyaguru, see Jean Filliozat, "Un chapitre du rgyud-bzi" (see 7.5.2[2]). And for a survey of the "Rites of Repentance in Worship of the Buddha Bhaisajyaguru," see M. W. de Visser, Ancient Buddhism in Japan (1.13.2.1[8]), pp. 239-308.

(10) ROBINSON, RICHARD. The Buddhist Religion (see 1.1.[8]), pp. 58-70.

(11) SAUNDERS, E. DALE. "A Note on Shakti and Dhyanibuddha." History of Religions, 1, no. 2 (Winter 1962), 300-306.

A brief article in which the author argues that the terms "shakti" and "dhyanibuddha" have been misused in Buddhist scholarship: that the former should be restricted to Hindu tantrism and that the latter should be replaced by "Tathagata" or "Jina" which, unlike "dhyanibuddha," occur in the original texts.

(12) TAJIMA, RYUJUN. Etude sur le Mahavairocana Sutra. See 2.6.2(9).

(13) VISSER, M. W. DE. "Rites of Repentance in Worship of the Buddha Amitabha," translated in his Ancient Buddhism in Japan (see 1.13.2.1[8]), pp. 318-350.

8.3   BODHISATTVAS

8.3.1   General Discussions

(1) BHATTACHARYYA, BENOYTOSH. The Indian Buddhist Iconography. London: Oxford, 1924, 220 pp.

This volume is basically a collection of Vajrayana materials from the eighth to the eleventh century. Bhattacharyya discusses Dhyanibuddhas, Bodhisattvas, and Bodhishakti emanations as they have been represented in iconography.

(2) "Bosatsukai," in Hobogirin: Dictionnaire Encyclopédique du Bouddhisme. Tokyo, 1930.

This article in the Franco-Japanese Hobogirin discusses a number of important Mahayana texts dealing with the morality of the Bodhisattva. It is extremely helpful for those who want references to original texts. It may also be supplemented by the more specific canonical passages cited in the notes of Etienne Lamotte's Traité de la Grande Vertu de Sagesse (see 3.3.1.2[6]), throughout the section dealing with morality (vol. 2, pp. 770-864).

(3) CONZE, EDWARD, trans. Astasahasrika Prajnaparamita (see 8.1.2.2[2]), pp. 1-18, 104-110, 121-129, 146-151.

These pages represent examples of how the Prajnaparamita understands the nature and functions of the Bodhisattva. Included are discussions as to the meaning of the word, the eight ways in which Bodhisattvas help beings, the danger of falling back, and the signs of "irreversibility."

(4) DAYAL, HAR. The Bodhisattva Doctrine in Buddhist Sanskrit Literature. Delhi: Motilal Banarsidass, 1970, 392 pp. (Originally published 1932.)

A standard, straightforward, and thorough discussion of all aspects of the bodhisattva and his path, with chapters on the origin and development of the doctrine, on bodhicitta, on the paramitas, on the Bhumis, and on the bodhisattva's last life and enlightenment. Useful for references to texts and to the works of other scholars on the subject. See, for example, the listing of opinions on the etymology of the word "boddhisattva" itself, p. 4 ff.

(5) FOUCHER, ALFRED. Etude sur l'iconographie bouddhique de l'Inde (see 1.2.2.3[5]), vol. 1, pp. 99-127; vol. 2, pp. 22-49.

Foucher discusses the cults, iconography, and texts associated with Bodhisattvas in late Indian Mahayana.

(6) GETTY, ALICE. The Gods of Northern Buddhism. Revised edition. Rutland, Vt.: C. E. Tuttle, 1962, 220 pp.

The primary focus of Getty's classic work is on the iconography of the various bodhisattvas which expresses the Mahayana conception of these figures.

8.3.1 Bodhisattvas

(7) LAMOTTE, ETIENNE, trans. Le traité de la grand vertu de Nagarjuna (see 3.3.1.2[6]), vol. 1, pp. 235-356, 428-430.

The three chapters included here present the standard Mahayana views of the Bodhisattva figure. Chapter 8 includes an etymology of the terms, a discussion concerning the differing conceptions of the Bodhisattva in the Mahayana and Hinayana schools, and the differences between a Bodhisattva and the Sravaka and Pratyekabuddha figures. Chapter 9 explains the meaning of "Mahasattva," a primary epithet for bodhisattvas. Chapter 10 refers to the eighteen qualities of the Bodhisattva. Pages 428-430 contain a list of twenty-two principal bodhisattvas and makes the interesting distinction between "lay" and "religious" bodhisattvas.

(8) LA VALLEE POUSSIN, LOUIS DE. "Bodhisattvas," in Encyclopedia of Religion and Ethics (see 1.15.1[9]), vol. 2, pp. 739-752.

This article could still be the best brief introductory piece on the subject. The author discusses the etymology of the word, the most significant meaning of the term for representative schools, and the typical career of the Bodhisattva.

(9) MATSUNAGA, ALICIA. The Buddhist Philosophy of Assimilation (see 4.1.4[6]).

(10) MIRONOV, N. D. "Buddhist Miscellanea." Journal of the Royal Asiatic Society of Great Britain and Ireland (1927), pp. 241-252.

A scholarly article focusing upon the etymological roots of the term "bodhisattva" from Sanskrit, Chinese, Tibetan, and Mongolian sources. The author has also attempted to trace the exact meaning of "Avalokitesvara" and "Avalokata isvari" in relation to the Chinese "Kuan-Yin."

(11) RAHULA, WALPOLA. "L'idéal du Bodhisattva dans le Theravada et le Mahayana." Journal asiatique, 259 (1971), 63-70.

An excellent introduction to the study of the bodhisattva notion in both Hinayana and Mahayana, something which is often neglected by scholars who see the former vehicle as solely preoccupied with notions of arhatship.

(12) ROBINSON, RICHARD. The Buddhist Religion (see 1.1[8]), pp. 58-70.

A basic and convenient source of general information about the major celestial Buddhas and Bodhisattvas.

(13) SANGHARAKSITA, BHIKSU. "Four Great Bodhisattvas." Aryan Path, 34, no. 6 (June 1963), 238-240; and "Three Family Protectors in Tibet," Aryan Path, 34, no. 2 (February 1963), 62-67.

In these two brief articles, Sangharaksita discusses in general fashion the significance of the following bodhisattvas: Maitreya, Kshitigarbha, Samantabhadra, Avalokitesvara, Manjusri, and Vajrapana.

(14) SARKISYANZ, E. Buddhist Backgrounds of the Burmese Revolution. See 1.4.2(15).

A study which underscores throughout the importance of the Bodhisattva ideal not only for Burmese kingship, but also for kingship in other Theravada countries. The author shows how kings were considered to be Bodhisattvas who have potential for becoming the future Buddha. He emphasizes the ethical implications this notion had for Buddhist kingship.

(15) SUZUKI, D. T. Outlines of Mahayana Buddhism (see 2.1[12]), pp. 242-307.

One of the earliest (1907) and still very useful general introductions to the Mahayana conception of the Bodhisattva.

(16) THOMAS, E. J. History of Buddhist Thought (see 2.1[14]), pp. 189-211.

A brief discussion, among others, concerned with the general nature of the Bodhisattva and a brief review of some careers.

8.3.2 Avalokitesvara/Kuan-yin

(1) BEAL, SAMUEL, trans. "The Liturgy of Kwan-Yin," in A Catena of Buddhist Scriptures from the Chinese (see 3.2.1.2[7]), pp. 396-409.

(2) BENVENISTE, EMILE, trans. "Avalokitesvarasya namastasataka stotra," in Textes sogdiens. Paris: P. Geuthner, 1940, pp. 105-115. (Mission Pelliot, No. 3.)

An interesting hymn of praise calling out and on the one hundred eight names of the Bodhisattva of Compassion, Avalokitesvara, translated from the Sogdian into French.

(3) CHAMBERLAYNE, JOHN H. "The Development of Kuan Yin: Chinese Goddess of Mercy," Numen, 9 (1962), 45-52.

A brief and not very original look at Kuan-yin (Avalokitesvara) within the context of other Chinese female deities, with some reference to the question of sex change.

(4) CHAPIN, HELEN B. "Yunnanese Images of Avalokitesvara." Harvard Journal of Asiatic Studies, 8 (1944-1945), 131-186.

Although the author is primarily interested in Avalokitesvara as he/she is represented in artistic expression, the reader will be able to draw the conclusion that the figure was received as a "dynastic talisman" during the time under consideration in Yunnan.

(5) DORE, HENRY. Researches into Chinese Superstitions (see 4.1.3[3]), vol. 6, pp. 134-234.

Though dated in both its approach and treatment, this still represents one of the most data-filled sources on the figure of Avalokitesvara (Kuan-yin) in China. As a background to the well known sex change of this bodhisattva, Dore gives a full account of the legend of the ancient Chinese princess Miao-shen, and then goes on to discuss various representations of Kuan-yin, emblems and symbols of the goddess (such as the willow branch), and, very briefly, worship and festivals of Kuan-yin.

(6) KERN, HENDRIK, trans. Saddharma-Pundarika or the Lotus of the True Law (see 3.3.5.1[2]), pp. 406-418.

This chapter of the "Lotus Sutra" is concerned with a description of the bodhisattva Avalokitesvara and the great advantage of relying upon this particular bodhisattva.

(7) LA VALLEE POUSSIN, LOUIS DE. "Avalokitesvara," in Encyclopaedia of Religion and Ethics (see 1.15.1[9]), vol. 2, pp. 256-261.

A readily available and still valuable scholarly introduction to the figure of the great bodhisattva Avalokitesvara. See also in the same encyclopedia (Volume 7, pp. 763-765) J. Takakusu's shorter article on "Kwan-yin."

(8) MALLMANN, MARIE-THERESE DE. Introduction à l'Etude d'Avalokitesvara. Annales du Musée Guimet, 57. Paris, 1948, 345 pp.

A thorough and now classic work which is indispensable to any serious study of this major bodhisattva. The book is divided into five sections. The first presents and discusses relevant textual materials from the Pure Land Sutras, the Lotus, the Lokesvara sataka, the Karanda-vyuha, and the Sadhanamala. Part 2 reviews all the theories about the etymology of Avalokitesvara's name. Part 3 is entitled "La place d'Avalokitesvara dans la pensée religieuse de l'Inde," and Parts 4 and 5 deal respectively with chronology and stylistics of images of the bodhisattva. See also on this work Jean Filliozat, "Avalokitesvara d'après un livre recent," Revue de l'Histoire des Religions, 137 (1950), 44-58.

(9) NANAYAKKARA, S. K. "Avalokitesvara," in Encyclopaedia of Buddhism (see 2.5.4[12]), vol. 2, pp. 407-415.

A good introductory article to all aspects of the study of this most important bodhisattva, in South and East Asia as well as in Tibet.

(10) PARANAVITANA, S. "Mahayanism in Ceylon." See 1.3.1(7).

One of the very few studies of the position of Avalokitesvara (and Tara) in Theravada Sri Lanka. Provides a helpful glimpse of the widespread popularity of this bodhisattva.

(11) STAEL-HOLSTEIN, A. VON. "Avalokita and Apalokita." Harvard Journal of Asiatic Studies, 1 (1936), 350-362.

A pedantic article in which the author seeks out the etymology of the term "Avalokita" by consulting primary and secondary sources.

(12) SUZUKI, D. T. "The Cult of Kwannon." See 7.8(12).

These pages are part of a larger article entitled "Impressions of Chinese Buddhism." Suzuki provides the reader with a general overview of Kwannon by listing the chief sources which deal with Avalokitesvara, gives a perspective on the significance of Kwannon from a Japanese Buddhist perspective (Pure Land), and then compares the figure to Amida.

(13) TUCCI, GIUSEPPE. "Buddhist Notes I: A propos Avalokitesvara." Mélanges chinois et bouddhique, 9 (1948-1951), 173-219.

One of the best sources available concerned with Avalokitesvara. Tucci discusses the possible origins of the figure and also the various ways in which Avalokitesvara has been represented.

(14) VAJRADATTA. Lokesvarasatakama. Translated by Suzanne Karpeles as "Cent strophes en l'honneur du seigneur du monde." Journal asiatique, 14 (1919), 357-465.

A translation with an edition of the Tibetan and Sanskrit texts of a long, 100 stanza invocation and praise of the Bodhisattva Avalokitesvara.

8.3.3 Tara

(1) BEYER, STEPHAN. The Cult of Tara: Magic and Ritual in Tibet. See 7.1.1(2).

Unquestionably the most thorough work in English on the cult and rituals associated with the goddess Tara, giving full descriptions of ritual practices, explanations, interpretations, and translations of cultic texts. At the same time the work is more than just a study of the cult of Tara, and seeks to illuminate the basic ritual structure and patterns that underlie other Tibetan rituals as well.

(2) SHASTRI. HIRANANDA. "Origin and Cult of Tara." See 7.8(10).

A basic, well done article in which the author discusses the problem of the origin and worship of the cult of Tara. The author contends that the Tara cult did not become established until some time after the fifth century.

(3) SIRCAR, DINESH CHANDRA, ed. The Shakti Cult and Tara. See 7.8(11).

This volume contains a collection of useful articles on the iconography and worship of Tara carried out by both Buddhist and Hindu Tantrics.

(4) WAYMAN, ALEX. "The Twenty-One Praises of Tara." See 7.8(18).

8.3.4 Maitreya

See also 9.1.4, The Coming of Maitreya.

(1) BARUCH, W. "Maitreya d'après les sources de Serinde." Revue de l'Histoire des Religions, 132 (1946), 67-92.

An examination and discussion of various Central Asian sources on the figure of Maitreya--artistic representations, literary documents, dedicatory inscriptions, and religious texts, especially the Maitreya-samiti which is treated in some detail. Also included is the translation of a Tibetan "Hymn to Maitreya."

(2) CHAPIN, HELEN B. "The Ch'an Master Putai." Journal of the American Oriental Society, 53 (1933), 47-52. See also 8.9.3[66].

(3) DEMIEVILLE, PAUL. "Maitreya l'inspirateur" and "Le paradis de Maitreya." Bulletin de l'Ecole française d'Extrême-Orient, 44 (1954), 376-387 and 387-395.

(4) FILLIOZAT, JEAN. "Maitreya l'invaincu." Journal asiatique, 238 (1950), 145-49.

A short discussion of Maitreya's epithet "Ajita," the "unconquered one," and of the parallelism that has been suggested between it and Mithra's epithet, "Sol Invictus." Filliozat cautiously seeks to undermine the arguments of Levi and Przyluski, and to suggest the possibility of influence operating in the other direction: from India on Iran.

(5) LAMOTTE, ETIENNE. Histoire du Bouddhisme Indien (see 1.2.1[10]), pp. 775-788.

The whole section is entitled "Le Messie Maitreya" and makes a fine summary of various sources and scholarly debates over the figure of Maitreya. Very useful as a substantial and serious introduction to the different aspects of the bodhisattva.

(6) LEVI, SYLVAIN. "Maitreya le consolateur," in Etudes d'Orientalisme Publiées par le Musée Guimet à la Mémoire de Raymond Linossier. Paris, 1932, vol. 2, pp. 360 ff.

A classic article on the figure of Maitreya, on the "eschatological" conceptions that surround him, and on the parallels between him and other figures such as Mithra, Mitra, etc. For a different view of the bodhisattva, see Jean Filliozat, "Maitreya l'invaincu" (above).

(7) Maitreyavyakarana. Translated by Edward Conze in Buddhist Scriptures (see 8.1.2.3[7]), pp. 237-242.

Translation of excerpts from the Maitreyavyakarana, one of the classic sources for the "prediction concerning Maitreya." Unfortunately Conze has not enlarged upon his rendition of the text.

(8) PRZYLUSKI, JEAN. "La Croyance au messie dans l'Inde et dans l'Iran." See 9.1.4(6).

8.3.5 Manjusri

(1) BHATTACHARYYA, BENOYTOSH. "Manjughosa," in Jha Commemoration Volume. Poona: Oriental Book Agency, 1937, pp. 59-68.

A brief but helpful discussion of the various aspects of the bodhisattva Manjusri (Manjughosa), based primarily on the Sadhanamala.

(2) LAMOTTE, ETIENNE. "Manjusri." T'oung Pao, 48 (1960), 1-96.

An excellent, authoritative study of the figure of the bodhisattva Manjusri, devoting separate chapters to the history of his cult, to his position in the cosmic scheme, and to his role in India, in Khotan and Nepal, and in China (where the focus is on Mt. Wu-t'ai and on the Avatamsaka sutra). Includes translations of important relevant passages from Chinese texts.

(3) MALLMAN, MARIE-THERESE DE. Etude Iconographique sur Manjusri. Paris: Ecole française d'Extrême-Orient, 1964, 285 pp.

Basically an iconographic study, but the only full-length book on this important bodhisattva, and a fundamental work on the subject. It makes a fine complement to Lamotte's article "Manjusri" (above).

8.3.6 Other Bodhisattvas

(1) DORE, HENRY. Researches into Chinese Superstitions (see 4.1.3[3]), vol. 7, pp. 235-249.

Dated in its approach, but useful for its information on various Chinese traditions concerning the important bodhisattva Kshitigarbha, known as Ti-tsang in China.

(2) HANDURUKANDE, RATNA, ed. and trans. "Manicudavadana," in F. Max Müller et al., Sacred Books of the East. Vol. 24, pp. 106-146.

The story of the bodhisattva Manicuda is an avadana (legend) presented in the form of a Jataka (birth stories of the Buddha). It extolls the virtue of selfless giving for the sake of enlightenment for all beings. The only dated manuscript of the story is of the late eighteenth century, but clearly the work is based upon much earlier material (possibly the fourth through eleventh centuries). Handurukande has rendered this version in prose and verse form.

(3) HOKEI, IDZUMI. "The Hymn on the Life and Vows of Samantabhadra." Eastern Buddhist, 5 (1930), 226-247.

Includes editing and translation of the so-called Bhadra-cari-pranidhana, a text dealing with the vows of the bodhisattva Samantabhadra, which was translated three times into Chinese, and incorporated into the Avatamsaka Sutra. For a different and partial translation entitled "The Great Vows of Samantabhadra," see Garma C. C. Chang, The Buddhist

Teaching of Totality (see 3.3.1.2[4]), pp. 187-196.

(4) LAMOTTE, ETIENNE. "Vajrapani en Inde," in Mélanges de Sinologie Offerts à M. Paul Demieville. Paris: Presses Universitaires, 1966, 1974, pp. 113-159.

A useful article on this important and widespread Bodhisattva figure. See also on this figure the rather diffuse article by Marcelle Lalou, "Four Notes on Vajrapani," Adyar Library Bulletin, 20 (1956), 287-293.

(5) LESSING, FERDINAND. "Bodhisattva Confucius." See 7.8(7).

(6) LU K'UAN-YU, trans. The Vimalakirti Nirdesa Sutra. See 3.3.2.1[35], pp. 57-61, 86-91.

In the first passage, Vimalakirti tells Manjusri how a Bodhisattva should behave when facing emptiness. The second passage contains Vimalakirti's song on the characteristics of the Bodhisattvas.

(7) SOGA, RYOJIN. "Dharmakara Bodhisattva." Translated and edited by Enyo Ito and Shojun Banjo. Eastern Buddhist, 1, no. 1 (September 1965), 64-78.

A scholarly treatment of Dharmakara (this is Amida in his stage of discipline) which also shows how the Pure Land tradition is a logical continuance of Mahayana. Further, the reader will find some remarks aimed at showing how Pure Land cannot be compared to Pauline-based Christian Protestantism.

(8) VISSER, MARINUS WILLEM DE. The Bodhisattva Akasagarbha (Kokuzo) in China and Japan. See 7.8(15).

(9) _____. The Bodhisattva Ti-tsang (Jizo) in China and Japan. See 7.8(16).

8.4 ARHATS (INCLUDING LOHANS)

(1) "Arahant," in Encyclopaedia of Buddhism (see 2.5.4[12]), vol. 2.

A fine and substantial introduction to the whole scope of meanings of the word and conception of arhats, in both Theravada and Mahayana Buddhism, written jointly by W. G. Weeraratne, G. P. Malalasekera, and Chou Shu-chia.

(2) AUNG, SHWE ZAN and C. A. F. RHYS-DAVIDS. Points of Controversy (The Katha-vatthu) (see 3.2.3.1[5]), pp. 64-70, 114-119 and 157-163.

In these passages and a few others in the text, the reader will find discussions concerned with the figure of the arhat. Among the controversial points that are settled are the questions: Can an arhat fall from arhatship? Does he ever have doubts about the truth? Is he always indifferent to his senses? Does he still accumulate merit? And, can a layman become an arhat?

(3) DORE, HENRY. Researches into Chinese Superstitions (see 4.1.3[3]), vol. 7, pp. 332-387.

Deals concisely with the various listings and descriptions of the lohans (arhats) in China. In addition to the usual groupings of sixteen and eighteen lohan, those of thirty-two, 108, 500, etc. are touched upon.

(4) EVOLA, GIULIO CESARE. The Doctrine of Awakening. Translated by H. E. Musson. London: Luzac, 1951, 310 pp.

An insightful presentation which examines the ideal of the arhat by focusing upon the regimen and goal of the practitioner. Translated from the original Italian.

(5) HOFINGER, MARCEL, trans. Le congrès du Lac Anavatapta (Vie de saints bouddhiques). See 3.2.1.2(1).

Hofinger has translated a portion of the Vinaya of the Mulasarvastivadins which deal principally with legends of thirty-six famous elders.

(6) HORNER, ISALINE BLEW. The Early Buddhist Theory of Man Perfected. London: Williams and Norgate, 1936, 327 pp.

A fine, highly recommended volume by a noted Pali scholar in which the conception of arhat is thoroughly discussed. The author draws her discussion from the Pali canon and often interjects her authoritative conjectures.

(7) _____. "The Four Ways and the Four Fruits of Buddhism." Indian Historical Quarterly, 10 (1934), 785-796.

A concise consideration of the development and elaboration of the notion of arhatship in early Buddhism with specific reference to the division of the path into stages of "stream-winner," "once-returner," "non-returner," and "arhatship."

(8) LAMOTTE, ETIENNE. Histoire du Bouddhisme Indien (see 1.2.1[10]), pp. 768 ff.

An extremely useful introduction to the various theories of the four, eight, sixteen, and eighteen arhats or lohans. Contains valuable references to untranslated materials, and is especially useful for tracing the origins and development of the doctrine. For a list of references to the conceptions of arhats, primarily within the Pali canon (and thus within translated texts), see Har Dayal, The Bodhisattva Doctrine in Buddhist Sanskrit Literature (8.3.1[4]), p. 319, no.1.

(9) _____. Le traité de la grand vertue de sagesse de Nagarjuna (see 3.3.1.2[6]), vol. 1, pp. 203-225.

In this passage, various etymologies of the word "arhat" are presented along with the Mahayana understanding of the terms. In addition, the reader will find an explanation as to why Ananda was not an arhat.

(10) LEVI, SYLVAIN and EDOUARD CHAVANNES. "Les seize arhat protecteurs de la Loi." See 3.3.8.2(6).

A masterful article by two well known scholars of the history of Buddhism, in which the relationship between the sixteen arhats and the "Mahayana canon" is explored. The authors show how and why the arhat rejects nirvana temporarily to stay in the world to protect and promote the law. There are also discussions on the iconographic representation of the sixteen arhats and on the question of sixteen or eighteen arhats.

(11) LEVY, PAUL. Buddhism: A Mystery Religion? (see 7.2.1[5]), pp. 82-96.

Levy here treats the rather unusual figure of Gavampati, the arhat in whom both human and animal seem to be intimately infused. It has been conjectured that Gavampati became the prototypical arhat for members of a Buddhist mystery cult which required special initiation apart from Sangha membership.

(12) PRIP-MOLLER, J. Chinese Buddhist Monasteries (see 7.2.1[7]), pp. 104-122.

Many of the larger Chinese monasteries contain Lo Han T'ang--halls in which are arranged statues of the 500 lo-hans (arhats), a very popular group in Chinese Buddhism. In surveying a number of these Lo-han t'ang, Prip-Moller discusses the interesting case of the incorporation of Marco Polo into the group, and includes a fascinating picture of a statue of the explorer in a monastery in Canton.

(13) RAHULA, WALPOLA. History of Buddhism in Ceylon (see 1.3.1[10]), pp. 217-229.

A discussion of arhats in Ceylon, with attention given both to the phenomenon in general and to specific arhats.

(14) RHYS-DAVIDS, C. A. F., trans. The Book of Kindred Sayings (Samyutta Nikaya) (see 2.7.7[10]), vol. 2, pp. 131-152.

This section of the Samyutta Nikaya contains much information on Maha-Kassapa, a disciple of the Buddha who is presented as exemplary of arhatship.

(15) The Sixteen Arhats and the Eighteen Arhats. Compiled by the Shah Shin Buddhist Institute. Peking: Buddhist Association of China, 1961.

This rare little book, published to commemorate the 1550th anniversary of Fa Hien's visit to Ceylon, contains a translation of the Record of the Abiding of the Dharma, a short text attributed to Nandimitra (a Ceylonese monk) and translated into Chinese by Hsuan Tsang during the T'ang dynasty. The text is an important source of information about the sixteen lohan (arhats) who were often portrayed in Chinese sculpture. The introductory piece explains how the sixteen lohan were expanded to eighteen in China.

(16) SUZUKI, D. T. Outlines of Mahayana Buddhism (see 2.1[12]), pp. 227-307.

Suzuki contrasts the ideal of Arhatship with the doctrine of Pratyekabuddhas and the Mahayanist attitude towards both.

(17) THOMAS, EDWARD J. "Epithets of an Arhat in the Divyavadana." Indian Historical Quarterly, 17 (1941), 104-107.

A discussion of the meaning of a sentence in the Divyavadana which describes an arhat. It is useful for the Hinayana but non-Theravada understanding of the nature of an arhat.

(18) VISSER, MARINUS WILLEM DE. "The Arhats in China and Japan." Ostasiatische Zeitschrift (April-September 1918), pp. 87-102; and (April-September 1920-1921), pp. 116-144.

The author discusses the change from arhat into bodhisattva.

8.5 PERFECTED YOGINS: SIDDHAS

(1) BAGCHI, P. C. "The Cult of the Buddhist Saddhacaryas," in The Cultural History of India. Edited by H. Bhattacharya. Calcutta: Ramakrishna Mission, 1956, pp. 273-279.

A very general article which would be good for undergraduates to look at.

(2) MONIER-WILLIAMS, MONIER. Buddhism, in Its Connection with Brahmanism, and in Its Contrast with Christianity. Second edition. Varanasi: Chowkhamba Sanskrit Series Office, 1964, pp. 223-252.

This is a decent presentation of the Mahayana beliefs concerning the magical powers of Yogis. The author supplements his presentation with frequent references to his first-hand observations of yogic practices.

(3) SCHMID, TONI. The Eighty-Five Siddhas. Stockholm: State Ethnographic Museum, 1958, 171 pp. and plates.

A presentation of iconographic depictions of the siddhas with some explanatory notes. Probably it is best used along with individual accounts of the lives of the siddhas.

(4) SHASTRI, J. "The Doctrinal Culture and Tradition of the Siddhas," in The Cultural Heritage of India. Edited by H. Bhattacharya. Calcutta: Ramakrishna Mission, 1937, vol. 2, pp. 303-319.

Another general article in which the character of Siddhas is discussed. It is of value as an introduction for the undergraduate student.

8.6 DEITIES OTHER THAN GAUTAMA AND BODHISATTVAS

(1) BHATTACHARYYA, BENOYTOSH. "The Cult of Bhutadharma." See 7.8(4).

A basic study of this tantric cult containing a wealth of information about the Buddhist deity Bhutadharma.

Cakravartins

(2) EVERS, HANS-DIETER. "Buddha and the Seven Gods." See 4.1.1(5).
This short article is basically a description of the dual organization of a Sinhalese temple which Evers then tries to analyze, showing the intimate connection between worship of the Buddha and worship with other deities.

(3) LESSING, FERDINAND D. Yung Ho Kung (see 7.5.3[3]), vol. 1, pp. 139-147.

(4) MONIER-WILLIAMS, MONIER. Buddhism, in Its Connection with Brahmanism and in Its Contrast with Christianity (see 8.5.2[2]), pp. 172-205.
These pages from Monier-Williams' work, which was originally published in 1889, give an account of the rise of Mahayana Buddhism, with special emphasis on the proliferation of ideal beings in the emerging Buddhist pantheon.

(5) PERI, NOEL. "Hariti, la mère des démons." See 9.2.2.5(9).

(6) REICHELT, KARL. Truth and Tradition in Chinese Buddhism (see 1.11.1[8]), pp. 171-205.
The reader will here find a rare detailed description of the Chinese Buddhist pantheon.

(7) TUCCI, GIUSEPPE. "Nomina, Numina," in Myths and Symbols: Studies in Honor of Mircea Eliade (see 8.1.2.2[1]), pp. 3-7.
This short but valuable article discusses the process of formation of many Vajrayana deities. Tucci is especially interested in the way in which practically any idea or object of importance in early Buddhism could be turned into a deity in the tantric vehicle.

(8) VAN GULIK, R. H. Hayagriva--The Mantrayanic Aspect of Horse-Cult in China and Japan. See 7.8(13).

(9) WADDELL, L. AUSTINE. Tibetan Buddhism (see 1.14.1[17]), pp. 324-386.
This is Waddell's attempt to present an orderly classification of what he calls "the disorderly mob" which is constitutive of the Lamaist pantheon. His general and descriptive list of this "chaotic crew" includes Buddhas, Bodhisats, Tutelaries, Defenders (of the faith--witches included), Brahmanical gods, country and personal gods.

8.7   CAKRAVARTINS

(1) ARCHAIMBAULT, C., trans. Les Trois Mondes (Traibhumi Brah R'van) (see 3.2.4.2[4]), pp. 86-111.
In the course of its description of "The Realm of Men," this important Thai cosmological text written in 1345 provides a long description of the cakkavatti, "la monarque universel," including separate sections devoted to each of his seven precious jewels.

(2) GOKHALE, B. G. "Early Buddhist Kingship." Journal of Asian Studies, 26, no. 1 (November 1966), 15-22.
This article includes a brief discussion of the influence of the cakravartin motif for Buddhist kingship.

(3) PRZYLUSKI, JEAN. "La ville du Cakravartin--influences babyloniennes sur la civilisation de l'Inde." Rocznik Orientalistyczny, 5 (1927), 165-185.
By a comparison of the city of the Cakravartin as described in the Mahusudassana sutta and of various other cities including Echatana, Przyluski tries to argue ultimately for a Babylonian origin to certain cakravartin motifs. Interesting, but for wary readers.

(4) RHYS-DAVIDS, T. W. and C. A. F. RHYS-DAVIDS, trans. Digha Nikaya (see 2.7.1[13]), vol. 2, pp. 192-232; vol. 3, pp. 53-76.
Contains the Mahasudassana sutta and the Cakkavatti Sihanada sutta, both extremely important to any study of the ideal figure of the cakravartin. The first sutta tells the story of the "great king of glory"--a cakravartin who ruled long ago in Kusinagara. His "seven jewels," his city, and his palace are all described. The second sutta considers the cakravartin's role in the cyclical ebb and flow of universal history.

(5) SARKISYANZ, EMANUEL. Buddhist Backgrounds of the Burmese Revolution. See 1.4.2(15).
A treatment that is useful for the beginning as well as the advanced student. Sarkisyanz reviews the poltiical history of Burma and traces its political and economic institutions (as well as the Sangha) back to the legends of Asoka. Specifically, his account of the revival of Buddhism in the early twentieth century is the best of its kind. A basic contention here, contrary to Max Weber, is that Buddhism is capable of generating rational economic activity.

(6) SENART, EMILE. Essai sur la Légende du Bouddha (see 8.1.2.3[28]), pp. 1-86.
In this first chapter of his work, Senart uses the cakravartin motif and symbol to bolster his interpretation of the figure of the Buddha in solar mythology terms. Though it should be read in light of later critiques of Senart's views, this remains an important discussion of the topic of cakravartins.

(7) SNELLGROVE, D. L. "The Notion of Divine Kingship in Tantric Buddhism." See 6.2.2.7(8).

(8) THIERRY, S. "La personne sacrée du roi dans la littérature populaire cambodienne." See 6.2.2.8(9).
The author examines the popular conceptions concerning kings found in Cambodian litera-

ture. The cakravartin motif is discussed in conjunction with the notion of a king's accumulation of merit.

8.8 BHIKSUS AND THE BUDDHA'S DISCIPLES

(1) Anguttara Nikaya. Translated by F. L. Woodward in The Book of the Gradual Sayings (see 3.2.2.1[1]), vol. 1, no. 14.
This sutra entitled the Etadaggavagga or "The Pre-eminent Ones" is a canonical listing of the Buddha's disciples with a brief statement concerning the fame of each. Woodward's translation is also useful for its cross references to stories about many of these disciples in other parts of the Pali Canon, especially the Theragatha and Therigatha.

(2) ASVAGHOSA. Saundarananda. See 3.2.4.1(2).

(3) BAREAU, ANDRE. Recherches sur la biographie du Bouddha dans les Sutrapitaka et les Vinayapitaka anciens. See 8.1.2.3(5).
A thorough study of the Sutra and Vinaya materials concerned with the life of the Buddha from his great departure to the conversions of Sariputa and Maudgalyayana. A valuable contribution to the study of the life of the Buddha.

(4) BODE, MABEL. "The Legend of Ratthapala in the Pali Apadana and Buddhaghosa's Commentary." See 4.2.3(7).

(5) EDKINS, JOSEPH. Chinese Buddhism. London: Trubner and Co., 1880, pp. 60-86.
In this chapter, entitled "The Patriarchs of the Northern Buddhist," Edkins gives the stories of the twenty-seven successive patriarchs of Buddhism, starting with Mahakasyapa and Ananda and ending with Bodhidharma (the twenty-eighth Indian patriarch but first Chinese patriarch). This account is based on the Chinese apocryphal text, the Fu fa-chang yin-yuan chuan, which was written in the sixth century. For a listing of the same patriarchs and the verses they uttered when transmitting the Dharma, see "The Forty Transmission Gathas," taken from The Transmission of the Lamp (Ching Te Ch'uan Teng Lu), translated by Lu K'uan Yu (below).

(6) HOCART, A. M. "Buddha and Devadatta." Indian Antiquary, 52 (1923), 267-272.
An analysis of Devadatta's antagonism towards the Buddha in terms of the friendly and ceremonial antagonism between cross-cousins which was traditional in certain kinds of kinship systems which Hocard hypothesizes to have predominated in the Buddha's time and place.

(7) LAMOTTE, ETIENNE. "Le Bouddha insulta-t-il Devadatta?" Bulletin of the School of Oriental and African Studies, 33 (1970), 107-115.

A study of the passages in the various Vinayas in which the Buddha calls Devadatta an "eater of spittle," and of the related passages in which Devadatta wins over King Ajatasatru by his magical powers.

(8) _____, trans. Le traité de la grande vertu de sagesse de Nagarjuna (see 3.3.1.2[6]), vol. 1, pp. 222-231.
This passage contains a Mahayanist version of the story of Ananda, Buddha's disciple. Particular emphasis is given to the reasons why Ananda was not an arhat and why he was called Ananda.

(9) _____. Le traité de la grande vertu de sagesse de Nagarjuna (see 3.3.1.2[6]), vol. 1, pp. 198-203.
Included are a number of etymologies of the word "bhiksu," followed by a brief discussion of the four kinds of assemblies of bhiksus (sanghas).

(10) _____. Le traité de la grande vertu de sagesse de Nagarjuna (see 3.3.1.2[6]), vol. 2, pp. 1001-1008, 621-640.
The first passage adds some details to the story of Yasodhara, the wife of the Buddha who attempted to win him back after his enlightenment. Lamotte notes other bibliographical references which can be used for further investigation of Yasodhara. The second section contains a full account of the story of Sariputra, one of the Buddha's earliest and most important disciples. The reader is treated to a full etymology of his name and can see the significance of this disciple from the Mahayanan point of view.

(11) _____. Le traité de la grande vertu de sagesse de Nagarjuna (see 3.3.1.2[6]), vol. 2, pp. 868-878.
An analytical account of Devadatta and his misdeeds, which is also useful for Lamotte's extensive footnote references to textual passages on Devadatta.

(12) LU K'UAN YU. Ch'an and Zen Teaching (see 2.5.7[16]), pp. 25-53.
This section of Lu's (Luk's) work is entitled "The Forty Transmission Gathas," and contains a translation of the verses that are attributed to the various patriarchs of Buddhism according to the Chinese tradition. It starts actually with the seven Buddhas of Antiquity, and then, beginning with Mahakasyapa and Ananda, lists the twenty-seven Indian patriarchs and their gathas. This is followed by the six Chinese patriarchs starting with Bodhidharma and ending with Hui Neng. For a fuller development of this list, see the annotation under Edkins (above).

(13) MIGOT, ANDRE. "Un grand disciple du Bouddha Sariputra." Bulletin de l'Ecole française d'Extrême-Orient, 46 (1954), 405-554.
This lengthy article is a major study, perhaps the best available, on the life, role,

Biography

and importance of Sariputra, a figure of major importance for the early history of Buddhism.

(14) MUKHERJEE, BISWADEH. Die Überlieferung von Devadatta, dem Widersacher des Buddha in den Kanonischen Schriften. Munich: Munchener Studien zur Sprachwissenschaft, 1966.

This is a study of the various sources and traditions relating to Devadatta in the Pali and Chinese canons and some Sanskrit Vinayas. At the same time it is a contribution to the literary history of the canons themselves. See the review by David S. Ruegg in T'oung Pao, 54 (1968), 164-168.

8.9 BIOGRAPHY

Note that some teachers (Naropa, etc.) were Indian teachers who became famous for their Buddhist works in other countries.

8.9.1 Great Buddhists of India

Ananda

(1) TSUKAMOTO, KEISHO. "Mahakasyapa's Precedence to Ananda in the Rajagrha Council." See 2.4.2(10).

(2) WITANACHCHI, C. "Ananda," in Encyclopaedia of Buddhism (see 2.5.4[12]), vol. 1, pp. 529-536.

One of the few substantive summaries of traditions dealing with the life of Ananda, cousin and personal attendant of the Buddha and one of his most important and interesting disciples. Seeks to cover all sources, but relies heavily on the Pali canon.

Ajatasatru

(3) LAMOTTE, ETIENNE. Histoire du Bouddhisme Indien (see 1.2.1[10]), pp. 100-102.

A short but helpful introduction to the intriguing figure of King Ajatasatru, useful especially for putting him into the context of Magadhan royalty and the Buddha's ministry.

(4) VAN ZEYST, H. G. A. "Ajatasattu," in Encyclopaedia of Buddhism (see 2.5.4[12]), vol. 1, pp. 315-321.

A substantive article on the various traditions relating to the curiously ambivalent figure of Ajatasattu, son of Bimbisara and king of Magadh during the last years of the Buddha's life. Attempts to deal with all sources but relies heavily on the Pali canon.

Aryadeva

(5) BU-STON. History of Buddhism (Chos 'byung) (see 1.14.1[2]), vol. 2, pp. 130-132.

A brief biography of the cofounder with Nagarjuna of the Madhyamika system, included in the fourteenth century History of Buddhism by Bu-sTon. For a later classic source also from the Tibetan tradition, see Taranatha, History of Buddhism in India (see 1.2.1[14]), pp. 123-129.

(6) SASTRI, P. S. "Nagarjuna and Aryadeva." Indian Historical Quarterly, 31 (1955), 193-202. See 8.9.1(41).

Asanga

(7) BU-STON. History of Buddhism (Chos 'byung) (see 1.14.1[2]), vol. 2, pp. 136-147.

The Tibetan histories tend to treat the biographies of the brothers Asanga and Vasubandhu together, and to see them as co-founders of the Yogacara school. Bu-sTon's account is a classic one dating from the fourteenth century. For a later version, also from the Tibetan tradition, see Taranatha, History of Buddhism in India, translated by Lama Chimpa and Alaka Chattopadhyaya (Simla, 1970), pp. 149-175. For works of both Asanga and Vasubandhu available in translation, see under 3.3.3.1.

(8) OBERMILLER, E. "The Sublime Science of the Great Vehicle to Salvation." See 3.3.2.1(23).

In his discussion of the authorship of the Ratnagotravibhaga, Obermiller touches on the matter of the relationship between Asanga and Maitreya, and takes issue with the views of H. Ui.

(9) RAHULA, WALPOLA. "Asanga." See 2.5.4(12).

A substantive article on the life, work, and thought of Asanga, the founder of the Yogacara system of Buddhism. Relies on all the principal sources and includes references to Western scholarship. For a shorter account by the same author, see Rahula, trans., Le Compendium de la Super Doctrine (Philosophie) (Abhidharmasamuccaya) d'Asanga (see 3.3.3.1[1]), pp. ix-xiv.

(10) TUCCI, GIUSEPPE. "Animadversiones Indicae: 1. On Maitreye, the Yogacara Doctor." Journal of the Asiatic Society of Bengal, n.s. 26 (1930), 125-128.

Tucci presents what he considers to be more evidence in support of Ui's view that there was a historical Maitreya, master of Asanga and author of several works. See also Tucci, On Some Aspects of the Doctrines of Maitreya (natha) and Asanga (2.5.4[18]), p. 9.

(11) UI, HAKUJU. "Maitreya as an Historical Personage," in Indian Studies in Honor of Charles Rockwell Lanman. Cambridge, Mass.: Harvard University Press, 1929, pp. 95 ff.

The locus classicus of the argument for a differentiation between Maitreya and Asanga as two separate historical personages. Ui even dates them at 270-350 A.D. and 310-390. Ui makes his argument on the bases of a number of texts which are said to have been written by or inspired by the bodhisattva Maitreya. His theory has received support from Tucci (above) and has been disputed by de La Vallée Poussin and Obermiller (above). See also H. Ui, "On the Author of Mahayanasutralamkara," Zeitschrift für Indologie und Iranistik, 6 (1928), 215-225.

Asoka

(12) <u>Asokavadana</u>. Translated by Jean Przyluski as <u>La Légende de l'Empereur Asoka dans les Textes Indiens et Chinois</u>. See 3.2.2.2(2).

(13) BARUA, BENI MADHAT. <u>Asoka and His Inscriptions</u>. Calcutta: New Ages Publishers, 1946, 2 vols.
   Chapters 2 and 4, "Personal History" and "Personal and Public Life," are especially relevant to Asoka's biography and are based both on the inscriptions and the legendary material (which Barua tends to discredit).

(14) DUTT, SUKUMAR. "A Comparison and Contrast between the Legends and the Edicts (of Asoka)." <u>Encyclopaedia of Buddhism</u>. Edited by G. P. Malalasekera (<u>see</u> 2.5.4[12]), Vol. 2, pp. 187-193.
   A brief discussion of the differences and parallels between the pictures of Asoka presented in his edicts and in the legends about him. It is preceded by a more general discussion of "Asoka" by H. G. A. Van Zeyst.

(15) EGGERMONT, P. H. L. <u>The Chronology of the Reign of Asoka Moriya</u>. See 1.2.2.2[2].

(16) GOKHALE, BALKRISHNA GOVIND. <u>Asoka Maurya</u>. New York: Twayne Publishers, 1966, 194 pp.
   A work specifically on Asoka and an attempt to analyze his personality and the influence of Buddhism on him. <u>See also</u> the same author's more general, earlier work, <u>Buddhism and Asoka</u> (<u>see</u> 1.2.2.2[3]).

(17) McKEON, RICHARD and N. A. NIKAM. <u>The Edicts of Asoka</u>. See 6.2.2.1[13].

(18) RHYS-DAVIDS, T. W. "Asoka and the Buddha Relics." See 8.1.2.4[16]).
   One of the few discussions in English of the well known tradition of Asoka's taking and spreading of the relics of the Buddha throughout the known world. Based on the <u>Asokavadana</u> and other references, for which <u>see</u> Przyluski's translation (above).

(19) SMITH, VINCENT A. <u>Asoka</u>. Oxford: Clarendon Press, 1920, 278 pp.
   Perhaps the most solid of a host of works simply entitled "Asoka" on the life, role, policy, thought, beliefs, etc. of the great Mauryan monarch. Although they vary greatly in quality, others which might be mentioned here include D. R. Bhandarkar, <u>Asoka</u> (Calcutta: University of Calcutta, <u>1955</u>), James M. MacPhail, <u>Asoka</u> (Calcutta: The Association Press, n.d.) and Radhakumud Mookerjee, <u>Asoka</u> (London: Macmillan, 1928).

(20) THAPAR, ROMILA. <u>Asoka and the Decline of the Mauryas</u> (<u>see</u> 1.2.2.2[4]), especially pp. 1-54.

Asvaghosa

(21) ANESAKI, MASAHARU. "Asvaghosa," in <u>Encyclopaedia of Religion and Ethics</u> (<u>see</u> 1.15.1[9]), vol. 2, pp. 159-160.
   Brief article on this important Buddhist author and contemporary of King Kaniska. Anesaki presents his article from the Chinese Mahayanist perspective which makes it useful to compare it with B. C. Law's monograph (below).

(22) LAW, BIMALA CHURN. <u>Asvaghosa</u>. Calcutta: Royal Asiatic Society of Bengal, 1946.
   Important monograph on the great second or third century A.D. Sanskrit Buddhist poet, Asvaghosa—his writings, life, art, and place in Buddhism. For a much shorter and perhaps more readily available article by the same author, <u>see</u> Law's "Asvaghosa," in <u>Encyclopaedia of Buddhism</u> (<u>see</u> 2.5.4[12]), vol. 2, pp. 292-298.

(23) LEVI, SYLVAIN. "Asvaghosa, le Sutralamkara et ses Sources." <u>Journal asiatique</u>, 12 (1908), 57-184.
   Still useful for review of the earlier scholarship, this piece examines the life of Asvaghosa and one of the principal works attributed to him. For a follow-up article by Levi, see his "Encore Asvaghosa," <u>Journal asiatique</u>, 213 (1928), 193.

Bimbisara

(24) VAN ZEYST, H. G. A. "Bimbisara," in <u>Encyclopaedia of Buddhism</u> (<u>see</u> 2.5.4[12]), vol. 3, pp. 115-118.
   Short summary of sources (mostly Pali) on the life of Bimbisara, who, as King of Magadha and contemporary of the Buddha, played an important role in the establishment and early development of Buddhism.

Buddhaghosa

(25) LAW, BIMALA CHURN. <u>The Life and Works of Buddhaghosa</u>. Calcutta: Thacker, Spink 1923, 183 pp.
   An overview using a variety of materials to form a composite account of this most important fifth century monk-commentator. For a brief account of Buddhaghosha, <u>see</u> T. W. Rhys-Davids, "Buddhaghosha," in <u>Encyclopedia of Religion and Ethics</u> (<u>see</u> 1.15.1[9]), vol. 2, pp. 885-887.

(26) GRAY, JAMES, trans. "Buddhaghosuppatti," in <u>Buddhaghosuppatti of The Historical Romance of the Rise and Career of Buddhaghosa</u>. London: Luzac, 1892, 2 vols.
   Contains a summary introduction and translation of a biography of the great fifth century commentator of the Pali scriptures, Buddhaghosa. The work, the date of which is uncertain, is attributed to one Mahamangala.

Biography

Candrakirti

(27) BU-STON. History of Buddhism (Chos 'byung) (see 1.14.1[2]), vol. 2, pp. 133-136.
Very brief biography of the great sixth-seventh century Madhyamika philosopher Candrakirti, included here within the History of Buddhism of the fourteenth century historian, Bu-sTon. For a later account of Candrakirti, also from the Tibetan tradition, see Taranatha, History of Buddhism in India (see 1.2.1[14]), pp. 198 ff. For a listing of Candrakirti's works available in translation, see 3.3.2.1.

Dharmakirti

(28) BU-STON. History of Buddhism (Chos 'byung) (see 1.14.1[2]), vol. 2, pp. 152-156.
A brief biography of the great seventh century logician and philosopher, Dharmakirti, a follower and reinterpreter of Dignaga. Bu-sTon's account is a classic one dating from the fourteenth century. For a later source, also from the Tibetan tradition, see Taranatha, History of Buddhism in India (see (1.2.1[14]), pp. 228 ff. For a listing of Dharmakirti's works available in translation, see 3.3.3.1.

Dignaga

(29) BU-STON. History of Buddhism (Chos 'byung) (see 1.14.1[2]), vol. 2, pp. 149-152.
Very little is known about the life history of the great sixth century Buddhist logician, Dignaga, and much of that comes from this biography, which the great Tibetan historian Bu-sTon (1290-1364) included here in his classic History of Buddhism. See also in this regard, the section entitled "Dignaga and His Works," in Masaaki Hattori, Dignaga on Perception (2.5.4[7]), pp. 1-12; and F. I. Stcherbatsky, Buddhist Logic (2.1[11]), vol. 1, pp. 31-34.

Kaniska

(30) BAILEY, H. W. "Kanaiska." See 4.2.3(5).

(31) BASHAM, A. L., ed. Papers on the Date of Kaniska Submitted to the Conference on the Date of Kaniska, London, 20-22 April 1960. Leiden: E. J. Brill, 1968, 478 pp.
A collection of nearly thirty articles, all by eminent Indologists, on different aspects of the controversial date and life of King Kaniska. References are from Indian, Chinese, Tibetan, and other sources. In addition, the volume includes summaries of the discussions held at the conference, and a bibliography of works dealing with the Kushans by Soviet scholars. One could wish for little more on this topic.

(32) "The Date of Kanishka." Journal of the Royal Asiatic Society (1913), pp. 911-1042.
A landmark discussion held at the Royal Asiatic Society on the question of the dates and life of King Kanishka. The debate was based on a paper presented by F. W. Thomas ("The Date of Kaniska," published in the same 1913 volume, pp. 627-650), in which he argues for a first century A.D. date. Participants in the discussion include Rapson, J. Kennedy, Vincent Smith, L. D. Barnett, L. A. Waddell, H. Longsworth Dames, Dr. Hoey, and J. F. Fleet. The latter's paper, "The Question of Kanishka," is also published in the 1913 volume (pp. 95-108). It is interesting to compare this discussion with the papers in the work edited by Basham (above).

(33) KENNEDY, J. "The Secret of Kanishka." Journal of the Royal Asiatic Society (1912), pp. 665-688, 981-1019.
Kennedy argues (wrongly) for placing Kaniska in the first century B.C., but in so doing presents an interesting number of sources. The second part of the article deals with Kaniska's coinage.

(34) LEVI, SYLVAIN. "Kaniska et Satavahana." Journal asiatique, 228 (1936), 61-121.
A posthumously published and uncompleted review of all the available sources on what Levi calls "Deux figures symboliques de l'Inde au premier siècle."

Matrceta

(35) TARANATHA. History of Buddhism in India (see 1.2.1[14]), pp. 130-136.
One of the classic sources (seventeenth century) on the life and works of the second century poet Matrceta, whose works attained great popularity throughout the Buddhist world. For a listing of some of the translations of his works, see 3.2.4.3.

Milinda (Menander)

(36) TAKAKUSU, J. "Chinese Translations of the Milinda Panha." See 3.2.3.4(11).
A brief article including translation of biographical materials on King Milinda from the Chinese. For a full scholarly account of these texts, see Paul Demieville, "Les Versions Chinoises du Milindapanha" (3.2.2.4[2]).

Nagarjuna

(37) BU-STON. History of Buddhism (Chos 'byung) (see 1.14.1[2]), vol. 2, pp. 122-130.
One of the classic sources for the "Life of Nagarjuna" is this biography, included in the fourteenth century Tibetan historian's History of Buddhism. For a later source, also from the Tibetan tradition, see Taranatha, History of Buddhism in India (1.2.1[14]).

(38) DAS, SARAT CHANDRA. "Contribution on the Religion of Tibet: 10. Life and Legend of Nagarjuna." Journal of the Asiatic Society of Bengal, 51 (1882), 115-120.
An unfortunately short but still useful account of some of the traditions surrounding the great Madhyamika philosopher, based on unnamed Tibetan sources.

(39) KARAMBELKAR, V. W. "The Problem of Nagarjuna." Journal of Indian History, 30 (1952), 21-33.

A discussion of the problem of the confusion between the various Nagarjunas, and the various sources dealing with them. The author seeks to distinguish between Nagarjuna the philosopher, the physician, the magician, and the alchemist.

(40) PATHAK, SUNITIKUMAR. "Life of Nagarjuna." Indian Historical Quarterly, 30 (1954), 93-95.

An interesting but very brief translation of some legends about Nagarjuna taken from a fragment of a Tibetan text entitled the Pag-Sam-Jon-Zang. The author, however, gives no further details or commentary on his translation.

(41) SASTRI, P. S. "Nagarjuna and Aryadeva." See 8.9.1(6).

In order to establish the historicity of Nagarjuna and his disciple, the author labors through literary sources to show that Nagarjuna was born in Andhra, that the great monastery in South Kosala is the same as Nagarjunikonda Mahacaitya, and that Nagarjuna was the teacher of the Satavahana rulers.

(42) TUCCI, GIUSEPPE. "Animadversiones Indicae: 4. A Sanskrit Biograpny of the Siddhas and Some Questions Connected with Nagarjuna." Journal of the Asiatic Society of Bengal, n.s. 26 (1930), 138-155.

Discussion and edition of a manuscript fragment of the Siddhas, which Tucci found in Nepal and which contains information on the birthplace of a certain "Nagarjuna." Tucci uses the opportunity to express his opinion on some aspects of the confused traditions concerning the many Nagarjunas.

(43) WALLESER, M. "The Life of Nagarjuna from Tibetan and Chinese Sources," in Hirth Anniversary Volume. Edited by Bruno Schindler. London: Probsthain, 1923, pp. 421-455.

A classic, still useful discussion of the various traditions about the various Nagarjunas. Translated from the original German by Arthur A. Probsthain.

(44) WINTERNITZ, MAURICE. A History of Indian Literature (see 3.1.1[5]), vol. 2, pp. 341-348.

A somewhat outdated but still useful summary of stories and legends about Nagarjuna. For other brief biographical treatments of Nagarjuna in more general works, see T. R. V. Murti, Central Philosophy of Buddhism (2.5.3[7]), pp. 87-89; and Etienne Lamotte, trans., Le Traité de la Grande Vertu de Sagesse (3.3.1.2[6]), vol. 1, pp. x-xiv, and his reexamination of the question in vol. 3, pp. xl, liii, 1373-1375.

(45) YUN-HUA, JAN. "Nagarjuna, One or More? A New Interpretation of Buddhist Hagiography." History of Religions, 2, no. 2 (November 1970), 139-155.

The basis of the article is an examination of the extant traditions in order to determine if the historicity of more than one Nagarjuna can be established. The reader will also find some cursory comments on the development of hagiography.

Santideva

(46) BU-STON. History of Buddhism (Chos 'byung) (see 1.14.1[2]), vol. 2, pp. 161-166.

This "Life of Santideva" represents one of the classic sources on legends and deeds attributed to the great eighth century Madhyamika poet and scholar. For a later source, also from the Tibetan tradition, see Taranatha, History of Buddhism in India (1.2.1[14]), pp. 215 ff. For a listing of the various translations of Santideva's works, see 3.3.2.1.

(47) DE JONG, J. W. "La Légende de Santideva." Indo-Iranian Journal, 16 (1975), 161-182.

An extended and critical review of Pezzali's book (below), but very useful for including De Jong's own translation of a Tibetan text giving the legend of the great Madhyamika poet and master. For a much earlier account of some of the legendary material, see also Haraprasad Sastri, "Santideva," Indian Antiquary, 42 (1913), 49-52.

(48) PEZZALI, AMALIA. Santideva, Mystique Bouddhiste des VIIème et VIIIème siècles. Florence: Vallechi, 1968.

The only full-length book on the life and work of this important Madhyamika scholar and poet. But see also De Jong's critical review listed above.

Sthiramati

(49) BU-STON. History of Buddhism (Chos 'byung) (see 1.14.1[2]), vol. 2, pp. 147-149.

A brief account of the life and work of the Yogacara scholar and philosopher Sthiramati, best known perhaps for his commentary on the work of Asanga (see 3.3.3.2).

Upagupta

(50) WADDELL, L. AUSTINE. "Upagupta, the Fourth Buddhist Patriarch and High Priest of Asoka." Journal of the Asiatic Society of Bengal, 66 (1897), 76-84.

A short and somewhat dated account of this important figure in the development of early Buddhism. The legendary tale of his conversion of Mara became well known and was developed especially in Southeast Asia, where Upagupta (Upagotta, Upakrut) came to be honored as a deity in his own right. In this regard, see C. Duroiselle, "Upagutta et Mara," Bulletin de l'Ecole française d'Extrême-Orient, 4 (1904), 414-428; S. J. Tambiah, Buddhism and

Biography

the Spirit Cults in Northeast Thailand (4.1.2[16]), pp. 168-178; and R. Grant Brown, "Rain-making in Burma" (7.5.1[4]).

Vasubandhu

(51) FRAUWALLNER, E. On the Date of the Buddhist Master of Law, Vasubandhu. Serie Orientale Roma, III. Rome: Istituto per il Medio ed Estremo Oriente, 1951, 69 pp.

This is the work which inspired Jaini's article (below). In this study, Frauwallner came to the conclusion that Kosakara Vasubandhu was neither a Mahayanist nor the author of the Vijnanavada, which he is often credited with writing.

(52) JAINI, P. "On the Theory of Two Vasabandhus." Bulletin of the School of Oriental and African Studies, 21 (1958), 48-53.

A summary of the scholarship concerned with the question of the two Vasubandhus. The article is an attempt to confirm Paramartha's account of Kosakara Vasubandhu's conversion to Mahayana and his authorship of several Mahayana works. For primary source material on the subject see Takakusu, "Life of Vasubandhu by Paramartha" (below).

(53) KIMURA, TAIHEN. "The Date of Vasubandhu Seen from the Abhidarmakosa," in Indian Studies in Honor of Charles Rockwell Lanman. Cambridge, Mass.: Harvard University Press, 1929, pp. 89-92.

A short article which supports Takakusu's dating of Vasubandhu at 420-500 A.D., but based strictly on the evidence of Abhidharma texts.

(54) ONO, GENMYO. "The Date of Vasubandhu Seen from the History of Buddhist Philosophy," in Indian Studies in Honor of Charles Rockwell Lanman. Cambridge, Mass.: Harvard University Press, 1929, pp. 93-94.

A short article offering further support to Takakusu's dating of Vasubandhu in the fifth century, but based on a study of the degree of development of the doctrine of the three bodies of the Buddha (trikaya) in Vasubandhu's and other writings.

(55) PERI, P. N. "A propos de la date du Vasubandhu." Bulletin de l'Ecole française d'Extrême-Orient, 11 (1911), 339-390.

After examining all of the available material of his time on this subject, Peri fixes the date of Vasubandhu around 350 A.D.

(56) TAKAKUSU, J. "The Date of Vasubandhu, the Great Buddhist Philosopher," in Indian Studies in Honor of Charles Rockwell Lanman. Cambridge, Mass.: Harvard University Press, 1929, pp. 79-88.

A short article in which the great Japanese scholar Takakusu reaffirms the dates (420-500 A.D.) which he proposed for Vasubandhu in his 1904 articles, and very cogently summarizes the scholarship on the issue in the meantime.

(57) _____. "The Life of Vasubandhu by Paramartha." T'oung Pao, 5 (1904), 269-296.

A translation from the Chinese of the canonical biography of the great Yogacara master Vasubandhu. This is one of the basic original sources on his life and should be read in conjunction with Takakusu's study of it (below).

(58) _____. "A Study of Paramartha's Life of Vasu-bandhu, and the Date of Vasu-bandhu." Journal of the Royal Asiatic Society (1905), pp. 33-53.

An analysis of the text translated by Takakusu in T'oung Pao (above) and an argument for the dates 420-500 A.D. for the life of the great Mahayana doctor. This along with the translation still remains one of the starting points for any study of the life of Vasubandhu.

8.9.2 Great Buddhists of Tibet

Atisa

(1) CHANG K'E-CH'IANG. "Atisa," in Encyclopaedia of Buddhism (see 2.5.4[12]), vol. 2, pp. 311-315.

An article on the life and work of the Indian monk, scholar, and traveler Atisa (982-1054), who was instrumental in restoring Buddhism to Tibet in the eleventh century.

(2) CHATTOPADHYAYA, ALAKA. Atisa and Tibet. See 1.14.2.2(3).

A work on the life and historical milieu of Atisa, the important eleventh century Indian monk largely responsible for important reforms in Tibetan Buddhism. Includes a catalogue of Atisa's works.

(3) SANKRITYAYAN, RAHUL. "Acarya Dipamkara Srijnana," in 2500 Years of Buddhism (see 1.2.1[1]), pp. 225-238.

A summary of the life history of Atisa (Dipamkara Srijnana) which does more than cover just the end of his life when he went to Tibet, dealing concisely with his education and travels in South and Southeast Asia as well.

Bu-sTon

(4) RUEGG, D. S. The Life of Bu-sTon Rinpoche. Serie Orientale Roma, No. 34. Rome: Istituto Italiano per il Medio ed Estremo Oriente, 1966, 192 pp.

An edition and translation of the Tibetan text of the Bu-sTon rNam thar, the biography of the Tibetan scholar monk Bu-sTon (1290-1364 A.D.), best known in the West as the author of the Chos 'byung (History of Buddhism), which has been translated by Obermiller (see 1.14.1[2]). The biography is preceded by an informative introduction.

Chos-skyabs dpal-bzang

See under 8.9.2, bSod-nams blo-gros.

Dalai Lamas

(5) BELL, CHARLES. *Portrait of the Dalai Lama.* See 1.14.2.3(1).

This volume shows a sympathetic treatment of the character and career of the thirteenth Dalai Lama (1876-1933). For another biography, though not of the caliber of Bell's, see Tokan Tada, *The Thirteenth Dalai Lama* (below).

(6) HOWARTH, DAVID, ed. *My Land and My People: The Autobiography of His Holiness the Dalai Lama of Tibet.* London: Pantheon, 1962, 254 pp.

This volume contains the present Dalai Lama's views concerning his own exile and his relationship with the Chinese.

(7) PETECH, LUCIANO. "The Dalai Lamas and Regents of Tibet: A Chronological Study." *T'oung Pao*, 47 (1959), 368-394.

A listing and discussion of the fourteen Dalai Lamas (up to the present) and the regents who filled in during periods of their minority or absence. Based on the important various Tibetan "Lives of the Dalai Lamas."

(8) TADA, TOKAN. *The Thirteenth Dalai Lama.* Tokyo: Centre for East Asian Cultural Studies, 1965, 115 pp.

A life history of the thirteenth Dalai Lama by a Japanese scholar who lived and studied in Tibet between 1913 and 1923, during which time he was a personal friend and advisor. Makes for a fascinating comparison with the account of the Dalai Lama written by his other "foreign friend," Charles Bell.

Marpa

(9) BACOT, JACQUES, trans. *La Vie de Marpa le "Traducteur."* Buddhica, No. 7. Paris: Paul Geuthner, 1937.

A translation from the Tibetan of a short life of Marpa, known as the "translator" for his many activities in transmitting Indian texts to Tibet, but perhaps better known still as the guru of Milarepa.

Milarepa

(10) BACOT, JACQUES, trans. *Milarepa, Ses Méfaits, Ses Epreuves, Son Illumination.* Paris: Fayard, 1971, 267 pp.

A re-edition of Bacot, *Le Poète Milarepa. Ses Crimes, Ses Epreuves, Son Nirvana* (Paris, 1925), this is a translation from the Tibetan of the *Mila Ras Pa'i rnam Thar*, an account of the life of Milarepa compiled by his disciple Ras Chung in the eleventh century.

(11) CHANG, GARMA C. C., trans. *The Hundred Thousand Songs of Milarepa.* See 4.3(12).

(12) EVANS-WENTZ, W. Y. *Tibet's Great Yogi Milarepa.* London: Oxford, 1928, 315 pp.

This is a translation of the *Jetsun Kahbum*, a very popular biography of the well known bka rGyud pa saint, Milarepa. In addition to its biographical and specific value, this volume is suitable for general use.

Naropa

(13) GUENTHER, HERBERT, trans. *The Life and Teachings of Naropa.* See 3.4.2(6).

The first 109 pages contain the English translation of Naropa's biography, which may be as old as the twelfth century. The signficance of Naropa's life is that it has been accorded "exemplary status" for those wishing to succeed in attaining "the overwhelming experience of the Real indirect knowledge." The rest of the book is a discussion of Naropa's teachings.

(14) SINGH, BIRESHWAR PRASAD. "Naropa: His Life and Activities." *Journal of the Bihar Research Society*, 53 (1967), 117-129.

A review of materials on the life of Naropa with discussion of chronology and dating.

(15) TUCCI, GIUSEPPE. "A Propos the Legend of Naropa." *Journal of the Royal Asiatic Society* (1935), 677-688.

A review article in which Tucci adds his own insights on the life of the guru of Marpa, and comments on A. Grünwedel's work, *Die Legenden des Naropa* (Leipzig: Otto Harrassowitz, 1933).

Padma Sambhava

(16) EVANS-WENTZ, W. Y. *The Tibetan Book of the Great Liberation* (see 3.4.2[3]), pp. 100-192.

A biographical presentation, based upon traditional sources of the great patriarch and transporter of Buddhism into Tibet, Padma-Sambhava. Padma-Sambhava's super-human feats are enumerated here.

(17) TOUSSAINT, GUSTAVE-CHARLES, trans. "Le Padma Than Yig." *Bulletin de l'Ecole française d'Extrême-Orient*, 20 (1920), 13-56 (for chapters 1, 12-22); *Journal asiatique*, 203 (1923), 257-328 (for chapters 2-11).

A French translation from the Tibetan of the life (or lives) of Padmasambhava, the colorful establisher of Buddhism in Tibet, whose image appears in temples throughout Tibet and is widely venerated as "Guru Rinpoche." Reportedly the whole work was published separately in translation as *Le Dict de Padma--Padma Thang yig* (Paris: Leroux, 1933).

dPal-ldan blo-gros

See under 8.9.2, bSod-nams blo-gros.

Panchen Lamas

(18) DAS, SARAT CHANDRA. "Contributions on the Religion of Tibet: 5. The Lives of the Panchen-Rinpoches or Tasi Lamas." *Journal of the Asiatic Society of Bengal*, 51 (1882), 15-52.

Biography

A compilation of biographical data from Tibetan sources on the various incarnations of the Panchen Lama (up to the sixth Panchen Lama, Paldan Yeses, in the eighteenth century) and including the earlier Indian incarnations.

bSod-nams, dbang-phyug

See under 8.9.2, bSod-nams blo-gros.

bSod-nams blo-gros

(19) SNELLGROVE, DAVID. Four Lamas of Dolpo. Cambridge, Mass.: Harvard University Press, 1967, pp. 81-123.

A translation of the biography of bSod-nams blo-gros (1945-1521), the abbot of dMar-sgom monastery in Dolpo, which is now part of Nepal but is culturally part of Tibet. Published with the three other biographies translated by Snellgrove: those of the abbots Chos-skyabs dpal-bang (1476-1565), pp. 127-182; dPal-ldan blo-gros (1467-1536), pp. 185-230; and bSod-nams dbang-phyug (1660-1731), pp. 233-273.

Sum-pa mKhan-po

(20) DAS, SARAT CHANDRA. "Life of Sum pa Khan-po. Also styled Yeses Dpal hboy, the Author of the Rehumig (Chronological Table)." Journal of the Asiatic Society of Bengal, 58 (1889), 37-84.

Most of the article is taken up by a translation of the valuable chronological table composed by this eighteenth century lama-historian, which is an important reference source on the history of Tibet between 1026 and 1745. The table is preceded by a short biographical study of its author.

(21) DE JONG, J. W. "Sum-pa mKan-po (1704-1788) and His Works." Harvard Journal of Asiatic Studies, 27 (1967), 208-217.

A review and correction of previous scholarship on the life and works of this important Tibetan historian of Buddhism.

Tson Kha pa

(22) DAS, SARAT CHANDRA. "Contributions on the Religion of Tibet: 6. Life and Legend of Tson Khapa, the Great Buddhist Reformer of Tibet." Journal of the Asiatic Society of Bengal, 51 (1882), 53-58.

A brief but still useful account of the life of Tsong Kha pa, the great scholar and founder of the Yellow Hat sect of Buddhism in Tibet. Based on unnamed Tibetan sources.

(23) OBERMILLER, EUGENE. "Tson-kha-pa le pandit." Mélanges chinois et boudhhiques, 3 (1935), 319-338.

Includes short reviews of sources that provide biographical material on Tsong Khapa.

8.9.3 Great Buddhists of China

(1) HUI-CHIAO. Kao seng chuan. Partial translation by Robert Shih in Biographies des Moines Eminents (Kao Seng Tchouan de Jouei-Kiao). Bibliothèque du Muséon, No. 54. Louvain: Institut Orientaliste, 1968.

An annotated translation of the first of ten sections of the Kao seng chuan, a compendium of biographies written by the sixth century scholar-monk Hui-chiao, and one of our most important sources on the lives of great early Buddhists in China. The section translated contains the biographies of thirty-five translators of Buddhist scriptures, many of them foreigners, thus making the work particularly important for the study of the introduction of Buddhism into China. Also on the Kao seng chuan see Arthur F. Wright, Hui-chiao's Lives of Eminent Monks: Silver Jubilee Volume of the Zinbun-Kagaku-Kenkyusyo (Kyoto: Kyoto University, 1954), pp. 383-432. On Hui-chiao, see A. Wright, "Hui-chiao as a Chinese Historian," Indogaku Bukkyogaku Kenkyu, 3, no. 1 (1954), 382-377 (sic).

Amoghavajra

(2) CHOU-YI-LIANG, trans. "The Biography of Amoghavajra of the Ta-Hsing-shan Temple of Ch'ang of the T'ang Dynasty," in his Tantrism in China. See 1.11.2.3(4).

A fully annotated translation from the Chinese of the biography of Amoghavajra (d. 774), whose Chinese name was Pu-k'ung-chin-kang. A native of Northern India, he was instrumental in the establishment of esoteric Buddhist traditions in China.

(3) KUO YUAN-HSING. "Amoghavajra," in Encyclopaedia of Buddhism (see 2.5.4[12]), vol. 1, pp. 482-487.

A summary of traditions on the eighth century scholar, monk, traveller, and translator, Amoghavajra, who made several trips to China, where he became patriarch of the esoteric school.

An-ling-shou

(4) WRIGHT, ARTHUR F. "Biography of the Nun An-ling-shou." See 1.11.2.2(14).

An Shih Kao

(5) HUI-CHIAO. Kao seng chuan (see 8.9.3[11]), pp. 4-12.

A translation of the biography of a second century Parthian monk who came to China and became a translator. For a compilation of biographical data from various sources in English, see also Lu ch'eng, "An shih kao," in Encyclopaedia of Buddhism (2.5.4[12]), vol. 1, pp. 725-729. For an assessment of his role within the history of Chinese Buddhism see E. Zurcher, The Buddhist Conquest of China (1.11.2.1[9]), vol. 1, pp. 32-34.

Buddhabhadra (Fo-t'o-po-t'o-lo)

(6) HUI-CHIAO. Kao seng chuan (see 8.9.3[1]), pp. 90-98.

Buddhajiva (Fo-t'o-Shih)

(7) HUI-CHIAO. Kao seng chuan (see 8.9.3[1]), p. 119.

Buddhavarman (Fo-t'o-po-mo)

(8) HUI-CHAO. Kao seng chuan (see 8.9.3[1]), pp. 119-120.

Buddhayasas (Fo-t'o-yeh-sheh)

(9) HUI-CHIAO. Kao seng chuan (see 8.9.3[1]), pp. 85-90.

Ch'eng Kuan

(10) CHANG, GARMA C. C. The Buddhist Teaching of Totality (see 3.3.1.2[4]), pp. 238-240.
A brief biography of the eighth and ninth century Hua-yen master, Ch'eng Kuan, author of the important work, "A prologue to Hua-yen."

Chih-I

(11) HURVITZ, LEON. "Chih-I (538-597): An Introduction to the Life and Ideas of a Chinese Buddhist Monk." Mélanges chinois et bouddhiques, 12 (1960-1962), 100-182.
Though Chih-I (538-597) is not traditionally held to be the founder of the T'ien T'ai school, he is in all probability the historical founder of the sect. These pages represent the most thorough account of his life that is available in English.

(Shih) Chih-meng

(12) CHAVANNES, EDOUARD. "Voyage de Song Yun dans l'Udyana et le Gandhara." See 1.2.2.3(1).

(13) HUI-CHIAO. Kao seng chuan (see 8.9.3.[1]), pp. 143-147.

(Shih) Chi-yen

(14) CHANG, GARMA C. C. The Buddhist Teaching of Totality (see 3.3.1.2[4]), pp. 234-237.
A short biography of the Chinese monk and writer Chih-yen (602-668), the successor of Tu-shun in the Hua-yen school. Includes translation from his canonical biography.

(15) HUI-CHIAO. Kao seng chuan (see 8.9.3[1]), pp. 120-123.

Chu fa-lan (Dharmaratna)

(16) HUI-CHIAO. Kao seng chuan (see 8.9.3[1]), pp. 2-4.

(17) MASPERO, H. "Le songe et l'ambassade de l'Empereur Ming." See 1.11.2.1(6).

Chu-Fo-nieh

(18) HUI-CHIAO. Kao seng chuan (see 8.9.3[1]), pp. 55-56.

Chu Tao-Sheng

(19) LIEBENTHAL, WALTER. "A Biography of Chu Tao-sheng." See 1.11.2.2(5).
A biographical sketch of Tao-sheng, a famous Chinese monk who was best known for his teaching of instantaneous enlightenment and the salvation of all beings, no matter how sinful or lowly they may be.

Dharmakala (T'an-k'o-ch'ia-lo)

(20) HUI-CHIAO. Kao seng chuan (see 8.9.3[1]), pp. 17-19.

Dharmaksema (T'an-wu-ch'an)

(21) HUI-CHIAO. Kao seng chuan (see 8.9.3[1]), pp. 98-107.

Dharmamitra (T'an-mo'mi-to)

(22) HUI-CHIAO. Kao seng chuan (see 8.9.3[1]), pp. 140-143.

Dharmanadin (T'an-mo-nan-ti)

(23) HUI-CHIAO. Kao seng chuan (see 8.9.3[1]), pp. 48-51.

Dharmaraksa (Chu T'an-mo-lo-ch'a)

(24) HUI-CHIAO. Kao seng chuan (see 8.9.3[1]), pp. 33-37.

(25) ZURCHER, E. The Buddhist Conquest of China (see 1.11.2.1[9]), vol. 1, pp. 65-70.

Dharmaruci (T'an-mo-liu-chih)

(26) HUI-CHIAO. Kao seng chuan (see 8.9.3[1]), pp. 82-84.

Dharmayasas (T'an mo-yeh She)

(27) HUI-CHIAO. Kao seng chuan (see 8.9.3[1]), pp. 57-59.

Fa-hsien

(28) HUI-CHIAO. Kao seng chuan (see 8.9.3[1]), pp. 108-115.
A brief biography of the famous monk pilgrim and translator Fa-hsien, who traveled to India and Ceylon at the turn of the fifth century A.D. For a translation of his account of his voyage, see Fa-hsien, A Record of Buddhistic Kingdoms (1.2.2.3[4]).

Fa-tsang

(29) CHANG, GARMA C. C. The Buddhist Teaching of Totality (see 3.3.1.2[4]), pp. 237-238.
An all too short biography of Fa Tsang (643-712), one of the most prolific and greatest of Chinese Hua-yen masters, and principal disciple of Chih-yen.

Biography

(30) LEE, PETER H. "Fa-tsang and Uisang." *Journal of the American Oriental Society*, 82 (1962), 56-62.

Fa Yen Wen I

(31) LU K'UAN YU. *Ch'an and Zen Teaching* (see 2.5.7[16]), pp. 215-228.
Fa Yen Wen I (885-958 A.D.), also called Ch'ing Liang Wen I, was the founder of the Fa Yen (Hogen) sect of Ch'an Buddhism. His anecdotal life-history is translated here from the "Transmission of the Lamp" (*Ching Te Ch'uan Teng Lu*). For another rendition of the same text, see also Chang Chung-Yuan, trans., *Original Teachings of Ch'an Buddhism* (3.3.6.1[2]), pp. 238-249.

Fo-t'u-teng

(32) WRIGHT, ARTHUR F. "Fo-t'u-teng--A Biography." See 1.11.2.2(16).

Gunabhadra (Ch'in-no-po-t'o-lo)

(33) HUI-CHIAO. *Kao seng chuan* (see 8.9.3[1]), pp. 148-156.

Gunavarman

(34) CHAVANNES, EDOUARD. "Gunavarman (367-431 A.D.)." *T'oung Pao*, 5 (1904), 193-206.

(35) HUI-CHIAO. *Kao seng chuan* (see 8.9.3[1]), pp. 125-137.

Gunavrddhi (Ch'iu-na-p'i-ti)

(36) HUI-CHIAO. *Kao seng chuan* (see 8.9.3[1]), pp. 156-157.

Hsieh Ling-yun

(37) FRODSHAM, J. D. "Hsieh Ling-yun's Contributions to Medieval Chinese Buddhism." See 2.5.7(7).

(38) MATHER, RICHARD. "The Landscape Buddhism of the Fifth Century Poet Hsieh Ling-yun." See 4.3(9).

Hsuan Tsang

(39) BEAL, SAMUEL. *Si-Yu-Ki: Buddhist Records of the Western World*. London: Trubner, 1884, 2 vols. (Reprinted: Delhi, 1969.) See 10.1.1(1).

(40) GROUSSET, RENE. *In the Footsteps of the Buddha*. Translated by J. A. Underwood. New York: Orion Press, 1971, 337 pp. (Originally published 1929.)
Grousset uses the lives and travels of the great Chinese pilgrims Hsuan Tsang and I-Ching to portray informally what he considers to be the "great age" of Buddhism in Asia--the sixth and seventh centuries.

(41) HUI LI. *The Life of Hsuan Tsang*. Translated by Li Yung-hsi. Peking: Chinese Buddhist Association, 1959.
A complete translation of the biography of the great Chinese monk, pilgrim and scholar Hsuan Tsang, written by one of his disciples. Unlike Samuel Beal's older and partial translation of the same text (Hui Li, *The Life of Hiuen-Tsiang* [London: Kegan, Paul, Trench and Trubner, 1911]), this rendition published under the auspices of the Chinese Buddhist Association has the advantage of including the chapters dealing with the life of Hsuan Tsang after his return from the West.

(42) MINH CHAU, THICH. *Hsuan Tsang: The Pilgrim and Scholar*. Nha-Trang: Vietnam Buddhist Institute, 1963, 139 pp.
A work on the great Chinese Tripitaka master and pilgrim by a Vietnamese scholar-monk. It aims at presenting the many sides of Hsuan Tsang's multifarious career, and devotes separate chapters to Hsuan Tsang as a pilgrim, a learner, a preacher, a translator, a debator, a writer, and a mystic.

(43) WALEY, ARTHUR. *The Real Tripitaka*. New York: Macmillan Co., 1952, pp. 9-130.
A biography of Hsuan Tsang designed as a historical complement to Waley's translation of the novel *Hsi yu-chi* (Monkey) (see 4.5[12]). This is followed on pages 131-168 by an account of Buddhism after Hsuan Tsang's death, somewhat misleadingly entitled "Ennin and Ensai."

(44) WATTERS, THOMAS, trans. and ed. *On Yuan Chwang's Travels in India*. See 1.2.2.3(14).

Huang-po

(45) DEMIEVILLE, PAUL. "Le recueil de la Salle des Patriarches--Tsou T'ang tsi." *T'oung Pao*, 56 (1970), 262-286, especially 271-278.
The *Chu T'ang chi*, compiled in 952, was a long lost text of the Southern school of Ch'an containing the stories of various Ch'an masters in the style of "The Transmission of the Lamp." By way of illustration, Demieville has here translated the anecdotes it contains about the ninth century master Huang-po. For a translation (much criticized by Demieville) of some of Huang-po's writings, which also contains biographical anecdotes, see John Blofeld, trans., *The Zen Teaching of Huang-po on the Transmission of Mind* (London: Rider and Co., 1938).

Hui Neng

(46) YAMPOLSKY, PHILIP B., trans. *The Platform Sutra of the Sixth Patriarch*. New York: Columbia University Press, 1967, pp. 48-88.
These pages in Yampolsky's introduction to the translation represent a discussion of the biographical materials relevant to the life of Hui Neng.

Hui-yuan

(47) LIEBENTHAL, WALTER. "Shih Hui-yuan's Buddhism as Set Forth in His Writings." See 2.5.8(12).

(48) MAKITA, TAIRYO. "Hui-yuan--His Life and Times." Translated by Philip Yampolsky. Zinbun (Kyoto), 6 (1962), 1-28.

A discussion of the fourth century monk Hui-yuan, his relationship to his master, Tao-an, and his role in relating Chinese traditional thought to early Chinese Buddhism. For a specific discussion of one aspect of Hui-yuan's life by another Japanese Buddhologist, see Koshiro Tamaki, "The Ultimate Enlightenment of Hui-yuan in Lu-shan," Indogaku Bukkyogaku Kenkyu/Journal of Indian and Buddhist Studies, 12, no. 2 (1964), 859-848 (sic).

(49) WAGNER, R. G. "The Original Structure of the Correspondence between Shih Hui-yuan and Kumarajiva." Harvard Journal of Asiatic Studies, 31 (1971), 28-48.

A study and reordering of the Ta-ch'eng ta-i chang, an interesting collection of letters exchanged between the great South China monk Hui-yuan and the Central Asian translator Kumarajiva, who arrived in Ch'ang-an in 402.

(50) ZURCHER, ERIK. The Buddhist Conquest of China (see 1.11.2.1[9]), pp. 204-253.

Pages 204-239 contain a detailed discussion of the life and role of the monk Hui-yuan (334-417) in the establishment and consolidation of Buddhism in China. This is followed on pages 240-253 by a translation of his canonical biography from the Chinese. An excellent source on this important figure.

I Ching

(51) I CHING. A Record of the Buddhist Religion as Practiced in India and the Malay Archipelago, by I-Tsing (see 1.2.2.3[8]), pp. xxv-xxxviii.

As a preface to his translation of I-Ching's text, Takakusu gives a brief but helpful biographical account of the "Life and Travels of I-Tsing."

Kalayasas (Chiang-liang-ye-She)

(52) HUI-CHIAO. Kao seng chuan (see 8.9.3[1]), pp. 147-148.

K'uei-chi

(53) WEINSTEIN, STANLEY. "A Biographical Study of Tz'u-en." Monumenta Nipponica, 15 (1959), 119-149.

A full biographical study of the life of Tz'u-en (632-682), better known as K'uei-chi, the founder of the Fa-hsiang (Japanese--Hosso) sect in China. One of the principal disciples of Hsuan Tsang, he was a great scholar-monk in his own right.

Kumarajiva

(54) HUI-CHIAO. Kao seng chuan (see 8.9.3[1]), pp. 60-81.

A translation of a basic biographical account of the life of one of the great prolific translators, who, through his works, did much to speed the spread of Buddhism in China. A native of Northwest India, he died in 409 A.D. in Ch'ang-an. A German translation of his biography may be found in Johannes Nobel, Kumarajiva (Leipzig: Otto Harrassowitz, 1937), 227 pp. See also Z. Tsukamoto, "The Dates of Kumarajiva and Seng-chao Re-examined," in Silver Jubilee Volume of the Zinbun-Kagaku-Kenkyusyo (Kyoto, 1954), part 1, pp. 568-584.

(55) WAGNER, R. G. "The Original Structure of the Correspondence between Shih Hui-yuan and Kumarajiva." See 8.9.3(49).

Lin-chi (Rinzai)

(56) DEMIEVILLE, PAUL. Entretiens de Lin-tsi. Paris: 1972.

A work of major significance on the life and teachings of the great Ch'an master, Lin-chi.

(57) LU K'UAN YU. Ch'an and Zen Teaching (see 2.5.7[16]), pp. 84-126.

Lin-chi (d. 866) was the founder of the Lin-chi (Rinzai) sect of Ch'an Buddhism. His life story (mostly anecdotal) given in these pages is taken from "The Five Lamps Meeting at the Source" (Wu Teng Hui Yuan) and the "Finger Pointing at the Moon" (Chih Yueh Lu). For a similar presentation translated from "The Transmission of the Lamp" (Ching Te Ch'uan Teng Lu), see Chang Chung-yuan, trans., Original Teachings of Ch'an Buddhism (see 3.3.6.1[2]), pp. 116-125.

(58) YANAGIDA, SEIZAN. "The Life of Lin-chi I-hsuan." Translated by Ruth Sasaki in Eastern Buddhist, 5, no. 2 (1972), 70-94.

A biographical study of the ninth century founder of Lin-chi (Rinzai), drawing on and evaluating all the basic sources for his life history. For a translation of the relevant portion of one of these sources--the Chu T'ang chi, see Paul Demieville, "Le Recueil de la Salle des Patriarches--Tsou T'ang tsi" (8.9.3[45]).

Ling-yu

(59) LU K'UAN YU. Ch'an and Zen Teaching (see 2.5.7[16]), pp. 57-68.

Not so much a formal biography as a series of anecdotes about the life of Ling-yu of Kuei Shan (771-853), who, along with his disciple Hui-chi of Yang-shan, was the founder of the Kuei Yang sect of Ch'an Buddhism (Ikyo Zen). The passage translated here is taken from "The Transmission of the Lamp" (Ching Te Ch'uan Teng Lu), and is followed on pages 69-83 by the "biography" of Hui-chi. A different translation of both texts may be found in Chang Chung-Yuan, Original Teachings of Ch'an Buddhism Selected from the Transmission of the Lamp (see 3.3.6.1[2]), pp. 200-209, 209-218.

Lokaksema (Chih Lou-chia-ch'an)

(60) HUI-CHIAO. Kao seng chuan (see 8.9.3[1]), pp. 13-17.

Biography

(61) ZURCHER, E. The Buddhist Conquest of China (see 1.11.2.1[9]), vol. 1, pp. 35-36.

Lu Hsi-Hsing

(62) LIU TS'UN-YAN. "Lu Hsi-Hsing: A Confucian Scholar, Taoist Priest, and Buddhist Devotee of the 16th Century." Asiatische Studien/Etudes Asiatiques, 18 (1965), 115-142.

A biographical study of a sixteenth century Chinese scholar and novelist who mixed the "three religions" in both his life and literary work.

(Shih) Pao-yun

(63) HUI-CHIAO. Kao seng chuan (see 8.9.3[1]), pp. 123-125.

Paramartha

(64) SASAKI, G. H. "Paramartha," in 2500 Years of Buddhism (see 1.2.1[1]), pp. 240-242.

Short but helpful account of the life and translating work of this great Central Asiatic monk who came to China.

Po Yuan

(65) HUI-CHIAO. Kao seng chuan (see 8.9.3[1]), pp. 37-42.

Pu-tai

(66) CHAPIN, HELEN B. "The Ch'an Master Pu-tai." See 8.3.4[2]).

Translation of the short Chinese biography of the monk Pu-tai from the Ching-te chuan teng lu which helps to show the transition made in China from a "tall well-formed Maitreya" to the fat, jolly "laughing Buddha."

Punyatara (Fu-jo-to-lo)

(67) HUI-CHIAO. Kao seng chuan (see 8.9.3[1]), p. 92.

Samghabhadra (Seng-ch'ieh-po-teng)

(68) HUI-CHIAO. Kao seng chuan (see 8.9.3[1]), pp. 46-48.

Samghadeva (Seng-ch'ieh-t'i-p'o)

(69) HUI-CHIAO. Kao seng chuan (see 8.9.3[1]), pp. 51-55.

Samghavarman (Seng ch'ieh-po-mo)

(70) HUI-CHIAO. Kao seng chuan (see 8.9.3[1]), pp. 138-140.

Seng-hui

(71) HUI-CHIAO. Kao seng chuan (see 8.9.3[1]), pp. 20-31.

Translation of a more than usually detailed biography of the Sogdian translator monk Seng-hui who died in 280 A.D. Other translations of the same text may be found in Edouard Chavannes, "Seng Houei," T'oung Pao, 10 (1909), 199-212, and in A. C. Soper, Literary Evidence for Early Buddhist Art in China (see 1.11.2.1[8]), pp. 5-6 (partial translation, but in English). See also E. Zurcher, The Buddhist Conquest of China (1.11.2.1[9]), vol. 1, pp. 51-55.

Shan-wu-wei

(72) CHOU YI-LIANG, trans. "The Biography of Shan-wu-wei of the Sheng-shan Temple of Lo-Yang of the T'ang Dynasty," in his "Tantrism in China" (see 1.11.2.3[4]).

Fully annotated translation from the Chinese of the biography of Shan-wu-wei (Subhakarasimha), a native of Central India who arrived in Ch'ang-an in 716 A.D. and was instrumental in the establishment of esoteric Buddhism in China.

She Mo-t'eng (Kasyapa Matanga??)

(73) HUI-CHIAO. Kao seng chuan (see 8.9.3[1]), pp. 1-2.

(74) MASPERO, H. "Le songe et l'ambassade de l'Empereur Ming." See 1.11.2.1[7].

Shen-hui

(75) GERNET, JACQUES. "Biographie du maître Chen-Houei de Ho-tso." See 2.5.7[8].

Srimitra (Po She-li-mi-to-lo)

(76) HUI-CHIAO. Kao seng chuan (see 8.9.3[1]), pp. 42-46.

T'ai Hsu

(77) CHOU HSIANG-KUANG. T'ai Hsu: His Life and Teaching. Allahabad: Indo-Chinese Literature Publications, 1957, 74 pp.

A short biographical study of a Chinese Buddhist abbot of a monastery during the revival of Buddhism in the late nineteenth century.

(78) WELCH, HOLMES. The Buddhist Revival in China (see 1.11.2.4[6]), pp. 51-71.

A chapter devoted to the figure of the great reformer T'ai Hsu which makes a fine introduction to the life, place, and importance of the man.

(Shih) T'an-wu'chieh (Dharmodgata??)

(79) CHAVANNES, EDOUARD. "Voyage de Song Yun dans l'Udyana et le Gandhara." See 1.2.2.3(1).

(80) HUI-CHIAO. Kao seng chuan (see 8.9.3[1]), pp. 115-118.

Tao An

(81) LINK, ARTHUR. "Biography of Shih Tao-an." See 1.11.2.2(7).

Tsung-mi

(82) JAN YUN-HUA. "Tsung-mi: His analysis of Ch'an Buddhism." See 2.5.7(13).

An account of the life and works of the early ninth century scholar Tsung-mi, and a study of his important and not fully exploited source for the history of Ch'an in China.

Tu Shun

(83) CHANG, GARMA C. C. The Buddhist Teaching of Totality (see 3.3.1.2[4]), pp. 231-234.
A short biography of Tu Shun (558-640), traditionally thought of as the first patriarch of Hua Yen Buddhism in China.

(84) LU K'UAN YU. Ch'an and Zen Teaching (see 2.5.7[16]), pp. 127-157.
An anecdotal life history translated from the "Finger Pointing at the Moon" (Chih Yueh Lu). Liang-chieh of Tung mountain, along with Pen chi of Ts'ao Shan (Ts'ao Shan, Pen-chi), was the founder of the Ts'ao Tung (Soto) sect of Ch'an. Ts'ao Shan's life history follows immediately on pages 127-157. The stories of both masters translated from "The Transmission of the Lamp" may be found in Chang Chun-Yuan, trans., Original Teachings of Ch'an Buddhism (see 3.3.6.1[2]), pp. 58-70, 71-83.

Tz'u-en

See under K'uei-chi.

Vajrabodhi

(85) CHOU YI-LIANG, trans. "The Biography of Vajrabodhi of the Kuang-fu Temple of Lo-yang of the T'ang Dynasty," in his "Tantrism in China." See 1.11.2.3(4).
A fully annotated translation of the life of Vajrabodhi, whose Chinese name was Chin-kang-chih. A native of South India, he arrived in Canton in 719 A.D. and was one of the foreign monks responsible for the establishment of esoteric Buddhism in China.

Vighna (Wei ch'i nan)

(86) HUI-CHIAO. Kao seng chuan (see 8.9.3[1]), pp. 31-32.

Vimalaksa (Pi-mo-lo-ch'a)

(87) HUI-CHIAO. Kao seng chuan (see 8.9.3[1]), pp. 84-85.

Wu-chen

(88) CHEN TSU-LUNG. La Vie et les Oeuvres de Wou-tchen (816-895): Contribution à l'Histoire Culturelle de Touen-houang. Paris: Ecole française d'Extrême-Orient, 1966, 169 pp.
An interesting and scholarly study of the little known life and work of the monk Wu-chen, who was rector of the Buddhist community at Tun huang. Especially valuable for its portrait of the relations between this outpost and the Chinese empire per se, during the exciting ninth century.

Yeh Lu Ch'u Ts'ai

(89) RACHEWILTZ, IGOR DE. "Yeh-Lu Ch'u-ts'ai (1189-1243), Buddhist Idealist and Confucian Statesman" (see 1.16.2[9]), pp. 189-216.

Yun Men Wen Yen

(90) LU K'UAN, YU. Ch'an and Zen Teaching (see 2.5.7[16]), pp. 181-214.
An anecdotal life history of Master Wen Yen (d. 949) of Yung Men mountain, the founder of the Yun Men sect of Ch'an, taken from the "Five Lamps Meeting at the Source" (Wu Teng Hui Yuan). For a version translated from "The Transmission of the Lamp," see Chang Chung-Yuan, trans., Original Teachings of Ch'an Buddhism (3.3.6.1[2]), pp. 283-295.

8.9.4 Great Buddhists of Japan

(1) SHIBATA, MASUMI. Les Maîtres du Zen au Japon. See 2.5.7(18).
This work is an attempt to view the development of Zen through biographical sketches of eighteen Zen masters and two important sermons. From these the reader can learn how practitioners of Zen view their own masters' teachings and achievements.

Bankei (b. 1622)

(2) SHIBATA, MASUMI. Les Maîtres du Zen au Japon. See 2.5.7(18).

Basho

(3) FOARD, JAMES. "The Loneliness of Masuo Basho," in The Biographical Process: Studies in the History and Psychology of Religion (see 8.1.2.3[23]), pp. 363-391.
A treatment of the relationship between the life of Basho and the cult which developed after his death. Foard shows the way in which religious resolution of Basho's loneliness was achieved but lost in his actual life, and how a new resolution not attained in his actual life was affirmed in the sacred biography which developed and sustained the cult.

Daio (b. 1235)

(4) SHIBATA, MASUMI. Les Maîtres du Zen au Japon. See 2.5.7(18).

Daito (b. 1281)

(5) SHIBATA, MASUMI. Les Maîtres du Zen au Japon. See 2.5.7(18).

Dogen

(6) SHIBATA, MASUMI. Les Maîtres du Zen au Japon (see 2.5.7[18]), pp. 25-48.
A substantial biography of the Zen master Dogen (b. 1200), who was primarily responsible for the establishment of Soto Zen in Japan. For a listing of the works of Dogen in translation, see 3.3.6.3. For another brief biographical account, see Hoang Thi Bich, Etude et Traduction du Gakudoyojin-shu (2.5.7[10]).

Biography

Eisai

(7) SHIBATA, MASUMI. *Les Maîtres du Zen au Japon.* See 2.5.7(18).

A brief but full biography of the twelfth century monk Eisai, who first introduced and established Zen Buddhism in Japan.

Ennin

(8) REISCHAUER, EDWIN O., trans. *Ennin's Diary: The Record of a Pilgrimage to China in Search of the Law.* See 1.11.2.3(6).

Hakuin (b. 1685)

(9) SHIBATA, MASUMI. *Les Maîtres du Zen au Japon* (see 2.5.7[18]), pp. 117-132.

A good introduction to the important Rinzai master Hakuin and some of his writings and anecdotes. Should be supplemented, however, by Philip Yampolsky's more complete account (below).

(10) YAMPOLSKY, PHILIP B., trans. *The Zen Master Hakuin: Selected Writings.* See 1.13.2.3(4).

Honen

(11) ANESAKI, MASAHARU. "Honen, The Pietist Saint of Japanese Buddhism." See 1.13.2.2(1).

A brief article which seeks to place Honen's significance in Japanese religious history. The article contains a brief biographical sketch and a resume of Honen's fundamental tenets of faith. For the beginning student.

(12) SHUNJO. *Honen, the Buddhist Saint.* See 1.13.2.2(12).

Ippen

(13) YANAGI, SOETSU. "Ippen Shonin." See 2.5.8(29).

Kanzan

(14) SHIBATA, MASUMI. *Les Maîtres du Zen au Japon.* See 2.5.7(18).

Keizan (b. 1268)

(15) SHIBATA, MASUMI. *Les Maîtres du Zen au Japon.* See 2.5.7(18).

Kukai

(16) BOHNER, HERMAN. "Kobo Daishi." See 1.13.2.2(5).

(17) CASAL, U. A. "The Saintly Kobo Daishi in Popular Lore (A.D. 774-835)." *Folklore Studies*, 18 (1959), 95-144.

A straightforward treatment of the life and thought of Kukai or Kobo Daishi, now largely superseded by the work of Yoshito Hakeda (below).

(18) HAKEDA, YOSHITO. *Kukai: Major Works* (see 2.6.2[4]), pp. 13-60.

In these pages, Hakeda provides the reader with a lucid account of what is known historically about the life of Kukai (Kobo Daishi), the eighth and ninth century Japanese Buddhist held to be the founder of the Shingon sect. The author attempts to make his biography strictly historical by leaving aside innumerable legends and stories.

(19) KITAGAWA, JOSEPH. "Master and Savior." See 2.5.2(3).

A reprint of an article that first appeared in *Studies of Esoteric Buddhism and Tantrism* (Koyasan: Koyasan University, 1965), pp. 1-26. It provides a review of the historical data we have concerning Kobo Daishi and the significance of beliefs about him for the popular tradition.

Muso (b. 1275)

(20) SHIBATA, MASUMI. *Les Maîtres du Zen au Japon.* See 2.5.7(18).

Nichiren

(21) ANESAKI, MASAHARU. *Nichiren, the Buddhist Prophet.* See 1.13.2.2(2).

Rennyo

(22) SUGIHIRA, SHIZUTOSHI. "Rennyo Shonin, Great Teacher of Shin Buddhism." See 1.13.2.3(13).

Saicho

(23) PETZOLD, BRUNO. "Dengyo Daishi." See 1.13.2.2(11).

Saigyo

(24) LaFLEUR, WILLIAM. "The Death and Lives of the Poet-Monk Saigyo: The Genesis of a Buddhist Sacred Biography," in *The Biographical Process: Studies in the History and Psychology of Religion* (see 8.1.2.3[24]), pp. 343-362.

This article discusses the influence of the Buddha as a model for the life of Saigyo, and the way in which Saigyo's life, as discerned from his poetic works, led to a new, specifically Japanese model of the ideal Buddhist life. May be supplemented by LaFleur's articles on Saigyo in the *History of Religions*, 13 (1974), 93-128, 227-248 (see 4.3[6]).

Shinran

(25) BLOOM, ALFRED. *The Life of Shinran Shonin: The Journey to Self Acceptance.* See 1.13.2.2(4).

(26) YAMAMOTO, KOSHO. *The Private Letters of Shinran Shonin.* See 3.3.7.2(6).

Shotoku

(27) ANESAKI, MASAHARU. *Prince Shotoku, the Sage Statesman.* See 1.13.2.1(1).

8.9.4 Biography

Daisetz Taro Suzuki

(28) NISHITANI, KEIJI and HIROSHI SAKAMATO, eds. Suzuki Memorial Volume. The Eastern Buddhist, 2 (August 1967).

This edition includes a chronology of Suzuki's life and a bibliography of his writings, as well as a number of panegyric articles.

Suzuki Shosan (b. 1579)

(29) SHIBATA, MASUMI. Les Maîtres du Zen au Japon. See 2.5.7(18).

Takuan (b. 1573)

(30) SHIBATA, MASUMI. Les Maîtres du Zen au Japon. See 2.5.7(18).

8.9.5 Great Buddhists of Southeast Asia and Sri Lanka

Buddhadasa

(1) SWEARER, DONALD. "Thai Buddhism: Two Responses to Modernity. See 1.5.2[22].

Buddhaghosa

(2) Buddhaghosuppatti. Edited and translated by James Gray in Buddhaghosuppatti of the Historical Romance of the Rise and Career of Buddhaghosa (see 8.9.1[26]).

Summary introduction, edition of the Pali text, and translation of a biography of the great fifth century commentator of the Pali scriptures, Buddhaghosa. The work, the date of which is uncertain but which seems to be fairly old, is attributed to one Mahamangala.

(3) FINOT, LOUIS. "La Légende de Buddhaghosa," in Cinquantenaire de l'Ecole Pratique des Hautes Etudes (Sciences Historiques et Philologiques), fasc. 239. Paris: Honoré Champion, 1921, pp. 101-119.

Thorough discussion of the available sources on the life of the great Buddhaghosa, and a serious questioning of the historicity of the figure himself. This article makes a good counterpart to the longer, but less critical, book on Buddhaghosa by Law (below).

(4) LAW, BIMALA CHURN. The Life and Works of Buddhaghosa. See 8.9.1(25).

An overview using the available materials to come up with a composite account of this most important fifth century monk-commentator. For a brief account of Buddhaghosa, see T. W. Rhys-Davids, "Buddhaghosa," in Encyclopaedia of Religion and Ethics (see 1.15.1[9]), vol. 2, pp. 885-887.

(5) SUBRAHMANIAM, R. and S. P. NAINAR. "Buddhaghosa: His Place of Birth." Journal of Oriental Research (Madras), 19 (1950), 278-284.

A review of the various theories of the origin of Buddhaghosa--Ceylon, Burma, Magadha --and then an argument for his birthplace in South India.

(6) TIN, PE MAUNG. "Buddhaghosa." Journal of the Burma Research Society, 12 (1922), 14-20.

Tries to see what can be found out about Buddhaghosa's life from his writings rather than from the legends about him. At the same time, Pe Maung Tin seeks to refute some of the arguments against the historicity of Buddhaghosa made by Finot (above).

Chulalongkorn

(7) Chulalongkorn the Great. See 1.5.2(6).

Dharmapala

(8) OBEYESEKERE, GANANATH. "Personal Identity and Cultural Crisis--The Case of Anagarika Dharmapala," in The Biographical Process: Studies in the History and Psychology of Religion (see 8.1.2.3[24]), pp. 221-252.

In this article Obeyesekere combines psychological, historical, and ethnological methods in order to depict the personal and social conflicts which informed the life of this modernist reformer in late nineteenth to early twentieth century Ceylon. Clearly the most interesting study of this figure presently available, it provides important insight into the "modernizing" process as such.

Mongkut

(9) GRISWOLD, ALEXANDER B. King Mongkut of Siam. See 1.5.2(10).

U Nu

(10) BUTWELL, RICHARD. U Nu of Burma. See 1.4.2(2).

8.9.6 Great Buddhists of Korea

(1) HONG, JUNG-SHIK. "The Thought and Life of Wonhyo." Translated by Paik Seung-gil in Buddhist Culture in Korea (see 1.12.1[1]), pp. 15-30.

A brief study of the life and times and writings of an important Korean Buddhist philosopher of the seventh century. Wonhyo was most noted for his writings in the Kishinnon (Awakening of Faith).

(2) KAKHUN, SOK. Lives of Eminent Korean Monks. See 1.12.1(4).

Includes a useful introduction and translation of available portions of this Korean classic. The work is a chief source of information for any student concerned with the general topic of Korean Buddhism.

(3) LEE, PETER H. "Fa-tsang and Uisang." See 8.9.3(30).

Translation of passsages from the Korean Samguk yuso giving the biography of the seventh century monk Uisang, the "founder" of the Hua Yen school in Korea (Silla). Uisang went to China where he met the Hua Yen patriarch Fa-tsang. Also included here is a translation

Biography

of a letter which Fa-tsang sent to Uisang after his return to Silla.

(4) _____. "The Life of the Korean Poet-Priest Kynyo." *Asiatische Studien* (1957/58), pp. 42-71.

9 Mythology
(Including Sacred History), Cosmology, and Basic Symbols

9.1 MYTHOLOGY (INCLUDING SACRED HISTORY)

See also 4.2.3, Avadanas.

9.1.1 General Discussions: Cycle and Length of Kalpas

(1) Cakkavatti sihanada sutta of Digha Nikaya. Translated by T. W. Rhys-Davids and C. A. F. Rhys-Davids in The Dialogues of the Buddha (see 2.7.1[13]), vol. 3, pp. 53-76.

The Cakkavatti Sihanada sutta, while dealing with the figure of the Cakravartin, also tells the "cosmic story" of one cycle of the world, beginning with the ideal "beginning" explaining the decline of the world and of the human life-span, its "recuperation," and finally the appearance of another cakravartin and the future Buddha Maitreya. It is an important source for any student concerned with these mythological themes.

(2) HARDY, R. SPENCE. A Manual of Buddhism. Varanasi: Chowkhamba Sanskrit Series, 1967, pp. 1-8, 28-35. (Originally published 1853.)

Hardy's Manual of Buddhism, which was based on his own firsthand acquaintance with Sinhala sources in the mid-nineteenth century, remains a valuable source of information on questions of mythology and cosmology. These pages contain a concise account of the length of an "asankhya" and of the duration and division of the various world cycles, including "the periodical destruction and renovation of the Universe."

(3) LA VALLEE POUSSIN, LOUIS DE. "Ages of the World (Buddhist)," in Encyclopaedia of Religion and Ethics (see 1.15.1[9]), vol. 1, pp. 187-190.

A fine, substantive introduction to the cycle of kalpas and their measurement, by one of the greatest Buddhologists of the Western world.

(4) McGOVERN, WILLIAM MONTGOMERY. A Manual of Buddhist Philosophy. Vol. 1: Cosmology. London: Kegan Paul, Trench, Trubner, 1923, pp. 39-48.

A clearly written introduction to the various numerical expressions of the length of time (from the smallest, the ksana, to the greatest, the mahakalpa). It is based, however, on a very late source, the deceptively useful Mahavyutpatti, a medieval Sanskrit-Tibetan-Chinese lexicon.

(5) VASUBANDHU. Abhidharmakosa (see 3.2.3.2[4]), vol. 3, pp. 181 ff.

The third chapter of Vasubandhu's monumental Abhidharmakosa is entirely devoted to a description of "the world." These pages (beginning with section 89d) deal extensively with the various types of kalpas and their duration, and have been extensively annotated by de La Vallée Poussin. They are closely related to the first chapter of the Sarvastivadin Prajnaptisastra, the Lokaprajnapti, which has been elsewhere analyzed by de La Vallée Poussin and forms a good introduction to be read in conjunction with the Abhidharmakosa passage. See Louis de La Vallée Poussin, "Bouddhisme: Etudes et matériaux. Cosmologie: le monde des êtres et le monde réceptacle" (9.1.2[4]).

9.1.2 Myths of the Renewed Creation of the World

(1) Agganna Sutta of Digha Nikaya. Translated by T. W. and C. A. F. Rhys-Davids in The Dialogues of the Buddha (see 2.7.1[13]), vol. 3, pp. 77-94.

The Agganna sutta, which the Rhys-Davids have here translated as "A Book of Genesis," is one of the classic Pali canonical accounts of the gradual loss of man's original paradisiacal situation and of his consequent need to choose the first king (Maha Sammata). A similar version of the story may be found in the Mahavastu (below). For a different, perhaps more popular version, collected by Hardy in mid-nineteenth century Ceylon, see R. Spence Hardy, A Manual of Buddhism (9.1.1[2]), pp. 63 ff. For a thorough study of the sutra, see Herbert Guenther, "Die Buddhistische Kosmogonie," Zeitschrift der deutschen morgenländischen Gesellschaft, 98 (1944), 44-83.

(2) CHEMPARATHY, GEORGE. "Two Early Buddhist Refutations of the Existence of Isvara as the Creator of the Universe." Wiener Zeitschrift für die Kunde Süd- und Ostasiens, 12-13 (1968-1969), 85-100.

A short analysis of the refutations of the argument for the existence of a creator as

Mythology (Including Sacred History)

found in the Yogacarabhumi and a short work known as the Visnorekakartrtvanirakaranam. Also contains a handy listing of textual refutations of the Isvara doctrine.

(3) COEDES, G. and C. ARCHAIMBAULT, trans. Les trois mondes (Traibhumi brah R'van) (see also 3.2.4.2[4]). Paris: Ecole française d'Extrême-Orient, 1973, pp. 216-232.
  Chapter 10 of this important Thai Buddhist cosmological text is entitled "The Interval between Two Mahakalpas," and deals in some detail with the topic of the destruction of the world at the end of one kalpa and of its regeneration at the beginning of the next. A helpful source on this important topic.

(4) LA VALLEE POUSSIN, LOUIS DE. "Bouddhisme: Etudes et matériaux. Cosmologie: le monde des êtres et le monde réceptacle." Mémoires de l'Academie royale de Belgique, classe des lettres et des sciences morales, 6 (1914-1919), 317 ff.
  An excellent description, taken from the Lokaprajnaptisastra (part of the Sarvastivadin Abhidharma text, the Prajnaptisastra) of the re-evolution of the world following its destruction by fire, wind or water. For a different version of the same re-evolution, see the great compendium of Theravada teachings, the Visuddhimagga of Buddhaghosa, translated by Maung Tin as The Path of Purity (3.2.4.2[1], pp. 483 ff. (paragraphs 417 ff.).

(5) LERCLERE, ADHEMARD. Le Bouddhisme au Cambodge (see 1.6.1[4]), pp. 35-50.
  Leclere's work is an important source for Cambodian Buddhist cosmogony. In this chapter, he discusses "L'origine première des choses" and describes his own attempts to find out from various persons and Cambodian works the answers to his Christian-oriented questions.

(6) Mahavastu (see 3.2.1.2[5]), vol. 1, pp. 285-301.
  This short passage, entitled the "Rajavamsa," tells the cosmic story of the regenesis of the world, the loss of the "initial" paradisiacal situation, the consequent selection of a first king from whom are descended the Sakyas--all of which is given as background to the birth of the Buddha. See also the Aggañña Sutta (above)

(7) Patika Sutta of Digha Nikaya. Translated by T. W. and C. A. F. Rhys-Davids in The Dialogues of the Buddhas (see 2.7.1[13]), vol. 3, pp. 25-32.
  In these pages, the subject of the Ultimate Beginnings of the world is touched upon, primarily in order to refute other (mistaken) doctrines of creation. The Buddhist argument (found in a number of other canonical and non-canonical texts) is that when the world-system begins to re-evolve, the first being reborn in the heaven of the Brahmas mistakenly assumes that he is a Brahma, the Creator of all things, and that Brahmins and others just share in his illusion.

(8) ROCKHILL, W. WOODVILLE, trans. The Life of the Buddha (see 3.2.1.2[11]), pp. 1-13.
  This is chapter 1 of Rockhill's work, entitled "History of the World from the Time of Its Renovation to the Reign of Suddhodana, Father of the Buddha," and contains an account of the re-evolution of the world and the early inhabitants' loss of their paradisiacal state, based on the Tibetan version of the Vinaya. It is interesting to compare this with the Theravada version in the Aggañña sutta (above), the Mahasanghika version of the Mahavastu (also above), and the late Chinese version in Samuel Beal, A Catena of Buddhist Scriptures (see 3.2.1.2[7]), pp. 109 ff.

(9) VASUBANDHU. Abhidharmakosa (see 3.2.3.2[4]), vol. 3, pp. 185 ff., 203 ff.
  In these passages of his Abhidharmakosa, Vasubandhu presents and discusses the events of the "kalpa of creation," during which the wind, water, earth, Mt. Meru, etc., gradually evolve, and (starting on page 203) how the beings inhabiting these regions gradually come into being and change.

(10) WAYMAN, ALEX. "Buddhist Genesis and the Tantric Tradition," in The Buddhist Tantras (see 2.6.1[15]), pp. 24-29.
  This is one of few recent articles on the Buddhist myth of the origins of the world. Wayman summarizes the myth and then discusses some of the writings of Tsong Kha pa which bring new information on the early inhabitants of the world, and new insights into the meaning of their story. This was originally published in Oriens Extremus, 9 (1962).

9.1.3 Myths of the Decline of Dharma and of the World

(1) BU-STON. History of Buddhism (Chos 'byung) (see 1.14.1[2]), pp. 171-180.
  The Tibetan historian Bu-sTon ends the India section of his great History of Buddhism with a chapter entitled "The Way How the Doctrine Will Cease to Exist," which represents an interesting compilation of sources current in the fourteenth century on the myth of the decline of the Dharma.

(2) COEDES, G. and C. ARCHAIMBAULT, trans. Les trois mondes. See 9.1.2(3).

(3) COEDES, GEORGES. "The Twenty-five Hundredth Anniversary of the Buddha." Diogenes, 15 (1956), 95-111.
  This provides an interesting insight into the mythology behind the Buddha Jayanti celebration of 1956. It discusses the present-day Buddhists' belief in the progressive decline of their religion and its final disappearance at a predetermined date, of which the Jayanti (in one tradition) marks the exact middle of the span of five thousand years.

9.1.3   Mythology (Including Sacred History)

(4) LAMOTTE, ETIENNE. L'Histoire du Bouddhisme indien (see 1.2.1[10]), pp. 210-222.

An excellent survey of the various traditions prophesying the disappearance of the Saddharma (good or true law). Lamotte provides ample references to original texts, and presents the different theories in a clear and concise manner. The same passage appeared later as an article entitled "Prophéties relatives à la disparition de la Bonne Loi," in Présence du Bouddhisme (see 1.5.1[6]), pp. 657-668.

(5) VASUBANDHU. Abhidharmakosa (see 3.2.3.2[4]), vol. 3, pp. 207-217.

The pages which end this important third chapter (on cosmology) of the Abhidharmakosa describe in detail the events that take place when the world has reached the limit of its declines and the lifespan of man is only ten years; it includes the different destructions by fire, water and wind, how often they occur, and their respective limits in the Rupadhatu.

9.1.4   The Coming of Maitreya and Other "Eschatological" Myths

(1) Cakkavatti sihanada sutta of Digha Nikaya (see 2.7.1[13]), vol. 3, pp. 53-76.

(2) CONZE, EDWARD. Buddhist Scriptures (see 8.1.2.3[7]), pp. 237-242.

In this section of his anthology of texts, under the title of "The Prophecy concerning Maitreya," Conze has translated excerpts from the Maitreyavyakarana, which present one version of the myth of the coming of Maitreya.

(3) FILLIOZAT, JEAN. "Maitreya l'invaincu." See 8.3.4(4).

A short discussion of Maitreya's epithet, "Ajita," of "the unconquered one," and of the parallelism that has been suggested between it and Mithra's epithet "Sol Invictus." Filliozat cautiously seeks to undermine the arguments of Levi and Przyluski (below), and suggests the possibility of influence operating in the other direction, from India on Iran.

(4) LEVI, SYLVAIN. "Maitreya le consolateur." See 8.3.4(6).

A classic article on the figure of Maitreya, on the "eschatological" conceptions surrounding him and on the parallels between him and other figures such as Mithra, Mitra, etc.

(5) MENDELSON, E. MICHAEL. "A Messianic Buddhist Association in Upper Burma." See 4.1.2(10).

A detailed description of the building and ceremonies of the Maheikdi gaing, a group whose millenarian expectations are hoped to be fulfilled with the coming of the future Buddha Maitreya. Also provides some comparative materials in his discussion of the movement.

(6) PRZYLUSKI, JEAN. "La croyance au messie dans l'Inde et dans l'Iran." Revue d'Histoire des Religions, 100 (1929), 1-12.

Przyluski uses an extended book review as a means of presenting his views on the parallels between "Maitreya Ajita" and "Mithra Sol Invictus," and for arguing in favor of an Iranian origin of the figure of Maitreya. See also his later article, "Un dieu iranien dans l'Inde," Rocznik Orientalistychy, 7 (1931), 1-9. For a parallel view, see the article by Levi (above), and for an undermining of both their views, see the article by Filliozat (above).

(7) SARKISYANZ, EMANUEL.. "Messianic Folk-Buddhism as Ideology of Peasant Revolts in Nineteenth and Early Twentieth Century Burma." Review of Religious Research, 10 (1968), 32-38.

An example of the "application" of Buddhist "eschatological" beliefs, including the belief in the coming of Metteya (Maitreya), to a particular situation. For further discussion of this topic, see pages 43-67 of Sarkisyanz, Buddhist Backgrounds of the Burmese Revolution (1.4.2[15]).

(8) SPIRO, MELFORD E. Buddhism and Society (see 6.2.1.1[42]), pp. 162-187.

This section of Spiro's work, entitled "A Religion of Chiliastic Expectations," discusses, on the basis of Burmese materials, the various Buddhist "eschatological" ideologies, and the manner in which they were interpreted and applied in a real situation. It is a good introduction to the subject.

9.1.5   Sacred Histories (National, Ecclesiastical, Doctrinal, etc.)

(1) BU-STON. History of Buddhism (Chos 'byung) (see 1.14.1[2]), vol. 2.

A fourteenth century work which includes, in its second volume, a narrative of the life of the Buddha, an account of the "rehearsals of the Scripture," biographies of Buddhist teachers, and a history of Buddhism in Tibet --doctrinal as well as chronological. It is a classic and important source of our knowledge of the history of Tibetan Buddhism.

(2) Camadevivamsa. Translated by Georges Coedes in "Documents sur l'histoire politique et religieuse du Laos occidental." See 1.7.1(2).

A book-size article in which Coedes translates texts pertaining to the history of Buddhism in Western Laos from two works: Ratanapanna's chronicle of Buddhism, the Jinakalamalini (circa 1516), and Bodhiramsi's Camadevivamsa, which traces the history of the city of Lamphoon from its earliest beginnings. An English translation of the Jinakalamalini may also be found in N. A. Jayawickrama, trans., The Sheaf of Garlands of the Epochs of the Conqueror (below).

(3) Culavamsa. See 1.3.1(3).

A late Sinhalese chronicle which attempts to "continue" the account of the Mahavamsa. Part I takes the narrative from the death of King Mahasena to the reign of Parakkamabahu I in the twelfth century. Part II focuses on Parakkamabahu I (pp. 1-124), Parakkambahu II (pp. 143-182), Vijayabahu IV (pp. 183-200), and carries the history of Sinhalese kingship to its demise in 1815. Like earlier chronicles, the Culavamsa is essential to an understanding of Sinhala Buddhism and culture.

(4) Dathavamsa. Translated by Bimala Churn Law as The Dathavamsa (A History of the Tooth-Relic of the Buddha). See 8.1.2.4(7).

The arrival of the tooth relic of the Buddha shortly after the reign of King Mahasena (334-361 A.D.) was an event of capital importance in the history of Ceylonese Buddhism. The Dathavamsa, originally composed in Sinhalese and translated into Pali in the thirteenth century, is a record of events and incidents surrounding the Tooth. A French summary of the text may be found in Victor Goloubew, "Le temple de la Dent à Kandy" (see 8.1.2.4[10]).

(5) Dipavamsa. See 1.3.1(4).

The first of the chronicles of Sri Lanka, written in the fourth century A.D., the Dipavamsa is an historical poem in Pali of considerable importance for an understanding of Buddhism up to the reign of Mahasena. Most of the poem deals with early Indian Buddhism, pre-Buddhist Ceylon, and the origins of Sinhala Buddhism. It should be read in conjunction with the Mahavamsa (translated by Geiger, above), a chronicle of the next century. For an older, long standard translation of the same text, see Hermann Oldenberg, The Dipavamsa (London, 1879).

(6) The Glass Palace Chronicle of the Kings of Burma. See 1.4.1(3).

Early in the nineteenth century, at the request of the king of Burma, a committee of "learned monks, brahmins and ministers" wrote a complete history of the kings of Burma based on all the "credible records" then available. Only a portion of the "Glass Palace Chronicle" (Hmannan Maha Yaza win taw kyi) has here been translated into English. The early section on Buddhism in India has been omitted, and the translation ends with the fall of Pagan. Nevertheless, it remains one of the few works in English in which the Western scholar can gain some idea of the contents of the many various ancient Burmese chronicles on which it is based.

(7) GOS LO-TSA-BA. Deb-ther-sngon-po. Translated by George N. Roerich as The Blue Annals. See 1.14.1(5).

An important, classic history of the origin, development and spread of Buddhism in Tibet, which unfortunately is not readily available.

(8) Jinakalamalini. Translated by N. A. Jayawickrama as The Sheaf of Garlands of the Epochs of the Conqueror. See 1.5.2(19).

The Jinakalamali was written by Ratapanna Thera about 1516 and is an important source of information about the political and religious history of Buddhism in Southeast Asia. As is usual for works of its kind, it starts with a rapid account of the life of the Buddha and the first three councils. This is followed by a short history of Buddhism in Ceylon, and then by more detailed accounts of the history of Haripunjaya (Lampoon) and Nabbisi (Chiengmai) in Northern Thailand and of the Sinhala form of Buddhism which was associated with those two centers.

(9) La-dvag-rgyal-rabs. Translated by A. H. Francke in Antiquities of Indian Tibet, vol. 2, The Chronicles of Ladakh. See 1.14.2.1(3).

(10) Mahavamsa. Translated by Wilhelm Geiger as The Mahavamsa or the Great Chronicle of Ceylon. See 1.3.1(6).

This fifth century chronicle, attributed to a monk named Mahanama, takes the narrative of Sinhalese history from its beginnings up to the reign of Mahasena in the early fourth century. Most of the Mahavamsa deals with the coming of Buddhism to Ceylon during the time of Devanampiyatissa in the third century B.C., and its further establishment under Dutthagamani two centuries later. This document is seminal for an understanding of the early self-image of Sinhalese Buddhism from the standpoint of the orthodox position of the Mahavihara.

(11) Saddhamma-Sangaha. Translated by Bimala Churn Law as A Manual of Buddhist Historical Traditions. Calcutta: University of Calcutta, 1941, 140 pp.

A late Pali chronicle of the history of Buddhism in Ceylon, drawing on other traditional materials, but interesting for its inclusion of the account of two Buddhist councils held in Ceylon under Devanampiyatissa and Vattagamani. It is also worthwhile as a supplement to the other Sinhala chronicles, the Mahavamsa and the Culavamsa.

(12) Sangitivamsa. Partially translated by Georges Coedes in "Une recension palie des Annales d'Ayuthia." See 1.5.2(7).

Coedes has here edited and translated the seventh chapter of the Sangitivamsa, a work written in Pali in 1789 by a monk named Vimaladhamma. The chapter translated deals with the history of thirty-six (or thirty-three) Buddhist kings of Ayuthya, the Thai capital until 1767.

(13) Sasanavamsa. Translated by Bimala Churn Law as The History of the Buddha's Religion. See 1.4.1(5).

The Sasanavamsa was written in 1861 by an eminent Burmese monk named Pannasami. It was done in the traditional style: like other works of its kind, it begins by dealing, briefly, with the life of the Buddha and the first three Buddhist councils. But its main concern is in tracing the history of the Buddhist religion in Burma, which it does from the time of the Asokan missionaries up to about 1850. It thus does for Burma what the Mahavamsa and Culvamasa do for Sri Lanka.

(14) bSOD NAMS GRAGS PA. Deb t'er dmar po gsar ma. See 1.14.1(14).

(15) TARANATHA. History of Buddhism in India. See 1.2.1(14).
An important, scholarly, and quite readable classic, all the more significant because it draws on a number of sources which were subsequently lost. Originally written in Tibetan in 1608, it was long available only in Vasiliev's Russian and Schiefner's German translation (F. Anton von Schiefner, trans., Taranatha's Geschichte des Buddhismus in Indien, St. Petersburg, 1869). Now in English, it should readily provide undergraduates with a fine example of a Buddhist's history of Buddhism.

(16) Thupavamsa. Translated by N. A. Jayawickrama as Chronicle of the Thupa. Pali Text Society Translation Series, No. 28. London: Pali Text Society, 1971.
The text and translation of a work important for stupa-symbolism which focuses on the history of the construction of Mahastupa at Anuradhapura in Sri Lanka, and recounts much of King Dutthagamani's dealings with it. Interesting for the advanced student.

(17) Vamsavali. Translated by Munshi Shew Shunker Singh and Shri Gunanand in History of Nepal. See 1.15.1(8).
The first seventy-five pages contain an introductory sketch by Wright (a surgeon who lived in Nepal for ten years in the 1860s and 1870s) which is an attempt to give the reader an overview of the then contemporary traditional life in Nepal. The rest of the volume contains the Vamsavali or a genealogical history of Nepal "according to the Buddhist recension." Hence, the reader is treated to the traditional account of the political and religious successes and failures according to the indigenous tradition.

9.2 COSMOLOGY (INCLUDING SACRED GEOGRAPHY)

9.2.1 Introductions and General Discussions: Structure and Size of the Universe

(1) BA HAN. "Burmese Cosmogony and Cosmology." Journal of the Burma Research Society, 48 (1965), 9-16.
A short article, which is useful for giving the Burmese perspective and presentation of the basic Buddhist themes.

(2) BEAL, SAMUEL, trans. A Catena of Buddhist Scriptures from the Chinese (see 3.2.1.2[7]), pp. 15-125.
The section is entitled "Fah-kai-on-lih-to: by Jin-Ch'au," which Beal translates as "The Buddhist Kosmos, with illustrations." It is a sort of compendium of Sino-Buddhist cosmological information which was written during the Ming Dynasty, circa 1583, and touches upon the measurements of the cosmos, the causes of earthquakes, the lands of the nagas, Asuras, and pretas, the various hot and cold hells, the palaces of the sun and moon, the rewards of the Trayastrimsa heaven, the longevity of the devas, and the duration of kalpas, etc.

(3) BHATTACHARYA, N. N. "Brahmanical, Buddhist and Jain Cosmography." Journal of History, 47 (1969), 43-64.
The article begins with a general overview of Vedic cosmology and post-Vedic transformations. It is within this Vedic context that the author understands the origins of Buddhist and Jain cosmologies. A decent introductory article.

(4) COEDES, G. and C. ARCHAIMBAULT, trans. Les trois mondes. See 9.1.2(3).
A French translation from the Thai of a basic Buddhist cosmological text, written in the fourteenth century but based on traditional materials, whose influence has been very great throughout Southeast Asia and which deals in detail with topics often neglected in other cosmologies.

(5) COEDES, GEORGES. "The Traibhumikath, Buddhist Cosmology and Treaty on Ethics. East and West, 7 (1957), 349-352.
An analysis of the most ancient systematic treatise on Buddhist cosmology composed in Thai, but based on Pali sources, by a king of the kingdom of Sukhothai.

(6) KIRFEL, W. Die Kosmographie der Inder. Bonn: K. Schroeder, 1920, pp. 178-208.
This classic study of various Indian cosmological notions, including the Buddhist, is valuable for reference purposes and for the comparison of Buddhist and Hindu and Jain cosmologies.

(7) LAMOTTE, ETIENNE. Histoire du Bouddhisme indien (see 1.2.1[10]), pp. 34-35.
Includes a very helpful chart, based on Sanskrit sources, which clarifies the relationship between the three dhatus (Kama-, Rupa-, and Arupya-dhatus), the five gatis (hells, animals, pretas, men, and gods) and distinguishes clearly which gods are in the Kamadhatu and which in the Rupadhatu.

(8) LA VALLEE POUSSIN, LOUIS DE. "Bouddhisme: études et matériaux. Cosmologie: Le monde des êtres et le monde réceptacle." See 9.1.2(4).

Cosmology (Including Sacred Geography)   9.2.2.1

A book-size "article" which remains one of the most substantial collections of original sources on Buddhist cosmology. In it, de La Vallée Poussin has translated the Tibetan text of Chapter 3 ("The world") of Vasubandhu's Abhidharmakosa (for a translation of the Chinese version, see Volume 3 of his later translation of L'Abhidharmakosa de Vasubandhu, below) and has edited and annotated the Sanskrit text of Yasomitra's commentary on this third chapter. He has also given an important and helpful summary and analysis of cosmological chapters of one of the seven Sarvastivadin Abhidharma works, the Prajnaptisastra.

(9) _____. "Cosmogony and Cosmology (Buddhist)," in Encyclopaedia of Religion and Ethics (see 1.15.1[9]), vol. 4, pp. 129-138.

A substantial introduction to the topic, by one of the greatest Buddhologists of all times, which includes references to original and translated materials, though of course the latter are out of date. This is a fine place for the serious student to begin a study of Buddhism cosmology.

(10) LECLERE, ADHEMARD. Le Bouddhisme au Cambodge (see 1.6.1[4]), pp. 65-171.

An extensive discussion of Buddhist cosmology, and one of the few that presents the particularly Cambodian interpretations of it. Presents an overall picture of the universe, and discusses specifically the planets and the stars, the various heavens and hells, and the inhabitants of the universe.

(11) McGOVERN, WILLIAM MONTGOMERY. A Manual of Buddhist Philosophy, Vol. 1: Cosmology (see 9.1.1[4]), pp. 1-80.

The introduction and Part I of this work by an English adventurer-scholar make a fair, if at times mixed survey of Buddhist cosmology: McGovern is more concerned with presenting material than with analyzing it or his sources. Parts 2 and 3 entitled "Cosmic Analysis" and "Cosmic Dynamics" deal respectively with Abhidharma classification and with the doctrine of Karma.

(12) MONIER-WILLIAMS, MONIER. Buddhism, in Its Connection with Brahmanism and Hinduism and in Its Contrast with Christianity. See 8.5(2).

Though the book as a whole is dated in both its methodology and opinions, these pages make not a bad general sketch of the cosmology of Indian Mahayana Buddhism and its relation to Hindu cosmology.

(13) VASUBANDHU. Abhidharmakosa. See 3.2.3.2(4).

This volume contains the French translation by de La Vallée Poussin of chapter 3 of Hsuan Tsang's Chinese rendition of Vasubandhu's great work, the Abhidharmakosa. The chapter is one of the most thorough classical works on Buddhist cosmology, starting with the division of everything into the Kama-, Rupa-, and Arupa-dhatus, and giving details and different opinions concerning each one's specific structure. The Tibetan text was earlier translated by de La Vallée Poussin in his "Bouddhisme, études et matériaux" (above).

(14) WADDELL, L. AUSTINE. Tibetan Buddhism (see 1.14.1[17]), pp. 77-105.

In this chapter on "The Metaphysical Sources of the Doctrine," Waddell presents, in his own vivid fashion, a description of the Tibetan Buddhist conceptions of the Universe--including the heavens of the various gods, the different hells (hot and cold), and other regions of rebirth and their inhabitants. Illustrated by charts and pictorial representations.

9.2.2 The Realm of Desire (Kamadhatu) and Its Inhabitants

9.2.2.1 General Discussions: Mt. Meru and the Four Continents

(1) BEYER, STEPHAN. The Cult of Tara (see 7.1.1[2]), pp. 167-170.

A fine description of the Tibetan practice of constructing and offering a "Mt. Meru Mandala," which includes representation of the four continents, the eight sub-continents, etc. The rite, which is an important one, offers one of the easiest ways of describing and teaching the structure of this cosmos. Other descriptions of it may be found in Alex Wayman, The Buddhist Tantras (see 2.6.1[15]), pp. 101-103; L. A. Waddell, Tibetan Buddhism (see 7.5.3[3]), pp. 398-405; F. D. Lessing, "Notes on the Thanksgiving Offering," Central Asiatic Journal, 2 (1956), 58-71; Lessing, Yung Ho Kung (see 7.5.3[3]), pp. 102-106; and, for more bibliographic references, Johaness Schubert, "Das Reis Mandala," in Asiatica (Festschrift Friedrich Weller; Leipzig: O. Harrassowitz).

(2) BUDDHAGHOSA. Atthasalini. Translated by Pe Maung Tin as The Expositor (see 3.2.3.3[3]), vol. 2, pp. 390-395.

This passage of Buddhaghosa's commentary on the first book of the Pali Abhidhamma pitaka contains some very precise statistics about the dimensions of the world-system, of Jambudvipa, of Mount Meru, etc.

(3) BURNOUF, EUGENE, trans. Le Lotus de la Bonne Loi (see 3.3.5.1[3]), vol. 2, pp. 844 ff.

An old but still valuable study of the seven mountain chains and Mt. Meru, presented as one of the appendices to Burnouf's translation of the Saddharma pundarka sutra.

(4) COEDES, G. and C. ARCHAIMBAULT, trans. Les trois mondes (see 9.1.2[3]), pp. 78-85, 190-215.

9.2.2.1   Cosmology (Including Sacred Geography)

These passages in the important Thai cosmological text represent a major source of information on Mt. Meru and the four continents, especially on Jambudvipa. See in particular pages 190-204, the discussion of Mt. Meru and astronomy, and pages 204 ff., the passage on the Himalaya and various forests. For a quite different approach to some of these questions, see Shoson Miyamoto, "The Geographical Expansion of the Indian Cultural Sphere Symbolized by the Metaphor of the Five Rivers of India and the Metaphor of the Four Rivers of Asia" (1.10.2[11]).

(5) HARDY, R. SPENCE. A Manual of Buddhism (see 9.1.1[2]), pp. 10-28.
A fine example of the mid-nineteenth century Ceylonese understanding of Mt. Meru and the surrounding mountains and continents, including the movement of the sun in relation to them. Though this should not be used as an introduction to the subject, as Hardy's spelling of terms is outdated and his explanations minimal, the more advanced student will find it an interesting additional source.

(6) LEVI, SYLVAIN. "Pour l'histoire du Ramayana." Journal asiatique, 11 (1918), 1-162.
A lengthy article which includes much information on Jambudvipa and the other continents, its rivers, mountains, etc., taken from Buddhist sources. Especially valuable for its long translation of relevant passages from the much neglected Saddharma-smrtyupasthana-sutra, and for its convenient tables of cosmological information.

(7) PRZYLUSKI, JEAN. "La Ville du Cakravartin--influences babyloniennes sur la civilisation de l'Inde" (see 8.7[3]).

(8) VASUBANDHU. Abhidharmakosa (see 3.2.3.2[4]), pp. 141-148.
A clear description of the location, size, shape, and color of Mt. Meru, the seven chains of mountains and seven seas surrounding it, and of the four continents. The order of the seven chains of mountains has been a matter of some variance from one source to another. For different listings, see, among others, Buddhaghosha, Atthasalini (above), vol. 2, p. 393; Mahavastu, translated by J. J. Jones (2.4.4[5]), vol. 2, p. 282; and Jataka, translated by E. B. Cowell (3.2.2.1[12]), vol. 6, p. 66.

9.2.2.2 Five and/or Six Gatis (General Discussions)
See also 9.3.2, The Wheel of Life.

(1) Katha-vatthu. Translated by Shwe zan Aung and C. A. F. Rhys-Davids as Points of Controversy (see 3.2.3.1[5]), pp. 211 ff.
The question of whether there were five or six realms of existence, i.e., of whether to include the Asuras as well as the hell-beings, animals, men, pretas, and gods, was one which was debated among Hinayanists themselves. In this passage the matter is one of controversy. Other parts of the Pali canon, however, seem to espouse the five gati theory (see, for example, Majjhima I: 98-102, Digha III: 234, Anguttara IV: 459, and Samyutta V: 474). Five gatis are also advocated by the Abhidharmakosa (see the de La Vallée Poussin translation, 3.2.3.2[4], p. 11), and in Nagarjuna's Letter to a Friend, translated by Stephan Beyer in The Buddhist Experience (see 3.3.2.1[18], p. 17. Elsewhere, however, Nagarjuna posits six gatis, as do the Mahavastu and parts of the Saddharmapundarika.

(2) LAMOTTE, ETIENNE. Histoire du Bouddhisme indien (see 1.2.1[10]), pp. 34-35, 697-698.
On pages 34 and 35, Lamotte discusses the five gatis and the repartition of their inhabitants in the kama and rupa-dhatus. On pages 697-698, he touches on the question of the origins of the theory of the sixth gati-- that of the Asuras. Helpful as an introduction, but no more than that.

(3) MUS, PAUL. La Lumière sur les six voies: Tableau de la transmigration bouddhique. Paris: Travaux et mémoires de l'Institut d'ethnologie, 1939.
An excellent, if somewhat involved, study of Buddhist cosmology which specifically tackles the question of the dual tradition of five or six realms of rebirth (gatis). Mus's discussion includes complex textual studies of two "Burmese" works, the Sadgatikarika and the Lokaprajnapti, and of the relation of the scheme of rebirths to Indian folklore. For advanced students only.

(4) WADDELL, L. AUSTINE. Tibetan Buddhism (see 1.14.1[17]), pp. 105-122.
On the wheel of life.

9.2.2.3 Hells, and the Realms of Animals, Pretas, and Asuras

(1) ANDREWS, ALLAN W. The Teachings Essential to Rebirth. See 2.5.8(1).
Genshin was one of the early advocates of the worship of Amida and the Nembutsu within Japanese Tendai. His work, which is here summarized, translated, and discussed, describes the torments of hell, the beauties of the Pure Land and the advantages of the Nembutsu. It was influential in the formative period of the Japanese Pure Land Sects. Another study of it may be found in A. K. Reschauer, "Genshin's Ojoyoshu," Transactions of the Asiatic Society of Japan, 2, no. 7 (December 1930), 16-97.

(2) BEAL, SAMUEL, trans. A Catena of Buddhist Scriptures from the Chinese. See 3.2.1.2(7).

(3) COEDES, G. and C. ARCHAIMBAULT, trans. Les trois mondes (see 9.1.2[3]), pp. 21-68.
The first four chapters of this basic Thai Buddhist cosmological text deal specifically

Cosmology (Including Sacred Geography)

world, the pretas, and the Asuras. For further discussion of the section on hells, see the article by Roeske (below).

(4) DORE, HENRI. Researches into Chinese Superstitions (see 4.1.3[3]), vol. 7, pp. 250-302.
A still valuable source for looking into the transformation of the notions of Buddhist hells in their particular Chinese interpretations. The bulk of the passage deals with the "ten Demon-rulers of Hades."

(5) FEER, LEON. "L'enfer indien." Journal asiatique (1892 and 1893), pp. 112-151.
A two-part article, which is dated but clearly and well presented, and one of the few that attempts a serious comparison between Buddhist and Hindu notions of hell.

(6) JAWORSKI, JAN. "L'Avalambanasutra de la Terre Pure." See 4.2.1(3).
The story of Mogallana's visit to the Buddhist hells became an extremely important one in China and Japan, where it is the basis of the so-called "Festival of All-Souls." This article gives a French translation of the story which includes vivid descriptions of the sufferings in those hells. For a description of the festival itself, see, among others, J. J. L. Duyvendak, "The Buddhistic Festival of the All-Souls in China and Japan" (7.3.2[4]).

(7) LAW, BIMALA CHURN. The Buddhist Conception of Spirits. London: Luzac and Co., 1936.
A study of the Buddhist belief in and traditions about the pretas, based primarily on Dhammapala's commentary on the Petavatthu. This includes many stories about individual pretas, some of which are here translated.

(8) _____. Heaven and Hell in Buddhist Perspective. Calcutta: Thacker and Spink, 1925.
An attempt to bring together, in as orderly a manner as possible, everything the Pali Canon and commentaries have to say about the Buddhist heavens and hells. The section on the hells should be supplemented by Daigan and Alicia Matsunaga's more recent The Buddhist Concept of Hell (below), which treats the topic more critically, and from a Mahayanist angle as well.

(9) LECLERE, ADHEMARD. Le Bouddhisme au Cambodge (see 1.6.1[4]), pp. 103-109.
A description of the Buddhist hells or "Norok," based on Cambodian sources. See also 9.2.1, and, for further details on Cambodian hells, Ch.-Henri Marchal, "Mythologie indochinoise," Mythologie asiatique illustrée (Paris: Librairie de France, 1928), pp. 170-179.

(10) Mahavastu (see 3.2.1.2[5]), vol. 1, pp. 6-25.
This passage of the Mahavastu consists largely of an account of Maha-Maudgalyayana's visit to the eight hells, and his description of the beings there. This is followed by shorter accounts of his trips to the worlds of the "brutes," the hungry ghosts, and the Asuras. The descriptions are graphic but by no means unique.

(11) MATSUNAGA, DAIGAN and ALICIA MATSUNAGA. The Buddhist Concept of Hell. New York: Philosophical Library, 1972.
A full study of the Buddhist notion and understanding of hell, especially from the Mahayana point of view. The authors begin by tracing the history of the notion of hell in Buddhism (beginning with the Vedic background), and then examine various philosophical interpretations of hell by Buddhist schools, especially the Madhyamikas and the Yogacarins. The work ends with a detailed description and discussion of the eight hells based on the otherwise untranslated but important Saddharma smrtyupasthana sutra. It is a fine complement to B. C. Law's Theravada-oriented Heaven and Hell in Buddhist Perspective (above).

(12) Peta Vatthu. Translated by Henry S. Gehman as Peta vatthu: Stories of the Departed. See 3.2.2.1(21).
The Peta vatthu is the seventh book of the Khuddaka Nikaya. It is a complementary work to the Vimana vatthu, telling, as it does, stories about pretas (the so-called "hungry ghosts") and their sufferings. Its main thrust is to prescribe the leading of the ethical life by illustrating the consequences of bad karma. Like the Vimana vatthu (above), it has long been neglected by Western scholarship.

(13) PRZYLUSKI, JEAN. La légende de l'empereur Asoka (see 3.2.2.2[2]), pp. 120-160.
As part of his introduction to one of the episodes contained in the various versions of the Asokavadana, Przyluski gives a fascinating study of the history and development of the Buddhist notion of hell, and the way in which the picture of hell may have evolved and changed. This is for students seriously interested in the subject.

(14) ROESKE, M. "L'enfer cambodgien d'après le Trai Phum, 'Les Trois Mondes.'" Journal asiatique (1914), pp. 587-606.
Translation and discussion of passages dealing with the various hells from the Trai Phum, an important Southeast Asian Buddhist cosmological text. For a further study of the conceptual influences at work here, see Paul Mus, "Note sur l'enfer bouddhique au Cambodge," appendix to his La Lumière sur les six voies (see 9.2.2.2.[3]).

(15) WADDELL, L. AUSTINE. Tibetan Buddhism (see 1.14.1[17]), pp. 89-100.

A graphic discussion of both the hot and the cold hells, and also of the land of the pretas, from the Tibetan perspective. It includes some interesting and frightening pictures.

9.2.2.4 Heavens and Gods of the Kama dhatu (Including the Guardians of the Four Quarters, Indra, Mara, etc.)

See also 9.3.5, Mara and Other Symbols of Evil

(1) BOYD, JAMES. "Symbols of Evil in Buddhism." Journal of Asian Studies, 31 (1971), 63-75.
This is one of the few studies to focus on the matter of the plurality of "Maras" referred to in both Pali and Sanskrit texts. Boyd discusses the relationship of Mara and the Maras and sets them in the context of Buddhist views of evil in general.

(2) COEDES, G. and C. ARCHAIMBAULT, trans. Les trois mondes (see 9.1.2[3]), pp. 151-169.
These pages (Chapter 6) of this basic Thai Buddhist cosmological text deal specifically with the gods of the realm of desire, and make a fine introduction to the subject. See especially the passages on the guardians of the four quarters, the trayastrimsa gods, and on the subject of the death of gods.

(3) DORE, HENRI. Researches into Chinese Superstitions (see 4.1.3[3]), vol. 7, pp. 394-408.
A brief treatment of the traditions of the "four heavenly kings," protectors of the four quarters within the Chinese context. Especially helpful for a comparison with a Taoist account of the four lokapalas.

(4) Katha-vatthu (see 3.2.3.1[5]), pp. 71-76.
This short passage deals with the nature of the religious life among the devas. The treatment of this question is especially interesting for its bearing on the parallel problem of the religious life of the laity, for both devas and laymen, although they do not renounce their respective "worlds," can nevertheless follow the Path.

(5) LAMOTTE, ETIENNE. Histoire du Bouddhisme indien (see 1.2.1[10]), pp. 759-761.
A short but illuminating discussion of a number of the different deities of the Kama dhatu: the guardians of the four quarters, the Trayastrimsa gods, led by Indra, the gods of Tusita heaven, and the Paranirmitavasavartin, whose leader is Mara, the sovereign of the Kama dhatu.

(6) LA VALLEE POUSSIN, LOUIS DE. "Bouddhisme: Etudes et matériaux: Cosmologie: Le monde des êtres et le monde réceptacle" (see 9.1.2[4]), pp. 301-306.
A detailed description of the various heavens of the Kama dhatu, based on the Lokaprajnapti sastra, an important commentary on a Sarvastivadin Abhidharma work. A more available text which follows similar lines, but in more chaotic fashion, may be found in de La Vallée Poussin's translation of the Abhidharmakosa (see 3.2.3.2[4]), pp. 160 ff. The latter includes, on page 169, a description of Yama's castle.

(7) LAW, BIMALA CHURN. Heaven and Hell in Buddhist Perspective. See 9.2.2.3(8).

(8) LESSING, FERDINAND. Yung Ho Kung. See 7.5.3(3).

(9) Mahavastu (see 3.2.1.2[5]), pp. 25-29.
A brief account of Maha Maudgalyayana's visit to the Caturmaharajika devas (guardians of the four quarters), to the Trayastrimsa devas, and a number of the other heavenly realms.

(10) "Vimana," in The Pali Text Society's Pali-English Dictionary. Edited by T. W. Rhys-Davids and W. Stede. London: Luzac and Co., 1921.
A substantial article on the different meanings of the word "Vimana," including many further textual references to passages in the Pali Canon.

(11) Vimanavatthu. Translated by Jean W. Kennedy as "Vimana Vatthu: Stories of the Mansions." See 3.2.2.1(30).

(12) WAYMAN, ALEX. "Studies in Yama and Mara." Indo-Iranian Journal, 3 (1959), 44 ff. and 112 ff.
A scholarly and difficult article on the figures of Yama and Mara, their background and relationship within Buddhism. Especially interesting is Wayman's discussion of the "four Maras."

9.2.2.5 Minor, Popular, Protective Deities of the Kamadhatu (Gandharvas, Nagas, Yaksas, etc.)

See also Category 4.1, Buddhism and Popular Beliefs, and Category 7.8, Cults and Rituals for Particular Buddhas, Bodhisattvas, Deities, Nagas, etc.

(1) COMBAZ, GISBERT. "Masques et dragons en Asie." Mélanges chinois et bouddhiques, 7 (n.d.), 1-328.
A book-length article covering the whole of Asia. After a study of apotropaic masks from Greek Gorgons to Japan, Combaz deals in detail with the makara in Indian, and various guardian figures in China, including nagas, dragons, aquatic elephants, etc.

(2) COOMARASWAMY, ANANDA K. Yaksas. New Delhi, 1971. (Originally published 1928-1931.)
A full study of yaksas, yaksis and their fundamental contribution to Buddhist mythology, iconography, cultic worship, ideas of reincarnation, and evaluation of Bodhisattva figures, especially in art. Coomaraswamy's

Cosmology (Including Sacred Geography)

thesis is that yaksa-yaksi worship reveals cults of local tutelary deities of fertility who were guardians of cities, towns or geographical features (mountains, rivers, etc.).

(3) FOUCHER, A. L'art gréco-bouddhique du Gandhara. Paris: E. Leroux, 1905-1922, vol. 2.

A very helpful and thorough study of the position and role of a number of minor deities, based on consideration of the pious imagery which developed around them.

(4) LALOU, MARCELLE. "Le culte des naga et la thérapeutique." See 7.8(6).

Text and translation of an important Tibetan ritual work dealing with methods of controlling nagas, the Klu'i gdon-las grol-bar-byed-pa sbrul 'jin gsan-po (Secret qui saisit le serpent, pour délivrer de l'emprise des naga). Also includes a description of a puja to eight nagas.

(5) LAMOTTE, ETIENNE. Histoire du Bouddhisme indien (see 1.2.1[10]), pp. 761-765.

This section is entitled "Les dieux dans la piété populaire," and, though not nearly as long as one might want, it makes a good introduction to the topic of "minor, popular" deities, paying attention to both their geographical distribution and to the social classes that worshipped them.

(6) LEVI, SYLVAIN. "Le catalogue géographique des Yaksas dans le Mahamayuri." Journal asiatique (1915), pp. 20-138.

An extensive discussion of the Mahamayuri, one of five famous Mahayana "Sutras of protection." The work is filled with mantras, but at the same time contains an invocation of a whole series of popular deities, group by group, and including the seven bodhi trees of the seven previous Buddhas, the four Maharajas, the son of Kubera, the yaksas protecting the cities, the twenty-eight Mahayaksasenapati, the dharmabrother of Vaisravana, the 108 nagarajas, Brahma, Indra, etc.

(7) Maha samaya sutta, in Digha Nikaya. Translated by T. W. Rhys-Davids in Dialogues of the Buddha (see 2.7.1[13]), vol. 2.

An important text listing several series of yaksas and gandharvas and other popular deities. Similar passages may be found and compared in the Samyutta Nikaya, translated by C. A. F. Rhys-Davids as The Book of Kindred Sayings (see 2.7.7[10]), vol. 3, chapters 29-32, and vol. 1, chapter 10, the so-called "Yakkha suttas."

(8) NEBESKEY-WOJKOWITZ, RENE DE. Oracles and Demons of Tibet. See 4.1.5(3).

Subtitled "The Cult and Iconography of the Tibetan Protective Deities," this is a substantial study of popular Tibetan deities, which are divided into two groups: the higher deities ('jig rten las 'das pa'i srung ma, including Sri Devi, Mahakala, Vaisravana, Yama, etc.) and the more this-worldly 'jig rten pa'i srung ma (which include Pe har, rDo rje shugs ldan, and mountain and protective deities, etc.). The book ends with a study of the "Cult of Protective Deities," including divination and oracles, and the cult of dharmapalas.

(9) PERI, NOEL. "Hariti, la mère des démons." Bulletin de l'Ecole française d'Extrême-Orient, 17 (1917), 1-102.

A substantial and critical study of the legends and cults surrounding the terrifying but popular yaksini, Hariti.

(10) PRZYLUSKI, JEAN and MARCELLE LALOU. "Notes de mythologie bouddhique." Harvard Journal of Asiatic Studies, 3 (1938), 40-46, 126-136; and 4 (1939), 69-76.

A three-part article dealing with yaksas and gandharvas in the Mahasamaya sutta of the Digha Nikaya, a parallel text from the Tibetan, and the list of the "sons of Brahma" in the same sutta.

(11) ROCK, JOSEPH F. The Na-Khi Naga Cult and Related Ceremonies. See 7.8(9).

Extensive and detailed descriptions of Nakhi religious rituals, with their interesting combination of Buddhist, Bon, and other elements. Rock's point of focus is the Ssu Ddu gv ceremony or great Naga cult.

(12) VISSER, MARINUS WILHELM DE. The Dragon in China and Japan. Amsterdam: Verhandelingen der Koninklijke Akademie van Wetenschappen te Amsterdam, 1913.

A study of the transformations of the myths and figure of the Naga, as it moved from India (mainly along Buddhist routes) to China and then to Japan. Helpful primarily for its survey of dragon lore in Chinese literature.

(13) ZIMMER, HEINRICH. Myths and Symbols in Indian Art and Civilisation. New York: Pantheon, 1946, pp. 59-68.

Zimmer investigates the nature of chthonic and aquatic guardian figures, yaksas and nagas, with a treatment of the harmony between the Buddha, who comes to conquer the bondage of nature, and the nagas representing chthonic bondage--a harmony best seen in the images of the Muchalinda Buddha.

9.2.3 The Realm of Form (Rupa Dhatu) and Its Inhabitants and the Realm Without Form (Arupa Dhatu)

See also Category 11.4.5 on Trance States.

(1) ANURUDDHA. Abhidhammattha Sangaha. Translated by Narada Thera as A Manual of Abhidhamma (see 3.2.3.3[2]), pp. 43-61.

These pages of this classic Theravada Abhidhamma manual contain scholastic explanations of the realm of form and the realm without form, relating them to the types of meditative consciousness they correspond to. Narada Thera's notes are helpful, but this is still for advanced students only. For another presentation along similar lines, see the translation of the Dhamma sangani (pp. 40-68, paragraphs 160-268).

(2) COEDES, G. and C. ARCHAIMBAULT, trans. Les trois mondes (see 9.1.2[3]), pp. 170-190.
Chapters 6 and 7 of this basic Thai cosmological text deal specifically and in more detail than usual with the topic of the gods of the realm of form and the gods of the realm without form. They make an important source on this topic which should be consulted by all doing serious work on it.

(3) Katha-vatthu (see 3.2.3.1[5]), pp. 153-156, 217-221, 310-311.
These passages of the Katha vatthu deal with certain questions concerning the nature of "existence" in the form and formless realms. Included are discussions of whether there is consciousness and whether there are senses in the rupa-sphere, whether there is any subtle matter in the arupa-sphere, whether the beings in these two realms have any desire for life, etc.

(4) LAMOTTE, ETIENNE. Histoire du Bouddhisme indien (see 1.2.1[10]), pp. 680-682.
A brief discussion, but very useful for correlating the levels of realization of the four noble truths with the status of the rupa and arupa dhatus. See also page 761 for a discussion of the types of deities in these two realms.

(5) VAN ZEYST, H. G. A. "Arupa loka," in Encyclopaedia of Buddhism (see 2.5.4[12]), vol. 2, pp. 103-164.
A short but very clear discussion of the major characteristics of the realm without form, from a Theravada perspective.

9.2.4 Buddha Fields (Buddha Ksetra)

See also Category 11.7.4, The Pure Land.

(1) BARUA, BENIMADHAB. "Buddhakhetta in the Apadana," in B. C. Law Volume. Poona: Bhandarkar Oriental Research Institute, 1946, vol. 2, pp. 183-190.
The question of the origins of the notions of the Pure Land is a complex one. In this fascinating article, Barua has translated a section of the Canonical Pali work, the Apadana, which deals primarily with the notion of the Buddha's field (Buddhakhetta)--the description of which is much akin to later descriptions of the Sukhavati of Amitatha.

(2) "Butsudo," in Hobogirin: dictionnaire encyclopédique du Bouddhisme (see 2.7.12[1]), pp. 198-203.
An excellent substantive article on the history and different meanings of the "Buddha field" concept--primarily in Mahayana, but also with some discussion of its Theravada antecedents. It is espeically valuable for its references to original texts.

(3) Maha prajnaparamita sastra. Translated by Etienne Lamotte as Le traité de la grande vertu de sagesse de Nagarjuna (see 3.3.1.2[6]), vol. 1, pp. 403-430.
The chapter deals specifically with the Buddha fields and is important not only as an example of a well developed Mahayana view of the topic, but also for Lamotte's extensive footnotes.

(4) ROWELL, TERESINA. "The Background and Early Use of the Buddha-ksetra Concept." Eastern Buddhist, 6 (1933), 199-246, 379-431; and 7 (1936), 131-145.
The concept of a Buddha's field (Buddhaksetra) is an important one in any understanding of the development of the doctrine of the Pure Land. In this article--one of the more substantial in English--Rowell seeks out the roots of this concept and exposes the point of doctrinal transition from emphasis on attaining a pure field for oneself by means of worshipping the Buddhas, to emphasis on the special ideal of being reborn in the Sukhavati of Amitabha.

(5) Vimalakirtinirdesa. Translated by Etienne Lamotte as L'enseignement de Vimalakirti (see 3.3.2.1[34]), pp. 395-404.
Chapter 1 of the Vimalakirti Nirdesa deals with the purification of the Buddha fields, but more important for the student is Lamotte's masterful appendix on the Buddhaksetra (pp. 395-404), which is full of indispensable references for the student of this topic.

9.2.5 Intermediate States (antarabhava/Bardo)

(1) EVANS-WENTZ, W. Y., ed. The Tibetan Book of the Dead or The After-Death Experiences on the Bardo Plane, According to Lama Dawa Samdup's English Rendering. See 3.4.2(2).
The most popular English rendition of the Tibetan Bardo Thodol, a ritual and doctrinal text dealing with the passage through the intermediate state between death and birth. The work has enjoyed a tremendous popularity in certain circles in the West, but its original import and place within Tibetan Buddhism is hard to estimate. The translation, which can hardly be called authoritative, is preceded by Evans-Wentz's long introduction, which is frustratingly unhelpful. The version by Freemantle (below) is far superior.

(2) FREEMANTLE, FRANCESCA and CHOGYAM TRUNGPA, trans. The Tibetan Book of the Dead. See 3.4.2(5).

(3) LA VALLEE POUSSIN, LOUIS DE. "The Buddhist Wheel of Life from a New Source." Journal of the Royal Asiatic Society (1897), pp. 463 ff.
A presentation of information from the Candamaha rosana tantra, which relates the theory of dependent origination and the doctrine of an intermediate state (antarabhava).

(4) VASUBANDHU. Abhidharmakosa (see 3.2.3.2[4]), pp. 31-53.

An extensive discussion of the pros and cons for the existence of the intermediate state between rebirths and of its nature. The question was one of debate among Theravadans. On this matter, see also de La Vallée Poussin, "Dogmatique bouddhique," Journal asiatique, 20 (1902), 295 ff.

(5) WAYMAN, ALEX. "The Intermediate State in Buddhism," in Buddhist Studies in Honour of I. B. Horner (see 1.2.2.4[11]), pp. 227-239.

A significant study of the different theories of the different schools about the intermediate state. In addition to reviewing the whole question, Wayman clarifies Nagarjuna's views on the subject and discusses the relation of the theory to Buddhist embryological theories. Much more helpful than the somewhat disappointing article by Edward Zonze, "The Intermediate World," The Eastern Buddhist, 7, no. 2 (1974), 22-31.

9.3 BASIC SYMBOLS

See also Category 5, Art. For mandalas, mudras, and also tantric symbolism, see 11.6.

9.3.1 The Wheel of Dharma

(1) AGRAWALA, VASUDEVA S. The Wheel Flag of India--Chakra Dhvaja. Banaras, 1964.

An unfortunately rare book, which contains a useful compendium of information and material on wheel symbolism. It is especially valuable for putting the Buddhist dharma cakra into its overall Indian context. An earlier and somewhat more specialized article which also helps in this regard is P. Horsch, "The Wheel: An Indian pattern of world interpretation," in Liebenthal Festschrift, edited by K. Roy (Santiniketan, 1957), pp. 62-79.

(2) Cakkavatti sihanada sutta of Digha Nikaya. See 2.7.1(13).

(3) COEDES, GEORGES. "Une roue de la loi avec inscription en Pali provenant du site de P'ra Pathom." Artibus Asiae, 19 (1956), 221-226.

A discussion of a fine specimen of a Dharma cakra from Cambodia, the inscriptions on which clearly relate the spokes to the Noble Truths.

(4) COOMARASWAMY, ANANDA K. Elements of Buddhist Iconography. Cambridge, Mass.: Harvard University Press, 1935, pp. 25-36.

A detailed discussion of what Coomaraswamy calls the "Word Wheel" (Dharma cakra), especlly valid for its presentation of some of the Indian background to this symbol.

(5) FOUCHER, A. The Life of the Buddha (see 2.7.6[5]), pp. 134-152.

A description of the setting and content of the Buddha's first sermon, the "setting in motion of the wheel of the Dharma," with helpful comments on the symbolism of the wheel.

(6) Lalitavistara. Translated by Philippe Edouard Foucaux as Développement des Jeux (see 3.3.8.1[2]), pp. 350-352.

This passage immediately follows the account of the Buddha's first Sermon at Sarnath, and contains a full "description" of the Wheel of the Dharma, with many epithets and explanations.

(7) MAJUMDAR, B. "Symbology of the Asoka pillar capital, Sarnath." Indian Culture, 2 (1935), 160-163.

The pillar capital at Sarnath has long been a subject of scholarly debate. In this article, Majumdar argues that the four wheels on the pillar represent dharmacakras, their twenty-four spokes being the twenty-four moments of causal relations.

(8) SIMPSON, WILLIAM. The Buddhist Praying Wheel: A Collection of Material Bearing upon the Symbolism of the Wheel and Circular Movements in Custom and Religious Ritual. London: Macmillan, 1896, pp. 40-65.

As a background to a general free-for-all discussion, this chapter deals with "The Wheel in Indian Buddhism." It is dated, but interesting.

9.3.2 The Wheel of Life

See also 2.7.6, Dependent Origination.

(1) BLOFELD, JOHN. The Tantric Mysticism of Tibet (see 2.6.1[3]), pp. 119-122.

A short but clear and adequate description of the Tibetan "Wheel of Life," including a diagram giving a "key to its symbolism."

(2) GOVINDA, ANAGARIKA. Foundations of Tibetan Mysticism (see 2.6.1[9]), pp. 234-257, 284-285.

Perhaps the finest readily available introduction to the "Wheel of Life" in its Tibetan form, which does not simply stop at explaining its various symbolic elements, but goes on to show its intimate relation to Avalokitesvara and the mantra "Om Mani Padme Hum."

(3) HARTMANN, GERDA. "Symbols of the Nidanas in Tibetan Drawings of the Wheel of Life." See 2.7.6(6).

Hartmann discusses briefly and specifically the symbols used in the outer rim of the Wheel of Life to depict the various links in the "chain of dependent origination."

(4) KARUNARATNE, T. B. The Buddhist Wheel Symbol. Wheel Publication, Nos. 137-138. Kandy: Buddhist Publication Society, 1969.

A fairly good discussion of the symbols of the ratnacakka of a cakravartin, the dhammacakka of Buddhism, the lakkhana cakka (one of the marks on the soles of a Buddha's feet) and the bhavacakka (wheel of life), with a number of interesting plates. For a fuller discussion, in the same series, of the last mentioned wheel, see Khantipalo, <u>The Wheel of Birth and Death</u> (Wheel Publications, Nos. 147-149, 1970), which includes a translation of an important and relevant passage from the Divyavidana.

(5) LA VALLEE POUSSIN, LOUIS DE. "Bouddhisme, Etudes et Matériaux." <u>See</u> 9.1.2(4).

A short article by a master Buddhologist, and one of the few which seeks to be somewhat analytical about the origins of the depiction of the wheel of life, and its relationship to other forms of the wheel in Buddhist iconography.

(6) PRZYLUSKI, JEAN. "La Roue de la Vie à Ajanta." <u>Journal asiatique</u>, 16 (1920), 313-331.

An interesting article which seeks to interpret the Wheel of Life depicted in one of the Ajanta caves in the light of instructions for making such wheels given by the Buddha in the <u>Divyavadana</u>. At the same time, Przyluski is critical of Waddell's interpretation in his article for the <u>Journal of the Asiatic Society of Bengal</u> (below).

(7) WADDELL, L. AUSTINE. "The Buddhist Pictorial Wheel of Life." <u>Journal of the Asiatic Society of Bengal</u>, 61 (1892), 133-155.

A classic article on the Ajanta Wheel of Life and the Tibetan version. It is especially valuable for showing the differentiation between the two kinds of Tibetan Wheels of Life: "old style" and "new style." For a disturbingly parallel treatment which does not even refer to Waddell, <u>see</u> Upali Karunaratna, "Bhavacakra," in <u>Encyclopaedia of Buddhism</u> (<u>see</u> 2.5.4[12]).

(8) _____. <u>Tibetan Buddhism</u> (<u>see</u> 1.14.1[17]), p. 122.

An illustration and explanation of the Tibetan version of the "bhavacakra" or wheel of becoming, which lays emphasis on the twelve links in the chain of dependent origination. Waddell's explanations are sometimes confused, but generally prefigure subsequent interpretations of this symbol. This passage of the book is largely based upon Waddell's earlier article in the <u>Journal of the Royal Asiatic Society</u> (above).

9.3.3 <u>The Lotus</u>

(1) BOSCH, F. D. K. <u>The Golden Germ: An Introduction to Indian Symbolism</u>. The Hague: Mouton, 1960.

Includes a most detailed and technical study of the cosmological significance of the frequently used Buddhist motif of the lotus rhizome.

(2) COOMARASWAMY, ANANDA K. <u>Elements of Buddhist Iconography</u> (<u>see</u> 9.3.1[4]), pp. 17-25, 39-59.

Considers both what Coomaraswamy calls the "Earth Lotus," and the "Lotus-throne." This is one of Coomaraswamy's better books: he discusses not only the symbolism and different iconographic uses of the lotus, but its Vedic and indigenous background. A shorter, more specialized discussion by the same author may be found in "Origins of the Lotus (so-called Bell-) Capital," <u>Indian Historical Quarterly</u>, 6 (1930), 373-375, which was taken up again by A. K. Mitra, "A further note on the origin of the Bell Capital," <u>Indian Historical Quarterly</u>, 10 (1934), 125-136.

(3) FOUCHER, A. "On the Iconography of the Buddha's Nativity," in <u>Memoirs of the Archaeological Survey of India</u>. No. 46. Delhi, 1934, p. 27.

Deals with the lotus as a symbol of the purity and nativity of the Buddha in pre- and non-Gandharan Buddhist art, where the other three "miracles"--enlightenment, first sermon, and death are represented respectively by tree, wheel, and mound.

(4) INAGAKI, HISAO. "Padma-symbolism in Pure Land Thought." <u>Indogaku Bukkyogaku Kenkyu/ Journal of Indian and Buddhist Studies</u>, 13, no. 1 (1965), 396-393 (sic).

Unfortunately a very short article on the lotus symbol in Pure Land traditions, with particular regard paid to modes of birth on earth and in the Pure Land.

(5) WADDELL, L. AUSTINE. "The Lotus (Buddhism)," in <u>Encyclopaedia of Religion and Ethics</u> (<u>see</u> 1.15.1[9]), vol. 8, pp. 142-144.

Waddell discusses the significance of the lotus in Buddhist symbolism. This should be compared with A. MacDonell's article in the same book on the general significance of the lotus in its Indian expression.

(6) _____. <u>Tibetan Buddhism</u> (<u>see</u> 1.14.1[17]), pp. 338-339, 388.

A very brief treatment of the significance of the lotus in Tibetan Buddhism, touching on the different colors and their relationships to various Buddhas and bodhisattvas.

(7) WARD, W. E. "The Lotus Symbol: Its Meaning in Buddhist Art and Philosophy." <u>Journal of Aesthetics and Art Criticism</u>, 11 (1953), 135-146.

A short but useful discussion of the lotus which tries to span its significance in several fields, including art history.

(8) ZIMMER, HEINRICH. <u>Myths and Symbols in Indian Art and Civilization</u> (<u>see</u> 9.2.2.5[13]), pp. 90-102.

This is useful for putting the lotus into the symbolic context of the whole of India, and also for discussing the Mahayana use of the lotus (in Padmapani) and in the Prajnaparamita texts. Another, extensive work on lotus symbolism by the same author may be found in Zimmer, <u>The Art of Indian Asia, Its Mythology and Transformation</u> (Bollingen Series, No. 34; New York: Pantheon, 1955), vol. 1, ch. 6.

Basic Symbols

9.3.4 Trees

(1) BOSCH, F. D. K. The Golden Germ: An Introduction to Indian Symbolism. See 9.3.3(1).

A detailed study of the wealth of accumulated literary and art-historical materials about the lotus as well as sacred Buddhist trees, and the associated tree-spirits, nagas and yaksas.

(2) MONIER-WILLIAMS, MONIER. Buddhism in Its Connection with Brahmanism and Hinduism and Its Contrast with Christianity (see 8.5[2]), pp. 515-520.

The book as a whole is severely dated, but these pages still contain a helpful overview of the various trees which figure in Buddhist symbolism, and their meaning, and connections with Hinduism.

(3) VIENNOT, ODETTE. Le culte de l'arbre dans l'Inde ancienne. Annales du Musée Guimet, No. 59. Paris, 1954, pp. 99-239.

A rich study of the fascinating subject of the role and symbolism of trees and tree worship in ancient Indian religions. The cited pages deal with the tree in Buddhist literature and iconography.

9.3.5 Mara and Other Symbols of Evil

See also 9.2.2.4, Heavens and Gods of the Kama dhatu. On Devadatta, see 8.8, Buddha's Disciples.

(1) Astasahasrika Prajnaparamita (see 8.1.2.2[2]), pp. 83-92, 152-157.

These passages reflect the role Mara plays in the Perfection of Wisdom literature: he seems to have given up his crude bombardment tactics and become a subtler devil. For example, it is said, "It is also a deed of Mara if, after one has written down the Prajnaparamita, one should either think that it IS the Prajnaparamita which is written down, or that it is NOT the Prajnaparamita which is written down."

(2) ASVAGHOSA. Buddhacarita. Translated by Samuel Beal as the Fo Sho Hing Tsan King--A Life of the Buddha (see 3.2.4.1[3]), pp. 147-156.

This account of Mara--his daughters and his hosts--and of their defeat by the Buddha under the Bodhi tree, is as graphic as any of those to be found in other biographies of the Buddha. Parallel passages may be found in the Lalita Vistara, translated into French by Philippe Edouard Foucaux (see 8.1.2.1[12]), where the comparison of the two attacks of Mara before and after the Buddha's enlightenment (pp. 257-286 and 314-317) can be interesting.

(3) BOYD, JAMES. "Symbols of Evil in Buddhism." See 9.2.2.4(1).

(4) DUROISELLE, CH. "Upagutta et Mara." Bulletin de l'Ecole française d'Extrême-Orient, 4 (1904), pp. 414-428.

The very important legend of the conversion to Buddhism of Mara by the sage Upagupta is known primarily from the Sanskrit Divyavadana. Here Duroiselle translates and discusses another version of the story from the Burmese Pali text, the Lokapannati.

(5) FOUCHER, A. The Life of the Buddha (see 2.7.6[5]), pp. 105-114, 129 ff.

A highly readable treatment of the symbolism and meaning of the Buddha's encounter, just before his enlightenment, with the assaults and temptations of Mara.

(6) LAW, B. C. "The Buddhist Conception of Mara," in Buddhistic Studies (see 2.4.2[7]), pp. 257-283.

A review of the Pali material about Mara--his various characters, his army, his daughters, etc.--which goes on to investigate the way in which he relates to monks, nuns and laymen. There is also a comparison of Mara and Kamadeva.

(7) LING, TREVOR O. Buddhism and the Mythology of Evil. London: Allen and Unwin, 1962.

A perceptive study of Mara in the Theravada tradition which argues that he is a myth to be transcended, so distinguishing him from the Christian Satan, who is said to be more integral to the Christian world view than Mara to the Buddhist.

(8) Mahaprajnaparamita sastra. Translated by Etienne Lamotte as Le traité de la grande vertu de sagesse de Nagarjuna (see 3.3.1.2[6]), vol. 2, pp. 868-878.

This passage contains the story of Devadatta, the Buddha's cousin who became a Buddhist personification of evil. The story covers his obtaining of supernatural powers, his three great crimes, and his fate in hell. Lamotte's notes also contain a bibliography of references which should assist anyone interested in Devadatta.

(9) Samyutta Nikaya. Translated by C. A. F. Rhys-Davids as The Book of Kindred Sayings (see 2.7.7[10]), vol. 1, pp. 128-170.

These two sections of the Samyutta Nikaya are valuable sources for any study of the symbolism of Mara. The first contains the "Mara suttas," records of a number of conversations between the Buddha (or various bhikkhus) and Mara, who adopts a number of guises. The other contains the "Suttas of Sisters," which record the dealings of various bhikkhunis with Mara.

9.3.6 Stupas

(1) BAREAU, ANDRE. "La construction et le culte du Stupa d'après le Vinayapitaka." Bulletin de l'Ecole française d'Extrême-Orient, 50 (1962), 229-274.

An important article dealing with the stupa as it is discussed and presented in Buddhist texts. It is preceded in the same volume by an archaeologically oriented article by Mireille Benisti, "Etude sur le Stupa dans l'Inde ancienne" (pp. 37-116).

(2) BARUA, B. M. "Stupa and Tomb." See 8.1.2.4(2).
A clear study of the relationship between the Buddhist stupa and non-Buddhist burial traditions and architectural forms. The author traces the stupa's origins to burial practices in ancient India and describes the stupa according to Buddhist Pali texts.

(3) COMBAZ, GISBERT. "L'évolution du stupa en Asie." Mélanges chinois et bouddhiques, 2: 163-302; 3: 93-144; 4: 1-123.
A three-part article, the last of which (in vol. 4) deals with the various symbolisms of the stupa. Part 1 is a rather helpful survey that traces the architectural fortunes of the stupa from India to South and Southeast Asia, China, Korea and Japan. The second and third parts are more informed, written under the impact of Van Erp's work and especially of Paul Mus's Barabudur (below), which was appearing serially at the same time.

(4) GOVINDA, ANAGARIKA. "The Historical and Symbolical Origin of the Chorten." Bulletin of Tibetology, 7, no. 3 (1970), 5-15.
A short but useful article on the development of the chorten--the Tibetan version of the stupa--and its particular symbolical meaning.

(5) LA VALLEE POUSSIN, LOUIS DE. "Staupikam." Harvard Journal of Asiatic Studies, 2 (1937), 276-280.
A miscellany of texts and information on the stupa, taken mostly from Chinese and Tibetan sources, by a great Buddhologist.

(6) MUS, PAUL. Barabudur: esquisse d'une histoire du Bouddhisme fondée sur la critique archéologique des textes. See 2.5.2(8).
This work shows the immense and exciting ramifications that can be generated by a broad and profound interpretation of the symbolism of the stupa. It is in two parts: a "foreword" (300 pp.) entitled "Les sources indiennes du Bouddhisme," in which Mus summarizes the methods, results, and implications of his work on Barabudur for the study of Buddhism as a whole. The second part (576 pp.) is subtitled "Les origines du stupa et la transmigration: Essai d'archéologie religieuse comparée." It contains five sections: 1) architectural interpretations; 2) religious interpretations; 3) the symbolism of Barabudur; 4) the problem of the five directions; and 5) the cosmic value of the stupa. To this is added an appendix on the seven steps of the Buddha and the doctrine of the Pure Lands. Unfortunately, the work has not been translated; its French is very difficult, and there is no index.

(7) PANT, SUSHILA. "The Origin and Development of Stupa Architecture in India." Journal of Indian History, 51, no. 3 (December 1973), pp. 471-478.
The author begins this article by noting that stupas were already in existence by the time of the Buddha. The author concludes that rock-cut stupas seem to have developed out of a primitive practice of building funeral monuments and then complexified under various socio-economic, politico-religious compulsions.

(8) PARANAVITANA, SENARAT. The Stupa in Ceylon. Colombo, 1946, 105 pp.
This volume represents a fine short essay by a noted scholar which can serve the student as an introductory piece on the nature of stupas and stupa worship.

(9) PRZYLUSKI, JEAN. "Les sept terrasses du Barabudur." Harvard Journal of Asiatic Studies, 1 (1936), 251-256.
In the wake of Mus's Barabudur, Przyluski attempts to reemphasize the similarities between Barabudur and ancient Babylonian ziggurats.

(10) Symbolisme cosmique des monuments religieux. Rome: Istituto Italiano per il Medio ed Estremo-Oriente, 1957.
The results of a symposium held on this topic, this is a series of articles which are useful for seeing the different expressions and dimensions of the symbolism which is caught in the stupa. Papers by R. A. Stein on China, J. Filliozat and J. Auboyer on India, and P. Levy on Southeast Asia are included.

(11) Thupavamsa. Translated by N. A. Jayawickrama as Chronicle of the Thupa. See 9.1.5(16).

(12) TUCCI, GIUSEPPE. "The Symbolism of the Temple of bSam yas." East and West, 6 (1956), 279-281.
A careful study of the temple and stupa complex of bSam yas, the first and in many ways the most important Buddhist architectural establishment in Tibet, dating from the eighth century. Tucci's study is based on firsthand observations.

9.3.7 Royal Symbols (Thrones, Cities, Monuments, Pillars, Seven Emblems of the Cakravartin, etc.)

(1) AUBOYER, JEANNINE. Le trône et son symbolisme dans l'Inde ancienne. Paris: Annales du Musée Guimet, 1949.
Part of this study analyzes the symbolic values of the royal throne, its cosmological significance, its own magical powers, etc. For a shorter, earlier study, in English, by the same author, see "The Symbolism of Sovereignty in India according to Iconography (Parasols, Thrones)," Indian Arts and Letters, 12 (1938), 26-36.

(2) Cakkavatti sihanada sutta, Digha Nikaya. See 2.7.1(13).

(3) COEDES, GEORGES. Pour mieux comprendre Angkor. Hanoi: Imprimerie d'Extrême-Orient, 1943.

A series of lectures which Coedes gave in Hanoi on the symbolism and cult of royalty at the old capital of the Khmer empire. Some of the same points can be found in English in Coedes' more general and introductory book, Angkor, an Introduction, translated by Emily Floyd Gardiner (New York: Oxford, 1963).

(4) FILLIOZAT, JEAN. "Le symbolisme du monument du Phnom Bakhen." Bulletin de l'Ecole française d'Extrême-Orient (1954), pp. 527-555.

Filliozat interprets one of the royal monuments at Angkor as a Mt. Meru.

(5) MAJUMDAR, B. "Symbology of the Asoka Pillar Capital, Sarnath" (see 9.3.1[7]).

(6) MUS, PAUL. "Angkor in the Time of Jayavarman VII." Indian Arts and Letters, 11 (1937), 65-75.

A reinterpretation of the symbolism of the balustrades of the bridges leading to the old royal capital of Angkor Thom. The figures of the Asuras and the Devas are generally thought of as churning the ocean, but Mus claims the bridge represents a rainbow which links the world of men with the world of the gods, symbolized by the royal city of Angkor Thom itself. His argument has been further developed and supported by Georges Coedes in "The Causeway of Giants of Angkor Thom," Indian Historical Quarterly, 14 (1938), 607-612.

(7) PRZYLUSKI, JEAN. "Le symbolisme du pillar de Sarnath," in Etudes d'orientalisme à la mémoire de Raymond Linossier. Paris: Leroux, 1932, pp. 481-489.

One of the important articles in a scholarly debate on the significance of the symbols of the "Asokan" pillar at Sarnath. Przyluski focuses on the cosmological signifiance of the four animals found on the pillar's capital.

(8) _____. "La ville du Cakravartin--influences babyloniennes sur la civilisation de l'Inde." See 8.7(3).

Przyluski gets a little carried away with his etymologies in attempting to show the parallel between Pataliputra, Patan, Potala, Ecbatana, etc., but he still points to some convincing relationships between the Babylonian and Asokan notions of royal cities.

(9) WAIDA, MANABUL. "Symbolism of 'Descent' in Tibetan Kingship and Some East Asian Parallels." Numen, 20, no. 1 (April 1973), 60-78.

After describing the central motif concerned with the descent of the first mythical Tibetan king from heaven to the summit of a mountain by a rope or ladder "in illo temporare," the author attempts to make the case that not only does the Tibetan myth of Kingship owe its origin to the Turco-Mongolian peoples, but that the myths of the foundation of kingship belonging to the Japanese and Korean peoples also belong to the mythological traditions of the pastoral peoples of Central Asia.

9.3.8 The Marks of the Mahapurusa

(1) Ambatthasutta, Digha Nikaya. Translated by T. W. Rhys-Davids in Dialogues of the Buddha (see 2.7.1[13]), vol. 1, pp. 130-136.

Two of the most mysterious of the thirty-two bodily signs of the Buddha (and other Mahapurusas) are his long tongue and the sheath which encloses his sexual organs. The Ambatthasutta tells the amusing story of the young Brahmin who doubted that the Buddha actually had these signs and how he found out that he was wrong.

(2) BANERJEE, J. N. "The Webbed Fingers of Buddha." Indian Historical Quarterly, 6 (1930), 717-727; 7 (1931), 654-656.

Another of the marks of the Buddha (and of other Mahapurusas) which has aroused the most scholarly controversy has been his reputed possession of "webbed" fingers and toes. This article by Banerjee elicited others: see M. B. F. Stutterheim, "Le jalalaksana de l'image du Bouddha," Acta Orientalia, 7 (1928), 232-237; and A. K. Coomaraswamy, "The Webbed Fingers of Buddha," Indian Historical Quarterly, 7 (1931), 365-366.

(3) BURNOUF, EUGENE. Le lotus de la bonne loi (see 3.3.5.1[3]), pp. 553-583.

In conjunction with his translation of the Saddharma pundarika sutra, Burnouf devoted a long discussion to the thirty-two major marks and eighty minor marks of the Mahapurusa. This work, by one of the great early Buddhologists, is dated but still valuable.

(4) COOMARASWAMY, A. K. "The Buddha's cuda, hair, usnisa, crown." Journal of the Royal Asiatic Society (1928), pp. 815-840.

Another of the thirty-two marks of the Mahapurusa that has been controversial in scholarly circles has been the proturbance on his head, the usnisa. Coomaraswamy discusses its possible origins and significance. See also J. N. Banerjee's "Usnisasiraskata in the Early Buddhist Images of India," Indian Historical Quarterly, 7 (1931), 499-514; and A. Foucher, Art gréco-bouddhique du Gandhara (see 9.2.2.5[3]), vol. 2, pp. 289-300.

(5) Lakkhanasutta, Digha Nikaya. Translated by T. W. Rhys-Davids in Dialogues of the Buddha (see 2.7.1[13]), vol. 3, pp. 136-153.

There are many listings of the thirty-two major marks of the "great man" (Mahapurusa). This one, preceded by a commentary by Rhys-Davids, is one of the basic ones. Others may be found in the Mahapadanasutta of Digha

Nikaya II, the Brahmayusutta of Majjhima Nikaya II, the Mahavastu (in Jones's translation, 3.2.1.2[5], vol. 1, p. 180). For a full listing, see Etienne Lamotte's translation of the Mahaprajnaparamita sastra (3.3.1.2[6]), vol. 1, p. 271. Of particular interest is Kathavatthu IV (p. 283), which discusses non-Mahapurusas who have some but not all of the thirty-two marks.

(6) SENART, EMILE. Essai sur la légende du Buddha (see 8.1.2.3[28]), pp. 87-160.

This chapter is entitled "The Mahapurusa." It contains a full analysis of the signs and symbols of that figure. Though the discussion is from Senart's solar mythology bias, this still forms a valuable treatment of the subject.

9.3.9 Light as a Symbol

(1) Amitayur-Dhyana-Sutra. Translated by J. Takakusu as "The Sutra of the Meditation on Amitayus," in Buddhist Mahayana Texts, Part 2. See 3.3.1.1(12).

The standard translation of one of the basic pure land sutras which is very popular in Japan. In it, the Buddha tells Queen Vaidehi the several ways of getting to the Pure Land, and instructs her in meditation techniques (including chanting the Nembutsu, and visualization) which will enable her to get a glimpse of that Western paradise. For a study of the visualization technique as explained by Shan Tao in his commentary on this sutra, see Julian Pas, "Shan Tao's Interpretation of the Meditative Vision of the Buddha Amitayus," History of Religions, 14 (1974), 96-116.

(2) EVANS-WENTZ, W. Y., ed. The Tibetan Book of the Dead. See 3.4.2(2).

(3) INGRAM, PAUL O. "The Symbolism of Light and Pure Land in Buddhist Soteriology." Japan Journal of Religious Studies, 1, no. 4 (December 1974), 331-349.

Using Mircea Eliade's morphological treatment of the subjective religious experience of light in Mephistopheles and Androgyne (New York: Sheed and Ward, 1965), pp. 19-77, the author comes to the following understanding of light symbolism in the Buddhist tradition: light symbolizes wisdom which a Buddha or bodhisattva possesses as a result of his experiences with "the structure of reality in all its 'suchness.'"

(4) Mahaprajnaparamitasastra. Translated by Etienne Lamotte as Le Traité de la Grande Vertu (see 3.3.1.2[6]), vol. 1, pp. 431-528.

The whole of this long chapter deals with the different sorts of light rays which the Buddha emits from his own body to cosmic distances. There are many details useful to those making a study of the subject.

(5) Saddharma pundarika. Translated by H. Kern as The Lotus of the True Law (see 4.2.1[6]), pp. 7 ff.

Develops the theme of the Buddha's emitting from his brow a ray of light which extends for yojanas and yojanas to all quarters, lighting up the cosmos.

(6) SOPER, ALEXANDER C. "Aspects of Light Symbolism in Gandharan Sculpture." Artibus Asiae, 12 (1949), 252-283, 314-330; 13 (1950), 63-85.

A major study which starts with a discussion of the popular legend of the Buddha leaving his shadow in a cave, and goes on to discuss light symbolism in Buddhism in North West India and in China, touching on solar symbolism, Iranian influences, the association of previous Buddhas with light, etc.

(7) SUZUKI, DAISETZ T. "Infinite Light." Eastern Buddhist, 4, no. 2 (1971), 1-24.

A posthumously published paper probably written around 1950 which still makes an adequate introduction to the whole question of light symbolism in Buddhism, but is based heavily on Pure Land materials. An interesting outline of the light of Amida as it exists in the Pure Land, in this world, and in the hells.

9.3.10 Other Symbols

(1) GOMBRICH, RICHARD. "Feminine Elements in Sinhalese Buddhism." See 4.2.3(15).

(2) LOFFLER, LORENZ G. "Beast, Bird and Fish: An Essay in South-East Asian Symbolism," in Folk Religion and the World View in the Southwestern Pacific. Edited by Nobuhiro and T. Mabuchi. Tokyo: Keio Institute of Cultural and Linguistic Studies, 1968, pp. 21-36.

This insightful article examines three Southeast Asian symbols and their codes which appear to present a tradition of life--prenatal, actual and post-mortal.

(3) MAQUET, JACQUES. "Expressive Space Theravada Values." Ethos, 6, no. 1 (1975), 1-23.

An attempt to analyze the spatial organization of a Sinhala monastery in which the author contends that the spaces created by buildings express the world view adhered to by those who live in them. Before examining this world view, the author describes the natural resources, techniques, and climactic factors which limit expression.

(4) OLSCHKI, LEONARDO. "The Crib of Christ and the Bowl of the Buddha." Journal of the American Oriental Society, 70 (1950), 161-164.

A short but fascinating discussion of an Uighur text of the "Adoration of the Magi" story which recounts that, in exchange for gifts of gold, frankincense and myrrh, the child Jesus gave the Magi a piece of rock which he broke off from his stone crib. The subsequent miraculous adventures of this piece of stone clearly reflect the tales surrounding the Buddha's begging bowl.

(5) PARANAVITANA, S. "The Significance of Sinhalese 'Moonstones.'" Artibus Asiae, 17 (1954), 197-231.

A masterful article by a great Ceylonese scholar which analyzes in detail the famous "moonstones" of Sri Lanka and explores the references to them in Buddhist literature.

(6) WADDELL, L. AUSTINE. Tibetan Buddhism (see 1.14.1[17]), pp. 387-419.

A rapid-fire account of various sacred emblems, signs, good luck charms, etc. that are found in Tibetan Buddhism. With good drawings, and a helpful listing of some materials not generally available elsewhere.

(7) WARD, W. E. "Selected Buddhist Symbols in Sinhalese Decorative Art." Artibus Asiae, 13 (1950), 270-296.

Ward deals with the significance of moonstones and Bodhi tree leaf motifs, garudas, kinnaras, the lotus, the goose, the parrot, etc., all found as decorative elements in Sinhala art.

(8) WAYMAN, ALEX. "Female Energy and Symbolism in the Buddhist Tantras." History of Religions, 2 (1962), 73-111.

A detailed analysis of female symbolism and related topics in selected Tantric Buddhist texts. Wayman's unnecessary defensiveness about the validity of the topic is dated, but the essay as a whole is interesting and illuminating.

(9) _____. "The Mirror as a Pan-Buddhist Metaphor-Simile." History of Religions, 13 (1973), 251-269.

A scholarly study of the multidimensional reflections of the metaphor of the mirror primarily in Mahayana Buddhism. Wayman first considers the meaning of the mirror in Yogacara and Madhyamika traditions before going on to other aspects of its symbolism.

10 Sacred Places

For all sections, see also Category 5, Art. For stupas, see 9.3.6. For construction of sacred places (monasteries, stupas, viharas), see 7.2.6.

10.1 PILGRIMS' AND TRAVELLERS' ACCOUNTS

10.1.1 Accounts Concerning India and Central Asia

(1) BEAL, SAMUEL. Si-Yu-Ki: Buddhist Records of the Western World. See 8.9.3(39).
Within these two volumes, the reader will find Beal's authoritative nineteenth century translations of Hsuan Tsang's Si-Yu-Ki, Fa-Hsien's Buddhist Country Records, and The Mission of Sung-Yun. The work has been considered a mine of information about Buddhism from 400-630 A.D. in India and proves to be handy because of its inclusion of the major pilgrims' accounts. The student needs only an account of I Ching's travels (below) to have a complete record.

(2) CHAVANNES, EDOUARD. Les religieux éminents qui allèrent chercher la Loi dans les pays d'occident. Paris: E. Leroux, 1910.
This work was originally composed by I Ching during the T'ang dynasty and consists of a series of biographies and recounting of voyages taken by Chinese pilgrims. An excellent introduction which fully describes the nature of the work is offered by Chavannes.

(3) _____, trans. "Voyage de Song Yun dans l'Udyana et le Ghandara." See 1.2.2.3(1).
This article is a French translation of the account of Song Yun's voyage to India at the beginning of the sixth century. In addition, Chavannes has included a scholarly introduction and an appendix listing the various Chinese works written about India prior to the T'ang dynasty.

(4) FA HSIEN. A Record of Buddhistic Kingdoms: Being an Account by the Chinese Monk Fa-hien of his Travels in India and Ceylon (A.D. 399-414) in Search of the Buddhist Books of Discipline. See 1.2.2.3(4).
This edition, translated by James Legge, is still the best translation of the travels of Fa-hien. Rich in footnotes and easily readable, it remains a good source for gathering materials concerned with the status of Buddhism in India in the early fifth century A.D. For other accounts of Fa-Hsien's travels, see H. A. Giles, The Travels of Fa-Hsien or a Record of Buddhistic Kingdoms (Cambridge: Cambridge University Press, 1923); Chinese Buddhist Association, A Record of Buddhist Countries (Peking, 1957); Samuel Beal, Si-Yu-Ki: Buddhist Records of the Western World (above); Samuel Beal, Travels of Fah-Hian and Sung-Yun (London: Trubner, 1869); and Abel Remusat, Foe Koue Ki (in French) (Paris: L'Imprimerie Royale).

(5) I CHING. A Record of the Buddhist Religion as Practiced in India and the Malay Archipelago. See 1.2.2.3(8).
A fine translation of the major pilgrim's account of Indian Buddhism in the seventh century A.D. Includes accounts of the major sacred places, their characters and conditions. An excellent source for the overall condition of Buddhism during the period.

(6) JAN, YUN-HUA. "South India in the VIII Century--Hui-Ch'ao's Description Re-examined." Oriens extremus, 15 (1968), 169-177.
This article represents a sequel to Jan's Hui-ch'ao's Memoirs of a Pilgrimage to the Five Regions of India. These memoirs belonged to an eighth century Korean monk (Hui-ch'ao), who, after completing his pilgrimage to India, returned to An-hsi, an important frontier city of T'ang Ching. The editors of the bibliography are not able, at this time, to locate Jan's Hui-ch'ao's Memoirs, but the reader is referred to the following articles by the same author: "Hui-ch'ao and His Works: A Reassessment," Indo-Asia Culture, 12 (1964), 177-190; "Some New Light on Kusinagara from the Memoirs of Hui-ch'ao," Oriens extremus, 12 (1965), 55-63; "West India According to Hui-ch'ao's Record," Indian Historical Quarterly, 39 (1963), 27-37; "The Korean Record of Varanasi and Sarnath," Vishveshvaranand Indological Journal, 4 (1966), 264-272; and "Some Fresh Reflections on Yasovarma of Kanauj and Muktapida of Kashmir," Journal of Indian History, 45 (1967), 161-179.

(7) JULIEN, STANISLAUS. Voyages des pèlerins bouddhistes. Paris: L'Imprimerie imperiale, 1853, 3 vols.

Pilgrims' and Travellers' Accounts 10.1.1

Julien's account of Hsuan Tsang must be listed separately from the others (see Beal, above), because of its early importance in Buddhist studies. Volume 1 is a history of the life (a biography?) of Hsuan Tsang, while volumes 2 and 3 comprise the pilgrim's own account of his travels (Si-Yu-Ki). For further reading in English, see F. Max Müller, Buddhism and Buddhist Pilgrims (London: Williams and Norgate, 1857), which is basically a review of Julien's work and some added biographical bits on Hsuan Tsang.

(8) LE COQ, ALBERT VON. Buried Treasures of Chinese Turkestan: An Account of the Activities and Adventures of the Second and Third Turfan Expeditions. Translated by Anna Barwell. London: G. Allen and Unwin, 1928, 180 pp.
A highly entertaining story of these German expeditions which focuses on the archeological remains of Buddhist sites in Chinese Turkestan. Provides a good background of archeological scholarship concerned with this area up until the 1920s.

(9) SASTRI, K. A. NILAKANTA. "Chinese Travelers," in 2500 Years of Buddhism (see 1.2.1[1]), pp. 254-274.
These pages contain short sketches of Fa-Hien, Hsuan Tsang, and I Ching. For the introductory student, this article is one of the better places to start as the reader can gain an overview of what these pilgrims' travels entailed.

(10) STEIN, MARK AUREL. On Ancient Central Asian Tracks. See 1.10.1(6).
Stein explored a great number of caves during his four expeditions into Central Asia. He devotes more space to the Tun-Huang caves than to any other, and there is an even more detailed account in Stein's The Thousand Buddhas (London: B. Quaritch, 1921), 65 pp. In this work, however, there are also interesting treatments of Wan-fu-hsia ("Valley of the Ten Thousand Buddhas"), Ma-ti-ssu in the Nan-Shan mountain ranges, the cave monasteries at Toyuk in Turfan, and the shrines of the Ming-oi ("The Thousand Houses") at Karashar.

(11) WATTERS, THOMAS. On Yuan Chwang's Travels in India. See 1.2.2.3(14).
A translation of Hsuan Tsang's account of his seventh century pilgrimage to and throughout India, which has the advantage of being accompanied by Watters' running commentary, from which the reader may gain many additional insights into the places visited by Hsuan Tsang and references to them in the accounts of other pilgrims or in Buddhist texts. Other treatments of this important work may be found in Jules Barthélemy Saint-Hilaire, Hiouen-Thsang in India, translated by Laura Ensor (Delhi: S. Gupta, 1952) and William Boulting, Four Pilgrims (London: K. Paul, Trench, Trubner, n.d.), pp. 1-64. See also the full translation of the work in Samuel Beal (above). For treatments of Hsuan Tsang's whole life, including his pilgrimage, see under 8.9.3.

10.1.2 Accounts Concerning China and Mongolia

(1) BLOFELD, JOHN. The Jewel in the Lotus: An Outline of Present Day Buddhism in China. London: Buddhist Society, 1948.
Captivating firsthand account of various sites of Buddhist importance in China which the author visited during troubled times before the Communist victory. See especially his accounts of Mt. Wu t'ai in Shansi province, and of Mt. Omei in Szechuan.

(2) ENNIN. Diary: The Record of a Pilgrimage to China in Search of the Law. See 1.11.2.3(6).
An excellent scholarly translation of a diary kept by Ennin, a Japanese Buddhist monk who made an extended pilgrimage to China between 838 and 847 A.D. It provides keen insight into the condition of Buddhism and its persecution under the T'ang. The companion volume by the same translator, Ennin's Travels in T'ang China (below [7]), is a marvelous supplement providing a mine of information on China in general and Buddhism in particular during this period.

(3) GILMOUR, JAMES. Among the Mongols. London: Religious Tract Society, 1883, 382 pp.
Chapters 12 and 13 of this work by a nineteenth century English missionary contain firsthand accounts of visits to Urga (present-day Ulan Bator) and also to Mt. Wu t'ai, sacred to the bodhisattva Manjusri. For other descriptions of Urga, see Beatrice Bulstrode, A Tour in Mongolia (London: Methuen, 1920), 237 pp.; and Harry Franck, Wandering in Northern China (New York: Century Press), ch. 9.

(4) HART, VIRGIL C. Western China: A Journey to the Great Buddhist Centre of Mount Omei. Boston: Ticknor, 1888, 302 pp.
A number of hardy Westerners visited the great Buddhist pilgrimage center of Mt. Omei during the nineteenth and early twentieth centuries. This is one of the more extensive accounts. For others, see Archibald Little, Mount Omei and Beyond (London: Heinemann, 1901), 272 pp.; Mrs. Archibald Little, Intimate China (London: Hutchinson, 1899), chapters 17-21; and E. G. Kemp, The Face of China (London: Chatto and Windus, 1909).

(5) HEDIN, SVEN. Jehol, City of Emperors. New York: E. P. Dutton, 1933, 273 pp.
A full firsthand description of Jehol in Inner Mongolia, the summer capital of the Manchu rulers, and famous for its Lamaist temples. For a somewhat later account of other sites in the same area, see Schuyler Cammann, The Land of the Camel: Tents and Temples of Inner Mongolia (New York: Ronald Press, 1951), 200 pp.

(6) PRATT, JAMES BISSET. *The Pilgrimage of Buddhism and a Buddhist Pilgrimage* (see 1.6.1[7]), pp. 272-416.

For descriptions of Buddhism during the Republican period, various firsthand accounts of Western travellers can be a valuable source, especially for small details and glimpses of particular places or events. The above pages of the always observant Pratt contain descriptions of temples, monks, laymen, and include a chapter on "The Buddhist Revival in China." Other works which might be consulted include Karl Reichelt, *Truth and Tradition in Chinese Buddhism* (see 1.11.1[8]), chapters 8-10; Hodous, *Buddhism and Buddhists in China* (see 1.11.1[7]); and the slightly earlier Reginald F. Johnston, *Buddhist China* (see 10.8.2[6]). One of the last and best personal accounts of Chinese Buddhism, just before the Communist victory, is John Blofeld's (above). Finally, Karl Reichelt, *The Transformed Abbot* (London: Lutterworth Press, 1954), tells the story of the Taiwanese monk Miao-chi (1895-1930), who studied and meditated under the great T'ai Hsu and ended up converting to Christianity; his biography also provides some informal and interesting glimpses into the Buddhism of the Republican era.

(7) REISCHAUER, EDWIN OLDFATHER. *Ennin's Travels in T'ang China*. See 1.11.2.3(13).

A companion volume to Reischauer's translation of Ennin's *Diary* (above), this is a highly readable account of the voyage of the Japanese pilgrim Ennin, and of the situation in China during his trip. It is especially useful for its description of the conditions and position of the Buddhist monks in Ch'ang-an in 842-845 just prior to the great persecution of Buddhism by the emperor Wu-tsung.

(8) VINCENT, IRENE VONGEHR. *The Sacred Oasis*. Chicago: University of Chicago Press, 1953, 114 pp.

The value of this work lies not so much in the author's expertise in treating the caves at Tun Huang, as in the references to Buddhist history which are interspersed throughout. They make this book a good supplement to Stein's treatments of Tun Huang (above).

10.1.3 Accounts Concerning Tibet and Himalaya

(1) BERNARD, THEOS. *Land of a Thousand Buddhas*. New York: Rider, 1952, 320 pp.

Of rather limited interest to the scholar. An American "becomes" a Tibetan Buddhist and describes his pilgrimage from Gyantse to Lhasa. His descriptions are good. Originally published in 1939 as *Penthouse of the Gods*.

(2) DAS, SARAT CHANDRA. *Indian Pandits in the Land of the Snow*. Calcutta: K. L. Mukhopadhyay, 1965, 101 pp.

This book is the text of four lectures given by the author which discuss Indian pandits in China, Chinese pilgrims in Tibet, Bengal pandits in Tibet, and the importance of Attissa for Tibetan Buddhism.

(3) DAVID-NEEL, ALEXANDRA. *My Journey to Lhasa*. New York: Harper and Bros., 1927, 310 pp.

During the course of ten centuries, Western adventurers, scholars, explorers, prisoners of war, etc., have entered Tibet from all points of the compass. David-Neel is certainly the best known to have come from the East, but like many of the others she does not quite know what to do or say once she reaches Lhasa. From the West came Heinrich Harrer, who wrote a fine but not very informative adventure book, *Seven Years in Tibet*, translated by Richard Graves (New York: E. P. Dutton, 1953), 314 pp. Much better on this is Martin Brauen, *Heinrich Harrers Impressionen aus Tibet* (Innsbruck: Penguin, 1974), 244 pp. Important on Western Tibet per se is Giuseppe Tucci and E. Ghersi, *Secrets of Tibet* (London: Blackie and Sons, 1935), 210 pp., which is a chronicle of the Italian West Tibet scientific expedition in 1933. For a lively account by Tucci's photographer of the Italians' later journey into Tibet from Sikkim, see Fosco Maraini, *Secret Tibet*, translated by Eric Mosbacher (New York: Grove Press, 1952), 306 pp. From all these and other works, descriptions and traditions about specific sacred places along the way may be gleaned.

(4) GOVINDA, ANAGARIKA BRAHMACARI. *The Way of the White Clouds*. London: Hutchinson, 1966, 305 pp.

A modern pilgrim describes his pilgrimage "of spirit and body" through Tibet.

(5) HEDIN, SVEN. *Trans-Himalaya: Discoveries and Adventure in Tibet*. New York: Macmillan, 1909, 2 vols.

The Swedish explorer par excellence, Sven Hedin, has added much to our geographical knowledge of former "terra incognita." This work is more useful for its accounts of well known Central Tibetan sites such as Shigatse and Tashi Lump. It also touches on his trip to Lake Manasarowa (Lake Anottata) at the foot of Mt. Kailas. On the lake and its significance through history, see also the important account in Sven Hedin, *Southern Tibet* (Stockholm: Lithographic Institute, n.d.), vols. 1-2, in which he compares his discoveries made there in 1906-1908 with all accounts of the sacred lake made previously.

(6) KAWAGUCHI, EKAI. *Three Years in Tibet*. Madras: Theosophist Office, 1909, 719 pp.

A long account of a Japanese Buddhist priest who visited Tibet in the early years of this century and entered the monastic college of Sera near Lhasa. This makes his work especially valuable for his discussions of Tibetan life--there and in Lhasa as well.

(7) MacGREGOR, JOHN. Tibet: A Chronicle of Exploration. New York: Praeger, 1970, 373 pp.

Because of its remoteness and romance, virtually every Western missionary, merchant, and imperialist who has ever entered Tibet has written a book about it. (Some have done so without even getting there.) Most of their accounts up to the British Younghusband expedition of 1904 are reviewed in this book by MacGregor. Among those perhaps most worth noting, from which information on specific sacred places may be gleaned, are: An eighteenth century account unfortunately not fully translated from the Italian but available in Filippo De Filippi, ed., An Account of Tibet: The Travels of Ippolito Desideri of Pistoia, S.J., 1712-1727 (London: Routledge and Sons, 1931); Clements R. Markham, ed., Narrative of the Mission of George Bogle to Tibet and of the Journey of Thomas Manning to Lhasa (New Delhi: Manjusri, 1971, originally published 1875), 360 pp., the latter being an eccentric who was the first Englishman to reach Lhasa; and the report of Warren Hasings' envoy Samuel Turner, An Account of an Embassy to the Court of the Teshoo Lama in Tibet (New Delhi: Manjusri, 1971, originally published 1800). The British invasion of 1904 engendered a host of reports, among which may be mentioned the following which are informative about Lhasa: Francis Younghusband, India and Tibet (London: J. Murray, 1910), 455 pp.; L. Austine Waddell, Lhasa and Its Mysteries (London: Methuen, 1905), 507 pp.; and Percival Landon, Lhasa (London: Hurst and Blackett, 1905), vol. 2. See also on this period and its immediate aftermath, David MacDonald, Twenty Years in Tibet (London: Seeley, Service, 1932), 318 pp.

(8) McGOVERN, WILLIAM MONTGOMERY. To Lhasa in Disguise. New York: Grosset and Dunlap, 1924, 462 pp.

McGovern's account of his trip to Lhasa well reflects his fanatical determination to get to the Tibetan capital, but it has the advantage of being one of the few such works written by someone who had a good knowledge of Buddhism.

(9) ROCKHILL, WILLIAM W. The Land of the Lamas. New York: Century, 1891, 399 pp.

The eminent Tibetologist Rockhill never made it to Central Tibet, but this and his other account of voyages in Northern and Eastern Tibet are useful for glimpses of sacred places (e.g., the Kumbum monastery) in those regions. See also his Diary of a Journey through Mongolia and Tibet (Washington: Smithsonian Institution, 1894), 410 pp.

(10) TUCCI, GIUSEPPE. Preliminary Report on Two Scientific Expeditions in Nepal. Rome: Istituto Italiano per il Medio ed Estremo Oriente, 1956.

The first volume in a series of reports emanating from Tucci's expeditions to Nepal. See especially, with regard to Buddhism, Chapter 1, "The Lamaist Area." For an older account of some of the sites of Nepal, as well as its history, culture, etc., see also Sylvain Levi, Le Nepal (Paris: E. Leroux, 1905), 3 vols.

10.1.4 Accounts Concerning Sri Lanka and Southeast Asia

(1) BOCK, CARL. Temples and Elephants. See 1.5.2(3).

The journal of an Englishman's trip in the 1880s through Northern Thailand and part of Laos, which can be useful for its descriptions of specific places. For a somewhat later account of the same area, see Reginald Le May, An Asian Arcady (1.5.2[13]), and for the reminiscences of a man who spent three years in Thailand at the turn of the century, see P. A. Thompson, Lotus Land (London: T. Werner Laurie, 1906), 307 pp.

(2) HULUGALLE, H. A. J. Ceylon of the Early Travellers. Colombo: Multipacks, 1965, 102 pp.

Convenient but not very critical review of the accounts of Sri Lanka by a series of travellers, starting with Chinese pilgrims and surveying the various Arabs and Portuguese up to Robert Knox (below).

(3) KNOX, ROBERT. An Historical Relation of Ceylon. See 1.3.2.1(8).

Originally published in 1681, this was the first book on Ceylon in English and remains an important source of information about the culture and religion in Kandy in the seventeenth century. The author was marooned on the island, captured by the Sinhalese, and held in Kandy for twenty years, during which time he became thoroughly familiar with the language, people and culture of the court and the capital. The book is his sensitive, observant and fascinating account, which he published after his "miraculous escape" (the Portuguese were more trouble to him than the Sinhalese). For an abridged version of the work, see E. F. C. Ludowyk, Robert Knox in the Kandyan Kingdom (Oxford: Oxford University Press, 1948).

(4) LA LOUBERE, SIMON DE. The Kingdom of Siam. See 1.5.2(12).

(5) PAVIE, AUGUSTE, et al. Mission Pavie en Indo-chine. Paris: E. Leroux, 1901, 6 vols.

A full report of a French scientific expedition which explored Indochina from 1879-1895 under the leadership of Auguste Pavie. The report contains descriptions and discussions of numerous sites of Buddhist importance. For another Frenchman's accounts of his late nineteenth century travels, see Etienne Aymonier, Le Cambodge (Paris: E. Leroux, 1900), 3 vols., and also his Voyage dans le Laos (Paris: E. Leroux, 1897), 2 vols.

10.1.4

(6) SANGERMANO, VINCENTIUS. *A Description of the Burmese Empire.* See 1.4.2(14).

An account of an early missionary to Burma, especially valuable for its description of the court and the capital. For a later account of the Burmese court, by an Englishman, see John Crawford, *The Court of Ava* (1.4.2[5]).

(7) SELKIRK, JAMES. *Recollection of Ceylon.* London: J. Hatchard, 1844, 544 pp.

Important work by an early missionary, especially valuable for its account of Kandy immediately after its British capture in 1815, and for its descriptions of many viharas visited by the author during his travels throughout Central Ceylon. For a slightly later account of Kandy, see Henry Charles Sirr, *Ceylon and the Cinghalese* (London: W. Shoberl, 1850), 2 vols., especially vol. 2.

(8) TENNENT, JAMES EMERSON. *Ceylon: An Account of the Island.* London: Longmans, Green, 1859, 2 vols.

Among the innumerable general works on Sri Lanka written by foreign visitors and residents on the island in the nineteenth and early twentieth centuries, many touch on the old capital cities of the kingdom: Anuradhapura, Sigiriya, Polonnaruwa; and all invariably refer to Adam's Peak. Volume 2 of Tennent's work contains some information on these. For other accounts, see Reginald Farrer, *In Old Ceylon* (London: E. Arnold, 1908), 350 pp.; Geraldine Mitton, *The Lost Cities of Ceylon* (London: J. Murray, 1917), 255 pp.

10.1.5 Accounts Concerning Korea and Japan

(1) COOPER, MICHAEL. *They Came to Japan: An Anthology of European Reports 1543-1640.* Berkeley: University of California Press, 1965, 439 pp.

An extremely useful compilation of the reports of various early travellers to Japan (mostly Portuguese) according to subjects discussed. See especially Chapter 16 on cities and travel, Chapter 18 on Buddhism, Chapter 19 on temples, and Chapter 20 on festivals.

(2) DICKSON, W. G. *Gleanings from Japan.* Edinburgh: W. Blackwood, 1889, 400 pp.

Almost every nineteenth and early twentieth century traveller to Japan had something to report on his visits to the ancient capitals of Nara and Kyoto and their many temples. Dickson's work also includes a chapter on a more rarely made trip to Koyasan, the headquarters of the Shingon sect. Also on Kyoto and Nara and Kamakura, see A. H. Edwards, *Kakemono: Japanese Sketches* (Chicago, 1906), 298 pp.; an account by Charles Hartshorne's niece, Anna Hartshorne, *Japan and Her People* (London: K. Paul, 1904), vol. 2; the report of the Swiss envoy Aime Humbert, *Japan and the Japanese*, translated by Mrs. Caskel Hoey (London: R. Bentley, 1874), 378 pp.; and

Pilgrims' and Travellers' Accounts

Edward Reed, *Japan, Its History, Traditions and Religions* (London: J. Murray, 1880), in volume 2 of which he tells of his visit to Nara in 1879.

(3) HEARN, LAFCADIO. *In Ghostly Japan.* London: K. Paul, Trench and Trubner, 1907, pp. 117-132.

One of the prolific Hearn's many musings, especially valuable here, however, for these pages on different Buddha's footprints that he has visited in Japan. For other accounts of his travels to Buddhist sites, see his *Glimpses of Unfamiliar Japan* (Boston: Houghton and Mifflin, 1894), 2 vols.

(4) PONSONBY-FANE, R. A. B. *Kyoto, the Old Capital of Japan (794-1869).* Kyoto: Ponsonby Memorial Society, 1956, 446 pp.

A full-length work on the history and importance of this ancient capital and its many prominent temples. For a less formal but very useful work on the city see also Gouverneur Mosher, *Kyoto, A Contemplative Guide* (Rutland, Vt. and Tokyo: C. Tuttle, 1964), 368 pp.

(5) TAKAKUSU, J., trans. "Le voyage de Kanshin en Orient (742-754) par Mabito Genkai (779)." *Bulletin de l'Ecole française d'Extrême-Orient* (1928-1929), pp. 28-29.

The translator has presented us with an account (written in the eighth century) of the Chinese pilgrim Kanshin, who did not go to India, but to Japan. After five adventurous, though unsuccessful, attempts to reach Nara, he finally succeeds and becomes an influential figure in Buddhist circles.

10.2 INDIA

10.2.1 General Discussions

(1) BAGCHI, P. C. "The Eight Great Caityas and Their Cult." See 7.1.3(2).

The eight stupas marking the major events in the life of the Buddha became, very early, important centers of pilgrimage and cult. They have remained so. As examples of the later cult paid to these eight caityas, Bagchi has translated here a Chinese text praising them (the *Fo shuo pa ta ling t'a hao king*, or *Buddhabhasita-asta-mahacaitya-nama-sutra*), and two Tibetan texts from the *bstan-'gyur* describing the worship of them. (Both texts are entitled *Gnas chen po brgyad kyi mchod rten la bstod pa* or *Astamaha sthana caitya-stotra*.)

(2) BARUA, DIPAK KUMAR. *Viharas in Ancient India.* Calcutta: Indian Publications, 1969, 248 pp.

An adequate treatment which consists of a descriptive survey of Buddhist viharas in ancient India. The author divides the subjects of his chapters according to geographical locale, which proves handy to the reader wishing to use this work as a source book.

(3) BHARATI, AGEHANANDA. "Pilgrimage Sites and Indian Civilization," in Chapters in Indian Civilization (see 2.2[8]), vol. 1, pp. 84-120.

A useful survey, although it deals with Hindu and Jain as well as Buddhist sites. Gives a map, but goes on to investigate the nature of pilgrimage sites as cultural phenomena, centers of links in civilization. Also includes a brief bibliography (pp. 230-231).

(4) BURGESS, JAMES. Report on the Buddhist Cave Temples and Their Inscriptions. London: Trubner, 1883, 140 pp.

This is a volume from the Archeological Survey of India. It can serve the reader as a general introduction and survey of the Buddhist cave temples of western India. The approach is strictly archeological. Nevertheless, its emphasis upon inscriptions provides the reader with a good line to the history of the specific west Indian locales of Buddhist activity. Perhaps its best use would be as a supplement to Fergusson's The Cave Temples of India (below). For more specific reading, see John Marshall, The Bagh Caves (London: India Society, 1927).

(5) CHAUDHURY, B. N. Buddhist Centers in Ancient India. Calcutta: Sanskrit College, 1969, 292 pp.

Chaudhury has organized his work according to the five traditional Buddhist geographical areas which comprise India. A chapter is devoted to each area in which the author has labored to mesh references in such diverse materials as the Vinaya, Puranas, Dipavamsa, Mahabharata, Digha Nikaya, and Buddhavamsa with contemporary archeological evidence in order to reconstruct Buddhist cultures within specific Buddhist centers, and their significances in Buddhist literature.

(6) CUNNINGHAM, ALEXANDER. Ancient Geography of India. Varanasi: Indological Book House, 1963, 481 pp.

A useful source book which is a discussion of the significance of the most important political and religious centers of ancient India. When dealing with important Buddhist sites, the author relied heavily upon the reports of Hsuan Tsang for specific details. However, the reader will find that many other sources, including Muslim and Greek, were used in order to provide the most comprehensive depictions of locales in various historical eras.

(7) DUTT, SUKUMAR. The Buddha and Five After Centuries (see 1.2.1[8]), pp. 163-197.

A very good discussion concerned with the rise of stupa worship and the essential symbolism of art connected to it. A good introduction.

(8) _____. Buddhist Monks and Monasteries in India. See 1.2.2.1(4).

Sections of this book are of great value to the student of Buddhism's sacred places. Pages 58-100 consist of a detailed treatment of the rise of the Sangharamas and avasas with the rise of monasteries. Pages 138-165 include a general discussion of the cave monasteries found in Western India (especially the Bagh Caves). Pages 126-137 discuss the artistic and historical significance of Nagarjunakonda. Finally, pages 319-380 consist of a survey of the architecture of Mahaviharas which functioned as universities (especially Nalanda).

(9) FERGUSSON, JAMES. Cave Temples of India. London: W. H. Allen, 1880, pp. 165-198.

Fergusson's study as a whole was a landmark work for the study of cave temples in general. Within these few pages, he discusses important Buddhist cave temples not only in relation to art and iconographic symbolism, but also in relation to local and national histories. A first-rate source.

(10) _____. History of Indian and Eastern Architecture. New edition. Delhi: Munishiram Manoharlal, 1967, 2 vols.

Originally published in 1876, this remains perhaps the best overall history and survey of Buddhist architecture. Pages 1-209 of Volume 1 comprise a comprehensive study of the most important stupas, rails, caves and viharas found in various geographical Indian locales. Without a doubt, these pages serve as an excellent introduction to the sacred Buddhist places of India.

(11) FOUCHER, ALFRED. The Life of the Buddha. See 2.7.6(5).

While Foucher does follow a chronological schema, The Life of the Buddha is primarily arranged according to the events which took place at the eight major pilgrimage sites in India within the life of the Buddha. Pages 91-94, 136-140, and 201-207 contain discussions concerning sacred geography as it is related to Buddhist pilgrimage and the life of the Buddha.

(12) GROUSSET, RENE. In the Footsteps of the Buddha. See 8.9.3(40).

Originally published in French in 1929, this is basically a rewriting of the accounts of Hsuan Tsang and other Chinese pilgrims, and a following of their journey to the different sacred places of India. See especially Chapter 7, "On to Holy Land of the Ganges"; Chapter 8, "The Holy Places of Buddhism"; Chapter 9, "A Journey Around the Deccan at the Time of Ajanta"; and Chapter 10, "Nalanda, the Monastic City."

(13) LAW, B. C. Geography of Early Buddhism. London: K. Paul, Trench, Trubner, 1932, 88 pp.

Law has taken references to specific locales mentioned in the traditional Pali literature and collated them according to traditional Buddhist geography. Fortunately, this book contains a useful index to aid the reader, for the locales are listed in essay form (each chapter being an essay on the important sites in general regions of traditional Buddhist geography). There are also descriptions of the most important cities, stupas, temples and mountains in Burma and Sri Lanka.

(14) MITRA, DEBALA. Buddhist Monuments. Calcutta: Sahitya Samsad, 1971, 307 pp.
A superb and detailed account of all the major and minor shrines in India. Though the focus of the approach is primarily architectural, Mitra's volume remains one of the best places to begin a study on sacred places of the Buddhists in India. Contains excellent plates.

(15) MONIER-WILLIAMS, MONIER. Buddhism in Its Connection with Brahmanism and Hinduism, and Its Contrast with Christianity (see 8.5[2]), pp. 493-528, 387-425.
Pages 493-528 contain an interesting discussion of the various sacred objects found at shrines, which leads to a consideration of what the Buddhists considered "sacred." Pages 387-425 are a discussion drawn from personal visits and the accounts of the Chinese pilgrims of Kapilavastu, Bodh Gaya, Sarnath, Sravasti, Rajagrha, Vesali and Kusinagara.

(16) ROWLAND, BENJAMIN. The Art and Architecture of India: Buddhist, Hindu, Jain. Third edition. New York: Penguin Books, 1967, 314 pp.
A straightforward approach to Indian art. The author briefly traces the changes which have taken place in the fundamental concept of Hindu and Buddhist art since the Mauryan period, while taking into account the historical causes for the changes. The reader will also find sketchy chapters on the history of art in Sri Lanka, Cambodia, Thailand, Burma and Indonesia. The strength of this introductory work is in the 216 pages of plates which include illustrations of all the major Buddhist shrines and stupas to be found in the Hinayana countries.

(17) WAUCHOPE, R. S. Buddhist Cave Temples of India. Calcutta: Calcutta General Print Co., 1933, 121 pp.
Wauchope has attempted "to give a more or less complete story of the growth of Buddhist cave architecture from the earliest times to the fall of Buddhism in India." The reader will note, however, that the author is also "more or less" interested in more general questions concerning the reasons for the rise and fall of Buddhism as an Indian religion. Nevertheless, he has devoted a chapter and illustrations to each of the fourteen cave sites which he discusses. Also includes a brief essay on the meaning of the primary symbols found in the cave temples surveyed.

10.2.2 Lumbini and Kapilavastu

(1) CARPENTIER, JARL. "Note on the Padariya or Rummindei Inscription." Indian Antiquary, 43 (1914), 17-20.
A rather technical discussion of the various forms of the word "Lumbini-Rummindei," but including helpful references to Buddhist texts which refer to this, the site of the Buddha's birth.

(2) FOUCHER, ALFRED. The Life of the Buddha (see 2.7.6[5]), pp. 13-82.
This first part of Foucher's life of the Buddha (which is organized according to the sites of pilgrimage in India) is entitled "The Kapilavastu Cycle," and provides an interesting account of the sacred places in and around the Buddha's hometown.

(3) LAW, BIMALA CHURN. Indological Studies. Allahabad: Ganganatha Jha Research Institute, 1954, pt. 3, pp. 1-6.
A short but useful article based on Pali and Sanskrit sources about the city of Kapilavastu.

(4) MITRA, SAIVENDRANATH. "The Lumbini Pilgrimage Record in Two Inscriptions." Indian Historical Quarterly, 5 (1929), 728-753.
This article includes a detailed description of the two inscriptions ascribed to Ashoka which he apparently had made upon his pilgrimage to Lumbini. The author goes on to discuss various interpretations which have been tendered by scholars concerning the authenticity and meaning of the inscriptions.

(5) MUKERJI, PURMA CHANDRA. "Antiquities in the Terai, Nepal: The Region of Kapilavastu," in Archaeological Survey of India, 1901.
A full archeological overview of the remains in the region of the Buddha's home, including the place of his birth, Lumbini. For a number of photographs of the same area, see Perceval Landon, Nepal (London, 1928), vol. 1, pp. 1-10.

10.2.3 Bodh Gaya

(1) BARUA, BENIMADHAB. Gaya and Buddha-Gaya. Calcutta: Chuckervetty Chatterjee, 1931, 2 vols.
Barua has offered the reader a complete and comprehensive account of the history and character of Bodh-Gaya. Happily, it is more readable than Cunningham's (below) or Mitra's Buddha-Gaya (below). The author has divided his work into five books which include general descriptions of the Bo Tree and the stone pillar erected by Ashoka, an analysis of the inscriptions, a study of the bas-reliefs in relation to the history of Buddhist piety, and a series of seventy-six plates.

(2) _____. "Old Shrines at Bodh-Gaya." Indian Historical Quarterly, 6 (1930), 1-31.
A scholarly article which is an attempt to collect and interpret the various inscriptions found at Bodh-Gaya. The author also discusses previous interpretations of the inscriptions and offers his own conjectures where he feels they are needed.

(3) BHATTACHARYA, TARAPADA. The Bodh Gaya Temple. Calcutta: K. L. Mukhopadhyaya, 1966, 40 pp.
A brief but adequate treatment of the historical significance of Bodh Gaya as a sacred Buddhist place of pilgrimage. The author seems to emphasize Bodh Gaya's sacredness for Hindus as well as Buddhists.

(4) BLOCH, T. "Notes on Bodh Gaya," in Archaeological Survey of India, 1908-1909, pp. 139-158.
A useful early article on different aspects of this most sacred spot of Buddhism. Discusses, along with references to the visits of Chinese pilgrims and to Buddhist texts, the Bodhi tree, Brahmanical worship at Bodh Gaya, and selected inscriptions which are translated, including those left by some pilgrims from Ceylon and one from Bengal.

(5) CHAVANNES, EDOUARD. "Les inscriptions chinoises de Bodh-gaya." See 8.1.3(3).
The text and translation of a number of inscriptions left by Chinese Buddhist pilgrims on their visits to Bodh Gaya. They form a fascinating record of what was foremost in the minds of these devout Buddhists during their stay at the holiest place of the religion.

(6) CUNNINGHAM, ALEXANDER. Mahabodhi. Varanasi: Indological Book House, 1961, 84 pp.
As is the case with all of Cunningham's efforts, very few details, if any, are overlooked. He has incorporated the reports of the Chinese pilgrims as well as the results of previous excavations in his own analysis. His well chosen illustrations and plates include a detailed sketch of the "great temple," a sketch of the entire Bodh-Gaya complex, plates of Indo-Scythian, Burmese, and Chinese inscriptions as well as plates illustrating the Buddha's Walk, and the Temple of Ashoka.

(7) MITRA, RAJENDRALALA. Buddha Gaya: The Great Buddhist Temple. Delhi: Indological Book House, 1972.
A worthwhile study of Bodh Gaya which consists basically of an historical sketch, a description of the architectural remains, sculpture and inscriptions, and fifty-one plates.

10.2.4 Sarnath

(1) BHATTACHARYA, B. C. The History of Sarnath or the Cradle of Buddhism. Benares: Ramashwar Pathak, 1924, 213 pp.
Beginning with the Pali sources and then with the inscriptions and architecture of the Sarnath monuments, Mitra traces the history of Sarnath in relation to the rule of Ashoka, the Sunga, the Sakas, and Guptas and subsequent dynasties. He then sketches the most important results of contemporary excavations, and finally gives an account of the present condition of the Sarnath inscriptions and monuments. For further reading about Sarnath, see J. Przyluski, "The Solar Wheel at Sarnath," Journal of the Indian Society of Oriental Art, 4 (1936), 45-51; B. Majumdar, "Symbology of the Asoka Pillar, Sarnath" (9.3.1[7]); and B. N. Sharma, "The Lion Capital of the Ashoka Pillar at Sarnath," Poona Orientalist, 1 (1936), 2-6.

(2) JONES, J. J., trans. and ed. The Mahavastu (see 3.2.1.2[5]), vol. 1, pp. 301-311.
These pages contain a short story about how Deer Park at Sarnath acquired its name. Particularly worth noting in the story is the connection made between noninjury and the sacredness of Deer Park.

(3) MAJUMDAR, BHAVATOSA. A Guide to Sarnath. Delhi: Manager of Publications, 1937, 122 pp.
The author begins by sketching the life of the Buddha and noting the significance of Sarnath as the place of the Buddha's first sermon (which he then summarizes). He follows with a history of Sarnath as it can be reconstructed from archeological findings and the comparative study of sculptural art. The reader is then provided with a description of the principal monuments and an interpretation of the symbolic animals which are carved on the Lion Capital. Finally, there are some philosophical explanations of the most important inscriptions. Overall, not a bad place to begin a study of Sarnath.

(4) MARSHALL, JOHN and STEN KONOW. "Excavations at Sarnath," in Archaeological Survey of India. Calcutta: Manager of Publications, 1904-1905, pp. 59-104; 1906-1907, pp. 68-101; 1907-1908, pp. 43-80; and 1914-1915, pp. 97-131.
A full archeological report on the findings at the site of the Buddha's first sermon at Sarnath. Especially valuable for its detailed plans of the site, its history of the place, including references to Buddhist texts and Chinese pilgrims, its lists and translations of some of the many inscriptions found there, or the sculpture left there, etc.

(5) SAHNI, DAYA RAM. Guide to the Buddhist Ruins of Sarnath. Delhi: Manager of Publications, 1933, 49 pp.
Though this guide is a bit dated and abbreviated, it does contain a useful, concise account of the archeological discoveries at Sarnath and their significance. The monuments (including seven monasteries, stupas, the main shrine, and the Ashoka pillar) are each individually discussed in historical as well as artistic terms.

10.2.5 Kusinara/Kusinagara

(1) <u>Mahaparinibbana Sutta</u>, in <u>Digha Nikaya (Dialogues of the Buddha)</u> (see 2.7.1[13]), chapters 5 and 6.

This is the canonical account of the establishment of sacred places and the types of reverence to be offered by the worshippers. The main discussion, however, is concerned with the shrine at Kusinagara.

(2) SMITH, V. A. "Kusinara, or Kusinagara and Other Buddhist Holy Places." <u>Journal of the Royal Asiatic Society</u> (1902), 139-163.

Though Smith's treatment of Kusinara is labored, it remains one of the few available. The reader will be presented with a rather standard discussion of the significance of Kusinara in the life of the Buddha and its consequent acquisition of "sacrality" as a major pilgrimage site.

(3) VOGEL, J. P., et al. "Excavations at Kasia," in <u>Archaeological Survey of India</u>. Calcutta: Manager of Publications, 1904-1905, pp. 42-58; 1905-1906, pp. 61-85; 1906-1907, pp. 44-67; 1911-1912, pp. 134 ff.; etc.

A series of archeological reports on the finds made at Kasia, the site of Kusinagara where the Buddha passed into Parinirvana. These reports, with their references to the accounts of Chinese pilgrims, to Buddhist texts, to inscriptions found on the site, and their precise detailed drawings of the remains, etc., are a mine of information on this, one of the four most sacred places of Buddhism.

10.2.6 Other Important Sites

10.2.6.1 In North India

(1) COOMARASWAMY, A. K. <u>Les sculptures de Bharhut</u>. Paris: Van Oest, 1956, 97 pp., 252 plates.

The author's chief intention here is to improve upon Cunningham's seminal work (below). Coomaraswamy pays much closer attention to the sculpture at Bharhut and notes his differing interpretations from those of B. M. Barua. An excellent study.

(2) CUNNINGHAM, ALEXANDER. <u>The Stupa of Bharhut</u>. Varanasi: Indological Book House, 1962, 143 pp.

Written from the point of view of the archeologist, this work offers enough detail and exactness to provide the intermediate and advanced student with raw materials needed to gain a perspective on the cultic activity which existed at this sacred place. In addition, V. S. Agrawala has written an excellent introduction to the volume which discusses the cosmological and architectural significance of stupas in general, and then of the particular significance of the stupa of Bharhut.

(3) LAW, BIMALA CHURN. <u>Indological Studies</u> (see 10.2.2[3]), pt. 3, pp. 27-46, 104-130, 131-147.

A series of articles based on Pali and Sanskrit sources, many of which treat Buddhist sacred places: in particular, the city of Mathura, famous among Hindus as well as Buddhists, and visited by Fa Hsien; Vaisali, the capital of the Licchavis and site of the second council; and Asoka's capital city, Pataliputra.

(4) _____. <u>Indological Studies</u> (see 10.2.2[3]), pt. 4, pp. 123-149, 150-166.

Two short articles based on Pali and Sanskrit texts and conveniently bringing together information about two important sacred places of Buddhism. The first deals with "Prince Jeta's Grove," the famous site of the monastery built for the Buddha by Anathapindika. The second concerns the River Nairanjana near Bodh Gaya.

(5) _____. <u>Sravasti in Indian Literature</u>. Delhi: Manager of Publications, Government of India, 1935, 39 pp.

This short essay is primarily a study of the archeology of Sravasti, with many references to the accounts of Fa-Hien and Hsuang.

(6) MARSHALL, JOHN. <u>Taxila</u>. Cambridge: Cambridge University Press, 1951, 3 vols., 895 pp.

A landmark work in Indian archeology. The three volumes (Volume 3 consists of plates only) record the findings of a thirty-one-year excavation (1913-1934). The reader will rarely find such a comprehensive study of this quality. Marshall's chief aim is to attempt a reconstruction of Taxila's once important cultural life. For an abridged account of the findings, see Marshall's <u>A Guide to Taxila</u> (Calcutta: Superintendent of Government Printing, 1918), 129 pp.

(7) SANKALIA, HASMUKH D. <u>The University of Nalanda</u>. See 6.2.5(24).

As the site of the great Buddhist university, Nalanda itself became an object of pilgrimage, as is clearly evidenced by the accounts of the Chinese pilgrims. This work recounts the history of the University and surveys its present archeological state. A not very inspiring but adequate treatment.

(8) SOMPURA, K. F. <u>Buddhist Monuments and Sculptures in Gujurat</u>. Hoshiapur: Vishveshvaranand Institute Publications, 1969, 38 pp.

A brief attempt to survey, from the standpoint of chronology, the Buddhist monuments supposedly ignored by the "classical" Indian archeologists. On the whole, descriptions are very short and, at its best, this book is of use only as a supplement for the purpose of dating the monuments.

(9) VOGEL, J. R. "Excavations at Sahet-Mahet," in <u>Archaeological Survey of India</u>. Calcutta: Manager of Publications, 19707-1908, pp. 81-131.

A detailed archeological report on the town which was known as Sravasti when it was an important secondary pilgrimage site of Buddhists. Includes plans and useful descriptions.

(10) WIN, LU PE. "Bharhut," in Encyclopedia of Buddhism (see 2.5.4[12]), vol. 2, pp. 696-700.
This brief article should only be consulted when the student is unable to find a copy of Cunningham's The Stupa of Bharhut (above). The discussion here is overly sympathetic to traditional significances, and not much effort has been made to comment upon the plates.

10.2.6.2 In Central India

(1) CUNNINGHAM, ALEXANDER. The Bhilsa Topes. London: Smith, Elder, 1854, 370 pp., 33 plates.
Once the reader has waded through the first twelve chapters (196 pp.), a rather dated history of Buddhism, he or she will benefit from Cunningham's first-rate descriptions of Sanchi, Bhojpur Satdhara and Andher, which follow. In addition, Chapter 13 is an essay concerned with the construction and dedication of Buddhist monuments in general.

(2) DHAVALIKAR, M. K. Sanchi: A Cultural History. Poona: Deccan College Postgraduate Research Institute, 1965, 84 pp.
This study is primarily concerned with the ornamental gateways of the "great stupa." Almost every element which appears in the gateways (from head-dresses to foot-stools) is examined in order to explain its significance in both the ancient and contemporary periods. Includes eight plates. For further reading, see also Debala Mitra, Sanchi (second edition; Delhi: Director General of Archeology in India, 1965).

(3) GUPTE, R. S. and B. D. MAHAJAN. Ajanta, Ellora, and the Aurangabad Caves. Bombay: D. B. Taraporevala, 1962, 288 pp.
The authors discuss "the story of the Buddha and the Buddha's teaching in addition to Buddhist iconography as an introduction" to the significance of the Ajanta caves. Similarly, they have discussed Hindu and Jain iconography while introducing Ellora.

(4) MAISEY, FREDERICK. Sanchi and Its Remains. London: K. Paul, Trench, Trubner, 1892, 142 pp.
Though less attention has been paid to Maisey, his work is of the same quality as that of Cunningham, Marshall, and Fergusson. He has attempted to describe the Sanchi remains in relation to the "religious system antecedent to what is now called Buddhism." Unfortunately, this approach has somewhat marred an otherwise brilliant depiction of the memorials. It was the author's contention that Buddhism represented an introduced reform of the "pre-existing semi-mithraic faith" around the beginning of the Christian era. Nevertheless, his descriptions are first-rate.

(5) MARSHALL, JOHN. A Guide to Sanchi. Third edition. Delhi: Manager of Publications, 1955, 168 pp.
The author, an eminent scholar, offers the reader the best treatment concerned with Sanchi. He begins his study with a historical sketch of Sanchi from the time of Asoka to the time of the first publication of this work. Then, in detailed fashion, he describes the history and architecture of the "great stupa," the pillars on the "main entrance," the adjacent temples and the monasteries. The author has made a brilliant attempt to relate the great number of carvings and reliefs to the episodes of the Buddha's life. A short, useful bibliography is appended.

(6) MARSHALL, JOHN and ALFRED FOUCHER. Monuments of Sanchi. London: Probsthain, 1940, 3 vols.
In this work, two outstanding scholars with complementary strengths have teamed up to present a masterful exposition. Marshall provides the archeological expertise and Foucher contributes an extensive knowledge of iconographic and literary materials. Volumes 2 and 3 contain only plates. Volume 1 concerns the historical significance of Sanchi for Buddhism and the significance of the artistic expression of Sanchi as a witness to the various stages of Buddhist piety and practice.

(7) ROWLAND, BENJAMIN. The Ajanta Caves. New York: Mentor-UNESCO Art Books, 1963.
A short but well done paperback which includes twenty-eight well-chosen color plates of the most outstanding frescoes. Though the approach used by the author is thoroughly of an artistic point of view, the reader can still benefit by gaining an overview of the significance of the Ajanta Caves in the development of the history of Buddhism in Western India. For further reading, see M. C. Dey, My Pilgrimages to Ajanta and Bagh (New York: G. H. Doran, 1925).

(8) SINGH, MADANJEET. Ajanta Paintings of the Sacred and Secular. Lausanne: E.D.I.T.A., 1956.
A fine examination which is primarily concerned with the artistic and historical significance of the frescoes found on the cave walls of Ajanta. Written by a prominent Indian art historian, the book is helpful for intermediate students.

(9) SIVARAMAMURTI, C. "Ajanta," in Encyclopedia of Buddhism (see 2.5.4[12]), vol. 1, pp. 754-765.
A very good short description of these Buddhist caves found in Western India. The uniqueness of the article lies in its attempt

to show how the cave paintings are related to themes within the Jatakas.

10.2.6.3 In South India

(1) AIYANPAN, A. and P. R. SRINAVASNA. *Guide to the Buddhist Antiquities*. Madras: Comptroller, Government of Madras, 1960, 60 pp.

This brief essay is primarily concerned with the history and sculpture of Amaravati. The remaining pages constitute an all too brief historical account of other fairly minor Buddhist sites around Amaravati.

(2) BURGESS, JAMES. *The Buddhist Stupas of Amaravati and Jaggayyapeta*. Varanasi: Indological Book House, 1970, 131 pp.

Although the author's approach is thoroughly archeological in its intent and scope, this effort remains extremely valuable for those students concerned with the period of Buddhist history around the time of Nagarjuna. The reader will also find the Dhauli and Jaugada versions of Ashoka's rock edicts at the end of this report.

(3) LONGHURST, H. *Buddhist Antiquities of Nagarjunakonda*. Delhi: Manager of Publications, Government of India, 1938, 67 pp.

A brief but well-done essay which presents the findings of the archeological dig at this third and fourth century stupa-monastery-university site. Suitable for the intermediate and advanced student.

(4) SASTRI, K. A. NILAKANTA. "Mahayana Buddhism in South India." *Bulletin of Tibetology*, 2, no. 3 (November 1965), 11-21.

This article is basically a survey of Mahayana remains in important Buddhist sites throughout South India. The author includes in his presentation short disucssions of the significance of Ajanta, Ellora, Nagarjunakonda, Ratnagiri, and Kanchipura.

10.3 SRI LANKA

10.3.1 The Royal Capitals and Their Special Sites

(1) DEVENDRA, D. T. "Abhayagiri," in *Encyclopedia of Buddhism* (see 2.5.4[12]), vol. 1, pp. 21-25.

A short article which provides the reader with a history and description of the operation of the Abhayagiri shrine. Photographs are included.

(2) _____. "Anuradhapura," in *Encyclopedia of Buddhism* (see 2.5.4[12]), vol. 1, pp. 754-765.

A useful article in that it provides the reader with a map designating the multiple shrines found at Anuradhapura and a brief description of each shrine.

(3) FERNANDO, W. D. MARCUS. *Ancient City of Anuradhapura*. Colombo: Government Press, 1965, 66 pp.

A useful pamphlet describing the oldest capital of Sri Lanka, with separate sections on its various viharas, the Bodhi tree, etc. A helpful introduction.

(4) GOLOUBEW, VICTOR. "Le temple de la Dent à Kandy." See 8.1.2.4(10).

Goloubew's article should be read as a supplement to Hocart's *The Temple of the Tooth* (below), as it mentions some aspects of the cult worship which are omitted in Hocart's account. A well-done article suitable to the intermediate and advanced student.

(5) HOCART, ARTHUR M. *The Temple of the Tooth in Kandy*. See 7.1.3(9).

Though it suffers from brevity, this study remains a worthwhile investment for any student interested in cultic worship in Southeast Asia. The author succinctly outlines the history of the temple, describes its architecture (mostly by means of drawings), depicts the various rituals conducted at the temple, and attempts to compare the plan of the temple with other Sinhalese temples and with Western monasteries.

(6) OLDENBERG, HERMAN, ed. and trans. *The Dipava*. London: Williams and Norgate, 1879, 227 pp.

The entire chronicle is useful for understanding the legendary account of the arrival and establishment of Buddhism. Of especial importance to the topic of sacred places are Chapters 13-16, in which Mahinda preaches the dhamma, the monastery is established, the shrine is built to encase the bodily relics of the Buddha, the veneration of the collar bone is initiated, and the branch of the Bodhi Tree is brought into the country.

(7) RAVEN-HART, R. *Ceylon History in Stone*. Colombo: Lake House, 1964, 320 pp.

Uses architecture and archaeology to describe the ancient Sinhalese capitals of Anuradhapura, Pollonaruwa and others. A useful introduction.

10.3.2 Other Important Sites

(1) LUDOWYK, EVELYN F. C. *The Footprint of the Buddha*. See 1.3.2.1[11].

Primarily an introductory work describing the beliefs and practices of Sinhala Buddhism; the author has combined sensitivity with scholarly insight in this description of the major sacred monuments of Sinhalese Buddhism. In addition to first-rate plates, the inclusion of a glossary adds to the value of the work.

(2) PARANAVITANA, S. *The God of Adam's Peak*. Ascona: Artibus Asiae Publishers, 1958, 78 pp., 15 plates.

When read in conjunction with the first chapter of the Mahavamsa, Paravitana's initial chapter concerned with the history and literature associated with Adam's Peak is informative and useful. However, the remainder of the essay consists of an attempt to argue through iconographic and literary comparison that the God of Adam's Peak (Saman) should be identified with the Hindu god Yama.

(3) WIRZ, PAUL. Kataragama: The Holiest Place in Ceylon. Colombo: Lake House Investments, 1966, 5 pp., 18 plates.

This fine little monograph describes the history and religious significance of Kataragama. The author describes the temples and shrines and the three major ceremonies which take place during the annual "great festival." In addition, he recounts the Hindu, Buddhist, and Islamic legends which lay claim to Kataragama as a sacred place.

10.4 BURMA

10.4.1 Pagan

(1) DAW THIN KYI. "The Old City of Pagan," in Essays Offered to G. H. Luce. Edited by Ba Ba Shih, Jean Boisselier, and A. B. Griswold. Ascona: Artibus Asiae, 1966, pp. 179-188.

By a thorough examination of the four sections of Pagan's city wall, the author attempts to make a statement concerning the progress of political and administrative organization around the eleventh and twelfth centuries.

(2) LUCE, G. H. Old Burma--Early Pagan. See 1.4.2(12).

An excellent presentation of the iconography and inscriptions of Pagan. Luce provides a fluid text which accompanies the large number of plates illustrating scenes from the Buddha's life, symbols, and various postures. Luce is careful throughout to observe the Brahmanical, Mahayanist and Tantric influences. Of use to the student of any level.

(3) SAHIAR, D. et al. "In Praise of the Buddhist Art in Burma." Marg, 9, no. 3 (June 1956), 1-60.

This excellent portfolio offers the reader an essay by Reginald Le May on "The Cultural Background of Burma," and an extensive analysis of the architecture, sculpture, and frescoes of the Ananda Temple at Pagan. The reader will also find excellent plates of other sites at Pagan. A good source to begin a study on sacred places in Burma. On the Ananda temple, see also Ch. Curoiselle, "The Ananda Temple at Pagan," Memoirs of the Archaeological Survey of India, 56 (1937), 24 pp.

(4) THAN TUN. "Religious Buildings of Burma, 100-1300." Journal of the Burma Research Society, 42 (1959), 71-80.

This brief article attempts to describe the most important structures at Pagan through the inscriptions left by the donors of the buildings. Of some use to the intermediate student.

(5) TIN, PE MAUNG. "Buddhism in the Inscriptions of Pagan." See 1.4.2(19).

A well-done article which begins by recounting the influence of Naga and Mon tendencies as well as the astrological influence of Brahmanic thought at Pagan. The rest of the article consists of an attempt to recall the "pure" Buddhist piety evidenced in the many inscriptions of the pagodas and monasteries. Of use to the intermediate and advanced student.

10.4.2 Other Important Sites

(1) FERGUSSON, JAMES. History of Indian and Eastern Architecture (see 10.2.1[10]), vol. 2, pp. 339-370.

An overview of the relationship between religious piety and its expression within the principles of Burmese architecture throughout history. The author specifically examines buildings found at Thaton, Prome, and Pagan. Monasteries are evaluated in general and the reader will also find a discussion comparing circular and square pagodas.

(2) MENDELSON, E. MICHAEL. "Observations on a Tour in the Region of Mount Popa." France-Asie, 19, no. 179, 786-807.

Like all of Mendelson's articles, this one contains materials unlikely to be found anywhere else. It contains specific discussions concerning the popular Buddhist religio-magical significance of Mount Popa as a holy place, not only for Buddhists but also for Nat propitiators. Mendelson gives an accounting of the pagodas, monks, and stories about "weikzas" which he encountered on his tour.

(3) SHORTO, HARRY. "The Thirty-Two Myos in the Medieval Mon Kingdom." Bulletin of the School of Oriental and African Studies, 26 (1963), 572-591.

A significant contribution to the study of notions of sacred places in the Mon kingdom of Lower Burma. Shorto re-examines the historical evidence for the division of the kingdom into thirty-two districts. This leads him to a new interpretation of the Burmese pantheon as well as providing insights into the origins of political organization of the region.

(4) TIN, PE MAUNG and G. H. LUCE. The Glass Palace Chronicles of the Kings of Burma (Hmannan maha yazawintawkyi). See 1.4.1(3).

The traditional history of the activities of the Burmese kings, this chronicle gives us the popular accounts of the building of the royal palace, the important pagodas of Shwezayan (pp. 84-86) and Shwezigon (pp. 87-88 and 108-110), and other important pagodas.

10.5 THAILAND

(1) ALABASTER, HENRY. The Wheel of the Law (see 8.1.2.1[2]), pp. 245-314.

This section of Alabaster's work includes a detailed description of a pilgrimage to see and venerate the "Phrabat" or Thai footprint of the Buddha. This is preceded by a general discussion of Buddha's footprints in stone, and is followed by detailed descriptions and explanations of its symbolism. Another description of the pilgrimage to the Prabat may be found in Ernest Young, The Kingdom of the Yellow Robe (see 7.2.5[8]), pp. 375-387.

(2) DAMRONG, RAJANUBHAB, PRINCE. A History of Buddhist Monuments in Siam. See 1.5.2(8).

This is an excellent, though dated, study of the introduction and further development of Buddhist scriptures, stupas and images in Siam. The specific study of these elements leads to a broader history of Buddhism in Siam. Recommended for the intermediate and advanced student.

(3) FERGUSSON, JAMES. History of Indian and Eastern Architecture (see 10.2.1[10]), vol. 2, pp. 404-413.

A brief but useful discussion concerned with the manner in which Buddhist piety has been expressed in the architectural principles of Thai temples.

(4) KEYES, CHARLES F. "Buddhist Pilgrimage Centers and the Twelve Year Cycle: Northern Thai Moral Orders in Space and Time." History of Religions, 15 (1975), 71-89.

An interesting article which relates the spatial organization of pilgrimage sites concentrically out from Northern Thailand to the calendrical cycle and to astrological determinations for individuals. Brings new light on the whole question of the overall organization of sacred places and pilgrimages to them in Buddhist Thailand.

(5) LE MAY, REGINALD. A Concise History of Buddhist Art in Siam. Cambridge: Cambridge University Press, 1938, 165 pp., 80 plates.

Though Le May is primarily interested in artistic style and thus organizes his book around the evolution of various schools of art in Siam, he does give enough attention to the history of Buddhist piety in Siam, so that the reader more specifically concerned with "sacred places" will be rewarded by his essay.

10.6 INDOCHINA AND INDONESIA

(1) BOISSELIER, J. Le Cambodge. Paris: A. and J. Picard, 1966, vol. 1, pt. 1, pp. 45-138.

These pages represent a masterful presentation of Cambodian architecture as it was expressed in the building of Buddhist temples through the post-Angkor period. A good overview, of use to the intermediate as well as the advanced student.

(2) COEDES, GEORGES. Angkor. Translated and edited by Emily F. Gardiner. New York: Oxford, 1963, 116 pp.

Although this work at first sight appears to be intended only for the general reader, it is perhaps the best single volume dedicated to the discussion of the historical and religious significance as well as the religious symbolism and cult practices associated with Angkor. For further reading, see Paul Mus, Angkor in the Time of Jayavarman VII (9.3.7[6]); H. Marchal, "Symbolisme des temples hindous et khmers," France-Asie, 12, no. 114-115 (1955), 339-344; H. Marchal, Angkor (les hauts lieux de l'histoire) (Paris: A. Guillot, 1955); and B. P. Groslier, Angkor, hommes et pierres (Paris: Arthaud, 1968, 245 pp.).

(3) DUMARCAY, JACQUES. Le Bayon: Histoire architecturale du temple. Paris: Ecole française d'Extrême-Orient, 1973, 326 pp.

An excellent and authoritative work on this temple at the center of the Buddhist capital city par excellence in the Angkor complex. It is profusely illustrated, and includes, over and beyond the architectural and archeological reports, a discussion of the temple as a mandala, of its place in history, and an edition by Bernard Groslier of all the inscriptions found on and near the Bayon itself.

(4) FERGUSSON, JAMES. History of Indian and Eastern Architecture (see 10.2.1[10]), vol. 2, pp. 371-403.

An overview of the relationship between religious piety and its expression within the principles of Cambodian architectural design. The author specifically concerns himself with Angkor Wat, Angkor Thom, Ta Prome and several other palaces. The second passage deals with Indonesia, primarily focusing on the expression of Buddhism found at Borobudur.

(5) FOUCHER, ALFRED. "Notes d'archéologie bouddhique." Bulletin de l'Ecole française d'Extrême-Orient, 9 (1909), 1-50.

One of the first French attempts to study in detail the significance of Borobudur, this article is basically separated into three main discussions: 1) the stupa of Borobudur; 2) the bas reliefs of Borobudur; and 3) a general discussion of Buddhist iconography in Java. A readable article which is of worth to those students who do not wish to tackle the monumental work by Paul Mus (below).

(6) KRASA, MILOSLAV. The Temples of Angkor. Translated by Joy Turner. London: A. Wingate, 1963, 61 pp.

The first third of Krasa's first-rate contribution recounts the religious and political history of Angkor, including a hypothetical reconstruction of everyday life at the site. The remaining portion of the book is dedicated to a survey of the principal artistic styles manifest in the temple design.

(7) MUS, PAUL. Barabudur. See 2.5.2(8).
This is one of the few books that spans just about every category in this bibliography. Though it was written in 1935, it remains exciting and seminal today. It is basically divided into two parts, a three-hundred-page "foreword" entitled "Les sources indiennes du Bouddhisme," in which Mus summarizes the methods, results, and implications of his work on Borobudur for the study of Buddhism as a whole, and a second part entitled "Les origines du stupa et la transmigration," containing five sections: architectural interpretations, religious interpretations, the symbolism of Barabudur, the cosmic value of the stupa, the problem of the five directions. To this is added an appendix on the seven steps of the Buddha and the doctrine of the "pure lands." Unfortunately, the work has never been translated into English, and its rather complicated style makes it readily handy only to those with a facility in French. For advanced students.

(8) WALES, HORACE G. Q. The Mountain of God: A Study in Early Religion and Kingship. London: B. Quaritch, 1953, pp. 131-170.
Wales' approach as a "diffusionist" tends to obscure the earlier chapters of the book which are concerned with China, India and Java. However, his final chapter on Khmer temple-mountains contains a worthwhile discussion on the origins of these temples which took place before the period of Hindu-Buddhist influence. After describing early Khmer religion, Wales discusses the history of the sacred mountain concept in Cambodia from Khmer times through the period of Hindu-Buddhist influence, showing how Khmer religion prepared Cambodians for the Hindu-Buddhist notion of "Mt. Meru."

10.7 TIBET AND HIMALAYA

(1) FERGUSSON, JAMES. History of Indian and Eastern Architecture (see 10.2.1[10]), vol. 1, pp. 273-301.
An overview of the relationship between religious piety and its expression within the principles of architecture found in the Himalayan countries of Tibet, Sikkim, and Nepal. The emphasis of the discussion is primarily on the plan, design, and ornament of the Buddhist monasteries.

(2) MKCYEN BRTSE. Mkcyen Brtse's Guide to the Holy Places of Central Tibet. Edited by Alfonsa Ferrari. Rome: Istituto italiano per il Medio ed Estremo Oriente, 1958, 198 pp.
This work is an autobiographical account of a nineteenth century Tibetan pilgrim's pilgrimage to the holy places of Central Tibet. The pilgrim is basically concerned with describing various temples and monasteries and, wherever possible, noting references to these holy places within Tibetan literature.

(3) SHRESTHA, C. B. Buddhist Geography of Ancient Nepal. Kathmandu: Fourth World Buddhist Conference, 1956(?), 11 pp.
This brief pamphlet lists sacred cities, temples, stupas, and lakes within Nepal and attempts to correlate their modern significances with traditional Buddhist sources.

(4) SNELLGROVE, DAVID. "Shrines and Temples of Nepal." Arts asiatiques, 8 (1961), 3-10, 93-120.
This well-done article begins with a discussion of the type of Buddhism transported into Nepal among the Newars and the consequent changes which followed. But the thrust of the article is concerned with the character of caityas, temples, and mandalas and how they reflect a small part of the culture of medieval India. See also Pratapaditya Pal, Buddhist Art in Lichham Nepal (Bombay: Marg Publications; Los Angeles: Los Angeles County Museum of Art, 1974), 39 pp.

(5) TUCCI, GIUSEPPE. Shrines of a Thousand Buddhas. New York: R. M. McBride, 1936, 272 pp.
The English edition of this book is vastly superior to its Italian counterpart, as it contains many illustrations, two fairly detailed maps, and a much improved index. The reader will be able to capture a bit of the style and flavor of Tibetan monastic art and life style. For the technical findings of Tucci's expedition, see his Indo-Tibetica.

(6) WADDELL, L. AUSTINE. Tibetan Buddhism (see 1.14.1[17]), pp. 255-323.
A well-done descriptive survey of the most important monasteries, shrines, "cathedrals," and other destinations of pilgrims in Tibet. Perhaps the highlight of this section of Waddell's book is his informative description of the "cathedral" at Lhasa.

10.8 CHINA

10.8.1 General Discussions

(1) ALABASTER, HENRY. The Wheel of the Law. See 8.1.2.1(2).

(2) BULLING, A. "Buddhist Temples in the T'ang Period." Oriental Art, 1 (1955), 115-122.
A worthwhile and well illustrated essay which treats the sociological role of the temple in T'ang society and the theological significance of the temple's design and decor. The author is sensitive to the differences between these Chinese temples and temples erected in Japan centuries later.

(3) KUPFER, CARL. Sacred Places in China. Cincinnati: Press of the Western Book Concern, 1911, pp. 9-69.
Though the author's main goal is not architectural, he does offer useful descriptions of monasteries in Hwang Mei, the

Nine-Lotus-Flower Mountain (Kiu Hua Shan) and Poot'oo (a sacred Chinese island). Kupfer accounts for the sacrality of these places by placing them within the context of popular Chinese history (most of which he seems to have garnered from Buddhist monks).

(4) PRIP-MOLLER, J. Chinese Buddhist Monasteries. See 7.2.1(7).
This is an attempt by a European architect to make some generalizations, from a study of various Chinese monasteries, about the role and character of Buddhist monasticism in Chinese history. In the first two chapters, he describes "the typical Buddhist monastery layout." The next two chapters are a specific discussion of the Hui Chu Ssu monastery. Finally, Prip-Moller attempts to reconstruct the typical life led by monks.

(5) SOPER, ALEXANDER and LAURENCE SICKMAN. The Art and Architecture of China. Baltimore: Penguin, 1956, 334 pp.
A general survey which attempts to give the reader an overview of the most important principles and influences expressed in Chinese art. The authors have provided the reader with a good general discussion of the changes effected by the introduction and maintenance of Buddhism upon artistic expression in general and have illustrated these changes in references to specific Buddhist shrines, caves, and monasteries. For further reading, see Soper's Literary Evidence for Early Buddhist Art in China (1.11.2.1[8]).

(6) TOKIWA, DAIJO and TADASHI SEKINO. Buddhist Monuments in China. See 1.11.2.2(11).
Each volume contains 100 or so pages of text explaining the massive number of plates, which accompany in a separate atlas. As a whole, the five volumes attempt to study the history of Buddhist culture during the Sui and T'ang dynasties by means of analysis of the archeological remains. Based on a series of seven expeditions to China during the first two decades of the twentieth century, the work seems to emphasize the significance of rock caves and the religious life centering on them. In addition, however, the authors have given a fairly comprehensive account of stupas and monasteries which apparently were of great importance. The basic arrangement of the volumes is chronological.

10.8.2 Caves, Mountains, and Other Specific Sites

(1) AKIYAMA, TERUKAZU and SABURO MATSUBARA. Arts of China: Buddhist Cave Temples. Tokyo: Kodansha, 1969, 247 pp.
A beautifully done volume with a great number of plates and excellent descriptions of the sculpture and paintings of the important Buddhist cave temples in China. The comprehensive scope of this work makes it one of the best sources on the subject.

(2) CHEN, KENNETH. Buddhism in China (see 1.11.1[1]), pp. 165-177.
In these pages, Chen outlines the character and historical significance of the Yun Kang and Lun Men caves. He considers these two caves typical of Chinese Buddhist caves, so the reader finds generalizations about the subject.

(3) ECKE, G. and PAUL DEMIEVILLE. The Twin Pagodas of Zayton. Cambridge, Mass.: Harvard University Press, 1935, 95 pp.
An excellent scholarly study of this specific Chinese Buddhist locale which contains a general discussion of the architectural and sculptural style in the first section and an iconographic and historical analysis of both eastern and western pagodas in the second section.

(4) GRAY, BASIL. Buddhist Cave Painting at Tun-Huang. See 1.10.2(7).
Gray's perspective is primarily artistic, but he indicates the religious significance of this important cave center in Western China.

(5) HUANG SHOU-FU and T'AN CHUN-YO. The Omei Illustrated Guide Book. Translated by D. L. Phelps. Cambridge, Mass.: Harvard Yenching Institute and West China Union University, 1936, 454 pp.
Originally written by two Chinese Buddhist monks in 1887, this "guide" begins with thirty-six poems and closes with twelve more. The overall theme of the poems is Mt. Omei. Between the two sections of poetry, the guide takes the reader on a step-by-step tour of Mt. Omei, emphasizing the significance of the many monasteries and recounting the many legends associated with the mountain.

(6) JOHNSTON, REGINALD FLEMING. Buddhist China. London: J. Murray, pp. 122-390.
An important contribution to our data on pilgrimage to sacred places in China. Chapter 7 contains a translation of sizeable excerpts of "A Pilgrim's Guide to the Four Famous Hills" (Ch'ao Ssu Ta-ming Shan Lu Yin). Chapters 8-13 are devoted to descriptions of two of those sacred mountains, Chiu-Hua Shan (and its patron divinity Ti-tsang/Jizo) and Putoshan (and Kuan-yin). Other brief treatments of the four mountains may be found in Reichelt, Truth and Tradition in Chinese Buddhism (see 1.11.1[8]), pp. 284-297; and in Welch, The Practice of Chinese Buddhism 1900-1950 (6.1.1[9]), pp. 305 ff.

(7) LITTLE, ARCHIBALD JOHN. Mount Omei and Beyond. London: W. Heinemann, 1901, pp. 51-105.
An interesting, detailed, firsthand account of pilgrims and temples at the great monastic center of Omei-shan in Szechuan Province.

(8) MIGOT, ANDRE. "Les temples bouddhiques du Mont O-Mei." Art asiatique, 4 (1957), 20-34, 131-142.

This fine article begins with a brief discussion of the four sacred mountains of China and the uniqueness of Mt. Omei. After a valuable account of the twenty-seven deities believed to reside on the mountain, Migot surveys Mt. Omei's twenty-seven monasteries and temples, focusing primarily on the iconographic and architectural significance of each. Unfortunately, he reports, his photos were either lost or stolen.

(9) MIZUNO, S. and T. NAGAHIRO. The Buddhist Cave Temples Honan and Hopei. Kyoto: Toho-Bunka-Gakuin Kyoto Kenkyusho, 1937, 157 pp.

Unfortunately, the bulk of this work has not been translated into English. There are, however, English annotations of sixty-six plates and forty-eight other illustrations, and a ten-page English synopsis of their findings. But the scenario is so blunt, straightforward, and technical that it provides little information about the history, piety, or doctrine connected with the caves examined.

(10) ROCK, J. F. The Amnye Ma-chhen Range and Adjacent Regions. Serie Orientale Roma, No. 12. Rome: Serie Orientale Roma, 1956, 194 pp.

A fine monograph on this region of Western China-Eastern Tibet, important here for its inclusion of details on the great Labrang Lamasery, a center of local pilgrimage.

(11) SULLIVAN, MICHAEL. The Cave Temples of Maichishan. Berkeley: University of California Press, 1969, 77 pp.

Sullivan's brief volume contains excellent and detailed annotations as well as a useful bibliography. However, the real strength of his work is a result of his ability to place the caves of Maichishan within a specific historical and cultural context.

10.9 JAPAN AND KOREA

(1) ARMSTRONG, R. C. An Introduction to Japanese Buddhist Sects. See 1.13.2.2(3).

References to specific Japanese Buddhist temples are made throughout the text of the book. Consult the index for these specific references.

(2) ELIOT, CHARLES. Japanese Buddhism (see 1.13.1[4]), pp. 135-141.

These pages represent a brief but informative essay on the Indian deities and personages which can be found in Japanese Buddhist temples (especially around Kyoto).

(3) KIDDER, JONATHAN E. Japanese Temples. London: Thames and Hudson, 1964, 554 pp.

A brilliant effort by an excellent scholar provides a comprehensive study of Japanese Buddhist (and Shinto) temples. The author also discusses sculpture, painting, and gardens, noting their religious significance.

For further reading on the history and sacred places of Buddhism from A.D. 645-794, see Kidder's Early Buddhist Japan (1.13.2.1[4]).

(4) PAINE, ROBERT and ALEXANDER SOPER. The Art and Architecture of Japan. Baltimore: Penguin, 1955, 316 pp.

Though one would not expect it from the title, the majority of this book is concerned with the historical influence of Buddhism on Japanese art. It is therefore a good place to begin a study of Japanese pagodas and shrines in general. For a more detailed study of Buddhist influence in Japanese architecture, see Soper, The Evolution of Buddhist Architecture in Japan (see 5.11.3[12]).

11 Soteriological Experience and Processes: Path and Goal

11.1 SURVEYS AND DESCRIPTIONS OF THE PATH (INCLUDING THE TEN BODHISATTVA BHUMIS, THE NOBLE EIGHTFOLD PATH, THE FIVE PATHS, ETC.)

For the practice of the Perfections (paramitas), see 11.5. For the Vajrayana shortcut, see 11.6.

(1) BEYER, STEPHAN. The Buddhist Experience: Sources and Interpretations. See 3.3.2.1(18).
This anthology of freshly translated texts makes readily available for the first time a number of important texts, some of which had never been translated, and many of which had been biding their time in obscure editions and scholarly journals. Selected from all three vehicles and organized into the traditional division of "Sila" (virtue), "Samadhi" (meditation) and "Prajna" (wisdom), these texts give the student a vivid and firsthand account of all aspects of the path, without omitting some of its often neglected features, such as worship, the magical use of charms, visualizations, etc.

(2) BUDDHAGHOSA. The Path of Purification (Visuddhimagga). See 3.2.4.2(1).
This magnum opus of the great fifth century exegete Buddhaghosa has enjoyed a tremendous reputation among Theravada Buddhists. On the one hand, it is a detailed meditation manual full of practical advice and instruction. On the other hand, it is an authoritative reference work which classically presents the Path to Nirvana, centering on three topics, "Sila" (virtue), "Samdhi" (concentration), and "Panna" (understanding, wisdom), and organized into seven stages of purification.

(3) DAYAL, HAR. The Bodhisattva Doctrine in Buddhist Sanskrit Literature (see 8.1.3[4]), chapter 4, pp. 80-164, and chapter 6.
Chapter 4 gives the important list of the "thirty-seven wings of enlightenment"--a classification scheme for describing the path which was developed by Theravadans and Mahayanists alike. The thirty-seven include the Four Fixings of Attention (Smrtyupasthana), the Four Correct Efforts (Samyakpradhana), the Four Foundations of Magical Power (rddhipada), the Five Faculties (indriya), the Five Powers (bala), the Seven Limbs of Enlightenment (Bodhyanga) and the Noble Eightfold Way (Aryastangamarga). Anyone doing extensive research on any of these topics may find another account of the thirty-seven Bodhipaksika, together with extensive cross-references to the various Buddhist canons, in Lamotte's translation of the Mahaprajnaparamitasastra (see 3.3.1.2[6]), vol. 3, pp. 1119-1207. Chapter 6 of Dayal's work is a comprehensive treatment of the ten bodhisattva stages (bhumis) and is especially useful for its summary of previous Western scholarship on the topic. The theory of the ten bhumis was not exclusively a Mahayanist one. For a "still-as-yet-Hinayanist" exposition of it, see J. J. Jones, trans., The Mahavastu (3.2.1.2[5]), vol. 1, pp. 53-124, in which each of the stages is illustrated by Jataka-like stories. For a Tibetan description of the bhumis, see The Jewel Ornament of Liberation (below, chapter 19), and for a presentation from the Hua Yen perspective, see Garma C. C. Chang, The Buddhist Teaching of Totality (3.3.1.2[4]), pp. 28-47.

(4) sGAM PO PA. The Jewel Ornament of Liberation. See 3.3.8.3(2).
In Tibetan there are many texts which deal with the stages of the path (Lam rim). This one, by one of Milarepa's disciples, is one of the most substantial yet translated into English. Though somewhat couched in Guenther's terminology, it still remains an excellent (and available) account of the Path as a whole, the way some Tibetan masters still teach it today--from the motives for taking refuge, through the development of Bodhicitta, the practice of the perfections, and all the bodhisattva levels to perfect Buddhahood. The classic Tibetan descriptions of the Path are, of course, Tsong Kha pa's Lam Rim, which, unfortunately, have not yet been definitively translated into English. However, one of Tsong Kha pa's letters, the Lam.gyi.rim.mud.tsam-du-bstanpa (A Brief Exposition of the Main Points of the Graded Course to Enlightenment) has been translated as The Graded Course to Enlightenment, by Sherpa and Khamlung Tulkus and Alexander Berzin (see 3.3.8.3[4]). It makes a fine short introduction to the Lam Rim literature for the advanced student.

(5) HORNER, ISALINE BLEW. *The Early Buddhist Theory of Man Perfected*. See 8.4(6).

In the course of this important study of the concept of the Arhat, Horner describes the entire Buddhist Path, but her work is especially valuable for its analysis of the final stages of the path. See, in particular, Chapter 6, "The Four Ways and the Four Fruits," which gives a lucid analysis based on Pali materials) of the four attainings of the four fruits of Stream-winning, once-returning, non-returning, and arhatship. This forms perhaps the most thorough introduction to this important subject.

(6) HSUAN TSANG. *Ch'eng Wei-shih Lun: The Doctrine of Mere Consciousness* (see 2.5.4[8]), pp. 669-809.

This section of Hsuan Tsang's major doctrinal compendium contains a full description of the five paths (or stages) from a Vijnanavada point of view. Separate sections are devoted to the Sambhara (merit), Prayoga (training), Darsana (illumination), Bhavana (contemplation) and Asaiksa (no moral training) margas. The same passage may be found in de La Vallée Poussin's annotated French translation of the text, *Vijnaptimatrata siddhi: La siddhi de Hiuan Tsang* (see 3.3.3.2[6]), pp. 562-719.

(7) HURVITZ, LEON. "The Road to Buddhist Salvation as Described by Vasubhadra." *Journal of the American Oriental Society*, 87 (1967), 434-486.

This is a translation, with copious notes, of a "quasi-abhidharma" text which was rendered into Chinese by Kumarabuddhi in 382 A.D. The work is interesting for its combination of various systems of describing the path, using an analysis of the Noble Eightfold Way together with the scheme of the Five Paths, a description of the kinds of beings who walk the path (sravakas, pratyekabuddhas, and Buddhas), and the cosmological division of the realms of desire, form and formlessness. Hurvitz's summary and diagram (pp. 465-470) are very helpful in sorting it all out.

(8) MATICS, MARION L. *Entering the Path of Enlightenment (The Bodhicaryavatava of the Buddhist poet Santideva)*. See 3.3.2.1(28).

The *Bodhicaryavatara* contains a complete and classic Madhyamika description of the Bodhisattva path, from the confession of Evil and the development of Bodhicitta, through the Paramitas to the perfection of wisdom. Available as it is in paperback, it makes a handy introduction to the subject, especially accompanied by Matics' fine introduction and notes. At times, however, the translation becomes difficult to use.

(9) OBERMILLER, EUGENE. "The Doctrine of Prajnaparamita as Exposed in the Abhisamalamkara of Maitreya." See 3.3.1.3(4).

Part 2 (pp. 14-47) of this article provides a fine introduction to the basic Mahayanist division of the way to Buddhahood into five paths. For the three points of view of sravakas, pratyekabuddhas, and bodhisattvas, Obermiller presents in turn: the path of accumulation of merit (sambhara-marga/tshogs-lam), the path of training (prayoga-marga/sbyor-lam), the path of illumination (darsana-marga/mthong-lam), the path of concentrated contemplation (bhavana-marga/sgom-lam), and the path of no more training (asaiksa-marga/mi slob-lam). For other treatments of this important scheme of the five paths, see sGam po pa, *The Jewel Ornament of Liberation* (above), Chapter 18; Tenzing Gyatsho, the 14th Dalai Lama, *The Opening of the Wisdom Eye* (Bangkok: Social Science Association Press, 1968), pp. 77-88; and Kamalasila's *Bhavanakrama*, translated by Stephan Beyer as "The Meditations of a Bodhisattva," in *The Buddhist Experience* (above), pp. 99-115.

(10) PIYADASSI. *The Buddha's Ancient Path*. London: Rider, 1964, pp. 77-218.

These pages are devoted entirely to a description of the Noble Eightfold Path. Chapter by chapter, they present an orthodox Theravadan interpretation of each of the limbs of the path (right understanding, right thought, right speech, right action, right livelihood, right effort, right mindfulness, right concentration). The book is not exactly inspiring but is of value as a stepping-stone because of its cross-references to and quotes from the Pali Canon. For a listing of the major textual references in Sanskrit (and Pali) to the Noble Eightfold Way, see Etienne Lamotte, trans., *Le traité de la grande vertu de sagesse* (3.3.1.2[6]), vol. 3, pp. 1129-1132.

(11) RAHULA, WALPOLA. *What the Buddha Taught* (see 2.1[10]), pp. 45-50.

A standard, concise, and supremely clear description of the fourth Noble Truth, "The Noble Eightfold Path." It is excellent as an introduction but lacks details and development, for which see Piyadassi Thera (above).

(12) SADDHATISSA, H. *The Buddha's Way*. London: Allen and Unwin, 1971, 133 pp.

This is a short, introductory work aimed at Westerners from a Theravada angle, designed to outline some of the moral, philosophical and meditational aspects of the Buddha's path. Helpful as a starting point but no more than that.

11.2 FAITH (SRADDHA) IN THE THREE REFUGES

(1) BARUA, B. M. "Faith in Buddhism," in *Buddhistic Studies* (see 2.4.2[7]), pp. 329-349.

A tremendously helpful article in showing the changing understandings of the meaning of "sraddha" as it is presented in various Buddhist texts. Distinguishing between "blindly professed faith" (saddha), "faith as a faculty" (saddhindriya), and "faith as a power" (saddhabala), Barua traces the varying combination of these elements as expressed in the Kathavatthu, the Netipakarana, the Milindapanha, the Atthasalini and Asvaghosa's Awakening of Faith. He also compares Buddhaghosa's view of faith with certain Hindu understandings of bhakti, and analyzes the relative positions of faith and reason as seen in the various classifications of eminent arhats. Altogether an important contribution to the study of sraddha in spite of Barua's view of faith as something calling up "a train of cowardly associations which befits a degenerated age."

(2) DUTT, NALINAKSHA. "Place of Faith in Buddhism." Indian Historical Quarterly, 16 (1940), 639-646.

An important article, analyzing the role and place of faith as presented in the whole range of the Pali Canonical texts. Dutt distinguishes between two functions of sraddha: the one as an antidote to delusion (moha) and to doubt about the excellence of the Buddha, Dharma and Sangha; the other as a self-confidence which produces virya (energy) in practice. Dutt then goes on to analyze the roles of faith for the layman and for the monk, and although he thinks it is more important for the former, he does point out its indispensability in the training of the latter and provides a fascinating analysis of the Vatthupama Sutta, in which a complete course of training is prescribed for monks who wish to make faith "their main prop for the attainment of liberation."

(3) HAKEDA, YOSHITO S., trans. "On Faith and Practice," in The Awakening of Faith Attributed to Asvaghosa (see 3.3.8.2[1]), pp. 92-102.

Here Asvaghosa distinguishes between four types of faith--faith in the Ultimate Source, faith in the numberless qualities of the Buddhas, faith in the great benefits of the Dharma, and faith in the Sangha. A good introduction to Mahayana conceptions of sraddha. A more developed Mahayana view of the merits of faith may be found in the last chapter of the Ratnagotravighaga. (See Jikido Tokasaki, A Study of the Ratnagotravibhaga. [Rome: Istituto Italiano per il Medio ed Estremo Orient, 1966], pp. 380-390.)

(4) LA VALLEE POUSSIN, LOUIS DE. Bouddhisme, opinions sur l'histoire de la dogmatique. Paris: G. Beauchesne, 1909, pp. 128-155.

The section is entitled "Foi, raison, et intuition" and contains an excellent discussion (supported by ample references to Pali and Sanskrit texts) of the place of faith in both monastic and lay Buddhism. De La Vallée Poussin's position here on the matter is that Buddhism is basically a religion of faith, that faith is the root of right views, and that reason plays a secondary role. This is a quite different way of looking at the situation than that chosen by Hardy and many of his ideological successors, who see the Buddhist Path as being entirely a rationally governed endeavor.

(5) _____. "La doctrine des refuges--Documents d'Abhidharma traduits et annotés." See 3.2.3.4(6).

Through a number of translations of Abhidharma texts, and his own introduction, de La Vallée Poussin presents the doctrine of the three-fold refuge, according to the Sarvastivadin school. He claims the early profession of faith was "Sakyamuni is truly the perfect Buddha, the Dharma has been well preached, the Sangha is on the right path," and shows this to be at the base of the trisarana formula. Also, he points to the interesting practice presented in the Vighasa of a mother taking refuge for a child even before its birth. The article as a whole is only for students wanting a quite scholastic account of the three refuges.

(6) MASAKI, HARUHIKO. "On the Problem of Prajna, Carya, and Sraddha." Indogaku Bukkyogaku Kenkyu/Journal of Indian and Buddhist Studies, 19 (1971), 993-984 (sic).

Unfortunately not fully developed but nevertheless an insightful and suggestive article on the relationship between various soteriologically oriented modes of action in Buddhism: wisdom, conduct, and faith.

(7) NYANAPONIKA, MAHATHERA. "The Threefold Refuge." The Wheel, no. 76 (1965), pp. 1-26.

A handy compilation of passages taken from the works of the great fifth century commentator Buddhaghosa dealing with the act of taking refuge in the Buddha, the Dharma, and the Sangha, and its preliminary which is sraddha. This is followed by Nyanaponika's own comments on the passages translated.

(8) SADDHATISSA, H. "The Significance of the Refuges," in Buddhist Ethics. London: Allen and Unwin, 1970, pp. 53-85.

Saddhatissa points out (and supports with canonical quotations) that sraddha really means "confidence" and represents an attitude that is directly opposed to that of "blind faith." The view is commonly espoused by modern educated Theravada Buddhists (who sometimes wish thereby to oppose Buddhism to Christianity). For another discussion along similar lines, see Nanamoli, "Does Saddha Mean Faith?" The Wheel, 52/53 (1963), 11-38.

11.3 MORAL DISCIPLINE AND ETHICS

See also section on moral observances under Merit-Making and Rituals of Piety, in Practices, Rituals and Popular Beliefs, 7.1.2.

(1) ANESAKI, MASAHARU. "Ethics and Morality (Buddhist)," in Encyclopedia of Religion and Ethics (see 1.15.1[9]).

A concise attempt by a great Japanese scholar to survey the whole of Buddhist

Moral Discipline and Ethics

personal ethics and relate them to practice and theory.

(2) BEYER, STEPHAN. *The Buddhist Experience* (see 3.3.2.1[18]), pt. 1, pp. 1-73.
This part of Beyer's anthology contains a selection of texts from all three vehicles to illustrate the notion of sila (virtue). The topics dealt with include "the model" (the Buddha), "personal morality," "worship," and living together.

(3) BUDDHAGHOSA. *The Path of Purification (Visuddhimagga)* (see 3.2.4.2[1]), pp. 1-83.
In the first of these two chapters, Buddhaghosa analyzes what is meant by virtue (sila), in theory and in practice. In the second, he describes the thirteen kinds of ascetic practices allowed by the Buddha. All of this is put in the persepctive of the overall development on the Path of Purification.

(4) CONZE, EDWARD, ed, and trans. "Morality," in *Buddhist Scriptures* (see 8.1.2.3[7]), pp. 69-97.
This selection of texts gives the basic precepts and a sense of the flavor of Buddhist "morality" for both monks and laymen. It may be used to complement the texts translated by Beyer in *The Buddhist Experience* (above).

(5) EBERHARD, WOLFRAM. *Guilt and Sin in Traditional China.* See 4.2.3(14).
A study of the popular legends contained in the pien wen texts found at Tun Huang, focusing on their importance as part of an effort of the elite to inculcate morality and a sense of sin into the masses of the time.

(6) GOMBRICH, RICHARD. *Precept and Practice* (see 4.1.1[7]), pp. 244-268.
Under the title "The Ethic of Intention," Gombrich discusses the relationship and discrepancies between the moral precepts, the understanding of the moral precepts, and the actual moral practices among Buddhist villagers in Central Ceylon.

(7) HORNER, ISALINE BLEW, trans. *The Book of the Discipline (Vinaya pitaka).* See 3.2.1.1[1]).

(8) _____. "Early Buddhism and the Taking of Life," in *B. C. Law Volume* (see 1.2.2.3[6]), vol. 1, pp. 436-455.

(9) JAYATILLEKE, K. N. *Ethics in Buddhist Perspective.* Wheel Publication, Nos. 175-176. Kandy: Buddhist Publication Society, 1972, 71 pp.
A series of talks originally delivered by the late professor of philosophy at the University of Ceylon in 1970. It is one of the few concise surveys of the topic which combines a thorough acquaintance with the Pali texts and knowledge of modern Western analytic philosophy. Includes discussions of the "basis of Buddhist ethics," the Buddhist ethical ideal, and the Buddhist conceptions of evil and of right and wrong.

(10) KHANTIPALO PHRA. *Tolerance: A Study from Buddhist Sources.* London: Rider, 1964, 190 pp.
Written by an English monk now living in Bangkok, this is a strange attempt to approach an essentially Western ethical concept through Buddhist categories and texts. It is not always successful, but is one of the few full studies to deal with a single specific topic of ethical import.

(11) KING, WINSTON L. *In the Hope of Nibbana: An Essay on Theravada Buddhist Ethics.* La Salle: Open Court, 1964, 298 pp.
This work is an important attempt to deal with the relationship of Buddhist ethics both to doctrine (especially the goal of Nibbana), and to the contemporary socio-political situation.

(12) KITAGAWA, JOSEPH M. "Buddhist Ethics and International Relations." *Indogaku Bukkyogaku Kenkyu/Journal of Indian and Buddhist Studies*, 8 (1960), 777-769 (sic).
A quick survey of Buddhist ethics and their relationship to social life, with special attention to the modern period throughout Asia.

(13) LAW, BIMALA CHURN. "The Concept of Morality in Buddhism and Jainism." *Journal of the Asiatic Society of Bombay*, n.s.34-35 (1959-1960), 1-21.
A good introductory article in which the author explains the nature of the concept of "sila" as it has been articulated in the canons of Jainism and Buddhism. Law explains respective classifications of "sila" and its relationship to wisdom, purity, and dharma.

(14) MORGAN, F. BRUCE. "Vocation of Monk and Layman: Signs of Change in Thai Buddhist Ethics." See 6.1.2(14).
The chief thrust of this article is to report certain strains and tensions in ethical thinking concerned with the traditional role distinction between monk and layman among present-day Thai. The author seeks to account for these tensions, which have blurred the traditional distinction.

(15) PACHOW, W. *A Comparative Study of the Pratimoksa.* See 3.2.1.4(6).
Though primarily a textual study, this work is of great importance for the understanding of the development of the rules of the pratimoksa which lie at the heart of the Buddhist monastic discipline.

(16) PREBISH, CHARLES. *Buddhist Monastic Discipline.* See 3.2.1.2(10).

(17) SADDHATISSA, H. *Buddhist Ethics.* See 11.2.(8).
This is perhaps the clearest and most comprehensive survey of this topic to date. It

is also one of the few works to deal significantly with the ethics of the laity. Its approach is from the Theravada perspective.

(18) TACHIBANA, S. *The Ethics of Buddhism*. London: Oxford, 1926, 288 pp.

Long the only work of its kind, this has now been surpassed by Saddhatissa (see above). Although Tachibana is more aware of certain Mahayana perspectives, he too focuses on Theravada ethics.

(19) WIJESEKERA, O. H. DE A. "Buddhist Ethics," in *Pathways of Buddhist Thought*. Edited by Nyanaponika. London: Allen and Unwin, 1971, pp. 49-67.

Originally published in the *Maha Bodhi* (December 1956) and in *The Wheel* (Publication No. 50), this essay remains one of the few attempts to put the ethics of early Buddhism in its Indian Brahmanic context.

11.4 MEDITATION

11.4.1 General Surveys and Introductions

(1) BEYER, STEPHAN. *The Buddhist Experience* (see 3.3.2.1[18]), pp. 74-146.

An interesting selection of texts taken from all Buddhist traditions which should do a lot to help change the usual notions of what meditation does and does not include.

(2) CONZE, EDWARD. *Buddhist Meditation*. See 2.7.5(2).

This is not Conze's best book, for his great enthusiasm for Buddhaghosa has resulted in an overdependence on the *Visuddhimagga* in his choice of texts and materials. Still, it can form a good introduction to Buddhist meditation in general, especially when it is put next to Chapter 2 (pp. 98-144) of his anthology *Buddhist Scriptures* (see 8.1.2.3[7]), which helps rectify the balance.

(3) EVOLA, GIULIO CESARE. *The Doctrine of Awakening: A Study of Buddhist Ascesis*. See 8.4(4).

Though Evola at times gets carried away with his interpretation of the word "Aryan" (see for example p. 16, n. 2, where he affirms the racial significance of the term), his book is a full-length study of meditation techniques and goals, based primarily on the Pali texts. It is especially valuable for its chapters on the preliminaries for meditation and the extraordinary powers resulting from it.

(4) KING, WINSTON L. *A Thousand Lives Away* (see 2.8[14]), pp. 180-235.

Though based on Burmese materials, this chapter provides a good short introduction to Buddhist meditation in general, as it is practiced today in South Asia. The discussion is followed by an appendix giving the author's personal account of "an experience in Buddhist meditation."

(5) LU K'UAN YU. *The Secrets of Chinese Meditation*. London: Rider, 1964, 240 pp.

Essentially a series of translations with essays, this book attempts to describe a number of different forms of Chinese Buddhist "self-cultivation," including those found in the *Surangama Sutra* and in the Ch'an, Pure Land, and T'ien T'ai schools. Also included is a chapter on Taoist practices.

(6) REICHELT, KARL LUDVIG. *Meditation and Piety in the Far East*. London: Lutterworth Press, 1953, 171 pp.

Written by a Lutheran missionary enthusiast of dialogue, this book attempts to put Buddhist meditation in China in the context of Taoist, Confucian and Mohist practices, and for this it is valuable. However, the reader should keep in mind Reichelt's particular point of view, which he outlines in the introduction.

(7) SWEARER, DONALD K. "Control and Freedom: The Structure of Buddhist Meditation in the Pali Suttas." *Philosophy East and West*, 23 (1973), 435-455.

A lucid description of Theravada meditation which can help the beginning student sort out the various practices involved in that tradition. Using the figure of an hourglass as a model, he sees consciousness as being refined by mindfulness (sati) and concentration (samadhi), by one-pointedness, and then expanding to hitherto unexperienced dimensions (jhanas) and reaching equanimity (upekkha) and the four unlimiteds. Swearer also includes a fine description of the attainment and use of magical powers (siddhi).

(8) _____, ed. *Secrets of the Lotus: Studies in Buddhist Meditation*. New York: Macmillan, 1971.

An outgrowth of a "meditation workshop" organized at Oberlin College in January 1969, this book contains lectures and instructions by the Ven. Chao Khin Sobhana Dhammasuddhi, a Theravada meditation master, and the Rev. Eshin Nishimura, a Zen monk. Together with a chapter by Swearer, an excerpt from the *Vimuttimagga*, and some translations by Nishimura, these form a mixed but successful introduction to Buddhist meditation through the Rinzai and Satipatthana traditions.

(9) VAJIRANANA PARAVAHERA, MAHATHERA. *Buddhist Meditation in Theory and Practice*. Colombo: Gunasena, 1962.

Probably the best exposition of contemplative practice by a learned Theravada monk. Based on the *Visuddhimagga*, it ranges over the entire Pali Canon and Theravadin tradition, and assembles any and every mention of meditation. Although no attempt is made to reconcile conflicting systems in a historical way, it remains the best single introduction to the topic.

Meditation

11.4.2 Meditation Manuals

(1) Amitayur-Dhyana-Sutra (The Sutra of the Meditation on Amitayus), translated by J. Takakusu, in Buddhist Mahayana Texts. See 3.3.1.1(12).

One of the basic Pure Land texts, this sutra is also a meditation manual in which the Buddha instructs Queen Vaidehi in the visualization techniques which will enable her to get a glimpse of the Western Paradise. Especially relevant portions of this work have also been translated in Beyer, The Buddhist Experience (see 3.3.2.1[18]), pp. 116-124.

(2) Buddhadhyana-samadhi-sagara-sutra, Ch. 9 of the Chinese version, translated by Paul Demieville, in "Notes sur le fragment sogdien du Buddhadhyanasamadhisagara sutra." See 3.3.8.2(3).

(3) BUDDHAGHOSA. The Path of Purification (Visuddhimagga). See 3.2.4.2(1).

Written by the great Theravadan scholar Buddhaghosa in the fifth century, this is the best known, greatest, and most systematic of all the meditation manuals--a classic in every sense. However, because of its length and detail, it has not always received the attention it deserves in introductory courses. First approaches to it might be made easier by reference to N. Dutt, "The Buddhist Meditation," The Indian Historical Quarterly, 11 (1935), 710-740, which summarizes Buddhaghosa's views on meditation; or by reference to Nyanatiloka, The Buddha's Path to Deliverance (Colombo, 1969), which is an anthology of canonical texts arranged according to the seven stages of purity outlined in the Visuddhimagga, and very useful for clarifying Buddhaghosa's abstract categories. There also exists another, but somewhat inferior English translation: Pe Maung Tin, The Path of Purity (see 3.2.4.2[1]). See also U. Dhammahatana, Guide Through the Vissudhimagga (Varanasi: Mahabodhi Secrets, 1965).

(4) CHIH I. "Samatha-Vipasyana for Beginners (T'ung Meng Chih Kuan)," in The Secrets of Chinese Meditation (see 11.4.1[5]), pp. 111-160.

One of four works written on "knowledge and wisdom" by the founder of the T'ien-t'ai school, this manual expounds T'ien-t'ai views of meditational techniques and goals. It may also be found translated in Dwight Goddard, and, in part, in Samuel Beal, A Catena of Buddhist Scriptures from the Chinese (see 3.2.1.2[7]), pp. 250-273.

(5) DEMIEVILLE, PAUL. "Le Yogacarabhumi de Sangharaksa." See 3.2.4.2(3).

This article contains a synopsis of the Yogacarabhumi by Sangharaksa, a contemporary and perhaps teacher of King Kanishka. Not to be confused with Asanga's great work of the same name, it is a treatise on meditation from the Sarvastivadin point of view. The Sanskrit original has been lost, and the Chinese translation here has received a sort of Mahayanist appendix.

(6) KAMALASILA. Bhavanakrama. Translated by Stephan Beyer in The Buddhist Experience (see 3.3.2.1[8]), pp. 99-115.

This eighth century meditation book, translated here under the title "The Meditations of a Bodhisattva," describes the whole of the bodhisattva path, showing the progress through the ten bhumis or stages. The Tibetan and Sanskrit versions, and an English synopsis of the complete text, may be found in Giuseppe Tucci, Minor Buddhist Texts (see 1.14.2.1[10]), vol. 2, pp. 157-282.

(7) Maha-satipatthana sutta in Dialogues of the Buddha (Digha Nikaya) (see 2.7.1[13]), vol. 2, pp. 323-346.

This is the oldest and perhaps the most important presentation of the method and purpose of mindfulness in the Pali Canon. It should be studied by everyone interested in Theravada meditation techniques. A more modern translation of it can be found in Beyer (see 3.3.2.1[18]), pp. 90-99; and yet another translation, together with excerpts from two of the classical commentaries on it, is in Soma, The Way of Mindfulness (Kandy: Buddhist Publication Society, 1967).

(8) MUKHERJEE, SUJIT KUMAR. "An Outline of Principal Methods of Meditation." Visva-Bharati Annals, 3 (1950), 110-149.

Contains an English rendition of an anonymous Chinese meditation treatise, the Sse wei yao leo fa. Said to have been translated into Chinese and perhaps compiled by Kumarajiva, it is a small compendium of advice to meditators.

(9) PAD-MA DKAR-PO. "Manual of the Spontaneous Great Symbol" (Chos-rje 'brug-pa'i lugs-kyi phyag-rgya chen-po lhan-cig skyes-sbyor-gyi khrid-yig), in The Buddhist Experience (see 3.3.2.1[18]), pp. 154-161.

These pages contain the instructions of Pad-ma dKar-po, a sixteenth century Tibetan monk, for twenty-one sessions in "The Practice of Calm." They form a good, concise example of Mahamudra techniques.

(10) Vimuktimarga Dhutaguna-Nirdesa. Translated by P. V. Bapat. Bombay: Asia Publishing House, 1964, 121 pp.

An edition and translation of a manual preserved only in Tibetan on the qualities of purification. It is akin to both the Visuddhimagga and the Vimuttimagga, both of which have been studied comparatively by Bapat, in his Vimuttimagga and Visuddhimagga: A Comparative Study (1938), which forms a useful background to this work.

(11) Vimuttimagga: The Path of Freedom. See 3.2.4.2(5).

Attributed to the monk Upatissa, the Vi-muttimagga is an earlier and less scholarly work than the Visuddhimagga, and it devotes comparatively more space to practical meditation instructions. It was reportedly written along the lines of Abhayagiri practice (while Buddhaghosa's work followed the Mahavihara), but the two works are so similar in structure and content that it is hard to believe Buddhaghosa did not have the former before him when he wrote the latter.

(12) WOODWARD, FRANK L., trans. Manual of a Mystic. See 3.2.4.2(5).
The original influence of this eighteenth century Ceylonese meditation manual is difficult to assess, and clearly its early publication and translation by the Pali Text Society have given it a more widespread fame than it might have attained on its own. Perhaps its final importance lies not so much in its contents per se as in what they reveal about the history and development of Theravada meditation: when compared to much earlier meditation discourses, it reflects a definite quasi-tantric yogic influence. D. B. Jayatilaka's appendix is also helpful in setting the text in its historical framework.

(13) "Zazen-gi" (On Zazen Meditation). Translated by Eshin Nishimura in Secrets of the Lotus (see 11.4.1[8]), pp. 161-189.
The "Zazen-gi" is a very brief (four pages) meditation manual dating back to eighth century China, but still important in Japan today. Its translation here is followed by a series of lectures on the text by Mumon Yamada Roshi.

11.4.3 Subjects of Meditation (Including Brahma Viharas)

For specifically tantric subjects of meditation, see 11.6.1 (Sadhanas), and 11.6.2 (Mandalas). For emptiness as a subject of meditation see Emptiness in 2.7.

(1) Anapanasati sutta, in Majjhima Nikaya ("Middle Length Sayings") (see 3.2.2.1[16]), vol. 3, sutta 118.
A clear, canonical exposition of the use of breathing as a subject for mindfulness and meditation.

(2) BUDDHAGHOSA. The Path of Purification (Visuddhimagga) (see 3.2.4.2[1]), pp. 84-408.
Without a doubt these chapters contain the most thorough description of the classic forty subjects of meditation, complete with practical advice. Chapters 4 and 5 deal with the ten kasinas (devices); Chapter 6 with the ten states of decomposition of a corpse; Chapter 7 with the Six Recollections (of the Buddha, the Dhamma, the Sangha, Virtue, Generosity and the Deities); Chapter 8 with the mindfulnesses of Death, the body, breathing, and peace; Chapter 9 with the four Brahmaviharas; Chapter 10 with the Four Immaterial States (space, infinite consciousness, nothingness, and neither perception nor non-perception); and Chapter 11 with the repulsiveness of food and with the Four Elements. Students who want a quick and clear introduction to all of this might refer to pages 144-150 of the Venerable Balangoda Ananda Maitreya's "Buddhism in Theravada Countries," in The Path of the Buddha (see 1.1[6]).

(3) _____. Visuddhimagga (see 3.2.4.2[1]), ch. 9.
This chapter contains Buddhaghosa's lucid exposition of the four Brahma viharas (love, compassion, sympathetic joy, and equanimity) and is especially useful for placing the contemplation and practice of these within Buddhist meditation. This is perhaps the most thorough Hinayanist treatment of this subject. Others may be found in Buddhaghosa's Atthasalini (The Expositor) (see 3.2.3.3[2]), vol. 1, pp. 258-263); and in Vasubandhu's Abhidharmakosa (see 3.2.3.2[4]).

(4) CONZE, EDWARD. Buddhist Thought in India (see 2.1[1]), pp. 80-91, pp. 217-218.
The chapter is entitled "The Cultivation of Social Emotions" and forms an excellent introduction to the four Brahmaviharas--maitri (which Conze translates "friendliness"), karuna ("compasssion"), mudita ("sympathetic joy"), and upeksa ("impartiality"). Probably the best single short survey of what these have meant in the Buddhist tradition. See pages 217-218 for the way in which the Brahmaviharas developed and were interpreted in the Mahayana.

(5) HAMILTON, CLARENCE H. "The Idea of Compassion in Mahayana Buddhism." Journal of the American Oriental Society, 70 (1950), 145-151.
A fine introductory survey of the meaning of compassion (karuna) in Buddhism. With an eye for Christian parallels, Hamilton examines the development of the notion in Pali canonical texts, in the Jatakas, and in the Mahayana sutras.

(6) Kayagatasati-sutta, in Majjhima Nikaya (Middle Length Sayings) (see 3.2.2.1[16]), vol. 3, sutta 119.
A clear, canonical exposition of the use of the parts of the body as subjects for mindfulness and meditation.

(7) LAMOTTE, ETIENNE. "La bienveillance bouddhique." Bulletin de la classe des lettres, Académie royale de Belgique, 38 (1952), 381-403.
An extensive discussion of the various meanings of the term Maitri, the first of the four Brahma viharas, and a comparison of it with Christian "love."

(8) _____, trans. La traité de la grande vertu de sagesse de Nagarjuna (Mahaprajnaparamitasastra) (see 3.3.1.2[6]), vol. 3, pp. 1329-1430.

Meditation

These pages contain what is without a doubt the most thorough account of the eight anusmrti ("commemorations") which form important subjects of meditation in Hinayana and Mahayana. They include remembrance-meditations on the Buddha, the Dharma, the Sangha, morality, abandonment, divinities, breathing and death. Lamotte's footnotes contain numerous references to textual passages dealing with these in the Pali, Sanskrit, Chinese and Tibetan canons.

11.4.4 Mindfulness

(1) BYLES, MARIE BEAUZEVILLE. Journey into Burmese Silence. London: Allen and Unwin, 1962.
An Australian's personal account of her experiences with Buddhism in Burma, this makes an informal but informative introduction to Satipatthana meditation. Also interesting, for comparative purposes, is her later book, Paths to Inner Calm (London: G. Allen and Unwin, 1965, 207 pp.), in which she recounts and evaluates her experiences with meditation in Japan and contrasts them to those she had in Burma.

(2) CONZE, EDWARD. "Mindfulness," in Buddhist Meditation (see 2.7.5[2]), pp. 62-107.
Conze's selection and discussion of passages taken mostly from Buddhaghosa's Visuddhimagga forms a fine standard introduction to the practice and purpose of mindfulness. See also his comments on pages 28-32.

(3) LOUNSBERY, G. CONSTANT. Buddhist Meditation in the Southern School. London: Luzac, 1936.
A dated but still valuable book which gives a clear and concise account of the practice of Mindfulness in Theravada countries.

(4) Maha-satipatthana sutta, in Dialogues of the Buddha (see 2.7.1[13]), vol. 2, pp. 323-346.

(5) Majjhima Nikaya (Middle Length Sayings) (see 3.2.2.1[16]), vol. 1, Satipatthana Sutta (sutta 10); vol. 3, Anapanasati Sutta (sutta 118); and Kayagatasati Sutta (sutta 119).
These three suttas deal specifically with the techniques and aims of mindfulness. The first is a classic presentation of the topic and is paralleled in the Digha Nikaya (see Mahasatipatthana Sutta, above). The second deals with mindfulness of breathing, and the third with that of the body. Another translation of the Anapanasati Sutta, together with extracts from relevant portions of the classical commentaries, may be found in Nanamoli, Mindfulness of Breathing (Kandy: Buddhist Publication Society, 1964).

(6) NYANAPONIKA. The Heart of Buddhist Meditation. New York: Citadel Press, 1969, 223 pp.

Written by a German Theravada monk now residing in Ceylon, this book is a major work on the methods and meaning of mindfulness. It is a lucid exposition, giving considerable detail, and has become a classic work on the subject. It also includes an anthology of texts.

(7) _____. The Power of Mindfulness. Wheel Publication, Nos. 121-122. Kandy: Buddhist Publication Society, 1968.
Probably one of the best publications of the Wheel Series, this pamphlet offers a good short introduction to and interpretation of Satipatthana. Another perhaps more accessible version appears in Pathways of Buddhist Thought (see 11.3[19]), pp. 101-148.

(8) SWEARER, DONALD K., ed. Secrets of the Lotus (see 11.4.1[8]), pp. 27-109.
The first of these two chapters, "Discourses on Mindfulness," contains fourteen informal practice-oriented lectures by the Venerable Chao Khun Sobhana Dhammasuddhi, a Theravada meditation teacher. Chapter 3, "The Foundation of Mindfulness," is a discussion of the Satipatthana Sutta by Donald Swearer, and helps put the preceding chapter into perspective.

11.4.5 Concentration and Trance States (Samadhi, Dhyana/Jhana)

(1) ANESAKI, M. and J. TAKAKUSU. "Shyana," in Encyclopedia of Religion and Ethics (see 1.15.1[9]), vol. 4, pp. 702-704.
A brief, handy description of the Buddhist levels of trance, based on Pali texts, and perhaps at times a bit clearer than it ought to be. Especially convenient is the table of correspondences between the four dhyanas and the sixteen heavens of the rupa-loka.

(2) BUGAULT, GUY. La notion de "Prajna" ou de sapience selon les perspectives du "Mahayana." Paris: E. de Boccard, 1968, 287 pp.
A scholarly, philosophically oriented study, technical at times but important for any advanced study of the topic. The author begins by reviewing the definition and relationship of prajna and dhyana ("sapience et recueillement"), then examines how prajna and dhyana are applied in various meditational practices such as the smrtyupasthana, the krtshayatana, and some samadhis, and finally addresses the whole question of the role and place of insight and wisdom in Buddhist practice.

(3) CONZE, EDWARD. "Trance," in Buddhist Meditation (see 2.7.5[2]), pp. 110-139.
Although this section of Conze's book forms an adequate introduction to the eight levels of trance and their application to the Stations of Brahma, it is not really comprehensive and must be read in conjunction with Conze's introduction to the subject on pages 17-22.

(4) DEMIEVILLE, PAUL. "Le chapitre de la Bodhisattvabhumi sur la perfection du Dhyana." Rocznik Orjentalistyczny, 21 (1957), 109-128.

A French translation, with copious notes, of the chapter of Asanga's Bodhisattvabhumi which deals with the perfection of meditation. The text is analytical and only for advanced students.

(5) DOGEN. "Shobogenzo Sammai O Zammai." Translated by Norman Waddell and Maseo Abe as "The King of Samadhis Samadhi." The Eastern Buddhist, n.s. 7 (1974), 118-124.

A translation of a very short sermon by Dogen on a particular kind of Samadhi practice. Of interest to students doing special work on Soto Zen.

(6) ELIADE, MIRCEA. Yoga, Immortality and Freedom. Second edition. Princeton: Bollingen, 1969, pp. 167-173. (Originally published 1958.)

A good short introduction to the Buddhist dhyanas and their relation to Yoga as a whole. See also his notes on pages 396-397.

(7) Katha-vatthu (Points of Controversy) (see 3.2.3.1[5]), pp. 120-123, 175-177, 190-191, 299-300, 327-332.

The nature of the trance states (jhana) was a matter of dispute even within the Theravada. These passages of the Katha-Vatthu provide examples of discussions on such questions as: whether one can utter articulate sounds while in jhana, whether hallucination occurs in jhana, whether one can hear sounds in jhana, whether a man can die in jhana, etc.

(8) LAMOTTE, ETIENNE. "La concentration de la marche héroïque (Suramgamasamadhisutra)." See 3.3.2.1(33).

In these pages of his "Introduction" to his translation of the Suramgamasamadhisutra, Lamotte reviews very concisely the various Theravada and Mahayana understandings of "Samadhi." Any interested student who reads French should take a look at it.

(9) _____, trans. Le traité de la grande vertu de sagesse de Nagarjuna (Mahaprajnaparamitasastra) (see 3.3.1.2[6]), vol. 2, pp. 1023-1057.

These pages of the massive Mahaprajnaparamitasastra contain precise and concise discussions of the different levels of trance, but the rich value of the passage (even to the non-French reader) lies in Lamotte's footnotes, which list all the major references to the Dhyanas in the Pali, Chinese, and Sanskrit canons.

(10) LA VALLEE POUSSIN, LOUIS DE. "Musila et Narada: Le chemin du Nirvana." Mélanges chinois et bouddhiques, 5 (1937), 189-222.

An important discussion of the relationship between the analytical discernment of vipasyana and the trances of samatha, personified here in the figures of Musil and Narada. De La Vallée Poussin examines the views of different traditions on this question. The same theme is also analyzed in his "Extase et spéculation," in Indian Studies in Honor of Charles Rockwell Lanman (Cambridge, Mass.: Harvard University Press, 1929), pp. 135-136.

(11) NGAWANG LOBSANG YISHEY TENZING GYATSO, THE 14TH DALAI LAMA. The Opening of the Wisdom-Eye. Bangkok: Social Science Press, 1968, pp. 53-69.

The Tibetans (and especially the great reformer Tsong Kha pa) developed an elaborate but very methodical technique for developing concentration (samadhi). It consists in a combination of "Six Powers," "Four Mental Activities," through "Nine States" of mind leading up to the first trance. The whole system receives what is perhaps its most concise description in English in these pages of the Dalai Lama's book. Another and perhaps more accessible analysis may be found in Yes-shes-rgyal-mtshan, "The Gold Refinery Bringing out the Very Essence of the Sutra and Tantra Paths," in Treasures on the Tibetan Middle Way, edited by H. V. Guenther (Berkely: Shambala, 196)), pp. 91 ff.

(12) RAHULA, WALPOLA. "A Comparative Study of Dhyanas According to Theravada, Sarvastivada and Mahayana." The Maha Bodhi, 70 (1962), 190-199.

A short and concise attempt to compare what the Pali Text, Vasubandhu's Abhidharmakosa, and Asanga's Abhidharmasamuccaya have to say about the four (or five) dhyanas.

(13) REGAMEY, K., trans. Three Chapters from the Samadhirajasutra. See 3.3.8.1(7).

(14) Samyutta Nikaya (The Book of Kindred Sayings) (see 2.7.7[10]), vol. 4, pp. 179-185.

An example of a short presentation of the various trances and stages gone through during the course of meditation and a warning about "getting stuck" at any one of those levels. The list appears in many places (see Lamotte, above) throughout the canon(s). This one is useful because of its conciseness.

11.4.6 The Development of Extraordinary Powers (Abhijna and Rddhi)

See also 8.1.2.2, Status, powers, and knowledge of the Buddha.

(1) BUDDHAGHOSA. The Path of Purification (Visuddhimagga) (see 3.2.4.2[1]), pp. 409-478.

These chapters deal in detail with the attainment of the extraordinary powers which are among the benefits of concentration. These include the ten kinds of psychic power (siddhi), the "divine" ear, divine eye, mind-reading, recollection of past births, etc.

For a selection of these passages which makes a good and much more concise introduction to the subject, see Conze, Buddhist Scriptures (8.1.2.3[7]), pp. 121-133.

(2) DAYAL, HAR. "The Bodhisattva Doctrine in Buddhist Sanskrit Literature" (see 8.3.1[4]), pp. 104-134.

A scholarly and fairly detailed discussion of the five (or six) abhijnas as they developed doctrinally, with numerous references to the Sanskrit texts. For extensive references to the Sanskrit, Pali, and Chinese sources, and the translation of the portion of the Mahaprajnaparamitasastra which deals with the abhijnas from a Mahayana perspective, see Etienne Lamotte, trans., Le traité de la grande vertu de sagesse (3.3.1.2[6]), vol. 1, pp. 328-333.

(3) DEMIEVILLE, PAUL. "La mémoire des existences antérieures." Bulletin de l'Ecole française d'Extrême-Orient, 27 (1927), 283-298.

A classic study of one of the "extraordinary" powers--that of remembering former births, and one of the few specific studies of this achievement.

(4) ELIADE, MIRCEA. Yoga, Immortality and Freedom (see 11.4.5[6]), pp. 177-185.

(5) EVOLA, J. The Doctrine of Awakening (see 8.4[4]), pp. 229-238.

One of the few works in English that attempt to discuss (as opposed to simply present) the meditator's claim to extraordinary powers. A more substantial work which studies the "extraordinary" powers within the framework of Yoga as a whole, and discusses them from a psychological point of view, is Sigurd Lindquist, Siddhi und Abhinna: Eine Studie über die klassischen Wunder des Yoga (Uppsala: Universitets Aarsskrift, 1935), 99 pp.

(6) LAMOTTE, ETIENNE, trans. Le traité de la grande vertu de sagesse de Nagarjuna (Mahaprajnaparamitasastra) (see 3.3.1.2[6]), vol. 3, pp. 1177-1179.

The spectacular nature of "magical" feats often eclipses the training that lies behind them. These few pages contain a short discussion of magical powers (rddhipada), and point to the need for a proper balance of wisdom, energy, and power of concentration. The rddhipada are among the thirty-seven factors of enlightenment.

(7) Patika Suttanta, in Digha Nikaya (Dialogues of the Buddha) (see 2.7.1[13]), vol. 3, pp. 1-25.

There are many passages in the Pali Canon that deal with the subject of extraordinary powers. The first part of the "Patika Sutta" is a good example of a canonical statement on the place which "mystic and supernatural" wonders occupy in the teaching of the Buddha: they are said to be the by-products which miss the main thrust of the Dharma, but then there they are, described in rather great detail. Other Pali suttas which might be consulted include the "Kevadha Sutta" in Digha Nikaya, vol. 1, pp. 272-284. For a concise list of the ten extraordinary powers, see the "Mahasihanada sutta," in Majjhima Nikaya (3.2.2.1[16]), vol. 1, sutta 12, pp. 93-97.

11.4.7 The Perfection of Insight (Vipasyana/Vipassana, Prajna/Panno)

For classification of dharmas, see 2.7, Buddhist Thought.

(1) BUDDHAGHOSA. The Path of Purification (Visuddhimagga) (see 3.2.4.2[1]), pt. 3.

The whole last section of Buddhaghosa's magnum opus contains one of the most thorough expositions on the topic of prajna (wisdom). It takes the meditator straight through from the analyses of the skandhas, ayatanas and dhatus, to dependent origination, the four noble truths and other subjects, arriving finally at the stages of knowledge (entering the stream, of once-returning, of non-returning and of arhatship).

(2) BUGAULT, GUY. La Notion de "Prajna." See 11.4.5(2).

(3) CONZE, EDWARD. "Wisdom," in Buddhist Meditation (see 2.7.5[2]), pp. 140-176.

The selections in these pages of Conze's anthology on meditation, when taken along with his introductory comments on wisdom on pages 22-24 and 33-36, form an adequate introduction to the subject of the perfection of insight. Topics covered include the aspects of the noble truths, the three marks of conditioned things, the eight cognitions of withdrawal from the world, and emptiness. A more systematic description of an analytical meditation on emptiness, organized around the five "levels" of the famous mantra of the Heart Sutra (Gate, gate, paragate, parasamgate, Bodhi Svaha) may be found in Conze's Buddhist Thought in India (see 2.1[1]), pp. 242-249.

(4) LA VALLEE POUSSIN, LOUIS DE. "Musila et Narada: Le chemin du Nirvana." See 11.4.5(10).

(5) MAHASI SAYADAW (SOBHANA). The Progress of Insight. Kandy: Forest Hermitage, 1965.

Originally written in Pali in 1950, and here translated into English by the Ven. Nyanaponika Thera, this is a modern treatise on Insight Meditation by a Burmese master. In it the description of the progress of insight is organized around Buddhaghosa's classical Seven Stages of Purification.

(6) SUZUKI, DAISETZ TEITARO. "Reason and Intuition in Buddhist Philosophy," in Essays in East-West Philosophy: An Attempt at World Philosophical Synthesis (see 2.5.1[6]), pp. 17-48.

A worthwhile essay in which Suzuki attempts to spell out the differences and relationship between prajna and vijnana in terms of method, ontology, and perception.

(7) SWEARER, DONALD K. "Two Types of Saving Knowledge in the Pali Suttas." Philosophy East and West, 22 (1972), 355-371.

A study of vinnana ("discriminating knowlege") and panna ("intuitive knowledge") as they appear in some Pali suttas. Swearer sees the two of them as distinct but related epistemological levels in the soteriological quest, vinnana being insight into the phenomenal and panna into the noumenal. This represents a different approach than the one drawing a radical distinction between prajna and dhyana as "rational" and "ecstatic" modes of knowledge, and is helpful as an opening into a broader discussion of the place of wisdom in Buddhist soteriological processes.

11.4.8 Ch'an/Zen Methods

See also under 2.5.7, Religious Thought, and 3.3.6, Authoritative texts.

11.4.8.1 General Discussions

(1) BLOFELD, JOHN, trans. The Zen Teaching of Hui Hai on Sudden Illumination. See 3.3.6.2(9).

(2) _____. The Wan-ling Record in the Zen Teaching of Huang Po on the Transmission of Mind. See 3.3.6.2(7).

(3) CHANG, GARMA C. C. The Practice of Zen. New York: Harper, 1959, 199 pp.

One of the more balanced books on Zen and the best available account of the Chinese practice of Ch'an meditation. It corrects some of the idiosyncrasies of D. T. Suzuki's writings. Pages 185-219 place Zen meditation neatly within other forms of Buddhist meditation. Perhaps the best single introduction to the topic.

(4) DUMOULIN, HEINRICH. "Technique and Personal Devotion in the Zen Exercise," in Studies in Japanese Culture (see 4.2.4[10]), pp. 17-40.

A study of the relation of personal devotion to special techniques in the enlightenment experience, as described in modern accounts. An excellent description and acute analysis of religious elements sometimes regarded as alien to Zen--piety, contrition, dependence on "other-power."

(5) FUKUNAGA, MITSUJI. "'No-mind' in Chuang-tzu and in Ch'an Buddhism." Zinbun, 12 (1969), 9-45.

A good article in which the author first lays out the concept of "no-mind" as understood by Chuang-tzu and then by the Ch'an masters Hui-neng, Hsi-yun, and I-hsuan. After comparing Chuang-tzu's articulation with the three Ch'an thinkers, the author concludes that Ch'an Buddhism became a distinctly Chinese enterprise because of its incorporation of Chuang-tzu's thought.

(6) KING, WINSTON L. "A Comparison of Theravada and Zen Buddhist Meditational Methods and Goals." History of Religions, 9 (1970), 304-315.

One of the few serious attempts at comparing two of the major traditions of meditation within Buddhism. An interesting exercise, useful in many respects, but open to methodological question.

(7) LU K'UAN YU. The Secrets of Chinese Meditation (see 11.4.1[5]), pp. 43-80.

In this chapter, which incorporates much material pertinent to meditation from his Ch'an and Zen Teachings (see 2.5.7[16]), Lu K'uan Yu (Charles Luk) informally surveys the various meditation techniques of Chinese Ch'an. Included are discussions of the Kung An (Koan), the Hua T'ou technique, and I Ch'ing (the feeling of doubt). For the practice of holding "Ch'an Weeks" (week-long periods of intensive meditation for both monks and laymen), see the translation of the Venerable Hsu Yun's "Daily Lectures at Two Ch'an Weeks," in Ch'an and Zen Teachings, Series 1, pp. 49-109. These Ch'an Weeks were held at the Jade Buddha Temple in Shanghai in 1953 and were perhaps among the last to be conducted on the mainland.

(8) MASUNAGA, REIHO. A Primer of Soto Zen. See 3.3.6.3(3).

(9) _____. The Soto Approach to Zen (see 2.5.7[17]), pp. 29-34, 100-187.

These pages, in what was one of the first books on Soto Zen in English, contain translations of passages relevant to meditation techniques from Dogen's great work, the Shobogenzo. Included are the "Fukanzazengi" (Rules for Zazen), the "Zazenyojinki" (Points to Watch in Zazen), the "Genjokoan" (on the koan expressed in daily life), the "Bendowa" (on zazen), and the "Shushogi" (True Meaning of Training and Enlightenment). Another translation of selections from Dogen's Shobogenzo may be found on pages 73-158 of Jiyu Kennett, Selling Water by the River (see 2.5.7[14]).

(10) PACHOW, W. "A Buddhist Discourse on Meditation from Tun-Huang." University of Ceylon Review, 21, no. 1 (April 1963), 47-62.

The author has provided an English translation of a text found at Tun-Huang by Aurel

Stein in 1907. The treatise turns out to be authored by Hung Jen, the teacher of Hui Neng, and has been dated around 713. Pachow has provided a brief but helpful introduction in which he discusses the text's historical as well as doctrinal importance to Ch'an thought.

(11) SEKIGUCHI, SENDAI. Zen: A Manual for Westerners. San Francisco: Japan Publications, 1970.

There are numerous books which attempt to explain the practice and techniques of Zen meditation to Westerners. This one, which is well illustrated, includes clear, detailed instructions on posture, bowing, walking and other procedures according to the Rinzai tradition. Shunryu Suzuki's Zen Mind, Beginner's Mind (New York: Weatherhill, 1970) contains sermons on difficulties of a more mental nature, from a Soto perspective. For an informal but sincere "brief account of zazen" by a Westerner, focusing on the fundamentals of zen practices, see Paul Wienpahl, The Matter of Zen (New York: University Press, 1964), 162 pp. Philip Kapleau, The Three Pillars of Zen (New York: Harper and Row, 1965), 363 pp., is a readily available popularized treatment of zen teaching, practice and enlightenment, designed to interest Westerners in the practice of meditation. Finally, H. M. Enomiya Lassalle, Zen Meditation for Christians (LaSalle: Open Court, 1974), is a recent attempt to encourage Christians in Zen practice by pointing to certain parallels with Christian mystical traditions.

(12) SUZUKI, DAISETZ TEITARO. The Training of the Zen Buddhist Monk. See 7.2.1(10).

(13) _____. "Zen and Jodo, Two Types of Buddhist Experience." The Eastern Buddhist, 4 (1927), 89-121.

An interesting and significant discussion of a topic which should have received more attention than it has. Suzuki, with his Shin and Zen sympathies, was the right person to write this article. Basically the distinction is that Zen is "jiriki" (self-power) while Jodo is "tariki" (other-power), and hence the one is easy to believe and difficult to practice while the other is difficult to believe and easy to practice. An interesting specification of this view in which Shin is "hearing" while Rinzai is "seeing" may be found in Kensho Yokogawa, "Shin Buddhism as the Religion of Hearing," The Eastern Buddhist, 7 (1939), 296-341.

(14) _____. Zen Buddhism (see 2.5.7[22]), pp. 111-133.

Suzuki has written often about Zen techniques and meditation, and almost any of his major works may be consulted for his views on the subject. In this chapter, entitled "Practical Methods of Zen Instruction," he outlines various "Verbal Methods" (including paradox, contradiction, affirmation, repetition, exclamation, etc.)

(15) SWEARER, DONALD K., ed. Secrets of the Lotus (see 11.4.1[8]), pp. 129-211.

Taken together, these three chapters form a good, varied introduction to the practice of Zen meditation in Japan. Chapter 5, "Zen Training," is an essay by Esshin Nishimura. Chapter 6, "Rules for Contemplation in Sitting," contains a translation of the Zazengi together with a modern commentary by Mumon Yamada Roshi. Chapter 7, "Perfection of Wisdom," includes the seventeenth century master Hakuin's marvellous "Venomous Commentary" on the "Heart Sutra."

(16) WELCH, HOLMES. The Practice of Chinese Buddhism 1900-1950 (see 6.1.1[29]), pp. 47-88, 426-441.

Chapter 2, "The Meditation Hall" (pp. 47-88), gives an excellent description of the physical setting and routine of meditation in the great Chinese meditation centers such as Chin Shan. Appendix 3 (pp. 426-441) is a model of clarity in providing exact details of the schedule of a meditation hall.

(17) WETERING, JAN WILLEM VAN DE. The Empty Mirror. Boston: Houghton Mifflin, 1974, 145 pp.

The books and articles written by Westerners about their encounters with Zen meditation are almost without number. The above is a recent, lively, personal, and perceptive account of one man's experiences in a Japanese Zen monastery. Others include Paul Wienpahl, Zen Diary (New York: Harper and Row, 1970), which was written as a companion volume to his Matter of Zen (1964); Philip Kapleau, The Three Pillars of Zen (New York: Harper and Row, 1965), which contains personal accounts by laymen and women of their experiences in meditation. John Blofeld, in The Wheel of Life (Berkeley: Shambala, 1972), pp. 156-174, tells of some of his experiments and experiences in a Chinese Buddhist monastery in Yunnan. Donald Swearer, ed., Secrets of the Lotus (above), pp. 212-235, contains a number of "responses" written by American college students just beginning to experiment with both Zen and Theravada meditation. Eugen Herrigel, Zen in the Art of Archery (New York: Pantheon, 1953) is a captivating account of a German's approach to Zen through the martial arts. Jack Huber, Through an Eastern Window (Boston: Houghton Mifflin, 1967), 121 pp., is an excellent comparison of a psychologist's experiences under Zen and Burmese masters.

(18) YOSHIHARU AKISHIGE, ed. Psychological Studies on Zen. Tokyo: Komazawa University, 1974, 280 pp. (Originally published in Bulletin of the Faculty of Literature of Kyushu University, 11 [1968].)

An excellent scientific analysis from the psychological perspective concerned with various aspects of Zen meditation. The volume begins with a very helpful historical survey of past psychological studies on Zen medita-

11.4.8.2   Meditation

tion and continues with eight articles focusing upon such topics as Zen posture, respiratory patterns, the relation between respiratory function and meditation, the differences between EEG and EKG rates before and after meditation, etc.

11.4.8.2 The Koan

See also 4.3.2, Poetry and Song: Japan.

(1) The Hekigan Roku (Blue Cliff Records). See 3.3.6.1(8).

(2) MIURA, ISSHU and RUTH FULLER SASAKI. Zen Dust. See 3.1.5(6).
One of the most important scholarly works on the Zen koan, this discusses the origin, history, classification and use of koans in the Rinzai (Lin-Chi) tradition. A shorter version of the book (without the extensive notes and valuable bibliography) has been published as The Zen Koan.

(3) The Mumonkan. Translated by Reginald H. Blyth in his Zen and Zen Classics (see 2.5.7[1]), vol. 4.

(4) SUZUKI, DAISETZ TEITARO. Essays in Zen Buddhism (Second Series) (see 2.5.7[20]), pp. 3-186.
Suzuki wrote often about the Zen koan, but this first essay of his second series of essays remains one of his more substantial contributions on the subject. It is in pure Suzuki style, and was one of the first introductions of the topic to the English reader. Of special interest is the often neglected subject of "The koan exercise and the Nembutsu," which is dealt with in part 2 of the essay. Shorter essays by Suzuki on Zen meditation and the koan technique may be found in his Zen Buddhism (see 2.5.7[22]), Living by Zen, The Training of the Zen Buddhist Monk (see 7.2.1[10]), etc.

11.4.8.3 Satori/Wu

(1) CHANG, GARMA C. C. The Practice of Zen. See 11.4.8.1(3).

(2) KISHIMOTO, KIDEO. "The Immediacy of Zen Experience and Its Cultural Background." Philosophical Studies of Japan, 3 (1962), 25-32.
An interesting article by a well known Japanese student of philosophy, which may be read profitably by either the beginning or the advanced student. Kishimoto's central argument is that culture conditions the categorial structures of the mind and that since Japanese culture nurtures an intuitive and "inner" approach to experience, the "immediacy" of Zen experience is a consequence. He goes on to describe the Zen satori as a religious experience which is pure, non-abstracted, and non-symbolically communicated.

Moreover, he holds that the nature of satori is mediated by "nothing."

(3) LINSSEN, ROBERT. Living Zen. Translated by Diana Abrahams-Curiel. New York: Macmillan, 1958, pp. 138-173.
A series of short chapters identifying satori with Nirvana and attempting to discuss its major characteristics in a popular and simple manner. Heavily dependent on the work of D. T. Suzuki, but more philosophically minded.

(4) MAUPIN, EDWARD W. "Zen Buddhism: A Psychological Review." Journal of Consulting Psychology, 26 (1962), 362-378.
A very handy survey of various interpretations of satori that have been made from the psychological and psychiatric standpoint. Includes reviews of the positions of Erich Fromm, H. Fingarette, and E. G. Schachter, as well as a number of other bibliographical references.

(5) MIURA, ISSHU and RUTH FULLER SASAKI. Zen Dust. See 3.1.5(6).
The index (see under "Wu") contains a detailed listing of the satori experiences of various Zen masters, and also references to short but balanced accounts of the place of satori in Zen, of its relation to Kensho, etc.

(6) SUZUKI, DAISETZ TEITARO. Zen Buddhism (see 2.5.7[22]), pp. 83-110.
In his extensive writings, Suzuki often dealt with the topic of satori--enlightenment. This chapter is perhaps one of his more helpful passages on the subject. Although in it he does not curb his anecdotal tendencies, he does provide a listing of eight "chief characteristics of satori" which makes a good introduction to Suzuki on Zen experience. For other similar accounts of satori by the same author, see Living by Zen (London: Rider, 1972), chapters 3-4; and Field of Zen (London: Buddhist Society, 1969), chapters 3, 7, 15. For a similar account by a different author, see Christmas Humphreys, Zen Buddhism (New York: Macmillan, 1971), chapters 8-9.

11.4.9 Hua Yen, T'ien-t'ai and Other Methods

See also 2.5.6, Religious Thought.

(1) CHANG, GARMA C. C. The Buddhist Teaching of Totality (see 3.3.1.2[4]), pp. 121-171, 207-223.
In the section entitled "The Philosophy of Totality" (pp. 121-171), Chang discusses the typically Hua Yen notions of "Mutual penetration" and "Mutual identity," and their relation to the doctrine of the four Dharmadhatus, which is one of the hallmarks of Hua Yen meditation. The second passage (pp. 207-223) contains a translation of the Hua Yen patriarch Tu Shun's "On the Meditation of Dharmadhatu" (Fa Chieh Kuan).

(2) CHIH I. "Samatha-Vapasyana for Beginners." See 11.4.2[4].

(3) HURVITZ, LEON. Chih-I (see 2.5.6[3]), pp. 183-331.
This section of Hurvitz's book (in English) discusses the basic doctrines of T'ien-t'ai Buddhism as seen in the works of its "founder" Chih I. Especially relevant in terms of T'ien-t'ai meditation are the chapters entitled "Viewing the Mind" (pp. 318-331) and "The Trischiliocosm in a Moment of Consciousness" (pp. 271-317).

(4) LU K'UAN YU. The Secrets of Chinese Meditation. See 11.4.1[5].
One of the few sources in English dealing with Chinese meditation techniques in T'ien-t'ai, Pure Land, the Surangama Sutra, as well as Taoism and Chinese yoga. Chapter 1 contains relevant excerpts from the Surangama Sutra in which Manjusri describes and rejects twenty-four methods of meditation before finally choosing that recommended by Avalokitesvara--the meditation on Sound. Chapter 3 deals with "self-cultivation according to the Pure Land school." Chapter 4 describes T'ien-t'ai techniques with the help of selections from Chih I's meditation treatises and the late Chian Wei Ch'iao's (Yin Shih Tsu) "Experimental Meditation for the Promotion of Health."

11.5 THE PRACTICE OF THE PERFECTIONS (PARAMITAS)

(1) "The Cariyapitaka: The Collection of Ways of Conduct" (see 3.2.2.1[3]), Pt. 3, pp. 95-127.
A translation of the fifteenth book of the Khuddaka-nikaya and one of the latest works in the Pali Canon. It is a collection of Jatakas retold in verse, intended to illustrate a number of the paramitas characteristic of a bodhisattva's conduct. Its importance lies in its being the only work in the Pali Canon which is concerned with a systematic presentation of the Paramitas as such.

(2) CONZE, EDWARD. Buddhist Thought in India (see 2.1[1]), pp. 211-217.
This section, entitled "The six perfections," is a discussion rather than an exposition of the Mahayana practices of giving, morality, patience, vigor, concentration and wisdom.

(3) DAYAL, HAR. "The Bodhisattva Doctrine in Buddhist Sanskrit Literature" (see 8.3.1[4]), pp. 165-269.
Probably the most thorough study in English of the six (and ten) perfections. It is systematically presented and contains many references for further study.

(4) DEMIEVILLE, PAUL. "Le chapitre de la Bodhisattvabhumi sur la perfection du Dhyana." See 11.4.5(4).

(5) LAMOTTE, ETIENNE, trans. Le traité de la grande vertu de sagesse de Nagarjuna (Mahaprajnaparamitasastra) (see 3.3.1.2[6]), vol. 2, pp. 658-1113.
The bulk of this second volume of the French translation of the Mahaprajnaparamitasastra is devoted to the six paramitas which are here presented in the light of the doctrine of sunyata. Chapters 18-20 deal with dana (giving), Chapters 21-23 with sila (moral conduct), Chapters 24-35 with ksanti (patience), Chapters 26-27 with virya (energy), Chapter 28 with dhyana (meditation), and Chapters 29-30 with prjna (wisdom). See Lamotte's notes throughout for references to the various canons.

(6) MATICS, MARION L. Entering the Path of Enlightenment (see 3.3.2.1[28]), pp. 47-140, 162-226.
Together, these passages form a good introduction to the practice of the six paramitas. Pages 47-140 contain Matics' lucid presentation of the subject, and pages 162-226 contain the relevant passages of his translation of the eighth century Madhyamika poet Santideva's Bodhicaryavatara.

11.6 MANTRA-/VAJRA-/TANTRA-YANA

See also 2.6, Religious Thought, and 2.4, Authoritative Texts.

11.6.1 Tantric Practices (Sadhanas)

(1) BEYER, STEPHAN. The Buddhist Experience (see 3.3.2.1[18]), pp. 124-130, 140-154, 155-161.
Three selections in Beyer's anthology readily illustrate different types of tantric techniques. They are all taken from works of Pad-ma dkar-po. The first, entitled "The Worship of the Fierce Lord," is an example of an evocation of a terrifying deity. The second, "The Meditator Becomes the God," well illustrates a tantric sadhana with its elaborate visualizations and powerful symbolism. The third, "Sessions on the Great Symbol," is an example of Mahamudra practice.

(2) _____. The Cult of Tara (see 7.1.1[2]), pp. 1-226.
The whole of this huge chapter of Beyer's important contribution to the study of Tibetan magic and ritual contains considerable detail on the practices associated with Tara, and on the philosophy and schematization of tantric meditation in general.

(3) BHARATI, AGEHANANDA. The Tantric Tradition (see 2.6.1[1]), pp. 228-278.
The chapter is entitled "Sadhaka and Sadhana: The Aspirant and the Observance." It is not entirely successful: Bharati's commendable attempt to treat the whole tantric tradition (Buddhist and Hindu) as a single movement is more successful when he deals

with history and theory than it is when he deals with practice, where it does not always make for clarity.

(4) _____. "Sakta and Vajrayana: Their Place in Indian Thought," in Studies of Esoteric Buddhism and Tantrism. Koya San: Koya San University, 1965, pp. 73-99.

A lively, impatient and modern discussion of the practice of seminal retention in tantric sadhanas, and some of the confusion that has arisen about it in Western and Eastern thought. Deals with both the Hindu and Buddhist traditions.

(5) BHATTACHARYYA, BENOYTOSH, ed. "Introduction," in Sadhanamala. Gaekwad's Oriental Series, No. 41. Baroda: Gaekwad's Oriental Series, 1928, vol. 2, pp. xi-clxxviii.

An extensive discussion of the history, doctrine and practice of tantric Buddhism as a background to the author's edition of the Sanskrit text of the important Sadhanamala. A free translation of one of the sadhanas of this work, the Kincitvistara Tara Sadhana, may be found in the same author's Introduction to Buddhist Esoterism (see 2.6.1[2]), pp. 104-108, and is further discussed by him in "The Psychic Process of Sadhana," in his Indian Buddhist Iconography (see 8.3.1[1]), pp. 17-23. The Tara Sadhana may also be found in Conze's Buddhist Meditation (see 2.7.5[2]), pp. 133-139.

(6) BLOFELD, JOHN. The Tantric Mysticism of Tibet. See 2.6.1(3).

"A practical guide to the theory, purpose, and techniques of Tantric meditation," this book contains clear descriptions of some of the many facets of Tantric practices, from initial aspiration and preliminaries to advanced yogic enterprises. Excellent for putting the Sadhanas and "Advanced Practices" (pp. 198-248) into the context of the Vajrayana as a whole.

(7) BROMAGE, BERNARD. Tibetan Yoga. New York: S. Weiser, 1952, 244 pp.

A worthwhile introduction to the general topic of Tibetan yoga, written in a straightforward manner. The author comprehensively concerns himself with the history and philosophy of yoga, yoga techniques, accounts of great Tibetan yogis, the Tibetan pantheon, magic, and art.

(8) CHANG, GARMA C. C. Teachings of Tibetan Yoga. New Hyde Park, N.Y.: University Books, 1963, 128 pp.

An introduction to the practices and theories of Tibetan yoga through translations of brief texts. Helpful as a supplement to Evans-Wentz (below), but demands careful reading.

(9) CONZE, EDWARD et al., eds. Buddhist Texts Through the Ages (see 3.3.1.1[19]), Pt. 3, pp. 221-268.

This section of the anthology is entitled "The Tantras" and was ably edited and translated by David Snellgrove. It includes selections from Saraha's Treasury of Songs, Anangavajra's The Attainment of the Realization of Wisdom and Means, and the biography of Milarepa, and altogether makes a good, available first introduction to the subject and variety of tantric practices.

(10) DASGUPTA, SHASHIBHUSAN. Obscure Religious Cults (see 2.6.1[6]), pp. 87-109.

This chapter is the classic treatment in English of the tantric practices of the Sahajiyas of Bengal--a late offshoot of Tantric Buddhism. Particular attention is paid to guru-vada, the esoteric sadhanas, and the state of supreme bliss (mahasukha). For the interested student only.

(11) ELIADE, MIRCEA. Yoga, Immortality and Freedom (see 11.4.5[6]), pp. 200-273.

One of the easiest and most readily available introductions to tantric practices and to the role yoga plays in them. It deals with both Hinduism and Buddhism, and contains basic bibliographies in the notes.

(12) EVANS-WENTZ, W. Y., ed. Tibetan Yoga and Secret Doctrines. See 3.4.2(4).

One of the four books transmitted to the West through the strange offices of Evans-Wentz, this is perhaps the most substantial; but the intrinsic difficulty of the seven texts that it "translates" is not lessened by the language and notes of the translator. The book should not be used as an introduction to Tibetan meditation, although it can repay the careful digging of the advanced student. Of special interest for tantric practices are Book 3, which includes the Kargyutpa techniques of Psychic Heat, Illusory Body, Bardo, and the Clear Light; Book 5, which contains a Nyingmapa "Yoga of Subduing the Lower Self"; and Book 6, "The Yoga of the Long Hum." The other books contain the "Precepts of the Gurus," a mahamudra practice, and a Prajnaparamita text.

(13) FINOT, LOUIS. "Manuscrits sanskrits de Sadhanas retrouvés en Chine." See 3.4.1(3).

An important article containing an introduction, Sanskrit edition and translation into French of the Hevajraskdaprakriya and seven other short tantric liturgical manuals, most of which are untitled but deal with the cult of Heruka and his consort Vajravarahi.

(14) GUENTHER, HERBERT V. The Life and Teaching of Naropa (see 3.4.2[6]), pp. 131-249.

This section, entitled "The Theoretical Content of Naropa's Training," contains a psycho-philosophical presentation of some of the tantric practices carried out by Naropa and his Kargyutpa followers. Included are discussions of the important Vajrasattva meditation, of Mystic Heat (gTummo), of Apparition (Mayakaya), of Radiant Light, Resurrection, Mahamudra, Bardo, etc. These are all useful aids for pondering Evans-Wentz's texts.

(15) ____. Tibetan Buddhism Without Mystification (see 3.4.2[9]), pp. 92-103, 136-148.
Two Tibetan texts dealing with tantric practices are translated. The first is the Tantra portion of "The Gold Refinery Bringing out the Very Essence of the Sutra and Tantra Paths." The second is entitled "The Instruction in the Essence of the Vajrayana Path." Guenther's translation of technical terms requires, as always, some effort on the part of the reader.

(16) ____. Yuganaddah: The Tantric View of Life. See 2.6.1(10).
Discusses at length the psychology and philosophy of tantric Buddhist "integration" and its various stages, and includes one of the few extended treatments in English of the karma-, dharma-, maha-, and samaya-mudras. It is a difficult book, not intended as an introduction.

(17) LALOU, MARCELLE. "Préliminaires d'une étude des Ganacakra," in Studies of Esoteric Buddhism and Tantrism (see 11.6.1[4]), pp. 41-46.
These so-called "Tantric Festivals" (ganacakra, chogs-kyi 'khor-lo) have received very little scholarly attention in the West. Lalou's article lists some of the principal ones that were held, what their main features were, and the primary sources for their study.

(18) LA VALLEE POUSSIN, LOUIS DE. Bouddhisme: Etudes et matériaux (see 9.1.2[4]), pp. 118-185.
An old work, and confused about the relations of Buddhist and Hindu Tantra, but one of the first on tantric rituals, and still valuable for the comments on Dharani, Maithuna, and Anuttarayoga. It also contains an introduction to, analysis and edition of a ritual manual, the Adikarmapradipa.

(19) SNELLGROVE, D. L., trans. The Hevajra Tantra (see 2.6.1[11]), Pt. 1, Introduction and Translation.
The Hevajra, which is an anuttarayoga-tantra text, is largely devoted to practical instruction in the performance of sadhanas, use of mantras and mandalas. Snellgrove's fine translation, preceded by an excellent introduction, may well be recommended as a "jumping-in place" for the student interested in tantric texts and practices.

(20) WAYMAN, ALEX. "The Five-fold Ritual Symbolism of Passion," in Studies of Esoteric Buddhism and Tantrism (see 11.6.1[4]), pp. 117-144.
An imaginative look at the rich symbolism of certain features of Sadhanas in order to suggest non-tantric backgrounds of certain Buddhist tantric ideas.

(21) WILLIS, JANICE DEAN. The Diamond Light. New York: Simon and Schuster, 1972.
A refreshingly clear exposition that simply sets forth the "how-to" of Tibetan Buddhist meditation, without any show or stage-effects. Texts from the four major schools of rNying ma pa, bKargyud pa, Saskya pa, and dGelugs pa are also presented. Also contains a section on the important samaya vows which underlie all Vajrayana initiation and practice.

11.6.2 The Use of Mandalas

(1) BEYER, STEPHAN. The Cult of Tara (see 7.1.1[2]), pp. 167-170.
The ritual construction and offering of a "Mt. Meru Mandala" out of piles of grain which are visualized as parts of the cosmos, is a common Vajrayanic practice. These pages contain the translation of a short Tibetan text describing the visualization. Other versions may be found, with diagrams, in Alex Wayman, The Buddhist Tantras (see 2.6.1[15]), pp. 101-103; L. A. Waddell, Tibetan Buddhism (see 1.14.1[17]), pp. 398-405; and F. D. Lessing, Yung Ho Kung (see 7.5.3[3]), pp. 102-106 (there are some mistakes in the numbering on the diagram in the latter). More extensive bibliographic references may be found in the notes of Johannes Schubert, "Das Reis Mandala," in Asiatica: Festschrift Friedrich Weller (Leipzig: O. Harrassowitz, 1954), pp. 584-609.

(2) BHATTACHARYA, B. Nispannayogavali. Gaekwad's Oriental Series, No. 109. Baroda: Oriental Institute, 1949, pp. 1-86.
This introduction summarizes the twenty-six main mandalas found in the text itself, which is a summary of some of the more important mandalas in the Vajrayana around the eleventh century. Very useful for exposing students to the variety of mandalas used in Tantric Buddhist cults. A much shorter introduction, showing the ritual use of mandalas, may be found in Marcelle Lalou, Les religions du Tibet (see 1.14.1[8]), pp. 26 ff.

(3) "Chakuji," in Hobogirin: Dictionnaire encyclopédique du Bouddhisme. Paris: A. Maisonneuve, 1937, vol. 3, p. 279.
A short treatment in French of the important but neglected practice of "choosing the ground" for the construction of a mandala.

(4) ELIADE, MIRCEA. Yoga, Immortality and Freedom (see 11.4.5[6]), pp. 219-227.
If an introduction to the use of the mandalas in a few pages is what is wanted, this is probably the clearest and most readily available. See also Eliade's bibliographical notes on pages 408-409.

(5) GOVINDA, ANAGARIKA. *Foundations of Tibetan Mysticism.* See 2.6.1(9).
Presents a vast amount of material on the mandala but presupposes a certain amount of knowledge. It should thus be given to the student interested in the mandala only after a sound knowledge of the image has already been obtained.

(6) JUNG, C. GUSTAV. *Mandala Symbolism.* Translated by R. F. C. Hull. Princeton: Bollingen, 1972.
This book handily collates (with illustrations) what Jung had to say about "Mandalas." However, it should be pointed out that when Jung is talking about the mandala, he is not necessarily referring to the Vajrayanist image. It is an unfortunate accident of history that Jung chose to call his quaternity images "mandalas." His images are no more like the Vajrayanist image than they are like any of the other quaternity symbols that manifest themselves in other world religions.

(7) KIYOTA, MINORU. "Shingon Mikkyo Mandala." *History of Religions*, 8 (1968-1969), 31-59.
One of the few brief studies of the Shingon mandalas (Vajradhatu and Garbhakosadhatu mandalas) in English, and their relation to esoteric Shingon. It is a little too compact to be useful as an introduction but can be helpful to the more advanced student.

(8) LESSING, FERDINAND D. *Yung Ho Kung* (see 7.5.3[3]), pp. 128-138.
A complete description of the making of a rajomandala of Samvara out of colored powder, as it used to be constructed in the Tantra Hall of the Yung Ho Kung Monastery in Peking. Includes a sketch and a photograph (Plate xxvi) of the finished work.

(9) MacDONALD, ARIANE. *Le Mandala du Manjusrimulakalpa.* See 3.4.2(10).
Chapters 2 and 3 of the *Manusrimulakalpa* which describe the rites and visualizations involved in making the text's mandala are here introduced and translated into French. Chapters 4-7, which describe the ritual making of pata (Paintings on cloth) may be found in French translation in Marcelle Lalou's *Iconographie des étoffes peintes (Pata) dans le Manjusrimulakalpa* (see 3.4.2[10]).

(10) POTT, P. H. *Yoga and Tantra.* The Hague: M. Nijhoff, 1966.
An often-quoted but difficult and confusing book, with which the author himself now feels uneasy. The argument is convoluted and the conclusions far from clear. Students interested in the mandala should be steered away from this book until they have a thorough grounding in their studies.

(11) SNELLGROVE, DAVID. *Buddhist Himalaya* (see 1.14.2.1[9]), pp. 64-90.
An excellent, short introduction to the ritual construction and symbolism of the mandala, especially useful when read in conjunction with volume 1, pages 27-39, of Snellgrove's *Hevajra Tantra* (see 2.6.1[11]).

(12) TAJIMA, RYUJUN. *Les deux grands Mandalas et la doctrine de l'ésotérisme Shingon.* See 2.6.2(8).

(13) TUCCI, GIUSEPPE. *The Theory and Practice of the Mandala.* Translated by Alan Brodrick. London: Rider, 1961, 146 pp.
A fine study of the Mandala, its meaning, symbolism and rites, which should remain the standard introduction to the topic. However, certain criticisms are possible. First, Tucci neglects history and historical differences; he lumps things together at points where this should not be done, and discusses the mandala as if there were not important differences regarding it in different Vajrayana traditions. Second, though he commendably attempts to deal with both Hindu and Buddhist Tantrism, he discusses them as if they were nearly interchangeable traditions. Such a view is not accepted by the adherents of the two traditions, and modern scholarship is beginning to accept the idea that they do very different things with some of the same symbols.

11.6.3 The Use of Sacred Sounds and Words (Mantras, Dharanis, Sandhabhasa)

(1) BEYER, STEPHAN. *The Cult of Tara.* See 7.1.1(2).
The whole of Beyer's book contains many illustrations of the use of mantras in Tibetan practices, especially those connected with Tara. The index has a thorough listing of specific cases.

(2) BHARATI, AGEHANANDA. *The Tantric Tradition* (see 2.5.1[1]), pp. 101-184.
Chapter 5 contains one of the most substantial recent attempts to deal with the whole question of mantra in both the Buddhist and Hindu tantric traditions. It is helpful for its survey of previous scholarship, distinguishes two kinds of use of mantra (in ritual and as "spontaneous meditation"), and offers a new scheme for the classification of mantras. Chapter 6 deals with sandhabhasa (intentional language), succinctly reviewing the scholarly debate about the meaning and purpose of sandhabhasa, and attempts to distinguish between "afferent" and "efferent" sandha-terms.

(3) BHATTACHARYYA, BENOYTOSH. *An Introduction to Buddhist Esoterism* (see 2.6.1[2]), pp. 55-61.
A short chapter devoted to a general discussion of mantras and their use in Vajrayana Buddhism, this is a reworking of pages lxvi-lxxiii of the "Introduction" to his edition of the *Sadhanamala* (see 11.6.1[5]).

(4) ELIADE, MIRCEA. Yoga, Immortality and Freedom (see 11.4.5[6]), pp. 212-216, 149-154.

These two passages contain short but adequate introductions to the subjects of Mantras, Dharanis, and Sandhabhasa in the tantric tradition in general. See also the bibliographical notes on pages 407-408 and 410-411.

(5) GOVINDA, ANAGARIKA. Foundations of Tibetan Mysticism. See 2.6.1(9).

The whole book is an exegesis and unfolding of the Mantra "Om Mani Padme Hum" and shows the extent to which Mantras can be taken. Based in part on the teachings of Govinda's teacher, Tomo Geshe Rimpoche, it is not an introductory work. A much shorter explanation of the same mantra can be found in John Blofeld, The Tantric Mysticism of Tibet (see 11.6.1[6]), pp. 194-197.

(6) The Saddharma-Pundarika or the Lotus of the True Law (see 3.3.5.1[2]), pp. 370-375.

Many important Mahayana sutras contain special chapters devoted to mantras and dharanis. The most readily available translation of a Mahayana Sutra with references to mantras and dharanis is this short chapter from the Lotus. Another is Chapter 9 (pp. 223-225) of the Lankavatara Sutra (see 3.3.3.1[15]).

(7) SAUNDERS, E. DALE. "Some Tantric Techniques," in Studies of Esoteric Buddhism and Tantrism (see 11.6.1[4]), pp. 167-177.

An excellent introduction to the specifically Buddhist use of dharanis and mantras in tantric meditations, with bibliographic suggestions. For a serious attempt to make comparisons in the use of sacred sounds outside of India, see J. W. Hauer, Die Dharani im nordlichen Buddhismus und ihre Parallelen in der sogennanten Mithrasliturgie (Stuttgart: W. Kohlhammer, 1927), 25 pp.

(8) WADDELL, L. AUSTINE. "The Dharani Cult in Buddhism, Its Origin, Deified Literature and Images." Östasiatische Zeitschrift, 1 (1912), 155-195.

An illustrated account of the important but neglected aspect of the use of mantras as protective deities. A related study of "deified dharanis" (pratisara) may be found in Sukumar Sen "On Dharani and Pratisara," in Studies of Esoteric Buddhism and Tantrism (see 11.6.1[4]), pp. 67-72.

(9) _____. "The Dharani or Indian Buddhist Protective Spell." Indian Antiquary, 43 (1914), 37-42, 49-54.

Translations from the Tibetan of a number of interesting texts containing dharanis of "protective spells." The first five concern the evocation of the Garuda Bird (one of these has also been translated in Beyer, The Buddhist Experience [see 3.3.2.1(18)]), pp. 134-136. But even more interesting and substantial is Text No. 6, the "White Umbrella-One of Buddha's Diadem" (Usnisa sitatapatra aparajita).

(10) WAYMAN, ALEX. The Buddhist Tantras (see 2.6.1[15]), pp. 128-135.

This chapter, entitled "Twilight Language and a Tantric Song," is a continuation of Wayman's essay on this subject in Mélanges d'indianisme à la mémoire de Louis Renou (Paris: E. de Boccard, 1968), pp. 789-796. Here he discusses the meaning of the expression "Sandhabhasa," arguing again for the translation "Twilight language," on the basis of its use by Candrakirti and Tsong Kha pa. He also offers some interesting illustrations of the use of Sandhabhasa.

11.6.4 The Use of Symbolic Gestures (Mudras)

(1) AUBOYER, JEANNINE. "Moudra et hasta." Oriental Art, 3 (1950-1951), 153-161.

Examines briefly the iconography of mudras and their use in esoteric rituals, and compares them with the hasta of Hindu dance.

(2) BEYER, STEPHAN. The Cult of Tara. See 7.1.1(2).

The entire book is filled with specific references to the use of mudras--the occasions of making them and their meaning. Numerous illustrations show what the gestures look like. This is one of the few places where the student of mudra can get beyond the basic gestures frozen in Buddhist iconography and see how mudras are used in ritual. See, for example, pages 146-164, which discuss the mudras made in accompaniment to the visualization of offerings; and check the index under "gesture" for references throughout the work.

(3) COOMARASWAMY, ANANDA K. "Mudra, mudda." Journal of the American Oriental Society, 48 (1928), 279-281.

A brief article reviewing the early scholarly debate about the meaning of the word, and appending a short bibliography on "the language of gesture." A more up-to-date bibliography may be found in Eliade's Yoga, Immortality and Freedom (see 11.4.5[6]), pp. 405-407.

(4) KLEEN, TYRA DE. Mudras: The Ritual Hand-Poses of the Buddha Priests and the Shiva Priests of Bali. New Hyde Park, N.Y.: University Books, 1970, 62 pp. (Originally published 1926.)

This is a re-issue of de Kleen's original study of Balinese hand-gestures. It is chiefly of value for its sixty annotated drawings of different mudras, and for being one of the few attempts to make a comparative study of this subject.

(5) PRZYLUSKI, JEAN. "Mudra." Indian Culture, 2 (1936), 715-719.

A good but unfortunately very short introduction to the different meanings and uses of mudras.

(6) SAUNDERS, ERNEST DALE. Mudra: A Study of Symbolic Gestures in Japanese Buddhist Sculptures. See 2.6.2(7).
This is the standard and most thorough work on mudra in English. It is well illustrated, provides details on the symbolism of the various gestures, and contains a large bibliography. It approaches mudra from the Japanese angle, and though it is largely based on iconographic representations, it does include a section on Tantrism and the use of mudras in rituals (see pp. 17-35).

(7) ____. "Symbolic Gestures in Buddhism." Artibus Asiae, 21 (1958), 47-63.
A short article by Saunders for those who cannot find the same author's Mudra (above). This specifically considers the "gesture of fearlessness" (abhayamudra), the "turning of the wheel of the law" (dharmacakramudra), and the specifically tantric "Mudra of Vairocana." It is primarily an iconographic study.

(8) VISSER, MARINUS WILLEM DE. Ancient Buddhism in Japan (see 1.13.2.1[8]), pp. 167-175.
These pages contain a description of the use of ten mudras in a Japanese "Tantric Ninno ceremony." The description is taken from a Tendai commentary to the Ninnokyo or "Sutra of the Benevolent Kings."

11.7 PURE LAND PRACTICES AND EXPERIENCES

See also 2.5.8, Religious Thought, and 3.3.7, Authoritative Texts.

11.7.1 General Discussions: Faith in Amida

(1) BLOOM, ALFRED. Shinran's Gospel of Pure Grace (see 2.5.8[4]), pp. 27-75.
A clear exposition of Shinran's understanding of faith--its importance in the "degenerate age of the Dharma," its grounding in "Other-poweredness" and its expression in the Nembutsu. A good introduction for the Western reader. Another version of it can be found in Bloom's "Shinran's Philosophy of Salvation by Absolute Other Power," Contemporary Religions in Japan, 5 (1964), 119-142.

(2) LU K'UAN YU. The Secrets of Chinese Meditation (see 11.4.1[5]), pp. 81-108.
The chapter entitled "Self-cultivation According to the Pure Land School" is the best introduction in English to Chinese techniques and expressions of faith in Amitabha. [Luk] distinguishes three methods of practice: repetition of Amitabha's name, repetition of his mantra, and the contemplation of the Buddha Amitayus. The latter is illustrated by a translation of the Amitayur Dhyana Sutra (Kuan Wu Liang Shou Ching).

(3) MIYAMATO, SHOSON. "A Study of Attainment (Sho) in Shinran's Kyogyoshinsho." Indogaku Bukkyogaku Kenkyu/Journal of Indian and Buddhist Studies, 20, no. 2 (1972), 1030-1009 (sic).
A helpful study of Shinran's interpretation of attainment (sho) and nirvana, as he presents it in his major doctrinal work, the Kyogyoshinsho (Teaching, Practice, Faith, and Attainment).

(4) SASAKI, GESSHO. A Study of Shin Buddhism (see 2.5.8[17]), pp. 46-93.
The two chapters deal respectively with "Knowledge, Faith, and Salvation by Faith" and "Shin and Moral Life," in each case putting these in the context of Mahayana practices in general.

(5) SUZUKI, DAISETZ TEITARO. A Miscellany on the Shin Teaching of Buddhism (see 2.5.8[23]).
In these two chapters, Suzuki illustrates the faith of Shin Buddhists through stories about the "wondrously happy men" (Myokonin) who are often illiterate and always pious, and through an account of the "Sayings of a Modern Tariki ("Other Power") Mystic," (Chapter 3).

(6) ____. "Zen and Jodo, Two Types of Buddhist Experience." See 11.4.8.1(13).

(7) YAMABE, SHUGAKU. "Amida as Saviour of the Soul" and "The Way to the Land of Bliss." The Eastern Buddhist, 1 (1921), 123-130, 337-340.
Two pietistic articles on Buddhist pietism, more interesting as expressions of faith than as descriptions of it.

(8) YAMAMOTO, KOSHO. An Introduction to Shin Buddhism (see 1.13.2.2[15]), pp. 119-141.
These pages contain a concise description of the "Easy Path."

(9) ____. The Private Letters of Shinran Shonin (see 3.3.7.2[6]), pp. 3-53.
These pages contain a translation of the "Mattosho," a collection of Shinran's letters to his followers. They form a good example of the kind of spiritual advice and practical instructions the founder of Shin Buddhism gave. Other examples may be gleaned from the collection of Shinran's sayings by Kakunyo (1270-1351), the "Tract on Steadily Holding to the Faith" (Shuji), translated in Suzuki, A Miscellany on the Shin Teaching of Buddhism (above), (originally published in The Eastern Buddhist, 7 [1938], 363-375).

11.7.2 The Nembutsu

(1) ANDREWS, ALLAN W. "Nembutsu in the Chinese Pure Land Tradition." The Eastern Buddhist, n.s. 3 (1970), 20-45.
A fairly detailed survey of Chinese Pure Land literature with special reference to the Nien-fo (Mebutsu) practice. A more specific study of the earliest known Chinese teaching on the Nien-fo may be found in Roger Corless,

Pure Land Practices and Experiences

"T'an-luan's Commentary of the Pure Land Discourse" (Unpublished Ph.D. dissertation, University of Wisconsin, 1973), pp. 218-226.

(2) ANDREWS, ALLAN W. The Teachings Essential to Rebirth: A Study of Genshin's Ojoyoshu. See 2.5.8(1).

(3) BANDO, SHOJUN. "The Significance of the Nembutsu." Contemporary Religions in Japan, 7 (1966), 193-208.

An article based on the "Practice" section of Shinran's Kyo-gyo-shin-sho, and explaining the Nembutsu as the culmination of Buddhist mantra tradition. It forms a good introduction to Shinran's view of the Nembutsu.

(4) SHUNJO, HOIN. Honen the Buddhist Saint (see 1.13.2.2[12]), pp. 36-41.

The whole of this massive study of Honen contains references to his views on and practice of the Nembutsu. Check the index under "Nembutsu" (pp. 832-833) for a detailed listing of references. Especially handy are pages 36-41, which survey the use of the Nembutsu in meditation within Tendai prior to Honen, and the special contributions of Genshin (942-1017), Ryonin (1072-1132), Kakuban (1095-1143), Yokwan (1032-1111) and Chingai (1091-1152).

(5) SUGIHIRA, SHIZUTOSHI. "Honen Shonin and Shinran Shonin: Their Nembutsu Doctrine." The Eastern Buddhist, 7 (1939), 342-3612.

A rather pietistic look at some of the differences and similarities between the views of the two great founders of Japanese Pure Land on the Nembutsu.

(6) _____. "The Teaching of Ippen Shonin (1239-1289)." The Eastern Buddhist, 6 (1932-1935), 287-300.

The article contains translations of some of the letters of the thirteenth century founder of the Ji subsect of the Pure Land school. Ippen believed that "beside reciting Na-mu-a-mi-da-butsu no mental equipment is necessary and that except saying this there is no faith." For another account of his life, see Soetsu Yanagi, "Ippen Shonin" (see 2.5.8[29]).

11.7.3 Other Techniques and Expressions (Meditative Visions, Amitayus and His Pure Land, Liturgy, Hymns, etc.)

(1) BEYER, STEPHAN. The Buddhist Experience (see 3.3.2.1[18]), pp. 116-124.

This section, entitled "The Vision of Paradise," translates excerpts from the "Kuan wu-liang-shou-fo-ching" (the Amitayur-dhyana-sutra), which is the basic text setting forth the techniques of meditation on the "Buddha of everlasting life." A full translation of the sutra may be found in Cowell, Müller and Takakusu, Buddhist Mahayana Texts (see 3.3.1.1[12]: "Amitayur-Dhyana-Sutra"), or in Lu K'uan Yu's Secrets of Chinese Meditation (see 11.4.1[5]), pp. 81-108.

(2) INGRAM, PAUL O. "The Symbolism of Light and Pure Land in Buddhist Soteriology." See 9.3.9(3).

Using Mircea Eliade's morphological treatment of the subjective religious experience of light in Mephistopheles and Androgyne (New York:: Sheed and Ward, 1965), pp. 19-77, Ingram comes to the following understanding of light symbolism in the Buddhist tradition: light symbolizes wisdom which a Buddha or bodhisattva possesses as a result of his experience with "the structure of reality in all its 'suchness.'"

(3) PAS, JULIAN F. "Shan-Tao's Interpretation of the Meditative Vision of Buddha Amitayus." History of Religions, 14 (1974), 96-116.

An analysis of the commentary of Pure Land Patriarch Shan Tao (613-681) on the Amitayur-Dhyana-Sutra, which makes a good introduction to the details of the techniques of the Amita vision. Includes a discussion of the preliminaries and progressive states of hsiang (visualization), kuan (inspection), chien (vision), and samadhi.

(4) ROBINSON, RICHARD, trans. Chinese Buddhist Verse. See 4.2.1(5).

A selection of passages from various texts, some of which are used in liturgies by the Pure Land sect, and others which are hymns of praise of the Buddha, often expressive of faith.

(5) VISSER, MARINUS WILLEM DE. Ancient Buddhism in Japan (see 1.13.2.1[8]), pp. 318-450.

Reviews the main features of Amitabha's cult in China, but especially in Japan, including a very interesting list of the sixteen types of meditation on Amitabha. Also provides details on the Ceremony of Repentance before Amitabha--the Amida Kekwa or Sembo.

11.7.4 The Pure Land

(1) ANDREWS, ALLEN. The Teachings Essential to Rebirth: A Study of Genshin's Ojoyoshu. See 2.5.8(1).

Genshin was one of the early advocates of the worship of Amida and the Nembutsu within Japanese Tendai. His work, which is here summarized, translated and discussed, includes a description of the beauties of the Pure Land and the advantages of the Nembutsu.

(2) BARUA, BENIMADHAB. "Buddhakhetta in the Apadana." See 9.2.4(1).

The question of the origins of the notions of the Pure Land is a complex one. In this fascinating article, Barua has translated a section of the Canonical Pali work, the Apadana, which deals primarily with the notion

11.7.4 Pure Land Practices and Experiences

of the Buddha's field (Buddhakhetta)--the description of which is much akin to later descriptions of the Sukhavati of Amitabha.

(3) BLOOM, ALFRED. Shinran's Gospel of Pure Grace (see 2.5.8[4]), pp. 77-85.

This section of Bloom's concise treatment of Shin doctrine deals with "The believer's destiny" and contains descriptions of the Pure Land of Amida. A fine introduction.

(4) HAYASHIMA KYOSHO. "A Study in the Thought of 'Hon-gan' or the Basic Vow of a Bodhisattva." Indogaku Bukkyogaku Kenkyu/ Journal of Indian and Buddhist Studies, 14 (1966), 935-920 (sic).

Contains a straightforward description of the various types of understanding of the Pure Land: as a Pure Land of meditation, as being in another direction (the West), as being future in this world.

(5) KANEKO, DAIER. "The Meaning of Salvation in the Doctrine of Pure Land Buddhism," adapted by Hiroshi Sakamoto. Eastern Buddhist, n.s. 1 (1965-1966), 48-63.

A good explanation of Pure Land's soteriology, based on and referring to the teachings of Honen and Shinran. Not bad as an introduction, although somewhat homiletical.

(6) MUS, PAUL. Barabudur (see 2.5.2[8]), vol. 2, pp. 475-576.

This "appendix," which in many ways is not an appendix at all but the culmination of the whole of Mus's monumental Barabudur, is entitled "Les sept pas du Buddha et la doctrine des Terres Pures." It is an important essay on the origins of the notion of the Pure Land, in which Mus creatively brings together the legends of the levelling of the earth which occurs during the seven steps taken by the Buddha at birth, the rise to the mystic pole of the universe which this implies, and the traditions of the cankrama or walkway at Bodhgaya, and connects these to the descriptions of the Pure Land of Amitabha and to his interpretation of the symbolism of the stupa of Barabudur. For advanced students only.

(7) PRUDEN, LEO, trans. "Ten Doubts Concerning the Pure Land (The Ching-t'u Shih-i-lun)." See 3.3.7.2(1).

An introduction to and translation of a short eighth century Chinese catechism once thought to be a minor work of Chih-i, the founder of Chinese T'ien-t'ai. The "doubts" raise and answer questions concerning the nature and direction of Amitabha's Pure Land, and its attainment by common lay people.

(8) ROWELL, TERESINA. "The Background and Early Use of the Buddha-ksetra Concept." See 9.2.4(4).

The concept of a Buddha's field (Buddha-ksetra) is an important one in any understanding of the development of the doctrine of the Pure Land. In this article--one of the more substantial in English--Rowell seeks out the roots of this concept and exposes the point of doctrinal transition from emphasis on attaining a pure field for oneself by means of worshipping the Buddhas, to emphasis on the special ideal of being reborn in the Sukhavati of Amitabha.

(9) SHUNJO, HOIN. Honen the Buddhist Saint (see 1.13.2.2[12]), pp. 39-40, 44, 56-57, 188.

Throughout this monumental work on the life and teaching of Honen, the diligent student can glean various descriptions and interpretations of the Pure Land of Amida. The above pages contain accounts of the Pure Land of Amida as a "mystical adornment" of the Palace of Vairocana, as being everywhere and the same as this world here and now, as interpreted by the patriarch Shogei (1341-1420), as viewed by the Hosso sect. See the index for further references.

(10) "The Larger Sukhavati-Vyuha" and "The Smaller Sukhavati-Vyuha," translated by F. Max Müller; Buddhist Mahayana Texts. See 3.3.1.1(12).

Basic texts of the Pure Land School which contain descriptions of the "Land of Bliss" of Amitabha. See also 3.3.7.1(1) through 3.3.7.1(3) for additional annotations.

11.8 NIRVANA/NIBBANA

For Charmakaya, Tathata, Tathatagatagarbha, Sunyata, etc., see 2.8, Religious Thought.

(1) JOHANSSON, RUNE E. A. The Psychology of Nirvana. London: Allen and Unwin, 1969, 141 pp.

A book written from a psychological and semantic, rather than a historical and philosophical perspective, and based primarily on the Pali tradition. It is interesting, but should be complemented by Welbon's The Buddhist Nirvana and Its Western Interpreters (below) and, if possible, de La Vallée Poussin's Nirvana (below).

(2) KING, WINSTON L. In the Hope of Nibbana. See 11.3(11).

Basically a study of Theravadan ethics, this work discusses the problems that arise when Nibbana, though remaining the religious ideal and goal, is no longer thought to be attainable in the conceivable future. In light of this, King touches briefly (pp. 226-229) on the important modern "reinterpretation" of Nibbana as "this worldly" and attainable "in this very life-time."

(3) LA VALLEE POUSSIN, LOUIS DE. "Documents d'Abhidharma, Première partie: Textes relatifs au Nirvana et aux Asamskrtas en général." See 2.7.7(7).

Through translations from the Vibhasa, one of the greatest experts on abhidharma of this century outlines the Sarvastivada-Sautrantika controversies over the nature of Nirvana.

(4) ____. *Nirvana*. Paris: G. Beauchesne, 1925, 194 pp.

Perhaps the most important statement on the subject by the great Belgian Buddhologist. In it, he treats Buddhism as a religion born in the historical context of Yoga, and not as a purely speculative systematic school of philosophy. He concludes that for early Buddhism at least, Nirvana was a reality--an immortal and ineffable refuge--and did not mean annihilation. He thereby criticizes the views of many of his contemporaries and predecessors, including his own as expressed in his earlier works on the subject: see his The Way to Nirvana (2.7.1[9]); and his "Nirvana," in Encyclopaedia of Religion and Ethics (see 1.15.1[9]), vol. 9, pp. 376-379. At the same time, he sparked a vivid reaction from Stcherbatsky (see his Conception of Buddhist Nirvana, below). For one of the last statements of de La Vallée Poussin's position, see his "Dernière note sur le Nirvana," in Etudes d'orientalisme publiées à la mémoire de R. Linossier (Paris: E. Leroux, 1932), vol. 2, pp. 329-354.

(5) ____. "Le Nirvana d'après Aryadeva." Mélanges chinois et bouddhiques, 1 (1932), 127-135.

A translation of two passages from Aryadeva's Satasastra and Catuhsataka which deal with Nirvana in the form of a debate between a Buddhist and a "foreigner." They present a Madhyamika view of the topic which warns against affirming either the existence or non-existence of Nirvana, and claims that the affirmation that there is a Nirvana is only made to condemn the views of those who deny it.

(6) LAW, BIMALA CHURN. "Aspects of Nirvana." Indian Culture, 2 (1935), 328-348.

A convenient review of some of the epithets and synonyms of Nirvana, as described in the Pali texts, especially the Nettipakarana. Then, proclaiming the need to look at the concept of Nirvana from all angles, Law approaches it, briefly, in its historical, eschatological, poetical, logical, psychical, and ethical aspects. Not a bad introduction.

(7) MUS, PAUL. Barabudur (see 2.5.2[8]), vol. 1, pp. 48-83.

A unique contribution to the study of the role and position of nirvana in the popular Buddhism of early India. The section is entitled "Le Nirvana et la survie du Buddha: Culte, dogme, et légende," and in it Mus synthesizes the positions of the "annihilationists" by showing the Nirvana of the Buddha to be an absence remediable by magical action as described generally in the Hindu Brahmanas and as realized, for example, in the cult or the stupa. (Page 74: "Disons que la magie ancienne avait élaboré une collection de recettes pour remédier à l'absence des objets ou des personnes, ou qu'ils fussent ou ne fussent plus, et pour agir sur eux à distance. Le nirvana a été traité comme un nouveau genre d'absence.") For advanced students only, as Mus's arguments and language are both convoluted.

(8) OBERMILLER, E. "Nirvana According to the Tibetan Tradition." Indian Historical Quarterly, 10 (1934), 211-257.

Obermiller seeks to add details from new sources in support of Stcherbatsky's view of Nirvana. In so doing he examines works of Tsong Kha pa and Jam-yang-shad-pa, and presents their analysis of the views of Nirvana according to the four schools (Vaibhasikas, Sautrantikas, Yogacaras, and Madhyamikas, both the Svatantrikas and Prasangikas). Of interest primarily to the student already familiar with these philosophical traditions.

(9) OLDENBERG, HERMANN. Buddha: His Life, His Doctrine, His Order (see 8.1.2.3[20]), pp. 263-285.

This is the section of Oldenberg's work that deals primarily with Nirvana. Because he has often been labelled an "annihilationist," his view deserves a more careful reading by the advanced student who may discover in him a more balanced opinion.

(10) SLATER, ROBERT LAWSON. Paradox and Nirvana: A Study of Religious Ultimates with Special Reference to Burmese Buddhism. Chicago: University of Chicago Press, 1951, 145 pp.

This work approaches the question of the nature of Nirvana, not primarily through the study of authoritative texts, but through the author's own investigations of the opinions of Burmese Buddhists. See especially Chapter 3, "Nibbana in Burmese Buddhism," in which he argues against the negativistic interpretation of Nirvana, concluding that the concept "eludes philosophy" while it inspires life.

(11) STCHERBATSKY, F. I. (THEODORE). The Conception of Buddhist Nirvana. See 2.5.3(12).

This is Stcherbatsky's major contribution to the theory of Nirvana, and it represents an important study of the evolution of the concept in the various philosophical schools. Stcherbatsky approaches Nirvana through the writings of the Vaibhasikas, the Sautrantikas, the Vijnanavadins, the Madhyamikas and others, and thus tries to give a total philosophical perspective. The work is also important for its translation of Chapters 1 and 25 of Candrakirti's Prasannapada, and as a landmark in the Stcherbatsky/de La Vallée Poussin debate. For more on the latter, see Stcherbatsky's "Review" (of de La Vallée Poussin's Nirvana), Bulletin of the School of Oriental Studies, 4 (1926-1928), 357-360.

(12) SUZUKI, DAISETZ TEITARO. Outlines of Mahayana Buddhism (see 2.1[12]), pp. 331-371.

In this chapter, Suzuki proposes to present the Mahayana view of Nirvana, and concludes that it is "not annihilation of life but its enlightenment." He disputes the works of various Pali scholars, and argues for a Vijnanavada distinction between "Absolute Nirvana" (i.e., Dharmakaya), Nirvana-with-remainder, Nirvana-without-remainder, and "the Nirvana that has no abode." For other Yogacara discussions of Nirvana, in which Nirvana is described as a "revulsion in the Alayavijnana" or as a "getting rid of the Manovijnana," see Suzuki, trans., The Lankavatara Sutra (3.3.3.1[15]), pp. 86-87, 108-109.

(13) THOMAS, E. J. "Nirvana and Parinirvana," in India Antiqua (Jean Philippe Vogen Festschrift). Leiden: E. J. Brill, 1947, pp. 294-295.

A brief but forceful note, in which Thomas complains about the persistence of the view that Parinirvana somehow means only final Nirvana at death. He argues tht the only distinction between Nirvana and Parinirvana is a purely grammatical one, in which Nirvana expresses the state and Parinirvana the attaining of the state. For a more complete presentation of Thomas's view on Nirvana, see Chapter 10, "Release and Nirvana" (pp. 107-132), of his The History of Buddhist Thought (2.1[14]).

(14) TUCCI, GIUSEPPE. "Un traité d'Aryadeva sur le 'Nirvana' des hérétiques." T'oung Pao, 24 (1925), 16-31.

A translation of a short treatise from the Chinese canon, attributed to Aryadeva, which explains and condemns the twenty various "heretical," i.e., non-Madhyamika, views of Nirvana. This parallels a similar passage in the Lankavatara sutra.

(15) WELBON, GUY RICHARD. The Buddhist Nirvana and Its Western Interpreters. See 2.9(43).

A very useful introduction to the history of the meaning of the word "Nirvana" among Western scholars. At the same time it is a statement regarding the difficulties and complexities lying in this central concept, the culture-specific interpretations of the West, and a general study of the difficulty one culture has in attempting to correctly understand another. It is especially helpful for its survey of the early scholarship's positions--Colebrooke, Hodgon, Csoma de Koros, Burnouf and his immediate followers, Max Müller, d'Alwis, and Childers--even Schopenhauer, Wagner, and Nietzsche. At the same time, it forms a solid introduction to the views of Oldenberg, Thomas and Caroline Rhys-Davids, and to the de La Vallée Poussin/Stcherbatsky debate. Altogether a fine introduction to the subject.

12 Research Aids

12.1 DICTIONARIES

(1) BUDDHADATTA, A. P. Concise Pali-English Dictionary. Second edition. Colombo: Colombo Apothecaries' Co., 1957.

　A fine, succinct dictionary which is suitable for working in the Pali Canon. See also Buddhadatta's English-Pali Dictionary (Colombo: Colombo Apothecaries' Co., 1955).

(2) DAS, SARAT CHANDRA. A Tibetan-English Dictionary with Sanskrit Synonyms. Edited by Graham Sandberg and A. William Heyde. Delhi: Motilal Banarsidass, 1970. (Originally published Calcutta, 1902.)

　Rather dated at times, but still useful, especially for its inclusion of the Sanskrit equivalents for Tibetan terms.

(3) EDGERTON, FRANKLIN. Buddhist Hybrid Sanskrit Grammar and Dictionary. Vol. 2: Dictionary. New Haven, Conn.: Yale University Press, 1953.

　An indispensable tool for reading any Buddhist hybrid Sanskrit text, and useful more generally for the specific Buddhist meanings of Sanskrit words.

(4) EITEL, ERNEST J. Hand-book of Chinese Buddhism: Being a Sanskrit-Chinese Dictionary. Tokyo: Sanshusha, 1904.

　A helpful work which also includes vocabularies of Buddhist terms in Pali, Sinhalese, Siamese, Burmese, Tibetan, Mongolian, and Japanese.

(5) HUMPRHEYS, CHRISTMAS. A Popular Dictionary of Buddhism. London: Arco, 1962.

　Exactly what the title says it is, this can be helpful for beginners' reference.

(6) LING, TREVOR O. A Dictionary of Buddhism. New York: C. Scribner's Sons, 1972.

　A recent, general reference work to Buddhist terms. Taken from A Dictionary of Comparative Religion (New York: Scribners, 1970).

(7) MONIER-WILLIAMS, MONIER. A Sanskrit-English Dictionary. Oxford: Clarendon, 1898.

　Still the basic general Sanskrit-English dictionary. For Buddhist texts, however, it should be supplemented by Edgerton's dictionary (above).

(8) NYANATILOKA. Buddhist Dictionary. Second edition. Colombo: Frewin, 1956.

　A very useful manual of Buddhist terms and doctrines, based on the Pali materials.

(9) RHYS-DAVIDS, T. W. and WILLIAM STEDE. The Pali Text Society's Pali-English Dictionary. London: Luzac, 1949.

　First published in 1921-1925, this is by one of the first great Pali scholars.

(10) ROSENBERG, OTTO. Introduction to the Study of Buddhism according to Material Preserved in Japan and China. Pt. 1: Vocabulary. Tokyo: Shueisha, 1916.

　A dated but still useful survey of Buddhist terms, which includes Japanese readings and Sanskrit equivalents.

(11) SOOTHILL, WILLIAM E. and LEWIS HODOUS, comps. A Dictionary of Chinese Buddhist Terms. London: K. Paul, Trench, Trubner, 1937.

　An important reference work for Chinese Buddhism, including Sanskrit and English equivalents.

(12) TRENCKNER, VILHELM. Critical Pali Dictionary. Copenhagen: Royal Danish Academy. and Society of Sciences and Letters, 1924-. Vol. 1, A-Asota (1924-1926); Epilegomena to vol. 1, by Helmer Smith (1948); vol. 2, fasc. 1-2, A-Appatik (1960-1962).

　A major work which has not progressed far enough to be generally useful.

(13) WOODWARD, FRANK LEE et al. Pali Tipitaka Concordance. London: Luzac, 1952-.

　Still in progress, but very helpful to the study of Pali texts and commentaries.

12.2 BIBLIOGRAPHIES

(1) BANDO SHOJUN. A Bibliography on Japanese Buddhism. Tokyo: CIIB Press, 1958.

　Over 1600 entries listing books and articles located in the various libraries of Japan as of 1958.

12.2 Bibliographies

(2) BEAUTRIX, PIERRE. Bibliographie du Bouddhisme. See 3.1.1(2).
A bibliography of Buddhist texts edited in their original languages. Volume 2, in preparation, will list translations of Buddhist texts into various Western languages.

(3) _____. Bibliographie du Bouddhisme Zen. Brussels: Institut belge des hautes études bouddhiques, 1971, 114 pp.
A helpful bibliography of books and articles arranged into basic categories.

(4) _____. Bibliographie de la littérature Prajnaparamita. See 3.3.1.3(1).

(5) BECHERT, HEINZ. Buddhismus, Staat und Gesellschaft in den Ländern des Theravada-Buddhismus. Wiesbaden: O. Harrassowitz, 1973, vol. 3, Bibliographie, Dokumente, Index, 662 pp.
This third volume of Bechert's magnum opus contains a fully indexed monumental bibliography of works by over 2000 authors. As such, it is an invaluable tool for detailed work on almost any aspect of Theravada Buddhism.

(6) Bibliographie bouddhique. Paris: Librairie orientaliste Paul Guethner, 1930-1933; and Paris: Librairie l'Amérique et Orient Adrien-Maisonneuve, 1934-1967, vols. 1-32, January 1928-May 1958.
A sporadically published, but very helpful bibliography including works in all major European languages and Japanese. All of the exceptionally important works are annotated critically. In sum, this work really is a catalogue of the major contributors to European studies of Buddhism.

(7) Bibliography of Asian Studies. Association for Asian Studies, 1946-.
A major yearly bibliographic effort published by the Journal of Asian Studies. Up until 1956 it was known as the Far Eastern Bibliography. It is a tool of fundamental importance for Buddhist studies, as well as all other fields of Asian studies, especially helpful for its reference to anthropological and social science materials which are not commonly covered in other places.

(8) GARD, RICHARD. "Buddhism," in A Reader's Guide to the Great Religions. Edited by Charles Adams. New York: Free Press, 1965, pp. 83-160.
An excellent bibliographical essay which covers comprehensively all major and many minor sources concerned with a myriad of topics within the scope of Buddhist studies. A new edition of this is due soon and should more than adequately supplement the 1965 edition. For "Buddhism in Japan," see Joseph Kitagawa, in this work, pages 161-190.

(9) HANAYAMA, SHINSHO. Bibliography on Buddhism. Edited by The Commemoration Committee for Professor Shinsho Hanayama's Sixty-first Birthday. Tokyo: Hokuseido, 1961.
This bibliography lists 15,073 books, articles and reviews. Publications in Western languages are covered extensively up until about 1925.

(10) HELD, HANS LUDWIG. Deutsche Bibliographie des Buddhismus. Munich: Hans Sachs, 1916.
A dated but still useful bibliography listing around 2500 books, articles, and reviews.

(11) MARCH, ARTHUR, comp. A Buddhism Bibliography. London: Buddhist Lodge, 1935.
A still useful bibliography of books and articles with a subject index. Annual supplements to the bibliography appeared during the first five years after 1935.

(12) MIURA, ISSHU and RUTH FULLER SASAKI. Zen Dust (see 3.1.5[6]), pp. 333-479.

(13) REGAMEY, CONSTANTIN. Buddhistische Philosophie. Bern: A. Francke, 1950, 86 pp.
This bibliography focuses almost exclusively upon philosophical books and articles which deal with Buddhist thought.

(14) REYNOLDS, FRANK E. "From Philology to Anthropology: A Bibliographical Essay on the Works Related to Early, Theravada and Sinhalese Buddhism," in The Two Wheels of Dhamma (see 1.3.1[11]), pp. 107-121; and "Tradition and Change in Theravada Buddhism: A Bibliographical Essay Focused on the Modern World," in Tradition and Change in Theravada Buddhism (see 6.2.1.1[40], pp. 91-104.
Two very helpful bibliographical essays which may be the first place a student should look for an overview of appropriate books and articles on the topic of Theravada Buddhism.

12.3 ENCYCLOPEDIAS

(1) DEMIEVILLE, PAUL, ed. Hobogirin: Dictionnaire encyclopédique du Bouddhisme après les sources chinoises et japonaises. See 2.7.12(1).
Unfortunately, this major work did not progress too far; but even so it is tremendously useful for major articles by top scholars on all topics of Buddhism it has covered. Especially valuable for its extensive references to Chinese tripitaka texts.

(2) HASTINGS, JAMES, ed. Encyclopaedia of Religion and Ethics. See 1.15.1(9).
Often dated, but still an invaluable encyclopedia. Check the index in Volume 13 for many articles on Buddhism, often of scholarly importance, and by great Buddhologists of the time.

(3) MALALASEKERA, G. P. Dictionary of Pali Proper Names. London: Luzac, 1960.
An invaluable reference work for finding out everything about almost anyone who appears in the Pali canon and commentaries.

Encyclopedias

(4) ____, ed. Encyclopaedia of Buddhism. See 2.5.4(12).

A major effort to compile a comprehensive Encyclopaedia of Buddhism, which unfortunately has not yet progressed very far. However, it is sure to be of some help on any topic in Buddhism beginning with A or B. It generally betrays a Theravada bent, though it tries to fight it.

Author/Title Index

Abe, Masao
 "Dogen on Buddha Nature," 2.7.14(1)
 "Zen and Nietzsche," 2.9(1)
Abhay, Thau Nhouy
 "Fêtes religieuses." See citations under Pierre S. Nginn.
Abhidharmakosa-karika, 3.2.3.2(1)
Abhiniskramanasutra, 3.2.4.1(1); 8.1.2.1(1)
Abhisamayalankara, 3.3.2.1(1)
Abhisamayalankara-nama-prajnaparamitopadesa-sastra, 3.3.1.2(1)
Acker, W. R. B.
 "Notes on Wall Paintings," 5.9.3(1)
Acton, Harold
 Famous Chinese Plays. See citations under Lewis Charles Arlington.
Adams, Charles
 A Reader's Guide to the Great Religions, 12.2(8)
Adhyardhasatika prajnaparamita, 3.3.1.1(1); 3.4.1(1)
Adikaram, E. W.
 Early History of Buddhism in Ceylon, 1.3.1(1)
Agganna Sutta, 9.1.2(1)
Agrawala, Prithiri Kumar
 Gupta Temple Architecture, 5.2.2(1); 5.2.8(1)
Agrawala, Vasudeva S.
 Gupta Art, 5.2.8(2)
 Indian Art, 5.2.1(1)
 Masterpieces of Mathura Sculpture, 5.2.4(1)
 The Wheel Flag of India, 9.3.1(1)
Ahmad, Zahiruddin
 Sino-Tibetan Relations in the Seventeenth Century, 1.14.2.2(1)
Ahn, Kye-Hyon
 "Buddha Images in Korean Tradition," 1.12.2(1)
Aiyanpan, A.
 Guide to Buddhist Antiquities, 10.2.6.3(1)
Akanuma, Chizen
 "The Triple Body of the Buddha," 8.1.3(1)
Akin Rabibhadana
 The Organization of Thai Society in the Early Bangkok Period, 1.5.2(1)
Akiyama, Terukazu
 Arts of China: Buddhist Cave Temples, 5.9.4(1); 10.8.2(1)
 Japanese Painting, 5.11.5(1)
"Akosobhya," 8.2.2(1)
Alabaster, Henry
 The Wheel of the Law, 8.1.2.1(2); 10.5(1); 10.8.1(1)
Alex, William
 Japanese Architecture, 5.11.3(1)

Altan Tobci, 1.16.2(1)
Ambatthasutta, 9.3.8(1)
Ambedkar, B. R.
 The Buddha and His Dhamma, 8.1.2.3(1)
Ames, Michael M.
 "Buddha and the Dancing Goblins," 4.1.1(1)
 "Ideological and Social Change in Ceylon," 6.2.1.1(1)
 "Magical-Animism and Buddhism," 4.1.1(2)
 "Ritual Prestations and the Structure of the Sinhalese Pantheon," 4.1.1(3)
Ames, Van Meter
 Zen and American Thought, 2.9(2)
"Amita," 8.2.2(2)
Amitayur-Dhyana-Sutra, 3.3.7.1(1); 9.3.9(1); 11.4.2(1)
Anand, Mulk Raj
 Ajanta, 5.2.6(1)
Anapanasati sutta, 11.4.3(1)
Anavataptagatha, 3.2.1.2(1); 4.2.3(1)
Anderson, Mary M.
 The Festivals of Nepal, 7.3.3(1)
Andrews, Allan
 "Nembutsu in the Chinese Pure Land Tradition," 11.7.2(1)
 The Teachings Essential for Rebirth, 2.5.8(1); 3.3.7.2(2); 9.2.2.3(1); 11.7.2(2); 11.7.4(1)
Andrews, Frederick Henry
 Catalogue of Wall Paintings. See citations under Aurel Stein.
 Descriptive Catalogue of Antiquities Recovered by Sir Aurel Stein, 1.10.2(1)
Anesaki, Masaharu
 "Asvaghosa," 8.9.1(21)
 Buddhist Art in its Relation to Buddhist Ideals, 5.11.1(1)
 "Docetism," 8.1.3(2)
 "Ethics and Morality (Buddhist)," 11.3(1)
 "The Foundation of Buddhist Culture in Japan," 6.2.1.2(1)
 History of Japanese Religion, 1.13.1(1)
 "Honen . . ., the Pietist Saint of Japanese Buddhism," 1.13.2.2(1); 8.9.4(11)
 Nichiren the Buddhist Prophet, 1.13.2.2(2); 2.5.9(1); 7.1.3(1); 8.9.4(21)
 Prince Shotoku, the Sage Statesman, 1.13.2.1(1); 8.9.4(27)
 "Shyana," 11.4.5(1)
Anguttara Nikaya, 3.2.2.1(1); 8.8(1)
Annales du Siam, 1.5.1(1)
Anuman Rajaton, Phraya
 Life and Ritual in Old Siam, 1.5.2(2); 7.3.1(1)

Anuruddha
    Abhidhammattha-sangaha, 3.2.3.3(1), (2); 9.2.3(1)
Aparimitayuh sutra, 3.3.8.4(1)
Appleton, G.
    Buddhism in Burma, 1.4.1(1)
"Arahant," 8.4(1)
Araki, James T.
    The Ballad-Drama of Medieval Japan, 5.12.2(1)
Arasaratnam, Sinnappah
    Ceylon, 1.3.1(2)
"Araya," 2.7.12(1)
Archaeological Survey of India
    Archaeological Remains, 5.2.1(2)
Archaimbault, Charles
    "Contributions à l'Étude du Rituel Funéraire Lao," 7.4.2(1)
    "La Fête du T'at à Louang Prabang," 7.3.1(2)
    "Les rites pour l'obtention de la pluie à Louang Prabang," 7.5.1(1)
    Les Trois Mondes, 3.2.4.2(4); 8.7(1). See also citations under Georges Coedes.
Ariyapala, M. B.
    Society in Mediaeval Ceylon, 1.3.2.1(1); 6.2.2.2(1); 6.2.5(1)
Arlington, Lewis Charles
    Famous Chinese Plays, 4.4(1)
Armbruster, Gisela
    Das Shigisan engi emaki, 5.11.5(2)
Armstrong, Robert Cornell
    "The Doctrine of the Tendai Sect," 2.5.6(1)
    An Introduction to Japanese Buddhist Sects, 1.13.2.2(3); 2.5.1(1); 10.9(1)
Arthapada sutra, 3.2.2.2(1)
Arthaud, Jacques
    Angkor: Art and Civilization. See citations under Bernard Groslier.
Arts Council of Ceylon
    Art and Architecture of Ceylon, 5.4.2(1)
Arya Mahabala-nama-mahayanasutra, 3.4.2(1)
Aryadeva
    Hastavalaprakarana, 3.3.2.1(2)
    Satasastra, 3.3.2.1(3)
Aryasura
    Jatakamala, 4.2.2(1); 8.1.1(1)
Asanga
    Abhidharmasamuccaya, 3.3.3.1(1)
    La Compendium de la Super-Doctrine, 2.7.5(1)
    Madhyantavibhanga, 3.3.3.1(2)
    Mahayanasamgraha, 3.3.3.1(3)
    Mahayanasutralankara, 3.3.3.1(4)
    Trisatikayah prajnaparamitayah karika Saptatih, 3.3.1.2(2); 3.3.3.1(5)
    Yogacarabhumi sastra, 3.3.3.1(6)
Ashikaga, Ensho
    "The Festival for the Spirits of the Dead in Japan," 7.4.2(2)
Ashton, Leigh
    An Introduction to the Study of Chinese Sculpture, 5.9.2(1)
Asiatica: Festschrift Friedrich Weller, 2.5.2(7)
Asoka
    Edicts, 1.2.2.2(1)
Asokavadana, 3.2.2.2(2); 4.2.3(2); 8.2.1(1); 8.9.1(12)
Asraya-prajnaptisastra, 3.2.3.2(2)
Astasahasrika Prajnaparamita, 2.7.10(1); 3.3.1.1(3); 9.3.5(1)
Astadasasahasrika prajnaparamitasutra, 3.3.1.1(2)
Asvaghosa
    Buddhacarita, 3.2.4.1(3), (4), (5); 8.1.2.1(3); 9.3.5(2)
    Saundarananda, 3.2.4.1(2); 8.8(2)
    Sutralamkara, 4.2.3(3)
Atanatiya sutta, 7.5.4(1)
Auboyer, Jeannine
    Indien und Sudostasien. See citations under Herbert Hartel
    Les Influences et les réminiscences étrangères au Kondo du Horyuji, 5.11.5(3)
    "Moudra et hasta," 11.6.4(1)
    Le trône et son symbolisme dans l'Inde ancienne, 9.3.7(1)
Audric, John
    Angkor and the Khmer Empire, 5.5.4(1)
Aung, Hla U
    "Some Aspects of Marriage," 6.2.7(1)
Aung, Shwe Zan
    "Abhidhamma Literature in Burma," 3.2.3.4(1)
    Compendium of Philosophy, 3.2.3.3(1)
    Points of Controversy, 3.2.3.1(5); 8.1.2.1(4); 8.4(2); 9.2.2.2(1); 9.2.2.4(4); 9.2.3(3); 11.4.5(7)
Avadanasataka, 3.2.2.2(3); 4.2.3(4); 8.2.1(2)
Avalokitasimha
    Dharmasamuccaya, 3.2.2.2(4)
Avatamsaka Sutra, 3.3.4.1(1); 3.3.4.1(2)
Awakawa, Yasuichi
    Zen Painting, 5.11.6(1)
Ayabe, Tsuneo
    "Dek Wat and Thai Education," 6.2.5(2)
Ayal, Eliezer B.
    "Value Systems and Economic Development in Japan and Thailand," 6.2.6(1)

Ba Han
    "Burmese Cosmogony and Cosmology," 9.2.1(1)
Ba Shih
    Essays Offered to G. H. Luce, 10.4.1(1)
Ba U
    My Burma, 1.4.2(1)
Babbitt, Irving
    Dhammapada, 3.2.2.1(4)
Bachhofer, Ludwig
    Early Indian Sculpture, 5.2.3(1)
Bacot, Jacques
    Le Bouddha, 3.3.1.1(14)
    Documents de Touen-Houang relatifs à l'histoire du Tibet, 1.14.2.1(1)
    "Drimedkundan, une version Tibétaine Dialoguée du Vessantara Jataka," 4.4.(4)
    Milarepa, 8.9.2(10)
    "Prajnaparamita-hrdaya-sutra," 3.3.1.1(14)
    "La table des présages signifiés par l'éclair," 7.6(1)
    Three Tibetan Mysteries, 4.4(2)
    La Vie de Marpa le "Traducteur," 8.9.2(9)
    Zuginima, 4.4(3)
Badaraev, Bal-Dorzhi
    "Notes on a List of the Various Editions of the Kanjur," 3.1.4(1)
Badgley, John
    "Theravada Polity of Burma," 6.2.2.3(1)
Bagchi, Prabodh Chandra
    "The Cult of the Buddhist Saddhacaryas," 8.5(1)
    "The Eight Great Caityas and Their Cult," 7.1.3(2); 10.2.1(1)
    India and Central Asia, 1.10.1(1)
    "New Materials for the Study of the Kumaratantra of Ravana," 7.5.2(1)
Bailey, H. W.
    "Kanaiska," 4.2.3(5); 8.9.1(30)
    "The pradaksina-sutra," 3.3.8.4(2); 7.1.3(3)

Author/Title Index

Bando, Shojun
    A Bibliography on Japanese Buddhism, 12.2(1)
    "Myoe's Criticism of Honen's Doctrine," 2.5.8(2)
    "Shinran's Indebtedness to T'an-luan," 2.5.8(3)
    "The Significance of the Nembutsu," 11.7.2(3)
Bannerjee, Anukul Chandra
    "Abhidharma Texts in Tibetan," 3.1.4(2)
    "Pratityasamutpada," 2.7.6(1)
    Sarvastivada Literature, 2.4.3(1); 3.1.3(1); 3.2.4(1)
    "The Vinaya pitaka--Tibetan Version," 3.2.1.4(2)
Banerjee, Jitendra Nath
    "Pratinalaksanam," 3.3.8.1(4)
    "The Webbed Fingers of Buddha," 9.3.8(2)
Banerjee, P.
    "Central Asia and its Early Buddhist and Other Remains," 1.10.2(2)
Banerji, Adris
    Origins of Early Buddhist Church Art, 5.2.1(3)
Banerji, R. D.
    Eastern School of Medieval Sculpture, 5.2.8(3)
Bankei Zenji Goroku, 3.3.6.2(1)
Bapat, Purushottam Vishvanath
    "The Arthapada sutra," 3.2.2.2(1)
    2500 Years of Buddhism, 1.2.1(1); 2.4.1(1); 2.5.1(2); 6.2.5(3); 8.1.2.3(2); 8.9.2(3); 8.9.3(64); 10.1.1(9)
    Vimuktimarga Dhutaguna-Nirdesa, 11.4.2(10)
Barborka, Geoffrey A.
    H. P. Blavatsky, Tibet and Tulku, 2.9(3)
Bareau, André
    L'Absolu en Philosophie Bouddhique, 2.7.7(1)
    "Le Bouddhisme Indien," 1.2.1(2)
    "La Construction et le culte du Stupa," 7.1.3(4); 9.3.6(1)
    "La Date du Nirvana," 8.1.2.3(3)
    "Les idées sous-jacentes aux pratiques cultuelles bouddhiques dans le Cambodge actuel," 7.1.1(1)
    "La Jeunesse du Bouddha dans les sutrapitaka et les Vinayapitaka Anciens," 8.1.2.3(4)
    "Les Origines du Sariputrabhidharmasastra," 3.2.3.4(2)
    "Le Parinirvana du Bouddha et la naissance de la religion bouddhique," 8.1.2.4(1)
    Les Premiers Conciles Bouddhiques, 2.4.2(1)
    "Quelques ermitages et centres de méditation bouddhiques au Cambodge," 6.1.1(1)
    Recherches sur la Biographie du Bouddha dans les Sutrapitaka et les Vinayapitaka Anciens, 8.1.2.3(5); 8.8(3)
    Les religions de l'Inde, 1.2.1(3); 3.1.1(1)
    Les Sectes bouddhiques du petit véhicule, 2.4.1(2)
    "The Superhuman Personality of the Buddha," 8.1.2.2(1)
    "Trois traités sur les sectes bouddhiques," 2.4.1(3)
    La vie et l'organisation des communautés bouddhiques modernes de Ceylan, 6.1.2(1); 7.2.2(1); 7.2.6(1)
Barnett, Lionel David
    The Path of Light, 3.3.2.1(26)
Barrett, Douglas
    Sculptures from Amaravati in the British Museum, 5.2.7(1)
Barthoux, Jules
    Les Fouilles de Hadda, 5.2.5(1)
Barua, Benimadhab
    Asoka and His Inscriptions, 8.9.1(13)
    Bharhut, 5.2.4(2)
    "Buddhakhetta in the Apadana," 9.2.4(1); 11.7.4(2)
    "Faith in Buddhism," 11.2(1)
    Gaya and Buddha-Gaya, 5.2.4(3); 10.2.3(1)
    The History of Pre-Buddhist Indian Philosophy, 2.2(1)
    "Old Shrines at Bodh-Gaya," 10.2.3(2)
    "Pratitya-samutpada as Basic Concept," 2.7.6(2)
    "Stupa and Tomb," 8.1.2.4(2); 9.3.6(2)
Barua, Dipak Kumar
    An Analytical Study of Four Nikayas, 3.2.2.4(1); 4.2.1(1)
    "Buddhism and Lay Worshippers," 6.1.2(2)
    "Origin of State: A Buddhist Approach," 6.2.2.1(1)
    "Secular Discourses of Buddha to the Laity," 6.1.2(3)
    Viharas in Ancient India, 10.2.1(2)
Barua, Promode Ranjan
    Early Buddhism and the Brahmanical Doctrines, 2.2(2)
Barua, Rabindra Bijay
    "The Marriage Ceremonies of the Buddhists," 7.4.1(1)
Baruch, Willy
    "Le cinquante-deuxième chapitre du mJans-blun," 4.2.3(6)
    "Maitreya d'après les sources de Serinde," 8.3.4(1)
Basham, Arthur Llewellyn
    History and Doctrines of the Ajivikas, 2.2(3)
    Papers on the Date of Kaniska, 8.9.1(31)
    "Society and State in Theravada Buddhism," 6.2.2.1(2)
    The Wonder That Was India, 1.2.1(4)
Bawden, Charles R.
    The Jebtsundamba Khutukhtus of Urga, 1.16.1(1)
Beal, Samuel
    A Catena of Buddhist Scriptures from the Chinese, 3.2.1.2(7); 3.3.8.2(9); 3.5(1); 7.2.2(2); 7.2.3(1); 7.8(1); 8.1.2.1(24); 8.3.2(1); 9.2.1(2); 9.2.2.3(2)
    Dhammapada, with Accompanying Narratives, 3.2.2.2(5)
    The Fo-sho-hing-tsan-king, 3.2.4.1(3); 8.1.2.1(5); 8.1.2.4(3); 9.3.5(2)
    The Romantic Legend of Sakya Buddha, 3.2.4.1(1); 8.1.2.1(1)
    Si-Yu-Ki: Buddhist Records of the Western World, 8.9.3(39); 10.1.1(1)
    "The Sutra of Forty-two Sections," 3.3.8.2(9)
    "Text and Commentary of the Memorial of Sakya Buddha Tathagata by Wong Phu," 8.1.2.1(6)
    "Vajrachchedika, . . . or Diamond Sutra," 3.3.1(24)
Beauce, Thierry de
    "Le Cambodge: Bouddhisme et développement," 1.6.2(1); 6.2.2.8(1)
Beautrix, Pierre
    Bibliographie du Bouddhisme, 3.1.1(2); 12.2(2)
    Bibliographie du Bouddhisme Zen, 12.2(3)
    Bibliographie de la Littérature Prajnaparamita, 3.3.1.3(1); 12.2(4)
Bechert, Heinz
    "Buddhism and Mass Politics in Burma and Ceylon," 6.2.2.2(2); 6.2.2.3(2)
    Buddhismus, Staat und Gesellschaft, 6.2.1.1(2); 12.2(5)
    "Religionssoziologie und Struktur des südasiatischen Buddhismus," 6.2.1.1(3)
    "Sangha, State, Society, 'Nation,'" 6.2.1.1(4)
    "Some Remarks on the Kathina Rite," 7.1.2(1)
    "Theravada Buddhist Sangha," 6.1.1(2)

Belenitskii, Aleksandr Markovich
  Central Asia, 1.10.1(2)
Bell, Charles Alfred
  Portrait of the Dalai Lama, 1.14.2.3(1); 8.9.2(5)
  The Religion of Tibet, 1.14.1(1); 3.1.4(3); 6.2.2.7(1)
Bellah, Robert Neelly
  Religion and Progress in Modern Asia, 6.2.1.1(38)
  Tokugawa Religion, 1.13.2.3(1); 6.2.2.6(1); 6.2.6(2)
Bendall, Cecil
  "Bodhisattva-Bhumi," 3.3.3.1(6)
  Siksha-samuccaya, 3.3.2.1(30)
Benisti, Mireille
  Evolution du style indien d'Amaravati. See citations under Philippe Stern.
Benveniste, Emile
  "Avalokitesvarasya namastasataka stotra," 8.3.2(2)
  "Notes sur le fragment sogdien," 3.3.8.2(3); 11.4.2(2)
  Textes Sogdiens, 3.3.8.4(3)
  Vessantara Jataka, 4.2.2(12); 8.1.1(15)
Beny, Roloff
  Island Ceylon, 5.4.1(1)
Benz, Ernst
  Buddhism or Communism, 2.8(1); 6.1.4(1)
Bernard, Theos
  Land of a Thousand Buddhas, 5.6(1); 10.1.3(1)
Bernier, Ronald M.
  The Temples of Nepal, 5.3(1)
Berry, Thomas Sterling
  Christianity and Buddhism, 2.9(4)
Berval, René de
  Kingdom of Laos, 6.1.1(22)
  Présence du Bouddhisme, 1.5.1(6); 1.7.2(5); 1.8.2(3); 1.9.1(2); 1.11.2.4(2); 1.17(1); 3.1.6(6); 3.3.6.4(1); 5.1.1(4)
  Présence du Cambodge, 1.6.2(13); 6.1.1(18)
  Présence du Royaume Lao, 1.7.1(1)
Bethel, Dayle M.
  Makiguchi, 6.2.5(4)
Beyer, Stephan
  The Buddhist Experience, 3.3.2.1(18); 3.4.2(12), (13); 3.5(2); 7.5.3(1); 11.1(1); 11.3(2); 11.4.1(1); 11.4.2(6), (9); 11.6.1(1); 11.7.3(1)
  The Cult of Tara: Magic and Ritual in Tibet, 5.6(2); 7.1.1(2); 7.8(2); 8.3.3(1); 9.2.2.1(1); 11.6.1(2); 11.6.2(1); 11.6.3(1); 11.6.4(2)
  "Manual of the Spontaneous Great Symbol," 3.4.2(11)
  "The Process of Generation of the Wishing Gem," 3.4.2(13)
  "The Worship of the Fierce Lord," 3.4.2(12)
Bezacier, Louis
  L'Art vietnamien, 5.5.5(1)
Bhadanta Santi, Bhiksu
  "Fa Fu T'i Hsin Chin Lun," 2.7.14(2)
Bhagvat, D. N.
  Early Buddhist Jurisprudence, 6.1.3(1); 6.2.7(2)
Bhaisajyagurusutra, 3.3.8.1(1); 7.8(3); 8.2.2(3)
Bhandarkar, D. R.
  B. C. Law Volume, 1.2.2.3(6); 2.7.1(12); 2.7.6(2); 3.1.5(4); 11.3(8)
Bharati, Agehananda
  "Pilgrimage Sites and Indian Civilization," 10.2.1(3)
  "Sakta and Vajrayana," 11.6.1(4)

The Tantric Tradition, 2.6.1(1); 11.6.1(3); 11.6.3(2)
Bhattacharya, Ajit Ranjan
  "Brahman of Sankara and Sunyata of Madhyamikas," 2.7.8(1)
Bhattacharya, B.
  Nispannayogarali, 11.6.2(2)
Bhattacharya, B. C.
  The History of Sarnath, 10.2.4(1)
Bhattacharya, H.
  The Cultural Heritage of India, 8.5(4)
Bhattacharya, Kamaleswar
  L'Atman-Brahman dans le Bouddhisme Ancien, 2.7.4(1)
  "The Dialectical Method of Nagarjuna," 3.3.2.1(19)
Bhattacharya, Karuna
  "Sankara's Criticism of Nagarjuna," 2.5.3(1)
Bhattacharya, N. N.
  "Brahmanical, Buddhist and Jain Cosmography," 9.2.1(3)
Bhattacharya, Tarapada
  The Bodgaya Temple, 5.2.4(4); 10.2.3(3)
  The Canons of Indian Art, 5.2.2(2)
Bhattacharya, Vidhushekhara
  "Evolution of Vijnanavada," 2.5.4(1)
Bhattacharyya, Benoytosh
  "The Cult of Bhutadharma," 7.8(4); 8.6(1)
  Guhyasamaja Tantra, 3.4.1(2)
  "Iconography of Heruka," 8.1.2.4(4)
  The Indian Buddhist Iconography, 5.2.8(4); 8.3.1(1)
  An Introduction to Buddhist Esoterism, 2.6.1(2); 5.2.8(5); 11.6.3(3)
  "Manjughosa," 8.3.5(1)
  Sadhanamala, 11.6.1(5)
  Two Vajrayana Works, 3.4.4(1)
Bhattasali, Nalini Kanta
  Introduction of the Buddhist and Brahmanical Sculptures in the Dacca Museum, 5.2.8(6)
Bhavasamkrantisutra, 3.3.2.1(4)
Bhavaviveka
  Karatalaratna, 3.3.2.1(5)
  Madhyamarthasamgraha, 2.7.9(1); 3.3.2.1(6)
Bibliographie bouddhique, 5.1.1; 12.2(6)
Bibliography of Asian Studies, 12.2(7)
Bigandet, Paul A.
  The Life or Legend of Gaudama the Buddha of the Burmese, 8.1.2.1(7)
Binsted, G. C.
  "Life in a Khalkha Steppe Lamasery," 6.2.3(1)
Binyon, Laurence
  The Spirit of Man in Asian Art, 5.1.4(1)
Bischoff, F. A.
  Arya Mahabala-nama-mahayanasutra, 3.4.2(1)
  "Preliminary Report on a Mongol Buddhist Text on Christian Teaching," 1.16.1(2)
Bitard, Pierre
  "Le monde du sorcier au Cambodge," 7.5.1(2)
  "Ordination de deux dignitaires bouddhiques." See citations under Pierre-Bernard Lafont.
Bivar, David
  "The Nomad Empires and the Expansion of Buddhism," 1.10.2(3)
Blacker, Carmen
  "Le Soka Gakkai japonais," 6.2.2.6(2)
Blaser, Werner
  Japanese Temples and Tea-houses, 5.11.3(2)
Bleeker, C. J.
  Historia Religionum, 1.1(9)
  Initiation, 7.2.1(6)

Bloch, T.
    "Notes on Bodh Gaya," 10.2.3(4)
Blofeld, John Eaton Calthorpe
    The Jewel in the Lotus, 10.1.2(1)
    Mahayana Buddhism in Southeast Asia, 6.1.4(2); 7.2.2(3)
    The Tantric Mysticism of Tibet, 2.6.1(3); 2.7.14(3); 9.3.2(1); 11.6.1(6)
    The Wan-ling Record, 3.3.6.2(7); 11.4.8.1(2)
    The Zen Teaching of Hui Hai, 3.3.6.2(9); 11.4.8.1(1)
Bloom, Alfred
    The Life of Shinran Shonin, 1.13.2.2(4); 8.9.4(25)
    Shinran's Gospel of Pure Grace, 2.5.8(4); 11.7.1(1); 11.7.4(3)
Bloss, Lowell W.
    "The Buddha and the Naga," 4.1.1(4)
Blyth, Reginald Horace
    Haiku, 4.3(1)
    Zen in English Literature and Oriental Classics, 2.9(5)
    Zen and Zen Classics, 2.5.7(1); 3.3.6.1(11); 11.4.8.2(3)
Bock, Carl
    Temples and Elephants, 1.5.2(3); 10.1.4(1)
Bode, Mabel Haynes
    "The Legend of Ratthapala," 4.2.3(7); 8.8(4)
    The Pali Literature of Burma, 3.1.2(1)
    "Women Leaders of the Buddhist Reformation," 6.1.3(2)
Bohner, Hermann
    "Kobo Daishi," 1.13.2.2(5); 8.9.4(16)
Boisselier, Jean
    Ba Shin, 4.2.2(11)
    Le Cambodge, 10.6(1)
    La Statuaire du Champa, 1.8.2(1); 5.5.5(2)
    La Statuaire khmère, 5.5.4(2)
Bolle, Kees W.
    "Devotion and Tantra," 2.6.1(14)
Bongard-Levin, G. M.
    "Buddhist Studies in the USSR," 1.10.2(4)
"Bosatsukai," 8.3.1(2)
Bosch, Frederik David Kan
    The Golden Germ, 5.1.3(1); 9.3.3(1); 9.3.4(1)
    India Antiqua, 1.14.1(16)
Bose, Phanindra Nath
    The Indian Teachers in China, 1.11.2.1(1)
Boston Museum of Fine Arts
    The Arts of India and Nepal, 5.1.4(2)
Bourlet, A.
    Funérailles chez les Thay," 7.4.2(3)
Boutsavath, Vongsavanh
    "Lao Popular Buddhism and Community Development," 6.2.3(2)
Bowers, Faubion
    Theater in the East, 5.12.1(1)
Bowie, Theodore
    The Arts of Thailand, 5.5.3(1)
    The Sculpture of Thailand, 5.5.3(2)
Bownas, Geoffrey
    Japanese Rainmaking and Other Folk Practices, 7.3.2(1); 7.5.1(3)
Boyd, James W.
    "Symbols of Evil in Buddhism," 9.2.2.4(1); 9.3.5(3)
Boyer, Martha
    "Omizutori," 7.1.4(1); 7.3.2(2)
Brandon, James E.
    Theater in Southeast Asia, 5.12.1(2)

Brazell, Karen
    The Confessions of Lady Nijo, 4.5(1)
Brear, Douglas
    "Early Assumptions in Western Buddhist Studies," 2.9(6)
Brett, Cecil
    "The Priest-Emperor Concept in Japanese Political Thought," 6.2.2.6(3)
Brewster, E. H.
    The Life of Gotama the Buddha, 8.1.2.3(6)
Briessen, Fritz van
    The Way of the Brush, 5.9.3(2)
Briggs, Lawrence Palmer
    "Dvaravati, The Most Ancient Kingdom of Siam," 1.5.2(4)
    "The Khmer Empire and the Malay Peninsula," 1.6.2(2)
    "The Syncretism of Religions in Southeast Asia," 1.6.1(1)
Brodbeck, Jean-Claude
    "L'Intronisation du Prince Héritier de Thailand," 7.7(1)
Brodrick, Alan Houghton
    Little Vehicle, 1.6.2(3); 1.7.2(1)
Brohm, John
    "Buddhism and Animism in a Burmese Village," 4.1.2(1)
Bromase, Richard
    Tibetan Yoga, 11.6.1(7)
Brogh, John
    "Comments on the Third-Century Shan-shan," 1.10.2(5)
    "The Language of the Buddhist Sanskrit Texts," 3.1.3(2)
    "Legends of Khotan and Nepal," 4.2.4(1)
    Nepalese Buddhist Rituals, 7.4.1(2)
Brown, Percy
    Indian Architecture, 5.2.2(3)
Brown, R. Grant
    "The Pre-Buddhist Religion of the Burmese," 4.1.2(2)
Bruce, Helen
    Nine Temples of Bangkok, 5.5.3(3)
Bryner, Edna
    Thirteen Tibetan Tankas, 5.6(3); 8.1.1(2)
The Buddha's Tooth Relic Pagoda, 8.1.2.4(5)
Buddhadasa, Bhikkhu
    Toward the Truth, 2.8(2)
Buddhadatta, A. P.
    Concise Pali-English Dictionary, 12.1(1)
Buddhadhyana-samadhi-sagara-sutra, 3.3.8.2(3); 11.4.2(2)
Buddhaghosa
    Atthasalini, 3.2.3.3(3); 3.2.3.4(3); 9.2.2.1(2)
    Kathavatthuppakarana-Atthakatha, 3.2.3.3(4)
    Paramatthajotika, 3.2.2.3(1)
    Samantapasadika, 3.2.1.3(1)
    Visuddhimagga, 3.2.4.2(1); 11.1(2); 11.3(3); 11.4.2(3); 11.4.3(2), (3); 11.4.6(1); 11.4.7(1)
Buddhaghosuppatti, 8.9.1(26); 8.9.5(2)
Buddharakkhita
    Jinalankara, 8.1.2.1(8)
Buddhavamsa, 3.2.2.1(2)
Buddhist Committee of Inquiry
    The Betrayal of Buddhism, 1.3.2.2(1); 6.2.1.1(5); 6.2.2(3)
Bugault, Guy
    La notion de "Prajna" ou de sapience selon les perspectives du "Mahayana," 11.4.5(2); 11.4.7(2)

Buhot, Jean
   Chinese and Japanese Art, 5.8(1); 5.10(1)
   Histoire des arts du Japon, 5.11.2(2)
Bukkokuji Temple, 5.10(2)
Bulling, Anneliese
   "Buddhist Temples in the T'ang Period," 5.9.3(3); 10.8.1(2)
Bunker, Emma C.
   "Early Chinese Representations of Vimala-kirti," 5.9.2(2)
Bunnag, Jane
   Buddhist Monk, Buddhist Layman?, 6.1.2(4); 7.2.1(1)
Burckhardt, Titus
   Sacred Art in East and West, 5.1.2(1)
Burgess, James
   The Buddhist Stupas of Amaravati and Jaggayyapeta, 5.2.7(2); 10.2.6.3(2)
   The Cave Temples of India. See citations under James Fergusson.
   Notes on the Bauddha Rock-temples of Ajanta, 5.2.6(2)
   Report on the Buddhist Cave Temples and Their Inscriptions, 5.2.6(3); 10.2.1(4)
Buribhand, Luang Boribal
   "Buddhism in Thailand," 1.5.1(2)
Burlingame, Eugene Watson
   Buddhist Legends, 3.2.2.3(2); 4.2.3(13)
   The Grateful Elephant and Other Stories, 4.2.2(2)
Burnouf, Eugène
   Le Lotus de la Bonne Loi, 3.3.5.1(3); 9.2.2.1(3); 9.3.8(3)
Burr, Angela
   "Religious Institutional Diversity, Social Structure and Conceptual Unity," 6.2.3(3)
Bush, Richard C.
   Religion in Communist China, 1.11.2.4(1)
Bussagli, Mario
   5000 Years of Indian Art, 5.2.1(4)
   Painting of Central Asia, 5.7(1)
Bu-ston Rin-chen-grub-pa
   History of Buddhism (Chos-'byung), 1.2.1(5); 1.14.1(2); 8.1.2.1(9); 8.9.1(5), (7), (27), (28), (29), (37), (46), (49); 9.1.3(1); 9.1.5(1)
"Butsudo," 9.2.4(2)
Buttinger, Joseph
   Vietnam: A Political History, 1.8.2(2)
Butwell, Richard A.
   U Nu of Burma, 1.4.2(2); 8.9.5(10)
Bya chos rin-chen 'phren-ba, 4.2.3(8)
Byles, Marie Beauzeville
   Journey into Burmese Silence, 11.4.4(1)

Cadière, Leopold Michel
   Croyances et pratiques religieuses des vietnamiennes, 1.8.1(1); 4.1.2(3)
Cady, John
   Political Institutions of Old Burma, 6.2.2.3(3)
Cahill, James
   Chinese Painting, 5.9.3(4)
Cakkavatti sihanada sutta, 9.1.1(1); 9.1.4(1); 9.3.1(2); 9.3.7(2)
Camadevivamsa, 9.1.5(2)
Campbell, Alexander
   "Education in Burma," 6.2.5(5)
Candrakirti
   Madhyamakavatara, 3.3.2.1(7)
   Prasannapada Madhyamakavrtti, 3.3.2.1(8)
Cariya pitaka, 3.2.2.1(3); 8.1.1(3); 11.5(1)

Carpenter, Frederic Ives
   Emerson and Asia, 2.9(7)
Carpentier, Jarl
   "Notes on the Padariya or Rummindei Inscription," 10.2.2(1)
Carrasco, Pedro
   Land and Polity in Tibet, 6.2.2.7(2); 6.2.6(3)
Carter, Dagny
   Four Thousand Years of China's Art, 5.9.1(1)
Carter, John Ross
   "Dharma as a Religious Concept," 2.4.3(2)
Carus, Paul
   Treatise of the Exalted One on Response and Retribution, 4.2.4(17)
Casal, U. A.
   "The Saintly Kobo Daishi in Popular Lore," 8.9.4(17)
Cassinelli, C. W.
   A Tibetan Principality, 1.14.2.2(2); 6.2.2.7(3)
Castile, Rand
   The Way of Tea, 5.11.8(1)
Catholic Church, Secretarius pro non-Christianis
   Towards the Meeting with Buddhism, 1.2.1(6)
"Chakuji," 11.6.2(3)
Chalmers, Robert
   Buddha's Teachings, 3.2.2.1(23)
   Further Dialogues of the Buddha, 3.2.2.1(15)
Chamberlayne, John H.
   "The Development of Kuan Yin," 8.3.2(3)
Chan, Wing-tsit
   The Great Asian Religions, 1.13.1(9)
   The Platform Scripture, 3.3.6.1(4)
   Religious Trends in Modern China, 6.2.1.2(2)
   A Source Book in Chinese Philosophy, 2.5.1(3)
   "Wang Yang-ming's Criticism of Buddhism," 6.2.1.2(3)
Chand, Emcee
   Thai Monumental Bronzes, 5.5.3(4)
Chandra, Lokesh
   "Buddhism in Mongolia," 1.16.2(2)
   "A Conspectus of the Mongolian Tanjur," 3.1.6(1)
   Sanskrit Bijas and Mantras in Japan. See citation under Raghu Vira.
Chandra, Pramod
   Stone Sculpture in the Allahabad Museum, 5.2.3(2)
Chandra, Pratap
   "Was Early Buddhism Influenced by the Upanishads?," 2.2(4)
Chandra, Ramprasad
   The Beginnings of Art in Eastern India, 5.2.4(5)
Ch'ang-ch'un
   The Travels of an Alchemist, 1.16.1(3)
Chang, Chung-yuan
   Original Teachings of Ch'an Buddhism, 3.3.6.1(2)
Chang, Garma C. C.
   The Buddhist Teaching of Totality, 2.5.5(1); 3.3.1.2(4); 3.3.4.1(1), (3), (4), (5); 3.3.4.2(1); 8.9.3(10), (14), (29), (83); 11.4.9(1)
   The Hundred Thousand Songs of Milarepa, 4.3(12); 8.9.2(11)
   The Practice of Zen, 11.4.8.1(3); 11.4.8.3(1)
   Teachings of Tibetan Yoga, 11.6.1(8)
Chang K'e-ch'iang
   "Atisa," 8.9.2(1)
Chao P'u-ch'u
   "Buddhism in China," 1.11.2.4(2); 6.1.4(3)
Chao Wei-pang
   "Secret Religious Societies in North China," 4.1.3(1)

Chao-lun, 3.3.6.1(1); 3.3.8.2(4)
Chapelier, George
"Lao Popular Buddhism and Community Development."
See citations under Vongsavanh Boutsavath.
Chapin, Helen B.
"The Ch'an Master Pu-tai," 8.3.4(2); 8.9.3(66)
"A Little Known Temple," 5.10(3)
A Long Roll of Buddhist Images, 5.9.3(5)
"Yunnanese Images of Avalokitesvara," 8.3.2(4)
Chapman, F. Spencer
Lhasa: The Holy City, 5.6(4)
Charters, Ann
Kerouac: A Biography, 1.17(2); 2.9(8)
Chatterjee, Ashok Kumar
The Yogacara Idealism, 2.5.4(2)
Chatterjee, H.
"Pratityasamutpada," 2.7.6(3)
Chatterjee, Sris Chandra
Magadha Architecture and Culture, 5.2.2(4)
Chatterji, Bijan Raj
Indian Cultural Influence in Cambodia, 1.6.2(4)
Chatterji, Durgacharan
"Hetucakranirnaya," 3.3.3.1(11)
Chatterji, S. K.
"Buddhist Survivals in Bengal," 1.2.2.4(1)
Chattopadhyaya, Alaka
Atisa and Tibet, 1.14.2.2(3); 8.9.2(2)
Chaudhury, Binayendranath
Buddhist Centers in Ancient India, 10.2.1(5)
"Pataliputra: Its Importance to the History of
Buddhism," 1.2.2.4(2)
Chavannes, Edouard
Cinq Cents Contes et Apologues Extraits du
Tripitaka Chinois, 4.2.3(9)
"Gunavarman," 8.9.3(34)
"Les Inscriptions Chinoises de Bodh-gaya,"
8.1.3(3); 10.2.3(5)
Les religieux éminents qui allèrent chercher la
loi dans les pays d'occident, 10.1.1(2)
"Les Seize Arhat protecteurs de la Loi." See
citations under Sylvain Levi.
Six monuments de la sculpture chinoise, 5.9.2(3)
"Voyage de Song-Yun," 1.2.2.3(1); 8.9.3(12),
(79); 10.1.1(3)
Chemparathy, George
"Two Early Buddhist Refutations of the Existence
of Isvara," 9.1.2(2)
Ch'en, Kenneth Kuan Sheng
"Anti-Buddhist Propaganda During the Nan-ch'ao,"
1.11.2.2(1); 6.2.2.5(1)
"A propos the Mendhaka Story," 4.2.3(10)
Buddhism in China, 1.11.1(1); 3.1.5(1); 4.1.3(2);
7.3.2(3); 10.8.2(2)
Buddhism: The Light of Asia, 1.1(1); 2.8(3)
The Chinese Transformation of Buddhism,
1.11.1(2); 6.2.1.2(4); 6.2.2.5(2); 6.2.5(6);
6.2.6(5)
"The Economic Background of the Hui-ch'ang
Suppression of Buddhism," 1.11.2.3(1);
6.2.6(4)
"Filial Piety in Chinese Buddhism," 6.2.3(4)
"Mahayana Buddhism and Chinese Culture,"
1.11.1(3); 6.2.1.2(5)
"Neo-Taoism and the Prajna School during the
Wei and Chin Dynasties," 1.11.2.2(2)
"The Role of Buddhist Monasteries in T'ang
China," 1.11.2.3(2)
"The Sale of Monk Certificates During the Sung
Dynasty," 1.11.2.3(3)

"A Study of the Svagata Story," 4.2.3(11)
"The Tibetan Tripitaka," 3.1.4(4)
Chen, Shou-yi
Chinese Literature: A Historical Introduction,
4.2.4(2)
Chen, Tsu-lung
"Table de concordance des numérotages,"
5.9.4(2)
La vie et les oeuvres de Woutchen, 1.10.2(6);
8.9.3(88)
Cheney, George
The Pre-revolutionary Culture of Outer Mongolia,
6.2.1.2(6)
Chih I
T'ung Meng Chih Kuan, 11.4.2(4); 11.4.9(2)
Ching-t'u Shih-i-lun, 2.5.8(5); 3.3.7.2(1)
Chogyam Trungpa
The Tibetan Book of the Dead. See citations
under Francesca Freemantle.
Chotisukharat, Sanguan
"Supernatural Beliefs and Practices in Chungmai,"
4.1.2(4)
Chou, Hsiang-Kuang
A History of Chinese Buddhism, 1.11.1(4)
T'ai Hsu: His Life and Teaching, 8.9.3(77)
Chou, Ta Kuan
Notes on the Customs of Cambodia, 1.6.2(5)
Chou Yi-liang
"Tantrism in China," 1.11.2.3(4); 2.6.2(1);
8.9.3(2), (72), (85)
Chowdury, R. P.
"Interpretation of the 'Anatta' Doctrine of
Buddhism," 2.7.4(2)
Christy, Arthur
The Orient in American Transcendentalism,
1.17(3); 2.9(9)
Ch'uan-teng lu, 3.3.6.1(2)
Chula, (Prince)
Lords of Life: The Paternal Monarchy of
Bangkok, 1.5.2(5)
Chulalongkorn the Great, 1.5.2(6); 8.9.5(7)
Chun, Shin-yong
Buddhist Culture in Korea, 1.12.1(1); 6.2.1.2(7);
8.9.6(1)
Clark, Charles Allen
Religions of Old Korea, 1.12.1(2); 7.1.4(2)
Cleaves, Francis Woodman
"The Bodistw-a cari-a awatar-un Tayilbur,"
3.3.2.1(9)
Cleveland, Harlan
The Ethics of Power. See citations under
Harold D. Lasswell.
Cochrane, Wilbur
"Shans and Buddhism of the Northern Canon,"
1.4.2(3)
Codrington, Kenneth de Burgh
Ancient India, 5.2.1(5)
Coedes, Georges
Angkor, 5.5.4(3); 10.6(2)
Les Collections archaeologiques du Musée
National de Bangkok, 5.5.3(5)
"Le culte de la rayauté divinisée," 7.7(2)
"Dhammakaya," 8.1.3(4)
"Documents sur l'histoire politique et
religieuse du Laos occidental," 1.7.1(2);
9.1.5(2)
The Indianized States of Southeast Asia,
1.8.1(2); 1.9.1(1)
"Note sur les ouvrages Palis composés en Pays
Thai," 3.1.2(2)

The Making of South East Asia, 1.4.1(2); 1.5.1(3); 1.6.1(2); 1.7.1(3); 1.8.1(3)
Pour mieux comprendre Angkor, 9.3.7(3)
"Une recension palie des Annales d'Ayuthya," 1.5.2(7); 9.1.5(12)
"Le Royaume de Çrivijaya," 1.9.2(1)
"The Traibhumikath," 9.2.1(5)
Les Trois Mondes, 3.2.4.2(4); 8.7(1); 9.1.2(3); 9.1.3(2); 9.2.1(4); 9.2.2.1(4); 9.2.2.3(3); 9.2.2.4(2); 9.2.3(2)
"The Twenty-five Hundredth Anniversary of the Buddha," 9.1.3(3)
"Une roue de la loi," 9.3.1(3)

Cohen, Jerome Alan
China Today and Her Ancient Treasures. See citations under Joan Lebold Cohen.

Cohen, Joan Lebold
China Today and Her Ancient Treasures, 5.9.1(2)

Cohn, William
Chinese Painting, 5.9.3(6)

Collis, Maurice
The Land of the Great Image, 1.4.2(4)

Combaz, Gisbert
"L'évolution du stupa en Asie," 5.2.2(5); 9.3.6(3)
L'Inde et l'Orient classique, 5.1.2(2)
"Masques et dragons en Asie," 9.2.2.5(1)

Condominas, Georges
"Notes sur le Bouddhisme populaire en milieu rural lao," 1.7.2(2); 6.2.3(5)

Conze, Edward
Abhisamayalankara, 3.3.1.2(1); 3.3.2.1(1)
Astasahasrika Prajnaparamita, 8.1.2.2(2); 8.1.2.4(6); 8.3.1(3); 9.3.5(1)
"The Blessed Perfection of Wisdom," 3.3.1.1(4)
The Buddha's Law Among the Birds, 4.2.3(8)
Buddhism: Its Essence and Development, 1.1(2); 2.7.2(1); 2.7.8(2); 2.7.12(2); 6.1.2(5)
Buddhist Meditation, 2.7.5(2); 3.4.1(5); 11.4.1(2); 11.4.4(2); 11.4.5(3); 11.4.7(3)
"Buddhist Philosophy and Its European Parallels," 2.9(10)
"Buddhist Prajna and Greek Sophia," 2.9(11)
Buddhist Scriptures, 8.1.2.3(7); 8.3.4(7); 9.1.4(2); 11.3(4)
Buddhist Texts Through the Ages, 3.3.1.1(19); 3.4.4(4); 3.5(3); 11.6.1(9)
Buddhist Thought in India, 2.1(1); 2.3(1); 2.4.3(3); 2.4.4(1); 2.5.1(4); 2.5.2(1); 2.5.3(2); 2.5.4(3); 2.7.3(1); 2.7.4(3); 2.7.6(4); 2.7.7(2); 2.7.8(3); 2.7.10(2); 2.7.13(1); 11.4.3(4); 11.5(2)
Buddhist Wisdom Books, 3.3.1.1(11)
"The Diamond Sutra," 3.3.1.1(22)
The Gilgit Manuscript, 3.3.1.1(2)
"The Heart Sutra," 3.3.1.1(11); 4.2.1(4)
"The 108 Names of Perfect Wisdom," 3.3.1.1(16); 3.4.2(14)
"The Ontology of the Prajnaparamita," 2.7.7(3)
"Perfect Wiscom and the Five Bodhisattvas," 3.3.1.1(10)
"The Perfection of Wiscom for Kausika," 3.3.1.1(5)
The Perfection of Wisdom in Eight Thousand Lines, 3.3.1.1(3)
"The Perfection of Wisdom in a Few Words," 3.3.1.1(21)
"The Perfection of Wisdom in 500 Lines," 3.3.1.1(8)
"The Perfection of Wisdom in 150 Lines," 3.3.1.1(1); 3.4.1(1)
"The Perfection of Wisdom in 700 Lines," 3.3.1.1(18)
The Prajnaparamita Literature, 2.5.2(2); 3.3.1.3(2)
"Prasastrasena's Arya-prajnaparamita-hrdaya-tika," 3.3.1.2(7)
"The Questions of Suvikrantavikramin," 3.3.1.1(20)
"Satasahasrika prajnaparamita-sutra," 3.3.1.1(19)
The Short Prajnaparamita Texts, 3.3.1.1(1)
"The Sutra on Perfect Wisdom," 3.3.1.1(7)
Thirty Years of Buddhist Studies, 2.5.1(5); 2.9(12)
"The 25 Doors to Perfect Wisdom," 3.3.1.1(9); 3.4.1(6)
"Verses on the Perfection of Wisdom," 3.3.1.1(17)

Cooke, Gerald
"Traditional Buddhist Sects and Modernization in Japan," 1.13.2.4(1)

Coomaraswamy, Ananda Kentish
The Arts and Crafts of India and Ceylon, 5.1.4(3)
Buddha and the Gospel of Buddhism, 1.2.1(7)
"The Buddha's Cuda, Hair, Usnisa, Crown," 9.3.8(4)
Christian and Oriental Philosophy of Art, 5.1.2(3)
"Early Indian Architecture," 5.2.2(6)
Elements of Buddhist Iconography, 5.2.3(3); 9.3.1(4); 9.3.3(2)
History of Indian and Indonesian Art, 5.1.4(4)
Introduction to Indian Art, 5.2.1(6)
"Mudra, mudda," 11.6.4(3)
The Origin of the Buddha Image, 5.2.3(4)
"Rebirth and Omniscience in Pali Buddhism," 2.7.1(1)
La sculpture de Bodhgaya, 5.2.4(6)
Les sculptures de Bharhut, 5.2.4(7); 10.2.6.1(1)
The Transformation of Nature in Art, 5.1.3(2)
Yaksas, 5.2.3(5); 9.2.2.5(2)

Cooper, Michael
They Came to Japan, 10.1.5(1)

Corea, J. C. A.
"One Hundred Years of Education in Ceylon," 6.2.5(7)

Corless, Roger
"Monotheistic Elements in Early Pure Land Buddhism," 2.5.8(6)

Cosgi, Odsir
Bodistw-a cari-a Awatar-un Tayilbur, 3.3.2.1(9)

Cousins, L.
Buddhist Studies in Honor of I. B. Horner, 1.2.2.4(11); 1.4.2(9); 2.5.4(10); 3.1.2(8); 3.3.1.2(7); 3.3.8.4(2); 8.1.2.2(6), (7); 9.2.5.(5)

Cowell, E. B.
Buddhist Mahayana Texts, 3.3.1.1(12), (23); 3.3.7.1(1), (2), (3); 9.3.9(1); 11.4.2(1); 11.7.4(10)
"The Buddhacarita of Asvaghosha," 3.2.4.1(4); 8.1.2.1(10)
The Jataka, 3.2.2.1(12); 3.2.2.3(3); 4.2.2(6); 8.1.1(10)

Crawford, John
Journal of an Embassy from the Governor General of India to the Court of Ava, 1.4.2(5)

Crosthwaite, Charles Haukes Todd
The Pacification of Burma, 1.4.2(6)

Csoma, Alexander
"Analyse du Kandjour," 3.1.4(5); 3.3.4.2(2)

Cuendet, Georges
"Textes sanscrits bouddhiques d'Asie centrale," 3.1.3(3)
Culavamsa: Being the More Recent Part of the Mahavamsa, 1.3.1(3); 9.1.5(3)
Cullavagga, 3.2.1.1(6)
Cunningham, Alexander
Ancient Geography of India, 10.2.1(6)
The Bhilsa Topes, 10.2.6.2(1)
Mahabodhi, 5.2.4(8); 5.2.8(7); 10.2.3(6)
The Stupa of Bharhut, 5.2.4(9); 10.2.6.1(2)

Damais, Louis-Charles
"Le Bouddhisme en Indonésie," 1.9.1(2)
Damrong Ranjanubhab, (Prince)
A History of Buddhist Monuments in Siam, 1.5.2(8); 10.5(2)
Dani, Ahmed Hasan
Buddhist Sculpture in East Pakistan, 5.2.3(6)
Darian, Steven
"Buddhism in Bihar from the Eighth to the Twelfth Century," 1.2.2.3(2)
Das, Sarat Chandra
"Contribution on the Religion of Tibet: 5. The Lives of the Panchhen-Rinpoches," 8.9.2(18)
"Contribution on the Religion of Tibet: 6. Life and Legend of Tson Khapa," 8.9.2(22)
"Contribution on the Religion of Tibet: 10. Life and Legend of Nagarjuna," 8.9.1(38)
Indian Pandits in the Land of the Snow, 10.1.3(2)
"Life of Sum pa Khan-po," 1.14.2.2(4); 8.9.2(20)
"Rise and Progress of Buddhism in Mongolia," 1.16.1(4)
"Rise and Progress of Buddhism in Tibet," 1.14.1(3)
A Tibetan-English Dictionary, 12.1(2)
Dasgupta, Shashibhusan
An Introduction to Tantric Buddhism, 2.6.1(5); 2.7.14(4)
Obscure Religious Cults, 2.6.1(6); 11.6.1(10)
Dasgupta, Surendranath
A History of Indian Philosophy, 2.2(5)
Indian Idealism, 2.5.4(4)
Dassanayake, M. B.
The Kandy Esala Perahera, 7.3.1(3)
"The Date of Kanishka," 8.9.1(32)
Dathavamsa, 8.1.2.4(7); 9.1.5(4)
Datta, Bupendranath
Indian Art and Its Relation to Culture, 5.2.1(7)
Dauer, Dorothea W.
Schopenhauer as Transmitter of Buddhist Ideas, 2.19(13)
David-Neel, Alexandra
La Connaissance Transcendente, 3.3.1.1(25)
Magic and Mystery in Tibet, 7.2.2(4)
My Journey to Lhasa, 10.1.3(3)
The Superhuman Life of Gesar of Ling, 4.2.4(3)
Textes Tibétains Inédits, 4.2.4(4); 4.3(2)
Davidson, J. LeRoy
The Lotus Sutra in Chinese Art, 5.9.4(3)
"Traces of Buddhist Evangelism in Early Chinese Art," 7.2.5(1)
Davis, Richard
"Tolerance and Intolerance of Ambiguity," 7.1.1(3)
Daw, Thin Kyi
"The Old City of Pagan," 10.4.1(1)
Dawson, Christopher Henry
Mission to Asia, 1.16.2(3)

Dawson, R.
The Legacy of China, 1.11.1(12)
Dayal, Har
"The Bodhisattva Doctrine in Buddhist Sanskrit Literature," 8.3.1(4); 11.1(3); 11.4.6(2); 11.5(3)
De, G.
Democracy in the Buddhist Sangha, 6.1.1(3)
De, Suskit Kumar
"The Buddhist Tantric Literature, Sanskrit, of Bengal," 3.4.4(2)
DeBary, William Theodore
The Buddhist Tradition in India, China and Japan, 1.11.1(5); 1.13.1(2); 2.5.7(2); 3.5(4)
Sources of Chinese Tradition, 2.5.8(7)
Sources of Indian Tradition, 6.2.2.1(2)
Dehejia, Vidya
Early Buddhist Rock Temples, 5.2.6(4)
DeJong, J. W.
"La Légende de Santideva," 8.9.1(47)
"Sum-pa nKhan-po," 8.9.2(21)
De Kleen, Tyra
Mudras, 5.5.6(1); 11.6.4(4)
Del Campana, Pier P.
"The Sutra of Meditation." See citations under Kojiro Miyasaka.
The Three Fold Lotus Sutra, 3.3.5.1(1)
Demieville, Paul.
"Le Bouddhisme: 1. Les sources." See citations under Jean Filliozat.
"Le Bouddhisme Chinois," 1.11.1(6)
"Le Bouddhisme et la guerre," 6.2.2.6(4)
"Busshin," 8.1.3(5)
"Le chapitre de la Bodhisattvabhumi sur la perfection du Dhyana," 11.4.5(4); 11.5(4)
Le concile de Lhasa, 1.14.2.1(2)
Entretiens de Lin-tsi, 8.9.3(56)
"Un Fragment Sanskrit de l'Abhidharma des Sarvastivadin," 3.2.3.2(3)
Hobogirin: Dictionnaire Encyclopédique du Bouddhisme, 2.7.12(1); 3.1.5(3); 9.2.4(2); 11.6.2(3); 12.3(1)
"Maitreya l'inspirateur," 8.3.4(3)
"La mémoire des existences antérieures," 11.4.6(3)
"Notes sur le fragment sogdien." See citations under Emile Benveniste.
"L'Origine des sectes bouddhiques d'après Paramartha," 2.4.1(4)
"Le paradis de Maitreya," 8.3.4(3)
"La pénétration du Bouddhisme dans la tradition philosophique chinoise," 1.11.2.1(2)
"A propos du concile de Vaisali," 2.4.2(2)
"Le recueil de la Salle des Patriarches-Tsou T'ang tsi," 8.9.3(45)
The Twin Pagodas of Zayton. See citations under G. Ecke.
"Les Versions Chinoises du Milindapanha," 3.2.2.4(2)
"Le Yogacarabhumi de Sangharaksa," 3.2.4.2(3); 11.4.2(5)
Deneck, M. M.
Indian Sculpture, 5.2.3(7)
Denis, Eugene
"L'Origine Cingalaise du P'rah Malay," 4.2.3(12)
De Silva, K. M.
"Buddhism and the British Government in Ceylon," 1.3.2.2(2); 6.2.2.2(4)
De Silva, S. P.
A Scientific Rationalization of Buddhism, 2.8(4)

Devendra, D. T.
    "Abhayagiri," 10.3.1(1)
    "Anuradhapura," 10.3.1(2)
    The Buddha Image and Ceylon, 5.4.2(2)
    Classical Sinhalese Sculpture, 5.4.2(3)
Dewaraja, Lorna Srimathie
    A Study of the Political, Administrative, and Social Structure of the Kandyan Kingdom of Ceylon, 1707-1760, 1.3.2.1(2)
Dey, Mukul
    My Pilgrimages to Ajanta and Bagh, 5.2.6(5)
Deydier, Henri
    Contribution à l'étude de l'art du Gandhara, 5.2.5(2)
    Introduction à la connaissance du Laos, 7.3.1(4)
De Zoete, Beryl
    Dance and Magic Drama in Ceylon, 5.12.1(3)
Dge-legs-dpal-bzan po
    Mkhas grub rje's Fundamentals of the Buddhist Tantra, 2.6.1(7)
Dhammakitti
    The Dathavamsa, 1.3.2.1(3)
Dhammapada, 3.2.2.1(4), (5), (6), (7), (8), (9)
Dhammapadatthakatha, 3.2.2.3(2); 4.2.3(13)
Dhamma-Sangani, 3.2.3.1(1)
Dhaninivat, H. H. Prince
    Monarchical Protection of the Buddhist Church, 6.2.2.4(1)
Dharmakirti
    Nyayabindu, 3.3.3.1(7)
    Pramanavarttika, 3.3.3.1(8); 3.3.3.2(1)
Dharmapala, Anagarika
    Return to Righteousness, 1.3.2.2(3); 2.8(5)
Dharmottara
    Nyayabindutika, 3.3.3.2(2)
Dhatu Katha, 3.2.3.1(3)
Dhavalikar, M. K.
    Sanchi: A Cultural History, 5.2.4(10); 10.2.6.2(2)
Dhirasekara, Jothiya
    "Women and the Religious Order of the Buddha," 6.1.3(3)
Dickson, J. F.
    "Notes Illustrative of Buddhism as the Daily Religion of the Buddhists of Ceylon," 7.1.1(4)
    "The Patimokkha," 7.2.4(1)
Dickson, W. G.
    Gleanings from Japan, 10.1.5(2)
Digha Nikaya, 3.2.2.1(10); 6.2.1.1(6); 6.2.4(1)
Dignaga
    Alambanapariksa, 3.3.3.1(9)
    Hastavalaprakarana, 3.3.3.1(10)
    Hetucakranirnaya, 3.3.3.1(11)
    Prajnaparamitapindartha, 3.3.1.2(3); 3.3.3.1(12), (13)
    Pramanasamuccaya, 3.3.3.1(14)
Dikshitar, V. R. R.
    "Buddhism in Andhradesa," 1.2.2.4(3)
(Dipavamsa) The Chronicle of the Island of Ceylon, 1.3.1(4); 9.1.5(5)
Doehring, Karl
    Buddhistische Tempelangen in Siam, 5.5.3(6)
Dogen
    Gakudoyojin-shu, 3.3.6.3(1)
    A Primer of Soto Zen, 2.5.7(3)
    Shobogenzo, 3.3.6.3(2)
    "Shobogenzo Sammi O Zammai," 11.4.5(5)
    Shobogenzo Zuimonki, 3.3.6.3(3)

Dore, Henri
    Researches into Chinese Superstitions, 4.1.3(3); 8.2.1(3); 8.3.2(5); 8.3.6(1); 8.4(3); 9.2.2.3(4); 9.2.2.4(3)
Dorson, Richard Mercer
    Folk Legends of Japan, 4.2.4(5)
Draeger, Donn F.
    Classical Budo, 5.11.6(2)
Drekmeier, Charles
    Kingship and Community in Early India, 1.2.2.1(1)
Dresden, Mark J.
    "The Jatakastava," 3.3.8.4(5); 4.2.2(5); 8.1.1(9)
Drexler, Arthur
    The Architecture of Japan, 5.11.3(3)
Dri med kun ldan-gye rnam-thar, 4.4(4)
Dubs, Homer H.
    "The 'Golden Man' of Former Han Time," 1.11.2.1(3)
Dumarcay, Jacques
    Le Bayon, 10.6(3)
Dumoulin, Heinrich
    Buddhism in the Modern World, 1.1(3); 2.8(6)
    The Development of Chinese Zen, 2.5.7(4)
    A History of Zen Buddhism, 1.13.2.2(6); 2.5.7(5)
    "Technique and Personal Devotion in the Zen Exercise," 11.4.8.1(4)
Duncan, Marion Herbert
    Harvest Festival Dramas of Tibet, 4.4(5)
    Love Songs and Proverbs of Tibet, 4.3(3)
Dupont, Pierre
    "Etudes sur l'Indochine ancienne," 1.6.2(6)
    "La propagation du Bouddhisme indien en Indochine occidentale," 1.6.2(7)
Durand, Maurice
    "Introduction du Bouddhisme au Vietnam," 1.8.2(3)
Duroiselle, Charles
    "Upagutta et Mara," 9.3.5(4)
Dutt, Nalinaksha
    Aspects of Mahayana Buddhism, 1.2.2.3(3); 2.1(2); 2.5.2(3); 2.7.9(2)
    "The Brahmajala Sutta," 3.2.2.4(3)
    "Brahminism and Buddhism," 2.2(6)
    "Buddhism in Kashmir," 1.2.2.4(4)
    Buddhist Sects in India, 2.4.1(5); 6.1.1(4)
    Development of Buddhism in Uttar Pradesh, 1.2.2.4(5)
    "The Dhammasangani," 3.2.3.4(4)
    "Doctrines of the Sammitiya School of Buddhism," 2.4.3(4)
    "Early History of the Spread of Buddhism and the Buddhist Schools," 1.2.2.1(2)
    Early Monastic Buddhism, 1.2.2.1(3); 6.1.1(5); 7.2.5(2); 8.1.2.3(8)
    Gilgit Manuscripts, 1.2.2.4(4); 3.2.1.4(3); 3.3.8.1(1); 7.8(3); 8.2.2(3)
    "Place of Faith in Buddhism," 11.2(2)
    "The Place of the Laity in Early Buddhism," 6.1.2(6)
    "The Second Buddhist Council," 2.4.2(3)
    "Tantric Buddhism," 2.6.1(8)
    "Tathagatagarbha," 2.7.11(1)
Dutt, Sukumar
    The Buddha and Five After-Centuries, 1.2.1(8); 2.4.1(6); 8.1.2.3(9); 8.1.2.4(8); 10.2.1(7)
    Buddhist Monks and Monasteries in India, 1.2.2.1(4); 5.2.2(7); 6.1.1(6); 6.1.2(7); 6.1.3(4); 10.2.1(8)

"A Comparison and Contrast between the Legends and the Edicts (of Asoka)," 8.9.1(14)
Early Buddhist Monachism, 6.1.1(7)
Duyvendak, J. J. L.
"The Buddhistic Festival of the All-Souls in China and Japan," 7.3.2(4)
Dvadasa graha santi, 7.5.2(1)
Dvadasamukhasastra, 3.3.2.1(10)

Earhart, H. Byron
Japanese Religion: Unity and Diversity, 1.13.1(3)
A Religious Study of the Mount Haguro Sect of Shugendo, 4.1.4(1)
"Shugendo, The Tradition of En no Gyoja," 2.6.2(2); 4.1.4(2)
Eberhard, Wolfram
Chinese Festivals, 7.3.2(5)
Folk Tales of China, 4.2.4(6)
Guilt and Sin in Traditional China, 4.2.3(14); 11.3(5)
"Temple-Building Activities in Medieval and Modern China," 1.11.2.3(5)
Ebihara, May
"Interrelations Between Buddhism and Social Systems in Cambodian Peasant Culture," 6.2.1(7); 6.2.6(6)
Ecke, G.
The Twin Pagodas of Zayton, 5.9.2(5); 10.8.2(3)
Eckhardt, Andreas
A History of Korean Art, 5.10(5)
Edgerton, Franklin
Buddhist Hybrid Sanskrit Grammar and Dictionary, 12.1(3)
Edkins, Joseph
Chinese Buddhism, 8.8(5)
Edmunds, Albert Joseph
Buddhist and Christian Gospels, 2.9(14)
Edmunds, Will H.
Pointers and Clues to the Subjects of Chinese and Japanese Art, 5.8(3)
Education in Ceylon (From the Sixth Century B.C. to the Present Day), 6.2.5(8)
Edwardes, Michael
A Life of the Buddha from a Burmese Manuscript, 8.1.2.1(11)
Egerod, Soren
Studia Serica Bernhard Karlgren Dedicata, 7.1.3(11)
Eggermont, Pierre Herman Leonard
The Chronology of the Reign of Asoka Moriya, 1.2.2.2(2); 8.9.1(15)
Ehara, N. R. H.
The Path of Freedom, 3.2.4.2(5); 11.4.2(11)
Eitel, Ernest J.
Hand-book of Chinese Buddhism, 12.1(4)
Ekvall, Robert V.
Religious Observances in Tibet, 5.6(5); 7.1.1(5); 7.1.3(5); 7.1.4(3); 7.6(2)
"Three Categories of Inmates Within Tibetan Monasteries," 6.1.1(8)
A Tibetan Principality. See citations under C. W. Cassinelli.
Elder, Joseph Walter
Chapters in Indian Civilization, 2.2(8); 2.5.3(11); 2.5.4(13); 10.2.1(3)
Eliade, Mircea
From Primitives to Zen, 8.1.2.3(10)
Yoga, Immortality and Freedom, 11.4.5(6); 11.4.6(4); 11.6.1(11); 11.6.2(4); 11.6.3(4)

Eliot, Charles Norton Edgecumbe
Hinduism and Buddhism: An Historical Sketch, 1.1(4); 1.5.1(4); 1.6.1(3); 1.8.1(4); 1.9.1(3); 1.10.1(3); 1.14.1(4)
Japanese Buddhism, 1.13.1(4); 10.9(2)
Ellawala, H.
Social History of Early Ceylon, 6.2.1.1(8)
Ellwood, Robert S.
"Percival Lowell's Journey to the East," 2.9(15)
Embree, John Fee
Suye Mura, 4.1.4(3); 6.2.3(6)
"Thailand--A Loosely Structured Social System," 6.2.1.1(9)
Eminent Orientalists, 1.17(4); 2.9(16)
Emmerick, R. E.
The Khotanese Surangamasamadhisutra, 3.3.2.1(32)
The Sutra of Golden Light, 3.3.8.1(8); 4.2.1(7); 7.5.2(5)
Encho Tamura
"The Influence of Silla Buddhism on Japan," 1.12.2(2); 1.13.2.1(2)
Encyclopedia of World Art, 5.1.1(3)
Ennin
Diary: The Record of a Pilgrimage to China, 1.11.2.3(6); 8.9.4(8); 10.1.2(2)
Ensink, Jacob
The Question of Rastrapala, 3.3.8.1(6)
Eshin, Nishimura
Unsui: A Diary of Zen Monastic Life. See citations under Giei Sato.
Evans-Wentz, Walter Yeeling
The Tibetan Book of the Dead, 3.4.2(2); 9.2.5(1); 9.3.9(2)
The Tibetan Book of the Great Liberation, 3.4.2(3); 8.9.2(16)
Tibetan Yoga and Secret Doctrine, 3.4.2(4); 11.6.1(12)
Tibet's Great Yogi Milarepa, 8.9.2(12)
Evers, Hans-Dieter
"Buddha and the Seven Gods," 4..1.1(5); 8.6(2)
"Buddhism and the British Colonial Policy in Ceylon," 6.2.2.2(5); 6.2.6(7)
"The Buddhist Sangha in Ceylon and Thailand," 6.2.1.1(10); 6.2.2.2(6); 6.2.2.4(2)
"Kingship and Property Rights in a Buddhist Monastery in Central Ceylon," 6.1.1(9); 6.2.6(8)
"Monastic Landlordism in Ceylon," 6.2.6(9)
Monks, Priests, and Peasants, 6.2.1.1(11); 6.2.6(10)
Evola, Giulio Cesare
The Doctrine of Awakening, 8.4(4); 11.4.1(3); 11.4.6(5)

Fa chu ching, 3.2.2.2(5)
Fa Hsien
A Record of Buddhistic Kingdoms, 1.2.2.3(4); 1.3.2.1(4); 10.1.1(4)
Fa Tsang
Chin-shih-tzu chang, 3.3.4.1(3)
A Commentary on the Heart Sutra, 3.3.1.2(4); 3.3.4.1(4)
Fachow, W.
"Development of Tripitaka-Translations in China," 3.1.5(4)
Fairweather, Ian
The Drunken Buddha, 4.5(2)
Falk, Maryla
"Nairatmya and Karman," 2.7.4(4)
Nama-rupa and Dharma-rupa, 2.3(2)

Falk, Nancy E.
    "Wilderness and Kingship in Ancient South Asia," 4.1.1(6)
Faure, Marie-Daniel
    "Fêtes religieuses." See citations under Pierre S. Nginn.
Fausboll, V.
    The Dhammapada and the Sutta-Nipata. See citations under Friedrich Max Müller.
Feer, Leon
    Avadana-çataka, 3.2.2.2(3); 4.2.3(4); 8.2.1(2)
    "L'enfer indien," 9.2.2.3(5)
    "Extraits du Paritta--textes et commentaires en Pali," 7.5.4(2)
    Fragments Extraits du Kandjour, 3.5(5)
    "Les Jatakas dans les mémoires de Hiouen-Thsang," 4.2.2(3)
    "Le Karma-sataka," 4.2.3(19)
    A Study of the Jatakas, 8.1.1(4)
Feng Chia-sheng
    "History of Chinese Society." See citations under Karl A. Wittfogel.
    "Religion under the Liao Dynasty." See citations under Karl A. Wittfogel.
Ferguson, John
    "The Quest for Legitimization by Burmese Monks and Kings," 1.4.2(7)
Fergusson, James
    Cave Temples of India, 5.2.6(6); 10.2.1(9)
    History of Indian and Eastern Architecture, 5.2.2(8); 10.2.1(10); 10.4.2(1); 10.5(3); 10.6(4); 10.7(1)
    Tree and Serpent Worship, 5.2.3(8); 5.2.7(3)
Fernando, P. Edwin Ebert
    "An Account of the Kandyan Mission sent to Siam in 1750 A.D.," 1.3.2.1(5)
Fernado, W. D. Marcus
    Ancient City of Anuradhapura, 10.3.1(3)
Filliozat, Jean
    "Le Bouddhisme, 1. Les Sources," 3.1.1(3); 3.1.3(4); 3.1.4(6)
    "Fragments du Vinaya des Sarvastivadin," 3.2.1.2(2)
    L'Inde classique. See citations under Louis Renou.
    "Maitreya l'invaincu," 8.3.4(4); 9.1.4(3)
    "La mort volontaire par le feu," 7.4.2(4)
    "Le symbolisme du monument du Phnom Bakhen," 9.3.7(4)
    "Un chapitre du rgyud-bzi sur les bases de la santé et des maladies," 7.5.2(2)
    "La vie du Buddha," 8.1.2.3(11)
Finot, Louis
    "La Légende de Buddhaghosa," 8.9.5(3)
    "Mahaparinibbanasutta et Cullavagga," 3.2.1.4(4); 3.2.2.4(4)
    "Manuscrits sanskrits de Sadhanas retrouvés en Chine," 3.4.1(3), (7); 11.6.1(13)
    "Notes on the Singhalese Tradition Relative to Buddha's Relics," 8.1.2.4(9)
    "Outlines of the History of Buddhism in Indo-China," 1.6.2(8); 1.7.2(3)
    "Le Pratimoksasutra des Sarvastivadins," 3.3.1.2(8)
    "Recherches sur la littérature laotienne," 3.1.6(2)
    "La religion des Chams d'après les monuments," 1.8.1(5)
Fiske, Adele
    "Religion and Buddhism among India's New Buddhists," 1.2.2.5(1); 6.2.4(2)

Foard, James
    "The Loneliness of Masuo Basho," 8.9.4(3)
Focillon, Henri
    L'Art Bouddhique, 5.1.4(5)
Fong, Wen
    The Lohans and a Bridge to Heaven, 5.9.3(7)
Fontein, Jan
    Ancient Indonesian Art, 5.5.6(3)
    China, Korea, Japan, 5.8(5); 5.10(6)
    The Pilgrimage of Sudhana, 5.5.6(2); 5.8(4)
    Zen Painting and Calligraphy, 5.9.3(8); 5.11.6(3)
Foucaux, Phillippe Edouard
    Développement des Jeux, 3.3.8.1(2); 9.3.1(6)
    Histoire du Bouddha sakya-mouni, 8.1.2.3(12)
    Le Lalita Vistara, 8.1.2.1(12); 8.1.2.2(3)
Foucher, Alfred Charles Auguste
    L'art gréco-bouddhique du Gandhara, 5.2.5(3); 9.2.2.5(3)
    Les Bas-reliefs du stupa de Sikri, 5.2.5(4)
    Etude sur l'iconographie bouddhique de l'Inde, 1.2.2.3(5); 8.1.2.3(13); 8.3.1(5)
    Etudes sur l'art bouddhique de l'Inde, 5.2.3(10)
    "Le grand miracle du Bouddha à Sravasti," 8.1.2.2(4)
    The Life of the Buddha," 2.7.6(5); 5.2.3(11); 8.1.2.3(14); 9.3.1(5); 9.3.5(5); 10.2.1(11); 10.2.2(2)
    Monuments of Sanchi. See citations under John Marshall.
    "Notes d'archéologie bouddhique," 10.6(5)
    "On the Iconography of the Buddha's Nativity," 5.2.3(12); 9.3.3(3)
    Les Vies Antérieures du Bouddha, 2.7.1(2); 4.2.2(4); 6.1.3(5); 8.1.1(5)
Fox, Douglas A.
    "Soteriology in Jodo Shin and Christianity," 2.9(17)
    The Vagrant Lotus, 2.1(3)
    "Zen and Ethics," 2.5.7(6)
Fozdar, Jamshed K.
    The God of Buddha, 2.2(7)
Francis, H. T.
    Jataka Tales, 8.1.1(6)
Francke, A. H.
    Antiquities of India and Tibet, 1.14.2.1(3); 9.1.5(9)
Frank, Bernard
    "Le Bouddhisme Japonais." See citations under Gaston Renondeau.
Franke, Rudolf Otto
    "The Buddhist Councils at Rajagaha and Vesali," 2.4.2(4)
Frauwallner, Erich
    "On the Date of the Buddhist Master of Law, Vasubandhu," 8.9.1(51)
    The Earliest Vinaya and the Beginnings of Buddhist Literature, 3.2.1.4(5)
    "The Historical Data We Possess on the Person and the Doctrine of the Buddha," 8.1.2.3(15)
Fredric, Louis
    The Arts of Southeast Asia, 5.5.1(1)
Freemantle, Francesca
    The Tibetan Book of the Dead, 3.4.2(5); 7.4.2(5); 8.2.2(4); 9.2.5(2)
Friedmann, David Lasar
    Sthiramati, Madhyantavibhagatika, 3.3.3.2(4)
Frodsham, J. D.
    "Hsieh Ling-yun's Contributions to Mediaeval Chinese Buddhism," 2.5.7(7); 8.9.3(37)

Fromm, Erich
    "Psychoanalysis and Zen," 2.8(7)
    Zen Buddhism and Psychoanalysis, 2.9(18)
Fujikawa, Asako
    Daughter of Shinran, 1.13.2.2(7)
Fujimoto, Ryuko
    An Outline of the Triple Sutra of Shin Buddhism, 2.5.8(8)
Fujioka, Ryoichi
    Tea Ceremony Utensils, 5.11.8(2)
Fujiwara, Hirotatsu
    I Denounce Soka Gakkai, 6.2.2.6(5)
Fujiwara, Ryusetsu
    The Way to Nirvana, 2.5.8(9)
Fujiyoshi, Jikai
    "Omizutori." See citations under Martha Boyer.
    "The Spirit of Criticism in Buddhism," 2.1(4)
Fukaura, Seibun
    "Alaya-Vijnana," 2.7.12(3)
Fukunaga, Mitsuji
    "'No-mind' in Chuang-tzu," 11.4.8.1(5)
Fung Yu-lan
    A History of Chinese Philosophy, 2.5.4(5); 2.5.5(2); 2.5.6(2)
    "The Rise of Neo-Confucianism and its Borrowings from Buddhism and Taoism," 1.11.2.3(7)
Furer-Haimendorf, Christoph von
    Morals and Merit, 4.1.5(1)
    "The Role of the Monastery in Sherpa Society," 6.2.1.2(8)
    The Sherpas of Nepal, 1.15.1(1)
Furnivall, John S.
    "Manu in Burma," 6.2.7(3)
Futagawa, Yukio
    The Roots of Japanese Architecture, 5.11.3(4)

sGam Po Pa, 3.3.8.3(2); 3.4.2(8); 11.1(4)
Gamble, Sydney D.
    Chinese Village Plays, 4.4(6)
Gandistotra, 3.3.8.2(5); 7.2.3(2)
Gangoly, O. C.
    The Antiquity of the Buddha Image, 5.2.3(13)
    The Art of Java, 5.5.6(4)
    Indian Architecture, 5.2.2(9)
Gangopadhyaya, Mrinalkanti
    Nyayabindu-tika, 3.3.3.2(7)
Gard, Richard
    Buddhism, 7.2.2(5)
    "Buddhism," 12.2(8)
    "Buddhism and Political Power," 6.2.2.1(3)
    "The Madhyamika in Korea," 2.5.3(3)
    The Role of Thailand in World Buddhism, 1.5.1(5)
    "Why Did the Madhyamika Decline?," 2.5.3(4)
Garfias, Robert
    Gagaku, 5.12.3(1)
Garnier, Francis
    "Chronique royale du Cambodge," 1.6.2(9)
Gauthiot, Robert
    Le Sutra des Causes et des Effets du Bien et du Mal, 2.7.1(3); 3.3.8.4(4)
Geden, A. S.
    "The Life of the Buddha," 8.1.2.3(16)
Gehman, Henry Snyder
    "Peta Vatthu," 3.2.2.1(21); 9.2.2.3(12)
Geiger, Wilhelm
    Culture of Ceylon in Mediaeval Times, 1.3.2.1(6); 6.2.1.1(12); 7.7(3)
    The Mahavamsa or the Great Chronicle of Ceylon, 1.3.1(6); 9.1.5(10)
    Pali Literature and Language, 3.1.2(3)

Gelder, Roma
    The Timely Rain: Travels in New Tibet. See citations under Stuart Gelder.
Gelder, Stuart
    The Timely Rain: Travels in New Tibet, 1.14.2.3(2)
Génies, Anges et Démons, 4.1.2(5)
Genshin
    Ojoyoshu, 3.3.7.2(2)
Gernet, Jacques
    Les aspects économiques du Bouddhisme dans la société chinoise du Ve au Xe siècle, 1.11.2.2(3); 6.2.6(11)
    "Biographie du Maître Chen-houei du Ho-tso," 2.5.7(8); 8.9.3(75)
    Entretiens du Maître de Dhyana Chen-houei du Ho-tso, 3.3.6.2(2)
    "Les Suicides par le feu," 7.4.2(6)
Gerschevitch, Ilya
    "On the Sogdian Vessantara Jataka," 8.1.1(7)
Gervaise, Nicolas
    The Nature and Political History of the Kingdom of Siam, 1.5.2(9)
Getty, Alice
    The Gods of Northern Buddhism, 5.2.3(14); 8.3.1(6)
Chine, Ohn
    "The Botatung Pagoda," 7.1.3(6)
Ghosh, N. N.
    "Did Pusyamitra Sunga Persecute the Buddhists?," 1.2.2.3(6)
Ghoshal, U. N.
    "The Ancient Indian Republic," 6.2.2.1(4)
    A History of Indian Political Ideas, 6.2.2.1(5)
    "Principle of Kings' Righteousness," 6.2.2.1(6); 6.2.7(4)
    Studies in Indian History and Culture, 6.2.2.1(4)
Giap, Tran-Van
    "Le Bouddhisme en Annam des origines au XIIIe siècle," 1.8.2(4)
Giles, Herbert Allan
    Strange Stories from a Chinese Studio, 4.2.4(13)
Giles, Lionel
    Descriptive Catalogue, 3.1.5(5)
Gilmour, James
    Among the Mongols, 10.1.2(3)
Gimaret, Daniel
    "Bouddha et les Bouddhistes dan la Tradition Musulmane," 4.1.5(2)
Ginsburg, Norton S.
    Area Handbook on Laos, 6.2.5.(11)
Giteau, Madeleine
    Le Bornage Rituel des Temples bouddhiques au Cambodge, 5.5.4(4); 7.2.6(2)
    Khmer Sculpture and the Angkor Civilization, 5.5.4(5)
Glahn, Else
    Studia Serica Bernhard Karlgren Dedicata. See citations under Soren Egerod.
Glasenapp, Helmuth von
    Buddhism and Christianity, 2.9(19)
Godakumbura, C. E.
    Sinhalese Literature, 3.1.6(3)
Godard, André
    Les Antiquités bouddhiques de Bamiyan, 5.2.5(5)
Goddard, Dwight
    A Buddhist Bible, 3.5(6)
    Was Jesus Influenced by Buddhism?, 2.9(20)
Goetz, Hermann
    The Art of India, 5.2.1(8)

Gogerly, Daniel John
   Ceylon Buddhism, 7.5.4(3)
Gokhale, Balkrishna Govind
   "Anagarika Dharmapala," 1.3.2.2(4); 6.2.2.2(7)
   Asoka Maurya, 8.9.1(16)
   Buddhism and Asoka, 1.2.2.2(3); 6.1.2(8); 6.2.5(9)
   "The Buddhist Social Ideals," 6.2.1.1(13)
   Development of Buddhism in Uttar Pradesh, 1.2.2.4(5)
   "Dhamma as a Political Concept in Early Buddhism," 6.2.2.1(7)
   "The Early Buddhist Elite," 6.1.2(9)
   "Early Buddhist Kingship," 8.7(2)
   "The Early Buddhist View of the State," 6.2.2.1(8)
   "Theravada Buddhism in Western India," 1.2.2.4(6)
Golay, Jacqueline
   "Pathos and Farce," 5.12.2(2)
Goloubew, Victor
   D'Ajanta, 5.2.6(7)
   "Le temple de la dent à Kandy," 8.1.2.4(10); 10.3.1(4)
Gombrich, Richard Francis
   "The Consecration of a Buddhist Image," 7.2.6(3)
   "Feminine Elements in a Sinhalese Buddhism," 4.2.3(15); 8.1.1(8); 9.3.10(1)
   "Merit Transfer in Sinhalese Buddhism," 7.1.1(6)
   Precept and Practice: Traditional Buddhism in the Rural Highlands of Ceylon, 4.1.1(7); 6.2.1.1(14); 6.2.3(7); 6.2.4(3); 7.1.1(7); 7.2.2(6); 11.3(6)
Gordon, Antoinette
   The Iconography of Tibetan Lamaism, 5.6(6)
   Tibetan Religious Art, 5.6(7)
Gordon, Elizabeth Anna
   "Some Recent Discoveries in Korean Temples," 1.12.2(3)
Gorer, Geoffrey
   "The Use of Thread-Crosses in Lepcha Lamaist Ceremonies." See citations under René de Nebesky-Wojkowitz.
Gos lo-tsa-ba
   Deb-ther-sngon-po (The Blue Annals), 1.14.1(5); 9.1.5(7)
Goswami, Kunja Govinda
   "Buddhism in the Sunga Period," 1.2.2.3(7)
Govinda, Anagarika Brahmacari
   Foundations of Tibetan Mysticism, 2.6.1(9); 9.3.2(2); 11.6.2(5); 11.6.3(5)
   "The Historical and Symbolical Origin of the Chorten," 9.3.6(4)
   The Psychological Attitude of Early Buddhist Philosophy, 2.7.5(3); 2.7.7(4); 3.2.3.4(5)
   The Way of the White Clouds, 10.1.3(4)
Grant Brown, R.
   "Rain-making in Burma," 7.5.1(4)
Gray, Basil
   Buddhist Cave Paintings at Tun-huang, 1.10.2(7); 5.9.4(4); 10.8.2(4)
Gray, James
   Buddhaghosuppatti, 8.9.1(26); 8.9.5(2)
   Embellishments of Buddha, 8.1.2.1(8)
Griffis, William Elliot
   The Religions of Japan from the Dawn of History to the Era of the Meiji, 1.13.1(5)
Grinstead, E. D.
   "The Manuscript Kanjur in the British Museum," 3.1.4(7)

Griswold, Alexander B.
   The Art of Burma, Korea, Tibet, 5.1.4(6); 5.6(8)
   Ba Shin. See citations under Jean Boisselier.
   Dated Buddhist Images of Northern Siam, 5.5.3(7)
   King Mongkut of Siam, 1.5.2(10); 8.9.5(9)
   "Prolegomena to the Study of the Buddha's Dress," 5.9.2(6)
   Towards a History of Sukhodaya Art, 1.5.2(11)
Groot, John J. M. de
   "Buddhist Masses for the Dead in Amoy," 7.4.2(7)
   Le code du Mahayana en Chine, 7.2.4(2); 7.2.5(3); 7.5.1(5)
   Les fêtes annuelles célébrées à Emoui (Amoy), 7.3.2(6)
   "Militant Spirit of the Buddhist Clergy in China," 6.2.2.5(3)
   Sectarianism and Religious Persecution in China, 6.2.2.5(4)
   Der Thupa, 5.9.2(7)
Groslier, Bernard Philippe
   Angkor: Art and Civilization, 5.5.4(6)
   The Art of Indochina, 5.5.5(3)
Groslier, George
   Arts et archéologie khmers, 5.5.4(7)
Grousset, René
   Chinese Art and Culture, 5.9.1(3)
   The Civilization of India, 5.2.1(9)
   The Civilizations of the East, 5.9.1(4)
   The Empire of the Steppes, 1.16.1(5)
   In the Footsteps of the Buddha, 8.9.3(40); 10.2.1(12)
Grunwedel, Albert
   Buddhist Art in India, 5.2.1(10); 5.2.5(6)
Guenther, Herbert V.
   Buddhist Philosophy in Theory and Practice, 2.1(5)
   sGam Po Pa, Jewel Ornament of Liberation, 3.3.8.3(2); 3.4.2(8); 11.1(4)
   The Life and Teaching of Naropa, 3.4.2(6); 8.9.2(13); 11.6.1(14)
   Philosophy and Psychology in the Abhidharma, 2.7.5(5)
   "The Psychology of the Three Kayas," 8.1.3(6)
   The Royal Song of Saraha, 3.4.2(7)
   The Tantric View of Life, 2.6.1(10); 11.6.1(16)
   Tibetan Buddhism without Mystification, 3.4.2(9); 11.6.1(15)
Gulik, Robert H. van
   Hayagriva, 7.8(13); 8.6.(18)
   "The Lore of the Chinese Lute," 5.12.3(2)
   Siddham: An Essay on the History of Sanskrit Studies in China and Japan, 1.11.2.1(4)
Gunji, Masakutsu
   Kabuki, 5.12.2(3)
Gupta, Kesab Chandra
   "Relics of Sariputta and Moggallana Arahans," 7.1.3(7)
Gupte, Ramesh Shankar
   Ajanta, Ellora, and the Aurangabad Caves, 5.2.6(8); 10.2.6.2(3)
   The Iconography of the Buddhist Sculptures of Ellora, 5.2.6(9)
Guruge, Ananda W. P.
   Facets of Buddhism, 2.8(8)

Haarh, Erik
    The Yar-Lun Dynasty, 1.14.2.1(4)
Hackin, Joseph
    Les Antiquités bouddhiques de Bamiyan. See citations under André Godard.
    Asiatic Mythology, 4.1.3(5); 5.1.3(3)
Hackman, Heinrich Friedrich
    Buddhism as a Religion, 1.12.2(4)
Hajek, Lubor
    Chinese Art, 5.9.1(5)
Hakeda, Yoshito S.
    The Awakening of Faith Attributed to Asvaghosa, 3.3.8.2(1); 11.2(3)
    Kukai: Major Works, 1.13.2.2(8); 2.6.2(4); 3.3.1.2(5); 3.4.3(1); 8.9.4(18)
    "The Religious Novel of Kukai," 4.5(3)
Hakuin Zenji
    Yasen Kanna, 3.3.6.2(3)
    Zazen Wasan, 3.3.6.2(4)
Haldar, Aruna
    "Doctrine of Sarvastivada," 2.4.3(5)
Haldar, Jnanranjan
    Links Between Early and Later Buddhist Mythology, 2.5.2(4)
Hallade, Madeleine
    Etudes d'art indien, 5.2.3(15)
    Gandharan Art of North India, 5.2.5(7)
Halpern, Joel Martin
    Government, Politics, and Social Structure in Laos, 1.7.2(4); 6.2.2.8(2)
    "Traditional Medicine and the Role of the Phi in Laos," 7.5.2(3)
Hambly, Gavin
    Central Asia, 1.10.2(3)
Hamilton, Clarence Herbert
    Buddhism: A Religion of Infinite Compassion, 3.5(7)
    "Encounter with Reality in Buddhist Madhyamika Philosophy," 2.7.8(4)
    "Hsuan Chuang and the Wei Shih Philosophy," 2.5.4(6)
    "The Idea of Compassion in Mahayana Buddhism," 11.4.3(5)
    Wei Shih Er Lun, 3.3.3.1(20)
Hamilton, James Russell
    Le Conte Bouddhique du Bon, 4.2.3(16)
Hammer, Raymond
    Japan's Religious Ferment, 1.13.2.4(2)
Han Sang-ryan
    "The Influence of Buddhism in Korea," 1.12.1(3)
Han Shan
    Chin-kang chueh-i, 3.3.6.2(6)
    Cold Mountain, 4.3(4)
    Pan-jp po-lo-mi-to hsin-ching chih-shuo, 3.3.6.2(5)
Hanayama, Shinsho
    Bibliography on Buddhism, 12.2(9)
    "Buddhism of the One Great Vehicle," 2.5.1(6)
Hanayama, Shoyu
    "A Summary of Various Research on the Prajnaparamita Literature by Japanese Scholars," 3.3.1.3(3)
Handurukande, Ratna
    "Manicudavadana," 8.3.6(2)
    The Manicudavadana and Lokananda, 4.2.3(22); 4.4(8)
Hanks, L. M., Jr.
    "Merit and Power in the Thai Social Order," 6.2.1.1(15); 6.2.5(10)

Hansford, Howard S.
    A Glossary of Chinese Art and Archaeology, 5.9.1(6)
Harada, Jiro
    A Glimpse of Japanese Ideals, 5.11.2(4)
    Masterpieces of Japanese Art. See citations under Seiroku Noma.
Hardy, R. Spence
    A Manuel of Buddhism, 9.1.1(2); 9.2.2.1(5)
Hare, E. M.
    The Book of Gradual Sayings. See citations under F. L. Woodward.
    Woven Cadences of Early Buddhists, 3.2.2.1(25)
Hare, William L.
    Religions of the Empire, 6.2.5(18)
Harich-Schneider, Eta
    "Roei," 5.12.3(3)
Harle, J. C.
    Gupta Sculpture, 5.2.8(8)
Harlez, Charles Joseph de
    "Prajnaparamita-hrdaya-sutra," 3.3.1.1(15)
    La religion nationale des Tartares orientaux, 1.16.1(6)
Harper, Edward B.
    Religion in South Asia, 4.1.1(2); 7.5.2(11)
Hart, Virgil C.
    Western China, 10.1.2(4)
Hartel, Herbert
    Indien und Sudostasien, 5.1.4(7)
Hartmann, Gerda
    "Symbols of the Nidanas," 2.7.6(6); 9.3.2(3)
Hassain, F. M.
    Buddhist Kashmir, 1.2.2.4(7)
Hastings, James
    Encyclopaedia of Religion and Ethics, 1.15.1(9); 3.3.5.2(2); 7.4.2(15); 8.1.2.3(16); 8.1.3(2); 8.2.1(7), (8); 8.3.1(8); 8.3.2(7); 8.9.1(21); 9.1.1(3); 9.2.1(8); 9.3.3(5); 11.3(1); 11.4.5(1); 12.3(2)
Hasumi, Toshimitsu
    Zen in Japanese Art, 5.11.6(4)
Hattori, Masaaki
    Dignaga on Perception, 2.5.4(7); 3.3.3.1(14)
Havell, Ernest B.
    The Ancient and Medieval Architecture of India, 5.2.2(10)
    The Art Heritage of India, 5.2.1(11)
    A Handbook of Indian Art, 5.2.1(12)
    The Himalayas in Indian Art, 5.1.3(4)
    Indian Sculpture and Painting, 5.2.3(16)
Hayakawa, Masao
    The Garden Art of Japan, 5.11.7(1)
Hayashima, Kyosho
    "From Sakyamuni to Shinran," 2.5.8(10)
    "A Study in the Thought of 'Hon-gan,'" 11.7.4(4)
Hayashiya, T.
    Japanese Arts and the Tea Ceremony, 5.11.8(3)
Hearn, Lafcadio
    In Ghostly Japan, 10.1.5(3)
    Gleanings in Buddha-Fields, 2.9(21); 4.3(5)
    Japan: An Attempt at Interpretation, 2.9(22)
    Oriental Articles, 2.9(23)
Hedin, Sven
    Jehol, City of Emperors, 10.1.2(5)
    Trans-Himalaya, 10.1.3(5)
Heine-Geldern, Robert
    Conceptions of State and Kingship in Southeast Asia, 6.2.2.1(9)
Held, Hans Ludwig
    Deutsche Bibliographie des Buddhismus, 12.2(10)

Hanpel, Rose
    China, Korea, Japan. See citations under Jon Fontein.
Henderson, Gregory
    "The Buddha of Seiryoji," 5.11.4(2)
Herold, A. Ferdinand
    The Life of Buddha, 8.1.2.3(17)
Herrigel, Eugen
    Zen in the Art of Archery, 5.11.6(5)
Hettiarachchy, Tilak
    History of Kingship in Ceylon, 6.2.2.2(8)
Hevajra Tantra, 3.4.1(4)
Hevajrasekaprakriya, 3.4.1(3)
Heyman, Alan
    "Historical Document in Sound: Korean Buddhist Ceremony Recorded in Its Entirety," 7.4.2(8)
    "Lunar Leap Year Offers Buddhist Ceremonial Music and Dance," 7.3.2(7)
Hickey, G. E.
    "Religion and Education," 6.2.5(11)
Hickman, Money
    Zen Painting and Calligraphy. See citations under Jon Fontein.
Hikato, Ryusho
    "On the author of Ta-chic-tu-lun," 3.3.2.2(1)
Hirai, Tomio
    Psychophysiology of Zen, 2.8(9)
Hirakawa, Akira
    "The Rise of Mahayana Buddhism," 2.5.2(5); 5.2.2(11); 7.1.3(8); 8.1.2.4(11)
    "The Two-Fold Structure of the Buddhist Sangha," 6.1.1(10)
Hirano, Umeyo
    Buddhist Plays from Japanese Literature, 5.12.2(4)
Hisamatsu, Shin'ichi
    "The Characteristics of Oriental Nothingness," 2.5.7(9)
    "The Nature of Sado Culture," 5.11.8(4)
    Zen and the Fine Arts, 5.11.6(6)
Hmannan Maha Yazawintawkyi, 1.4.1(3); 9.1.5(6); 10.4.2(4)
Ho, Wai-Kam
    Chinese Art under the Mongols. See citations under Sherman E. Lee.
Hoang-thi-bich
    Etude et Traduction du Gakudo-yojin-shu, 2.5.7(10); 3.3.6.3(1); 10.3.1(5)
Hocart, A. M.
    "Buddha and Devadatta," 8.8(6)
    The Temple of the Tooth in Kandy, 7.1.3(9); 8.1.2.4(12)
Hodous, Lewis
    Buddhists and Buddhism in China, 1.11.1(7)
    A Dictionary of Chinese Buddhist Terms. See citations under William E. Soothill.
Hoernle, A. F. Rudolf
    Manuscript Remains of Buddhist Literature, 3.2.1.2(3); 3.2.2.2(6); 3.3.1.1(27); 3.3.8.4(1)
Hoffman, Helmut
    Die Religionen Tibets, 6.2.2.7(4)
    The Religions of Tibet, 1.14.1(6)
    Symbolik der Tibetischen Religionen, 5.6(9)
Hofinger, Marcel
    "L'action missionnaire du Bouddhisme ancien," 7.2.5(4)
    Le Congrès du Lac Anavatapta, 3.2.1.2(1); 4.2.3(1); 8.4(5)
    Etude sur le Concile de Vaisali, 2.4.2(5)

Hokei Idzumi
    "The Hymn on the Life and Vows of Samantabhadra," 8.3.6(3)
    "Vimalakirti's Discourse on Emancipation," 3.3.2.1(36)
Holck, Fredrick
    Death and Eastern Thought, 7.4.2(9)
Holt, Claire
    Art in Indonesia, 5.5.6(5)
Honda, Yasuji
    "Yamabushi Kagura and Bangaku," 5.12.3(4)
Hong, Jung-shik
    "The Thought and Life of Wonhyo," 8.9.6(1)
Hooykaas, C.
    "Buddhism in Bali," 1.9.2(2)
Hori, Ichiro
    "On the Concept of Hijiri," 4.1.4(5)
    Folk Religion in Japan, 4.1.4(4); 5.12.3(5)
    "Self-mummified Buddhas in Japan," 7.4.2(10)
Horner, Isaline Blew
    The Book of the Discipline, 3.2.1.1(1), (3), (5), (6), (7); 6.2.7(5); 7.2.1(12); 11.3(7)
    "Buddhavamsa," 3.2.2.1(2)
    "Cariya-pitaka," 3.2.2.1(3)
    "Early Buddhism and the Taking of Life," 11.3(8)
    The Early Buddhist Theory of Man Perfected, 8.4(6); 11.1(5)
    "The Four Ways and the Four Fruits of Buddhism," 8.4(7)
    Majjhima Nikaya (The Middle Length Sayings), 3.2.2.1(16); 8.1.2.1(13); 11.4.3(1), (6); 11.4.4(5)
    Milinda's Questions, 3.2.2.1(17)
    "Vimana Vatthu," 3.2.2.1(30)
    Vinaya Pitaka, 8.1.2.1(14)
    Women Under Primitive Buddhism, 6.1.3(6)
Howarth, David
    My Land and My People, 8.9.2(6)
Hrdlickova, V.
    "The First Translations of Buddhist Sutras into Chinese Literature," 4.2.1(2); 4.2.3(17)
Hsieh Chih-Lu
    Tung-huang I-shu Hsu-lu, 5.9.4(5)
Hsiung, Shih-i
    "Drama," 5.12.1(4)
Hsu, Francis L. K.
    Under the Ancestors' Shadow, 4.1.3(4); 6.2.3(8)
Hsuan Tsang
    Ch'en Wei-shih Lun, 2.5.4(8); 2.7.12(4); 2.7.13(2); 3.3.3.2(3); 11.1(6)
Htin Aung, Maung
    Burmese Drama, 5.12.1(5)
    Burmese History Before 1287, 1.4.1(4)
    "Burmese Initiation Ceremonies," 7.4.1(3)
    "Customary Law in Burma," 6.2.7(6)
Htin Aung, U.
    Burmese Monk's Tales, 4.2.3(18); 4.2.4(7); 7.2.5(5)
    Folk Elements in Burmese Buddhism, 4.1.2(6)
Ho Shih
    "Buddhist Influence on Chinese Religious Life," 6.2.1.2(9)
    "Development of Zen Buddhism in China," 2.5.7(11)
    "The Indianization of China," 6.2.1.2(10)
Huang-po Tuan-chi ch'an-shih Wan-ling lu, 3.3.6.2(7)
Huang Shou-fu
    The Omei Illustrated Guide Book, 10.8.2(5)

Author/Title Index

Huber, Edouard
  Açvaghosa, Sutralamkara, 3.3.8.2(8); 4.2.3(3)
  "Le Pratimoksusutra des Sarvastivadins." See citations under Louis Finot.
Hui Li
  The Life of Hsuan Tsang, 8.9.3(41)
Hui-chiao
  Kao seng chuan, 8.9.3(1), (5), (6), (7), (8), (9), (13), (15), (16), (18), (20), (21), (22), (23), (24), (26), (27), (28), (33), (35), (36), (52), (64), (60), (63), (65), (67), (68), (69), (70), (71), (73), (76), (80), (86), (87)
Hullugalle, H. A. J.
  Ceylon of the Early Travellers, 10.1.4(2)
Hummel, Siegbert
  Geschichte der Tibetischen Kunst, 5.6(11)
  Die Lamaistische Kunst, 5.6(10)
Humphreys, Christmas
  A Popular Dictionary of Buddhism, 12.1(5)
  Sixty Years of Buddhism in England, 1.17(5)
  The Way of Action, 2.7.1(4)
Hunter, Louise H.
  Buddhism in Hawaii, 1.17(6)
Hurvitz, Leon Nahum
  "The Buddha of Seiroji." See citations under Gregory Henderson.
  Chih I, 2.5.6(3); 11.4.9(3)
  "Chih I," 8.9.3(11)
  "Render Unto Caesar," 6.2.2.5(5)
  "The Road to Buddhist Salvation as Described by Vasubhadra," 11.1(7)
Hyers, Conrad
  Zen and the Comic Spirit, 2.5.7(12)

I Ching
  A Record of the Buddhist Religion, 1.2.2.3(8); 1.9.2(3); 7.1.3(10); 7.1.4(4); 7.2.1(2); 7.2.2(7); 7.2.4(3); 8.9.3(51); 10.1.1(5)
Ichiro, Hari
  Japanese Religion, 1.13.1(6)
Ienaga, Saburo
  "Japan's Modernization and Buddhism," 6.2.2.6(6)
  Painting in the Yamato Style, 5.11.5(4)
Iggleden, R. E. W.
  "Short Survey of Buddhism in the West," 1.17(7)
Inada, Kenneth
  "Whitehead's 'Actual Entity' and the Buddha's Anatman," 2.9(24)
Inagaki, Hisao
  The Kyo Gyo Shisho, 3.3.7.2(5)
  "Padma-Symbolism in Pure Land Thought," 9.3.3(4)
Ingersoll, Jasper
  "The Priest Role in Central Village Thailand," 6.1.2(10); 6.2.3(9)
  "Theravada Buddhism and Village Economic Behavior," 6.2.3(10); 6.2.6(12)
Ingholt, Harald
  Gandharan Art in Pakistan, 5.2.5(8)
Ingram, Paul O.
  "Soka Gakkai and the Komeito," 6.2.2.6(7)
  "The Symbolism of Light and Pure Land," 9.3.9(3); 11.7.3(2)
Inoue, Mitsusada
  "Eizon Ninsho and the Saidai-ji Order," 1.13.2.2(9)
Irwin, John
  "Asokan Pillars," 5.2.4(11)
Isaacs, Harold R.
  India's Ex-Untouchables, 1.2.2.4(2); 6.2.4(4)

Ishida, Mitsyki
  "Tendai Elements in the Doctrinal Systems of Honen's Disciples," 2.5.8(11)
Ishida, Mosaku
  Japanese Buddhist Prints, 5.11.5(5)
Ishii, Yoneo
  "Thailand: Church and State," 6.2.2.4(3)
Itivuttaka, 3.2.2.1(11)
Ito, Teiji
  The Japanese Garden, 5.11.7(2)
  Space and Illusion in the Japanese Garden, 5.11.7(3)
Izumida, Junjo
  Shinranism in Mahayana Buddhism. See citations under Takeichi Takahashi.

Jackson, Carl T.
  "The Orient in Post-Bellum American Thought," 2.9(25)
Jagchid, Sechin
  "Buddhism in Mongolia after the Collapse of the Yuan Dynasty," 1.16.2(4)
Jahn, Karl
  "Kamalashri-Rashid al-Din's 'Life and Teaching of Buddha," 1.10.2(8)
Jaini, Padmarabh S.
  "Buddha's Prolongation of Life," 8.1.2.2(5)
  "On the Sarvajnatva (Omniscience) of Mahavira and the Buddha," 8.1.2.2(6)
  "Sramanas: Their Conflict with Brahmanical Society," 2.2(8)
  "On the Theory of Two Vasubandhus," 8.9.1(52)
James, J. M.
  "Descriptive Notes on the Rosaries (jiu-dzu) as Used by the Different Sects of Buddhism in Japan," 7.1.4(5)
Jan, Yun-hua
  "Buddhist Relations Between India and Sung China," 1.11.2.3(8)
  "Buddhist Self-immolation in Medieval China," 7.4.2(11)
  A Chronicle of Buddhism in China, 1.11.2.2(4); 1.11.2.3(9)
  "South India in the VIII Century," 10.1.1(6)
  "Tsung-mi: His Analysis of Ch'an Buddhism," 2.5.7(13); 8.9.3(82)
Jardine, John
  "Buddhist Law," 6.2.7(7)
Jataka, 3.2.2.1(12)
Jatakastava, 3.3.8.4(5); 4.2.2(5); 8.1.1(9)
Jatakatthakatha, 3.2.2.3(3); 4.2.2(6); 8.1.1(10)
Jatava, D. R.
  The Buddha and Karl Marx, 2.8(10)
Jaworski, Jan
  "L'Avalambanasutra de la Terre Pure," 4.2.1(3); 9.2.2.3(6)
Jayasekera, U. D.
  Early History of Education in Ceylon, 6.2.5(12)
Jayaswal, Kashi Prasad
  Hindu Polity, 6.2.2.1(10)
  "Republican Origin of the Buddhist Sangha," 6.2.2.1(10)
Jayatilleke, Kashi Nath
  The Message of the Buddha, 2.1(6)
Jayatilleke, Kulatissa Nanda
  Aspects of Buddhist Social Philosophy, 6.2.4(5)
  Buddhist Attitude to Other Religions, 2.8(11)
  "Buddhist Relativity and the One-World Concept," 2.8(12)
  Early Buddhist Theory of Knowledge, 2.2(9)
  Ethics in Buddhist Perspective, 11.3(9)

Jayaweera, Swarna
    "Religious Organizations and the State in Ceylonese Education," 6.2.5(13)

Jayawickrama, N. A.
    "Buddhaghosa and the Traditional Classifications of the Pali Canon," 3.1.2(4)
    Chronicle of the Thupa, 9.1.5(16); 9.3.6(11)
    The Inception of Discipline, 3.2.1.3(1); 8.1.2.4(13)
    The Sheaf of Garlands of the Epochs of the Conqueror. See citations under Thera Ratanapanya.

Jayewardene, Junius Richard
    Buddhism and Marxism, 2.8(13)

Jennings, J. G.
    The Vedantic Buddhism of the Buddha, 2.3(3)

Jerstad, Luther G.
    Mani-Rimdu, 5.12.1(6)

Jha, Ganganatha
    The Tattvasangraha of Santaraksita, 3.3.2.1(11), (25)

Jinacarita, 3.2.4.1(6); 8.1.2.1(15)

Jinakalamalini, 9.1.5(8)

Jinaratana, Mahasthavira Neluwe
    "Buddhist Festivals," 7.3.1(5)

Jisl, Lumir
    Tibetan Art, 5.6(12)

Jivaka, Lobsang
    "Le Bouddhisme tibétain," 1.14.1(7)

Johansson, Rune E. A.
    The Psychology of Nirvana, 11.8(1)

Johnston, Edward Hamilton
    The Buddhacarita, 3.2.4.1(5); 8.1.2.1(3)
    Saundarananda, 3.2.4.1(2); 8.8(2)

Johnston, E. J.
    "The Lands of the Gong," 3.3.8.2(5); 7.2.3(2)

Johnston, Reginald Fleming
    Buddhist China, 10.8.2(6)

Jones, G. H.
    "Korea's Colossal Image of Buddha," 1.12.2(5)

Jones, J. Garrett
    "The Four Truths and the Three Marks," 2.7.5(4)

Jones, J. J.
    Mahavastu, 3.2.1.2(5); 3.2.4.1(7); 8.1.1(12); 8.1.2.1(16); 8.2.1(4); 9.1.2(6); 9.2.2.3(10); 9.2.2.4(9); 10.2.4(2)

Jong, Jan Willem de
    "The Background of Early Buddhism," 2.2(10)
    "A Brief History of Buddhist Studies in Europe and America," 1.17(8); 2.9(26)
    "Le Problème de l'absolu dans l'école Madhyamika," 2.7.8(5)

Joseph, Marietta B.
    "The Viharas of the Kathmandu Valley," 6.1.1(11)

Joshi, Lal Mani
    Studies in the Buddhistic Culture of India, 1.2.2.3(9); 2.3(4); 6.2.5(14); 6.2.6(13)

Julien, Stanislaus
    Voyages des pèlerins bouddhistes, 10.1.1(7)

Jung, Gustav C.
    Mandala Symbolism, 11.6.2(6)

Jurji, Edward J.
    Religious Pluralism and the World Community, 2.8(12); 6.2.7(15)

Kadokawa, Shoten
    A Pictorial Encyclopedia of the Oriental Arts: China, 5.9.1(7)
    A Pictorial Encyclopedia of the Oriental Arts: Japan, 5.11.2(5)
    A Pictorial Encyclopedia of the Oriental Arts: Korea, 5.10(7)

Kakhun
    Lives of Eminent Korean Monks, 1.12.1(4); 8.9.6(2)

Kalupahana, David J.
    Buddhist Philosophy, 2.1(7)
    "Schools of Buddhism in Ceylon," 1.3.2.1(7)

Kamalasila
    Bhavanakrama, 11.4.2(6)
    Tattvasamgrahapanjika, 3.3.2.1(11)

Kamstra, J. H.
    Encounter or Syncretism: The Initial Growth of Japanese Buddhism, 1.13.2.1(3)

Kanaoka, Shuyu
    "Vairocana in Tathagata Form," 8.2.2(5)

Kaneko, Daier
    "The Meaning of Salvation in the Doctrine of Pure Land Buddhism," 11.7.4(5)

Kao Kuan-ju
    "Avatamsaka Sutra," 3.3.4.2(3)

Karambelkar, V. W.
    "Matsyendranatha and His Yogini Cult," 7.8(5)
    "The Problem of Nagarjuna," 8.9.1(39)

Kariyanwasam, A. G. S.
    "Amoghasiddhi," 8.2.2(6)

Karma-sataka, 4.2.3(19)

Karpeles, Suzanne
    "Cent strophes en l'honneur du seigneur du monde," 8.3.2(14)

Karunaratne, T. B.
    The Buddhist Wheel Symbol, 9.3.2(4)

Karunatillake, W. S.
    "Avatamsaka School," 2.5.5(3)

Kathavattu, 2.4.1(7); 2.7.1(5); 2.7.2(2); 2.7.3(2); 2.7.4(5); 3.2.3.1(5); 9.2.2.2(1); 9.2.2.4(4); 9.2.3(3)

Kathinavastu, 3.2.1.2(4)

Kato, Bunno
    Myoho-Renge-Kyo, 3.3.5.1(5)

Katz, Nathan
    "An Appraisal of the Svatantrika-Prasanghika Debates," 2.5.3(5)

Kaufman, Howard Keva
    Bangkhuad: A Community Study in Thailand, 7.1.2(2)

Kaufman, Walter
    "The Mudras in Samavedic Chant," 5.12.3(6)

Kausika prajnaparamita-sutra, 3.3.1.1(5)

Kawaguchi, Ekai
    Three Years in Tibet, 10.1.3(6)

Kayagatasati-sutta, 11.4.3(6)

Kearney, Robert
    "Sinhalese Nationalism and Social Conflict in Ceylon," 6.2.2.2(9)

Keay, F. B.
    Ancient Indian Education, 6.2.5(15)

Keene, Donald
    Landscapes and Portraits, 5.12.2(5)
    No, 5.12.2(6)
    Twenty Plays of the No Theatre, 5.12.2(7)

Keith, Arthur Berriedale
    Buddhist Philosophy in India and Ceylon, 2.1(8); 2.5.2(6)
    "Pre-canonical Buddhism," 2.3(5)
    The Sanskrit Drama, 5.12.1(7)

Kemp, Jeremy
    Aspects of Siamese Kingship in the Seventeenth Century, 6.2.2.4(4)

Kempers, A. J. Bernet
    Ancient Indonesian Art, 5.5.6(6)

Kennedy, Jean W.
"The Secret of Kanishka," 8.9.1(33)
"Vimana Vatthu," 3.2.2.1(30); 9.2.2.4(11)
Kennett, Jiyu
Selling Water by the River, 2.5.7(14)
Kern, Hendrik
Der Buddhismus und seine Geschichte in Indien, 1.2.1(9)
Histoire du Bouddhisme dans l'Inde, 1.2.1(9)
The Lotus of the True Law, 4.2.1(6); 7.1.3(13); 9.3.9(5)
Manual of Indian Buddhism, 1.2.1(9); 6.1.1(12)
The Saddharma-Pundarika, 3.3.5.1(2); 8.1.2.1(17); 8.3.2(6); 11.6.3(6)
Kerouac, John (Jack)
The Dharma Bums, 1.17(9); 2.9(27)
Kessle, Gun
Angkor. See citations under Jan Myrdal.
Keyes, Charles F.
"Buddhism and National Integration in Thailand," 6.2.1.1(16)
"Buddhist Pilgrimage Centers and the Twelve Year Cycle," 7.3.1(6); 10.5(4)
Khan, F. A.
Architecture and Art Treasures in Pakistan, 5.2.5(9)
Khantipalo Phra
Tolerance: A Study from Buddhist Sources, 11.3(10)
Khosla, Sarla
History of Buddhism in Kashmir, 1.2.2.4(8)
Khuddaka-patha, 3.2.2.1(13), (14)
Kidder, Jonathan Edward, Jr.
Early Buddhist Japan, 1.13.2.1(4); 5.11.3(5)
Japanese Temples, 5.11.3(6); 10.9(3)
Masterpieces of Japanese Sculpture, 5.11.4(3)
Kim, Chewon
The Arts of Korea, 5.10(8)
"The Stone Pagoda of Kuo Huang Li," 5.10(9)
Treasures of Korean Art, 5.10(11)
"Treasures from the Songyimsa Temple," 5.10(10)
Kim, Wong-Yong
Treasures of Korean Art. See citations under Chewon Kim.
Kimura, Ryukan
Introduction to the History of Early Buddhist Schools, 2.4.1(8)
Kimura, Taihen
"The Date of Vasubandhu," 8.9.1(53)
Kincitvistara Tara Sadhana, 3.4.1(5)
King, Winston Lee
Buddhism and Christianity, 2.9(28)
"Buddhism and Political Power in Burma," 6.2.2.3(4)
"A Comparison of Theravada and Zen Buddhist Meditational Methods and Goals," 11.4.8.1(6)
In the Hope of Nibbana, 11.3(11); 11.8(2)
"Practicing Dying," 7.4.2(12)
"Split Selves and Fractured Karma," 2.7.1(6)
A Thousand Lives Away, 2.8(14); 4.1.2(7); 11.4.1(4)
Kirby, John B., Jr.
From Castle to Teahouse, 5.11.3(7)
Kirfel, W.
Die Kosmographie der Inder, 9.2.1(6)
Kirsch, A. Thomas
Change and Peristence in Thai Society. See citations under G. William Skinner.
Kishibe, Shigeo
The Traditional Music of Japan, 5.12.3(7)

Kishimoto, Kideo
"The Immediacy of Zen Experience," 5.11.6(7); 11.4.8.3(2)
Kitagawa, Joseph Mitsuo
"Buddhism in America," 1.17(10)
"Buddhism and Asian Politics," 6.2.2.1(11)
"Buddhism, History of," 1.1(5)
"Buddhism in Taiwan Today," 1.11.2.4(3)
"Buddhist Ethics and International Relations," 11.3(12)
"The Buddhist Transformation in Japan," 1.13.1(7)
"The Contemporary Religious Situation in Japan," 1.13.2.4(3)
"Master and Savior," 2.6.2(3); 8.9.4(19)
Religion in Japanese History, 1.13.1(8); 6.2.1.2(11)
Religions of the East, 6.1.1(13); 6.2.1.2(13)
"Religions of Japan," 1.13.1(9); 6.2.1.2(12)
"Religious and Cultural Ethos of Modern Japan," 6.2.1.2(14)
Kiyota, Minoru
"Buddhism in Postwar Japan," 1.13.2.4(4)
"Buddhism and Social Change in Southeast Asia," 6.2.1.1(17)
"Introduction to the Hizo-Hoyaku," 3.4.3(2)
"Meiji Buddhism: Religion and Patriotism," 1.13.2.4(5); 6.2.2.6(8)
"Shingon Mikkyo Mandala," 11.6.2(7)
"The Structure and Meaning of Tendai Thought," 2.5.6(4)
"The Three Modes of Encompassing," 2.7.13(3)
Klaproth, Julius Heinrich
"Vie de Bouddha d'après les livres mongols," 8.1.2.1(18)
Klausner, William J.
"Popular Buddhism in Northeast Thailand," 6.2.3(11)
Kloppenborg, Ria
The Paccekabuddha, Buddhist Ascetic, 8.2.1(5)
Knox, Robert
"An Historical Relationship of Ceylon," 1.3.2.1(8); 10.1.4(3)
Kokusai Bunka Shinkokai
Tradition of Japanese Garden, 5.11.7(4)
Kolarz, Walter
Religion in the Soviet Union, 1.10.2(9); 1.16.2(5)
Kolmas, Josef
"Notes on the Kanjur and Tanjur in Prague," 3.1.4(8)
Know, Sten
"Aparimitayuh sutra," 3.3.8.4(1)
"Excavations at Sarnath." See citations under John Marshall.
"Vajracchedika prajnaparamita-sutra," 3.3.1.1(27)
Kosambi, Damodar Dharmanand
Ancient India, 1.2.2.1(5)
The Culture and Civilization of Ancient India in Historical Outline, 6.2.1.1(18)
Koshelinko, G.
"The Beginning of Buddhism in Margiana," 1.10.2(10)
Kramrisch, Stella
The Art of India, 5.2.1(13)
The Art of Nepal, 5.3(2)
"Die Figurale Plastik der Guptazeit," 5.2.8(9)
Indian Sculpture, 5.2.1(14)
"Pala and Sena Sculptures," 5.2.8(10)
A Survey of Painting in the Deccan, 5.2.6(10)

Krasa, Miloslav
   The Temples of Angkor, 10.6(6)
Krishnan, Y.
   "Was it Permissible for a Samnyasi (Monk) to Revert to Lay Life?," 6.1.2(11)
   "Was There Any Conflict Between the Brahmins and the Buddhists?," 6.2.4(6)
Krom, Nicolas J.
   The Life of the Buddha on the Stupa of Barabudur, 5.5.6(7); 8.1.2.4(14)
Kuan-p'u-hsien-p'u-sa-hsing-fa-ching, 3.3.5.1(1)
Kubo, Noritada
   "Prolegomena on the Study of Controversies between Buddhists and Taoists in the Yuan Period," 1.11.2.3(10)
Kuck, Loraine
   The World of the Japanese Garden, 5.11.7(5)
Kukai
   Major Works, 2.6.2(4)
   The Secret Key to the Heart Sutra, 3.3.1.2(5)
Kun Chang
   A Comparative Study of the Kathinavastu, 3.2.1.2(4)
Kung-hsien Shih-k'u-ssu, 5.9.4(6)
Kuno, Horyu
   "Fragments du Vinaya des Sarvastivadin." See citations under Jean Filliozat.
Kuno, Takeshi
   A Guide to Japanese Sculpture, 5.11.4(4)
   Kanto chokoku no kenkyu, 5.11.4(5)
Kunst, A.
   Buddhist Studies in Honour of I. B. Horner. See citations under L. Cousins.
Kuo Yuan-hsing
   See Kao Kuan-ju.
Kupfer, Carl
   Sacred Places in China, 10.8.1(3)
Kurata, Hyakuzo
   The Priest and His Disciples, 4.4(7)
   Shinran, 4.5(4)
Kusalasaya, Karuna
   "Buddhism in Siam," 1.5.1(6)
Kvarne, Per
   "Aspects of the Origin of the Buddhist Tradition in Tibet," 1.14.2.1(5)
Kwon Sang-no
   "History of Korean Buddhism," 1.12.1(5)

Lach, Donald Frederick
   Asia in the Making of Europe, 1.17(11); 2.9(29)
La-dvag-rgyal-rabs, 9.1.5(9)
LaFleur, William R.
   "The Death and Lives of the Poet-Monk Saigyo," 8.9.4(24)
   "Saigyo and the Buddhist Value of Nature," 4.3(6)
Lafont, Pierre-Bernard
   "Les écritures du Pali au Laos," 3.1.2(5)
   "Introduction du Bouddhisme au Laos," 1.7.2(5)
   "Ordination de deux dignitaires bouddhiques," 7.2.1(3)
La Fuente, Marguerite
   Pirit Nula, 7.5.4(4)
Lai, T'ien-ch'ang
   Selected Chinese Sayings, 4.2.4(8)
Lakkhanasutta, 9.3.8(5)
Lal, P.
   Dhammapada, 3.2.2.1(6)
Lalitavistara, 3.3.8.1(2); 9.3.1(6)

Lalou, Marcelle
   "Le culte des naga et la thérapeutique," 7.8(6); 9.2.2.5(4)
   "Deux Prières de Caravaniers Tibétains," 7.1.4(6)
   "Document tibétain sur l'expansion du Dhyana chinois," 2.5.7(15)
   Iconographie des Etoffes Peintes (Pata) dans le Manjusrimulakalpa, 3.4.2(10); 5.6(13)
   "Manjusrimulakalpa et Taramulakalpa," 3.4.4(3)
   "Notes à propos d'une amulette de Touen Houang," 7.5.3(2)
   "Notes de mythologie bouddhique." See citations under Jean Przyluski.
   "Préliminaires d'une étude des Ganacakra," 11.6.1(17)
   "Récits Populaires et Contes Bouddhiques." See citations under Jean Przyluski.
   Les religions du Tibet, 1.14.1(8)
La Loubere, Simon de
   The Kingdom of Siam, 1.5.2(12); 10.1.4(4)
Lamotte, Etienne
   "L'Alayavijnana (Le Réceptacle) dans le Mahayanasamgraha," 2.7.12(5)
   "Alexandre et le Bouddhisme," 1.2.2.3(10)
   "La bienveillance bouddhique," 11.4.3(7)
   "Le Bouddha insulta-t-il Devadatta?," 8.8(7)
   "Buddhist Controversy over the Five Propositions," 2.4.4(3)
   "La Concentration de la Marche Héroïque," 3.3.2.1(33); 11.4.5(8)
   L'Enseignement de Vimalakirti, 3.3.2.1(34); 4.2.1(8); 9.2.4(5)
   Histoire du Bouddhisme indien, 1.2.1(10); 2.4.1(9); 2.7.7(6); 8.3.4(5); 8.4(8); 8.9.1(3); 9.1.3(4); 9.2.1(7); 9.2.2.2(2); 9.2.2.4(5); 9.2.2.5(5); 9.2.3(4)
   "Khuddaka-nikaya and Ksudrakapitaka," 3.2.2.4(5)
   "La légende du Bouddha," 8.1.2.3(18)
   "Manjusri," 8.3.5(2)
   "Passions and Impregnations of the Passions in Buddhism," 8.1.2.2(7)
   Samdhinirmocana Sutra, 3.3.3.1(17)
   La Somme du Grand Véhicule d'Asanga Mahayanasamgraha, 3.3.3.1(3)
   "Le suicide religieux dans le bouddhisme ancien," 7.4.2(13)
   "Sur la Formation du Mahayana," 2.5.2(7)
   "Le traité de l'acte de Vasubandhu," 2.4.3(6); 2.7.1(7); 3.2.3.2(5)
   Le Traité de la Grande Vertu, 3.3.1.2(6); 3.3.2.1(12); 6.1.1(14); 8.1.2.2(8), (9); 8.2.1(6); 8.3.1(7); 8.4(9); 8.8(8), (9), (10), (11); 9.2.4(3); 9.3.5(8); 9.3.9(4); 11.4.3(8); 11.4.5(9); 11.4.6(6); 11.5(5)
   "Vajrapani en Inde," 8.3.6(4)
Lancashire, Douglas
   "Buddhist Reaction to Christianity in Late Ming China," 2.9(30)
Lancaster, L.
   "The Questions of Nagasri," 3.3.1.1(6)
Lane, George S.
   "The Tocharian Punyavantajataka," 4.2.2(7)
Lang, M. E.
   "La Mahajjatakamala," 4.2.2(9)
Lankavatarasutra, 2.7.13(4); 3.3.3.1(15); 3.3.6.1(3)
Lasswell, Harold D.
   The Ethics of Power, 6.2.2.1(3)
Lattimore, Owen
   "Religion and Revolution in Mongolia," 1.16.2(6); 6.2.2.9(1)

Author/Title Index

La Vallée Poussin, Louis de
  L'Abhidharmakosa de Vasubandhu, 3.2.3.2(4);
    9.1.1(5); 9.1.2(9); 9.1.3(5); 9.2.1(13);
    9.2.2.1(8); 9.2.5(4)
  "Adi Buddha," 8.2.1(7)
  "Ages of the World (Buddhist)," 9.1.1(3)
  "The Atman in the Pali Canon," 2.7.4(6)
  "Avalokitesvara," 8.3.2(7)
  Bodhicaryavatara, 3.3.2.1(27)
  "Bodhisattva-Bhumi." See citations under Cecil
    Bendall.
  "Bodhisattvas," 8.3.1(8)
  "Bouddhisme: Etudes et matériaux," 9.1.2(4);
    9.2.1(8); 9.2.2.4(6); 9.3.2(5); 11.6.1(18)
  Bouddhisme, opinions sur l'histoire de la
    dogmatique, 11.2(4)
  "The Buddhist Councils," 2.4.2(6)
  "The Buddhist Wheel of Life from a New Source,"
    9.2.5(3)
  "Cosmogony and Cosmology (Buddhist)," 9.2.1(9)
  "Death and Disposal of the Dead (Buddhist),"
    2.7.1(8)
  "Les deux, les quatre, les trois vérités,"
    2.7.9(3)
  "Documents d'Abhidharma," 2.7.7(7); 3.2.3.4(7);
    11.8(3)
  "Documents d'Abhidharma, la Controverse du
    Temps," 2.7.3(3)
  "Documents d'Abhidharma, traduits et annotés,"
    3.2.3.4(6); 11.2(5)
  "Les fidèles laïcs ou Upasaka," 6.1.2(12)
  "The Five Points of Mahadeva," 2.4.4(4)
  "Le Joyau dans la Main," 3.3.2.1(5)
  "Lotus of the True Law," 3.3.5.2(2)
  "Madhyamakavatara," 3.3.2.1(7)
  "Musila et Narada: Le chemin du Nirvana,"
    11.4.5(10); 11.4.7(4)
  Nirvana, 11.8(4)
  "Le Nirvana d'après Aryadeva," 11.8(5)
  "Note sur l'Alayavijnana," 2.7.12(6)
  "Le Petit Traité de Vasubandhu-Nagarjuna,"
    3.3.3.1(19)
  "Pratyekabuddha," 8.2.1(8)
  "Les Quatres Odes de Nagarjuna," 3.3.2.1(14)
  "Reflexions sur le Madhyamika," 2.5.3(6)
  "Sautrantikas," 2.4.3(7)
  "Staupikam," 9.3.6(5)
  "Studies in Buddhist Dogma: The Three Bodies
    of a Buddha," 8.1.3(7)
  "Traité des Vingt Slokas," 3.3.3.1(22)
  Vijnaptimatratasiddhi, 3.3.3.2(6)
  "Vyadhisutra on the Four Aryasatyas," 2.7.5(5)
  The Way to Nirvana, 2.7.1(9)
Law, Bimala Churn
  "Aspects of Nirvana," 11.8(6)
  Asvaghosa, 8.9.1(22)
  "Buddha's Activities at Anga-Magadha,"
    8.1.2.3(19)
  The Buddhist Conception of Spirits, 9.2.2.3(7)
  "Buddhavamsa," 3.2.2.1(2); 8.1.2.1(19)
  Buddhistic Studies, 2.4.2(7); 6.2.5(26);
    7.3.1(11); 9.3.5(6); 11.2(1)
  "Cariya-pitaka," 3.2.2.1(3); 8.1.1(3)
  "The Concept of Morality in Buddhism and
    Jainism," 11.3(13)
  The Dathavamsa: A History of the Tooth-Relic of
    the Buddha, 8.1.2.4(7); 9.1.5(4)
  The Debates Commentary, 3.2.3.3(4)
  Designation of Human Types, 3.2.3.1(4)
  "Formulation of Pratityasamutpada," 2.7.6(7)
  Geography of Early Buddhism, 10.2.1(13)
  Heaven and Hell in Buddhist Perspective,
    5.2.3(17); 9.2.2.3(8); 9.2.2.4(7)
  Historical Gleanings, 1.2.2.1(6); 2.2(11)
  The History of the Buddha's Religion, 1.4.1(15);
    9.1.5(13)
  A History of Pali Literature, 3.1.2(6)
  Indological Studies, 10.2.2(3); 10.2.6.1(3), (4)
  "Karma," 2.7.1(10)
  Ksatriya Clans in Buddhist India, 1.2.2.1(7)
  The Life and Works of Buddhaghosa, 1.3.2.1(9);
    8.9.1(25); 8.9.5(4)
  A Manual of Buddhist Historical Traditions,
    9.1.5(11)
  "A Short Account of the Wandering Ascetics,"
    6.1.1(15)
  "Some Observations on the Jatakas," 4.2.2(8);
    8.1.1(11)
  Sravasti in Indian Literature, 10.2.6.1(5)
  "Tirukkural et Dhammapada," 3.2.2.4(6)
Law, Narendra Nath
  Louis de La Vallée Poussin Memorial Volume,
    2.7.4(4)
Layman, Emma McCloy
  Buddhism in America, 1.17(12)
Le Hu'o'ng
  "Les sectes bouddhiques au Sud Viet-nam,"
    1.8.1(6)
Leach, Bernard
  Kenzan and his Tradition, 5.11.6(8)
Leach, Edmund Ronald
  "Buddhism in the Post-Colonial Political Order
    in Burma and Ceylon," 6.2.2.2(10);
    6.2.3(5)
  Dialectic in Practical Religion, 6.1.2(15);
    6.2.3(19)
  "Pulleyar and the Lord Buddha," 4.1.1(8)
Le Bar, Frank M.
  Laos: Its People, its Society, its Culture,
    1.7.1(4); 6.2.1.1(19)
Leclere, Adhemard
  Le Bouddhisme au Cambodge, 1.6.1(4); 6.1.1(16);
    6.2.1.1(20); 7.1.4(7); 7.2.1(4); 7.2.2(8);
    7.2.4(4); 7.2.6(4); 7.3.1(7); 9.1.2(5);
    9.2.1(10); 9.2.2.3(9)
  Cambodge: Festes Civiles et Religieuses,
    7.3.1(2)
  Les crémations et les rites funéraires au
    Cambodge, 7.4.2(14)
  Les Livres Sacres du Cambodge, 3.1.6(4);
    8.1.2.1(20)
Le Coq, Albert von
  Buried Treasures of Chinese Turkestan, 10.1.1(8)
Ledyard, Carl
  "Cultural and Political Aspects of Traditional
    Korean Buddhism," 1.12.2(6); 6.2.2.9(2)
Lee, Orlan
  "From Acts--to Non-Action--to Acts," 2.7.1(11)
  Cases Under Burmese Law, 6.2.7(8)
Lee, Peter H.
  "Fa-tsang and Uisang," 1.12.2(7); 8.9.3(30);
    8.9.6(3)
  "The Life of the Korean Poet-Priest Kyunyo,"
    1.12.2(8); 8.9.6(4)
Lee, Sherman E.
  Ancient Cambodian Sculpture, 5.5.4(8)
  Chinese Art under the Mongols, 5.9.1(8)
  A History of Far Eastern Art, 5.1.4(8); 5.8(6)
  "Six of the 500 Rakan," 5.11.4(6)
  Tea Taste in Japanese Art, 5.11.8(5)

Leland, C. G.
   Fusang or the Discovery of America by Chinese Buddhist Priests, 1.17(13)

Le May, Reginald
   An Asian Arcady: The Land and People of Northern Siam, 1.5.2(13)
   The Concise History of Buddhist Art in Siam, 5.5.3(8); 10.5(5)
   The Culture of South-East Asia, 6.2.1.1(21)

Lessing, Ferdinand D.
   "Bodhisattva Confucius," 7.8(7); 8.3.6(5)
   "Structure and Meaning of the Rite Called the Bath of the Buddha," 7.1.3(11)
   Yung-ho-kung, 5.9.2(8); 7.5.3(3); 7.8(8); 8.6(3); 9.2.2.4(8); 11.6.2(8)

Lester, Robert
   Theravada Buddhism in Southeast Asia, 6.1.1(17); 6.1.2(13); 6.2.2.1(12)

Levi, Sylvain
   Asanga: Mahayana-sutralamkara, 3.3.3.1(4)
   "Asvaghosa, le Sutralamkara et ses Sources," 8.9.1(23)
   "Le catalogue géographique des Yaksas dans le Mahamayuri," 7.5.3(4); 9.2.2.5(6)
   "Les Eléments de Formation du Divyavadana," 4.2.3(20)
   Fragments des textes Koutchéens, 3.2.2.3(4)
   "Kaniska et Satavahana," 8.9.1(34)
   "Maitreya le consolateur," 8.3.4(6); 9.1.4(4)
   Matériaux pour l'Etude du Système Vijnaptimatra, 3.3.3.1(18)
   "Pour l'histoire du Ramayana," 9.2.2.1(6)
   "Les Seize Arhat protecteurs de la Loi," 3.3.8.2(6); 8.4(10)
   Un Système de Philosophie Bouddhique, 2.5.4(9); 2.7.12(7); 3.3.3.3(1)
   "La Trentaine," 3.3.3.1(18)
   "La Vingtaine," 3.3.3.1(22)

Levine, Deborah Brown
   "Aurangabad," 5.2.6(11)

Levy, Howard S.
   Translations from Po Chu-i's Collected Works, 4.3(7)

Levy, Paul
   Buddhism: A Mystery Religion?, 7.2.1(5); 8.4(11)
   "Les traces de l'introduction du Bouddhisme à Luang Prabang," 1.7.2(6)

Li, An-che
   "The Bkah-Brgyud Sect of Lamaism," 1.14.2.2(5)
   "The Lamasery as an Educational Institution," 6.2.5(16)
   "Rnin-ma-pa: The Early Form of Lamaism," 1.14.2.1(6); 6.2.5(17)

Li, T'ieh-cheng
   Tibet, Today and Yesterday, 1.14.1(9)

Liebenthal, Walter
   "A Biography of Chu Tao-sheng," 1.11.2.2(5); 8.9.3(19)
   The Book of Chao, 3.3.6.1(1); 3.3.8.2(4)
   "Chinese Buddhism During the 4th and 5th Centuries," 1.11.2.2(6)
   "Shih Hui-yuan's Buddhism," 2.5.8(12); 8.9.3(47)

Lienhard, Siegfried
   Manicudavadanoddhrta: A Buddhist Rebirth Story, 4.2.3(21)
   Nevarigitimanjari: Religious and Secular Poetry, 4.3(8)

Lin Li-Kouang
   Dharmasamuccaya, 3.2.2.2(4)

Ling, R.
   "Buddhist Factors in Population Growth and Control," 6.2.3(12)

Ling, Trevor
   The Buddha: Buddhist civilization in India and Ceylon, 1.2.1(11); 1.3.1(5)
   Buddha, Marx, and God, 2.8(15)
   Buddhism and the Mythology of Evil, 9.3.5(7)
   A Dictionary of Buddhism, 12.1(6)
   "The Social Dimension of Theravada Buddhism in Burma," 6.2.1.1(22)

Lingat, Robert
   "The Buddhist Manu," 6.2.7(9)
   "La Conception du droit dans l'Indochine Hinayaniste," 6.2.7(10)
   "La double crise de l'Eglise Bouddhique au Siam," 1.5.2(14)
   "Evolution of the Conception of Law in Burma and Siam," 1.4.2(8); 1.5.2(15); 6.2.7(11)
   "La vie religieuse du roi Mongkut," 1.5.2(16)
   "Vinaya et droit laïque," 6.2.7(12)

Link, Arthur E.
   "Biography of Shih Tao-an," 1.11.2.2(7); 8.9.3(81)

Linssen, Robert
   Living Zen, 11.4.8.3(3)

Lion-Goldschmidt, Daisy
   Chinese Art, 5.9.1(9)

Li-Tai Ming Hua Chi
   Some T'ang and Pre-T'ang Texts on Chinese Painting, 5.9.3(1)

Little, Archibald John
   Mount Omei and Beyond, 10.8.2(7)

Litvinsky, Boris Anatolevich
   "Outline History of Buddhism in Central Asia," 1.10.1(4)

Liu Ts'un-yan
   "Lu Hsi-Hsing," 8.9.3(62)

Liu-tsu t'an-ching, 3.3.6.1(4), (5), (6), (7)

Livingston, Helen H.
   Cross-Cultural Understanding. See citations under F. S. C. Northrop.

Liyanagamage, Amaradasa
   The Decline of Polonnaruwa and the Rise of Dambadeniya, 1.3.2.1(10)

Lloyd, Arthur
   The Creed of Half Japan, 1.12.2(9); 1.13.1(10); 2.5.9(2)
   "Death and the Disposal of the Dead (Japanese)," 7.4.2(15)
   "Development of Japanese Buddhism," 2.6.2(5)
   The Praises of Amida, 7.2.5(7)

Loffler, Lorenz G.
   "Beast, Bird and Fish," 9.3.10(2)

Lokananda, 4.4(8)

Long, Charles
   Myths and Symbols. See citations under Joseph Mitsuo Kitagawa.

Longhurst, H.
   The Buddhist Antiquities of Nagarjunakonda, 5.2.7(4); 10.2.6.3(3)

Lorgeou, M. E.
   "Notice sur un manuscript siamois contenant la relation de deux missions religieuses envoyées de Siam à Ceylan au milieu de xviii-e siècle," 1.5.2(17)

Louis-Frédéric (pseud.)
   Japan: Art and Civilization, 5.11.2(6)

Lounsbery, G. Constant
   Buddhist Meditation in the Southern School, 11.4.4(3)

Lowell, Percival
    The Soul of the Far East, 2.9(31)
Lu K'uan Yu
    Ch'an and Zen Teaching, 2.5.7(16); 3.3.6.1(5);
        3.3.6.2(5), (6); 3.3.6.3(5); 8.8(12);
        8.9.3(31), (57), (59), (84), (90)
    The Secrets of Chinese Meditation, 11.4.1(5);
        11.4.2(4); 11.4.8.1(7); 11.4.9(4); 11.7.1(2)
    The Vimalakirti Nirdesa Sutra, 3.3.2.1(35);
        8.3.6(6)
de Lubac, Henri
    La Rencontre du Bouddhisme et de l'Occident,
        2.9(32)
Luce, Gordon H.
    "The Advent of Buddhism in Burma," 1.4.2(9)
    "The Ancient Pyu," 1.4.2(10)
    "Burma's Debt to Pagan," 1.4.2(11)
    "Economic Life of the Early Burman," 6.2.6(14)
    Old Burma: Early Pagan, 1.4.2(12); 5.5.2(1);
        10.4.1(2)
Ludowyk, Evelyn Fredrick Charles
    The Footprint of the Buddha, 1.3.2(11);
        5.4.1(2); 10.3.2(1)
Luk, Charles
    See citations under Lu K'uan Yu.
Lutter, Henry M.
    A Manual of Buddhist Law, 6.2.7(13)
Lyons, Islay
    Gandharan Art in Pakistan. See citations under
        Harald Ingholt.

Mabuchi, T.
    Folk Religion and the World View in the South-
        western Pacific. See citations under
        Nobuhiro Matsumoto.
MacDonald, Alexandre W.
    Matériaux pour l'Etude de la Littérature
        Populaire Tibétaine, 4.2.4(9)
    "La notion du sambhogakaya à la lumière de
        quelques faits ethnographiques," 8.1.3(8)
MacDonald, Ariane
    Le Mandala du Manjusrimulakalpa, 3.4.2(10);
        11.6.2(9)
MacGregor, John
    Tibet: A Chronicle of Exploration, 10.1.3(7)
Mackenzie, Donald Alexander
    Buddhism in Pre-Christian Britain, 1.17(14)
Mahajan, B. D.
    Ajanta, Ellora, and the Aurangabad Caves. See
        citations under R. S. Gupte.
Mahajjatakamala, 4.2.2(9)
Mahanama
    The Mahavamsa, 1.3.1(6); 9.1.5(10)
"Maha-nidana Suttanta," 2.7.6(8)
Mahaparinirvana sutra, 3.3.8.2(7); 10.2.5(1)
Mahaprajnaparamitasastra, 3.3.1.2(6); 9.2.4(3);
    9.3.5(8); 9.3.9(4)
Mahaprajnaparamitopadesa, 3.3.2.1(12)
Maha samaya sutta, 9.2.2.5(7)
Maha-satipatthana sutta, 11.4.2(7); 11.4.4(4)
Mahasi Sayadaw
    The Progress of Insight, 11.4.7(5)
Mahavagga, 3.2.1.1(5)
Mahavastu, 2.4.4(5); 3.2.1.2(5); 3.2.4.1(7);
    8.1.1(12); 9.1.2(6); 9.2.2.3(10); 9.2.2.4(9)
Mahayana-Vimsaka, 3.3.2.1(13)
Maisey, Frederick C.
    Sanchi and Its Remains, 5.2.4(12); 10.2.6.2(4)
Mai-Tho-Truyen, Chanh-tri
    Le Bouddhisme au Vietnam, 1.8.1(7)

Maitreyavyakarana, 8.3.4(7)
Majjhimanikaya, 2.7.8(6); 3.2.2.1(15), (16)
Majumdar, Bhavatosa
    A Guide to Sarnath, 10,2.4(3)
    "Symbology of the Asoka Pillar Capital,
        Sarnath," 9.3.1(7); 9.3.7(5)
Majumdar, Ramesh Chandra
    "The Buddhist Councils," 2.4.2(7)
    Hindu Colonies in the Far East, 1.6.2(10);
        1.8.1(8); 1.9.1(4)
    The History and Culture of the Indian People,
        1.2.1(12)
Majumder, Prabhas Chandra
    "The Karandavyuha," 3.3.8.1(3)
Makita, Tairyo
    "Hui-yuan," 8.9.3(48)
Malalasekera, George Peiris
    "Anatta," 2.7.4(7)
    Dictionary of Pali Proper Names, 12.3(3)
    Encyclopaedia of Buddhism, 2.5.4(12); 2.7.3(5);
        2.7.4(7); 2.7.12(3); 2.7.14(5); 3.3.4.2(3);
        8.2.2(1), (2), (6), (9); 8.3.2(9); 8.4(1);
        8.9.1(2), (4), (14), (24); 8.9.2(1);
        8.9.3(3); 9.2.3(5); 10.2.6.1(10); 10.2.6.2(9);
        10.3.1(1), (2); 12.3(4)
    "The Influence of Busshism on Education in
        Ceylon," 6.2.5(18)
    The Pali Literature of Ceylon, 1.3.2(12);
        3.1.2(7)
    "The Status of the Individual in Theravada
        Buddhism," 2.7.4(8)
Malalgoda, Kitsiri
    Buddhism in Sinhalese Society, 1.3.2.1(13)
    "Millennialism in Relation to Buddhism,"
        4.1.2(8)
Mallmann, Marie-Thérèse de
    Etude Iconographique sur Manjusri, 8.3.5(3)
    Introduction à l'Etude d'Avalokiteçvara,
        5.2.3(18); 8.3.2(8)
Malm, William P.
    Japanese Music and Musical Instruments,
        5.12.3(8)
Manicudavadana, 4.2.3(22)
Manjusrimulakalpa, 3.4.2(10)
Maquet, Jacques
    "Expressive Space Theravada Values," 9.3.10(3)
Maraldo, John C.
    Buddhism in the Modern World, 1.1(3)
March, Arthur
    A Buddhism Bibliography, 12.2(11)
Marchal, Henri
    Guide to Angkor, 5.5.4(9)
    Les Temples d'Angkor, 5.5.4(10)
Marshall, John
    The Bagh Caves in Gwalior State, 5.2.6(12)
    The Buddhist Art of Gandhara, 5.2.5(10)
    "Excavations at Sarnath," 10.2.4(4)
    A Guide to Sanchi, 5.2.4(13); 10.2.6.2(5)
    A Guide to Taxila, 5.2.5(11)
    Monuments of Sanchi, 5.2.4(14); 10.2.6.2(6)
    Taxila, 10.2.6.1(6)
Martini, Francis
    "Le bonne cambodgiés," 6.1.1(18)
    "Organisation du clergé bouddhique," 6.1.1(18)
Martini, G.
    "Valukacetiya," 7.3.1(9)
Masaki, Haruhiko
    "On the Problem of Prajna, Carya, and Sraddha,"
        11.2(6)

Masao, Abe
"The King of Samadhis Samadhi." See citations under Norman Waddell.
Maspero, Georges
Un empire colonial français: l'Indochine, 1.8.2(5)
Maspero, Henri
"Communautés et moines bouddhistes chinois au 2e et 3e siècles," 1.11.2.1(5); 6.1.1(19)
"Mélanges posthumes sur les religions et l'histoire de la Chine," 1.11.2.1(6)
"The Mythology of Modern China," 4.1.3(5)
"Le songe et l'ambassade de l'empereur Ming," 1.11.2.1(7); 8.9.3(17), (74)
Masson-Oursel, Paul
"Les Trois corps du Bouddha," 8.1.3(9)
Masuda, Jiryo
Origin and Doctrines of Early Indian Buddhist Schools, 2.4.1(10)
Masunaga, Reiho
A Primer of Soto Zen, 3.3.6.3(3); 11.4.8.1(8)
The Soto Approach to Zen, 2.5.7(17); 3.3.6.3(2), (4); 11.4.8.1(9)
Mather, Richard B.
"The Conflict of Buddhism with Native Chinese Ideology," 6.2.1.2(15)
"The Landscape Buddhism of the Fifth Century Poet Hsieh Ling-yun," 4.3(9); 8.9.3(38)
"Vimalakirti and Gentry Buddhism," 1.11.2.2(8)
Matics, Marion L.
Entering the Path of Enlightenment, 3.3.2.1(28); 11.1(8); 11.5(6)
Matilal, Bimal Krishna
"A Critique of Buddhist Idealism," 2.5.4(10)
Matrceta
Maharajakanikalekha, 3.2.4.3(1)
Satapancasatka, 3.2.4.3(2); 7.1.4(8)
Varnarhavarna Stotra, 3.2.4.3(3); 7.1.4(9)
Matsubara, Saburo
Arts of China: Buddhist Cave Temples. See citations under Terukazu Akiyama.
Chugoku bukkyo chokoku-shi kenkyu, zotei, 5.9.2(9)
Matsumoto, Nobuhiro
Folk Religion and the World View in the Southwestern Pacific, 9.3.10(2)
Matsunaga, Alicia
The Buddhist Concept of Hell. See citations under Daigan Matsunaga.
The Buddhist Philosophy of Assimilation, 4.1.4(6); 6.2.1.2(16); 8.3.1(9)
Matsunaga, Daigan
The Buddhist Concept of Hell, 9.2.2.3(11)
Matsunaga, Yukei
"Tantric Buddhism and Shingon Buddhism," 2.6.2(6)
Matsuo, Basho
Back Roads to Far Towns, 4.3(10)
The Narrow Road to the Deep North, 4.3(11)
Maung, Maung
Burma and General Ne Win, 6.2.2.3(6)
Maung, Mya
"Cultural Value and Economic Change in Burma," 6.2.6(15)
Maupin, Edward W.
"Zen Buddhism," 11.4.8.3(4)
May, Jacques
"La philosophie bouddhique idéaliste," 2.5.4(11)
"La philosophie bouddhique de la vacuité," 2.7.8(7)

Maybon, Charles
Lectures sur l'histoire moderne et contemporaine du pays d'Annam de 1428 à 1926, 1.8.2(6)
Mayer, Fanny Hagin
"Religious Elements in Japanese Folk Tales," 4.2.4(10)
McCallum, Donald P.
"The Sculpture of Enku," 5.11.4(7)
McCune, Evelyn
The Arts of Korea, 5.10(13)
McDermott, A. C. Senape
An Eleventh-Century Buddhist Logic of Exists, 3.3.3.1(16)
McDougal, Colin
Buddhism in Malaya, 1.9.2(4)
McGovern, William Montgomery
To Lhasa in Disguise, 10.1.3(8)
A Manual of Buddhist Philosophy, 9.1.1(4); 9.2.1(11)
McKeon, Richard P.
The Edicts of Asoka, 1.2.2.2(1); 6.2.2.1(13); 8.9.1(17)
Mehta, Ratilal
"Crime and Punishment in the Jatakas," 6.2.7(14)
Mélanges chinois et bouddhiques, 5.1.1(2)
Mendelson, E. Michael
"Buddhism and the Buddhist Establishment," 6.2.2.3(7)
"Initiation and Paradox of Power," 7.2.1(6)
"The King of the Weaving Mountain," 4.1.2(9)
"A Messianic Buddhist Association in Upper Burma," 4.1.2(10); 9.1.4(5)
"Observations on a Tour in the Region of Mount Popa," 4.1.2(11); 10.4.2(2)
Sangha and State in Burma, 1.4.2(13)
"The Uses of Religious Skepticism in Modern Burma," 4.1.2(12)
Merillat, Herbert C.
Sculpture in East and West, 5.1.2(4)
Merton, Thomas
Mystics and Zen Masters, 2.9(33)
Meunie
Shotorak, 5.2.5(12)
Meuwese, Catherine
L'Inde du Bouddha, 1.2.2.3(11)
Mibu, Taishun
"On the Theory of Five Buddhas," 8.2.2(7)
Migot, André
"Le Bouddhisme en Indochine," 1.6.1(5); 1.7.1(5)
"Un grand disciple du Buddha Sariputra," 8.8(13)
"Les temples bouddhique du Mont O-Mei," 10.8.2(8)
Mikisaburo, Mori
"Chuang Tzu and Buddhism," 6.2.1.2(17)
Mila mgur 'bum, 4.3(12)
Milindapanha, 3.2.2.1(17), (18)
Miller, Beatrice O.
"On Two Bhutanese New Year's Celebrations." See citations under Robert J. Miller.
"The Web of Tibetan Monasticism," 6.2.1.2(18)
Miller, Margaret
"Educational Practices of Tibetan Lama Training," 6.2.5(19)
Miller, Robert James
"Buddhist Monastic Economy," 6.2.6(16)
Monasteries and Culture Change in Inner Mongolia, 1.16.1(7); 6.2.1.2(19)
"They Will Not Die Hindus," 1.2.2.4(3); 6.2.4(7)
"On Two Bhutanese New Year's Celebrations," 7.3.3(2)

Minami, Atsumi
"A Buddhist Prayer Against Sickness." See citations under Ilza Veith.
Minh Chau
Hsuan Tsang, 8.9.3(42)
Ministry of Information and Broadcasting, Government of India
The Way of the Buddha, 5.2.3(19)
Mironov, N. D.
"Buddhist Miscellanea," 8.3.1(10)
Mishima, Yukio
The Temple of the Golden Pavilion, 4.5(5)
Mishra, Ramakanta
"The Pratimoksa Sutra of the Mahasanghikas." See citations under W. Pachow.
Misra, G. S. P.
The Age of Vinaya, 5.2.1(15)
Misra, S. S. P.
"The Ideal of Education in Early Buddhism," 6.2.5(20)
Mitra, Debala
Buddhist Monuments, 5.2.2(12); 10.2.1(14)
Mitra, R. C.
The Decline of Buddhism in India, 1.2.2.3(12); 6.2.2.1(14)
Mitra, Rajendralala
Buddha Gaya, 5.2.4(15); 10.2.3(7)
The Lalitavistara, 8.1.2.1(21)
The Sanskrit Buddhist Literature of Nepal, 3.1.3(5)
Mitra, Saivendranath
"The Lumbini Pilgrimage Record in Two Inscriptions," 10.2.2(4)
Mitton, Geraldine E.
The Lost Cities of Ceylon, 5.4.1(3)
Miura, Isshu
Zen Dust, 3.1.5(6); 3.3.4.2(4); 3.3.6.2(4); 3.3.6.3(6); 11.4.8.2(2); 11.4.8.3(5); 12.2(12)
Miyamoto, Shoson
"The Geographical Expansion of the Indian Cultural Sphere," 1.10.2(11)
"A Study of Attainment," 11.7.1(3)
"Time and Eternity in Buddhism," 2.7.3(4)
Miyasaka, Kojiro
"The Sutra of Meditation," 3.3.5.1(1)
Miyazawa, Kenji
Spring and Asura, 4.3(13)
Mizuno, Kogen
Primitive Buddhism, 1.2.2.1(8); 2.2(12); 2.3(6)
Mizuno, Seiichi
Bronze and Stone Sculpture in China, 5.9.2(10)
The Buddhist Cave Temples Honan and Hopei, 10.8.2(9)
The Buddhist Cave Temples of Hsiang-T'ang-ssu, 5.9.4(7)
A Study of the Buddhist Cave Temples at Lung-men, 5.9.4(8)
Yun-kang, 5.9.4(9)
Mkcyen Brtse
Mkcyen Brtse's Guide to the Holy Places of Central Tibet, 10.7(2)
Mode, Heinz
Die buddhistische Plastik auf Ceylon, 5.4.2(4)
Moerman, Michael
"Ban Ping's Temple," 6.2.1.1(23); 6.2.3(13)
"Le monastère bouddhique de Tep Pranam à Oudong," 6.1.1(20)

Monier-Williams, Monier
Buddhism, in Its Connection with Brahmanism, and in Its Contrast with Christianity, 8.5(2); 8.6(4); 9.2.1(12); 9.3.4(2); 10.2.1(15)
A Sanskrit-English Dictionary, 12.1(7)
Mookerjee, S.
The Pramanavarttikam of Dharmakirti, 3.3.3.1(8); 3.3.3.2(1)
Mookerji, Radha Kumud
Ancient Indian Education, 6.2.5(21)
Hindu Civilization, 1.2.2.1(9)
Moore, Charles Alexander
Essays in East-West Philosophy, 2.5.1(6); 11.4.7(6)
Philosophy East and West, 2.7.10(5)
Moran, Sherwood F.
"Ashura," 5.11.4(8)
"Certain Features of Kichijoten Statue," 5.11.4(9)
"The Death of the Buddha," 5.11.5(6)
"Early Heian Sculpture," 5.11.4(10)
"The Statue of Miroku Bosatsu," 5.11.4(11)
"Structural Features of Clay Sculpture," 5.11.4(12)
Moreau-Gobard, Jean-Claude
Chinese Art. See citations under Daisy Lion-Goldschmidt.
Morgan, F. Bruce
"Vocation of Monk and Layman," 6.1.2(14); 11.3(14)
Morgan, Kenneth William
"The Buddhists," 6.2.1.1(24)
The Path of the Buddha, 1.1(6); 1.11.1(10); 2.1(9)
Mori, Hisashi
Sculpture of the Kamakura Period, 5.11.4(13)
Morioka, Kiyoma
"Buddhist Orders and the Japanese Family System," 6.2.3(14)
Morrell, Robert E.
"The Buddhist Poetry in the Goshuishu," 4.3(14)
Morris, Ivan
The Pillow Book of Sei Shonagon, 4.5(6)
Morris, John
Living with Lepchas, 1.15.1(2)
Mudiyanse, Nandasena
The Art and Architecture of the Gampola Period, 5.4.2(5)
Mahayana Monuments in Ceylon, 5.4.2(6)
Müller, Friedrich Max
Dhammapada, 3.2.2.1(7)
The Dhammapada and the Sutta-Nipata, 3.2.2.1(24)
"The Larger Sukhavati-vyuha," 3.3.7.1(3); 11.7.4(10)
"The Prajnaparamita-hrdaya-sutra," 3.3.1.1(12)
"The Smaller Sukhavati-vyuha," 3.3.7.1(2); 11.7.4(10)
"The Vagrakkhedika, or Diamond Cutter," 3.3.1.1(23)
Mukerji, Purma Chandra
"Antiquities in the Terai, Nepal," 10.2.2(5)
Mukherjee, Biswadeb
Die Überlieferung von Devadatta, 8.8(14)
Mukherjee, Prabhat Kumar
"The Dhammapada and the Udanavarga," 3.2.2.4(7)
Mukherjee, Radhakamal
The Cosmic Art of India, 5.2.1(16)
The Culture and Art of India, 5.2.1(17)
The Flowering of Indian Art, 5.2.1(18)

Mukherjee, Sujit Kumar
    "An Outline of Principal Methods of Meditation,"
       11.4.2(8)
Mukhopadhyaya, Sujitkumar
    The Vajrasuci of Asvaghosa, 3.2.4.3(4); 6.2.4(8)
Mulder, J. A. Niels
    "A Comparative Note on the Thai and Javanese
       World View," 6.2.1.1(25)
    Monks, Merit and Motivation, 6.2.1.1(26)
Munsterberg, Hugo
    Art of the Far East, 5.8(7)
    Art of India and Southeast Asia, 5.1.4(9)
    The Arts of Japan, 5.11.2(7)
    Chinese Buddhist Bronzes, 5.9.2(11)
    A Short History of Chinese Art, 5.9.1(10)
    Zen and Oriental Art, 5.11.6(9)
Muramatsu, Yuji
    "Some Themes in Chinese Rebel Ideologies,"
       4.1.3(6)
Murasaki, Shikibu
    The Tale of Genji, 4.5(7)
Murase, Miyeko
    Japanese Art, 5.11.2(8)
Murata, Kiyoaki
    Japan's New Buddhism, 1.13.2.4(6)
Murthy, M. Chidananda
    "Buddhism in Karnataka," 1.2.2.4(9)
Murti, Tirupattur Ramaseshayyer Vankatachala
    The Central Philosophy of Buddhism, 2.5.3(7);
       2.7.8(8); 2.7.9(4); 3.3.2.2(2)
Mus, Paul
    "Angkor in the Time of Jayavarman VII, "
       9.3.7(6)
    "Ankor vu du Japon," 1.6.2(11); 6.2.2.8(3)
    Barabudur, 2.5.2(8); 5.5.6(8); 8.2.2(8);
       9.3.6(6); 10.6(7); 11.7.4(6); 11.8(7)
    "Le Bouddha Paré," 3.3.5.2(3); 8.1.3(10)
    "Buddhism in Vietnamese History and Society,"
       1.8.2(7); 6.2.2.8(4)
    La Lumière sur les six voies, 9.2.2.2(3)
Musée Guimet
    Guide-Catalogue du Musée Guimet, 5.1.4(10)
Myer, Prudence
    "The Great Temple at Bodh-Gaya," 5.2.4(16)
Myrdal, Jan
    Angkor: An Essay on Art and Imperialism,
       5.5.4(11)

Nagahiro, Toshio
    The Buddhist Cave Temples Honan and Hopei. See
       citations under S. Mizuno.
    The Buddhist Cave Temples of Hsiang-T'ang-ssu.
       See citations under Seiichi Mizuno.
    A Study of the Buddhist Cave Temples at Lung-
       men. See citations under Seiichi Mizuno.
    "On Wei-ch'ih I-seng," 5.9.3(9)
    Yun-kang. See citations under Seiichi Mizuno.
Nagao, Gadjin
    "On the Theory of the Buddha-Body," 8.1.2.2(10);
       8.1.3(11)
Nagarjuna
    Catuhstava, 3.3.2.1(14), (15); 8.1.1(13);
       8.1.3(12)
    Mulamadhyamakakarikas, 3.3.2.1(16)
    Ratnavali, 3.3.2.1(17)
    Suhrilekha, 3.3.2.1(18)
    La Traité de Grande Vertu, 2.7.4(9)
    Vigrahavyavartani, 3.3.2.1(19), (20), (21), (22)

Nagasaki, Hojun
    The Pramanavarttikam of Dharmakirti. See
       citations under S. Mookerjee.
Nagasri-pariprccha prajnaparamitasutra, 3.3.1.1(6)
Nainar, S. P.
    "Buddhaghosa: His Place of Birth." See
       citations under R. Subrahmaniam.
Naito, Toichiro
    The Wall Paintings of Horyu-ji, 5.11.5(7)
Nakamura, Hajime
    "The Indian and Buddhist Concept of Law,"
       6.2.7(15)
Nakamura, Kyoko Motomochi
    "Miraculous Stories from the Japanese," 4.2.3(23)
Nanamoli, Bhikkhu
    "Anicca," 2.7.3(5)
    The Guide, 3.2.2.1(19)
    The Illustrator of Ultimate Meaning, 3.2.2.3(1)
    The Minor Readings in the Minor Readings,
       3.2.2.1(14)
    The Path of Purification, 3.2.4.2(1); 11.1(2);
       11.3(3); 11.4.2(3); 11.4.3(2), (3);
       11.4.6(1); 11.4.7(1)
    The Patimokkha, 7.2.4(5)
    The Pitaka-Disclosure, 3.2.2.1(20)
Nanayakkara, S. K.
    "Avalokitesvara," 8.3.2(9)
    "Bhaisajyaguru," 8.2.2(9)
    "Bodhicitta," 2.7.14(5)
Nanjio, Bunyiu
    A Short History of the Twelve Japanese Buddhist
       Sects, 1.13.2.2(10)
Narada, Thera
    Dhammapada, 3.2.2.1(8)
    "Kamma or the Buddhist Law of Causation,"
       2.7.1(12)
    A Manual of Abhidhamma, 3.2.3.3(2); 9.2.3(1)
Narada, U.
    Conditional Relations, 3.2.3.1(6)
    Discourse on Elements, 3.2.3.1(3)
Nash, June C.
    "Living with Nats," 4.1.2(13); 6.2.3(15)
Nash, Manning
    Anthropological Studies in Theravada Buddhism,
       4.1.1(3); 4.1.2(13); 7.1.1(8)
    The Golden Road to Modernity, 4.1.2(14);
       6.2.3(16); 6.2.6(17)
    "Ritual and Ceremonial Cycle in Upper Burma,"
       7.1.1(8)
Natsagdorji, Sh.
    "The Introduction of Buddhism into Mongolia,"
       1.16.2(7)
Naudou, Jean
    Les bouddhistes kasmiriens au moyen âge,
       1.2.2.4(10)
Nebesky-Wojkowitz, René de
    "Ancient Funeral Ceremonies of the Lepchas,"
       7.4.2(16)
    Oracles and Demons of Tibet, 4.1.5(3); 5.6(14);
       9.2.2.5(8)
    "Tibetan Drum Divination," 7.6(3)
    "The Use of Thread-Crosses in Lepcha Lamaist
       Ceremonies," 7.5.3(7)
Nettippakarana, 3.2.2.1(19)
Ngawang Lobsang Yishey Tenzing Cyatso
    My Land and My People, 1.14.2.3(3)
    The Opening of the Wisdom-Eye, 11.4.5(11)
Nghiem-Dang
    Vietnam: Politics and Public Administration,
       1.8.2(8)

Nginn, Pierre S.
    "Fêtes religieuses," 7.3.1(10)
Nhat-Hanh, Thich
    Vietnam: Lotus in a Sea of Fire, 1.8.2(9); 6.2.2.8(5)
Nichiren
    The Awakening to the Truth, 2.5.9(3); 3.3.5.2(4)
    Hokke-Shuyo-Sho, 3.3.5.2(5)
Niehoff, Arthur
    "Theravada Buddhism: A Vehicle for Technical Change," 6.2.3(17)
Nielson, Thomas P.
    The T'ang Poet-Monk Chiao-jan, 4.3(15)
Nikam, N. H.
    The Edicts of Asoka. See citations under Richard P. McKeon.
Ninno Prajnaparamita-sutra, 3.3.1.1(7)
Nishitani, Keiji
    Suzuki Memorial Volume, 8.9.4(28)
Nishitsunoi, Masayoshi
    "Religious Music and Drama in Japan," 5.12.3(9)
Niwa, Fumio
    The Buddha Tree, 4.5(8)
Niyogi, Phushpa
    "Organization of Buddhist Monasteries in Ancient Bengal and Bihar," 6.1.1(21)
Noburi, Asaji
    A Philosophy of the Japanese Noh Drama, 5.12.2(8)
Nogami, Toyoichiro
    Zeami and His Theories on Noh, 5.12.2(9)
Noma, Seiroku
    The Arts of Japan, 5.11.2(9)
    Early Japanese Bronze Sculpture, 5.11.4(14)
    Masterpieces of Japanese Art, 5.11.4(15)
Norman, K. R.
    Buddhist Studies in Honour of I. B. Horner. See citations under L. Cousins.
    The Elders' Verses I, 3.2.2.1(26)
    The Elders' Verses II, 3.2.2.1(27)
Northrop, F. S. C.
    Cross-Cultural Understanding, 6.2.3(11)
Nyanaponika, Thera
    Abhidhamma Studies, 3.2.3.4(8)
    The Heart of Buddhist Meditation, 11.4.4(6)
    Pathways of Buddhist Thought, 11.3(19)
    The Power of Mindfulness, 11.4.4(7)
    "The Three-Fold Refuge," 11.2(7)
Nyanasatta, C. Thera
    "Buddhism in the West," 1.17(15)
Nyanatiloka, Mahathera
    Buddhist Dictionary, 12.1(8)
    Guide to the Abhidhamma Pitaka, 2.4.1(11); 3.2.3.4(9)
Nyaya-Tarkatirtha, A. D.
    "Nirodha-satya," 2.7.7(8)

Obermiller, Eugene
    "The Doctrine of Prajnaparamita," 3.3.1.3(4); 11.1(9)
    "Nirvana According to the Tibetan Tradition," 11.8(8)
    "A Study of the Twenty Aspects of Sunyata," 2.7.8(9); 3.3.2.2(3)
    "The Sublime Science of the Great Vehicle to Salvation," 3.3.2.1(23); 8.9.1(8)
    "Tson-kha-pa le pandit," 8.9.2(23)

Obeyesekere, Gananath
    "The Great Tradition and the Little in the Perspective of Sinhalese Buddhism," 4.1.1(9)
    "Personal Identity and Cultural Crisis," 8.9.5(8)
    "The Ritual Drama of the Sanni Demons," 7.5.2(4)
    "Sin, Theodicy, and Salvation," 6.1.2(15)
    "Structure of a Sinhalese Ritual," 7.1.1(9)
Offner, Clark B.
    Modern Japanese Religions with Special Emphasis on Their Doctrines of Healing, 1.13.2.4(7)
Ogata, Sohaku
    Zen for the West, 3.3.6.1(12)
Okakura, Kakuzo
    The Book of Tea, 1.13.2.4(8); 5.11.8(6)
Okudaira, Hideo
    Narrative Picture Scrolls, 5.11.5(8)
Okusa, Yejitsu
    Principal Teaching of the True Sect of Pure Land, 2.5.8(13)
Oldenberg, Hermann
    Buddha: His Life, His Order, His Doctrine, 8.1.2.3(20); 11.8(9)
    Dipavamsa, 10.3.1(6)
    Vinaya Texts. See citations under Thomas William Rhys-Davids.
d'Oldenburg, Serge
    "On the Buddhist Jatakas," 4.2.2(10)
Olschki, Leonardo
    "The Crib of Christ and the Bowl of the Buddha," 9.3.10(4)
Oltramare, Paul Jean
    La Formule Bouddhique des Douze Causes, 2.7.6(9)
O'Neill, Herbert S.
    "Religious Influence in Thai Culture," 6.2.1.1(27)
O'Neill, Patrick Geoffrey
    Early No Drama, 5.12.2(10)
Ono, Genmyo
    "The Date of Vasubandhu," 8.9.1(54)
    "On the Pure Land Doctrine of Tz'u-min," 2.5.8(14)
Ooka, Minoru
    Temples of Nara and Their Art, 5.11.3(8)
Opie, John Lindsay
    Island Ceylon. See citations under Roloff Beny.
Opper, Conrad
    "Educational Development in Thailand," 6.2.5(22)
Overmeyer, Daniel L.
    "Folk-Buddhist Religion: Creation and Eschatology in Medieval China," 1.11.2.3(11); 4.1.3(7)

Pachow, W.
    "Ancient Cultural Relations Between Ceylon and China," 1.11.2.3(12)
    "A Buddhist Discourse on Meditation," 11.4.8.1(10)
    A Comparative Study of the Pratimoksa, 3.2.1.4(6); 7.2.4(6); 11.3(15)
    "Legal Dealings Between the Buddhist Sangha and the Laity," 6.1.2(16); 6.2.7(16)
    "The Pratimoksa sutra of the Mahasanghikas," 3.2.1.2(6)

Pad-ma dkar-po
    Chos-rje 'brug-pa'i lugs-kyi phyag-rgya chen-po lhan-cig skyes-sbyor-gyi khrid-yig, 3.4.2(11); 11.4.2(9)
    Mgon-po mchod-pa, 3.4.2(12)
    Snyan-rgyud yid bzhin nor-bu'i bskeyd-pa'i rim-pa rgyas-pa 'dod-pa'i re-skong znes bya-pa, 3.4.2(13)

Paik, Nak Choon
    "Tripitaka Koreana," 3.1.6(5)

Paine, Robert Treat
    The Art and Architecture of Japan, 5.11.2(10); 5.11.3(9); 10.9(4)

Pal, Pratapaditya
    The Art of Tibet, 5.6(15)
    The Arts of Nepal, 5.3(3)
    Aspects of Indian Art, 5.2.1(19)
    Bronzes of Kashmir, 5.2.8(11)
    Lamaist Art, 5.6(16)
    Nepal: Where the Gods are Young, 5.3(4)

Pallis, Marco
    Peaks and Lamas, 5.6(17)

Palmer, Arvin
    Buddhist Politics: Japan's Clean Government Party, 6.2.2.6(9)

Palmer, Spencer J.
    "The New Religions of Korea," 1.12.2(10)

Pancasatika Prajnaparamitasutra, 3.3.1.1(8)
Pancavimsati-prajnaparamitamukha, 3.3.1.1(9); 3.4.1(6)

Pande, Govind Chandra
    Studies in the Origins of Buddhism, 1.2.2.1(10); 2.2(13); 2.3(7); 2.7.5(6); 3.2.2.4(8)

Pandeya, Ram Chandra
    "The Madhyamika Philosophy," 2.5.3(8)

Pandita, Vincent
    "Buddhism during the Polonnaruywa Period," 1.3.2.1(14)

P'ang chu-shih yu-lu, 3.3.6.2(8)

Pang Khat
    "Le Bouddhisme au Cambodge," 1.6.1(6)

Pannasami
    (Sasanavamsa) The History of the Buddha's Religion, 1.4.1(5); 9.1.5(13)

Pannasiri, Bhadanta
    "Sigalovada-sutta," 3.2.2.2(8)

Pant, Sushila
    "The Origin and Development of Stupa Architecture in India," 9.3.6(7)

Paranavitana, Senarat
    Art of the Ancient Sinhales, 5.4.2(7)
    "Buddhist Revivals in Ceylon," 7.3.1(11)
    The God of Adam's Peak, 5.4.1(4); 10.3.2(2)
    "Mahayanism in Ceylon," 1.3.1(7); 8.3.2(10)
    "New Light on the Buddhist Era in Ceylon," 1.3.2.1(15)
    "The Religious Intercourse between Ceylon and Siam in the Thirteenth to Fifteenth Centuries," 1.3.2.1(16); 1.5.2(18)
    "The Significance of Sinhalese 'Moonstones,'" 9.3.10(5)
    The Story of Sigiri, 1.3.2.1(17)
    The Stupa in Ceylon, 5.4.2(8); 9.3.6(8)
    The University of Ceylon History of Ceylon, 1.3.1(8)

Pardue, Peter
    Buddhism, 6.2.1.1(28)

Parivara, 3.2.1.1(7)

Parmentier, Henri
    L'Art Khmer classique, 5.5.4(12)
    L'Art du Laos, 5.5.5(4)
    "Sentences et Proverbes Cambodgiens," 4.2.4(11)

Pas, Julian F.
    "Shan-Tao's Interpretation of the Meditative Vision of Buddha Amitayus," 11.7.3(3)

Pasadiko, Bhikkhu
    The Wisdom Gone Beyond, 3.3.3.1(12)

Pathak, Sunitikumar
    "Life of Nagarjuna," 8.9.1(40)

Pathoumxad, Krough
    "Organization of the Sangha," 6.1.1(22)

Patika Sutta, 9.1.2(7)
Patimokkha, 3.2.1.1(4)
Patthana, 3.2.3.1(6)

Pauly, Bernard
    "Fragments Sanskrits de Haute Asie," 3.2.2.2(7)

Pavie, Auguste
    Mission Pavie en Indo-chine, 10.1.4(5)

"Payasi Suttanta," 2.7.1(13)

Pelliot, Paul
    Les Grottes de Touen-houang, 5.9.4(10)
    Le Sutra des Causes et des Effets du Bien et du Mal. See citations under Robert Gauthiot.

Perara, E.
    "Sinhala Culture and Buddhism," 6.2.1.1(29)

Perara, H. R.
    Buddhism in Ceylon, 1.3.1(9)

Perera, Arthur A.
    "The Daily Ritual at the Dalada Maligava," 7.1.3(12)

Peri, Noel
    "Les femmes de Sakya-muni," 8.1.2.3(21)
    "Hariti, la mère des démons," 8.6(5); 9.2.2.5(9)
    "A propos de la date du Vasubandhu," 8.9.1(55)

Perry, Edmund F.
    The Sangha of the Tri-ratana, 6.1.1(23)

Petakopadesa, 3.2.2.1(20)
Peta vatthu, 3.2.2.1(21); 9.2.2.3(12)

Petech, Luciano
    China and Tibet in the Early 18th Century, 1.14.2.2(6)
    "The Dalai Lamas and Regents of Tibet," 8.9.2(7)
    "A Study on the Chronicles of Ladakh," 1.14.2.1(7)

Petzold, Bruno
    "The Chinese Tendai Teaching," 2.5.6(5)
    "Dengyo Daishi . . .: The Founder of the Japanese Tendai Sect," 1.13.2.2(11); 8.9.4(23)

Pe Win, U Lu
    "The Jatakas in Burma," 4.2.2(11)

Pezzali, Amalia
    Santideva, Mystique Bouddhiste des VIIème et VIIIème siècles, 8.9.1(48)

Pfanner, David
    "The Buddhist Monk in Rural Burmese Society," 6.2.1.1(30)
    "Theravada Buddhism and Village Economic Behavior." See citations under Jasper Ingersoll.

Phimmasone, Phouvang
    "La Littérature bouddhique lao," 3.1.6(6)

Pier, Garrett Chatfield
    Temple Treasures of Japan, 5.11.2(11)

Pieris, Ralph
    Sinhalese Social Organization, 6.2.1.1(31); 6.2.6(18)

Piker, Steven
"Buddhism and Modernization in Contemporary Thailand," 6.2.1.1(32)
"Comments on the Integration of Thai Religion," 6.2.1.1(33)
"The Relationship of Belief Systems to Behavior in Rural Thai Society," 6.2.3(18)
Pilgrim, Richard
"Some Aspects of Kokuro in Zeami," 5.12.2(11)
"Some Considerations of Yugen and Sabi," 5.11.1(3)
"Zeami and the Way of No," 5.12.2(12)
Piyadassi
The Buddha's Ancient Path, 11.1(10)
Pi-yen lu, 3.3.6.1(8)
Plopper, Clifford H.
Chinese Religion Seen through the Proverb, 4.2.4(12)
Ponsonby-Fane, R. A. B.
Kyoto, the Old Capital of Japan, 10.1.5(4)
Poppe, Nicholas
"The Destruction of Buddhism in the U.S.S.R.," 1.16.2(8)
"A Fragment of the Bodhicaryavatara," 3.3.2.1(29)
Three Mongolian Versions of the Vajracchedika Prajnaparamita Texts, 3.3.1.1(26)
The Twelve Deeds of Buddha, 3.3.8.4(6); 8.1.2.3(22)
Poree-Maspero, Eveline
"La Cérémonie de l'appel des esprits vitaux chez les cambodgiens," 7.5.3(6)
Etude sur les rites agraires des cambodgiens, 1.6.2(12); 7.3.1(12)
Pott, P. H.
"Le Bouddhisme de Java et l'ancienne civilisation javanaise," 1.9.1(5)
Yoga and Tantra, 5.2.8(12); 11.6.2(10)
Prajnaparamita-hrdaya-sutra, 3.3.1.1(11), (12), (13), (14), (15); 4.2.1(4)
Prajnaparamita-nama-astasataka, 3.3.1.1(16); 3.4.2(14)
Prajnaparamita-ratnagunasamcayagatha, 3.3.1.1(17)
Pramoj, Kukrit
Red Bamboo, 4.5(9)
Prastastrasena
Arya-prajnaparamita-hrdaya-tika, 3.3.1.2(7)
Pratimalaksanam, 3.3.8.1(4)
Pratimoksa, 3.2.1.2(7), (8), (9)
Pratt, James Bissett
The Pilgrimage of Buddhism and a Buddhist Pilgrimage, 1.6.1(7); 1.11.2.4(4); 1.12.1(6); 1.13.1(11); 10.1.2(6)
Prebish, Charles S.
Buddhism: A Modern Perspective, 1.1(7)
Buddhist Monastic Discipline, 3.2.1.2(10); 3.2.1.4(7); 11.3(16)
"A Review of Scholarship on the Buddhist Councils," 2.4.2(8)
Presler, Henry
"The Neo-Buddhist Stir in India," 1.2.2.5(4); 6.2.4(9)
Prip-Moller, J.
Chinese Buddhist Monasteries, 5.9.2(12); 7.2.1(7); 7.2.2(9); 8.4(12); 10.8.1(4)
Pruden, Leo
"Ten Doubts Concerning the Pure Land," 3.3.7.2(1); 11.7.4(7)

Prusek, Jaroslav
"The Narrators of Buddhist Scriptures and Religious Tales in the Sung Period," 4.2.3(24); 7.2.5(6)
Przyluski, Jean
Le Concile de Rajagrha, 2.4.2(9)
"La croyance au messie dans l'Inde et dans l'Iran," 8.3.4(8); 9.1.4(6)
"Darstantika, Sautrantika and Sarvastivadin," 2.4.3(8)
La Légende de l'Empereur Açoka, 3.2.2.2(2); 4.2.3(2); 8.2.1(1); 8.9.1(12); 9.2.2.3(13)
"Mudra," 11.6.4(5)
"Notes de mythologie bouddhique," 9.2.2.5(10)
"Le Parinirvana et les Funérailles du Buddha," 8.1.23(23)
"Le partage des reliques du Buddha," 8.1.2.4(15)
"Récits Populaires et Contes Bouddhiques," 4.2.3(25)
"La Roue de la Vie à Ajanta," 9.3.2(6)
"Les sept terrasses du Barabudur," 9.3.6(9)
"Le symbolisme du pilier de Sarnath," 9.3.7(7)
"Uposatha," 7.2.4(7)
"La ville du Cakravartin," 8.7(3); 9.2.2.1(7); 9.3.7(8)
P'u Sung-ling
Liao Chai Chih i, 4.2.4(13)
Puggala Pannatti, 3.2.3.1(4)
Puri, Baijnath
"Buddhism in Ancient Kambujadesa," 1.6.2(14)
Python, Pierre
Vinaya-viniscaya-Upali-pariprccha, 3.3.8.1(5)

Queneau, Raymond
Histoire des littératures, 3.1.6(7)

Rachewiltz, Igor de
"Yeh-Lu Ch'u-Ts'ai (1189-1243)," 1.16.2(9); 8.9.3(89)
Radhakrishnan, Sarvepalli
Dhammapada, 3.2.2.1(9)
Rahul, Ram
The Government and Politics of Tibet, 6.2.2.7(5)
Modern Bhutan, 1.15.1(3)
"The Role of Lamas in Central Asian Politics," 6.2.2.9(3)
Rahula, Walpola
"Asanga," 2.5.4(12); 8.9.1(9)
"A Comparative Study of Dhyanas," 11.4.5(12)
Le Compendium de la Super-Doctrine Philosophie, 3.3.3.1(1)
"Duhkha-Satya," 2.7.2(3)
History of Buddhism in Ceylon: The Anuradhapura Period, 1.3.1(10); 6.1.1(24); 6.2.1.1(34); 6.2.2.2(11); 6.2.4(10); 6.2.5(23); 7.2.2(10); 8.4(13)
"L'idéal du Bodhisattva dans le Theravada et le Mahayana," 8.3.1(11)
What the Buddha Taught, 2.1(10); 2.4.3(9); 2.7.4(10); 2.7.5(7); 11.1(11)
Ramachandra Rao, P. R.
The Art of Nagarjunikonda, 5.2.7(7)
Ramachandran, T. N.
Buddhist Sculptures from a Stupa Near Goli Village, 5.2.7(5)
The Nagapattinam, 5.2.8(13)
Nagarjunakonda, 5.2.7(6)

Ramanan, K. Venkata
    Nagarjuna's Philosophy, 2.5.3(9); 3.3.2.2(4)
Ranasinghe, C. P.
    The Buddha's Explanation of the Universe, 2.7.7(9)
Ras-chun
    Tibet's Great Yogi, Milarepa, 1.14.2.2(7)
Rastrapalapariprccha, 3.3.8.1(6)
Ratanapanya, Thera
    The Sheaf of Garlands of the Epochs of the Conqueror, 1.5.2(19); 9.1.5(8)
Ratnagotravibhaga Mahayana-Uttaratantra, 3.3.2.1(23), (24)
Ratnakirti
    Ksanabhangasiddhih Vyatirekatmika, 3.3.3.1(16)
Ratnapala, Nandasena
    The Katikavatas, 6.2.1.1(35)
Ratnayaka, Shanta
    The Sangha of the Tri-ratana. See citations under Edmund F. Perry.
Ratti, Oscar
    Secrets of the Samurai, 1.13.2.3(2)
Raven-Hart, R.
    Ceylon: History in Stone, 5.4.1(5); 10.3.1(7)
Rawson, Philip
    The Art of Southeast Asia, 5.5.1(2)
    The Art of Tantra, 5.2.8(14)
    Tantra, 5.2.8(15)
Ray, Niharranjan
    An Introduction to the Study of Theravada Buddhism in Burma, 1.4.1(6)
    Maurya and Sunga Art, 5.2.1(20); 5.2.4(17)
    Sanskrit Buddhism in Burma, 1.4.1(7)
Ray, Reginald
    "Demystifying Demystification," 2.9(35)
Rea, Alexander
    South Indian Buddhist Antiquities, 5.2.7(8)
Read, Herbert
    "Suzuki: Zen and Art," 5.11.6(10)
Regamey, Constantin
    Buddhistische Philosophie, 12.2(13)
    Three Chapters From the Samadhirajasutra, 3.3.8.1(7); 11.4.5(13)
    "Le problème du bouddhisme primitif," 2.3(8)
Reichelt, Karl Ludwig
    Meditation and Piety in the Far East, 11.4.1(6)
    Truth and Tradition in Chinese Buddhism, 1.11.1(8); 7.4.2(17); 8.6(6)
Reischauer, August Karl
    "A Catechism of the Shin Sect," 2.5.8(15)
    Studies in Japanese Buddhism, 1.13.1(12)
Reischauer, Edwin Oldfather
    Ennin's Travels in T'ang China, 1.11.2.3(13); 10.1.2(7)
Rennyo
    Anjinketsujosho, 3.3.7.2(3)
    The Words of St. Rennyo, 2.5.8(16)
Rennyoshonin-Goichidaiki-kikigaki, 3.3.7.2(4)
Renondeau, Gaston
    "Le Bouddhisme japonais," 1.13.1(13)
    Le Bouddhisme dans les No, 5.12.2(13)
    "Le Date de l'Introduction du Bouddhisme au Japon," 1.13.2.1(5)
    La Doctrine de Nichiren, 2.5.9(4); 3.3.5.2(5)
Renou, Louis
    L'Inde classique, 1.2.2.1(11); 3.1.3(4); 3.1.5(2); 8.1.2.3(11)
Reps, Paul
    Zen Flesh, Zen Bones, 3.3.6.1(9), (13)

Revertegat, Bruno
    "Le Bouddhisme et les bonzes au Sud-Vietnam," 1.8.2(10); 6.2.2.8(6)
Reynolds, C. H. B.
    An Anthology of Sinhalese Literature, 4.2.4(14)
    "Buddhism and the Maldivian Language," 1.2.2.4(11)
Reynolds, Frank E.
    The Biographical Process, 8.1.2.3(24); 8.9.4(3), (24); 8.9.5(8)
    "Buddhism as Universal Religion and as Civic Religion," 6.2.1.1(36)
    "The Holy Emerald Jewel," 1.5.2(20)
    "The Many Lives of Buddha," 8.1.2.3(24)
    "From Philology to Anthropology," 12.2(14)
    Religious Encounters With Death," 7.4.2(12)
    "Ritual and Social Hierarchy: An Aspect of Traditional Religion in Buddhist Laos," 1.7.2(7); 6.2.1.1(37)
    "Sacral Kingship and National Development: The Case of Thailand," 6.2.2.4(5)
    "Tradition and Change in Theravada Buddhism," 12.2(14)
Rhie, Marilyn
    "The Sculpture of T'ien Lung-shan." See citations under Harry Vanderstrappen.
Rhys-Davids, Caroline Augusta Foley
    A Buddhist Manual of Psychological Ethics, 3.2.3.1(1)
    Compendium of Philosophy. See citations under Shwe Zan Aung.
    Dhammapada, 3.2.2.1(5)
    Gotama the Man, 8.1.2.3(25)
    "Khuddaka-pathaka," 3.2.2.1(13)
    Points of Controversy. See citations under Shwe Zan Aung.
    Psalms of the Brethren, 3.2.2.1(26)
    Psalms of the Early Buddhists, 3.2.2.1(26), (27)
    Psalms of the Sisters, 3.2.2.1(27); 6.1.3(7)
    "The Relations Between Early Buddhism and Brahmanism," 2.2(14)
    Sakya or Buddhist Origins, 2.3(9)
    Samyutta Nikaya: The Book of Kindred Sayings, 2.7.7(10); 3.2.2.1(22); 8.4(14); 9.3.5(9); 11.4.5(14)
    Sigalovada suttanta. See citations under Thomas William Rhys-Davids.
Rhys-Davids, Thomas William
    "Asoka and the Buddha Relics," 8.1.2.4(16); 8.9.1(18)
    Buddhist India, 1.2.2.1(12); 8.1.1(14)
    Dialogues of the Buddha (Digha Nikaya), 2.7.1(13); 2.7.6(8); 3.2.2.1(10); 6.2.1.1(6); 6.2.4(1); 7.5.4(1); 8.1.2.1(22); 8.2.1(9); 8.7(4); 9.1.1(1); 9.1.2(1), (7); 9.1.4(1); 9.2.2.5(7); 9.3.1(2); 9.3.7(2); 9.3.8(1), (5); 10.2.5(1); 11.4.2(7); 11.4.4(4); 11.4.6(7)
    Pali-English Dictionary, 9.2.2.4(10); 12.1(9)
    The Questions of King Milinda, 3.2.2.1(18)
    "The Sects of the Buddhists," 2.4.1(12)
    Sigalovada Suttantra, 6.1.2(19)
    Vinaya Texts, 3.2.1.1(2); 3.2.1.1(4), (5), (6); 7.2.4(8)
Rice, Tamara Talbot
    Ancient Arts of Central Asia, 5.7(2)

Richardson, Hugh E.
   A Cultural History of Tibet. See citations under David Snellgrove.
   "The Karma-pa Sect," 1.14.2.2(8)
   "Tibetan Inscriptions at Zva-hi Lha Khan," 1.14.2.1(8)
Robertson, Alec
   The Triple Gem and the Uposatha, 7.2.4(9)
Robinson, G. W.
   Poems of Wang Wei, 4.3(16)
Robinson, Richard H.
   "Buddhism: In China and Japan," 1.11.1(9)
   The Buddhist Religion, 1.1(8); 2.5.1(7); 8.1.2.3(26); 8.2.2(10); 8.3.1(12)
   Chinese Buddhist Verse, 4.2.1(5); 4.3(17); 11.7.3(4)
   "Madhyamika," 2.5.3(11)
   Early Madhyamika in India and China, 1.11.2.2(9); 2.5.3(10); 3.3.2.2(5)
   "Vijnanavada," 2.5.4(13)
Rock, Joseph F.
   The Amnye Ma-chhen Range and Adjacent Regions, 10.8.2(10)
   "Excerpts from a History of Sikkim," 1.15.2(1)
   The Na-Khi Naga Cult and Related Ceremonies, 7.8(9); 9.2.2.5(11)
Rockhill, William Woodville
   "The Dalai Lamas of Lhasa," 6.2.2.7(6)
   The Land of the Lamas, 10.1.3(9)
   The Life of the Buddha and the Early History of His Order, 3.2.1.2(11); 8.1.2.1(23); 8.1.2.3(27); 8.1.3(13); 9.1.2(8)
   Udanavarga, 3.2.2.2(10)
Roerich, George N.
   Deb-ther-sngon-po (*The Blue Annals*), 1.14.1(5); 9.1.5(7)
Roeske, M.
   "L'enfer cambodgien d'après le Trai Phum, 'Les Trois Mondes,'" 9.2.2.3(14)
Rogers, Henry Thomas
   Buddhaghosha's Parables, 4.2.3(26)
Roggendorf, Joseph
   Studies in Japanese Culture, 4.2.4(10)
Rosenberg, Otto
   Introduction to the Study of Buddhism, 12.1(10)
Rosenfield, John M.
   "On the Dated Carvings of Sarnath," 5.2.8(16)
   The Dynastic Arts of the Kushans, 5.2.5(13)
   Japanese Arts of the Heian Period, 5.11.2(12); 5.11.5(9)
   Traditions of Japanese Art, 5.11.2(13)
Ross, Nancy Wilson
   Three Ways of Ancient Wisdom, 5.1.4(11)
Rouse, William Henry Denham
   "Jinacarita," 3.2.4.1(6); 8.1.2.1(15)
   Siksha-samuccaya. See citations under Cecil Bendall.
Rowell, Teresina
   "The Background and Early Use of the Buddha-ksetra Concept," 9.2.4(4); 11.7.4(8)
Rowland, Benjamin
   The Ajanta Caves, 10.2.6.2(7)
   Ancient Art from Afghanistan, 5.2.5(14)
   Art in Afghanistan, 5.2.5(15)
   The Art and Architecture of India, 5.2.1(21); 10.2.1(16)
   The Art of Central Asia, 5.7(3)
   Art in East and West, 5.1.2(5)
   The Evolution of the Buddha Image, 5.2.3(20)
   Gandharan Sculpture from Pakistan Museums, 5.2.5(16)
   The Harvard Outline and Reading Lists for Oriental Art, 5.1.1(5)
   The Wall-Paintings of India, Central Asia, and Ceylon, 5.1.4(12); 5.7(4)
Roy, Choudhury, P. C.
   Temples and Legends of Bengal, 5.2.8(17)
Royal India Society
   Studies in Chinese Art, 5.9.1(11)
Ruegg, David Seyfort
   "The Jo nan pas," 1.14.2.2(9)
   The Life of Bu ston Rinpoche, 8.9.2(4)
   La Théorie du Tathagatagarbha, 2.7.11(2)
   La Traité du Tathagatagarbha, 2.7.11(3); 3.3.8.3(1)
Russier, Henri
   Lectures sur l'histoire moderne. See citations under Charles Maybon.

Sacks, I. Milton
   "Some Religious Components in Vietnamese Politics," 6.2.2.8(7)
Saddhamma-Sangaha, 9.1.5(11)
Saddharmapundarika sutra, 3.3.5.1(2), (3), (4), (5), 4.2.1(6); 7.1.3(13); 9.3.9(5)
Saddhatissa, H.
   The Buddha's Way, 11.1(12)
   Buddhist Ethics, 11.2(8); 11.3(17)
   "Pali Literature of Thailand," 3.1.2(8)
Sadler, Arthur
   Cha-no-yu, 5.11.8(7)
   "Engakuji and Kenchoji," 6.1.2(17)
   "Pagoda and Monastery," 6.1.2(18)
   A Short History of Japanese Architecture, 5.11.3(10)
Saha, Kshanika
   Buddhism and Buddhist Literature in Central Asia, 1.10.1(5)
Sahiar, D.
   "In Praise of the Buddhist Art in Burma," 10.4.1(3)
Sahni, Daya Ram
   Catalogue of the Museum of Archaeology at Sarnath, 5.2.8(18)
   Guide to the Buddhist Ruins at Sarnath, 10.2.4(5)
Saigusa, Mitsuyoshi
   "Henri Bergson and Buddhist Thought," 2.9(36)
Saito, Katsuo
   Magic of Trees and Stones, 5.11.7(6)
Sakamoto, Hiroshi
   Suzuki Memorial Volume. See citations under Keiji Nishitani.
Salmory, Alfred
   Sculpture in Siam, 5.5.3(9)
Samadhinirmocanasutra, 3.3.3.1(17)
Samadhirajasutra, 3.3.8.1(7)
Samgharaksa
   Yogacarabhumi, 3.2.4.2(3)
Samyutta Nikaya, 2.7.7(10); 3.2.2.1(22); 9.3.5(9); 11.4.5(14)
Sangermano, Vicentius
   A Description of the Burmese Empire, 1.4.2(14); 10.1.4(6)
Sangharaksita, Bhiksu
   "Four Great Bodhisattvas," 8.3.1(13)
   "Ordination and Initiation in the Three Yanas of Buddhism," 7.2.1(8)
   "Three Family Protectors in Tibet," 8.3.1(13)
   The Three Jewels, 6.1.1(25)
Sangitivamsa, 9.1.5(12)

Sankalia, Hasmukh D.
    The University of Nalanda, 5.2.8(19); 6.2.5(24); 10.2.6.1(7)
Sankrityayan, Rahul
    "Acarya Dipamkara Srijnana," 8.9.2(3)
    Buddhism: The Marxist Approach, 2.8(16)
Sansom, George Bailey
    A History of Japan, 1.13.1(14)
    Japan: A Short Cultural History, 1.13.1(15)
Santaraksita
    Tattvasamgraha, 3.3.2.1(25)
Santideva
    Bodhicaryavatara, 3.3.2.1(26), (27), (28), (29)
    Entering the Path of Enlightenment, 2.7.9(5); 2.7.14(6)
    Siksasamuccaya, 3.3.2.1(30)
Saptasatika prajnaparamita-sutra, 3.3.1.1(18)
Sarachchandra, Ediriweera R.
    The Folk Drama of Ceylon, 4.4(9)
    "Traditional Values and the Modernization of a Buddhist Society," 6.2.1.1(38); 6.2.2.2(12)
Saraswati, S. K.
    A Survey of Indian Sculpture, 5.2.3(21)
Sargent, Galen Eugene
    "Tchou Hi contre le Bouddhisme," 1.11.2.3(14)
Sarkar, Himansu Bhushan
    "The Evolution of the Siva-Buddha Cult in Java," 1.9.2(5)
    Studies in Early Buddhist Architecture of India, 5.2.2(13)
Sarkisyanz, Emanuel
    Buddhist Backgrounds of the Burmese Revolution, 1.4.2(15); 6.2.2.3(8); 6.2.6(19); 8.3.1(14); 8.7(5)
    "Communism and Utopianism in Central Asia," 6.2.2.9(4)
    "Messianic Folk-Buddhism as Ideology of Peasant Revolts in Nineteenth and Early Twentieth Century Burma," 9.1.4(7)
    "On the Place of U Nu's Socialism in Burma's History of Ideas," 6.2.2.3(9)
    "The Social Ethics of Buddhism," 6.2.2.1(15); 6.2.6(20)
Sasaki, G. H.
    "Paramartha," 8.9.3(64)
Sasaki, Genjun Kidemaru
    "The Concept of Kamma in Buddhist Philosophy," 2.7.1(14)
Sasaki, Gessho
    A Study of Shin Buddhism, 2.5.8(17); 11.7.1(4)
Sasaki, Ruth Fuller
    The Recorded Sayings of Layman P'ang, 3.3.6.2(8)
    Zen Dust. See citations under Isshu Miura.
Sastri, D. A. Nilakanta
    "Sri Vijaya," 1.9.2(6)
Sastri, K. A. Nilakanta
    "Chinese Travelers," 10.1(9)
    "Mahayana Buddhism in South India," 10.2.6.3(4)
    "Nalanda," 6.2.5(25)
Sastri, N. Aiyaswami
    "Abhidharmakosa-karika," 3.2.3.2(1)
    "Bhavasamkrantisutra," 3.3.2.1(4)
    "Dvadasamukhasastra of Nagarjuna," 3.3.2.1(10)
    "Madhyamarthasamgraha of Bhavaviveka," 2.7.9(1); 3.3.2.1(6)
    "Sramana of Non-Brahmanical Sects," 2.2(15)
Sastri, P. S.
    "Nagarjuna and Aryadeva," 8.9.1(6), (41)
    "The Rise and Growth of Buddhism in Andhra," 1.2.2.4(12)
Satasahasrika prajnaparamitasutra, 3.3.1.1(19)

Sato, Giei
    Unsui: A Diary of Zen Monastic Life, 5.11.6(11); 7.2.2(11)
Satomi, Kishio
    Japanese Civilization, Its Significance and Realization, 2.5.9(5)
Satow, Ernest Mason
    "History of the Introduction of Buddhism into Japan," 1.13.2.1(6)
Saunders, Ernest Dale
    Buddhism in Japan, 1.13.1(16)
    Mudra: A Study of Symbolic Gestures, 2.6.2(7); 5.11.4(16); 11.6.4(6)
    "A Note on Shakti and Dhyanibuddha," 8.2.2(11)
    "Some Tantric Techniques," 11.6.3(7)
    "Symbolic Gestures in Buddhism," 11.6.4(7)
Saunders, Kenneth James
    Buddhist Ideals, 2.9(37)
Sawa, Takaaki
    Art in Japanese Esoteric Buddhism, 5.11.3(11)
Schayer, Stanislaus
    "Pre-canonical Buddhism," 2.3(10)
Schecter, Jerrold
    The New Face of Buddha, 6.2.2.1(16)
    "The New Face of Buddhism in Asia," 6.2.2.1(17)
von Schiefner, F. Anton
    Tibetan Tales, Derived from Indian Sources, 4.2.3(27)
Schiffer, Wilhelm
    "A Chat on a Boat in the Evening." See citations under R. D. M. Shaw.
Schindler, Bruno
    Hirth Anniversary Volume, 8.9.1(43)
Schlagintweit, Emil
    Buddhism in Tibet, 5.6(18)
Schmid, Toni
    The Eighty-Five Siddhas, 5.6(19); 8.5(3)
Schram, Louis M. J.
    The Mongours of the Kansu-Tibetan Frontier, 1.16.2(10); 7.3.3(3); 7.4.2(18); 7.5.1(6)
Schwab, Raymond
    La Renaissance Orientale, 2.9(38)
Scigliano, Robert
    "Vietnam: Politics and Religion," 6.2.2.8(8)
Scott, Adolfe C.
    The Classical Theatre in China, 5.12.1(8)
Scott, James George
    "Buddhism in the Shan States," 1.4.2(16)
    The Burman: His Life and Notions, 1.4.2(17)
Seckel, Dietrich
    The Art of Buddhism, 5.1.4(13); 5.8(8); 5.9.1(12); 5.10(14)
    Emakimono, 5.11.5(10)
Sekiguchi, Sendai
    Zen: A Manual for Westerners, 11.4.8.1(11)
Sekino, Tadashi
    Buddhist Monuments in China. See citations under Daijo Tokiwa.
Selkirk, James
    Recollection of Ceylon, 10.1.4(7)
Senart, Emile
    Essai sur la Légende du Buddha, 8.1.2.3(28); 8.7(6); 9.3.8(6)
Seneviratne, H. L.
    "The Asala Perahara in Kandy," 7.3.1(13)
Seng-chao
    Chao lun, 1.11.2.2(10)
Sengupta, P. C.
    "Dates of Principal Events in the Buddha's Life," 8.1.2.3(29)

Author/Title Index

Sengupta, Sudha
    "Buddhism in the Classical Age," 1.2.2.3(13)
Serruys, Henry
    "Early Lamaism in Mongolia," 1.16.1(8)
    "A Mongol Lamaist Prayer," 7.1.4(10)
Shackleton-Bailey, David Roy
    The Satapanca-satka of Matrceta, 3.2.4.3(2); 7.1.4(8)
    "The Varnarhavarna Stotra of Matrceta," 3.2.4.3(3); 7.1.4(9)
Shakabpa, Tsepon W. D.
    Tibet: A Political History, 1.14.1(10); 6.2.2.7(7)
Shastri, Ajay M.
    An Outline of Early Buddhism, 6.1.1(26)
Shastri, Hirananda
    The Origin and Cult of Tara, 7.8(10); 8.3.3(2)
Shastri, J.
    "The Doctrinal Culture and Tradition of the Siddhas," 8.4(4)
Shaw, R. D. M.
    The Blue Cliff Records, 3.3.6.1(8); 11.4.8.2(1)
    "A Chat on a Boat in the Evening," 3.3.6.2(3)
Shibata, Masumi
    Les Maîtres du Zen au Japon, 2.5.7(18); 8.9.4(1), (2), (4), (5), (6), (7), (9), (14), (15), (20), (29), (30)
    "Sermon sur le Bouddhisme Zen," 3.3.6.4(1)
Shih, Robert
    Biographies des Moines Eminents, 8.9.3(1)
Shih-niu-t'u sung, 3.3.6.1(9), (10)
Shimada, Shujiro
    Traditions of Japanese Art. See citations under John M. Rosenfield.
Shinran
    Kyo Gyo Shisho, 3.3.7.2(5)
    Mattosho, 3.3.7.2(6)
    The Private Letters of Shinran Shonin, 2.5.8(18)
    Shuji, 3.3.7.2(7)
    Wasan, 3.3.7.2(8)
Shiveley, Donald H.
    "Buddhahood for the Non-sentient," 4.4(10); 5.12.2(14)
Shorto, Harry
    "The Thirty-Two Myos in the Medieval Mon Kingdom," 10.4.2(3)
Shosoin Jimusho
    Treasures of the Shosoin, 5.11.2(14); 5.11.5(11)
Shrestha, C. B.
    Buddhist Geography of Ancient Nepal, 10.7(3)
Shunjo, Hoin
    Honen, The Buddhist Saint, 1.13.2.2(12); 2.5.8(19); 8.9.4(12); 11.7.2(4); 11.7.4(9)
Sickman, Laurence
    The Art and Architecture of China, 5.9.1(13); 5.9.2(13); 10.8.1(5)
Sigalovada-sutta, 3.2.2.2(8)
Sigalovada Suttanta, 6.1.2(19)
Silva-Vigier, Anil de
    The Art of Chinese Landscape Painting, 5.9.4(11)
    The Life of the Buddha, 5.2.3(22)
Simpson, William
    The Buddhist Praying Wheel, 9.3.1(8)
Singh, Bhupal
    A Survey of Anglo-Indian Fiction, 2.9(39)
Singh, Bireshwar Prasad
    "Naropa: His Life and Activities," 8.9.2(14)
Singh, Madan Mohan
    "Life in the Buddhist Monastery During the 6th Century B.C.," 6.1.1(27)

Singh, Madanjeet
    Ajanta, 5.2.6(13)
    Ajanta Paintings of the Sacred and Secular, 10.2.6.2(8)
    Himalayan Art, 5.2.8(20)
Singh, Ram Jee
    World Perspectives in Philosophy, Religion, and Culture, 6.2.1.2(3)
Sircar, Dinesh Chandra
    The Sakti Cult and Tara, 7.8(11); 8.3.3(3)
    Studies in the Religious Life of Ancient and Medieval India, 1.2.2.4(13)
Siren, Osvald
    "Central Asian Influences," 5.7(5); 5.9.3(10)
    Chinese Painting, 5.9.3(11)
    Chinese Sculpture from the Fifth to the Fourteenth Century, 5.9.2(14)
    A History of Early Chinese Art, 5.9.1(14)
    A History of Early Chinese Paintings, 5.9.3(12)
Sivaramamurti, Calembus
    "Ajanta," 10.2.6.2(9)
    Amaravati Sculptures, 5.2.7(9)
    5000 Years of Indian Art. See citations under Mario Bussagli.
    Le Stupa du Barabudur, 5.5.6(9)
The Sixteen Arhats and the Eighteen Arhats, 8.4(15)
Skinner, G. William
    Change and Persistence in Thai Society, 1.5.2(21)
Slater, Robert Lawson
    Paradox and Nirvana, 11.8(10)
Smith, Bardwell L.
    Religion and Political Legitimization in Southeast Asia, 1.4.2(7)
    "Toward a Buddhist Anthropology," 6.2.1.1(39)
    Tradition and Change in Theravada Buddhism, 1.3.2.2(4); 1.5.2(22); 6.1.2(14); 6.2.1.1(32), (40); 6.2.2.4(5); 12.2(14)
    The Two Wheels of Dhamma, 1.3.1(11); 6.2.1.1(41)
Smith, Bradley
    China: A History in Art, 5.9.1(15)
    Japan: A History in Art, 5.11.2(15)
Smith, Donald Eugene
    "The Political Monks of Burma and Ceylon," 6.2.2.2(13); 6.2.2.3(10)
    Religion and Political Development, 6.2.2.1(18)
    Religion and Political Modernization, 6.2.2.2(2)
    South Asian Politics and Religion, 1.2.2.4(5); 1.3.2.2(5); 6.2.2.2(14); 6.2.4(11)
Smith, Vincent A.
    Asoka, 8.9.1(19)
    A History of Fine Art in India and Ceylon, 5.1.4(14)
    "Kusinara, or Kusinagara and Other Buddhist Holy Places," 10.2.5(2)
    The Oxford History of India, 1.2.1(13)
Snellgrove, David L.
    Buddhist Himalaya, 1.14.2.1(9); 1.15.1(4); 11.6.2(11)
    A Cultural History of Tibet, 1.14.1(11)
    Four Lamas of Dolpo, 8.9.2(19)
    The Hevajra Tantra, 2.6.1(11); 3.4.1(4); 11.6.1(19)
    "The Notion of Divine Kingship in Tantric Buddhism," 6.2.2.7(8); 8.7(7)
    "Saraha's Treasury of Songs," 3.4.4(4)
    "Shrines and Temples of Nepal," 10.7(4)
Sobhana
    See citations under Mahasi Sayadaw.
bSod nams grags pa
    Deb t'er dmar po gsar ma, 9.1.5(14)

Soga, Ryojin
"Dharmakara Bodhisattva," 8.3.6(7)
Sok, Do-Ryun
"Modern Sun Buddhism in Korea," 1.12.2(11); 2.5.7(19)
"Sun Buddhism in Korea," 1.12.2(12)
Sompura, K. F.
Buddhist Monuments and Sculptures in Gujurat, 10.2.6.1(8)
Soothill, William Edward
A Dictionary of Chinese Buddhist Terms, 12.1(11)
The Lotus of the Wonderful Law, 3.3.5.1(4)
Soper, Alexander C.
The Art and Architecture of China, 10.8.1(5)
The Art and Architecture of Japan. See citations under Robert Paine.
"Aspects of Light Symbolism in Gandharan Sculpture," 9.3.9(6)
Chinese, Korean, and Japanese Bronzes, 5.8(9); 5.9.2(15); 5.10(15); 5.11.4(17)
"Early Buddhist Attitudes Toward the Art of Painting," 5.9.3(13)
The Evolution of Buddhist Architecture in Japan, 5.11.3(12)
"The Fire in the Horyuji Kondo," 5.11.5(12)
"Imperial Cave-chapels of the Northern Dynasties," 5.9.4(12)
"Japanese Evidence for the History of Architecture," 5.9.2(16)
Kuo Jo-hsu's Experiences in Painting, 5.9.3(14)
Literary Evidence for Early Buddhist Art in China, 1.11.2.1(8); 5.9.1(16)
"Northern Wei and Northern Liang," 5.7(6); 5.9.4(13)
"Notes on Horyuji," 5.11.4(18)
"A Pictorial Biography of Prince Shotoku," 5.11.5(13)
"Representations of Famous Images," 5.9.3(15)
"Some Late Chinese Bronze Images," 5.9.2(17)
"South Chinese Influence," 5.9.4(14)
"T'ang Ch'ao Ming Hua Lu," 5.9.3(16)
"Two Stelae and a Pagoda," 5.9.2(18)
"A 'Wei Style' Bronze," 5.9.2(19)
Sourys-Rolland, A.
"Les procédés magiques d'immunisation chez les cambodgiens," 7.5.3(7)
Soymie, Michel
"L'Entrevue de Confucius et de Hiang T'o," 4.2.4(15)
Speiser, Werner
The Art of China, 5.9.1(17)
Oriental Architecture in Colour, 5.1.4(15)
Spencer, Robert F.
Religion and Change in Contemporary Asia, 1.11.2.4(7); 6.2.2.8(7)
Speyer, J. S.
The Gatakamala, or Garland of Birth Stories, 4.2.2(1); 8.1.1(1)
Spink, Walter
Ajanta to Ellora, 5.2.6(14)
Spiro, Melford E.
"Buddhism and Economic Action in Burma," 6.2.6(21)
Buddhism and Society, 6.2.1.1(42); 6.2.2.1(19); 7.1.1(10); 7.1.2(3); 7.2.1(9); 7.3.1(14); 7.4.1(4); 7.4.2(19); 7.5.4(5); 9.1.4(8)
Buddhist Supernaturalism, 4.1.2(15)
Sprung, Mervin
The Problem of Two Truths in Buddhism and Vedanta, 2.7.9(6)

Srimala-devi-simhanada-sutra, 2.7.11(4); 3.2.2.2(9); 3.3.2.1(31)
Srinavasna, P. R.
Guide to Buddhist Antiquities. See citations under A. Aiyanpan.
Ssu-shih-erh-chang-ching, 3.3.8.2(9)
von Stael-Holstein, A.
"Avalokita and Apalokita," 8.3.2(11)
Standard Buddhist Gathas and Services, 7.2.3(3)
Stargardt, Janic
"Social and Religious Aspects of Royal Power in Medieval Burma," 6.2.2.3(11)
Starr, Frederick
Korean Buddhism: History, Condition, Art, 1.12.1(7)
Stcherbatsky, Fedor Ippolitovich (Theodore)
Buddhist Logic, 2.1(11); 2.2(16); 2.3(11); 2.5.4(14); 3.3.3.1(7); 3.3.3.2(2)
The Central Conception of Buddhism, 2.7.7(11); 3.2.3.4(10)
The Conception of Buddhist Nirvana, 2.5.3(12); 11.8(11)
"The 'Dharmas' of the Buddhists," 2.7.7(12)
"The Doctrine of the Buddha," 2.3(12)
"La littérature Yogacara d'après Bouston," 3.3.3.3(2)
Madhyanta-Vibhanga, 3.3.3.1(2); 3.3.3.2(5)
The Soul Theory of the Buddhists, 2.7.4(11)
Stein, Aurel
On Ancient Central-Asian Tracks, 1.10.1(6); 10.1.1(10)
Ancient Khotan, 5.7(7)
Catalogue of Wall-Paintings, 5.7(11)
Innermost Asia, 5.7(8)
Ruins of Cathay, 5.7(9)
Serindia, 5.7(10); 5.9.3(17)
Stein, Otto
"Notes on the Trikaya-Doctrine," 8.1.3(14)
Stein, Rolf Alfred
L'Epopée Tibétaine de Gesar dans sa version Lamaïque de Ling, 4.2.4(16)
Tibetan Civilization, 1.14.1(12)
"Trente-trois fiches de divination tibétaines," 7.6(4)
Vie et chante de 'Brug-Pa Kun-Legs le Yogin, 4.3(18)
Steinberg, David J.
Cambodia: Its People, Its Society, Its Culture, 1.6.1(8)
Steinilber-Oberlin, Eamile
The Buddhist Sects of Japan, 1.13.2.2(13); 2.5.5(4)
Stern, Philippe
L'Art du Champa, 5.5.5(5)
Evolution du style indien d'Amaravati, 5.2.7(10)
Les Monuments Khmers, 5.5.4(13)
Stern, Theodore
"Ariya and the Golden Book," 1.4.2(18)
Sthiramati
Madhyantavibhagatika, 3.3.3.2(4)
Story, Francis
The Case for Rebirth, 2.8(17)
Streng, Frederick J.
Emptiness, 2.5.3(13); 2.7.6(10); 2.7.8(10); 2.7.9(7); 3.3.2.1(16), (20)
Strong, D. M.
The Udana, 3.2.2.1(29)
Subrahmaniam, R.
"Buddhaghosa: His Place of Birth," 8.9.5(5)

Suddard, Adrienne
    Laos: Its People, its Society, its Culture.
        See citations under Frank M. LeBar.
Sugihira, Shizutoshi
    "Honen Shonin and Shinran Shonin," 11.7.2(5)
    "Rennyo Shonin, the Great Teacher of Shin
        Buddhism," 1.13.2.3(3); 8.9.4(22)
    "A Study in the Pure Land Doctrine," 2.5.8(20)
    "The Teaching of Ippen Shonin," 11.7.2(6)
Sukhavati vyuha, 3.3.7.1(2), (3)
Sullivan, Michael
    The Arts of China, 5.9.1(18)
    The Cave Temples of Maichishan, 5.9.4(15);
        10.8.2(11)
    An Introduction to Chinese Art, 5.9.1(19)
Suramgamasamadhisutra, 3.3.2.1(32), (33)
Sutralamkara, 3.3.8.2(8)
Sutta-Nipata, 3.2.2.1(23), (24), (25)
Sutta-vibhanga, 3.2.1.1(3)
Suvarnabhasottamasutra, 3.3.8.1(8); 4.2.1(7);
    7.5.2(5)
Suvikrantavikrami-pariprccha prajnaparamita-sutra,
    3.3.1.1(20)
Suzuki, Beatrice Lane
    "Ceremonies for Lay Buddhists at Koya-san,"
        7.1.4(11); 7.2.3(4)
    "Honen Shonin and the Jodo Ideal," 2.5.8(21)
    Mahayana Buddhism, 2.5.1(8)
    Nogaku, 5.12.2(15)
    "An Outline of the Avatamsakasutra," 3.3.4.2(5)
    "The Songs of Shinran Shonin," 3.3.7.2(8)
Suzuki, Daisetz Teitaro
    Asvaghosha's Discourse on the Awakening of
        Faith, 3.3.8.2(2)
    "Avatamsaka Sutra," 3.3.4.1(2)
    Collected Writings on Shin Buddhism, 2.5.8(22)
    "The Cult of Kwannon," 7.8(12); 8.3.2(12)
    Essays in Zen Buddhism, 2.5.5(5); 2.5.7(20);
        3.3.4.2(6); 11.4.8.2(4); 11.8(12)
    On Indian Mahayana Buddhism, 2.5.5(6);
        3.3.4.1(6); 3.3.4.2(7)
    "Infinite Light," 9.3.9(7)
    Japanese Buddhism, 1.13.1(17)
    The Lankavatara Sutra, 3.3.3.1(15); 3.3.6.1(3)
    Manual of Zen Buddhism, 2.5.7(21); 3.3.1.1(13);
        3.3.6.1(10); 7.2.3(5)
    A Miscellany on the Shin Teaching of Buddhism,
        2.5.8(23); 3.3.7.2(7), (8); 11.7.1(5)
    Mysticism: Christian and Buddhist, 2.9(40)
    Outlines of Mahayana Buddhism, 2.1(12);
        2.5.1(9); 2.7.9(8); 2.7.10(4); 2.7.11(5);
        2.7.12(8); 2.7.13(5); 2.7.14(7); 8.1.2.2(11);
        8.1.3(15); 8.3.1(15); 8.4(16)
    "Philosophy of the Yogacara," 2.5.4(15)
    "The Prajnaparamita-hrdaya-sutra," 3.3.1.1(13)
    "Reason and Intuition," 11.4.7(6)
    Sengai: The Zen Master, 5.11.6(12)
    Studies in the Lankavatara Sutra, 3.3.3.3(3);
        8.1.2.2(12)
    The Training of the Zen Buddhist Monk, 7.2.1(10);
        7.2.2(12); 7.2.3(6); 11.4.8.1(12)
    Treatise of the Exalted One on Response and
        Retribution. See citations under Paul Carus.
    Zen Buddhism: Selected Writings, 2.5.7(22);
        11.4.8.1(14); 11.4.8.3(6)
    Zen and Japanese Culture, 5.11.6(13); 6.2.1.2(20)
    "Zen and Jodo," 11.4.8.1(13); 11.7.1(6)
Svalpaksara prajnaparamita-sutra, 3.3.1.1(21)

Swann, Peter C.
    The Art of Japan, 5.11.2(16)
    Arts of China, Korea, and Japan, 5.8(10);
        5.10(16)
    Chinese Monumental Art, 5.9.4(16)
    Chinese Painting, 5.9.3(18)
    An Introduction to the Arts of Japan, 5.11.2(17)
Swann, Winn
    Lost Cities of Asia, 5.2.2(14)
Swaramamurti, C.
    "Buddhism in Sikkim, Ladakh, and Bhutan,"
        1.15.1(5)
Swearer, Donald K.
    Buddhism in Transition, 2.8(18); 6.1.4(4);
        6.2.1.1(43)
    "Control and Freedom," 11.4.1(7)
    "Lay Buddhism and the Buddhist Revival in
        Ceylon," 1.3.2.2(6); 6.1.2(20)
    Secrets of the Lotus, 11.4.1(8); 11.4.2(13);
        11.4.4(8); 11.4.8.1(15)
    "Thai Buddhism: Two Responses to Modernity,"
        1.5.2(22); 8.9.5(1)
    "Two Types of Saving Knowledge," 11.4.7(7)
    Wat Haripunjaya, 1.5.2(23)
Symbolisme cosmique des monuments religieux,
    9.3.6(10)
"Symposium on Buddhism and Society in Thailand,"
    1.5.2(24)

Tachibana, S.
    The Ethics of Buddhism, 11.3(18)
Tada Kanai
    Shudo Kowa, 7.2.5(7)
Tada, Tokan
    The Thirteenth Dalai Lama, 8.9.2(8)
T'ai-shang kan-ying p'ien, 4.2.4(17)
Tajima, Ryujun
    Les Deux Grands Mandalas et la Doctrine de
        l'Esotérisme Shingon, 2.6.2(8); 11.6.2(12)
    Etude sur le Mahavairocanasutra, 2.6.2(9);
        3.4.3(3); 8.2.2(10)
Takahashi, Shinkichi
    Afterimages: Zen Poems, 4.3(19)
Takahashi, Takeichi
    Shinranism in Mahayana Buddhism, 2.5.8(24)
Takakusu, Junjiro
    "On the Abhidharma Literature of the
        Sarvastivadins," 2.4.3(10); 3.2.3.4(12)
    "Buddhism as a Philosophy of 'Thusness,'"
        2.7.10(5)
    "Chinese Translations of the Milinda Panha,"
        3.2.3.4(11); 8.9.1(36)
    "The Date of Vasubandhu," 8.9.1(56)
    The Essentials of Buddhist Philosophy, 2.1(13);
        2.4.1(13); 2.5.1(10); 2.5.3(14); 2.5.4(16);
        2.5.5(7); 2.5.6(6); 2.5.7(23); 2.5.9(6)
    "The Life of Vasubandhu," 8.9.1(57)
    "Sarvastivadins," 2.4.3(11)
    "Shyana." See citations under Masaharu Anesaki.
    "A Study of Paramartha's Life of Vasu-bandhu,"
        8.9.1(58)
    "The Sutra of the Meditation on Amitayus,"
        3.3.7(1); 9.3.9(1)
    "Le voyage de Kanshin en Orient," 10.1.5(5)
Takakuwa, Gisei
    Japanese Garden Revisited, 5.11.7(7)

Takasaki, Jikido
    "Dharmata, Dharmadhatu, Dharmakaya, and
        Buddhadhatu," 2.7.10(6)
    A Study on the Ratnagotravibhaga, 2.7.11(6);
        3.3.2.1(24)
Takata, Osamu
    Ajanta, 5.2.6(15)
    Takao Mandara, 5.11.5(14)
Takeda, Choshu
    "Ancestor Worship," 4.1.4(7)
Takeyama, Michio
    Harp of Burma, 4.5(10)
Taki, Seiichi
    Japanese Fine Art, 5.11.2(18)
Talim, M. V.
    "Buddhist Nuns and Disciplinary Rules," 6.1.3(8)
Tamaki, Koshiro
    "The Position of Dogen in the History of
        Buddhist Thought," 2.5.7(24)
Tambiah, Stanley J.
    Buddhism and the Spirit Cults in North-East
        Thailand, 4.1.2(16); 7.1.1(11); 7.2.1(11);
        7.2.2(13); 7.3.1(15); 7.4.2(20); 7.5.2(6);
        7.5.4(6)
    "Buddhism and This Worldly Activity,"
        6.2.1.1(44)
    "The Ideology of Merit and the Social Correlates
        of Buddhism in a Thai Village," 6.2.3(19)
    "The Persistence and Transformation of Tradition
        in Southeast Asia," 6.2.1.1(45)
    World Conqueror and World Renouncer, 1.5.1(7)
Tamura, Yoshiro
    "The New Buddhism of Kamakura Nichiren,"
        2.5.6(7)
    "The Sutra of Innumerable Meanings," 3.3.5.1(6)
T'an Chun-yo
    The Omei Illustrated Guide Book. See citations
        under Huang Shou-fu.
bsTan 'dzin Chos rgyal
    Lho'i chos-'byung, 1.15.1(6)
Tanabe, Hisao
    Japanese Music, 5.12.3(10)
Tanaka, Ichimatsu
    Japanese Ink Painting, 5.11.5(15)
Tanaka, Sen'o
    The Tea Ceremony, 5.11.8(8)
Tao-yuan, Shih
    Original Teachings of Ch'an Buddhism, 2.5.7(25)
Tapingkae, Amnuay
    Education in Thailand, 6.2.5(26)
Taranatha
    History of Buddhism in India, 1.2.1(14);
        8.9.1(35); 9.1.5(15)
Taut, Bruno
    Houses and People of Japan, 5.11.3(13)
Tennent, James Emerson
    Ceylon: An Account of the Island, 10.1.4(8)
Tenzin, Gyatso
    The Buddhism of Tibet, 2.7.8(11)
    "The Key to the Middle Way," 2.7.8(11)
Than, U Aung
    "Relation Between the Sangha and State and
        Laity," 6.1.2(21); 6.2.2.3(12)
Than Tun
    "Religious Buildings of Burma, 100-1300,"
        10.4.1(4)
Thapar, Romila
    Asoka and the Decline of the Mauryas, 1.2.2.2(4);
        8.9.1(20)

Thaung, U
    "Burmese Kingship in Theory and Practice,"
        6.2.2.3(13)
Theragatha, 3.2.2.1(26)
Therigatha, 3.2.2.1(27)
Thien-an, Thich
    Buddhism and Zen in Vietnam, 1.8.1(9)
Thierry, Solange
    "La personne sacrée du Roi dans la littérature
        populaire cambodgienne," 6.2.2.8(9); 7.7(4);
        8.7(8)
Thittila, U.
    The Book of Analysis, 3.2.3.1(2)
Thomas, Edward Joseph
    "Buddhist Education in Pali and Sanskrit
        Schools," 6.2.5(27)
    "Epithets of an Arhat in the Divyavadana,"
        8.4(17)
    The History of Buddhist Thought, 2.1(14);
        8.3.1(16)
    Jataka Tales. See citations under H. T.
        Francis.
    The Life of the Buddha as Legend and History,
        8.1.2.3(30)
    "Nirvana and Parinivana," 11.8(13)
Thomas, Frederick William
    Documents de Touen-Houang relatifs à l'histoire
        du Tibet. See citations under Jacques Bacot.
    "The Hand Treatise," 3.3.2.1(2); 3.3.3.1(10)
    "Matriceta and the Maharajakanikalekha,"
        3.2.4.3(1)
    Tibetan Literary Texts, 3.3.8.3(3)
The Three Basic Facts of Existence: 1. Impermanence,
    2.7.3(6)
Thubten Jigme Norbu
    Tibet, 1.14.1(13)
Thupavamsa, 9.1.5(16); 9.3.6(11)
Tibetans in Exile, 1.14.2.3(4)
Tin, Pe Maung
    "Buddhaghosa," 8.9.5(6)
    "Buddhism in the Inscriptions at Pagan,"
        1.4.2(19); 10.4.1(5)
    Buddhist Devotion and Meditation, 7.1.1(12)
    The Expositor, 3.2.3.3(3); 3.2.3.4(3);
        9.2.2.1(2)
    The Glass Palace Chronicles. See citations
        under Hmannan Maha Yazawintawkyi.
    The Path of Purity, 3.2.4.2(1)
Toda, Josei
    Lecture on the Sutra, 3.3.5.2(6)
Toda, Kenji
    "The Shitennoji Albums," 5.11.5(16)
Tokiwa, Daijo
    Buddhist Monuments in China, 1.11.2.2(11);
        1.11.2.3(15); 5.9.2(20); 5.9.4(17); 10.8.1(6)
Totten, George O.
    "Buddhism and Socialism in Japan and Burma,"
        6.2.2.3(14); 6.2.2.6(10)
Toussaint, Gustave-Charles
    Documents de Touen-Houang relatifs à l'histoire
        du Tibet. See citations under Jacques Bacot.
    "Le Padma Than Yig," 8.9.2(17)
Traeger, Frank
    Burma: From Kingdom to Republic, 6.2.2.3(15)
Traibhumi Brah R'van, 3.2.4.2(4)
Trenckner, Vilhelm
    Critical Pali Dictionary, 12.1(12)
Tripathi, Chhote Lal
    The Problem of Knowledge in Yogacara Buddhism,
        2.5.4(17)

Trisvabhavanirdesa, 2.7.13(6)
Trollope, Mark Napier
   "Introduction to the Study of Buddhism in Corea," 1.12.1(8)
Tsao, Hsueh-chin
   Dream of the Red Chamber, 4.5(11)
Tseng, Hsien-ch'i
   Lamaist Art. See citations under Pratapadihya Pol.
Tsong Khapa
   The Graded Course to Enlightenment, 3.3.8.3(4)
Tsuda, Noritake
   Handbook of Japanese Art, 5.11.2(19)
Tsukamoto, Keisho
   "Mahakasyapa's Precedence to Ananda in the Rajagrha Council," 2.4.2(10); 8.9.1(1)
Tsukamoto, Zenryu
   "Buddhism in the Asuka-Nara Period," 1.13.2.1(7)
   "Buddhism in China and Korea," 1.11.1(10)
   "The Sramana Superintendent T'an-yao and his Time," 1.11.2.2(12)
Tsunoda, Ryusaku
   Sources of the Japanese Tradition, 2.5.8(25)
Tu Shun
   Fa Chieh Kuan, 3.3.4.1(5)
Tucci, Guiseppe
   "Animadversiones Indicae: 1. On Maitreye," 8.9.1(10)
   "Animadversiones Indicae: 4. A Sanskrit Biography of the Siddhas and Some Questions Connected with Nagarjuna," 8.9.1(42)
   "A Brief History of Tibetan Religious Literature," 3.1.4(9)
   "Buddhist Notes I: A propos Avalokitesvara," 8.3.2(13)
   Deb t'er dmar po gsar ma Tibetan Chronicles by bSod nams grags pa, 1.14.1(14); 9.1.5(14)
   Gyantse ed i suoi Monasteri, 5.6(20)
   Minor Buddhist Texts, 1.14.2.1(10); 3.3.1.2(2); 3.3.3.1(5)
   "Nomina, Numina," 8.6(7)
   "The Prajnaparamita pindartha of Dignaga," 3.3.1.2(3); 3.3.3.1(13)
   Pre-Dignaga Buddhist Texts on Logic, 3.3.2.1(3), (21)
   Preliminary Report on Two Scientific Expeditions in Nepal, 10.1.3(10)
   "A propos the Legend of Naropa," 8.9.2(15)
   "The Ratnavali of Nagarjuna," 3.3.2.1(17)
   Shrines of a Thousand Buddhas, 5.6(21); 10.7(5)
   On Some Aspects of the Doctrines of Maitreya and Asanga, 2.5.4(18)
   "The Symbolism of the Temple of bSam yas," 9.3.6(12)
   The Theory and Practice of the Mandala, 11.6.2(13)
   Tibet: Land of Snows, 1.14.1(15); 5.6(22)
   Tibetan Folk Songs, 4.3(20)
   "Tibetan Notes 2: The Diffusion of the Yellow Church: Western Tibet," 1.14.2.2(10)
   Tibetan Painted Scrolls, 1.14.2.2(11); 2.6.1(12); 3.1.4(9)
   The Tombs of the Tibetan Kings, 1.14.2.1(11)
   "Un Traité d'Aryadeva sur le 'Nirvana' des hérétiques," 11.8(14)
   "Two Hymns of the Catuhstava of Nagarjuna," 3.3.2.1(15); 8.1.1(13); 8.1.3(12)
   "The Validity of Tibetan Historical Tradition," 1.14.1(16)
   "The Wives of Sron btsan sgam po," 1.14.2.1(12)

Tuladhar, Kuladharma Ratna
   Buddhism and Nepal, 1.15.1(7)
Tung-shan
   Pao-ching San-Mei, 3.3.6.3(4), (5)
   Wu-wei sung, 3.3.6.3(6)
Tun-huang Pi-hua, 5.9.4(18)
Tun-wu ju-tao yao-men lun, 3.3.6.2(9)
Turnbull, Colin M.
   Tibet. See citations under Thubten Jigme Norbu.
Twitchett, Denis C.
   Confucian Personalities. See citations under Arthur F. Wright.
   "The Monasteries and China's Economy in Medieval Times," 6.2.6(23)
   "Monastic Estates in T'ang China," 1.11.2.3(16); 6.2.6(22)

Udana, 3.2.2.1(28), (29)
Udanavarga, 3.2.2.2(10)
Ueda, Yoshifumi
   "Thinking in Buddhist Philosophy," 2.7.4(12)
   "Two Main Streams of Thought in Yogacara Philosophy," 2.5.4(19)
Ui, Hakuju
   "The Hand Treatise." See citations under Frederick William Thomas.
   "Maitreya As an Historical Personage," 8.9.1(11)
   "A Study of Japanese Tendai Buddhism," 1.13.2.2(14); 2.5.6(8)
Umehara, Rakeshi
   "Heidegger and Buddhism," 2.9(41)
University of Ceylon
   History of Ceylon, 5.4.2(9)
Upadhyaya, Kashi Nath
   Early Buddhism and the Bhagavadgita, 2.2(17)
Upatissa
   Vimuttimagga, 3.2.4.2(5); 11.4.2(11)
Utsuki, Nishu
   The Shin Sect, 2.5.8(26)

Vajiranana Paravahera, Mahathera
   Buddhist Meditation in Theory and Practice, 11.4.1(9)
Vajracchedika prajnaparamita-sutra, 3.3.1.1(22), (23), (24), (25), (26), (27)
Vajradatta
   Lokasvasasatakam, 8.3.2(14)
Vajrasuci, 3.2.4.3(4)
Vamsavali, 1.15.1(8); 9.1.5(17)
Vanderstrappen, Harry
   "The Sculpture of T'ien Lung-shan," 5.9.4(19)
Van Gulik, R. H.
   Hayagriva, 7.8(13); 8.6(8)
Van Lohuizen-de Leeuw, J. E.
   The "Scythian" Period, 5.2.4(18); 5.2.5(17)
Van Straelen, Henry
   Modern Japanese Religions with Special Emphasis on Their Doctrines of Healing. See citations under Clark B. Offner.
Van Zeyst, H. G. A.
   "Ajatasattu," 8.9.1(4)
   "Arupa loka," 9.2.3(5)
   "Bimbisara," 8.9.1(24)
Varma, Vishwanath Prasad
   Early Buddhism and its Origins, 1.2.2.1(13); 2.2(18); 6.2.1.1(46)
   "The Origins and Sociology of the Early Buddhist Philosophy of Moral Determinism," 2.7.1(15)
   "Studies in Hindu Political Thought," 6.2.2.1(20)

Vasubandhu
    Abhidharmakosa, 3.2.3.2(4); 9.1.1(5); 9.1.2(9); 9.1.3(5); 9.2.1(13); 9.2.2.1(8); 9.2.5(4)
    Karmasiddhiprakarana, 3.2.3.2(5)
    Madhyantavibhangabhasya, 3.3.3.2(5)
    Trimsika karika prakarana, 3.3.3.1(18)
    Trisvabhavanirdesa, 3.3.3.1(19)
    Vimsika karika prakarana, 3.3.3.1(20), (21), (22)
Vasubandhu, 2.7.10(3)
Veith, Ilza
    "A Buddhist Prayer Against Sickness," 7.5.2(7)
Venkataramanan, K.
    "Sammitiya-nikaya-sastra," 3.2.3.2(2)
Vessantara Jataka, 4.2.2(12); 8.1.1(15)
Vibhanga, 3.2.3.1(2)
Vidhisamgraha, 3.4.1(7)
Vidyabhushan, Satis Chandra
    "A Descriptive List of Works on the Madhyamika Philosophy," 3.3.2.2(6)
    "So-sor-thar-pa," 3.2.1.2(9)
Viennot, Odette
    Le culte de l'arbre dans l'Inde ancienne, 9.3.4(3)
Vijayavardhana, D. C.
    The Revolt in the Temple, Composed to Commemorate 2500 Years of the Land, the Race and the Faith, 1.3.2.2(7); 2.8(19); 6.2.2.2(15)
Vijnaptimatratasiddhi, 3.3.3.2(6)
Vimaladhamma
    Sangitivamsa, 9.1.5(12)
Vimalakirti Nirdesa sutra, 3.3.2.1(34), (35), (36); 4.2.1(8); 9.2.4(5)
Vimalapanda, Tennakoon
    The State and Religion in Ceylon since 1815, 1.3.2.2(8); 6.2.2.2(16)
"Vimana," 9.2.2.4(10)
Vimana vatthu, 3.2.2.1(30); 9.2.2.4(11)
Vimuktimarga Dhutaguna-Nirdesa, 11.4.2(10)
Vinaya pitaka, 3.2.1.1(1), (2); 7.2.1(12)
Vincent, Irene Vongehr
    The Sacred Oasis, 5.9.4(20); 10.1.2(8)
Vinitad-va
    Nyayabindu-tika, 3.3.3.2(7)
Vira, Raghu
    Sanskrit Bijas and Mantras in Japan, 5.11.5(19)
Visser, Marinus Willem de
    Ancient Buddhism in Japan, 1.13.2.1(8); 5.11.2(20); 7.1.2(4); 7.2.3(7); 7.3.2(8); 7.4.2(21); 7.5.2(8); 7.7(5); 7.8(14); 8.2.2(13); 11.6.4(8); 11.7.3(5)
    "The Arhats in China and Japan," 8.4(18)
    The Arhats in China and Japan, 5.8(11)
    The Bodhisattva Akasagarbha (Kokuzo) in China and Japan, 5.8(12); 7.8(15); 8.3.6(8)
    The Bodhisattva Ti-tsang (Jizo) in China and Japan, 5.8(13); 7.8(16); 8.3.6(9)
    The Dragon in China and Japan, 5.8(14); 9.2.2.5(12)
Vo, H. P.
    "Religion and Education." See citations under G. E. Hickey.
Vogel, Jean Philippe
    Buddhist Art in India, Ceylon, and Java, 5.1.4(16)
    Catalogue of the Museum of Archaeology at Sarnath. See citations under Daya Ram Sahni.
    "Excavations at Kasia," 10.2.5(3)
    "Excavations at Sahet-Mahet," 10.2.6.1(9)
    La Sculpture de Mathura, 5.2.4(19)
Von der Mehden, Fred
    "The Changing Pattern of Religion and Politics in Burma," 6.2.2.3(16)

Wada, Saidaij
    Magic of Trees and Stones. See citations under Katsuo Saito.
Waddell, Lawrence Austine
    "Bhutan, Buddhism in," 1.15.1(9)
    The Buddhism of Tibet, 5.6(23)
    "The Buddhist Pictorial Wheel of Life," 9.3.2(7)
    "Demonolatry in Sikhim Lamaism," 4.1.5(4)
    "The Dharani Cult in Buddhism," 11.6.3(8)
    "The Dharani or Indian Buddhist Protective Spell," 11.6.3(9)
    "The Indian Buddhist Cult of Avalokita," 7.8(17)
    "Lamaic Rosaries," 7.1.4(12)
    "The Lotus (Buddhism)," 9.3.3(5)
    Tibetan Buddhism, 1.14.1(17); 1.15.1(7); 4.4(11); 7.2.1(13); 7.2.3(8); 7.5.3(8); 7.6(5); 8.6(9); 9.2.1(14); 9.2.2.2(4); 9.2.2.3(15); 9.3.2(8); 9.3.3(6); 9.3.10(6); 10.7(6)
    "Upagupta," 8.9.1(50)
Waddell, Norman
    "The King of Samadhis Samadhi," 11.4.5(5)
    "The Zen Sermons of Bankei Yotaku," 3.3.6.2(1)
Wagle, N. K.
    "Social Groups and Ranking," 6.2.1.1(47)
Wagner, Fritz
    Indonesia: The Art of an Island Group, 5.5.6(10)
Wagner, R. C.
    "The Original Structure of the Correspondence Between Shih Hui-yuan and Kumarajiva," 8.9.3(49), (55)
Waida, Manabul
    "Symbolism of 'Descent' in Tibetan Kingship," 9.3.7(9)
Wai-lim Yip
    Hiding the Universe, 4.3(21)
Waldschmidt, Ernst
    "A Fragment from the Samyuktagama," 3.2.2.2(11)
    Nepal: Art Treasures from the Himalayas, 5.3(5)
    "Sutra 25 of the Nidanasamyukta," 3.2.2.2(12)
Waldschmidt, Rose
    Nepal: Art Treasures from the Himalayas. See citations under Ernest Waldschmidt.
Wales, Horace Geoffrey Quaritch
    Ancient Siamese Government and Administration, 6.2.2.4(6)
    Dvaravati: The Earliest Kingdom of Siam, 1.5.2(25); 5.5.3(10)
    Early Burma--Old Siam, 5.5.2(2)
    The Mountain of God, 10.6(8)
    Siamese State Ceremonies, 7.7(6)
Waley, Arthur
    Ballads and Stories from Tun-Huang, 4.2.3(28)
    A Catalogue of Paintings, 5.9.4(21)
    An Introduction to the Study of Chinese Painting, 5.9.3(19)
    Monkey, 4.5(12)
    The No Plays of Japan, 4.4(12); 5.12.2(16)
    The Real Tripitaka, 8.9.3(43)
Walleser, Max
    "The Life of Nagarjuna," 8.9.1(43)
Wang Puh
    Shing Tan ki, 8.1.2.1(24)

Author/Title Index

Wangyal, Geshe Thupten
    The Door of Liberation, 2.6.1(13)
Ward, W. E.
    "The Lotus Symbol," 9.3.3(7)
    "Selected Buddhist Symbols in Sinhalese Decorative Art," 9.3.10(7)
Ward, William Alfred Rae
    A History of Siam, 1.5.1(8)
Warder, Anthony Kennedy
    Indian Buddhism, 1.2.1(15); 2.1(15); 2.4.1(14); 2.4.4(6); 2.5.3(15); 2.5.4(20); 2.6.1(14); 3.4.1(8); 6.2.1.1(48); 8.1.2.3(31)
    "On the Relationship Between Early Buddhism and Other Contemporary Systems," 2.2(19); 2.3(13)
Ware, James Roland
    "Studies in the Divyavadana," 4.2.3(29)
    "Wei Shou on Buddhism," 1.11.2.2(13)
Warner, Langdon
    Buddhist Wall-paintings, 5.9.4(22)
    The Craft of the Japanese Sculptor, 5.11.4(20)
    The Enduring Art of Japan, 5.11.2(21)
    Japanese Sculpture of the Suiko Period, 5.11.4(21)
    Japanese Sculpture of the Tempyo Period, 5.11.4(22)
    "A Tun-huang Statue," 5.9.2(21); 5.9.4(23)
Warren, Henry Clarke
    Buddhism in Translations, 2.7.1(16); 2.7.7(13); 3.5(8); 7.2.1(14)
Warren, William
    The House on the Klong, 5.5.3(11)
Watson, William
    Sculpture of Japan, 5.11.4(23)
Watsuji Tetsuro
    "The Reception of Buddhism in the Suiko Period," 1.13.2.1(9); 6.2.1.2(21)
Watters, Thomas
    On Yuan Chwang's Travels in India, 1.2.2.3(14); 8.9.3(44); 10.1.1(11)
Watts, Alan Wilson
    In My Own Way, 1.17(16); 2.9(42)
Wauchope, R. S.
    Buddhist Cave Temples of India, 10.2.1(17)
Wayman, Alex
    Analysis of the Sravakabhumi Manuscript, 3.3.3.1(6); 3.3.3.3(4)
    "Buddhism," 1.1(9)
    "Buddhist Dependent Origination," 2.7.6(11)
    The Buddhist Tantras, 2.6.1(15); 3.4.4(5); 9.1.2(10); 11.6.3(10)
    "The Concept of Poison in Buddhism," 7.5.2(9)
    "Contributions to the Madhyamika School of Buddhism," 2.5.3(15)
    "Female Energy and Symbolism in the Buddhist Tantras," 9.3.10(8)
    "The Five-fold Ritual Symbolism of Passion," 11.6.1(20)
    "The Intermediate State in Buddhism," 9.2.5(5)
    "Introduction to Tson Kha pa's Lam rim chen mo," 3.3.8.3(5)
    The Lion's Roar of Queen Srimala, 3.2.2.2(9); 3.3.2.1(31)
    "The Mirror as a Pan-Buddhist Metaphor-Simile," 9.3.10(9)
    "A Report on the Sravaka-bhumi," 3.3.3.3(5)
    "Studies in Yama and Mara," 9.2.2.4(12)
    "The Twenty-One Praises of Tara," 7.8(18); 8.3.3(4)
    "The Yogacara Idealism," 2.5.4(21)
Wayman, Hideko
    The Lion's Roar of Queen Srimala. See citations under Alex Wayman.
Weber, Max
    The Religion of India, 6.2.1.1(49)
Weeramantry, Lucian G.
    Assassination of a Prime Minister, 1.3.2.2(9)
Weeraratne, Amarasiri
    "The Bhikkhuni Order in Ceylon," 6.1.3(9)
Weerasooriya, Hubert E.
    Voices in Stones, 5.4.1(6)
Weiner, Sheila L.
    "From Gupta to Pala Sculpture," 5.2.8(21)
Weinstein, Stanley
    "The Alaya-vijnana in Early Yogacara Buddhism," 2.7.12(9)
    "A Biographical Study of Tz'u-en," 8.9.3(53)
Welbon, Guy Richard
    The Buddhist Nirvana and Its Western Interpreters, 2.9(43); 11.8(15)
Welch, Holmes H.
    Buddhism under Mao, 1.11.2.4(5); 2.8(20); 6.2.2.5(6)
    "Buddhist Organizations in Hong Kong," 6.1.4(5)
    The Buddhist Revival in China, 1.11.2.4(6); 6.1.4(6); 6.2.1.2(22); 6.2.5(28); 8.9.3(78)
    "Dharma Scrolls and the Succession of Abbots in Chinese Monasteries," 6.1.1(28)
    The Practice of Chinese Buddhism, 1900 to 1950, 6.1.1(29); 7.1.1(13); 7.1.4(13); 7.2.1(15); 7.2.2(14); 7.4.2(22); 11.4.8.1(16)
Wells, Henry W.
    The Classical Drama of the Orient, 5.12.1(10)
Wells, Kenneth Elmer
    Thai Buddhism: Its Rites and Activities, 1.5.1(9); 7.1.2(5); 7.1.4(14); 7.2.1(16); 7.2.2(15); 7.2.3(9); 7.2.4(10); 7.2.6(5); 7.3.1(16); 7.4.1(5); 7.4.2(23); 7.5.1(7); 7.5.4(7)
Westbrook, Adele
    Secrets of the Samurai. See citations under Oscar Ratti.
Wetering, Jan Willem van de
    The Empty Mirror, 11.4.8.1(17)
Wettimuny, R. G. de S.
    Buddhism and Its Relation to Religion and Science, 2.8(21)
White, James W.
    The Sokagakkai and Mass Society, 1.13.2.4(9); 6.2.2.6(11)
White, William Charles
    Chinese Temple Frescoes, 5.9.3(20)
Wickramasinghe, Martin
    Buddhism and Art, 5.4.2(10)
    Buddhism and Culture, 2.8(22)
    Landmarks of Sinhalese Literature, 4.2.4(18)
Wickremeratne, L. A.
    "Religion, Nationalism, and Social Change in Ceylon," 1.3.2.2(10); 6.2.1.1(50)
Widengreen, George
    Historia Religionum, 1.1(9)
Wieger, Leon
    Bouddhisme chinois, 7.2.1(17)
    "Les Vies Chinoises du Buddha," 8.1.2.1(25)
Wigmore, John Henry
    A Panorama of the World's Legal Systems, 6.2.7(17)
Wijesekera, Nandadeva
    Early Sinhalese Painting, 5.4.2(11)
    Early Sinhalese Sculpture, 5.4.2(12)

Wijesekera, O. H. De A.
"Buddhist Ethics," 11.3(19)
Wijosuparto, R. M. S.
"The Role of Buddhism of South India on the Development of Buddhist Thought in Indonesia," 1.9.2(7)
Wilkinson, William Cleaver
Edwin Arnold as Poetizer and as Paganizer, 2.9(44)
Willets, William
Chinese Art, 5.9.1(20)
Foundations of Chinese Art, 5.9.1(21)
Williams, Gertrude Leavenworth
Priestess of the Occult, Madame Blavatsky, 2.9(45)
Willis, Janice Dean
The Diamond Light, 11.6.1(21)
Wilson, David A.
Politics in Thailand, 1.5.2(26); 6.2.2.4(7)
Wilson, H. H.
"Buddha and Buddhism," 8.1.2.3(32)
Win, Lu Pe
"Gharhut," 10.2.6.1(10)
Winternitz, Moriz (Maurice)
A History of Indian Literature, 3.1.1(5); 8.9.1(44)
"Problems of Buddhism," 2.3(14)
Wirz, Paul
Exorcism and the Art of Healing in Ceylon, 7.5.2(10)
Kataragama: The Holiest Place in Ceylon, 10.3.2(3)
Witanachchi, C.
"Ananda," 8.9.1(2)
Wittfogel, Karl A.
"History of Chinese Society," 1.11.2.3(17)
"Religion under the Liao Dynasty," 6.2.2.5(7)
Wong mu-lam
The Sutra of Wei-lang, 3.3.6.1(6)
Woodcock, George
The Greeks in India, 1.2.2.3(15)
Woodward, Frank Lee
The Book of Gradual Sayings, 3.2.2.1(1); 8.8(1)
Buddhist Stories, 4.2.3(30)
"Itivuttaka," 3.2.2.1(11)
Manual of a Mystic, 3.2.4.2(2); 11.4.2(12)
Pali Tipitaka Concordance, 12.1(13)
Samyutta Nikaya: The Book of Kindred Sayings. See citations under Caroline Augusta Foley Rhys-Davids.
"Udana," 3.2.2.1(28)
Wray, Elizabeth
Ten Lives of the Buddha, 5.5.3(12); 8.1.1(16)
Wriggins, W. Howard
Ceylon: Dilemmas of a New Nation, 6.2.2.2(17); 6.2.6(24)
Wright, Arthur Frederick
"Biography of the Nun An-ling-shou," 1.11.2.2(14); 8.9.3(4)
"Buddhism and Chinese Culture," 6.2.1.2(23)
Buddhism in Chinese History, 1.11.1(11)
"Buddhism in Modern and Contemporary China," 1.11.2.4(7); 6.2.1.2(24)
Confucian Personalities, 1.16.2(9)
The Confucian Persuasion, 4.1.3(6)
"The Economic Role of Buddhism in China," 6.2.6(25)
"The Formation of Sui Ideology," 1.11.2.2(15); 6.2.2.5(8)

"Fo-t'u-teng: A Biography," 1.11.2.2(16); 8.9.3(32)
"Fu I and the Rejection of Buddhism," 1.11.2.2(17); 6.2.1.2(25)
Wu, Cheng-en
Hsi-yu chi, 4.5(12)
Wu, Ching-Hsiung
The Golden Age of Zen, 2.5.7(26)
Wu, Chi-yu
"A Study of Han-shan," 4.3(22)
Wu-liang-i-ching, 3.3.5.1(6)
Wu-men-kuan, 3.3.6.1(11), (12), (13)
Wylie, Turrell
"Mortuary Customs at Sa-skya, Tibet," 7.4.2(24)

Yalman, Nur
"The Ascetic Monks of Ceylon," 6.1.1(30)
"Some Binary Categories in Sinhalese Religious Thought," 4.1.1(10)
"The Structuring of Sinhalese Healing Rituals," 7.5.2(11)
Yamabe, Shugaku
"Amida as Savior of the Soul," 11.7.1(7)
"The Way to the Land of Bliss," 11.7.1(7)
Yamaguchi, Susumu
"Dignaga: Examen de l'objet de la connaissance," 3.3.3.1(9)
"Nagarjuna's Mahayana-Vimsaka," 3.3.2.1(13)
"Traité de Nagarjuna . . .," 3.3.2.1(22)
Yamamoto, Kosho
An Introduction to Shin Buddhism, 1.13.2.2(15); 2.5.8(27); 11.7.1(8)
The Mahayana Mahaparinirvana-Sutra, 3.3.8.2(7)
The Private Letters of Shinran Shonin, 3.3.7.2(6); 8.9.4(26); 11.7.1(9)
The Shinshu Seitin, 2.5.8(28)
The Words of St. Rennyo, 3.3.7.2(3), (4)
Yampolsky, Philip B.
The Platform Sutra of the Sixth Patriarch, 3.3.6.1(7); 8.9.3(46)
The Zen Master Hakuin, 1.13.2.3(4); 2.5.7(27); 3.3.6.2(10); 3.3.6.3(7); 8.9.4(10)
Yanagi, Soetsu
"Ippen Shonin," 2.5.8(29); 8.9.4(13)
The Unknown Craftsman, 5.11.1(4)
Yanagida, Seizan
"The Life of Lin-chi I-hsuan," 8.9.3(58)
Yang, Lien-sheng
"Buddhist Monasteries and Four Money Raising Institutions in China," 6.2.6(26)
Yang, Ming-che
"China Reinterprets Buddhism," 6.2.1.2(26)
Yashpal
"Surgery and Medicine in the Days of Gautama," 7.5.2(12)
Yazdani, Ghulam
Ajanta, 5.2.6(16)
Yetts, W. Percival
"Notes on the Disposal of Buddhist Dead in China," 7.4.2(25)
Yimsiri, Khien
Thai Monumental Bronzes. See citations under Emcee Chand.
Yokagawa, Kensho
"The Tract on Steadily Holding to the Faith," 3.3.7.2(7)
Yongden
The Superhuman Life of Gesar of Ling. See citations under Alexandra David-Neel.

Yoshida, Kenko
    Essays in Idleness, 4.5(13)
Yoshiharu Akishige
    Psychological Studies on Zen, 11.4.8.1(18)
Young, Ernest
    The Kingdom of the Yellow Robe, 7.2.5(8)
Yu, David C.
    "Buddhism in Communist China," 1.11.2.4(8)
Yun-hua, Jan
    "Nagarjuna, One or More?," 8.9.1(45)
Yusuf, S. F.
    "The Early Contacts between Islam and Buddhism," 1.2.2.3(16)

Zaehner, R. C.
    The Concise Encyclopaedia of Living Faiths, 1.11.1(9); 2.5.1(5)
Zarina, Xenia
    Classical Dances of the Orient, 5.12.1(11)

"Zazen-gi," 11.4.2(13)
Zelliot, Eleanor
    "Buddhism and Politics in Maharashtra," 1.2.2.4(5); 6.2.4(11)
    Dr. Ambedkar and the Mahar Movement, 1.2.2.4(6); 6.2.4(12)
    "The Revival of Buddhism in India," 1.2.2.4(7); 6.2.4(13)
Zetland, Lawrence John Lumley Dundas
    Lands of the Thunderbolt, 1.15.1(8)
Zimmer, Heinrich
    The Art of Indian Asia, 5.1.3(5)
    Myths and Symbols in Indian Art and Civilization, 5.1.3(6); 9.2.2.5(13); 9.3.3(8)
Zurcher, Erik
    "Buddhism in China," 1.11.1(12)
    Buddhism: Its Origin and Spread, 1.1(10)
    The Buddhist Conquest of China, 1.11.2.1(9); 6.2.1.2(27); 8.9.3(25), (50), (61)

Subject Index

Abhidharma (See also Skandhas, Sautrantikas, Sarvastivada) 2.4.1(11) Hinayana; 2.4.3(10) Sarvastivadins, cf. 3.1.3; 2.7.1 Kathavatthu; 2.7.3 Kathavatthu; 2.7.5(1) Mahayana, cf. 3.3.3.1; 2.7.6 Abhidharmakosa, cf. 3.2.3.2, 11.4.5; 2.7.7 Dharmas; 3.1.3(1) Sarvastivadins; 3.1.4(2) Tibetan Texts; 3.2.3.1 Outline of Abhidharma Pitaka; 3.2.3.2(4) Abhidharmakosa; 3.3.1.1(1) and Prajnaparamita school; 8.9.1(53); 9.2.1(11); 9.2.2.1(2); 9.2.2.4(6); 9.2.3(1); 11.2(4) Refuges; 11.4.5(12) Abhidharmakosa

Abhijna (See also Powers, Siddhi) 9.4.6; 11.4.6

Abhisamayalankara (See also Prajnaparamita) 2.7.8(9) Thought; 3.3.1.1(2), (3) Texts, cf. 3.3.1.2; 3.3.1.2(1) Texts; 3.3.1.3(4); 3.3.2.1

Absolute (See also Truths, Atman, Nirvana) 2.7.8(1), (8) Madhyamika; 2.7.10(2) Suchness

Aesthetics 4.5(13) Japanese, cf. 5.11.1; 5.1.2 Comparative; 5.2.3(21) in sculpture; 5.6(15) in Tibetan Art; 5.11.1 Japanese; 5.11.6(6) in Zen

Ajanta (See also Caves) 5.2.1(19); 5.2.6; 10.2.1(12); 10.2.6.2(3), (8), (9); 10.2.6.3(4)

Ajivakas 2.2(3), (9)

Alayavijnana (See also Store Consciousness, Vijnanavada) 2.5.4(9); 2.7.11(5) and Tathagatagarbha; 2.7.12 Doctrine of; 3.3.3.2(6) and Prajnaparamita literature; 11.8(12) and Nirvana

Alchemy 8.9.1(39) and Nagarjuna

Amaravati (See also Stupa) 5.2.7

Amitabha/Amida (See also Bodhisattvas, Ching T'u, Nembutsu, Pure Land, Western Paradise) 1.12.2(1) Buddha images; 2.5.8(1), (10), (25); 2.5.9(6); 7.2.5(7); 8.2.2; 8.3.2(12) and cult of Kwannon); 9.2.2.3(1); 11.6.3 Meditative visions of Amitayus; 11.7.1 Meditative visions of Amitayus; 11.7.3 Meditative visions of Amitayus; 11.7.4(6) and stupa symbolism

Amitayus (See Amitabha)

Amulets (See also Spells, Protection) 7.5.3 Protective; 9.3.10(6) Protective

Anatman (See also Atman) 2.7.1(14) and karma; 2.7.4; 2.7.8(2) and dharmas, and skandhas, and emptiness; 3.3.2.1(8) in the wisdom literature

Ancestors (See also Cults, Filial Piety) 4.1.2 in Burmese village; 4.1.3(4) in China, cf. 6.2.3; 4.1.4(7) in Japan; 6.2.3 in China; 7.4.2(2); 9.1.2(8) Primordial; 9.2.1(10) Inhabitants

Angkor (See also City, Royal Capitals, Cosmology) 5.5.4 Art and architecture; 10.6

Animals (See also Divination, Dragons, Folk Religion, Jatakas) 4.1.1 Burmese village; 4.2.3(8) Dharma in animal kingdom; 4.2.4 in literature; 4.4(10) No drama; 7.5.3 Protection from; 7.6 Divination; 9.2 Jatakas; 9.2.1(2), (8) Jatakas; 9.2.2.5(1) Jatakas; 9.3.7(8) Jatakas; 9.3.10(7) Jatakas

Animism (See Folklore, Magic) 1.5.2(10), (13); 1.8.2(5); 4.1.1(2) Magical; 4.1.2(1), (2), (8); 6.2.1.1(27); 6.2.3(11) in village, (15) and Nats

Anitya (See Impermanence)

Annam (See also Vietnam) 1.8; 1.8.1(1); 1.8.2(5); 5.5.5(5) Art and architecture

Antarabhava (See Bardo)

Archaeology (See also Art, Architecture, City) 1.2.2.2(1) Ashokan Edicts; 1.2.2.3(13); 1.5.2(8), (25); 1.6.1(1); 1.6.2(4), (6), (7), (8), (14); 1.7.2(6); 1.8.1(4); 1.9.2(1), (6); 1.10.1(2), (4), (5); 1.10.2(1), (2), (10); 1.11.2.2(11); 1.11.2.3(17); 1.13.2.1(4); 1.14.2.1(8), (11); 2.5.7(15); 5.1.1(1); 5.2.8 Tantra and Yoga; 10.2.6.1(6) Taxila

Architecture (See also Art, City, Royal Capitals, Stupa) 1.6.2(3) cf. 5.5.4; 5.2.1(4), (21); 5.2.2; 5.2.8; 5.4.2 of Sri Lanka; 5.5.2 of Burma; 5.5.3 of Thailand; 5.5.6 of Indonesia; 5.6(12) of Tibet; 5.8; 5.9 of China; 5.9.2 of China; 5.10 of Korea; 5.11.2(4) of Japan; 5.11.3 of Japan; 5.11.6(9) of Japan

Arhat 2.4.4(3), (4) According to Mahasamghikas; 3.3.8.2(6); 4.2.3 Arhati, cf. 6.1.3; 5.8(11) and art; 5.9 and art; 6.1.3(3) Arhati; 8.1.2.2(9) and Buddhas, cf. 11.1; 8.4; 11.1(5) Status of, (7) and Buddhas, and Pratyekabuddhas

397

Subject Index

Art (See Category 5; See also Architecture, Art Motifs, Stupa, Drama, Folk Art, Jatakas) 1.5.2(11), (25); 1.6.2(13); 1.7.1(1) Laos; 1.8.2(1) Vietnam; 1.9.2(6) Indonesia, cf. 10.6; 1.10.2(2) Central Asia, (7) Central Asia; 1.11.2.1(8) China; 1.12.1(7) Korea; 1.12.2(1) Korea; 1.13.2.1(7) Japan; 1.14.2.2(11) Tibetan scrolls; 2.5.2(8) Representation of doctrine; 6.2.1.1(21); 8.1.1(2) Tibet; 8.1.2.4(12) Sri Lanka, (14) Indonesia; 9.2.2.5(3) Schools of and Influences; 10.2.1(10), (16) in cave temples; 10.5 Thailand; 10.6 Champa (Vietnam), Indonesia, Laos

Art Motifs (See Category 5; See also Artists, Aesthetics, Architecture, Caves, Iconography) 1.1(1); 1.3.2.1(11); 1.4.2(12); 1.5.2(11); 1.6.2(13) Cambodia; 1.7.1(1) Laos; 1.10.2(2) Central Asia, (4) Central Asia; 1.11.2.1(3), (8); 1.11.2.2(11) Caves and stupas; 1.12.1(1) Korea, (7) Korea; 1.12.2(1) Korean Buddha images; 3.3.8.2(3) Buddha image; 4.2.2(11) in Jatakas; 4.3.1 Landscape poetry; 7.2.6(2) on boundary markers; 8.1.2.4(8) Stupa; 9.1.5(16); 9.2.2.5(1) Masks; 9.3.1(1), (4); 9.3.2(5); 9.3.3 Lotus; 10.1.1(10) Caves; 10.2.1 Gen. discussion of art and architecture; 10.2.3 Bodh Gaya; 10.2.4 Sarnath; 10.2.6 Indian sites; 10.4; 10.5(1) Buddha's footprints; 10.9 Stupas and temples in Japan; 11.6.2 Mandalas; 11.6.4(6) Mudras and symbolic gestures

Artists 1.9.2(6) Srivijaya; 2.6.1(12) Tibetan scrolls; 5.1.1(2); 5.2.5 Gandharan school; 5.4 Ceylon; 5.5 Southeast Asia; 5.8(3) East Asia; 5.9.1(1), (13), (17) Chinese and Ch'an; 5.9.3(9) Wei-Ch'ih, I-Seng, (11) various masters, (14), (16) of T'ang; 5.9.4(14) of six dynasties; 5.11.2(17) Print masters, surveys-Japanese; 5.11.4(7) on Enku, (13), (20) Japanese sculpture; 5.11.6(1) Zen

Arupadhatu (See also Realms) 2.7.7(11), (12) Dhatus

Arya Deva (See also Vijnanavada) 3.3.2.1(3); 3.3.2.2(2); 3.3.3.2 Dignaga, Hastavalaprakarana; 8.9.1 and Nagarjuna; 11.8(5), (14) on Nirvana

Asanga 2.5.4 Yogacara school; 2.7.5 Abhidharma-samuccaya, cf. 3.3.3.1; 3.3.1.1 Vajraccedika commentaries; 3.3.1.2(2); 3.3.3.1 Abhidharma-samuccaya; 3.3.3.3(5) Life of

Asceticism 2.7.1 and Buddhism; 6.1.1(30); 8.2.1(5), (8) and the paccekabuddha

Asoka (See also Archaeology, Councils) 1.2.1(8) and Buddhism, cf. 8.9.1; 1.2.2.2; 1.2.2.2(1) Edicts, cf. 8.9.1; 6.2.2.1(15) as model of kingship and state; 8.1.2.4(16) and the Buddha's relics; 8.9.1

Astrology 1.16.2(9)

Asuras 9.2.2.3 in Realm of Desire

Asvaghosa 3.2.4.1; 3.2.4.3(4); 3.3.8.2 Awakening of Faith, Sutralamkara; 6.2.4(8) on caste, Vajrasuchi; 8.9.1

Atisa 8.9.2; 10.1.3

Atman (See also Anatman) 2.2(1), (2), (6); 2.7.3 3.3.3.2(6) Yogacarin notions

Avadanas 2.4.2(9) and the council accounts; 4.2.3

Avalokitesvara (See also Kuan Yin, Bodhisattvas) 1.12.2(1) Korea; 3.3.8.1(3); 3.3.8.4(3) 108 names of; 4.2.4(10) in Japan; 5.2.8(5) in art; 5.11.3(11) Iconography of; 5.11.4(10) Kannon statues; 7.8(1), (5), (17); 8.3.1(14); 8.3.2; 9.3.2(2); 11.4.9(4)

Avatamsaka/Hua Yen 2.5.5; 2.5.7(20), (21), (22), (23) Relation to Zen; 2.5.8(2), (3) Opposition to Shin; 3.3.1.2 View of Prajnaparamita; 3.3.4.1(1), (2) Sutra, Third Patriarch, Tu-Shun, Meditative Texts; 4.2.1(5) Sutra; 5.8(5) and art; 8.3.5(2) and Manjusri; 8.3.6(3) and Samanta Bhadra; 8.9.5(4) Influences on Korean poetry; 9.4.9 Meditation methods

Ayatana (Sense Fields) 2.7.7(11), (12); 3.2.3.1(2), (3)

Bardo 3.4.2(2); 9.2.5; 11.6

Bhaisajya 1.12.2(1); 3.3.8.1(1); 3.3.8.4(3); 7.5.2(2); 7.8(14); 8.2.2(9)

Bhakti 1.2.1(8) Influence on Buddhism, cf. 11.2; 2.6.1(4) Relation to Tantrism; 8.1.2.4(8) and Stupa cult; 11.2(1) Influence on Buddhism

Bharhut 1.2.2.3(7); 5.1.2(2); 5.2.4(6); 10.2.6.1(1)

Bhavaviveka (See also Truths, Madhyamika) 2.5.3(5); 2.7.9 and the Two Truths; 3.3.2.1(5), (6); 3.3.2.2(2)

Bhutan (See also Himalayan Kingdoms) 1.15.1 History; 5.6(10) Buddhist art; 6.2.2.9(13) Lamas and politics; 6.2.6(16) Monastic economy; 7.5.3 Calendrical rituals

Bibliographies 5.1.1; 12

Biography 1.5.2(6) Chulalongkorn; 1.11.2.1(8) Chinese Monks; 1.11.2.2(6), (12), (15); 1.11.2.4(4) Miao-chi; 1.12.1(4) Korean Monks; 1.13.2.1(1) Shotoku; 1.13.2.2(1) Honen, (4) Shinran, cf. 2.5.8, 11.7.2; 1.14.2.3 13th and 14th Dalai Lamas; 1.16.2 Yeh Lu ch'u Ts'ai; 1.17 of Kerouac, Eminent Orientalists, of Watts cf. 2.9; 2.5.6(3) of Chia-I; 2.5.7 Zen masters; 2.5.8 of Shinran, Ippen Shonin and Shin sect leaders; 2.5.9(1) of Nichiren; 2.6.2(1) Tantric monks in China; 2.9 of Kerouac, Eminent Orientalists, of Watts; 3.1.2(2) of Buddha, cf. 3.2.4, 4.2.2, 8.1; 3.2.1.2(1) of elders, Jatakas and Buddha; 3.2.4.1(3), (4), (5) Buddhacarita, of Buddha; 3.3.6.1 Chan patriarchs; 3.3.8.1 Lalitavistara; 3.4.2(4) of Padmasambava, Naropa; 4.2.2 of Buddha; 5.11.5(13) Pictorial biography of Shotoku; 5.11.6(1) of Zen artists; 5.11.8(7) Tea masters; 8.1 Buddha; 8.9.1 Great Buddhists of India; 8.9.2 Great Buddhists of Tibet; 8.9.3 Great Buddhists of China; 8.9.4 Great Buddhists of Japan; 8.9.5 Great Buddhists of Korea; 8.9.6 Great Buddhists of Sri Lanka and Southeast Asia; 9.1.5(1), (7) Teachers; 11.4.6(3) and powers; 11.6.1(9) Milarepa; 11.7.2(5) of Shinran

Subject Index

Bodhagaya 1.2.2.3(7); 5.2.4(3), (4), (7), (15), (16); 10.2.3

Bodhicaryavatara (by Santideva) 2.7.9(9); 3.3.2.1(9)

Bodhicitta 2.5.8 and Shin; 2.7.8(8) and Madhyamika; 2.7.14; 3.3.2.1(26), (27), (28), (29); 3.3.8.1(6); 8.3.1(4) and Bodhisattvas

Bodhisattvas 1.3.1(7) Ceylon; 1.6.2(11) Cambodia, King as; 1.12.2(1) Korea; 2.1(2) Stages of, Doctrine of; 3.3.1.1(20) "Five"; 3.3.2.1(30) Path of; 3.3.3.1(4) Path of; 3.3.8.1(5) Discipline of; 4.2.3 in Avadhana literature; 4.2.4(16) Gesar as; 4.4 Manicuda, in drama, Avadhana literature; 5.2.1(10) Images of, cf. 5.2.8; 5.2.3(14) Iconography of; 5.2.5(3) Legends in art; 5.2.8(5) Images of; 5.6(6) Tibetan; 5.9.1(6), (8), (16) in Chinese art; 5.10(13) in Korean art; 5.11.4(10) Kannon, cf. 7.1.4; 5.11.5(3), (7); 6.1.3(5) and women; 6.2.1.2(16) China and Japan; 6.2.2.5(4) and military; 6.2.2.8(3) and kingship; 7.1.4(1), (11) Kannon; 7.2.1(8) Vows and ordination; 7.2.4(2) Pratimoksa for; 7.3.2(5); 7.4.2 Suicide by; 7.8 Avalokitesvara/Kuan Yin, Bhai Sajya, Ksitigarbha, Akasagarbha; 8.1.1 Gautama, Jatakas; 8.1.3(13) Ksitigarbha; 8.2.2 Vairocana, Kanoaka; 8.3.1; 8.3.2 Avalokitesvara/Kuan Yin; 8.3.3 Tara; 8.3.4 Maitreya; 8.3.5 Manjusri; 8.3.6; 9.3.3(6); 9.3.9(3) Wisdom of; 11.5 Training of and Paramitas; 11.7.3 Amitayus; 11.7.4(4) Vows

Bon (See also Tibet) 1.14.1(8); 1.14.2.1(5); 4.4(5) and mystery plays; 9.2.2.5(8), (11)

Borobudur (See also Stupa) 2.5.2(8); 5.5.6(9), (10); 5.8(5); 8.1.2.4(14); 9.3.6(9); 10.6(4), (5)

Boundary Demarcation 7.2.6(2), (4), (5)

Brahmanism 1.2.2.3(7) Influences of at Buddhist centers; 1.6.2(14) Cambodia; 2.2(1), (2), (6), (8), (10) as background of Buddhism; 2.7.1(10) and Buddhist karma, as background of Buddhism

Buddha, Gautama (See also Jataka) 1.1(8) Life of, cf. 8.1.2.3; 1.2.1(8) Life of; 1.2.2.1(3) Ministry of, Disciples of, cf. 8.8, 8.9; 3.2.2.1 Previous lives, cf. 4.2.2, 8.1; 3.3.8.1(2) Biographies of, cf. 8.1; 4.2.2 Previous lives; 7.2.3(2) and Mara, cf. 9.3.5; 7.8 Cults of; 8.1.2; 8.1.2.2 Status of; 8.1.2.2(8) Epithets of; 8.1.2.3 Life of; 8.1.2.3(13) Status of; 8.1.2.4 Relics of; 8.8 Disciples of; 8.9 Disciples of; 9.3.3(3) Symbols of; 9.3.5(2), (5), (9) and Mara

Buddha Bodies (See also Tri-Kaya) 2.5.2(4) as mythic motif; 3.3.2.1(15); 3.4.2(9); 8.1.2.2(10) Theory of; 8.1.3

Buddha Fields (See also Buddhaksetra) 2.9(21); 9.2.4; 11.7.4(2), (8) Pure Land

Buddhaghosa 1.3.2.1(9); 2.7.7 Abhidharma discussions, cf. 3.2.3.3; 3.1.2(4), (6) and Pali canon; 3.2.1.3(1) Vinaya commentaries; 3.2.3.3(3), (4) Abhidharma discussions; 3.2.4.2 Visuddhimagga (Path of Purification); 8.9.1; 8.9.5; 11.2(7)

Buddhaksetra (See also Buddha Fields) 11.7.4(8) and Pure Land

Buddhas 2.5.9 Eternality of 2.7.1(2) Previous lives, cf. 8.1.2.3; 3.2.1.2(11) Jatakas, etc., Sakyamuni's life, cf. 3.2.41, 3.3.5.2; 3.2.2.1(2) Previous lineages; 3.2.4.1 Sakyamuni's life; 3.3.5.2(3) Sakyamuni's life; 3.3.6.1(12) Seven Buddhas of the past; 5.2.3(12) on nativity; 5.9.1(8), (16) in Chinese art; 5.10(13) in Korean art; 6.2.1.2(16) China and Japan; 7.8 Cults of; 8.1.2.2(3); 8.1.2.3(7) Previous lives, (12) of Mahyana Buddhism; 8.2.1(1) Pratyeka, (3) Dipamkara, (4) Previous 500; 8.2.2; 8.3.1(1) Dhyani; 8.3.4 Future; 9.3.9(6) and light; 11.2(4) Refuge in; 11.3(2) as ethical model; 11.4.3 as subject of meditation; 11.7.1 Amida

Buddhism (See also specific countries, Theravada, Hinayana, Mahayana) 1.1 Historical overview, (4) Pali; 1.2.1 Early development of, cf. 2.2; 1.2.2.1 Early development of; 1.2.2.3(12) Decline of, cf. 1.11.2.3, 1.12.2, 1.16.2, 6.1.1; (16) and Islam; 1.2.2.4(11) and Islam; 1.2.2.5 in modern India; 1.3.2.1(7) Schools of; 1.4.1(7) Sanskrit, cf. 3.1.3; 1.6.2(12) Sanskrit; 1.11.2(6), (10), (13) and Taoism, cf. 4.1.2, 4.1.3, 6.2.1.2, 6.2.2.5; 1.11.2.3(3) Decline of, (5), (7), (10) and Taoism, (14) and Neo-Confucianism, cf. 4.1.2, 6.2.2.5; 1.11.2.4 and Modern China, cf. 6.2.1.2; 1.12.2(12) Decline of; 1.14.1(9) and Bon religion; 1.14.2.1(5), (11) and Bon Religion; 1.16.2(4), (6), (7), (8) Decline of; 1.17 and the West, cf. 2.8, 2.9; 2.1(8) Pali; 2.2(18) "Primitive Buddhism", Early development of; 2.3(6) "Primitive Buddhism"; 2.7.1(1) Pali; 2.8 and the West, and Christianity; 2.9 and the West, and Christianity; 3.1.2 Pali; 3.1.3 Sanskrit; 3.1.4 Tibetan texts; 3.1.5 Chinese texts; 4.1.2; 4.1.3(6) and Taoism; 4.1.4(2) Esoteric; 6.1.1(6) Decline of; 6.1.2(5), (6), (8) and laity; 6.1.4 and laity; 6.2.1.2(2) and modern China, (9) Taoism; 6.2.2.5(8) and Taoism, and Neo-Confucianism; 9.1.5 Myths about the spread of

Buddhist Schools and Sects (See also names of individual founders, schools and sects, Theravada, Hinayana, Mahayana) 1.13.2.2(3), (10), (13); 1.13.2.4(1); 1.14.2.1(6); 1.14.2.2; 2.1(7), (13); 2.5.1(3), (4), (5); 4.1.4(1) Shugindo (Mt. Haguro sect); 6.1.1(4) Early schisms and sects

Burma (See also Chronicles, Colonialism, Politics) 1.4; 1.4.1(3) Inception of Buddhism; 3.1.2(1) Pali literature; 3.1.6(7) Literature; 5.5.2; 5.12.1(5) Drama; 6.2.2.3 Politics; 8.9.5 Politics; 10.1.4(6) Travellers' accounts; 10.4 Sacred Places; 10.4.1 Royal capital

Cakravartin (See also Kingship) 8.1.2.2(1) Symbolism, cf. 9.3.1, 9.3.2; 8.7; 9.1.1; 9.3.1(2) Symbolism; 9.3.2(4) Symbolism

Calligraphy 5.9.1 Painting and willets; 5.9.3(8) and Zen; 5.11.5; 5.11.6 and Zen

Cambodia 1.1(4) Historical overview; 1.6; 1.6.2(4) Hindu influences, (6), (7), (12) Spread of Buddhism; 3.1.6(4), (7) Literature; 5.5.4

(Cambodia)
Sacred places, cf. 10.1, 10.6, art and architecture; 5.12.1 Drama; 6.2.2.8; 10.1 Sacred places; 10.1.4 Travellers' accounts: 10.6 Sacred places

Candrakirti 2.5.3(7) and Madhyamika; 3.3.2.1 on Bhavasamkrantisutra, Madhyamakavatara, Prasannapada; 3.3.2.2(2); 8.9.1(27); 11.6.3(10); 11.8(11) on Nirvana

Canon (See also Councils) 1.13.1(12); 1.14.1(2), (5); 2.1(8) Pali, cf. 2.7.4, 3.1.2; 2.3(5), (6) and "primitive" Buddhism; 2.4.2(9) and the councils; 2.7.4(6) Pali; 3.1.1(3); 3.1.2 Pali; 3.1.3 Sanskrit; 3.1.4 Tibetan; 3.1.5 Chinese; 3.2.2.4(5); 4.2.2(6) Jatakas; 8.8(14)

Caste (See also Monks, Monasteries) 2.2.(1); 6.2.1.1; 6.2.4

Causality (See also Dependent Origination) 2.7.1(3), (12) and karma; 2.7.6 Pratitya Samutpada; 3.3.2.1(8) Prasannapada 18-22

Cave Paintings 1.10.2(7); 5.1.4(6); 5.2.6; 5.9.3; 5.9.4; 5.10; 9.3.2(6); 10.2.1(9)

Caves and Cave Temples (See also Iconography) 1.2.2.3(13); 1.11.2.1(8) in China; 1.11.2.2(11); 2.5.7(15); 5.2.1(5); 5.2.6; 5.7(3); 5.8; 5.9; 5.9.3 Cave of the 1000 Buddhas (Tun-huang); 5.9.4; 10.1.1(10); 10.1.2(8); 10.2.1(4), (8), (9), (17); 10.2.6.2(3); 10.8.2

Central Asia 1.10.1; 1.10.2 Archaeological finds; 1.16.1 Mongolia; 3.1.3(3) Sanskrit texts; 4.2.4 Folk literature in; 5.1.1(5) Art history; 5.7 Art and architecture, (5) Influence on T'ang, cf. 5.9.3: 5.8(1) Buddhist art in; 5.9.1(11) Buddhist art in; 5.9.3(10) Influence on T'ang; 5.9.4(13) Cave paintings; 6.2.1.2 Samgha in; 6.2.2.9 Politics in; 8.3.4(1) Maitreya; 8.9.3(49), (55) Kumarajiva and Hui Yuan; 10.7 Tibet and Himalaya; 11.4.2 Meditation manual

Ch'an/Zen (See also Soto Zen, Zen, Zen Masters, Zazen, Kegon, Koan) 1.13.2.2; 2.5.7; 3.3.6; 8.8(12); 11.4.8 Methods

Ch'an Masters 3.3.6.2(5), (6) Han Shan; 8.3.4(2)

Chanting 2.5.8 Nembutsu, cf. 11.7.2; 3.3.6.2(4) in Zen; 4.2.1(5) Buddhist hymns; 5.12.3(6) Vedic and Japanese; 7.1.4 Practice and Rosaries of sutras; 7.2.2 Recitation of sutras; 7.2.3; 7.2.4 of Pratimoksa; 7.3.1(16) in Thai festivals; 7.5.1 for rain; 9.3.9 Amitayur-Dhyanasutra; 11.6.1(12) Yogic; 11.6.3 Mantras; 11.7.1 Amida's name; 11.7.2 Nembutsu

China 1.8.2(4) and Vietnam; 1.10.1 Central Asian expansion; 1.11; 1.11.2.1 Buddhism; 1.11.2.3 Medieval community; 1.11.2.4 Buddhism, modern; 1.14.2.3 Dalai Lama and; 1.16.1 Travellers; 1.16.2(10) in Mongolia; 1.17(13) Monks in America; 2.5.1(2), (3) Mahayana in; 2.5.3(10) Madhyamika in; 2.5.4 Hsuan-Tsang and Yogacara; 2.5.5 Avatamsaka in; 2.5.6 T'ien T'ai; 2.5.8 Pure Land; 2.6.2 Tantrism in; 2.7.11 Doctrine of Alaya-Vijnana; 3.1.5(1) Texts; 4.1.3 Popular beliefs; 4.2.3 Avadana literature; 4.2.4 Folk literature; 4.3.2 Poets; 4.4.3 Village plays; 4.5 Popular novels; 5.9.1(1) Cave sites; 5.8 Architecture and sculpture; 5.9 Architecture and sculpture; 5.9.2 Architecture and sculpture; 5.9.3 Painting; 5.12.1 Drama; 6.1.1(28), (29) Sangha, Political, etc.; 6.2.1.2(6) Monasteries; 6.2.3(4) Filial piety; 6.2.5(28) Buddhist education; 6.2.6(5), (11), (16), (22), (23), (26) Economies and monasteries; 7.1.1(13) Rituals; 7.1.3 Bathing Buddha; 7.2.2 Daily monastic routine; 7.2.3 Chanting; 7.2.4 Pratimoksa; 7.3.2 Calendrical festivals; 7.4.2 Funerary practices; 7.5.1(5) Rainmaking; 8.1.3 Buddha bodies; 8.4(3), (18) Lohans/Arhats; 8.9.3 Great Buddhists of; 10.1.2 Sacred places by travellers and pilgrims; 10.8.2 Temples and mountains; 11.4.1(5) Meditation; 11.4.8.1 Zen meditation; 12.1(4), (10), (11) Dictionaries; 12.3(1) Tripitaka

Ch'ing T'u (See Pure Land, Amitabha) 2.5.8 in China, Japan; 3.3.7.1 Sutras; 4.1.3 and secred societies; 7.2.3 Chants of "standard Buddhist . . ."; 7.3.2(4); 11.7.3 Visions and liturgy; 11.7.4 Rebirth into

Christianity 1.2.1 "Catholic church"; 1.11.2.4(4); 1.12.2; 1.13.2.4 and "new religions"; 1.16.1(2) in Mongolian texts; 1.16.2(3) Understanding of Mongolian Buddhism; 2.1; 2.5.7(4), (5) and Zen; 2.5.8(22), (23) and Shin; 5.1.2(3) Art; 6.2.2.2(16) in Ceylon; 6.2.5(12) Schools, (21) Missions and Buddhist education; 8.1.2.3(28); 8.3.6(7); 8.5(2); 8.6(4); 9.1.2(5); 9.2.1(12); 9.3.5(7) Satan; 11.17.1 and Pure Land

Chronicles 1.3.1(3), (4), (6), (11) Sinhalese, cf. 3.1.2; 1.3.2.1(2) Sinhalese; 1.4.1(3), (4), (5) Burmese; 1.5.1(1) Thai; 1.5.2(19), (20) Thai; 1.6.2(9) Cambodian; 1.11.2.2(4) Chinese; 1.14.1(5), (14) Tibetan; 1.14.2.1(1), (3), (7) Tibetan; 1.15.1(6) Bhutan; 1.16.2(1) Mongolia; 3.1.2(6), (7) Sinhalese; 9.1.5

Chronologies 1.1(2); 1.2.2.1(11); 1.3.2.1(17) Sri Lanka; 1.6.2(13) Cambodia; 1.11.2.1(1) China; 2.3(7) Early Buddhist; 3.1.2(6) of the Pali canon

City (See also Architecture, Royal Capitals, specific countries) 5.2.2(6), (14) Architecture; 5.4.1(3) in Sri Lanka; 5.5.4 in Cambodia; 5.6(4) in Tibet; 5.11.2(3) in Japan; 8.7(3) of the Cakravartin; 9.2.2.5(2) Guardians of; 9.3.7(4) as Mt. Meru; 10.1.2(5) of Emperors; 10.2.1(12) Monastic; 10.3.1 Capitals

Colonialism (See also Nationalism, specific countries) 1.3.2.2 in Sri Lanka, cf. 6.2.2.2; 1.6.2(1) Cambodia; 6.2.2.2(5) British use of Buddhist idiom, (6) in Sri Lanka; 6.2.2.3 in Burma; 6.2.5(12) and education

Communism (See also Mao tse-tung, Marxism, specific countries) 1.11.2.4 and Buddhism in China; 1.16.2 USSR and Central Asia; 2.8 and Buddhist dialogue; 6.1.4(1)

Subject Index

Community (See category 6; See also Sangha, Monasticism, etc.) 1.1(1) Pan-Asian development; 1.2.1 in India; 1.2.2.1 Early development; 1.2.2.3 Post Mauryan development; 1.3.1 in Ceylon; 1.4.2 Burma; 1.5.2 Thailand; 1.6.1 Cambodia; 1.7.2(2), (4) Education and monarchy; 1.8.2 Vietnam; 1.10.2; 1.11.2.1(5) Early monastic, cf. 1.14.2.1; 1.11.2.2(12); 1.11.2.4 in China, and Communism; 1.13.1 in Japan; 1.14.2.1(5) Early monastic; 1.17(10) in America; 2.3(9); 2.4.1 Hinayana sects, 18 schools, 2.4.2 Councils; 2.7.6 Pratityas; 3.1.2(5); 3.2.1.1(1), (2), (3), (4) Vinaya rules, Pratimokkha rules; 3.2.2.1(18) and state; 3.2.3.4(6) Abhidharma literature; 5.2.1(15) and early arts; 5.2.2(7); 7.1.1(9) Social organization; 7.1.2 Gifts to; 7.2.1 Reception into; 7.2.2 Daily monastic routine; 7.2.4 Rules of discipline; 7.2.5 Preaching; 7.2.6; 7.3.1(15); 7.3.2 Chinese and Japanese festivals; 7.5.2 Medicinal practices; 7.5.4 Exorcisms; 8.1.2 After Buddha's death; 8.1.3(8); 11.2(2) and faith; 11.3 Ethical roles; 11.4.3 as subject of meditation; 11.4.8.1 Zen monastic

Compassion (See also Brahmavittaras) 3.5(7); 8.1.2.1(4); 8.1.2.2(12); 8.3.2(2); 11.4.3 in meditation

Concentration (See also Dhyana, Samadhi) 2.5.7 in Zen, cf. 11.4.8.1; 3.3.2.1(33); 11.4.1(7); 11.4.5 in Theravada; 11.4.8.1 in Zen; 11.5(2) as Paramita

Confucianism 1.8.2(5) in Vietnam; 1.11.2.1(7); 1.11.2.2(1) Opposition to Buddhism, cf. 6.2.2.5; 1.11.2.3(7) Neo-; 1.12.2 in Korea; 1.11.2.3 Effects of Samurai; 1.16.2 Yeh-Lu Ch'u-Ts'ai, cf. 8.9.3; 4.1.2 and popular religion; 4.1.3 Popular beliefs in China; 4.5(3) in Kukai's novel; 6.2.1.2; 6.2.2.5(2) Opposition to Buddhism, (8) Sui ideology; 6.2.2.6(1), (3) in Tokugawa Japan; 6.2.2.8(7) in Vietnam; 6.2.2.9(2) in Korea; 6.2.3(4) and Filial piety; 7.3.2 and all souls festival; 7.8 Confucius as Buddhist deity; 8.3.6 Confucius as Buddhist deity; 11.4.1(6) Meditative practices

Consciousness (See also Abhidharma) 2.5.1(3) Consciousness only, school of; 2.5.4 Consciousness only, school of; 2.7.7 Factors and functions of Govinda; 2.7.11 Store house; 3.2.3.1(1) States of; 3.2.3.3 Anuruddha; 9.2.3 Anuruddha; 9.2.5(1) After death; 11.4.1(7) Meditative; 11.4.3(3)

Conversion 1.2.2.5(1), (3), (5), (6), (7) in modern India; 1.16.1(7) Mongolia; 1.17(5) and the West; 7.2.5(4) of the masses; 8.1.2.2(4) of the masses, by the Buddha; 8.8(3) by the Buddha, of Sariputra; 9.3.5(4) of Mara

Corpses 7.4.2 Disposal; 9.2.5(1); 11.4.3(3)

Cosmology (See also Abhidharma, Stupa, Angkor, Mandala, Lotus, Karma, Dharma, Transmigration, Mt. Meru) 3.2.2.1(21) Hells, (30) Heavens, cf. 4.2.3; 3.2.3.2(4) in Abhidharma texts; 4.1.2(3) Vietnamese; 4.2.3(12) Heavens and hells, (28) Hells; 5.2.1(16) Art; 5.2.3(4) Art; 5.5.4 Art; 5.5.6 and stupas, cf. 10.6; 6.2.2.1(9) and kingship and state; 8.3.1(12) Celestial Buddhas; 9.2; 10.6(7) and stupas, (18) and temples; 11.1(7)

Cosmos 6.2.2.1(9) as archetype; 9.1.1 Creation myths

Councils (See also Chronicles, Hinayana, Mahasanghikas, Mulasarvastivadins, Sthaviravadins) 2.4.2; 3.2.1.3(1)

Cults 1.2.2.4(1); 1.9.2(5) of Shiva, of Buddha; 1.14.1(17); 2.6.1(6) Sahajya; 3.4.1 of Heruka, cf. 11.6; 4.1.1(4) of Nagas, relics, etc.; 4.1.3 Ancestral, imperial shrines, popular; 4.1.4 Japanese; 4.1.5(3) in Tibet; 5.2.1; 5.2.3; 5.9.3(7) of Lohans; 5.9.4(3) Paradise; 5.11.3(5) Relics; 5.11.5(13) of Shotoku; 6.1.2 in Ceylon; 6.2.1.2(16) China and Japan; 6.2.2.4(5) of Holy Emerald Jewel; 6.2.2.8(9) Royal Cambodian; 6.2.3(5) Phiban, Laos; 7.1.3 of stupas and relics; 7.2.6(1) of stupas and relics; 7.3.1 Calendrical; 7.4.2 of the dead; 7.7 Royal; 7.8(5) Yogini; 8.1.2.3(24); 8.3.2 of Kwannon; 8.3.3(1) of Tara, cf. 11.6.3, (3) of Tara and Shakti; 8.3.4(3) of Maitreya; 8.3.5(2) of Manjusri; 8.5(1) of Saddhacaryas; 8.6(1) of Bhutadharma, (8) Horse; 8.9.4(3) and Basho; 9.1.5(4) of the tooth relic, of Gos Lo tsa-ba; 9.2.2.5; 9.3.4(3) of trees; 11.6(13) of Heruka; 11.6.3 of Tara; 11.7.3 of Amitabha; 11.8(7) of stupa and Nirvana

Dakini 4.1.5(4) in Tibet

Dalai Lama 1.14.2.3 13th and 14th; 1.14.1(17); 2.7.8 14th on Sunyata; 4.3(2) Love songs of 6th; 6.2.1.2(18), (19) and Sangha; 6.2.2.7(1) as deity, (5), (7) and government; 8.9.2(8) 13th, (6) 14th; 11.1(9) 14th on "path"

Dana (Giving) (See also Merit-Making) 4.2.3(22); 7.1.1(4); 7.1.2

Dance (See also Folk Art, Drama) 5.5.6(5) Indonesia; 5.11.2(14) Japan; 5.12; 5.12.3 Japan

Death (See also Antarabhava, Bardo, Funerary Rites) 2.7.1(8); 3.4.2(2); 6.2.4(7); 7.4.2 Rites of; 8.1.2.4(1) of Buddha; 9.2.2.4(2), (12) Death of Gods; 9.3.10(2) Masks

Debates 1.11.2.3 Taoist vs. Buddhist, Buddhist vs. Confucian; 1.14.2.1(2) in Tibet, under Kri'-srong-lde-behn, (10) on first Bhavanakrama; 2.3 on original Buddhism; 2.4.1 Between 18 schools; 2.4.2 Over historicity of councils; 2.4.3(6) Mahasanghika; 2.5.2(7) over north/south origin of Mahayana; 2.5.3 on Madhyamika; 2.5.7(11), (20), (21), (22) on Zen; 2.7.1(7) on nature of Karma, cf. 3.2.3.2; 2.7.2(2) on Dukkha; 2.7.3 on impermance and time; 3.2.2.4(5) over Hinayana canon; 3.2.3.1(5) Debates commentary; 3.2.3.2(5) on nature of Karma; 3.3.3.3(4), (5) Rules of Sravaka Bhumi; 6.2.5(5) as educative device; 8.1.2.1(4) on nature of Buddha; 9.1.5 Gos Lo-tsa-ba; 9.2.2 on 5 or 6 Gatis; 11.4.5(7) on Jnana; 11.8(15) on nature of Nirvana

Subject Index

Deities (See also Asuras) 1.3.1 in Ceylon; 2.5.2(4) Mahayana and Hinayana compared; 3.4.2(12) Fierce; 4.1.1(1), (5), (8); 4.1.2; 4.1.3 in China; 4.1.5(3), (4) in Tibet; 4.2.4(6), (17) Taoist; 5.1.3(4) Mountains as; 5.2.1(19) Protective goddesses; 5.2.8(4), (5) Images; 5.4.1(4) of Adam's Peak; 5.6(14) Protective, cf. 9.2.2.5; 5.11.3(11) Japanese esoteric; 5.11.4(8) Ashuras, (22), (23) in Japanese sculpture; 6.2.2.7(1) Dalai Lama as; 7.1.4(10) Prayers to; 7.5.2 and Health; 8.1.2.4(4) Heruka; 8.6; 9.2.2.4 of Desire Realm; 9.2.2.5 of Desire Realm, (5), (6), (7) Popular; 11.4.3 as subjects of meditation; 11.6.2(8); 11.6.3 Mantras as

Dependent Origination (See also Pratityasamutpada) 2.5.3; 2.7.5; 2.7.6; 3.2.3.1(2); 9.2.5(3), 9.3.2(3), (7); 11.4.7(1)

Dharanis (See also Amulets, Folk Religion, Magic Protection) 2.5.7(21); 3.3.8.1(8); 3.3.8.4(1); 7.1.4 Rosaries; 7.2.2(2); 7.5.2; 9.6.3; 11.6(18) 11.6.3

Dharma (See also Skandha, Buddha bodies) 1.3.1(11) Theravada; 2.4.3(5) Sarvastivadin; 2.7.7 Analysis and classification of, cf. 3.2.3.4; 2.7.8(2) and anatman doctrine; 3.2.3.4 Analysis and classification of; 4.2.3(8) Myths of, cf. 9.1.3, 11.7.1; 6.1.1(28) Scrolls; 6.2.7 and law; 8.1.2.5 Body of the; 9.1.3 Myths of; 9.3.1 Wheel of; 11.7.1(1) Myths of

Dharmakaya (See also Buddha Bodies, Tri-kaya) 8.1.3(4), (9); 11.8

Dharmakirti 2.5.4(14); 3.3.3.1; 3.3.3.2(1), (7); 8.9.1

Dhatu (Elements) (See also Dharma, Skandha, Ayatana) 2.7.7(10) Abhidhamma; 3.2.3.2(4); 9.2.2.5(5)

Dhyana (See also Samadhi, Concentration, Trances) 2.5.7; 11.4.5 Stages of; 11.4.7(1), (7); 11.4.8.1; 11.5

Diamond Sutra (See also Prajnaparamita) 2.7.8; 3.3.1.1; 3.3.6.2 Han Shan's commentary; 11.4.8.1(15)

Dignaga 2.1(11); 2.5.4(7), (17) and Yogacara/Vijnanavada philosophy; 3.3.1.1(3) Commentary on Prajnaparamita; 3.3.1.2(3) Commentary on Prajnaparamita; 3.3.2.1 Hand treatise; 3.3.3.2 Treatises; 8.9.1(29)

Divination (See also Magic) 7.6

Dogen (See also Soto Zen) 2.5.7(3), (10), (17), (24); 2.7.4(12) and Anatomy; 2.7.14(1) and the Buddha-nature; 3.3.6.3; 8.9.4; 11.4.5(5)

Dragons 5.8(14) in art (China and Japan)

Drama 4.4 Buddhist influences in; 5.5.6(5) Indonesian; 5.12.1; 5.12.2; 6.2.5(5) as education

Duhkha 2.7.2; 2.7.5 Four truths

Economic(s) 1.2.2.1(12), (13) Context of early Buddhism; 1.2.2.2(3), (4) under Mauryans, Asoka; 1.5.2(21) Change; 1.6.2(13) Cambodia; 1.7.1(1) Laos; 1.7.2(2) Temple/Wat, cf. 1.11.2.3; 1.11.1(2) China; 1.11.2.2(3) China; 1.11.2.3(1), (16), (17) China, (5) Temple/Wat; 1.13.2.3(1) Japan; 6.2.1.1; 6.2.2.1; 6.2.2.7 Tibet; 6.2.3(10) Burma, Thailand; 6.2.6

Education 1.7.1(1) in Laos; 1.7.2(2) of community; 1.11.1(2) in China; 1.13.1(11) Monks and lay in Japan; 6.2.1.1(27) in Thailand; 6.2.1.1(43) and Wat, cf. 6.2.3; 6.2.1.2(5) and Chinese monasteries, (6) in Mongolia; 6.2.2.3(17) in Burma, Monastic; 6.2.2.9(2) in Korea; 6.2.3(5) and Wat; 6.2.5; 7.2.5 Sermons and preaching methods; 11.3(5) Ethical

Ego (See also Atman, Anatman) 2.7.4(5)

Ekayana (One Vehicle Doctrine) 3.3.5.1 in the Lotus (Saddharmapundarika) Sutra

Elders (See also Theravada School) 3.2.1.2(1) Legends of; 3.2.2.1(26) "Verses"; 6.2.5(11) as outstanding teachers; 8.4(5) 36 famous

Emanations 8.3.1(1) Represented in iconography

Emptiness (See also Sunya) 2.5.3(13) Madhyamika; 2.5.5 and Hua yen Chang; 2.5.7(9) Mu; 2.7.6(10) and Pratityasamutpada; 2.7.8; 11.4.7(3) Meditation on; 11.5(5) Sunyata and Paramitas

Enlightenment (See also Nirvana/Nibbana, Bodh Gaya) 2.5.7(7), (8) Sudden, cf. 3.3.6.2; 2.7.6(5) of Buddha; 2.7.7(5) in the Abhidharma; 3.3.6.2(2) Sudden; 11.1(3) 37 wings

Epistemology (See also Dignaga, Dharmakirti) 2.2(9); 2.5.4(17); 2.7.13(5) Trilaksana (Outlines); 3.3.3.1(8)

Eschatology (See also Maitreya) 8.3.4(6); 9.1.1(1); 9.1.3(3), (4), (5)

Ethics (See also Vinaya, Merit) 2.5.7(6) and Zen; 2.7.9(5) and Madhyamika; 3.2.2.2(8) of the laity, cf. 4.2.1, 6.1.2; 3.2.3.1(1) Abhidharma/dhamma; 3.3.8.1(8) in the Sutra of Golden Light; 4.2.1(1) of the laity; 6.1.2(14) of the laity, of the monks; 6.2.1.1(20) in Cambodian Buddhism; 6.2.2.1(15) Social Ethics; 11.2(8); 11.3

Etymology 8.1.2.2(2) of Tathagata; 8.3.1(3), (8) of Bodhisattva; 8.3.2(8) of Avalokitesvara; 8.4 of Arhat "Encyclopaedia . . ."; 8.8(9) of Bhiksu

Exile 1.14.2.3(3) Tibetan

Exorcism 7.5.2

Fa-hsien 1.2.2.3; 1.2.2.4; 1.3.2.1; 2.4.1(12); 2.5.4; 6.2.5(14); 7.2.2; 8.4 and 16 Lohans; 8.9.3 Life of; 10.1.1(1)

Subject Index

Fa-tsang 1.12.2(7) Korea; 2.5.5 and Hua-yen; 3.3.1.2 Heart Sutra commentary; 3.3.4.1 Treatise on gold lion, Third Hua yen patriarch; 8.9.3(29), (30) Life; 8.9.6(3) and Uisang

Faith (Sraddha) 2.5.8 in Amida; 3.2.3.4(6); 3.3.7.2 Rennyo, Shinran; 5.6(5); 6.2.5 Propagation in China; 8.9.4(11) Honen; 9.2 Refuges; 11.7.1 in Pure Land; 11.7.2 Nembutsu practice; 11.7.3 Hymns

Family (See also Ancestors) 1.11.1(7) China; 4.1.2(3) Vietnam; 6.2.1.1; 6.2.3

Fertility 5.8(14) and Nagas, Rites; 7.5.1 Rites

Festivals 1.3.1(10) Lay in Ceylon; 1.5.2(2) Thai; 1.6.2(3) Cambodian; 1.7.2(7) Laotian New Year; 4.4.1 Harvest festivals and dramas in Tibet; 5.11.2(20) on Buddha's birth, in Japan; 6.1.1(12) Monastic; 6.2.5(5) of propagation or faith; 7.1.2 Rainy season; 7.2.4 Uposatha; 7.3.1 Calendrical, Tooth Relic, Wat, Southeast and South Asia; 7.3.2 All Souls, calendrical in China and Japan; 7.4.2 of the dead; 8.3.2 of Kuan Yin; 9.1.3(3) Buddha Jayanti; 9.1.4(5) Millenarian; 9.2.2.3(6) All Souls; 10.1.5(1); 11.6.1(17) Tantric

Filial Piety 6.2.3(4)

Folk Art (See also Dance, Art) 5.6(10), (11), (12) of Tibet; 5.11.1(2) of Japan; 5.11.4(20) of Japan; 5.12; 5.12.2 of Japan; 5.12.3 of Japan

Folk Literature 3.2.2.1 Jatakas; 4.2.2 Jatakas; 4.2.3(18) Monk's tales, (17), (24), (25) Story telling; 4.2.8; 8.1.1 Jatakas

Folk Religion (See also Buddhism, Ancestors) 1.11.2.3(11) in China; 1.13.1(3), (7), (8) in Japan; 4.1; 4.1.1 in South Asia; 6.2.3 in South Asia, in Southeast Asia; 8.1.2.4(2), (8) and Stupa worship

Folklore (See also Legends, Jatakas, Death) 1.6.2(13) Cambodian, cf. 4.2.4; 1.7.1(1) Laotian; 1.14.2.1(5) Tibetan, cf. 4.2.4; 4.2.4

Founders (of Religious Schools) 1.2.1 Buddha, cf. 2.1; 1.2.2.5 Ambedkar; 2.1(10) Buddha; 2.2(15), (16) Ajivikas, Jains, Sceptics, Materialists; 2.5.6(3) of T'ien T'ai, cf. 8.9.3; 2.5.8 Pure Land and Shin; 2.5.9 Nichiren; 2.6.2(1) Tantrism in China; 2.7.14 Dogen, Soto sect; 3.3.6.2 Dogen, Soto sect; 4.1.4 Shugendo; 8.9.1(5), (6), (37), (38), (39), (40), (41), (42), (43), (44), (45) Madhyamika, (7), (8), (9), (10), (11), (51), (52), (53), (54), (55), (56), (57), (58) Yogacara; 8.9.3(53) Fa-hsiang/Hosso

Frescoes 5.9.3(20) in Chinese temples

Funerary Rites (See also Death, Bardo, Cults) 1.5.2(9); 1.11.1(8); 4.1.2(3); 4.1.3(4); 5.11.3(6); 7.4.2; 8.1.2.3(5), (22); 8.1.2.4(2), (15)

Gandharvas 9.2.2.5 in Realm of Desire

Gandhavyuha 2.5.5(5), (6); 2.5.7(20); 3.3.4.2(5) Influence on Avatamsaka; 5.5.6(2); 5.8(5)

Gardens 5.9.1(1); 5.11.2(21); 5.11.3(4), (6); 5.11.6(9); 5.11.7; 5.11.8(1), (8) Tea

Gatis (See Realms)

Genealogies 1.14.1(1) Tibetan; 1.14.2.1(1), (3) Tibetan; 3.2.2.1 Buddhavamsa; 9.1.5 of kings and monks

Genghis Khan 1.16.1(3); 1.16.2(7), (9); as benevolent patriarch, Altan tobci

Geography 1.1(10) Maps; 1.2.2.3(9) Survey of Buddhism, cf. 1.6.2, 10.2.1; 1.6.1(2) Southeast Asian, cf. 1.7.1; 1.6.2(13) Survey of Buddhism; 1.7.1(1) Southeast Asian; 1.10.1(5) Central Asian; 1.16.1(5) Central Asian; 6.2.2.1(9) Sacred; 9.2 Sacred; 10.2.1(13) Survey of Buddhism

Gilgit Manuscripts 1.2.2.4(4); 3.2.1.4(3); 3.3.1.1(3) Astadasasahasrika Prajnaparamita; 3.3.5.2(1); 3.3.8.1(1); 8.1.2.3(8)

Grammars 3.1.2(2), (6); 3.1.6(2); 9.1.1(4)

Han Shan (See also Poetry) 3.3.1.1; 3.3.6.2 17th century, Heart and Diamond Sutra commentaries; 4.3.1(4), (22)

Healing (See also Medicine, Bhaisajya) 3.3.6.2(3); 4.1.2; 7.5.2 Rites

Heavens (See also Cosmology, Realms) 8.3.1(12) Celestial Buddhas; 9.2.2.4

Hells (See also Cosmology, Realms) 9.2.2.3

Himalayan Kingdoms (See also Bhutan, Kashmir, Sikkim) 1.15.1 History; 5.2.2(8) Art; 5.2.8(21) Art; 5.6(10) Art; 6.2.2 Politics; 6.2.7 Politics; 6.2.9 Politics; 7.4.2; 10.1.3 Travellers' accounts; 10.7 Travellers' accounts

Hinayana (See also Sthaviravadin, Theravada, Buddhist Sects) 1.2.2.3(3) and Mahayana; 1.8.1(6) and Mahayana in Vietnam; 1.9.2(5) and Mahayana in Indonesia; 2.1(1), (8), (15); 2.4; 2.4.1(6), (14) Propagation and diffusion; 2.7.6(3) Dependent origination; 2.7.8(6) and Emptiness; 2.7.9(3) and the Truths; 2.7.10(5) and Suchness; 2.7.12(1) and Store-consciousness (Alaya-vijnana); 3.2 Texts; 3.2.2.2 Texts; 3.2.4.2 Meditation

History (See also Chronicles, Genealogies) 1.2.2.1(5) from Marxist stance, cf. 1.3.2.2; 1.2.2.3(13) and Archaeology; 1.3.2.2(7) from Marxist stance; 9.1.5 Sacred (National, ecclesiastical, doctrinal)

Holy Man (See also Arhat, Bodhisattva) 1.13.1(6); 2.6.2(2) Shugendo; 4.1.2; 4.1.4(2), (5) Hijiri; 4.2.4 in popular literature; 4.4.2 Plays about; 7.2.1 Ordination and initiation; 7.5.2 Medicine man; 11.1 Bodhisattvas; 11.4.6 Powers of

403

Subject Index

Honen (Founder of Jodo Sect) (See also Jodo, Nembutsu) 1.13.2.2(1), (12); 2.5.8(2), (11), (19), (20), (25); 8.9.4; 11.7.2(6)

Hosso (Consciousness Only School) 2.5.4; 8.9.3(53) K'uei-chi, Chinese founder of; 11.7.4(9)

Hsuan Tsang 1.2.2.3 in India; 1.2.2.4 in India; 2.4.1(10), (12) on Hinayana sects, 2.5.1(3) on Consciousness Only school; 2.5.4(5) Yogacara; 2.7.10(3) Vijnaptimatratasiddhi; 3.2.3.2(1), (3), (4) Abhidharmakosa-karika; 3.3.1.1(13) Version of Heart Sutra; 3.3.2.1 Bhavaviveka's "Jewel in the Hand"; 3.3.3.1 Translations of Vasubandhu; 3.3.3.2(3), (6) Ch'eng-wei-shih Lun; 3.3.8.2(6); 4.2.2 Version of Jatakas; 4.5 in Hsu Yuchi; 5.2.3(10) Itinerary; 5.11.4(2) on Udayana Buddhist image; 6.1.1(21) on Indian monasteries; 6.2.5(14) on education, (24) on Nalanda; 8.4 and 16 Lohans; 8.9.3(39), (40), (41), (42), (43), (44) Life of, (53) and his disciples; 10.1.1(11); 11.1 from Vijnaptimatratasiddhi, on path

Hua Yen (See also Avatamsaka) 2.5.5; 2.5.7(24) and Zen; 3.3.4; 4.2.1(5) (Sutra); 8.9.3(29) Lives of masters; 8.9.6(3) in Korea; 11.1(3) Path and stages; 11.4.9 Meditative methods

Hui-yuan 1.11.2.2(5), (7); 2.5.3(10) and Madhyamika; 6.2.2.5(5); 8.9.3(47) Life of, Writings

Iconography (See also Mandala, Images, Art) 1.2.2.3(5); 1.12.2(1), (5); 1.17(14); 3.3.8.1(4); 3.4.4(3) in Vajrayana texts, cf. 8.3.1; 4.1.5(3); 5.1.4(6); 5.2.1(14) Schools of (Sculpture); 5.2.3(12) of Buddha's nativity, (14) Mahayana, cf. 5.6; 5.5.6 Mahayana, Stupas, cf. 9.3.6, 10.2.1, 10.2.6.2; 5.6(7), (12); 5.8(5) in cave temples, cf. 10.2.1, 10.2.6.2; 5.8(11) Arhats, cf. 8.4; 5.9 Arhats, in cave temples; 5.10 in cave temples; 5.11.5(6) of Buddha's parinirvana; 8.1.2.2(4); 8.1.2.4(4) of Heruka; 8.3.1(1) in Vajrayana texts, (5), (6); 8.3.3(3) of Tara; 9.2.2.5(2) Yaksas, (8) Protective deities; 9.3.1(4); 9.3.2(5), (7) Wheel in; 9.3.4(3) Trees; 9.3.6 Stupas; 9.3.7 Royal symbols; 10.2.1(7) Stupas, in cave temples; 10.2.6.2(5), (6) Stupas, (3) in cave temples

Idealism 1.13.2.1(1) of Shotoku; 2.1(11), (15); 2.4.3(5) Sarvastivadins characterized as; 2.5.1(3) Hsuan tsang and Consciousness Only; 2.5.3(8) Critique of Madhyamika as; 2.5.4 Yogacara as; 2.6.7; 3.3.3.1(16); 5.1.4(5)

Images (See also Iconography) 1.2.2.3(13) Archaeological studies; 1.5.2(8) Archaeological studies; 1.11.2.1(8) Archaeological studies; 1.12.2(1), (5) Buddha images, cf. 5.1.2, 5.2.3, 5.4.2, 8.3.1; 1.13.2.1(7) Buddha images; 3.3.8.1(4) Construction and consecration of, cf. 7.2.6; 3.3.8.2(3) Contemplation and veneration, cf. 7.1.3; 5.1.2(1) Buddha images; 5.2.1(3), (10) Artistic and cultic development, cf. 5.2.3, 5.2.5, 5.4.2, 5.5.3, 5.5.6, 5.6, 5.7, 5.8, 5.9, 5.9.2, 5.9.3, 5.10, 5.11.4; 5.2.3; 5.2.5(5) Artistic and cultic development; 5.4.2(3) Artistic and cultic development, Buddha images; 5.5.3(7) Artistic and cultic development; 5.5.6 Artistic and cultic development; 5.6(6), (7), (9), (13) Artistic and cultic development; 5.7(11) Artistic and cultic development; 5.8 Artistic and cultic development; 5.9 Artistic and cultic development; 5.9.2 Artistic and cultic development; 5.9.3(5) Artistic and cultic development; 5.10 Artistic and cultic development; 5.11.4 Artistic and cultic development; 7.1.3 Contemplation and veneration of; 7.2.6 Construction and consecration of; 8.3.1(1) Buddha images; 8.3.2(4) of Avalokitesvara

Impermanence (Anitya/Anicca) 2.7.3; (6) and suffering

India (See also specific places) 1.2; 1.2.2.3(12) Decline of Buddhism; 1.2.2.5 Modern Buddhist movements; 2.2 as background for Buddhist thought; 5.2.1 Art; 5.12.1 Drama; 6.2.2.1 Politics; 10.1.1 Sacred places, Travellers' accounts; 10.2 Sacred places

Indonesia and Malaya 1.1(4); 1.9; 1.9.1; 1.9.2(4) Inception and development of Buddhism; 5.5.6 Art and architecture, Sacred places; 5.12.1 Drama; 6.2.2 Politics; 10.1.4 Sacred places, Travellers' accounts; 10.6 Sacred places

Indra (See Kingship)

Inscriptions 1.2.2.2 of Ashoka, cf. 8.9.1, 10.2.6.2; 1.2.2.4 in Bengal; 1.3.2.1 Paranavitana; 1.4.2(19) at Pagan, cf. 6.2.6, 10.4.1, 1.6.2(13) Cambodian; 1.7.2(6) at Luang Prabang; 1.9.2(1) at Kota Kapur; 1.10.2 Sogdian; 1.12.2(5) Korean; 1.14.2.1(8), (11) Tibetan; 5.8 in East Asian art, (1) on Buddhist bronzes; 5.9.1(16) in China; 6.1.1(26) on founding of order; 6.2.2.3 on royal power in Burma; 6.2.6(14) at Pagan; 7.6(4) for divination; 8.3.4 on Maitreya; 8.9.1 of Ashoka; 10.2.2 on Lumbini pilgrimage; 10.2.3 at Bodh-Gaya; 10.2.5 at Sarnath; 10.2.6.2 of Ashoka; 10.4.1 at Pagan; 10.6(5) at Borobudur

Insight 12.4.7 Perfection of Vipasyana

Intuition 2.5.7(23) in Zen; 2.8; 11.4.7(7)

Invocation (and Evocation) (See also Deities, Rituals) 7.1.4(10) of Lamaist Deities; 7.5.1 of rain; 7.5.3 Health and protection, of Tara; 7.8(2) of Tara; 9.2.2.5(6); 11.6(1) Fierce deities

Jains 2.2(9), (10), (11), (13), (16); 2.7.1(10) Notion of Karma, cf. 11.3; 8.1.2.2(6) Notion of omniscience; 11.3(13) Notion of Karma

Japan 1.6.2(11); 1.11.2.3 Ennin in China; 1.12.2(2) and Silla; 1.13.1 History; 1.13.2.1 Nara period; 1.13.3.3 Founding of sects, Tokugawa period; 1.13.2.4 Modern; 2.1(13) Buddhist philosophers; 2.3(6); 2.5.1(1) Sects; 2.5.3(14) Madhyamika in; 2.5.5 Kegon in; 2.5.6(8) Tendai in; 2.5.7 Zen in; 2.5.8 Shin and Jodo; 2.5.9 Nichiren; 2.6.2 Shingon; 3.4.3 Shingon texts; 4.1.4 Popular beliefs; 4.3.2 Haiku; 4.4.3 No plays; 4.5 Genji and other diaries, Poetry; 5.1.1(5) Art history; 5.8 Arts in; 5.11.1 Aesthetics; 5.11.2 Temple treasures; 5.11.3 Architecture; Gardens; 5.12.1 Drama; 5.12.2 Drama; 5.12.3 Dance; 6.2.1.2(11),

Subject Index

(12), (13), (14) Buddhism and social order; 6.2.2.8(3) Bodhisattva and kingship; 6.2.3(14) Orders; 6.2.6(1), (2) Economics; 7.1.2(4) Feasts for Samgha; 7.1.4(1), (5) Ceremonies; 7.3.2 Calendrical festivals; 7.5.1 Rain making; 8.4(18) Arhats; 8.9.4 Great Buddhists of; 10.1.5 Sacred places, Travellers' accounts; 10.9 Temples and Stupas in; 11.4.8.3(2) Zen and culture; 12.1(4), (10) Reference materials, vocabulary and terminology; 12.2 Bibliographies and encyclopaedias

Jatakas (See also Buddha, Gautama, Folklore) 2.7.1(2); 3.2.2.1; 4.2.2; 5.2.4(2) and art; 5.5.3(12) and art; 5.5.6 and art; 5.6(3) and art; 8.1.1; 11.5(1) and practice of the perfections

Jewels (See also Refuges) 5.2.5(7) in art; 6.1.1(25) Three; 6.2.2.4(5) Holy emerald; 8.7(1) 7 jewels of the Cakravartins

Jodo (See also Honen) 2.5.8(3), (11), (19), (21); 2.9(17) and Christianity; 7.1.4 Use of rosaries

Kalpas (See Time)

Kamadhatu (See also Realms) 2.7.7(11) on Dhatus

Kamalasila (See also Debates) 1.14.2.1(2), (10); 2.5.3(5) Madhyamika; 3.3.2.1 Santaraksita, Tattvasamgrahapanjika; 3.3.2.2(2); 11.1(9) Bodhisattva stages; 11.4.2 Bodhisattva stages

Kaniska (See also Kushana Hegemony) 3.2.4.3(1); 3.3.2.1(18) and Nagarjuna; 4.2.3(3), (5) Legend of; 5.1.3(4) Relic casket; 5.2.5(12); 8.9.1(21) and Asvaghosa, (30), (31), (32), (33), (34) Story of; 11.4.2(5)

Kanjur (See also Tibet, Tripitaka) 1.10.2(8) Mongolian, cf. 1.3.6; 3.2.2.2(10) Version of Dharmapada; 3.4.4(5); 3.5(5) Translation from; 4.2.3 Avadanas; 7.1.3 Eight Caityas; 8.1.2 Bu-ston; 8.1.2.3(26) Life of Buddha; 8.1.3 Tri-kaya; 9.1.2(8) "History of World"

Kapilavastu (See also India [Sacred Places]) 10.2.2 Pilgrimage sites

Karma (See also Causality) 2.2 Indian context; 2.7.1 Theory; 2.8 and science story; 3.2.2.1(21); 3.2.3.2; 3.2.3.3(3), (4); 3.3.2.1(7), (8); 3.3.8.4(4); 4.1.2 Supplanted by belief in spirits; 7.1.1(7) in Ceylon; 9.2.2.3(12) Consequences of bad Karma; 11.6.1(15) and Mudra

Kashmir (See also Himalayan Kingdoms) 1.15.1; 5.1.1(5) Art history; 5.2.8(11) Bronzes

Kassapa 1.3.2.1; 2.4.2(10) and Ananda at 1st council; 8.8(5), (12) Mahakasyapa

Kegon (See also Avatamsaka, Hua Yen, Gandhavyuha, Zen) 2.5.5; 2.4.7(23)

Kingship (See also Cakravartin, Asoka) 1.2.1(8) and Buddhism's development; 1.5.2(5), (7), (26) Thai, cf. 6.2.2.4; 1.6.2(11) Cambodian; 1.12.2(6) Korean; 1.14.2.1(3), (4), (9), (11) Tibetan, cf. 6.2.2.7; 4.1.1(6) and order, cf. 6.2.2.1, 6.2.2.4, 9.2.2.4; 4.2.4(3) in legends and chronicles, cf. 9.1.5; 5.8(14) Dragon-kings; 6.2.2; 6.2.2.1 and Sangha, (9) and order; 6.2.2.2 and Sangha; 6.2.2.6(3) Japanese; 6.2.2.7 Tibetan; 7.7 Rituals of; 9.1.5 in legends and chronicles; 9.2.2.4(3) and order; 9.3.1 Symbols of

Kingship 1.5.2; 4.1.3(4) Chinese popular beliefs; 6.2.6(9) Ceylon, property rites

Koan 2.5.7(4), (14), (20); 3.1.5(6); 3.3.6.1(9), (10) 10 bulls, Texts; 3.3.6.3(1), (4), (5), (6), (7); 11.3.8.2

Kobo Daishi (Kukai) 1.13.2.2(5); 3.3.1.2(5) Heart Sutra; 3.4.3(1), (2); 4.5(3) Sango-shiki; 5.11.5(14), (19) and art; 8.9.4

Korea 1.12.1 History; 1.12.2 Specific studies; 2.5.3(3), (4) Madhyamika in; 2.5.7(19) Sun Buddhism; 3.1.6(5) Tripitaka; 5.1.4(6), (8) Arts; 5.8 Arts; 5.10 Arts; 6.2.1.2(7) Culture and politics; 6.2.2.9 Kingship; 8.9.5 Great Buddhists (Eminent monks); 10.1.5 Sacred places and Travellers' accounts

Kuan Yin (See also Avalokitesvara, Bodhisattvas) 7.8; 8.3.1(10); 8.3.2

Kushana Hegemony 1.10.1(1), (2) Buddhism and; 1.10.2(3); 5.1.4(9) Arts under; 5.2.4(9) Mathuran art; 5.2.5(12), (13); 5.2.8(18)

Kusinara/Kusinagara 10.3.5

Laity 1.2.2.1(6); 1.3.1(10) in Ceylon; 1.5.2(22) Meditation of; 1.11.2.1(8) Masses for; 3.2.2.2; 3.2.2.4(1) Discourse to, cf. 6.1.2; 3.3.1.1 Vajracchedika Prajnaparamita; 4.2.1(1) in Nikayas; 4.2.3; 4.2.4 in popular literature; 6.1.2; 6.1.4(4) Modern associations, (6) Revival in China; 6.2.2.2 and politics, Ceylon and Burma; 6.2.2.3 Attempt to control Sangha; 6.2.3(11) Conceptions of monks and doctrine; 6.2.4(3) and caste; 6.2.5(5) Lay societies; 6.2.6(9); 6.2.7(16); 7.1.1 Rituals of; 7.1.2 Gifts to Sangha; 7.1.3(11) Use of prayers and rosaries; 7.2.1(17) Vows; 7.2.5(5); 7.2.6; 7.3.1 and calendrical festivals; 7.4.1 Life cycle rites; 7.5.1 Rainmaking; 8.3.1(7) Bodhisattva; 8.4(2) and Arhatship; 9.2.2.4(4) and deities; 9.3.5(6); 11.2(2); 11.3(17) Ethics of; 11.4.8.1(17); 11.7.1(5) in Pure Land; 11.7.4(7) in Pure Land

Laksana (See Three Characteristics, Tri-laksana)

Lamaism 1.14.1 History; 1.14.2.1 Sects; 1.14.2.3 Contemporary status; 1.16.1(7); 1.16.2(6); 4.1.5(4) in Sikkim; 4.2.4(3); 5.1.3(3) Mythology; 5.6; 6.2.1.2(19) in Mongolia; 6.2.2.9(3) and Central Asian politics; 7.1.4 Rosaries; 7.2.1 Tibetan ordinations; 7.4.2(16) Funerary practices; 7.5.3 Health rituals; 7.6 Astrology; 7.8 Rituals for particular deities; 8.6(9) Pantheon of; 10.1.3

Lamasery (See also Monasteries, Sangha, Tibet) 1.16.2(8) USSR; 5.6(20), (21); 5.9.2(8) Cathedral in Peking; 6.1.1 Inmates of; 6.2.3(1)

Subject Index

(Lamasery)
Mongolian; 6.2.5(16), (19) Entrance and Training; 7.2.2(4), (5) Daily life; 9.2.2.1(1); 10.1.2(5) in Jehol; 10.1.3(6), (10); 10.8.1 Tibet and Himalayas

Laos 1.7; 1.7.1(2) Historical overview; 1.7.2(5), (6) Inception of Buddhism; 3.1.2(5) Pali texts of; 3.1.6(2), (6), (7) Literature of; 5.5.5 Art and architecture, Sacred places; 10.1.4 Sacred places, Travellers' accounts; 10.6 Sacred places

Law (See also Dharma) 1.5.2(16); 1.11.2.3(6) of the Buddhist order; 6.1.2(16); 6.2.7; 8.1.2.2(4) Preaching of

Legends 1.11.2.1(5), (6), (7) of origins of Mahayana in China; 1.12.2(5) in art; 1.14.2.1(4) Tibetan; 4.2; 4.2.2 of Gautama Buddha's lives, cf. 8.1; 8.1 of Gautama Buddha's lives; 8.2 of other Buddhas' lives; 9.1.2 Origins of world and beings

Letters 2.5.8 of Shin Ran, cf. 3.3.7.2, 8.9.4; 2.5.9(4) of Nichiren; 3.2.4.3(1) Nagarjuna to Kaneska; 3.3.2.1(18) Nagarjuna to Kaneska; 3.3.6.2(10) Zen masters; 8.9.4(26) of Shin Ran

Light 5.11.2(20) Festival, Japan; 9.3.9; 11.7.3(12) in Pure Land

Logic (See also Dignaga) 2.1(11); 2.2(16); 3.3.2.1(21) Nagarjuna; 3.3.3.1(7), (9), (11), (13), (14) Epistemology; 8.9.1 Bu-ston on Dignaga; 11.8(5) and Nirvana

Lohans (See also Arhats) 8.4

Lotus (See also Art Motif) 9.3.3 as symbol

Lotus Sutra 3.3.5; 5.9.4(3) in art; 7.2.5(1) Teaching/preaching; 8.1.2.1(17); 8.1.3(10)

Lumbini 4.3(8) Poem of; 10.2.2

Madhyamika (See also Nagarjuna) 1.2.2.3(5); 1.11.2.2(9); 2.1(15); 2.5.1(3) in China, (4) in India; 2.7.6(10) and causality; 2.7.7(1) and Dharmas; 2.7.8 View of Sunyata; 2.7.9 Two Truths; 3.3.1.2(7) Commentary on Heart Sutra; 3.3.2.1 Texts; 3.3.2.2 Studies; (5), (6) India and China; 3.3.6.1(1); 8.9.1 Candrakirti, Nagarjuna, Santideva; 9.2.2.3(11) Interpretation of hell; 9.3.10(9) Mirror; 11.1(8) Description of Path; 11.5(6) Paramitas; 11.8(8), (11), (14) on Nirvana

Magic 4.1.1(1); 5.12.1(3) and art; 6.2.3(18); 7.1(2); 7.2.2(4); 7.5 Protection; 8.1.2.2(4) Performed by the Buddha; 8.5(2) Power of Yogis; 8.8(11) Power of Devadatta; 11.1(1), (3) Foundations of

Mahasanghikas 1.2.2.4(12) Emergence of; 2.4.2(3), (5) and the second council; 2.4.4; 3.2.1.2(5), (6), (10)

Mahayana 1.1 Development of, cf. 2.5.1; 1.2.1 in India; 1.2.2.3 Post Mauryan; 1.3.1 in Ceylon, cf. 8.3.2; 1.4.2(16); 1.5.1(6); 1.6.2(8); 1.8.1(6) in Vietnam; 1.14.1(7); 2.1(1) Rise of thought; 2.4.3(3) and Mahasangikas; 2.5.1 Development of; 2.5.2(7) Origins; 2.5.3 Madhyamika; 2.5.4 Yogacara; 2.5.5 Avatamsaka; 2.5.7(6) and Zen subjectivism; 2.5.8(18), (26); 2.5.9(6) Nichiren; 2.6.1 Vajrayana; 2.7.5 Four Truths; 2.7.6(3) and Hinayana on causality; 2.7.8 View of Sunyata; 2.7.9 and Two Truths; 2.7.11(2) Spiritual lineage, Tathagatagarbha; 2.7.12 Alayavijnana, on Bodhicitta; 3.3 Texts in translation; 3.3.1.2(1) Five-fold Path; 3.3.2.1 Madhyamika texts; 3.3.3.1 Yogacara texts; 5.2.3(14) Iconography of; 5.4.2(6) in Ceylon; 5.5.6(8) Beginnings of Buddhology; 6.1.4(2) Modern associations in Southeast Asia; 7.2.1 Ordination, Bodhisattva Samvara; 7.2.4 Uposatha and Pratimoksa; 7.5.3(4) Sutras for protection; 8.1.2.1(17) on Buddha's enlightenment; 8.1.2.4(11) Stupas and rise of Mahayana, cf. 9.3.6; 8.1.3(14) rise of Mahayana; 8.2.1(6) on plurality of Buddhas; 8.3.1(6), (7), (15) in Ceylon, Bodhisattva iconography; 8.4(10) Concept of arhat; 8.9.1(57), (58) Translation of Milindapanha, View of Asvaghosa; 9.3.6 Stupas and rise of Mahayana; 11.1 Path, Bodhisattva stages; 11.2(3) Faith; 11.3(18) Ethics; 11.4 Meditation manuals; 11.4.3(4) Subjects of meditation; 11.4.5 Trance levels; 11.4.6 View of Siddhis and powers; 11.5 Prajnaparamitas

Maitreya (See also Bodhisattvas) 1.12.2(1) in Korea; 2.5.4(18) of Yogacara school; 3.3.1.2(1) Abhisamayalankara commentary, cf. 11.1; 3.3.1.3(4) Abhisamayalankara commentary; 3.3.2.1(23), (24); 3.3.3.1(2); 4.1.2 Cults of, Southeast Asia, in China; 5.9.3(20) Painting of Maitreya's paradise; 8.3.4; 8.9.1 and Vasubandhu; 8.9.3 and Pu-tai; 9.1.1(1) "Cakkavatti"; 10.8.2 Associated with mountains in China; 10.10.2 Associated with mountains in China; 11.1 Abhisamayalankara commentary

Malaya (See Indonesia and Malaya)

Mandala 2.6.2(8) in Shingon, cf. 3.4.3; 3.4.1(4) Use of, cf. 3.4.4; 3.4.2(10) Construction of, cf. 9.2.2.1; 3.4.3(3) in Shingon; 3.4.4(3) Use of; 5.6(20) as art; 5.11.3(11) as art; 5.11.5(14) as art; 7.1.3(1) Veneration of; 9.2.2.1(1) Construction of, and cosmology; 10.6 and temple construction; 11.6.2

Manjusri (See also Bodhisattvas) 3.3.1.1(18), (19) Saptasatika Prajnaparamita; 8.3.1(14); 8.3.5(2) Cult of, (3) Iconography; 8.3.6(6) and Vimalakirti; 10.1.2(3) Visit to Wu-t'ai shan; 11.6.2(9) Mulakalpa, Mandala

Mantras (See also Dharanis) 2.6.1(9) in Vajrayana; 3.3.1.1(21) in Prajnaparamita; 3.4.1 in Tantric texts; 3.5(5); 5.2.8(14), (15); 5.5.6(1) Indonesian and Mudras; 5.11.5(19) Japan; 7.1.4(6) Prayers of laity; 7.5.3(4) Protection, cf. 9.2.2.5; 7.8(13) Horse cult and; 9.2.2.5 Protection; 9.3.2(2); 11.6.1(18); 11.6.3 Tantrism; 11.7.2(4) Nembutsu as

Mantrayana (See also Vajrayana) 1.1(9) Historical overview; 3.4.1(7) Historical overview; 3.4.2(1), (8) Texts

Subject Index

Mao-tse-tung 1.11.2.4(5); 1.14.2.4 and 14th Dalai Lama; 6.2.2.5(6)

Mara 8.1.2.3(21) "Evil one"; 8.9.1(50) and Upagupta; 9.2.2.4(1), (5), (12); 9.3.5

Marriage 7.4.1(1), (5) Ceremony

Martial Arts 1.13.2.3(2) Samurai

Marxism and Socialism 2.8; 6.2.2.2(14) and Buddhist coalition in Ceylon; 6.2.2.3(6) Modern Burma, (9); 6.2.2.6(10) Japan and Burma

Maya (Illusion) 2.7.9(5) and the Two Truths

Medicine (See also Bhaisajya) 1.7.1(1) Laos; 3.2.1.1(5) Mahavagga; 3.3.6 Zen sickness and cure; 3.3.8.1(8); 6.2.1.2(4) in China; 7.5.2 Use of amulets and charms; 7.5.3 Use of amulets and charm

Meditation 1.5.2(22) Lay; 1.13.2.2 in Japanese sects; 2.1(1); 2.5.3(2) on emptiness, cf. 3.3.4.1; 2.5.6(4) in T'ien T'ai; 2.5.7 in Zen; 2.6.1 in Vajrayana, 2.7.3(5) on impermanence; 3.2.2.4(3); 3.2.3.1(1) Manuals; 3.3.4.1 on emptiness; 3.3.7.1 on Amitayus; 3.4.1 Tantric; 6.1.1(1) Hermitages; 7.2.2(12) in daily monastic life; 9.2.3 Anuruddha, Types of consciousness; 9.3.9 in Amitayur-Dhyana-Sutra; 11.1 on path; 11.4.4 Sattipatthana, on mindfulness; 11.4.5 Dhyana, 11.4.7 Perfection of insight; 11.4.8.1 Zen/Ch'an; 11.4.8.2 Koan; 11.4.9 in Hua Yen and T'ien T'ai; 11.5(5) Dhyana and Paramita; 11.6 Tantric Sadhanas; 11.6.2(13) on Mandalas; 11.6.3 and Mantras; 11.7.3 and Pure Land teachings

Merit-making (See also Karma, Dana) 4.2.3(19) Stories of, cf. 8.2.1; 6.1.2(12); 6.2.1.1(7), (14) in Cambodia; 6.2.2.1(19) in Burma; 6.2.3(7) in Sri Lanka, cf. 7.1.1, (10), (19) in Thailand; 7.1; 7.1.1(4), (7) in Sri Lanka; 8.2.1(2) Stories of

Milarepa (See also Yogin) 1.14.2.3 and "white sect"; 4.3.3 Songs of; 8.9.2 Biography; 11.6.1(9) Biography

Millennarian Movements 1.4.2(18) Burma; 4.1.2(8), (9), (10), (11) Burma; 8.3.4(3) Surrounding Maitreya; 9.1.4 Surrounding Maitreya, Eschatological myths

Mind (Citta) 2.4.3(5) Sarvastivadin doctrine of; 2.5.4 Mind only (Yogacara) school; 2.5.7; 2.7.14 of enlightenment (Bodhicitta); 3.3.3.1(15) Only, (22) Vasubandhu

Mindfulness 3.2.3.1(2); 11.1(10) Right mindfulness/ 8-fold path; 11.4.1(7); 11.4.3(3) of death; 11.4.8.1 in Zen

Missionary Movements 1.2.2.1(2) Early Buddhist, cf. 7.2.5; 1.3.2.1(5), (16) Within Theravada countries; 1.5.2(17) Within Theravada countries; 7.2.5(4) Early Buddhist, Preaching

Mithra 8.3.4(6) Parallels with Maitreya; 9.1.4 Parallels with Maitreya

Modernity 1.2.2.4 Buddhist revival in India; 1.3.2.2(4) and Anagarika Dharmapala, cf. 6.2.2.2; 1.5.2(22) Thailand; 1.7.2(2); 1.13.2.4 in Japan, cf. 6.2.1.2, 6.2.2.6; 1.14.2.3 in Tibet, cf. 6.2.7.7; 2.5.7(18) and Zen; 2.5.9(5) Nichirenism; 2.8; 3.1.2 Pali literature in Burma, cf. 6.2.3; 4.5(9); 5.11.2(19) Temples and museums in Japan; 6.1.2(1) in Ceylon; 6.2.1.1(2) The Sangha in, (25), (32), (40) Thailand and Java; 6.2.1.2(24) in China, (14) in Japan; 6.2.2.2 and Anagarika Dharmapala; 6.2.2.3(8) and Buddhist kingship; 6.2.2.6(6) in Japan; 6.2.3(16) Pali literature in Burma; 6.2.7.7 in Tibet

Monastery (See also Lamasery, Education, Economics) 1.11.2.1(6) White Horse, China; 1.11.2.2(3) (11) China; 1.11.2.3(2), (16), (17) China; 1.12.2(4) Korea; 1.14.1(15), (17) Tibet; 1.16.1(7) Mongolia; 5.1.4(13) and art; 5.2.2 and art; 6.1.1; 6.2.5 Universities; 7.2.6 Building and consecration

Monasticism (See also Sangha, Lamaism) 1.3.1(10) in Sri Lanka; 1.3.2.1(5), (17) Renewal of ordination; 1.10.1(5) in Central Asia; 1.11.2.2(3) in China; 1.11.2.3(2), (16) in China; 1.11.2.4(6) in China; 1.12.2(4) in Korea; 1.14.1(17) in Tibet, cf. 6.2.1.2; 3.2.1 Rules; 6.1.1; 6.1.2(2) Rituals and practices; 6.2.1(10) Rituals and practices; 6.2.1.2(18), (19) in Tibet; 7.2; 7.2.2; 7.2.1 Ordination

Mongolia 1.10.2 Kanjur; 1.16.1(7); 3.1.6(1) Tanjur; 5.6(10) Arts; 6.2.1.2(6) Social order, (19) Lamaism, Social stability; 6.2.2.5(7); 6.2.2.9(1) Political, (3) Lamas and politics; 6.2.3(1) Lamasery; 6.2.6(16) Monastic economy; 8.1.2 Life of Buddha; 8.1.2.3(21) Life of Buddha; 10.1.2 Travellers' accounts; 10.4 Sacred places

Monk (See also Monasteries, Sangha) 1.8.2(10) and politics; 1.11.2.2(15) Biographies of; 1.11.2.3(4) Biographies of, (3), (6), (8), (13) China; 1.12.1(4) Biographies of; 1.12.2(4) and laity, cf. 4.2.3, 6.1.2, Korea; 1.13.1(11) and laity, Japan; 1.14.1(1), (17) Tibet; 3.2.1 Vinaya, cf. 7.2.2; 4.2.3(18) and laity, Tales; 4.2.4(6), (13) Tales; 6.1.1(6) India, (8) Tibet, (9) Kinship and lineage; 6.1.2 and laity; 7.2.2 Vinaya

Moonstones 9.2.10(5), (7)

Moral Discipline (See Vinaya, Ethics)

Mount Meru 9.2.2.1; 11.6.2(1) as mandala

Mountains 4.1.4(1) and Shugendo; 5.1.3(4) in art, as deities; 5.4.1(4) Adam's peak; 5.9.2(18) Mt. Sung, 5.9.3(7) T'ien T'ai and Rock Bridge; 7.3.1(9) Cosmic significance of Southeast Asia and mts.; 9.1.2(9) Mt. Meru; 9.2.2.1; 9.2.2.5(8) Deities of

Mudra 3.4.2(11) in Tantrism, cf. 5.6, 11.6, 11.6.4; 5.5.6(1) in art; 5.6(6) in Tantrism, in art; 5.9.1(21) in art; 5.12.3 in art, in Japan; 11.6 in Tantrism; 11.6.4 in Tantrism

Subject Index

Mulasarvastivadin 2.4.2(3) and the 2nd council; 3.2.1.2(4), (7), (8), (9), (10) Vinaya; 3.2.1.4(3) Vinaya; 3.2.2.2(4) Sutra

Music (See Category 5)

Mysticism 2.5.3(10); 2.5.7(5) Zen, cf. 11.4.8.2; 2.6.1(9) Tantric; 2.7.14 and Bochicitta; 8.9.1(48) and Santideva; 8.9.3(42) and Hsuan Tsang; 11.4.2(12)

Mythology (See also Jatakas) 1.17(14) Comparative, East and West; 2.5.2(4), (7), (8) of Hinayana and Mahayana; 4.1.3(5) of China; 4.4(11) of Tibet; 5.1.3; 8.1 Surrounding the Buddha; 9.1; 9.2.2.5(2) Yaksas

Myths (See also specific entries, e.g. Dharma, Maitreya, Buddhism, Kingship) 1.14.2.1(4) Tibetan, cf. 4.4.1; 2.5.2(7) of the origin of Mahayana; 4.1.1(4) and Nagas, cf. 5.8; 4.4(11) Tibetan; 5.1.3 in art; 5.8(14) and Nagas, of dragons; 6.2.1.1(37) and ritual; 7.1.1(3) and ritual

Naga (See also Art Motifs, Fertility) 3.3.2.1; 4.1.1(4) Popular beliefs in; 4.1.2(2) Snake worship; 5.1.3(6) Art; 5.2.3(8); 5.8(14) Dragon; 7.8 Cult and rituals, cf. 9.2.2.5; 9.2.1(2); 9.2.2 in desire realm; 9.2.2.5(4), (11) Cult and rituals, (1)

Nagarjuna (See also Madhyamika) 2.7.3(3) Three Natures; 2.7.4 Mahaprajnaparamita Sutra; 2.7.6(10) on Pratityasamutpada, cf. 3.3.1.2, 9.2.4; 2.9(24) and white head; 3.2.2.4(3); 3.3.1.2(6) on Pratityasamutpada; 3.3.2.1; 3.3.2.2(1), (2), (4); 5.2.7 Nagarjunakonda; 8.1.1 Catuhstava (poetry); 8.9.1(37), (38), (39), (40), (41), (42), (43), (44), (45); 9.2.4 on Pratityasamutpada; 9.2.5(5)

Narrative Literature 3.2.2.4(4); 3.2.4.1 Works, including Buddha biographies; 4.2.1(2) Popular tales; 4.2.2 Jatakas; 4.2.3 Avadanas; 4.4 Dramas; 4.5; 5.11.5(8) Picture scrolls; 8.1.2.3(21) Mongolian, Life of Buddha

Nationalism (See also Colonialism) 1.3.2.2 in Sri Lanka, cf. 6.1.2; 1.4.2(15) in Burma; 1.12.2(6) in Korea; 1.13.1(7), (8) in Japan, cf. 2.5.9; 1.13.2.1(1) in Japan; 1.13.2.4(5) in Japan; 1.14.1(11) in Tibet; 2.5.9(5) in Japan; 6.1.2(20) in Sri Lanka; 6.2.1; 6.2.2.1; 6.2.2.2

Nativity (See also Jatakas) 4.2.2 Jatakas; 9.3.3(3); 10.6(7) Seven steps

Nembutsu (See also Pure Land, Amitabha, Folk Religion) 1.13.2.2(9); 2.5.8(1), (20), (29); 3.3.7.1(1); 4.1.4(4) and folk religion; 9.2.2.3(1) and rebirth; 11.4.8.2 and the koan exercise; 11.7.1(1); 11.7.2; 11.7.4(1)

Nepal (See also Himalayan Kingdoms) 1.14 History; 5.1.1(5) Art history; 5.1.4 Arts; 5.3 Arts; 5.6(10) Arts; 6.2.2.9 Politics of; 8.9.2(19); 10.2.2 Region of Kapilavastu

New Religions 1.12.2(10) Korea; 1.13.2.4(6), (9) Soka Gakkai, (6), (7) Japan; 6.2.2.6(2) Soka Gakkai, Japan

Nichiren (See also Soka Gakkai) 1.13.2.2(2), 2.5.6(7); 2.5.7(23); 2.5.9; 6.2.2.6(2) and Soka Gakkai; 8.9.4

Nidanas (See also Dependent Origination) 2.7.6

Nihilism (See also Emptiness, Nagarjuna, Madhyamika) 2.7.8(8), (10); 3.3.2.1(8); 3.3.3.1(2)

Nikaya 2.3(7) Chronology of; 2.4.1; 2.5.2(3) Mahayana traces in; 2.7.6 Dighanikaya on causality; 2.7.7 Samyutta; 2.7.8 Majjhimanikaya, on Sunyata; 3.2.2.1 Outline of various Nikayas; 3.2.3.4 Studies of Digha; 4.2.1(1) on laity; 4.2.2 Jatakas; 6.2.1.1 on Buddhist morality; 6.2.4 Dighanikaya on caste; 7.5.4(2) Texts for warding off evil; 11.4.2 Maha-satipatthanasutra, Majjhimanikaya subjects for meditation; 11.4.4 Majjhimanikaya mindfulness; 11.4.6 Patika Suttarta, special powers; 11.5 Khuddaka, on Paramitas

Nirmanakaya (See Tri-kaya)

Nirvana/Nibbana 2.1(7), (11); 2.5.3(12); 2.5.8(9); 2.7.1(9); 2.7.8(8) and Emptiness; 5.11.5 and art; 6.1.1(5) Early monastic notions; 11.4.8.3(3) and satori/wu; 11.8

Nuns 1.11.2.2(17) China, cf. 4.2.4; 3.2.1 Monastic rule-Vinaya, cf. 6.1.3; 4.2.4(13) China, Tales; 6.1.3 Monastic rule

Obaku (Sect of Zen) 3.3.6.4(1)

Ontology 2.5.1(4) of Mahayana; 2.5.4 Yogacara; 2.5.7 Mahayana and Zen; 2.7.7(11) on Dharma; 2.7.8 Two Truths; 9.1.2

Oracles (See also Divination) 4.1.5(3) Popular use of; 7.6(1) Divination-bird and lightning; 9.2.2.5(8)

Oral Tradition 2.7.8 Tenzin Gyatso--on Sunyata; 4.2.1(2) Storytelling in China; 4.2.2(3) Jatakas, oral versions through Hsuan Tsang; 4.4 Plays and dramas; 7.2.5 Sermon and preaching

Padmasambhava 1.15.2 Progenitor of Sikkimese kings?; 8.9.2(16) Biography

Pagoda (See also Temple, Art, Architecture) 4.1.2(7) Religion; 5.1.4(13) Art and architecture, cf. 6.2.1.1, 10.4.2; 5.5.2 Art and architecture; 5.5.5 Art and architecture; 5.9 Art and architecture; 5.9.2(5) Art and architecture, (7) Symbolism of; 5.10 Art and architecture; 5.11.3 Art and architecture; 6.1.2(17), (18) Social morphology; 6.2.1.1(21) Art and architecture; 7.1.3(6) of the hair relic; 8.1.2.4 of the tooth relic; 10.4.2(1), (4) Art and architecture

Painting(s) 2.6.1(12) Tibetan scrolls; 2.7.6(6) Tibetan Nidana symbols; 5.1.1(2); 5.2.1(11) Wall and mural; 5.2.6 Cave, at Ajanta, Ellora, etc., cf. 10.2.6.2; 5.2.8 Gupta period; 5.4.2(11) Sinhalese; 5.5.3(1) Thai, (12) in Jatakas;

5.6(13), (17), (20) Tankas, rules of painting, Pata; 5.7(1), (11) Central Asian, (4) India; 5.9.1(1) Chinese; 5.9.3; 5.9.4(12) at Tun Huang, Lungmen, etc.; 5.10(13) Korean; 5.11.2(7), (10), (18) Japanese; 5.11.3(11) of esoteric schools; 5.11.5; 5.11.6 Zen; 8.1.1(16) Last ten Jatakas; 9.3.10(7); 10.4.1 At Pagan

Pali (See also Canon, Vinaya, Sutra, Abhidharma) 1.1(4) Buddhism; 1.3.1(1) Commentaries; 2.1(8) Canon, cf. 3.1.1; 2.7.4(6) Canon; 2.7.6(8) Canon on dependent origination; 3.1.1(3) Canon; 3.1.2 Texts; 3.2.1 Vinaya; 3.2.2.1 Sutta Pitaka

Palladia 1.3.2.1(2) of Sri Lanka, cf. 10.3; 7.1.3(9) of Sri Lanka; 10.3 of Sri Lanka

Pantheon (See also Deities, Art Motifs) 4.1.1(1) Sinhalese; 4.1.2 Southeast Asian; 4.1.3(3) Chinese; 5.2.3(6) Evolution of; 5.6(6) in Tibetan art; 5.11.3(11) in Japanese esotericism; 8.6(6) Chinese, (9) Lamaist; 9.2.2.5(3); 11.6.1(7) Tibetan

Paramitas (See also Dana, Prajna, Bodhisattvas, etc.) 8.3.1(4); 11.1 Path and matics; 11.5 Practice and description

Parinirvana (Parinibbana) 3.2.2.4(4) Mahaparinibbanasutta; 3.3.8.2(7) Mahaparinirvanasutta; 5.11.5(6) Japanese painting; 8.1.2.3(5), (23) of Buddha; 8.1.2.4(1), (15) and relics

Paritta Texts 7.5.4

Parthia 1.10.2(10)

Pataliputra (See also Councils) 1.2.2.4(2)

Path 3.2.3.1 Vibhanga; 3.3.1.1(3) of Bodhisattva, "8000" Prajnaparamita; 3.3.1.2(1) Five fold, Abhisamayalankara; 3.3.2.1(7) Bodhisattva; 3.3.3.1(1) in Yogacara; 3.3.8.3(5) Tsongkha pa; 8.1.2.3(10) of Buddha; 8.3.1(4); 11.1 Descriptions; 11.4.1 Meditative; 11.7.1 Easy

Patriarchs 2.5.7 Zen, cf. 4.2.1; 2.5.8 Pure Land and Shin, cf. 3.3.7.1; 3.3.4.1 Hua yen, Fa tsang; 3.3.6.1(2) Ch'an, (7) Ch'an--6th (Hui Neng); 3.3.7.1 Pure Land and Shin; 4.2.1 Zen; 8.9.1 Upagupta; 8.9.6(3) Hua yen in Korea

Perfection of Wisdom (See also Prajnaparamita) 3.3.1; 3.3.1.1; 11.4.7

Persecution 1.10.2(9) Central Asia; 1.11.2.2(1), (12), (16) China, cf. 6.2.2.5; 1.11.2.3(1), (6), (13), (14) China; 1.14.2.2(3) Tibet; 6.2.2.5(4) China; 6.2.2.6(8) Japan

Physiology 2.8(9) Psychophysiology of Zen; 7.5.2 and medicinal practice

Pilgrimage 1.11.2.3(6) Accounts of, cf. 7.1.3; 6.1.2(2); 7.1.1(13); 7.1.3(2), (10) Accounts of; 8.1.2.3(13); 10.1; 10.2.1(3); 10.2.2 to Lumbini

Pilgrims 1.2.2.3(4), (8), (11), (14) Accounts of, cf. 7.1.3.1, 10.1; 1.11.2.3(6), (13) Accounts of; 2.5.4(6) Hsuan Tsang; 7.1.3(10) Accounts of; 10.1 Accounts of

Pillar 5.2.2(1) in Buddhist art; 5.2.4(11) in Buddhist art, Pillar of Asoka; 5.9.2(5) in Buddhist art

Platform Sutra (Sutra of the Sixth Patriarch) 2.5.7(16); 3.3.6.1(2), (7)

Poetry 3.1.6(3) Sinhalese; 3.2.2.1(4), (5), (6), (7), (8), (9), (26), (27) Thera and Theri Gathas; 3.2.4.1(2), (3); 3.2.4.3(2) Praises of Buddha, cf. 8.9.1; 3.3.2.1(17) of Nagarjuna, Santideva, cf. 8.9.1; 3.3.8.2(1) The Awakening of Faith; 4.2.1(5); 4.2.3(28); 4.3.1 Chinese popular; 4.3.2 Haiku; 4.3.3 Tibetan; 8.1.2(12); 8.9.1 Praises of Buddha, Santideva; 8.9.2(11) of Milarepa; 8.9.3(38) of Hsieh Ling-yun; 8.9.4(24) of Saigyo; 8.9.6(3) of Kyunyo; 11.7.3(4) Pure Land; 11.8(6) and Nirvana

Politics (See also specific countries, Persecution, Nationalism, Colonialism, Economics, Kingship) 1.3.2.2(5); 1.5.2(21), (26); 1.6.2(2); 1.7.2(4); 1.8.2(2), (7), (8), (1.13.2.1(1); 1.14.1(1), (9), (10), (11); 1.14.2.1(9); 1.14.2.3(1), (2); 1.16.2(6); 4.1.3(6); 5.2.1(7), (20) and art; 5.5.2(2) and art; 5.11.2(6) and art; 6.2.2; 6.2.2.7(5)

Popular Beliefs (See also Myths, Legends) 1.6.2(13); 1.7.2(2) in Laos; 1.8.1(1) in Vietnam; 1.12.1(2); 1.14.2.1(4) Tibetan; 3.5(2); 4.1.1 in Southern Asia; 4.1.2 Spirit cults, Nats, in Southern Asia; 4.1.4 Holy men, Japan; 4.1.5 Gods, Demons, etc. in Tibet; 4.2.1 Sutra passages on; 4.2.2 Jataka stories; 4.2.3 Avadana literature; 6.1.1(25) Worship; 6.2.1.1(12) in Ceylon; 6.2.3; 7.1.4 Use of prayers and invocations; 7.3.2 Merit; 7.4.2 Funerary practices; 7.5.1(2) Rainmaking; 7.5.3 Amulets and charms; 7.6 Divination; 8.9.4(19) and Kukai; 9.2.2.5(5); 10.8.2 and mountains in China; 11.3(5) Pien-wen and ethics; 11.8(7) Stupa and Nirvana

Power (See Category 6) (See also Abhijna, Siddhi) 3.3.7.2 Rennyo; 4.2.3 of vows, gifts, Avadana literature; 8.1.2.2(5) of Buddha; 8.1.3(8); 9.3.7(1) of stupa; 11.1(3) Magical, of Bodhisattva, cf. 11.5; 11.4.6 Extraordinary; 11.5 Magical, of Bodhisattva; 11.6.1(12) Yogic; 11.7.1(8) "Self" and "Other"

Prajna 9.3.9(3) and light; 11.4.7

Prajnaparamita (See also Perfection of Wisdom) 2.5.2(2) South Indian origins; 2.5.3(9) Mahayanasutra; 2.7.4(9) Mahayanasutra; 2.7.10(2) "8000 Lines"; 3.3.1.1(9) 25 doors to; 3.3.1.2 Prajnaparamita commentaries; 3.3.3.1(12), (13) Yogacara views of; 4.2.1(4) Hrdaya (Heart) Sutra; 8.1.2.2(2) on the Tathagata; 8.1.2.4(6) and relics; 8.3.1(3) and nature of Bodhisattva; 9.3.3(8); 9.3.5(1); 11.4.3(7) Subjects of meditation; 11.4.6 Subjects of meditation; 12.2(4) Bibliography of Prajnaparamita literature

Pranayama (Breathing) 11.4.3(7) Use of in meditation

Prasangika (See also Madhyamika) 2.5.3(5) Debates

Subject Index

Pratimoksha 3.2.1; 3.2.1.4(6) Comparative study, cf. 7.2.1; 3.3.8.1(5) for Bodhisattvas; 6.1.1(7); 7.2.1(8) Comparative study; 7.2.4 Recitation of

Pratityasamutpada (See also Dependent Origination) 3.2.3.4(9); 3.3.2.1(25)

Prayer 7.1.1(5) Wheels; 7.1.4 Use of

Prayer Forms (See also Prayer, Devotion) 2.5.8 Nembutsu as; 2.6.2(7), (9) and Mudras; 2.9(28) (33) and meditative techniques; 7.1.4 Rosaries; 7.2.2(12) in monastic life; 7.8 in rituals to Bodhisattvas; 11.6.3 Mantras

Pretas (See also Hells, Cosmology) 3.2.2.1(21) Petavatthu; 4.2.3(28); 7.3.2 All-Souls festival in China; 9.2.1(2); 9.2.2.3(7), (15) Tibetan view

Protection 4.1.5(3) Deities of; 5.6(14) Rites of; 7.5.1 Rites of; 7.5.3 Rites of; 7.5.4 Rites of

Psychology (See also Therapy, Abhidharma) 2.5.9(1) Religious, Nichiren; 2.7.7(4), (5) Early Buddhist; 2.8(7) Psychoanalysis and Zen, cf. 11.4.8.3; 2.9 Zen and meditation; 3.2.3.3 Primer of Anuruddha; 3.2.3.4(5); 4.1.1(8); 5.2.5(13) Value of images; 6.2.1.1(33) Thai village; 6.2.2.1(20) Buddhist kingship; 6.2.2.6(11) Soka Gakkai; 7.5.2(9) Medicinal; 8.1.3 Tri-kaya; 11.4.8.3(4) Psychoanalysis and Zen; 11.6.1(15) and Tantra; 11.8(1) of Nirvana

Pure Land 1.11.2.2(8); 2.5.8 History; 3.3.7.1 Sutras; 3.3.7.2 Abbots and patriarchs; 4.5 Novel of Shin priest; 5.11.2(2) Arts of; 5.11.3(14) and arts in Japan; 7.2.5(7) Sermons; 8.1.2(25) and Sakyamuni; 8.3.2(8) and Avalokitesvara; 8.3.6(7) and Mahayana; 9.2.2.3(1) Genshin and beauties of; 9.2.4; 9.3.3(4); 9.3.6(6); 9.3.9(7) Amitayur-Dhyana sutra; 10.6(7); 11.7.1 Faith; 11.7.2 Practice; 11.7.3 Visualization techniques; 11.7.4 Attainment to

Purification 7.1.4(1) of sins; 11.1(2) Path of

Rajagrha (See Councils)

Realms 2.7.7(11) Dhatus; 2.7.10(6) Dharma and Buddha Dhatus; 7.8(14) of rebirth; 9.2.1(7); 9.2.1(13); 9.2.2 Kamadhatu (Desire realm); 9.2.3 Rupadhatu (Form realm), Arupadhatu (Formless realm)

Rebirth (See also Karma, Pratityasamutpada) 2.5.8(1) in Shin, Chinese and Indian conception of; 2.7.1 Karma and; 2.7.6 Pratityasamutpada and; 2.8(17) and science; 3.2.2.1(30); 4.2.2 of Buddha; 11.7.4(8) in Pure Land

Refuge 6.1.2(2); 11.2(4) Faith in 3 refuges; 11.8(5) Nirvana as

Relics (See also Chronicles, Pagoda) 1.3.2.1(2) in Sri Lanka; 6.1.1(12) Veneration of; 7.1.3; 7.3.1(3), (11), (13); 8.1.2.4; 9.1.5

Remembrance (Recollections) 8.1.2.3(10) of past lives; 11.4.3(3) in meditation; 11.4.6(3) of former rebirths

Rennyo Shonin (8th Abbot of Shin Buddhism) 1.13.2.3(3); 2.5.8(16); 3.3.7.2(3); 8.9.4

Renunciation 2.2(4); 2.7.1(11); 6.1.3(8) and the religious life of women

Revival 1.3.2.2(3), (4), (5), (7) in Sri Lanka, cf. 6.1.2, 7.3.1; 1.11.2.2(16) in China; 1.11.2.4(4), (7) in China; 1.12.2(11), (12) in Korea; 1.13.2.4(1) in Japan; 2.8(1) in the modern world, cf. 6.2.1.1; 6.1.2(20) in Sri Lanka; 6.2.1.1 in the modern world; 6.2.4 in India; 7.3.1(11) in Sri Lanka

Ritual (See also Funerary Rites) 1.5.2(13) Daily Thai monastic, cf. 7.2.2; 1.6.1(4) Cambodian; 1.11.2.4(5) Chinese monastic; 1.12.2(10) of Korea and new religions; 1.13.2.1(4) Sites in Nara; 1.13.2.2 Various Japanese sects; 1.13.2.4 Tea ceremony; 1.14.1 Tibetan, cf. 4.1.5; 1.15.1(5); 2.2(2) Buddhist use of Brahmanic; 2.5.7(21) Zen; 2.5.9 Chanting of Lotus; 3.2.1.1(4) Pratimokkha; 3.3.8.1(1) for Bhaisajyaguru; 4.1.1(1) Sinhalese; 4.1.2 Popular shrines in Southeast Asia; 4.1.3 Popular in China; 4.1.4(3) in Japanese village; 4.1.5(4) Tibetan; 5.5.4(4) in Cambodian temple art; 5.9.2(8) at Lamaist cathedral; 5.12.3(1) Japanese imperial; 6.1.1; 6.1.2(2) of laity; 6.1.3(1) of Bhikkhunis; 6.2.1.1(37) Thai myth and ritual, (41) Ceylon; 6.2.2.8(2) and social hierarchy; 6.2.3(1) Lamaistic, (15) Propitiation of Nats; 6.2.6(9) Property rites; 7.1.1 for merit-making; 7.1.2 of gifts to Sangha; 7.1.3(11) Bathing Buddha; 7.2.2 Daily Thai monastic; 7.2.3 Chanting; 7.2.4 Uposatha; 7.2.6 for new monastery; 7.3.1 Calendrical and seasonal in Southeast Asia; 7.3.2 Calendrical in East Asia; 7.4.1(4) Life cycle; 7.5.1 for rain; 7.5.2 of healing; 7.5.3(3) Protective; 7.5.4 Paritta texts; 7.6 of divination; 7.7 Royal; 7.8 to various Bodhisattvas and deities; 8.1.2.3(23) Funeral of Buddha; 8.3.3(1) of Tara; 9.2.2.5(4) Pujas; 10.2.1 of temples and stupa worship; 10.3.1(4), (15) of tooth relic; 10.5 of Buddha footprints, alabaster; 10.6(2) at Angkor; 10.8.1(4) Monastic; 11.2 of refuge and faith; 11.4.8.1(16) Zen; 11.6 Tantric; 11.6.2(11) and Mandalas

Ritual Actions 2.5.8 the Nembutsu as, cf. 11.7.2; 2.5.9 Chanting the Lotus; 2.6.2(7), (9) Mudras and gestures, cf. 11.6.4; 4.1.1 Prestations; 5.5.6(1) Mudras, Indonesian; 7.1.3 Circumambulation of stupa, Cleansing, I-Tsing; 7.1.4 Rosaries and chanting; 7.2.1 Scarification; 7.2.2 in monastic setting; 7.2.6 Painting; 7.3.1(11) Renewing stupa whitewash; 7.3.3 Archery as; 7.4.2 Funerary; 7.5.3 Ingesting charms; 7.6 Divination; 10.2.1 Stupa worship; 11.6.3 Mantras; 11.6.4 Mudras and gestures; 11.7.1 Homages to Amida; 11.7.2 the Nembutsu as

Ritual Vehicles (See also Chanting, Dharanis, Amulets) 2.5.2(5) Stupas and rise of Mahayana; 5.6(6), (12) Tibetan, (14) Threat Crosses, etc.; 5.9.1(14) Altars; 5.10(5) Altars; 7.1.2 Gifts; 7.1.4 Rosaries; 7.5.3 Dharanis and charms; 7.6 Dice and tally; 11.6.2 Mandalas

Subject Index

Royal Capitals (See also City) 1.3.2.1(3) Sri Lanka, cf. 10.3.1; 1.4.2(11), (12) Pagan, Burma, cf. 10.4; 1.5.2(4), (25) Thailand; 1.6.2(11) Cambodia; 4.1.2(3) Vietnam; 10.3.1 Sri Lanka; 10.4 Burma

Rupa (Rupakaya) 2.3(2) Namarupa and Dharmarupa; 3.2.3.3(2); 3.3.1.1(8) Prajnaparamita

Rupadhatu (See also Realms) 2.7.7(11) Dhatus

Rupakaya (See also Buddha Bodies) 2.7.15

Sacred Places (See Category 10) (See also Royal Capitals, Temples, Pilgrimage) 6.1.2(17) Social morphology of temples

Sacrifice 2.2(2) Buddhist transformation; 2.5.2(8) Buddhist transformation

Sadhana 3.4.1 Tantric texts; 9.6.1 in Tantrism; 11.6

Sahajiyas 2.6.1(6) in Bengal; 11.6.1(10)

Saicho 1.13.2.2(11); 2.5.6(7); 8.9.4

Samadhi (See also Dhyana, Concentration, Meditation) 2.8.1 Journal; 3.3.2.1(12); 3.3.8.1(7) Anecdotes about; 11.4.1(7) One-pointedness; 11.4.5 Types of

Sambhogakaya (See also Tri-kaya) 2.7.15; 8.1.3(8), (9)

Samkhya 2.2(5), (13), (16); 2.7.6(3) and the doctrine of dependent origination; 2.7.7(12) Gunas vs. dharmas

Sanchi 5.2.4(10), (12), (13), (14); 10.2.6.2

Sangha (See also Monastery, Monasticism, Monk, Temple) 1.2.1(8) Emergence of; 1.2.2.1(2), (3), (14) Emergence of, (13) Economic support of; 1.7.2(4); 1.11.2.3(16) China; 1.17(7) and the West; 2.4 Schisms; 2.7.1(5), (13) Early notions of karma; 2.7.2(2) Early notions of duhkha; 2.7.3 Early notions of time and impermanence; 3.2.1 Textual regulations (Vinaya); 6.1; 6.1.1; 6.1.2(1) Modern organization of; 6.1.4 Modern organization of; 6.2.1.1(7) Cambodia; 6.2.1.2(18) Authority structure; 6.2.2.1 and kingship, and state; 6.2.2.2 and kingship, and state

Santideva 2.7.9(5); 3.3.2.1(9); 3.3.2.2(2); 8.9.1

Saraha (See also Yogins, Songs, Poetry) 3.4.2(7); 11.6(9) Songs of

Sarnath 1.2.2.3(7) under Sunga rulers; 5.2.8(18); 10.2.4

Sarvastivada (See also Sthaviravadin) 2.4.3(10) and Abhidharma, cf. 3.2.3.2, 3.2.3.4, Doctrine; 2.7.1(7) on Karma; 2.7.7(1), (11), (12) on dharmas; 3.1.3(1) and Vinaya, Literature, cf. 3.2.2.2; 3.2.1.2(2), (7), (8), (9) and Vinaya; 3.2.2.2 Literature; 3.2.3.2 and Abhidharma; 3.2.3.4(6) and Abhidharma

Satipatthana 3.2.2.1(10) Mahasatipatthanasutta Dighanikaya; 11.4.2 Mahasatipatthanasutta, 11.4.4 Techniques and subject of

Satori/wu (See also Enlightenment, Nirvana, Pure Land, Zen) 11.4.8.3

Sautrantikas 1.3.2.1(7); 2.4.1(13); 2.4.3 Doctrines, etc.; 2.7.1(7) Karma; 2.7.3 Debates over impermanence; 3.2.3.2(4), (5) Karmasiddhiprakarana; 11.8(4), (8) on Nirvana

Schism (or "sect") 1.2.2.1 in early Buddhism; 2.4.1(3), (7) "18 schools"; 2.4.3(7) Mahasangika; 4.1.3(7); 6.2.2.3(7) in Burma; 6.2.2.5(3) in China; 6.2.2.6(2) Soka Gakkai; 6.2.5(16) Tibet, "Red Sect"; 9.1.4(7) Peasant Revolts

Science 2.8 and Buddhism, contemporary; 3.2.2.1(29); 7.5.2 Medicinal and healing

Sculpture (See Category 5) (See also Art) 1.6.2(11) of Cambodia; 1.7.2(6) of Laos; 1.12.1(1) of Korea; 2.6.2(7) of Japan

Seng-chao 1.11.2.2(6); 2.5.1(3) Doctrine of Reality; 3.3.6.1(1)

Sermons 2.5.7(2) of Lin Chi; 3.3.6.2(1) Rinzai masters; 3.3.6.2(7) of Huang Po, Hui, Hai; 3.3.6.4 Obakuzen sect, tetsugen; 4.2.1 Discourses in Nikayas; 4.2.2 Jatakamala; 7.2.5(5) Burmese, on Jatakas; 8.1.2.1(13) of Buddha, cf. 9.3.1; 8.9.4(1) Japanese Zen masters; 9.3.1(5) of Buddha; 9.3.3(3); 10.2.6.1 at Sravasti; 11.4.4(4) on Satipatthana

Shin 1.13.2.2 Founding of; 1.13.2.3(2) Restoration; 2.5.8; 3.3.7.2 Rennyo; 4.5 Novel; 7.1.4(5) Rosaries in; 7.2.5 Contemporary sermons; 11.7.1; 11.7.4(3) Pure Land

Shingon (See also Kobo Daishi, Mandala) 2.6.2(3), (4), (5), (6), (8) Kukai, founder, (6), (8) Relation to Indo-Tibetan Tantra; 3.4.3(3); 7.1.4(5) Use of rosaries, (11) Ceremonies of

Shinran 1.13.2.2 Biography and history; 2.5.8 Letter; 3.3.7.2 Songs; 4.4.2 Story of, drama; 8.9.4(25) Life, (26) Letters of; 11.7.1

Shin shu 1.13.2.2(4) Historical accounts; 2.5.8 History; 11.7.1 Meditation techniques

Shinto 4.1.4(3); 4.2.4(10) Folk tales; 5.11.3 and art and architecture; 6.2.1.2(14); 6.2.2.6(3) and kingship

Shugendo 2.6.2(2)

Siddhas (Perfected Ones) 5.6(19) the 85; 8.5(4) the 85; 8.9.1(42) and Nagarjuna

Siddhi (Power) (Rddhi) (See also Abhijna, Powers) 9.3.5 Mahaprajnaparamita; 11.1 Vijnaptimatrata, of Hsuan tsang; 11.4.1(7) Powers; 11.4.6 Types of; 11.6.1(12) Yogic

Subject Index

Sikkim (See also Himalayan Kingdoms) 4.1.5(4) Popular beliefs and rituals; 5.6(10) Buddhist art; 6.2.2.9 Lamas and politics; 6.2.6(16) Monastic economy; 10.1.3(3) Maraini

Sinicization 1.11.1(1), (2), (3); 1.11.2.1(4) of Buddhism; 2.5.3(8), (10) of Madhyamika; 6.2.2.5(1) of Sangha

Skandha (Aggregates) (See also Dharma, Dhatu, Abhidharma, Ayatanas) 2.7.2(3) and duhkha; 2.7.4(10) and anatman; 2.7.7(note)(10) and dharmas

Soka Gakkai (See also New Religions, Nichiren) 1.13.2.4(6), (9); 6.2.2.6(2), (5), (7), (9), (11); 6.2.5(3) and education

Songs (See also Poetry, Chanting) 2.5.7(16) of Zen Enlightenment; 3.2.2.1(26), (27) Thera and Theri Gathas; 3.3.6.2(4) Zazen; 3.4.2(7) of Saraha, cf. 11.6; 4.2.1(5) Popular hymns; 4.3.3 Milarepa, Sharapa, folksongs, marriage songs, etc.; 6.1.3(7) Nuns; 8.3.6(6) of Vimalakirti; 11.6 of Saraha; 11.7.3(4) Pilgrimage hymns

Soteriology 2.5.1(5) in Mahayana; 2.7.8 Sunyata; 2.7.11(2) Tathagatagarbha theory; 2.9(17) in Todo Shin and Christianity, cf. 11.7.1; 6.2.6(21) Merit and economics; 7.1.1 Merit and economics; 7.4.2 and funerary rites; 9.1.4 Path and stages; 11.4.7(7) Prajna/wisdom; 11.4.8.3 in Zen; 11.7.1 in Todo Shin and Christianity, 11.7.4 Pure Land

Soto Zen 2.5.7(8), (10), (14), (17), (24); 2.7.14(1) Notions of Buddha nature; 3.3.6.3 Masters, Masters' works, Dogen, cf. 11.4.5; 5.8(11) and veneration of arhats; 11.4.5(5); 11.4.8.1

Spells (See also Mantra, Sutra) 7.5.3

Sramanas 2.2(8), (15) and early Buddhism; 6.1.2(7) Anatre Sangha; 6.1.3(8) and nuns; 7.2.2(2) Daily life of "Shaman"

Sravaka 1.2.1 Catholic church; 8.3.1(7) Bodhisattvas; 11.1(9) Path of

Sri Lanka (Ceylon) (See also Chronicles, Canon) 1.3; 1.3.1 Inception of Buddhism; 1.3.2.1(11) Inception of Buddhism; 3.1.6(3) Literature of; 5.4 Art; 5.4.1 Sacred places, cf. 10.1.4, 10.3; 5.12.1 Dance and magic; 6.2.2.2 Politics; 8.3.2(10) Mahayana influences; 10.1.4 Sacred places, Travellers' accounts; 10.3 Sacred places, Royal capitals

Sthaviravadin 2.1(1) Historical survey; 2.4.1; 2.4.2(5) and the 2nd council; 2.4.3; 2.4.4(6) Schism; 3.1.3 Literature of; 3.2.1.2(1) Vinaya

Sthiramati 2.5.3(15); 2.7.14(7) on Bodhicitta; 3.3.3.1(2) and other schools, (18) on Bodhicitta; 3.3.3.2

Store(house) Consciousness (See also Alaya-vijnana) 2.7.12

Stupa 1.2.1(8) Veneration of, cf. 1.11.2.2, 2.5.2, 6.1.2, 7.1.3, 8.1.2.4, 9.3.6, 10.2.1; 1.2.2.3(13) Archaeological studies of, 1.11.2.2; 1.5.2(3) Archaeological studies, in Thailand; 1.11.2.2(11) Archaeological studies, Veneration of; 2.5.2(5), (8); 4.2.3(5) Great Stupa of Kaniska; 5.1.1(2) General discussion, Symbolism on, cf. 10.2.1; 5.1.4(6), (13) Symbolism on; 5.2.1(11), (12) Symbolism on; 5.2.2(5), (8) Symbolism on; 5.2.4(2) Symbolism on, at Bharhut, cf. 10.2.6.1; 5.2.7 at Amaravati, cf. 10.2.6.3; 5.4.2(8) in Sri Lanka; 5.5.6 of Borobodur; 5.9.2(5) in China; 6.1.2(2) Veneration of; 7.1.3 Veneration of; 8.1.2.4(2), (8) Veneration of; 9.1.5(16) Chronicle of; 9.3.6 Veneration of, as symbol, Construction and consecration, cf. 10.2.6.1; 10.2.1(1) Veneration of, (7) Symbolism; 10.2.6.1(2) Construction and consecration, as symbol, at Bharhut; 10.2.6.2(2), (5), (6) at Sanchi; 10.2.6.3 at Amaravati

Suchness (See also Tathata) 2.7.10(2); 8.1.2.2(2)

Suffering (See also Duhkha) 2.7.2 Duhkha; 7.5.2 Healing of and causes; 9.1.2(8) Loss of paradisal state; 9.2.2.3(12) in hell

Sukhavati (See also Western Paradise) 3.3.7.1

Sunya 2.7.8; 3.3.2.2(3) Aspects of; 11.5(5) and Paramitas

Sutra 3.2.2; 3.3.2.1 Pali sutta pitaka; 3.3 Mahayana texts; 3.3.1.1 Prajnaparamita, Mahayana texts; 3.3.6 Ch'an/Zen texts; 7.1.4; 7.2.3 Repetition of; 7.5.3(4) of protection; 7.5.4 of protection

Svabhava (See Tri-laksana/Tri-Svabhava)

Symbols (See also specific references, Art Motifs) 2.5.2(8) of cosmos, cf. 6.2.2.1; 4.1.1(4) Serpent, (6) Wilderness; 4.2.3(15) Feminine, cf. 9.3.10; 5.1.3 in art; 5.9.3(7) Bridge, cf. 9.3.7; 6.2.2.1(9) of cosmos, of state and kingship, cf. 9.3.1, 9.3.7; 8.1.2.2(1) of state and kingship; 9.2.2.3 of enlightenment, cf. 9.3.5; 9.2.2.4(1) of enlightenment; 9.2.2.5(1), (2); 9.3; 9.3.1(2) of state and kingship; 9.3.5 of enlightenment; 9.3.7(6) Bridge, of state and kingship; 9.3.10(9) Feminine; 1.6.1(20) of passion; 11.7.3(2) of light

Syncretism (See also Folk Religion, Drama, Shinto) 1.6.1(1); 1.7.2(2) Laos; 1.8.2(5) Annam (Vietnam); 1.11.2.3(11) China, cf. 4.4.2; 1.13.2.1(3) Japan; 4.1.1(8); 4.4(6) China; 4.4.(9); 7.8(5) (7), (9), (13) of cult and ritual

T'an luan (Patriarch) (See also Shinran, Pure Land) 2.5.8(3); 11.7.2(1)

Tankas (See also Painting, Tibet) 5.6(3) of Jatakamala, (19) of 85 Siddhas; 8.1.1 of Jatakamala; 10.7 Temples and art

Tantras 1.11.2.3(4) in China; 3.4.1 Guhyasamaja, etc.; 5.2.8 Arts, (4), (5) Pantheon of, (14), (15) Art of; 5.11.4(16) Mudras; 5.12.1 Dance/Drama; 7.5.2(2) and healing; 8.2.2(7) Guhyasamaja; 9.2.5(3); 9.3.10(9) Female symbolism; 11.6 Practice of Sadhanas

Tantrayana (See Vajrayana)

Taoism 1.11.2.2(6), (10), (13); 1.11.2.3(5), (7), (10); 4.2.4(17) Deities, and Karma; 5.1.4(1) and art

Tara (See also Deities) 3.3.1.1(3) 108 names, Prajnaparamitanama Astasataka; 3.4.1(5) Sadhana of; 8.3.3; 9.2.2.1(1); 11.6.1(2) Practices; 11.6.3(1) Mantras of; 11.6.4(2) Mudras of

Tathagata 2.7.11; 2.7.12(8) and Alayavijnana; 3.2.2.2(7) Hymns to, (9) Theory and text; 3.3.2.1(8) Prasannapada, (23), (24), (31) Srimala, Ratnagotravibhaga; 3.3.8.3(1); 8.1.2.1(6) Sakya, (24)

Tathata 1.11.2.2(2) and "Tao"; 2.7.10; 9.3.9(3) and light

Tea Ceremony 5.11.1(2) Japan, cf. 5.11.8; 5.11.2(9), (21) Japan; 5.11.3(2), (14) Japan, (2) Teahouses; 5.11.6(13) Japan; 5.11.7 Tea-gardens; 5.11.8 Japan

Teachers 1.11.2.1(1) in China; 1.14.1(2) Biographies of, cf. 9.1.5; 1.14.2.1 in Tibetan monastery; 1.15.2 Sikkimise; 2.2(11), (15) Contemporary with Buddha; 2.5.6 of T'ien T'ai; 2.5.7 of Zen; 7.2.5 of Dhamma, Sermons; 8.1.1 Buddha biographies; 8.1.2 Buddha biographies; 9.1.5 Biographies of

Teaching/Preaching (See also Sarnath) 3.2.4 Manuals of; 7.2.5 in monastic context; 8.1.2.2(4) the Law; 11.2(5) the Law

Temples (See also Monasteries, Ritual, Cave) 1.5.2(24) Wat, cf. 5.5.3; 1.7.2(2) Wat; 1.11.2.3(5), (16), (17); 1.12.2(3) Korea, cf. 5.8, 5.10; 1.13.1 Japan, cf. 5.8, 5.11.2, 5.11.3, 6.1.2; 5.1.4(13) Art and architecture, cf. 8.1.1, 10.6; 5.2.2 Art and architecture; 5.3 of Nepal; 5.5.3(12) Wat; 5.5.4 Cambodia; 5.5.5 of Indochina (incl. Laos, Champa, Vietnam); 5.6(1), (3), (20) of Tibet; 5.7 of Central Asia; 5.8(11) Japan, China; 5.9 China; 5.9.2 China; 5.9.4 China; 5.10 Korea; 5.11.2 Japan; 5.11.3 Japan; 6.1.2(17), (18) Japan, Cultural implications; 6.2.1.1(7), (10), (11), (21); 7.1.3(9) of Sri Lanka; 8.1.1(16) Art and architecture; 10.2.3 of Bodh-Gaya, of India; 10.6(8) Art and architecture, and cosmology

Tendai (See T'ien t'ai/Tendai)

Therapy 4.1.1(3) Reciprocal prestations and; 7.5.3 by charms and amulets; 7.8(6) Naga cult; 9.2.2.5(4) Methods of controlling nagas

Thailand (See also Chronicles) 1.1(4) Historical overview, cf. 1.8.1; 1.5; 1.5.1(2) Inception of Buddhism; 1.5.2(5) Inception of Buddhism; 1.8.1(2), (3) Historical overview; 3.1.2(2), (8) Pali texts of; 5.5.2(2) Politics, cf. 6.2.2.4; 5.5.3 Art and architecture, Sacred places, cf. 10.1.4, 10.5; 5.12.1 Drama; 6.2.2.4 Politics; 8.9.5 King Mongkut, King Chulalongkorn; 10.1.4 Sacred places, Travellers' accounts; 10.5 Sacred places

Theravada (See also Sthaviravadin, Hinayana, Buddhaghosa) 2.7.7(1) Notions of dharmas, (5) Abhidharma discussions; 3.2.1.3(1) Vinaya commentaries

Three Characteristics (See also Tri-laksana/Tri-svabhava) 2.7.13(1), (5); 3.3.3.1(17)

Throne (See also Cakkavatti, Lotus, Art Motifs) 9.3.7

Tibet 1.14.1 History, cf. 8.1.2; 1.14.2.1 Sects; 2.1(5) Thought; 2.7.6(6) Symbolism; 2.7.8 14th Dalai Lama; 2.7.14(3) Bodhicitta doctrine; 3.1.2 Texts; 3.2.1.2(9) Pratimoksa; 4.1.5 Popular beliefs; 4.4 Stories, tales, drama; 5.1.4(6) Arts; 5.6 Arts; 5.12.1(6) Drama; 6.1.1(8) Monks; 6.2.1.2(18) Monasticism, cf. 7.2.2; 6.2.2.7 Politics in; 6.2.2.9 and Mongolia, Lamas and politics; 6.2.5(19) Education, (17) Red Sect; 6.2.6(3) Land and polity; 7.2.1 Ordination ceremonies; 7.5.3 Use of charms and amulets; 7.8 Bodhisattvas and deities; 8.1.2.1(23) Buddha biographies; 8.1.2.3 Buddha biographies; 8.3.3(1) Ritual structure; 8.9.1(38) Nagarjuna; 8.9.2 on Atisa, on Buston, Biographies of Dalai Lamas, Marpa, Milarepa, Naropa, Padmasambhava, Panchen Lamas, Tsongkhapa; 10.1.3 Sacred places, Travellers' accounts; 10.7 Sacred places, Travellers' accounts

T'ien T'ai/Tendai 1.11.2.2(4) Fo tsu T'ung Chi; 1.13.2.2 Saicho; 2.5.6; 2.5.7(24) and Zen; 8.9.3(11); 10.8.2 Mt. T'ien T'ai; 11.4.2(4) Meditation manuals; 11.7.2(4) Use of Nembutsu

Time 2.4.3(5) Sarvastivadin; 2.7.3; 3.3.2.1(8) in the Wisdom literature, Mahayana notions; 3.3.6.3(2) in Soto Zen; 8.7 and Cakravartins

Tombs (See also Funerary Rites) 1.13.2.1(4) Kofun; 9.3.6

Totality 2.5.5(1) Doctrine of, and Hua yen; 3.3.4.1(5) Meditation on

Trance 11.4.5 Kinds and levels

Transcendences (See Paramitas)

Transformation of Concepts and Symbols 1.14.2.1(5) Buddhism and Bon; 1.17 in European and Indian iconography; 2.2(2) Atman, caste, etc.; 2.5.1(5) Mahayana; 2.5.3(11) Madhyamika in China; 2.7.6(6) Wheel of life; 2.7.9 Two Truths; 2.8(20) Buddhism under Mao; 4.1.1(4), (6) Nagas, Wilderness; 5.1.3(2), (4) Nature in art; 5.2.1(16) Indian art; 5.9.4 Lotus Sutra; 6.2.2.3(4) Sacred kingship; 8.1.1(8) Feminine symbolism; 8.1.2.2 the superhuman; 8.1.2.3(27) Solar imagery; 8.7(6) Buddha and Cakravartin; 9.1.2(9) Transformation of Beings; 9.1.5(10); 9.2.1(3) and Vedic tradition; 9.2.2.3(4) Notion of Chinese hells, (13) Notion of hell; 9.2.2.5(12) Nagas; 9.3.6(3) Evolution of stupa; 11.6 of Tantric practice; 11.7.4(6) Stupa and Pure Land

Subject Index

Translation (See Category 3 for translations of specific Buddhist texts) 1.11.2.1(4) from Sanskrit to Chinese; 1.12.1(2) of Korean texts; 1.14.1 of Tibetan texts; 2.5.9(4) Nichiren; 2.7.11(4) Chinese, Japanese and Tibetan, Srimalasutra; 3.1.2(6) Summary of untranslated Pali; 3.1.5(1) Chinse Tripitaka, (4) History of translation; 3.2.3.4(12) Chinese; 3.2.4.2 Samgharaksa; 4.7.4 of Popular literature; 12.2(2)

Transmigration 2.7.1 Karma and rebirth; 2.7.4 and soul; 5.5.6(8) Origin of stupa and; 7.4.2(17); 9.2.5(1), (4); 9.3.6(6)

Transmission (See also Chronicles, Genealogies) 1.13.1(7) of Buddhism, cf. 6.2.1.2; 1.13.2.1(2) of Buddhism; 2.5.7(4) of Zen masters; 4.2.3(17), (24) Story-telling; 4.2.4(18) and the role of art and literature; 6.1.1(28) of Abbots; 6.2.1.2(5), (10) of Buddhism

Transmission of the Lamp (See also Ch'an/Zen) 2.5.7(25); 3.3.6.1(2)

Trees (See also Art Motifs) 4.1.2(3) Cult of; 5.1.3(1) as symbols; 9.3.4 as symbols; 10.2.3(1) Bodhi-tree

Tri-Kaya (See also Buddha Bodies) 2.1(2) Doctrine of, cf. 8.1.2.2; 2.7.5; 8.1.2.2 Doctrine of; 8.1.3(3), (6), (7), (9); 8.9.1(54); 9.2.5(1)

Tri-laksana/Tri-svabbhava 2.7.13(1)

Tripitaka (See Abhidharma, Sutra, Vinaya)

Truths 2.1(2) Two Truths, cf. 2.7.9; 2.7.5 Four Noble Truths, and path, and healing; 2.7.6(3) and dependent origination; 2.7.9 Two Truths; 3.2.3.1(2) Four Truths; 3.3.2.1 Bhavaviveka; 9.2.3(4) Four Truths correlated with realms; 9.3.1(3)

Tsong-kha-pa 1.14.1 Jivaka; 3.3.8.3(4), (5); 7.2.2(4) the Kumbum monastery; 8.9.2(22) Life; 9.1.2(10); 11.6.3(10); 11.8(8) on Nirvana

Tu-Shun (Founder of Hua Yen School) 3.3.4.1 Meditation; 8.9.3(83) Biography, Chih-yen, his disciple, (84) Biography

Upagupta 8.2.1(1) and 500 Pratyeka Buddhas; 8.9.1(50) and Mara; 9.3.5(4) Conversion of Mara

Upava (See Paramita)

Vairocana (the Shining B) 1.12.2(1) B-images; 1.13.2.1(7); 8.2.2(5)

Vaisali (See also Councils) 2.4.2; 3.2.1.1(3) Council

Vajrayana (See also Tantras) 1.2.1(3); 1.4.1(7) in Burma; 1.4.2(12) in Burma; 2.1(1), (15); 2.6.1 in India and Tibet; 2.6.2 in China, Japan; 2.7.14(3) in Tibet, and Bodhicitta; 3.3.1.2(5) View of Prajnaparamita; 3.4.1 Texts and studies; 5.2.8 Pantheon; 5.11.4(10) Art of, in Japan; 6.2.2.7 and divine kingship in Tibet; 8.3.1(1) on Bodhisattvas; 8.6(1) and Bhutadharma; 8.6(8) and Horse cult, (7) Various deities; 8.7(7) of divine kingship; 8.9.3 and Shan-wu-wei, and Vajrabodhi; 8.9.4(19) on Kukai; 11.6 Practice and Sadhana; 11.6.2 Use of Mandala; 11.6.3 Use of Mantras

Vasubandhu (See also Sautrantika, Asanga, Founder of Yogacara) 2.5.4(19); 2.5.8(3), (7) Pure Land; 2.7.1(7) and Karma; 2.7.4(11) and Anatman; 2.7.7(note) and Dharmas, (5), (11) Abhidharma discussions; 3.2.3.2(4), (5) Abhidharma discussions; 3.3; 3.3.3.1(2), (18), (19), (20), (21), (22); 8.9.1

Vedanta 2.2(5); 2.7.8(1)

Veneration of Sacred Objects 7.1.3; 8.1.2.4

Vietnam (Champa and Annam) (See also Politics) 1.1(4) Historical overview, cf. 1.8.1; 1.8; 1.8.1(2), (3) Historical overview, (4), (8) Hindu influence, (6) Spread of Buddhism; 5.5.5 Art and architecture, Sacred places, cf. 10.1.4, 10.6; 5.8(1) Art and architecture; 6.2.2.8; 10.1.4 Sacred places, Travellers' accounts; 10.6 Sacred places

Vijnanavada (See also Yogacara/Vijnanavada) 2.5.4; 2.7.5(1) Abhidharmasamuccaya; 2.7.13 Theory of Tri-Laksana; 11.1(6) View of Path

Village Life 4.1.1(9) Sinhalese; 4.1.3(4) in China; 4.1.4(3) in Japan; 4.4 Dramas and plays; 5.11.2(9) Art remains in Japan; 6.2.1.1 Economics and merit-making; 6.2.3; 6.2.6(12) Economic behavior, (14) in Burma; 7.1.1 Rituals; 7.1.2 and Samgha; 7.3.1 Southeast Asia, Calendrical rituals, Wats; 7.5.1(2); 7.5.2 Medicinal practices; 9.1.5(17) in Nepal; 11.3(6) Ethical practices, in Ceylon

Vimalakirti 3.3.2.1(34), (35), (36) Nirdesa sutra; 5.9.2 Depicted in art; 7.2.5(1) Teaching

Vinaya (See also Monasticism, Monk, Sangha) 3.1.3(1) Sarvastivada; 3.2.1; 3.2.1.4(5) History of, cf. 6.1.1; 5.2.1(15) and art; 6.1.1(7) History of; 7.2.1 Ordination

Vipasyana 11.4.2(4) Samathavipasyana

Visualization 3.3.7.1 in Pure Land, Amitayur Dhyana Sutra, cf. 9.3.9, 11.4.2; 3.4.2(10) of Mandalas; 9.3.9 in Pure Land, Amitayur Dhyana Sutra; 11.4.2 in Pure Land, Amitayur Dhyana Sutra; 11.6.1(2); 11.6.4(2) and Mudras; 11.7.3 in Pure Land

Visuddhimaga (Path of Purification) (See also Buddhaghosa) 3.2.4.2

Vows 7.1.1(13) Lay; 7.1.4(11) Bodhisattva; 7.2.1(8) Samaya (Vajrayana)

War(s) (See also Colonialism) 6.2.2.3(8) Revolution, cf. 6.2.2.9; 6.2.2.6(4); 6.2.2.9(1) Revolution

Weberian Analyses 1.13.2.3(1); 6.2.1.1(28), (44), (49)

Western Paradise (See also Sukhavati) 3.3.7.1 Amitayur Dhyana Sutra, cf. 9.3.6, Larger Sukhavati Vyuha, cf. 9.3.9; 4.1.3 in Chinese popular beliefs, Secret societies and millennial; 9.3.9 Amitayur Dhyana Sutra; Larger Sukhavati Vyuha; 11.4.3; 11.7.4 Description of

Wheel (See also Art Motifs) 2.7.6(6) of Life; 9.3.1 of Dharma; 9.3.2

Wisdom (See also Prajna) 11.4.5(2) Relation to Dhyana; 11.5(5) Paramita

Wives 1.14.2.1(12) of Sron-btsan Sgam po (Tibetan king); 6.1.3(6); 8.1.2.3(21) of Buddha

Women 1.11.2.2(17) Nuns; 3.2.1.1(3) Bikkhuni Vibhanga; 3.2.2.1(27) Psalms of; 6.1.2(12) Laity; 6.1.3; 7.1.3(11) Bathing Buddha; 8.9.3(4) Anling-shou

Worship (See Categories 7, 10 and 11) (See also Ritual Art, Iconography) 1.3.1(10) in Sri Lanka; 1.5.1(9) in Thailand, 1.5.2(2), (22) in Thailand; 1.7.1(1) in Laos; 1.7.2(7) in Laos; 1.8.1(1), (5) in Vietnam, cf. 4.1.1; 1.9.2(5) in Indonesia, cf. 2.5.2; 1.12.2(10) in Korea; 1.13.2.1 in Japan, cf. 8.3.2; 1.13.2.2(3) in Japan; 1.14.1(17) in Tibet, cf. 5.6; 2.5.2(8) in Indonesia; 2.5.7(14), (21) in Zen; 4.1.2(3) in Vietnam; 5.6 in Tibet; 8.1.2.4 of relics; 8.3.2(5) in China, (12) in Japan

Wu (See Satori/Wu)

Yaksas/Yaksinis (See also Art Motifs) 4.1.1(6) and kingship; 9.2.2.5(2), (7), (9), (10), (13) in Realm of Desire; 9.3.4(1) and trees

Yoga (See Asceticism) 2.6.1(12) and Tantras; 5.2.8(12) and Tantra in archaeology; 11.6 Tantric; 11.8(4) Early Buddhism, Yogic context

Yogacara/Vijnanavada (See also Idealism, Mind) 2.5.4 Development and history; 2.5.5(1) Mind-only; 2.7.5(1) Abhidharmasamuccaya; 2.7.7(1) on Dharmas; 2.7.11 Doctrine of Alaya-Vijnana; 2.7.13 Doctrine of Tri-Laksana; 3.3.3.1 Literature and texts; 3.3.2.2; 3.3.3.3 Studies of; 3.3.4.2 Yogacarabhumi; 8.9.1 Founders of, Asanga and Vasubandhu; 9.2.2.3(11) Interpretation of Hell; 9.3.10(9) Mirror

Yogin/Yogini (See also Siddhas) 3.3.3.1(6) Yogacarabhumi; 4.3 Songs of, Milarepa, Brug-pa kun-legs; 7.8 Matsyendrantha; 8.5(2) Magical powers; 8.9.2(12) Milarepa; 11.6.1(9) Milarepa, Saraha

Zazen 2.5.7(14); 3.3.6.2(4); 3.3.6.3(2)

Zen (See also Ch'an/Zen, Transmission of the Lamp, Soto, Koan, Meditation) 1.13.2.4(8) and art, cf. 5.1.4, 5.8, 5.11.2, 5.11.4, 5.11.6, Rituals of, cf. 7.1.4, 7.2.1; 2.5.5(5), (6) and Gandhavyuha, Influences on Avatamsaka; 2.5.7; 2.8(7), (9) and psychology, cf. 11.4.8.3; 2.9(18) and psychology; 3.3.6.1; 5.1.4(1) and art; 5.8(7) and art; 5.11.2 and art; 5.11.4 and art; 5.11.6 and art; 6.2.1.2(20); 7.1.4(5) Rituals of; 7.2.1(10) Rituals of; 11.4.8.1(11), (12), (13), (14), (15), (17), (18); 11.4.8.3(4) and psychology, and Satori/wu

Zen Masters (See also Soto, Koan, Satori) 1.13.2.3(4) Hakuin (18th century) rinzai, cf. 3.3.6.3, 8.9.4, 11.4.8.1; 2.5.7(4), (12), (14), (17), (18) Soto masters, cf. 3.3.6.3; 3.3.6.1(8); 3.3.6.2; 3.3.6.3(10) Hakuin (18th century) rinzai, Soto masters; 5.11.6(12) and art; 8.9.4(4) Hakuin (18th century) rinzai; 11.4.8.1(15) Hakuin (18th century) rinzai; 11.4.8.3(5) Satori experiences

Ref
Z
7860
R48